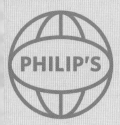

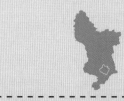

T0319300

LOCAL EXPLORER

DERBYSHIRE

www.philips-maps.co.uk

Published by Philip's, a division of
Octopus Publishing Group Ltd
www.octopusbooks.co.uk
Carmelite House, 50 Victoria Embankment,
London EC4Y 0DZ
An Hachette UK Company
www.hachette.co.uk

First edition 2023
First impression 2023
DBYFA

ISBN 978-1-84907-638-8

© Philip's 2023

This product
includes mapping
data licensed from
Ordnance Survey®
with the permission
of the Controller of His Majesty's Stationery
Office. © Crown copyright 2023. All rights
reserved. Licence number 100011710.

Photographic acknowledgements:
Alamy Stock Photo: /darren ball II top; /Terry
Mathews II bottom right; /Transportimage
Picture Library III; /travellinglight front cover.
Dreamstime.com: /Krzysztof Nahlik II
bottom left.

Printed in China

CONTENTS

II **Best places to visit**

IV **Key to map pages**

VI **Route planning**

X **Key to map symbols**

1 **Street maps** at 3½ inches to 1 mile

266 **Street maps** of Chesterfield and Derby at
7 inches to 1 mile

268 **Index** of towns, villages, streets, hospitals, industrial
estates, railway stations, schools, shopping centres,
universities and places of interest

Best places to visit

Outdoors

Arbor Low Neolithic stone circle or henge, comprising 50 limestone slabs (none standing) surrounded by earthworks and a ditch. Its central stone 'cove' indicates that it was a very important sacred site in pre-historic times. **Gib Hill Barrow** – a large burial mound – is nearby. *Monyash* 🖥 www.english-heritage.org.uk **123 E4**

Carsington Water Large reservoir with visitor centre, popular for its watersports courses and fishing. Bike hire is available and there are off-road cycling and walking routes around the reservoir and further afield. The paths link to the longer-distance Tissington and High Peak trails. *Ashbourne* 🖥 www.carsingtonwater.com **164 C4**

Creswell Crags Archaeological park, centred on a dramatic limestone gorge dotted with caves on the border between Derbyshire and Nottinghamshire. The caves, first excavated in the 19th century, were lived in by early humans during the Ice Age. Tools have been discovered as well as the earliest cave art in the UK, plus bones from woolly mammoths, bears and reindeer. The museum has an important collection of finds from here and elsewhere in the UK. There are walking trails in the woodland and by the lake. *Creswell* 🖥 www.creswell-crags.org.uk **82 A1**

Elvaston Country Park Over 300 acres of parkland, woodland and nature reserve with formal gardens and a peaceful, traditional English walled garden, centred on Gothic revival Elvaston Castle (private). There are walking and cycling routes and the lakeside walk is popular for bird watching. *Derby*. www.derbyshire.gov.uk **233 F6**

Foremark Large nature reserve and reservoir, with waymarked walks through woodland, grassland and heath. Water sports are available on the reservoir, and there is an orienteering course and playground. Wildlife includes birds of prey, waterfowl and deer. Carver's Rocks is a Site of Special Scientific Interest for its rare lowland heath geology and plant life. *Derby* 🖥 www.nationaltrust.org.uk **250 C5**

Heights of Abraham Large hilltop country park with a cable car up to the summit, from where there are excellent views over the surrounding countryside. Visitors can tour two show caverns and see exhibitions and films about their history. There are adventure playgrounds, a willow sculpture trail, heritage and

▲ *Mam Tor*

▶ *Buxton Opera House*

nature-themed walks, as well as special events. *Matlock Bath* 🖥 www.heightsofabraham.com **143 A2**

Peak District National park covering 555 square miles mainly within Derbyshire. **The Dark Peak** (or High Peak) area in the north and east is characterised by dramatic gritstone cliffs, moorland and steep-sided valleys. It is the location of **Kinder Scout**, the highest point in the Peak District, famous not only for the views from its plateau but also for the 'mass trespass' of 1932, which helped pave the way for 'right to roam' legislation. Kinder Scout is a challenging walk, accessible from Edale or Hayfield. **Stanage Edge**, a gritstone escarpment or 'edge' approximately 4 miles long, is a natural landmark within the Dark Peak popular for dramatic views over the moorlands. On the border between the Dark Peak and White Peak is the hill known as **Mam Tor**, famous for its beautiful surroundings. The **White Peak** is an area of limestone plateau with steep dales. It is where the national nature reserve **Dovedale**, a limestone valley, can be found. In the Upper Dove Valley are Chrome Hill and Parkhouse peaks, together known as the 'Dragon's Back'. Dovedale is popular with walkers for its steep crags, woodland and wildlife, renowned for its stepping stone crossing over the River Dove. There are several reservoirs within the Peak District, the three largest being **Howden**, **Derwent** and **Ladybower**, which are linked together. Derwent reservoir and dam were used by the RAF for 'bouncing bomb' practice in World War 2. For further places of interest within the Peak District, see individual listings. There are visitor centres in Bakewell, Castleton, Derwent and Edale. 🖥 www.peakdistrict.gov.uk 🖥 www.visitpeakdistrict.com

Renishaw Gardens Italianate gardens surrounding the 17th-century manor house Renishaw Hall, built for the Sitwell family. The gardens were designed in the late 19th century and have been carefully developed since. Among the many features are a picturesque lake, rose gardens, exotic plants and a woodland area. The history of the Sitwell family, and their writing, is displayed in the Sitwell Museum, within the grounds. *Eckington* 🖥 https://renishaw-hall.co.uk/ **59 F2**

Staunton Harold park and reservoir Over 150 acres of countryside around a large reservoir with nature

reserves and walking trails through various habitats. These include woodland and wildflower meadows as well as evidence of industrial activity, including the remains of limestone kilns. Tower Windmill overlooks the reservoir. Watersports and fishing can be arranged and there is a children's playground. *Melbourne* 🖥 www.nationaltrust.org.uk/visit/peak-district-derbyshire/staunton-harold **251 F5**

Towns & villages

Ashbourne Attractive market town on the southern edge of the Peak District with many listed buildings. St Oswald's Church dates from the 12th century and has a strikingly tall, slender spire dating from the early 14th. Also of historical interest are the Old Grammar School, founded in 1586; 17th- and 18th-century almshouses; and many Georgian inns and townhouses, the most impressive of which is known simply as 'the mansion'. The Tissington Trail – a traffic-free walking and cycling route – links Ashbourne to the moorlands and the High Peak Trail. **173 C2**

Bakewell Attractive, historic market town with a 14th-century stone bridge over the River Wye. The largest town within the Peak District National Park, it is famous for Bakewell Pudding, still made to a secret recipe. All Saints Church, dates principally from the 13th and 14th centuries and has an unusual octagonal tower. Nearby is **Bakewell Old House Museum**, housed in a Tudor building that started life as a tax collector's cottage, became a grander house in Elizabethan times, and then mill workers' cottages during the Industrial Revolution. The Old Market Hall houses a tourist information centre and small exhibition. 🖥 www.oldhousemuseum.org.uk **109 C5**

Belper Town on the River Derwent, prominent during the Industrial Revolution as a centre for textile manufacturing. From the 14th to the 18th centuries, Belper was known for ironworking, particularly the manufacture of nails, but this was eclipsed when Jedediah Strutt built one of the world's first water-powered cotton mills here. Of the large complex of mills that developed, North Mill and East Mill remain landmarks within the town and are part of the **Derwent Valley Mills world heritage site**. Also of interest are the 13th-century St John's Chapel, old nail-makers' houses and Belper River Gardens. **179 B3**

Buxton Historic spa town on the River Wye. It grew up around a natural thermal spring known to the Romans as Aquae Arnemetiae. The elegant Georgian Buxton Crescent now houses the **Buxton Crescent Experience**, which tells the story of the thermal baths, and of the building itself. Opposite the Crescent is St Anne's Well, where visitors can sample the warm mineral water. **Buxton Museum and Art Gallery** displays collections relating to the Peak District – its geology, archaeology and art. There are changing exhibitions and family activities. Nearby are the Victorian **Pavilion Gardens,** with a boating lake and playgrounds, and **Buxton Opera House**.

There are events and entertainment in the Octagon Hall. On the edge of the town is **Buxton Country Park** which was created in the early 19th century to screen limestone quarries from visitors to the spa. At the top of the hill is the Victorian folly Solomon's Temple. Within the park are woodland trails with plentiful wildlife and **Poole's Cavern**, an impressive system of limestone caverns. **85 A7**

Castleton Small village in the heart of the Peak District National Park, a popular centre for walkers overlooked by Mam Tor ('shivering mountain'). The village has a long history, with evidence of Celtic settlement on Mam Tor, and lead mining since Roman times. The ruined Norman fortress of **Peveril Castle** has impressive views over the Hope Valley. The village is famous for its caverns. The ornamental blue fluorspar Blue John is mined in **Blue John Cavern** and **Treak Cliff Cavern**. Visitors can tour the impressive caverns and see old mining equipment. **Peak Cavern** differs in that it is almost entirely natural and was inhabited until the early 20th-century by rope makers. **Speedwell Cavern**, an old lead mine, can only be entered by boat, with tunnels leading towards a large underground cavern and lake. Castleton Visitor Centre provides tourist information and houses a small museum and café.

The nearby village of **Edale** is the starting point for the long-distance footpath the **Pennine Way**. **38 C2**

Cromford Village known for its industrial heritage, site of the pioneering industrialist Richard Arkwright's first water-powered cotton mill, built in 1771. Cromford is part of the **Derwent Valley Mills world heritage site**, which aims to preserve the industrial heritage of the region. At **Cromford Mills** visitors can tour the mill complex and learn about Arkwright, Jedediah Strutt and the millworkers. The village itself has fine examples of purpose-built industrial housing.

An attractive walk beside Cromford Canal, starting from Cromford Wharf by the mill, leads to **High Peak Junction Visitor Centre**, where the canal once met the former Cromford and High Peak Railway. The canal can be explored further and is known for its abundant wildlife. **Leawood Pumphouse** nearby was built in 1849 and used steam power to pump water from the River Derwent to the canal. It has been fully restored and can be visited on certain days. The long-distance walking route High Peak Trail begins at the visitor centre.

🖥 www.derwentvalleymills.org **155 A6**

Derby City on the River Derwent, settled by Romans and later Vikings. It came to prominence in the 18th century as a centre of the Industrial Revolution. **Derby Museum of Making** incorporates what remains of Derby's Silk Mill, one of the world's first factories. Its artefacts range widely over all of Derby's manufacturing industries. There are activities and events for all ages. **Derby Museum and Art Gallery** displays an important collection of works by the 19th-century artist Joseph Wright, known as Wright of Derby. There are also extensive displays of locally made ceramics, military and natural history and interesting objects from around the world. There are frequent events. **Pickford's House**, the family home of Georgian architect Joseph Pickford, is a museum of domestic life, with rooms furnished from periods between the 18th and 20th centuries. There is an important collection of toy theatres. All Saints Church became **Derby Cathedral** in 1927. The building is largely neo-Classical in style, but with a strikingly tall Perpendicular Gothic tower, which can be climbed, dating from the early 16th century. Interesting features include the wrought-iron Bakewell Screen, made by iron-worker Robert Bakewell in the 1720s, and the tomb of Bess of Hardwick. **267 C4**

Hathersage Attractive village in the Hope Valley. It is best known for its association with the writer Charlotte Brontë, who used locations from the village in her novel Jane Eyre. The village is also linked to the legends of Robin Hood, with Little John said to be buried in the churchyard of St Michaels and All Angels. Nearby is the gritstone escarpment **Stanage Edge**, popular with walkers and rock climbers. **53 B7**

Wirksworth Market town in the Derbyshire Dales, a former centre of lead mining and stone quarrying also important in the textile trade. **Haarlem Mill**, an imposing building on the edge of the town, was built in 1780 by Richard Arkwright to mill cotton. The parish church of St Mary's dates mainly from the 13th century, but fragments of an older church remain, including an Anglo-Saxon coffin lid dating from 800. The **Wirksworth Heritage Centre** contains a museum of local history, exploring the industries, traditions and people of the area. Outside the town is the **National Stone Centre**, set within six former limestone quarries and known for its interesting geological formations. There is a fossil trail, activities, courses and a play area.
🖥 www.wirksworthheritage.co.uk
🖥 www.nationalstonecentre.org.uk
165 E8

▼ *Hardwick Old Hall*

Buildings

Bolsover Castle Stuart mansion built in the 17th century for pleasure rather than defence, with a spectacular hilltop setting. The castle's state rooms can be made out in the ruins of the grand Terrace Range. The turreted Little Castle is well preserved, with grand marble fireplaces, and richly decorated walls and ceilings. Visitors can enjoy the views from the walls and explore the elegant gardens. There is a Riding School, where horses have been trained in dressage since the 17th century. *Bolsover.* 🖥 www.english-heritage.org.uk **99 A2**

Calke Abbey Manor house built on the site of a former priory in the early 18th century and now preserved as it was in the 1980s – a country house in decline. The decoration is crumbling, but there are interesting wall hangings, taxidermy and other collections, and a colourful walled garden. Within the large surrounding area of parkland are walking and cycling trails, bird hides, a deer park and an area of ancient trees. *Ticknall.*
🖥 www.nationaltrust.org.uk **251 D2**

Chatsworth Imposing manor house dating from the 16th century, when it was owned by Bess of Hardwick, one of the most powerful women in England, but largely rebuilt in the 17th. An important collection of art and sculpture, ranging from ancient Egyptian to the present day is displayed within magnificent state rooms. The house is set in 100 acres of gardens, with rare trees and shrubs, rose and cottage gardens, as well as streams, ponds and fountains. There are special events, activities, and a large area of parkland with walking trails. Chatsworth farmyard and adventure playground are popular with families; there are daily hands-on activities. *Bakewell.* www.chatsworth.org **92 A1**

Hardwick Hall Manor house built in the 16th century in the Italian Renaissance style for Bess of Hardwick. The house was particularly impressive at the time for the large size of its windows. It houses an internationally important collection of 16th- and 17th-century needlework, as well as much of its original decoration. Within the formal gardens are a herb garden and two orchards, and there is a large area of surrounding parkland, with walking routes, woodland and wetland habitats. **Stainsby Mill**, a Victorian water mill, is within Hardwick Estate. *Chesterfield.* 🖥 www.nationaltrust.org. uk **133 E4**

Hardwick Old Hall Ruined 16th-century manor house, home to Bess of Hardwick while the adjacent Hardwick Hall was being built. Although now open to the elements, it is still possible to appre-

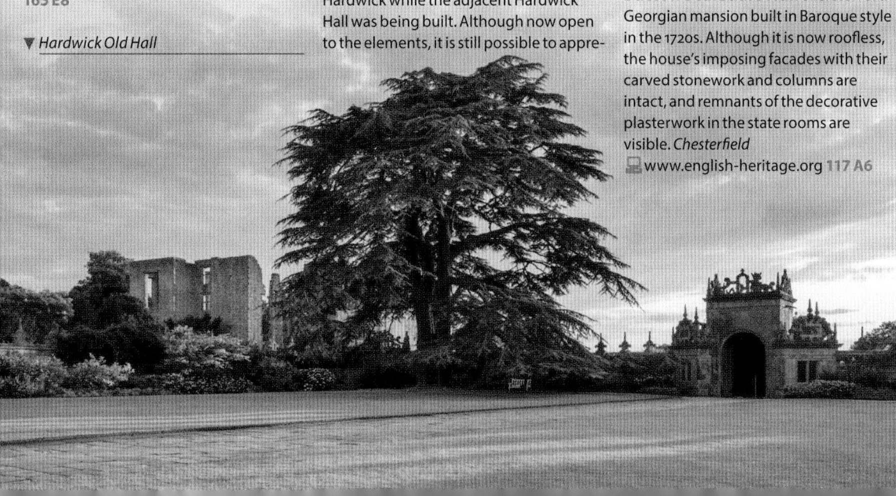
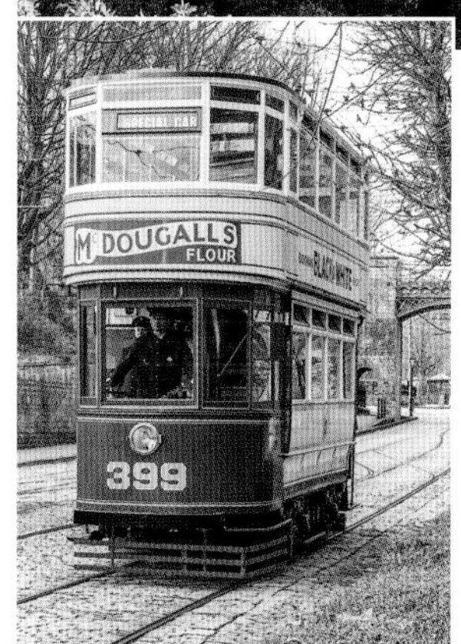

▲ *Bolsover Castle*

◀ *Crich Tramway Village*

ciate the grandeur of the state rooms, and to climb up to the fourth floor for far-reaching views over the countryside and to see the original plaster friezes at close range. *Chesterfield*
🖥 www.english-heritage.org.uk **133 E4**

Heage Windmill Historic windmill, built in 1797 and restored to full working order. Visitors can tour the windmill and learn about its history and the traditional method of milling flour. There is also a display in the windmill's undercroft and a visitor centre where the stoneground flour can be bought. *Belper*
🖥 www.heagewindmill.org.uk **168 D2**

Kedleston Hall Grand country house built in 1765 for the Curzon family, designed for entertaining and showcasing the family's wealth rather than as a home. The impressive state rooms display fine art and furniture, and there is a Museum of Asian Artefacts. The house's architect, Robert Adam, also designed the gardens and parkland. Highlights of the garden include statues, an orangery and hermitage. There are walking routes and an orienteering course in the parkland, a lake and wilderness area. *Derby*
🖥 www.nationaltrust.org.uk **203 E5**

Sutton Scarsdale Hall Skeleton of a Georgian mansion built in Baroque style in the 1720s. Although it is now roofless, the house's imposing facades with their carved stonework and columns are intact, and remnants of the decorative plasterwork in the state rooms are visible. *Chesterfield*
🖥 www.english-heritage.org **117 A6**

Museums & galleries

Crich Tramway Village Museum centred around the National Tramway Museum's collection. The Great Exhibition Hall displays the trams and relates their history, from horse-drawn through to electric. There are further exhibitions in the Stephenson Discovery Centre and elsewhere on site. Outside is a recreated period street, with buildings rescued from around the country. There are tram rides, woodland walks and a sculpture trail. *Matlock* 🖥 www.tramway.co.uk **156 E2**

Great British Car Journey Museum detailing the rise and fall of the British car industry. Nearly 130 cars are on display, from the earliest models of the 1920s to some of the last cars produced when the industry died out in the Midlands in the late 20th century. The interactive exhibition features the British pioneers William Morris and Herbert Austin, as well as cars with unusual stories. *Ambergate*
🖥 https://greatbritishcarjourney.com **167 E5**

Peak District Lead Mining Museum Museum exploring the history of lead mining and the lives of lead-mining families in Derbyshire,. Exhibits range from a large pumping engine and climbing tunnels to mineral specimens. Next to the museum is Temple Mine, where lead and fluorspar was mined in the 1920s. Visitors can see the mine workings and the equipment used, and a 1930s locomotive. *Matlock Bath* 🖥 https:// peakdistrictleadminingmuseum.co.uk **143 A1**

Pleasley Pit Mine and Country Park Coal mine active from 1870 to 1983, now surrounded by a country park. The mine shaft has been filled in, but visitors can see the two headstocks, winding engines, cages and other equipment. The surrounding area is now a nature reserve, with ponds, reed beds, limestone grassland and recently planted woodland. *Mansfield* 🖥 www.pleasleypittrust.org.uk **134 E6**

Sharpe's Pottery Museum Victorian coal-fired 'bottle' kiln (named after its shape rather than its products) and original workshops. Although it also produced functional kitchen ceramics, Sharpe's became best known for its sanitary ware, including products of the family's own design. Visitors can see large displays of vintage ceramics, from here and elsewhere, and learn about their production. *Swadlincote*
🖥 www.sharpespotterymuseum.org.uk **256 B4**

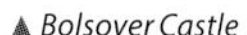

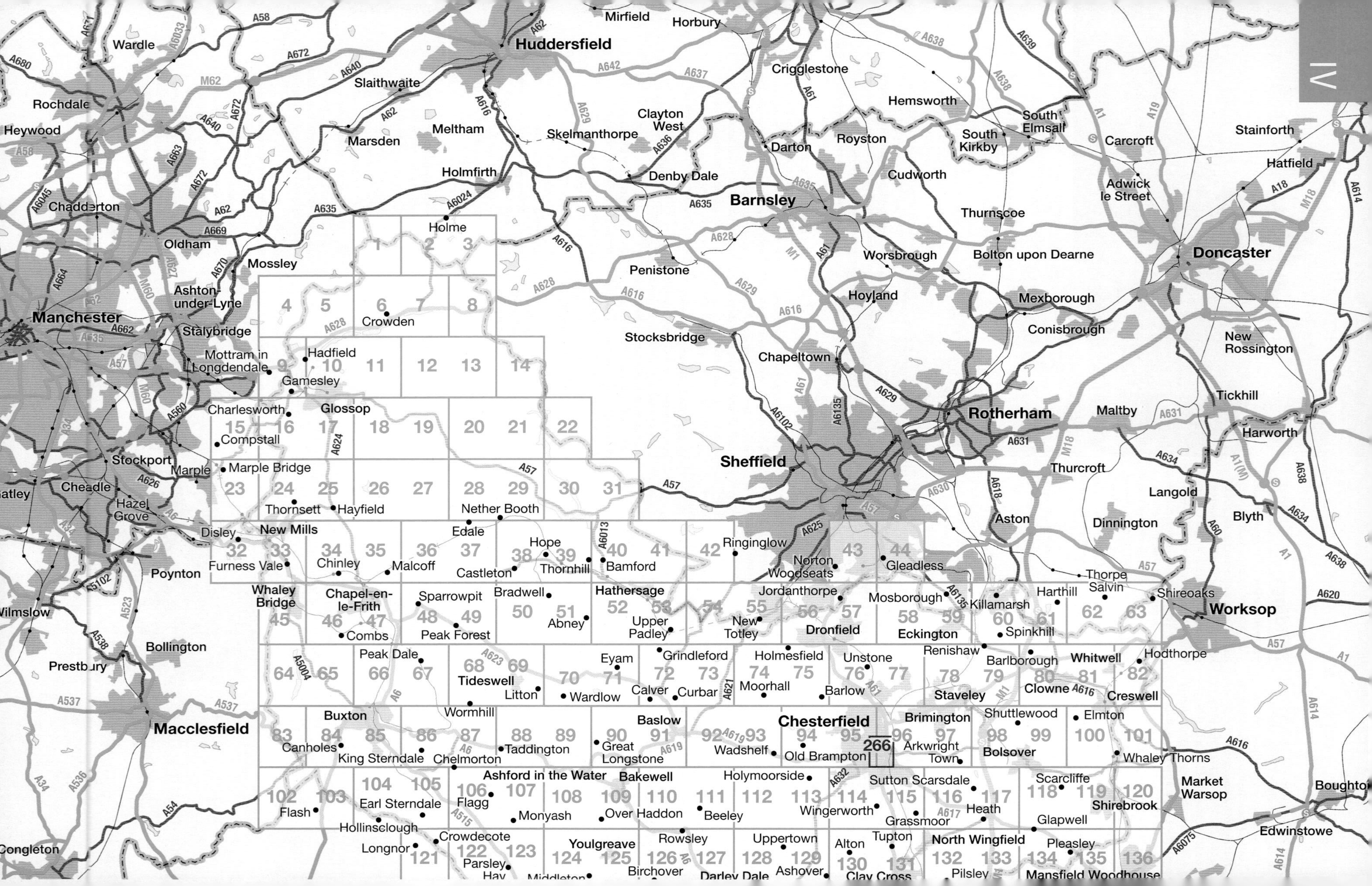
Mirfield
Horbury
Huddersfield
Wardle
Rochdale
Heywood
Slaithwaite
Crigglestone
Hemsworth
South Elmsall
South Kirkby
Carcroft
Stainforth
Hatfield
Meltham
Marsden
Skelmanthorpe
Clayton West
Darton
Royston
Adwick le Street
Holmfirth
Denby Dale
Cudworth
Chadderton
Barnsley
Thurnscoe
Oldham
Holme
Mossley
Penistone
Worsbrough
Bolton upon Dearne
Doncaster
Ashton-under-Lyne
Manchester
Crowden
Hoyland
Mexborough
Stalybridge
Conisbrough
New Rossington
Mottram in Longdendale
Hadfield
Gamesley
Stocksbridge
Chapeltown
Tickhill
Charlesworth
Glossop
Rotherham
Maltby
Harworth
Compstall
Stockport
Marple
Marple Bridge
Sheffield
Thurcroft
Cheadle
Hazel Grove
Thornsett
Hayfield
Nether Booth
Langold
Blyth
Disley
New Mills
Edale
Aston
Dinnington
Hope
Ringinglow
Furness Vale
Chinley
Malcoff
Castleton
Thornhill
Bamford
Norton Woodseats
Gleadless
Thorpe Salvin
Poynton
Whaley Bridge
Chapel-en-le-Frith
Sparrowpit
Bradwell
Hathersage
Jordanthorpe
Mosborough
Killamarsh
Harthill
Shireoaks
Worksop
Wilmslow
Combs
Peak Forest
Abney
Upper Padley
New Totley
Dronfield
Eckington
Spinkhill
Bollington
Peak Dale
Eyam
Grindleford
Holmesfield
Unstone
Renishaw
Barlborough
Whitwell
Hodthorpe
Prestbury
Tideswell
Litton
Wardlow
Calver
Curbar
Moorhall
Barlow
Staveley
Clowne
Creswell
Macclesfield
Buxton
Wormhill
Baslow
Chesterfield
Brimington
Shuttlewood
Elmton
Canholes
King Sterndale
Chelmorton
Taddington
Great Longstone
Wadshelf
Old Brampton
266
Arkwright Town
Bolsover
Whaley Thorns
Ashford in the Water
Bakewell
Holymoorside
Sutton Scarsdale
Scarcliffe
Market Warsop
Boughton
Flash
Earl Sterndale
Flagg
Monyash
Over Haddon
Beeley
Wingerworth
Heath
Grassmoor
Glapwell
Shirebrook
Hollinsclough
Crowdecote
Longnor
Youlgreave
Rowsley
Uppertown
Alton
Tupton
North Wingfield
Pleasley
Edwinstowe
Congleton
Parsley Hay
Birchover
Darley Dale
Ashover
Clay Cross
Pilsley
Mansfield Woodhouse

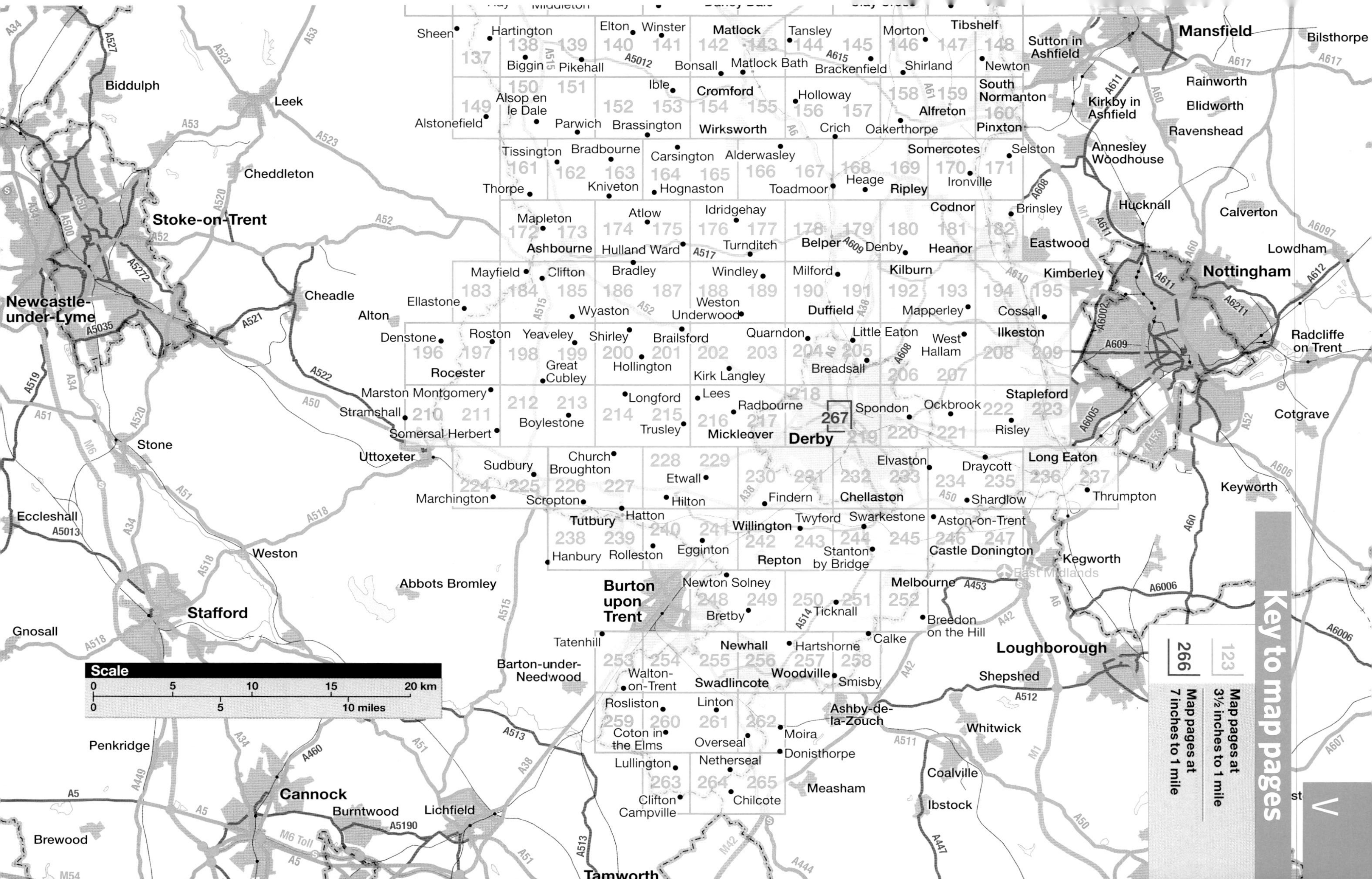

Key to map pages

| 123 | Map pages at 3½ inches to 1 mile |
| 266 | Map pages at 7 inches to 1 mile |

Scale

0   5   10   15   20 km

0   5   10 miles

Route planning

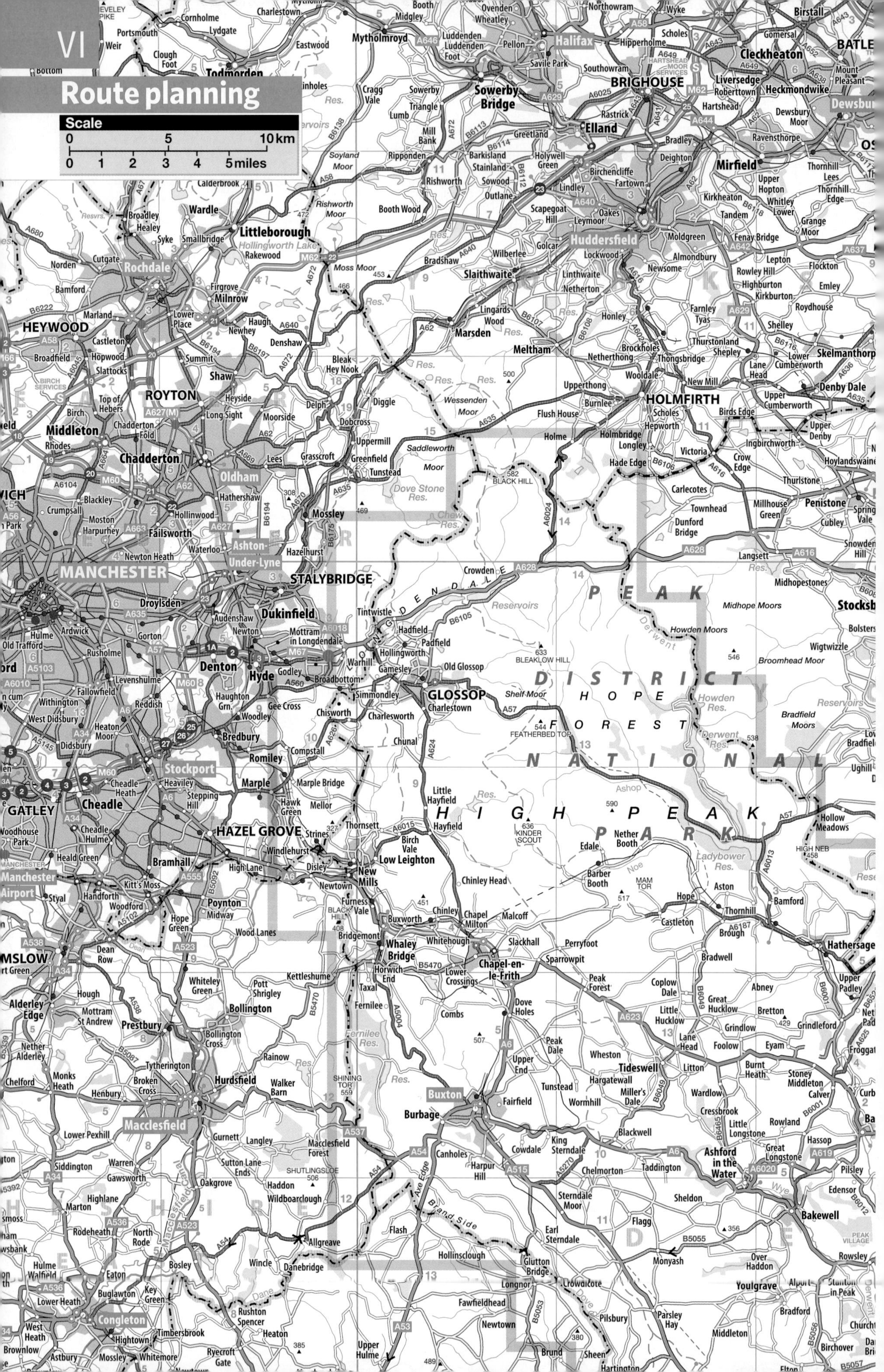
Scale
0
5
10 km
0
1
2
3
4
5 miles
Portsmouth
Weir
Cornholme
Lydgate
Charlestown
Clough Foot
Todmorden
Eastwood
Mytholmroyd
Midgley
Booth
Luddenden
Luddenden Foot
Ovenden
Wheatley
Pellon
Halifax
Savile Park
Northowram
Hipperholme
Wyke
Scholes
Birstall
Gomersal
Cleckheaton
BATLE
Liversedge
Robertown
Heckmondwike
Mount Pleasant
Dewsbu
Southowram
BRIGHOUSE
Rastrick
Elland
Hartshead
Dewsbury Moor
Ravensthorpe
Sowerby
Sowerby Bridge
Triangle
Cragg Vale
Lumb
Mill Bank
Ripponden
Barkisland
Stainland
Greetland
Holywell Green
Birchencliffe
Fartown
Bradley
Deighton
Mirfield
Thornhill
Thornhill Lees
Thornhill Edge
Upper Hopton
Whitley Lower
Kirkheaton
Grange Moor
Tandem
Soyland Moor
Rishworth
Sowood
Outlane
Lindley
Scapegoat Hill
Leymoor
Oakes
Huddersfield
Moldgreen
Fenay Bridge
Almondbury
Lepton
Flockton
Lockwood
Golcar
Wilberlee
Bradshaw
Slaithwaite
Linthwaite
Netherton
Newsome
Rowley Hill
Highburton
Kirkburton
Emley
Roydhouse
Calderbrook
Wardle
Broadley
Healey
Syke
Smallbridge
Littleborough
Hollingworth Lake
Rakewood
Rishworth Moor
Booth Wood
Moss Moor
Norden
Cutgate
Rochdale
Bamford
Firgrove
Milnrow
Lower Place
Newhey
Haugh
Denshaw
Marland
HEYWOOD
Castleton
Hopwood
Broadfield
Slattocks
Summit
Shaw
Bleak Hey Nook
Lingards Wood
Marsden
Meltham
Honley
Farnley Tyas
Brockholes
Thurstonland
Shepley
Shelley
Lower Cumberworth
Skelmanthorp
Netherthong
Thongsbridge
Lane Head
Wooldale
New Mill
Denby Dale
Upperthong
Burnlee
HOLMFIRTH
Upper Cumberworth
Birds Edge
Scholes
Hepworth
Holmbridge
Longley
Flush House
Holme
Wessenden Moor
Upper Denby
Ingbirchworth
Hade Edge
Victoria
Crow Edge
Hoylandswaine
Thurlstone
Top of Hebers
ROYTON
Heyside
Long Sight
Birch
Middleton
Rhodes
Chadderton Fold
Chadderton
Moorside
Delph
Diggle
Dobcross
Uppermill
Grasscroft
Greenfield
Tunstead
Lees
Oldham
Saddleworth Moor
BLACK HILL
Dove Stone Res.
Hathershaw
Hollinwood
Blackley
Crumpsall
Moston
Harpurhey
Failsworth
Mossley
Carlecotes
Townhead
Millhouse Green
Penistone
Dunford Bridge
Cubley
Spring Vale
Newton Heath
Waterloo
Ashton-Under-Lyne
Hazelhurst
Langsett
Snowden Hill
MANCHESTER
STALYBRIDGE
Crowden
LONGDENDALE
Midhopestones
Droylsden
Dukinfield
Tintwistle
PEAK
Midhope Moors
Stocksb
Audenshaw
Newton
Hadfield
Padfield
Reservoirs
Howden Moors
Bolsters
Ardwick
Hulme
Old Trafford
Rusholme
Gorton
Denton
Hyde
Mottram in Longdendale
Hollingworth
BLEAKLOW HILL
Broomhead Moor
Wigtwizzle
Levenshulme
Godley
Warhill
Gamesley
Old Glossop
DISTRICT
Broadbottom
GLOSSOP
Charlestown
Shelf Moor
HOPE
Fallowfield
Withington
Reddish
Haughton Grn.
Gee Cross
Simmondley
Chisworth
Charlesworth
FEATHERBED TOP
FOREST
Howden Res.
Bradfield Moors
Reservoirs
West Didsbury
Heaton Moor
Woodley
Bredbury
Compstall
Chunal
Derwent Res.
Didsbury
Romiley
Stockport
NATIONAL
Cheadle Heath
Heaviley
Marple
Marple Bridge
Stepping Hill
Ashop
Little Hayfield
Mellor
Hawk Green
GATLEY
Cheadle
HIGH
KINDER SCOUT
PEAK
Hollow Meadows
Woodhouse Park
Cheadle Hulme
HAZEL GROVE
Strines
Thornsett
Hayfield
Birch Vale
Nether Booth
Edale
PARK
HIGH NEB
Heald Green
Windlehurst
Bramhall
High Lane
Disley
Low Leighton
New Mills
Ladybower Res.
Manchester Airport
Kitt's Moss
Barber Booth
MAM TOR
Chinley Head
Styal
Handforth
Newtown
Furness Vale
Aston
Woodford
Poynton
Midway
BLACK HILL
Chinley
Chapel Milton
Malcoff
Hope
Bamford
Thornhill
Castleton
Hope Green
Buxworth
Wood Lanes
Bridgemont
Whitehough
Whaley Bridge
Slackhall
Perryfoot
Brough
Hathersage
Dean Row
Sparrowpit
Bradwell
MSLOW
Horwich End
Lower Crossings
Chapel-en-le-Frith
Kettleshume
Peak Forest
Coplow Dale
Abney
Upper Padley
Whiteley Green
Pott Shrigley
Taxal
Hough
Alderley Edge
Mottram St Andrew
Bollington
Fernilee
Combs
Dove Holes
Great Hucklow
Little Hucklow
Bretton
Grindlow
Grindleford
Prestbury
Fernilee Res.
Bollington Cross
Nether Alderley
Rainow
Peak Dale
Wheston
Lane Head
Foolow
Eyam
Froggat
Upper End
Tytherington
Tideswell
Litton
Burnt Heath
Stoney Middleton
Chelford
Monks Heath
Broken Cross
Hurdsfield
Walker Barn
SHINING TOR
Hargatewall
Tunstead
Miller's Dale
Calver
Henbury
Buxton
Fairfield
Wormhill
Wardlow
Macclesfield
Burbage
Cressbrook
Little Longstone
Rowland
Lower Pexhill
Gurnett
Langley
Macclesfield Forest
Blackwell
King Sterndale
Cowdale
Hassop
Great Longstone
Warren
Siddington
Gawsworth
Sutton Lane Ends
Canholes
Harpur Hill
Chelmorton
Taddington
Ashford in the Water
Pilsley
SHUTLINGSLOE
Oakgrove
Haddon
Edensor
Highlane
Marton
Wildboarclough
Axe Edge
Sterndale Moor
Sheldon
Bakewell
Rodeheath
North Rode
Brand Side
Flash
Earl Sterndale
Flagg
Allgreave
Hollinsclough
Monyash
Rowsley
Hulme Walfield
Eaton
Bosley
Wincle
Danebridge
Glutton Bridge
Over Haddon
Lower Heath
Buglawton
Key Green
Longnor
Crowdicote
Youlgrave
Alport
Stanton in Peak
Congleton
Rushton Spencer
Fawfieldhead
Parsley Hay
Bradford
West Heath
Timbersbrook
Heaton
Pilsbury
Newtown
Middleton
Hightown
Brownlow
Astbury
Mossley
Whitemore
Ryecroft Gate
Upper Hulme
Brund
Sheen
Hartington
Birchover

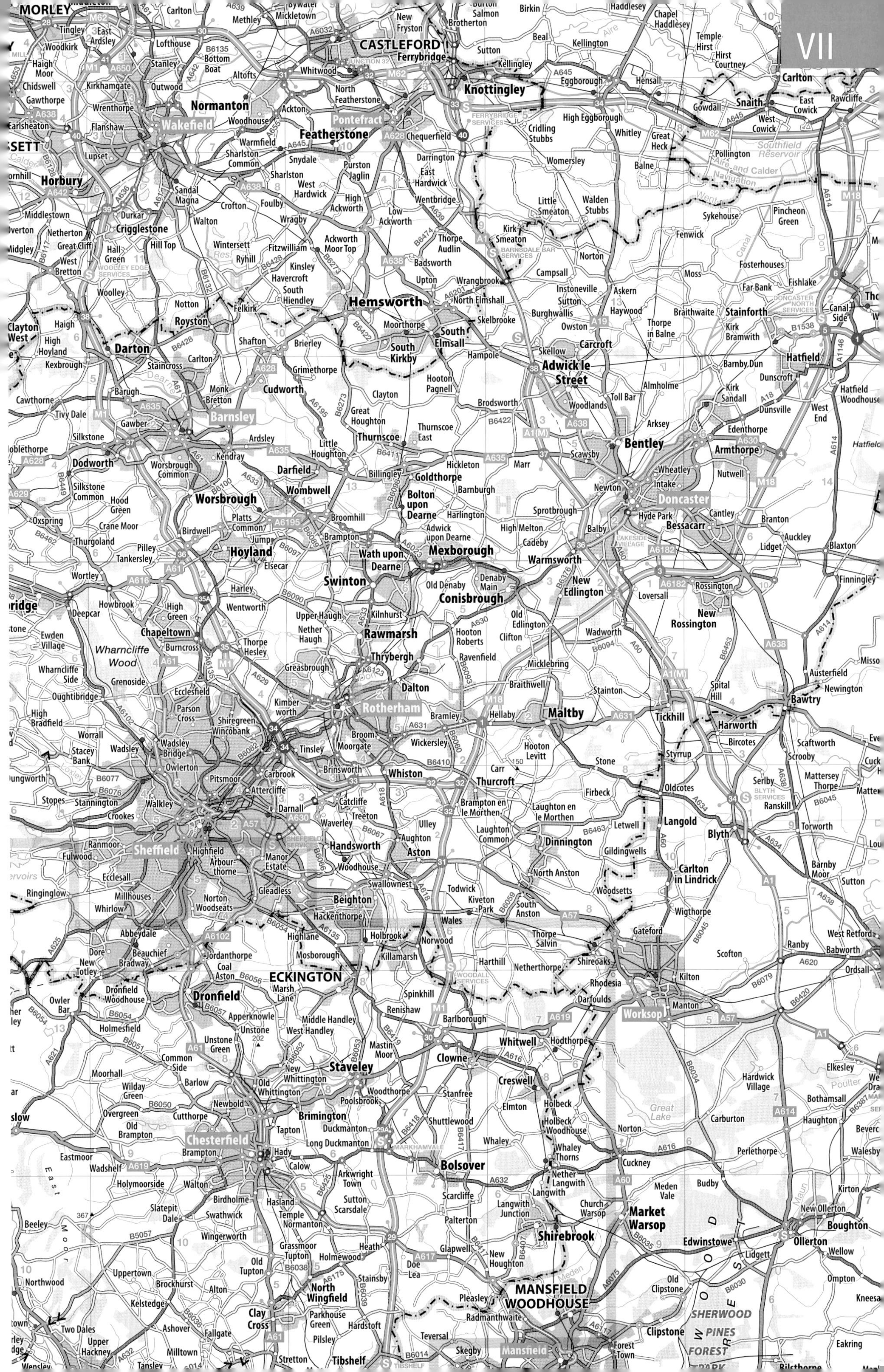
VII
MORLEY
Tingley
East Ardsley
Woodkirk
Haigh Moor
Chidswell
Kirkhamgate
Gawthorpe
Earlsheaton
Wrenthorpe
Flanshaw
Wakefield
Lupset
Horbury
Lofthouse
Stanley
Outwood
Carlton
Methley
Mickletown
Bywater
Normanton
Altofts
Bottom Boat
Woodhouse
Warmfield
Sharlston Common
Sharlston
Sandal Magna
Crofton
Foulby
Featherstone
North Featherstone
Ackton
Whitwood
Castleford
Ferrybridge
Junction 32
Pontefract
Chequerfield
New Fryston
Brotherton
Burton Salmon
Birkin
Knottingley
Kellingley
Sutton
Beal
Kellington
Eggborough
High Eggborough
Ferrybridge Services
Cridling Stubbs
Whitley
Great Heck
Hensall
Temple Hirst
Hirst Courtney
Chapel Haddlesey
Haddlesey
Aire
Gowdall
Snaith
Carlton
East Cowick
West Cowick
Rawcliffe
Pollington
Southfield Reservoir
Balne
Aire and Calder Navigation
Womersley
Darrington
East Hardwick
Wentbridge
Purston Jaglin
Snydale
West Hardwick
High Ackworth
Low Ackworth
Little Smeaton
Walden Stubbs
Kirk Smeaton
Barnsdale Bar Services
Thorpe Audlin
Norton
Sykehouse
Pincheon Green
Fenwick
Fosterhouses
Moss
Fishlake
Far Bank
Stainforth
Doncaster North Services
Canal Side
Thorne
Middlestown
Netherton
Overton
Midgley
Great Cliff
Crigglestone
Durkar
Walton
Hall Green
West Bretton
Woolley Edge Services
Hill Top
Wintersett Res
Ryhill
Fitzwilliam
Ackworth Moor Top
Wragby
Kinsley
Havercroft
South Hiendley
Badsworth
Upton
Wrangbrook
North Elmshall
Campsall
Instoneville
Sutton
Askern
Haywood
Burghwallis
Owston
Thorpe in Balne
Braithwaite
Kirk Bramwith
Hatfield
Woolley
Notton
Royston
Felkirk
Hemsworth
Moorthorpe
South Elmsall
Skelbrooke
Skellow
Carcroft
Adwick le Street
Barnby Dun
Dunscroft
Clayton West
High Hoyland
Haigh
Darton
Kexbrough
Staincross
Carlton
Shafton
Brierley
Grimethorpe
South Kirkby
Hampole
Hooton Pagnell
Almholme
Kirk Sandall
Hatfield Woodhouse
Cawthorne
Barugh
Monk Bretton
Cudworth
Tivy Dale
Gawber
Barnsley
Clayton
Great Houghton
Brodsworth
Woodlands
Toll Bar
Arksey
Dunsville
Edenthorpe
West End
Silkstone
Noblethorpe
Dodworth
Ardsley
Kendray
Worsbrough Common
Darfield
Little Houghton
Thurnscoe
Thurnscoe East
Billingley
Hickleton
Goldthorpe
Marr
Scawsby
Bentley
Armthorpe
Wheatley
Intake
Nutwell
Doncaster
Newton
Hatfield
Silkstone Common
Hood Green
Worsbrough
Wombwell
Bolton upon Dearne
Barnburgh
Harlington
Sprotbrough
Hyde Park
Bessacarr
Cantley
Branton
Oxspring
Crane Moor
Birdwell
Platts Common
Broomhill
Adwick upon Dearne
High Melton
Cadeby
Balby
Lakeside Village
Auckley
Blaxton
Thurgoland
Pilley
Tankersley
Jump
Hoyland
Elsecar
Brampton
Wath upon Dearne
Mexborough
Warmsworth
Lidget
Wortley
Harley
Swinton
Old Denaby
Denaby Main
Conisbrough
New Edlington
Loversall
Rossington
Finningley
Deepcar
Howbrook
High Green
Wentworth
Upper Haugh
Kilnhurst
Old Edlington
New Rossington
Ewden Village
Chapeltown
Burncross
Thorpe Hesley
Nether Haugh
Rawmarsh
Hooton Roberts
Clifton
Wadworth
Wharncliffe Wood
Wharncliffe Side
Thrybergh
Ravenfield
Micklebring
Greasbrough
Dalton
Braithwell
Stainton
Austerfield
Newington
Grenoside
Oughtibridge
Ecclesfield
Parson Cross
Kimberworth
Rotherham
Bramley
Hellaby
Maltby
Tickhill
Spital Hill
Bawtry
High Bradfield
Shiregreen
Wincobank
Worrall
Wadsley
Wadsley Bridge
Stacey Bank
Tinsley
Broom
Moorgate
Wickersley
Hooton Levitt
Harworth
Bircotes
Scaftworth
Styrrup
Scrooby
Owlerton
Carbrook
Brinsworth
Whiston
Carr
Thurcroft
Stone
Firbeck
Oldcotes
Serlby
Mattersey Thorpe
Blyth Services
Ranskill
Dungworth
Pitsmoor
Attercliffe
Catcliffe
Brampton en le Morthen
Laughton en le Morthen
Langold
Blyth
Torworth
Stopes
Stannington
Walkley
Crookes
Darnall
Treeton
Waverley
Ulley
Laughton Common
Letwell
Dinnington
Gildingwells
Carlton in Lindrick
Barnby Moor
Sutton
Ranmoor
Sheffield
Highfield
Sheffield Services
Handsworth
Aughton
Aston
Fulwood
Ecclesall
Arbourthorne
Manor Estate
Woodhouse
North Anston
Woodsetts
Wigthorpe
Ringinglow
Millhouses
Norton Woodseats
Gleadless
Swallownest
Beighton
Todwick
Kiveton Park
South Anston
Whirlow
Hackenthorpe
Wales
Thorpe Salvin
Gateford
West Retford
Abbeydale
Dore
Beauchief
Bradway
Highlane
Holbrook
Norwood
Harthill
Netherthorpe
Shireoaks
Ranby
Babworth
Scofton
Ordsall
New Totley
Jordanthorpe
Coal Aston
Mosborough
Killamarsh
Woodall Services
Rhodesia
Kilton
Dronfield Woodhouse
Dronfield
Eckington
Marsh Lane
Spinkhill
Renishaw
Darfoulds
Worksop
Manton
Owler Bar
Holmesfield
Apperknowle
Unstone
Middle Handley
West Handley
Barlborough
Whitwell
Hodthorpe
Unstone Green
Common Side
Mastin Moor
Clowne
Creswell
Hardwick Village
Elkesley
Moorhall
Barlow
New Whittington
Old Whittington
Staveley
Woodthorpe
Stanfree
Elmton
Holbeck
Holbeck Woodhouse
Great Lake
Bothamsall
Haughton
Wilday Green
Newbold
Poolsbrook
Brimington
Shuttlewood
Carburton
Overgreen
Cutthorpe
Old Brampton
Chesterfield
Tapton
Duckmanton
Long Duckmanton
Markham Vale
Whaley
Whaley Thorns
Norton
Perlethorpe
Eastmoor
Brampton
Hady
Calow
Arkwright Town
Bolsover
Cuckney
Wadshelf
Holymoorside
Walton
Nether Langwith
Langwith
Meden Vale
Budby
Kirton
Birdholme
Hasland
Sutton Scarsdale
Scarcliffe
Langwith Junction
Church Warsop
Market Warsop
New Ollerton
Boughton
Slatepit Dale
Swathwick
Temple Normanton
Palterton
Shirebrook
Edwinstowe
Ollerton
Beeley
Wingerworth
Grassmoor
Tupton
Heath
Glapwell
New Houghton
Wellow
Holmewood
Doe Lea
Lidgett
Old Tupton
Uppertown
Northwood
Brockhurst
Stainsby
North Wingfield
Mansfield Woodhouse
Old Clipstone
Ompton
Alton
Kelstedge
Clay Cross
Parkhouse Green
Hardstoft
Pleasley
Radmanthwaite
Sherwood Pines Forest Park
Clipstone
Forest Town
Kneesall
Two Dales
Ashover
Fallgate
Upper Hackney
Milltown
Pilsley
Teversal
Skegby
Mansfield
Eakring
Wensley
Tansley
Stretton
Tibshelf
Tibshelf Services
Bilsthorpe
Sherwood Forest
East Moor
Meden
Maun
Poulter
Don
Dearne
Went
Canal

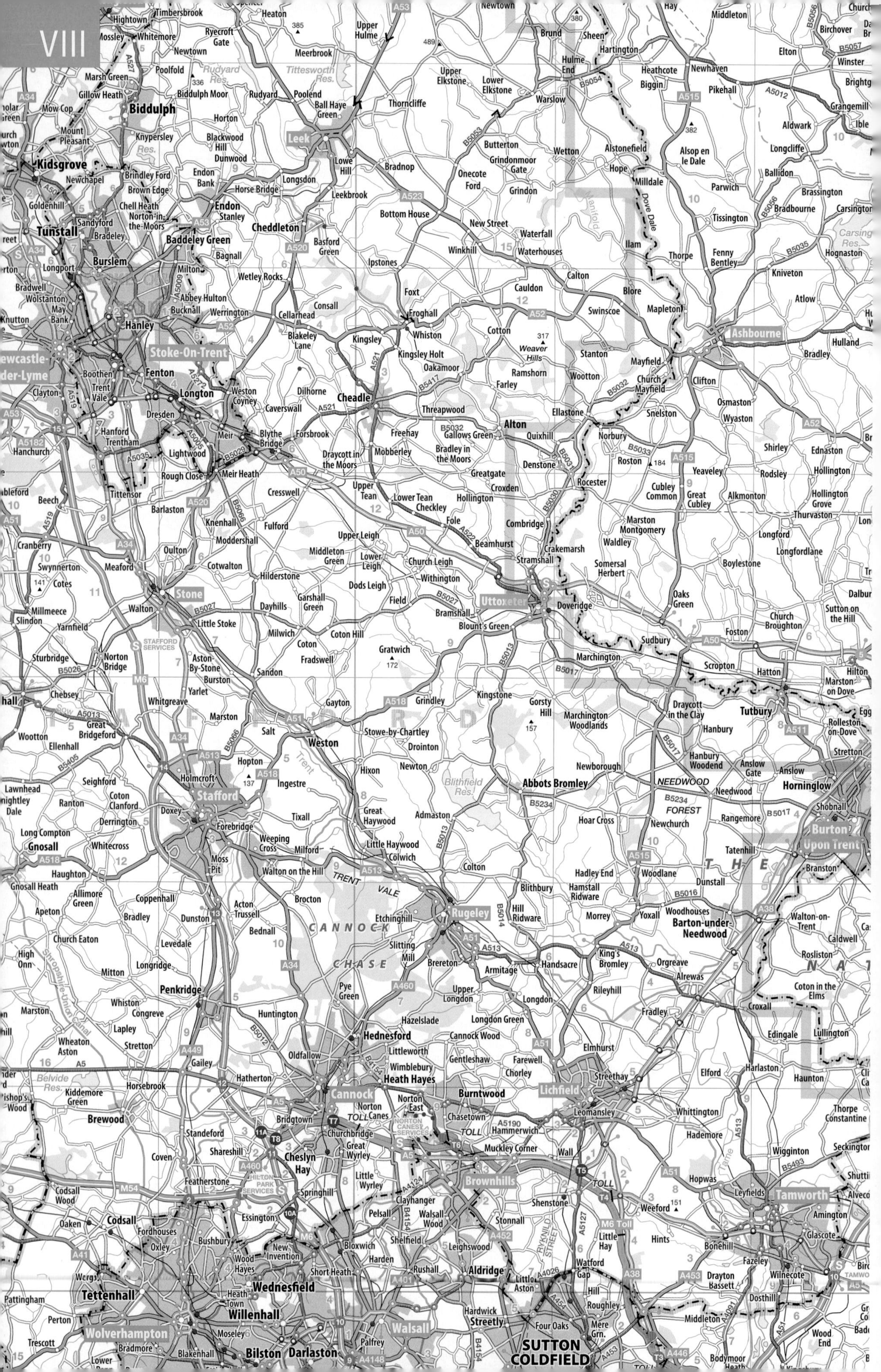
Hightown
Timbersbrook
Heaton
Upper Hulme
Newtown
Brund
Sheen
Hartington
Middleton
Birchover
Elton
Winster
Mossley
Whitemore
Ryecroft Gate
Meerbrook
Newtown
Poolfold
Rudyard Res.
Tittesworth Res.
Upper Elkstone
Lower Elkstone
Hulme End
Heathcote
Biggin
Newhaven
Pikehall
Marsh Green
Gillow Heath
Biddulph Moor
Rudyard
Poolend
Ball Haye Green
Thorncliffe
Warslow
Grangemill
Mow Cop
Biddulph
Horton
Aldwark
Mount Pleasant
Knypersley
Blackwood Hill
Leek
Lowe Hill
Butterton
Grindonmoor Gate
Wetton
Alstonefield
Alsop en le Dale
Longcliffe
Dunwood
Kidsgrove
Brindley Ford
Endon Bank
Bradnop
Onecote
Ford
Hope
Ballidon
Newchapel
Brown Edge
Horse Bridge
Longsdon
Grindon
Milldale
Parwich
Brassington
Goldenhill
Chell Heath
Norton-in-the-Moors
Endon
Stanley
Leekbrook
Bottom House
Dove Dale
Bradbourne
Carsington
Sandyford
Tunstall
Bradeley
Baddeley Green
Cheddleton
New Street
Waterfall
Tissington
Basford Green
Winkhill
Waterhouses
Ilam
Thorpe
Fenny Bentley
Hognaston
Burslem
Bagnall
Ipstones
Longport
Milton
Wetley Rocks
Calton
Kniveton
Bradwell
Wolstanton
Abbey Hulton
Foxt
Cauldon
Blore
Atlow
May Bank
Bucknall
Werrington
Consall
Cellarhead
Froghall
Swinscoe
Mapleton
Knutton
Hanley
Blakeley Lane
Kingsley
Whiston
Cotton
Weaver Hills
Ashbourne
Hulland
Newcastle-under-Lyme
Stoke-On-Trent
Kingsley Holt
Oakamoor
Stanton
Ramshorn
Mayfield
Bradley
Fenton
Boothen
Trent Vale
Dilhorne
Farley
Wootton
Church Mayfield
Clifton
Clayton
Longton
Weston Coyney
Caverswall
Cheadle
Threapwood
Ellastone
Snelston
Osmaston
Wyaston
Dresden
Meir
Blythe Bridge
Forsbrook
Freehay
Gallows Green
Alton
Quixhill
Norbury
Hanchurch
Hanford
Trentham
Lightwood
Draycott in the Moors
Mobberley
Bradley in the Moors
Denstone
Roston
Shirley
Ednaston
Yeaveley
Rodsley
Hollington
Rough Close
Meir Heath
Greatgate
Croxden
Rocester
Cubley Common
Great Cubley
Alkmonton
Hollington Grove
Tittensor
Cresswell
Upper Tean
Lower Tean
Checkley
Hollington
Beech
Barlaston
Thurvaston
Fole
Combridge
Marston Montgomery
Longford
Knenhall
Fulford
Waldley
Cranberry
Moddershall
Upper Leigh
Beamhurst
Crakemarsh
Longfordlane
Swynnerton
Oulton
Middleton Green
Lower Leigh
Church Leigh
Stramshall
Somersal Herbert
Boylestone
Meaford
Cotwalton
Hilderstone
Withington
Cotes
Stone
Garshall Green
Dods Leigh
Field
Uttoxeter
Doveridge
Oaks Green
Dalbury
Millmeece
Slindon
Walton
Dayhills
Bramshall
Sutton on the Hill
Church Broughton
Yarnfield
Little Stoke
Milwich
Coton Hill
Blount's Green
Stafford Services
Coton
Gratwich
Sudbury
Foston
Sturbridge
Norton Bridge
Aston-By-Stone
Fradswell
Marchington
Scropton
Hatton
Hilton
Burston
Sandon
Marston on Dove
Chebsey
Yarlet
Whitgreave
Gayton
Grindley
Kingstone
Gorsty Hill
Draycott in the Clay
Tutbury
Marston
Marchington Woodlands
Great Bridgeford
Salt
Weston
Stowe-by-Chartley
Drointon
Hanbury
Rolleston-on-Dove
Wootton
Ellenhall
Stretton
Hopton
Trent
Hixon
Newton
Hanbury Woodend
Anslow Gate
Anslow
Holmcroft
Ingestre
Blithfield Res.
Newborough
Needwood
Horninglow
Seighford
Stafford
Abbots Bromley
Lawnhead
Ranton
Coton Clanford
Tixall
Great Haywood
Admaston
Forest
Shobnall
Derrington
Doxey
Forebridge
Hoar Cross
Newchurch
Rangemore
Burton Upon Trent
Long Compton
Weeping Cross
Milford
Little Haywood
Colwich
Tatenhill
Gnosall
Whitecross
Moss Pit
Walton on the Hill
Trent Vale
Colton
Woodlane
Dunstall
Branston
Haughton
Hadley End
Hamstall Ridware
Gnosall Heath
Allimore Green
Coppenhall
Brocton
Blithbury
Apeton
Acton Trussell
Etchinghill
Rugeley
Hill Ridware
Morrey
Yoxall
Woodhouses
Barton-under-Needwood
Walton-on-Trent
Bradley
Dunston
Cannock
Church Eaton
Bednall
Levedale
Slitting Mill
Brereton
Handsacre
King's Bromley
Orgreave
Rosliston
High Onn
Longridge
Chase
Armitage
Alrewas
Coton in the Elms
Mitton
Penkridge
Pye Green
Upper Longdon
Longdon
Rileyhill
Whiston
Congreve
Huntington
Hazelslade
Longdon Green
Fradley
Croxall
Marston
Lapley
Edingale
Lullington
Wheaton Aston
Stretton
Hednesford
Cannock Wood
Elmhurst
Shropshire Union Canal
Gailey
Littleworth
Gentleshaw
Farewell
Oldfallow
Wimblebury
Chorley
Harlaston
Belvide Res.
Hatherton
Heath Hayes
Burntwood
Streethay
Elford
Haunton
Kiddemore Green
Horsebrook
Lichfield
Norton East
Chasetown
Leomansley
Whittington
Thorpe Constantine
Brewood
Bridgtown
Norton Canes
Norton Canes Services
Toll
Hammerwich
Standeford
Churchbridge
Hademore
Shareshill
Great Wyrley
Muckley Corner
Wall
Wigginton
Seckington
Coven
Cheslyn Hay
Brownhills
Hopwas
Featherstone
Hilton Park Services
Little Wyrley
Leyfields
Tamworth
Codsall Wood
Springhill
Shenstone
Weeford
Alvecote
Oaken
Codsall
Essington
Clayhanger
Pelsall
Walsall Wood
Stonnall
Amington
Fordhouses
Bushbury
Oxley
New Invention
Shelfield
Bloxwich
Little Hay
Hints
Bonehill
Glascote
Wood Hayes
Leighswood
Ryknild Street
Fazeley
Wergs
Harden
Short Heath
Rushall
Aldridge
Watford Gap
Drayton Bassett
Wilnecote
Pattingham
Tettenhall
Wednesfield
Heath Town
Little Aston
Hill
Roughley
Dosthill
Perton
Willenhall
Hardwick
Streetly
Middleton
Wolverhampton
Walsall
Four Oaks
Mere Grn.
Trescott
Moseley
Bradmore
Blakenhall
Bilston
Darlaston
Palfrey
Sutton Coldfield
Wood End
Bodymoor Heath
Lower

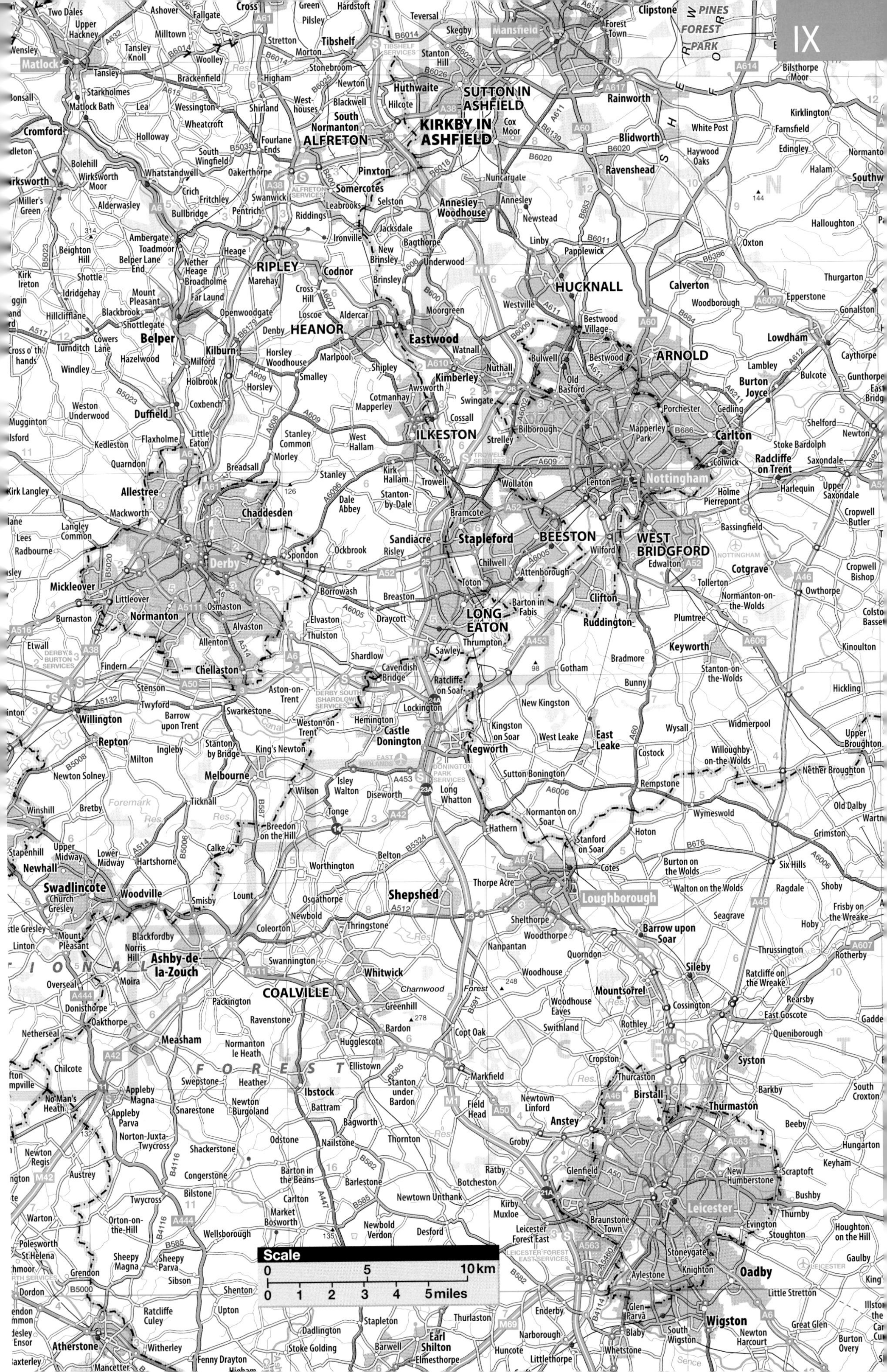
Two Dales
Upper Hackney
Ashover
Fallgate
Cross
Green
Pilsley
Hardstoft
Teversal
Skegby
Mansfield
Forest Town
Clipstone
PINES FOREST PARK
Matlock
Tansley Knoll
Tansley
Milltown
Woolley
Stretton
Tibshelf
Morton
Stonebroom
TIBSHELF SERVICES
Stanton Hill
Brackenfield
Higham
Newton
Huthwaite
SUTTON IN ASHFIELD
Rainworth
Bilsthorpe Moor
Bonsall
Starkholmes
Matlock Bath
Lea
Wessington
Shirland
West-houses
Blackwell
Hilcote
South Normanton
KIRKBY IN ASHFIELD
Cox Moor
Kirklington
Farnsfield
Cromford
Holloway
Wheatcroft
Fourlane Ends
ALFRETON
Blidworth
White Post
Edingley
South Wingfield
Haywood Oaks
Normanton
Bolehill
Wirksworth Moor
Whatstandwell
Oakerthorpe
Pinxton
Ravenshead
Halam
Southwell
Wirksworth
Crich
Fritchley
Swanwick
ALFRETON SERVICES
Somercotes
Nuncargate
Miller's Green
Alderwasley
Bullbridge
Pentrich
Riddings
Leabrooks
Selston
Annesley Woodhouse
Annesley
Newstead
Halloughton
Ambergate
Toadmoor
Ironville
Jacksdale
Bagthorpe
Linby
Papplewick
Oxton
Beighton Hill
Belper Lane End
Heage
Nether Heage
Broadholme
RIPLEY
Codnor
New Brinsley
Underwood
Kirk Ireton
Shottle
Marehay
Cross Hill
Brinsley
HUCKNALL
Calverton
Thurgarton
Idridgehay
Mount Pleasant
Far Laund
Woodborough
Epperstone
Blackbrook
Openwoodgate
Loscoe
Aldercar
Moorgreen
Westville
Gonalston
Hillcliffiane
Shottlegate
Bestwood Village
Cowers Lane
Belper
Denby
HEANOR
Eastwood
Lowdham
Turnditch
Kilburn
Horsley Woodhouse
Marlpool
Watnall
Bestwood
ARNOLD
Caythorpe
Cross o' th' hands
Hazelwood
Milford
Shipley
Nuthall
Bulwell
Lambley
Gunthorpe
Windley
Holbrook
Horsley
Smalley
Kimberley
Old Basford
Burton Joyce
Bulcote
Awsworth
Cotmanhay
Mapperley
Swingate
Porchester
Gedling
Weston Underwood
Duffield
Coxbench
Cossall
Bilborough
Mugginton
Little Eaton
Flaxholme
Stanley Common
West Hallam
ILKESTON
Strelley
Mapperley Park
Carlton
Shelford
Newton
Kedleston
Morley
TROWELL SERVICES
Stoke Bardolph
Quarndon
Breadsall
Stanley
Kirk Hallam
Trowell
Wollaton
Lenton
Nottingham
Colwick
Radcliffe on Trent
Saxondale
Kirk Langley
Allestree
Harlequin
Upper Saxondale
Holme Pierrepont
Mackworth
Chaddesden
Dale Abbey
Stanton-by-Dale
Bramcote
Cropwell Butler
Langley Common
Bassingfield
Lees
Sandiacre
Stapleford
BEESTON
WEST BRIDGFORD
Radbourne
Derby
Spondon
Ockbrook
Risley
Chilwell
Wilford
NOTTINGHAM
Cotgrave
Cropwell Bishop
Attenborough
Edwalton
Mickleover
Borrowash
Toton
Tollerton
Owthorpe
Littleover
Osmaston
Breaston
LONG EATON
Barton in Fabis
Clifton
Normanton-on-the-Wolds
Colston Bassett
Burnaston
Normanton
Alvaston
Elvaston
Draycott
Ruddington
Plumtree
Thulston
Thrumpton
Etwall
DERBY & BURTON SERVICES
Allenton
Shardlow
Sawley
Keyworth
Kinoulton
Findern
Chellaston
Cavendish Bridge
Gotham
Bradmore
Stanton-on-the-Wolds
Stenson
Aston-on-Trent
Ratcliffe on Soar
Bunny
Hickling
Twyford
DERBY SOUTH (SHARDLOW) SERVICES
Lockington
New Kingston
Willington
Barrow upon Trent
Swarkestone
Weston-on-Trent
Hemington
Kingston on Soar
West Leake
East Leake
Wysall
Widmerpool
Upper Broughton
Repton
Stanton by Bridge
Ingleby
King's Newton
Castle Donington
Kegworth
Costock
Willoughby-on-the-Wolds
Milton
EAST MIDLANDS
DONINGTON PARK SERVICES
Sutton Bonington
Nether Broughton
Newton Solney
Melbourne
Isley Walton
Rempstone
Foremark
Wilson
Diseworth
Long Whatton
Bretby
Ticknall
Old Dalby
Winshill
Tonge
Normanton on Soar
Wymeswold
Breedon on the Hill
Hathern
Hoton
Grimston
Stapenhill
Upper Midway
Lower Midway
Calke
Stanford on Soar
Newhall
Hartshorne
Worthington
Belton
Burton on the Wolds
Six Hills
Thorpe Acre
Cotes
Swadlincote
Church Gresley
Woodville
Shepshed
Loughborough
Walton on the Wolds
Ragdale
Shoby
Smisby
Lount
Osgathorpe
Frisby on the Wreake
Newbold
Shelthorpe
Barrow upon Soar
Hoby
Castle Gresley
Mount Pleasant
Blackfordby
Coleorton
Thringstone
Seagrave
Linton
Norris Hill
Ashby-de-la-Zouch
Nanpantan
Woodthorpe
Thrussington
Rotherby
Swannington
Quorndon
Sileby
Overseal
Moira
Whitwick
Woodhouse
Ratcliffe on the Wreake
COALVILLE
Charnwood
Forest
Mountsorrel
Donisthorpe
Packington
Greenhill
Woodhouse Eaves
Cossington
Rearsby
Oakthorpe
Ravenstone
East Goscote
Gaddesby
Netherseal
Measham
Bardon
Swithland
Rothley
Queniborough
Normanton le Heath
Hugglescote
Copt Oak
Chilcote
FOREST
Ellistown
Cropston
Syston
Markfield
Thurcaston
Appleby Magna
Swepstone
Heather
Stanton under Bardon
Barkby
South Croxton
No Man's Heath
Ibstock
Birstall
Newton Burgoland
Field Head
Newtown Linford
Appleby Parva
Snarestone
Battram
Thurmaston
Beeby
Anstey
Norton-Juxta-Twycross
Bagworth
Thornton
Groby
Hungarton
Newton Regis
Shackerstone
Odstone
Nailstone
Austrey
Congerstone
Barton in the Beans
Barlestone
Ratby
Glenfield
Scraptoft
Keyham
New Humberstone
Bilstone
Botcheston
Twycross
Carlton
Newtown Unthank
Bushby
Warton
Orton-on-the-Hill
Market Bosworth
Kirby Muxloe
Leicester
Thurnby
Wellsborough
Braunstone Town
Evington
Houghton on the Hill
Polesworth
St Helena
Newbold Verdon
Desford
Leicester Forest East
Stoughton
Sheepy Magna
Sheepy Parva
LEICESTER FOREST EAST SERVICES
Stoneygate
Gaulby
Grendon
Sibson
Aylestone
Knighton
Oadby
LEICESTER
Dordon
Shenton
King's Norton
Little Stretton
Upton
Thurlaston
Enderby
Glen Parva
Wigston
Illston on the Hill
Ratcliffe Culey
Stapleton
Great Glen
Dadlington
Earl Shilton
Narborough
Blaby
South Wigston
Newton Harcourt
Burton Overy
Atherstone
Witherley
Stoke Golding
Barwell
Huncote
Whetstone
Mancetter
Fenny Drayton
Elmesthorpe
Littlethorpe
Sence
Scale
0 5 10 km
0 1 2 3 4 5 miles

Key to map symbols

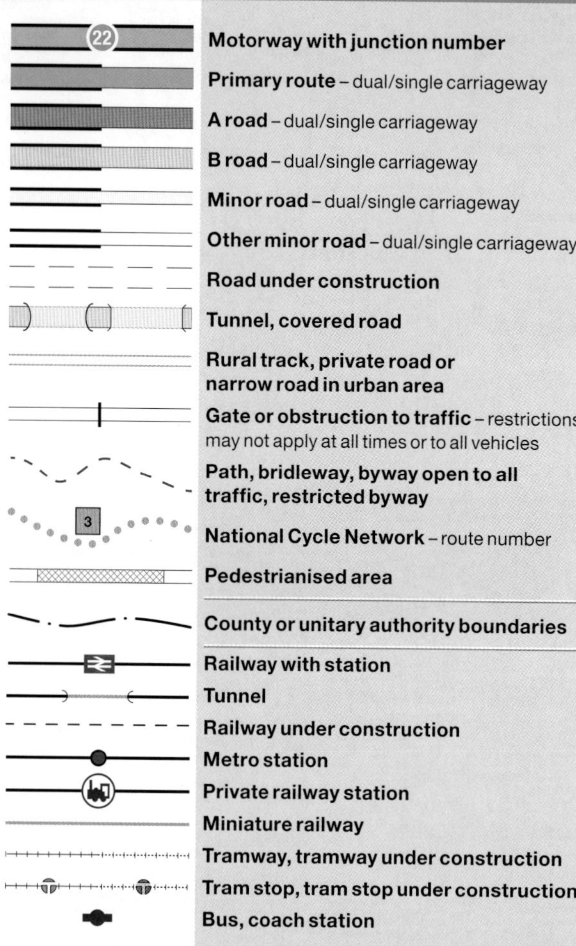

	Motorway with junction number
	Primary route – dual/single carriageway
	A road – dual/single carriageway
	B road – dual/single carriageway
	Minor road – dual/single carriageway
	Other minor road – dual/single carriageway
	Road under construction
	Tunnel, covered road
	Rural track, private road or narrow road in urban area
	Gate or obstruction to traffic – restrictions may not apply at all times or to all vehicles
	Path, bridleway, byway open to all traffic, restricted byway
	National Cycle Network – route number
	Pedestrianised area
	County or unitary authority boundaries
	Railway with station
	Tunnel
	Railway under construction
	Metro station
	Private railway station
	Miniature railway
	Tramway, tramway under construction
	Tram stop, tram stop under construction
	Bus, coach station

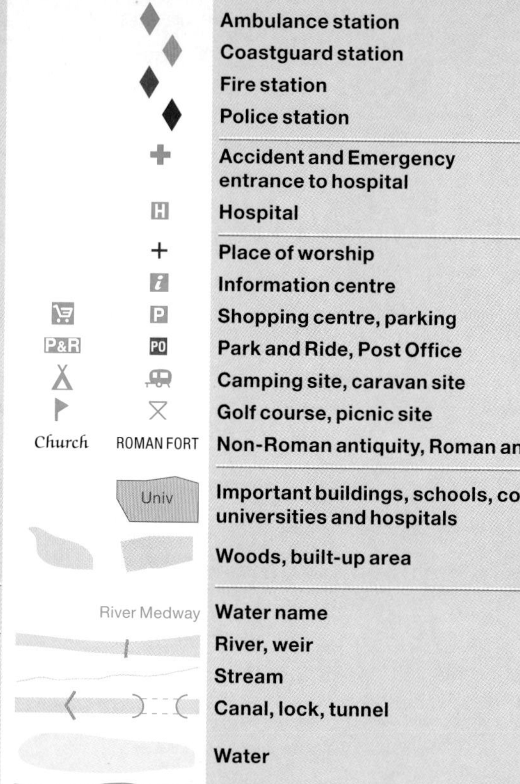

	Ambulance station
	Coastguard station
	Fire station
	Police station
	Accident and Emergency entrance to hospital
H	Hospital
+	Place of worship
i	Information centre
	Shopping centre, parking
P&R PO	Park and Ride, Post Office
	Camping site, caravan site
	Golf course, picnic site
Church ROMAN FORT	Non-Roman antiquity, Roman antiquity
Univ	Important buildings, schools, colleges, universities and hospitals
	Woods, built-up area
River Medway	Water name
	River, weir
	Stream
	Canal, lock, tunnel
	Water
	Tidal water

Adjoining page indicators and overlap bands – the colour of the arrow and band indicates the scale of the adjoining or overlapping page (see scales below)

The dark grey border on the inside edge of some pages indicates that the mapping does not continue onto the adjacent page

The small numbers around the edges of the maps identify the 1-kilometre National Grid lines

Enlarged maps only

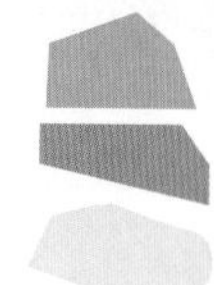

	Railway or bus station building
	Place of interest
	Parkland

Abbreviations

Acad	Academy	Meml	Memorial
Allot Gdns	Allotments	Mon	Monument
Cemy	Cemetery	Mus	Museum
C Ctr	Civic centre	Obsy	Observatory
CH	Club house	Pal	Royal palace
Coll	College	PH	Public house
Crem	Crematorium	Recn Gd	Recreation ground
Ent	Enterprise		
Ex H	Exhibition hall	Resr	Reservoir
Ind Est	Industrial Estate	Ret Pk	Retail park
IRB Sta	Inshore rescue boat station	Sch	School
		Sh Ctr	Shopping centre
Inst	Institute	TH	Town hall / house
Ct	Law court	Trad Est	Trading estate
L Ctr	Leisure centre	Univ	University
LC	Level crossing	W Twr	Water tower
Liby	Library	Wks	Works
Mkt	Market	YH	Youth hostel

The map scale on the pages numbered in blue is 3½ inches to 1 mile
5.52 cm to 1 km • 1:18 103

0	¼ mile	½ mile	¾ mile	1 mile

0	250m	500m	750m	1km

The map scale on the pages numbered in red is 7 inches to 1 mile
11.04 cm to 1 km • 1:9051

0	220yds	440yds	660yds	½ mile

0	125m	250m	375m	500m

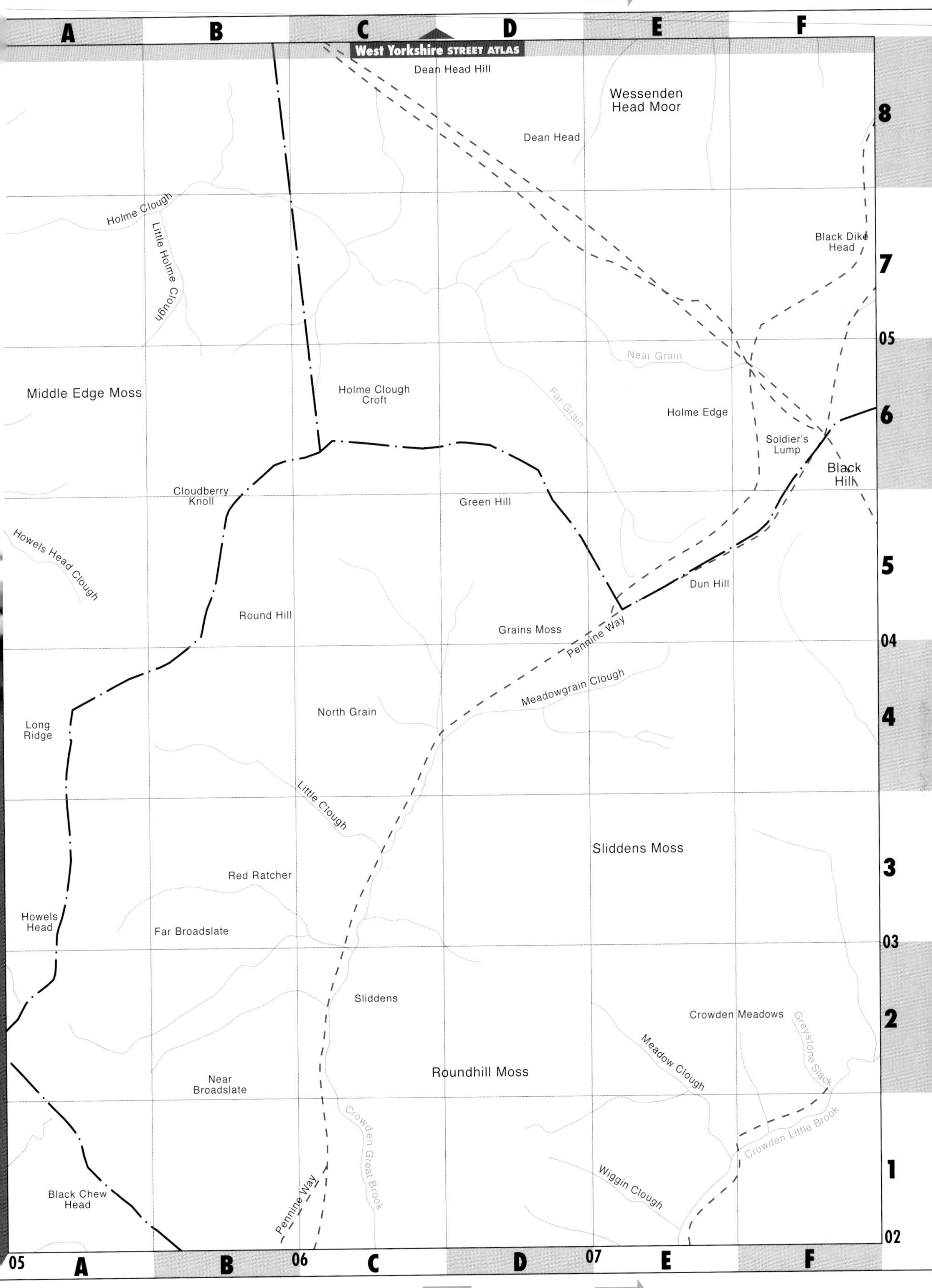

West Yorkshire STREET ATLAS

A B C D E F

8

Dean Head Hill

Wessenden
Head Moor

Dean Head

Black Dike
Head

7

Holme Clough

Little Holme Clough

05

Near Grain

Middle Edge Moss

Holme Clough
Croft

Far Grain

Holme Edge

6

Soldier's
Lump

Black
Hill

Cloudberry
Knoll

Green Hill

Howels Head Clough

Round Hill

Dun Hill

5

Grains Moss

Pennine Way

04

Meadowgrain Clough

Long
Ridge

North Grain

4

Little Clough

Sliddens Moss

3

Red Ratcher

Howels
Head

Far Broadslate

03

Sliddens

Crowden Meadows

2

Meadow Clough

Greystone Slack

Near
Broadslate

Roundhill Moss

Crowden Great Brook

Crowden Little Brook

1

Pennine Way

Wiggin Clough

Black Chew
Head

02

05   A   B   06   C   D   07   E   F

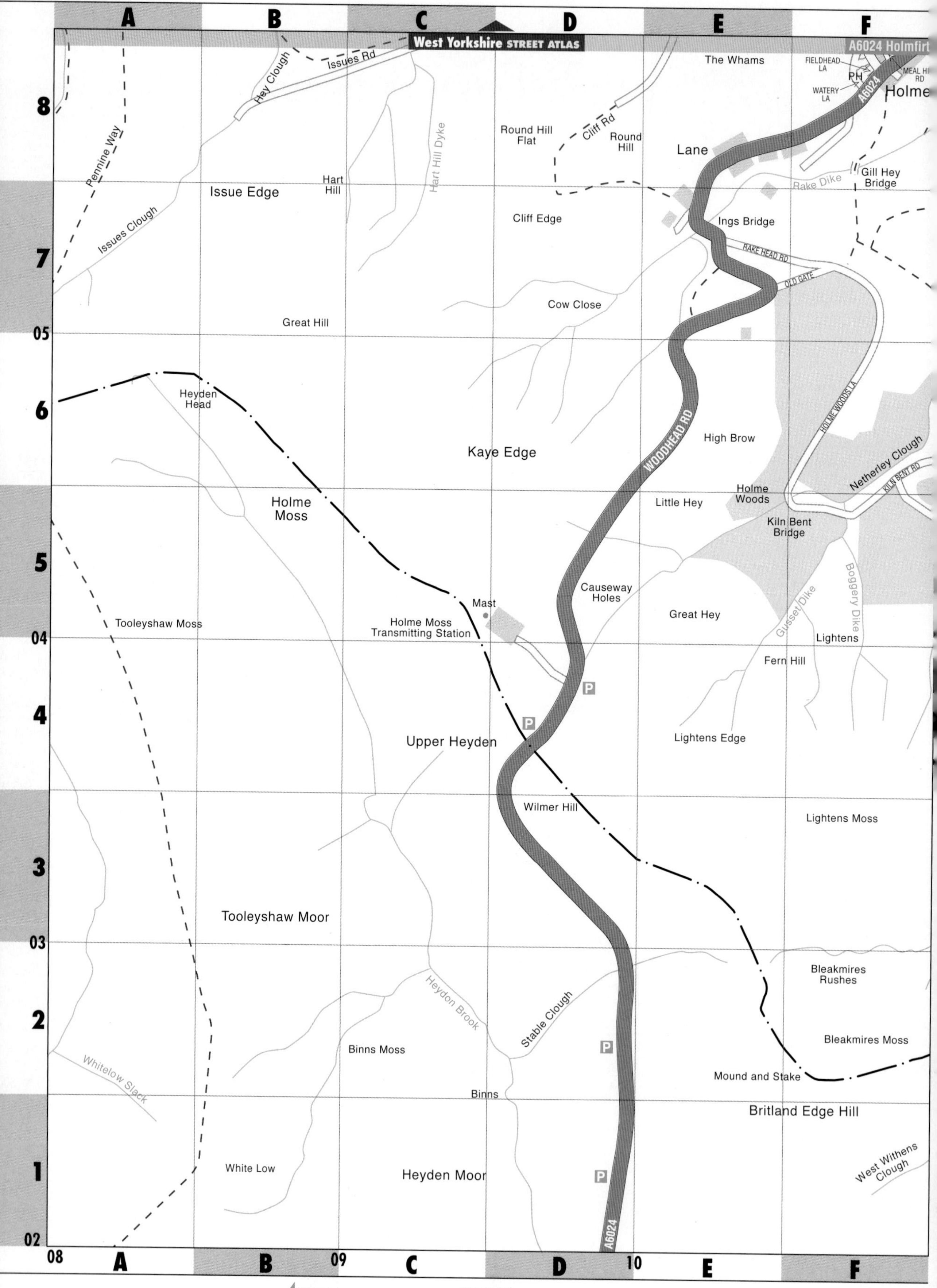

West Yorkshire STREET ATLAS

A6024 Holmfirt

A   B   C   D   E   F

The Whams

FIELDHEAD LA
PH
WATERY LA
MEAL HI RD
Holme

8

Hey Clough
Issues Rd

Cliff Rd
Round Hill Flat
Round Hill
Lane

A6024

Rake Dike

Gill Hey Bridge

Issue Edge
Hart Hill
Hart Hill Dyke

Cliff Edge
Ings Bridge

RAKE HEAD RD

Pennine Way

7

Issues Clough

Great Hill

Cow Close

OLD GATE

05

HOLME WOODS LA

Heyden Head

6

Kaye Edge

High Brow

Netherley Clough

WOODHEAD RD

Holme Moss

Little Hey

Holme Woods

KILN BENT RD

Kiln Bent Bridge

Boggery Dike

5

Tooleyshaw Moss

Causeway Holes

Great Hey

Gusset Dike

Lightens

Mast

04

Holme Moss Transmitting Station

Fern Hill

4

Upper Heyden

P

P

Lightens Edge

Lightens Moss

3

Wilmer Hill

03

Tooleyshaw Moor

Bleakmires Rushes

Heydon Brook

Stable Clough

2

Binns Moss

P

Bleakmires Moss

Whitelow Slack

Binns

Mound and Stake

Britland Edge Hill

1

White Low

Heyden Moor

P

A6024

West Withens Clough

02

08   A   B   09   C   D   10   E   F

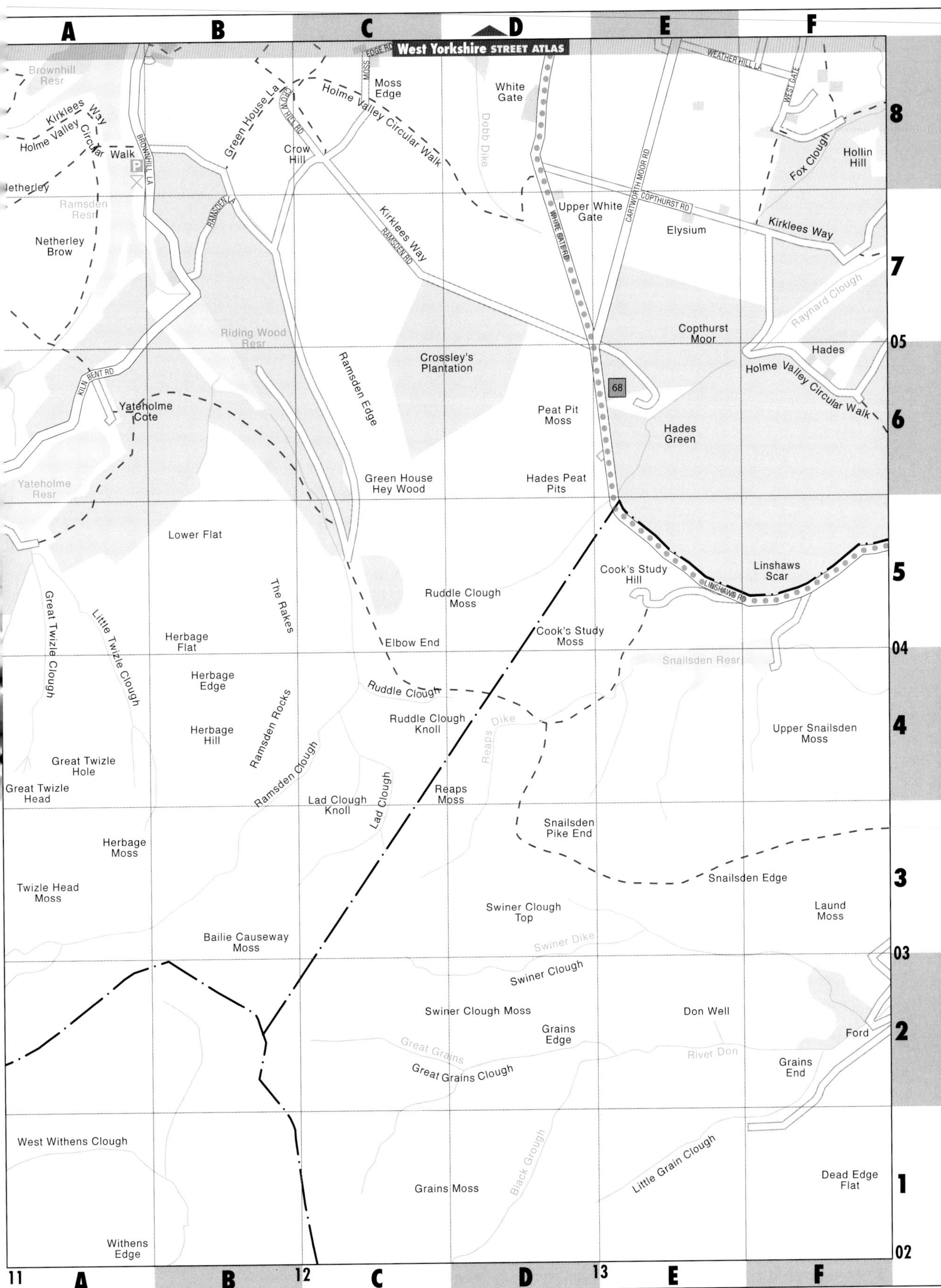

West Yorkshire STREET ATLAS

Brownhill Resr

Kirklees Way
Holme Valley Circular Walk

Netherley

Ramsden Resr

Netherley Brow

Kiln Bent Rd

Yateholme Cote

Yateholme Resr

Green House La

Edge Rd

Moss Edge

Crow Hill

Holme Valley Circular Walk

Dobb Dike

White Gate

Upper White Gate

Weather Hill La

West Gate

Fox Clough

Hollin Hill

Kirklees Way

Elysium

Copthurst Rd

Cartworth Moor Rd

White Gate Rd

Kirklees Way

Ramsden La

Brownhill La

Edge Rd

Eyton Hill Rd

Ramsden Rd

Kirklees Way

Crossley's Plantation

Ramsden Edge

Riding Wood Resr

68

Copthurst Moor

Raynard Clough

Hades

Holme Valley Circular Walk

05

Peat Pit Moss

Hades Green

6

Green House Hey Wood

Hades Peat Pits

Lower Flat

Great Twizle Clough

Little Twizle Clough

The Rakes

Herbage Flat

Herbage Edge

Herbage Hill

Ramsden Rocks

Ruddle Clough Moss

Elbow End

Ruddle Clough

Ruddle Clough Knoll

Cook's Study Moss

Cook's Study Hill

Linshaws Scar

Linshaws Rd

5

Snailsden Resr

04

Reaps Dike

Upper Snailsden Moss

4

Great Twizle Hole

Great Twizle Head

Ramsden Clough

Lad Clough Knoll

Lad Clough

Reaps Moss

Snailsden Pike End

Herbage Moss

Twizle Head Moss

Bailie Causeway Moss

Swiner Clough Top

Swiner Dike

Snailsden Edge

Laund Moss

3

03

Swiner Clough

Swiner Clough Moss

Don Well

River Don

Ford

2

Great Grains

Grains Edge

Great Grains Clough

Grains End

West Withens Clough

Black Grough

Little Grain Clough

Dead Edge Flat

1

Grains Moss

Withens Edge

02

8

05
7
6
5
4
3
2
8

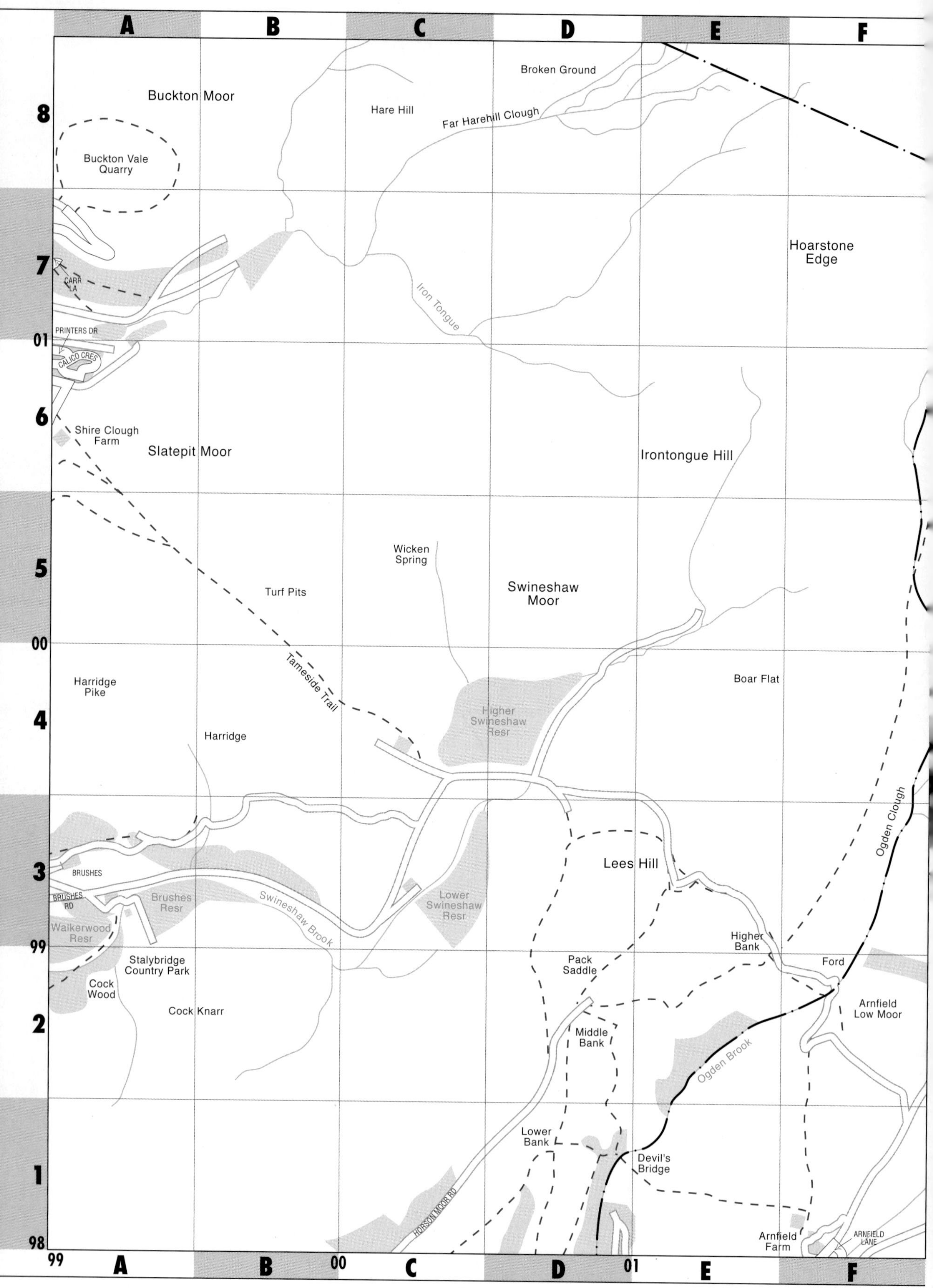

A B C D E F

8

7

01

6

01

6

5

00

4

3

99

2

1

98

Buckton Moor

Buckton Vale
Quarry

Broken Ground

Hare Hill

Far Harehill Clough

Hoarstone
Edge

CARR
LA

PRINTERS DR

CALICO CRES

Iron Tongue

Shire Clough
Farm

Slatepit Moor

Irontongue Hill

Wicken
Spring

Swineshaw
Moor

Turf Pits

Tameside Trail

Harridge
Pike

Boar Flat

Higher
Swineshaw
Resr

Harridge

BRUSHES

BRUSHES
RD

Brushes
Resr

Swineshaw Brook

Lower
Swineshaw
Resr

Lees Hill

Higher
Bank

Ford

Walkerwood
Resr

Ogden Clough

Stalybridge
Country Park

Pack
Saddle

Arnfield
Low Moor

Cock
Wood

Cock Knarr

Middle
Bank

Ogden Brook

Lower
Bank

Devil's
Bridge

HOBSON MOOR RD

Arnfield
Farm

ARNFIELD
LANE

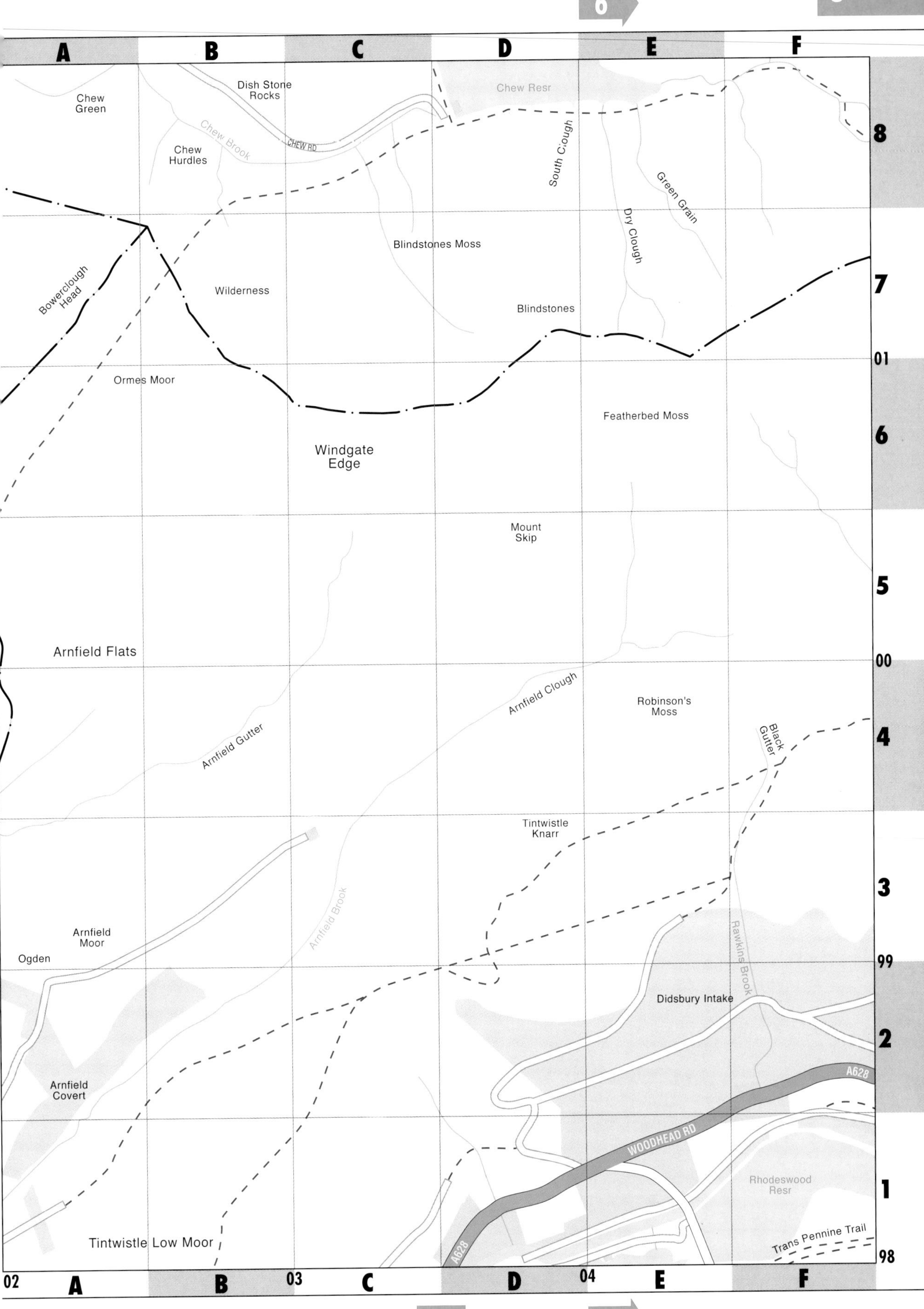

Chew Green

Dish Stone Rocks

Chew Hurdles

Chew Brook

CHEW RD

Chew Resr

8

South Clough

Green Grain

Dry Clough

Blindstones Moss

Bowerclough Head

Wilderness

Blindstones

7

01

Ormes Moor

Windgate Edge

Featherbed Moss

6

Mount Skip

5

Arnfield Flats

00

Arnfield Clough

Robinson's Moss

Black Gutter

4

Arnfield Gutter

Tintwistle Knarr

Rawkins Brook

3

Arnfield Brook

Arnfield Moor

99

Ogden

Didsbury Intake

2

Arnfield Covert

A628

WOODHEAD RD

Rhodeswood Resr

1

Tintwistle Low Moor

A628

Trans Pennine Trail

98

A **B** **C** **D** **E** **F**

8

Laddow
Moss

Laddow
Rocks

Black Hill
End

Crowden Little Moor

7

Oaken
Clough

Bareholme Moss

Hey Moss

01

Oakenclough Brook

Crowden Great Brook

Crowden Little Brook

Rakes Moss

6

Rakes
Rocks

Span

Pennine Way

5

Black
Tor

Loft
Intake

00

Millstone
Rocks

Lad's
Leap

Ford

4

Coombes Clough

Highstone
Rocks

YH

3

X

P

Crowden

A628

B6105

99

Highstones

Hollins Clough

2

Quiet Shepherd
Farm

The
Hollins

A628

Trans Pennine Trail

Torside Resr

62

Rollick
Stones

P

1

Rhodeswood
Resr

Visitor
Ctr

98

WOODHEAD RD

Torside
Bridge

B6105

05 **A** **B** **06** **C** **D** **07** **E** **F**

2
8

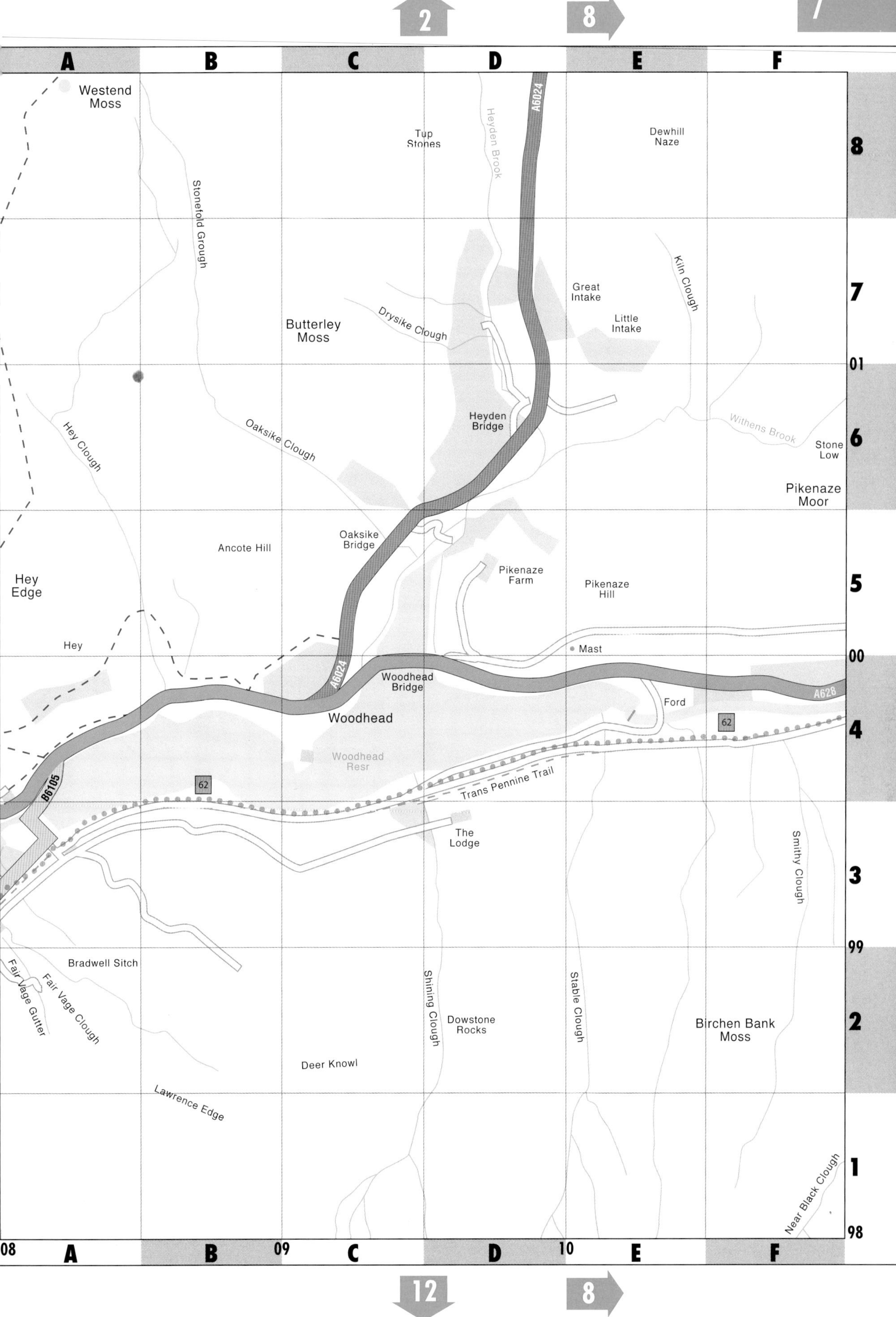
A
B
C
D
E
F
Westend Moss
Tup Stones
Heyden Brook
A6024
Dewhill Naze
8
Stonefold Grough
Kiln Clough
Great Intake
Little Intake
7
Butterley Moss
Drysike Clough
01
Heyden Bridge
Withens Brook
Stone Low
6
Hey Clough
Oaksike Clough
Pikenaze Moor
Oaksike Bridge
Ancote Hill
Pikenaze Farm
Pikenaze Hill
Hey Edge
5
Hey
Mast
00
Woodhead Bridge
Woodhead
Ford
A628
62
4
Woodhead Resr
B6105
Trans Pennine Trail
The Lodge
Smithy Clough
3
99
Bradwell Sitch
Fair Vage Gutter
Fair Vage Clough
Shining Clough
Stable Clough
Dowstone Rocks
Birchen Bank Moss
2
Deer Knowl
Lawrence Edge
1
Near Black Clough
98
08
09
10

12
8

A B C D E F

Withens Moor

8

Dead Edge End

Upper Dead Edge

Dead Edge Moss

Withens Brook

Wike Head

Cat Clough

Upper Head Moss

7

Upper Head

Pillar

Smallden Clough Head

Red Hole

01

Upper Head Dike

Air Shaft

Wike

Wike Edge

Round Hill

6

Air Shaft

Salter's Brook

Longside Moss

Pikenaze Moor

Netherhead Clough

Audernshaw Clough

Woodhead Tunnel (dis)

Salter's Brook Bridge

Salter's Brook Moss

5

Ford

Longside Edge

Hawthorn Clough

P

Salter's Brook

00

P

62

Round Hill Nick

A628

Ironbower Moss

Longdendale Trail

62

4

Long Side

Longside End

River Etherow

Ford

Near Small Clough

Birchen Bank Wood

Far Small Clough

Middle Small Clough

Shooting Cabins

3

Swan Clough

Rose Clough

99

Middle Small Clough Head

Near Black Clough

2

Far Small Clough Head

Middle Small Clough Head

Middle Black Clough

Far Black Clough

Dean Head

1

Featherbed Moss

Swains Head

98

River Derwent

11 A B 12 C D 13 E F

A628 Barnsley

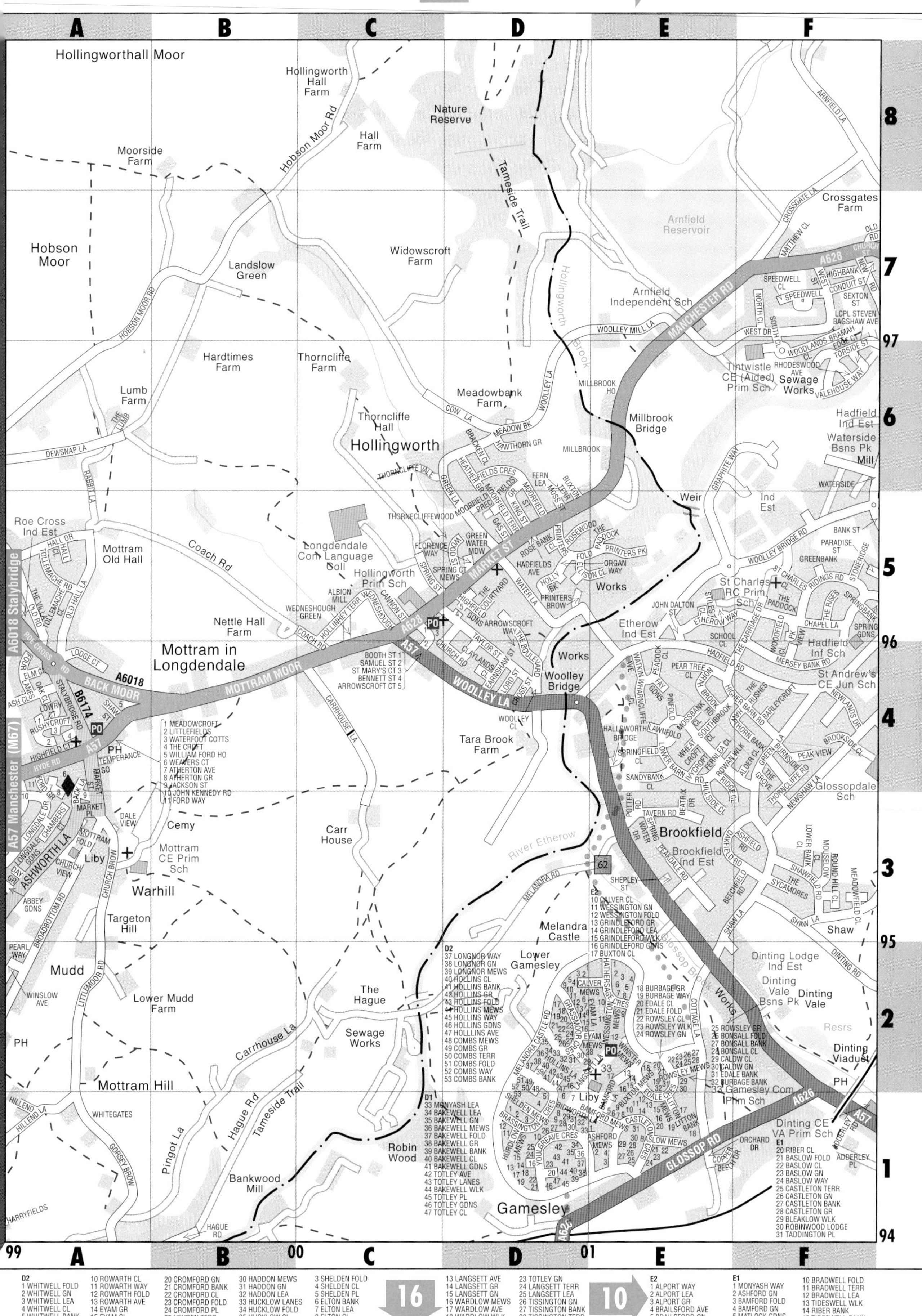

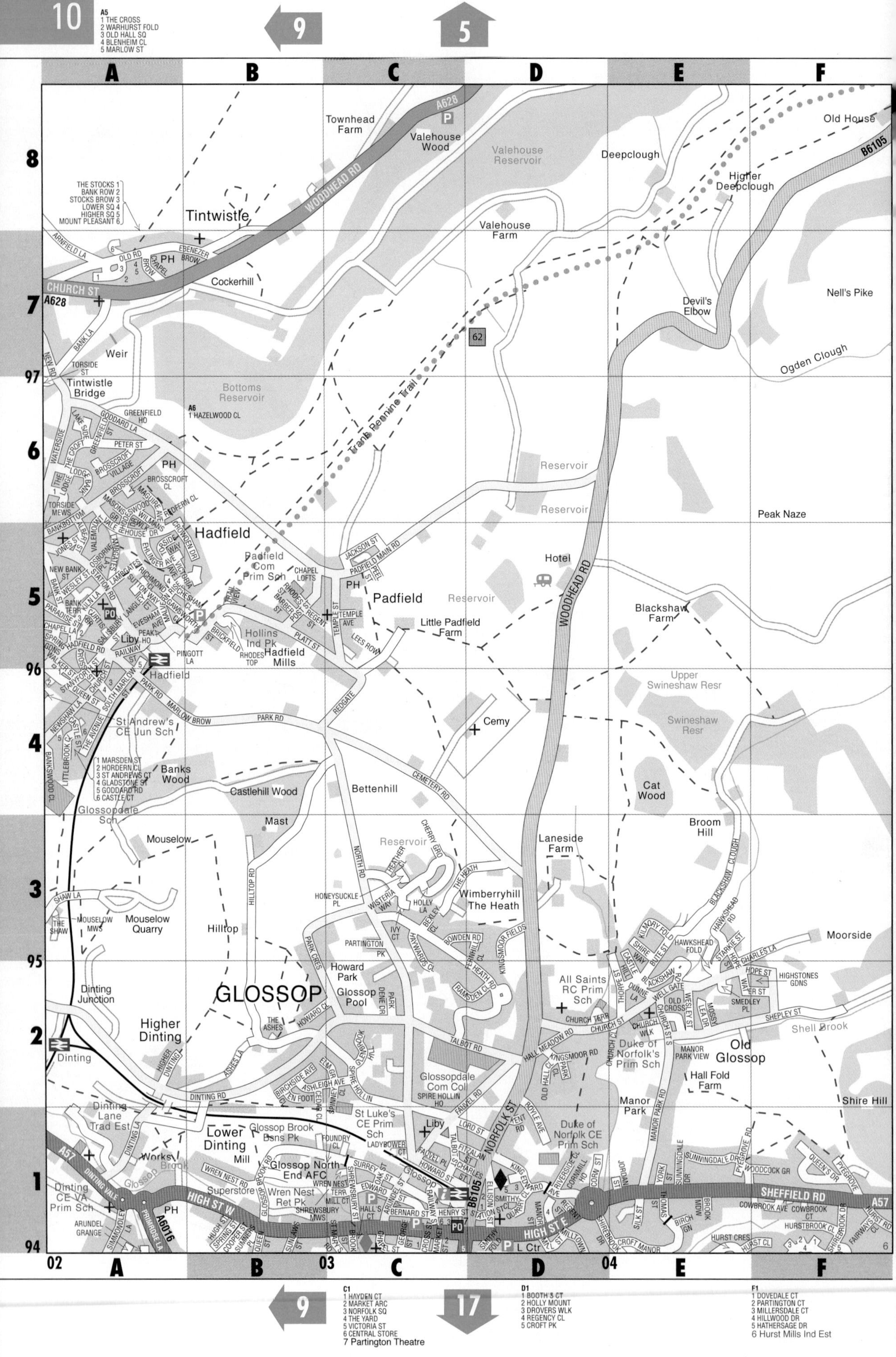

A B C D E F

8

THE STOCKS 1
BANK ROW 2
STOCKS BROW 3
LOWER SQ 4
HIGHER SQ 5
MOUNT PLEASANT 6

Townhead Farm
Valehouse Wood
Valehouse Reservoir
Deepclough
Old House
B6105

Tintwistle
WOODHEAD RD
Valehouse Farm
Higher Deepclough

7

A628
CHURCH ST
Cockerhill
Weir
Devil's Elbow
Nell's Pike

Tintwistle Bridge
97
Bottoms Reservoir
Trans Pennine Trail
62
Ogden Clough

A6
1 HAZELWOOD CL

6
Greenfield HO
Hadfield
Reservoir
Reservoir
Peak Naze

5
Padfield Com Prim Sch
Chapel Lofts
PH
Padfield
Reservoir
Hotel
Little Padfield Farm
Blackshaw Farm

Liby
Hollins Ind Pk
Hadfield Mills
96
Hadfield
Upper Swineshaw Resr

Park Rd
Redgate
Cemy
Swineshaw Resr

4
St Andrew's CE Jun Sch
1 MARSDEN ST
2 HORDERN CL
3 ST ANDREWS CT
4 GLADSTONE ST
5 GODDARD RD
6 CASTLE CT
Banks Wood
Castlehill Wood
Bettenhill
Cat Wood
Broom Hill

Glossopdale Sch
Mouselow
Mast
Reservoir
Laneside Farm

3
Shaw La
Mouselow Quarry
Hilltop
The Heath
Wimberryhill
Moorside

Hawkshead Fold

2
Dinting Junction
Higher Dinting
Howard Park
Glossop Pool
All Saints RC Prim Sch
Duke of Norfolk's Prim Sch
Old Glossop

Dinting
GLOSSOP
The Ashes
Church Terr
Manor Park View
Hall Fold Farm
Shell Brook

95
Dinting Rd
Glossopdale Com Coll
Manor Park
Shire Hill

St Luke's CE Prim Sch
Liby

1
Dinting Lane Trad Est
Lower Dinting Mill
Glossop Brook Bsns Pk
Glossop North End AFC
Wren Nest Ret Pk
Duke of Norfolk CE Prim Sch

Works
A57
HIGH ST W
Superstore
NORFOLK ST
HIGH ST E
SHEFFIELD RD
A57

Dinting CE VA Prim Sch
A6016
PH
B6105
Cowbrook Ave Cowbrook Ct
Hurstbrook Cl

94
ARUNDEL GRANGE
L Ctr
Hurst Cres
6

02 A 03 B C 04 D E F

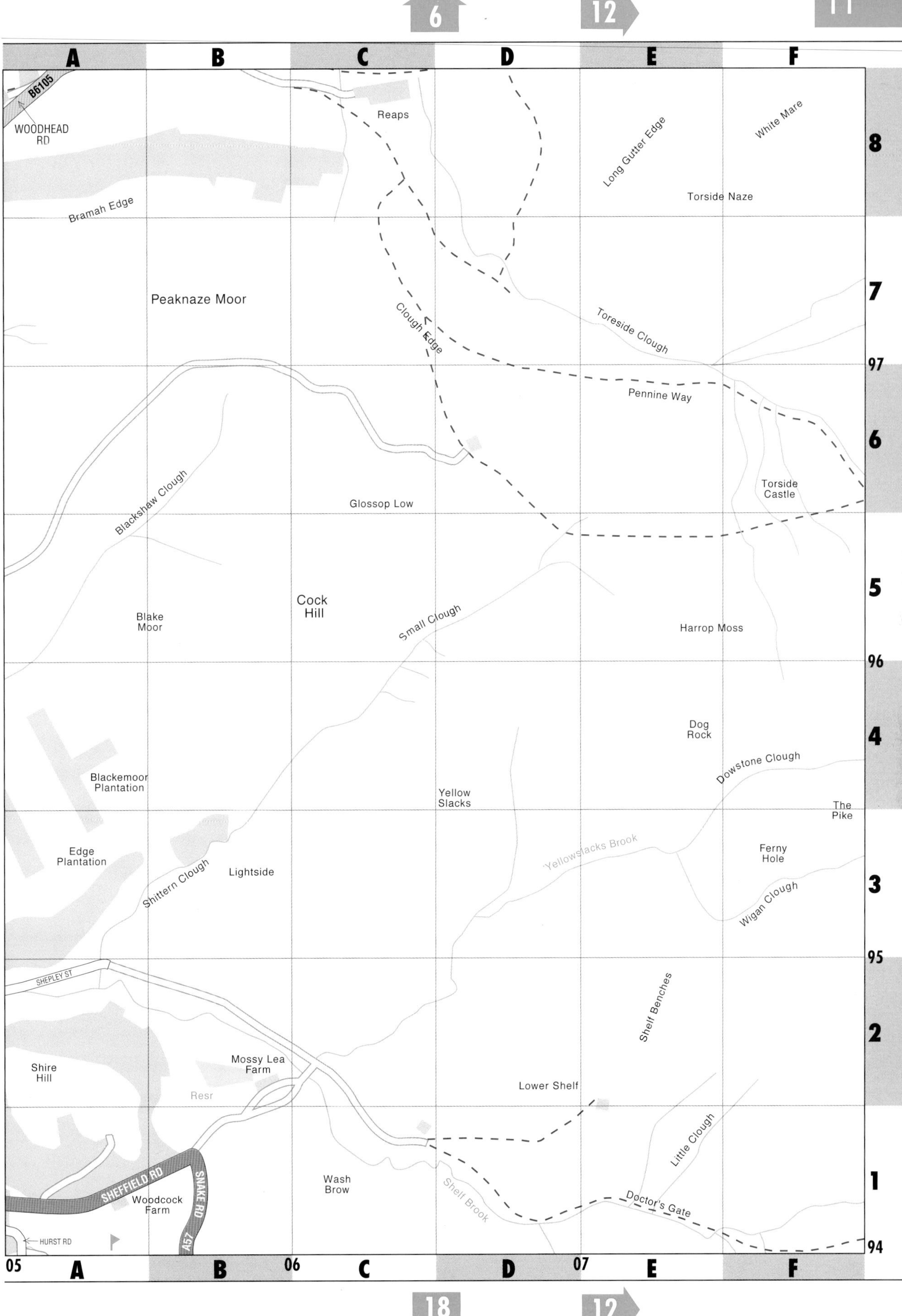

A B C D E F

8
7
97
6
5
96
4
95
3
2
1
94

WOODHEAD RD

B6105

Bramah Edge

Peaknaze Moor

Reaps

Clough Edge

Long Gutter Edge

White Mare

Torside Naze

Toreside Clough

Pennine Way

Blackshaw Clough

Glossop Low

Torside Castle

Cock Hill

Blake Moor

Small Clough

Harrop Moss

Dog Rock

Dowstone Clough

The Pike

Blackemoor Plantation

Yellow Slacks

Yellowslacks Brook

Ferny Hole

Edge Plantation

Shittern Clough

Lightside

Wigan Clough

SHEPLEY ST

Shelf Benches

Shire Hill

Mossy Lea Farm

Resr

Lower Shelf

Little Clough

SHEFFIELD RD

SNAKE RD

A57

Woodcock Farm

HURST RD

Wash Brow

Shelf Brook

Doctor's Gate

05 A 06 B C 07 D E F

A   B   C   D   E   F

8

Wildboar Clough

Round
Hill

Shining Clough
Moss

7

Near Black Clough

Bleaklow
Meadows

Sykes Moor

97

Near Bleaklow
Stones

6

Far
Moss

Bleaklow

Wildboar Grain

Bleaklow
Hill

5

Joseph
Patch

Alport
Head

96

Bleaklow
Head

Wain Stones

4

Pennine Way

Dowstone Clough

Shelf Moss

Near Fork Grain

Far Fork Grain

Hern Stones

95

The
Swamp

Shelf Moor

Grains
in the Water

2

Lower Shelf
Stones

Hern Clough

Higher Shelf
Stones

Alport
Low

Ashton Clough

Crooked Clough

1

White Clough

Devil's Dike

Gathering
Hill

94

08   A   B   09   C   D   10   E   F

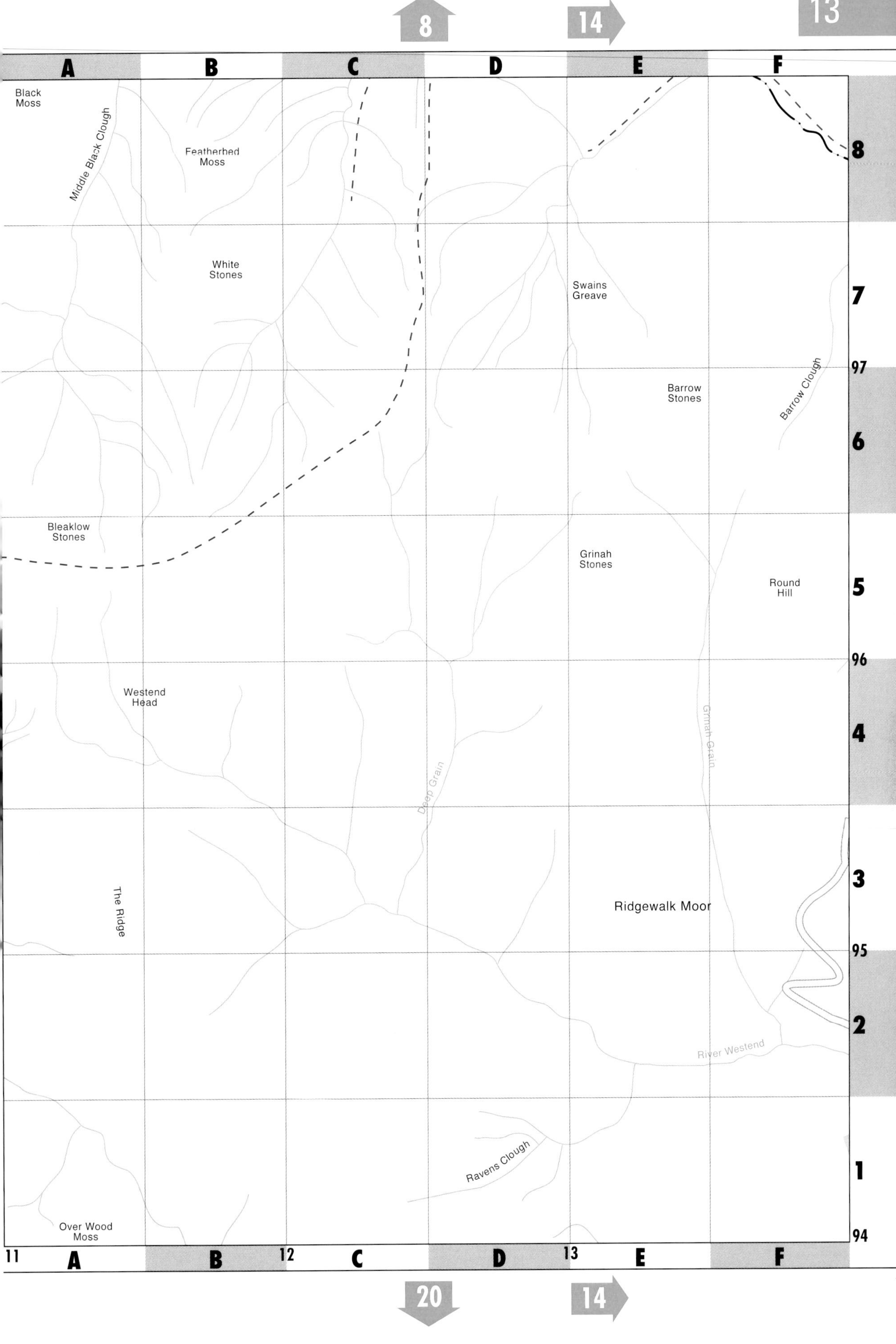

| A | B | C | D | E | F |

Black Moss

Middle Black Clough

Featherbed Moss

8

White Stones

Swains Greave

7

97

Barrow Stones

Barrow Clough

6

Bleaklow Stones

Grinah Stones

Round Hill

5

96

Westend Head

Grinah Grain

4

Deep Grain

The Ridge

Ridgewalk Moor

3

95

2

River Westend

1

Ravens Clough

Over Wood Moss

94

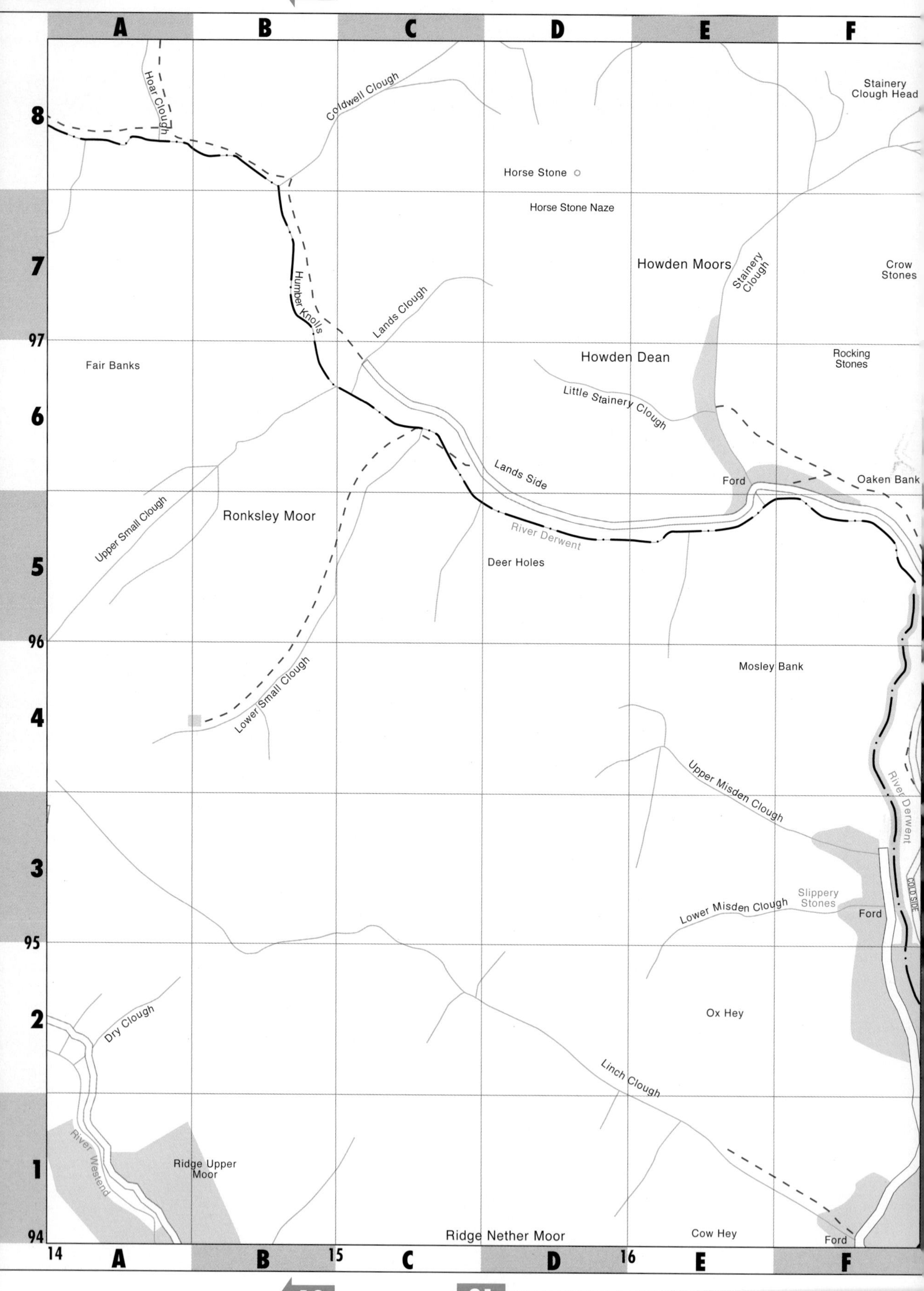

Hoar Clough

Coldwell Clough

Stainery
Clough Head

8

Horse Stone ○

Horse Stone Naze

Howden Moors

Crow
Stones

Humber Knolls

Stainery
Clough

7

Lands Clough

97

Fair Banks

Howden Dean

Rocking
Stones

Little Stainery Clough

6

Lands Side

Ford

Oaken Bank

Upper Small Clough

Ronksley Moor

River Derwent

5

Deer Holes

96

Mosley Bank

Lower Small Clough

4

Upper Misden Clough

River Derwent

3

Lower Misden Clough

Slippery
Stones

Ford

COLD SIDE

95

Dry Clough

Ox Hey

2

Linch Clough

River Westend

1

Ridge Upper
Moor

94

Ridge Nether Moor

Cow Hey

Ford

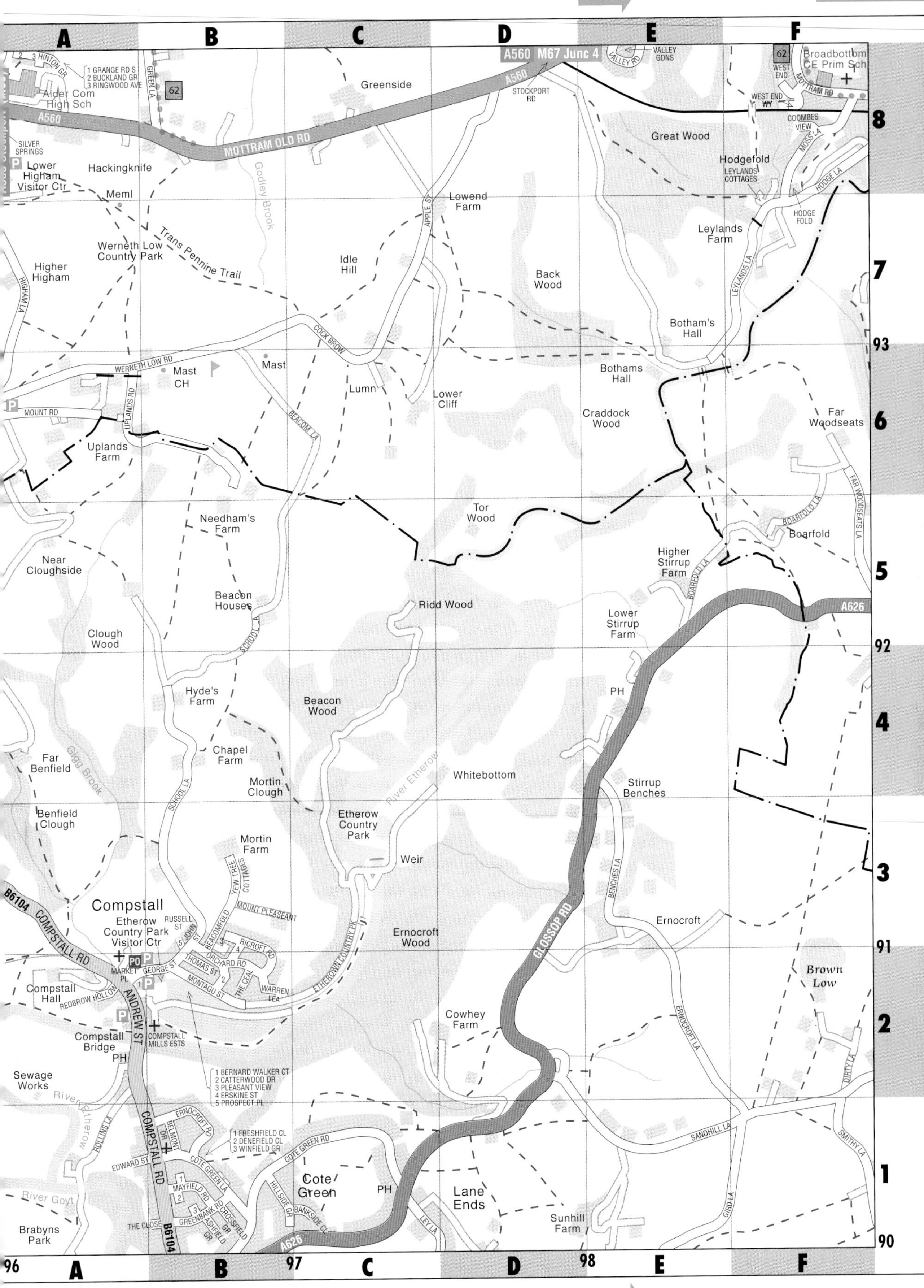

A   B   C   D   E   F

1 GRANGE RD S
2 BUCKLAND GR
3 RINGWOOD AVE

62

Greenside

A560 M67 Junc 4
VALLEY GDNS

62 WEST END
Broadbottom CE Prim Sch

VALLEY RD

STOCKPORT RD

Alder Com High Sch
A560

SILVER SPRINGS

COOMBES VIEW

WEST END WY

8

Lower Higham Visitor Ctr

Hackingknife

MOTTRAM OLD RD

Great Wood

Hodgefold
LEYLANDS COTTAGES

HODGE FOLD

HODGE LA

Meml

Godley Brook

APPLE ST

Lowend Farm

Leylands Farm

7

Trans Pennine Trail

Higher Higham

Werneth Low Country Park

Idle Hill

Back Wood

LEYLANDS LA

93

Mast CH

WERNETH LOW RD

Mast

COCK BROW

Lumn

Lower Cliff

Botham's Hall

MOSS LA

Bothams Hall

Craddock Wood

Far Woodseats

6

UPLANDS RD

BEACOM LA

Uplands Farm

Tor Wood

Higher Stirrup Farm

Boarfold

BOARFOLD LA

FAR WOODSEATS LA

Near Cloughside

Needham's Farm

Lower Stirrup Farm

A626

5

Clough Wood

Beacon Houses

SCHOOL LA

Ridd Wood

PH

92

Far Benfield

Gigg Brook

Hyde's Farm

Beacon Wood

BOARFOLD LA

4

Benfield Clough

Chapel Farm

Mortin Clough

River Etherow

Whitebottom

Stirrup Benches

Mortin Farm

Etherow Country Park

Weir

BENCHES LA

GLOSSOP RD

3

B6104

COMPSTALL RD

FEW TREE COTTAGES

MOUNT PLEASANT

Ernocroft Wood

Ernocroft

Compstall
Etherow Country Park Visitor Ctr

RUSSELL ST

BEACONFIELD

RICROFT RD

ST JOHN

ETHEROW COUNTRY CK

ERNOCROFT LA

Brown Low

91

MARKET PL

THOMAS ST

ORCHARD RD

GEORGE ST

WARREN LEA

2

Compstall Hall

REDBROW HOLLOW

MONTAGU ST

1 BERNARD WALKER CT
2 CATTERWOOD DR
3 PLEASANT VIEW
4 ERSKINE ST
5 PROSPECT PL

ANDREW ST

Compstall Bridge
PH

Compstall Mills Ests

Cowhey Farm

SANDHILL LA

GRID LA

SMITHY LA

DIRTY LA

Sewage Works

River Etherow

ROLLINS LA

ERNOCROFT RD

BELMONT CTR

1 FRESHFIELD CL
2 DENEFIELD CL
3 WINFIELD GR

Sunhill Farm

1

EDWARD ST

COMPSTALL RD

COTE GREEN LA

COTE GREEN RD

Cote Green

PH

Lane Ends

River Goyt

THE CLOSE

B6104

MAYFIELD RD

GREENBANK RD

CASTLE RD

HILLSIDE GR

BANKSIDE CL

LEYLA

Brabyns Park

A626

90

96   A   B   97   C   D   98   E   F

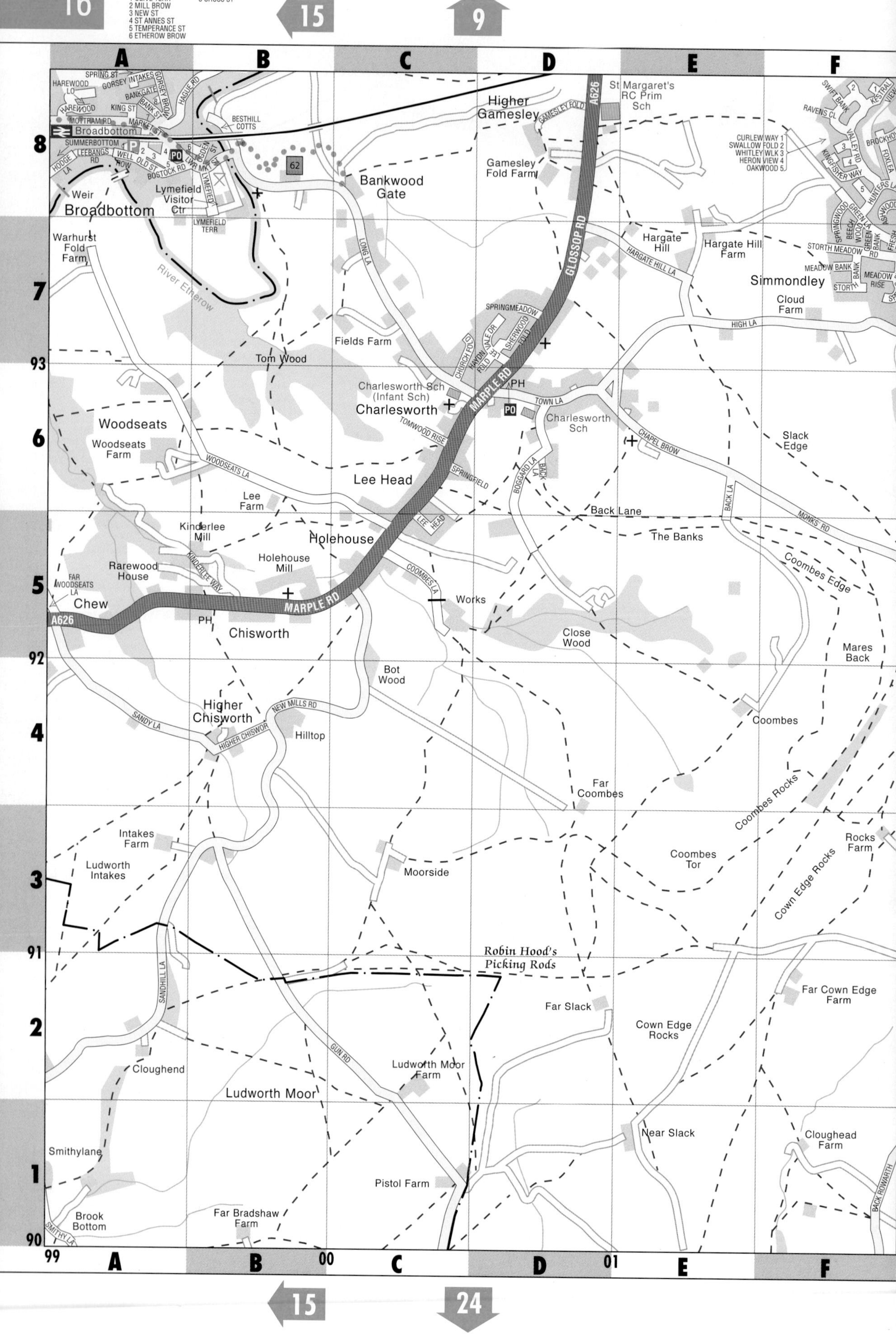

16

A8
1 OLIVE TERR
2 MILL BROW
3 NEW ST
4 ST ANNES ST
5 TEMPERANCE ST
6 ETHEROW BROW
7 GARDEN ST
8 CROSS ST

15   9

A   B   C   D   E   F

8

7

93

6

5

92

4

3

91

2

1

90

SPRING ST
HAREWOOD LO
HAREWOOD
GORSEY INTAKES
BANKGATE
KING ST
HASLE RD
MOTTRAM RD
HOOD LA
SUMMERBOTTOM
LEEBANGS RD
WELL OLD ST
BOSTOCK RD
Broadbottom
Weir
Broadbottom
Lymefield Visitor Ctr
LYMEFIELD TERR

BESTHILL COTTS

62

Bankwood Gate

Higher Gamesley

St Margaret's RC Prim Sch

GAMESLEY FOLD

GLOSSOP RD
A626

Gamesley Fold Farm

Hargate Hill

HARGATE HILL LA

Hargate Hill Farm

Simmondley

SWIFT BANK
RAVENS CL
KESTRAL
VIEW

CURLEW WAY 1
SWALLOW FOLD 2
WHITLEY WLK 3
HERON VIEW 4
OAKWOOD 5

KINGFISHER WAY
VALLEY RD
SPRINGWOOD GREEN
BROCKHOLE
FOX LEA
STORTH MEADOW
MEADOW BANK
MEADOW RISE
STORTH

Cloud Farm

HIGH LA

Warhurst Fold Farm

River Etherow

Tom Wood

Fields Farm

LONG LA

SPRINGMEADOW
CHURCH FOLD
SHERWOOD
MARION VALE DR

Charlesworth Sch (Infant Sch)
Charlesworth
TOWN LA
PH
PO
Charlesworth Sch
CHAPEL BROW

Slack Edge

Woodseats
Woodseats Farm

WOODSEATS LA

Lee Head
TOMWOOD RISE
MARPLE RD

SPRINGFIELD

BOGGARD LA
BACK LA

Back Lane
BACK LA
MONKS RD

The Banks

Coombes Edge

Lee Farm

Kinderlee Mill
KINDERLEE WAY

Rarewood House

Holehouse Mill
Holehouse

LEE HEAD

COOMBES LA
Works

Close Wood

Mares Back

FAR WOODSEATS LA
Chew
A626
MARPLE RD
PH
Chisworth

Bot Wood

Coombes

Higher Chisworth
SANDY LA
HIGHER CHISWOR
NEW MILLS RD
Hilltop

Coombes Rocks

Rocks Farm

Far Coombes

Intakes Farm

Ludworth Intakes

Moorside

Coombes Tor

COWN EDGE ROCKS

Robin Hood's Picking Rods

Far Cown Edge Farm

SANDHILL LA

GUN RD

Far Slack

Cown Edge Rocks

Cloughend

Ludworth Moor Farm

Ludworth Moor

Near Slack

Cloughead Farm

BACK ROWARTH

Smithylane

Pistol Farm

Brook Bottom

Far Bradshaw Farm

SMITHY LA

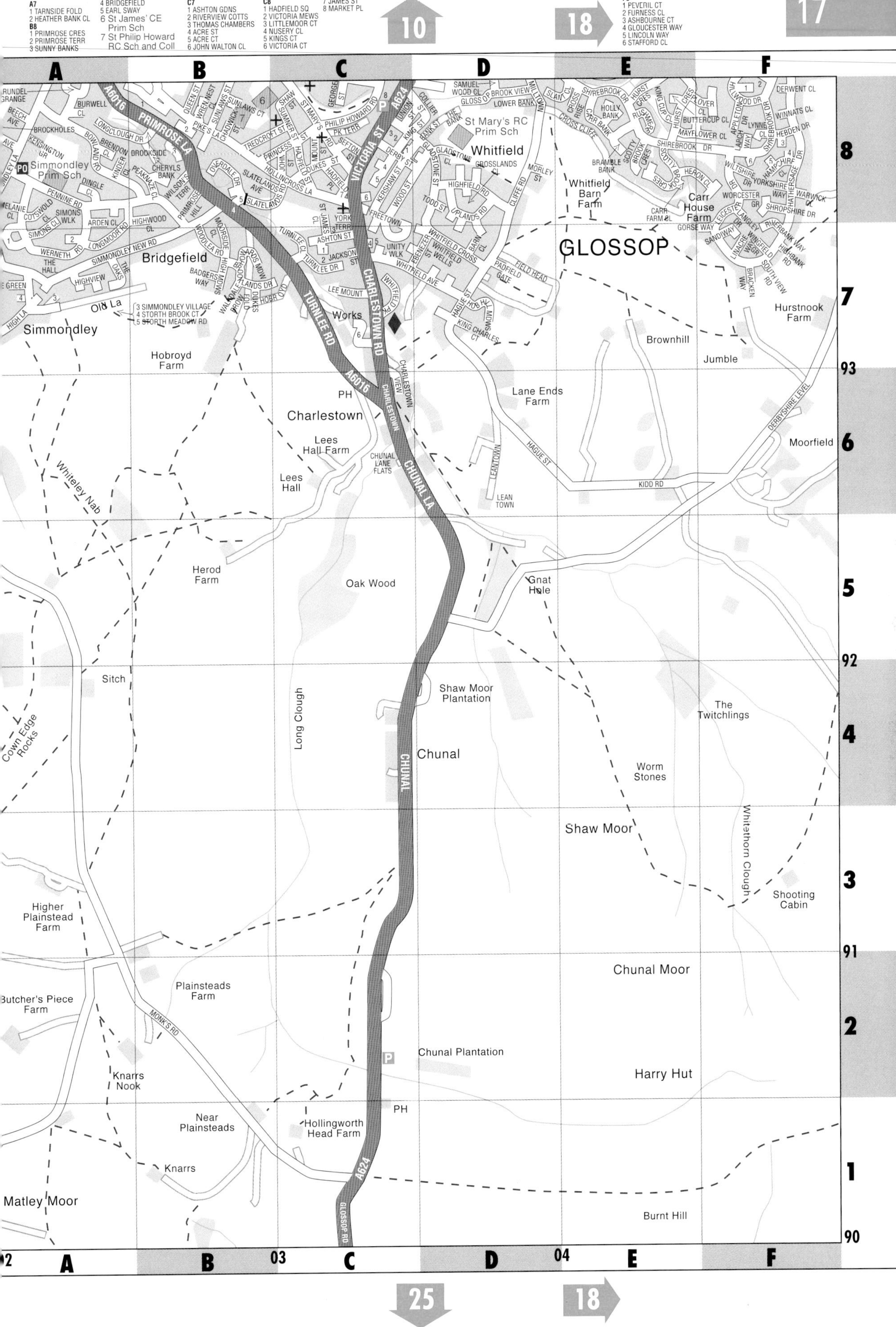
A7
1 TARNSIDE FOLD
2 HEATHER BANK CL
B8
1 PRIMROSE CRES
2 PRIMROSE TERR
3 SUNNY BANKS
4 BRIDGEFIELD
5 EARL SWAY
6 St James' CE Prim Sch
7 St Philip Howard RC Sch and Coll
C7
1 ASHTON GDNS
2 RIVERVIEW COTTS
3 THOMAS CHAMBERS
4 ACRE ST
5 ACRE CT
6 JOHN WALTON CL
C8
1 HADFIELD SQ
2 VICTORIA MEWS
3 LITTLEMOOR CT
4 NUSERY CL
5 KINGS CT
6 VICTORIA CT
7 JAMES ST
8 MARKET PL
10
18
F8
1 PEVERIL CT
2 FURNESS CL
3 ASHBOURNE CT
4 GLOUCESTER WAY
5 LINCOLN WAY
6 STAFFORD CL
Simmondley Prim Sch
Simmondley
Bridgefield
Hobroyd Farm
Charlestown
Lees Hall Farm
Lees Hall
St Mary's RC Prim Sch
Whitfield
Whitfield Barn Farm
Carr House Farm
GLOSSOP
Hurstnook Farm
Brownhill
Jumble
Lane Ends Farm
Moorfield
Works
PH
Whiteley Nab
Herod Farm
Oak Wood
Gnat Hole
Sitch
Shaw Moor Plantation
The Twitchlings
Cown Edge Rocks
Long Clough
Chunal
Worm Stones
Shaw Moor
Whitethorn Clough
Higher Plainstead Farm
Shooting Cabin
Chunal Moor
Plainsteads Farm
Butcher's Piece Farm
Chunal Plantation
Knarrs Nook
Harry Hut
Near Plainsteads
Hollingworth Head Farm
Knarrs
Matley Moor
Burnt Hill
A6016
A624
PRIMROSE LA
TURNLEE RD
CHARLESTOWN RD
VICTORIA ST
CHUNAL LA
CHUNAL
GLOSSOP RD
KIDD RD
HAGUE ST
DERBYSHIRE LEVEL
MONK'S RD
LEANTOWN
LEAN TOWN
Old La
3 SIMMONDLEY VILLAGE
4 STORTH BROOK CT
5 STORTH MEADOW RD
A B C D E F
8 7 6 5 4 3 2 1
93 92 91 90
03 04
25
18

A   B   C   D   E   F

8

CH

Hill End
Farm

Hurst
Resr

Lordship
Hill

Hey
Clough

Old Dike

Birchen Orchard Clough

Lower Ridge

DERBYSHIRE LEVEL

A57

Hurst Brook

S N A K E   R D

Ramsley Clough

Coldharbour Moor

7

Cabin Clough

93

Ramsley
Moor

Span Moor

Span Clough

Higher Rd

6

MOORFIELD

Holden Clough

Hurst Moor

A5

5

Wood's
Cabin

Bostock
Plantation

Highmoor
Pits

92

Black Moor

Bray Clough

Fairvage Clough

Moss
Castle

Pennine Way

4

Bakestone Delph Clough

Glead
Hill

Pennine Way

3

Within Clough

91

2

Snake Path

Ashop
Head

River Ashop

Mill Hill

1

Pennine Way

90

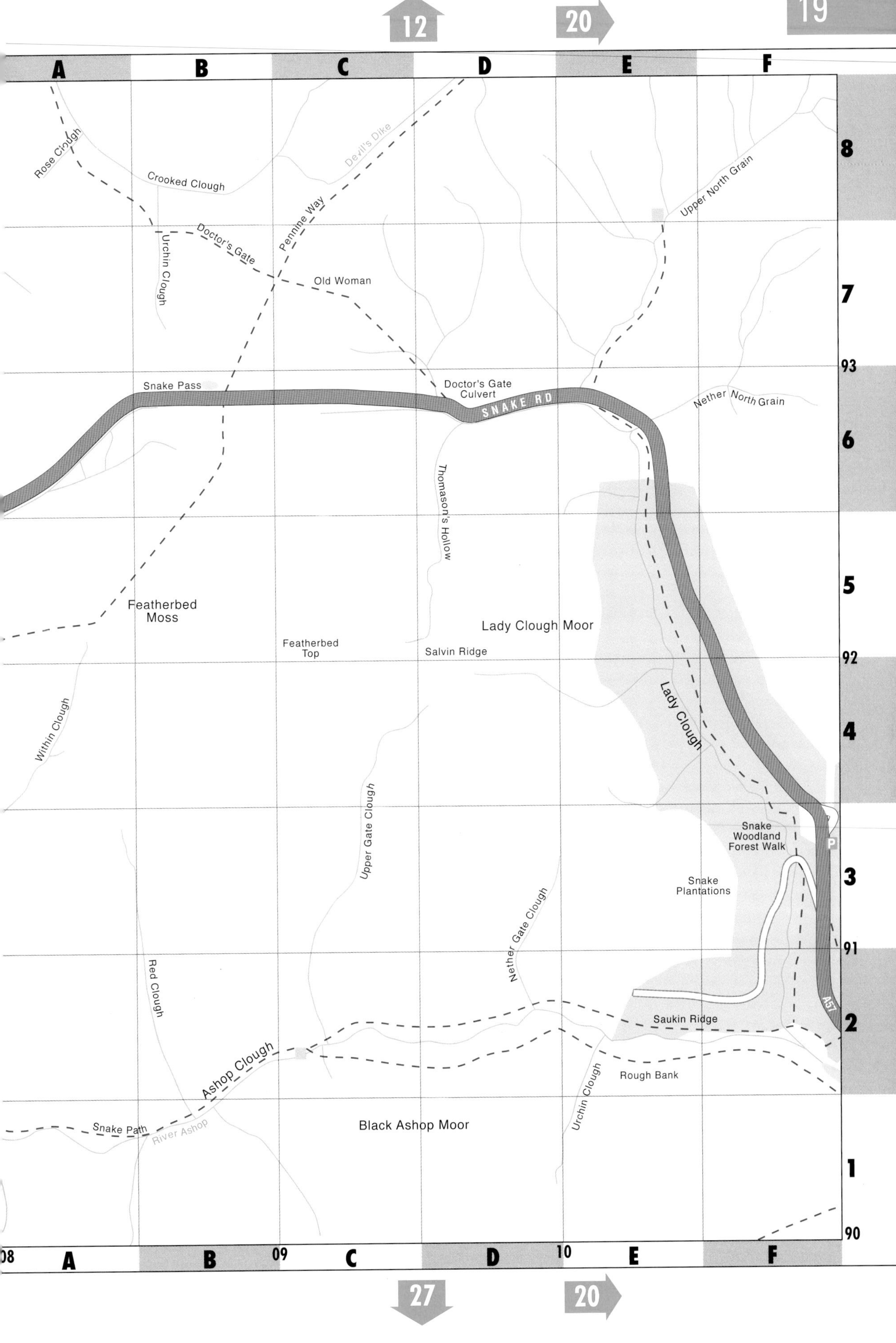

12
20

A B C D E F

Rose Clough

Crooked Clough

Devil's Dike

Upper North Grain

8

Urchin Clough

Doctor's Gate

Pennine Way

Old Woman

7

93

Snake Pass

SNAKE RD

Doctor's Gate
Culvert

Nether North Grain

6

Thomason's Hollow

Featherbed
Moss

Lady Clough Moor

Lady Clough

5

92

Featherbed
Top

Salvin Ridge

4

Within Clough

Upper Gate Clough

Snake
Woodland
Forest Walk

P

3

Snake
Plantations

Red Clough

Nether Gate Clough

91

A57

Ashop Clough

Saukin Ridge

2

Snake Path

River Ashop

Black Ashop Moor

Urchin Clough

Rough Bank

1

90

08 A B 09 C D 10 E F

19
13

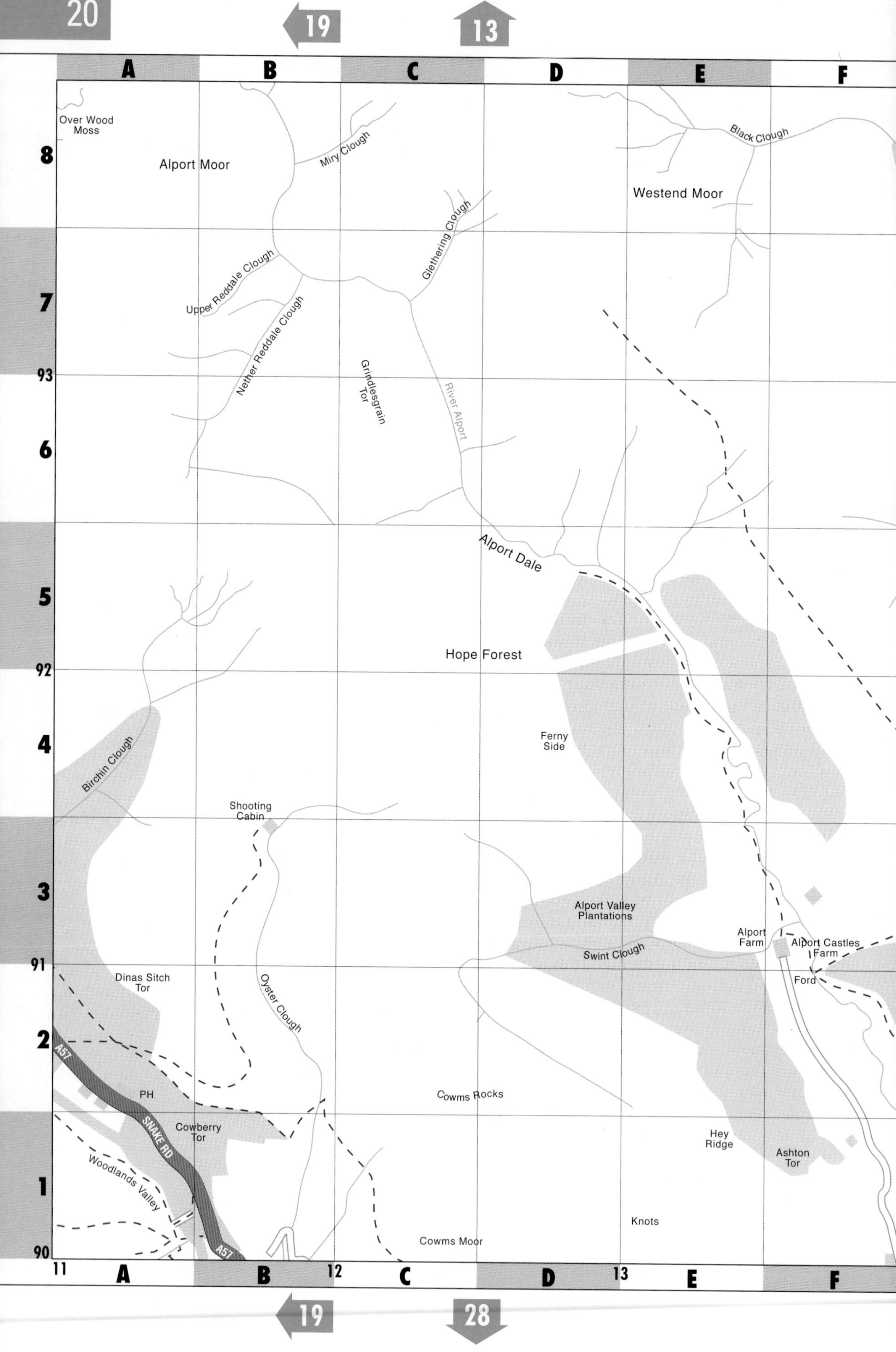

A **B** **C** **D** **E** **F**

8

Over Wood
Moss

Alport Moor

Miry Clough

Black Clough

Westend Moor

7

Upper Reddale Clough

Nether Reddale Clough

Glethering Clough

93

Grindlesgrain Tor

River Alport

6

Alport Dale

5

Hope Forest

92

Ferny
Side

4

Birchin Clough

Shooting
Cabin

3

Alport Valley
Plantations

Alport
Farm

Alport Castles
Farm

91

Dinas Sitch
Tor

Oyster Clough

Swint Clough

Ford

2

A57

PH

SNAKE RD

Cowberry
Tor

Cowms Rocks

Hey
Ridge

Ashton
Tor

1

Woodlands Valley

A57

Cowms Moor

Knots

90

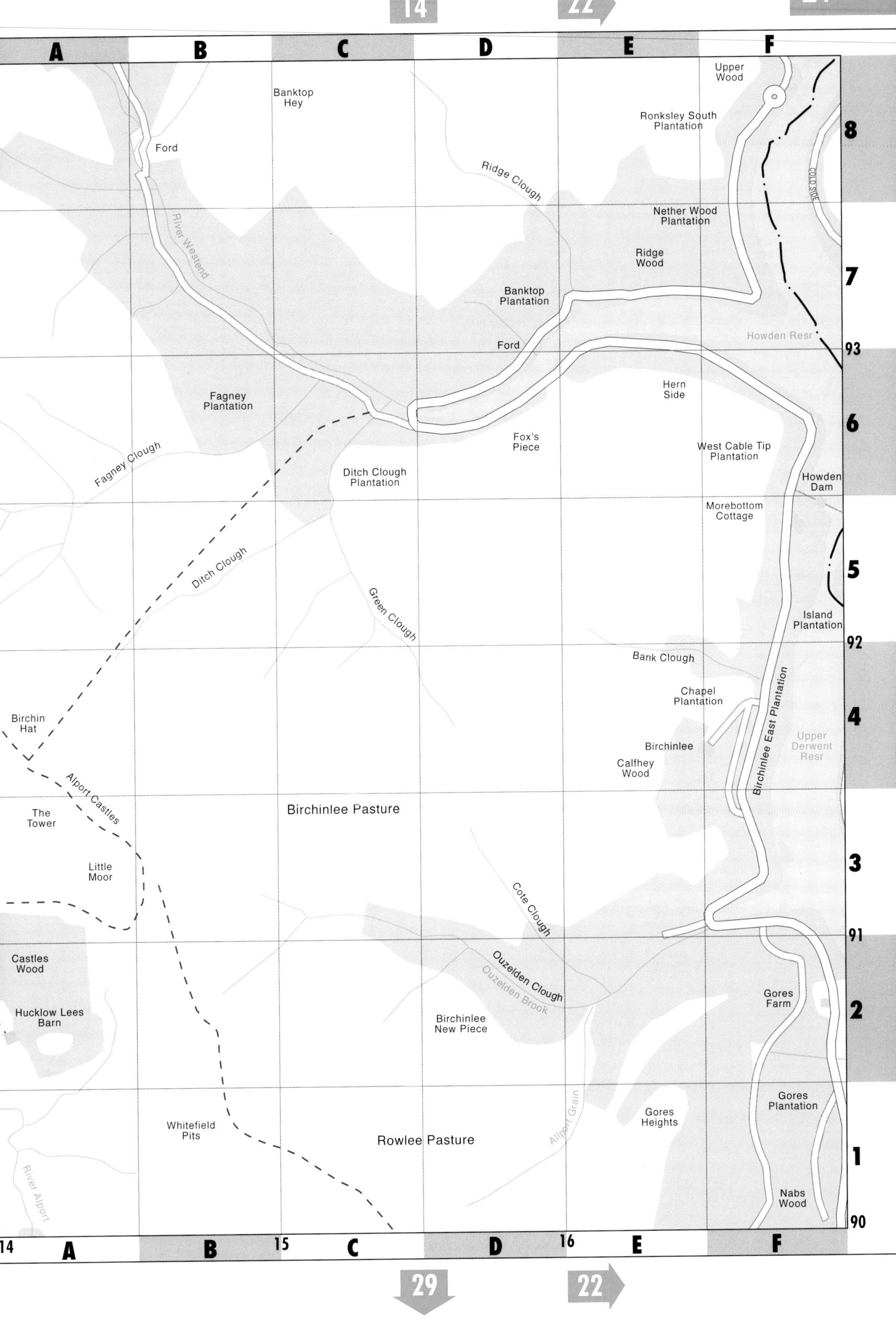

A B C D E F

Upper
Wood

Ronksley South
Plantation

8

Banktop
Hey

Ford

Ridge Clough

COLD SIDE

River Westend

Nether Wood
Plantation

Ridge
Wood

7

Banktop
Plantation

Ford

Howden Resr

93

Fagney
Plantation

Fox's
Piece

Hern
Side

West Cable Tip
Plantation

6

Fagney Clough

Ditch Clough
Plantation

Howden
Dam

Morebottom
Cottage

Ditch Clough

Green Clough

5

Island
Plantation

92

Bank Clough

Birchinlee East Plantation

Birchin
Hat

Chapel
Plantation

Birchinlee

Upper
Derwent
Resr

4

Alport Castles

Calfhey
Wood

The
Tower

Birchinlee Pasture

Little
Moor

Cote Clough

3

91

Castles
Wood

Ouzelden Clough

Ouzelden Brook

Gores
Farm

2

Hucklow Lees
Barn

Birchinlee
New Piece

Whitefield
Pits

Rowlee Pasture

Allport Grain

Gores
Heights

Gores
Plantation

1

River Alport

Nabs
Wood

90

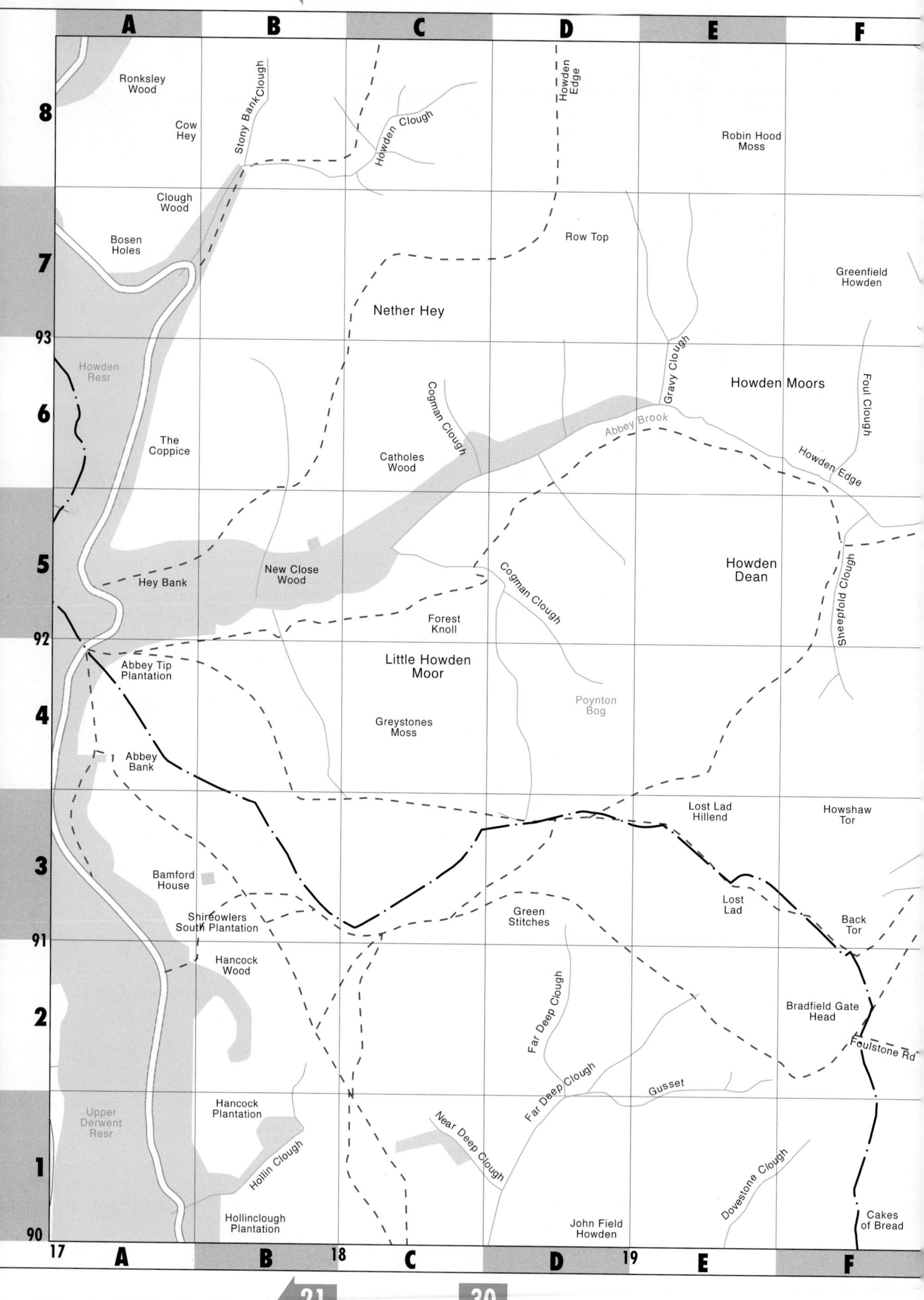

A **B** **C** **D** **E** **F**

8
Ronksley Wood
Cow Hey
Stony Bank Clough
Howden Clough
Howden Edge
Robin Hood Moss

Clough Wood

7
Bosen Holes
Greenfield Howden

Row Top

93
Howden Resr
Nether Hey

Gravy Clough

6
The Coppice
Cogman Clough
Catholes Wood
Abbey Brook
Howden Moors
Foul Clough
Howden Edge

5
Hey Bank
New Close Wood
Cogman Clough
Howden Dean
Sheepfold Clough

92
Forest Knoll
Abbey Tip Plantation
Little Howden Moor
Poynton Bog

4
Abbey Bank
Greystones Moss

Lost Lad Hillend
Howshaw Tor

3
Bamford House
Green Stitches
Lost Lad
Back Tor

Shireowlers South Plantation

91
Hancock Wood
Bradfield Gate Head
Foulstone Rd

2
Far Deep Clough
Far Deep Clough
Gusset

Hancock Plantation
Near Deep Clough
Dovestone Clough

1
Upper Derwent Resr
Hollin Clough
Cakes of Bread

90
Hollinclough Plantation
John Field Howden

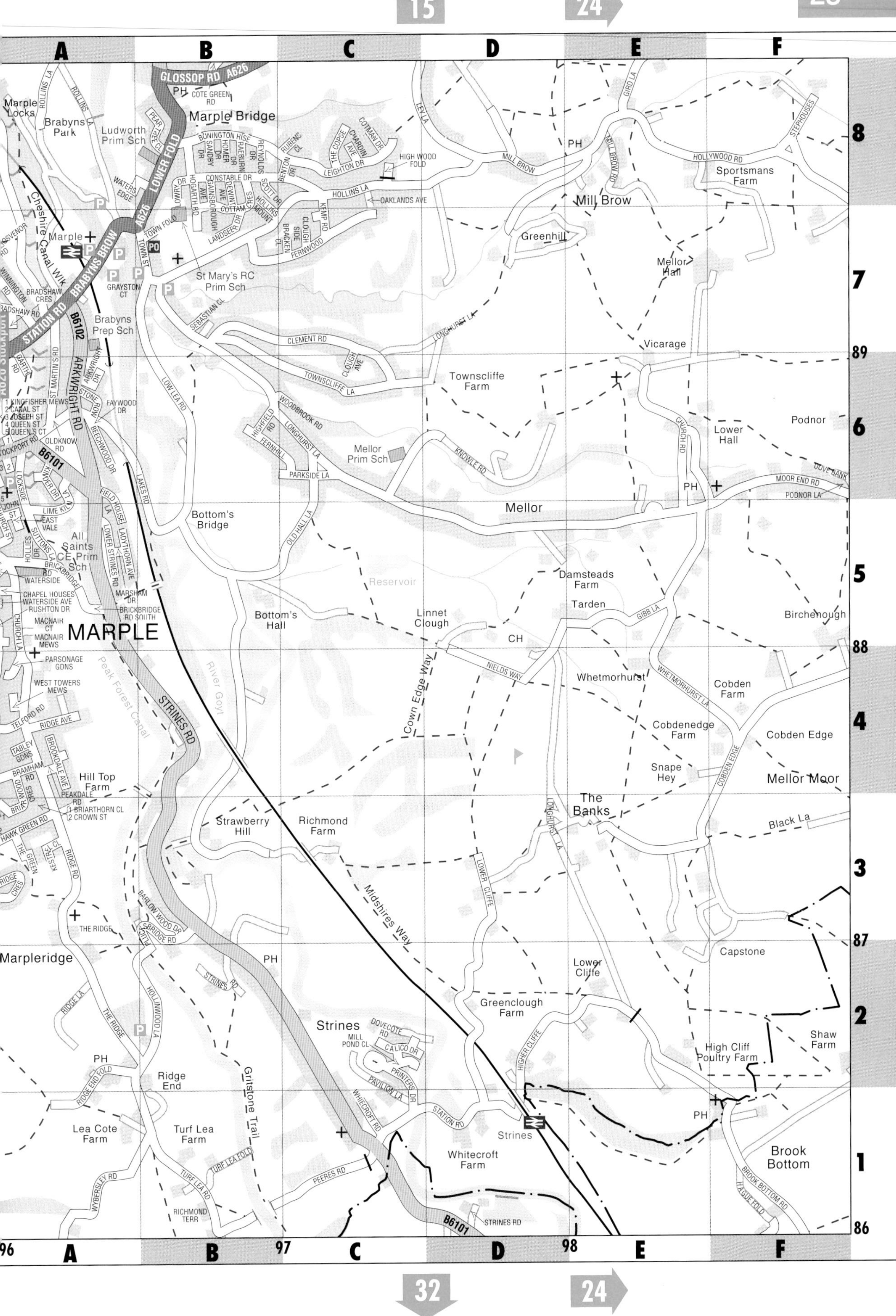
15
24
A
B
C
D
E
F
8
7
89
6
5
88
4
3
87
2
1
86
96
97
98
32
24
Marple Bridge
Mill Brow
Marple
MARPLE
Mellor
Strines
Marpleridge
Brook Bottom
Mellor Moor
GLOSSOP RD A626
LOWER FOLD
BRABYNS BROW
STATION RD
B6102
B6101
STRINES RD
Cheshire Canal Wlk
Peak Forest Canal
River Goyt
Midshires Way
Cown Edge Way
Gritstone Trail
Reservoir
Brabyns Park
Ludworth Prim Sch
Brabyns Prep Sch
St Mary's RC Prim Sch
Mellor Prim Sch
All Saints CE Prim Sch
Sportsmans Farm
Mellor Hall
Vicarage
Townscliffe Farm
Lower Hall
Podnor
Bottom's Bridge
Bottom's Hall
Damsteads Farm
Tarden
Linnet Clough
Birchenough
Whetmorhurst
Cobden Farm
Cobdenedge Farm
Cobden Edge
Snape Hey
The Banks
Hill Top Farm
Strawberry Hill
Richmond Farm
Capstone
Lower Cliffe
Greenclough Farm
Shaw Farm
High Cliff Poultry Farm
Ridge End
Lea Cote Farm
Turf Lea Farm
Whitecroft Farm
Greenhill
Black La
Marple Locks
PH
CH
PO

23
16

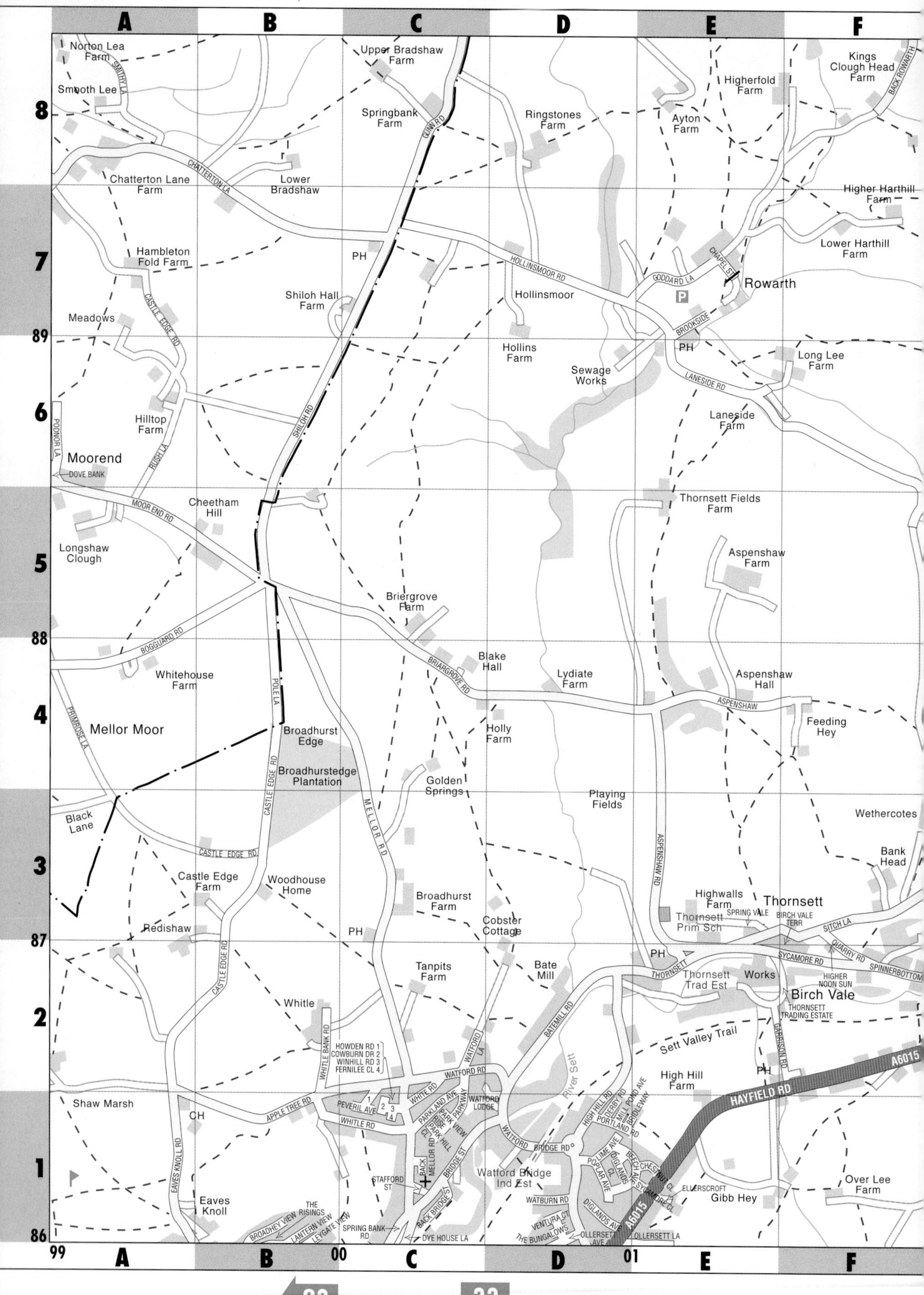
Norton Lea Farm
Smooth Lee
Upper Bradshaw Farm
Springbank Farm
Ringstones Farm
Higherfold Farm
Ayton Farm
Kings Clough Head Farm
Chatterton Lane Farm
Lower Bradshaw
Higher Harthill Farm
Lower Harthill Farm
Hambleton Fold Farm
Shiloh Hall Farm
Hollinsmoor
Rowarth
Meadows
Hollins Farm
Sewage Works
Long Lee Farm
Hilltop Farm
Laneside Farm
Moorend
Cheetham Hill
Thornsett Fields Farm
Longshaw Clough
Aspenshaw Farm
Briergrove Farm
Whitehouse Farm
Blake Hall
Lydiate Farm
Aspenshaw Hall
Mellor Moor
Broadhurst Edge
Broadhurstedge Plantation
Holly Farm
Feeding Hey
Golden Springs
Playing Fields
Black Lane
Wethercotes
Castle Edge Farm
Woodhouse Home
Broadhurst Farm
Highwalls Farm
Thornsett
Thornsett Prim Sch
Bank Head
Redishaw
Cobster Cottage
Tanpits Farm
Bate Mill
Thornsett Trad Est
Works
Birch Vale
White
Sett Valley Trail
High Hill Farm
Shaw Marsh
River Sett
Watford Bridge Ind Est
Eaves Knoll
Gibb Hey
Over Lee Farm
HAYFIELD RD
A6015
99
00
01
86
87
88
89
A B C D E F
1 2 3 4 5 6 7 8

23
33

17
26

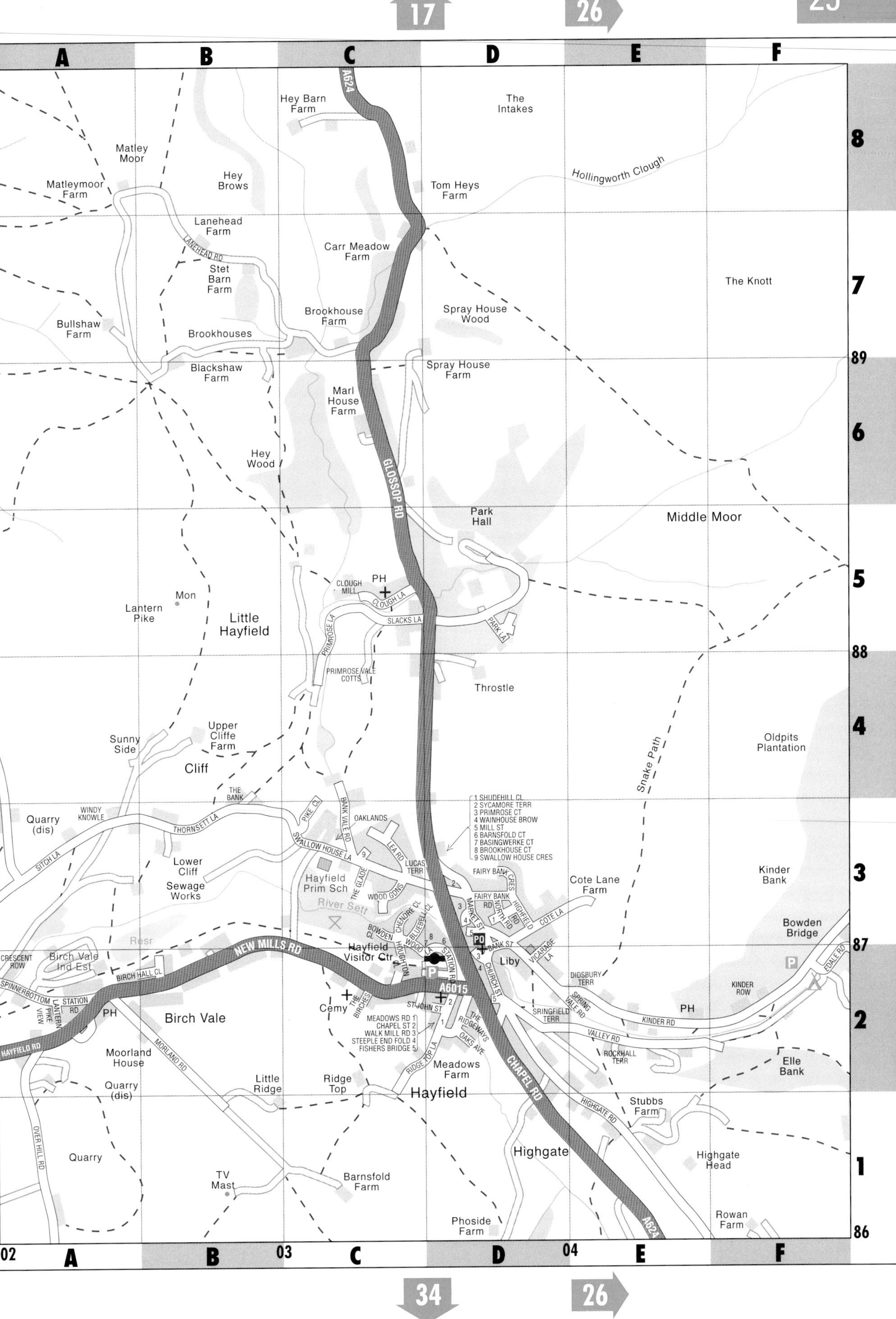
A
B
C
D
E
F
8
7
89
6
5
88
4
3
87
2
1
86
02
03
04
A624
Hey Barn Farm
The Intakes
Matley Moor
Hey Brows
Matleymoor Farm
Tom Heys Farm
Hollingworth Clough
Lanehead Farm
LANEHEAD RD
Carr Meadow Farm
Stet Barn Farm
The Knott
Bullshaw Farm
Brookhouse Farm
Spray House Wood
Brookhouses
Blackshaw Farm
Spray House Farm
Marl House Farm
Hey Wood
GLOSSOP RD
Park Hall
Middle Moor
CLOUGH MILL
PH
CLOUGH LA
Mon
Lantern Pike
Little Hayfield
SLACKS LA
PARK LA
PRIMROSE LA
PRIMROSE VALE COTTS
Throstle
Sunny Side
Upper Cliffe Farm
Cliff
Oldpits Plantation
Snake Path
THE BANK
Quarry (dis)
WINDY KNOWLE
PIKE CL
BANK VALE RD
OAKLANDS
THORNSETT LA
SWALLOW HOUSE LA
LEA RD
1 SHUDEHILL CL
2 SYCAMORE TERR
3 PRIMROSE CT
4 WAINHOUSE BROW
5 MILL ST
6 BARNSFOLD CT
7 BASINGWERKE CT
8 BROOKHOUSE CT
9 SWALLOW HOUSE CRES
SITCH LA
Lower Cliff
LUCAS TERR
FAIRY BANK CRES
Hayfield Prim Sch
Sewage Works
THE GLADE
FAIRY BANK RD
Cote Lane Farm
Kinder Bank
WOOD GDNS
River Sett
NORTH RD
HIGHFIELD RD
COTE LA
MARKET ST
CHENDRE CL
BLUEBELL CL
Bowden Bridge
Resr
BOWDEN CL
HOUGHTON
WOOD LA
PO
BANK ST
Hayfield Visitor Ctr
STATION RD
VICARAGE LA
Liby
CRESCENT ROW
Birch Vale Ind Est
NEW MILLS RD
P
EDALE RD
BIRCH HALL CL
A6015
CHURCH ST
DIDSBURY TERR
KINDER ROW
SPINNERBOTTOM
STATION RD
LANTERN PIKE VIEW
THE BIRCHES
ST JOHN ST
SPRING VALE RD
Cemy
SRINGFIELD TERR
PH
KINDER RD
Birch Vale
MEADOWS RD 1
CHAPEL ST 2
WALK MILL RD 3
STEEPLE END FOLD 4
FISHERS BRIDGE 5
THE RIDGEWAYS
OAKS AVE
VALLEY RD
HAYFIELD RD
ROCKHALL TERR
Moorland House
MORLAND RD
RIDGE TOP LA
Meadows Farm
CHAPEL RD
Elle Bank
Little Ridge
Ridge Top
Quarry (dis)
Hayfield
HIGHGATE RD
Stubbs Farm
OVER HILL RD
Quarry
Highgate
Highgate Head
TV Mast
Barnsfold Farm
Phoside Farm
Rowan Farm

34
26

A B C D E F

8

7

89

6

5

88

4

3

87

2

1

86

Leygatehead Moor

William Clough

Pennine Way

Sandy Heys

Nab Brow

Mermaid's Pool

White Brow

Hollin Head

River Kinder

Kinder Reservoir

Red Brook

Blackshaws

Kinder Head

Upper Moor

Marepiece Wood

Upper House

Farlands

Booth

River Kinder

Cluther Rocks

OLD KINDER

The Cote

Broad Clough

Kinder Low

Hill Houses

The Three Knolls

Pennine Way

EDALE RD

Tunstead Clough Farm

Tunstead House

River Sett

Stones House

Kinderlow End

The Ashes

Oaken Clough

Swine's Back

Harry Moor

Edale Cross

05 A B 06 C D 07 E F

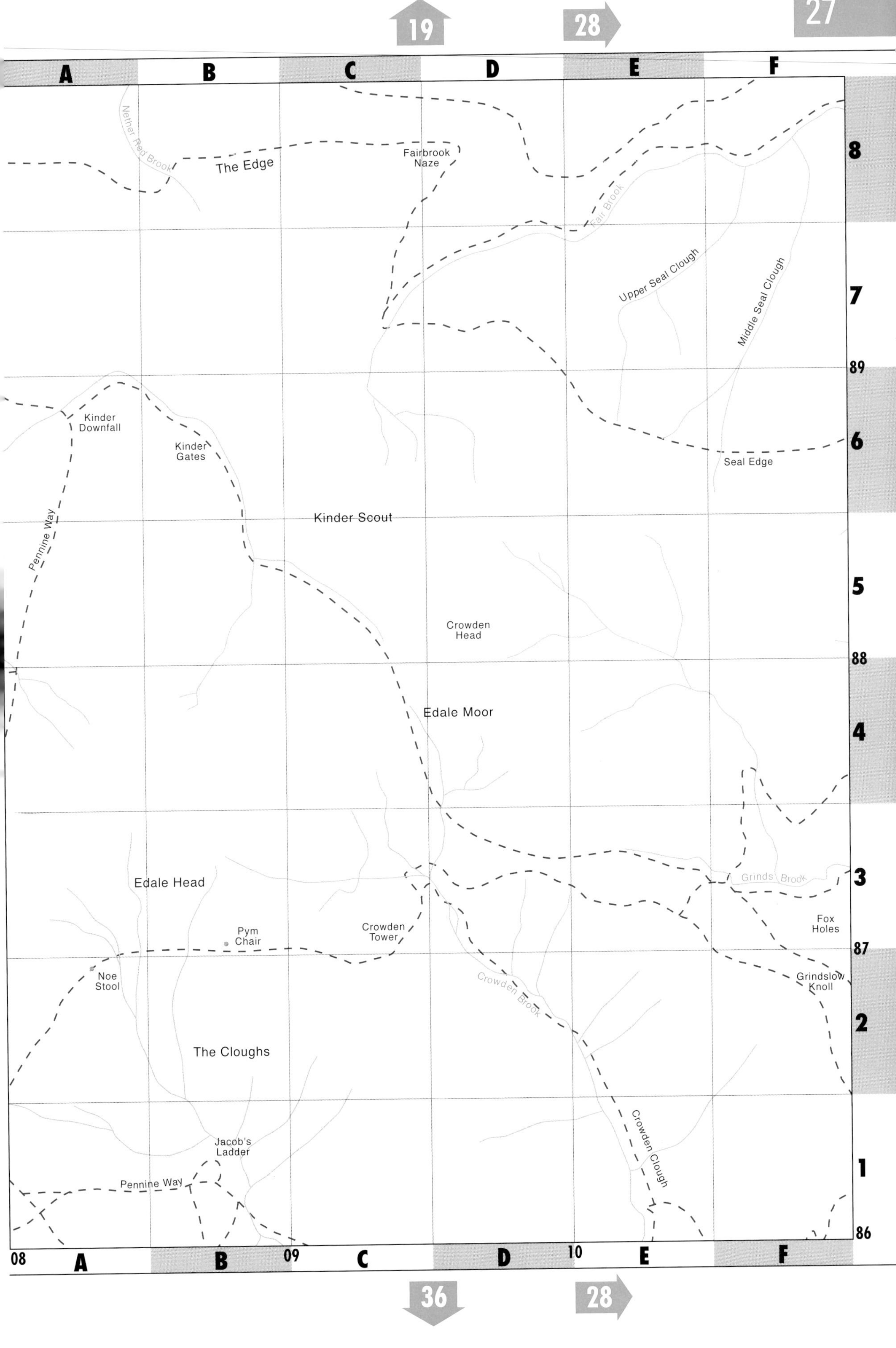

A   B   C   D   E   F

8

Nether Red Brook

The Edge

Fairbrook Naze

Fair Brook

7

Upper Seal Clough

Middle Seal Clough

89

Kinder Downfall

6

Kinder Gates

Seal Edge

Kinder Scout

Pennine Way

5

Crowden Head

88

Edale Moor

4

Edale Head

Grinds Brook

3

Pym Chair

Crowden Tower

Fox Holes

87

Noe Stool

Crowden Brook

Grindslow Knoll

2

The Cloughs

Crowden Clough

Jacob's Ladder

1

Pennine Way

86

08   A   B   09   C   D   10   E   F

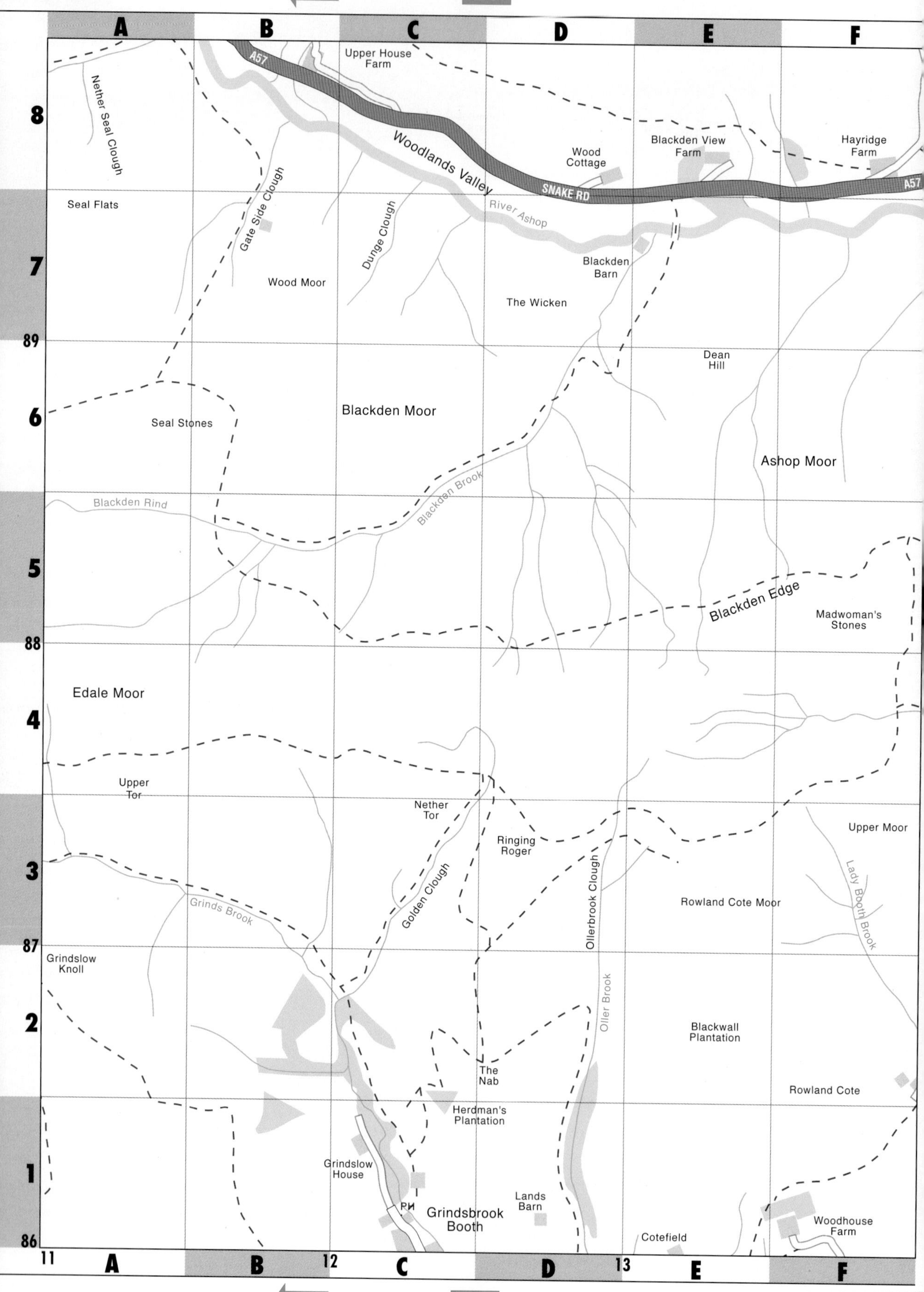

A B C D E F

8

Nether Seal Clough

Upper House Farm

Woodlands Valley

Wood Cottage

Blackden View Farm

Hayridge Farm

Seal Flats

Gate Side Clough

Dunge Clough

SNAKE RD

River Ashop

A57

7

Wood Moor

Blackden Barn

The Wicken

Blackden Moor

Dean Hill

89

6

Seal Stones

Blackden Brook

Ashop Moor

Blackden Rind

5

Blackden Edge

Madwoman's Stones

88

Edale Moor

4

Upper Tor

Nether Tor

Upper Moor

Ringing Roger

Lady Booth Brook

3

Grinds Brook

Golden Clough

Ollerbrook Clough

Rowland Cote Moor

Grindslow Knoll

87

Oller Brook

2

Blackwall Plantation

The Nab

Rowland Cote

Herdman's Plantation

Grindslow House

Lands Barn

1

P

Grindsbrook Booth

Cotefield

Woodhouse Farm

86

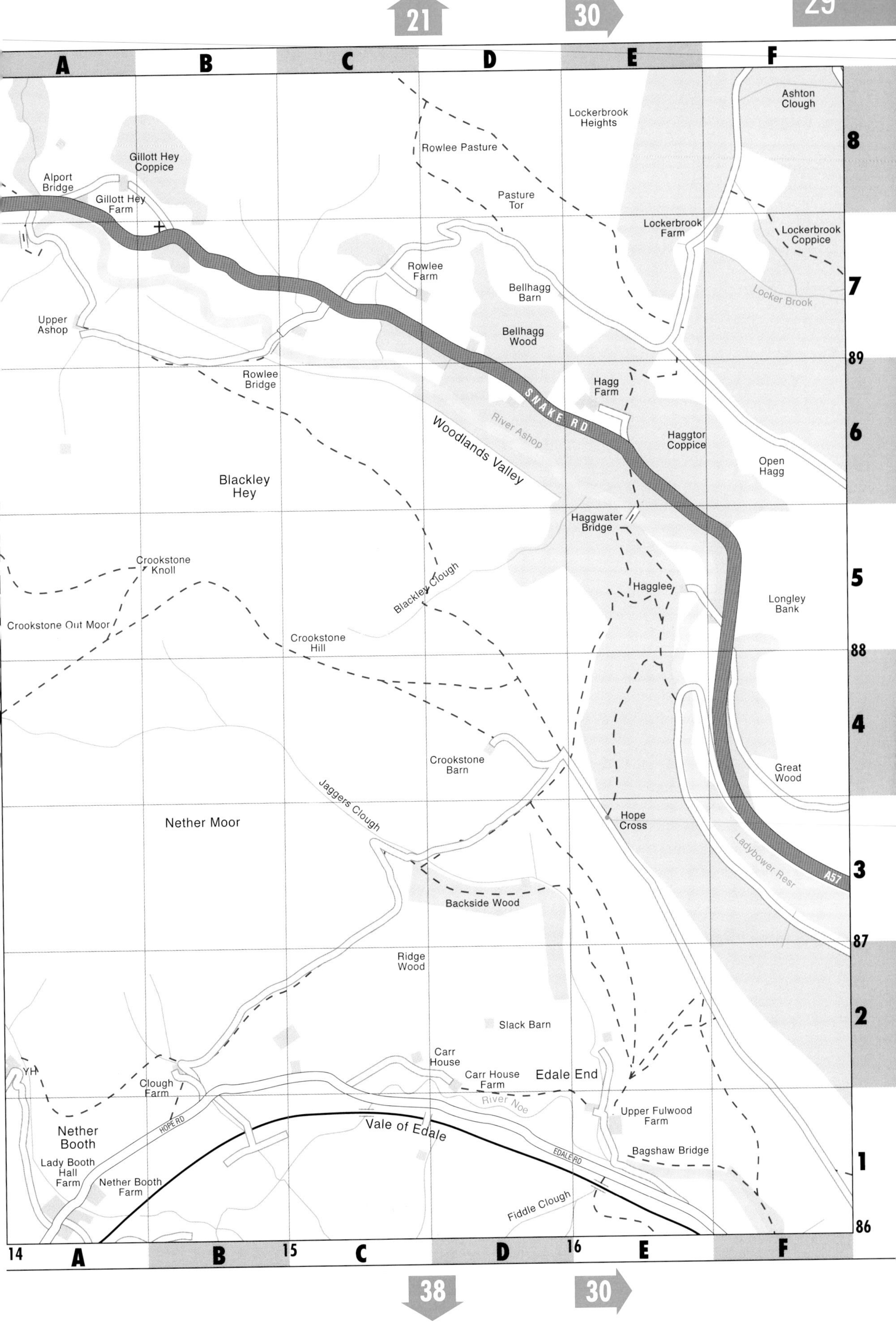

A B C D E F

8

Ashton
Clough

Lockerbrook
Heights

Rowlee Pasture

Gillott Hey
Coppice

Alport
Bridge

Gillott Hey
Farm

Pasture
Tor

Lockerbrook
Farm

Lockerbrook
Coppice

7

Rowlee
Farm

Bellhagg
Barn

Locker Brook

Upper
Ashop

Rowlee
Bridge

Bellhagg
Wood

89

SNAKE RD

Hagg
Farm

6

River Ashop

Woodlands Valley

Haggtor
Coppice

Open
Hagg

Blackley
Hey

Haggwater
Bridge

Crookstone
Knoll

Blackley Clough

Hagglee

Longley
Bank

5

Crookstone Out Moor

Crookstone
Hill

88

Crookstone
Barn

Great
Wood

4

Jaggers Clough

Hope
Cross

Ladybower Resr

A57

3

Nether Moor

Backside Wood

87

Ridge
Wood

Slack Barn

2

Carr
House

YH

Clough
Farm

Carr House
Farm

Edale End

River Noe

Upper Fulwood
Farm

HOPE RD

Nether
Booth

Vale of Edale

EDALE RD

Bagshaw Bridge

1

Lady Booth
Hall
Farm

Nether Booth
Farm

Fiddle Clough

86

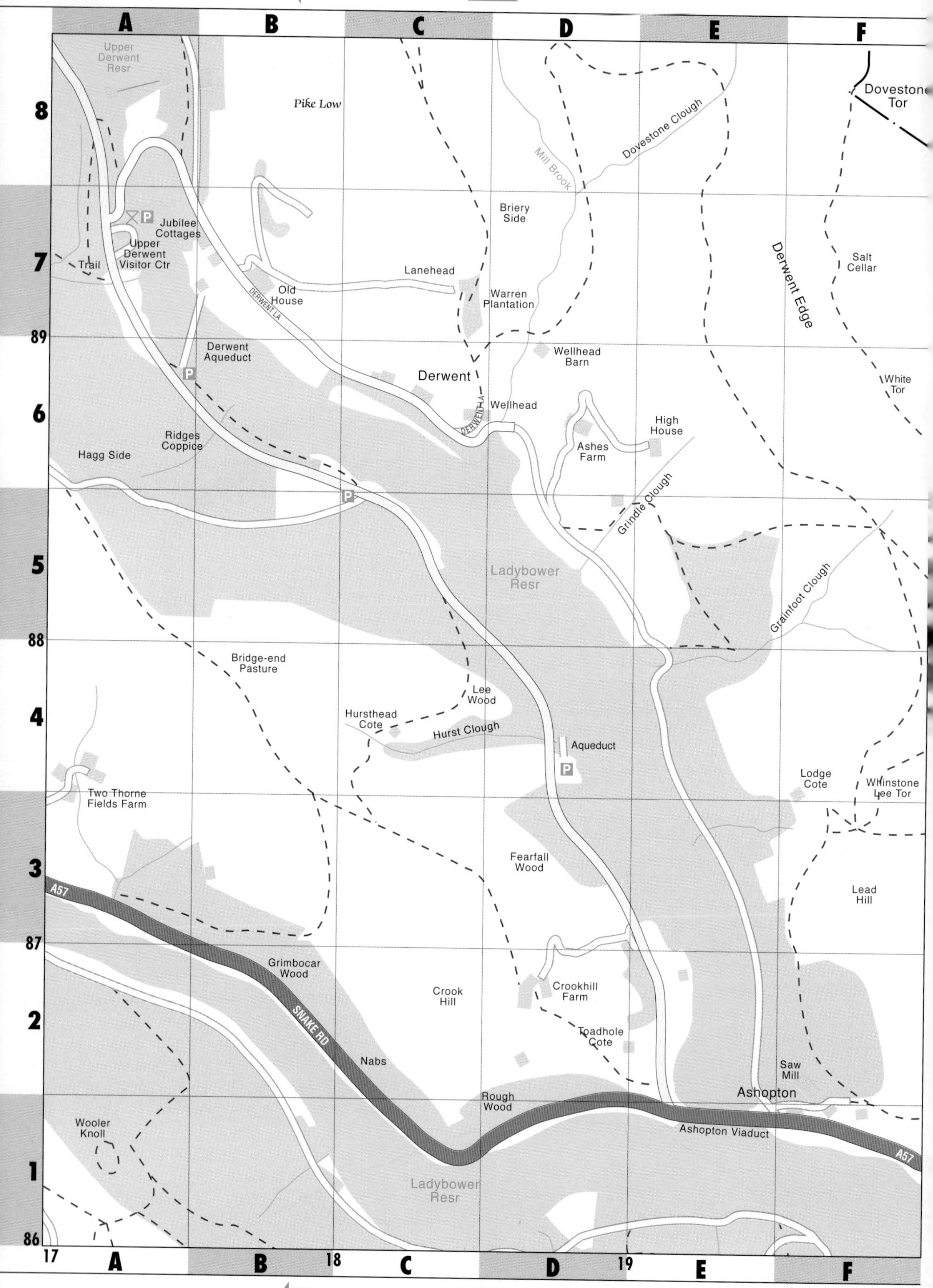

29
22

A   B   C   D   E   F

8   Upper
     Derwent
     Resr

     Pike Low

                                        Mill Brook   Dovestone Clough

                                                                              Dovestone
                                                                              Tor

                              Briery
                              Side   Derwent Edge   Salt
                                                                                     Cellar
7   P Jubilee
        Cottages
     Upper   Lanehead
     Derwent   Old
     Visitor Ctr   House   Warren
  Trail   Plantation
                          DERWENT LA

                                                                                          White
89   Wellhead   Tor
        Derwent   Derwent   Barn
        Aqueduct   DERWENT LA

     P   Derwent
6   Wellhead   High
                                                            House
        Ridges   Ashes
     Hagg Side Coppice   Farm
                                                   Grindle Clough

                   P
5   Ladybower
                                  Resr   Grainfoot Clough

88
        Bridge-end
        Pasture
                                  Lee
                                  Wood
4   Hursthead   Lodge
     Cote   Hurst Clough   Aqueduct   Cote   Whinstone
                                                                    Lee Tor
     Two Thorne   P
     Fields Farm
                                                                    Lead
3 A57   Fearfall   Hill
                                        Wood
87
        Grimbocar   Crookhill
        Wood   Crook   Farm
2   Hill
        SNAKE RD   Toadhole   Saw
                 Nabs   Cote   Mill
                          Rough   Ashopton
                          Wood
     Wooler   Ashopton Viaduct   A57
     Knoll
1   Ladybower
                                  Resr

86
17   A   B   18   C   D   19   E   F

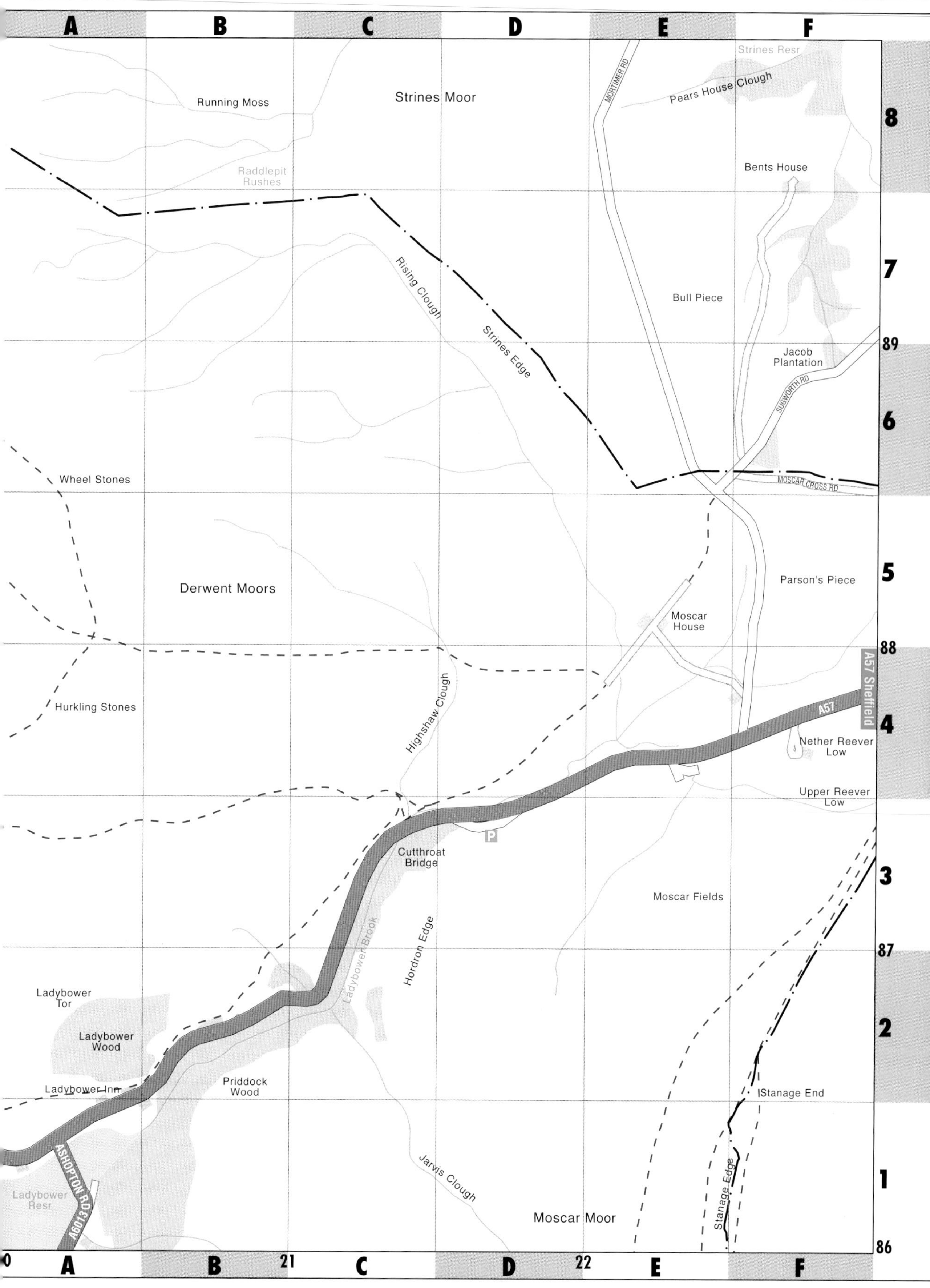

A B C D E F

Running Moss

Strines Moor

Pears House Clough

Strines Resr

Bents House

Raddlepit
Rushes

Rising Clough

Strines Edge

MORTIMER RD

Bull Piece

Jacob
Plantation

SUGWORTH RD

MOSCAR CROSS RD

Wheel Stones

Derwent Moors

Parson's Piece

Moscar
House

A57 Sheffield

A57

Hurkling Stones

Highshaw Clough

Nether Reever
Low

Upper Reever
Low

Cutthroat
Bridge

P

Moscar Fields

Ladybower Brook

Hordron Edge

Ladybower
Tor

Ladybower
Wood

Priddock
Wood

Ladybower Inn

IStanage End

Stanage Edge

ASHOPTON RD B6013 A6013

Ladybower
Resr

Jarvis Clough

Moscar Moor

23

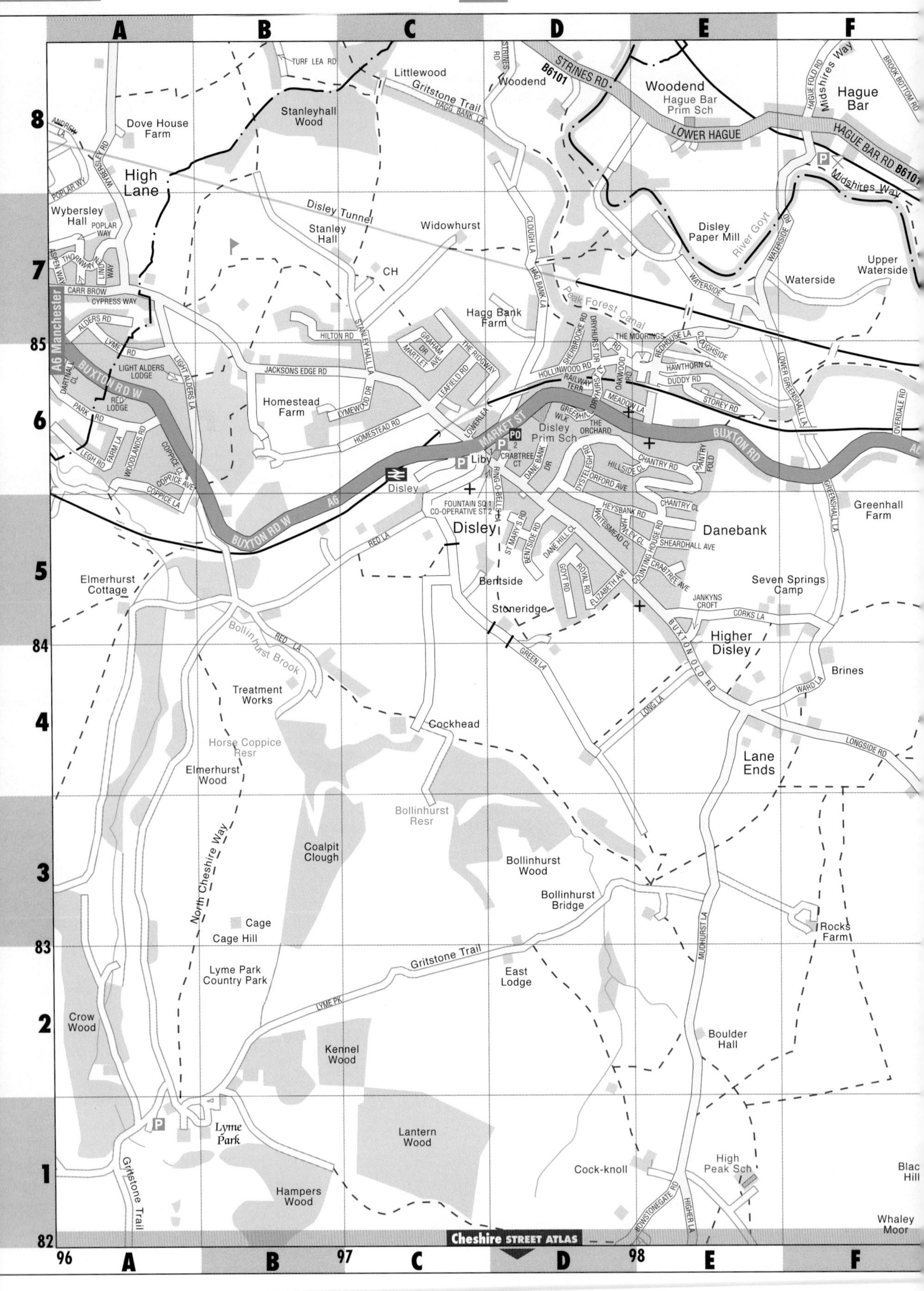
A
B
C
D
E
F
8
7
85
6
5
84
4
3
83
2
1
82
96
97
98
Dove House Farm
High Lane
Wybersley Hall
Stanleyhall Wood
Littlewood
Gritstone Trail
Woodend
STRINES RD
B6101
Woodend
Hague Bar Prim Sch
LOWER HAGUE
Hague Bar
HAGUE BAR RD B6101
Midshires Way
Disley Tunnel
Stanley Hall
Widowhurst
CH
Disley Paper Mill
River Goyt
Upper Waterside
Waterside
Peak Forest Canal
Hagg Bank Farm
HILTON RD
JACKSONS EDGE RD
Homestead Farm
HOMESTEAD RD
A6 Manchester
BUXTON RD W
LIGHT ALDERS LODGE
RED LODGE
Disley
Disley Prim Sch
Liby
MARKET ST
BUXTON RD
Danebank
Greenhall Farm
Elmerhurst Cottage
Bentside
Stoneridge
Seven Springs Camp
Higher Disley
Brines
GREEN LA
RED LA
Bollinhurst Brook
Treatment Works
Horse Coppice Resr
Cockhead
Elmerhurst Wood
Lane Ends
Bollinhurst Resr
Coalpit Clough
Bollinhurst Wood
Bollinhurst Bridge
North Cheshire Way
Cage
Cage Hill
Rocks Farm
Lyme Park Country Park
East Lodge
Crow Wood
Kennel Wood
Boulder Hall
Lyme Park
Lantern Wood
Hampers Wood
Cock-knoll
High Peak Sch
Whaley Moor
MUDHURST LA
LONGSIDE RD
BUXTON OLD RD

C7
1 FOUNDRY CT
2 LOWER ROCK ST
3 BACK UNION RD
4 LEES MILL

C8
1 New Mills Sch
and Sixth From Ctr

24

34

33

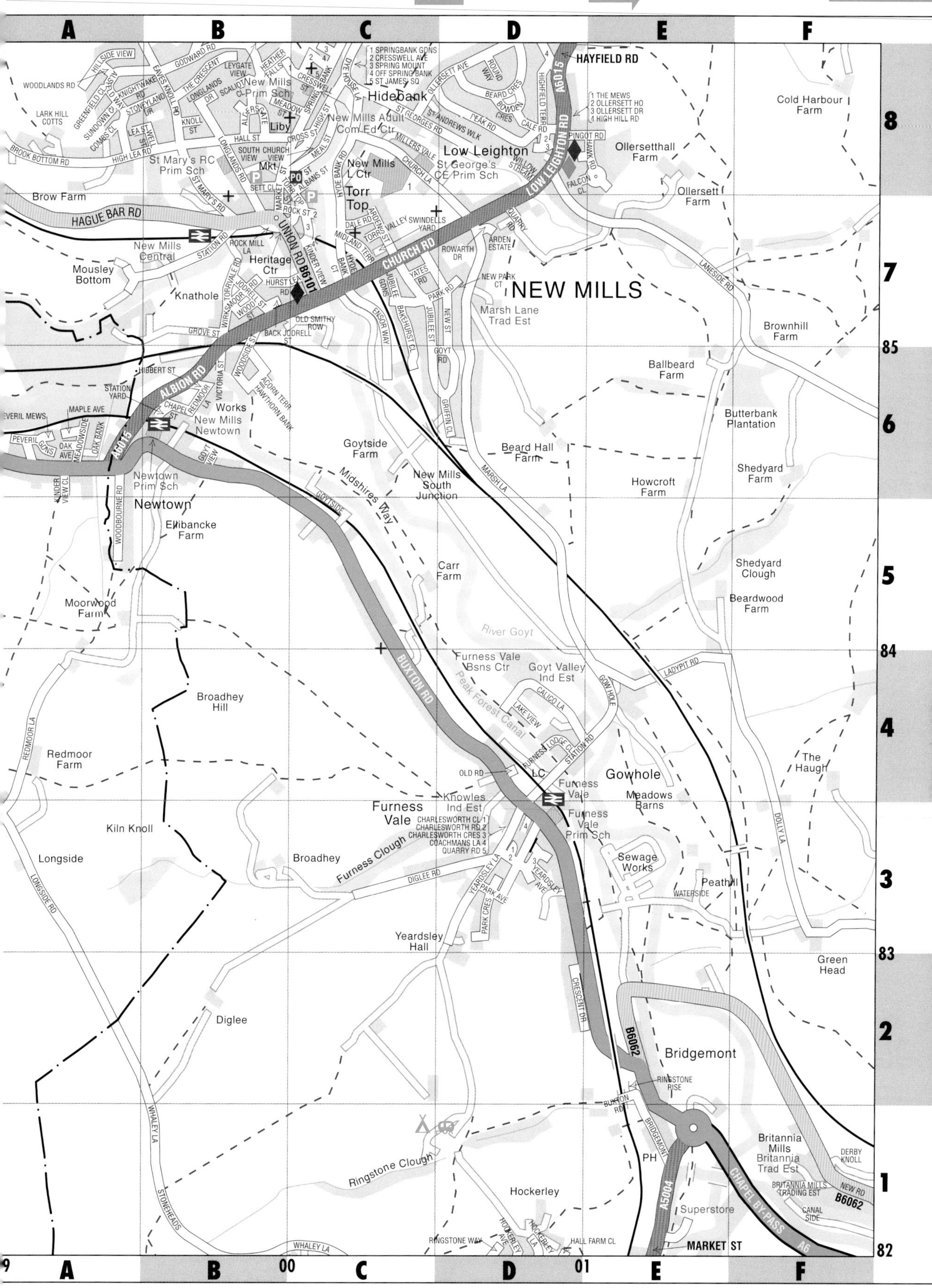

33
25

A B C D E F

8
Ollersett
Foxholes Clough
Far Phoside
Newhouse Farm
A624
HIGHGATE RD
The Heys
CHAPEL RD
OVER HILL RD
Moor Lodge
7
Higher Heys Farm
Piece Farm
Peep-O-Day
85
Higher Hills Farm
6
LANESIDE RD
Whiterakes
Red Mires
Higher Ashen Clough
Chinley Head
HAYFIELD RD
Lower Ashen Clough
New Allotments
Shedyard Piece
5
MAYNESTONE RD
OVER HILL RD
Monk's Meadows
84
Greenacres Farm
4
Clappersgate
Otter Brook
Chinley Churn
Hollands
Cloughhead
Cracken Edge
The Naze
Throstle Bank
3
Laneside Farm
Hill Farm
Mosley House
Alders Farm
83
Dryclough
Ancoats
THE SIDINGS 1
CHINLEY LODGE 2
ST MARY'S CL 3
BELLE VUE 4
LYME PARK
ALDERS LA
2
DOLLY LA
Chinley Houses
Cotebank
Tithe Barn
Stubbins
Mast
STUBBINS LA
RUTLAND WAY
ALPHA RD
ALDER BROOK
ALDERS MEADOW
Hotel
BUXTON RD
Chinley
STATION RD
PORTLAND
MANNERS CL
CRACKEN CL
PRINCES RD
PIKE VIEW CL
ALDERS AVE
Peak Sch
Brierley Green
DOLLY WOOD CL
BRIERLEY PK
Hollin Wood
Buxworth
Knowltop
LEADEN KNOWLE
B6062
LOWER LA
DEVONSHIRE DR
RHUDDLAN PL
DERWENT SQ
GREEN LA
BELGRADE AVE
DERWENT DR
STOCKTON DR
Chinley Prim Sch
White Hall
HAWTHORN CL
ASH GR
Chinley
1
B6062
NEW RD
STATION RD
Buxworth Prim Sch
ROSEYBANK
JANE LA
Works
Black Brook
WHITEHALL TERR
HUNTERS GREEN CL
FORGE RD
HARTINGTON DR
GRANBY AVE
HADFIELD DR
MILLPOND CL
BLACKBROOK DR
FORGE TERR
Mill
OUTRAM W
MILL CL
PH
WHITEHOUGH HEAD LA
MARRIOTT PL
BROOKSIDE
PH
A6
82
02 A B 03 C D 04 E F

33
46

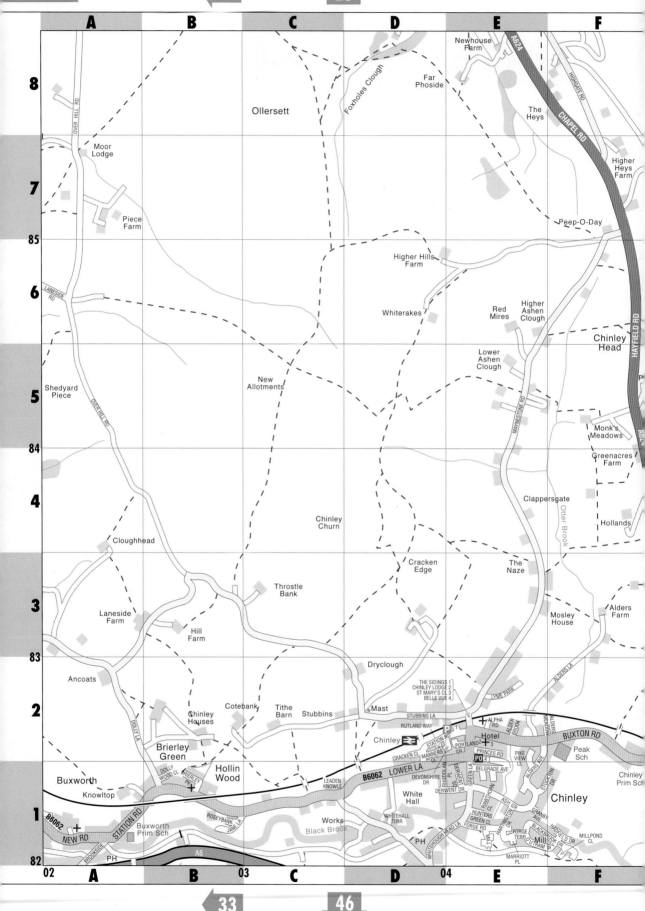

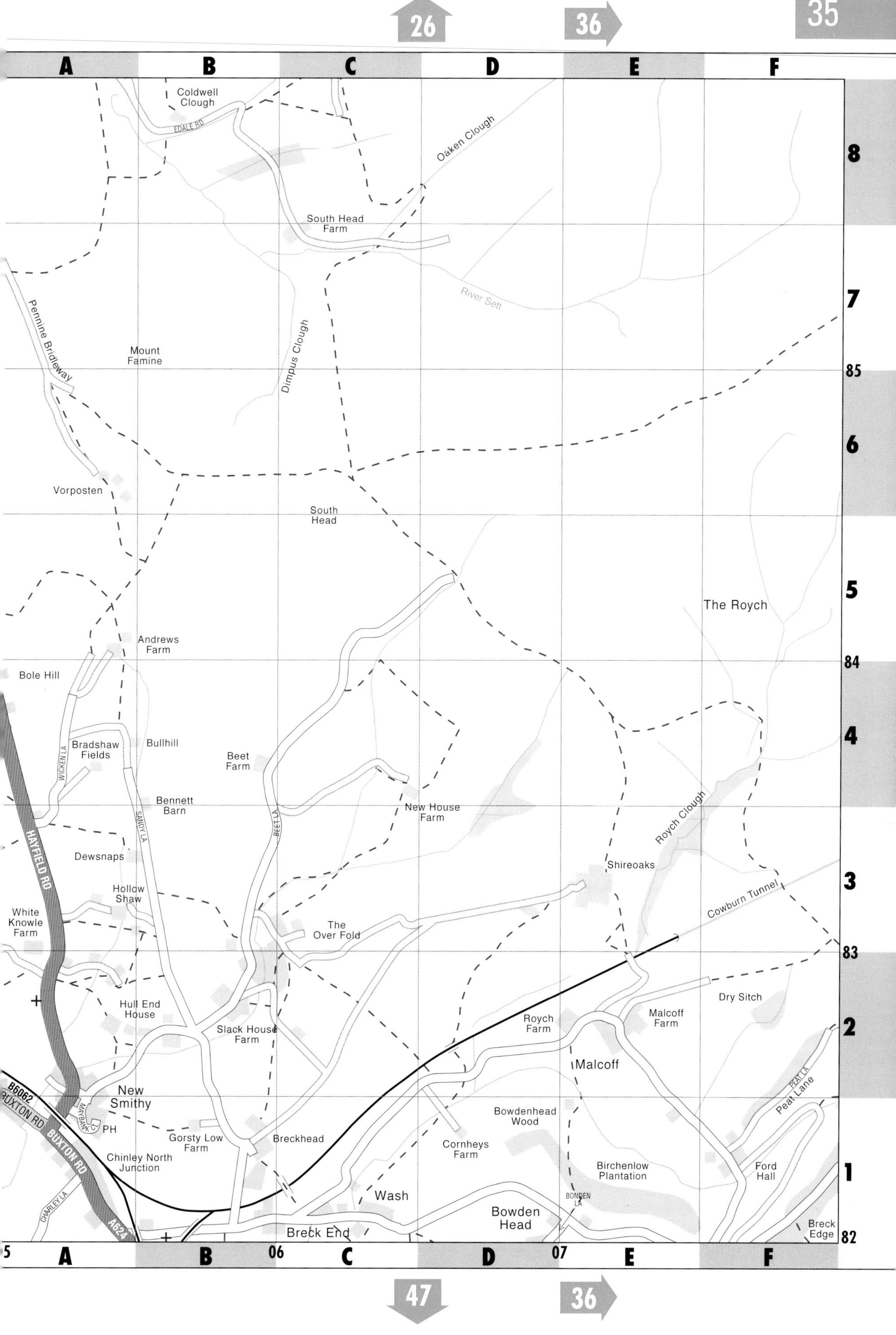

A   B   C   D   E   F

8

Coldwell
Clough

EDALE RD

Oaken Clough

South Head
Farm

River Sett

7

85

Mount
Famine

Dimpus Clough

Pennine Bridleway

6

Vorposten

South
Head

5

The Roych

Andrews
Farm

84

Bole Hill

4

Bradshaw
Fields

Bullhill

WICKEN LA

Beet
Farm

SANDY LA

Bennett
Barn

BEET LA

New House
Farm

Roych Clough

Dewsnaps

Shireoaks

3

Hollow
Shaw

Cowburn Tunnel

White
Knowle
Farm

HAYFIELD RD

The
Over Fold

83

+

Hull End
House

Roych
Farm

Malcoff
Farm

Dry Sitch

2

Slack House
Farm

Malcoff

B6062

New
Smithy

BUXTON RD

MAYBANK

Bowdenhead
Wood

Peat Lane

PEAT LA

BUXTON RD

PH

Gorsty Low
Farm

Breckhead

Cornheys
Farm

Birchenlow
Plantation

Ford
Hall

1

Chinley North
Junction

Wash

BONDEN
LA

CHARLEY LA

A624

+

Breck End

Bowden
Head

Breck
Edge

82

5   A   B   06   C   D   07   E   F

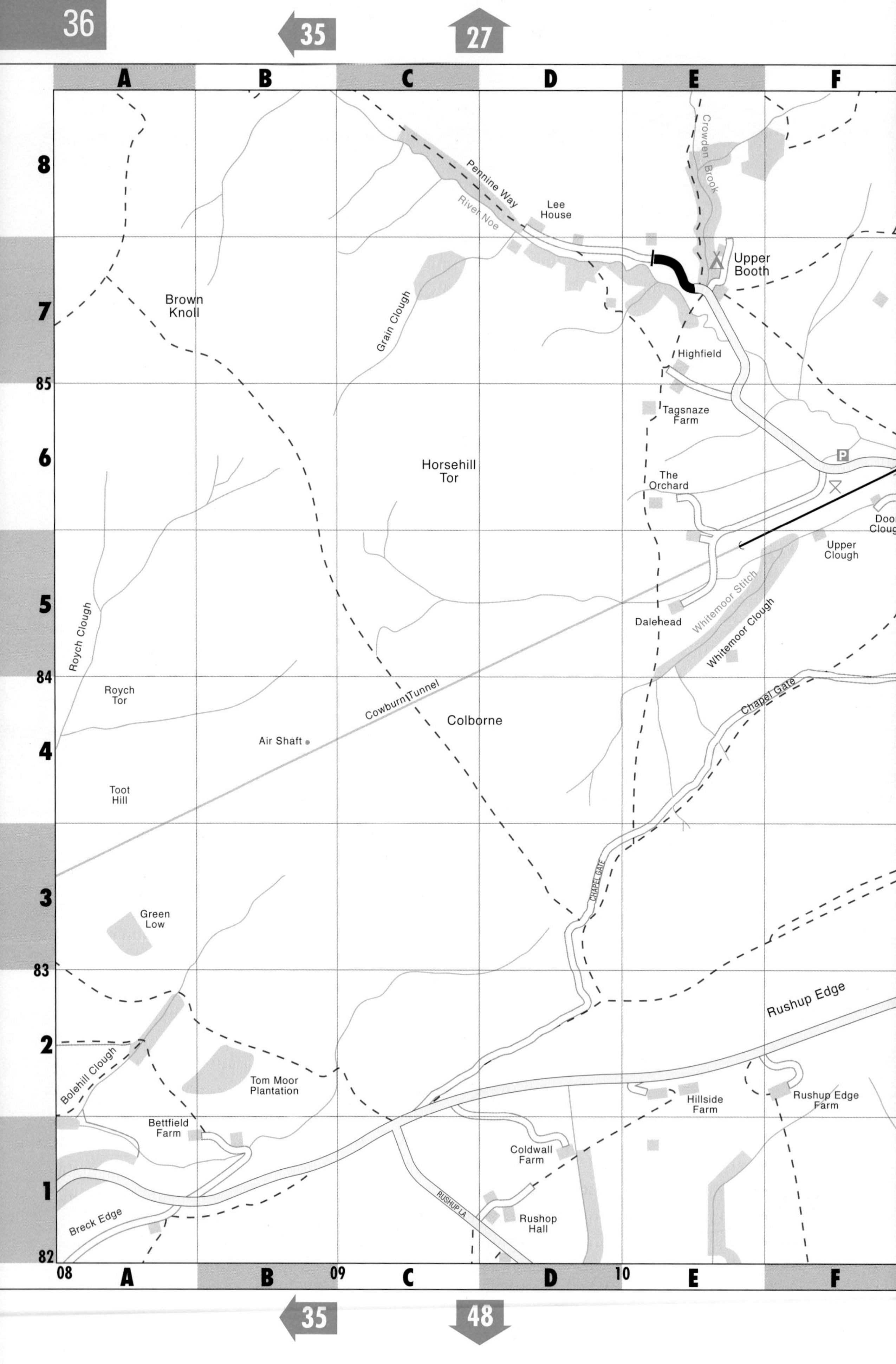

A B C D E F

8

Pennine Way

Crowden Brook

River Noe

Lee House

Upper Booth

7

Brown Knoll

Grain Clough

Highfield

85

Tagsnaze Farm

6

Horsehill Tor

The Orchard

P

Door Clough

Upper Clough

Whitemoor Stitch

5

Roych Clough

Dalehead

Whitemoor Clough

84

Roych Tor

Cowburn Tunnel

Colborne

Chapel Gate

4

Air Shaft

Toot Hill

3

Green Low

83

Chapel Gate

Rushup Edge

2

Bolehill Clough

Tom Moor Plantation

Hillside Farm

Rushup Edge Farm

Bettfield Farm

Coldwall Farm

1

Breck Edge

RUSHUP LA

Rushop Hall

82

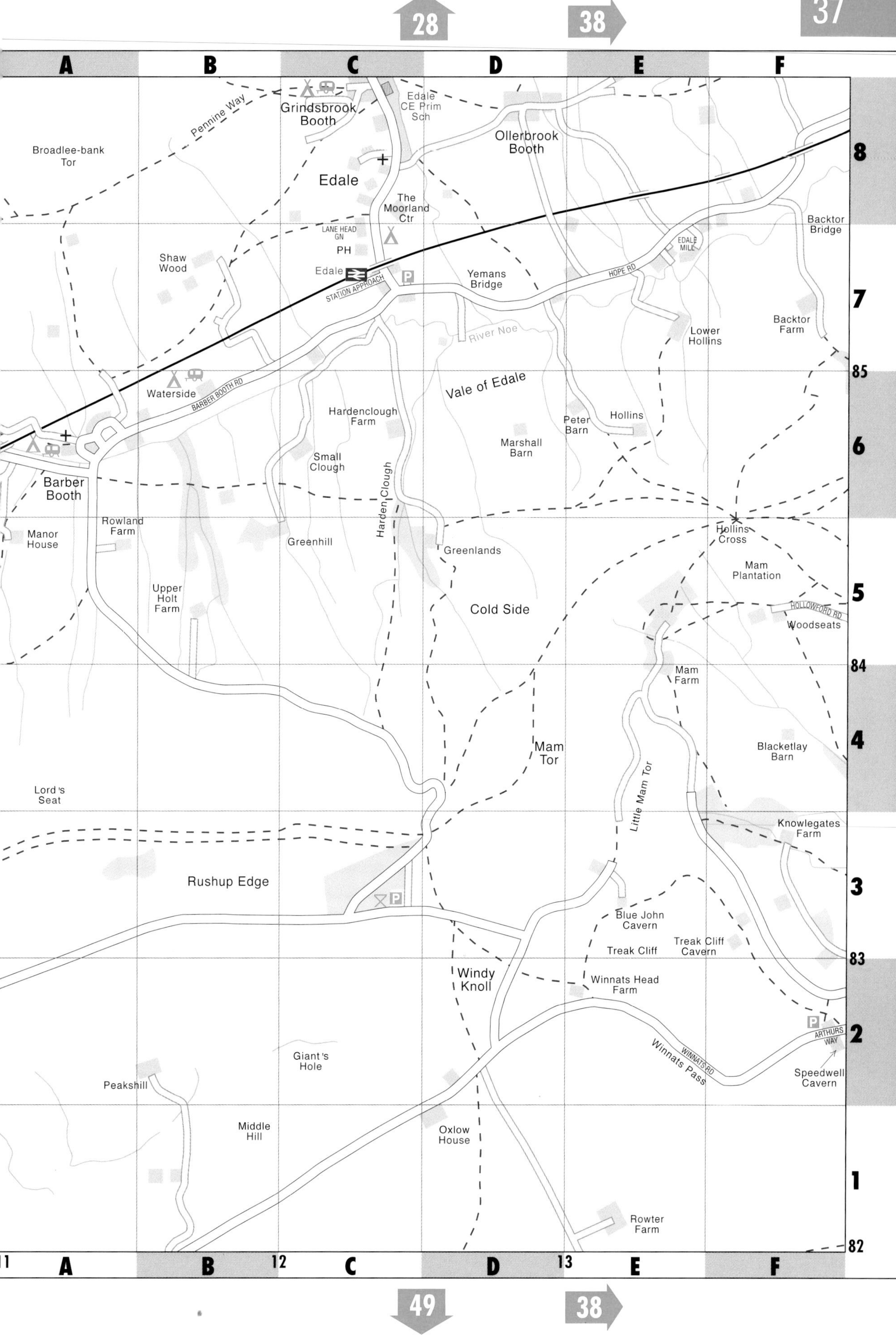

A B C D E F

Broadlee-bank Tor

Grindsbrook Booth

Edale CE Prim Sch

Ollerbrook Booth

Edale

The Moorland Ctr

LANE HEAD GN
PH

Shaw Wood

Edale
STATION APPROACH

Yemans Bridge

HOPE RD

EDALE MILL

Backtor Bridge

Lower Hollins

Backtor Farm

River Noe

Vale of Edale

Waterside

BARBER BOOTH RD

Hardenclough Farm

Peter Barn

Hollins

Small Clough

Marshall Barn

Harden Clough

Barber Booth

Manor House

Rowland Farm

Greenhill

Greenlands

Hollins Cross

Mam Plantation

HOLLOWFORD RD

Woodseats

Upper Holt Farm

Cold Side

Mam Farm

Lord's Seat

Mam Tor

Little Mam Tor

Blacketlay Barn

Knowlegates Farm

Rushup Edge

Blue John Cavern

Treak Cliff

Treak Cliff Cavern

Windy Knoll

Winnats Head Farm

ARTHURS WAY

Peakshill

Giant's Hole

WINNATS RD

Winnats Pass

Speedwell Cavern

Middle Hill

Oxlow House

Rowter Farm

85 8 7 85 6 5 84 4 3 83 2 1 82

37
29

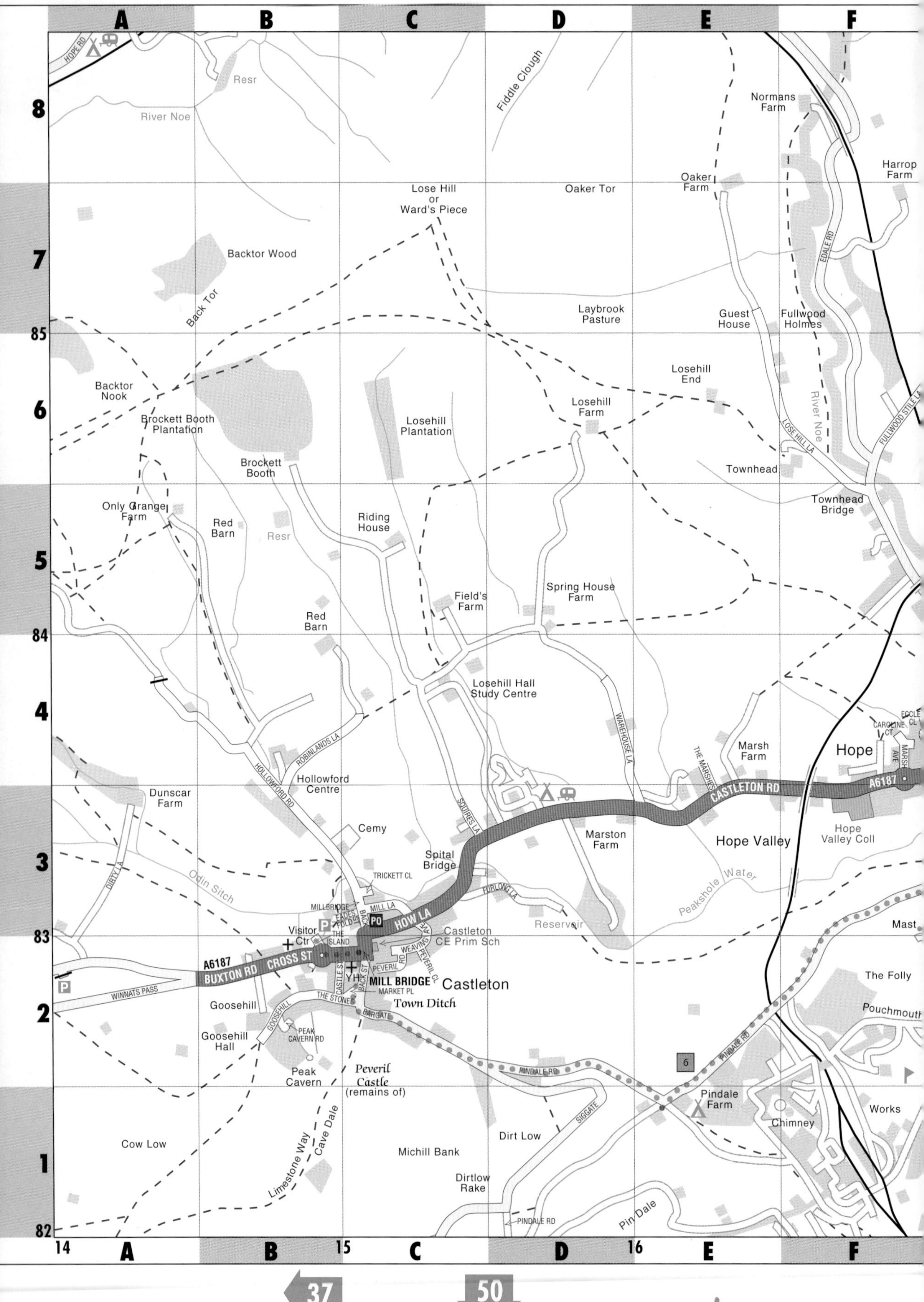
A
B
C
D
E
F
8
7
85
6
5
84
4
3
83
2
1
82
14
15
16
HOPE RD
Resr
River Noe
Fiddle Clough
Normans Farm
Harrop Farm
Lose Hill or Ward's Piece
Oaker Tor
Oaker Farm
Backtor Wood
Back Tor
EDALE RD
Laybrook Pasture
Guest House
Fullwood Holmes
Losehill End
Backtor Nook
Brockett Booth Plantation
Losehill Farm
Losehill Plantation
River Noe
FULLWOOD STILE LA
LOSE HILL LA
Brockett Booth
Townhead
Townhead Bridge
Only Grange Farm
Red Barn
Resr
Riding House
Spring House Farm
Field's Farm
Red Barn
Losehill Hall Study Centre
WAREHOUSE LA
ROBINLANDS LA
Marsh Farm
THE MARSHES
CAROLINE CT
ECCLES CL
Hope
MARSH AVE
Hollowford Centre
HOLLOWFORD RD
CASTLETON RD
A6187
Dunscar Farm
Cemy
SQUIRES LA
Marston Farm
Hope Valley
Hope Valley Coll
Spital Bridge
TRICKETT CL
Odin Sitch
DIRTY LA
Peakshole Water
MILLBRIDGE
EADES FOLD
BACK
MILL LA
PO
HOW LA
FURLONG LA
Reservoir
Mast
Visitor Ctr
THE ISLAND
Castleton CE Prim Sch
A6187
CROSS ST
BUXTON RD
WEAVING
PEVERIL
RD
PEVERIL CL
YH
MILL BRIDGE
Castleton
CASTLE ST
BACK ST
MARKET PL
Town Ditch
The Folly
WINNATS PASS
Goosehill
THE STONES
BARGATE
Pouchmouth
GOOSEHILL
Goosehill Hall
PEAK CAVERN RD
PINDALE RD
6
Peak Cavern
Peveril Castle (remains of)
PINDALE RD
Pindale Farm
Works
SIGGATE
Chimney
Cave Dale
Cow Low
Limestone Way
Dirt Low
Michill Bank
Dirtlow Rake
Pin Dale
PINDALE RD

37
50

30 40

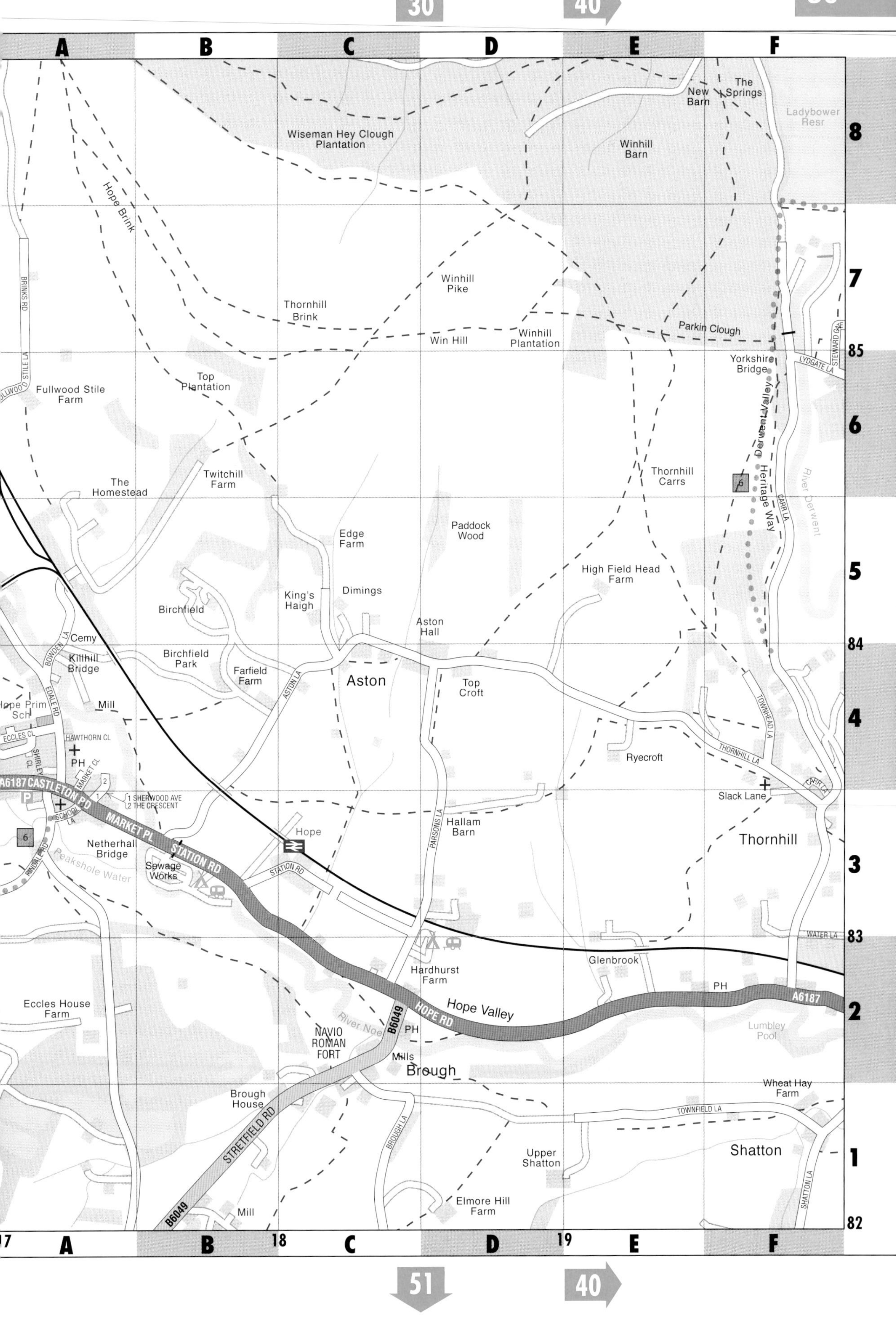

Wiseman Hey Clough Plantation
New Barn
The Springs
Ladybower Resr
Winhill Barn
Hope Brink
BRINKS RD
Winhill Pike
Thornhill Brink
Win Hill
Winhill Plantation
Parkin Clough
Yorkshire Bridge
LYDGATE LA
STEWARD GA
FULLWOOD STILE LA
Fullwood Stile Farm
Top Plantation
Derwent Valley Heritage Way
Twitchill Farm
The Homestead
Thornhill Carrs
CARR LA
River Derwent
Edge Farm
Paddock Wood
High Field Head Farm
King's Haigh
Dimings
Birchfield
Aston Hall
Cemy
BOWDEN LA
Killhill Bridge
Birchfield Park
Farfield Farm
ASTON LA
Aston
Top Croft
Hope Prim Sch
EDALE RD
Mill
TOWNHEAD LA
ECCLES CL
HAWTHORN CL
SHIRLEY CL
PH
MARKET CL
Ryecroft
THORNHILL LA
CARR LA
A6187 CASTLETON RD
1 SHERWOOD AVE
2 THE CRESCENT
Slack Lane
SCHOOL LA
MARKET PL
Hope
PARSONS LA
Hallam Barn
Thornhill
Netherhall Bridge
STATION RD
Sewage Works
STATION RD
Peakshole Water
PINDALE RD
WATER LA
Glenbrook
Hardhurst Farm
PH
A6187
Hope Valley
HOPE RD
Eccles House Farm
River Noe
B6049
PH
Lumbley Pool
NAVIO ROMAN FORT
Mills
Brough
Wheat Hay Farm
Brough House
TOWNFIELD LA
STRETFIELD RD
BROUGH LA
Upper Shatton
Shatton
SHATTON LA
Elmore Hill Farm
Mill
B6049
A B C D E F
8 7 85 6 5 84 4 3 83 2 1 82
17 18 19

51 40

39
31

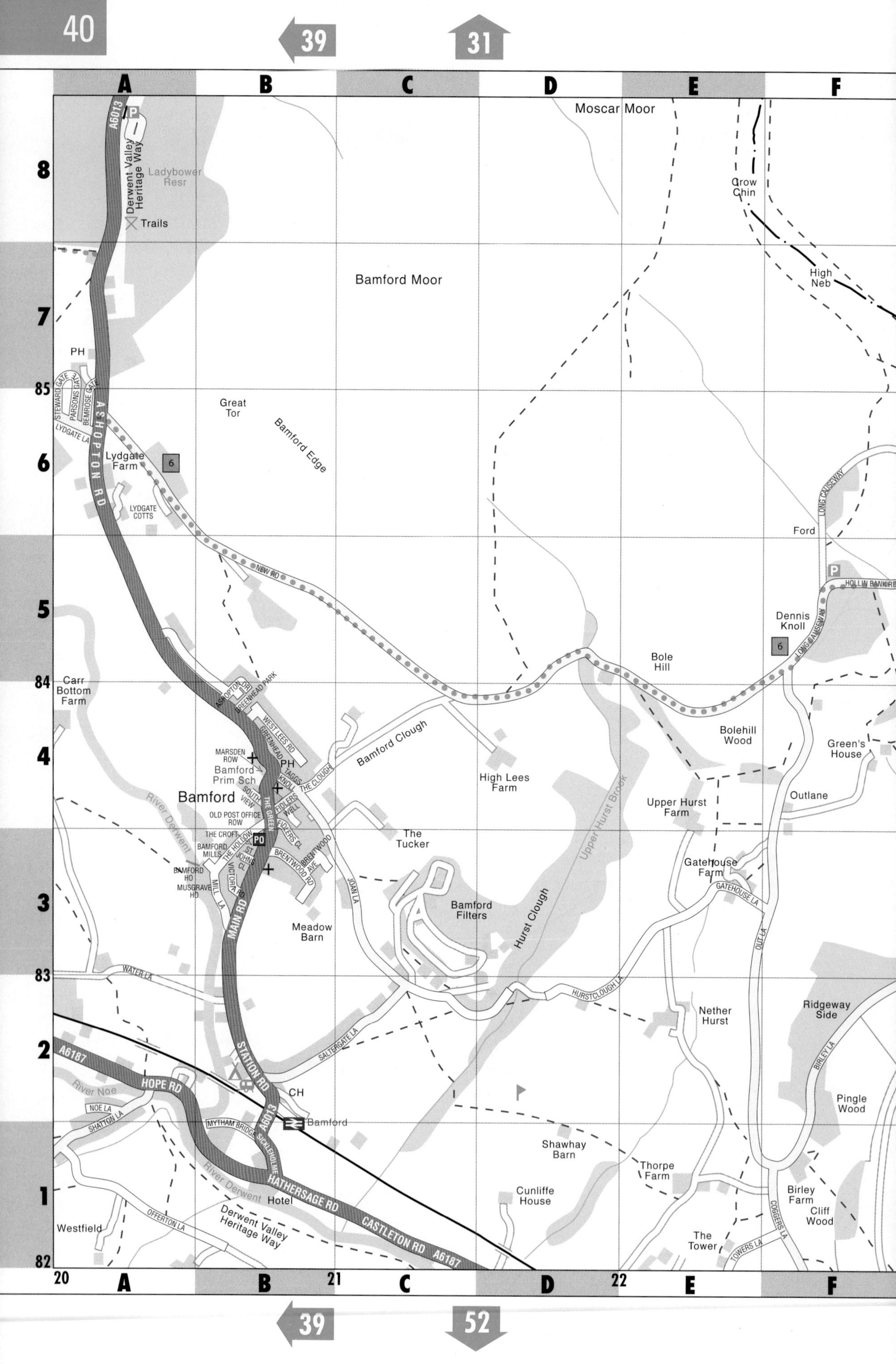
A
B
C
D
E
F
8
7
85
6
5
84
4
3
83
2
1
82
20
21
22
Moscar Moor
Ladybower Resr
Derwent Valley Heritage Way
Trails
Crow Chin
High Neb
Bamford Moor
PH
Great Tor
Bamford Edge
Lydgate Farm
LYDGATE COTTS
ASHOPTON RD
A6013
NEW RD
Ford
LONG CAUSEWAY
HOLLIN BANK RD
Dennis Knoll
Bole Hill
Carr Bottom Farm
Bolehill Wood
Green's House
Bamford Clough
High Lees Farm
Upper Hurst Farm
Outlane
Bamford
Bamford Prim Sch
River Derwent
The Tucker
Upper Hurst Brook
Gatehouse Farm
GATEHOUSE LA
Bamford Filters
Hurst Clough
MAIN RD
Meadow Barn
JOAN LA
WATER LA
HURSTCLOUGH LA
OUT LA
Ridgeway Side
Nether Hurst
SALTERGATE LA
STATION RD
A6187
HOPE RD
River Noe
NOE LA
SHATTON LA
CH
Bamford
MYTHAM BRIDGE
BIRLEY LA
Pingle Wood
Shawhay Barn
Thorpe Farm
Cunliffe House
Birley Farm
Cliff Wood
HATHERSAGE RD
CASTLETON RD
Hotel
Westfield
OFFERTON LA
The Tower
TOWERS LA
COGGERS LA

39
52

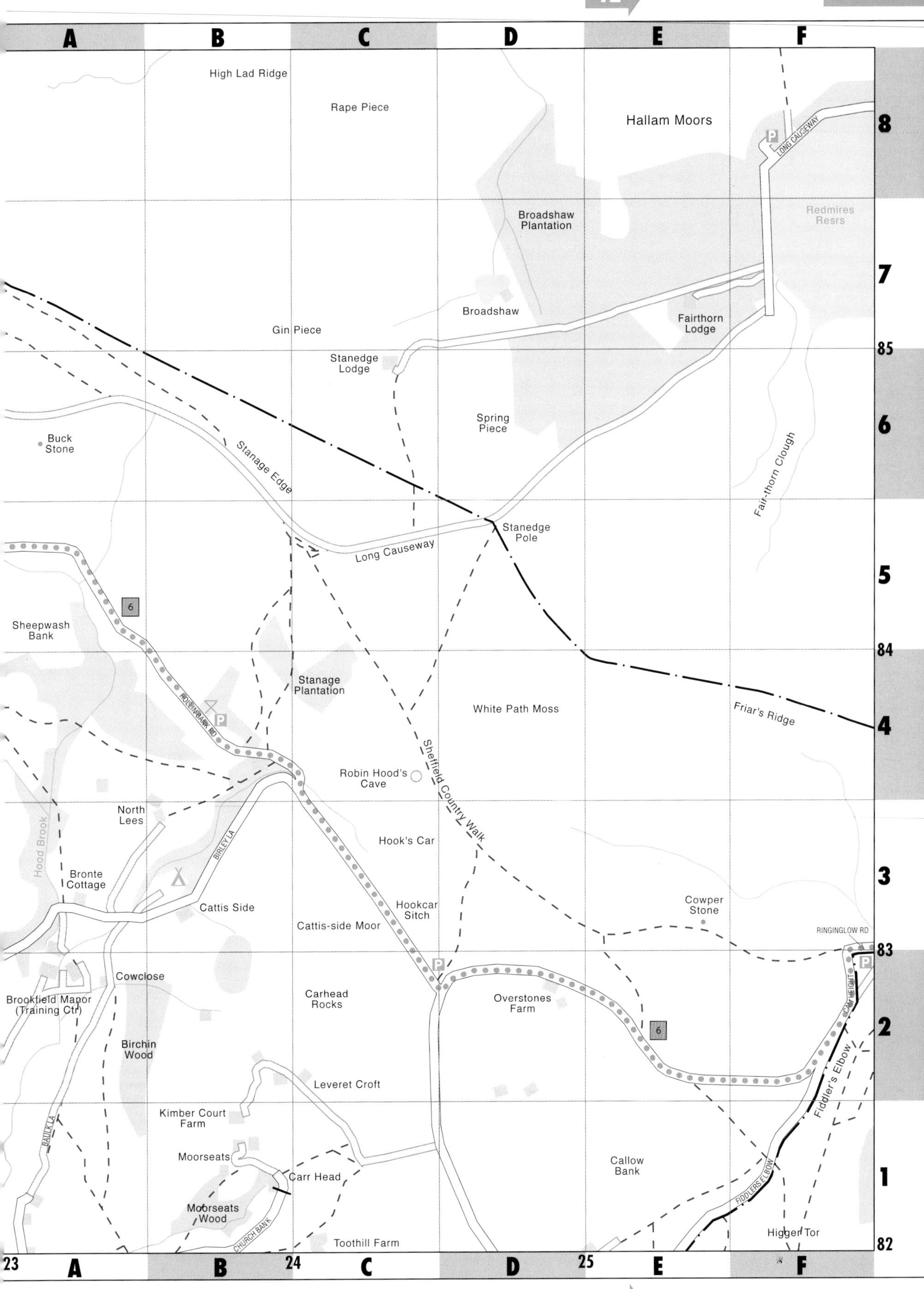

A   B   C   D   E   F

High Lad Ridge

Rape Piece

Hallam Moors

8

Broadshaw
Plantation

Redmires
Resrs

7

Broadshaw

85

Gin Piece

Fairthorn
Lodge

Stanedge
Lodge

6

Buck
Stone

Spring
Piece

Stanage Edge

Fair-thorn Clough

Long Causeway

Stanedge
Pole

5

Sheepwash
Bank

6

84

Stanage
Plantation

White Path Moss

Friar's Ridge

4

RIVELIN PARK RD

P

Robin Hood's
Cave

Sheffield Country Walk

North
Lees

Hook's Car

Cowper
Stone

RINGINGLOW RD

3

Hood Brook

Bronte
Cottage

BIRLEY LA

Hookcar
Sitch

83

Cattis Side

Cattis-side Moor

P

P

Cowclose

Carhead
Rocks

Overstones
Farm

6

CARR HEIGHTS

2

Brookfield Manor
(Training Ctr)

Birchin
Wood

Leveret Croft

Fiddler's Elbow

BAULK LA

Kimber Court
Farm

Callow
Bank

FIDDLERS ELBOW

1

Moorseats

Carr Head

CHURCH BANK

Moorseats
Wood

Higger Tor

82

Toothill Farm

23   A   B   24   C   D   25   E   F

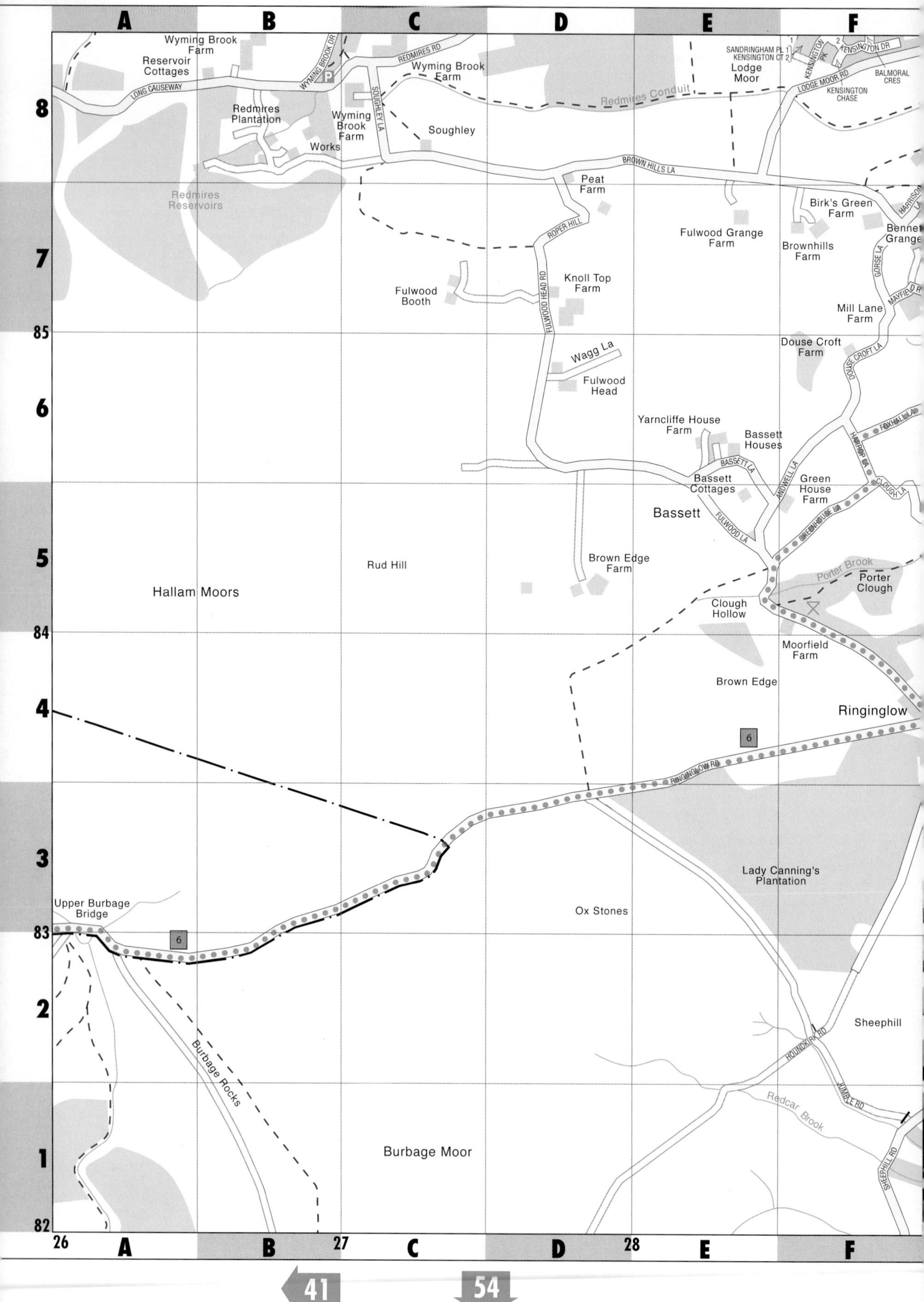

A B C D E F

8

Wyming Brook
Farm
Reservoir
Cottages
LONG CAUSEWAY
Redmires
Plantation
Wyming
Brook
Farm
Works
WYMING BROOK DR
P
REDMIRES RD
SOUGHLEY LA
Wyming Brook
Farm
Soughley
Redmires Conduit
Lodge
Moor
SANDRINGHAM PL 1
KENSINGTON CT 2
1
2
KENSINGTON DR
KENSINGTON PK
LODGE MOOR RD
KENSINGTON
CHASE
BALMORAL
CRES
HARRISON

Redmires
Reservoirs
BROWN HILLS LA
Peat
Farm
Fulwood Grange
Farm
Birk's Green
Farm
Brownhills
Farm
Bennet
Grange
GORSE LA
MAYFIELD R

7

Fulwood
Booth
ROPER HILL
Knoll Top
Farm
Mill Lane
Farm

85

FULWOOD HEAD RD
Wagg La
Fulwood
Head
Douse Croft
Farm
DOUSE CROFT LA

6

Yarncliffe House
Farm
Bassett
Houses
Bassett
Cottages
BASSETT LA
FOXHALL HEAD
LANCROFT LA
Green
House
Farm
AKDWELL LA
CLOUGH

Bassett

5

Hallam Moors
Rud Hill
Brown Edge
Farm
Clough
Hollow
FULWOOD LA
GREENHOUSE LA
Porter Brook
Porter
Clough

84

Moorfield
Farm

4

Brown Edge
Ringinglow
6
RINGINGLOW RD

Upper Burbage
Bridge

3

Lady Canning's
Plantation
Ox Stones

83

6

2

Burbage Rocks
Sheephill
HOUNDKIRK RD
JUMBLE RD
Redcar Brook
SHEEPHILL RD

1

Burbage Moor

82

26 A B 27 C D 28 E F

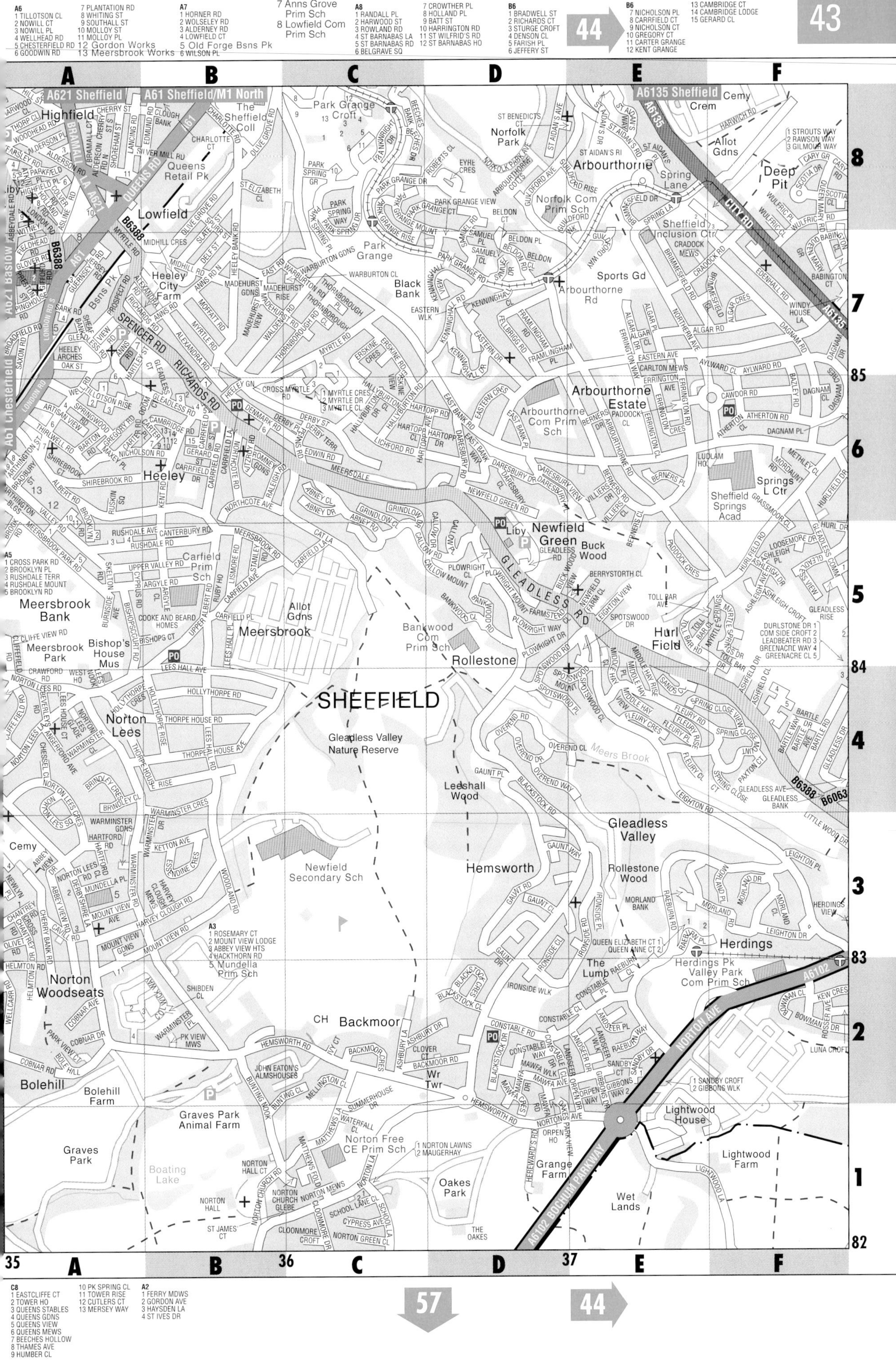

43
A6
1 TILLOTSON CL
2 NOWILL CT
3 NOWILL PL
4 WELLHEAD RD
5 CHESTERFIELD RD
6 GOODWIN RD
7 PLANTATION RD
8 WHITING ST
9 SOUTHALL ST
10 MOLLOY ST
11 MOLLOY PL
12 Gordon Works
13 Meersbrook Works
A7
1 HORNER RD
2 WOLSELEY RD
3 ALDERNEY RD
4 LOWFIELD CT
5 Old Forge Bsns Pk
6 WILSON PL
7 Anns Grove Prim Sch
8 Lowfield Com Prim Sch
A8
1 RANDALL PL
2 HARWOOD ST
3 ROWLAND RD
4 ST BARNABAS LA
5 ST BARNABAS RD
6 BELGRAVE SQ
7 CROWTHER PL
8 HOLLAND PL
9 BATT ST
10 HARRINGTON RD
11 ST WILFRID'S RD
12 ST BARNABAS HO
B6
1 BRADWELL ST
2 RICHARDS CT
3 STURGE CROFT
4 DENSON CL
5 FARISH PL
6 JEFFERY ST
44
B6
7 NICHOLSON PL
8 CARRFIELD CT
9 NICHOLSON CT
10 GREGORY CT
11 CARTER GRANGE
12 KENT GRANGE
13 CAMBRIDGE CT
14 CAMBRIDGE LODGE
15 GERARD CL
A B C D E F
8 7 6 5 4 3 2 1
85 84 83 82
35 36 37
A621 Sheffield
A61 Sheffield/M1 North
A6135 Sheffield
A61 Chesterfield
A621 Baslow
Highfield
The Sheffield Coll
Park Grange Croft
Norfolk Park
Arbourthorne
Cemy
Crem
Allot Gdns
Deep Pit
Queens Retail Pk
Lowfield
Spring Lane
Norfolk Com Prim Sch
Sheffield Inclusion Ctr
Park Grange
Heeley City Farm
Black Bank
Sports Gd
Arbourthorne Rd
Arbourthorne Estate
Arbourthorne Com Prim Sch
Heeley
Springs L Ctr
Sheffield Springs Acad
Newfield Green
Buck Wood
Carfield Prim Sch
Allot Gdns
Meersbrook
Meersbrook Bank
Bankwood Com Prim Sch
Bishop's House Mus
Meersbrook Park
Rollestone
Hurl Field
SHEFFIELD
Norton Lees
Gleadless Valley Nature Reserve
Meers Brook
Leeshall Wood
Cemy
Gleadless Valley
Newfield Secondary Sch
Hemsworth
Rollestone Wood
Herdings
The Lump
Herdings Pk Valley Park Com Prim Sch
Norton Woodseats
Backmoor
Bolehill
Bolehill Farm
Wr Twr
Graves Park Animal Farm
Lightwood House
Graves Park
Norton Free CE Prim Sch
Lightwood Farm
Boating Lake
Oakes Park
Grange Farm
Wet Lands
Norton Hall
A5
1 CROSS PARK RD
2 BROOKLYN PL
3 RUSHDALE TERR
4 RUSHDALE MOUNT
5 BROOKLYN RD
A3
1 ROSEMARY CT
2 MOUNT VIEW LODGE
3 ABBEY VIEW HTS
4 HACKTHORN RD
5 Mundella Prim Sch
1 STROUTS WAY
2 RAWSON WAY
3 GILMOUR WAY
DURLSTONE DR 1
COM SIDE CROFT 2
LEADBEATER RD 3
GREENACRE WAY 4
GREENACRE CL 5
1 SANDBY CROFT
2 GIBBONS WLK
1 NORTON LAWNS
2 MAUGERHAY
A6135
A6102
B6388
B6063
A6102 BOCHUM PARKWAY
NORTON AVE
GLEADLESS RD
SPENCER RD
RICHARDS RD
CITY RD
QUEENS RD
C8
1 EASTCLIFFE CT
2 TOWER HO
3 QUEENS STABLES
4 QUEENS GDNS
5 QUEENS VIEW
6 QUEENS MEWS
7 BEECHES HOLLOW
8 THAMES AVE
9 HUMBER CL
10 PK SPRING CL
11 TOWER RISE
12 CUTLERS CT
13 MERSEY WAY
A2
1 FERRY MDWS
2 GORDON AVE
3 HAYSDEN LA
4 ST IVES DR
57
44

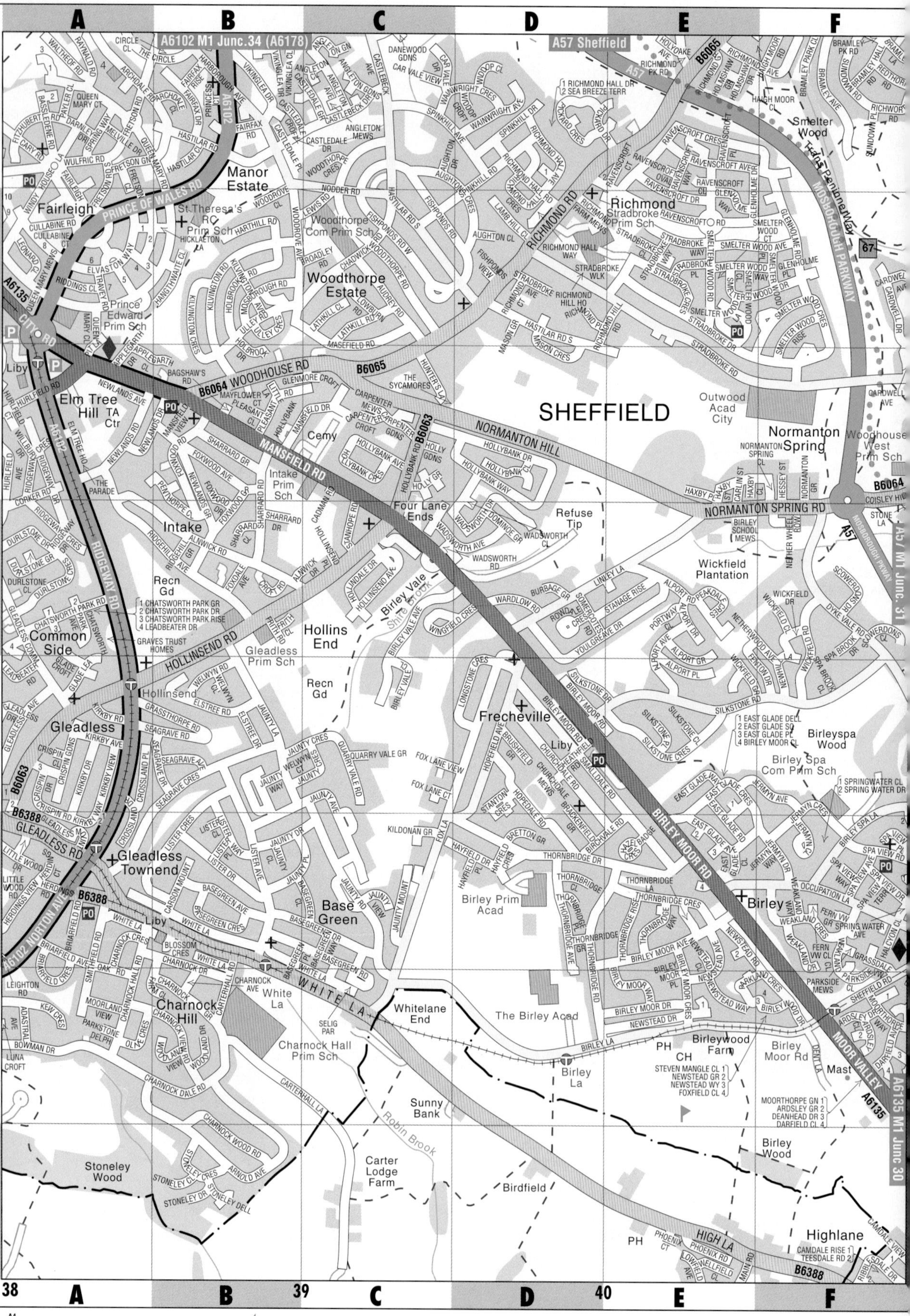

A8
1 Queen Mary Cres
2 Bassledene Ct
3 Queen Mary Ri
4 Norfolk Park Sch

B8
1 Tickhill Dr
2 Skellow Cl
3 Dobroyd Ave
4 Ravensworth Cl
5 Mackworth Cl
6 Ayton Cl

7 Ayton Cl
8 Fitzhubert Rd
9 Babington Ct
10 Babington Cl

SHEFFIELD

A4
1 Gleadless Bank
2 Hollinsend Rd
3 Crispin Rd

A3
1 Gleadless Rise
2 Gleadless View

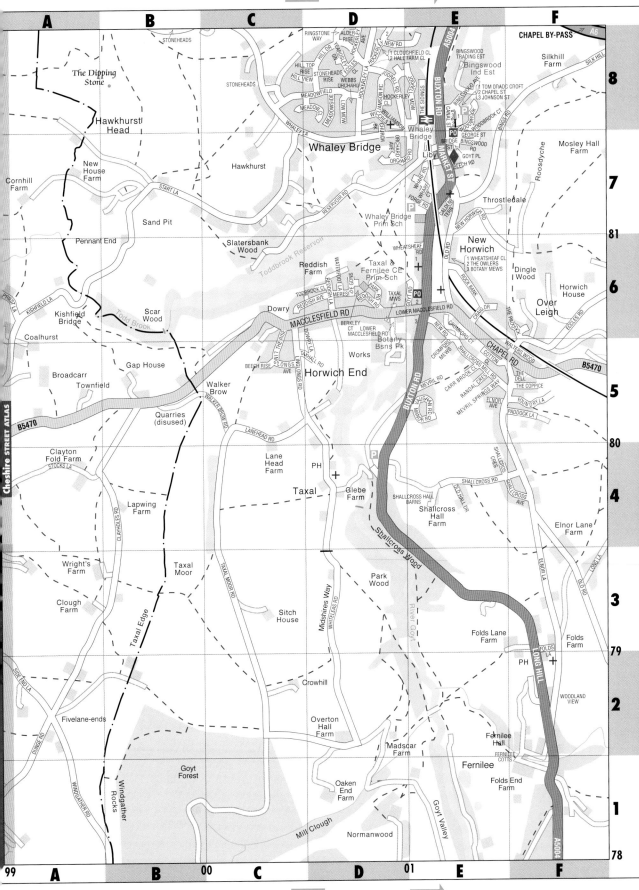
45

33
46

A B C D E F

CHAPEL BY-PASS
A6
A5004
8
7
81
6
5
80
4
3
79
2
1
78

STONEHEADS
The Dipping Stone
Hawkhurst Head
RINGSTONE WAY
ALDER RISE
HILL DR
YEARDSLEY GN
ECCLES CL
HOCKERLEY AVE
NEW RD
1 CLOUGHFIELD CL
2 HALL FARM CL
HILL TOP RISE
HILL VIEW
STONEHEADS RISE
WEBBS ORCHARD
MEADOWFIELD
MEADOW CL
MEADOWSIDE
LOW MDW
HOCKERLEY LA
JODRELL RD
JODRELL MDW
THE SIDINGS
HOCKERLEY CL
WILLIAMSON RD
WILLIAMSON CRES
CHURCH AVE
BK
WHALEY LA
ORCHARD AVE
ORCHARD RD
Whaley Bridge
Whaley Bridge
Liby
BUXTON RD
MARKET ST
BINGSWOOD TRADING EST
Bingswood Ind Est
BINGSWOOD AVE
1 TOM BRADC CROFT
2 CHAPEL ST
3 JOHNSON ST
CANAL ST
WOODBROOK
WOODBROOK CT
GEORGE ST
BRIDGE ST
BINGSWOOD RD
GOYT PL
BEECH RD
BINGS RD
SILK HILL
Silkhill Farm
Mosley Hall Farm
Roosdyche
Cornhill Farm
New House Farm
Hawkhurst
START LA
RESERVOIR RD
WHARF RD
WHARF CT
FORGE RD
CALDENE TERR
Throstledale
Sand Pit
Whaley Bridge Prim Sch
NEW HORWICH RD
New Horwich
1 WHEATSHEAF CL
2 THE OWLERS
3 BOTANY MEWS
OLD RD
Pennant End
Slatersbank Wood
Toddbrook Reservoir
WHEATSHEAF RD
Reddish Farm
WATERFOOT LA
Taxal & Fernilee CE Prim Sch
Dingle Wood
ROCK BANK
Horwich House
Over Leigh
PRIEST LA
KISHFIELD LA
Kishfield Bridge
TODBROOK CL
REDDISH LA
MERES GDNS
REDDISH AVE
MERES CT
PARK RD
REDDISH RD
TAXAL MWS
GOYT RD
PO
Scar Wood
Todd Brook
Dowry
MACCLESFIELD RD
LOWER MACCLESFIELD RD
CRAIG DR
THE PADDOCK
ECCLES RD
Coalhurst
BERKLEY CT
LOWER MACCLESFIELD RD
Botany Bsns Pk
NEW RD
CROMFORD CT
CHAPEL RD
WALTERS WOOD
B5470
THE RISE
DOWRY LA
TAXHALL RD
Works
CROMFORD MEWS
SHALLCROSS MILL RD
COTTON CL
Gap House
BEECH RISE
CLONGS AVE
LINGLONGS RD
Horwich End
CARR BROOK CL
RANDAL CRES
THE DELL
THE COPPICE
Broadcarr
Townfield
Walker Brow
MEVRIL RD
MEVRIL SPRINGS WAY
ELNOR AVE
FOUNDRY LA
VAUGHAN RD
MANOR RD
PADDOCK LA
B5470
Quarries (disused)
WALKER BROW RD
LANEHEAD RD
Clayton Fold Farm
STOCKS LA
Lane Head Farm
PH
SHALLCROSS CRES
SHALLCROSS RD
SHALLCROSS AVE
Taxal
Glebe Farm
SHALLCROSS HALL BARNS
OLD HALL DR
Lapwing Farm
CLAYHOLES RD
Shallcross Hall Farm
Elnor Lane Farm
Shallcross Wood
Wright's Farm
Taxal Moor
TAXAL MOOR RD
Park Wood
ELNOR LA
OLD RD
LONG LA
Clough Farm
Midshires Way
WHITELEAS RD
Sitch House
River Goyt
Taxal Edge
Folds Lane Farm
Folds Farm
FOLDS LA
LONG HILL
SIDE END LA
Crowhill
WOODLAND VIEW
Fivelane-ends
Overton Hall Farm
Fernilee Hall
DUNGE RD
Madscar Farm
FERNILEE COTTS
Fernilee
Goyt Forest
Folds End Farm
WINDGATHER RD
Windgather Rocks
Oaken End Farm
Goyt Valley
Mill Clough
Normanwood
A5004

99 A B 00 C D 01 E F

64
46

45
34

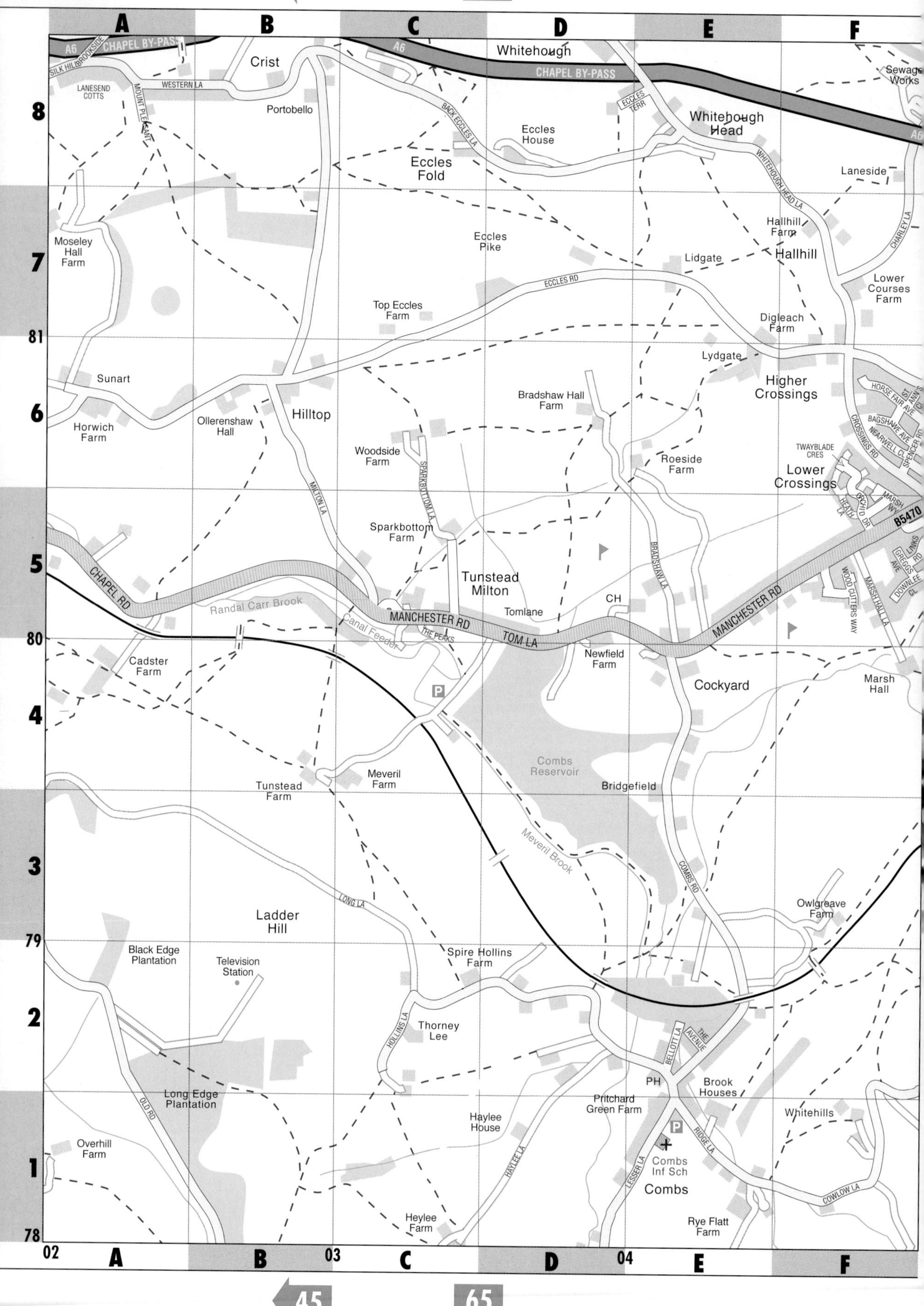
A
B
C
D
E
F
8
7
81
6
5
80
4
3
79
2
1
78
02
03
04
A6
CHAPEL BY-PASS
SILK HILL
BROOKSIDE
LANESEND COTTS
MOUNT PLEASANT
WESTERN LA
Crist
Portobello
Whitehough
BACK ECCLES LA
Eccles House
Eccles Fold
ECCLES TERR
Whitehough Head
Sewage Works
Laneside
WHITEHOUGH HEAD LA
Hallhill Farm
Hallhill
CHARLEY LA
Lidgate
Moseley Hall Farm
Eccles Pike
ECCLES RD
Lower Courses Farm
Top Eccles Farm
Digleach Farm
Lydgate
Sunart
Higher Crossings
Bradshaw Hall Farm
Horwich Farm
Ollerenshaw Hall
Hilltop
Woodside Farm
SPARKBOTTOM LA
MILTON LA
Roeside Farm
TWAYBLADE CRES
Lower Crossings
HORSE FAIR AVE
ST ANN'S CL
BAGSHAWE AVE
NEARWELL CL
SPENCER RD
CROSSINGS RD
HEATH LA
ORCHID DR
MARSH WY
B5470
Sparkbottom Farm
LINKS RD
GREGGS AVE
DOWNLEE CL
WOOD CUTTERS WAY
MARSH HALL LA
CHAPEL RD
Tunstead Milton
BRADSHAW LA
Randal Carr Brook
Canal Feeder
MANCHESTER RD
Tomlane
CH
THE PEAKS
TOM LA
Newfield Farm
Cadster Farm
P
Cockyard
Marsh Hall
Combs Reservoir
Tunstead Farm
Meveril Farm
Bridgefield
Meveril Brook
COMBS RD
Owlgreave Farm
LONG LA
Ladder Hill
Black Edge Plantation
Television Station
Spire Hollins Farm
HOLLINS LA
Thorney Lee
BELLOTT LA
THE AVENUE
PH
Brook Houses
Long Edge Plantation
OLD RD
Pritchard Green Farm
Haylee House
Whitehills
Overhill Farm
HAYLEE LA
LESSER LA
Combs Inf Sch
RIDGE LA
COWLOW LA
Combs
Heylee Farm
Rye Flatt Farm

45
65

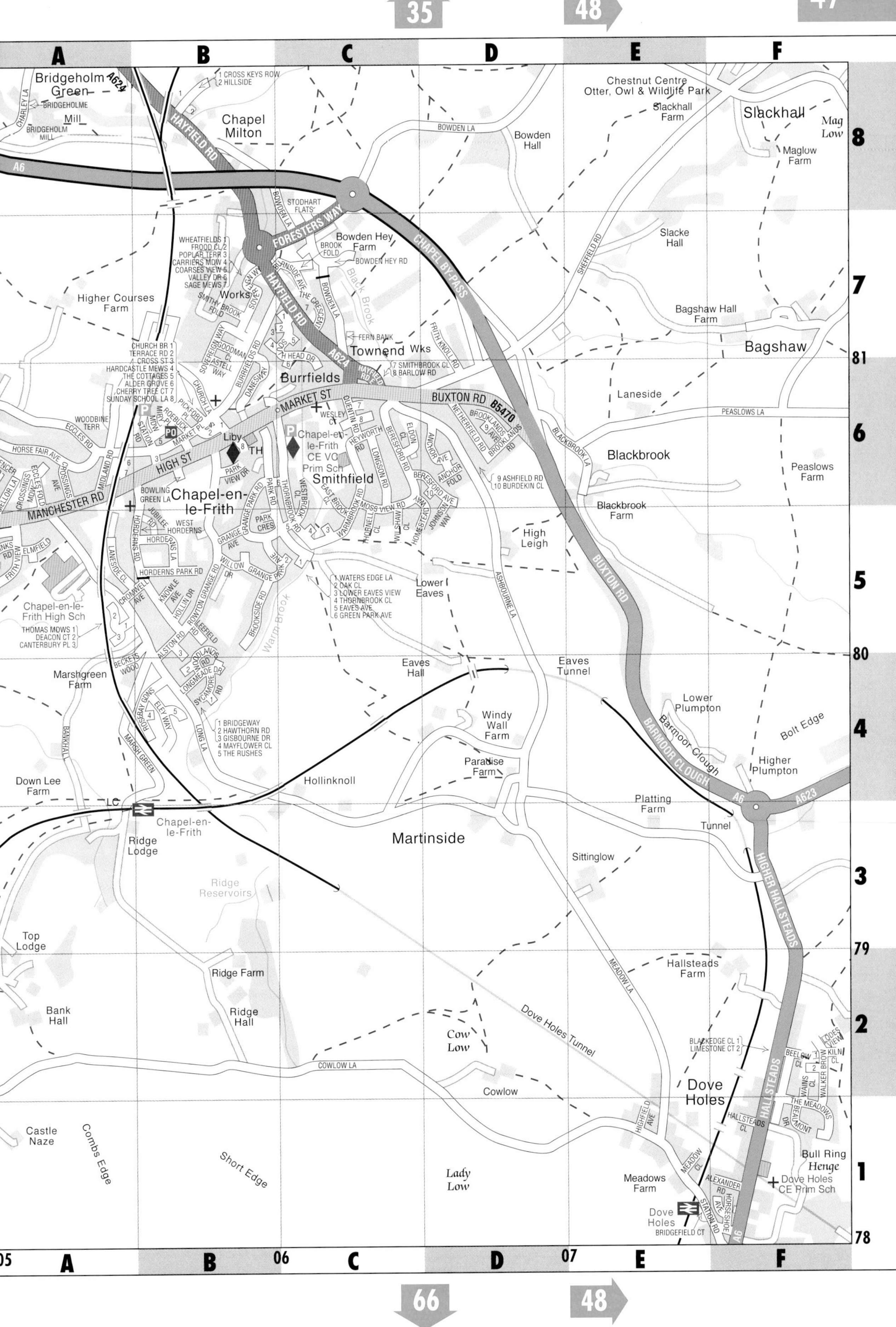

A B C D E F

Bridgeholm Green
A624
BRIDGEHOLME Mill
BRIDGEHOLM MILL
A6
CHARLEY LA

1 CROSS KEYS ROW
2 HILLSIDE
Chapel Milton
HAYFIELD RD

Chestnut Centre
Otter, Owl & Wildlife Park
Slackhall Farm
Slackhall
Mag Low

BOWDEN LA
Bowden Hall
Maglow Farm

8

STODHART FLATS
FORESTERS WAY
BOWDEN LA
Bowden Hey Farm
BROOK FOLD
BOWDEN HEY RD
CHAPEL BI-PASS
SHEFFIELD RD
Slacke Hall

WHEATFIELDS 1
FROOD CL 2
POPLAR TERR 3
CARRIERS MDW 4
COARSES VIEW 5
VALLEY DR 6
SAGE MEWS 7
Higher Courses Farm
SMITHY FOLD
Works
Bagshaw Hall Farm

7

Bagshaw
81

CHURCH BR 1
TERRACE RD 2
CROSS ST 3
HARDCASTLE MEWS 4
THE COTTAGES 5
ALDER GROVE 6
CHERRY TREE CT 7
SUNDAY SCHOOL LA 8
WOODBINE TERR
HORSE FAIR LA
ECCLES FOLD
FERN BANK
Townend
Wks
7 SMITHBROOK CL
8 BARLOW RD
BUXTON RD
B5470
BROOKLANDS
Laneside

PEASLOWS LA

Burrfields
MARKET ST
WESLEY CT
Libry
TH
Chapel-en-le-Frith CE VC
Prim Sch
Smithfield
9 ASHFIELD RD
10 BURDEKIN CL
Blackbrook
Blackbrook
6

HIGH ST
PARK VIEW DR
Chapel-en-le-Frith
Blackbrook Farm
Peaslows Farm

MANCHESTER RD
PENCER
ECCLES FOLD
CHESSMOSS
MELLOR LA
MIDLAND RD
HORDERNS RD
BOWLING GREEN LA
WEST HORDERNS
THORNBROOK RD
PARK CRES
High Leigh
Peaslows Farm

HORSE FAIR LA
LINKS RD
FRITH VIEW
ELMFIELD
LANESIDE CL
HORDERNS PARK RD
GRANGE PARK RD
GRANGE AVE
WILLOW DR
1 WATERS EDGE LA
2 OAK CL
3 LOWER EAVES VIEW
4 THORNBROOK CL
5 EAVES AVE
6 GREEN PARK AVE
Lower Eaves
ASHBOURNE LA

5

Chapel-en-le-Frith High Sch
THOMAS MDWS 1
DEACON CT 2
CANTERBURY PL 3
KNOWLE AVE
HOLLIN DR
BOWDEN GRANGE RD
BROOKSIDE RD
Eaves Hall
Eaves Tunnel
BUXTON RD
80

Marshgreen Farm
BECKET'S WOOD
GROWMILL AVE
BILSTON RD
LONGMEADE DG
SYCAMORE RD
LONG LA
Windy Wall Farm
Lower Plumpton
Bolt Edge

4

1 BRIDGEWAY
2 HAWTHORN RD
3 GISBOURNE DR
4 MAYFLOWER CL
5 THE RUSHES
Paradise Farm
BARMOOR CLOUGH
A6
A623
Higher Plumpton

Down Lee Farm
LC
Chapel-en-le-Frith
Ridge Lodge
Hollinknoll
Martinside
Platting Farm
Tunnel
HIGHER HALLSTEADS

3

Ridge Reservoirs
Sittinglow
79

Top Lodge
Ridge Farm
Ridge Hall
MEADOW LA
Hallsteads Farm
BLACKEDGE CL 1
LIMESTONE CT 2
ODDES VIEW
BEELOW
BEELOW KILN
WALKER BROW
SWANN'S BRIDGE
2

Bank Hall
Cow Low
Dove Holes Tunnel
Dove Holes
THE MEADOWS
BEAUMONT
HALLSTEADS CL

Castle Naze
Combs Edge
Short Edge
COWLOW LA
Cowlow
Lady Low
Meadows Farm
MEADOW CL
ALEXANDER RD
Bull Ring Henge
Dove Holes CE Prim Sch
HORSESHOE
SANTON RD
HIGHFIELD AVE
1

Dove Holes
BRIDGEFIELD CT
78

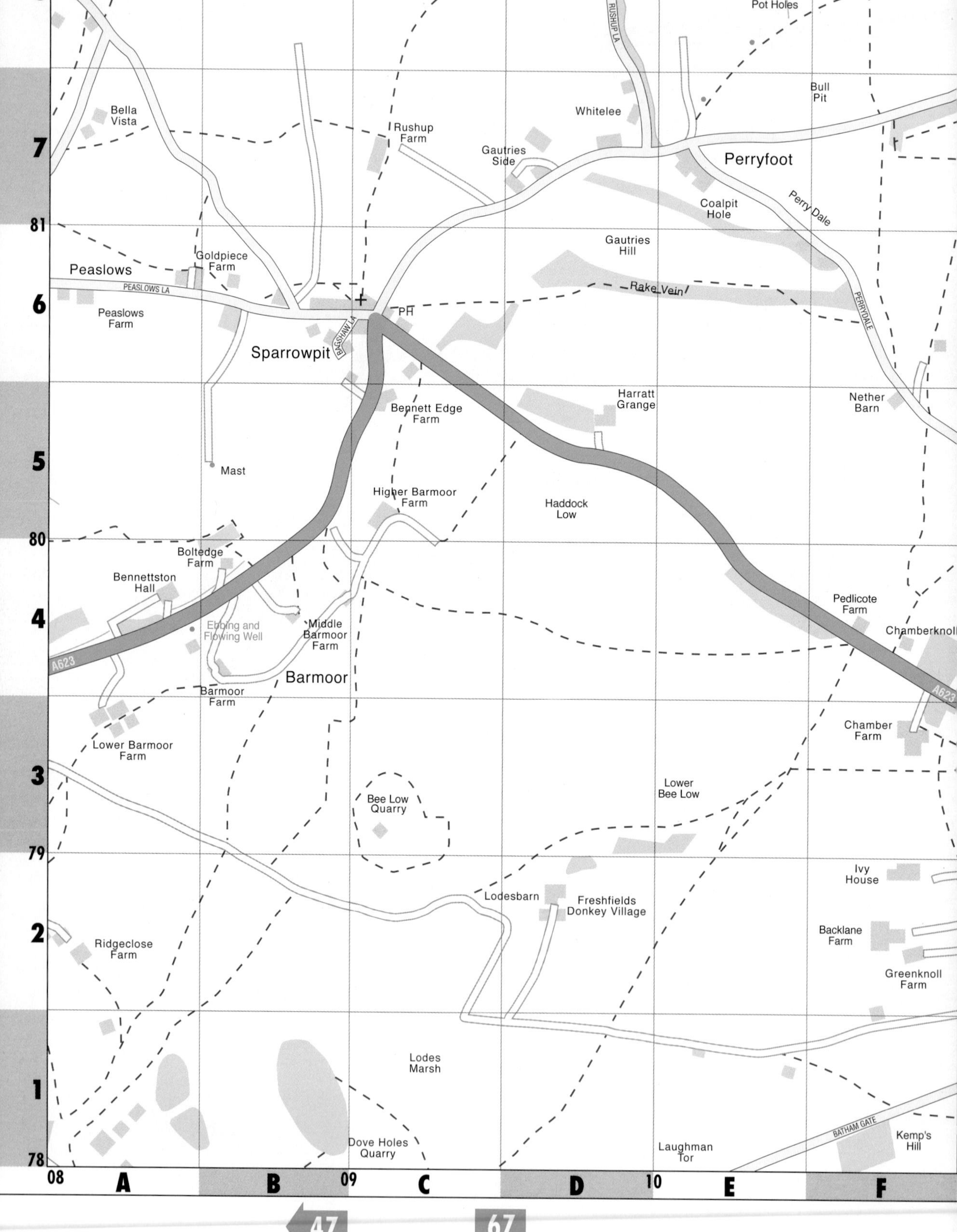

A B C D E F

8

Stonyford

Pot Holes

Bull Pit

7

Bella Vista

Rushup Farm

Gautries Side

Whitelee

Perryfoot

81

Coalpit Hole

Perry Dale

Peaslows

Goldpiece Farm

PEASLOWS LA

Gautries Hill

PERRYDALE

6

Peaslows Farm

BAGSHAW LA

PH

Rake Vein

Sparrowpit

Harratt Grange

Nether Barn

Bennett Edge Farm

5

Mast

Higher Barmoor Farm

Haddock Low

80

Boltedge Farm

Bennettston Hall

Ebbing and Flowing Well

Middle Barmoor Farm

Pedlicote Farm

4

A623

Barmoor Farm

Barmoor

Chamberknoll

Lower Barmoor Farm

A623

Chamber Farm

3

Bee Low Quarry

Lower Bee Low

79

Lodesbarn

Freshfields Donkey Village

Ivy House

2

Ridgeclose Farm

Backlane Farm

Greenknoll Farm

Lodes Marsh

1

Dove Holes Quarry

Laughman Tor

BATHAM GATE

Kemp's Hill

78

08 A B 09 C D 10 E F

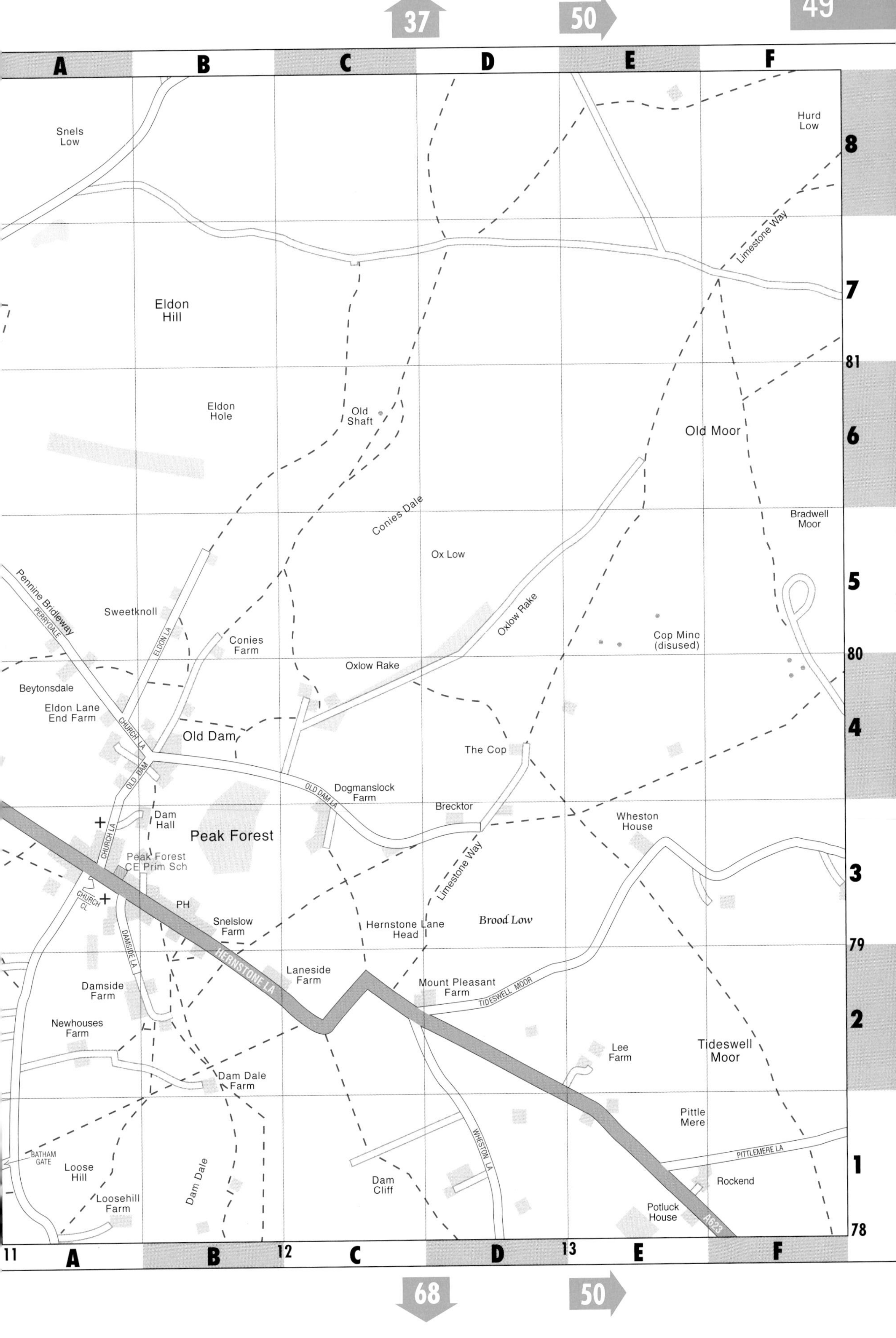
37
50
A
B
C
D
E
F
Snels Low
Hurd Low
Eldon Hill
Eldon Hole
Old Shaft
Old Moor
Limestone Way
Conies Dale
Ox Low
Bradwell Moor
Pennine Bridleway
PERRYDALE
Sweetknoll
ELDON LA
Conies Farm
Oxlow Rake
Cop Mine (disused)
Beytonsdale
Eldon Lane End Farm
CHURCH LA
Old Dam
The Cop
OLD DAM
Dogmanslock Farm
OLD DAM LA
Brecktor
Dam Hall
Peak Forest
Wheston House
Peak Forest CE Prim Sch
CHURCH CL
PH
Snelslow Farm
Hernstone Lane Head
Brood Low
DAMSIDE LA
HERNSTONE LA
Laneside Farm
Damside Farm
Mount Pleasant Farm
TIDESWELL MOOR
Newhouses Farm
Lee Farm
Tideswell Moor
Dam Dale Farm
Pittle Mere
BATHAM GATE
Loose Hill
Dam Dale
Dam Cliff
WHESTON LA
PITTLEMERE LA
Rockend
Loosehill Farm
Potluck House
A623
8
7
81
6
5
80
4
3
79
2
1
78
11
12
13
68

49 38

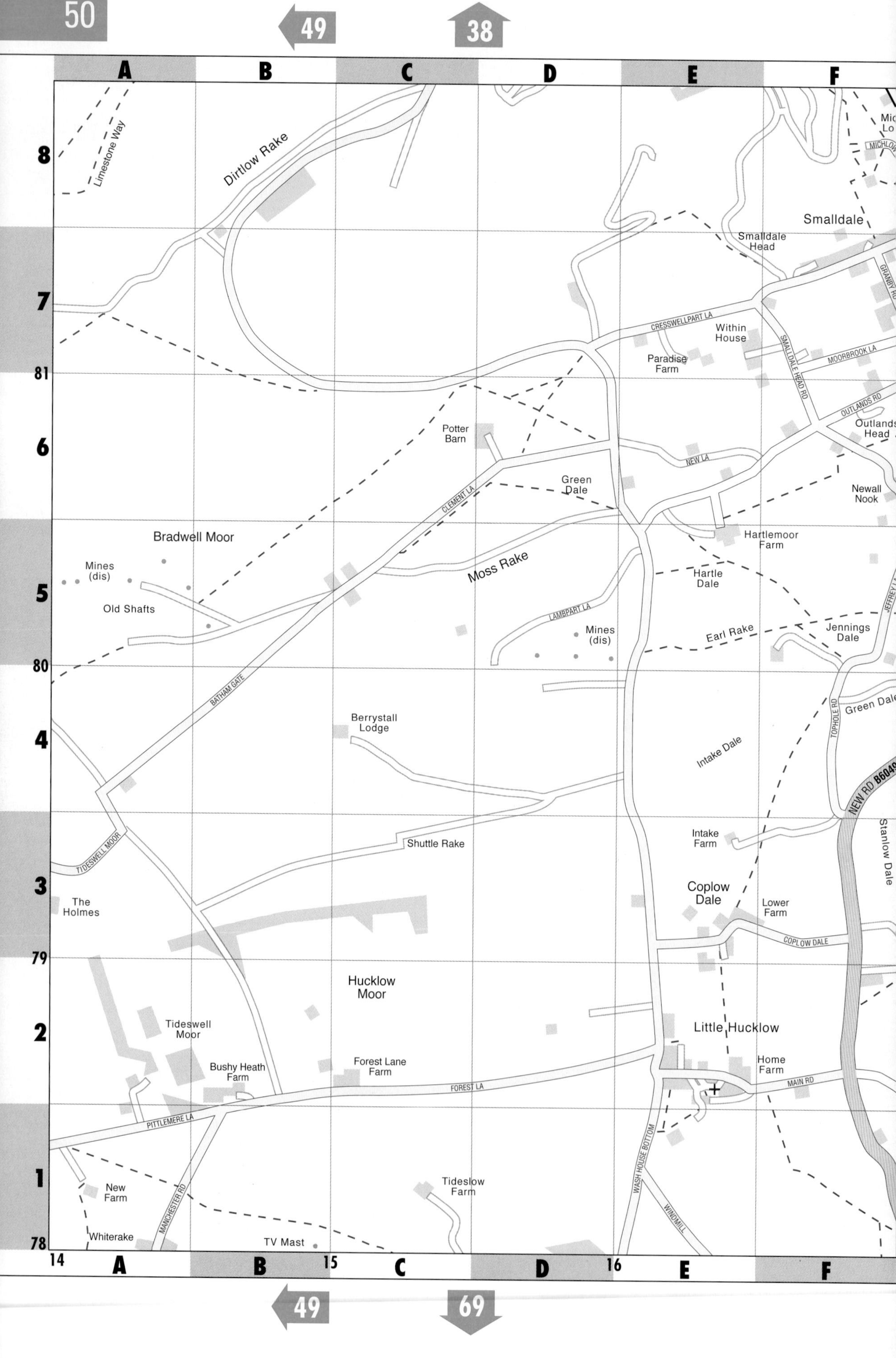

Limestone Way
Dirtlow Rake
Smalldale
Smalldale Head
GRANBY RD
CRESSWELLPART LA
Within House
Paradise Farm
SMALLDALE HEAD RD
MOORBROOK LA
OUTLANDS RD
Outlands Head
Potter Barn
NEW LA
Green Dale
Newall Nook
CLEMENT LA
Bradwell Moor
Hartlemoor Farm
Mines (dis)
Moss Rake
Hartle Dale
Old Shafts
LAMBPART LA
Mines (dis)
Earl Rake
Jennings Dale
JEFFREY LA
BATHAM GATE
Berrystall Lodge
TOPHOLE RD
Green Dale
Intake Dale
NEW RD B6049
Stanlow Dale
TIDESWELL MOOR
Shuttle Rake
Intake Farm
The Holmes
Coplow Dale
Lower Farm
COPLOW DALE
Hucklow Moor
Tideswell Moor
Little Hucklow
Bushy Heath Farm
Forest Lane Farm
Home Farm
FOREST LA
MAIN RD
PITTLEMERE LA
WASH HOUSE BOTTOM
New Farm
MANCHESTER RD
Tideslow Farm
WINDMILL
Whiterake
TV Mast

49 69

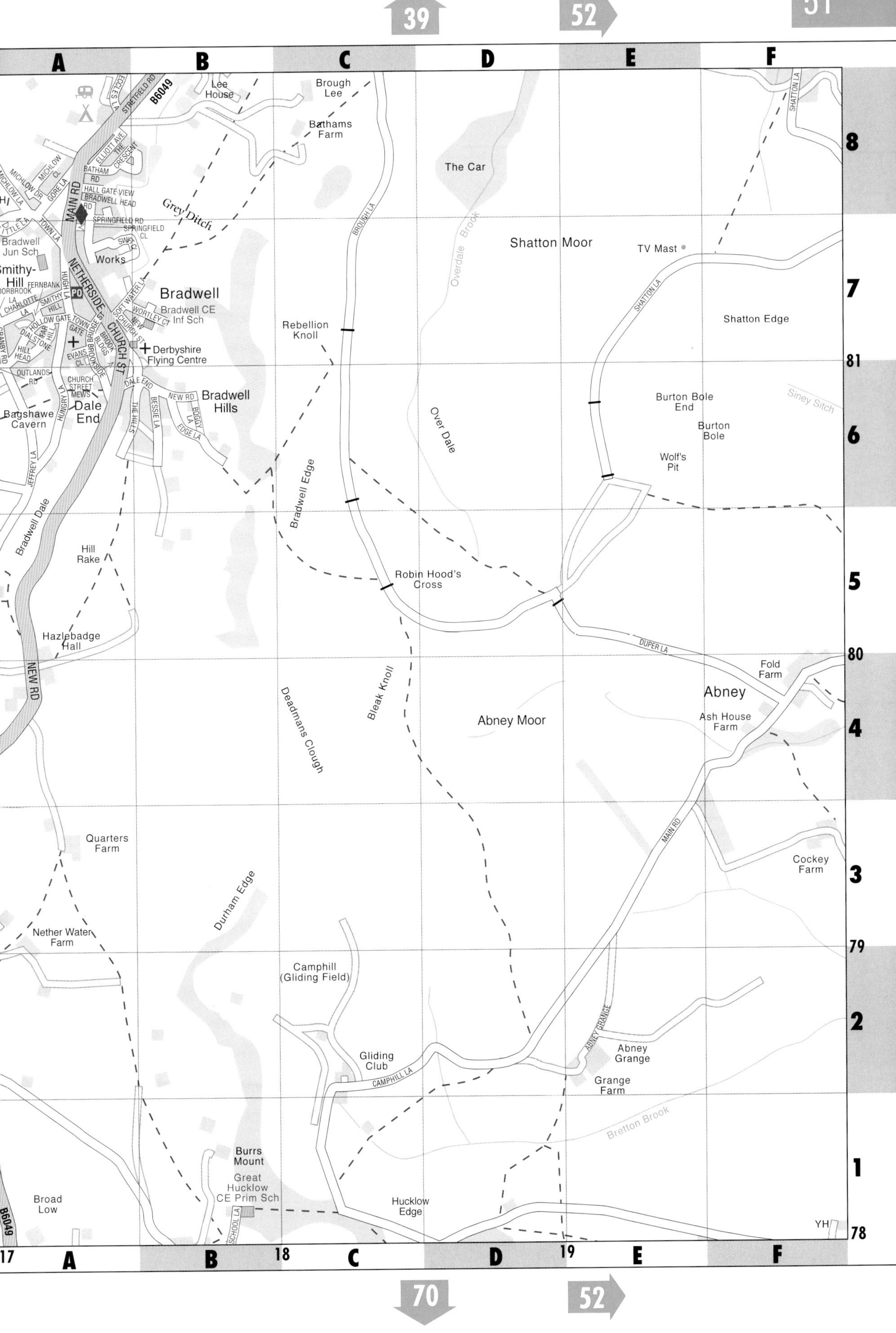
39
52
A
B
C
D
E
F
Lee House
Brough Lee
Bathams Farm
B6049
STRETFIELD RD
ECCLES LA
ELLIOTT AVE
THE CRESCENT
MICHLOW CL
MICHLOW DR
MICHLOW LA
GORE LA
BATHAM RD
HALL GATE VIEW
BRADWELL HEAD RD
MAIN RD
SPRINGFIELD RD
SPRINGFIELD CL
TOWN LA
Grey Ditch
Bradwell Jun Sch
Works
Smithy-Hill
FERNBANK
HUGH LA
PO
NETHERSIDE
CHURCH ST
SOFT WATER LA
WORTLEY CT
Bradwell
Bradwell CE Inf Sch
Derbyshire Flying Centre
CHARLOTTE LA
SMITHY HILL
HOLLOW GATE
TOWN GATE
DIALSTONE
HILL HEAD
EVANS CL
BROOK BLDGS
BROOKSIDE
OUTLANDS RD
CHURCH STREET MEWS
DALE END
Dale End
HUNGRY LA
NEW RD
Bradwell Hills
BESSIE LA
THE HILLS
BOGGY LA
EDGE LA
Bagshawe Cavern
JEFFREY LA
Bradwell Dale
Hill Rake
Hazlebadge Hall
NEW RD
Quarters Farm
Nether Water Farm
Broad Low
B6049
The Car
Shatton Moor
Overdale Brook
TV Mast
SHATTON LA
BROUGH LA
Rebellion Knoll
Shatton Edge
Burton Bole End
Burton Bole
Siney Sitch
Over Dale
Wolf's Pit
Bradwell Edge
Robin Hood's Cross
DUPER LA
Fold Farm
Abney
Ash House Farm
Bleak Knoll
Deadmans Clough
Abney Moor
MAIN RD
Cockey Farm
Durham Edge
Camphill (Gliding Field)
Gliding Club
CAMPHILL LA
ABNEY GRANGE
Abney Grange
Grange Farm
Bretton Brook
Burrs Mount
Great Hucklow CE Prim Sch
SCHOOL LA
Hucklow Edge
YH
8
7
81
6
5
80
4
3
79
2
1
78
17
18
19
70
52

51
40

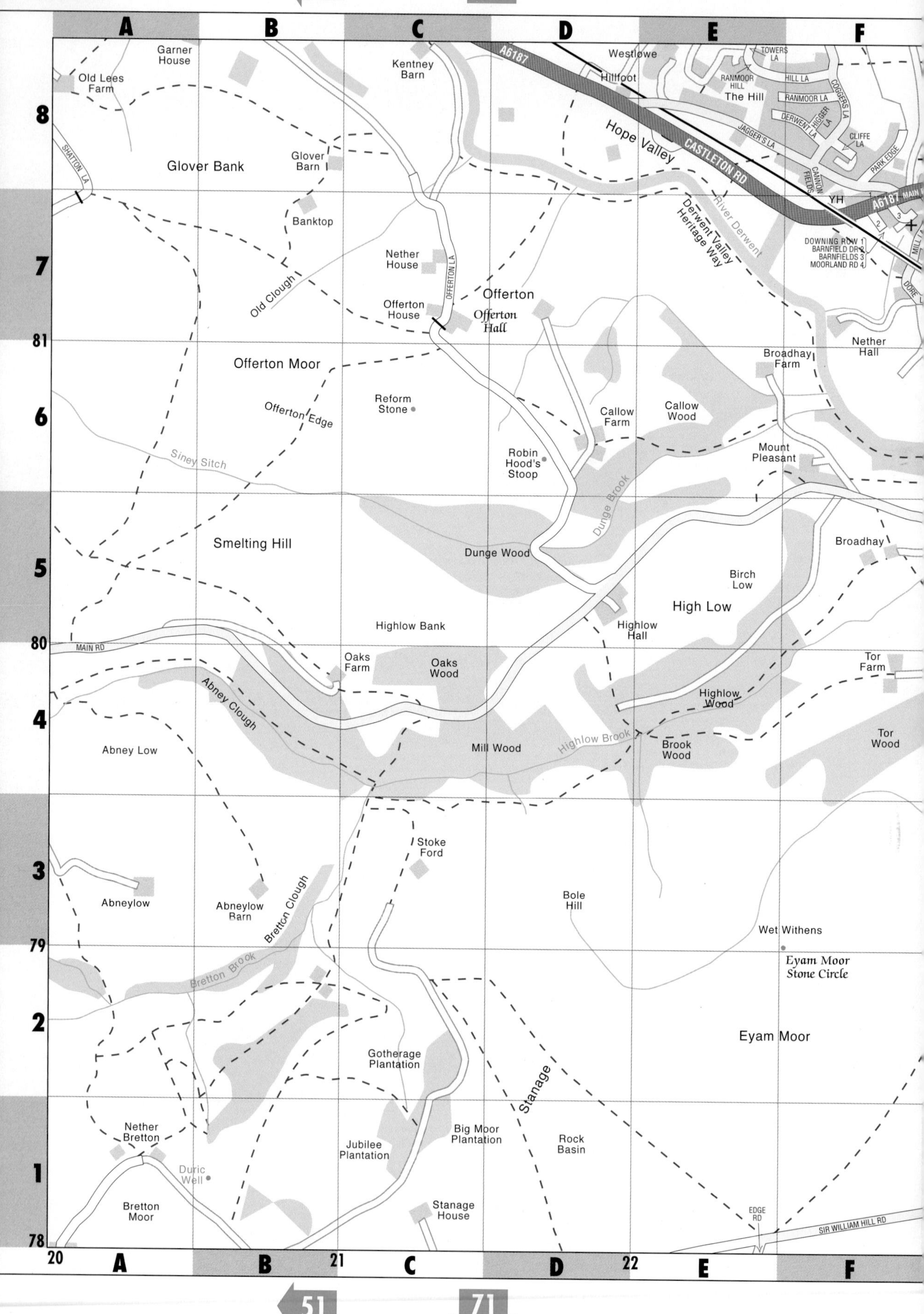
A
B
C
D
E
F
8
7
81
6
5
80
4
3
79
2
1
78
20
21
22
Garner House
Old Lees Farm
Kentney Barn
Westlowe
Hillfoot
A6187
TOWERS LA
RANMOOR HILL
HILL LA
The Hill
RANMOOR LA
COGGERS LA
HIGGER LA
DERWENT LA
JAGGER'S LA
CLIFFE LA
PARK EDGE
CANNON FIELDS
Hope Valley
CASTLETON RD
SHATTON LA
Glover Bank
Glover Barn
Banktop
YH
A6187 MAIN
River Derwent
Derwent Valley Heritage Way
DOWNING ROW 1
BARNFIELD DR 2
BARNFIELDS 3
MOORLAND RD 4
Nether House
OFFERTON LA
Old Clough
Offerton
Offerton House
Offerton Hall
DORE
Nether Hall
Offerton Moor
Broadhay Farm
Reform Stone
Offerton Edge
Callow Farm
Callow Wood
Siney Sitch
Robin Hood's Stoop
Mount Pleasant
Dunge Brook
Smelting Hill
Dunge Wood
Broadhay
Birch Low
High Low
Highlow Bank
Highlow Hall
MAIN RD
Oaks Farm
Oaks Wood
Tor Farm
Abney Clough
Highlow Wood
Highlow Brook
Brook Wood
Tor Wood
Abney Low
Mill Wood
Stoke Ford
Abneylow
Abneylow Barn
Bretton Clough
Bole Hill
Wet Withens
Eyam Moor Stone Circle
Bretton Brook
Eyam Moor
Gotherage Plantation
Stanage
Nether Bretton
Big Moor Plantation
Rock Basin
Jubilee Plantation
Duric Well
Bretton Moor
Stanage House
EDGE RD
SIR WILLIAM HILL RD

51
71

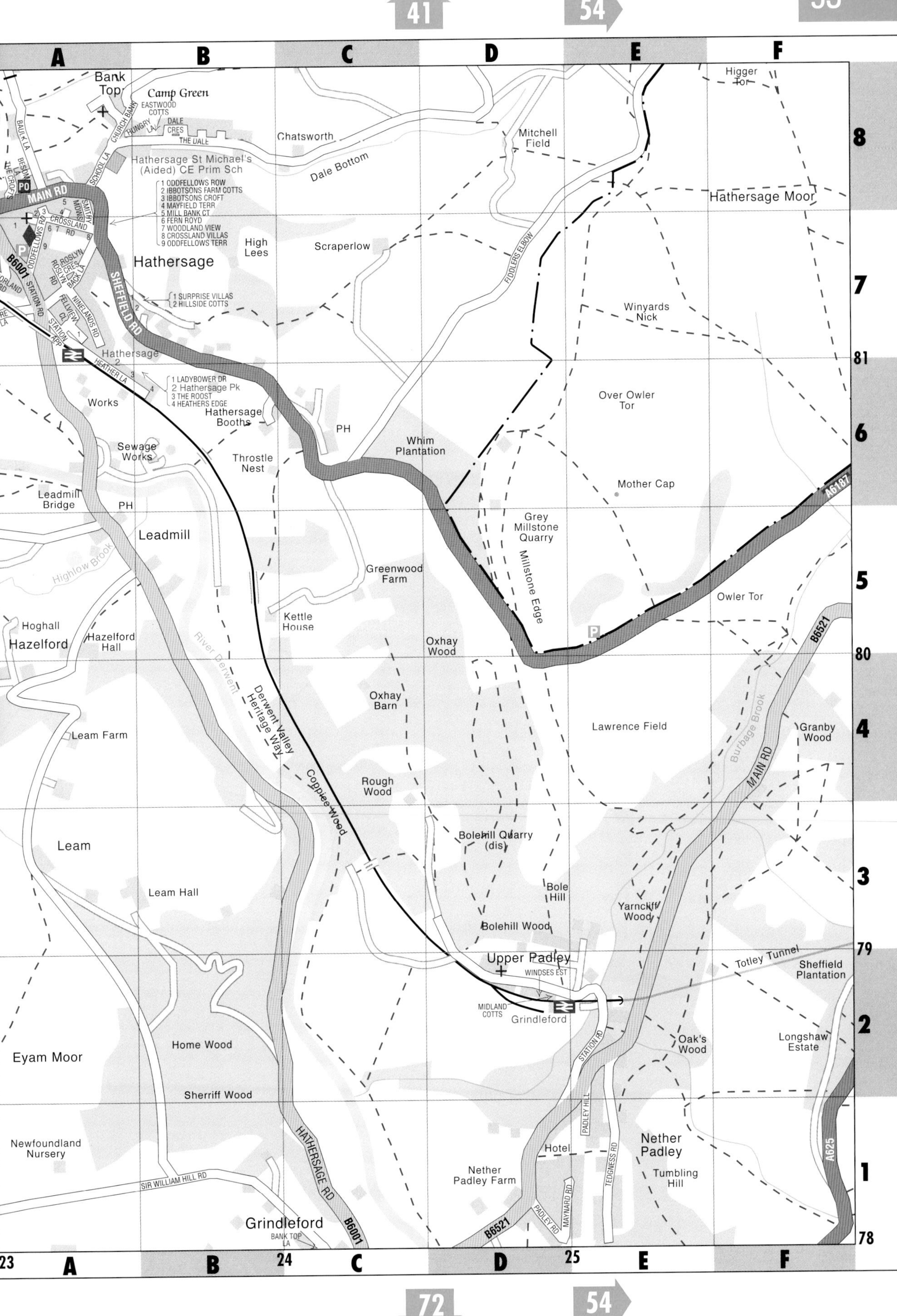
41
54
A
B
C
D
E
F
Bank Top
Camp Green
EASTWOOD COTTS
HUNGRY LA
DALE CRES
THE DALE
CHURCH BANK
SCHOOL LA
Chatsworth
Mitchell Field
Hathersage St Michael's (Aided) CE Prim Sch
1 ODDFELLOWS ROW
2 IBBOTSONS FARM COTTS
3 IBBOTSONS CROFT
4 MAYFIELD TERR
5 MILL BANK CT
6 FERN ROYD
7 WOODLAND VIEW
8 CROSSLAND VILLAS
9 ODDFELLOWS TERR
Dale Bottom
Hathersage Moor
BAULK LA
BESOM LA
THE CROFTS
MAIN RD
SMITHY MDWS
CROSSLAND RD
ODDFELLOWS RD
ROSLYN CRES
ROSLYN RD
BACK LA
B6001
STATION RD
DORLAND RD
FELLVIEW CL
NINELANDS RD
STATION APP
High Lees
Hathersage
Scraperlow
SHEFFIELD RD
FIDDLERS ELBOW
1 SURPRISE VILLAS
2 HILLSIDE COTTS
Winyards Nick
Hathersage
HEATHER LA
1 LADYBOWER DR
2 Hathersage Pk
3 THE ROOST
4 HEATHERS EDGE
Works
Hathersage Booths
Over Owler Tor
PH
Sewage Works
Throstle Nest
Whim Plantation
Mother Cap
A6187
Leadmill Bridge
PH
Leadmill
Grey Millstone Quarry
Highlow Brook
Greenwood Farm
Millstone Edge
Owler Tor
Hoghall
Hazelford
Hazelford Hall
River Derwent
Kettle House
Oxhay Wood
B6521
Derwent Valley Heritage Way
Oxhay Barn
Lawrence Field
Leam Farm
Burbage Brook
Granby Wood
MAIN RD
Coppice Wood
Rough Wood
Leam
Bolehill Quarry (dis)
Leam Hall
Bole Hill
Yarncliff Wood
Bolehill Wood
Upper Padley
Totley Tunnel
Sheffield Plantation
WINDSES EST
MIDLAND COTTS
Grindleford
Eyam Moor
Oak's Wood
Longshaw Estate
Home Wood
STATION RD
Sherriff Wood
PADLEY HILL
Newfoundland Nursery
HATHERSAGE RD
Hotel
Nether Padley
TEDGNESS RD
A625
Nether Padley Farm
Tumbling Hill
SIR WILLIAM HILL RD
MAYNARD RD
PADLEY RD
Grindleford
BANK TOP LA
B6001
B6521
8
7
81
6
5
80
4
3
79
2
1
78
23
24
25
72
54

A   B   C   D   E   F

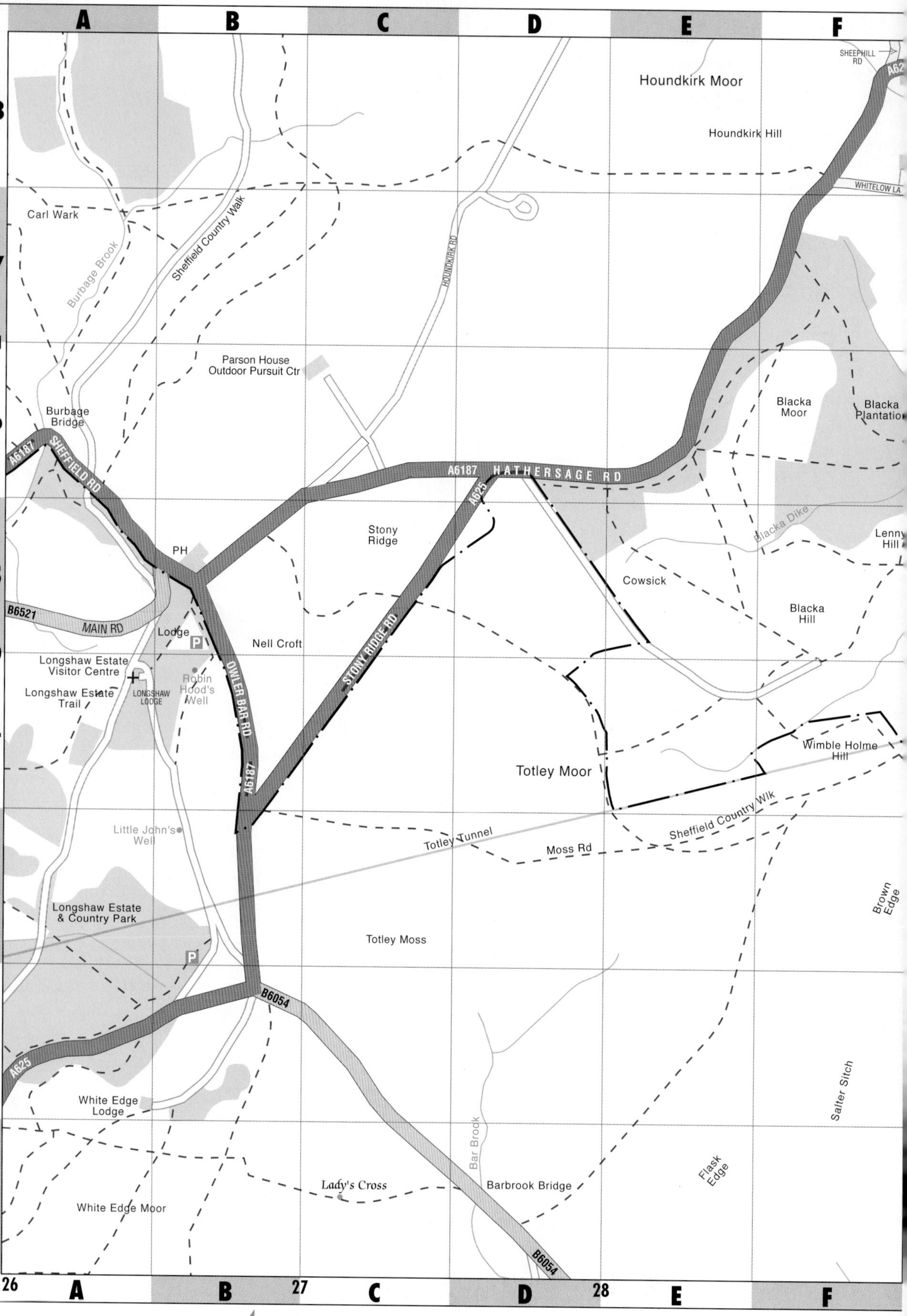

8

Houndkirk Moor

SHEEPHILL RD

A62

Houndkirk Hill

WHITELOW LA

Carl Wark

Sheffield Country Walk

7

Burbage Brook

HOUNDKIRK RD

81

Parson House
Outdoor Pursuit Ctr

Blacka
Moor

Blacka
Plantation

6

Burbage
Bridge

A6187   SHEFFIELD RD

A6187   HATHERSAGE RD

A625

Blacka Dike

Lenny
Hill

PH

Stony
Ridge

Cowsick

Blacka
Hill

5

B6521   MAIN RD

Lodge

P

Nell Croft

STONY RIDGE RD

80

Longshaw Estate
Visitor Centre

Robin
Hood's
Well

LONGSHAW
LODGE

Wimble Holme
Hill

Longshaw Estate
Trail

OWLER BAR RD   A6187

Totley Moor

4

Little John's
Well

Sheffield Country Wlk

Totley Tunnel

Moss Rd

Brown
Edge

3

Longshaw Estate
& Country Park

P

Totley Moss

79

B6054

2

A625

White Edge
Lodge

Bar Brook

Flask
Edge

Salter Sitch

Lady's Cross

Barbrook Bridge

1

White Edge Moor

B6054

78

26   A   B   27   C   D   28   E   F

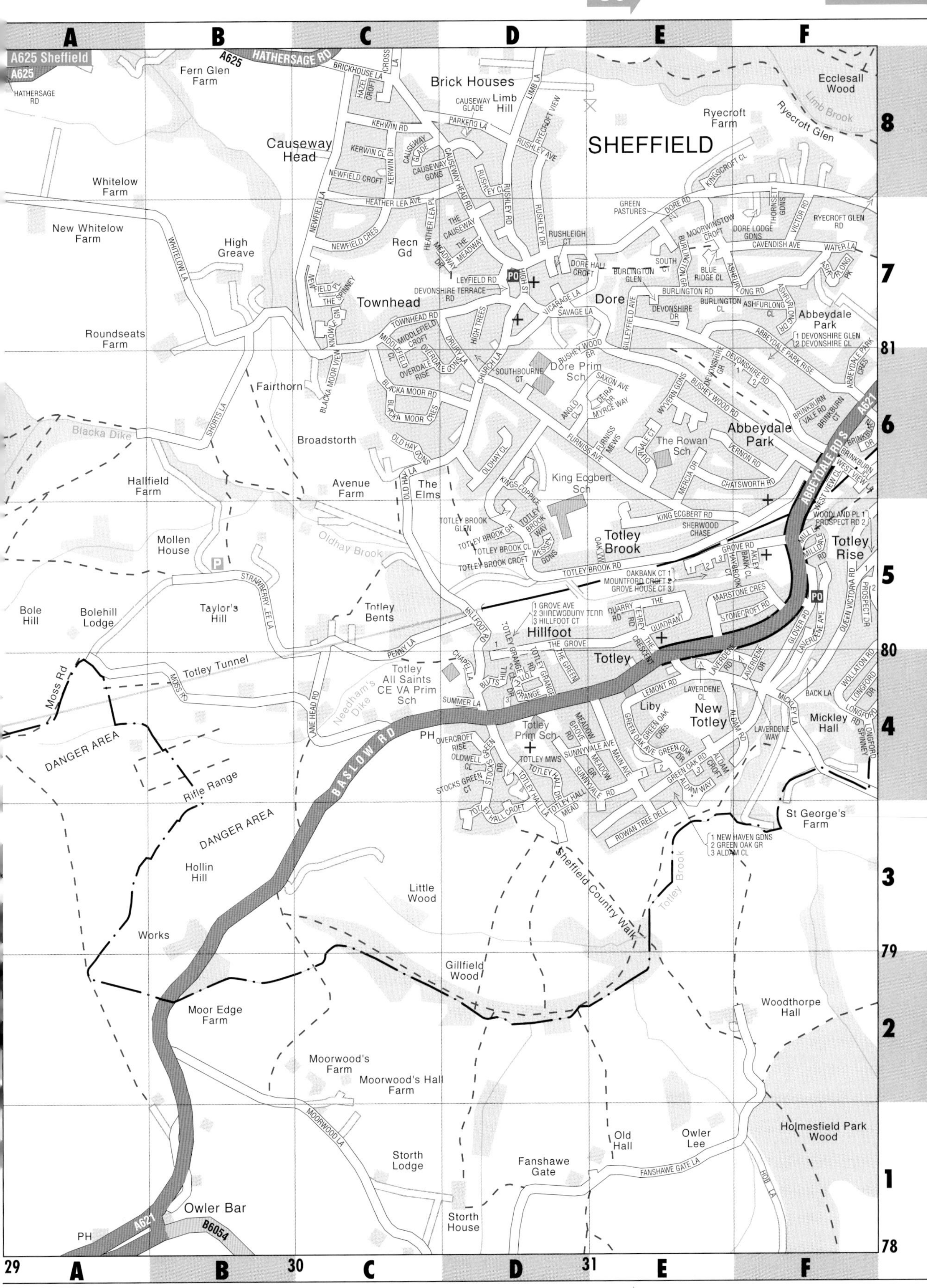

A625 Sheffield
A625
HATHERSAGE RD
A625

HATHERSAGE RD

Fern Glen Farm

Brickhouse La

CROSS

Brick Houses

Limb La

Limb Hill

SHEFFIELD

Ecclesall Wood

Limb Brook

Ryecroft Farm

Ryecroft Glen

Whitelow Farm

Causeway Head

Kehwin Rd

Kerwin Cl

Kerwin Dr

Newfield La

Causeway Glade

Limb Hill

Rushley Ave

Green Pastures

Kingscroft Cl

Dore Rd

Moorwinstow Croft

Dore Lodge Gdns

Thornsett Gdns

Ryecroft Glen Rd

Victor Rd

New Whitelow Farm

High Greave

Heather Lea Ave

Newfield Croft

Causeway Gdns

Causeway Head Rd

Meadway

The Meadway

Rushley Dr

PO

Burlington Glen

Burlington Rd

South Ct

Blue Ridge Cl

Ashford Rd

Water La

Cavendish Ave

Water La

Roundseats Farm

Newfield Cres

Townhead Rd

Middlefield Croft

Townhead

Drury La

High Trees

Leyfield Rd

Devonshire Terrace Rd

Vicarage La

Savage La

Dore

Dore Hall Ct

Burlington Ct

Devonshire Dr

Burlington Rd

Ashfurlong Cl

Abbeydale Park

1 Devonshire Glen
2 Devonshire Cl

Fairthorn

Blacka Moor View

Overdale Rise

Overdale Rd

Church La

Southbourne Ct

Dore Prim Sch

Anglo

Derra Rd

Saxon Ave

Myrtle Way

Furniss Ave

Wern Gdns

Bushey Wood Rd

Devonshire Glen

Abbeydale Park Rise

Abbeydale Glen

Brinkburn Vale Rd

Brinkburn Cl

A621

Blacka Dike

Blacka Moor Rd

Blacka Moor Cres

Old Hay Gdns

Old Hay La

Kings Coppice

The Elms

Furniss Mews

Furniss Ave

The Rowan Sch

Pernon Rd

Mercia Dr

Chatsworth Rd

Abbeydale Park

West View

West View

Abbeydale Rd S

Brinkburn

Hallfield Farm

Broadstorth

Avenue Farm

Shorts La

King Egbert Sch

King Egbert Rd

Sherwood Chase

Totley Brook

Grove Rd

Bushey Wood

Woodland Pl 1
Prospect Rd 2

Totley Rise

Mollen House

P

Strawberry Lea La

Oldhay Brook

Totley Brook Glen

Totley Brook Gr

Totley Brook Cl

Totley Brook Rd

Totley Brook Croft

Brook Way

Totley Brook Gdns

Oak La

Oakbank Ct 1
Mountford Croft 2
Grove House Ct 3

1 2 3

Bank Cl

Grove Rd

Riley Ave

Glover Rd

Prospect Dr

5

Bole Hill

Bolehill Lodge

Taylor's Hill

Totley Bents

Totley Bents

Hillfoot Rd

1 Grove Ave
2 Shrewsbury Road
3 Hillfoot Ct

Hillfoot

The Grove

Quarry Rd

Terry Rd

The Quadrant

Marstone Cres

Stonecroft Rd

Back La

Queen Victoria Rd

PO

Wollaton Rd

Longford Rd

80

Moss Rd

Moss Rd

Totley Tunnel

Vane Head Rd

Penny La

Chapel La

Needham's Dike

Totley All Saints CE VA Prim Sch

Summer La

Totley Grange Rd

Blacks La

Totley Grange Dr

Totley Grange Cl

The Green

Totley

Lemont Rd

Laverdene Rd

Laverdene Dr

Aldam Rd

Mickley La

Laverdene Way

Mickley Hall

Back La

Longford Spinney

4

Danger Area

Rifle Range

Danger Area

Hollin Hill

Baslow Rd

PH

Overcroft Rise

Oldwell Cl

Stocks Green Ct

Stocks Green Dr

Totley Hall La

Totley Prim Sch

Sunnyvale Ave

Sunnyvale Rd

Totley Mws

Meadow Grove Rd

Main Ave

Green Oak Rd

Green Oak Cres

Liby

New Totley

Green Oak Ave

Green Oak Croft

Aldam Way

Aldam Cl

St George's Farm

1 New Haven Gdns
2 Green Oak Gr
3 Aldam Cl

Woodthorpe Hall

3

Works

Little Wood

Sheffield Country Walk

Rowan Tree Dell

Totley Hall Croft

Totley Hall Mead

Totley Brook

79

Moor Edge Farm

Gillfield Wood

2

Moorwood's Farm

Moorwood's Hall Farm

Moorwood La

Storth Lodge

Fanshawe Gate

Old Hall

Owler Lee

Fanshawe Gate La

Holmesfield Park Wood

Hob La

1

PH

A621

B6054

Owler Bar

Storth House

Storth House

78

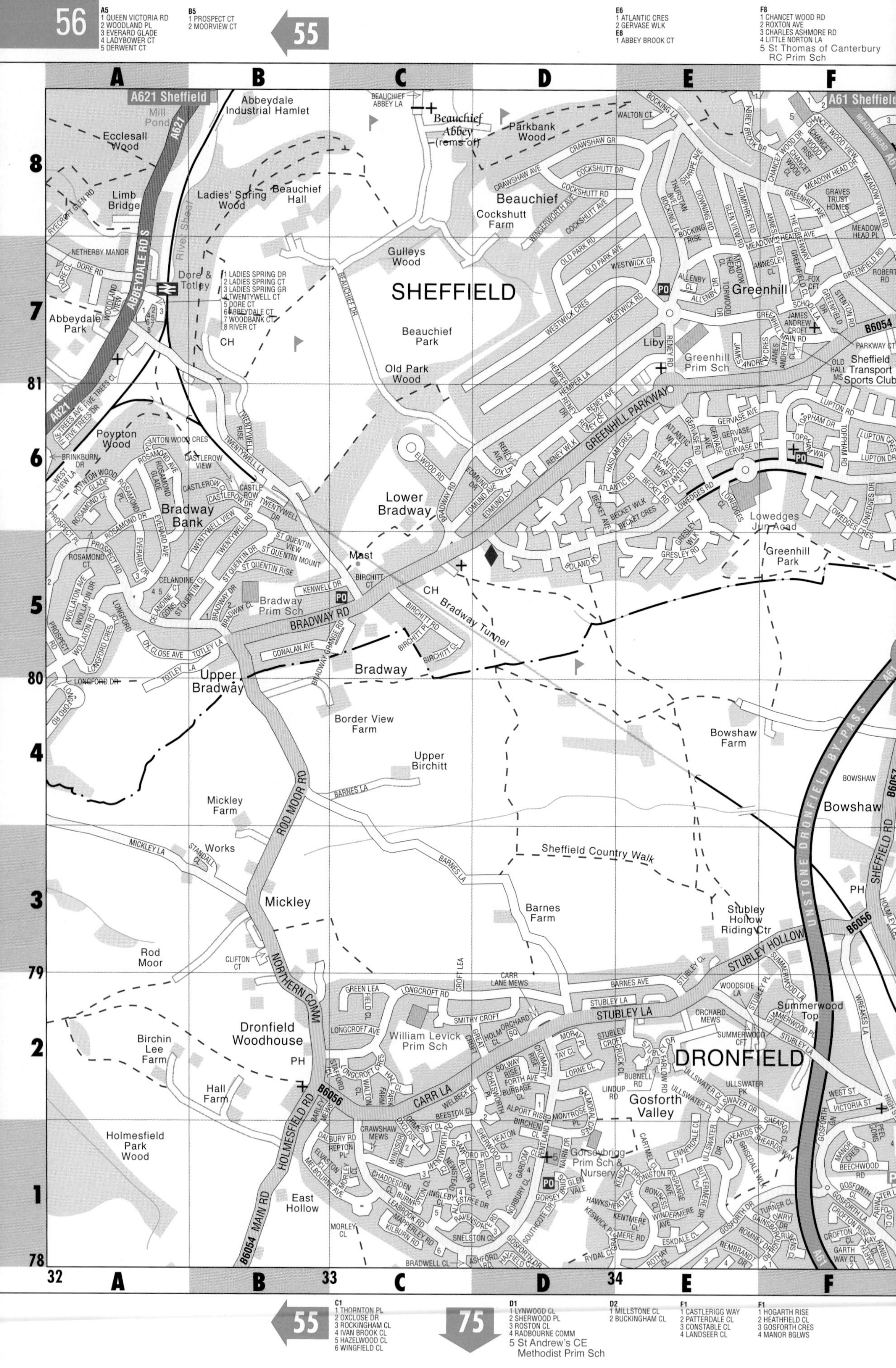
56
A5
1 QUEEN VICTORIA RD
2 WOODLAND PL
3 EVERARD GLADE
4 LADYBOWER CT
5 DERWENT CT
B5
1 PROSPECT CT
2 MOORVIEW CT
55
E6
1 ATLANTIC CRES
2 GERVASE WLK
E8
1 ABBEY BROOK CT
F8
1 CHANCET WOOD RD
2 ROXTON AVE
3 CHARLES ASHMORE RD
4 LITTLE NORTON LA
5 St Thomas of Canterbury RC Prim Sch
A
B
C
D
E
F
A621 Sheffield
A61 Sheffield
Abbeydale Industrial Hamlet
Mill Pond
Ecclesall Wood
Beauchief Abbey (rems of)
Parkbank Wood
Limb Bridge
Ladies' Spring Wood
Beauchief Hall
Beauchief
Cockshutt Farm
Gulleys Wood
SHEFFIELD
Greenhill
Dore & Totley
1 LADIES SPRING DR
2 LADIES SPRING CT
3 LADIES SPRING GR
4 TWENTYWELL CT
5 DORE CT
6 ABBEYDALE CT
7 WOODBANK CT
8 RIVER CT
Abbeydale Park
Beauchief Park
Old Park Wood
Liby
Greenhill Prim Sch
Sheffield Transport Sports Club
Poynton Wood
Bradway Bank
Lower Bradway
Lowedges Jun Acad
Greenhill Park
Mast
Bradway Prim Sch
Bradway Tunnel
Upper Bradway
Bradway
Border View Farm
Upper Birchitt
Bowshaw Farm
Mickley Farm
Works
Bowshaw
Sheffield Country Walk
Mickley
Barnes Farm
Stubley Hollow Riding Ctr
Rod Moor
Summerwood Top
Dronfield Woodhouse
William Levick Prim Sch
DRONFIELD
Birchin Lee Farm
Hall Farm
Gosforth Valley
Holmesfield Park Wood
Gorseybrig Prim Sch & Nursery
East Hollow
UNSTONE DRONFIELD BY-PASS
8
7
81
6
5
80
4
3
79
2
1
78
32
33
34
55
75
C1
1 THORNTON PL
2 OXCLOSE DR
3 ROCKINGHAM CL
4 IVAN BROOK CL
5 HAZELWOOD CL
6 WINGFIELD CL
D1
1 LYNWOOD CL
2 SHERWOOD PL
3 ROSTON CL
4 RADBOURNE COMM
5 St Andrew's CE Methodist Prim Sch
D2
1 MILLSTONE CL
2 BUCKINGHAM CL
E1
1 CASTLERIGG WAY
2 PATTERDALE CL
3 CONSTABLE CL
4 LANDSEER CL
F1
1 HOGARTH RISE
2 HEATHFIELD CL
3 GOSFORTH CRES
4 MANOR BGLWS

A1
1 GOSFORTH LA
2 HILLSIDE AVE
3 NETHERDENE RD
4 PEMBROKE RD
5 UPPER SCHOOL LA
6 HIGHDALE FOLD

B1
1 SCARSDALE CROSS
2 SCARSDALE RD
3 PALMER CRES

57 44

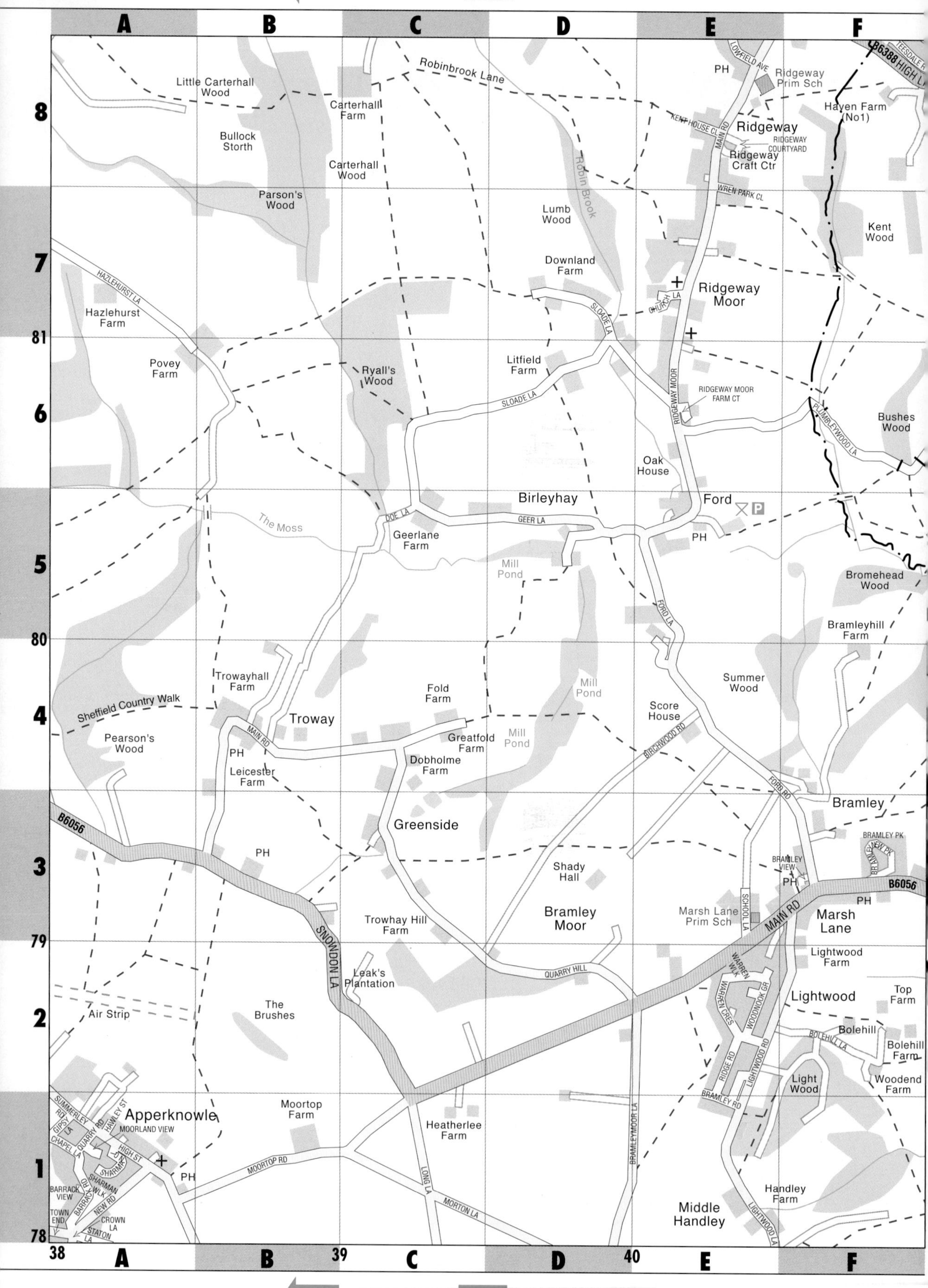

A B C D E F
8 7 81 6 5 80 4 3 79 2 1 78
38 39 40
Robinbrook Lane
Little Carterhall Wood
Carterhall Farm
Bullock Storth
Carterhall Wood
Parson's Wood
Ridgeway
Ridgeway Prim Sch
Ridgeway Courtyard
Ridgeway Craft Ctr
Hayen Farm (No1)
Kent Wood
Lumb Wood
Robin Brook
Downland Farm
Ridgeway Moor
Hazlehurst Farm
Povey Farm
Ryall's Wood
Litfield Farm
Sloade La
Ridgeway Moor Farm Ct
Bushes Wood
Oak House
Birleyhay
Ford
The Moss
Geerlane Farm
Geer La
Doe La
Mill Pond
Bromehead Wood
Bramleyhill Farm
Trowayhall Farm
Fold Farm
Summer Wood
Sheffield Country Walk
Troway
Score House
Pearson's Wood
Greatfold Farm
Dobholme Farm
Leicester Farm
Birchwood Rd
Ford Rd
Bramley
Bramley Pk
Bramley View
B6056
Greenside
Shady Hall
Marsh Lane
Marsh Lane Prim Sch
Trowhay Hill Farm
Bramley Moor
Snowdon La
Quarry Hill
Main Rd
Lightwood Farm
Leak's Plantation
Lightwood
Top Farm
Air Strip
The Brushes
Bolehill
Bolehill Farm
Bolehill La
Light Wood
Woodend Farm
Moortop Farm
Apperknowle
Moorland View
Heatherlee Farm
Moortop Rd
Long La
Morton La
Bramleymoor La
Handley Farm
Middle Handley
Lightwood La
Lightwood Rd
Ridge Rd
Bramley Rd
Warren Walk
Warren Cres
Woodnook Gr
School La
Summerley Rd
Gipsy La
Chapel La
Quarry Rd
Hawley St
High St
Sharman Wlk
Barrack View
Barrack Rd
New Rd
Town End
Crown La
Station La
Plumbley Wood La
Kent House Cl
Wren Park Cl
Church La
Lowfield Ave
Hazlehurst La
B6388 High La
Teesdale Rd
PH

57 77

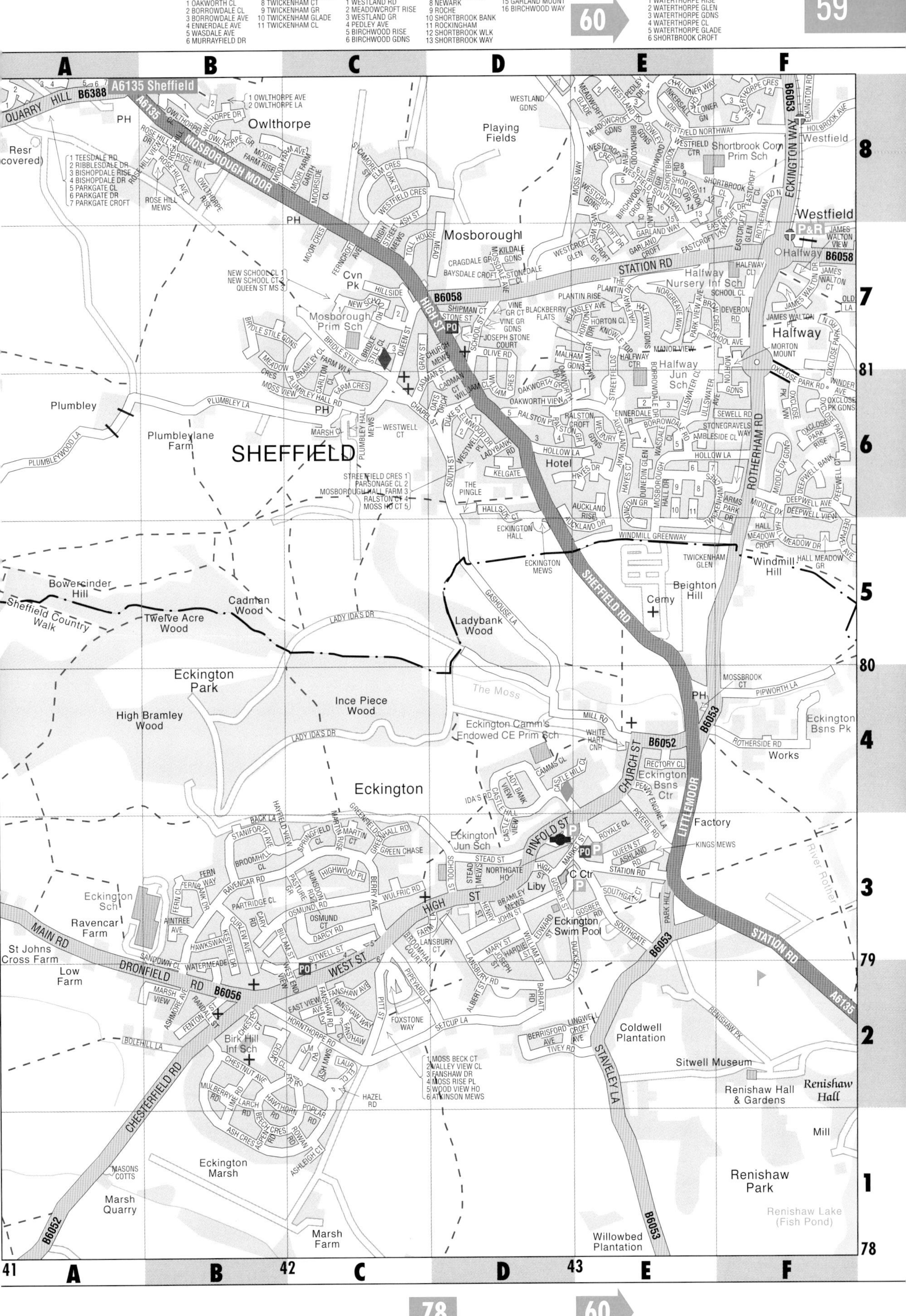

E6
1 OAKWORTH CL
2 BORROWDALE CL
3 BORROWDALE AVE
4 ENNERDALE AVE
5 WASDALE AVE
6 MURRAYFIELD DR
7 STONEGRAVELS CROFT
8 TWICKENHAM CT
9 TWICKENHAM GR
10 TWICKENHAM GLADE
11 TWICKENHAM CL

E8
1 WESTLAND RD
2 MEADOWCROFT RISE
3 WESTLAND GR
4 PEDLEY AVE
5 BIRCHWOOD RISE
6 BIRCHWOOD GDNS
7 BIRCHWOOD CL
8 NEWARK
9 ROCHE
10 SHORTBROOK BANK
11 ROCKINGHAM
12 SHORTBROOK WLK
13 SHORTBROOK WAY
14 SITWELL
15 GARLAND MOUNT
16 BIRCHWOOD WAY

F8
1 WATERTHORPE RISE
2 WATERTHORPE GLEN
3 WATERTHORPE GDNS
4 WATERTHORPE CL
5 WATERTHORPE GLADE
6 SHORTBROOK CROFT
7 EASTCROFT WAY

60

59

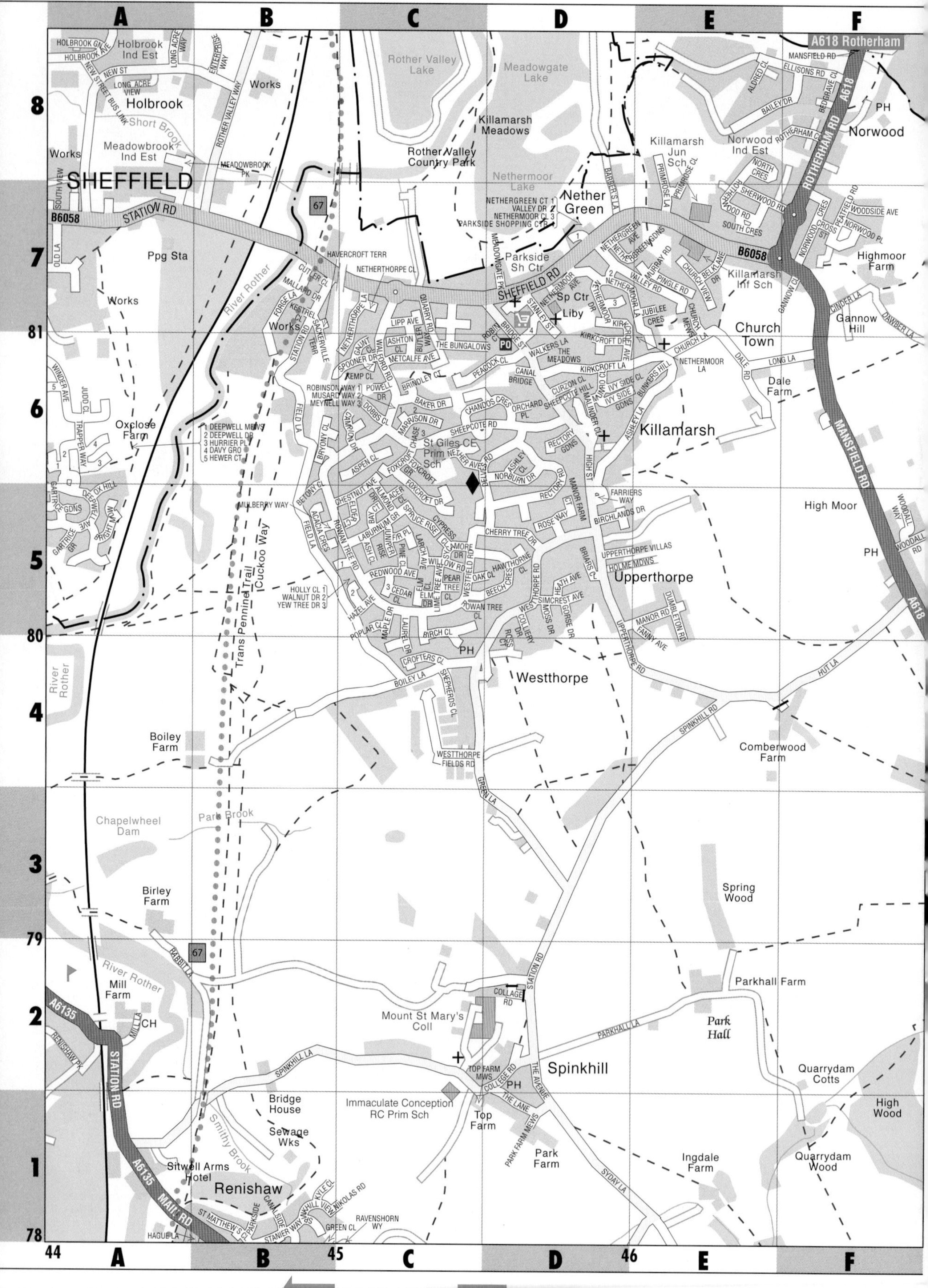
A
B
C
D
E
F
8
7
81
6
5
80
4
3
79
2
1
78
44
45
46
A618 Rotherham
Holbrook Ind Est
Holbrook
Works
Short Brook
Meadowbrook Ind Est
SHEFFIELD
B6058
STATION RD
Ppg Sta
Works
River Rother
Oxclose Farm
1 DEEPWELL MEWS
2 DEEPWELL DR
3 HURRIER PL
4 DAVY GRO
5 HEWER CT
MULBERRY WAY
Trans Pennine Trail
Cuckoo Way
Rother Valley Lake
Meadowgate Lake
Killamarsh Meadows
Rother Valley Country Park
Nethermoor Lake
NETHERGREEN CT 1
VALLEY DR 2
NETHERMOOR CL 3
PARKSIDE SHOPPING CTR 4
Nether Green
Parkside Sh Ctr
SHEFFIELD RD
HAVERCROFT TERR
NETHERTHORPE CL
Sp Ctr
Liby
THE BUNGALOWS
PO
THE MEADOWS
CANAL BRIDGE
St Giles CE Prim Sch
ROBINSON WAY 1
MUSARD WAY 2
MEYNELL WAY 3
Killamarsh Jun Sch
Norwood Ind Est
Norwood
PH
ROTHERHAM RD
A618
Killamarsh Inf Sch
B6058
Highmoor Farm
Church Town
Gannow Hill
Dale Farm
Killamarsh
MANSFIELD RD
High Moor
PH
FARRIERS WAY
BIRCHLANDS DR
UPPERTHORPE VILLAS
HOLME MDWS
Upperthorpe
HOLLY CL 1
WALNUT DR 2
YEW TREE DR 3
PH
Westthorpe
BOILEY LA
WESTTHORPE FIELDS RD
Boiley Farm
Comberwood Farm
SPINKHILL RD
HUT LA
Chapelwheel Dam
Park Brook
Spring Wood
Birley Farm
River Rother
Mill Farm
CH
A6135
STATION RD
Mount St Mary's Coll
COLLAGE RD
PARKHALL LA
Parkhall Farm
Park Hall
Spinkhill
TOP FARM MWS
PH
Quarrydam Cotts
Bridge House
Immaculate Conception RC Prim Sch
Top Farm
High Wood
Sewage Wks
Park Farm
Ingdale Farm
Quarrydam Wood
Sitwell Arms Hotel
Renishaw
SYDAY LA
RAVENSHORN WY
GREEN CL
HAGUE LA
ST MATTHEW'S CL
MAIN RD
67
67

59
79

62

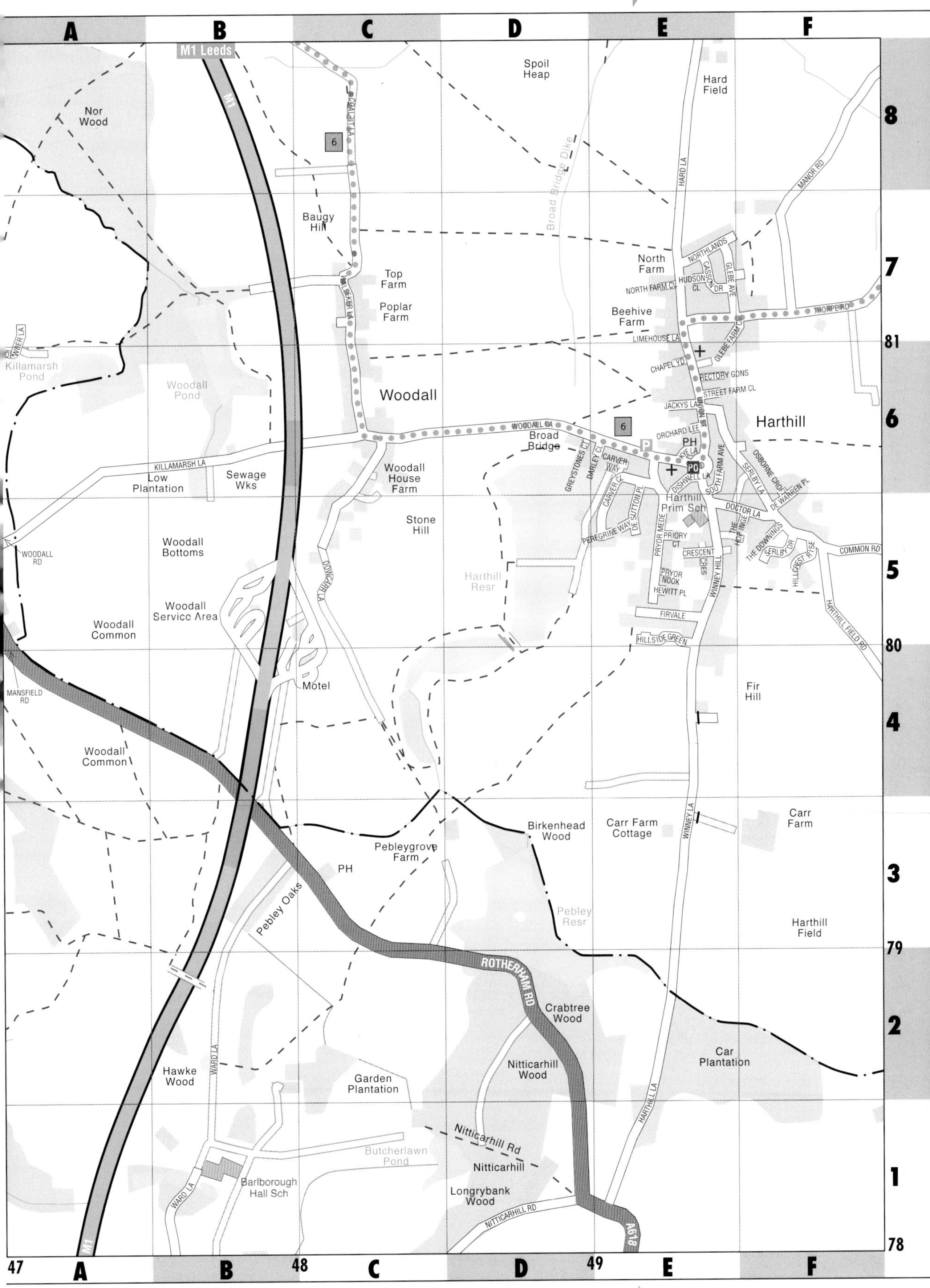
M1 Leeds
Nor Wood
Spoil Heap
Hard Field
Baugy Hill
Top Farm
Poplar Farm
North Farm
Beehive Farm
Killamarsh Pond
Woodall Pond
Woodall
Harthill
Broad Bridge
Low Plantation
Sewage Wks
Woodall House Farm
Stone Hill
Woodall Bottoms
Harthill Resr
Woodall Service Area
Woodall Common
Motel
Fir Hill
Birkenhead Wood
Carr Farm Cottage
Carr Farm
Pebleygrove Farm
PH
Pebley Oaks
Pebley Resr
Harthill Field
ROTHERHAM RD
Crabtree Wood
Nitticarhill Wood
Car Plantation
Hawke Wood
Garden Plantation
Nitticarhill Rd
Butcherlawn Pond
Nitticarhill
Barlborough Hall Sch
Longrybank Wood
NITTICARHILL RD
A618
Harthill Prim Sch
KILLAMARSH LA
WOODALL RD
MANSFIELD RD
WARD LA
HARD LA
MANOR RD
THORPE RD
WINNEY LA
HARTHILL LA
COMMON RD
HARTHILL FIELD RD
DONCASTER LA
WOODALL LA
Broad Bridge Dike

80

62

61

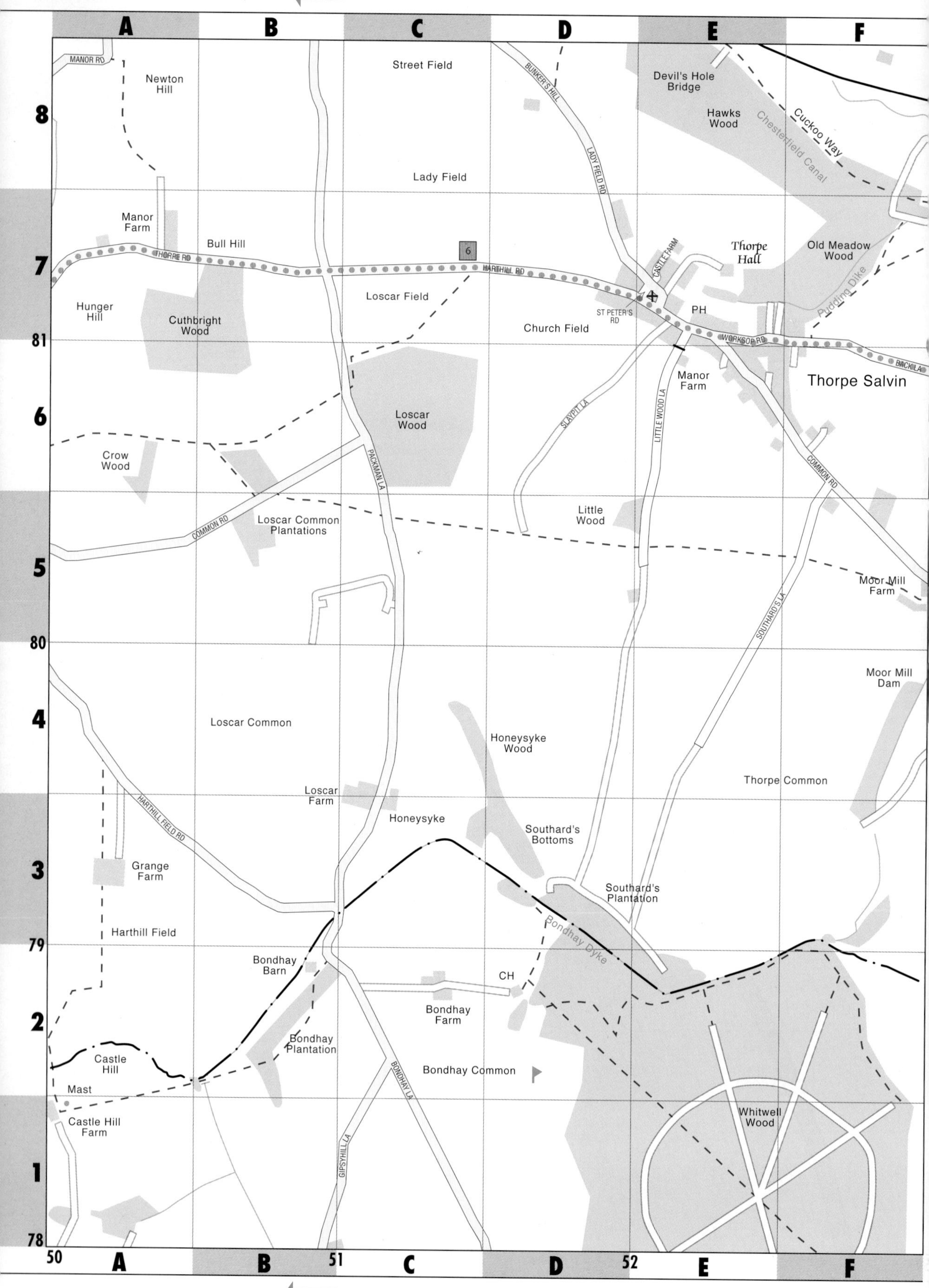
A
B
C
D
E
F
8
7
81
6
5
80
4
3
79
2
1
78
50
51
52
MANOR RD
Newton Hill
Street Field
BUNKER'S HILL
Devil's Hole Bridge
Hawks Wood
Chesterfield Canal
Cuckoo Way
LADY FIELD RD
Lady Field
Manor Farm
Bull Hill
THORPE RD
HARTHILL RD
CASTLE FARM
Thorpe Hall
Old Meadow Wood
Pudding Dike
Hunger Hill
Cuthbright Wood
Loscar Field
ST PETER'S RD
PH
Church Field
WORKSOP RD
BACK LA
Manor Farm
Thorpe Salvin
SLAYPIT LA
LITTLE WOOD LA
Loscar Wood
Crow Wood
PACKMAN LA
COMMON RD
Loscar Common Plantations
COMMON RD
Little Wood
Moor Mill Farm
SOUTHARD'S LA
Moor Mill Dam
Loscar Common
Honeysyke Wood
Thorpe Common
Loscar Farm
HARTHILL FIELD RD
Honeysyke
Southard's Bottoms
Grange Farm
Southard's Plantation
Bondhay Dyke
Harthill Field
Bondhay Barn
CH
Bondhay Farm
Bondhay Plantation
Castle Hill
BONDHAY LA
Bondhay Common
Mast
Castle Hill Farm
Whitwell Wood
GIPSYHILL LA
A
B
C
D
E
F

61
81

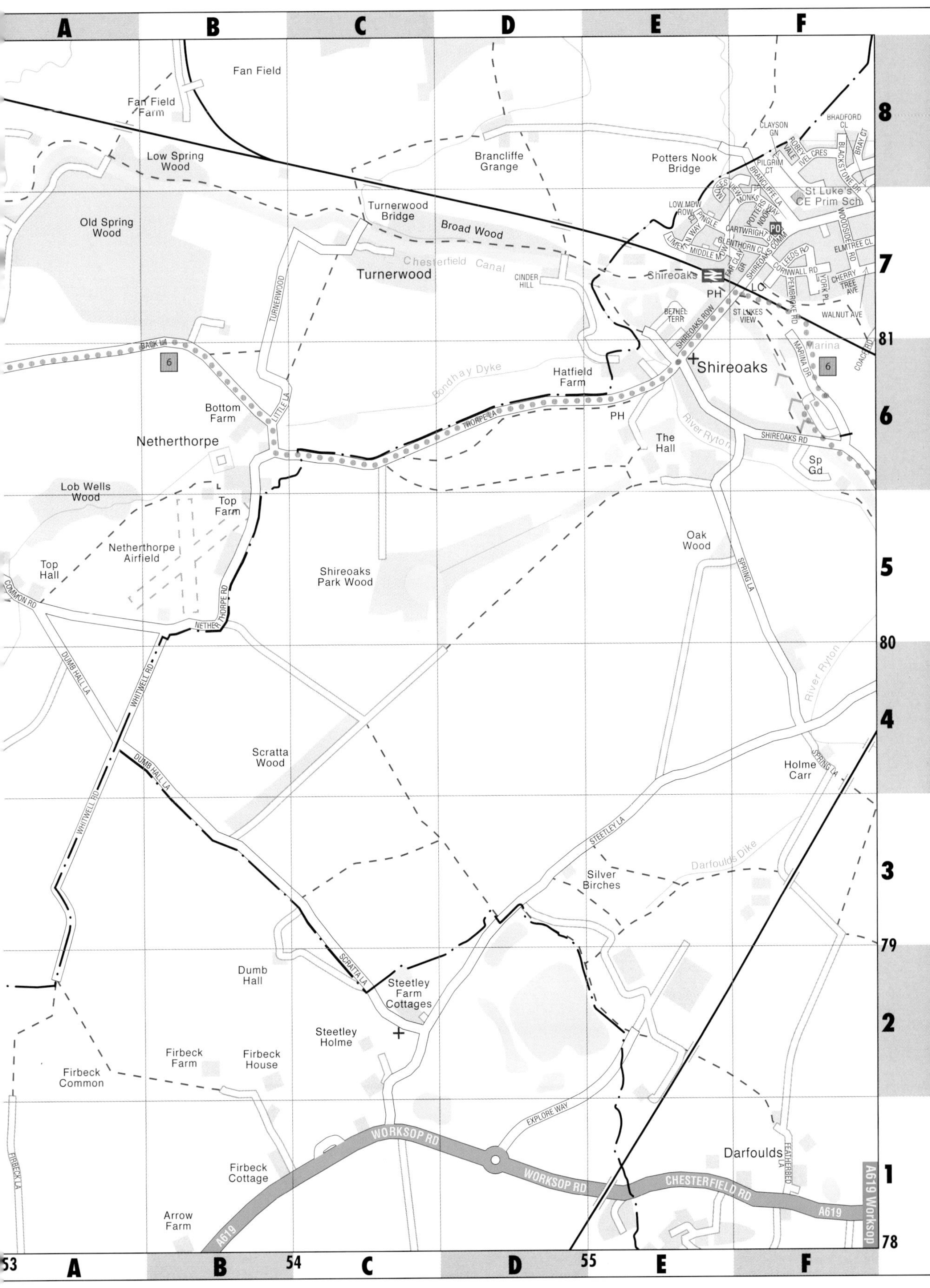

Fan Field

Fan Field Farm

Low Spring Wood

Old Spring Wood

Brancliffe Grange

Potters Nook Bridge

CLAYSON GN

BRADFORD CL

PILGRIM CT

St Luke's CE Prim Sch

Turnerwood Bridge

Broad Wood

Chesterfield Canal

Turnerwood

CINDER HILL

LOW MDW ROW

MONKS CL

BRANCLIFFE LA

CARTWRIGHT

Shireoaks

PH

LC

Shireoaks Row

BETHEL TERR

St Lukes View

WALNUT AVE

CHERRY TREE AVE

Marina

MARINA DR

6

BACK LA

6

Bondhay Dyke

THORPE LA

Hatfield Farm

PH

Shireoaks

River Ryton

SHIREOAKS RD

Sp Gd

Bottom Farm

LITTLE LA

Netherthorpe

The Hall

Lob Wells Wood

Top Farm

NETHER

THORPE RD

Shireoaks Park Wood

Oak Wood

SPRING LA

Top Hall

Netherthorpe Airfield

COMMON RD

DUMB HALL LA

WHITWELL RD

Scratta Wood

Holme Carr

SPRING LA

Steetley La

Darfoulds Dike

Silver Birches

SCRATTA LA

Dumb Hall

Steetley Farm Cottages

Steetley Holme

Firbeck Common

Firbeck Farm

Firbeck House

EXPLORE WAY

WORKSOP RD

Darfoulds

FEATHERBED

Firbeck Cottage

WORKSOP RD

CHESTERFIELD RD

A619 Worksop

Arrow Farm

A619

A619

FIRBECK LA

45

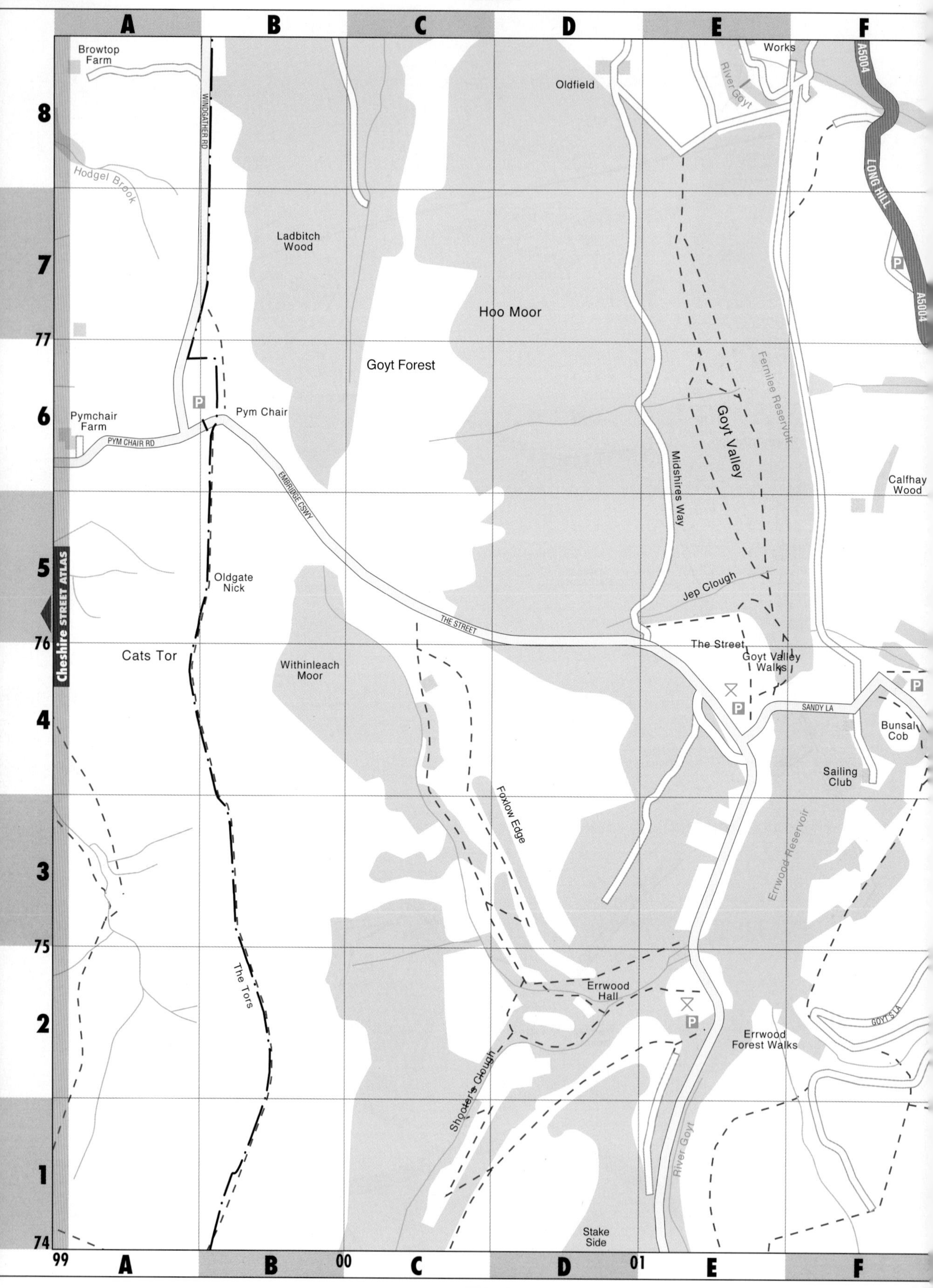
A
B
C
D
E
F
8
7
77
6
5
76
4
3
75
2
1
74
99
00
01
Cheshire STREET ATLAS
Browtop Farm
WINDGATHER RD
Hodgel Brook
Ladbitch Wood
Oldfield
Works
River Goyt
A5004
LONG HILL
Hoo Moor
Goyt Forest
Pymchair Farm
PYM CHAIR RD
Pym Chair
EMBRIDGE CSWY
Goyt Valley
Fernilee Reservoir
Midshires Way
Calfhay Wood
Oldgate Nick
Jep Clough
THE STREET
The Street
Goyt Valley Walks
Cats Tor
Withinleach Moor
SANDY LA
Bunsal Cob
Sailing Club
Foxlow Edge
Errwood Reservoir
The Tors
Errwood Hall
Errwood Forest Walks
GOYT'S LA
Shooter's Clough
River Goyt
Stake Side

83

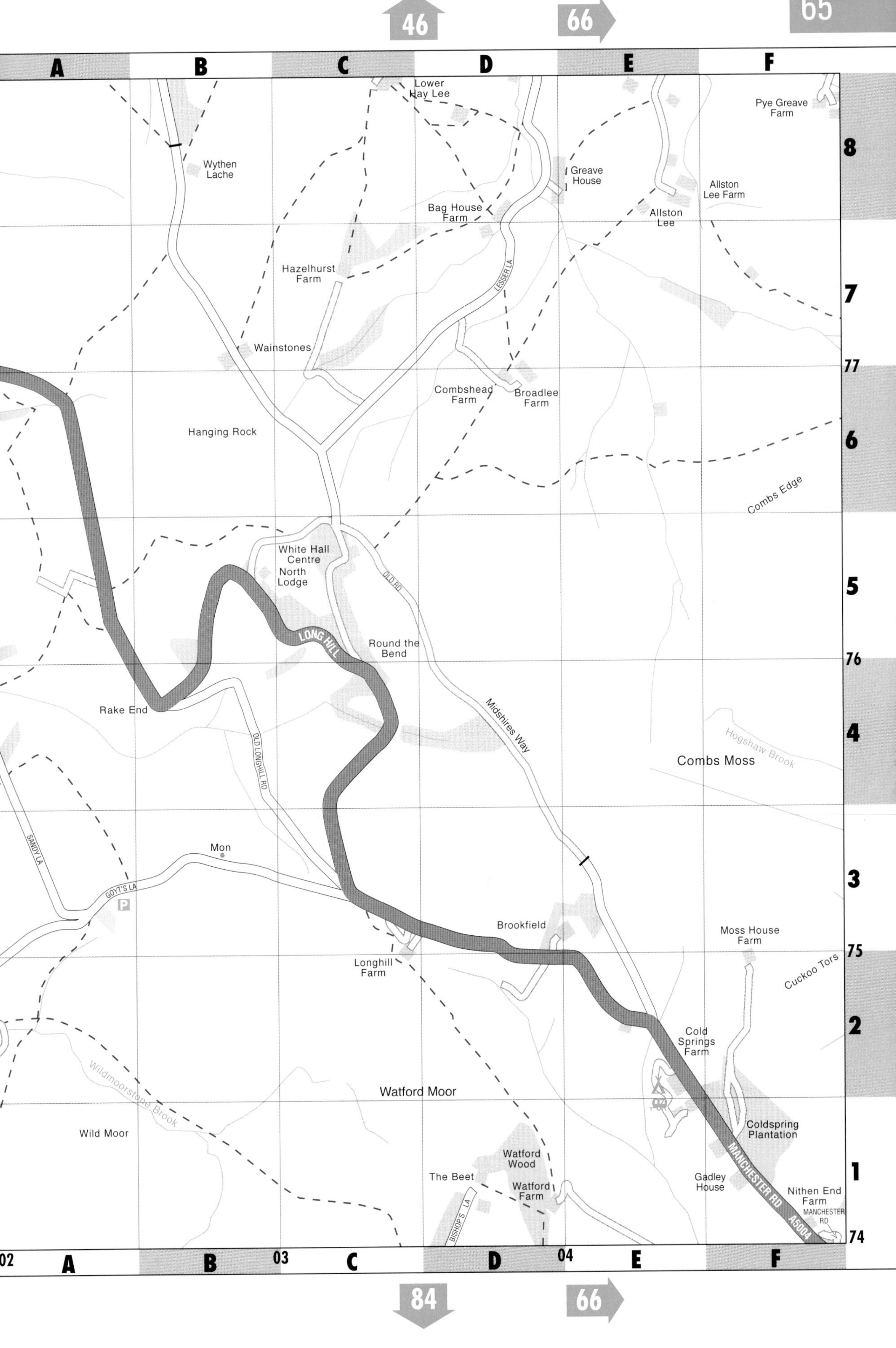

A   B   C   D   E   F

8

Pye Greave
Farm

Lower
Hay Lee

Greave
House

Allston
Lee Farm

Wythen
Lache

Bag House
Farm

Allston
Lee

7

Hazelhurst
Farm

LESSER LA

77

Wainstones

Combshead
Farm

Broadlee
Farm

6

Hanging Rock

Combs Edge

OLD RD

5

White Hall
Centre
North
Lodge

LONG HILL

Round the
Bend

76

Rake End

Midshires Way

Hogshaw Brook

4

Combs Moss

OLD LONGHILL RD

SANDY LA

Mon

3

GOYT'S LA

P

Brookfield

Moss House
Farm

75

Cuckoo Tors

Longhill
Farm

2

Cold
Springs
Farm

Watford Moor

Coldspring
Plantation

Wild Moor

Wildmoorstone Brook

Watford
Wood

The Beet

Watford
Farm

Gadley
House

Nithen End
Farm

MANCHESTER RD

MANCHESTER
RD

A5004

BISHOP'S LA

1

74

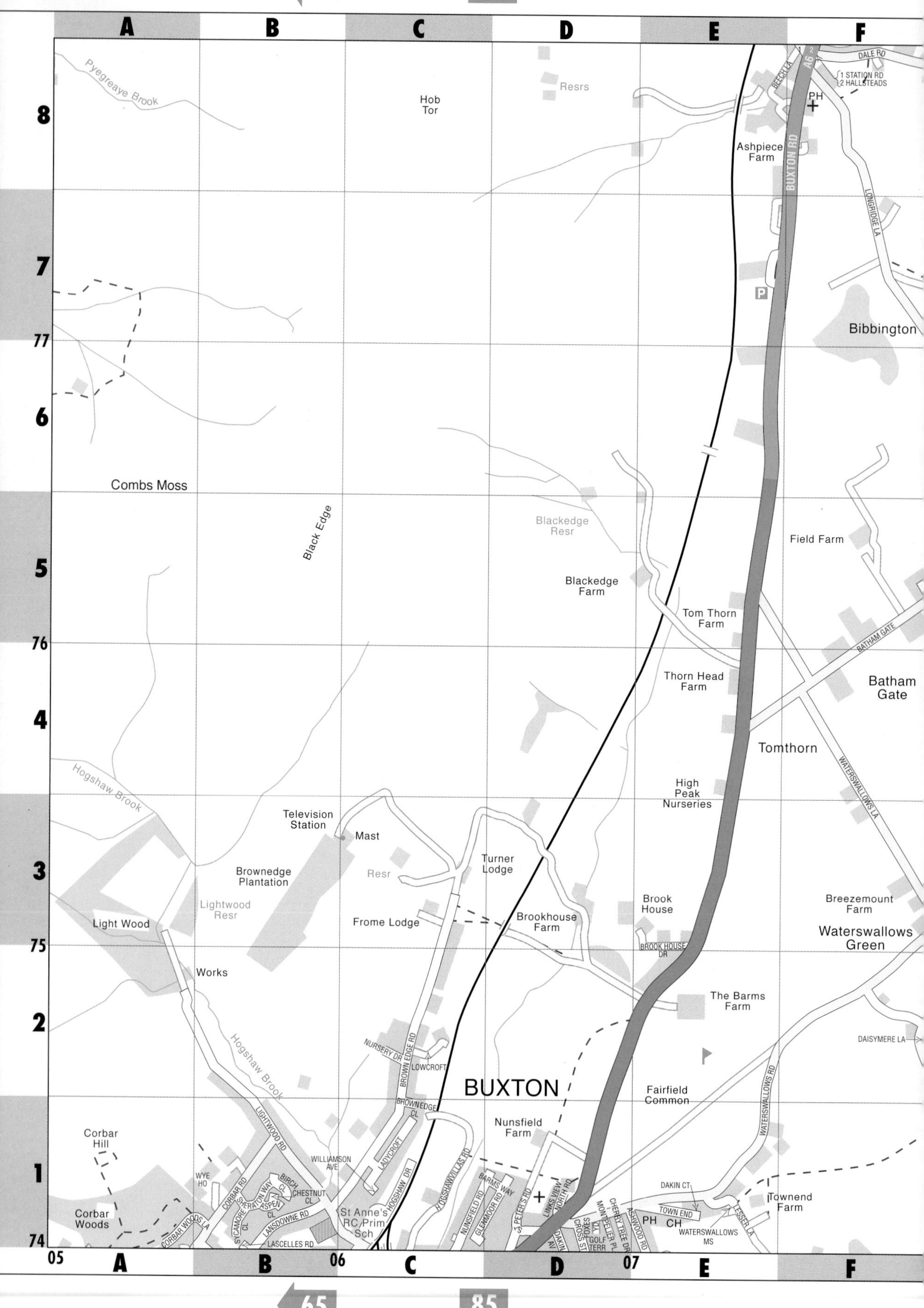

A　　B　　C　　D　　E　　F

8

Pyegreave Brook

Hob Tor

Resrs

DALE RD
1 STATION RD
2 HALLSTEADS

BEECH

PH

Ashpiece Farm

BUXTON RD

7

P

Bibbington

77

6

Combs Moss

Black Edge

Blackedge Resr

Blackedge Farm

Field Farm

5

76

Tom Thorn Farm

Thorn Head Farm

BATHAM GATE

Batham Gate

4

Hogshaw Brook

Tomthorn

WATERSWALLOWS LA

Television Station

Mast

Resr

Turner Lodge

High Peak Nurseries

Breezemount Farm

3

Brownedge Plantation

Frome Lodge

Brookhouse Farm

Brook House

Waterswallows Green

Lightwood Resr

BROOK HOUSE DR

Light Wood

75

Works

The Barms Farm

2

Hogshaw Brook

NURSERY DR

BROWN EDGE RD

LOWCROFT

Fairfield Common

WATERSWALLOWS RD

DAISYMERE LA

BROWNEDGE CL

BUXTON

Nunsfield Farm

Corbar Hill

LIGHTWOOD RD

CORBAR RD

WILLIAMSON AVE

LADYCROFT

BARMS WAY

DAKIN CT

Townend Farm

1

WYE HO

SYCAMORE CL
FERNTON WAY
ASPEN
BIRCH CL
CHESTNUT CL

FOSSTON VILLAS RD

NUNSFIELD RD

GLENMOOR RD

ST PETERS RD

LINKS VIEW

NORTH RD

CHERRY TREE DR

MONPELLIER PL

ASHWOOD RD

GOLF TERR

CROSS ST

TOWN END

PH

CH

LESSELL LA

Corbar Woods

CORBAR WOODS LA

LANSDOWNE RD

LASCELLES RD

St Anne's RC Prim Sch

DAKIN

WATERSWALLOWS MS

74

05　　A　　B　　06　　C　　D　　07　　E　　F

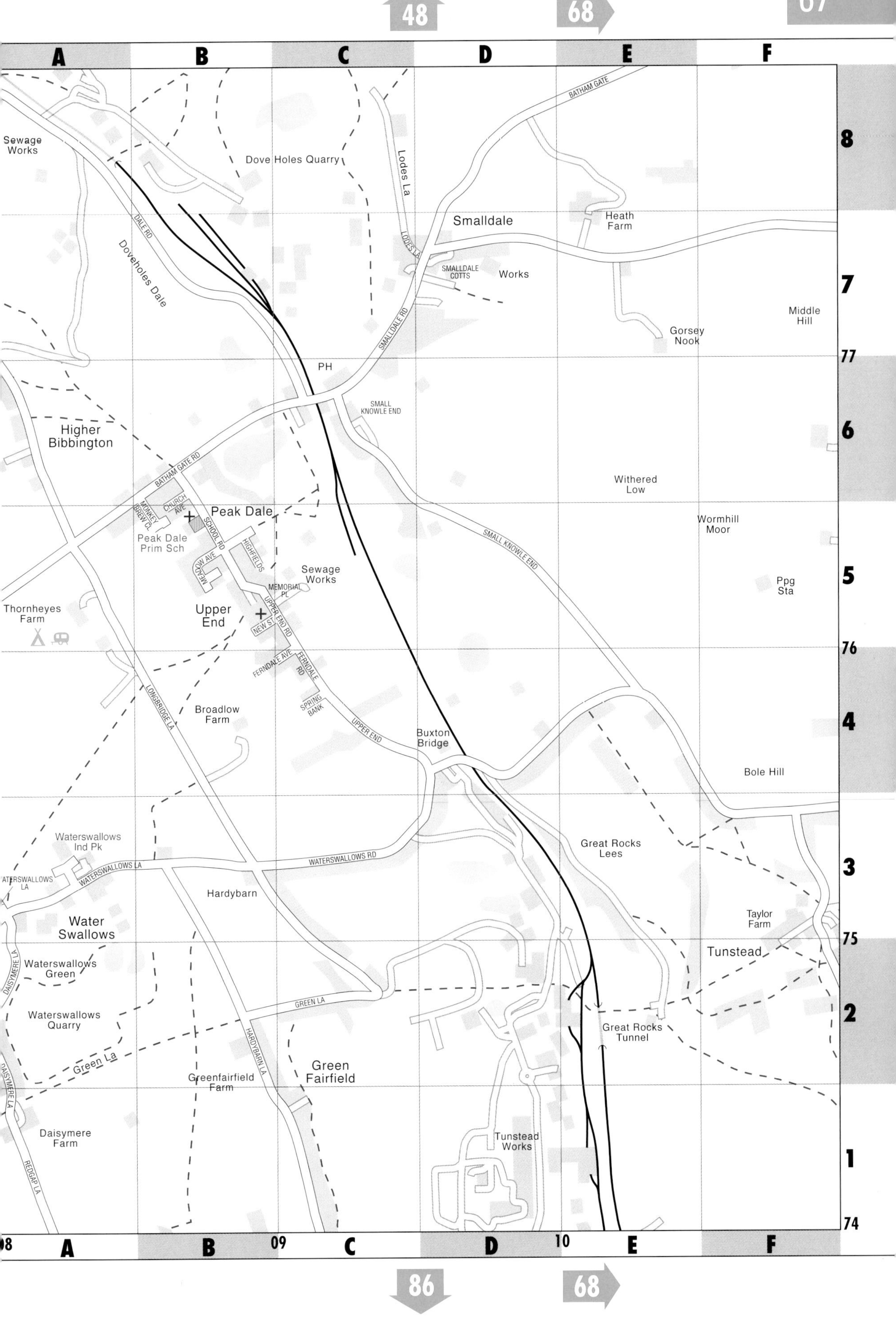

48
68

A B C D E F

8
Sewage Works
Dove Holes Quarry
Lodes La
Smalldale
Heath Farm
7
Doveholes Dale
Dale Rd
Smalldale Rd
SMALLDALE COTTS
Works
Gorsey Nook
Middle Hill
77
PH
SMALL KNOWLE END
6
Higher Bibbington
Withered Low
Wormhill Moor
Batham Gate Rd
Peak Dale
Peak Dale Prim Sch
Church Ave
School Rd
Highfield
Small Knowle End
Ppg Sta
5
Thornheyes Farm
Meadow Ave
Memorial Pl
Sewage Works
Upper End
New St
Upper End Rd
76
Ferndale Ave
Ferndale Rd
Broadlow Farm
Sipping Bank
Upper End
Buxton Bridge
Bole Hill
4
Longbridge La
Waterswallows Ind Pk
Waterswallows La
Waterswallows Rd
Great Rocks Lees
3
Waterswallows La
Hardybarn
Taylor Farm
75
Water Swallows
Tunstead
Waterswallows Green
Green La
2
Daisymere La
Waterswallows Quarry
Green La
Hardybarn La
Greenfairfield Farm
Green Fairfield
Great Rocks Tunnel
Redgap La
Daisymere Farm
Tunstead Works
1
74

A B 09 C D 10 E F

86
68

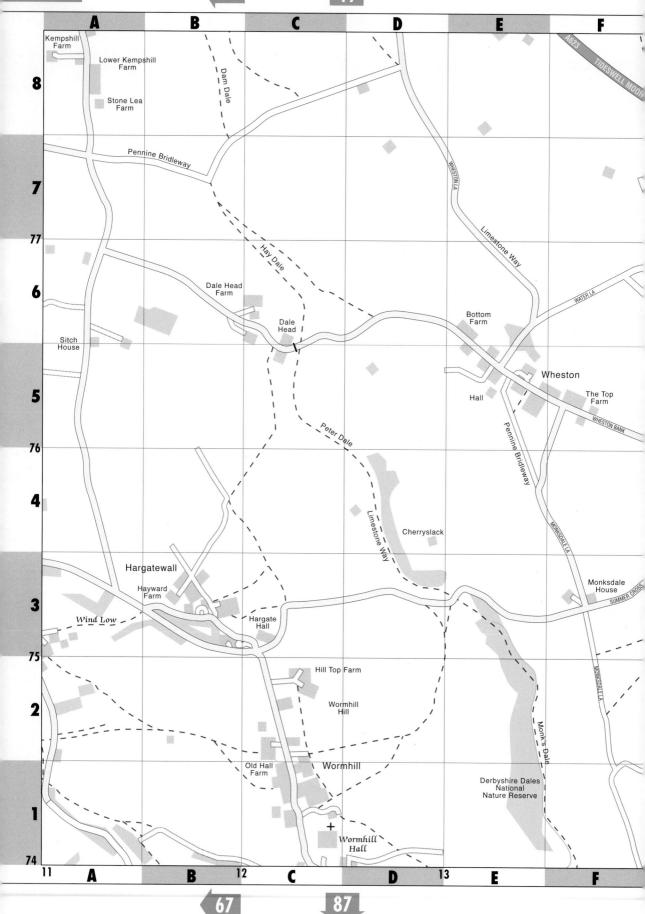

A B C D E F

8

7

77

6

5

76

4

3

75

2

1

74

Kempshill Farm

Lower Kempshill Farm

Stone Lea Farm

Dam Dale

Pennine Bridleway

A623

TIDESWELL MOOR

WHESTON LA

Limestone Way

WATER LA

Hay Dale

Dale Head Farm

Dale Head

Bottom Farm

Wheston

Sitch House

Hall

The Top Farm

WHESTON BANK

Peter Dale

Pennine Bridleway

Limestone Way

Cherryslack

MONKSDALE LA

Monksdale House

Hargatewall

SUMMER CROSS

Hayward Farm

Wind Low

Hargate Hall

Hill Top Farm

MONKSDALE LA

Wormhill Hill

Monk's Dale

Old Hall Farm

Wormhill

Derbyshire Dales National Nature Reserve

Wormhill Hall

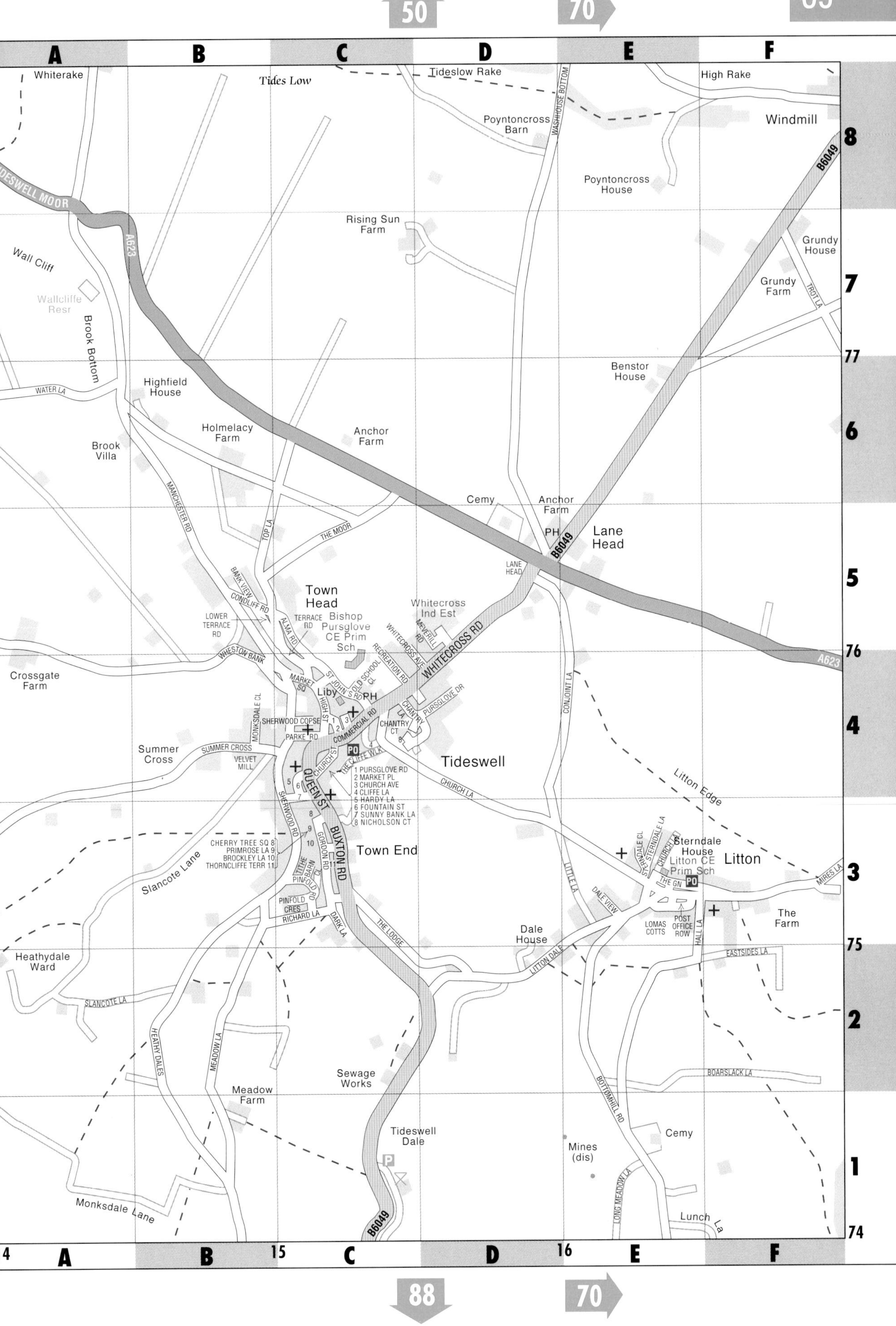

A B C D E F

Whiterake

Tides Low

Tideslow Rake

Poyntoncross Barn

WASHHOUSE BOTTOM

High Rake

Windmill

8

Poyntoncross House

B6049

Rising Sun Farm

Grundy House

7

Wall Cliff

Grundy Farm

TROT LA

Wallcliffe Resr

77

TIDESWELL MOOR

A623

Brook Bottom

Benstor House

WATER LA

Highfield House

6

Brook Villa

Holmelacy Farm

MANCHESTER RD

TOP LA

THE MOOR

Anchor Farm

Cemy

Anchor Farm

PH

Lane Head

B6049

5

BANK VIEW

CONDLIFF RD

WHESTON BANK

Town Head

Whitecross Ind Est

LANE HEAD

Crossgate Farm

LOWER TERRACE RD

TERRACE RD

ALMA RD

Bishop Pursglove CE Prim Sch

WHITECROSS LA

RECREATION RD

MILL HILL

WHITECROSS RD

A623

76

ST JOHN'S RD

OLD SCHOOL CT

HIGH ST

MARKET SQ

Liby

PH

CHANTRY

PURSGLOVE DR

CONJOINT LA

Litton Edge

4

MONKSDALE CL

SHERWOOD COPSE

PARKE RD

CHURCH ST

1 2

1 3

CHANTRY CT

Tideswell

Summer Cross

SUMMER CROSS

VELVET MILL

THE CLIFFE WLK

CHURCH LA

PO

1 PURSGLOVE RD
2 MARKET PL
3 CHURCH AVE
4 CLIFFE LA
5 HARDY LA
6 FOUNTAIN ST
7 SUNNY BANK LA
8 NICHOLSON CT

SHERWOOD RD

QUEEN'S ST

5 6

7

STERNDALE CL

STERNDALE LA

Sterndale House

Litton CE Prim Sch

Litton

MIRES LA

3

GORDON RD

BUXTON RD

9

10

Town End

LITTLE LA

DALE VIEW

CHURCH LA

THE GN

PO

The Farm

CHERRY TREE SQ 8
PRIMROSE LA 9
BROCKLEY LA 10
THORNCLIFFE TERR 11

PINFOLD RD

THE BARN

Slancote Lane

RICHARD LA

PINFOLD CRES

DARK LA

THE LODGE

Dale House

Lomas Cotts

HALL LA

POST OFFICE ROW

EASTSIDES LA

75

Heathydale Ward

SLANCOTE LA

LITTON DALE

2

HEATH DALES

MEADOW LA

Meadow Farm

Sewage Works

Mines (dis)

BOTTOMMILL RD

BOARSLACK LA

Cemy

Monksdale Lane

Tideswell Dale

P

B6049

LONG MEADOW LA

Lunch La

1

74

69
51

A B C D E F

8

WINDMILL

SIR WILLIAM HILL

Bretton Mount

B6049

Artis Farm

Great Hucklow

MAIN RD

SCHOOL LA

PH

Shepherd's Park

DIRTY LA

I Rose Farm

Grindlow

Hall Farm

7

GRINDLOW

77

Roods Farm

FOOLOW RD

Waterf Farm

BRADSHAW LA

Stanleymoor Farm

MAIN RD

Manor Farm

Foolow

6

Stanley Moor

Silly Dale

Little Moor

Old Hall Farm

Linen Dale

TROTT LA

Stanley Lodge

Brosterfield Farm

HOUSLEY RD

Opencast Workings

Tideswell Lane

5

Stanley House

MIDDLETON DALE

A62

76

A623

Housley

Housley House

Littonfields

PH

Somerset House Farm

Watergrove

BAKEWELL RD

4

MIRES LA

B6465

Wardlow Mires

Castlegate Stud Farm

Peter's Stone

THUNDERPIT LA

3

Meadow Farm

NARROWGATE LA

Mines (dis)

75

Manor Farm

White House Farm

Gregory Farm

LONG LA

White Rake

2

Tansley Dale

Wardlow

PH

Cressbrook Dale

MOOR RD

Hall Farm

1

Wardlow Hay Farm

MAIN RD

Longstone Moor

74

B6465

17 A 18 B C 19 D E F

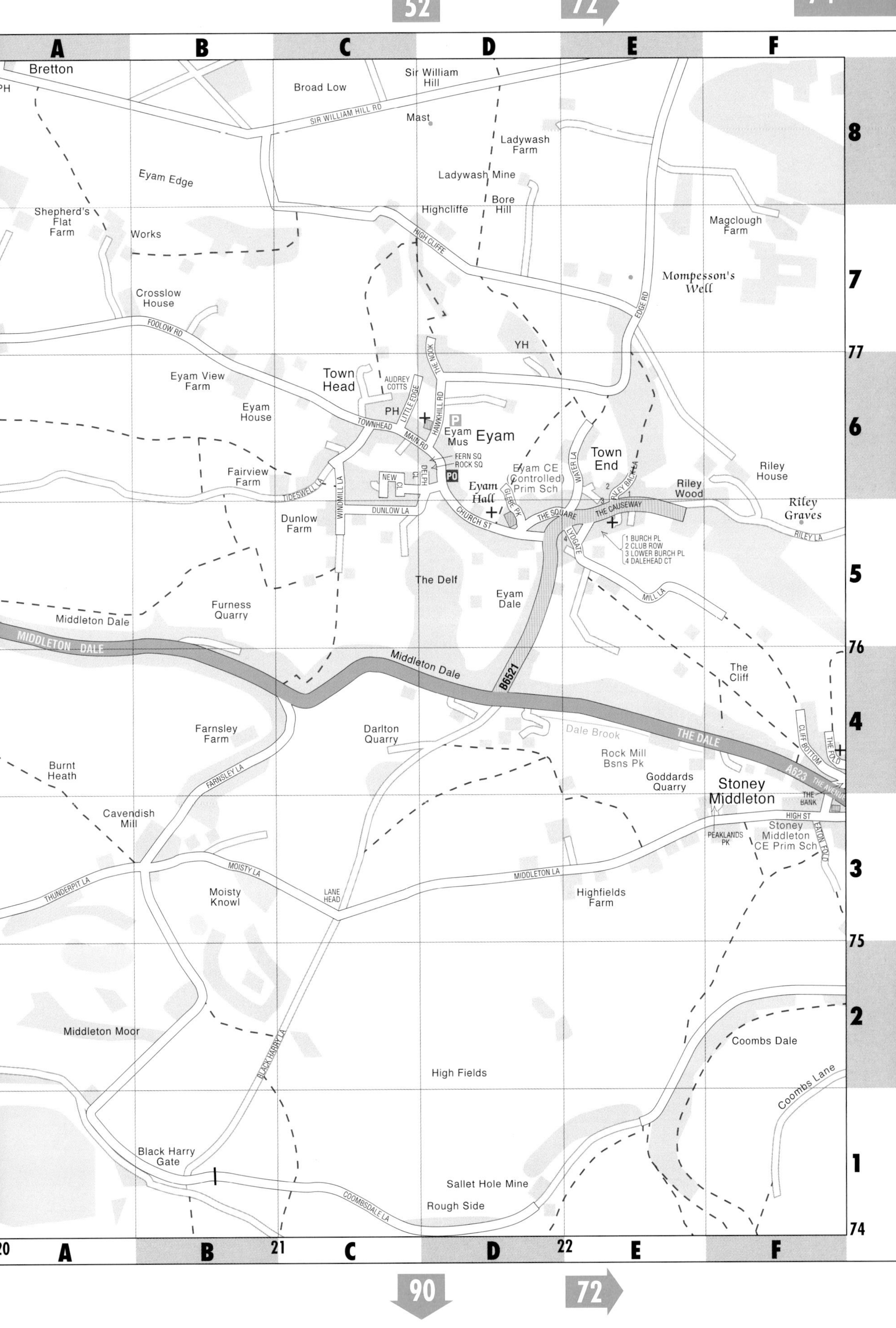
52
72
A
B
C
D
E
F
8
7
77
6
5
76
4
3
75
2
1
74
Bretton
PH
Broad Low
Sir William Hill
SIR WILLIAM HILL RD
Mast
Ladywash Farm
Ladywash Mine
Bore Hill
Highcliffe
Eyam Edge
Shepherd's Flat Farm
Works
HIGH CLIFFE
Magclough Farm
Mompesson's Well
Crosslow House
FOOLOW RD
EDGE RD
YH
Town Head
AUDREY COTTS
THE NOOK
LITTLE EDGE
HAWKHILL RD
Eyam View Farm
Eyam House
PH
TOWNHEAD
MAIN RD
P
Eyam Mus
Eyam
FERN SQ
ROCK SQ
PO
DELPH CL
NEW CL
Fairview Farm
TIDESWELL LA
WINDMILL LA
DUNLOW LA
Dunlow Farm
Eyam Hall
Eyam CE (Controlled) Prim Sch
WATER LA
Town End
RILEY BACK LA
THE CAUSEWAY
THE SQUARE
CHURCH ST
GLEBE PK
LYDGATE
1 BURCH PL
2 CLUB ROW
3 LOWER BURCH PL
4 DALEHEAD CT
Riley Wood
Riley House
Riley Graves
RILEY LA
The Delf
Eyam Dale
MILL LA
Furness Quarry
Middleton Dale
MIDDLETON DALE
Middleton Dale
B6521
The Cliff
Farnsley Farm
Darlton Quarry
Dale Brook
THE DALE
Rock Mill Bsns Pk
Goddards Quarry
Stoney Middleton
CLIFF BOTTOM
THE FOLD
A623
THE AVENUE
THE BANK
HIGH ST
Burnt Heath
FARNSLEY LA
Cavendish Mill
PEAKLANDS PK
Stoney Middleton CE Prim Sch
EATON FOLD
THUNDERPIT LA
MOISTY LA
Moisty Knowl
LANE HEAD
MIDDLETON LA
Highfields Farm
Middleton Moor
BLACK HARRY LA
High Fields
Coombs Dale
Coombs Lane
Black Harry Gate
Sallet Hole Mine
Rough Side
COOMBSDALE LA
20
21
22
90
72

71
53

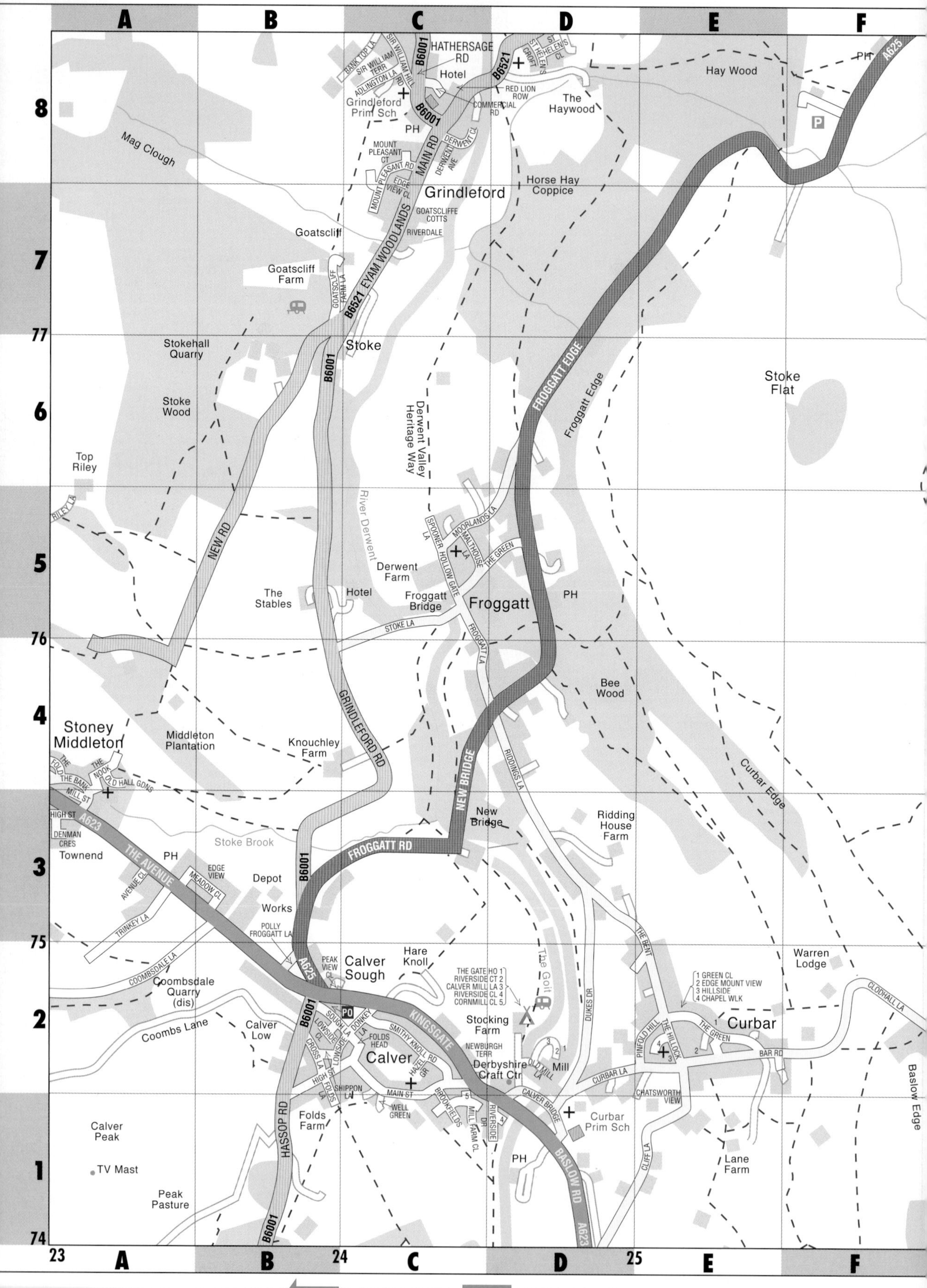
Grindleford
Grindleford Prim Sch
Hathersage Rd
Hotel
Main Rd
Eyam Woodlands
Goatscliff
Goatscliff Farm
Stoke
Stokehall Quarry
Stoke Wood
Top Riley
New Rd
Mag Clough
Hay Wood
The Haywood
Horse Hay Coppice
Froggatt Edge
Stoke Flat
Derwent Valley Heritage Way
River Derwent
Derwent Farm
The Stables
Hotel
Froggatt Bridge
Froggatt
PH
Stoke La
Bee Wood
Stoney Middleton
Middleton Plantation
Knouchley Farm
Grindleford Rd
Curbar Edge
New Bridge
Ridding House Farm
Froggatt Rd
Townend
The Avenue
Stoke Brook
Depot
Works
Calver Sough
Hare Knoll
Warren Lodge
Coombsdale Quarry (dis)
Coombs Lane
Calver Low
Calver
Stocking Farm
Derbyshire Craft Ctr
Mill
Curbar
Kingsgate
Folds Farm
Curbar Prim Sch
Calver Peak
TV Mast
Peak Pasture
Lane Farm
Baslow Edge
Baslow Rd
Hassop Rd
A623
A625
B6001
B6521

71
91

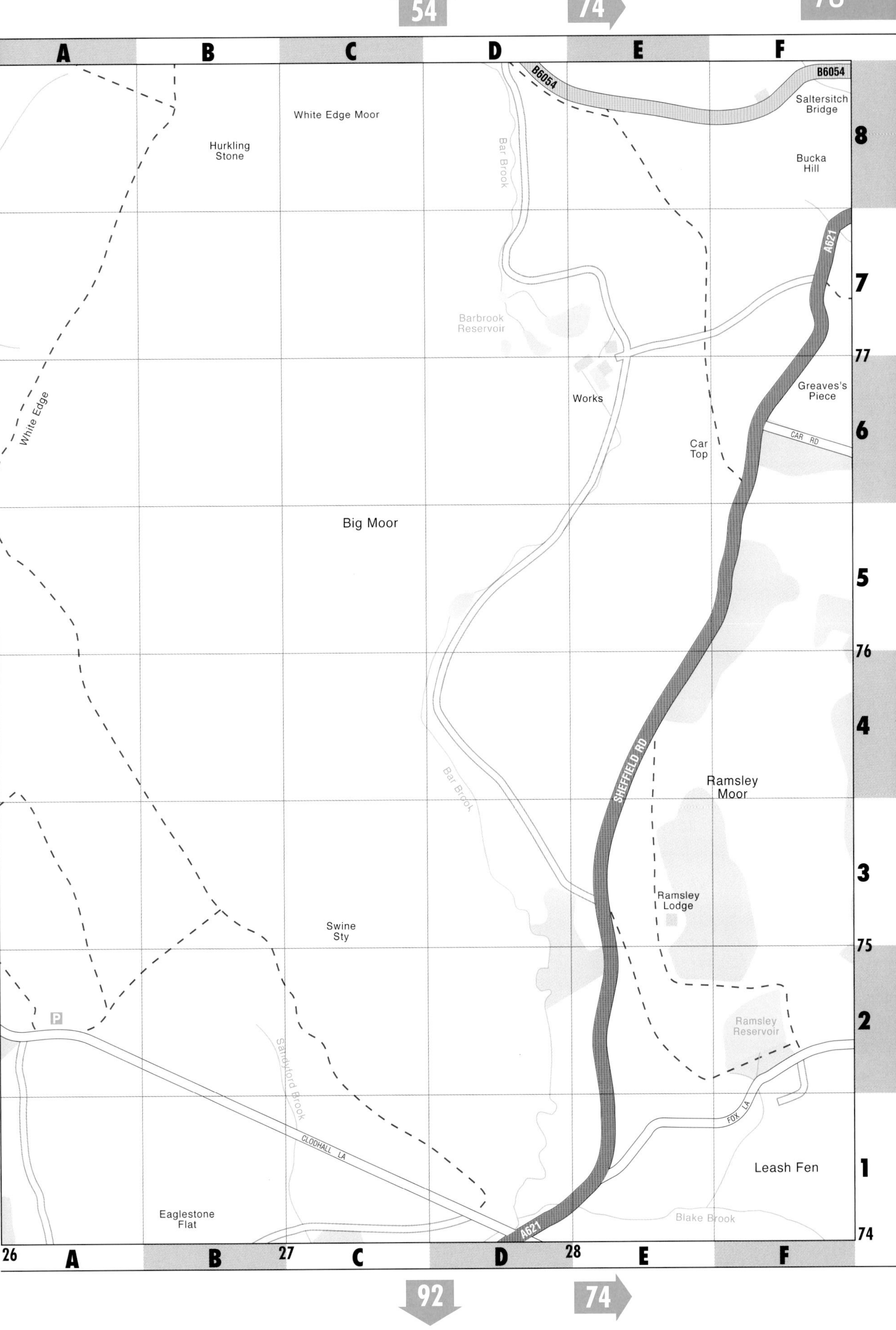

A B C D E F

B6054
B6054

Saltersitch
Bridge

8

Bucka
Hill

White Edge Moor

Hurkling
Stone

Bar Brook

A621

7

77

Barbrook
Reservoir

Greaves's
Piece

Works

6
CAR RD

Car
Top

White Edge

Big Moor

5

76

SHEFFIELD RD

4

Bar Brook

Ramsley
Moor

3

Swine
Sty

Ramsley
Lodge

75

P

Ramsley
Reservoir

2

Sandyford Brook

FOX LA

CLODHALL LA

Leash Fen

1

Eaglestone
Flat

A621

Blake Brook

74

26 A B 27 C D 28 E F

73
55

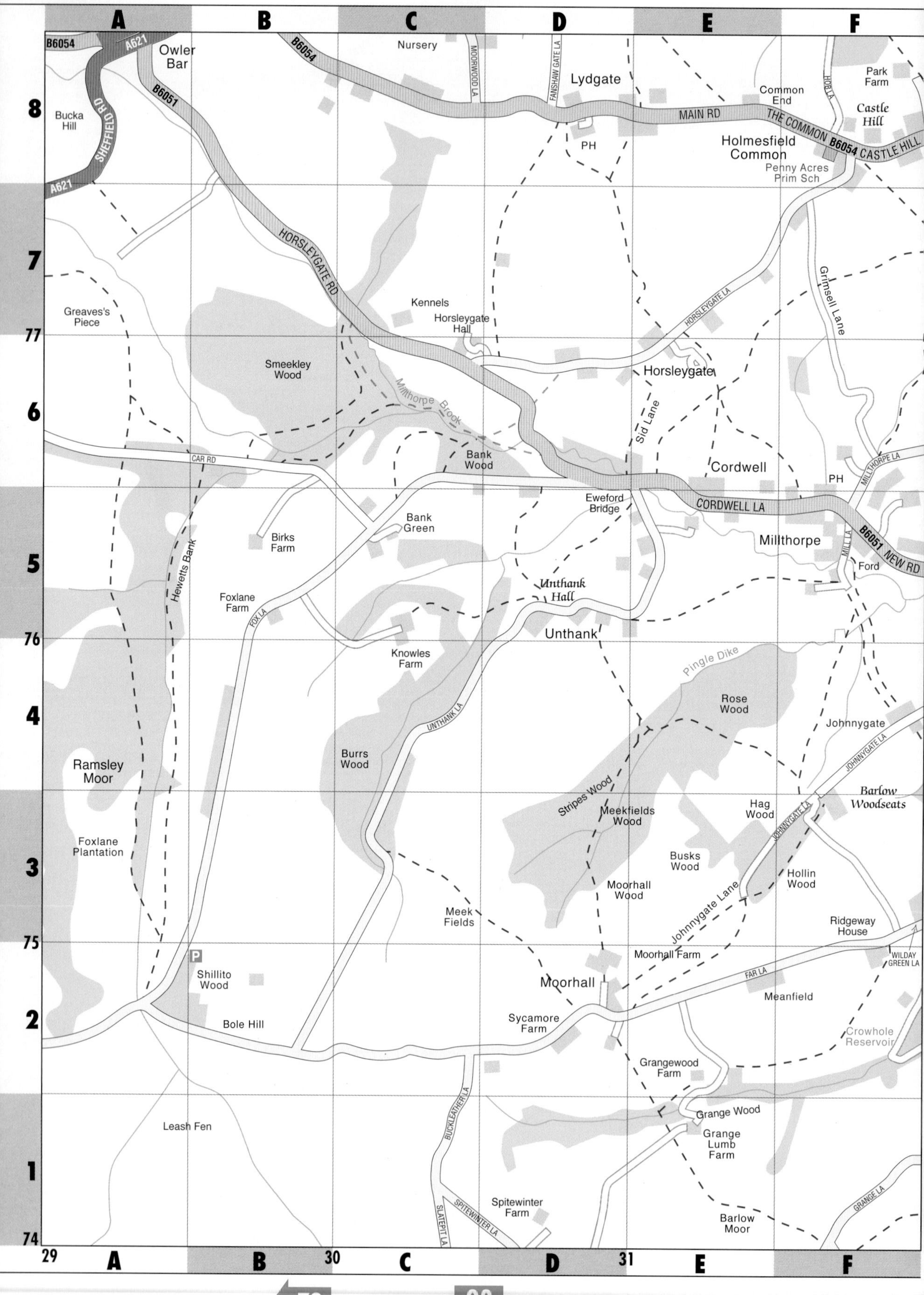
A
B
C
D
E
F
8
7
77
6
5
76
4
3
75
2
1
74
29
30
31
B6054
A621
Owler Bar
Nursery
MOORWOOD LA
FANSHAW GATE LA
Lydgate
Common End
HOBB LA
Park Farm
Castle Hill
Bucka Hill
SHEFFIELD RD
B6051
MAIN RD
THE COMMON
B6054
CASTLE HILL
PH
Holmesfield Common
Penny Acres Prim Sch
HORSLEYGATE RD
Grimsell Lane
Greaves's Piece
Kennels
Horsleygate Hall
HORSLEYGATE LA
Smeekley Wood
Horsleygate
Millthorpe Brook
Sid Lane
CAR RD
Bank Wood
Cordwell
MILLTHORPE LA
PH
Eweford Bridge
CORDWELL LA
Bank Green
Birks Farm
Millthorpe
MILL LA
B6051
NEW RD
Hewetts Bank
Ford
Foxlane Farm
FOX LA
Unthank Hall
Unthank
Knowles Farm
Pingle Dike
Rose Wood
UNTHANK LA
Johnnygate
JOHNNYGATE LA
Ramsley Moor
Burrs Wood
Stripes Wood
Barlow Woodseats
Hag Wood
Meekfields Wood
JOHNNYGATE LA
Foxlane Plantation
Busks Wood
Hollin Wood
Moorhall Wood
Johnnygate Lane
Meek Fields
Ridgeway House
Moorhall Farm
P
WILDAY GREEN LA
Shillito Wood
FAR LA
Moorhall
Meanfield
Sycamore Farm
Bole Hill
Crowhole Reservoir
Grangewood Farm
Grange Wood
BUCKLEATHER LA
Leash Fen
Grange Lumb Farm
SPITEWINTER LA
Spitewinter Farm
GRANGE LA
SLATEPIT LA
Barlow Moor

73
93

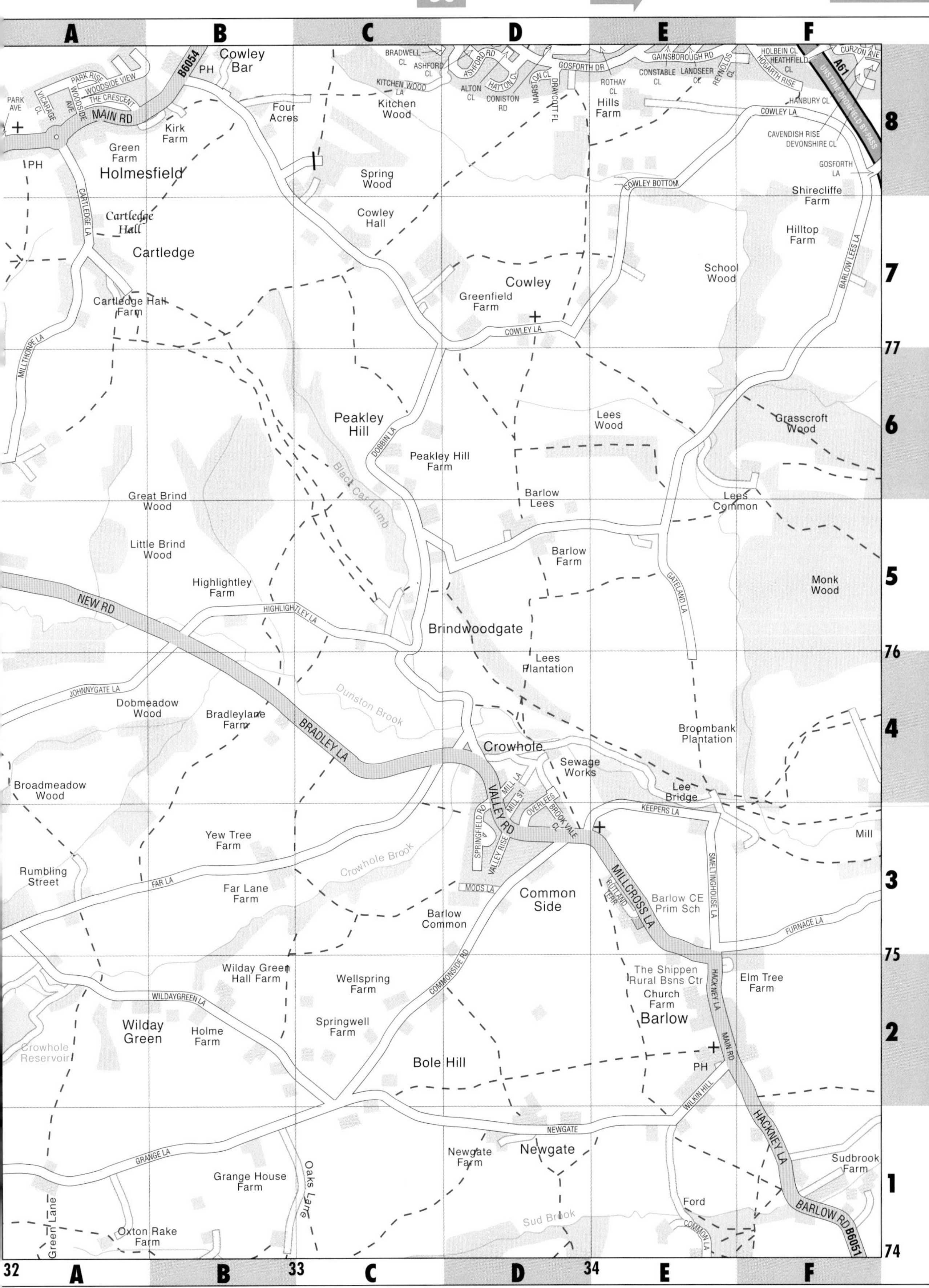

56
76
A
B
C
D
E
F
8
7
77
6
5
76
4
3
75
2
1
74
32
33
34
Cowley Bar
PH
B6054
MAIN RD
Holmesfield
Kirk Farm
Green Farm
Cartledge Hall
Cartledge
Cartledge Hall Farm
Four Acres
Kitchen Wood
Spring Wood
Cowley Hall
Cowley
Greenfield Farm
COWLEY LA
Hills Farm
COWLEY BOTTOM
Shirecliffe Farm
Hilltop Farm
School Wood
BARLOW LEES LA
A61
Peakley Hill
Peakley Hill Farm
DOBBIN LA
Black Car Lumb
Lees Wood
Barlow Lees
Grasscroft Wood
Lees Common
Great Brind Wood
Little Brind Wood
Barlow Farm
Monk Wood
GATELAND LA
Highlightley Farm
HIGHLIGHTLEY LA
NEW RD
Brindwoodgate
Lees Plantation
JOHNNYGATE LA
Dobmeadow Wood
Bradleylane Farm
Dunston Brook
BRADLEY LA
Broombank Plantation
Crowhole
Sewage Works
Lee Bridge
Broadmeadow Wood
VALLEY RD
KEEPERS LA
Mill
Yew Tree Farm
Rumbling Street
Crowhole Brook
FAR LA
Far Lane Farm
MODS LA
Common Side
MILLCROSS LA
Barlow CE Prim Sch
SMELTINGHOUSE LA
FURNACE LA
Barlow Common
Wilday Green Hall Farm
Wellspring Farm
COMMONSIDE RD
The Shippen Rural Bsns Ctr
Church Farm
Barlow
Elm Tree Farm
HACKNEY LA
MAIN RD
WILDAYGREEN LA
Wilday Green
Holme Farm
Springwell Farm
Crowhole Reservoir
Bole Hill
PH
WILKIN HILL
NEWGATE
Newgate Farm
Newgate
GRANGE LA
Grange House Farm
Oaks Lane
Ford
Sudbrook Farm
BARLOW RD B6051
Sud Brook
COMMON LA
Green Lane
Oxton Rake Farm
94
76

75
57

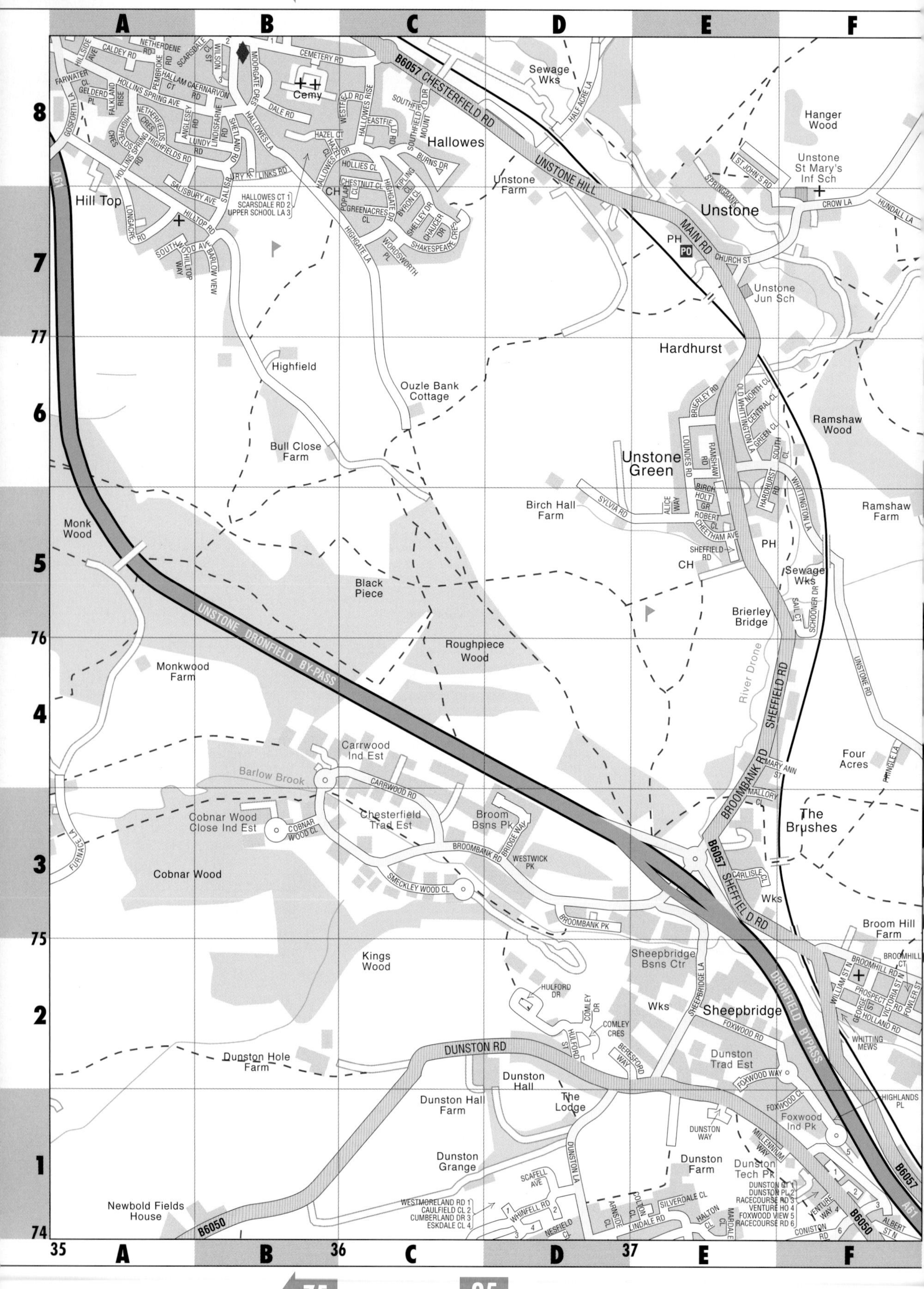
A
B
C
D
E
F
8
7
77
6
5
76
4
3
75
2
1
74
35
36
37
Hill Top
Hallowes
Cemy
Sewage Wks
Unstone Farm
Unstone
Hanger Wood
Unstone St Mary's Inf Sch
Unstone Jun Sch
Hardhurst
Highfield
Ouzle Bank Cottage
Bull Close Farm
Ramshaw Wood
Unstone Green
Birch Hall Farm
Ramshaw Farm
Monk Wood
Black Piece
Brierley Bridge
Sewage Wks
Roughpiece Wood
Monkwood Farm
River Drone
Four Acres
Carrwood Ind Est
Barlow Brook
Cobnar Wood Close Ind Est
Chesterfield Trad Est
Broom Bsns Pk
The Brushes
Cobnar Wood
Broom Hill Farm
Kings Wood
Sheepbridge Bsns Ctr
Wks
Sheepbridge
Dunston Hole Farm
Dunston Trad Est
Dunston Hall
The Lodge
Dunston Hall Farm
Foxwood Ind Pk
Dunston Grange
Dunston Farm
Dunston Tech Pk
Newbold Fields House
B6057 CHESTERFIELD RD
UNSTONE HILL
MAIN RD
UNSTONE DRONFIELD BY-PASS
SHEFFIELD RD
BROOMBANK RD
DRONFIELD BYPASS
DUNSTON RD
B6050
A61
B6057
HALLOWES CT 1
SCARSDALE RD 2
UPPER SCHOOL LA 3
WESTMORELAND RD 1
CAULFIELD CL 2
CUMBERLAND DR 3
ESKDALE CL 4
DUNSTON CT 1
DUNSTON PL 2
RACECOURSE RD 3
VENTURE HO 4
FOXWOOD VIEW 5
RACECOURSE RD 6

75
95

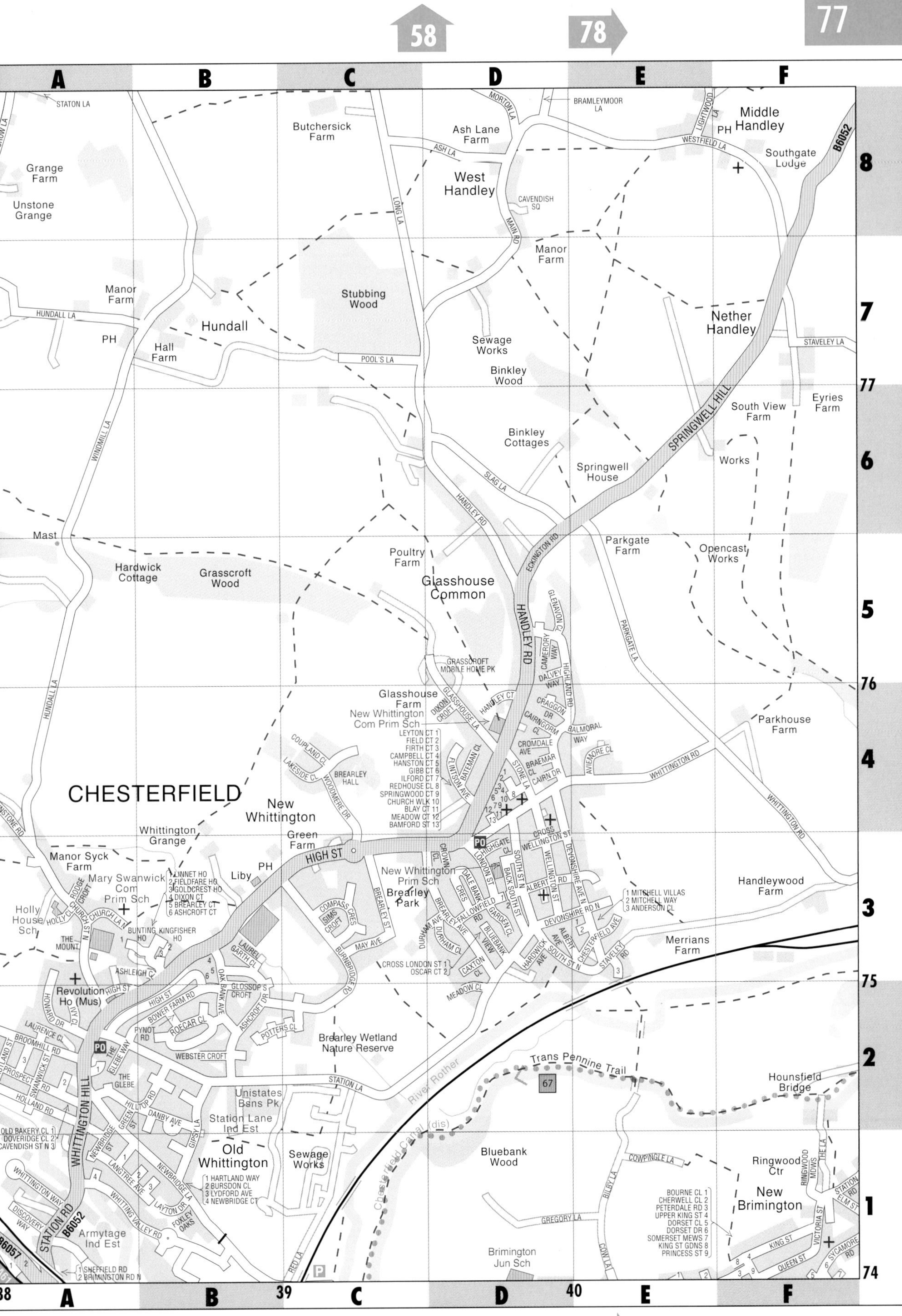
58
78
A
B
C
D
E
F
CHESTERFIELD
Middle Handley
West Handley
Hundall
Nether Handley
Glasshouse Common
New Whittington
Old Whittington
New Brimington
Grange Farm
Unstone Grange
Butchersick Farm
Ash Lane Farm
Southgate Lodge
Manor Farm
Stubbing Wood
Hall Farm
Sewage Works
Binkley Wood
South View Farm
Eyries Farm
Binkley Cottages
Springwell House
Works
Mast
Hardwick Cottage
Grasscroft Wood
Poultry Farm
Parkgate Farm
Opencast Works
Glasshouse Farm
New Whittington Com Prim Sch
Parkhouse Farm
Brearley Hall
Whittington Grange
Green Farm
Manor Syck Farm
Mary Swanwick Com Prim Sch
Liby
Holly House Sch
New Whittington Prim Sch
Brearley Park
Handleywood Farm
Merrians Farm
Revolution Ho (Mus)
Brearley Wetland Nature Reserve
Trans Pennine Trail
River Rother
Hounsfield Bridge
Unistates Bsns Pk
Station Lane Ind Est
Sewage Works
Chesterfield Canal (dis)
Bluebank Wood
Ringwood Ctr
Armytage Ind Est
Brimington Jun Sch
HIGH ST
HANDLEY RD
SPRINGWELL HILL
WHITTINGTON HILL
STATION RD
B6052
B6057
LEYTON CT 1
FIELD CT 2
FIRTH CT 3
CAMPBELL CT 4
HANSTON CT 5
GIBB CT 6
ILFORD CT 7
REDHOUSE CL 8
SPRINGWOOD CT 9
CHURCH WLK 10
BLAY CT 11
MEADOW CT 12
BAMFORD ST 13
1 LINNET HO
2 FIELDFARE HO
3 GOLDCREST HO
4 DIXON CT
5 BREARLEY CT
6 ASHCROFT CT
1 MITCHELL VILLAS
2 MITCHELL WAY
3 ANDERSON CL
CROSS LONDON ST 1
OSCAR CT 2
OLD BAKERY CL 1
DOVERIDGE CL 2
CAVENDISH ST N 3
1 HARTLAND WAY
2 BURSDON CL
3 LYDFORD AVE
4 NEWBRIDGE CT
BOURNE CL 1
CHERWELL CL 2
PETERDALE RD 3
UPPER KING ST 4
DORSET CL 5
DORSET DR 6
SOMERSET MEWS 7
KING ST GDNS 8
PRINCESS ST 9
1 SHEFFIELD RD
2 BRIMINGTON RD N
38
39
40
74
75
76
77
8
7
6
5
4
3
2
1
96
78

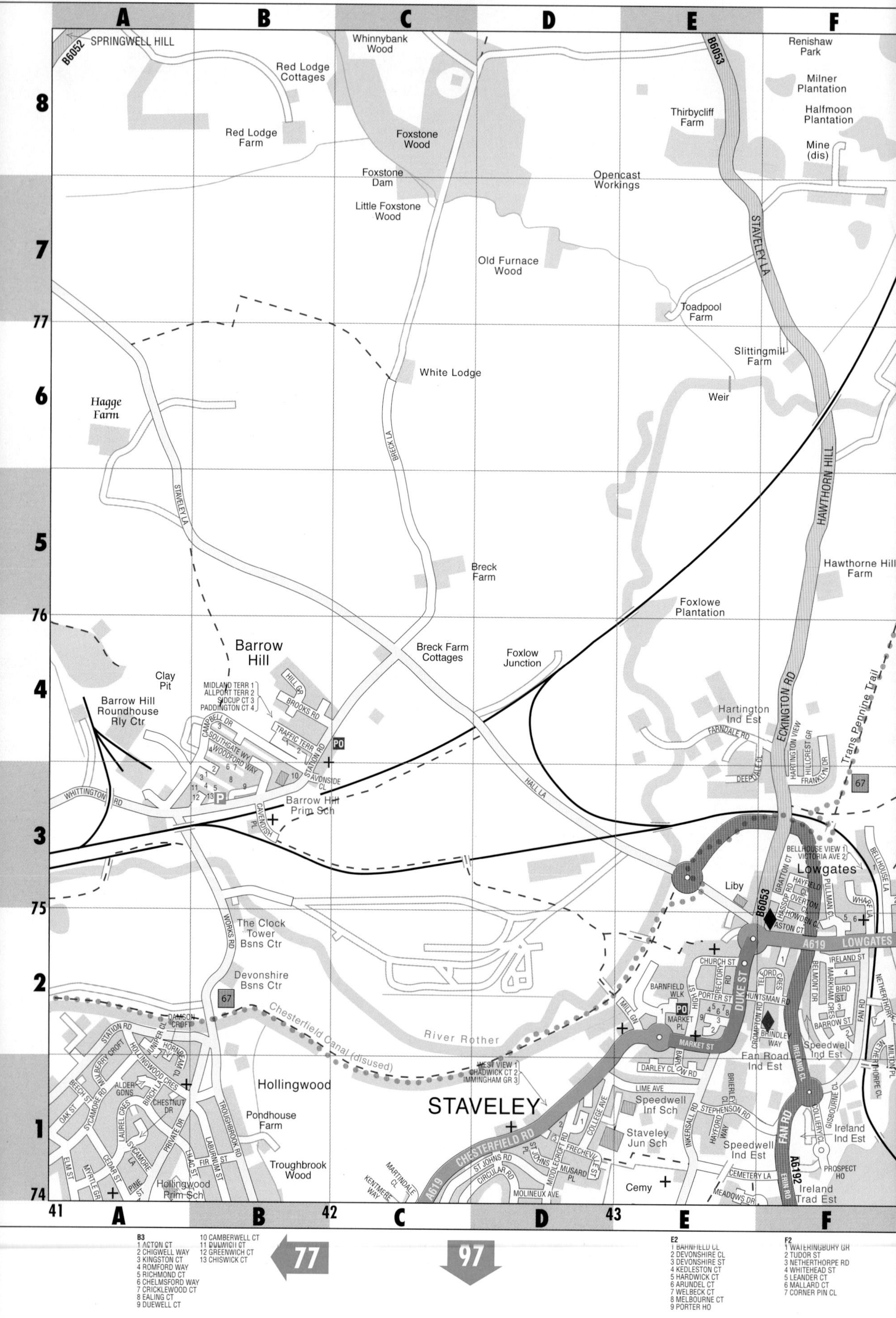

	A	B	C	D	E	F

SPRINGWELL HILL
B6052
B6053

Whinnybank Wood
Red Lodge Cottages
Red Lodge Farm
Foxstone Wood
Foxstone Dam
Little Foxstone Wood
Renishaw Park
Milner Plantation
Halfmoon Plantation
Mine (dis)
Thirbycliff Farm
Opencast Workings
STAVELEY LA

Old Furnace Wood
Toadpool Farm
Slittingmill Farm
Weir
White Lodge

Hagge Farm
HAWTHORN HILL
Hawthorne Hill Farm

Breck Farm
BRECK LA
STAVELEY LA
Foxlowe Plantation

Barrow Hill
Clay Pit
Breck Farm Cottages
Foxlow Junction
Hartington Ind Est
FARNDALE RD
Trans Pennine Trail
ECKINGTON RD

Barrow Hill Roundhouse Rly Ctr
MIDLAND TERR 1
ALLPORT TERR 2
SIDCUP CT 3
PADDINGTON CT 4
HILL GR
BROOKS RD
CAMPBELL DR
SOUTHGATE WY
WOODFORD WAY
TRAFFIC TERR
STATION RD
PO
HALL LA
Hartington View
HILLCREST GR
FRANK LN
DEEP DALE CL
67

WHITTINGTON RD
CAVENDISH PL
AVONSIDE CL
Barrow Hill Prim Sch
BELLHOUSE VIEW 1
VICTORIA AVE 2
Lowgates
Liby
BISHOP CL
GRAFTON CL
PULLMAN CL
HAYFIELD CL
OVERTON CL
CHOWDER CL
ASTON CL
B6053
BELLHOUSE LA
WHARF

WORKS RD
The Clock Tower Bsns Ctr
CHURCH ST
RECTORY CL
PORTER ST
FORD CL
Huntsman Rd
CRAMPTON ND
BRINDLEY WAY
A619 LOWGATES
IRELAND ST
MARKHAM CRES
BIRD CL
FAN RD
BELMONT DR
Speedwell Ind Est
NETHERTHORPE PL

Devonshire Bsns Ctr
67
DAMSON CROFT
Chesterfield Canal (disused)
Barnfield WLK
PO Market PL
DUKE ST
MILL CL
MARKET ST
Fan Road Ind Est
IRELAND CL
GISBOURNE CL

Hollingwood
STATION RD
HORNE LA
MULBERRY CROFT
WINTER CL
TROUGHBROOK RD
HOLLINGWOOD CRES
HAWTHORN RD
River Rother
WEST VIEW 1
CHADWICK CT 2
IMMINGHAM GR 3
COW RD
DARLEY CL
BRIERLEY CL
LIME AVE
Speedwell Inf Sch
STEPHENSON RD
Speedwell Ind Est
FAN RD
Ireland Ind Est

Pondhouse Farm
Troughbrook Wood
BEECH ST
OAK ST
SYCAMORE RD
ALDER GDNS
LAUREL GDNS
CHESTNUT DR
PRIVET DR
BIRCH LA
LABURNUM ST
LILAC ST
FIR ST
PINE ST
SYCAMORE LA
ELM ST
MYRTLE ST
GEORGE ST
STAVELEY
Hollingwood Prim Sch
Pondhouse Farm
Troughbrook Wood
MARTINDALE CL
KENTMERE WAY
CHESTERFIELD RD
A619
ST JOHNS RD
CIRCULAR RD
ST JOHNS RD
MUSARD PL
FRECHEVILLE ST
Staveley Jun Sch
Cemy
INNERSALL RD
CEMETERY LA
MEADOWS DR
A6192
Ireland Trad Est
PROSPECT HO
MOLINEUX AVE

	A	B	C	D	E	F

41 42 43

B3
1 ACTON CT
2 CHIGWELL WAY
3 KINGSTON CT
4 ROMFORD WAY
5 RICHMOND CT
6 CHELMSFORD CT
7 CRICKLEWOOD CT
8 EALING CT
9 DUEWELL CT
10 CAMBERWELL CT
11 DULWICH CT
12 GREENWICH CT
13 CHISWICK CT

E2
1 BARNFIELD CL
2 DEVONSHIRE CL
3 DEVONSHIRE ST
4 KEDLESTON CT
5 HARDWICK CT
6 ARUNDEL CT
7 WELBECK CT
8 MELBOURNE CT
9 PORTER HO

F2
1 WATERINGBURY GR
2 TUDOR ST
3 NETHERTHORPE RD
4 WHITEHEAD ST
5 LEANDER CT
6 MALLARD CT
7 CORNER PIN CL

60
80

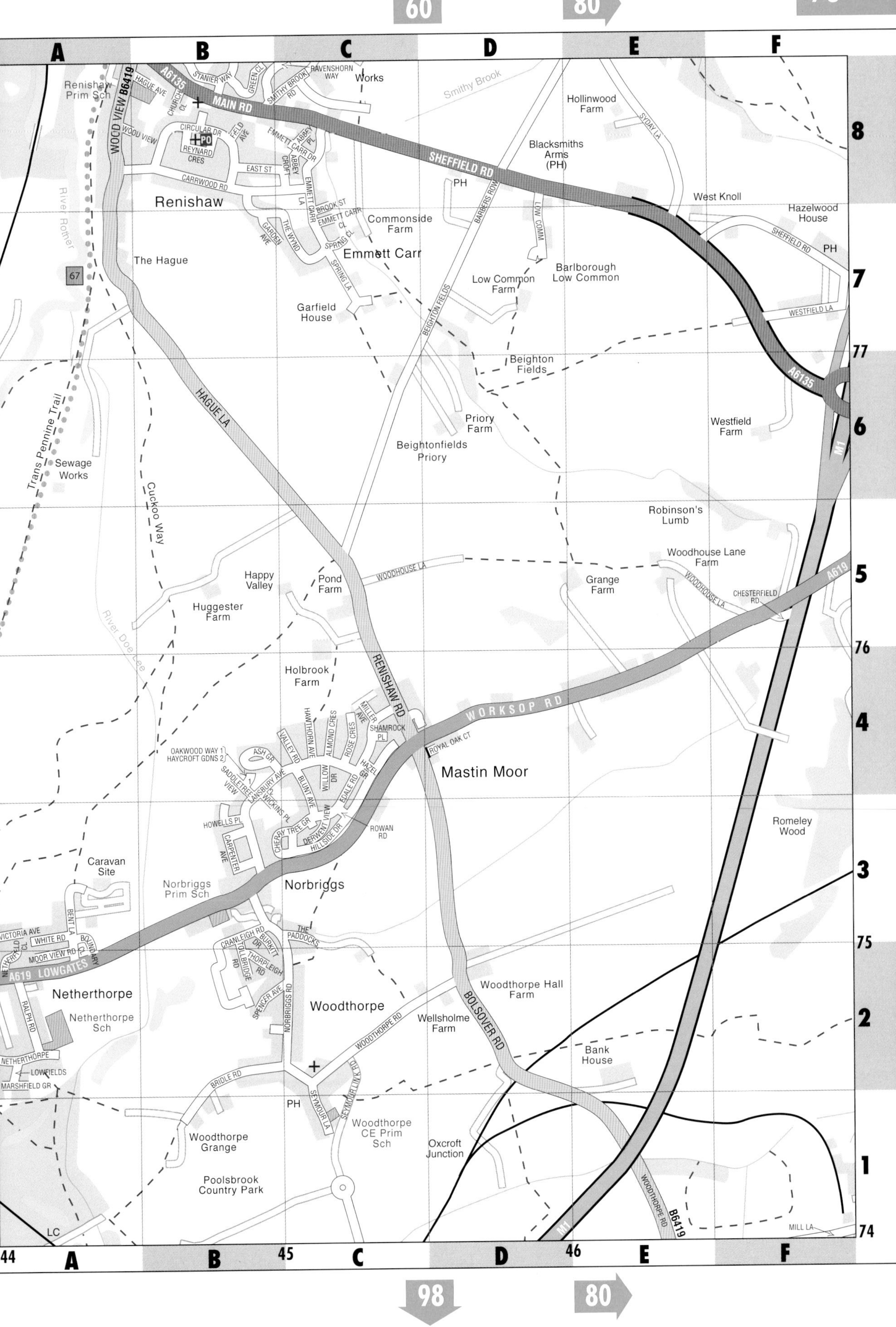
A
B
C
D
E
F
Renishaw Prim Sch
WOOD VIEW B6419
HAGUE AVE
STANIER WAY
GREEN CL
RAVENSHORN WAY
Works
SMITHY BROOK RD
A6135
MAIN RD
CHURCH CL
Smithy Brook
Hollinwood Farm
SYDAY LA
CIRCULAR DR
FIELD AVE
REYNARD CRES
EMMETT CARR DR
ABBEY PL
ABBEY CROFT
EAST ST
CARRWOOD RD
Blacksmiths Arms (PH)
SHEFFIELD RD
PH
BARBERS ROW
LOW COMM
Renishaw
River Rother
BROOK ST
EMMETT CARR CL
Commonside Farm
SPRING CL
West Knoll
Hazelwood House
GARDEN AVE
THE WYND
Emmett Carr
The Hague
67
Low Common Farm
Barlborough Low Common
SPRING LA
Garfield House
BEIGHTON FIELDS
WESTFIELD LA
Beighton Fields
A6135
Westfield Farm
Priory Farm
Beightonfields Priory
HAGUE LA
Trans Pennine Trail
Sewage Works
M1
Cuckoo Way
Robinson's Lumb
Woodhouse Lane Farm
WOODHOUSE LA
Happy Valley
Pond Farm
Grange Farm
CHESTERFIELD RD
A619
Huggester Farm
River Doe Lee
Holbrook Farm
RENISHAW RD
WORKSOP RD
HAWTHORN AVE
ALMOND CRES
ROSE CRES
MILLER AVE
SHAMROCK PL
ROYAL OAK CT
OAKWOOD WAY 1
HAYCROFT GDNS 2
ASH GR
VALLEY RD
SADDLETREE VIEW
LANSBURY AVE
WICKINS PL
BLUNT AVE
WILLOW DR
EGALE RD
HAZEL GR
Mastin Moor
HOWELLS PL
CARPENTER AVE
CHERRY TREE GR
DERWENT VIEW
HILLSIDE DR
ROWAN RD
Romeley Wood
Caravan Site
Norbriggs Prim Sch
Norbriggs
VICTORIA AVE
BENT LA
WHITE RD
BOUNDARY CL
MOOR VIEW RD
NETHERFIELD CL
A619 LOWGATES
CRANLEIGH RD
BURKITT DR
TOLLBRIDGE RD
THORPLEIGH RD
THE PADDOCKS
Woodthorpe Hall Farm
Netherthorpe
Netherthorpe Sch
RALPH RD
SPENCER AVE
NORBRIGGS RD
Woodthorpe
BOLSOVER RD
Wellsholme Farm
WOODTHORPE RD
NETHERTHORPE
LOWFIELDS
MARSHFIELD GR
BRIDLE RD
SEYMOUR LINK RD
Bank House
PH
SEYMOUR LA
Woodthorpe CE Prim Sch
Woodthorpe Grange
Oxcroft Junction
Poolsbrook Country Park
WOODTHORPE RD
B6419
M1
LC
MILL LA
8
7
77
6
5
76
4
3
75
2
1
74
44
45
46

98
80

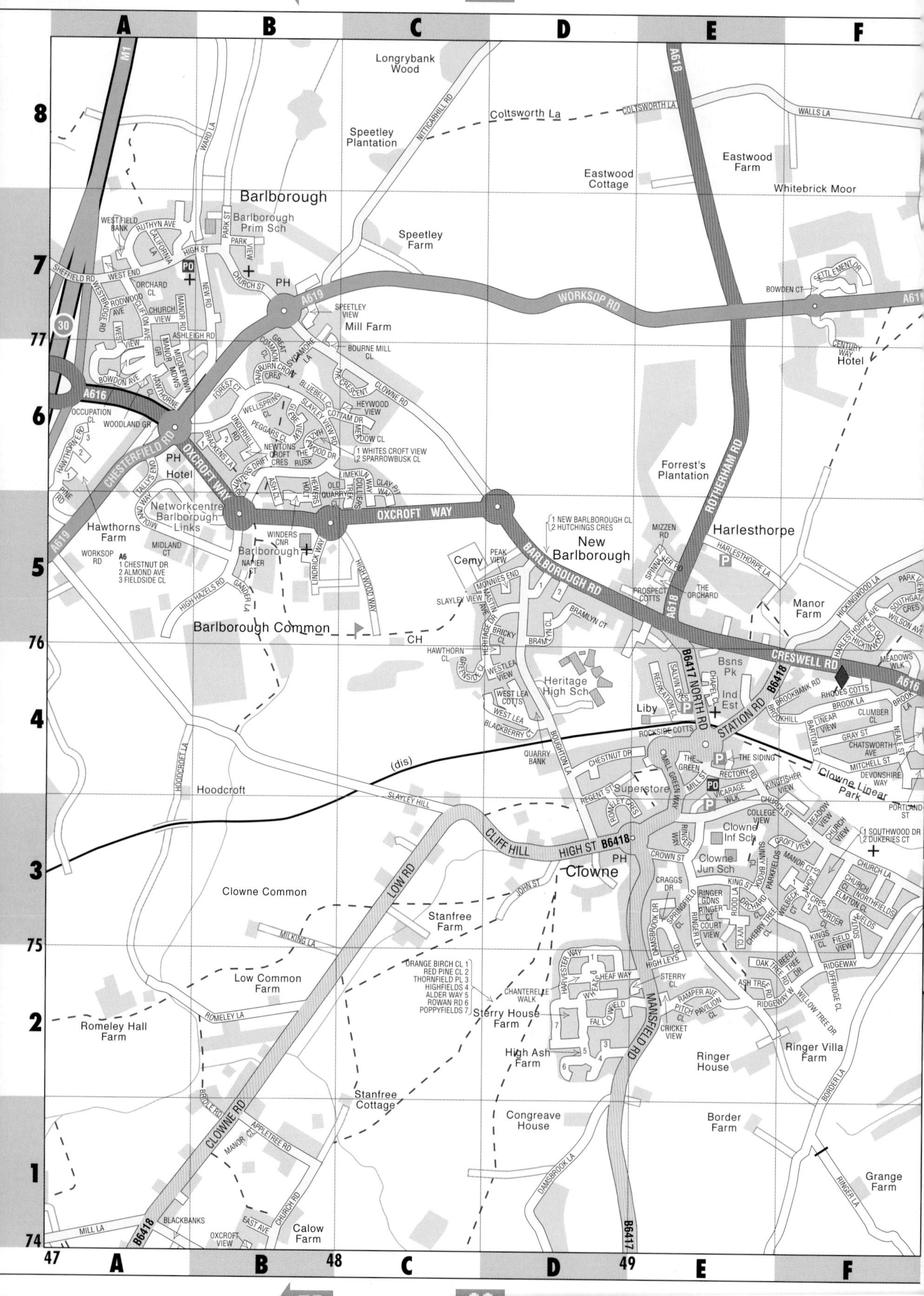
79
61
Barlborough
Barlborough Prim Sch
Longrybank Wood
Speetley Plantation
Speetley Farm
Coltsworth La
Eastwood Cottage
Eastwood Farm
Whitebrick Moor
WORKSOP RD
Mill Farm
OXCROFT WAY
Forrest's Plantation
ROTHERHAM RD
Harlesthorpe
New Barlborough
BARLBOROUGH RD
Manor Farm
CRESWELL RD
Networkcentre Barlborough Links
Hawthorns Farm
Barlborough Common
Heritage High Sch
Hoodcroft
Clowne Common
CLIFF HILL
HIGH ST B6418
Clowne
Clowne Linear Park
Superstore
Clowne Inf Sch
Clowne Jun Sch
Stanfree Farm
Low Common Farm
Romeley Hall Farm
Sterry House Farm
High Ash Farm
MANSFIELD RD
Ringer House
Ringer Villa Farm
Stanfree Cottage
Congreave House
Border Farm
Grange Farm
Calow Farm
CLOWNE RD
LOW RD
A
B
C
D
E
F
47
48
49
74
75
76
77
1
2
3
4
5
6
7
8
79
99

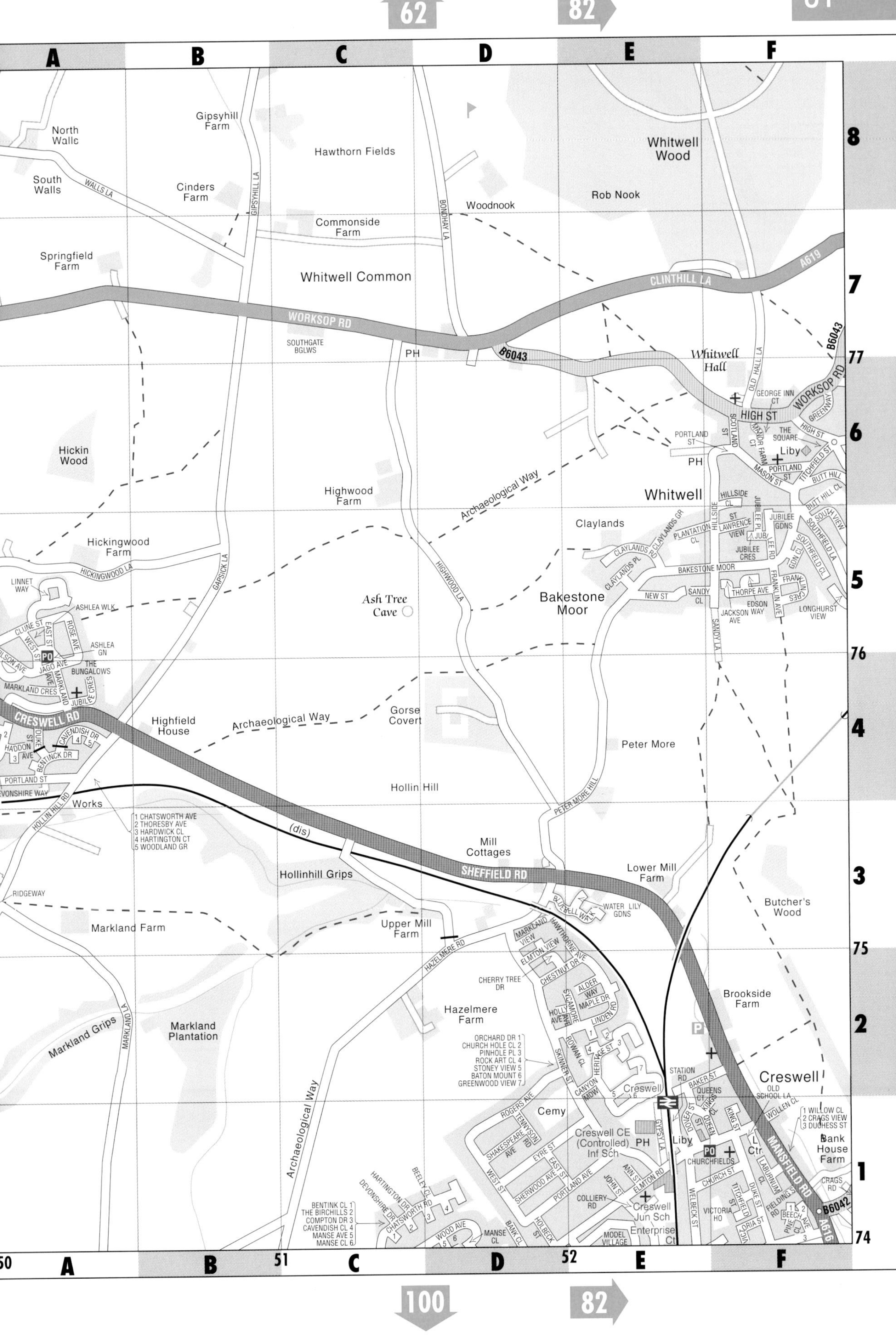

A B C D E F

8

North Walls

South Walls

WALLS LA

Springfield Farm

Gipsyhill Farm

GIPSYHILL LA

Cinders Farm

Hawthorn Fields

Commonside Farm

BONDHAY LA

Woodnook

Whitwell Wood

Rob Nook

Whitwell Common

7

CLINTHILL LA

A619

WORKSOP RD

B6043

SOUTHGATE BGLWS

PH

Whitwell Hall

77

B6043

WORKSOP RD

GREENWAY

George Inn Ct

HIGH ST

MASON FARM

SCOTLAND ST

OLD HILL

HIGH ST

THE SQUARE

Liby

PORTLAND ST

6

Hickin Wood

Highwood Farm

Archaeological Way

PH

PORTLAND ST

MASON ST

TITCHFIELD ST

BUTT HILL

Whitwell

Claylands

HILLSIDE CL

ST LAWRENCE VIEW

JUB

JUBILEE GDNS

LEE RD

SOUTHVIEW

BUTT HILL CL

SOUTHFIELD LA

Hickingwood Farm

HICKINGWOOD LA

GIPSICK LA

CLAYLANDS PL

CLAYLANDS RD

PLANTATION CL

HILLSIDE ST

JUBILEE CRES

THORPE AVE

FRANKLIN AVE

FRANKLIN CRES

SOUTHFIELD CL

5

Ash Tree Cave

HIGHWOOD LA

Bakestone Moor

BAKESTONE MOOR

NEW ST

SANDY CL

JACKSON AVE

EDSON WAY

LONGHURST VIEW

LINNET WAY

ASHLEA WLK

CLINE ST

EAST ST

WEST ST

ROSE AVE

ASHLEA GN

JAGO AVE

JANE AVE

MARKLAND

JUBILEE CRES

PO

THE BUNGALOWS

MARKLAND CRES

76

SANDY LA

Highfield House

Archaeological Way

Gorse Covert

Peter More

4

CRESWELL RD

HADDON AVE

DUKE ST

CAVENDISH DR

BENTINCK DR

PORTLAND ST

EVONSHIRE WAY

PETER MORE HILL

HOLLIN HILL RD

Works

Hollin Hill

1 CHATSWORTH AVE
2 THORESBY AVE
3 HARDWICK CL
4 HARTINGTON CT
5 WOODLAND GR

(dis)

Mill Cottages

Lower Mill Farm

Butcher's Wood

3

SHEFFIELD RD

RIDGEWAY

Hollinhill Grips

Markland Farm

WATER LILY GDNS

ROZELL WAY

MARKLAND VIEW

HAWTHORNE AVE

75

Upper Mill Farm

HAZELMERE RD

ELMTON VIEW

CHESTNUT DR

ALDER WAY

MAPLE DR

Brookside Farm

P

2

Markland Grips

MARKLAND LA

Markland Plantation

Hazelmere Farm

CHERRY TREE DR

SYCAMORE AVE

HOLLY AVE

ROWAN AVE

LINDEN

SKINNER ST

CANYON

MDW

MAPLE DR

HERITAGE

ORCHARD DR 1
CHURCH HOLE CL 2
PINHOLE PL 3
ROCK ART CL 4
STONEY VIEW 5
BATON MOUNT 6
GREENWOOD VIEW 7

STATION RD

BAKER ST

QUEENS CT

KINGS

OLD SCHOOL LA

Creswell

WOLLEN CL

1 WILLOW CL
2 CRAGS VIEW
3 DUCHESS ST

Bank House Farm

MANSFIELD RD

Archaeological Way

Cemy

ROGERS AVE

TENNYSON

SHAKESPEARE AVE

EYRE ST

SHERWOOD AVE

PORTLAND AVE

Creswell CE (Controlled) Inf Sch

PH

GYPSY LA

Liby

PO

ELMTON RD

ANN ST

CHURCHFIELDS

CHURCH ST

VICTORIA HO

L Ctr

DUKE ST

TITCHFIELD RD

FIELDINGS

CRAGS RD

B6042

1

BENTINK CL 1
THE BIRCHILLS 2
COMPTON DR 3
CAVENDISH CL 4
MANSE AVE 5
MANSE CL 6

HARTINGTON DR

DEVONSHIRE DR

CHATSWORTH RD

BEELEY RD

WEST ST

WOOD AVE

MANSE CL

SHERWOOD AVE

PORTLAND AVE

JOHN ST

BANK CL

HOLBECK

COLLIERY RD

WELBECK RD

Creswell Jun Sch

Enterprise Ct

Model Village

ORIA ST

BEECH

A616

74

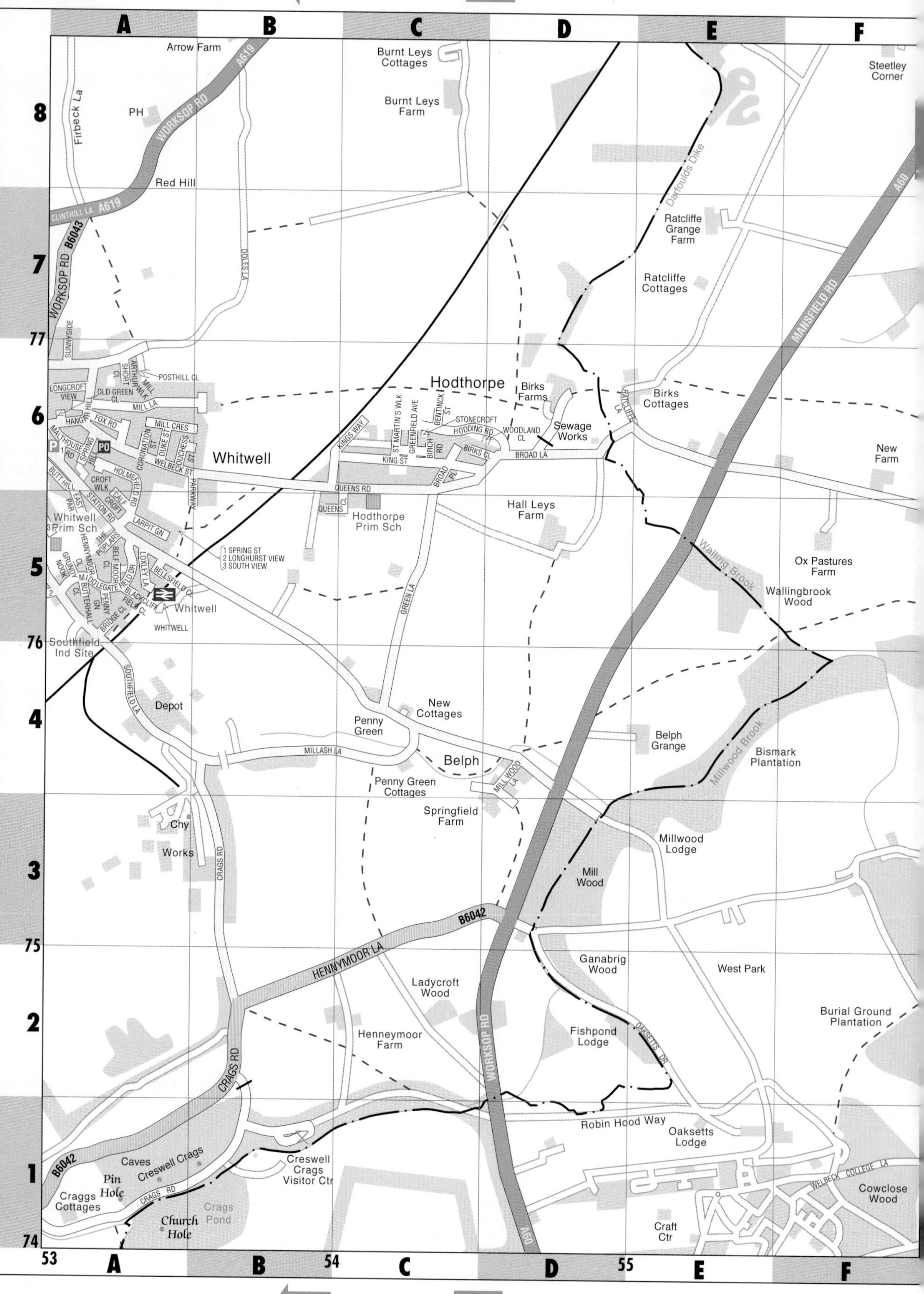

A B C D E F

8

7

77

6

Hodthorpe

Whitwell

5

76

4

3

75

2

1

74

53 A B 54 C D 55 E F

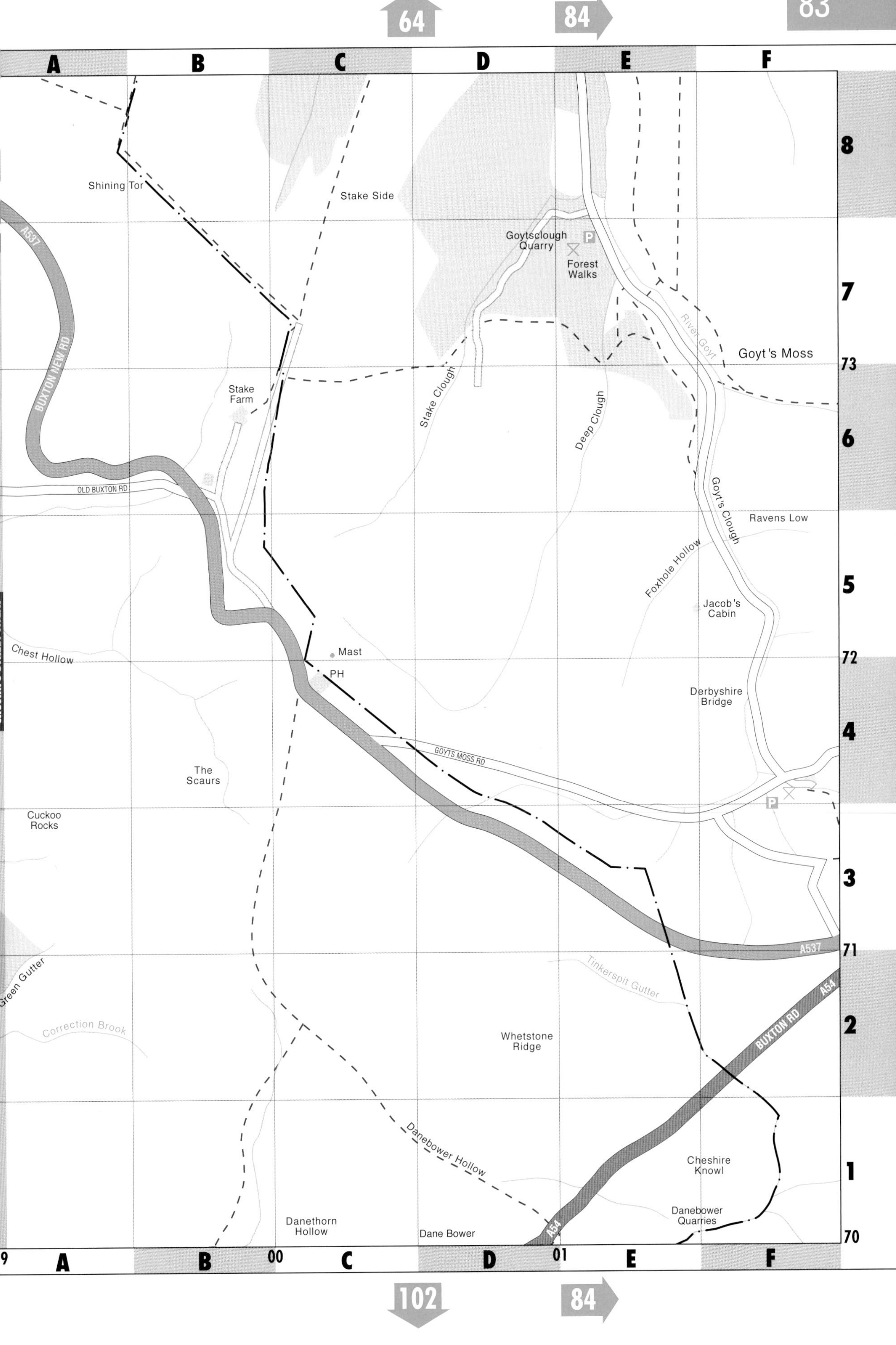

A B C D E F

8
7
73
6
5
72
4
3
71
2
1
70

Shining Tor
Stake Side
Goytsclough Quarry
P
Forest Walks
River Goyt
Goyt's Moss

A537
BUXTON NEW RD
Stake Farm
OLD BUXTON RD
Stake Clough
Deep Clough
Goyt's Clough
Ravens Low
Foxhole Hollow
Jacob's Cabin
Derbyshire Bridge

Chest Hollow
Mast
PH
GOYTS MOSS RD
P

The Scaurs
Cuckoo Rocks

A537

Green Gutter
Correction Brook
Tinkerspit Gutter
BUXTON RD
A54

Whetstone Ridge
Cheshire Knowl

Danebower Hollow
Danebower Quarries
A54
Danethorn Hollow
Dane Bower

A B 00 C D 01 E F
'9

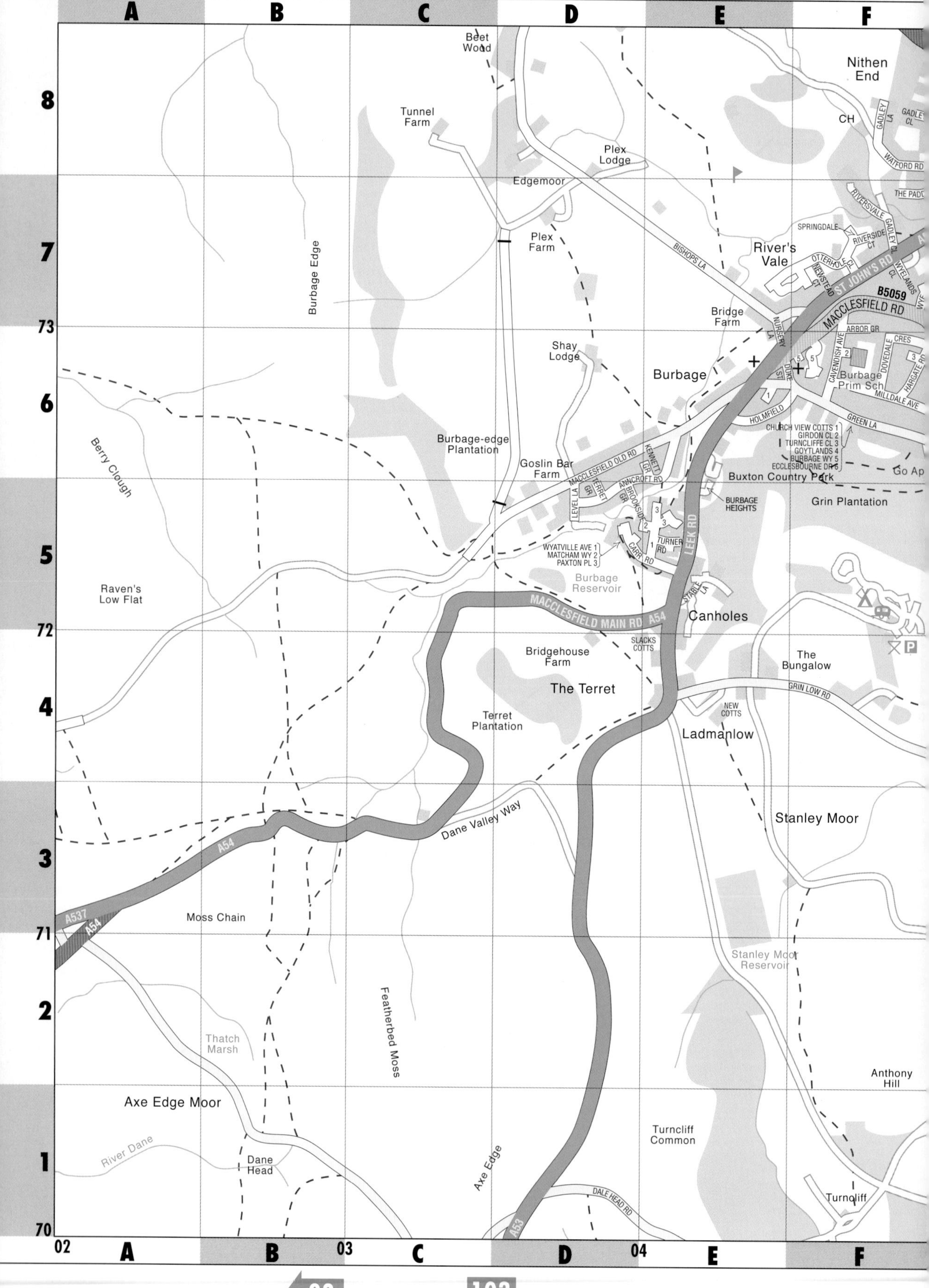

A B C D E F

8

7

73

6

5

72

4

3

71

2

1

70

02 A B 03 C D 04 E F

Beet Wood

Nithen End

CH

GADLEY LA

GADLE CL

Tunnel Farm

Plex Lodge

WATFORD RD

THE PADC

RIVERSVALE

GADLEY CL

Edgemoor

Burbage Edge

Plex Farm

BISHOPS LA

River's Vale

SPRINGDALE

RIVERSIDE CT

OTTERHOLE

St John's Rd

MACCLESFIELD RD

B5059

ARBOR GR

Shay Lodge

Bridge Farm

NURSERY

Burbage

CAVENDISH AVE

DOVEDALE

CRES

MARGATE RD

Berry Clough

Burbage-edge Plantation

Goslin Bar Farm

MACCLESFIELD OLD RD

LEVEL LA

TERRET GR

KENNETT

ANNCROFT RD

BROOKSIDE GR

Burbage Prim Sch

MILLDALE AVE

CHURCH VIEW COTTS 1
GIRDON CL 2
TURNCLIFFE CL 3
GOYTLANDS 4
BURBAGE WY 5
ECCLESBOURNE DR 6

Go Ap

HOLMFIELD

GREEN LA

Buxton Country Park

Grin Plantation

Raven's Low Flat

WYATVILLE AVE 1
MATCHAM WY 2
PAXTON PL 3

CARR RD

TURNER RD

BURBAGE HEIGHTS

LEEK RD

Burbage Reservoir

STABLE LA

MACCLESFIELD MAIN RD A54

Canholes

P

72

Bridgehouse Farm

SLACKS COTTS

The Bungalow

The Terret

GRIN LOW RD

Terret Plantation

NEW COTTS

Ladmanlow

A54

Dane Valley Way

Stanley Moor

Moss Chain

A537

A54

Stanley Moor Reservoir

Thatch Marsh

Featherbed Moss

Axe Edge Moor

River Dane

Dane Head

Axe Edge

Turncliff Common

Anthony Hill

DALE HEAD RD

A53

Turncliff

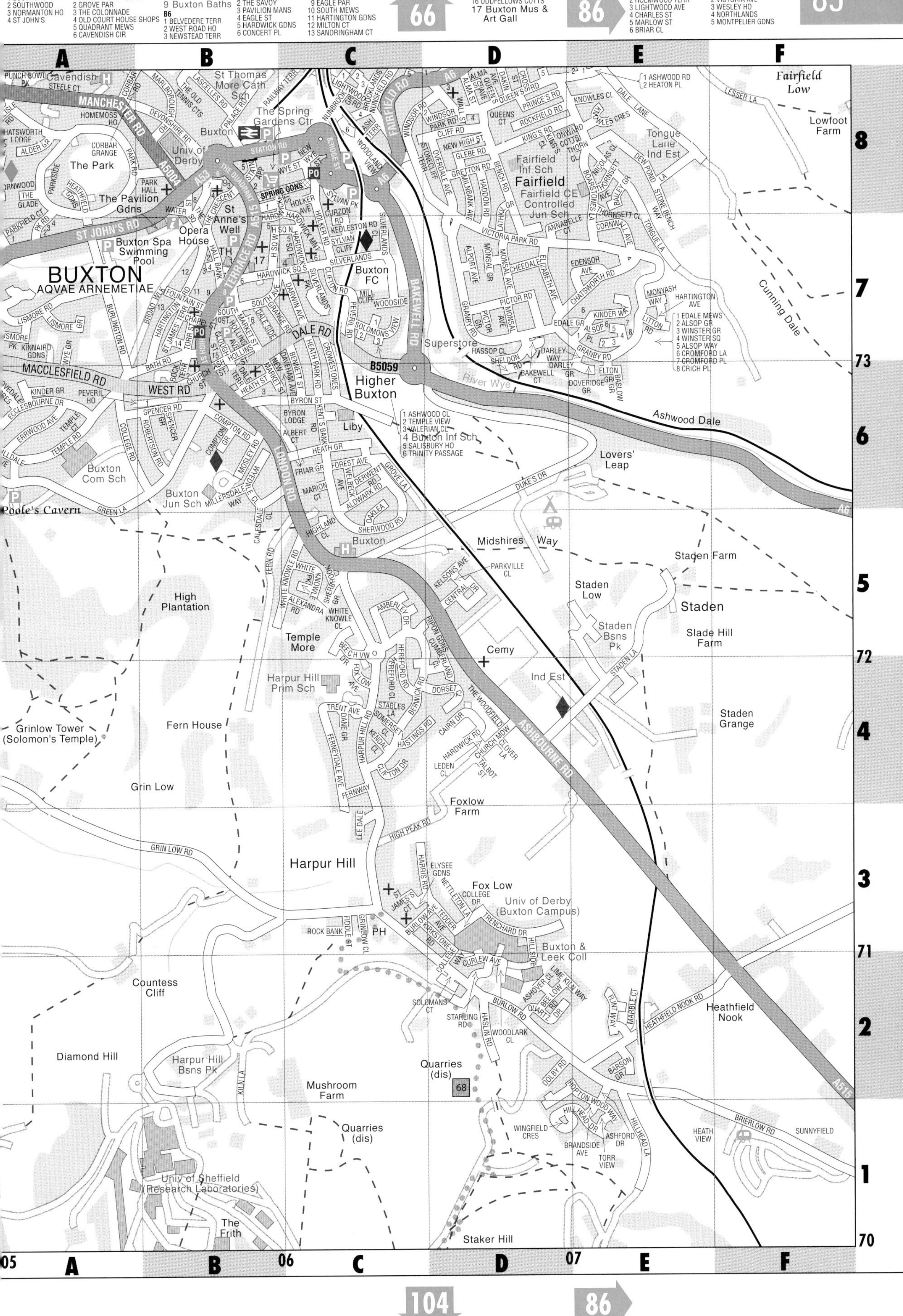

85
67

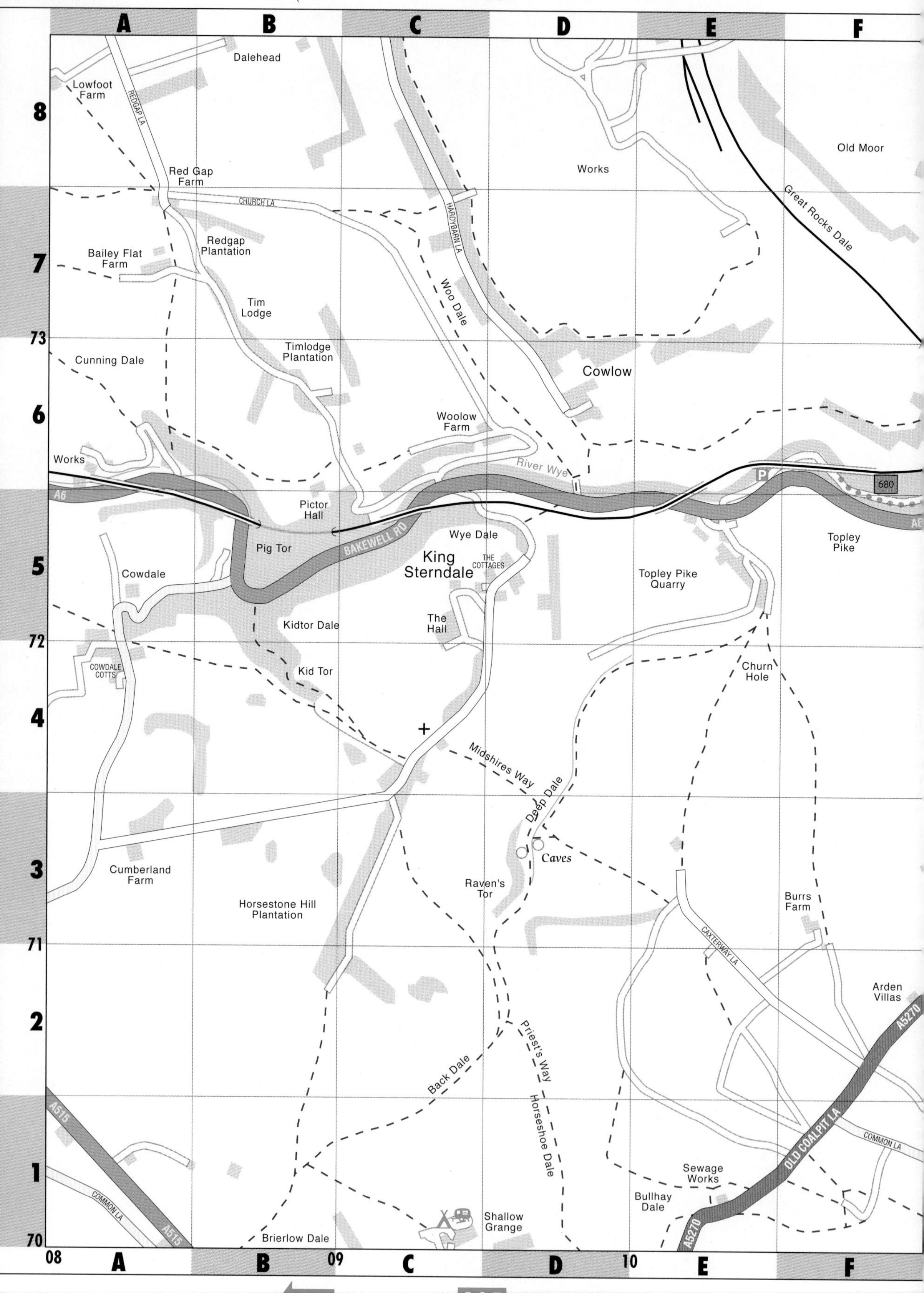
A
B
C
D
E
F
Dalehead
Lowfoot Farm
REDGAP LA
Red Gap Farm
CHURCH LA
Bailey Flat Farm
Redgap Plantation
Tim Lodge
Timlodge Plantation
Cunning Dale
HARDYBARN LA
Woo Dale
Works
Old Moor
Great Rocks Dale
Cowlow
Woolow Farm
Works
River Wye
A6
680
Pictor Hall
Pig Tor
BAKEWELL RD
Wye Dale
King Sterndale
THE COTTAGES
Topley Pike
Topley Pike Quarry
Cowdale
Kidtor Dale
The Hall
COWDALE COTTS
Kid Tor
Churn Hole
Midshires Way
Deep Dale
Caves
Cumberland Farm
Horsestone Hill Plantation
Raven's Tor
Burrs Farm
CAXTERWAY LA
Arden Villas
A5270
Priest's Way
Back Dale
Horseshoe Dale
A515
COMMON LA
OLD COALPIT LA
Sewage Works
Bullhay Dale
Shallow Grange
Brierlow Dale
8
7
73
6
5
72
4
3
71
2
1
70
08
09
10

85
105

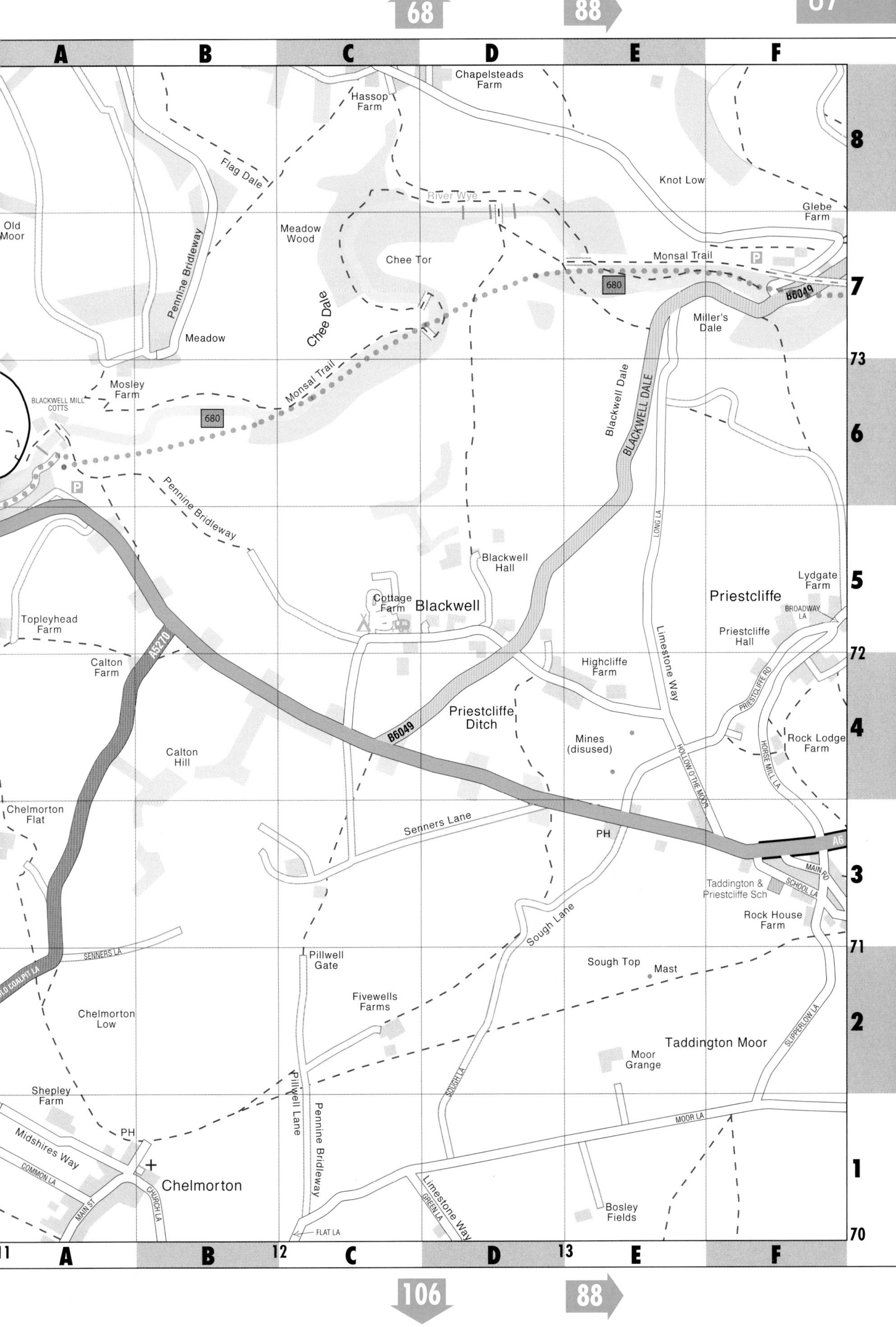
68
88
A
B
C
D
E
F
Chapelsteads Farm
Hassop Farm
Flag Dale
Knot Low
Glebe Farm
Old Moor
Meadow Wood
River Wye
Chee Tor
Pennine Bridleway
Monsal Trail
Chee Dale
680
Miller's Dale
B6049
Meadow
Mosley Farm
BLACKWELL MILL COTTS
Blackwell Dale
BLACKWELL DALE
Pennine Bridleway
LONG LA
Blackwell Hall
Lydgate Farm
Priestcliffe
BROADWAY LA
Cottage Farm
Blackwell
Topleyhead Farm
Priestcliffe Hall
Calton Farm
A5270
Highcliffe Farm
Limestone Way
PRIESTCLIFFE RD
Priestcliffe Ditch
Calton Hill
Mines (disused)
HOLLOW O'THE MOOR
HORSE MILL LA
Rock Lodge Farm
Chelmorton Flat
Senners Lane
PH
A6
MAIN RD
SCHOOL LA
Taddington & Priestcliffe Sch
Rock House Farm
Sough Lane
SENNERS LA
OLD COALPIT LA
Pillwell Gate
Sough Top
Mast
Fivewells Farms
Chelmorton Low
Taddington Moor
SLIPPERLOW LA
Moor Grange
Shepley Farm
Pillwell Lane
Pennine Bridleway
SOUGH LA
MOOR LA
PH
Midshires Way
COMMON LA
Chelmorton
MAIN ST
CHURCH LA
Limestone Way
GREEN LA
FLAT LA
Bosley Fields
8
7
73
6
5
72
4
3
71
2
1
70
11
12
13
106
88

87
69

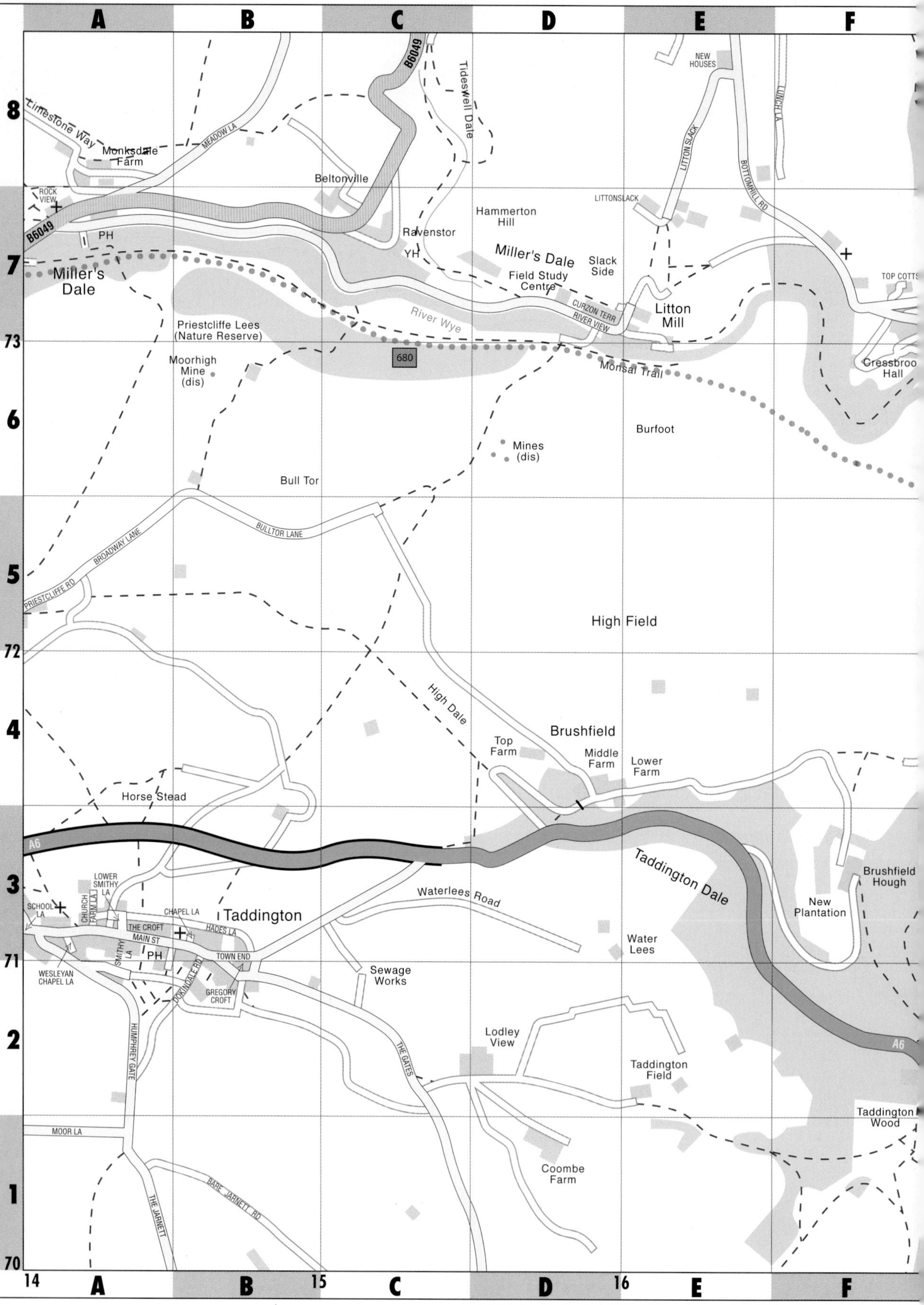

A   B   C   D   E   F

8

Limestone Way

Monksdale Farm

MEADOW LA

Beltonville

B6049

Tideswell Dale

NEW HOUSES

LITTON SLACK

BOTTOMMILL RD

LUNCH LA

ROCK VIEW

+

PH

B6049

Hammerton Hill

Ravenstor

YH

LITTONSLACK

7

Miller's Dale

Miller's Dale

Field Study Centre

Slack Side

TOP COTTS

+

River Wye

CURZON TERR

RIVER VIEW

Litton Mill

Priestcliffe Lees (Nature Reserve)

73

680

Monsal Trail

Gressbrook Hall

Moorhigh Mine (dis)

Burfoot

6

Mines (dis)

Bull Tor

BULLTOR LANE

BROADWAY LANE

5

PRIESTCLIFFE RD

High Field

72

High Dale

Brushfield

4

Top Farm

Middle Farm

Lower Farm

Horse Stead

A6

3

LOWER SMITHY LA

Taddington

Waterlees Road

Taddington Dale

Brushfield Hough

SCHOOL LA

+

CHURCH FARM LA

CHAPEL LA

THE CROFT

+

HADES LA

New Plantation

MAIN ST

SMITHY LA

71

PH

TOWN END

Water Lees

WESLEYAN CHAPEL LA

DOKIMGATE RD

GREGORY CROFT

Sewage Works

HUMPHREY GATE

2

THE GATES

Lodley View

Taddington Field

A6

MOOR LA

Taddington Wood

BARE JARNETT RD

1

Coombe Farm

THE JARNETT

70

14   A   B   15   C   D   16   E   F

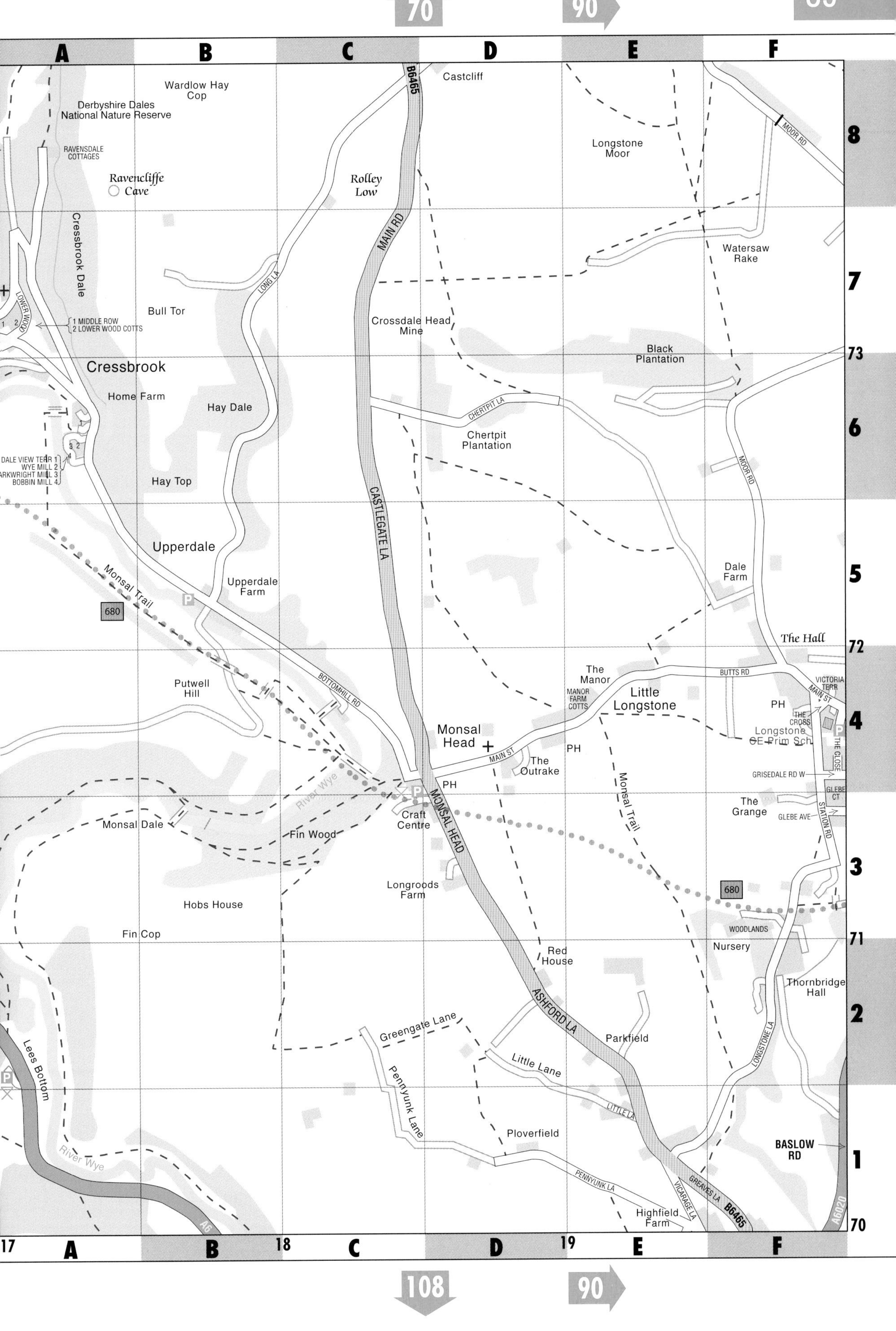

A · B · C · D · E · F

8
7
73
6
5
72
4
3
71
2
1
70

B6465

Castcliff

Derbyshire Dales
National Nature Reserve

Wardlow Hay
Cop

RAVENSDALE
COTTAGES

Ravencliffe
Cave

Rolley
Low

Longstone
Moor

MOOR RD

MAIN RD

Cressbrook Dale

LOWER WOOD

Bull Tor

1 MIDDLE ROW
2 LOWER WOOD COTTS

Cressbrook

LONG LA

Crossdale Head
Mine

Watersaw
Rake

Home Farm

Hay Dale

CHERTPIT LA

Chertpit
Plantation

Black
Plantation

MOOR RD

DALE VIEW TERR 1
WYE MILL 2
ARKWRIGHT MILL 3
BOBBIN MILL 4

Hay Top

Hay Dale

CASTLEGATE LA

Dale
Farm

Upperdale

Monsal Trail

Upperdale
Farm

The Hall

680

P

The Manor

BUTTS RD

VICTORIA
TERR

Putwell
Hill

BOTTOMHILL RD

MANOR
FARM
COTTS

Little
Longstone

PH

THE
CROSS

MAIN ST

Monsal
Head

MAIN ST

The Outrake

Longstone
CE Prim Sch

THE CLOSE

P

GRISEDALE RD W

GLEBE
CT

River Wye

Monsal Dale

Fin Wood

Craft
Centre

PH

MONSAL HEAD

PH

Monsal Trail

The
Grange

GLEBE AVE

STATION RD

680

Hobs House

Longroods
Farm

WOODLANDS

Nursery

71

Fin Cop

Red
House

Thornbridge
Hall

Lees Bottom

P

Greengate Lane

ASHFORD LA

Parkfield

LONGSTONE LA

Pennyunk Lane

Little Lane

LITTLE LA

Ploverfield

PENNYUNK LA

Highfield
Farm

VICARAGE LA

GREAVES LA

B6465

BASLOW
RD

A6020

River Wye

A6

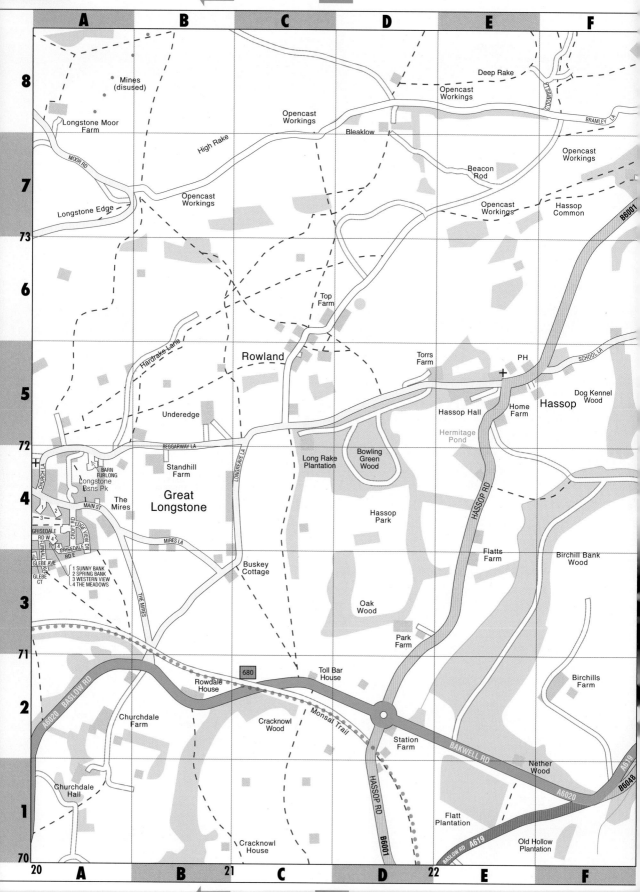

A   B   C   D   E   F

8

Mines
(disused)

Deep Rake

Opencast
Workings

Longstone Moor
Farm

Opencast
Workings

High Rake

MOOR RD

Opencast
Workings

Bleaklow

COOMBS LA

BRAMLEY LA

7

Beacon
Rod

Opencast
Workings

Longstone Edge

Opencast
Workings

Opencast
Workings

Hassop
Common

B6001

73

6

Top
Farm

Hardrake Lane

Rowland

Torrs
Farm

PH

SCHOOL LA

Dog Kennel
Wood

5

Underedge

Hassop Hall

Home
Farm

Hassop

Hermitage
Pond

72

Beggarway La

LONGREAVE LA

Long Rake
Plantation

Bowling
Green
Wood

HASSOP RD

CHURCH LA

BARN
FURLONG

Longstone
Bsns Pk

Standhill
Farm

4

1 2
3
GRISEDALE
RD W 4
FURNIVAL
4
GLEBE AVE
GLEBE
CT

The Mires

CROFT RD

EDGE VIEW LA

GRISEDALE
RD E

MAIN ST

Great
Longstone

MIRES LA

Hassop
Park

Flatts
Farm

Birchill Bank
Wood

1 SUNNY BANK
2 SPRING BANK
3 WESTERN VIEW
4 THE MEADOWS

Buskey
Cottage

3

THE MIRES

Oak
Wood

Park
Farm

Birchills
Farm

71

A6020 BASLOW RD

Rowdale
House

680

Toll Bar
House

Monsal Trail

2

Churchdale
Farm

Cracknowl
Wood

Station
Farm

BAKWELL RD

Nether
Wood

A619

B604B

HASSOP RD

B6001

A6020

1

Churchdale
Hall

Cracknowl
House

Flatt
Plantation

BASLOW RD A619

Old Hollow
Plantation

70

72
92

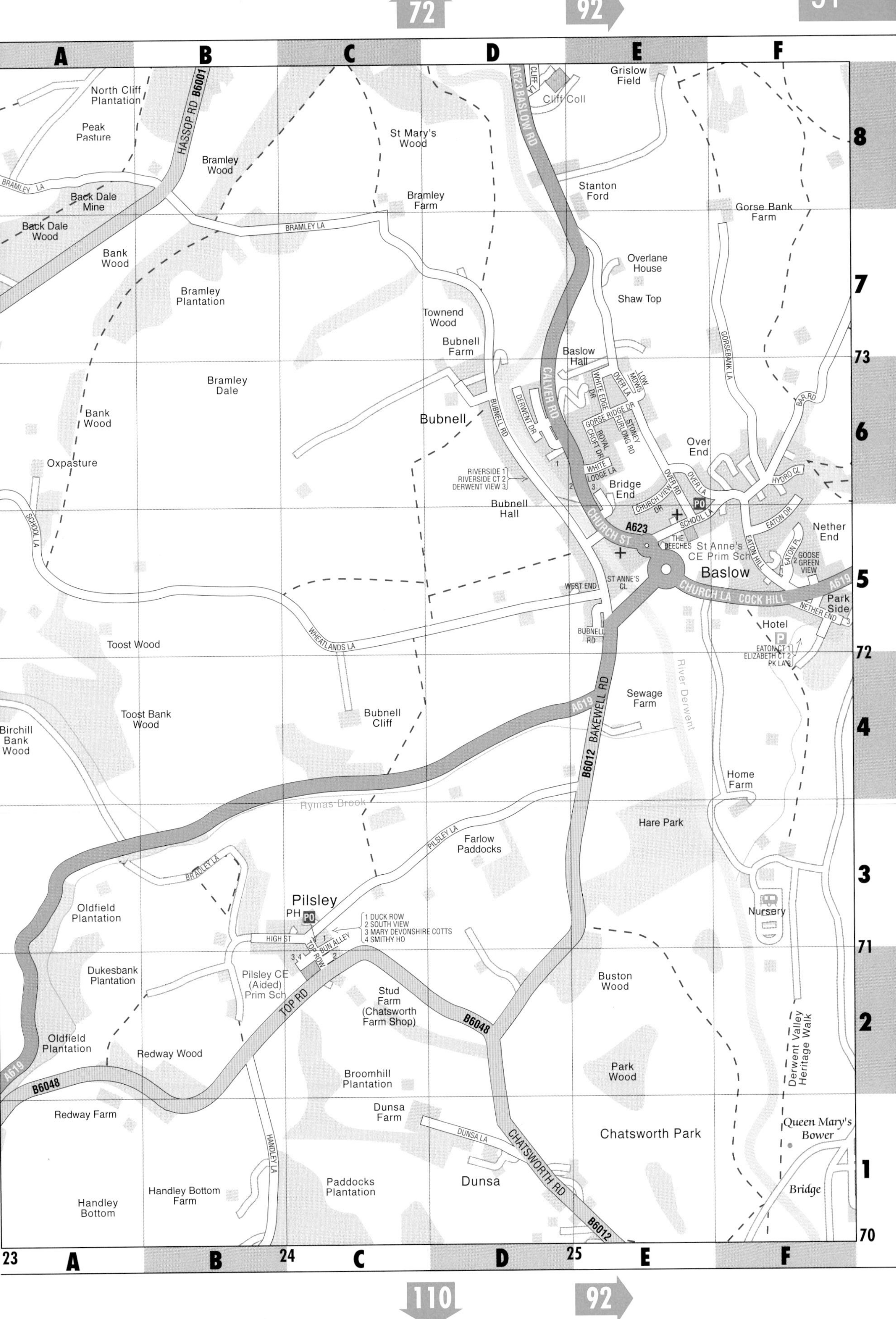
North Cliff Plantation
Peak Pasture
HASSOP RD B6001
Bramley Wood
BRAMLEY LA
Back Dale Mine
Back Dale Wood
Bank Wood
Bramley Plantation
St Mary's Wood
Bramley Farm
Townend Wood
Bubnell Farm
Bramley Dale
Bank Wood
Bubnell
Oxpasture
SCHOOL LA
BUBNELL RD
RIVERSIDE 1
RIVERSIDE CT 2
DERWENT VIEW 3
Bubnell Hall
WHEATLANDS LA
Toost Wood
Toost Bank Wood
Birchill Bank Wood
Bubnell Cliff
A619
Rymas Brook
Grislow Field
Cliff Coll
A623 BASLOW RD
Stanton Ford
Overlane House
Shaw Top
Baslow Hall
CALVER RD
DERWENT DR
WHITE EDGE DR
OVER LA
LOW MDWS
GORSE RIDGE DR
ROYAL CROFT DR
FURLONG RD
STONEY
WHITE LODGE LA
Bridge End
CHURCH VIEW DR
OVER LA
OVER RD
SCHOOL LA
CHURCH ST
A623
THE BEECHES
St Anne's CE Prim Sch
ST ANNE'S CL
WEST END
BUBNELL RD
Baslow
CHURCH LA
COCK HILL
Gorse Bank Farm
GORSEBANK LA
BAR RD
Over End
HYDRO CL
EATON DR
EATON HILL
EATON PL
Nether End
GOOSE GREEN VIEW
Park Side
NETHER END
Hotel
EATON CT 1
ELIZABETH CT 2
PK LA 3
Sewage Farm
River Derwent
BAKEWELL RD B6012
Home Farm
Hare Park
Farlow Paddocks
PILSLEY LA
BRADLEY LA
Oldfield Plantation
Pilsley
PH
PO
HIGH ST
TOP ROW
BUN ALLEY
1 DUCK ROW
2 SOUTH VIEW
3 MARY DEVONSHIRE COTTS
4 SMITHY HO
Nursery
Dukesbank Plantation
Pilsley CE (Aided) Prim Sch
TOP RD
Stud Farm (Chatsworth Farm Shop)
B6048
Buston Wood
Oldfield Plantation
Redway Wood
Broomhill Plantation
Park Wood
Derwent Valley Heritage Walk
Redway Farm
Dunsa Farm
DUNSA LA
Chatsworth Park
Queen Mary's Bower
HANDLEY LA
CHATSWORTH RD
B6012
Dunsa
Paddocks Plantation
Handley Bottom Farm
Handley Bottom
Bridge

110
92

91
73

A B C D E F

8
7
73
6
5
72
4
3
71
2
1
70

Bar Brook
A621
CLODHALL LA
Wellington's Monument
Jack Flat
SHEFFIELD RD
Gardom's Edge
BAR RD
Baslow Bar
Raddowhole Plantation
Bar Brook
Nelson's Monument
Yeld Wood
Birchen Edge
Yeldwood Farm
Far End
Moorside Farm
East Moor
A621
Yeld Farm
A619 NETHER END
OLD BRAMPTON RD
Newbridge Farm
PH
Jumble Coppice
Robin Hood
CHESTERFIELD RD
P
Robin Hood Farm
PK LA
B6050
Park Lodge
Saw Mill
Heathy Lea Brook
B6050
Chatsworth Park
BASLOW RD
STONELOW
Robin Hood Plantations
Stone Low
Dobb Edge
Emperor Stream
A619
Gibbet Wood
Parkgate
Umberley Brook
The Hunting Tower
Gibbet Moor
Bunker's Hill Wood
Emperor Lake
P
Stand Wood
Swiss Cottage
Chatsworth House
Swiss Lake

26 A B 27 C D 28 E F

91
111

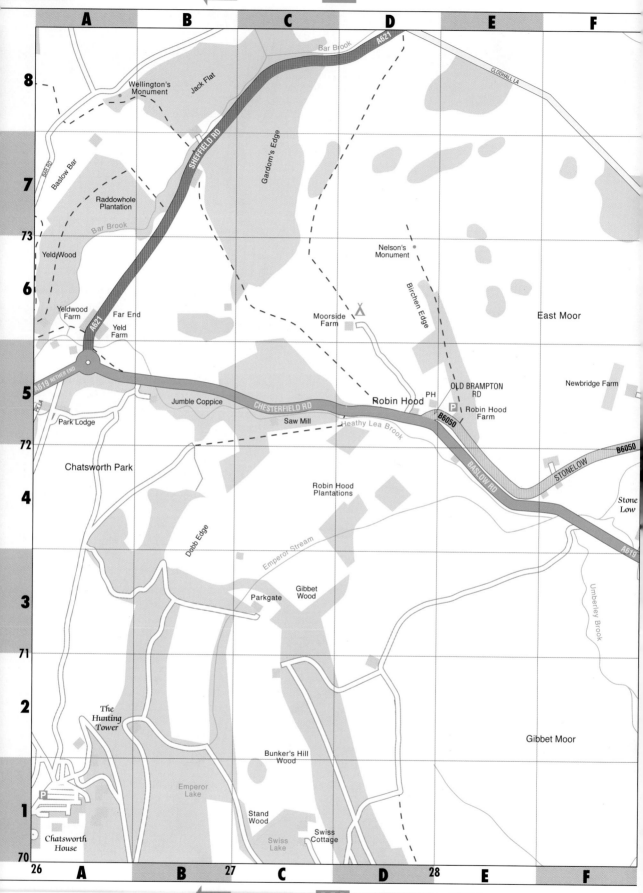

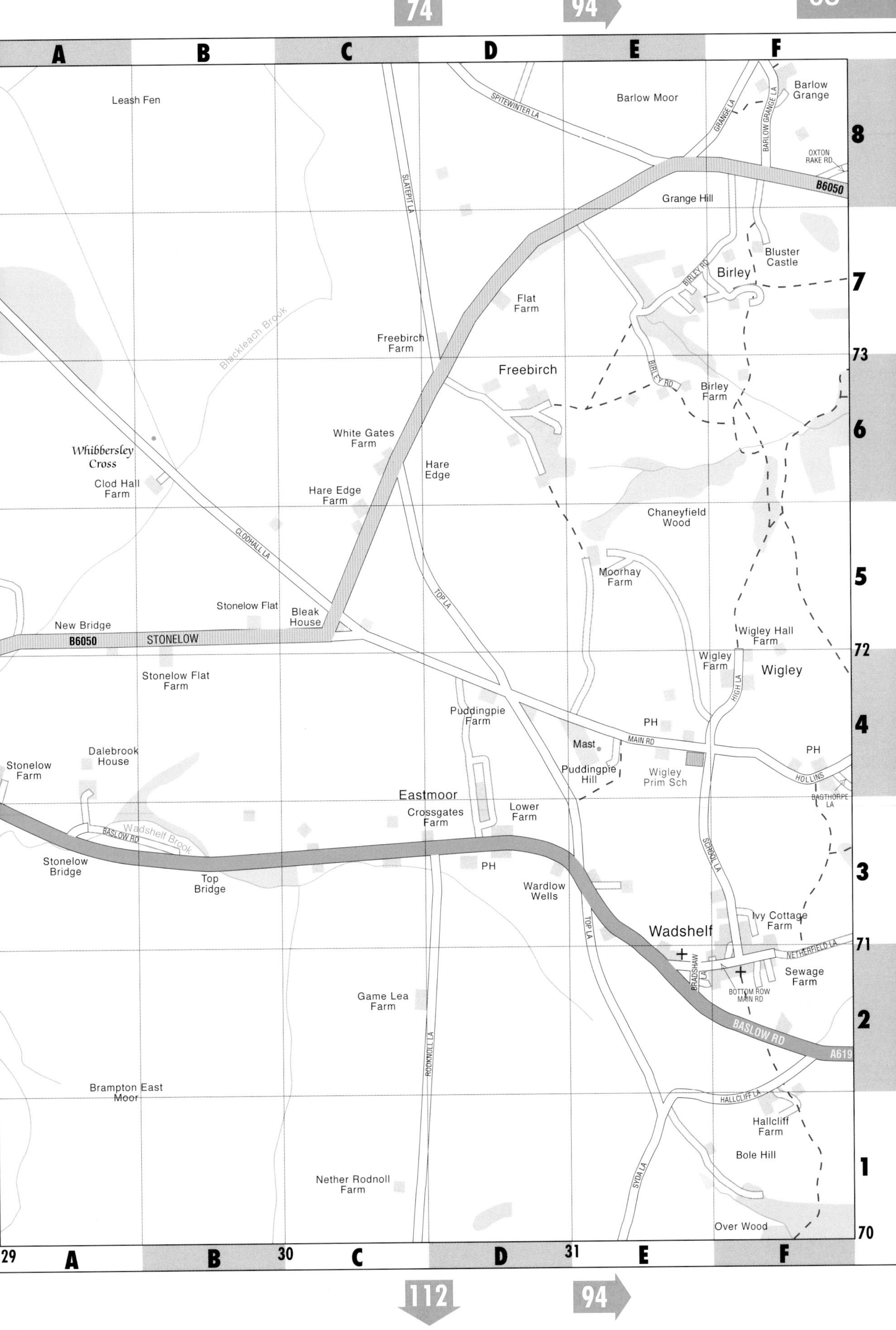

74
94
112
94
29
30
31

A   B   C   D   E   F

8
7
73
6
5
72
4
3
71
2
70
1

Leash Fen

SPITEWINTER LA

Barlow Moor

BARLOW GRANGE LA

Barlow Grange

GRANGE LA

OXTON RAKE RD

B6050

Grange Hill

SLATEPIT LA

Bluster Castle

Birley

BIRLEY RD

Flat Farm

Freebirch Farm

Freebirch

BIRLEY RD

Birley Farm

Brackleach Brook

White Gates Farm

Hare Edge

Whibbersley Cross

Clod Hall Farm

Hare Edge Farm

Chaneyfield Wood

CLODHALL LA

Moorhay Farm

TOP LA

Wigley Hall Farm

Stonelow Flat

Bleak House

Wigley Farm

Wigley

HIGH LA

New Bridge

B6050   STONELOW

72

Stonelow Flat Farm

Puddingpie Farm

PH

Main RD

PH

HOLLINS

Dalebrook House

Mast

Puddingpie Hill

Wigley Prim Sch

BAGTHORPE LA

Stonelow Farm

Eastmoor

Crossgates Farm

Lower Farm

Wadshelf Brook

BASLOW RD

SORROLL LA

Stonelow Bridge

Top Bridge

PH

Wardlow Wells

Ivy Cottage Farm

NETHERFIELD LA

Wadshelf

71

BRADSHAW LA

Sewage Farm

Game Lea Farm

TOP LA

BOTTOM ROW MAIN RD

RODNOLL LA

BASLOW RD

A619

2

Brampton East Moor

HALLCLIFF LA

Hallcliff Farm

SYDA LA

Bole Hill

Nether Rodnoll Farm

Over Wood

70

A   B   C   D   E   F

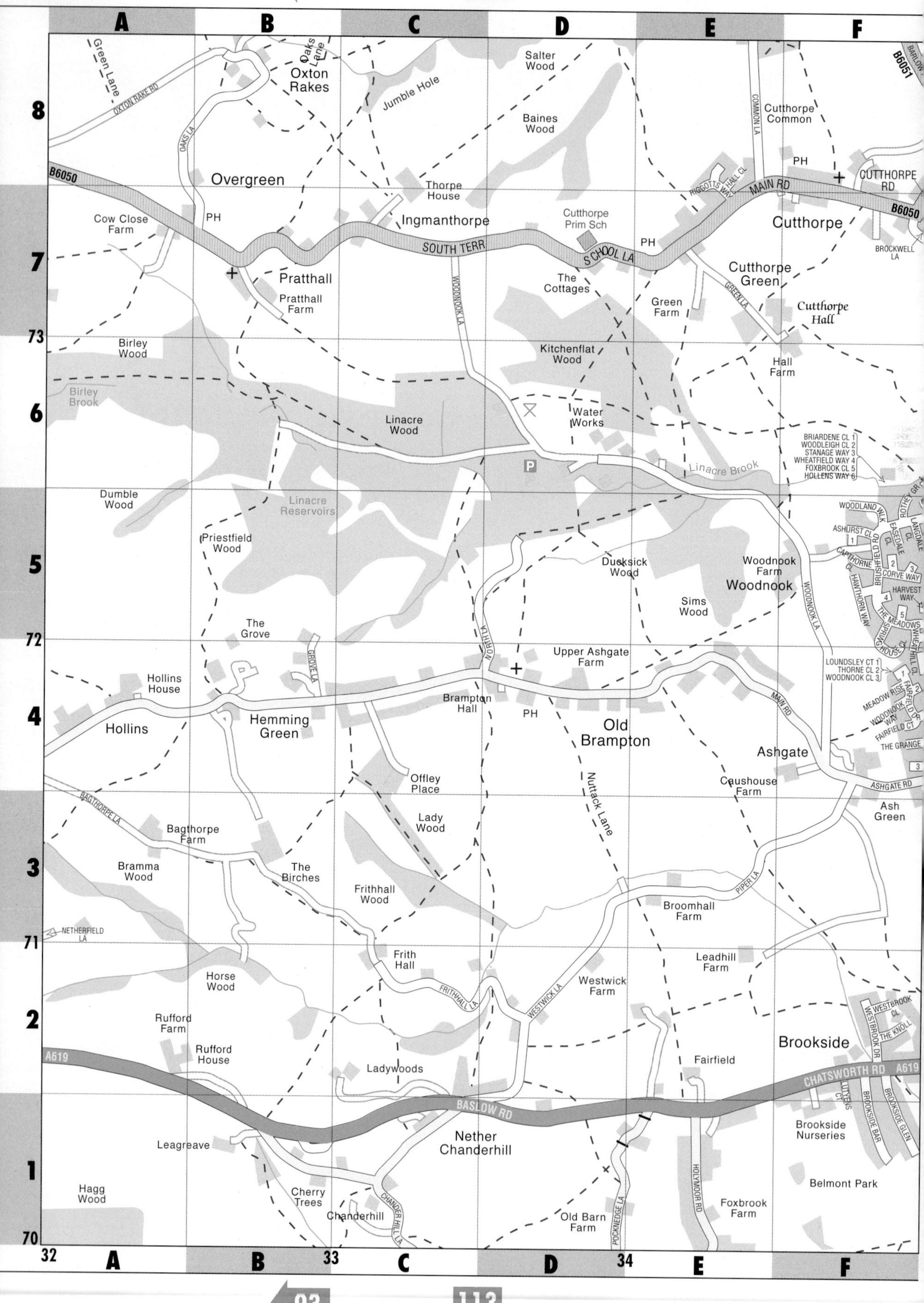

A **B** **C** **D** **E** **F**

8

Green Lane

Oxton
Rakes

Oaks Lane

Jumble Hole

Salter
Wood

Baines
Wood

Cutthorpe
Common

COMMON LA

B6051

B6050

Overgreen

OXTON RAKE RD

OAKS LA

PH

Thorpe
House

Cutthorpe
Prim Sch

PH

PIGEOTTS WAY

HALL CL

MAIN RD

PH

CUTTHORPE
RD

Cutthorpe

B6050

BROCKWELL
LA

7

Cow Close
Farm

Ingmanthorpe

SOUTH TERR

SCHOOL LA

Cutthorpe
Green

Pratthall

Pratthall
Farm

WOODNOOK LA

The
Cottages

GREEN LA

Green
Farm

Cutthorpe
Hall

73

Birley
Wood

Kitchenflat
Wood

Hall
Farm

6

Birley
Brook

Linacre
Wood

Water
Works

Linacre Brook

BRIARDENE CL 1
WOODLEIGH CL 2
STANAGE WAY 3
WHEATFIELD WAY 4
FOXBROOK CL 5
HOLLENS WAY 6

P

Dumble
Wood

Linacre
Reservoirs

WOODLAND WLK

ROTTIE GRT 4

LANGDALE

BASEDALE

ASHURST CL

CALTHORPE

CORVE WAY

5

Priestfield
Wood

Dusksick
Wood

Sims
Wood

Woodnook
Farm

Woodnook

WOODNOOK LA

HAWTHORN WAY

HARVEST
WAY.

THE MEADOWS

WHEATHILL CL

THE GRANGE

72

The
Grove

Upper Ashgate
Farm

LOUNDSLEY CT 1
THORNE CL 2
WOODNOOK CL 3

MEADOW RISE

FAIRFIELD CT

4

Hollins
House

GROVE LA

Brampton
Hall

PH

NORTH LA

MAIN RD

Old
Brampton

Ashgate

MEADOW
WOODNOOK
WAY
FAIRFIELD CT

Hollins

Hemming
Green

Offley
Place

Caushouse
Farm

ASHGATE RD

Ash
Green

BAGTHORPE LA

Bagthorpe
Farm

Lady
Wood

PIPER LA

3

Bramma
Wood

The
Birches

Frithhall
Wood

Broomhall
Farm

71

NETHERFIELD
LA

Horse
Wood

Frith
Hall

FRITHHALL LA

WESTWICK LA

Westwick
Farm

Leadhill
Farm

WESTBROOK
CL

WESTBROOK DR

THE KNOLL

2

Rufford
Farm

Rufford
House

NUTTACK LANE

Brookside

CHATSWORTH RD A619

A619

Leagreave

Ladywoods

BASLOW RD

Fairfield

HOLYMOOR RD

BROOKSIDE GLEN

Brookside
Bar

Brookside
Nurseries

1

Hagg
Wood

Cherry
Trees

Chanderhill

Nether
Chanderhill

CHANDER HILL LA

Old Barn
Farm

POCKNEDGE LA

Foxbrook
Farm

Belmont Park

70

A **B** **C** **D** **E** **F**

32 33 34

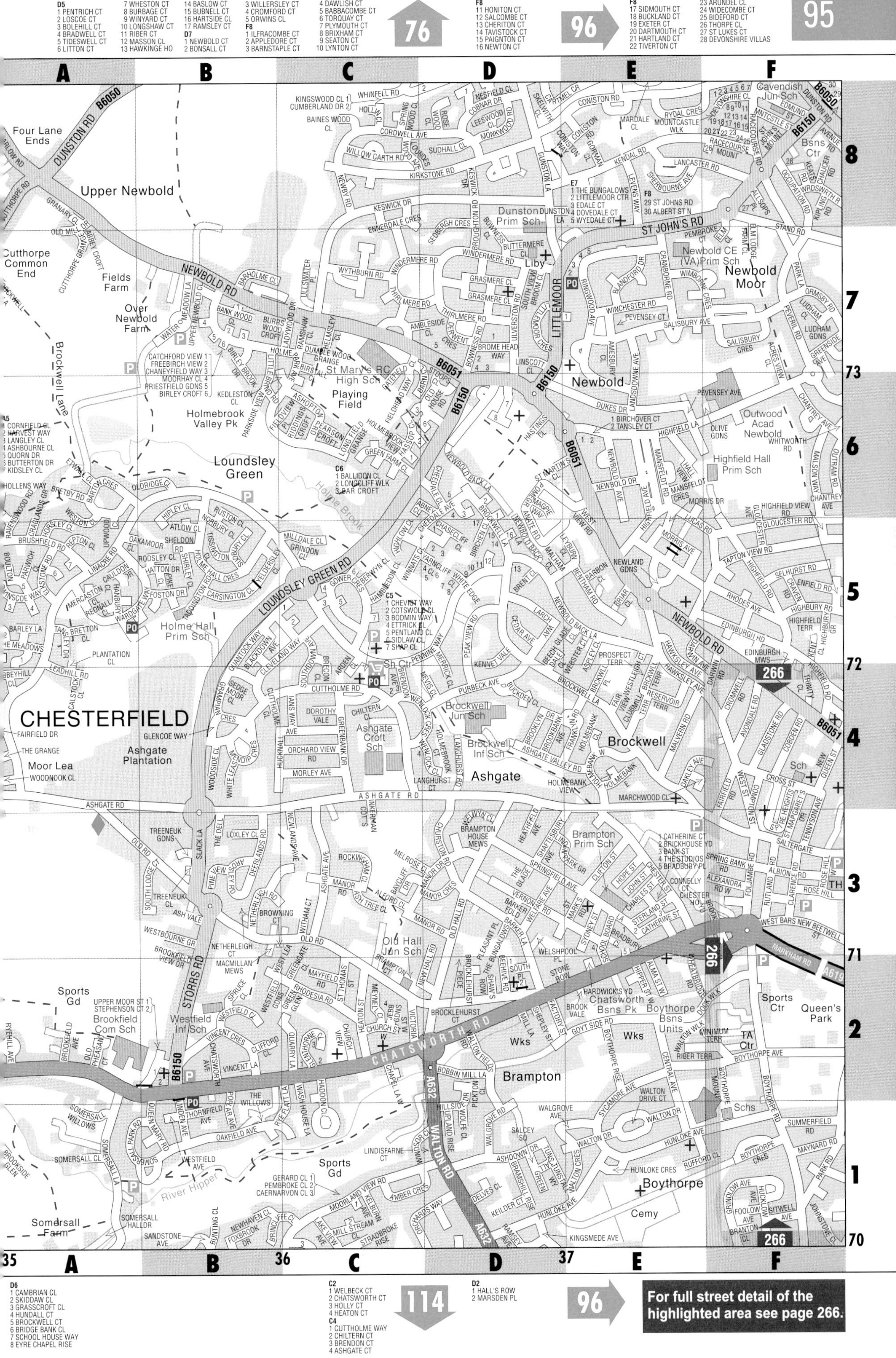

D5
1 PENTRICH CT
2 LOSCOE CT
3 BOLEHILL CT
4 BRADWELL CT
5 TIDESWELL CT
6 LITTON CT
7 WHESTON CT
8 BURBAGE CT
9 WINYARD CT
10 LONGSHAW CT
11 RIBER CT
12 MASSON CL
13 HAWKINGE HO
14 BASLOW CT
15 BUBNELL CT
16 HARTSIDE CL
17 RAMSLEY CT
D7
1 NEWBOLD CT
2 BONSALL CT
3 WILLERSLEY CT
4 CROMFORD CT
5 ORWINS CL
F8
1 ILFRACOMBE CT
2 APPLEDORE CT
3 BARNSTAPLE CT
4 DAWLISH CT
5 BABBACOMBE CT
6 TORQUAY CT
7 PLYMOUTH CT
8 BRIXHAM CT
9 SEATON CT
10 LYNTON CT
76
F8
11 HONITON CT
12 SALCOMBE CT
13 CHERITON CT
14 TAVISTOCK CT
15 PAIGNTON CT
16 NEWTON CT
96
F8
17 SIDMOUTH CT
18 BUCKLAND CT
19 EXETER CT
20 DARTMOUTH CT
21 HARTLAND CT
22 TIVERTON CT
23 ARUNDEL CL
24 WIDECOMBE CT
25 BIDEFORD CT
26 THORPE CL
27 ST LUKES CT
28 DEVONSHIRE VILLAS
95
A B C D E F
Four Lane Ends
Upper Newbold
Cutthorpe Common End
Fields Farm
Over Newbold Farm
Brockwell Lane
Holmebrook Valley Pk
Loundsley Green
St Mary's RC High Sch
Playing Field
Dunston Prim Sch
Liby
Newbold CE (VA) Prim Sch
Newbold Moor
Newbold
Outwood Acad Newbold
Highfield Hall Prim Sch
Holme Hall Prim Sch
CHESTERFIELD
Ashgate Plantation
Moor Lea
Ashgate Croft Sch
Brockwell Jun Sch
Brockwell Inf Sch
Ashgate
Brockwell
Brampton Prim Sch
Old Hall Jun Sch
Westfield Inf Sch
Brookfield Com Sch
Sports Gd
Chatsworth Bsns Pk
Boythorpe Bsns Units
Wks
Brampton
TA Ctr
Sports Ctr
Queen's Park
Schs
Boythorpe
Cemy
Somersall Farm
River Hipper
Holme Brook
NEWBOLD RD
LOUNDSLEY GREEN RD
CHATSWORTH RD
WALTON RD
ASHGATE RD
STORRS RD
ST JOHN'S RD
LITTLEMOOR
DUNSTON RD
B6050
B6051
B6150
A632
A619
266
8 7 73 6 5 72 4 3 71 2 1 70
35 36 37
C6
1 BALLIDON CL
2 LONGCLIFF WLK
3 BAR CROFT
C5
1 CHEVIOT WAY
2 COTSWOLD CL
3 BODMIN WAY
4 ETTRICK CL
5 PENTLAND CL
6 SIDLAW CL
7 SHAP CL
E7
1 THE BUNGALOWS
2 LITTLEMOOR CTR
3 EDALE CT
4 DOVEDALE CT
5 WYEDALE CT
F8
29 ST JOHNS RD
30 ALBERT ST N
D6
1 CAMBRIAN CL
2 SKIDDAW CL
3 GRASSCROFT CL
4 HUNDALL CT
5 BROCKWELL CT
6 BRIDGE BANK CL
7 SCHOOL HOUSE WAY
8 EYRE CHAPEL RISE
C2
1 WELBECK CT
2 CHATSWORTH CT
3 HOLLY CT
4 HEATON CT
C4
1 CUTTHOLME WAY
2 CHILTERN CT
3 BRENDON CT
4 ASHGATE CT
114
D2
1 HALL'S ROW
2 MARSDEN PL
96
For full street detail of the highlighted area see page 266.

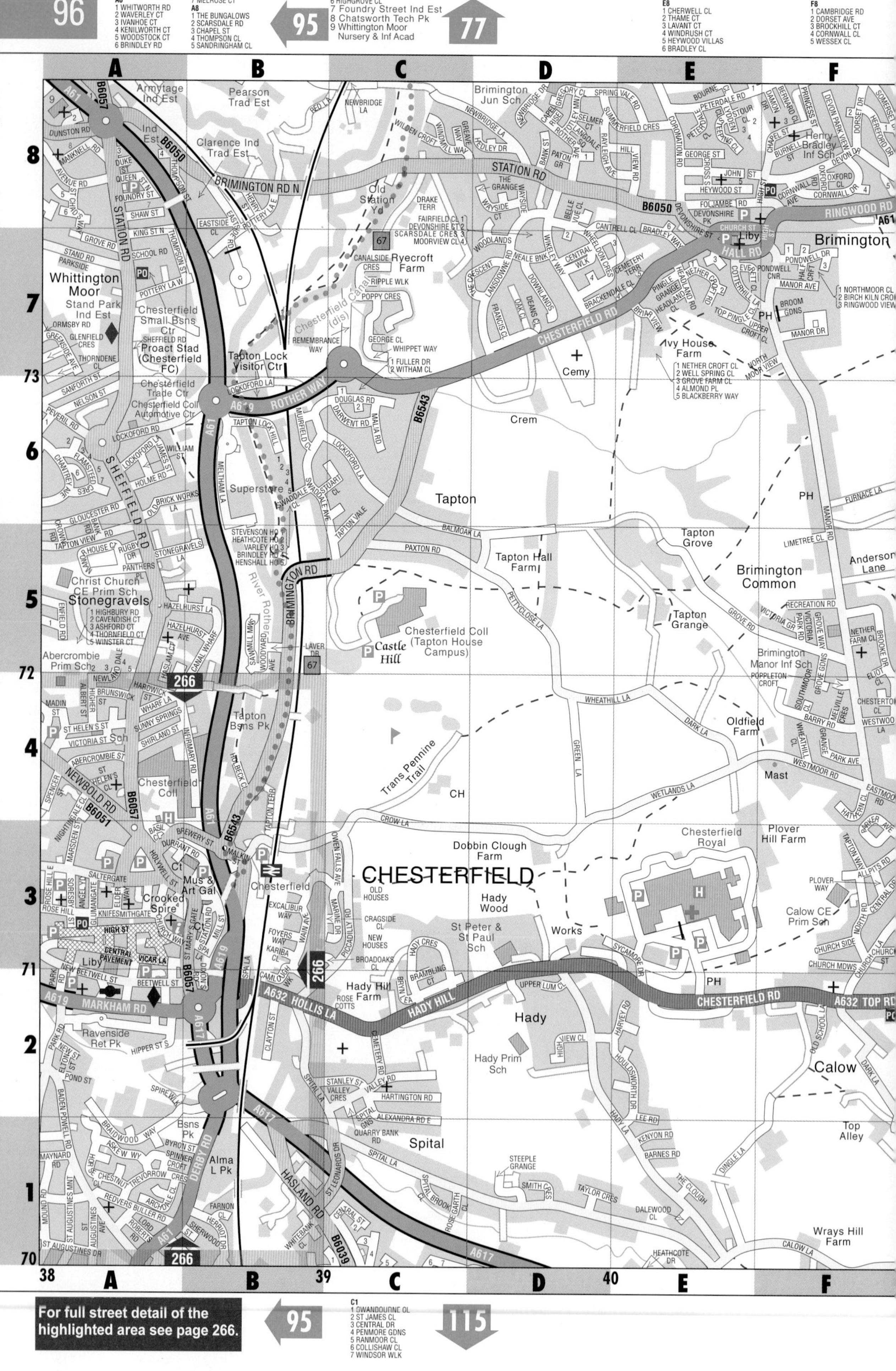
96
A6
1 WHITWORTH RD
2 WAVERLEY CT
3 IVANHOE CT
4 KENILWORTH CT
5 WOODSTOCK CT
6 BRINDLEY RD
7 MELROSE CT
A8
1 THE BUNGALOWS
2 SCARSDALE RD
3 CHAPEL ST
4 THOMPSON CL
5 SANDRINGHAM CL
95
6 HIGHGROVE CL
7 Foundry Street Ind Est
8 Chatsworth Tech Pk
9 Whittington Moor Nursery & Inf Acad
77
E8
1 CHERWELL CL
2 THAME CT
3 LAVANT CT
4 WINDRUSH CT
5 HEYWOOD VILLAS
6 BRADLEY CL
F8
1 CAMBRIDGE RD
2 DORSET AVE
3 BROCKHILL CT
4 CORNWALL CL
5 WESSEX CL
Armytage Ind Est
Pearson Trad Est
Brimington Jun Sch
Clarence Ind Trad Est
BRIMINGTON RD N
STATION RD
Old Station Yd
Ryecroft Farm
Whittington Moor
Stand Park Ind Est
Chesterfield Small Bsns Ctr
Proact Stad (Chesterfield FC)
Chesterfield Trade Ctr
Chesterfield Coll Automotive Ctr
Tapton Lock Visitor Ctr
Chesterfield Canal (dis)
ROTHER WAY
CHESTERFIELD RD
Ivy House Farm
1 NETHER CROFT CL
2 WELL SPRING CL
3 GROVE FARM CL
4 ALMOND PL
5 BLACKBERRY WAY
Brimington
1 NORTHMOOR CL
2 BIRCH KILN CROFT
3 RINGWOOD VIEW
RINGWOOD RD
Cemy
Crem
Superstore
Tapton
SHEFFIELD RD
Tapton Grove
Tapton Hall Farm
Brimington Common
Anderson Lane
Christ Church CE Prim Sch
Stonegravels
1 HIGHBURY RD
2 CAVENDISH CT
3 ASHFORD CT
4 THORNFIELD CT
5 WINSTER CT
River Rother
BRIMINGTON RD
Chesterfield Coll (Tapton House Campus)
Castle Hill
Tapton Grange
Brimington Manor Inf Sch
Abercrombie Prim Sch
266
Tapton Bsns Pk
Oldfield Farm
Trans Pennine Trail
Chesterfield Coll
CH
Mast
Plover Hill Farm
Chesterfield Royal
Dobbin Clough Farm
CHESTERFIELD
Mus & Art Gal
Crooked Spire
Chesterfield
Hady Wood
Works
Calow CE Prim Sch
St Peter & St Paul Sch
Liby
Hady Hill Farm
HOLLIS LA
HADY HILL
MARKHAM RD
Hady
Ravenside Ret Pk
Hady Prim Sch
Calow
Spital
Bsns Pk
Alma L Pk
Top Alley
DERBY RD
HASLAND RD
Wrays Hill Farm
38
39
40
70
71
72
73
1
2
3
4
5
6
7
8
A
B
C
D
E
F
For full street detail of the highlighted area see page 266.
95
115
C1
1 SWANBOURNE CL
2 ST JAMES CL
3 CENTRAL DR
4 PENMORE GDNS
5 RANMOOR CL
6 COLLISHAW CL
7 WINDSOR WLK

78 98

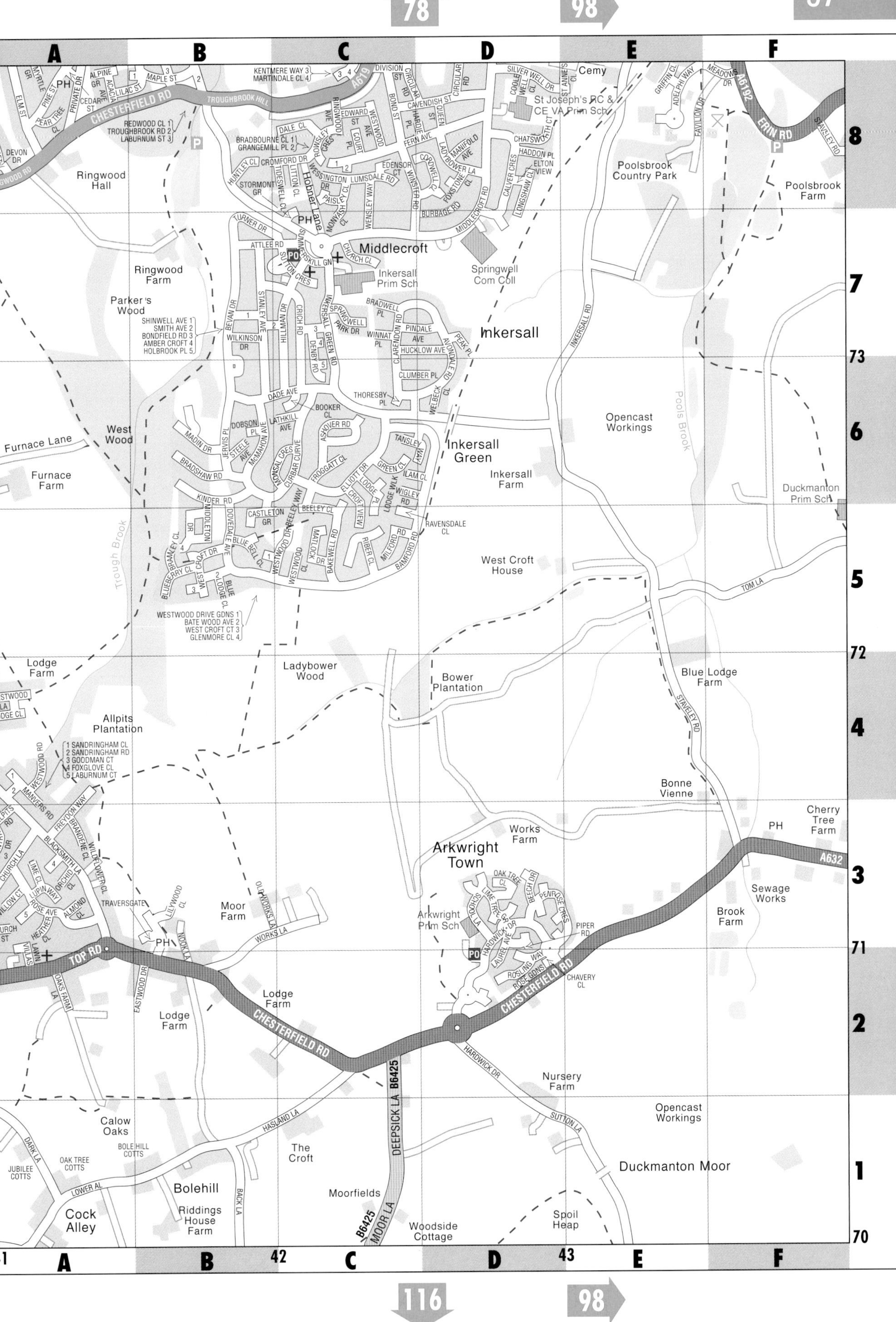

A
B
C
D
E
F
8
7
73
6
5
72
4
3
71
2
1
70
41
42
43
CHESTERFIELD RD
TROUGHBROOK HILL
A619
KENTMERE WAY 3
MARTINDALE CL 4
DIVISION ST
CIRCULAR RD
Cemy
SILVER WELL DR
ST ANNE'S CL
St Joseph's RC & CE VA Prim Sch
GRIFFIN CL
ADELPHI WAY
MEADOWS DR
A6192
ERIN RD
STAVELEY RD
PAVILION DR
MYRTLE GR
PINE ST
PEAR TREE CL
PRIVATE DR
ALPINE GR
CEDAR ST
ACACIA AVE
LILAC ST
MAPLE ST
ELM ST
DEVON DR
PH
REDWOOD CL 1
TROUGHBROOK RD 2
LABURNUM ST 3
BRADBOURNE CL 1
GRANGEMILL PL 2
DALE CL
EDWARD ST
CAVENDISH ST
BOND ST
HARDIE PL
QUEEN ST
RINGWOOD AVE
COURT PL
WESTWOOD AVE
FERN AVE
LADYBOWER LA
MANIFOLD AVE
CHATSWORTH CT
HADDON PL
ELTON VIEW
CALVER CRES
LONGSHAW CL
CROMFORD DR
HUNTLEY CL
STORMONT GR
TIDESWELL CL
LITTON CL
Hobner Lane
WESSINGTON LA
LUMSDALE RD
EDENSOR CT
COPPERWELL CL
FOXSTONE CL
MIDDLECROFT RD
BURBAGE RD
PAISLEY CL
MONYASH CL
WENSLEY WAY
WINSTER RD
Ringwood Hall
Poolsbrook Country Park
Poolsbrook Farm
TURNER DR
ATTLEE RD
SUMMERSKILL GN
SUTTON CRES
CHURCH CL
Middlecroft
Inkersall Prim Sch
Springwell Com Coll
Ringwood Farm
Parker's Wood
SHINWELL AVE 1
SMITH AVE 2
BONDFIELD RD 3
AMBER CROFT 4
HOLBROOK PL 5
BEVAN DR
STANLEY AVE
HILLMAN DR
CRICH RD
INKERSALL GREEN RD
SPRINGWELL PARK DR
BRADWELL PL
WINNAT PL
CLARENDON RD
PINDALE AVE
HUCKLOW AVE
PEAK PL
AVONDALE RD
Inkersall
INKERSALL RD
WILKINSON DR
DENBY RD
CLUMBER PL
THORESBY PL
WELBECK CL
DADE AVE
LATHKILL AVE
BOOKER CL
ASHOVER RD
DOBSON PL
MADIN DR
JERVIS PL
STEELE AVE
McMAHON AVE
MONSAL CRES
CURBAR CURVE
FROGGATT CL
TANSLEY WAY
GREEN CL
ILAM CL
WIGLEY RD
ELLIOTT DR
LODGE WLK
CROFT VIEW
Inkersall Green
Inkersall Farm
Opencast Workings
Pools Brook
Furnace Lane
West Wood
Furnace Farm
BRADSHAW RD
KINDER RD
CASTLETON GR
BEELEY CL
BEELEY WAY
Duckmanton Prim Sch
Trough Brook
MIDDLETON DR
DOVEDALE AVE
BLUE BELL CL
WESTWOOD DR
MATLOCK DR
BAKEWELL RD
RIBER CL
MILFORD RD
BAMFORD RD
RAVENSDALE CL
BLUEBERRY CL
BRAMLEY CL
WEST CROFT DR
BLUE LODGE CL
West Croft House
TOM LA
WESTWOOD DRIVE GDNS 1
BATE WOOD AVE 2
WEST CROFT CT 3
GLENMORE CL 4
Lodge Farm
Ladybower Wood
Bower Plantation
Blue Lodge Farm
Allpits Plantation
1 SANDRINGHAM CL
2 SANDRINGHAM RD
3 GOODMAN CT
4 FOXGLOVE CL
5 LABURNUM CT
WESTWOOD RD
MANVERS RD
FREYDON WAY
BRAMDENE CL
BLACKSMITH LA
WILDFLOWER CL
CHURCH LA
LIME CL
ORCHID CL
LUPIN WAY
ROSE AVE
ALMOND CL
WILLOW CT
HEATHER CL
LAWN VILLAS
Bonne Vienne
Cherry Tree Farm
PH
Works Farm
Arkwright Town
A632
OAK TREE CL
BEECH DR
PENROSE CRES
LIME TREE GR
HARDWICK DR
LAUREL AVE
Sewage Works
Brook Farm
TRAVERSGATE
LILYWOOD CL
Moor Farm
OLD WORKS LA
WORKS LA
Arkwright Prim Sch
PIPER RD
TOP RD
NOOK LA
ROSLING WAY
ROSE GDNS
CHAVERY CL
OAKS FARM LA
EASTWOOD DR
Lodge Farm
Nursery Farm
HARDWICK DR
DEEPSICK LA B6425
Calow Oaks
HASLAND LA
SUTTON LA
Opencast Workings
BOLE HILL COTTS
The Croft
DARK LA
OAK TREE COTTS
JUBILEE COTTS
LOWER AL
Duckmanton Moor
Bolehill
Moorfields
Riddings House Farm
BACK LA
Cock Alley
B6425 MOOR LA
Woodside Cottage
Spoil Heap

116 98

97
79

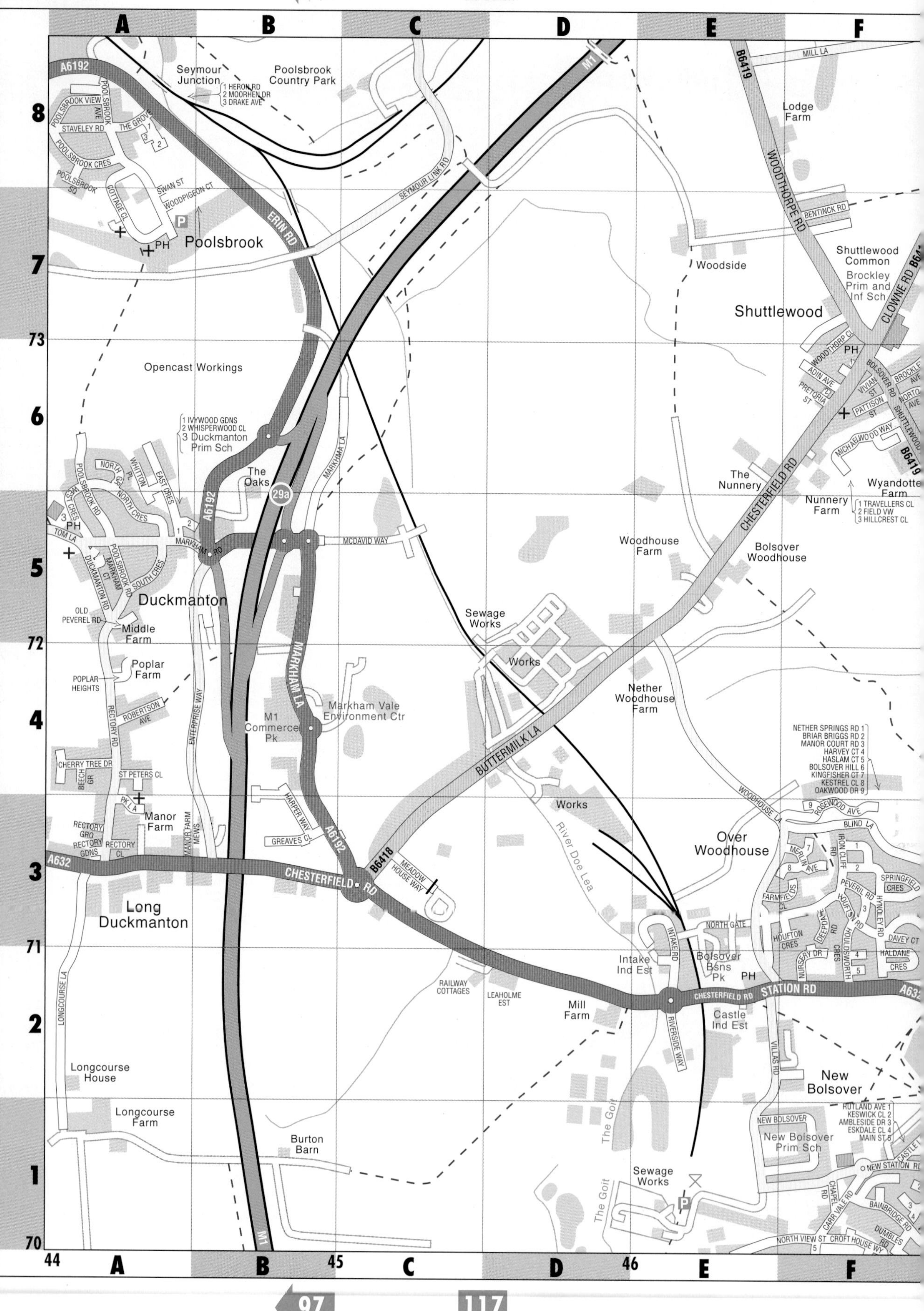
A
B
C
D
E
F
A6192
Seymour Junction
1 HERON RD
2 MOORHEN DR
3 DRAKE AVE
Poolsbrook Country Park
M1
B6419
MILL LA
POOLSBROOK VIEW
POOLSBROOK AVE
STAVELEY RD
THE GROVE
POOLSBROOK CRES
POOLSBROOK SQ
COTTAGE CL
SWAN ST
WOODPIGEON CT
SEYMOUR LINK RD
ERIN RD
PH
Poolsbrook
Lodge Farm
WOODTHORPE RD
BENTINCK RD
Woodside
Shuttlewood Common
Brockley Prim and Inf Sch
CLOWNE RD
Shuttlewood
Opencast Workings
WOODTHORPE CL
ADIN AVE
PRETORIA ST
BOLSOVER RD
VIVIAN ST
PATTISON ST
MICHAELWOOD WAY
SHUTTLEWOOD RD
1 IVYWOOD GDNS
2 WHISPERWOOD CL
3 Duckmanton Prim Sch
The Oaks
29a
MARKHAM LA
NORTH GR
WHITTON PL
EAST CRES
NORTH CRES
POOLSBROOK RD
WEST CRES
TOM LA
A6192
MARKHAM RD
MCDAVID WAY
The Nunnery
CHESTERFIELD RD
Nunnery Farm
Wyandotte Farm
1 TRAVELLERS CL
2 FIELD VW
3 HILLCREST CL
Woodhouse Farm
Bolsover Woodhouse
DUCKMANTON RD
MARKHAM CT
SOUTH CRES
Duckmanton
OLD PEVEREL RD
Middle Farm
Sewage Works
Works
Poplar Farm
POPLAR HEIGHTS
ROBERTSON AVE
ENTERPRISE WAY
MARKHAM LA
Markham Vale Environment Ctr
M1 Commerce Pk
Nether Woodhouse Farm
RECTORY RD
CHERRY TREE DR
BEECH GR
ST PETERS CL
PK LA
Manor Farm
MANOR FARM MEWS
HARPER WAY
BUTTERMILK LA
NETHER SPRINGS RD 1
BRIAR BRIGGS RD 2
MANOR COURT RD 3
HARVEY CT 4
HASLAM CT 5
BOLSOVER HILL 6
KINGFISHER CT 7
KESTREL CL 8
OAKWOOD DR 9
WOODHOUSE LA
ROSEWOOD AVE
BLIND LA
Works
River Doe Lea
Over Woodhouse
RECTORY GRO
RECTORY GDNS
RECTORY CL
GREAVES CL
A632
CHESTERFIELD RD
B6418
MEADOW HOUSE WAY
MERLIN AVE
IRON CLIFF RD
SPRINGFIELD CRES
PEVERIL RD
HYNDLEY RD
FARMFIELDS CL
HOUFTON RD
DAVEY CT
Long Duckmanton
NORTH GATE
INTAKE RD
HOUFTON CRES
DEEPDALE RD
HOULDSWORTH CRES
HALDANE CRES
NURSERY DR
Intake Ind Est
Bolsover Bsns Pk
PH
RAILWAY COTTAGES
LEAHOLME EST
Mill Farm
CHESTERFIELD RD
STATION RD
A632
LONGCOURSE LA
RIVERSIDE WAY
Castle Ind Est
VILLAS RD
Longcourse House
New Bolsover
RUTLAND AVE 1
KESWICK CL 2
AMBLESIDE DR 3
ESKDALE CL 4
MAIN ST 5
Longcourse Farm
NEW BOLSOVER
New Bolsover Prim Sch
Burton Barn
The Goit
Sewage Works
NEW STATION RD
CHAPEL RD
CARR VALE RD
BAINBRIDGE RD
DUMBLES RD
NORTH VIEW ST
CROFT HOUSE WY
M1
8
7
73
6
5
72
4
3
71
2
1
70
44
45
46

97
117

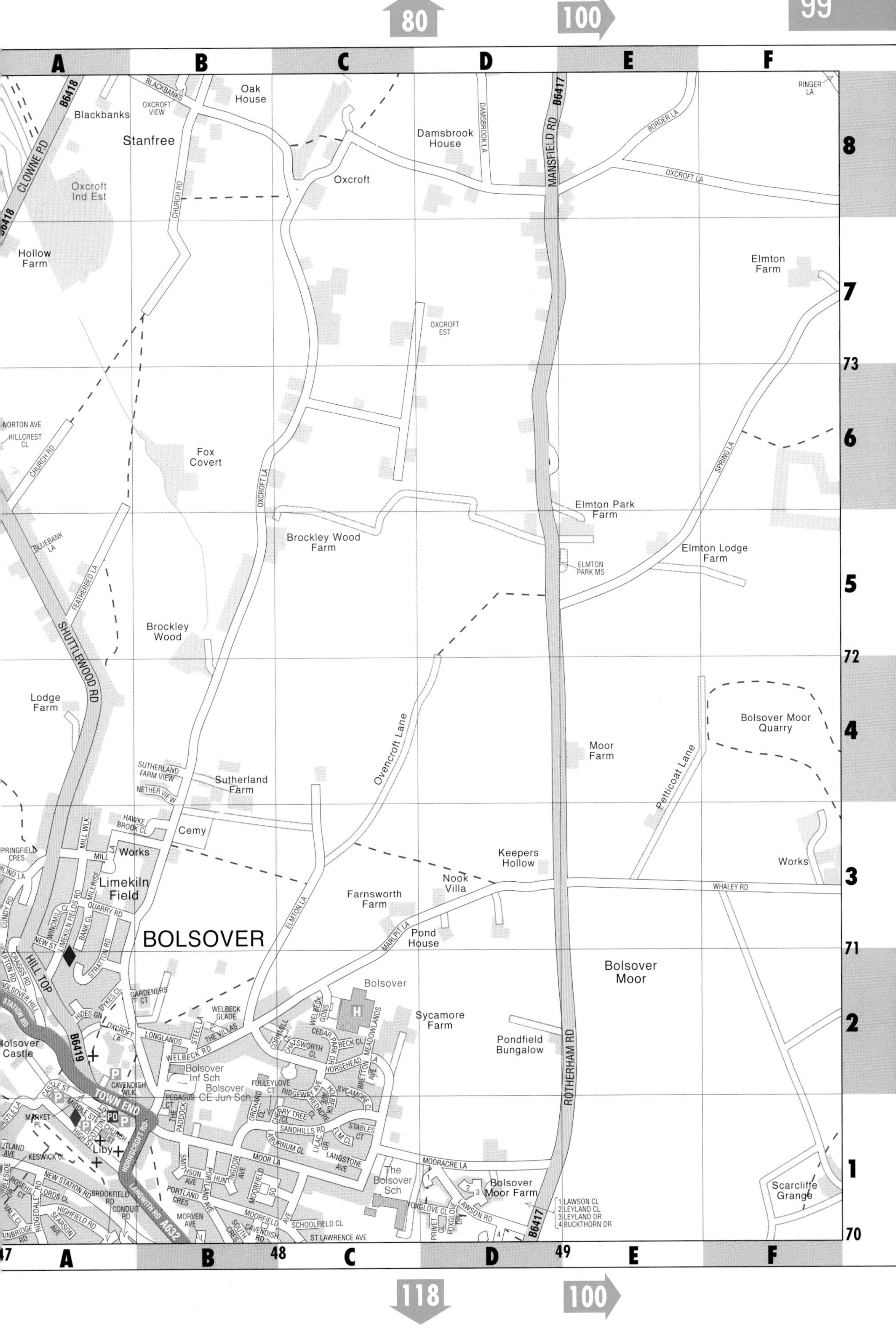
80
100
Blackbanks
Stanfree
Oak House
Oxcroft Ind Est
Hollow Farm
Damsbrook House
Oxcroft
Elmton Farm
OXCROFT EST
Fox Covert
Elmton Park Farm
Brockley Wood Farm
Elmton Lodge Farm
ELMTON PARK MS
Brockley Wood
Lodge Farm
Bolsover Moor Quarry
Moor Farm
Sutherland Farm
Cemy
Works
Limekiln Field
Keepers Hollow
Nook Villa
Farnsworth Farm
BOLSOVER
Pond House
Bolsover Moor
Bolsover
Sycamore Farm
Pondfield Bungalow
Bolsover Castle
Bolsover Inf Sch
Bolsover CE Jun Sch
The Bolsover Sch
Bolsover Moor Farm
Scarcliffe Grange
Ovencroft Lane
Petticoat Lane
MANSFIELD RD
ROTHERHAM RD
SHUTTLEWOOD RD
OXCROFT LA
WHALEY RD
MARLPIT LA
TOWN END
1 LAWSON CL
2 LEYLAND CL
3 LEYLAND DR
4 BUCKTHORN DR
118
100

99
81

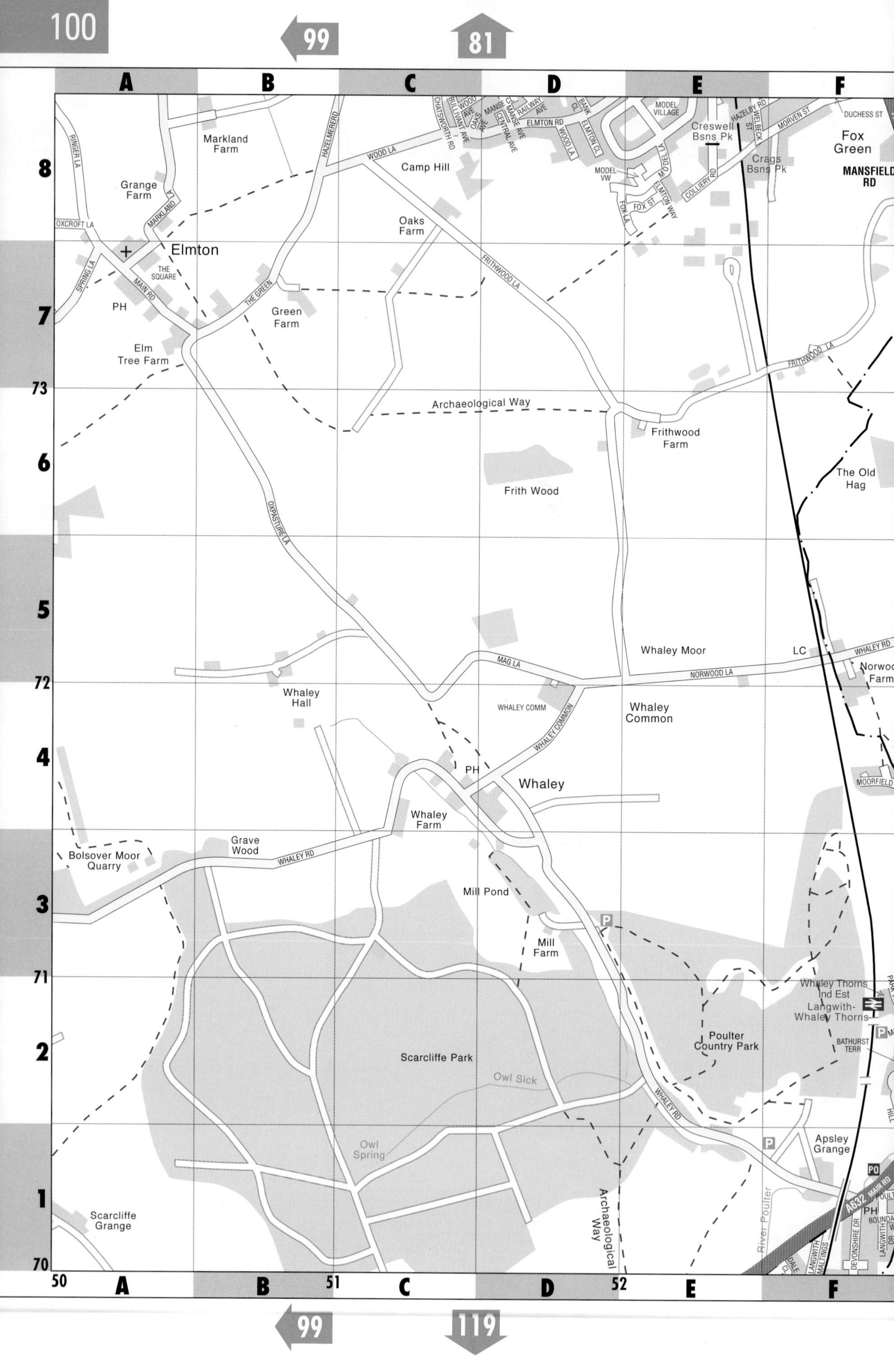
Markland Farm
Grange Farm
Camp Hill
Oaks Farm
Elmton
THE SQUARE
PH
Green Farm
Elm Tree Farm
Creswell Bsns Pk
Crags Bsns Pk
Fox Green
MANSFIELD RD
MODEL VILLAGE
Archaeological Way
Frithwood Farm
Frith Wood
The Old Hag
Whaley Moor
LC
Norwood Farm
Whaley Hall
WHALEY COMM
Whaley Common
PH
Whaley
Whaley Farm
Grave Wood
Bolsover Moor Quarry
Mill Pond
Mill Farm
Whaley Thorns Ind Est
Langwith-Whaley Thorns
Poulter Country Park
Scarcliffe Park
Owl Sick
Owl Spring
Apsley Grange
Scarcliffe Grange
Archaeological Way
River Poulter
RINGER LA
OXCROFT LA
SPRING LA
MARKLAND LA
MAIN RD
THE GREEN
HAZELMERE RD
WOOD LA
CHATSWORTH RD
ELMTON RD
FRITHWOOD LA
OXPASTURE LA
MAG LA
NORWOOD LA
WHALEY RD
WHALEY COMMON
MORVEN ST
DUCHESS ST
COLLIERY RD
FOX ST
FOX LA
ELMTON WAY
MOORFIELD
BATHURST TERR
A632 MAIN RD
DEVONSHIRE DR
LANGWITH MALTINGS
8
7
73
6
5
72
4
3
71
2
1
70
50
51
52
A
B
C
D
E
F

99
119

82

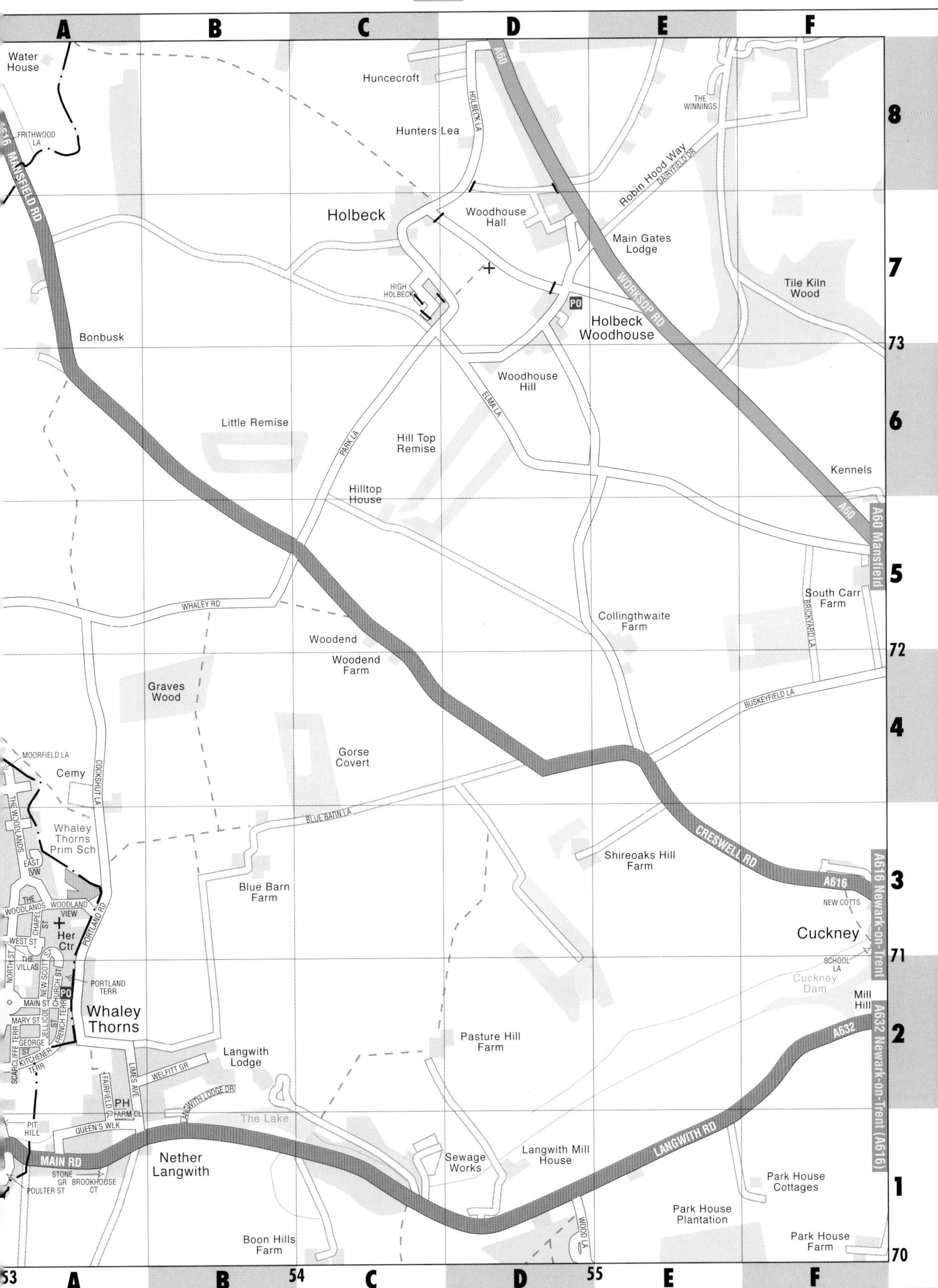

Water House
Huncecroft
Hunters Lea
HOLBECK LA
A60
THE WINNINGS
FRITHWOOD LA
A616 MANSFIELD RD
Robin Hood Way
DAIRYFIELD DR
Holbeck
Woodhouse Hall
Main Gates Lodge
HIGH HOLBECK
PO
Holbeck Woodhouse
WORKSOP RD
Tile Kiln Wood
Bonbusk
Woodhouse Hill
ELMA LA
Little Remise
Hill Top Remise
PARK LA
Kennels
Hilltop House
A60 Mansfield
South Carr Farm
WHALEY RD
BRICKYARD LA
Collingthwaite Farm
Woodend
Woodend Farm
Graves Wood
BUSKEYFIELD LA
Gorse Covert
MOORFIELD LA
Cemy
COCKSHUT LA
THE WOODLANDS
BLUE BARN LA
Whaley Thorns Prim Sch
EAST VW
CRESWELL RD
Shireoaks Hill Farm
A616
A616 Newark-on-Trent
NEW COTTS
Blue Barn Farm
THE WOODLANDS
WOODLAND VIEW
CHAPEL ST
Her Ctr
PORTLAND RD
WEST ST
Cuckney
THE VILLAS
SCHOOL LA
NORTH ST
NEW SCOTT ST
CHURCH ST
PORTLAND TERR
Cuckney Dam
MAIN ST
JELLICOE ST
FRENCH TERR
Whaley Thorns
Mill Hill
MARY ST
GEORGE ST
A632 Newark-on-Trent (A616)
A632
KITCHENER TERR
SCARCLIFFE TERR
Pasture Hill Farm
Langwith Lodge
LIMES AVE
WELFITT GR
FAIRFIELD CL
PH
FARM CL
LANGWITH LODGE DR
PIT HILL
QUEEN'S WLK
The Lake
MAIN RD
Nether Langwith
Sewage Works
Langwith Mill House
LANGWITH RD
STONE GR
BROOKHOUSE CT
POULTER ST
Park House Cottages
Park House Plantation
WOOD LA
Boon Hills Farm
Park House Farm
A
B
C
D
E
F
8
7
73
6
5
72
4
3
71
2
1
70
53
54
55

120

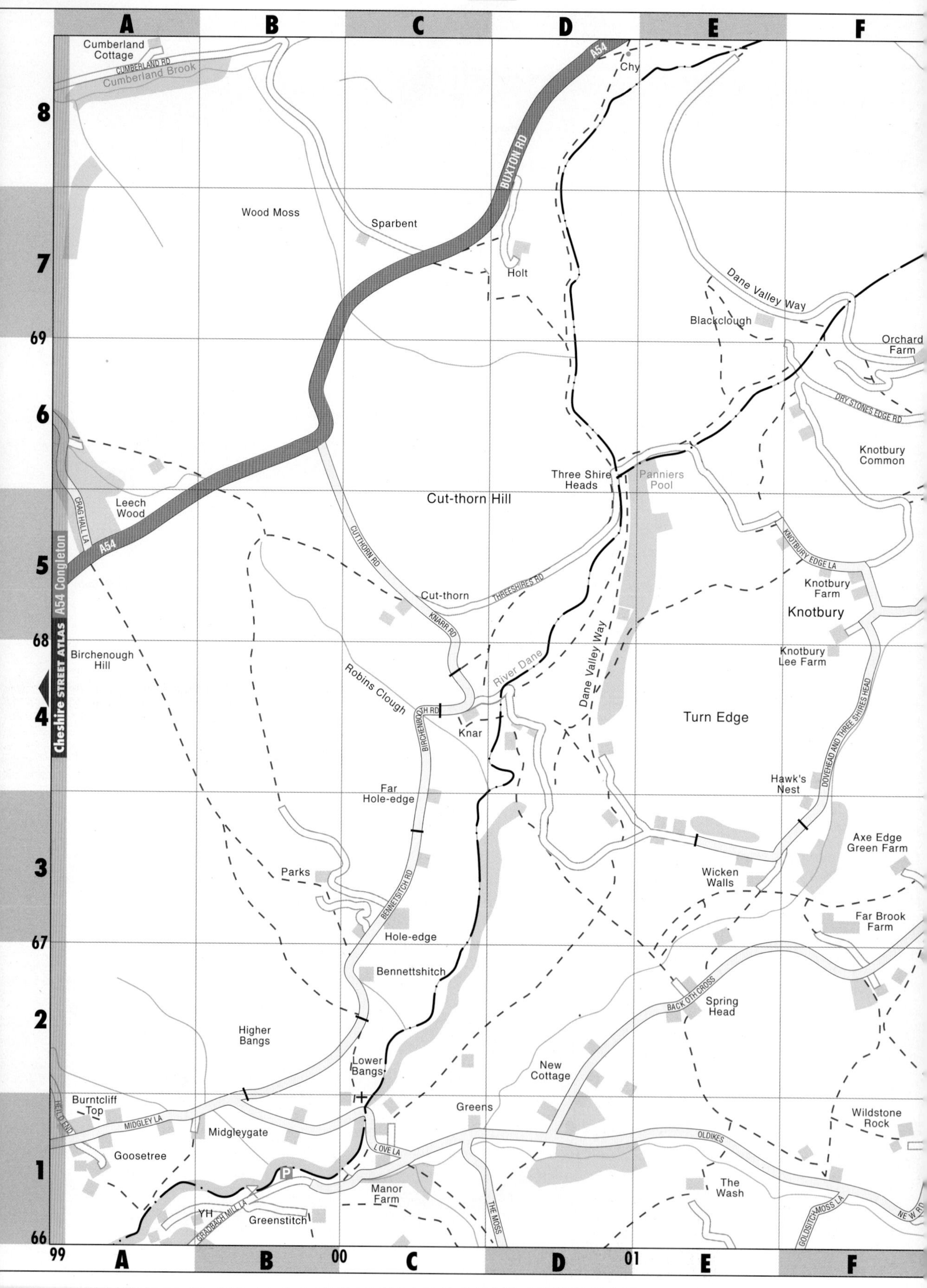

83

Cumberland Cottage
CUMBERLAND RD
Cumberland Brook

Wood Moss

Sparbent

BUXTON RD
A54

Chy

Holt

Dane Valley Way

Blackclough

Orchard Farm

DRY STONES EDGE RD

Knotbury Common

Leech Wood

CRAG HALL LA

A54

Three Shire Heads

Panniers Pool

Cut-thorn Hill

CUTTHORN RD

Knotbury Edge LA

Knotbury Farm

Knotbury

Birchenough Hill

Cut-thorn

KNARR RD

THREESHIRES RD

Dane Valley Way

Knotbury Lee Farm

Robins Clough

River Dane

Turn Edge

Knar

BIRCHENBROOK RD

Far Hole-edge

Hawk's Nest

DOVEHEAD AND THREE SHIRES HEAD

Axe Edge Green Farm

Parks

Wicken Walls

Far Brook Farm

Hole-edge

BENNETTSITCH RD

Bennettshitch

BACK O'TH CROSS

Spring Head

Higher Bangs

Lower Bangs

New Cottage

Greens

OLDIKES

Wildstone Rock

Burntcliff Top

HELL'S END

MIDGLEY LA

Midgleygate

LOVE LA

Manor Farm

THE MOSS

The Wash

GOLDSITCH MOSS LA

NEW RD

Goosetree

YH

GRADBACH MILL LA

Greenstitch

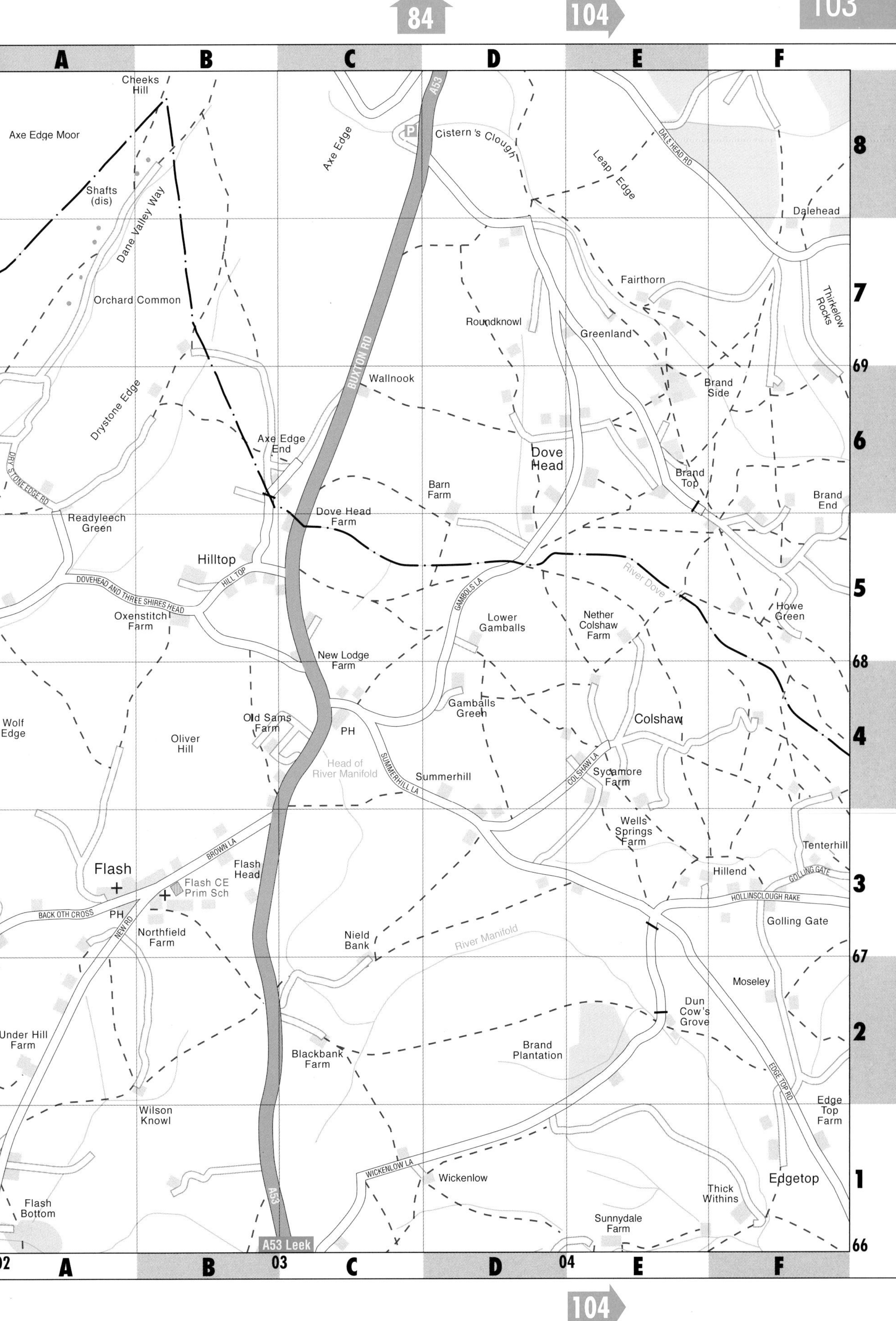

A B C D E F

Cheeks Hill

Axe Edge Moor

Shafts (dis)

Dane Valley Way

Orchard Common

Cistern's Clough

Axe Edge

Leap Edge

DALE HEAD RD

8

Dalehead

Fairthorn

Thirkelow Rocks

7

Drystone Edge

Wallnook

Roundknowl

Greenland

Brand Side

69

DRY STONE EDGE RD

Axe Edge End

Dove Head

Brand Top

6

Readyleech Green

Dove Head Farm

Barn Farm

Brand End

Hilltop

DOVEHEAD AND THREE SHIRES HEAD

HILL TOP

River Dove

Howe Green

5

Oxenstitch Farm

GAMBOLS LA

Lower Gamballs

Nether Colshaw Farm

68

Wolf Edge

New Lodge Farm

Old Sams Farm

PH

Gamballs Green

Colshaw

4

Oliver Hill

Head of River Manifold

SUMMERHILL LA

Summerhill

COLSHAW LA

Sycamore Farm

Wells Springs Farm

Tenterhill

BROWN LA

Flash Head

Hillend

GOLLING GATE

3

Flash

Flash CE Prim Sch

HOLLINSCLOUGH RAKE

Golling Gate

BACK OTH CROSS

PH

Northfield Farm

Nield Bank

River Manifold

67

Moseley

NEW RD

Dun Cow's Grove

Under Hill Farm

Brand Plantation

2

EDGE TOP RD

Edge Top Farm

Blackbank Farm

Wilson Knowl

WICKENLOW LA

Wickenlow

Thick Withins

Edgetop

1

Flash Bottom

Sunnydale Farm

A53 Leek

66

103
85

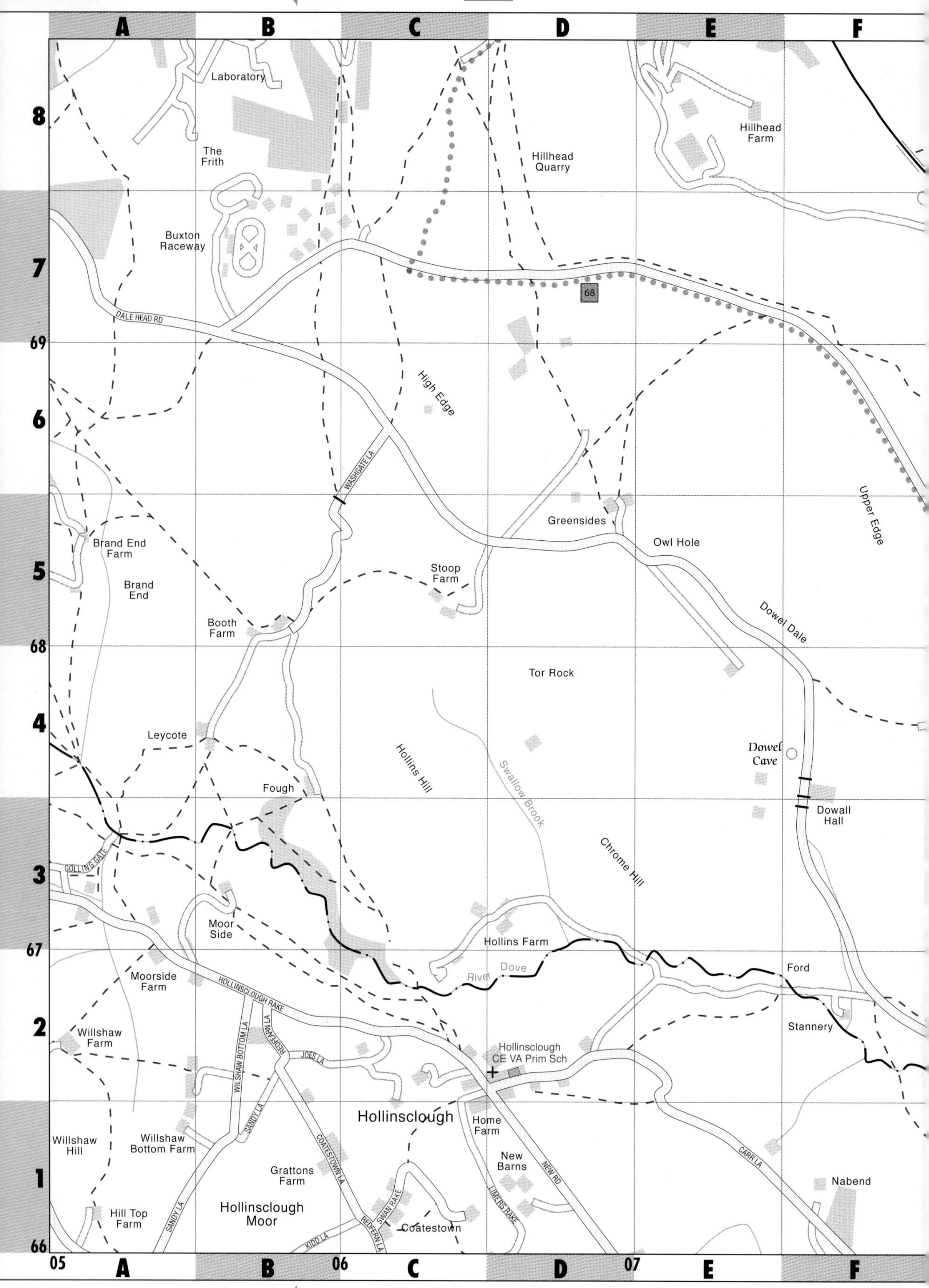

A B C D E F

8

Laboratory

Hillhead
Quarry

Hillhead
Farm

The
Frith

Buxton
Raceway

7

69

DALE HEAD RD

High Edge

68

6

WASHGATE LA

Greensides

Owl Hole

Upper Edge

5

Brand End
Farm

Stoop
Farm

Dowel Dale

Brand
End

Booth
Farm

68

Tor Rock

4

Leycote

Hollins Hill

Swallow Brook

Dowel
Cave

Fough

Dowall
Hall

Chrome Hill

3

GOLLING GATE

Moor
Side

Hollins Farm

67

River Dove

Ford

Moorside
Farm

HOLLINSCLOUGH RAKE

Stannery

2

Willshaw
Farm

WILSHAW BOTTOM LA

HEATHFIELD LA

JOES LA

Hollinsclough
CE VA Prim Sch

Willshaw
Hill

Willshaw
Bottom Farm

SANDY LA

COATESTOWN LA

Hollinsclough

Home
Farm

New
Barns

NEW RD

CARR LA

Nabend

1

Grattons
Farm

LIMERS RAKE

Hill Top
Farm

SANDY LA

Hollinsclough
Moor

KIDD LA

REDFERN LA

SWAIN RAKE

Coatestown

66

05 A B 06 C D 07 E F

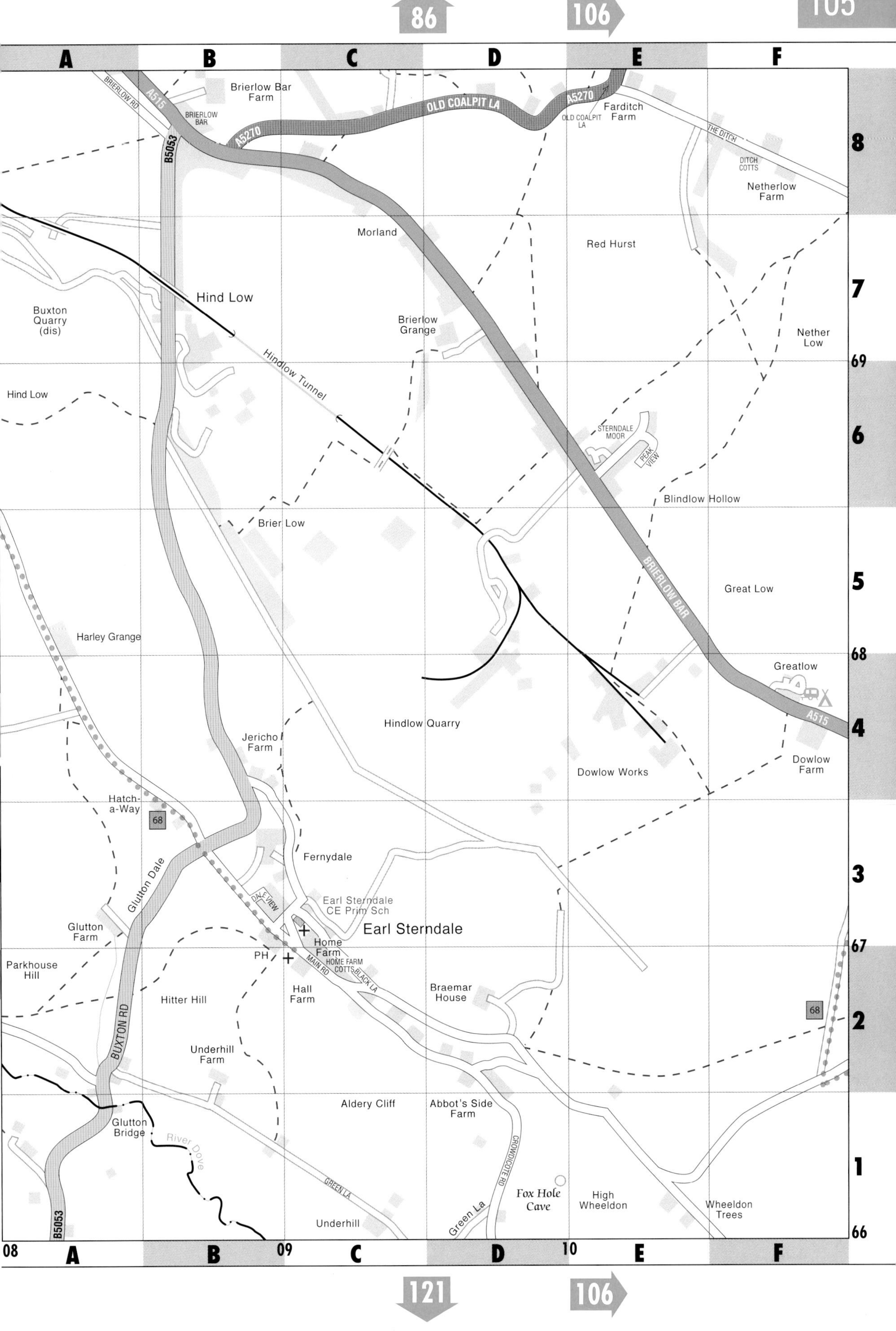

A B C D E F

8
7
69
6
5
68
4
3
67
2
1
66

BRIERLOW RD
A515
B5053
A5270
BRIERLOW BAR
OLD COALPIT LA
Brierlow Bar Farm
BRIERLOW BAR
A5270
OLD COALPIT LA
Farditch Farm
THE DITCH
DITCH COTTS
Netherlow Farm
Morland
Red Hurst
Hind Low
Buxton Quarry (dis)
Brierlow Grange
Nether Low
Hindlow Tunnel
Hind Low
STERNDALE MOOR
PEAK VIEW
Blindlow Hollow
Brier Low
Great Low
Harley Grange
BRIERLOW BAR
A515
Greatlow
68
Hindlow Quarry
Jericho Farm
Dowlow Works
Dowlow Farm
Hatch-a-Way
68
Glutton Dale
Fernydale
DALE VIEW
Earl Sterndale CE Prim Sch
Earl Sterndale
Glutton Farm
PH
Home Farm
HOME FARM COTTS
BLACK LA
MAIN RD
67
Parkhouse Hill
Hitter Hill
Hall Farm
Braemar House
68
BUXTON RD
Underhill Farm
2
Aldery Cliff
Abbot's Side Farm
CROWDICOTE RD
Glutton Bridge
River Dove
GREEN LA
Fox Hole Cave
High Wheeldon
Wheeldon Trees
B5053
Green La
Underhill

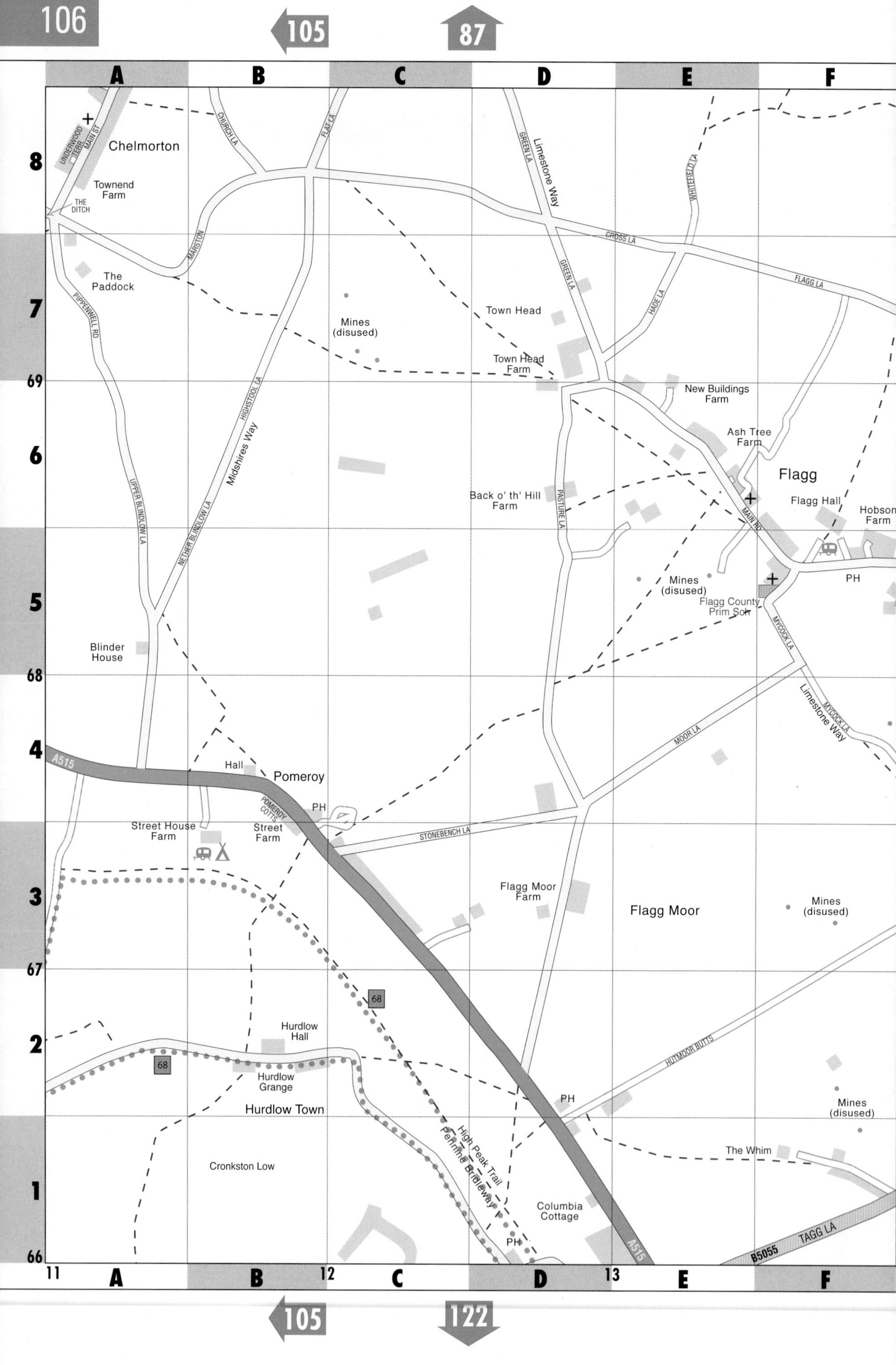
105
87
A
B
C
D
E
F
8
7
69
6
5
68
4
3
67
2
1
66
11
12
13
Chelmorton
UNDERWOOD TERR
MAIN ST
Townend Farm
THE DITCH
CHURCH LA
FLAT LA
GREEN LA
Limestone Way
WHITEFIELD LA
CROSS LA
FLAGG LA
MARSTON
The Paddock
PIPPENWELL RD
Mines (disused)
Town Head
Town Head Farm
HADE LA
New Buildings Farm
Ash Tree Farm
Flagg
Flagg Hall
Hobson Farm
HIGHSTOOL LA
Midshires Way
UPPER BLINDLOW LA
NETHER BLINDLOW LA
Back o' th' Hill Farm
PASTURE LA
MAIN RD
Mines (disused)
Flagg County Prim Sch
PH
MYCOCK LA
Blinder House
Limestone Way
MYCOCK LA
MOOR LA
A515
Hall
Pomeroy
POMEROY COTTS
PH
Street House Farm
Street Farm
STONEBENCH LA
Flagg Moor Farm
Flagg Moor
Mines (disused)
68
Hurdlow Hall
68
Hurdlow Grange
Hurdlow Town
HUTMOOR BUTTS
PH
Mines (disused)
High Peak Trail
Pennine Bridleway
The Whim
Cronkston Low
Columbia Cottage
PH
A515
B5055
TAGG LA
105
122

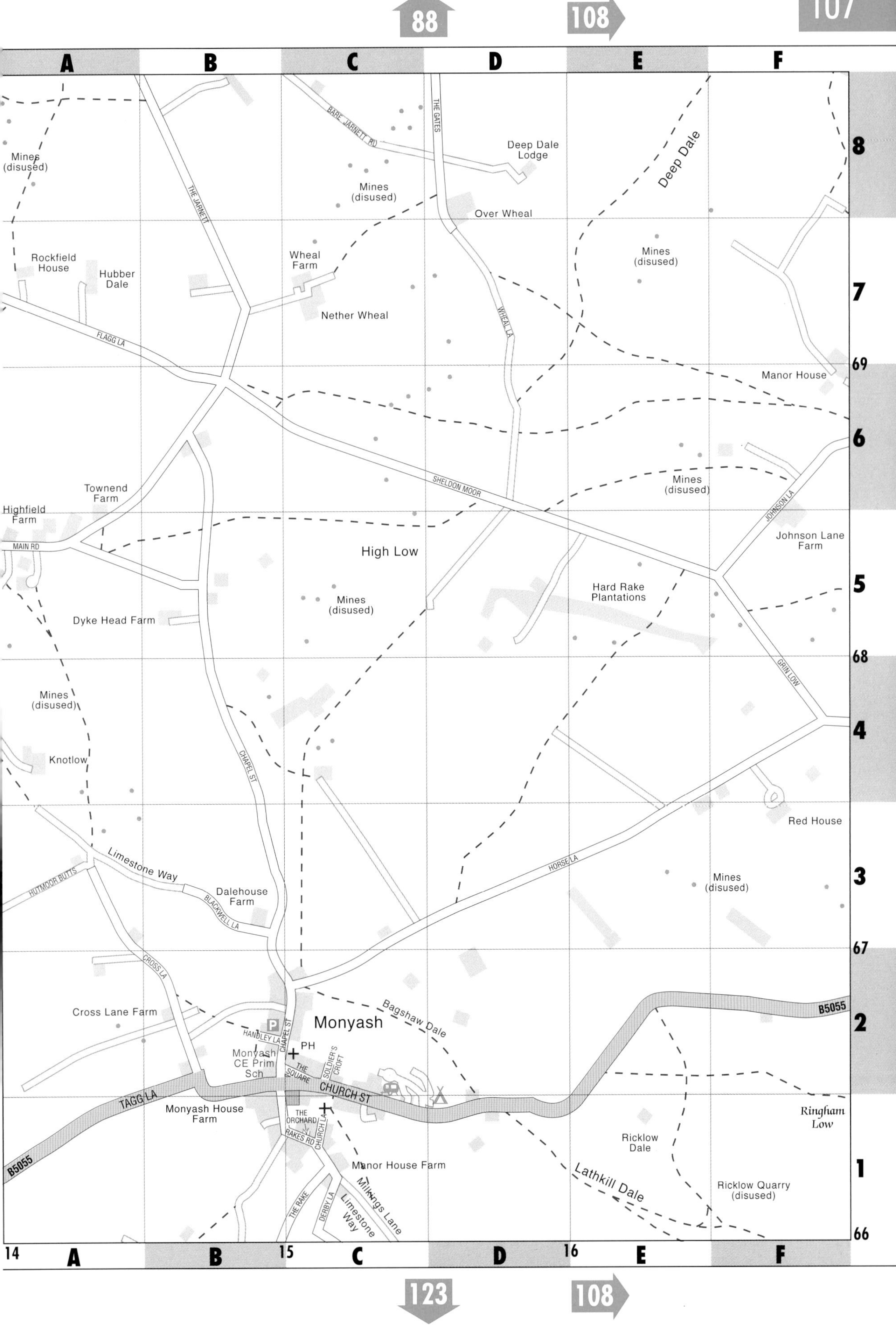

88
108

A B C D E F

8

Mines
(disused)

Deep Dale Lodge

Deep Dale

Over Wheal

Mines
(disused)

7

Rockfield House

Hubber Dale

Wheal Farm

Nether Wheal

Manor House

69

FLAGG LA

THE JARNETT

BARE JARNETT RD

THE GATES

WHEAL LA

6

Townend Farm

SHELDON MOOR

Mines
(disused)

JOHNSON LA

Highfield Farm

MAIN RD

High Low

Johnson Lane Farm

5

Dyke Head Farm

Mines
(disused)

Hard Rake Plantations

68

GRIN LOW

Mines
(disused)

4

Knotlow

Red House

Limestone Way

HUTMOOR BUTTS

Dalehouse Farm

BLACKWELL LA

CHAPEL ST

HORSE LA

Mines
(disused)

3

67

CROSS LA

Cross Lane Farm

Bagshaw Dale

B5055

2

P

HANDLEY LA

Monyash

Monyash CE Prim Sch

PH

THE SQUARE

SOLDIER'S CROFT

CHURCH ST

Ringham Low

TAGG LA

Monyash House Farm

THE ORCHARD

RAKES RD

CHURCH LA

Manor House Farm

Millings Lane

Limestone Way

Ricklow Dale

Lathkill Dale

Ricklow Quarry
(disused)

1

B5055

THE RAKE

DERBY LA

66

14 A 15 B C 16 D E F

107
89

A B C D E F
8 7 69 6 5 68 4 3 67 2 1 66
17 18 19
A6
Great Shacklow Wood
Weir
River Wye
Little Shacklow Wood
HIGHFIELD
VICARAGE LA
HILL CROSS
GREAVES LA
HALL END LA
A6020
TRINITY CL
COURT LA
FENNEL ST
CHURCH ST
WATTS GN
CHERRY CL
B6465
PH
BETTY LA
NEW RD (BASLOW RD)
BUXTON RD
MILL LA
Mill
THE DUKE S DR
DUKES DR
A6
THE ASHFORD RD
MOUNT PLEASANT
Ashford in the Water
CORNBROOK 1
HILLMORTON 2
MILLSTONE LA
JOHN BANK LA
Mast
Arrock Plantation
KIRK DALE
Opencast Workings
Rose Farm
MAIN ST
JOHNSON LA
CHURCH LA
Lower Farm
MAIN ST
PH
Top Farm
Sheldon
Opencast Workings
Dirtlow Farm
SHELDON LA
Woodbine Farm
Dirtlow Plantations
Kirk Dale
Cowden Plantations
Magpie Mine (disused)
Truebell Lane
TRUEBLUE LA
Opencast Workings
Green Cowden Farm
GRIN LOW
GREEN COWDEN
B5055
BOLE HILL
Shafts (dis)
Bole Hill
Bole Hill Farm
Blores Barn Farm
GREEN LA
Melbourne Farm
Haddon Grove Farm
B5055
CHURCH ST
Opencast Workings
Organ Ground
MONYASH RD
Mandale Rake
Haddon Grove
HADDON GROVE
Mines (dis)
Haddon Grove Farm
Twin Dales
Weir
River Lathkill

107
124

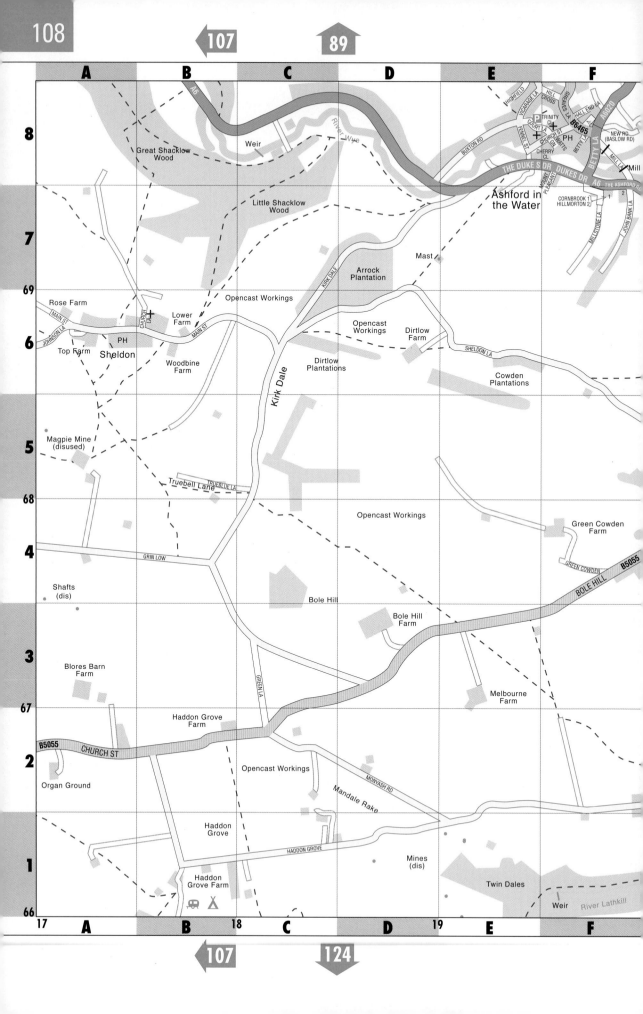

90
110

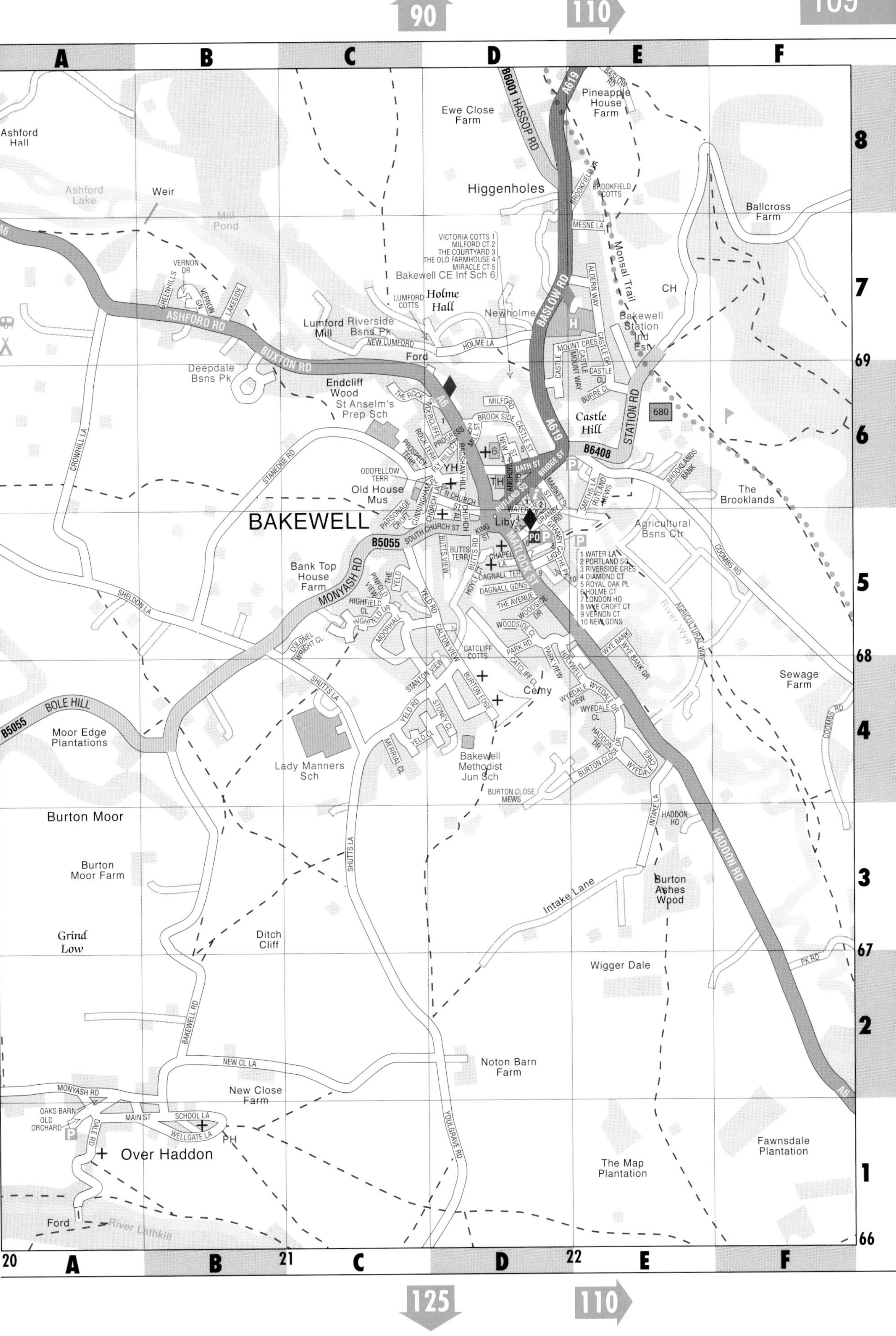
BAKEWELL
Ashford Hall
Ashford Lake
Weir
Mill Pond
Higgenholes
Ewe Close Farm
Pineapple House Farm
Ballcross Farm
Holme Hall
Newholme
Lumford Mill
Riverside Bsns Pk
Deepdale Bsns Pk
Endcliff Wood
St Anselm's Prep Sch
Old House Mus
Bakewell Station Ind Est
Castle Hill
The Brooklands
Agricultural Bsns Ctr
Bank Top House Farm
Sewage Farm
Moor Edge Plantations
Lady Manners Sch
Bakewell Methodist Jun Sch
Burton Moor
Burton Moor Farm
Burton Ashes Wood
Grind Low
Ditch Cliff
Wigger Dale
Noton Barn Farm
New Close Farm
Over Haddon
The Map Plantation
Fawnsdale Plantation
River Lathkill
River Wye
Monsal Trail
Intake Lane
VICTORIA COTTS 1
MILFORD CT 2
THE COURTYARD 3
THE OLD FARMHOUSE 4
MIRACLE CT 5
Bakewell CE Inf Sch 6
1 WATER LA
2 PORTLAND SQ
3 RIVERSIDE CRES
4 DIAMOND CT
5 ROYAL OAK PL
6 HOLME CT
7 LONDON HO
8 WYE CROFT CT
9 VERNON CT
10 NEW GDNS
A6
A619
B6001 HASSOP RD
B5055
B6408
ASHFORD RD
BUXTON RD
BASLOW RD
MATLOCK ST
HADDON RD
MONYASH RD
BOLE HILL
STATION RD
COOMBS RD
YOULGRAVE RD
BAKEWELL RD
SHUTTS LA
NEW CL LA
A B C D E F
8 7 6 5 4 3 2 1
69 68 67 66
20 21 22

125
110

109
91

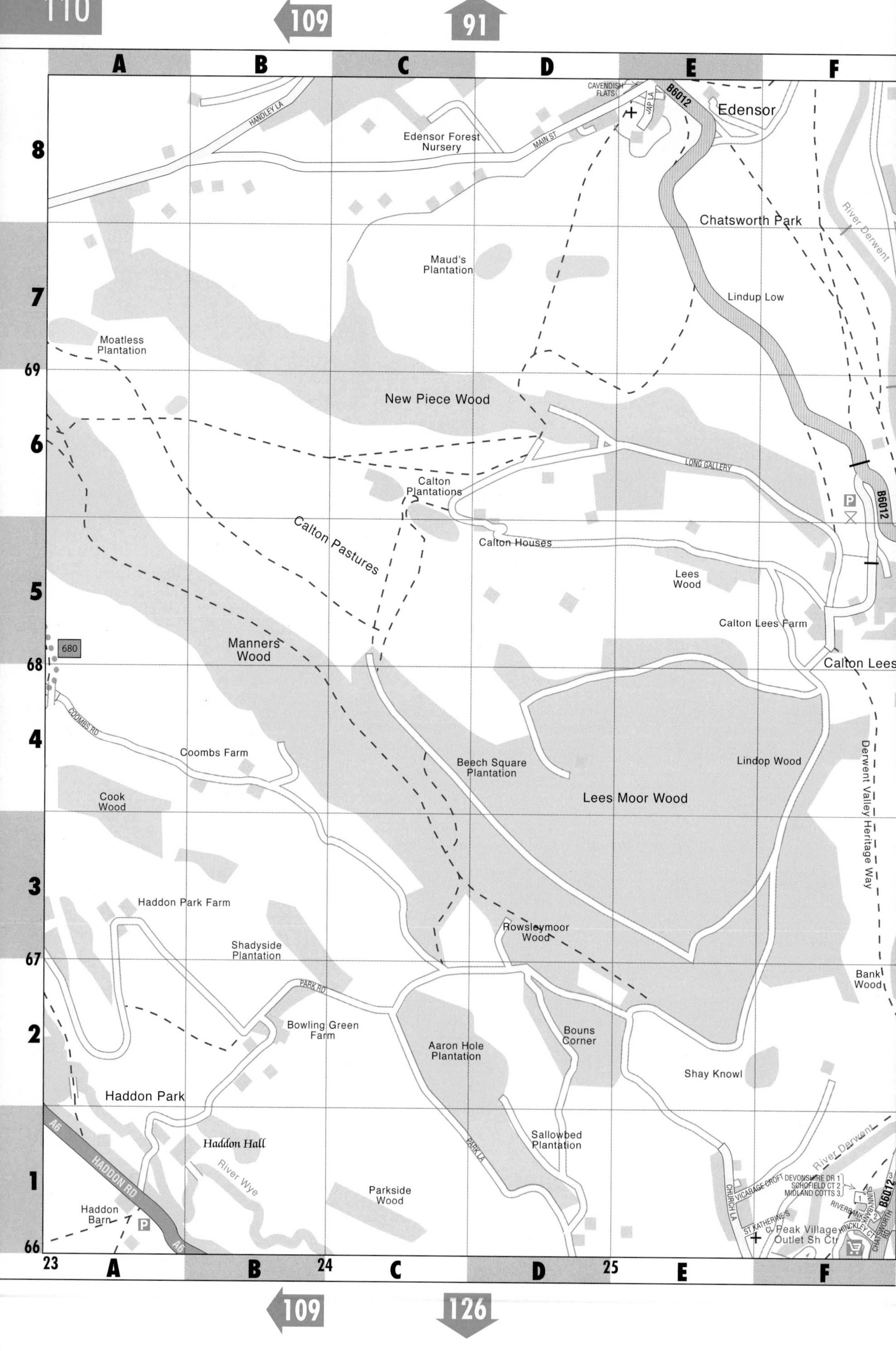
A
B
C
D
E
F
8
7
69
6
5
68
4
3
67
2
1
66
23
24
25
CAVENDISH FLATS
JAP LA
B6012
Edensor
HANDLEY LA
Edensor Forest Nursery
MAIN ST
Chatsworth Park
River Derwent
Maud's Plantation
Lindup Low
Moatless Plantation
New Piece Wood
LONG GALLERY
Calton Plantations
B6012
Calton Pastures
Calton Houses
Lees Wood
Calton Lees Farm
680
Manners Wood
Calton Lees
COOMBS RD
Coombs Farm
Beech Square Plantation
Lindop Wood
Derwent Valley Heritage Way
Lees Moor Wood
Cook Wood
Haddon Park Farm
Rowsleymoor Wood
Shadyside Plantation
Bank Wood
PARK RD
Bowling Green Farm
Bouns Corner
Aaron Hole Plantation
Shay Knowl
Haddon Park
Sallowbed Plantation
A6
HADDON RD
Haddon Hall
River Wye
PARK LA
River Derwent
CHURCH LA
VICARAGE CROFT
DEVONSHIRE DR 1
SCHOFIELD CT 2
MIDLAND COTTS 3
RIVERBANK
B6012
Parkside Wood
Haddon Barn
ST KATHERINE'S CL
Peak Village Outlet Sh Ctr
A6

109
126

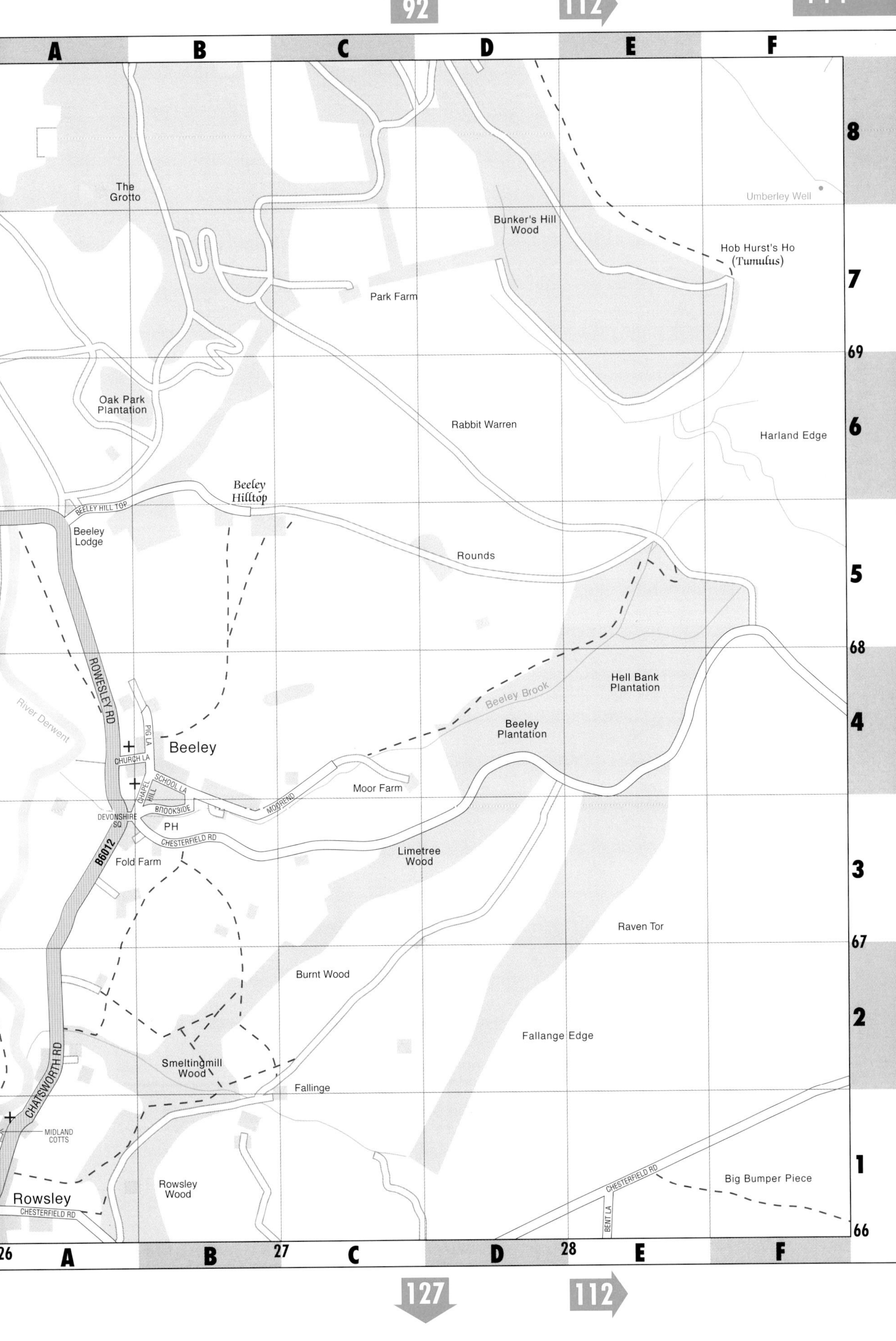
92
112
A
B
C
D
E
F
8
7
69
6
5
68
4
3
67
2
1
66
26
27
28
The Grotto
Bunker's Hill Wood
Umberley Well
Hob Hurst's Ho (Tumulus)
Park Farm
Oak Park Plantation
Rabbit Warren
Harland Edge
Beeley Hilltop
BEELEY HILL TOP
Beeley Lodge
Rounds
ROWSLEY RD
River Derwent
Beeley Brook
Hell Bank Plantation
Beeley Plantation
Beeley
PIG LA
CHURCH LA
SCHOOL LA
CHAPEL HILL
BROOKSIDE
MOOREND
Moor Farm
DEVONSHIRE SQ
PH
CHESTERFIELD RD
B6012
Fold Farm
Limetree Wood
Raven Tor
Burnt Wood
Fallange Edge
Smeltingmill Wood
Falling
CHATSWORTH RD
MIDLAND COTTS
Rowsley Wood
Rowsley
CHESTERFIELD RD
BENT LA
CHESTERFIELD RD
Big Bumper Piece
127
112

111
93

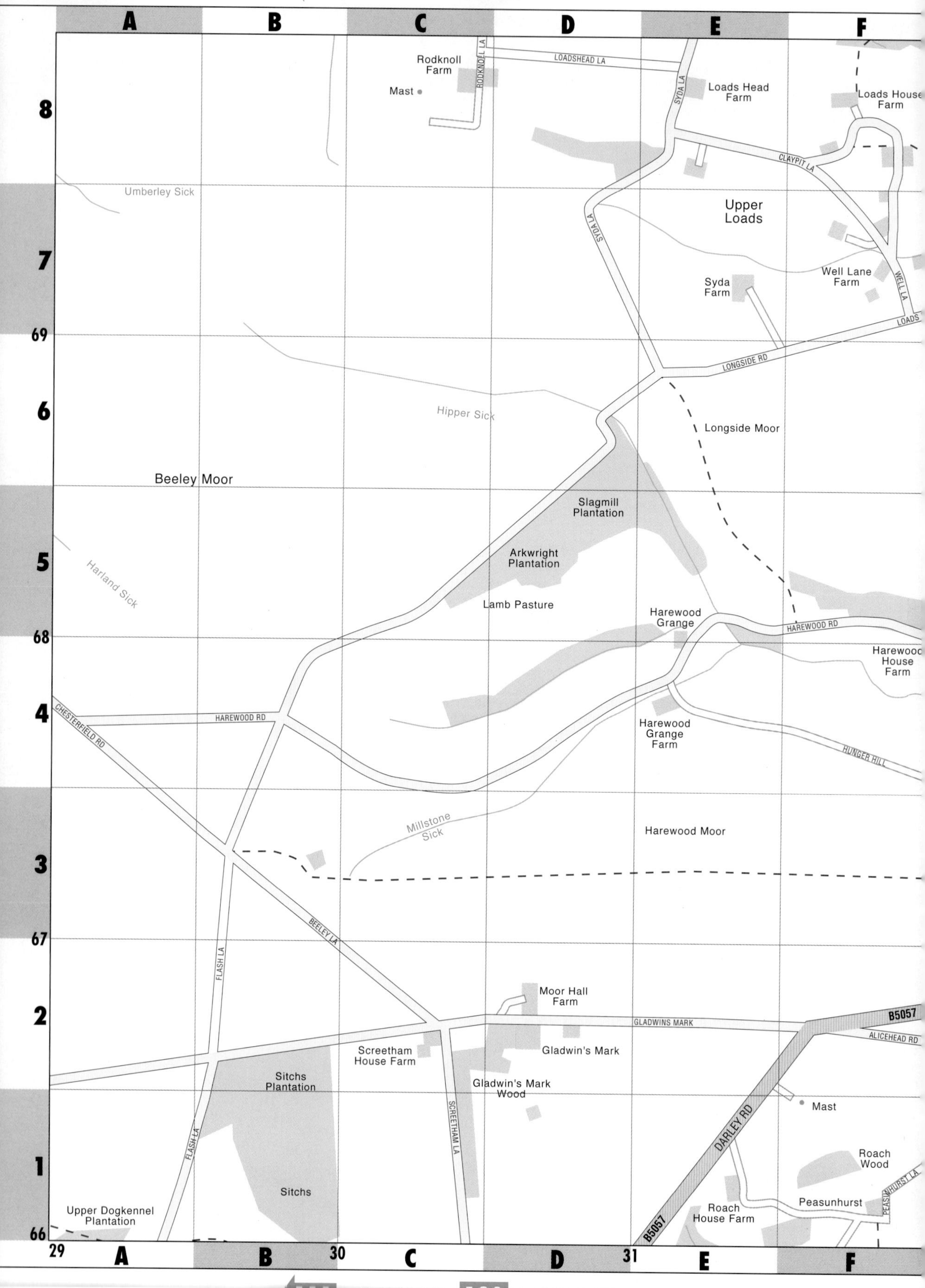
Rodknoll Farm
Mast
RODKNOLL LA
LOADSHEAD LA
SYDA LA
Loads Head Farm
Loads House Farm
CLAYPIT LA
Umberley Sick
Upper Loads
Syda Farm
Well Lane Farm
WELL LA
LOADS
LONGSIDE RD
Hipper Sick
Longside Moor
Beeley Moor
Slagmill Plantation
Arkwright Plantation
Harland Sick
Lamb Pasture
Harewood Grange
HAREWOOD RD
Harewood House Farm
CHESTERFIELD RD
Harewood Grange Farm
HUNGER HILL
Millstone Sick
Harewood Moor
BEELEY LA
FLASH LA
Moor Hall Farm
GLADWINS MARK
B5057
ALICEHEAD RD
Screetham House Farm
Gladwin's Mark
Sitchs Plantation
Gladwin's Mark Wood
SCREETHAM LA
DARLEY RD
Mast
Roach Wood
Sitchs
Peasunhurst
PEASUNHURST LA
Upper Dogkennel Plantation
Roach House Farm
A
B
C
D
E
F
8
7
69
6
5
68
4
3
67
2
1
66
29
30
31

111
128

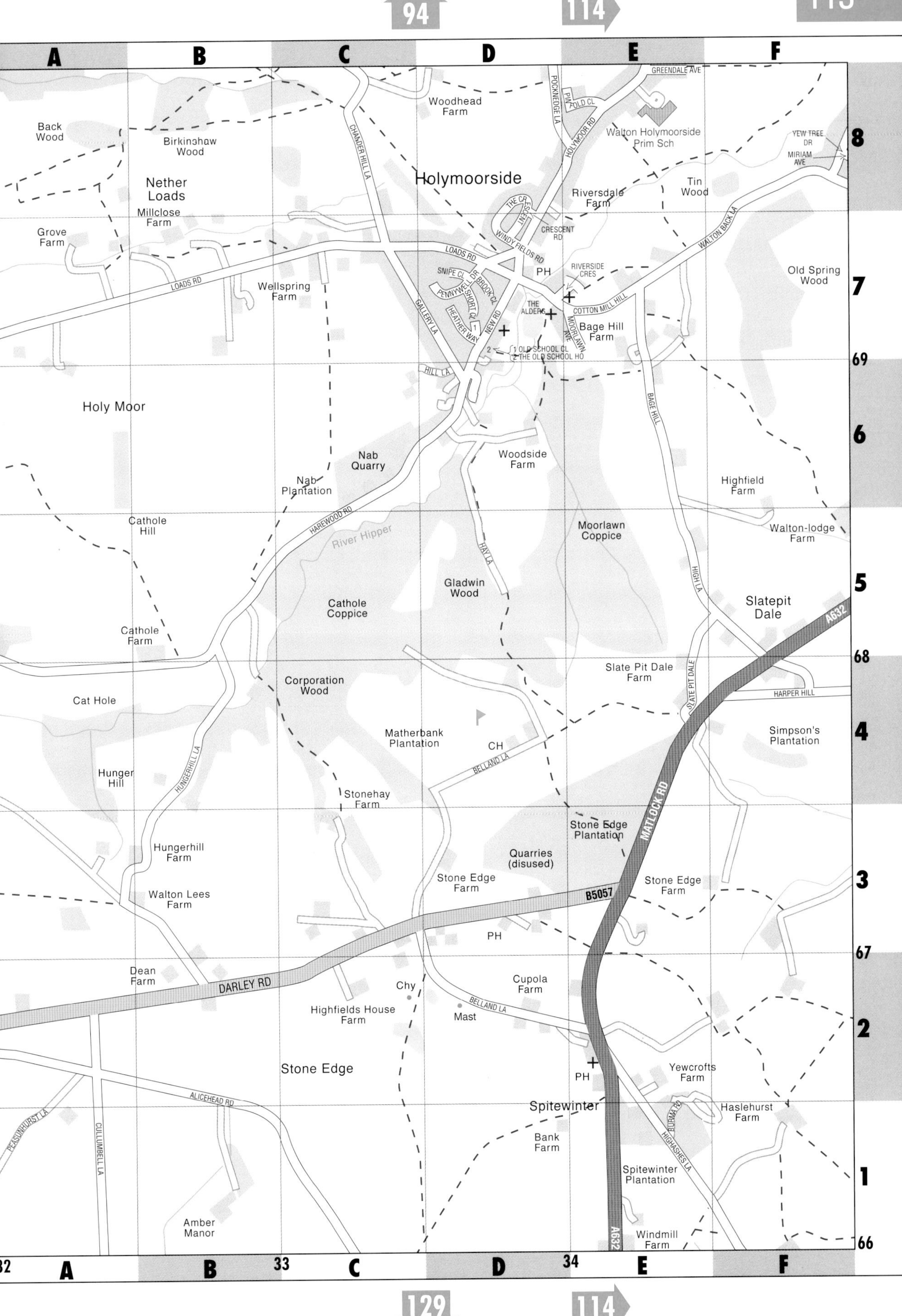

A B C D E F

8

GREENDALE AVE

Back
Wood

Birkinshaw
Wood

Woodhead
Farm

POLD CL

Walton Holymoorside
Prim Sch

YEW TREE
DR

Nether
Loads

Millclose
Farm

HOLY MOOR RD

POCKNEDGE LA

MIRIAM
AVE

Holymoorside

Riversdale
Farm

Tin
Wood

Old Spring
Wood

7

Grove
Farm

CHANDER HILL LA

LOADS RD

Wellspring
Farm

Snipe Cl

DE BROOK CL

SHORT CL

PENNYWELL

GALLERY LA

HEATHER WAY

LOADS RD

WINDY FIELDS RD

THE CRESCENT

CRESCENT
RD

PH

THE
ALDERN

Bage Hill
Farm

COTTON MILL HILL

MOORLAWN

MOOR LANE

RIVERSIDE
CRES

WALTON BACK LA

69

HILL LA

HEY RD

1 OLD SCHOOL CL
2 THE OLD SCHOOL HO

Holy Moor

Nab
Quarry

Nab
Plantation

Woodside
Farm

Moorlawn
Coppice

BAGE HILL

Highfield
Farm

Walton-lodge
Farm

6

Cathole
Hill

HAREWOOD RD

River Hipper

HAY LA

Gladwin
Wood

Moorlawn
Coppice

HIGH LA

Slatepit
Dale

A632

5

Cathole
Farm

Cathole
Coppice

Slate Pit Dale
Farm

68

Cat Hole

HUNGERHILL LA

Corporation
Wood

Matherbank
Plantation

CH

BELLAND LA

Stone Edge
Plantation

SLATE PIT DALE

MATLOCK RD

HARPER HILL

Simpson's
Plantation

4

Hunger
Hill

Hungerhill
Farm

Walton Lees
Farm

Stonehay
Farm

Quarries
(disused)

Stone Edge
Farm

B5057

Stone Edge
Farm

3

67

Dean
Farm

DARLEY RD

Highfields House
Farm

Chy

Mast

BELLAND LA

Cupola
Farm

PH

2

Stone Edge

ALICEHEAD RD

PH

Spitewinter

Yewcrofts
Farm

Haslehurst
Farm

PERKINHURST LA

CULLUMBELL LA

Amber
Manor

Bank
Farm

HIGHASHES LA

BUBNAB RD

Spitewinter
Plantation

A632

Windmill
Farm

1

66

32 A B 33 C D 34 E F

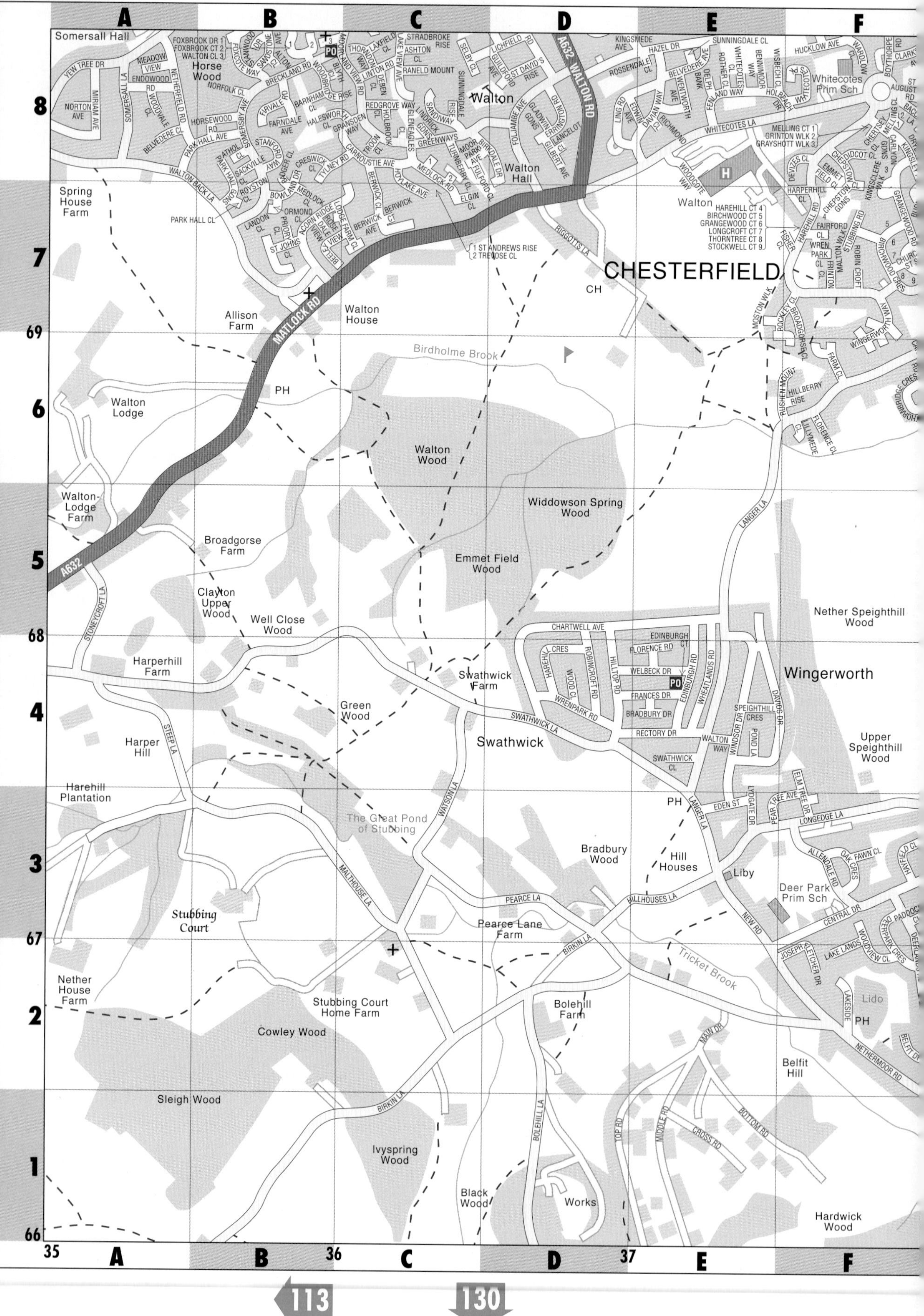

Somersall Hall

FOXBROOK DR 1
FOXBROOK CT 2
WALTON CL 3

Horse Wood

Walton

Walton Hall

Kingsmede

Whitecotes Prim Sch

Walton

HAREHILL CT 4
BIRCHWOOD CT 5
GRANGEWOOD CT 6
LONGCROFT CT 7
THORNTREE CT 8
STOCKWELL CT 9

Spring House Farm

Allison Farm

Walton House

Birdholme Brook

CHESTERFIELD

CH

PH

Walton Lodge

Walton Wood

Widdowson Spring Wood

Nether Speighthill Wood

Walton Lodge Farm

Broadgorse Farm

Emmet Field Wood

Clayton Upper Wood

Well Close Wood

Wingerworth

CHARTWELL AVE

Edinburgh

Nether Speighthill Wood

Harperhill Farm

Swathwick Farm

Green Wood

Upper Speighthill Wood

Harper Hill

Swathwick

Harehill Plantation

The Great Pond of Stubbing

PH

Bradbury Wood

Hill Houses

Liby

Deer Park Prim Sch

Stubbing Court

Pearce Lane Farm

Tricket Brook

Nether House Farm

Stubbing Court Home Farm

Bolehill Farm

Lido
PH

Cowley Wood

Belfit Hill

Sleigh Wood

Ivyspring Wood

Black Wood

Works

Hardwick Wood

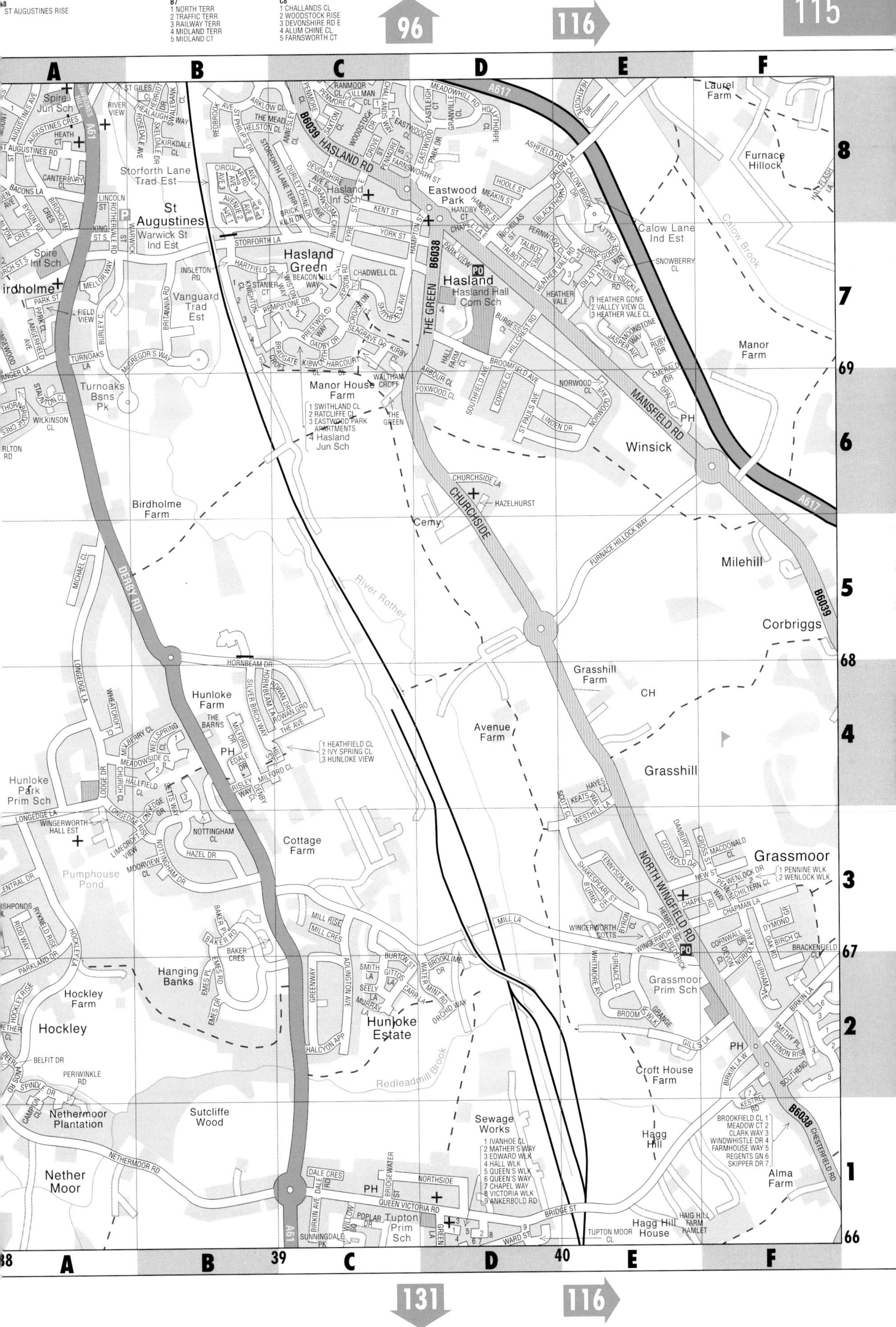

115
97

A B C D E F

8

7

69

6

5

68

4

3

67

2

1

66

Nether House Farm

HALL FLASH LA
CALOW LA

Calow Green

Calowgreen Farm

BACK LA

MOOR LA

B6425

Spoil Heap

Sutton Lane Farm

SUTTON LA

Bull Paddock Farm

Woodnook Farm

Calow Brook

HASSOCKY LA

Sutton Springs Wood

SUTTON SPRING WOOD

Hall Farm

ROCK LA

Yewtree Farm

A617

RAILWAY COTTS

Hill Farm

B6425

B6039

Muster Brook

Springwood Farm

SHIRE LA

Temple Normanton Bsns Pk

Bond's Main

MANSFIELD RD

SPRINGWOOD ST
ELM ST

Temple Normanton Prim Sch

POSTMANS LA

High House Farm

Grassmoor Country Park

MILL LA

SUTTON VIEW

P

Cemy

+

CHURCH LA

Temple Normanton

Musterbrook Bridge

Mansfield Road

A617

BIRKIN LA

CHURCH FARM MEWS

Philadelphia

67

CLARK WAY

CHESTERFIELD RD

Five Pits Trail

Williamthorpe Pends

MOORLAND DR
SLACK LA
LILAC CL

MEADOW CT

FARMHOUSE WAY

Lings Farm

High Top Poultry Farm

WILLIAMS WAY

Holmewood Bsns Pk

Williamthorpe Ind Pk

Enterprise Dr

UPTON WAY

WOODSOME PK

MOORE CL

Sewage Works

Holmewood Ind Pk

GORSE BANK

HEATHER CL
BRACKEN CL
BRAMBLE AVE

Heat Prim Sch

CHESTERFIELD RD

B6038

P

COLLIERY CT 1
BLUEBERRY CT 2
POPPY CT 3
KESTREL CT 4

FIELD LA

B6039

SNELLEY

SHAW ST
TENNYSON
LAWRENCE

HESTER WATERS

DICKENS DR

PARK RD

Pavilion Workshops

Works

WOOD ST

DUKES CL
HUNLOKE RD

QUEENS WLK

CAVENDISH

DEVONSHIRE TERR
QUEENSWAY

Holmewood

RAILWAY COTTS

A6175

HARDWICK VIEW RD

Holmewoo Ind Est

ASTWITH CL

HIGH
SANDBY

SHAKESPEARE ST
MASEFIELD AVE

COMPTON ST

FERN CT
AVE

41 42 43

A B C D E F

D1
1 POETG CL
2 ROSEBUD WAY
E1
1 MASEFIELD PL
2 COLLIERS WAY

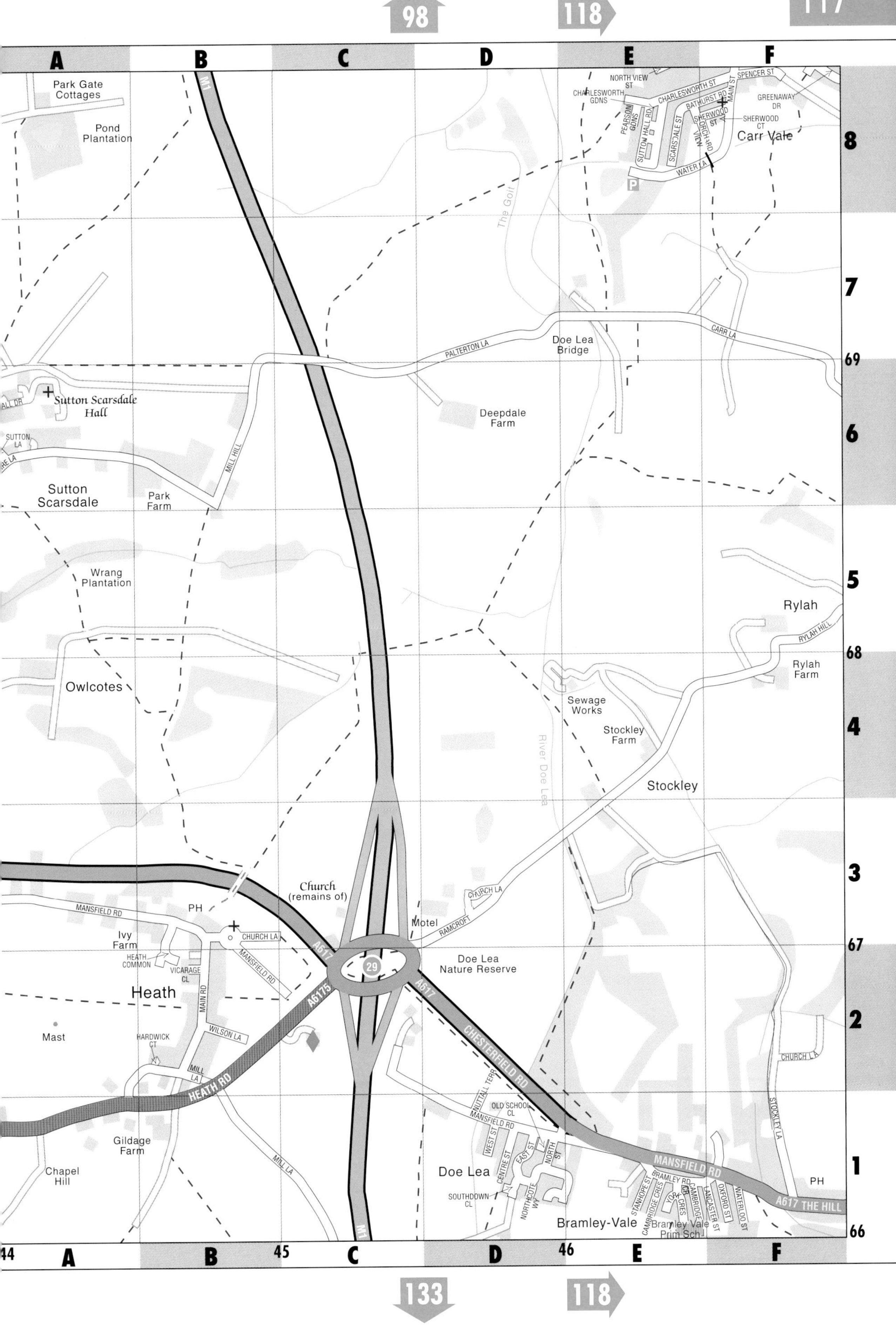

A B C D E F

8
7
69
6
5
68
4
3
67
2
1
66

Park Gate Cottages

Pond Plantation

NORTH VIEW ST
CHARLESWORTH GDNS
CHARLESWORTH ST
SPENCER ST
GREENAWAY DR
PEARSON GDNS
SUTTON HALL RD
SCARSDALE ST
BATHURST RD
SHERWOOD ST
MAIN ST
SHERWOOD CT
WATER LA
Carr Vale

P

The Golf

PALTERTON LA
Doe Lea Bridge
CARR LA

Sutton Scarsdale Hall

HALL DR

SUTTON LA
Deepdale Farm

Sutton Scarsdale

Park Farm

MILL HILL

Wrang Plantation

Rylah

RYLAH HILL

Owlcotes

Rylah Farm

Sewage Works

Stockley Farm

River Doe Lea

Stockley

Church (remains of)

MANSFIELD RD
PH
CHURCH LA
CHURCH LA
Motel
RAMCROFT
Doe Lea Nature Reserve

Ivy Farm
HEATH COMMON
VICARAGE CL
CHURCH LA
MANSFIELD RD
29

Heath

Mast
HARDWICK CT
MAIN RD
WILSON LA
A6175
A617

MILL LA
HEATH RD
CHESTERFIELD RD
CHURCH LA
STOCKLEY LA

Gildage Farm

MN LA

MANSFIELD RD
NUTTALL TERR
OLD SCHOOL CL
WEST ST
POST ST
NORTH ST
CENTRE ST
Doe Lea
SOUTHDOWN CL
NORTHCOTE WY
Bramley-Vale
STANHOPE ST
CAMBRIDGE CRES
BRAMLEY RD
YORK CRES
OXFORD RD
CAMBRIDGE ST
LANCASTER ST
WATERLOO ST
MANSFIELD RD
PH
A617 THE HILL
Bramley Vale Prim Sch

Chapel Hill

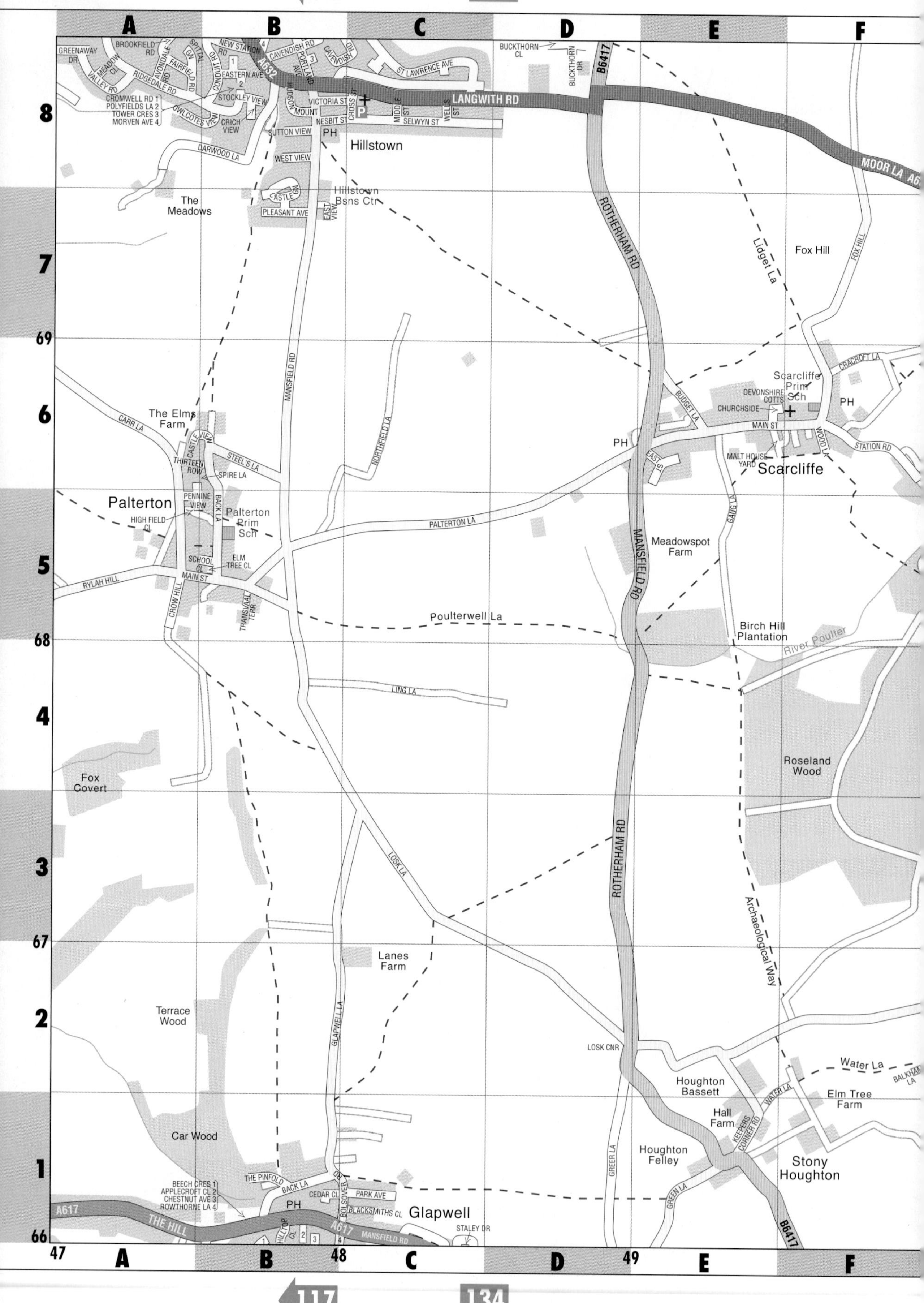

Hillstown

Palterton

Scarcliffe

Glapwell

Stony Houghton

Houghton Bassett

Houghton Felley

The Meadows

The Elms Farm

Meadowspot Farm

Birch Hill Plantation

Roseland Wood

Fox Hill

Fox Covert

Terrace Wood

Car Wood

Lanes Farm

Scarcliffe Prim Sch

Palterton Prim Sch

Hall Farm

Elm Tree Farm

River Poulter

Archaeological Way

ROTHERHAM RD

MANSFIELD RD

LANGWITH RD

MOOR LA A6

B6417

A617

THE HILL

100
120

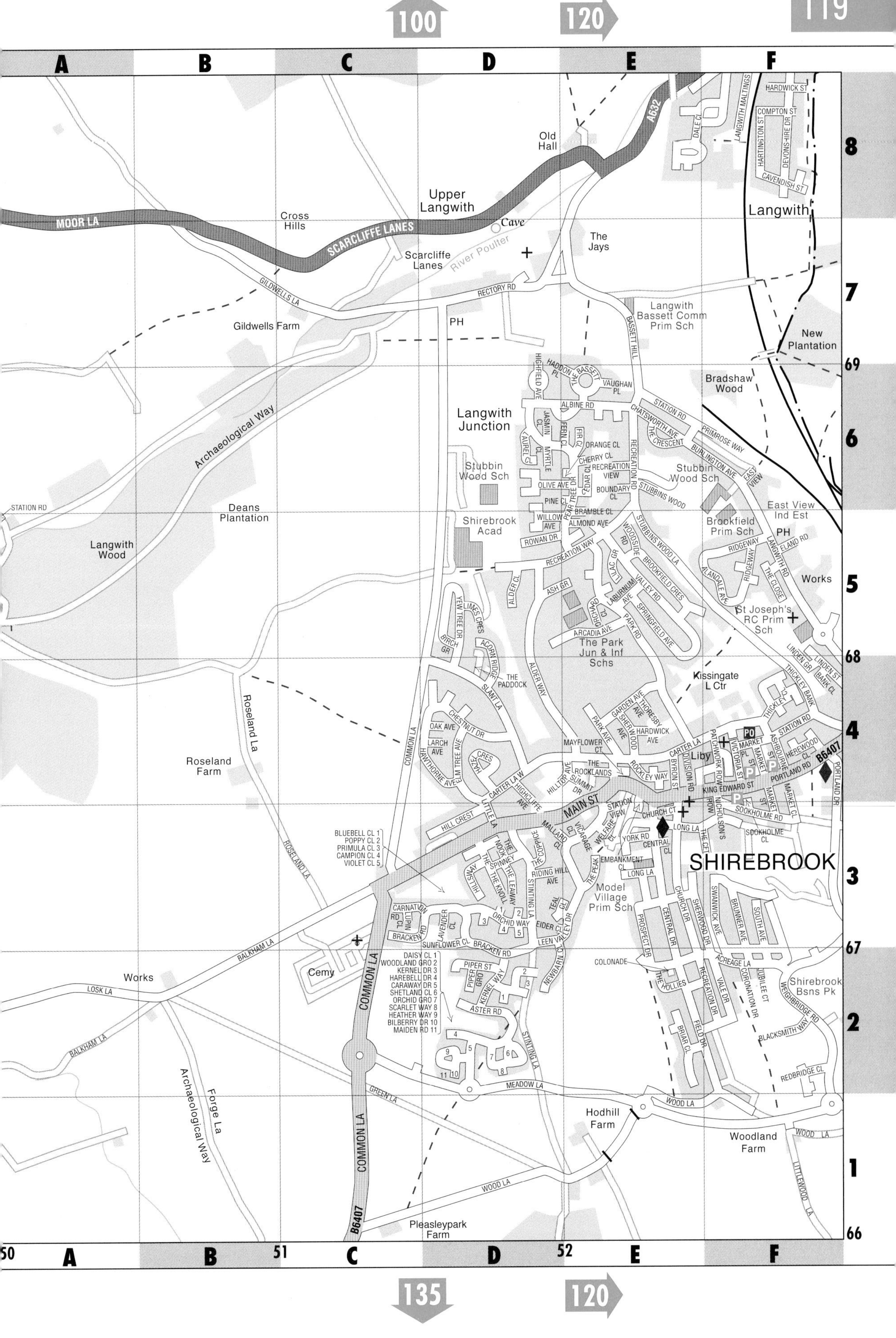
A
B
C
D
E
F
8
7
69
6
5
68
4
3
67
2
1
66
50
51
52
Old Hall
A632
Upper Langwith
MOOR LA
Cross Hills
SCARCLIFFE LANES
Cave
River Poulter
Scarcliffe Lanes
The Jays
Langwith
HARDWICK ST
COMPTON ST
HARTINGTON ST
DEVONSHIRE DR
CAVENDISH ST
LANGWITH MALTINGS
DALE CL
GILDWELLS LA
RECTORY RD
Gildwells Farm
PH
Langwith Bassett Comm Prim Sch
BASSETT HILL
New Plantation
Bradshaw Wood
HADDON PL
THE BASSETT
VAUGHAN PL
HIGHFIELD AVE
ALBINE RD
STATION RD
CHATSWORTH AVE
THE CRESCENT
PRIMROSE WAY
BURLINGTON AVE
EAST VIEW
Langwith Junction
Archaeological Way
JASMIN CL
FERN CL
FIR CL
ORANGE CL
CHERRY CL
RECREATION VIEW
RECREATION RD
LAUREL CL
MYRTLE CL
Stubbin Wood Sch
OLIVE AVE
CEDAR CL
PEAR TREE DR
BOUNDARY CL
STUBBINS WOOD
PINE CL
BRAMBLE CL
WILLOW AVE
ALMOND AVE
East View Ind Est
Brookfield Prim Sch
STATION RD
Deans Plantation
Shirebrook Acad
ROWAN DR
RECREATION WAY
WOODSIDE RD
STUBBINS WOOD LA
BROOKFIELD CRES
RIDGEWAY
LANGWITH RD
ELAND RD
PH
Langwith Wood
ALDER CL
LILAC GR
LABURNUM AVE
VALLEY RD
ALANDALE AVE
THE CLOSE
Works
ASH GR
ORCHARD CL
SPRINGFIELD AVE
St Joseph's RC Prim Sch
YEW TREE DR
LIMES CRES
ARCADIA AVE
PARK RD
BIRCH GR
ACORN RIDGE
The Park Jun & Inf Schs
LINDEN GR
LINDEN ST
BANK CL
THICKLEY BANK
THE PADDOCK
ALDER WAY
Kissingate L Ctr
SLANT LA
THICKLEY CL
Roseland La
CHESTNUT DR
GARDEN AVE
THORESBY AVE
SHERWOOD AVE
PARK AVE
HARDWICK AVE
STATION RD
PO
OAK AVE
COMMON LA
LARCH AVE
MAYFLOWER CT
CARTER LA
PATCHWORK ROW
MARKET PL
ASHBOURNE ST
HEREWOOD CL
B6407
Roseland Farm
HAWTHORNE AVE
ELM TREE AVE
HAZEL CRES
THE ROCKLANDS
ROCKLEY WAY
BYRON ST
DIVISION RD
Liby
VICTORIA ST
MARKET ST
PORTLAND RD
PORTLAND DR
CARTER LA W
HIGHCLIFFE AVE
HILLTOP AVE
SUMMIT DR
KING EDWARD ST
NICHOLSON'S ROW
SOOKHOLME RD
MARKET CL
P
HILL CREST
LITTLE LA
MAIN ST
STATION VIEW
CHURCH CT
LONG LA
SOOKHOLME CL
BLUEBELL CL 1
POPPY CL 2
PRIMULA CL 3
CAMPION CL 4
VIOLET CL 5
ROSELAND LA
THE NOOK
THE COPPICE
MALLARD CL
VICARAGE CL
WELFARE CL
YORK RD
CENTRAL CL
THE CROFT
SHIREBROOK
HILLSWAY
THE SPINNEY
THE KNOLL
THE LEAWAY
RIDING HILL AVE
THE PEAK
EMBANKMENT CL
LONG LA
STINTING LA
TEAL CL
Model Village Prim Sch
CHURCH DR
SHERWOOD DR
SWANWICK AVE
BRUNNER AVE
SOUTH AVE
CARNATION RD
LUPIN CL
LAVENDER CL
ORCHID WAY
EIDER CL
BRACKEN RD
SUNFLOWER CL
BRACKEN RD
LEEN VALLEY DR
CENTRAL DR
PROSPECT DR
NEWBARN CL
ACREAGE LA
BALKHAM LA
DAISY CL 1
WOODLAND GRO 2
KERNEL DR 3
HAREBELL DR 4
CARAWAY DR 5
SHETLAND CL 6
ORCHID GRO 7
SCARLET WAY 8
HEATHER WAY 9
BILBERRY DR 10
MAIDEN RD 11
COLONADE
THE COLLIES
Shirebrook Bsns Pk
Works
Cemy
PIPER ST
PIPER GRO
KERNEL WAY
RECREATION DR
VALE DR
CORONATION DR
JUBILEE CT
WEIGHBRIDGE RD
LOSK LA
COMMON LA
ASTER RD
BRIAR CL
FIELD DR
BLACKSMITH WAY
BALKHAM LA
STINTING LA
REDBRIDGE CL
GREEN LA
MEADOW LA
WOOD LA
Hodhill Farm
Archaeological Way
Forge La
Woodland Farm
WOOD LA
COMMON LA
LITTLEWOOD LA
WOOD LA
B6407
Pleasleypark Farm

135
120

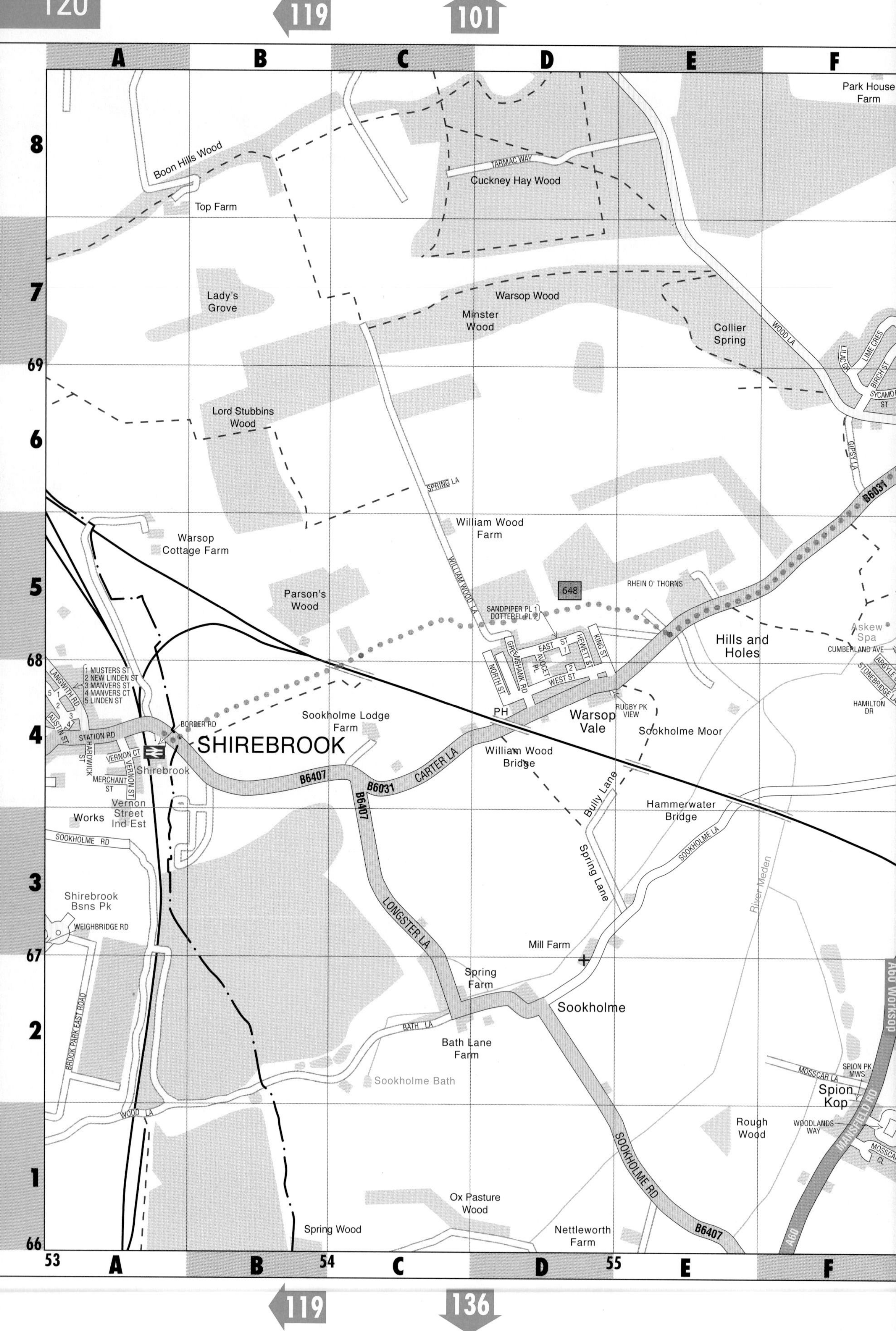

A　　B　　C　　D　　E　　F

8

Park House Farm

Boon Hills Wood

TARMAC WAY

Cuckney Hay Wood

Top Farm

7

Warsop Wood

Lady's Grove

Minster Wood

Collier Spring

WOOD LA

LIME CRES

LLWDR

69

BIRCH ST

SYCAMO

ST

Lord Stubbins Wood

6

GIPSY LA

B6031

SPRING LA

William Wood Farm

5

Warsop Cottage Farm

WILLIAM WOOD LA

648

RHEIN O' THORNS

Askew Spa

Parson's Wood

SANDPIPER PL

DOTTEREL PL

Hills and Holes

CUMBERLAND AVE

ARGYLE

STONEBRIDGE

68

EAST ST

HEWETT ST

KING ST

HAMILTON DR

GROVEHAVEN RD

NORTH ST

ADGET PL

1 MUSTERS ST
2 NEW LINDEN ST
3 MANVERS ST
4 MANVERS CT
5 LINDEN ST

WEST ST

LANGWITH RD

AUSTIN ST

BORDER RD

Sookholme Lodge Farm

PH

Warsop Vale

RUGBY PK VIEW

Sookholme Moor

4

STATION RD

HARDWICK ST

VERNON CT

VERNON ST

SHIREBROOK

Shirebrook

William Wood Bridge

CARTER LA

Bully Lane

Hammerwater Bridge

SOOKHOLME LA

MERCHANT ST

Vernon Street Ind Est

Works

B6407

B6031

B6407

Spring Lane

River Meden

SOOKHOLME RD

3

Shirebrook Bsns Pk

WEIGHBRIDGE RD

LONGSTER LA

Mill Farm

67

Spring Farm

Sookholme

A60 Worksop

2

BATH LA

Bath Lane Farm

MOSSCAR LA

Spion Pk MWS

SPION PK

BROOK PARK EAST ROAD

Sookholme Bath

Spion Kop

WOODLANDS WAY

WOOD LA

Rough Wood

MOSSCAR CL

MANSFIELD RD

A60

1

Ox Pasture Wood

Spring Wood

Nettleworth Farm

B6407

66

53　　A　　B　　54　　C　　D　　55　　E　　F

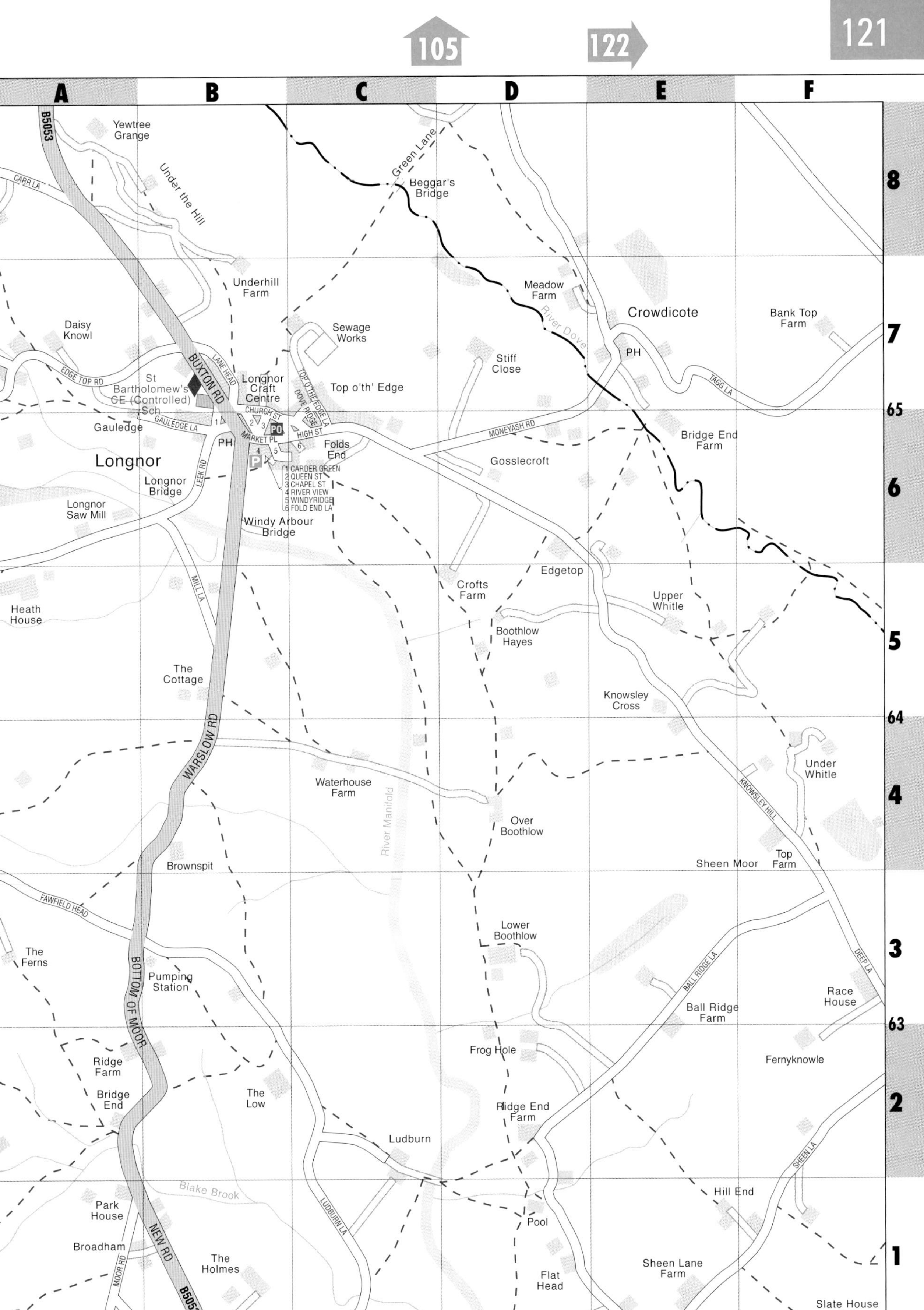

A   B   C   D   E   F

8

B5053

Yewtree Grange

Under the Hill

CARR LA

Green Lane

Beggar's Bridge

7

Daisy Knowl

Underhill Farm

Meadow Farm

River Dove

Crowdicote

PH

Bank Top Farm

EDGE TOP RD

St Bartholomew's CE (Controlled) Sch

BUXTON RD

LANE HEAD

Longnor Craft Centre

Sewage Works

Stiff Close

65

Gauledge

GAULEDGE LA

CHURCH ST

Top o'th' Edge

TOP O'TH EDGE LA

DOVE RIDGE LA

MONEYASH RD

Bridge End Farm

Longnor

PH

MARKET PL

HIGH ST

Folds End

Gosslecroft

TAGG LA

6

LEEK RD

1 CARDER GREEN
2 QUEEN ST
3 CHAPEL ST
4 RIVER VIEW
5 WINDYRIDGE
6 FOLD END LA

Longnor Saw Mill

Longnor Bridge

Windy Arbour Bridge

Crofts Farm

Edgetop

Upper Whitle

Heath House

MILL LA

The Cottage

Boothlow Hayes

5

Knowsley Cross

64

WARSLOW RD

Waterhouse Farm

River Manifold

Over Boothlow

KNOWSLEY HILL

Under Whitle

4

Brownspit

Sheen Moor

Top Farm

FAWFIELD HEAD

Lower Boothlow

BALL RIDGE LA

DEEP LA

3

The Ferns

BOTTOM OF MOOR

Pumping Station

Ball Ridge Farm

Race House

63

Ridge Farm

Frog Hole

Fernyknowle

Bridge End

The Low

Ridge End Farm

2

Ludburn

Park House

Blake Brook

LUDBURN LA

SHEEN LA

Hill End

Broadham

NEW RD

The Holmes

B5053

Pool

Flat Head

Sheen Lane Farm

1

Slate House Farm

62

MOOR RD

SCHOOL LA

08   A   B   09   C   D   10   E   F

122

121
106

A B C D E F
8
7
65
6
5
64
4
3
63
2
1
62
Sparklow
TAGG LA
B5055
A515
Endmoor
68
Needham Grange
Cronkston Grange
High Needham
Mines (dis)
ASHBOURNE RD
Middle Street Farm
Clemonseats Plantation
Cronkston Lodge
549
Waggon Low
Mine (dis)
Midshires Way
Cotesfield Farm
Mosey Low
Custard Field Farm
Pilsbury Castle Hills
Pilsbury Lodge
Sand Pit
Pilsbury
Broadmeadow Hall
River Dove
Vincent House
Parks Barn
SHEEN LA
Mines (dis)
Sheen Hill
Carder Low
Long Dale
High Sheen Farm
DEEP LA
Ludwell Farm
HIDE LA
Harris Close
Mines (dis)
11 A B 12 C D 13 E F

121
137

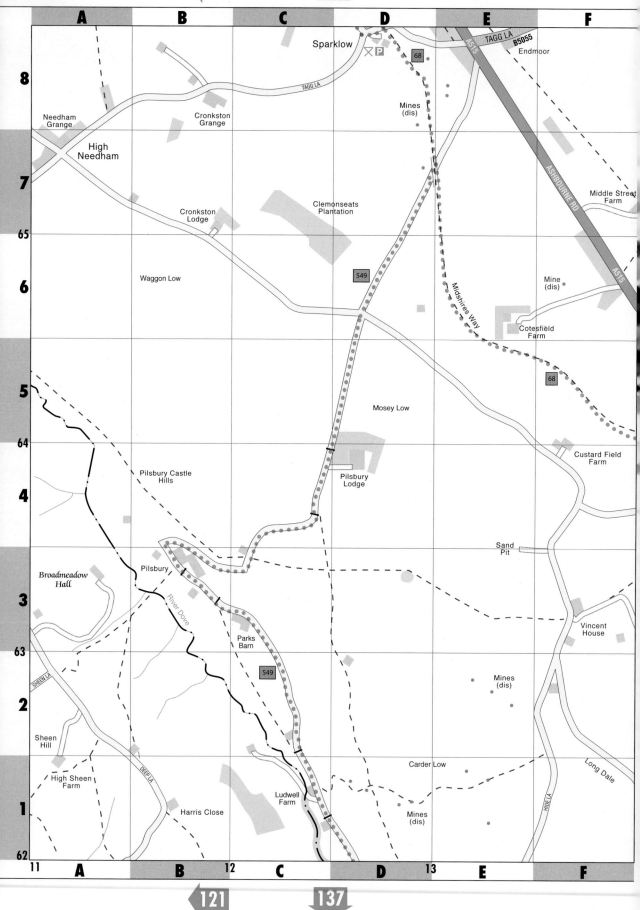

107
124

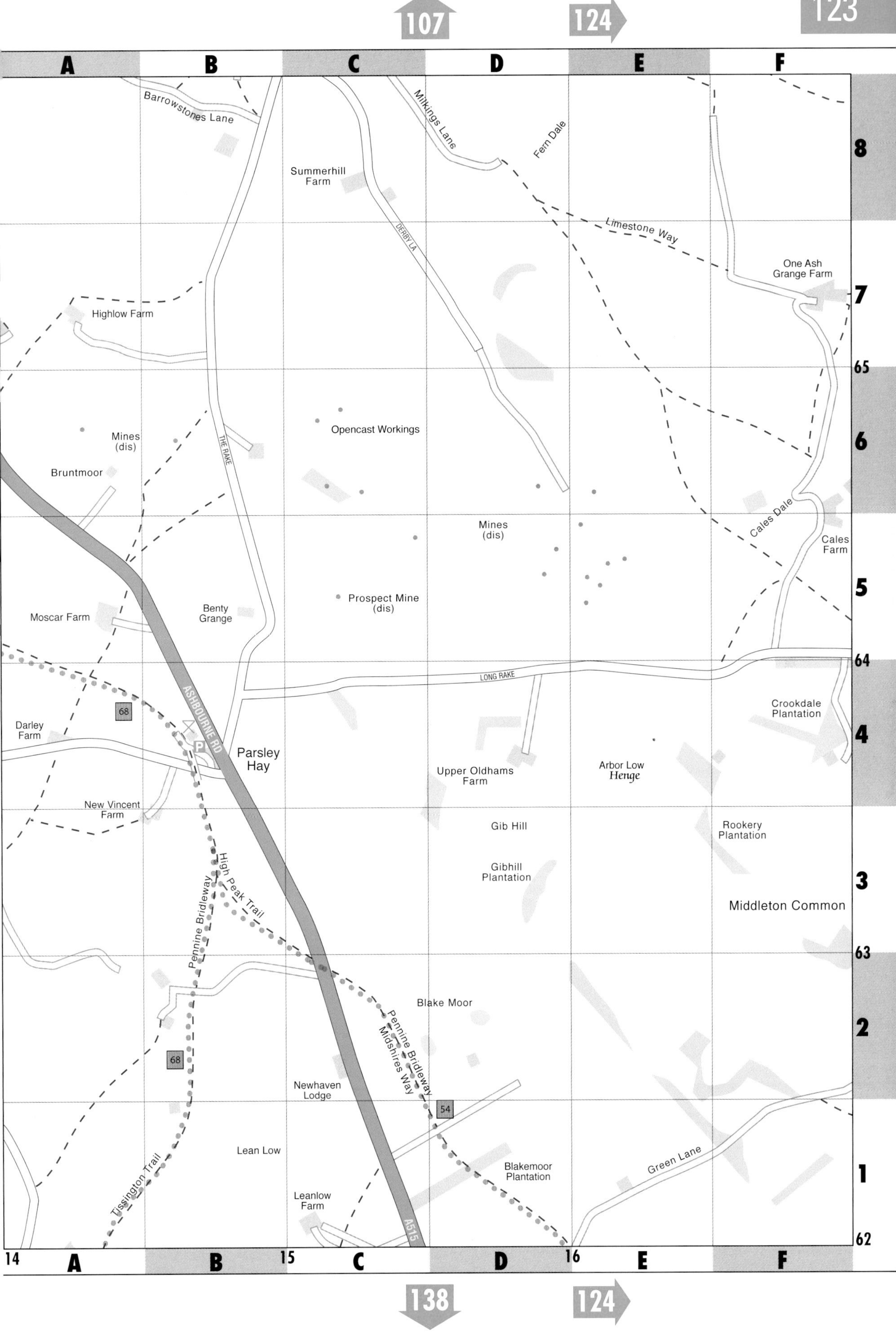
A
B
C
D
E
F
Barrowstones Lane
Milkings Lane
Fern Dale
Summerhill Farm
Limestone Way
DERBY LA
One Ash Grange Farm
Highlow Farm
Mines (dis)
Opencast Workings
Bruntmoor
THE RAKE
Cales Dale
Mines (dis)
Cales Farm
Prospect Mine (dis)
Moscar Farm
Benty Grange
LONG RAKE
ASHBOURNE RD
68
Darley Farm
Parsley Hay
Crookdale Plantation
Upper Oldhams Farm
Arbor Low
Henge
New Vincent Farm
Gib Hill
Rookery Plantation
High Peak Trail
Gibhill Plantation
Middleton Common
Pennine Bridleway
Blake Moor
Pennine Bridleway
Midshires Way
68
Newhaven Lodge
54
Lean Low
Blakemoor Plantation
Green Lane
Tissington Trail
Leanlow Farm
A515
8
7
65
6
5
64
4
3
63
2
1
62
14
15
16

138
124

123
108

A **B** **C** **D** **E** **F**

Palmerston Wood

River Lathkill

Meadow Place
Wood

8

Lathkill Dale

Low Wood

Derbyshire Dales
National Nature
Reserve

Mines
(dis)

Calling Low
Dale

Bee Low Wood

7

Cales Dale

Calling Low

65

Limestone Way

BACK LA

6

Bee Low

Low Moor
Plantation

MOOR LA

P

CALLIN LOW

Mine

Mines
(dis)

5

LONG RAKE

Works

Lomberdale
Hall

64

Crossflat
Plantation

4

River Bradford

Castle
Farm

Greenseats
Plantation

Flax Dale

Middleton

Castle
(remains of)

3

Middleton Common

FRIDEN RD

Bushey
Wood

DALE RD

THE SQUARE

THE PINFOLD

Thorntree

RAKE LA

Rake
Wood

Middleton
Hall

63

Mere Farm

WEADOW LA

2

Green Lane

WHITFIELD LA

Woodside
Farm

1

Kenslow
Farm

Kenslow
Wood

62

Little Rookery
Plantation

17 **A** **B** **18** **C** **D** **19** **E** **F**

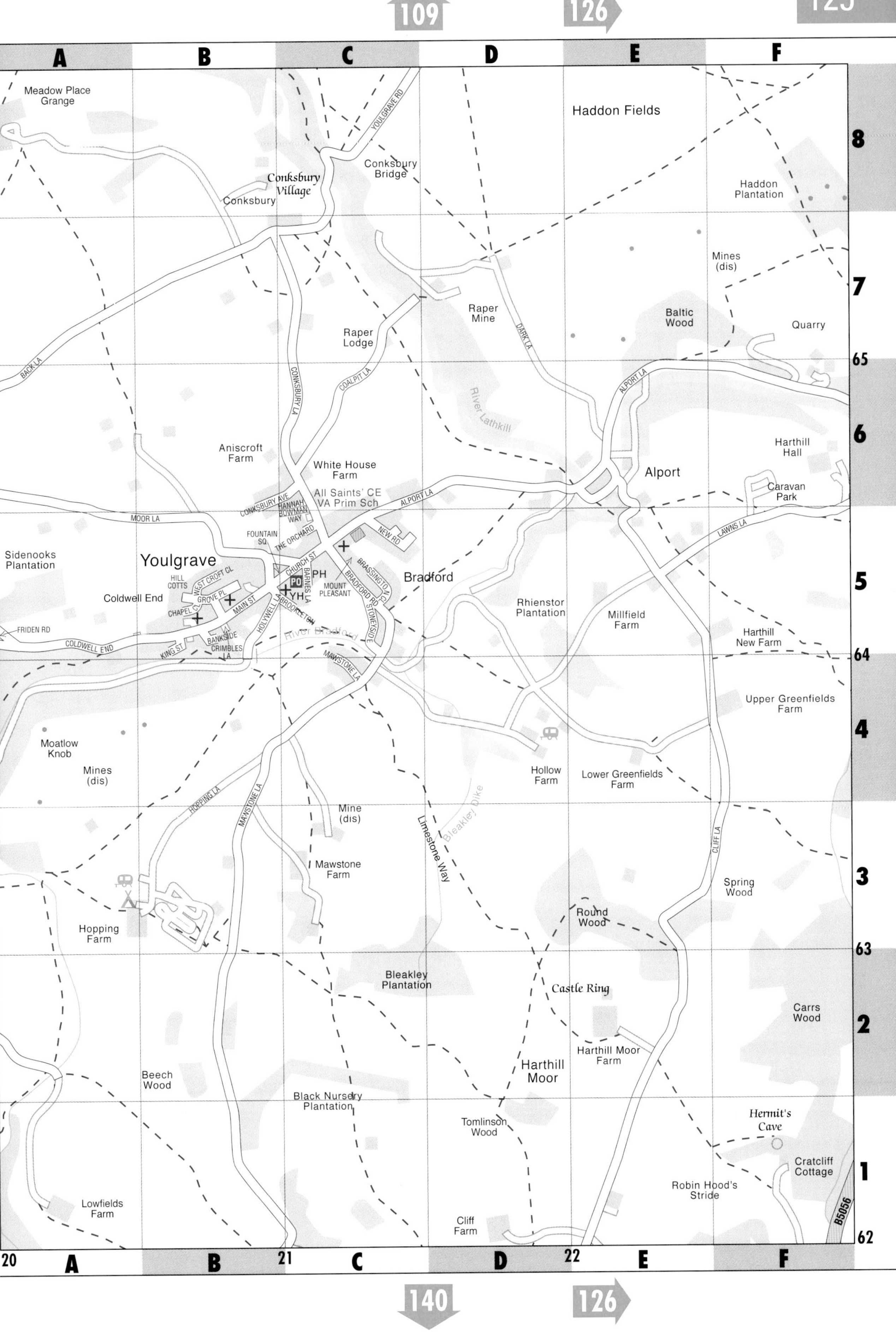

Meadow Place Grange

Haddon Fields

Conksbury Village
Conksbury Bridge
Conksbury

Haddon Plantation

Mines (dis)

Raper Mine

Baltic Wood

Quarry

Raper Lodge

65

BACK LA

River Lathkill

Harthill Hall

6

Aniscroft Farm

White House Farm

Alport

Caravan Park

All Saints' CE VA Prim Sch

MOOR LA

Sidenooks Plantation

Youlgrave

Bradford

LAWNS LA

HILL COTTS
WEST CROFT CL
Coldwell End
GROVE PL
CHAPEL
MAIN ST
BANKSIDE
CRIMBLES LA
KING ST
Mount Pleasant

Rhienstor Plantation

Millfield Farm

Harthill New Farm

5

FRIDEN RD

COLDWELL END

River Bradford

MAWSTONE LA

64

Upper Greenfields Farm

4

Moatlow Knob

Mines (dis)

Hollow Farm

Lower Greenfields Farm

HOPPING LA

MAWSTONE LA

Mine (dis)

Limestone Way

Bleakley Dike

CLIFF LA

Spring Wood

3

Mawstone Farm

Round Wood

63

Hopping Farm

Bleakley Plantation

Castle Ring

Carrs Wood

2

Beech Wood

Harthill Moor Farm

Harthill Moor

Black Nursery Plantation

Tomlinson Wood

Hermit's Cave

Cratcliff Cottage

1

Lowfields Farm

Robin Hood's Stride

B5056

Cliff Farm

62

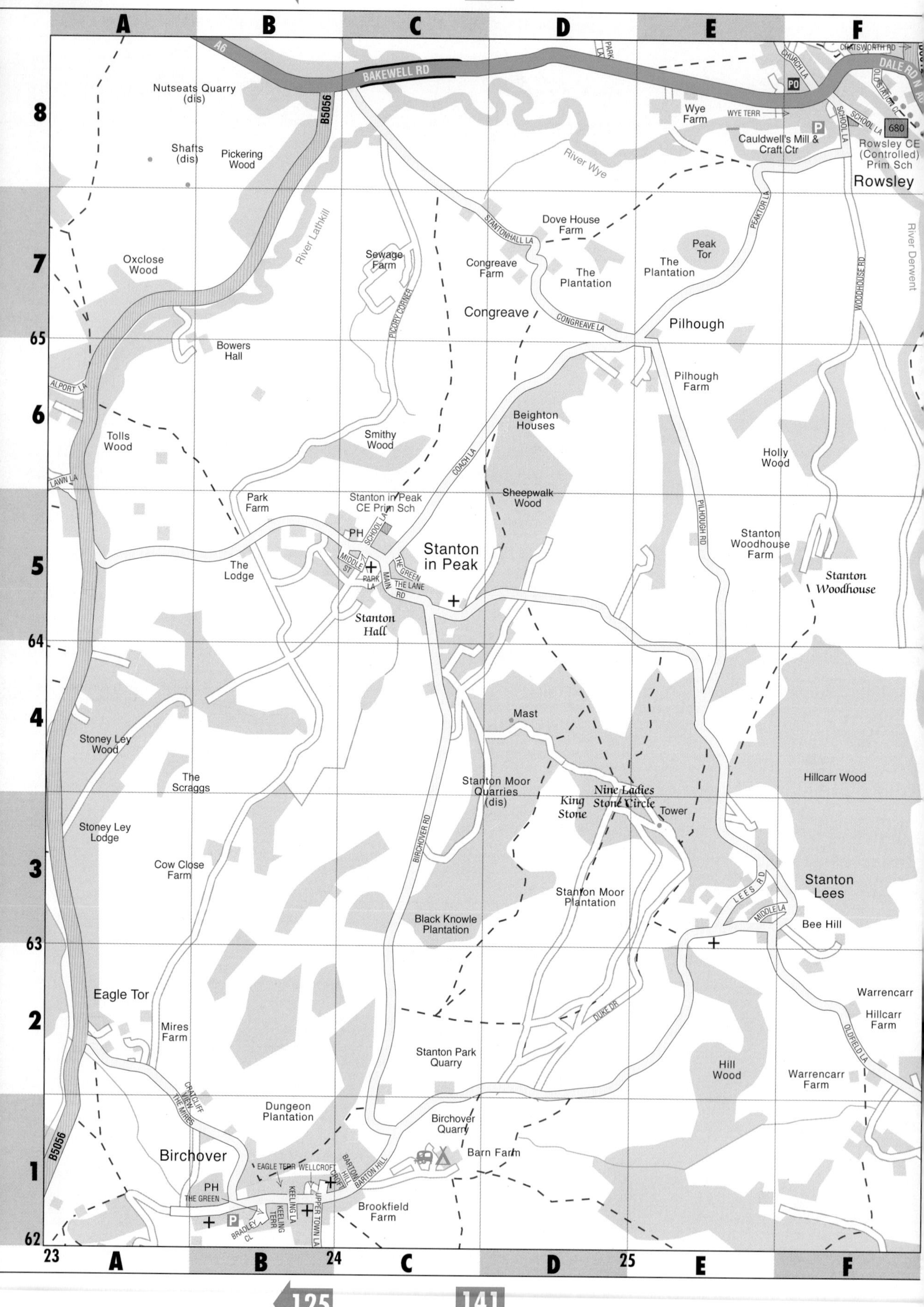

125
110

A6

BAKEWELL RD

B5056

Nutseats Quarry (dis)

Shafts (dis)

Pickering Wood

Wye Farm

WYE TERR

PO

Cauldwell's Mill & Craft Ctr

P

CHATSWORTH RD

CHURCHILL LA

OLD STATION CL

DALE RD N

SCHOOL LA

Rowsley CE (Controlled) Prim Sch

680

SCHOOL LA

Rowsley

River Wye

River Derwent

WOODHOUSE RD

Oxclose Wood

River Lathkill

Sewage Farm

PICORY CORNER

STANTONHALL LA

Dove House Farm

Congreave Farm

Congreave

The Plantation

CONGREAVE LA

Peak Tor

The Plantation

Pilhough

PEAKTOR LA

Bowers Hall

Smithy Wood

Beighton Houses

Pilhough Farm

Holly Wood

ALPORT LA

Tolls Wood

Park Farm

Stanton in Peak CE Prim Sch

COACH LA

Sheepwalk Wood

PILHOUGH RD

Stanton Woodhouse Farm

LAWN LA

PH

MIDDLE ST

SCHOOL LA

PARK LA

THE GREEN

MAIN RD

Stanton in Peak

Stanton Woodhouse

The Lodge

THE LANE

Stanton Hall

Stoney Ley Wood

Mast

Hillcarr Wood

The Scraggs

Stanton Moor Quarries (dis)

King Stone

Nine Ladies Stone Circle

Tower

Stanton Lees

Stoney Ley Lodge

BIRCHOVER RD

LEES RD

MIDDLE LA

Cow Close Farm

Stanton Moor Plantation

Bee Hill

Black Knowle Plantation

Eagle Tor

Warrencarr

Mires Farm

DUKE DR

Stanton Park Quarry

Hill Wood

Hillcarr Farm

B5056

CANCLIF

THE MIRES

Dungeon Plantation

Birchover Quarry

OLDFIELD LA

Warrencarr Farm

Birchover

EAGLE TERR

WELLCROFT

BARTON HILL

Barton Hill

Barn Farm

PH

THE GREEN

KEELING LA

KEELING TERR

UPPER TOWN LA

P

BRADLEY CL

Brookfield Farm

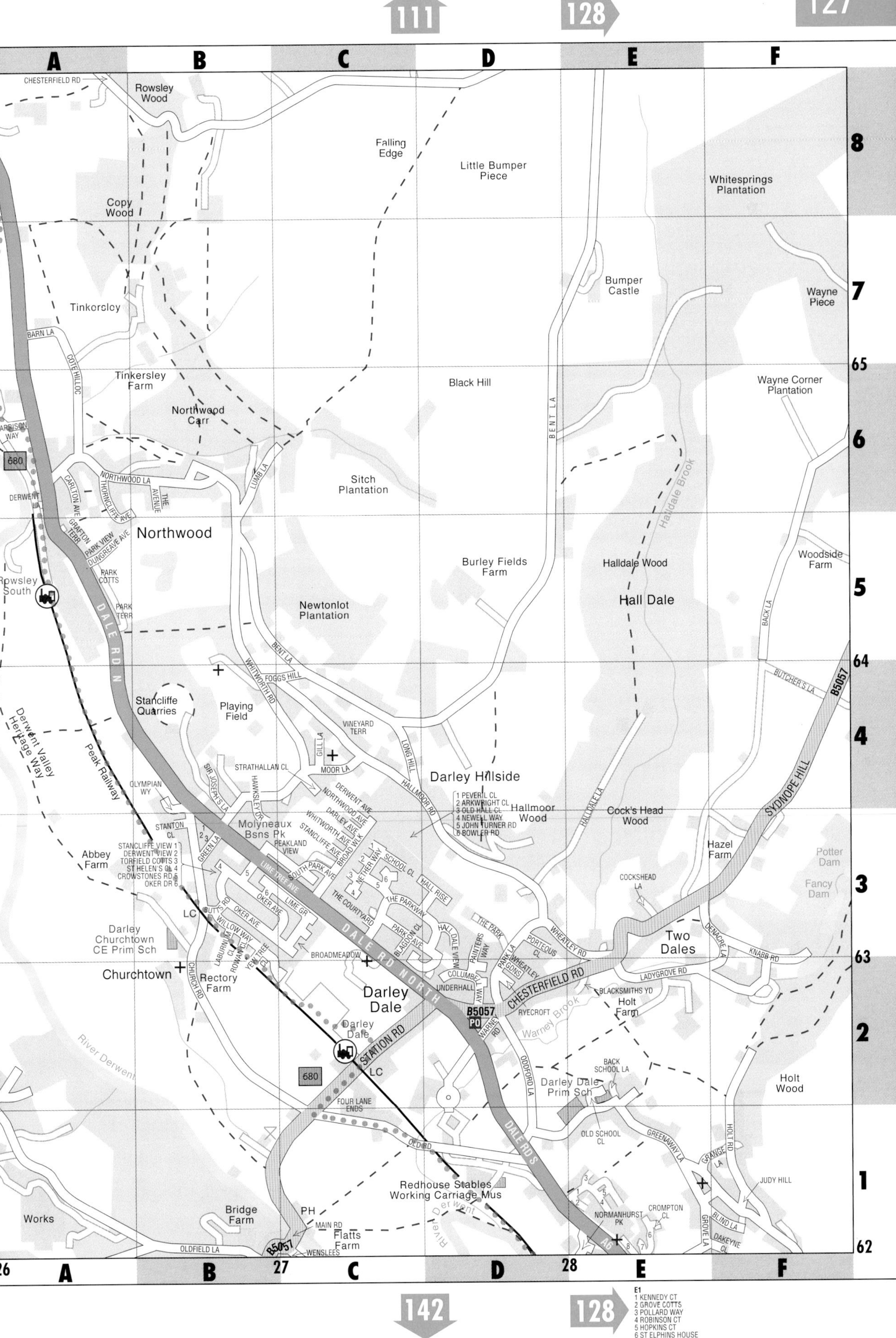

111
128

A B C D E F

8

7

65

6

5

64

4

3

63

2

1

62

CHESTERFIELD RD

Rowsley Wood

Copy Wood

Falling Edge

Little Bumper Piece

Whitesprings Plantation

Tinkersley

Bumper Castle

Wayne Piece

BARN LA

Tinkersley Farm

Black Hill

Wayne Corner Plantation

HARRISON WAY

Northwood Carr

Haldale Brook

680

DERWENT

NORTHWOOD LA
THORNCLIFFE AVE
THE AVENUE

Northwood

Sitch Plantation

Woodside Farm

DALE RD N
CARLTON AVE
GRAFTON TERR
DUNGREAVE AVE
PARK VIEW

PARK COTTS
PARK TERR

Burley Fields Farm

Halldale Wood

Hall Dale

BACK LA

Rowsley South

Newtonlot Plantation

BENT LA

BUTCHER'S LA

B5057

64

Derwent Valley Heritage Way

Stancliffe Quarries

Foggs Hill

Playing Field

Vineyard Terr

LONG HILL

HALLMOOR RD

Darley Hillside

Cock's Head Wood

SYDNOPE HILL

Peak Railway

OLYMPIAN WY

STRATHALLAN CL

MOOR LA

NORTHWOOD AVE
DARLEY AVE
WHITWORTH AVE
STANCLIFFE AVE

1 PEVERIL CL
2 ARKWRIGHT CL
3 OLD HALL CL
4 NEWELL WAY
5 JOHN TURNER RD
6 BOWLER RD

Hallmoor Wood

HALLCROFT LA

Hazel Farm

Potter Dam

Fancy Dam

Abbey Farm

STANTON CL

HAWKSLEY DR
SIR JOSEPH'S LA
GREEN LA

Molyneaux Bsns Pk

1 STANCLIFFE VIEW 1
2 DERWENT VIEW 2
3 TORFIELD COTTS 3
4 ST HELEN'S CL 4
5 CROWSTONES RD 5
6 OKER DR 6

PEAKLAND VIEW

BROOK LA

NETHER WAY

SCHOOL CL

HALL RISE

THE PARKWAY

PAINTERS WAY

WHEATLEY RD

PORTEOUS

Two Dales

Cockshead LA

DENACRE LA

KNABB RD

LC

OKER AVE

LIME TREE AVE
SOUTH PARK AVE
LIME GR

THE COURTYARD

HALL DALE VIEW
PARK CL
PARK AVE

PARK WHEATLEY
GDNS

LADYGROVE RD

Darley Churchtown CE Prim Sch

WILLOW WAY
LABURNUM RD
ROMAN RD
YEW TREE

BROADMEADOW

UNDERHALL

CHESTERFIELD RD

BLACKSMITHS YD

Holt Farm

Holt Wood

Churchtown

CHURCH RD

Rectory Farm

Darley Dale

HALL DALE LA

RYECROFT

Warney Brook

BACK SCHOOL LA

Darley Dale Prim Sch

River Derwent

Darley Dale

680

STATION RD

LC

B5057
PO

MANSE RD

ODDFORD LA

DALE RD S

OLD SCHOOL CL

GREENAWAY LA

GRANGE LA

HOLT RD

JUDY HILL

FOUR LANE ENDS

OLD RD

Redhouse Stables Working Carriage Mus

River Derwent

NORMANHURST PK

CROMPTON CL

BLIND LA

GROVE CL

DAKEYNE CL

Works

Bridge Farm

MAIN RD

PH

Flatts Farm

B5057

OLDFIELD LA

WENSLEES

A B C D E F

26 27 28

E1
1 KENNEDY CT
2 GROVE COTTS
3 POLLARD WAY
4 ROBINSON CT
5 HOPKINS CT
6 ST ELPHINS HOUSE
7 HUDSON PL
8 CHAPEL MWS

127
112

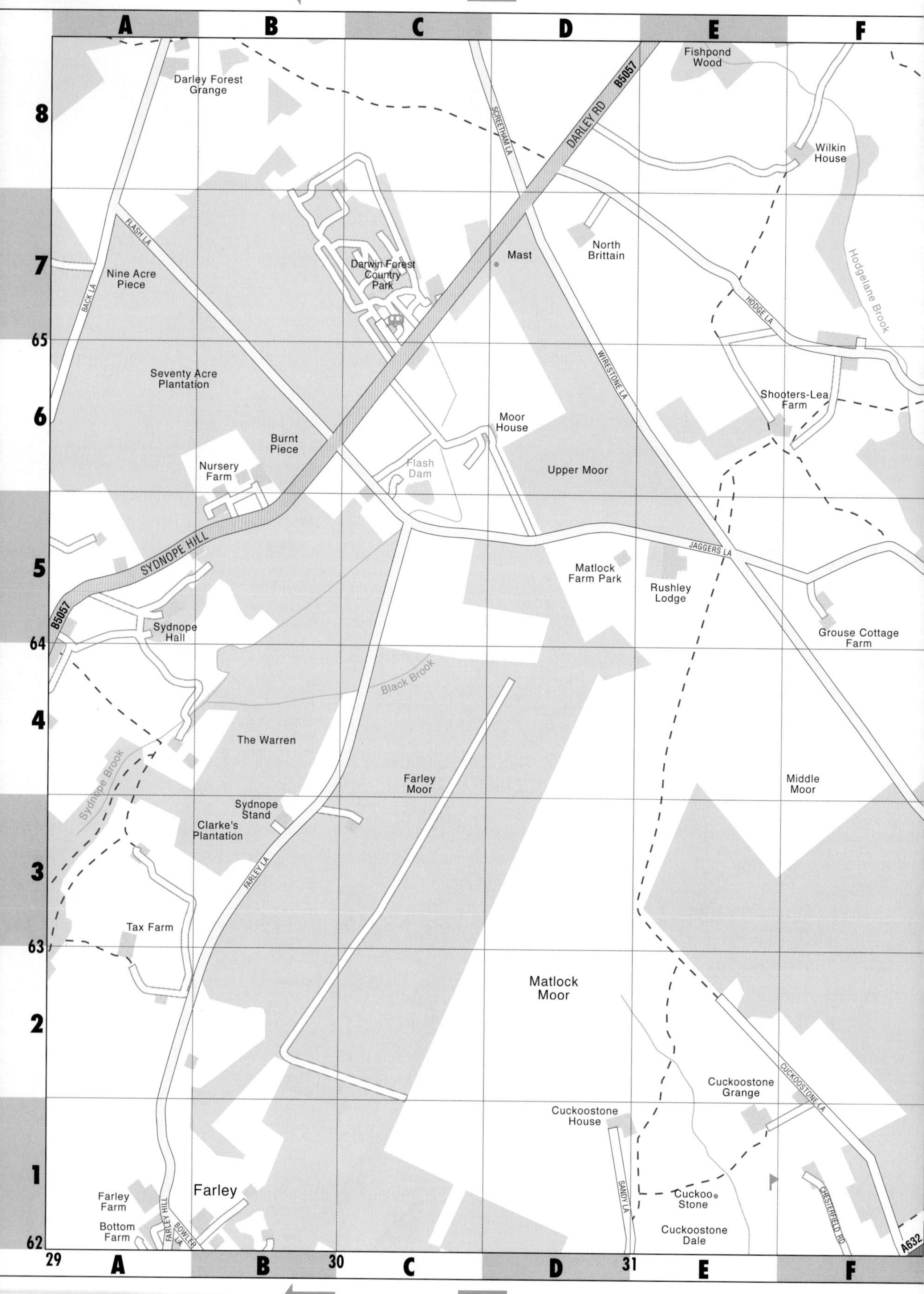
A
B
C
D
E
F
8
7
65
6
5
64
4
3
63
2
1
62
29
30
31
Darley Forest Grange
Fishpond Wood
B5057
DARLEY RD
SCREETHAM LA
Wilkin House
FLASH LA
Darwin Forest Country Park
Mast
North Brittain
Hodgelane Brook
HODGE LA
Nine Acre Piece
BACK LA
Seventy Acre Plantation
WIRESTONE LA
Shooters-Lea Farm
Moor House
Burnt Piece
Nursery Farm
Flash Dam
Upper Moor
JAGGERS LA
SYDNOPE HILL
Matlock Farm Park
Rushley Lodge
Grouse Cottage Farm
Sydnope Hall
Black Brook
The Warren
Sydnope Brook
Farley Moor
Middle Moor
Sydnope Stand
Clarke's Plantation
FARLEY LA
Tax Farm
Matlock Moor
Cuckoostone Grange
CUCKOOSTONE LA
Cuckoostone House
Farley
Farley Farm
Bottom Farm
FARLEY HILL
BOWLER LA
SANDY LA
Cuckoo Stone
Cuckoostone Dale
CHESTERFIELD RD
A632

127
143

113
130

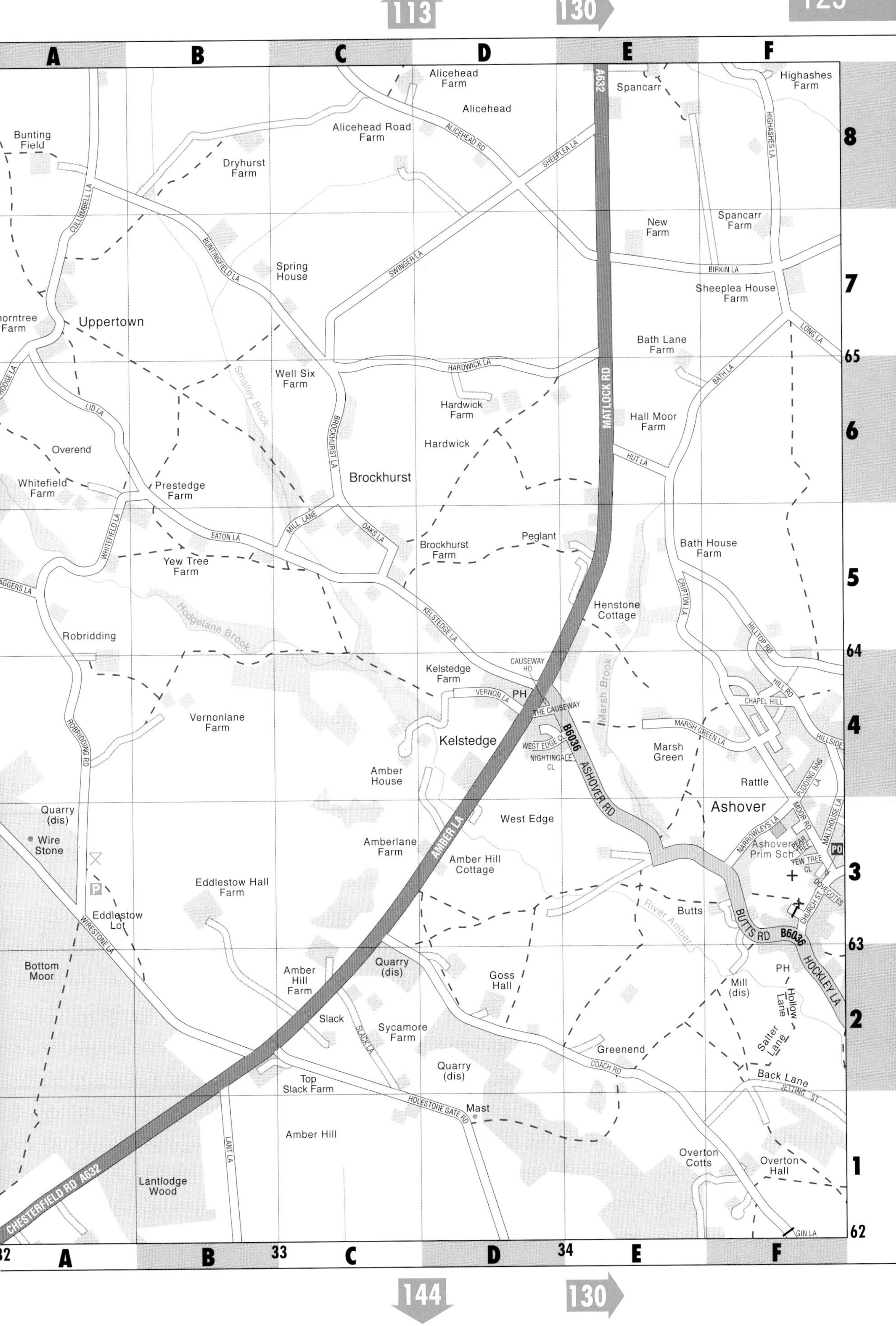
A
B
C
D
E
F
8
7
6
5
4
3
2
1
65
64
63
62
33
34
Alicehead Farm
Alicehead
Alicehead Road Farm
Spancarr
Highashes Farm
Bunting Field
Dryhurst Farm
Spring House
New Farm
Spancarr Farm
Sheeplea House Farm
Uppertown
Well Six Farm
Bath Lane Farm
Hardwick Farm
Hardwick
Hall Moor Farm
Overend
Whitefield Farm
Prestedge Farm
Brockhurst
Brockhurst Farm
Peglant
Bath House Farm
Yew Tree Farm
Henstone Cottage
Robridding
Kelstedge Farm
Vernonlane Farm
Kelstedge
Marsh Green
Rattle
Amber House
Ashover
Quarry (dis)
Wire Stone
West Edge
Amberlane Farm
Ashover Prim Sch
Amber Hill Cottage
Eddlestow Hall Farm
Eddlestow Lot
Butts
Bottom Moor
Amber Hill Farm
Quarry (dis)
Goss Hall
Mill (dis)
Slack
Sycamore Farm
Greenend
Quarry (dis)
Top Slack Farm
Back Lane
Mast
Amber Hill
Overton Cotts
Overton Hall
Lantlodge Wood
A632
MATLOCK RD
AMBER LA
CHESTERFIELD RD A632
B6036
ASHOVER RD
BUTTS RD
HOCKLEY LA
ALICEHEAD RD
SHEEPLEA LA
SWINGER LA
BIRKIN LA
HIGHASHES LA
LONG LA
BATH LA
HARDWICK LA
CULLUMBELL LA
BUNTINGFIELD LA
BROCKHURST LA
HUT LA
LID LA
WHITEFIELD LA
EATON LA
MILL LANE
OAKS LA
KELSTEDGE LA
CRIPTON LA
HILLTOP RD
HILL RD
CHAPEL HILL
MARSH GREEN LA
VERNON LA
THE CAUSEWAY
CAUSEWAY HO
PH
WEST EDGE CL
NIGHTINGALE CL
ROBRIDDING RD
WIRESTONE LA
HILLSIDE
PUDDING BAG LA
MOOR RD
MALTHOUSE LA
NARROWLEYS LA
PEAR TREE
YEW TREE CL
PO
DOVECOTES
CHURCH ST
Smalley Brook
Hodgelane Brook
Marsh Brook
River Amber
Hollow Lane
Salter Lane
SLACK LA
COACH RD
HOLESTONE GATE RD
LANT LA
JETTING ST
GIN LA
PH

144
130

129
114

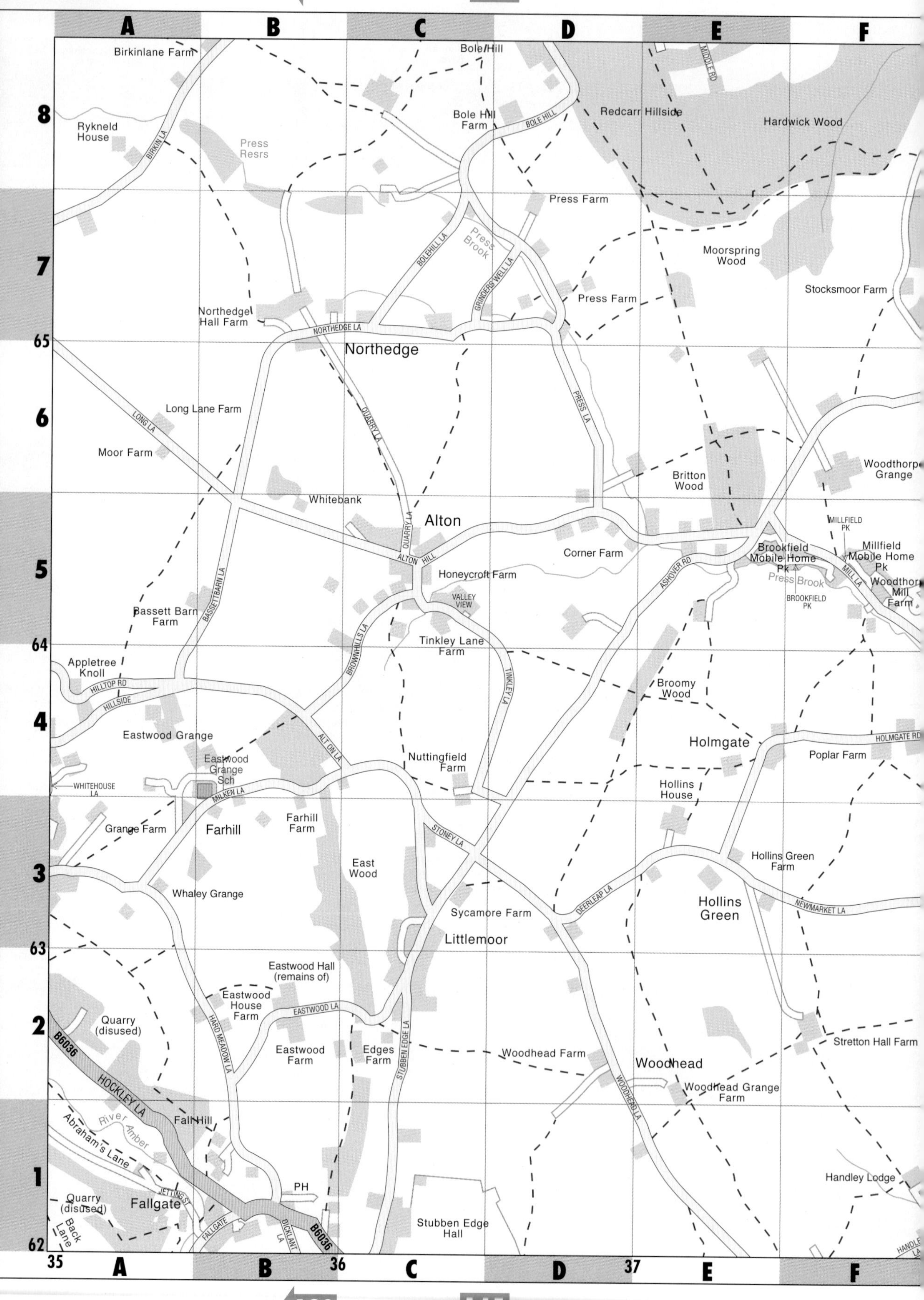
A
B
C
D
E
F
8
7
65
6
5
64
4
3
63
2
1
62
35
36
37
Birkinlane Farm
Bole Hill
Rykneld House
Press Resrs
Bole Hill Farm
BOLE HILL
Redcarr Hillside
Hardwick Wood
Press Farm
Press Brook
Moorspring Wood
Stocksmoor Farm
Press Farm
Northedge Hall Farm
NORTHEDGE LA
Northedge
Long Lane Farm
Moor Farm
LONG LA
QUARRY LA
PRESS LA
Britton Wood
Woodthorpe Grange
Whitebank
Alton
ALTON HILL
Corner Farm
Brookfield Mobile Home Pk
Millfield Mobile Home Pk
MILLFIELD PK
BROOKFIELD PK
Woodthorpe Mill Farm
MILL LA
ASHOVER RD
Honeycroft Farm
VALLEY VIEW
Bassett Barn Farm
BASSETTBARN LA
Tinkley Lane Farm
TINKLEY LA
BROWNHILLS LA
Appletree Knoll
HILLTOP RD
HILLSIDE
Broomy Wood
Holmgate
HOLMGATE RD
Poplar Farm
Eastwood Grange
Eastwood Grange Sch
ALTON LA
Nuttingfield Farm
Hollins House
WHITEHOUSE LA
MILKEN LA
Grange Farm
Farhill
Farhill Farm
STONEY LA
East Wood
Hollins Green Farm
Whaley Grange
Sycamore Farm
DEERLEAP LA
Hollins Green
NEWMARKET LA
Littlemoor
Eastwood Hall (remains of)
Eastwood House Farm
EASTWOOD LA
Quarry (disused)
HARD MEADOW LA
STUBBEN EDGE LA
Eastwood Farm
Edges Farm
Woodhead Farm
Woodhead
Stretton Hall Farm
Woodhead Grange Farm
WOODHEAD LA
B6036
HOCKLEY LA
River Amber
Abraham's Lane
Fall Hill
PH
Handley Lodge
Quarry (disused)
Fallgate
JETTING ST
FALLGATE
DICKLANT LA
Back Lane
Stubben Edge Hall
HANDLEY LA

129
145

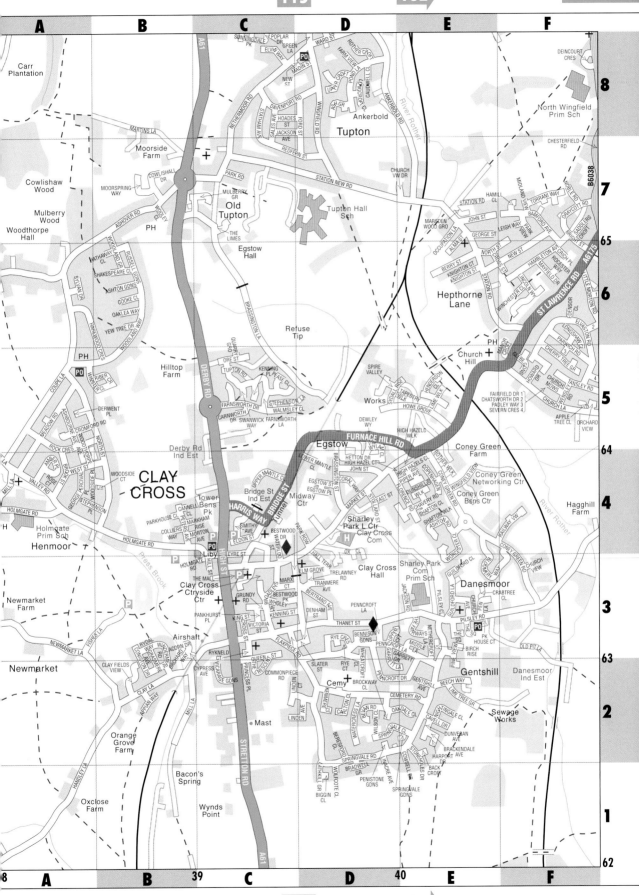
115
132
131

A B C D E F

8 7 65 6 5 64 4 3 63 2 1 62

Carr Plantation
Cowlishaw Wood
Mulberry Wood
Woodthorpe Hall
Moorside Farm
Old Tupton
Egstow Hall
Tupton
Ankerbold
Tupton Hall Sch
Refuse Tip
North Wingfield Prim Sch
Hepthorne Lane
Church Hill
Hilltop Farm
Spire Valley Works
Egstow
Coney Green Farm
Coney Green Networking Ctr
Coney Green Bsns Ctr
Hagghill Farm
Derby Rd Ind Est
CLAY CROSS
Tower Bsns Pk
Bridge St Ind Est
Midway Ctr
Tunnel
Sharley Park L Ctr
Clay Cross Com
Clay Cross Hall
Sharley Park Com Prim Sch
Danesmoor
Holmgate Prim Sch
Henmoor
Newmarket Farm
Clay Cross Ctryside Ctr
Airshaft
Newmarket
Gentshill
Danesmoor Ind Est
Sewage Works
Cemy
Mast
Orange Grove Farm
Bacon's Spring
Wynds Point
Oxclose Farm
River Rother
Press Brook

A61
DERBY RD
HIGH ST
STRETTON RD
A6175
ST LAWRENCE RD
B6038
FURNACE HILL RD
HARRIS WAY
BRIDGE ST
STATION NEW RD
MARTINS LA
ASHOVER RD
HOLMGATE RD
NEWMARKET LA
THANET ST
PILSLEY RD
CHESTERFIELD RD
NETHERMOOR RD
WINGFIELD RD
ANKERBOLD RD
BRASSINGTON LA
MILL LA
HANDLEY LA
CLAY LA
APPIAN WAY
FISHES LA
OLD PIT LA

FAIRFIELD DR 1
CHATSWORTH DR 2
PADLEY WAY 3
SEVERN CRES 4

8 A 39 C D 40 E F

131
116

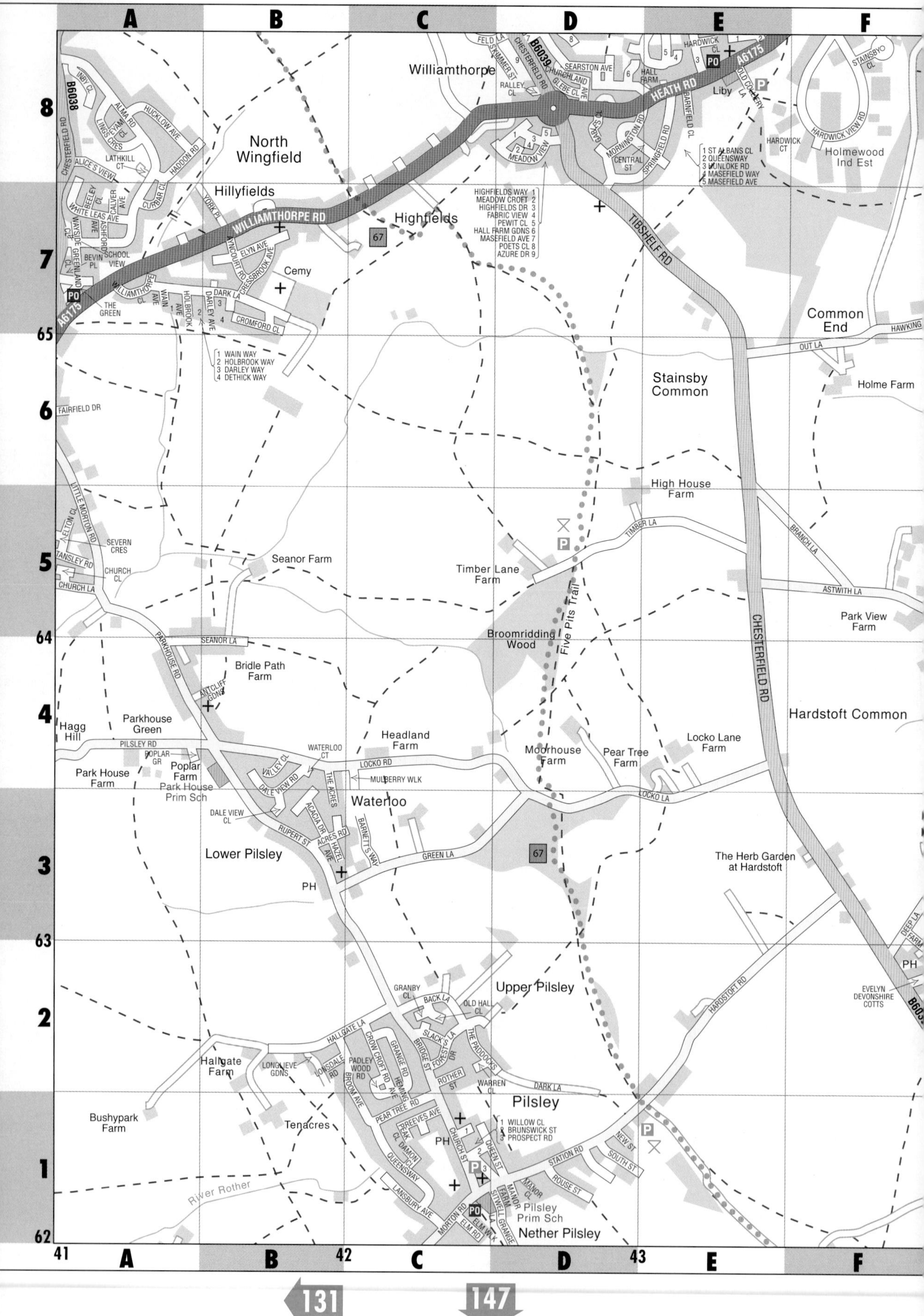
A
B
C
D
E
F
8
7
65
6
5
64
4
3
63
2
1
62
41
42
43
North Wingfield
Hillyfields
Williamthorpe
Highfields
Cemy
Liby
Holmewood Ind Est
Common End
Stainsby Common
Holme Farm
High House Farm
Timber Lane Farm
Broomridding Wood
Five Pits Trail
Seanor Farm
Park View Farm
Hardstoft Common
Bridle Path Farm
Hagg Hill
Parkhouse Green
Park House Farm
Poplar Farm
Park House Prim Sch
Headland Farm
Moorhouse Farm
Pear Tree Farm
Locko Lane Farm
Waterloo
Lower Pilsley
PH
The Herb Garden at Hardstoft
Upper Pilsley
Hallgate Farm
Bushypark Farm
Tenacres
Pilsley
Pilsley Prim Sch
Nether Pilsley
River Rother
WILLIAMTHORPE RD
HEATH RD
A6175
B6038
B6039
TIBSHELF RD
CHESTERFIELD RD
HARDWICK CL
OLD COLLIERY LA
STAINSBY CL
HARDWICK VIEW RD
HARDWICK CT
SEARSTON AVE
CHURCHLAND AVE
GLEBE CL
HALL FARM
GARDEN CL
MORNINGTON RD
CENTRAL ST
SPRINGFIELD RD
BARNFIELD CL
FELD LA
SKIMMER ST
RALLEY CL
MEADOW VIEW
1 ST ALBANS CL
2 QUEENSWAY
3 DUNLOKE RD
4 MASEFIELD WAY
5 MASEFIELD AVE
HIGHFIELDS WAY 1
MEADOW CROFT 2
HIGHFIELDS DR 3
FABRIC VIEW 4
PEWIT CL 5
HALL FARM GDNS 6
MASEFIELD AVE 7
POETS CL 8
AZURE DR 9
INBY CL
ALMA RD
HUCKLOW AVE
EYAM CL
LINGS CRES
HADDON RD
LATHKILL CT
ALICE'S VIEW
BEELEY CL
CALVER AVE
CURBAR CL
WHITE LEAS AVE
ASHFORD AVE
WAYSIDE CL
GREENLAND CL
BEVIN PL
SCHOOL VIEW
THE GREEN
YORK PL
AYNCOURT RD
ELYN AVE
CRESSBROOK AVE
DARK LA
WAIN AVE
HOLBROOK AVE
DARLEY AVE
CROMFORD CL
1 WAIN WAY
2 HOLBROOK WAY
3 DARLEY WAY
4 DETHICK WAY
OUT LA
HAWKING
FAIRFIELD DR
LITTLE MORTON RD
ELTON CL
SEVERN CRES
TANSLEY RD
CHURCH CL
CHURCH LA
TIMBER LA
BRANCH LA
ASTWITH LA
SEANOR LA
PARKHOUSE RD
ANTCLIFF GDNS
PILSLEY RD
POPLAR GR
WATERLOO CT
LOCKO RD
MULBERRY WLK
VALLEY CL
DALE VIEW RD
THE ACRES
DALE VIEW CL
ACACIA DR
ACRES RD
HAZEL AVE
BARNETT'S WAY
RUPERT ST
GREEN LA
LOCKO LA
DEEP LA
FARM
EVELYN DEVONSHIRE COTTS
HARDSTOFT RD
GRANBY CL
BACK LA
OLD HALL CL
HALLGATE LA
SLACK'S LA
FORSTER'S DR
THE PADDOCKS
CROW CROFT RD
GRANGE RD
BRIDGE ST
HEMMING AVE
LONGLIEVE GDNS
LONSDALE RD
PADLEY WOOD RD
BROOM AVE
ROTHER ST
WARREN CL
DARK LA
PEAR TREE RD
BREEVES AVE
PEAK CL
DAMON CL
QUEENSWAY
CHURCH ST
OWEN ST
1 WILLOW CL
2 BRUNSWICK ST
3 PROSPECT RD
STATION RD
NEW ST
SOUTH ST
ROUSE ST
MANOR CL
FARM CL
STILWELL GRANGE
LANSBURY AVE
MORTON RD
ELM RD
ELM WLK
PO
P
67

131
147

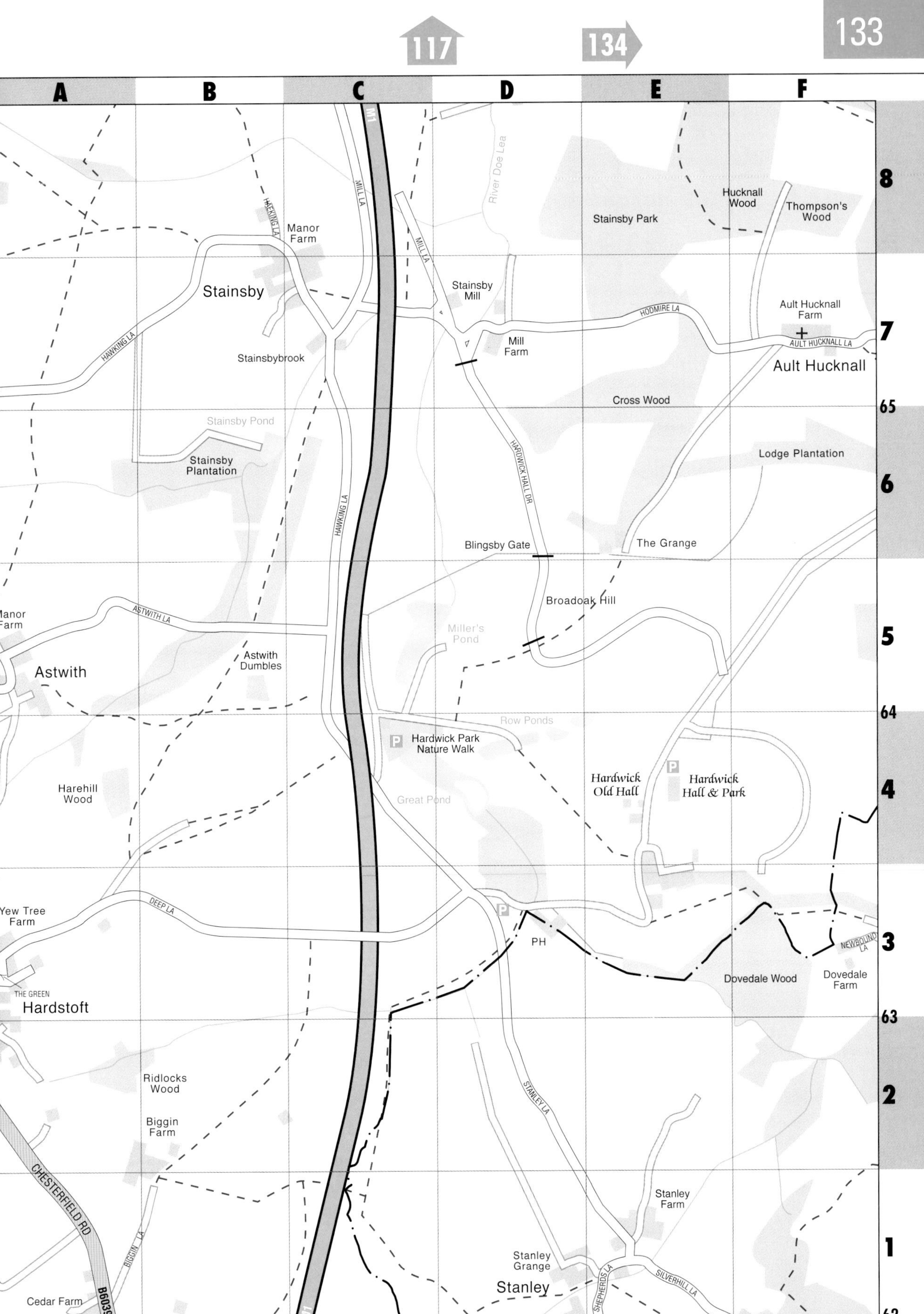

117
134

A B C D E F

8
7
65
6
5
64
4
3
63
2
1
62

Manor Farm

Stainsby

Stainsbybrook

Stainsby Pond

Stainsby Plantation

HERRING LA

HAWKING LA

MILL LA

MILL LA

River Doe Lea

Stainsby Mill

Mill Farm

Stainsby Park

Hucknall Wood

Thompson's Wood

Ault Hucknall Farm

HODMIRE LA

AULT HUCKNALL LA

Ault Hucknall

Cross Wood

HARDWICK HALL DR

Lodge Plantation

Blingsby Gate

The Grange

Broadoak Hill

Manor Farm

ASTWITH LA

Astwith

Astwith Dumbles

Miller's Pond

Row Ponds

P Hardwick Park Nature Walk

Great Pond

Hardwick Old Hall

P Hardwick Hall & Park

Harehill Wood

Yew Tree Farm

DEEP LA

THE GREEN

Hardstoft

Ridlocks Wood

Biggin Farm

CHESTERFIELD RD

BIGGIN LA

B6039

Cedar Farm

P
PH

STANLEY LA

NEWBOUND LA

Dovedale Wood

Dovedale Farm

Stanley Farm

Stanley Grange

Stanley

SHEPHERDS LA

SILVERHILL LA

44 A B 45 C D 46 E F

148
134

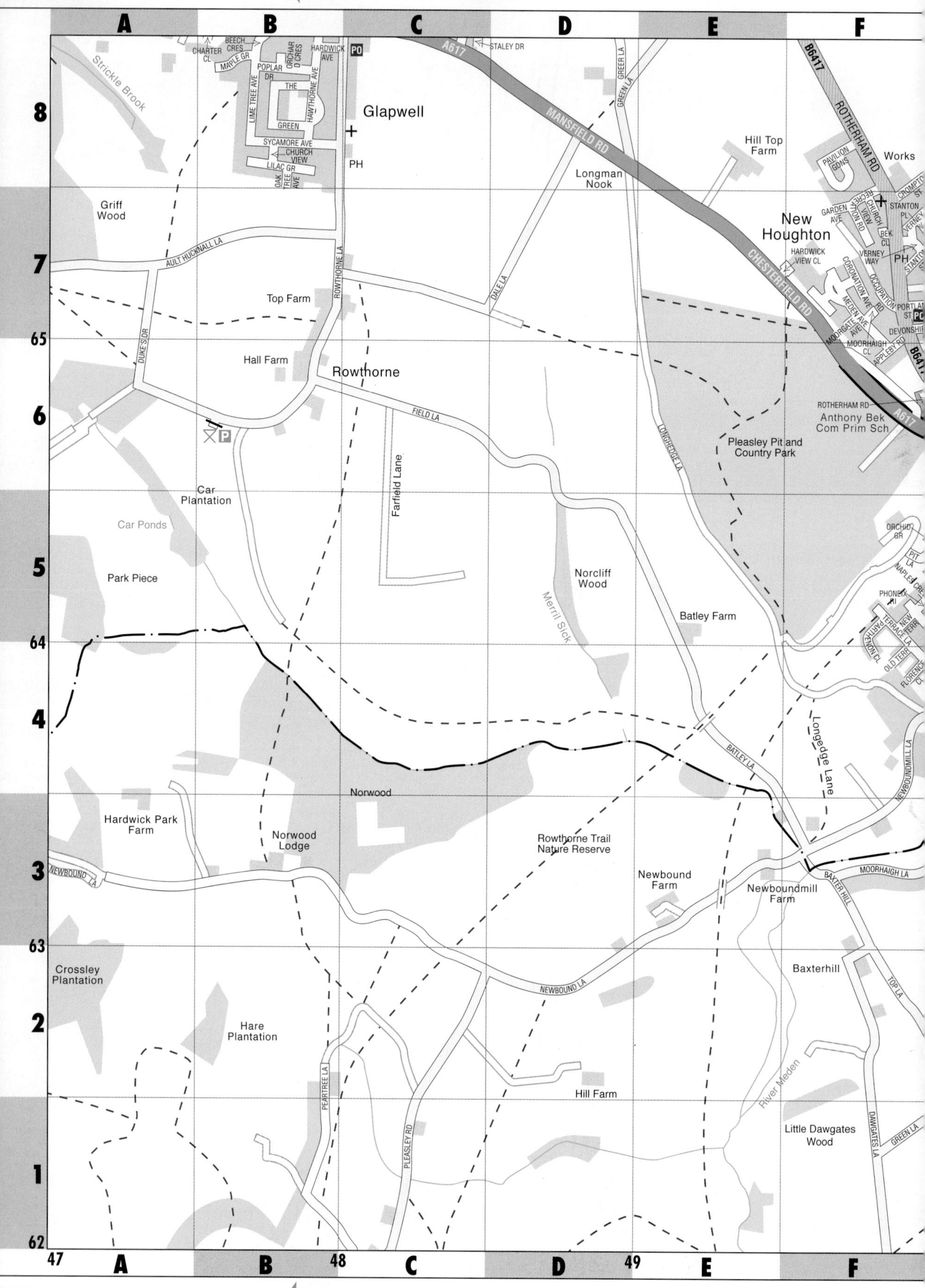

A   B   C   D   E   F

8

Strickle Brook

CHARTER CL
BEECH CRES
MAPLE GR
ORCHAR D CRES
HARDWICK AVE
PO
A617
STALEY DR
GREEN LA

LIME TREE AVE
POPLAR DR
THE
GREEN
HAWTHORNE AVE

Glapwell

MANSFIELD RD

Longman Nook

Hill Top
Farm

PAVILION GDNS

Works

CROMPTON ST

SYCAMORE AVE
CHURCH
VIEW
LILAC GR
OAK TREE AVE
+
PH

GARDEN AVE
CHURCH VIEW
CHURCH RD
STANTON RD
STANTON PL
VERNEY

New
Houghton

BEK CL
VERNEY WAY
PH
STANTON

Griff
Wood

7

AULT HUCKNALL LA

DUKE'S DR

Top Farm

ROWTHORNE LA

DALE LA

HARDWICK VIEW CL

MOORGATE AVE
PEVERIL AVE
MOORHAIGH
APPLEBY RD

PORTLAND ST
PC
DEVONSHIRE

65

Hall Farm

Rowthorne

FIELD LA

CHESTERFIELD RD

ROTHERHAM RD

Anthony Bek
Com Prim Sch

ORCHID GR
PIT LA
MAPLE CL

6

A617
P
X

Car
Plantation

Farfield Lane

LONGEDGE LA

Pleasley Pit and
Country Park

PHOENIX
TERRACE PANTILE
OLD TERR
FLORENCE
PHOENIX CL

Car Ponds

Park Piece

Merril Sick

Norcliff
Wood

Batley Farm

5

64

Norwood

BATLEY LA

Longedge Lane

NEWBOUNDMILL LA

4

Hardwick Park
Farm

Norwood
Lodge

Rowthorne Trail
Nature Reserve

Newbound
Farm

Newboundmill
Farm

BAXTER HILL

MOORHAIGH LA

3

NEWBOUND LA

63

Crossley
Plantation

Hare
Plantation

PEARTREE LA

NEWBOUND LA

Hill Farm

River Meden

Baxterhill

TOP LA

2

PLEASLEY RD

Little Dawgates
Wood

DAWGATES LA
GREEN LA

1

62

47   A   B   48   C   D   49   E   F

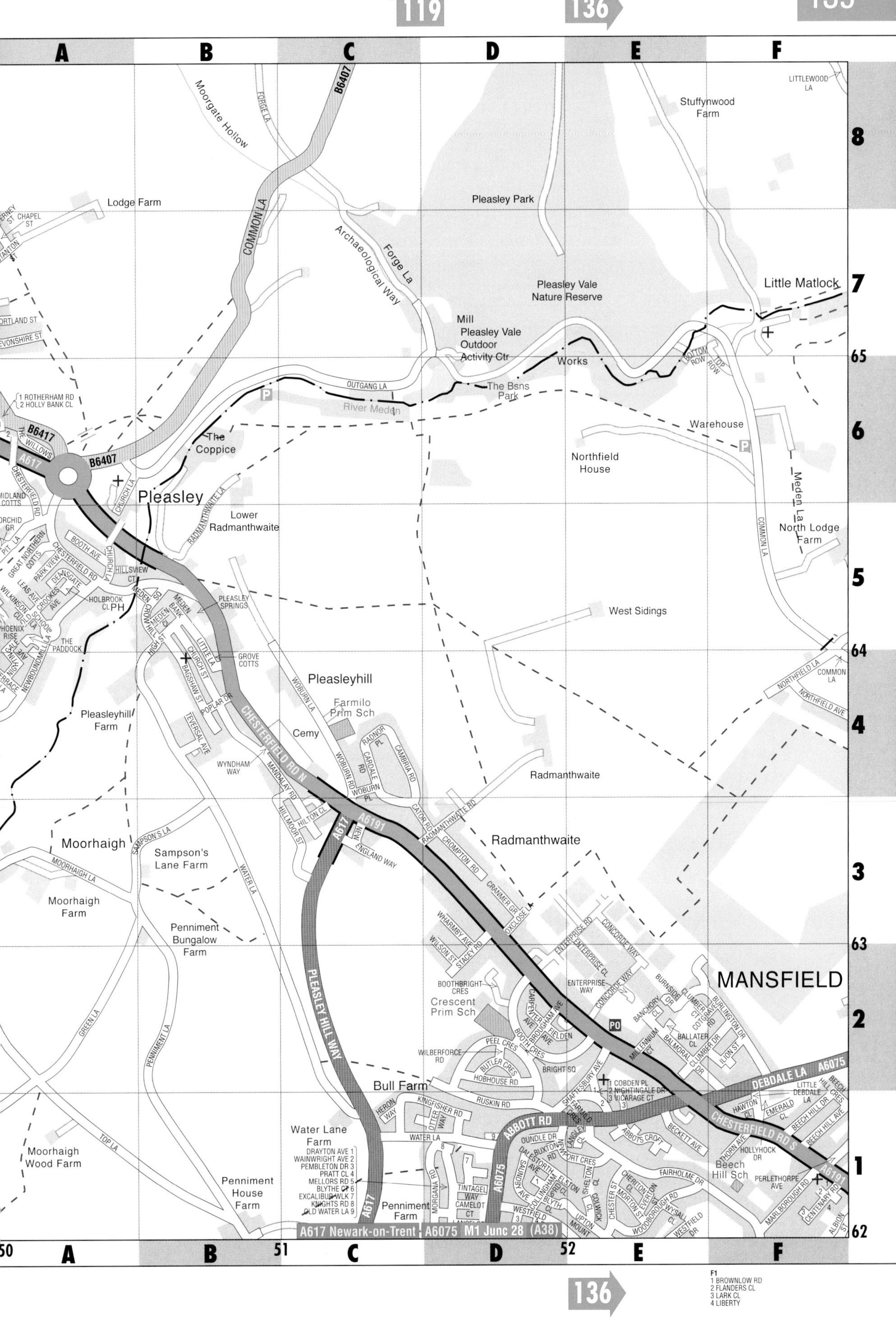

A   B   C   D   E   F

8
7
65
6
5
64
4
63
3
2
1
62

LITTLEWOOD LA

Stuffynwood Farm

Moorgate Hollow

FORGE LA

B6407

Lodge Farm

PORTLAND ST
DEVONSHIRE ST

Archaeological Way

Forge La

COMMON LA

Pleasley Park

Pleasley Vale Nature Reserve

Little Matlock

Mill
Pleasley Vale Outdoor Activity Ctr

Works

BOTTOM ROW

OUTGANG LA

The Bsns Park

1 ROTHERHAM RD
2 HOLLY BANK CL

River Meden

Warehouse

P

THE WILLOWS

B6417

A617

B6407

The Coppice

CHURCH LA

Northfield House

Meden La

Common La

North Lodge Farm

MIDLAND COTTS
ORCHID GR
PIT LA

Pleasley

Lower Radmanthwaite

CHESTERFIELD RD

GREAT NORTHERN AVE
BOOTH AVE
PARK VIEW AVE
BAGGALY AVE
WILKINSON CL
LEAS AV
CROOKES AV
HOLBROOK CL PH
PHOENIX RISE
THE PADDOCK
NEWBOUND LA

RADMANTHWAITE LA

Pleasley Springs

HILLSVIEW CT

MEDEN SQ
MILL CL
MEDEN CL
CHURCH ST
HIGH ST

West Sidings

Pleasleyhill

GROVE COTTS

CHURCH LA
LITTLE LA
POPLAR
TEVERSAL AVE

Pleasleyhill Farm

Farmilo Prim Sch

Cemy

WOBURN LA

WOBURN RD

RADNOR PL
CARDALE RD
CAMBRIA RD

NORTHFIELD LA
NORTHFIELD AVE
COMMON LA

CHESTERFIELD RD N

WYNDHAM WAY

MANDALAY ST
HILLMOOR ST
HILTON CL

Radmanthwaite

Moorhaigh

MOORHAIGH LA

Sampson's Lane Farm

WATER LA

A617
A6191
FEN ENGLAND WAY

RADMANTHWAITE RD
CROMPTON RD
CRANMER GR
OXCLOSE LA

Moorhaigh Farm

Penniment Bungalow Farm

MANSFIELD

WHARMBY AVE
WILSON ST
STACEY RD

ENTERPRISE RD
ENTERPRISE CL

CONCORDE WAY

Enterprise Way

BURNSIDE DR
PLUMBER DR
CLUMBER DR
BURLINGTON DR

PLEASLEY HILL WAY

GREEN LA

PENNIMENT LA

BOOTHBRIGHT CRES

Crescent Prim Sch

CARPEN
BOOTH CRES
FIELDEN

MILLENNIUM CT
BANCROFT
BALMORAL
BALLATER CL
CLUMBER DR
TILTON ST

PO

DEBDALE LA
A6075

WILBERFORCE RD

PEEL CRES

BRIGHT SQ

SHAFTESBURY AVE
CLARA
FARM CL

HAWTON
EMERALD CL
DEBDALE LA
BEECH HILL DR

HEATH CL

Bull Farm

BUTLER CRES
HOBHOUSE RD
RUSKIN RD

1 COBDEN PL
2 NIGHTINGALE DR
3 VICARAGE CT

CHESTERFIELD RD S

BECKETT AVE

HOLLYHOCK DR

Beech Hill Sch

HERON WAY
KINGFISHER RD

OTTER WAY

Water Lane Farm

DRAYTON AVE 1
WAINWRIGHT AVE 2
PEMBLETON DR 3
PRATT CL 4
MELLORS RD 5
BLYTHE CT 6
EXCALIBUR WLK 7
KNIGHTS RD 8
OLD WATER LA 9

Water La

ABBOTT RD

MORGANA RD

OUNDLE LA
TINTAGEL WAY
CAMELOT CT

A6075

OAKFORD
BUXTON
IMPORT CRES
ELSTON
SHIRLEY
LANGDON
BLYTH

OAKHAM
CHESTER ST

A617
A6075

ABBOTS CROFT

CHERITON RD
FAIRHOLME DR
UPTON CL
MORTON CL
WOODBOROUGH RD
WYSALL
CENTENARY RD
PERLETHORPE AVE
MARLBOROUGH RD
ALBION

Moorhaigh Wood Farm

TOP LA

Penniment House Farm

CRISWICK
WESTFIELD
MOUNT

Penniment Farm

F1
1 BROWNLOW RD
2 FLANDERS CL
3 LARK CL
4 LIBERTY

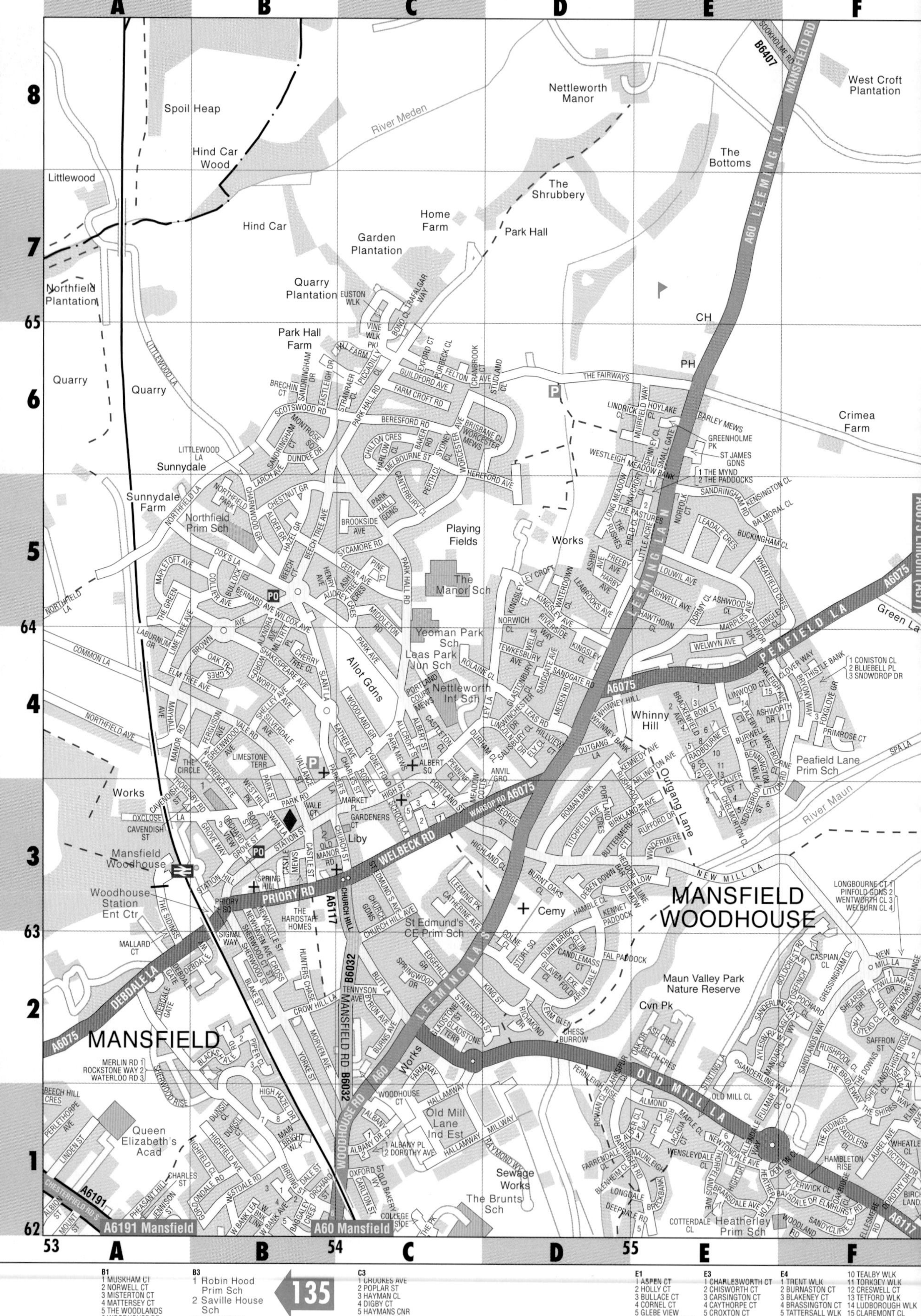

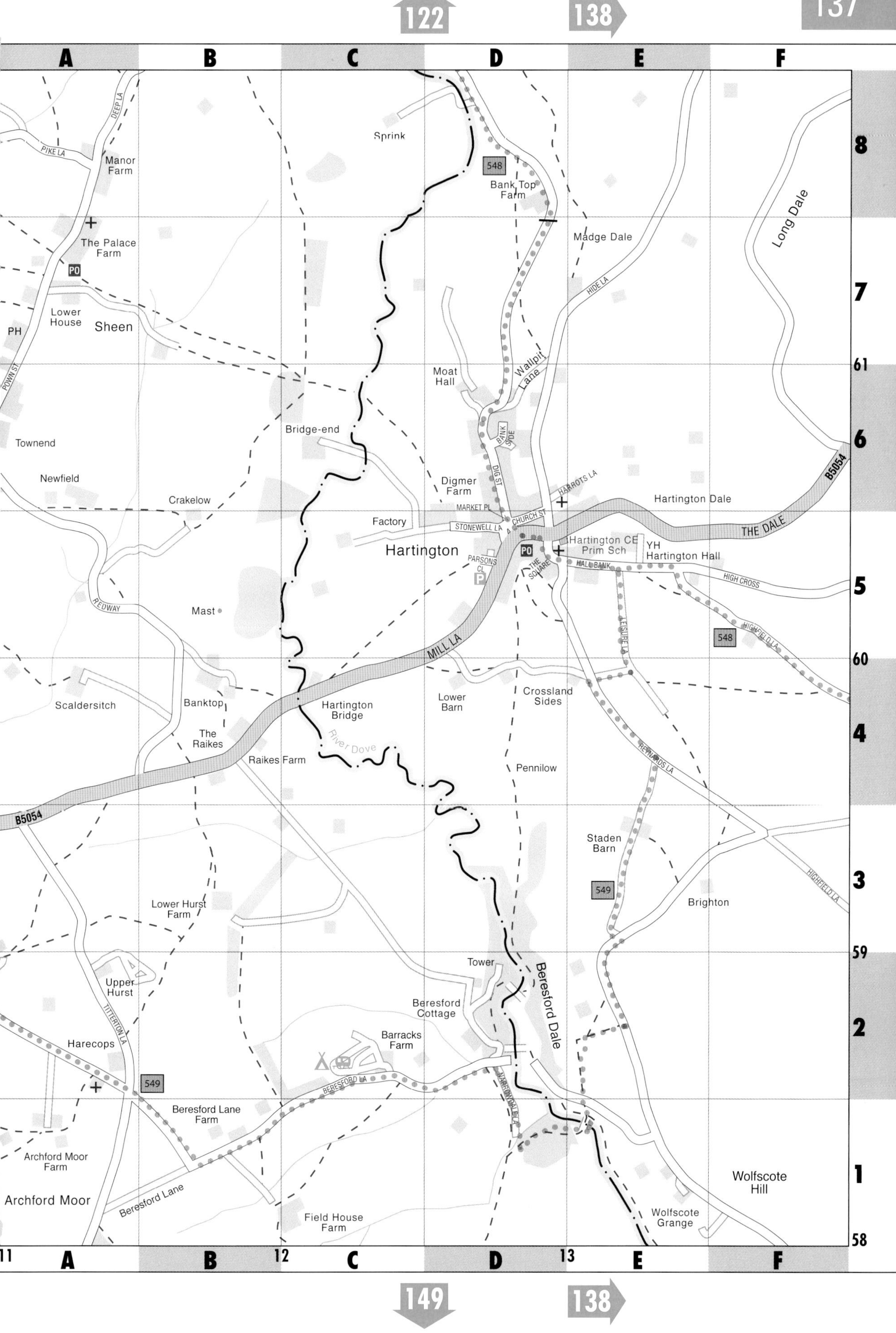

8

Sprink

548

Bank Top
Farm

Madge Dale

Long Dale

7

Manor
Farm

The Palace
Farm

PO

Lower
House

PH

Sheen

Moat
Hall

Wallpit Lane

HIDE LA

61

6

Townend

Bridge-end

BANK SIDE

DIG ST

HARROTS LA

B5054

Newfield

Digmer
Farm

Hartington Dale

Crakelow

MARKET PL

Factory

Stonewell LA

CHURCH ST

Hartington CE
Prim Sch

YH
Hartington Hall

THE DALE

5

Hartington

PARSONS
CL

PO

THE SQUARE

HALL BANK

HIGH CROSS

P

REDWAY

Mast

MILL LA

Lower
Barn

Crossland
Sides

HIGHFIELD LA

548

60

Scaldersitch

Banktop

Hartington
Bridge

River Dove

Raikes Farm

The
Raikes

Lower
Barn

Pennilow

REDFERNS LA

LEISURE LA

4

B5054

Staden
Barn

HIGHFIELD LA

3

Lower Hurst
Farm

549

Brighton

59

Tower

Beresford Dale

Upper
Hurst

TITTERTON LA

Harecops

549

Beresford
Cottage

Barracks
Farm

2

Beresford Lane
Farm

BERESFORD LA

NARREN DALE LA

Wolfscote
Hill

1

Archford Moor
Farm

Archford Moor

Beresford Lane

Field House
Farm

Wolfscote
Grange

58

137
123

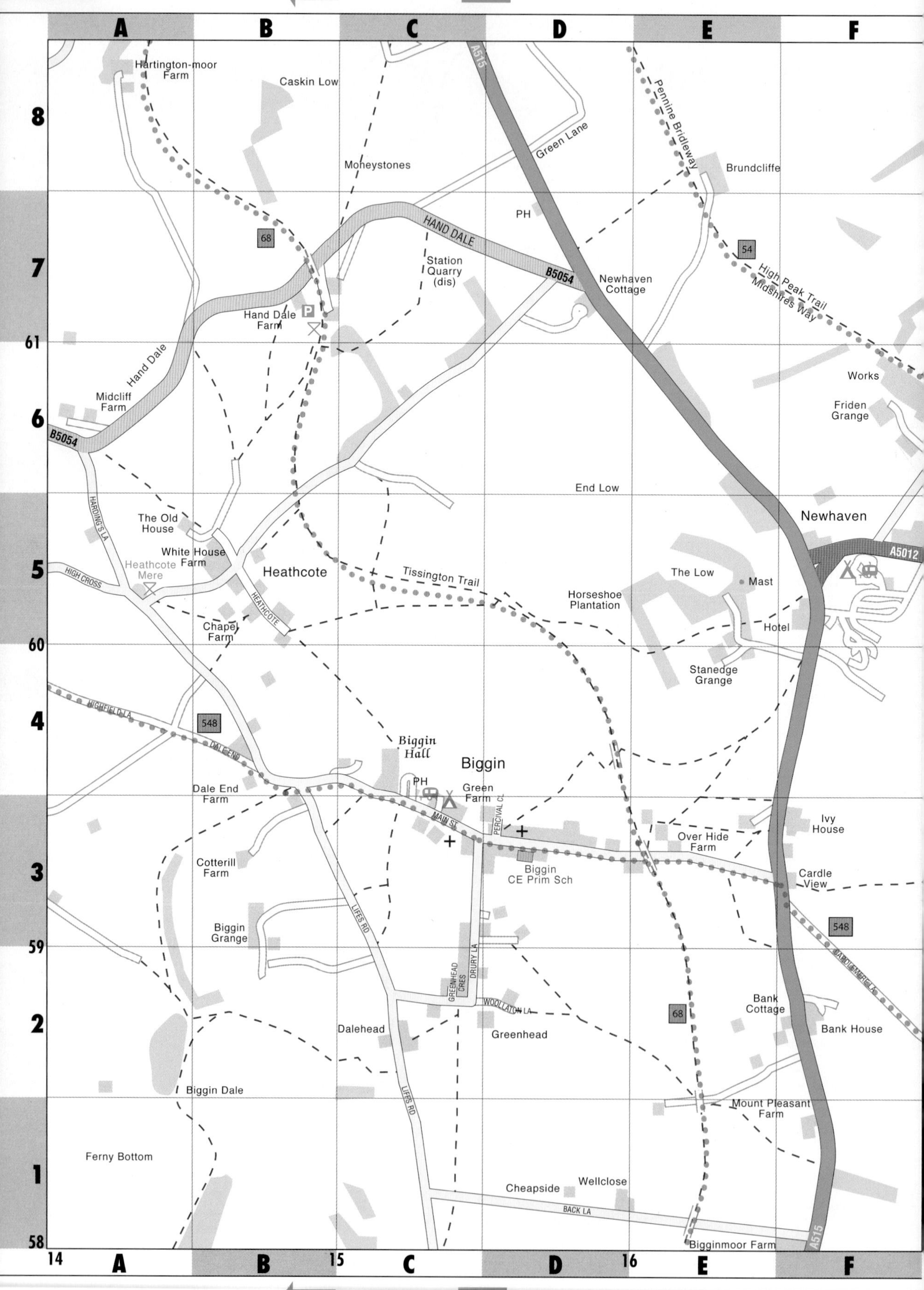
A
B
C
D
E
F
8
7
61
6
5
60
4
3
59
2
1
58
14
15
16
Hartington-moor Farm
Caskin Low
A515
Green Lane
Pennine Bridleway
Moneystones
Brundcliffe
PH
68
HAND DALE
Station Quarry (dis)
B5054
Newhaven Cottage
54
High Peak Trail
Midshires Way
Hand Dale Farm
Hand Dale
Midcliff Farm
Works
Friden Grange
End Low
The Old House
Newhaven
White House Farm
Heathcote Mere
Heathcote
Tissington Trail
The Low
Mast
A5012
HIGH CROSS
HARDING'S LA
HEATHCOTE
Horseshoe Plantation
Chapel Farm
Hotel
Stanedge Grange
HIGHFIELD LA
548
DALE END
Biggin Hall
Biggin
Dale End Farm
PH
Green Farm
MAIN ST
PERCIVAL CL
Ivy House
Over Hide Farm
Cotterill Farm
Biggin CE Prim Sch
Cardle View
Biggin Grange
LIFES RD
GREENHEAD CRES
DRURY LA
CARDLEMERE LA
WOOLLATON LA
Bank Cottage
Dalehead
Greenhead
Bank House
Biggin Dale
Mount Pleasant Farm
Ferny Bottom
Cheapside
Wellclose
BACK LA
Bigginmoor Farm

137
150

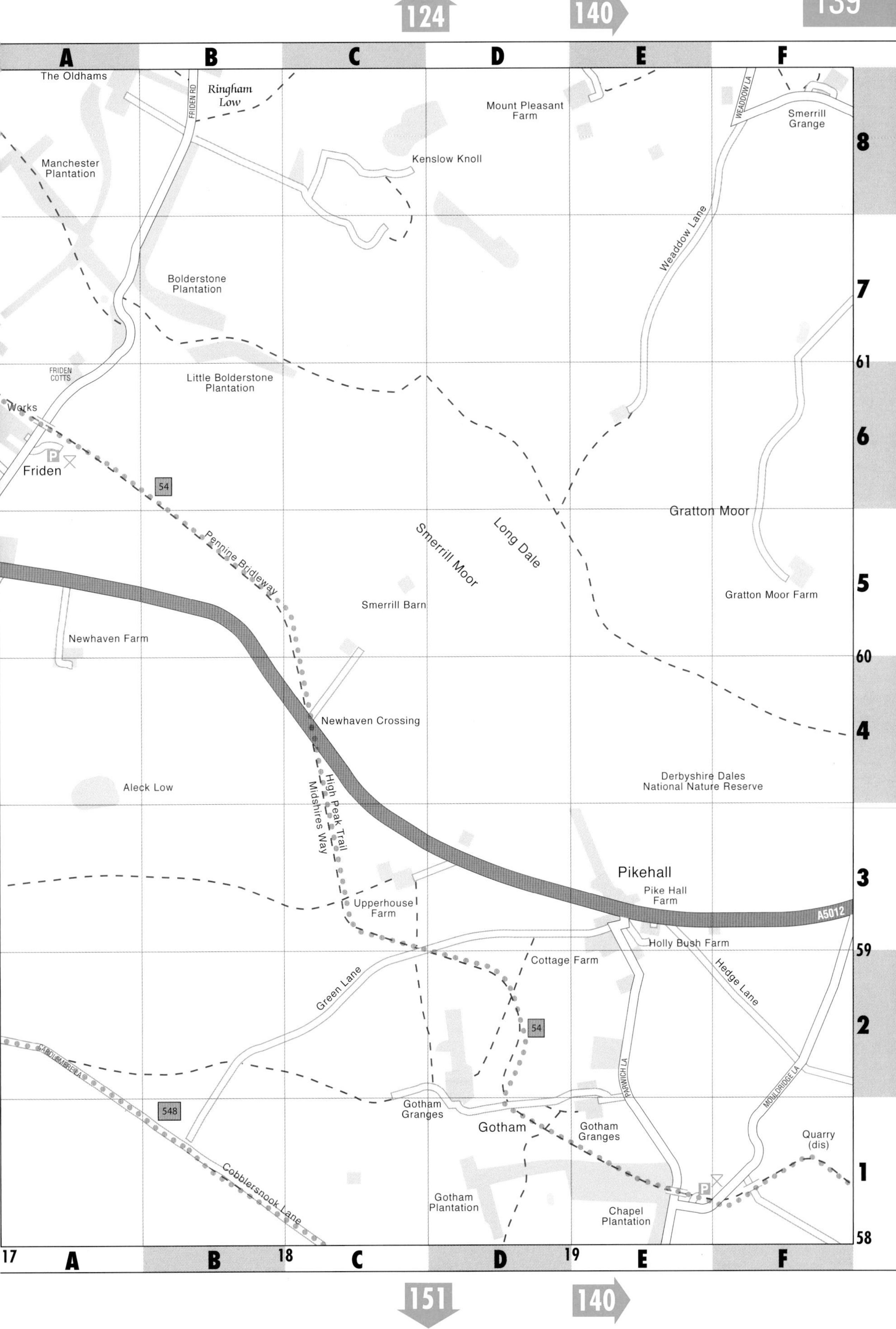

A B C D E F

8
7
61
6
5
60
4
3
59
2
1
58

The Oldhams

Manchester
Plantation

FRIDEN RD
Ringham
Low

Bolderstone
Plantation

Kenslow Knoll

Mount Pleasant
Farm

WEADDOW LA

Smerrill
Grange

Weaddow Lane

FRIDEN
COTTS

Little Bolderstone
Plantation

Works

P

Friden

54

Pennine Bridleway

Smerrill Moor

Long Dale

Gratton Moor

Gratton Moor Farm

Smerrill Barn

Newhaven Farm

Newhaven Crossing

High Peak Trail
Midshires Way

Aleck Low

Derbyshire Dales
National Nature Reserve

Pikehall

Pike Hall
Farm

A5012

Upperhouse
Farm

Green Lane

Cottage Farm

Holly Bush Farm

Hedge Lane

59

CARDLEMERE LA

54

PARWICH LA

MOUDRIDGE LA

548

Gotham
Granges

Gotham

Gotham
Granges

Quarry
(dis)

Cobblersnook Lane

Gotham
Plantation

P

Chapel
Plantation

139
125

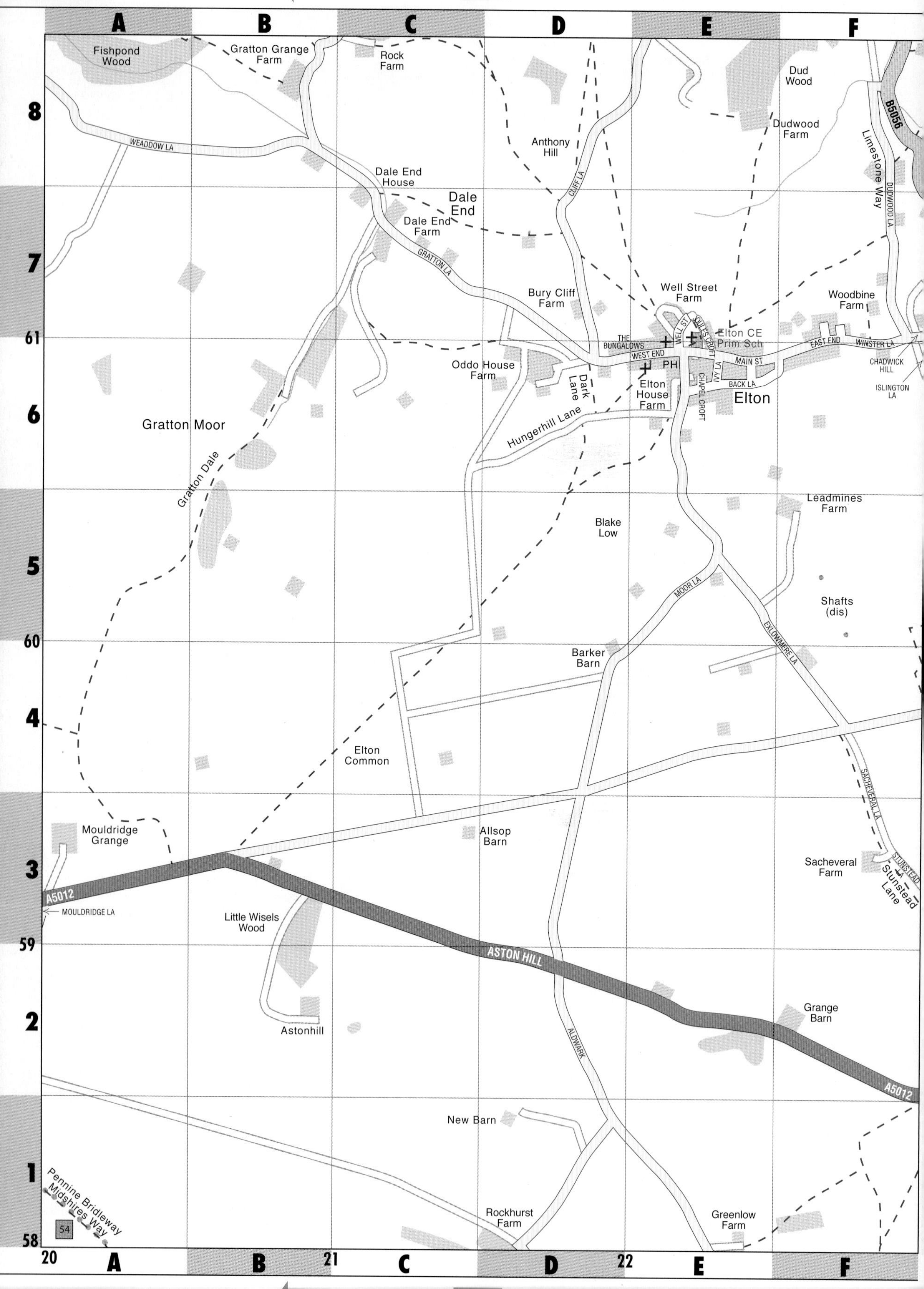
A
B
C
D
E
F
8
7
61
6
5
60
4
3
59
2
1
58
20
21
22
Fishpond Wood
Gratton Grange Farm
Rock Farm
Dud Wood
Dudwood Farm
B5056
Limestone Way
DUDWOOD LA
WEADDOW LA
Anthony Hill
Dale End House
Dale End
Dale End Farm
CLIFF LA
GRATTON LA
Bury Cliff Farm
Well Street Farm
Woodbine Farm
THE BUNGALOWS
WELL ST
Elton CE Prim Sch
EAST END
WINSTER LA
WEST END
PH
MAIN ST
CHADWICK HILL
ISLINGTON LA
Oddo House Farm
Dark Lane
Elton House Farm
CHAPEL CROFT
IVY LA
BACK LA
Elton
Gratton Moor
Hungerhill Lane
Gratton Dale
Leadmines Farm
Blake Low
MOOR LA
Shafts (dis)
EXLOWMERE LA
Barker Barn
Elton Common
SACHEVERAL LA
Mouldridge Grange
Allsop Barn
Sacheveral Farm
Stunstead Lane
A5012
MOULDRIDGE LA
Little Wisels Wood
ASTON HILL
Grange Barn
Astonhill
ALDWARK
A5012
New Barn
Pennine Bridleway
Midshires Way
54
Rockhurst Farm
Greenlow Farm

139
152

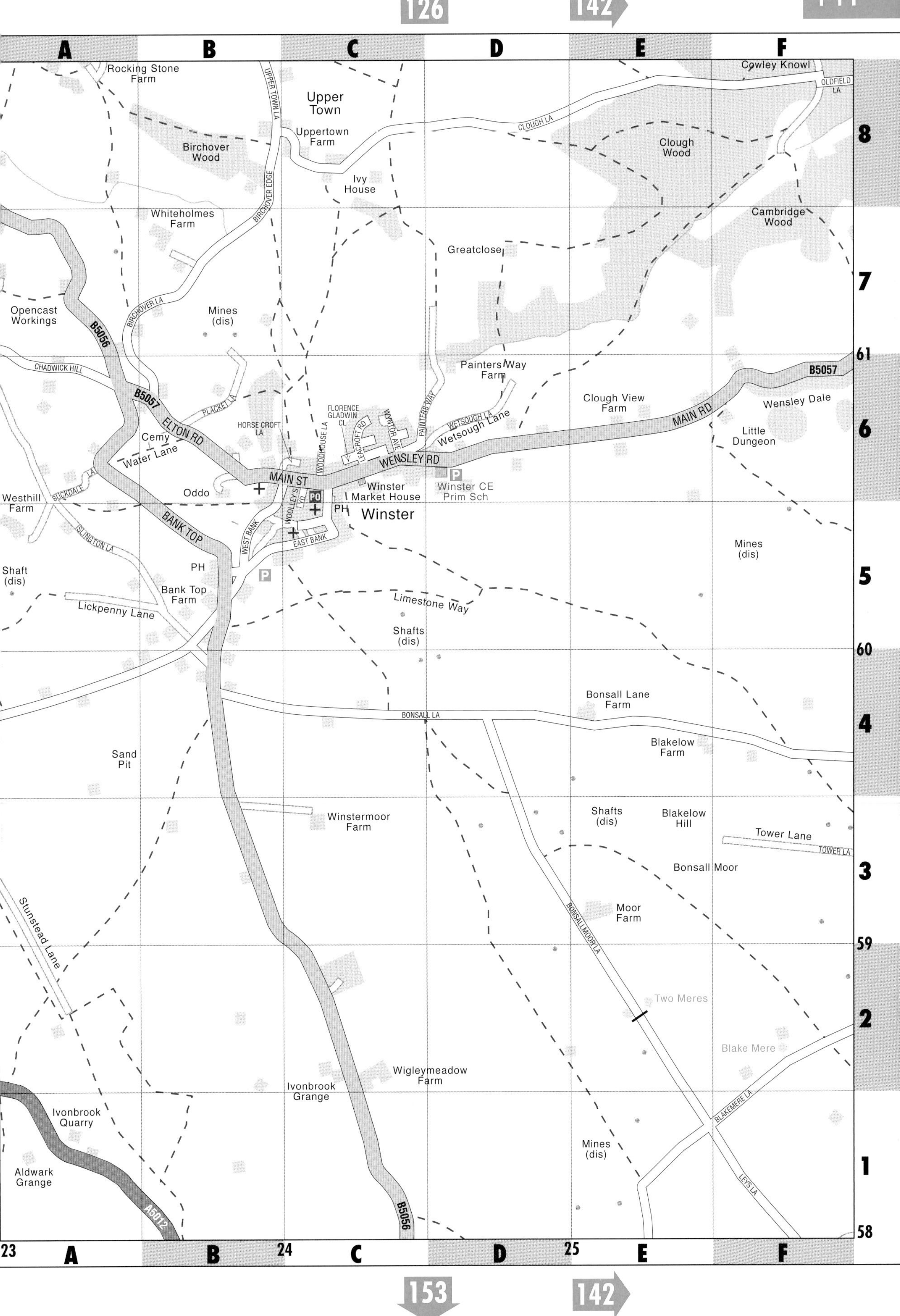

Rocking Stone Farm

Upper Town

Uppertown Farm

Birchover Wood

Ivy House

Whiteholmes Farm

Clough Wood

Cowley Knowl

OLDFIELD LA

CLOUGH LA

Cambridge Wood

Greatclose

Opencast Workings

Mines (dis)

BIRCHOVER LA

B5056

CHADWICK HILL

B5057

ELTON RD

PLACKET LA

HORSE CROFT LA

Cemy

Water Lane

BUCKDALE LA

Oddo

BANK TOP

WEST BANK

EAST BANK

PH

Westhill Farm

Shaft (dis)

Lickpenny Lane

ISLINGTON LA

PH

Bank Top Farm

Sand Pit

Stunstead Lane

Ivonbrook Quarry

Aldwark Grange

A6012

B5056

Ivonbrook Grange

Wigleymeadow Farm

Winstermoor Farm

Limestone Way

Shafts (dis)

Painters Way Farm

PAINTERS WAY

WYNDON AVE

LEACROFT RD

WOODHOUSE LA

FLORENCE GLADWIN CL

WENSLEY RD

WETSOUGH LA

Wetsough Lane

MAIN ST

Winster Market House

WOOLLEY'S YD

PO

PH

Winster

Winster CE Prim Sch

P

Clough View Farm

B5057

MAIN RD

Wensley Dale

Little Dungeon

Mines (dis)

Bonsall Lane Farm

BONSALL LA

Blakelow Farm

Shafts (dis)

Blakelow Hill

Tower Lane

TOWER LA

Bonsall Moor

BONSALL MOOR LA

Moor Farm

Two Meres

Blake Mere

BLAKEMERE LA

LEYS LA

Mines (dis)

8

7

61

6

5

60

4

3

59

2

58

1

23

24

25

A B C D E F

141
127

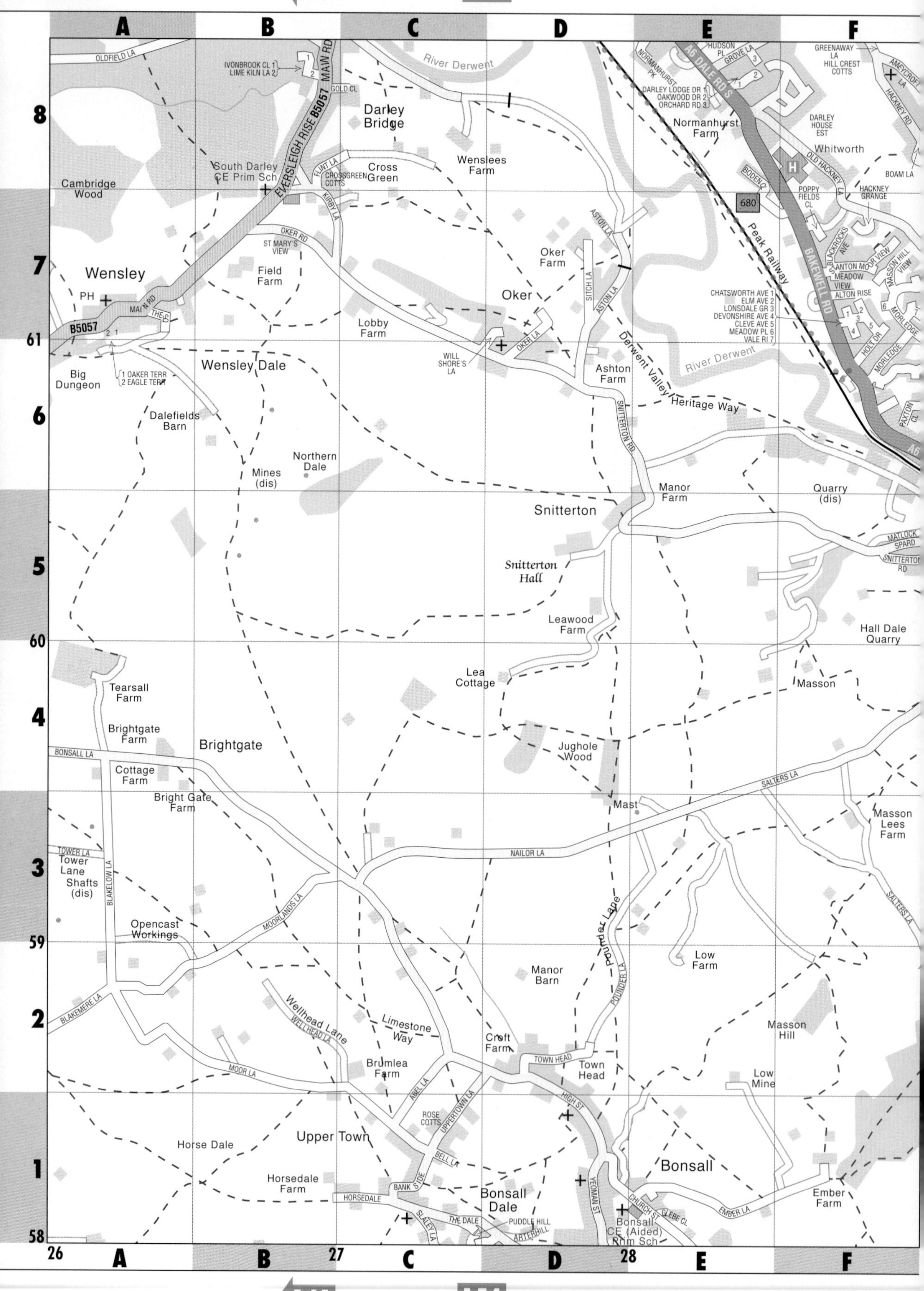
A
B
C
D
E
F
OLDFIELD LA
IVONBROOK CL 1
LIME KILN LA 2
MAIN RD
GOLD CL
River Derwent
Darley Bridge
HUDSON PL
GROVE LA
NORMANHURST PK
A6 DALE RD S
DARLEY LODGE DR 1
OAKWOOD DR 2
ORCHARD RD 3
GREENAWAY LA
HILL CREST COTTS
AMEYCROFT LA
HACKNEY RD
DARLEY HOUSE EST
Normanhurst Farm
Whitworth
OLD HACKNEY LA
BOAM LA
Wenslees Farm
Cross Green
FLINT LA
CROSSGREEN COTTS
South Darley CE Prim Sch
EVERSLEIGH RISE B5057
Cambridge Wood
KIRBY LA
BODEN CL
POPPY FIELDS CL
HACKNEY GRANGE
680
Peak Railway
OKER RD
ST MARY'S VIEW
ASTON LA
Oker Farm
BLACKROCKS AVE
BAKEWELL RD
ANTON MOOR VIEW
MEADOW VIEW
MASSON HILL VIEW
ALTON RISE
Wensley
Field Farm
Oker
SITCH LA
ASTON LA
CHATSWORTH AVE 1
ELM AVE 2
LONSDALE GR 3
DEVONSHIRE AVE 4
CLEVE AVE 5
MEADOW PL 6
VALE RI 7
MORLEDGE
HOLT DR
PH
MAIN RD
THE SQ
Lobby Farm
B5057
OKER LA
WILL SHORE'S LA
Derwent Valley Heritage Way
River Derwent
Big Dungeon
1 OAKER TERR
2 EAGLE TERR
Wensley Dale
Ashton Farm
Dalefields Barn
SNITTERTON RD
PAXTON CL
A6
Northern Dale
Mines (dis)
Manor Farm
Quarry (dis)
Snitterton
MATLOCK SPA RD
SNITTERTON RD
Snitterton Hall
Leawood Farm
Hall Dale Quarry
Lea Cottage
Tearsall Farm
Masson
Brightgate Farm
Brightgate
Jughole Wood
BONSALL LA
Cottage Farm
Bright Gate Farm
SALTERS LA
Mast
Masson Lees Farm
TOWER LA
Tower Lane Shafts (dis)
BLAKELOW LA
NAILOR LA
SALTERS LA
MOORLANDS LA
Opencast Workings
Pounder Lane
POUNDER LA
Low Farm
Manor Barn
BLAKEMERE LA
Wellhead Lane
WELLHEAD LA
Limestone Way
Croft Farm
Masson Hill
TOWN HEAD
Town Head
MOOR LA
Brumlea Farm
Low Mine
ABEL LA
ROSE COTTS
UPPERTOWN LA
HIGH ST
Horse Dale
Upper Town
BELL LA
Bonsall
Horsedale Farm
BANK SIDE
Bonsall Dale
YEOMAN ST
CHURCH ST
GLEBE CL
EMBER LA
Ember Farm
HORSEDALE
SLALEY LA
THE DALE
PUDDLE HILL
ARTERHILL
Bonsall CE (Aided) Prim Sch
8
7
61
6
5
60
4
3
59
2
1
58
26
27
28

141
154

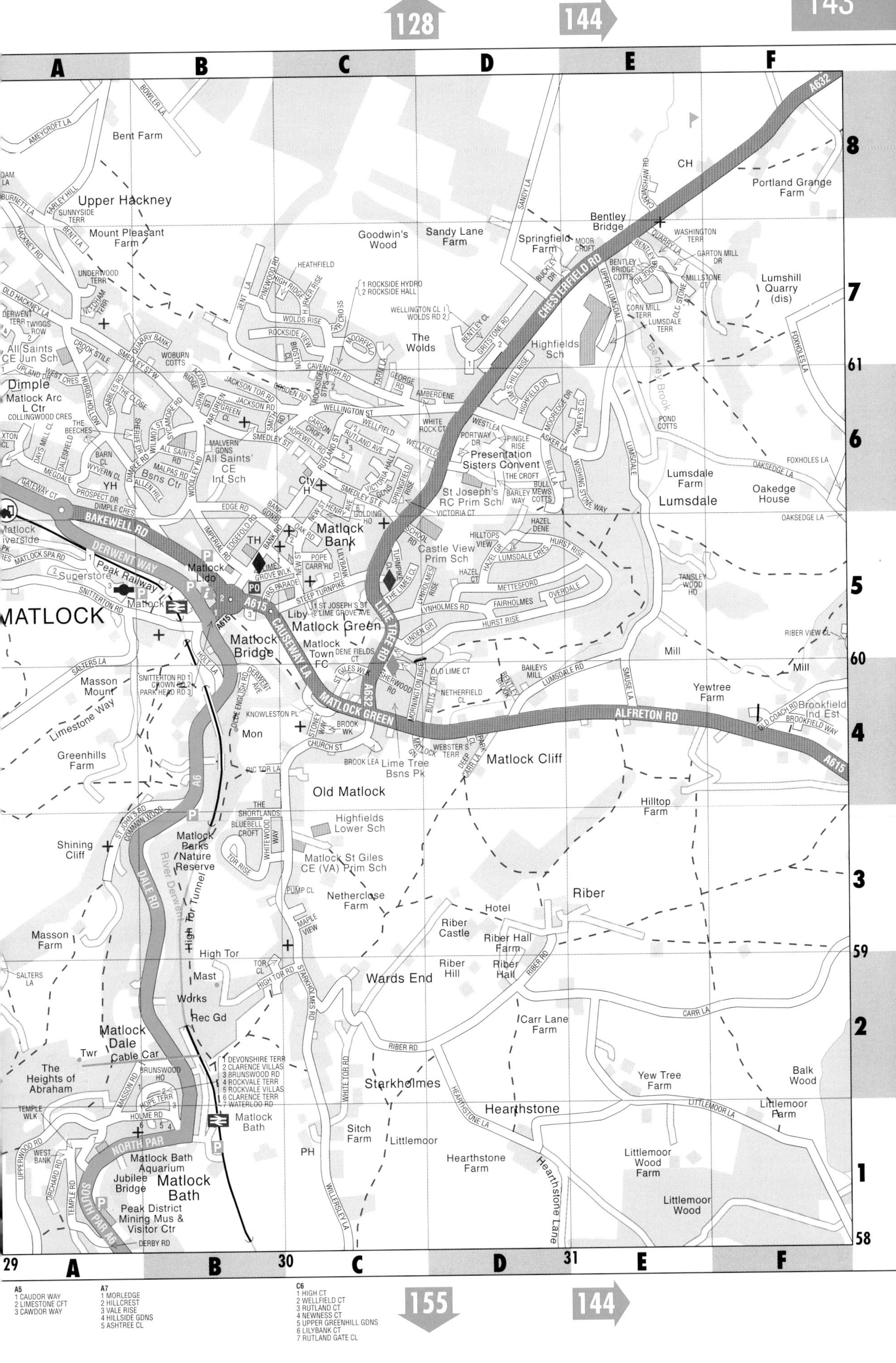

128
144
A
B
C
D
E
F
8
7
61
6
5
60
4
3
59
2
1
58
29
30
31
Bent Farm
Upper Hackney
Mount Pleasant Farm
Goodwin's Wood
Sandy Lane Farm
Springfield Farm
Bentley Bridge
CH
Portland Grange Farm
Lumshill Quarry (dis)
The Wolds
Highfields Sch
All Saints CE Jun Sch
Dimple
Matlock Arc L Ctr
All Saints' CE Inf Sch
Bsns Ctr
YH
Presentation Sisters Convent
St Joseph's RC Prim Sch
Lumsdale Farm
Lumsdale
Oakedge House
Matlock Bank
Castle View Prim Sch
Matlock Lido
Superstore
Peak Railway
Matlock
MATLOCK
Matlock Bridge
Matlock Green
Matlock Town FC
Liby
Mill
Yewtree Farm
Brookfield Ind Est
Masson Mount
Limestone Way
Greenhills Farm
Mon
Lime Tree Bsns Pk
Matlock Cliff
Old Matlock
Hilltop Farm
Highfields Lower Sch
Shining Cliff
Matlock Parks Nature Reserve
Matlock St Giles CE (VA) Prim Sch
Netherclose Farm
Riber
Hotel
Riber Castle
Riber Hall Farm
Masson Farm
High Tor
High Tor Tunnel
River Derwent
Mast
Riber Hill
Riber Hall
Wards End
Works
Rec Gd
Carr Lane Farm
Matlock Dale
Twr
Cable Car
The Heights of Abraham
Starkholmes
Yew Tree Farm
Balk Wood
Hearthstone
Littlemoor Farm
Matlock Bath
Sitch Farm
Littlemoor
PH
Hearthstone Farm
Hearthstone Lane
Littlemoor Wood Farm
Littlemoor Wood
Matlock Bath Aquarium
Jubilee Bridge
Peak District Mining Mus & Visitor Ctr
CHESTERFIELD RD
A632
BAKEWELL RD
DERWENT WAY
A615
CAUSEWAY LA
LIME TREE RD
MATLOCK GREEN
ALFRETON RD
A6
DALE RD
NORTH PAR
SOUTH PAR
CARR LA
RIBER RD
LITTLEMOOR LA
HEARTHSTONE LA
STARKHOLMES RD
WILLERSLEY LA
WHITE TOR RD
SMEDLEY ST
WELLINGTON ST
CAVENDISH RD
JACKSON RD
LUMSDALE
UPPER LUMSDALE
FOXHOLES LA
OAKEDGE LA
SALTERS LA
1 ROCKSIDE HYDRO
2 ROCKSIDE HALL
1 DEVONSHIRE TERR
2 CLARENCE VILLAS
3 BRUNSWOOD RD
4 ROCKVALE TERR
5 ROCKVALE VILLAS
6 CLARENCE TERR
7 WATERLOO RD
155
144
A5
1 CAUDOR WAY
2 LIMESTONE CFT
3 CAWDOR WAY
A7
1 MORLEDGE
2 HILLCREST
3 VALE RISE
4 HILLSIDE GDNS
5 ASHTREE CL
C6
1 HIGH CT
2 WELLFIELD CT
3 RUTLAND CT
4 NEWNESS CT
5 UPPER GREENHILL GDNS
6 LILYBANK CT
7 RUTLAND GATE CL

143
129

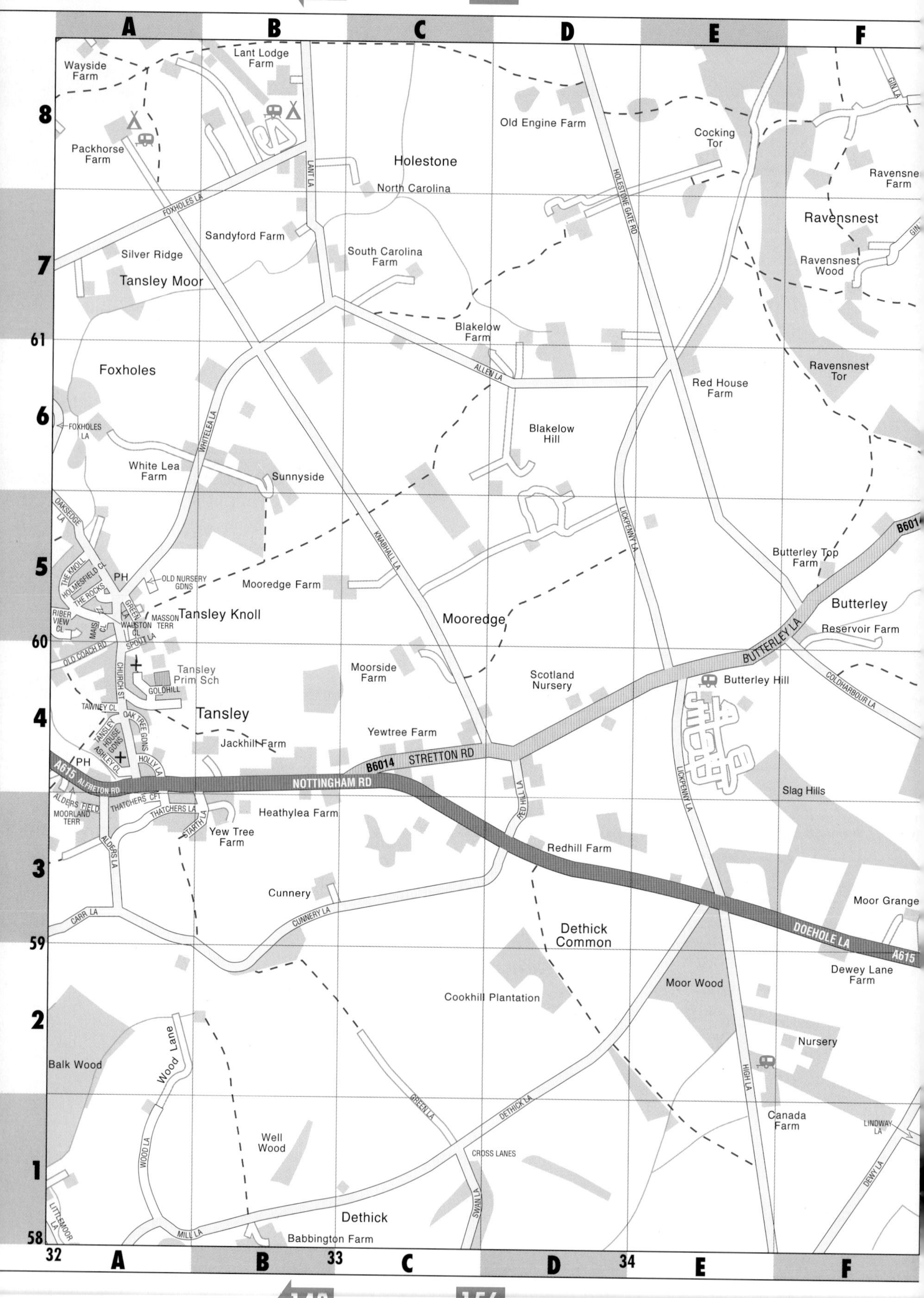
Wayside Farm
Lant Lodge Farm
Packhorse Farm
Old Engine Farm
Cocking Tor
Holestone
North Carolina
Ravensnest Farm
Ravensnest
Sandyford Farm
Silver Ridge
Tansley Moor
South Carolina Farm
Ravensnest Wood
Blakelow Farm
Foxholes
Ravensnest Tor
Red House Farm
Blakelow Hill
White Lea Farm
Sunnyside
Butterley Top Farm
Mooredge Farm
Butterley
Tansley Knoll
Mooredge
Reservoir Farm
Moorside Farm
Tansley Prim Sch
Scotland Nursery
Butterley Hill
Tansley
Yewtree Farm
Jackhill Farm
STRETTON RD
NOTTINGHAM RD
Slag Hills
Heathylea Farm
Yew Tree Farm
Redhill Farm
Cunnery
Moor Grange
Dethick Common
DOEHOLE LA
Dewey Lane Farm
Moor Wood
Cookhill Plantation
Nursery
Balk Wood
Wood Lane
Canada Farm
Well Wood
CROSS LANES
Dethick
Babbington Farm
FOXHOLES LA
LANT LA
HOLESTONE GATE RD
ALLEN LA
WHITELEA LA
KNABHALL LA
LICKPENNY LA
BUTTERLEY LA
COLDHARBOUR LA
RED HILL LA
CUNNERY LA
CARR LA
ALDERS LA
GREEN LA
DETHICK LA
SWAN LA
MILL LA
WOOD LA
HIGH LA
DEWY LA
LINDWAY LA
LITTLEMOOR LA
A615
B6014
B601
PH

143
156

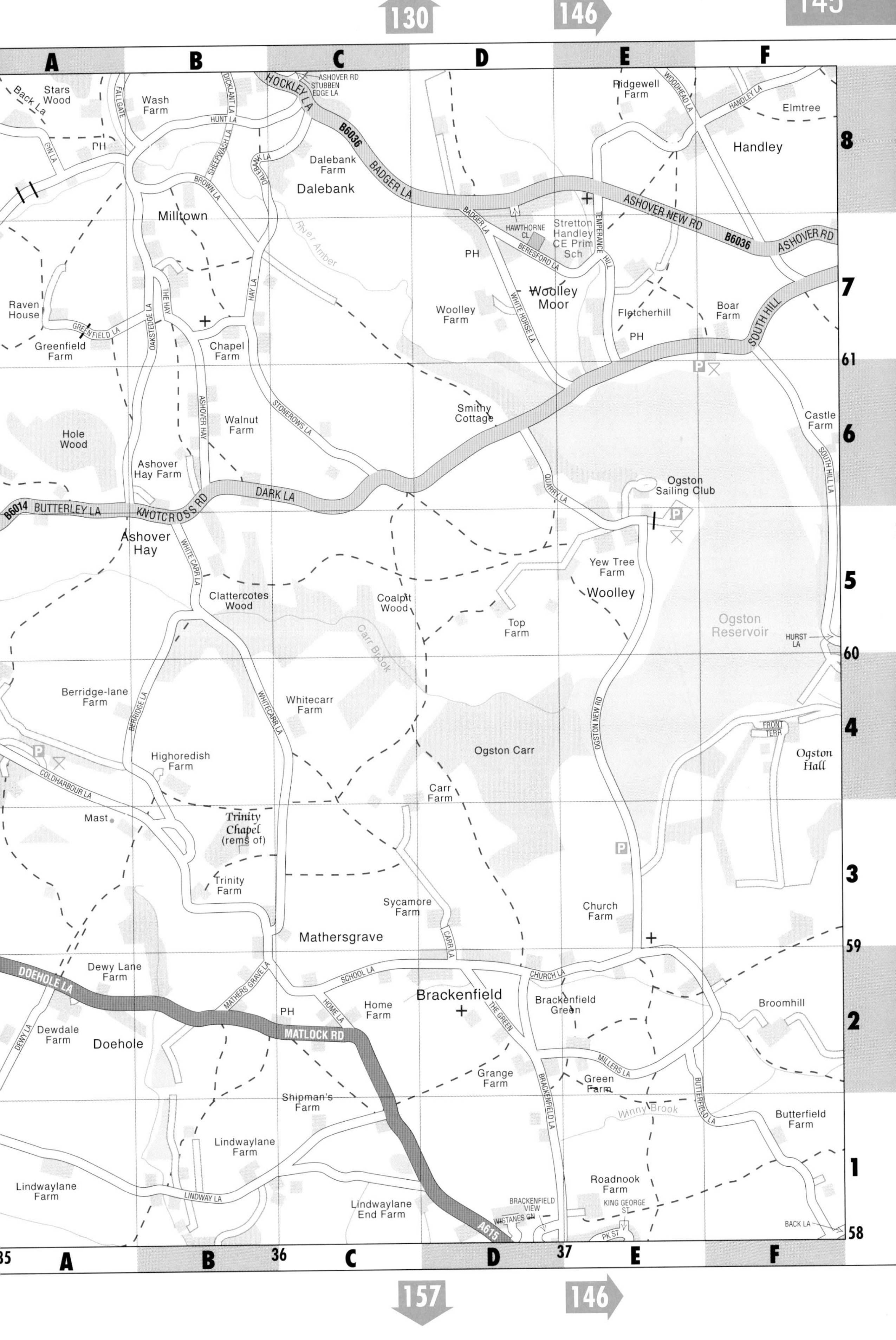

A B C D E F

8 7 61 6 5 60 4 3 59 2 1 58

Stars Wood
Back La
CN LA
PH
FALLGATE
Wash Farm
DUCKLANT LA
HOCKLEY LA
Ashover Rd
STUBBEN EDGE LA
SHEEPWASH LA
HUNT LA
B6036
BADGER LA
Ridgewell Farm
WOODHEAD LA
HANDLEY LA
Elmtree
Handley
Dalebank Farm
Dalebank
Milltown
BROWN LA
HAY LA
WELL LA
River Amber
BADGER LA
Hawthorne Cl
BERESFORD LA
Stretton Handley CE Prim Sch
TEMPERANCE HILL
ASHOVER NEW RD
B6036
ASHOVER RD

Raven House
GREENFIELD LA
THE HAY
OAKSTEDE LA
Greenfield Farm
Chapel Farm
Woolley Farm
PH
Woolley Moor
WHITE HORSE LA
Fletcherhill
PH
Boar Farm
SOUTH HILL
P

Hole Wood
ASHOVER HAY
Walnut Farm
STONEROWS LA
Smithy Cottage
Castle Farm
SOUTH HILL LA

Ashover Hay Farm
DARK LA
QUARRY LA
Ogston Sailing Club
P

B6014 BUTTERLEY LA
KNOTCROSS RD
Ashover Hay
WHITE CARR LA
Yew Tree Farm
Woolley
Ogston Reservoir

Clattercotes Wood
Coalpit Wood
Top Farm
HURST LA

Berridge-lane Farm
BERRIDGE LA
WHITECARR LA
Whitecarr Farm
Carr Brook
FRONT TERR
Ogston Hall

P
Highoredish Farm
Ogston Carr
OGSTON MAIN RD

Coldharbour La
Mast
Trinity Chapel (rems of)
Carr Farm
CARR LA

Trinity Farm
Sycamore Farm
Church Farm
P

Mathersgrave
DEWY LA
Dewy Lane Farm
MATHERS GRAVE LA
PH
SCHOOL LA
HOME LA
Home Farm
Brackenfield
CHURCH LA
Brackenfield Green
THE GREEN
Broomhill

DOEHOLE LA
Dewdale Farm
Doehole
MATLOCK RD
Grange Farm
Green Farm
MILLERS LA
BRACKENFIELD LA
BUTTERFIELD LA
Butterfield Farm

Shipman's Farm
Lindwaylane Farm
Lindwaylane Farm
LINDWAY LA
Lindwaylane End Farm
A615
BRACKENFIELD VIEW
WSTANES GN
Roadnook Farm
KING GEORGE ST
PK ST
Winny Brook
BACK LA

145
131

A B C D E F

8 7 6 5 4 3 2 1

61 60 59 58

Menel Farm
Stretton House
HIGHSTAIRS LA
A61 STRETTON RD
Top Farm
STRAW LA
Ain Moor
Padley Wood
Opencast Workings
Cemy
B6036
ASHOVER RD
Stretton Farm
B6014
SOUTH HILL
Smithy Moor
Sidness Farm
SMITHS LA
Stretton
Averill Farm
PH
Hillside Farm
Hilltop Farm
MORTON ROAD
South Hill
CROW LA
PEGGY LA
Smithy Brook
EVERSHILL LA
South Hill Farm
Stretton Plantation
Fold House Farm
BURNSHAW ST
Stretton Hillside
MALTBY AVE
SITWELL VILLAS
OAK VIEW GDNS
STRETTON RD
EVERSHILL CL
Haver Hill Farm
MAIN RD
SHERWOOD ST
CEDAR ST
Northedge Farm
HOLLAND CL
BACK LA
HAWTHORNE AVE
BRONTE ST
PRIESTLEY AVE
TENNYSON ST
MICKLEY LA
Morton
PH
MAIN RD
B60
HURST LA
RESERVOIR HOS
Mickley Estate
CLAYTON CL
CHURCH LA
Ogston
FIR TREE AVE
SHAKESPEARE AVE
Yew Tree Farm
CHURCH RISE
MILTON AVE
Mickley Inf Sch
HIGHAM LA
DALE VIEW
BLUEBELL HILL
SYCAMORE CL
Ogston Bridge
OGSTON LA
Mickley Farm
Stonebroom Prim Sch
Pingle Farm
Stonebroom
SCHOOL CL
QUARRY LA
WEST ST
HIGH ST
DOUBLE VILLAS
PH
JULIA CRES
CARLYLE RD
PH
WELL LA
COMMON LA
CHURCH VIEW CL
SCOTT CRES
THACKERAY RD
WESLEY RD
BIRKINSTYLE LA
ADDISON RD
Goosegreen
BIRKINSTYLE AVE
QUEENSWAY
BRIERLEY RD
KEATS RD
B6013
CHESTERFIELD RD
THE WILLOWS
FERN LEA
FERNWOOD CL
THE BUNGALOWS
CLEVELAND RD
BUNYAN CRES
KINGSLEY CRES
Higham
River Amber
GOOSE GREEN LA
DE PEVEREL CT
KEATS WLK
SHELLEY GR
BYRON GR
THE CROFT
NORTHFIELD
PH
STRETTEA LA
PO
NEW ST
SCHOOL CL
TOWN END
MEADOW VIEW
New Higham
DOG LA
WELLINGTON MEWS
Shirland
WELLINGTON PK
MAIN RD
PINEWOOD DR
PINEWOOD CL
THE FOX HOLLIES
AMBER CL
CHURCH ST
BELPER RD
Higham Dairy Farm
WILLOW ST
BURNSIDE AVE
ROWAN DR
LILAC WAY
ASPEN RISE
PH
PH
Shirland Prim Sch
ELM TREE AVE
BYRON ST
BURNS ST
HALLFIELDS RISE
HALLFIELDGATE LA
BUMPMILL LA
CLAY ST
GREAVES ST
BEVAN ST
ST LEONARDS PL
PARK CL
PARK LA
BEVAN CT
Hallfield Gate
CHESTERFIELD RD A61
OAK LA
Hallfield Hall
PIT LA
BACK LA
Carr Hill Farm
B6013
CROSS LA

38 A B 39 C D 40 E F

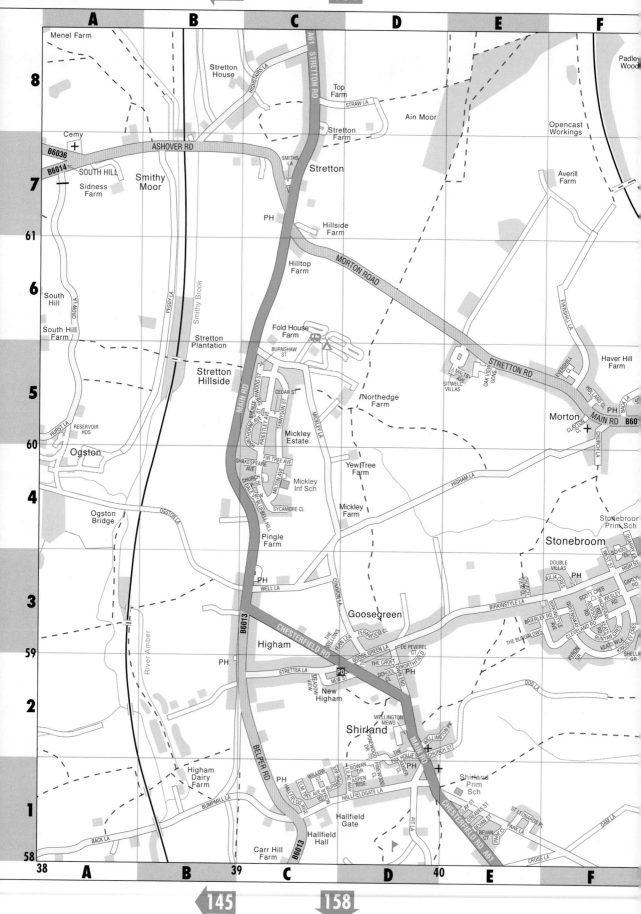

145
158

132
148

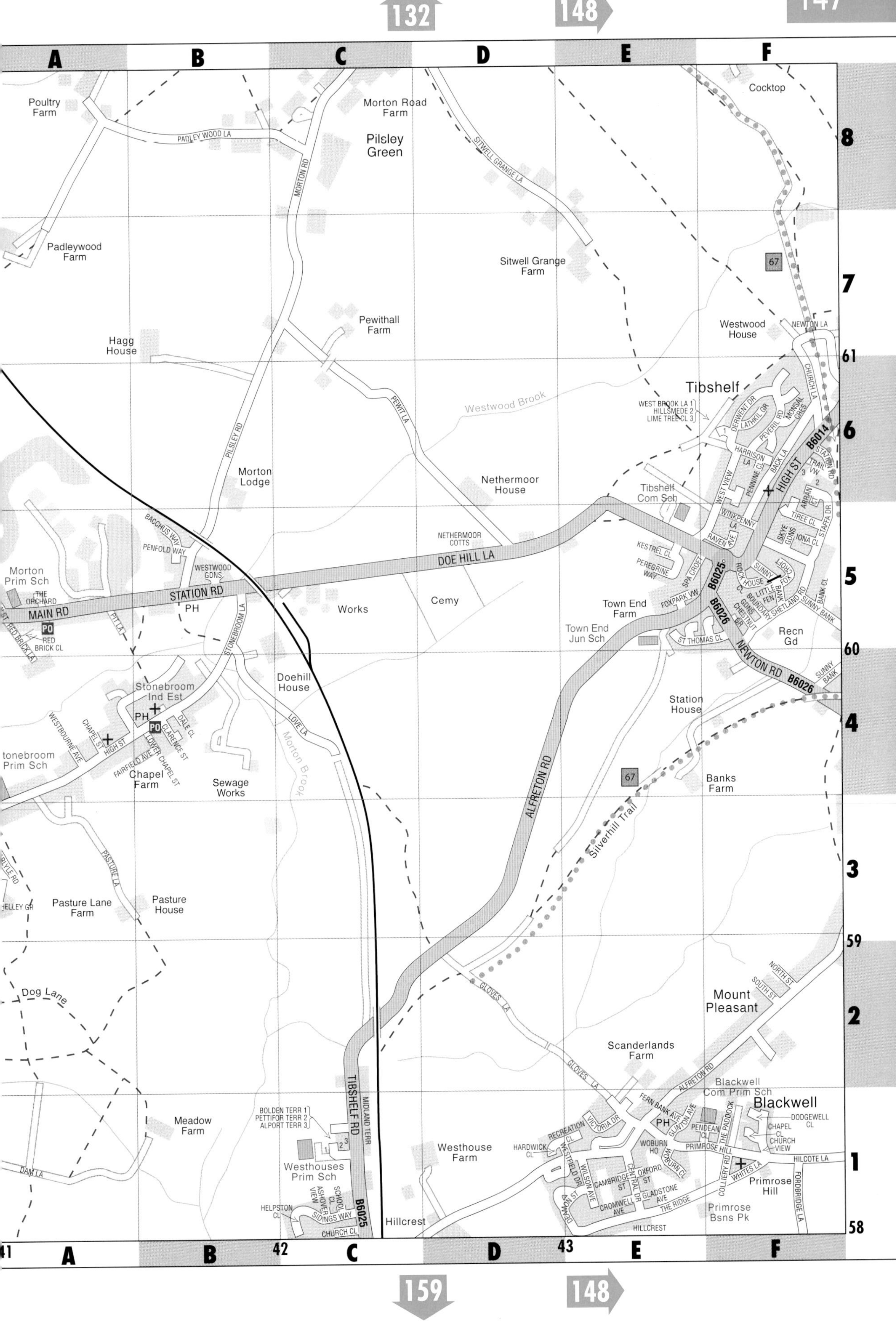
A
B
C
D
E
F
Poultry Farm
PADLEY WOOD LA
MORTON RD
Morton Road Farm
Pilsley Green
SITWELL GRANGE LA
Cocktop
Padleywood Farm
Sitwell Grange Farm
67
Pewithall Farm
Hagg House
Westwood House
NEWTON LA
Tibshelf
WEST BROOK LA 1
HILLSMEDE 2
LIME TREE CL 3
Westwood Brook
PEWIT LA
PILSLEY RD
CHURCH LA
B6014
HIGH ST
Morton Lodge
Nethermoor House
Tibshelf Com Sch
BACCHUS WAY
PENFOLD WAY
NETHERMOOR COTTS
DOE HILL LA
Morton Prim Sch
WESTWOOD GDNS
THE ORCHARD
STATION RD
MAIN RD
PH
Works
Cemy
Town End Farm
Town End Jun Sch
PO
RED BRICK CL
PIT LA
STONEBROOM LA
Doehill House
ST THOMAS CL
NEWTON RD
B6026
B6025
Recn Gd
Stonebroom Ind Est
Station House
WESTBOURNE AVE
CHAPEL ST
HIGH ST
DALE CL
CLARENCE ST
LOVE LA
Morton Brook
ALFRETON RD
Stonebroom Prim Sch
FAIRFIELD AVE
LOWER CHAPEL ST
Chapel Farm
Sewage Works
Banks Farm
Silverhill Trail
PASTURE LA
Pasture Lane Farm
Pasture House
Dog Lane
Mount Pleasant
NORTH ST
SOUTH ST
GLOVES LA
Scanderlands Farm
TIBSHELF RD
MIDLAND TERR
BOLDEN TERR 1
PETTIFOR TERR 2
ALPORT TERR 3
Meadow Farm
Blackwell Com Prim Sch
Blackwell
DODGEWELL CL
CHAPEL CL
CHURCH VIEW
HILCOTE LA
Westhouse Farm
Westhouses Prim Sch
HARDWICK CL
RECREATION CL
VICTORIA DR
PRIMROSE HILL
WHITES LA
Primrose Hill
DAM LA
HELPSTON CL
ASHOVER VIEW
SCHOOL CL
SIDINGS WAY
CHURCH CL
Hillcrest
WESTFIELD DR
WILSON AVE
CAMBRIDGE ST
OXFORD ST
CENTRAL DR
GLADSTONE AVE
THE RIDGE
CROMWELL AVE
HILLCREST
COLLIERY RD
Primrose Bsns Pk
FORDBRIDGE LA
8
7
61
6
5
60
4
3
59
2
1
58
41
42
43

159
148

147
133

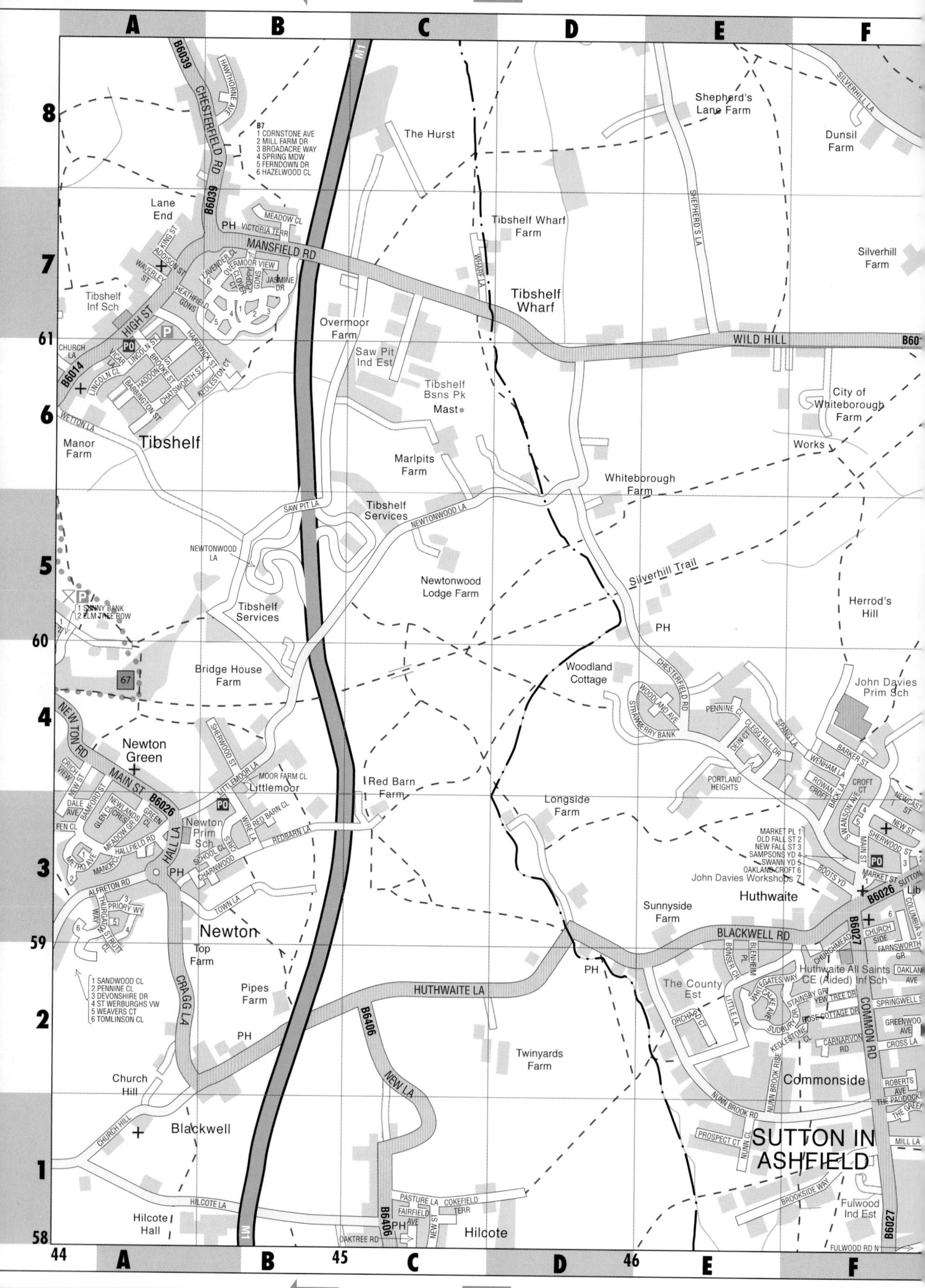
A
B
C
D
E
F
8
7
61
6
5
60
4
3
59
2
1
58
44
45
46
B6039
CHESTERFIELD RD
HAWTHORNE AVE
B7
1 CORNSTONE AVE
2 MILL FARM DR
3 BROADACRE WAY
4 SPRING MDW
5 FERNDOWN DR
6 HAZELWOOD CL
M1
The Hurst
Shepherd's
Lane Farm
SILVERHILL LA
Dunsil
Farm
Lane
End
MEADOW CL
PH
VICTORIA TERR
MANSFIELD RD
KING ST
ADDISON ST
WAVERLEY ST
LAVENDER CL
OVERMOOR VIEW
CLOVER CT
POPPY GDNS
JASMINE DR
HEATHFIELD GDNS
Tibshelf
Inf Sch
HIGH ST
Tibshelf Wharf
Farm
WHARF LA
SHEPHERD'S LA
Silverhill
Farm
Tibshelf
Wharf
Overmoor
Farm
WILD HILL
B60
CHURCH LA
VICAR LA
LINCOLN ST
BROOKE ST
HARDWICK ST
HADDON ST
KEDLESTON CT
CHATSWORTH ST
BABBINGTON ST
LINCOLN CL
B6014
Saw Pit
Ind Est
Tibshelf
Bsns Pk
Mast
City of
Whiteborough
Farm
WETTON LA
Manor
Farm
Tibshelf
Marlpits
Farm
Works
Whiteborough
Farm
SAW PIT LA
Tibshelf
Services
NEWTONWOOD LA
NEWTONWOOD LA
Newtonwood
Lodge Farm
Silverhill Trail
Herrod's
Hill
1 SUNNY BANK
2 ELM TREE ROW
Tibshelf
Services
PH
Bridge House
Farm
67
Woodland
Cottage
CHESTERFIELD RD
WOODLAND AVE
STRAWBERRY BANK
John Davies
Prim Sch
PENNINE CL
CLEGG HILL DR
SPRING LA
NEWTON RD
Newton
Green
SHERWOOD ST
MAIN ST
CRICH VIEW
NEW ST
DALE AVE
BAMFORD ST
GLEN CL
NEWLANDS CRES
MEADOW GR
GREEN CL
B6026
LITTLEMOOR LA
MOOR FARM CL
Littlemoor
Red Barn
Farm
DEIN CT
PORTLAND HEIGHTS
WENHAM LA
BARKER ST
ROWAN CROFT
BACK LA
CROFT CT
NEWCASTLE ST
Longside
Farm
FEN CL
HALLFIELD RD
HALL LA
Newton
Prim
Sch
RED BARN CL
WIRE LA
REDBARN LA
SCHOOL CL
CHARNWOOD
METRO AVE
MANOR CL
PH
MARKET PL 1
OLD FALL ST 2
NEW FALL ST 3
SAMPSONS YD 4
SWANN YD 5
OAKLAND CROFT 6
John Davies Workshops 7
SWANSON AVE
MAIN ST
NEW ST
SHERWOOD ST
BOOTS YD
MARKET ST
ALFRETON RD
PRIORY WY
THURGATON WAY
STRUTT CL
TOWN LA
Newton
Sunnyside
Farm
Huthwaite
B6026
SUTTON
Lib
B6027
CHURCH SIDE
FARNSWORTH GR
COLUMBIA ST
Top
Farm
BLACKWELL RD
CHURCHMEAD
PH
Huthwaite All Saints
CE (Aided) Inf Sch
OAKLANDS AVE
1 SANDWOOD CL
2 PENNINE CL
3 DEVONSHIRE DR
4 ST WERBURGHS VW
5 WEAVERS CT
6 TOMLINSON CL
Pipes
Farm
HUTHWAITE LA
B6406
BONSER CR
BLENHEIM PL
The County
Est
WHITEGATES WAY
LAKE AVE
STAINSBY GR
YEW TREE DR
SPRINGWELL ST
CRAGG LA
PH
LITTLE LA
ORCHARD CT
SUDBURY CT
ROSE COTTAGE DR
GREENWOOD AVE
KEDLESTONE CL
CARNARVON RD
COMMON RD
CROSS LA
Twinyards
Farm
Church
Hill
NEW LA
NUNN BROOK RISE
Commonside
ROBERTS AVE
THE PADDOCKS
THE GREEN
NUNN BROOK RD
CHURCH HILL
Blackwell
PROSPECT CT
NUNN CL
SUTTON IN
ASHFIELD
MILL LA
BROOKSIDE WAY
Fulwood
Ind Est
HILCOTE LA
PASTURE LA
COKEFIELD TERR
FAIRFIELD AVE
NEW ST
Hilcote
Hall
B6406
PH
Hilcote
OAKTREE RD
FULWOOD RD N
B6027

147
160

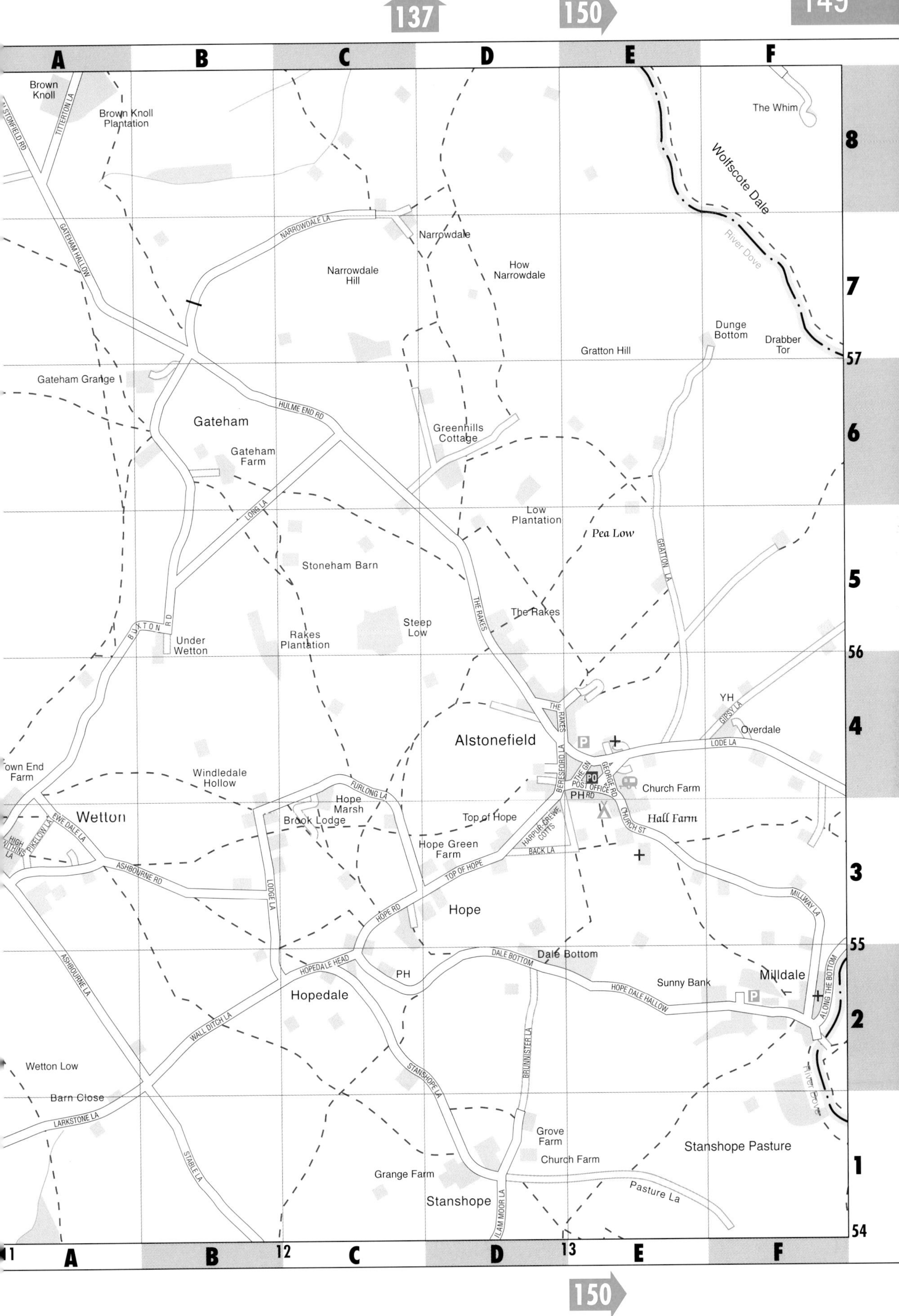

137
150

A B C D E F

8
7
57
6
5
56
4
3
55
2
1
54

Brown Knoll
Brown Knoll Plantation
The Whim
Wolfscote Dale
River Dove

STONEFIELD RD
TITTERTON LA
GATEHAM HALLOW

NARROWDALE LA
Narrowdale
Narrowdale Hill
How Narrowdale
Gratton Hill
Dunge Bottom
Drabber Tor

Gateham Grange
Gateham
HULME END RD
Greenhills Cottage
Gateham Farm
LONG LA
BUXTON RD

Low Plantation
Pea Low
GRATTON LA

Stoneham Barn
Steep Low
THE RAKES
The Rakes

Rakes Plantation
Under Wetton

YH
GIPSY LA
Overdale
LODE LA

THE RAKES
Alstonefield
P
Church Farm
BETHEL RD
CHURCH LA
GEORGE RD
PO
POST OFFICE
PH
Hall Farm
CHURCH ST

Town End Farm
Windledale Hollow
FURLONG LA
Hope Marsh
Brook Lodge
Top of Hope
Hope Green Farm
HARPUR CREWE COTTS
BACK LA
MILLWAY LA

Wetton
HIGH VIEW LA
PIXCLOW LA
EWE DALE LA
ASHBOURNE RD
LODGE LA
HOPE RD
TOP OF HOPE
Hope

Dale Bottom
Sunny Bank
Milldale
ALONG THE BOTTOM
P

HOPEDALE HEAD
PH
Hopedale
HOPE DALE HALLOW

ASHBOURNE LA
WALL DITCH LA
STANSHOPE LA
BRUNNISTER LA

Wetton Low
Barn Close
LARKSTONE LA
River Dove

STABLE LA
Grove Farm
Church Farm
Stanshope Pasture

Grange Farm
Stanshope
PASTURE LA
LLAM MOOR LA

150

149
138

A **B** **C** **D** **E** **F**

8

Biggin Dale

The Liffs

Greenrake Plantation

7

Johnson's Knoll

Tissington Trail

68

A515

PARWICH DALE

Alsop Moor Plantation

57

Cave

LIFFS RD

COLD EATON

6

Coldeaton

Lees Barn

Rivendale Caravan Pk

Dove Top Farm

Gipsy Bank

Iron Tors

Tissington Trail

5

Gipsy La

Nettly Knowe

Oulds Barn

GREENLOW

P

CROSSLOW LA

ALSOP MOOR GUTS

Oxdales Farm

Coldeaton Bridge

56

Pine View

Eatondale Wood

4

Lode House

Pinelow Plantation

Oxdales House

River Dove

Crosslow Bank Farm

Cross Low

3

Lode Plantation

Greenlowfield

LODE LA

Alsop en le Dale Hall

Manor Farm

Alsop en le Dale

68

OAM LA

55

ALONG THE BOTTOM

Mill Dale

Shining Tor

THE PINCH

OXCLOSE LA

Church Farm

Stonepit Plantation

2

P

New Inns

GREEN LA

New Hanson Grange

BUXTON RD

1

River Dove

Baley Hill

G4G LA

Moat Low

A515

54

14 **A** **B** **15** **C** **D** **16** **E** **F**

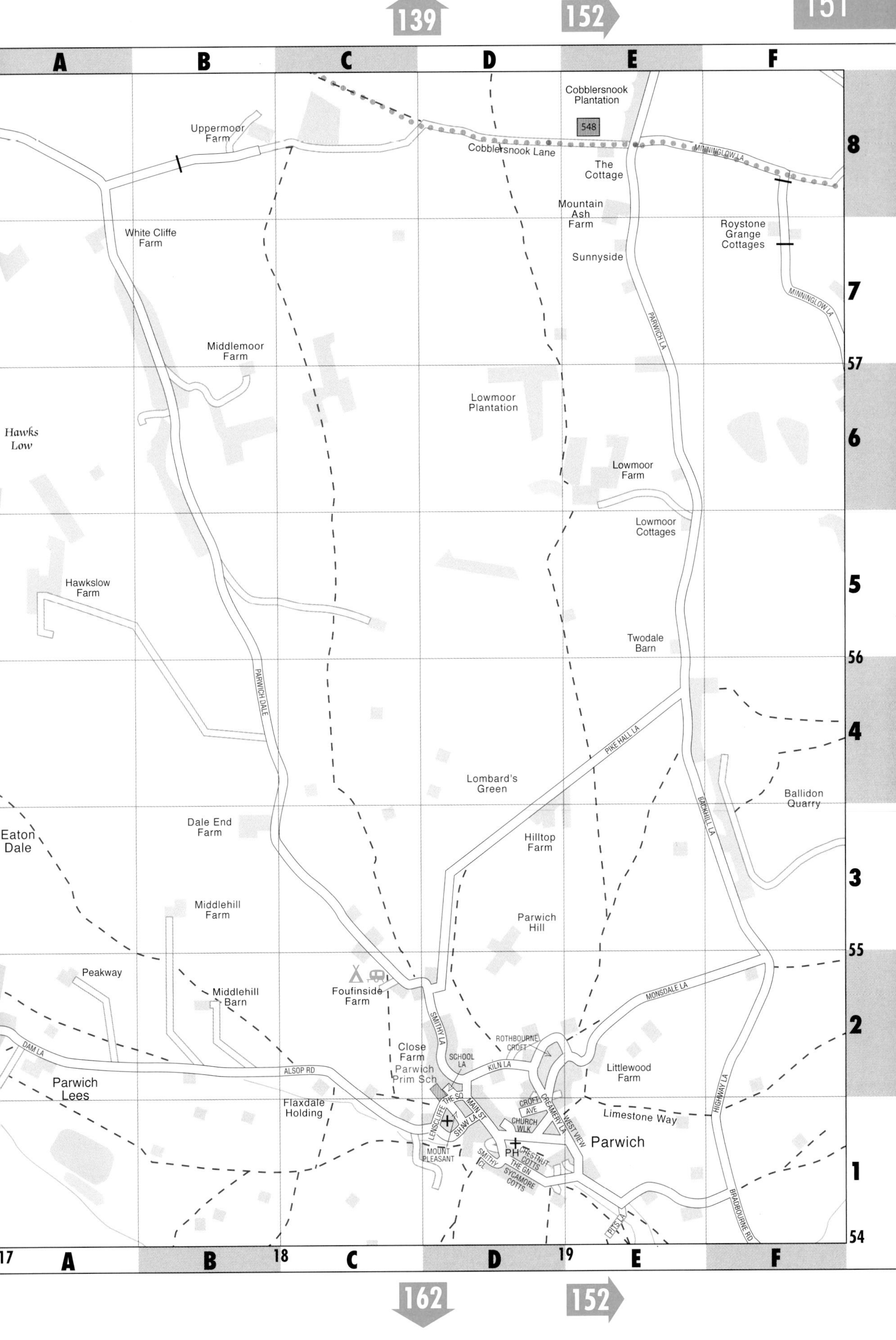

A **B** **C** **D** **E** **F**

8
7
57
6
5
56
4
3
55
2
1
54

Cobblersnook
Plantation

548

Cobblersnook Lane

The Cottage

Mountain
Ash
Farm

Sunnyside

Roystone
Grange
Cottages

MINNINGLOW LA

MINNINGLOW LA

Uppermoor
Farm

White Cliffe
Farm

Middlemoor
Farm

Hawks
Low

Lowmoor
Plantation

Lowmoor
Farm

Lowmoor
Cottages

PARWICH LA

Hawkslow
Farm

Twodale
Barn

PARWICH DALE

PIKE HALL LA

Lombard's
Green

Ballidon
Quarry

BACKHILL LA

Eaton
Dale

Dale End
Farm

Hilltop
Farm

Parwich
Hill

Middlehill
Farm

Peakway

Middlehill
Barn

Foufinside
Farm

MONSDALE LA

Littlewood
Farm

DAM LA

ALSOP RD

Close
Farm
Parwich
Prim Sch

SMITH LA

SCHOOL
LA

KILN LA

ROTHBOURNE
CROFT

CREAMERY LA

Limestone Way

HIGHWAY LA

Parwich
Lees

Flaxdale
Holding

LENSCLIFFE

THE SQ

SHAW LA

MAIN ST

CROFTS
AVE

CHURCH
WLK

WEST VIEW

Parwich

MOUNT
PLEASANT

SMITHY
CL

PH

CHESTNUT
COTTS

THE GN
SYCAMORE
COTTS

PH

BRADBOURNE RD

PITS LA

A **B** **C** **D** **E** **F**

17   18   19

A B C D E F

8
Minninglow
Grange

Longedge
Plantation

Rockhurst
Farm

ALDWARK

Lidgate
Farm

548

54

Works

Green
Farm
Aldwark

Hilltop
Farm

Shafts
(dis)

7

Minninglow
La

Minning
Low

Minninglow
Hill

Tithe
Farm

57

Slipper
Low

Minninglow La

Slipper Low
Farm

6
Roystone
Grange

Gallowlow La

ALDWARK

Daisy
Bank

Pennine Bridleway

Haven Hoe
Farm

5

High Peak Trail
Midshires Way

56

Hoe
Grange

PINDERS LA

Longcliffe
Farm

54

B5056

4

Ballidon
Quarry

BALLIDON MOOR

Ballidonmoor

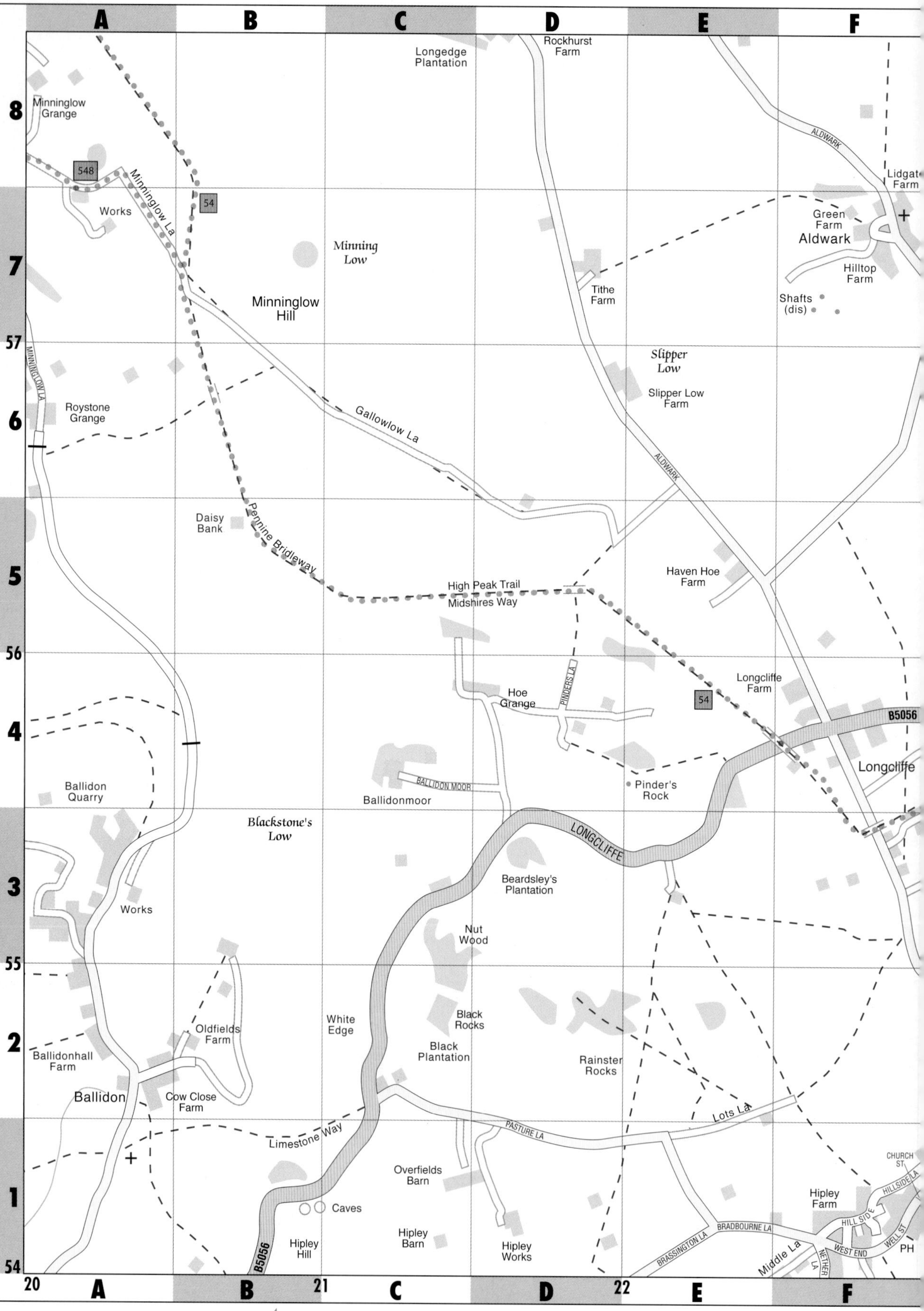

Pinder's
Rock

Longcliffe

Blackstone's
Low

LONGCLIFFE

3

Works

Beardsley's
Plantation

Nut
Wood

55

2

Oldfields
Farm

White
Edge

Black
Rocks

Black
Plantation

Rainster
Rocks

Lots La

Ballidonhall
Farm

Ballidon

Cow Close
Farm

Limestone Way

PASTURE LA

CHURCH
ST

Hipley
Farm

HILLSIDE LA

HILL SIDE

1

Overfields
Barn

Caves

B5056

Hipley
Hill

Hipley
Barn

Hipley
Works

BRADBOURNE LA

BRASSINGTON LA

Middle La

NETHER LA

WEST END

WELL ST

PH

54

20 A 21 B C 22 D E F

141
154

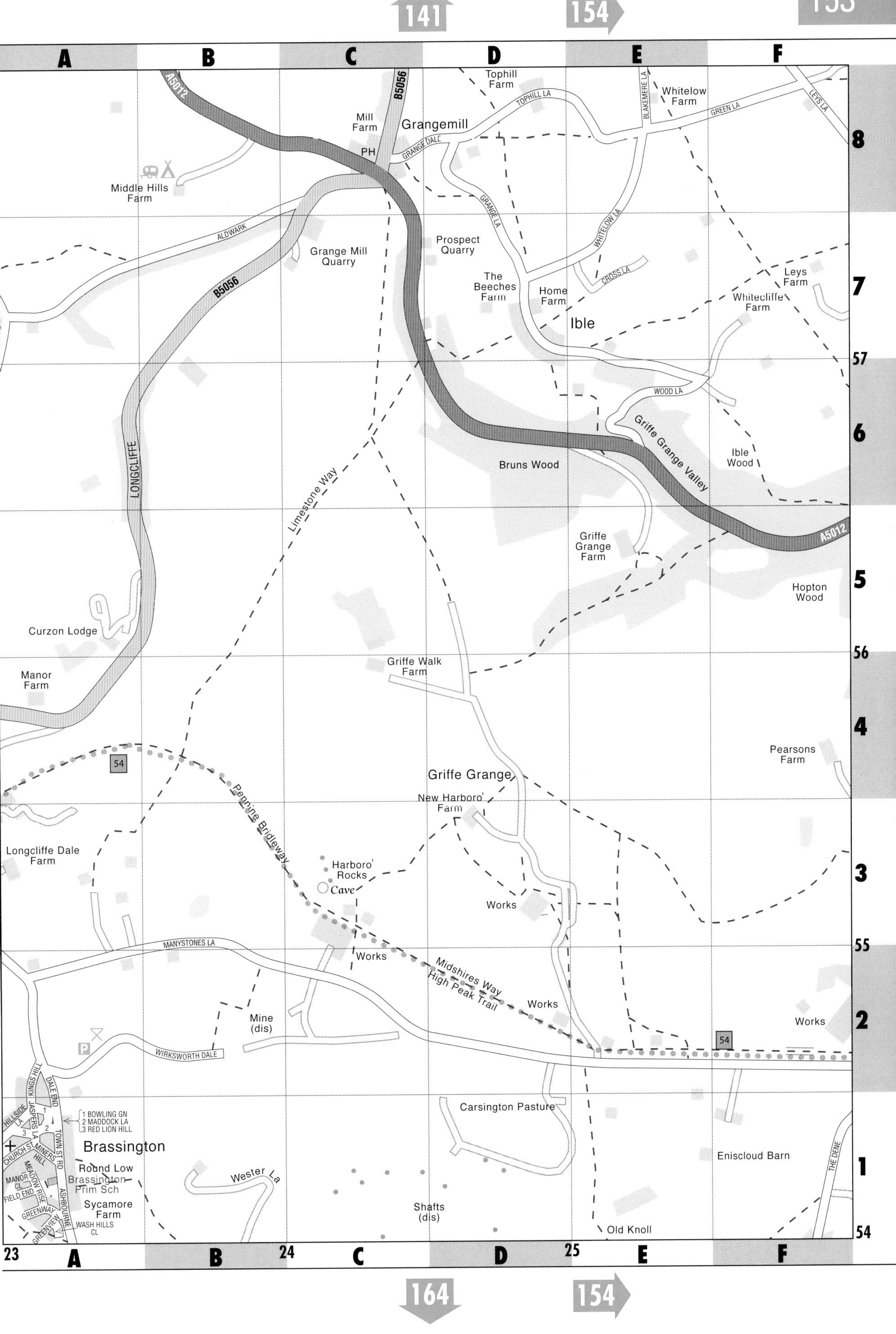
A
B
C
D
E
F
A5012
B5056
Tophill Farm
Whitelow Farm
TOPHILL LA
BLAKEMERE LA
GREEN LA
LEYS LA
Mill Farm
Grangemill
PH
GRANGE DALE
8
Middle Hills Farm
GRANGE LA
WHITELOW LA
ALDWARK
Prospect Quarry
Grange Mill Quarry
B5056
The Beeches Farm
Home Farm
CROSS LA
Leys Farm
Whitecliffe Farm
7
Ible
57
WOOD LA
LONGCLIFFE
Griffe Grange Valley
Ible Wood
6
Bruns Wood
Limestone Way
Griffe Grange Farm
A5012
5
Hopton Wood
Curzon Lodge
56
Griffe Walk Farm
Manor Farm
4
Pearsons Farm
54
Griffe Grange
Pennine Bridleway
New Harboro' Farm
Longcliffe Dale Farm
Harboro' Rocks
Cave
3
Works
55
MANYSTONES LA
Works
Midshires Way
High Peak Trail
Works
Works
2
Mine (dis)
54
WIRKSWORTH DALE
P
KINGS HILL
DALE END
HILLSIDE
JASPERS LA
1 BOWLING GN
2 MADDOCK LA
3 RED LION HILL
TOWN ST RD
Carsington Pasture
CHURCH ST
MINERS HILL
Brassington
Eniscloud Barn
THE DENE
1
Round Low
Brassington Prim Sch
MANOR CL
MEADOW RISE
FIELD END
Wester La
ASHBOURNE
Sycamore Farm
GREENWAY
Shafts (dis)
WASH HILLS CL
GREENVIEW
Old Knoll
54
23
A
B
24
C
D
25
E
F

164
154

A **B** **C** **D** **E** **F**

8

Leys

Limestone Way

Bonsall
Mines
(dis)

Slaley
Farm

Sunnyside
Farm

Slaley

BYEWAYS LA

SLALEY LA

Fairy Lane

PUDDLE HILL

DALE CL

THE DALE

STUDY DR

Study
Farm

Town End
Farm

CHURCH ST

Black
Tor

BLACK TOR RD

CLATTERWAY

Mill
Pond

Via Gellia
Mill

Balleye
Quarry

7

LEYS LA

Bonsall Wood

VIA GELLIA RD

Works

Dunsley Meadows
Nature Reserve

Groaning
Tor

Bonsall
Hollow

Slinter
Wood

A 5012

Sunnyside
Farm

57

Via Gellia

Middleton
Wood

Alabaster
Lane

6

Griffe
Grange
Valley

A5012

B5023

NEW RD

Cemy

CROFT
MEADOW

BURROWS LA

CHAPEL CROFT

LONGLOAD LA

Dean
Hollow

5

Hopton
Wood

HALLCROFT

THE
HALL

DUKE ST

THE GN

KING ST

STILE
CROFT

CHURCHILL
AVE

HALLICAR LA

56

THE
WATER

THE MOOR

QUEEN ST

CHAPEL LA

Willowdene
Farm

HOPTONWOOD
CL

THE FIELDS

OAKERTHORPE
RD

4

Hopton
Quarries

DOGROD'E LA

RAIN'S LA

HILLSIDE

MAIN ST

Middleton

Middleton Com
Prim Sch

Works

Steeple
Grange Light Riy

DARK LA

CROMFORD HILL

B5035

Cemy

Middleton Moor

Rise End

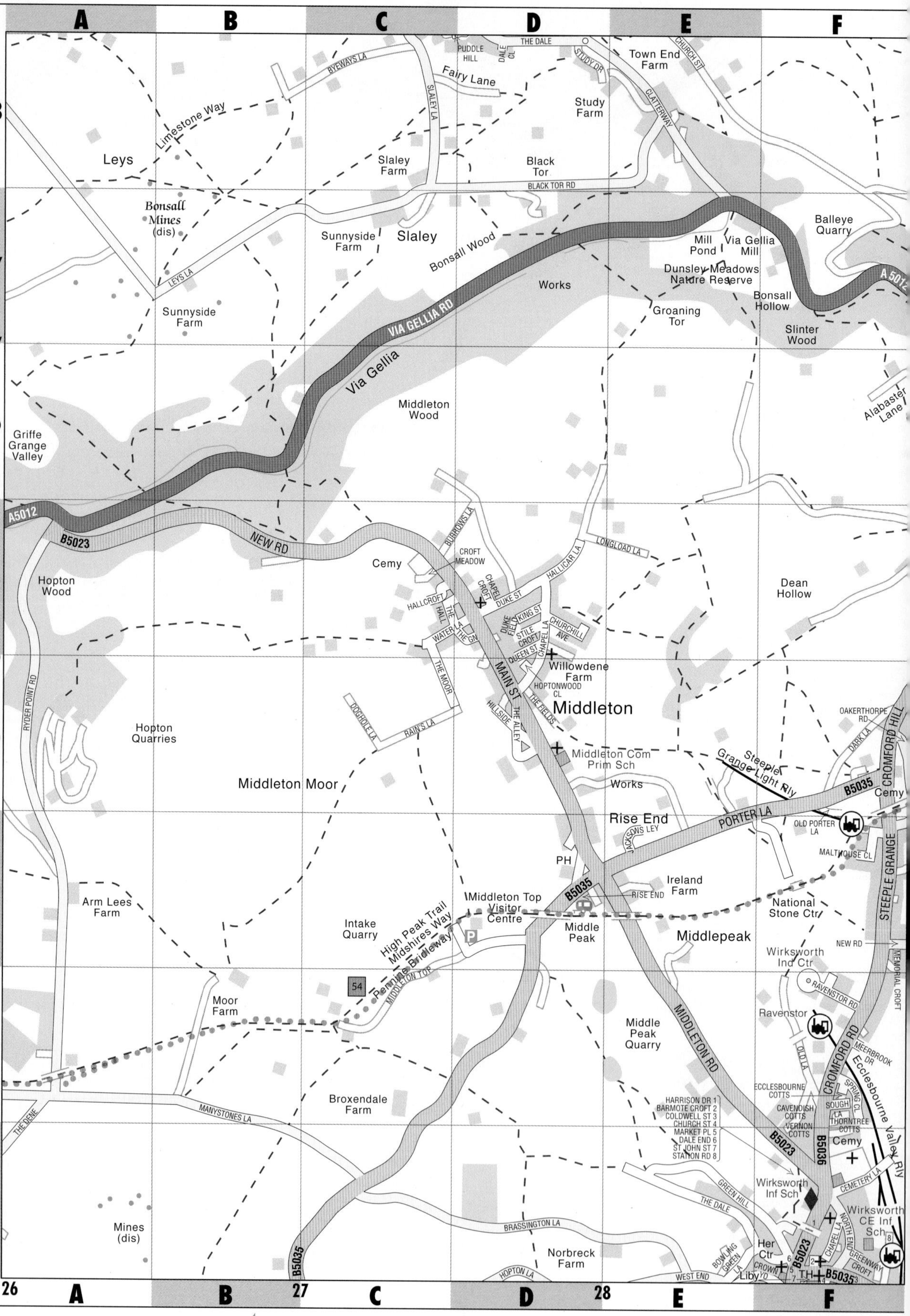

PORTER LA

Old Porter
LA

3

Arm Lees
Farm

Intake
Quarry

High Peak Trail
Midshires Way

Pennine Bridleway

Middleton Top
Visitor
Centre

P

JACKSONS LEY

PH

B5035

Middle
Peak

RISE END

Ireland
Farm

National
Stone Ctr

MALTHOUSE CL

STEEPLE GRANGE

55

54

MIDDLETON TOP

Middlepeak

NEW RD

Wirksworth
Ind Ctr

RAVENSTOR RD

MEMORIAL CROFT

2

THE NILE

Moor
Farm

Broxendale
Farm

MANYSTONES LA

Middle
Peak
Quarry

MIDDLETON RD

HARRISON DR 1
BARMOTE CROFT 2
COLDWELL ST 3
CHURCH ST 4
MARKET PL 5
DALE END 6
ST JOHN ST 7
STATION RD 8

ECCLESBOURNE
COTTS

CAVENDISH
COTTS

VERNON
COTTS

Ravenstor

MEERBROOK
DR

SOUGH
LA

THORNTREE
COTTS

CROMFORD RD

Ecclesbourne Valley Riv

Cemy

1

Mines
(dis)

BRASSINGTON LA

Norbreck
Farm

THE DALE

GREEN HILL

Wirksworth
Inf Sch

B5023

B5036

CEMETERY LA

Her
Ctr

Liby

BOWLING
GREEN

CROWN
YD

WEST END

HOPTON LA

NORTH END

B5035

B5023

CHAPEL LA

GREENWAY
CROFT

Wirksworth
CE Inf
Sch

B5035

54

B5035

26 **27** **28**

A **B** **C** **D** **E** **F**

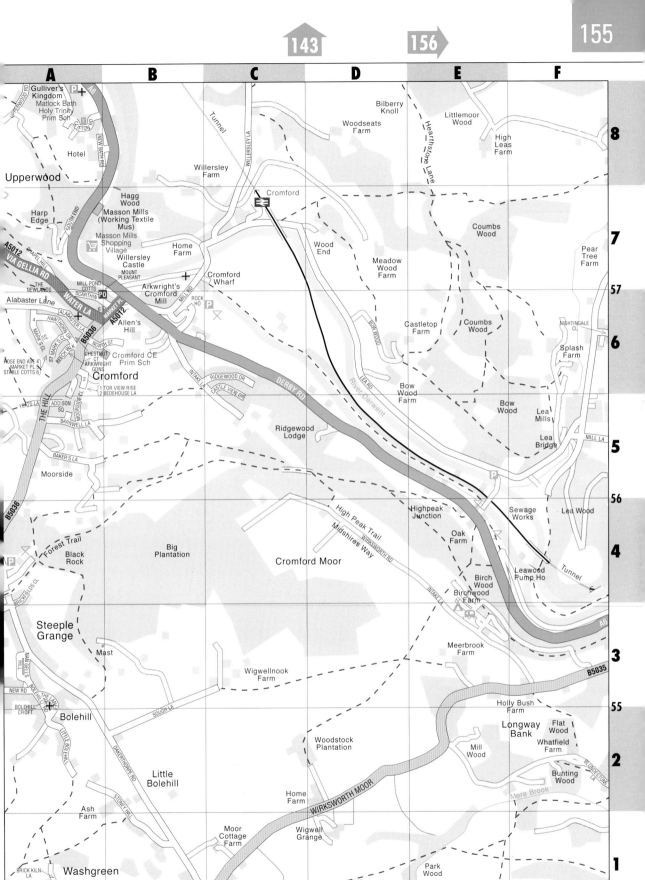
143
156
155

A B C D E F

8
7
57
6
5
56
4
3
55
2
1
54

Gulliver's Kingdom
Matlock Bath Holy Trinity Prim Sch
UPPERWOOD RD
CLIFTON RD
NEW BATH RD
A6
Hotel
Upperwood
Tunnel
WILLERSLEY LA
Willersley Farm
Bilberry Knoll
Woodseats Farm
Hearthstone Lane
Littlemoor Wood
High Leas Farm
Hagg Wood
Masson Mills (Working Textile Mus)
Masson Mills Shopping Village
Harp Edge
SOUTH END
Cromford
Home Farm
Willersley Castle
Coumbs Wood
Wood End
Meadow Wood Farm
Pear Tree Farm
A5012
CHAPEL HILL
VIA GELLIA RD
THE NEWLANDS
MILL POND COTTS
SCARTHIN
PO
WATER LA
MOUNT PLEASANT
Cromford Wharf
Arkwright's Cromford Mill
MILL RD
ROCK HO
Alabaster Lane
ALABASTER LA
HAWTHORN DR
ST MARK'S CL
ST MARK'S CL
BEECH WLK
MARKET PL
A5012
B5036
Allen's Hill
NORTH ST
CHESTNUT CT
ARKWRIGHT GDNS
Cromford CE Prim Sch
Cromford
ROSE END AVE 4
MARKET PL 5
STABLE COTTS 6
1 TOR VIEW RISE
2 BEDEHOUSE LA
INTAKE LA
RIDGEWOOD DR
CASTLE VIEW DR
DERBY RD
BOW WOOD
Castletop Farm
Coumbs Wood
NIGHTINGALE CL
Splash Farm
LEA RD
River Derwent
Bow Wood Farm
Bow Wood
Lea Mills
YEATS LA
ADDISON SQ
MOORSIDE CL
THE HILL
BARNWELL LA
Ridgewood Lodge
Lea Bridge
MILL LA
BAKER'S LA
Moorside
B5036
High Peak Trail
Midshires Way
WIRKSWORTH RD
Highpeak Junction
Sewage Works
Lea Wood
Oak Farm
Forest Trail
Black Rock
Big Plantation
Cromford Moor
Leawood Pump Ho
Tunnel
BRICKFIELDS CL
INTAKE LA
Birch Wood
Birchwood Farm
Steeple Grange
Mast
A6
Meerbrook Farm
NAN GELLS HILL
NEW RD
BOLEHILL RD
THE LANES
BOLEHILL CROFT
Bolehill
Wigwellnook Farm
SOUGH LA
B5035
Holly Bush Farm
Longway Bank
Flat Wood
Whatfield Farm
LITTLE BOLEHILL
OAKERTHORPE RD
Woodstock Plantation
Mill Wood
Little Bolehill
BLINDESTONE LA
Bunting Wood
Mere Brook
Ash Farm
STONEY HILL
Home Farm
WIRKSWORTH MOOR
Moor Cottage Farm
Wigwell Grange
Park Wood
BRICK KILN LA
Washgreen
Wirksworth Jun Sch
B5035
WASH GREEN
1 KING EDWARD ST
2 QUEEN ELIZABETHS CL
3 NETHER MILL CT
PH
B5035
WASH GREEN
BREAMFIELD LA
Moor Farm
GREEN LA
Wirksworth Moor
Long Wood

29 A B 30 C D 31 E F

155
144

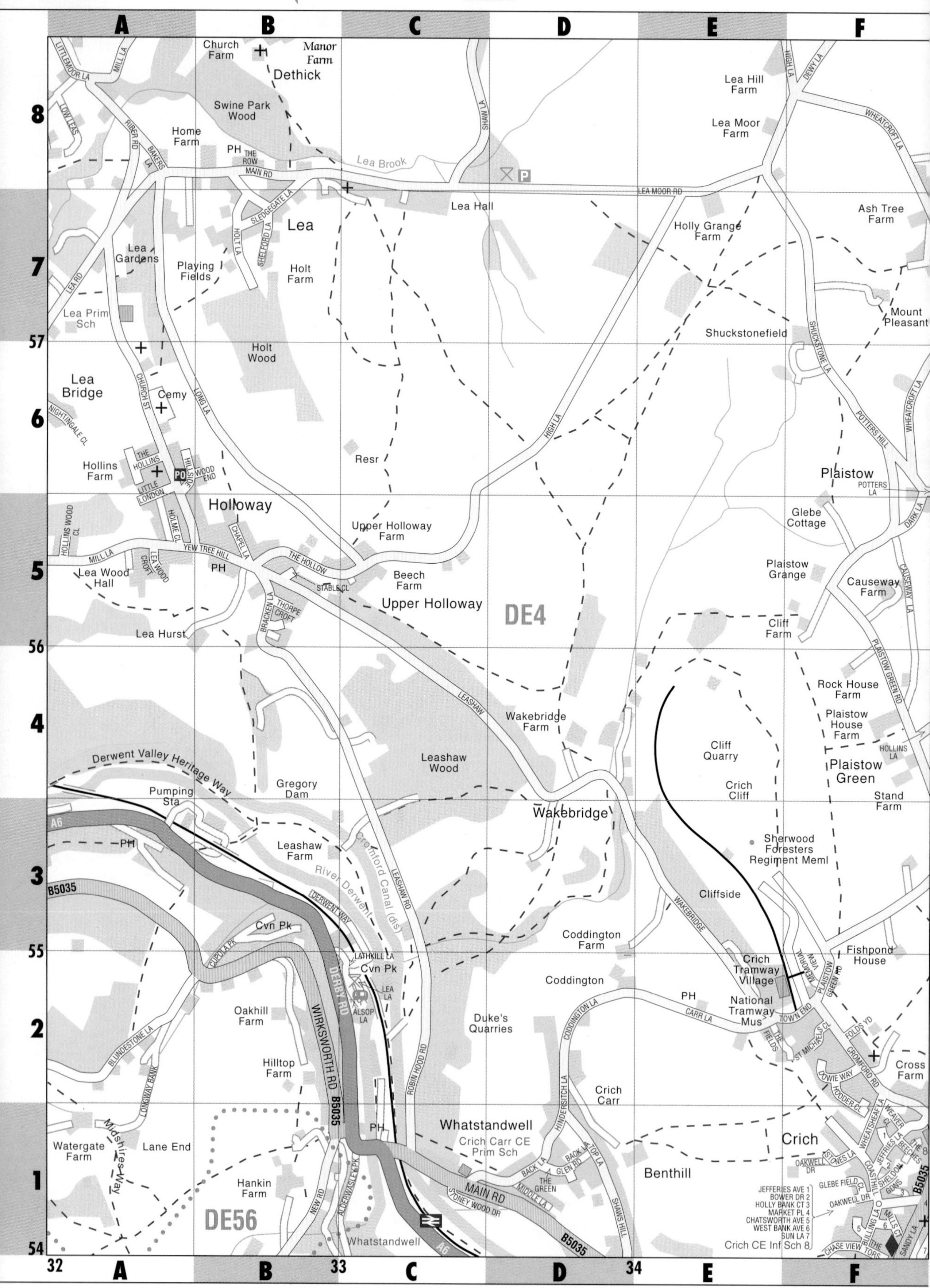
A
B
C
D
E
F
8
7
57
6
5
56
4
3
55
2
1
54
32
33
34
Church Farm
Manor Farm
Dethick
Swine Park Wood
Home Farm
PH
THE ROW
MAIN RD
Lea Brook
Lea Hill Farm
Lea Moor Farm
LEA MOOR RD
Lea Hall
Lea
Holly Grange Farm
Ash Tree Farm
Lea Gardens
Playing Fields
Holt Farm
Lea Prim Sch
Mount Pleasant
Shuckstonefield
Holt Wood
Lea Bridge
Cemy
Hollins Farm
PO
Holloway
Resr
Plaistow
Glebe Cottage
Upper Holloway Farm
Beech Farm
Upper Holloway
Plaistow Grange
Causeway Farm
Lea Wood Hall
PH
Lea Hurst
DE4
Cliff Farm
Rock House Farm
Plaistow House Farm
Wakebridge Farm
Leashaw Wood
Cliff Quarry
Plaistow Green
Derwent Valley Heritage Way
Gregory Dam
Pumping Sta
Crich Cliff
Stand Farm
Wakebridge
A6
PH
Leashaw Farm
Sherwood Foresters Regiment Meml
River Derwent
Cromford Canal (dis)
B5035
Cliffside
Cvn Pk
Coddington Farm
Cvn Pk
Fishpond House
Crich Tramway Village
Coddington
PH
National Tramway Mus
Oakhill Farm
Duke's Quarries
Hilltop Farm
Cross Farm
Crich Carr
Whatstandwell
Crich Carr CE Prim Sch
PH
Watergate Farm
Lane End
Midshires Way
Crich
Benthill
Hankin Farm
DE56
Whatstandwell
JEFFERIES AVE 1
BOWER DR 2
HOLLY BANK CT 3
MARKET PL 4
CHATSWORTH AVE 5
WEST BANK AVE 6
SUN LA 7
Crich CE Inf Sch 8
LITTLEMOOR LA
MILL LA
LOW LEYS
RIBER RD
BAKERS LA
SLEDGEGATE LA
HOLT LA
SHELFORD LA
SHAW LA
HIGH LA
DEWY LA
WHEATCROFT LA
LEA RD
CHURCH ST
LONG LA
NIGHTINGALE CL
THE HOLLINS
HILLSIDE
WOOD END
LITTLE LONDON
HOLLINS WOOD CL
HOLME CL
CHAPEL LA
YEW TREE HILL
MILL LA
LEA WOOD CROFT
LEA WOOD
THE HOLLOW
STABLE CL
BRACKEN LA
THORPE CROFT
LEASHAW
HIGH LA
SHUCKSTONE LA
POTTERS HILL
WHEATCROFT LA
POTTERS LA
DARK LA
CAUSEWAY LA
PLAISTOW GREEN RD
HOLLINS LA
DERWENT WAY
LEASHAW RD
WAKEBRIDGE
CUPOLA PK
LATHKILL LA
DERBY RD
LEA LA
ALSOP LA
WIRKSWORTH RD
BLUNDESTONE LA
LONGWAY BANK
ROBIN HOOD RD
CODDINGTON LA
CARR LA
MEMORIAL VIEW
PLAISTOW GREEN RD
TOWN END
THE FIELDS
ST MICHAELS CL
FOLDS YD
CROMFORD RD
DOWIE WAY
HODDER CL
WHEATSHEAF LA
WEAVER CL
HINDERSITCH LA
TOP LA
BACK LA
GLEN RD
THE GREEN
MIDDLE LA
SHAWS HILL
MAIN RD
STONEY WOOD DR
B5035
B5035
NEW RD
ALDERWASLEY PK
A6
STONES LA
OAKWELL DR
GLEBE FIELD CL
OAKWELL DR
JEFFRIES LA
BEECHES
COASTHILL
SHELDON GDNS
BULLING LA
MILLS CT
SANDY LA
CHASE VIEW
THE TORS
B5035

155
167

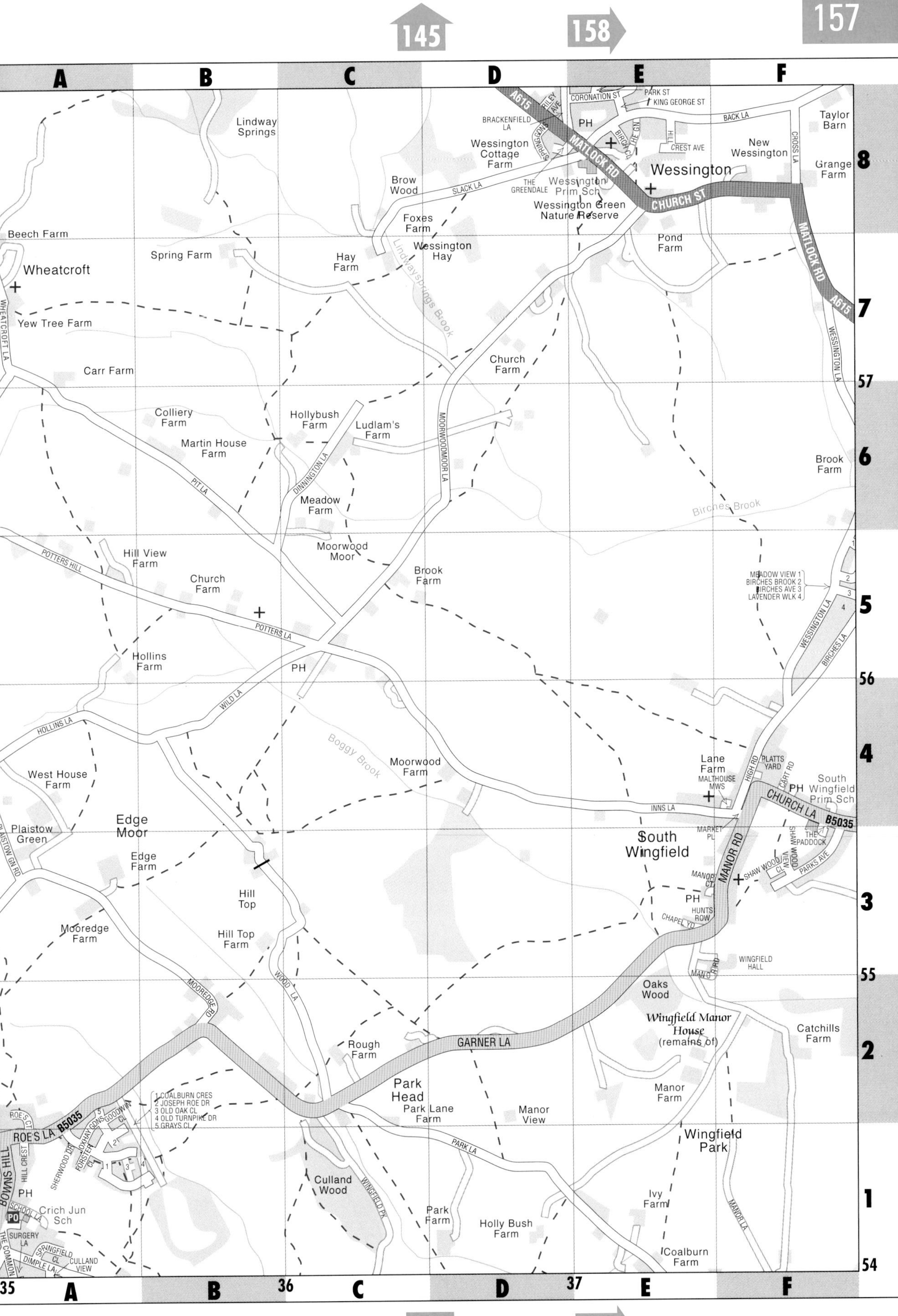

A B C D E F

8
7
57
6
5
56
4
55
2
54

35 A B 36 C D 37 E F

Lindway Springs
Wessington Cottage Farm
Brow Wood
SLACK LA
THE GREENDALE
Foxes Farm
Wessington Hay
Wessington Prim Sch
Wessington Green Nature Reserve
BRACKENFIELD LA
MATLOCK RD A615
CORONATION ST
PARK ST
KING GEORGE ST
CREST AVE
BACK LA
New Wessington
Taylor Barn
Grange Farm
Wessington
CHURCH ST
Pond Farm
MATLOCK RD A615
WESSINGTON LA

Beech Farm
Wheatcroft
Spring Farm
Hay Farm
WHEATCROFT LA
Yew Tree Farm
Carr Farm
Colliery Farm
Hollybush Farm
Ludlam's Farm
Church Farm
Brook Farm
LINDWAYSPRINGS BROOK
MOORWOODMOOR LA
Birches Brook
DINNINGTON LA
PIT LA
Martin House Farm
Meadow Farm
Moorwood Moor
Brook Farm
Hill View Farm
Church Farm
POTTERS HILL
POTTERS LA
MEADOW VIEW 1
BIRCHES BROOK 2
BIRCHES AVE 3
LAVENDER WLK 4
WESSINGTON LA
BIRCHES BROOK
Hollins Farm
PH
WILD LA
HOLLINS LA
Boggy Brook
Moorwood Farm
West House Farm
Edge Moor
Plaistow Green
Edge Farm
PLAISTOW GRN RD
Hill Top
MOOREDGE RD
Mooredge Farm
Hill Top Farm
WOOD LA
Lane Farm
MALTHOUSE MWS
INNS LA
HIGH RD
PLATTS YARD
CART RD
PH
South Wingfield Prim Sch
CHURCH LA
B5035
MARKET PL
MANOR RD
South Wingfield
THE PADDOCK
SHAW WOOD VIEW
SHAW WOOD
PARKS AVE
MANOR CT
PH
HUNTS ROW
CHAPEL YD
Rough Farm
Park Head
Park Lane Farm
GARNER LA
Manor View
Oaks Wood
MAWD
Wingfield Hall
Wingfield Manor House (remains of)
Catchills Farm
Manor Farm
1 COALBURN CRES
2 JOSEPH ROE DR
3 OLD OAK CL
4 OLD TURNPIKE DR
5 GRAYS CL
ROES LA
B5035
BOWNS HILL
SHERWOOD DR
FOSTER CL
GOODWIN
HILL CREST
SCHOOL LA
PO
PH
Crich Jun Sch
SURGERY LA
SPRINGFIELD CL
DIMPLE LA
THE COMMON
Culland View
WINGFIELD CK
Culland Wood
Park Farm
PARK LA
Holly Bush Farm
Wingfield Park
Ivy Farm
MANOR LA
Coalburn Farm
Manor View

157
146

A B C D E F

8 7 57 6 5 56 4 3 55 2 1 54

Carr Hill
CROSS LA
PARK LA
Sebastopol Farm
SHEEP LA
PIT LA
Adastra
CH
Upper Delves Farm
Shirland Lodge
Lower Delves Farm
Shirland Lodge Farm
Amber Farm
PH
Toadhole Furnace
MATLOCK RD
Broom House
AMBER GREEN
Alfreton Brook
Hall's Plantation
CHESTERFIELD RD
B6025 ALFRETON RD
WESSINGTON LA
Brook Farm
AMBER TERR
MEADOW VIEW
BIRCHES BROOK
BIRCHES LA
Dale Bridge
Pond Wood
Long Plantation
BIRCHES AVE
DALE HILL
B6013
Ufton Fields Farm
BISHOP ST
HARDY ST
Dale House
Wren Wood
ARTHUR ST
CHARLES ST
ROWLAND CT
Peacock Hotel
Ufton Fields
LAWMAN GDNS
LINBERY CL
BONSALL LA
MELROSE WAY
Lane Farm
HIGH ST
CHURCH ST
HILLSIDE PK
ST MARTINS CT
MARKET PL
B6008
HOLM LA
B5035
Fourlane Ends
Alfreton Park Com Specl Sch
Alfreton L Ctr
NEW ST
Mill
River Amber
Alfreton Park
Genesis Bsns & Con Ctr
CHURCH LA
Parkwood Ctr
GRANGE ST
CHATSWORTH CL
KING ST
HALL ST
Superstore
HIGHFIELD COTTS
1 JOHNO WOOD CL
2 PARKWOOD CL
3 CHAWORTH CL
4 COPTHORNE DR
5 HIGHFIELDS CL
HADDON CL
LINCOLN ST
INDEPENDENT HILL
ALFRED ST
David's Hill
LISSET CL
Oakerthorpe
GLADSTONE RD
PARK ST
WINGFIELD RD
A615
COOKER LA
PH
Oakerthorpe Nature Reserve
CH
MILLPOND CL
BLOOMERY CL
PROVIDENCE PL
NUTTALL CL
Hollybank House
HOLLY BANK CL
BACH WELL LA
WATCHORN COTTS
LONG MEADOW RD
Shaw Wood
HOLLBANK COTTS
DAMSTEAD PK AVE
DAM CL
AMBER GR
EWART LA
DERWENT GR
Oakerthorpe Manor Farm
Damstead Wood
A61 DERBY RD
WATCHORN LA
WATCHORN LAWNS
A38
Chestnut Farm
Alfreton Services
Shaw Wood Farm
Turnpike Bsns Pk
SWANWICK CT
TURNPIKE CL
B6179
SHAWWOOD DR
MILLSTONE LA
Longcroft
Lily Street Farm
OLD SWANWICK COLLIERY RD
Lily Cottage
TURNERS CL 1
LILYSTREET FARMWAY 2
HILLTOP DR 3
DERBY RD
Sleetmoor House
TAYLOR WAY
Castle Hill
JACKSON'S LA
GORDON RD
SLEETMOOR LA

38 A B 39 C D 40 E F

157
169

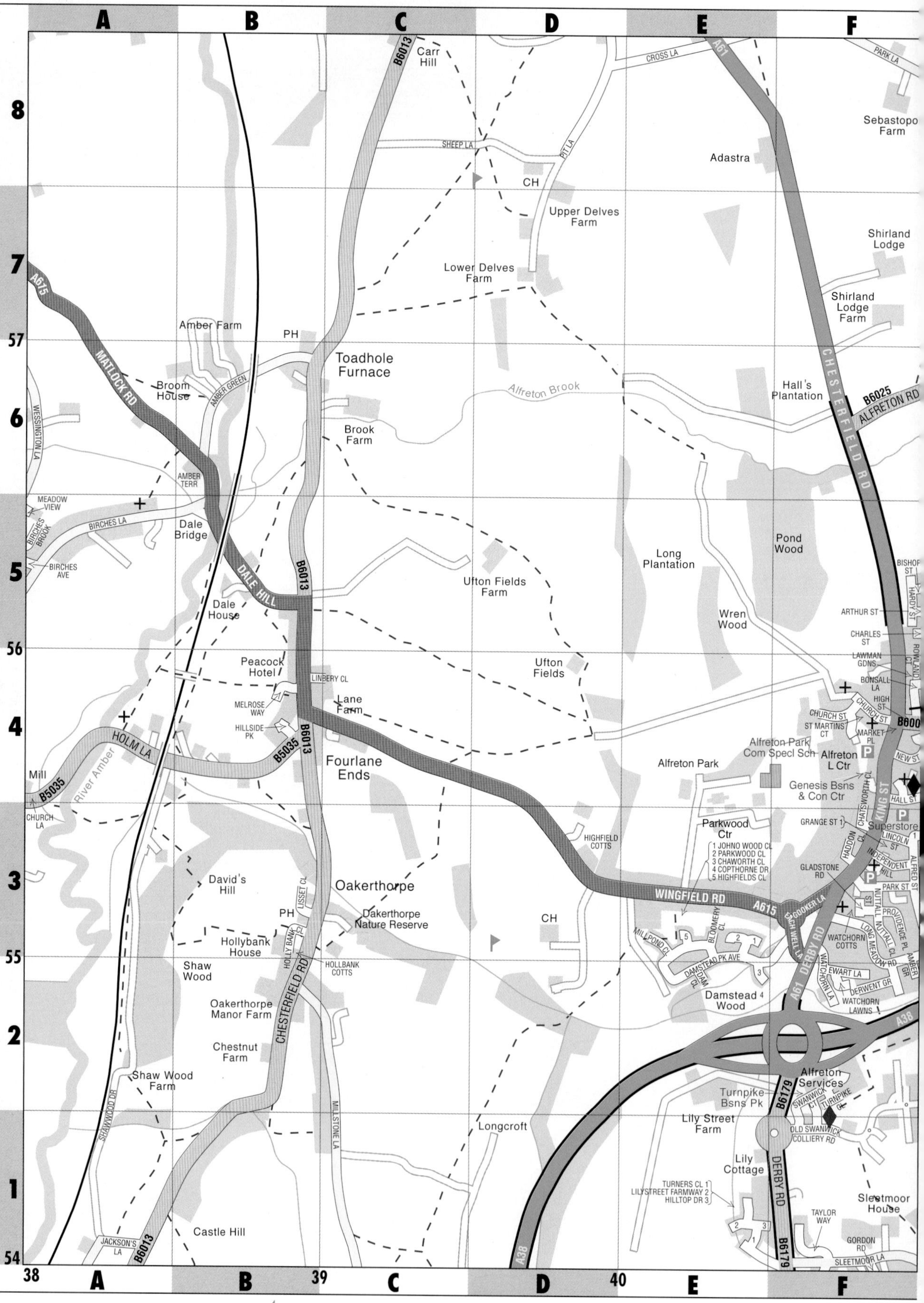

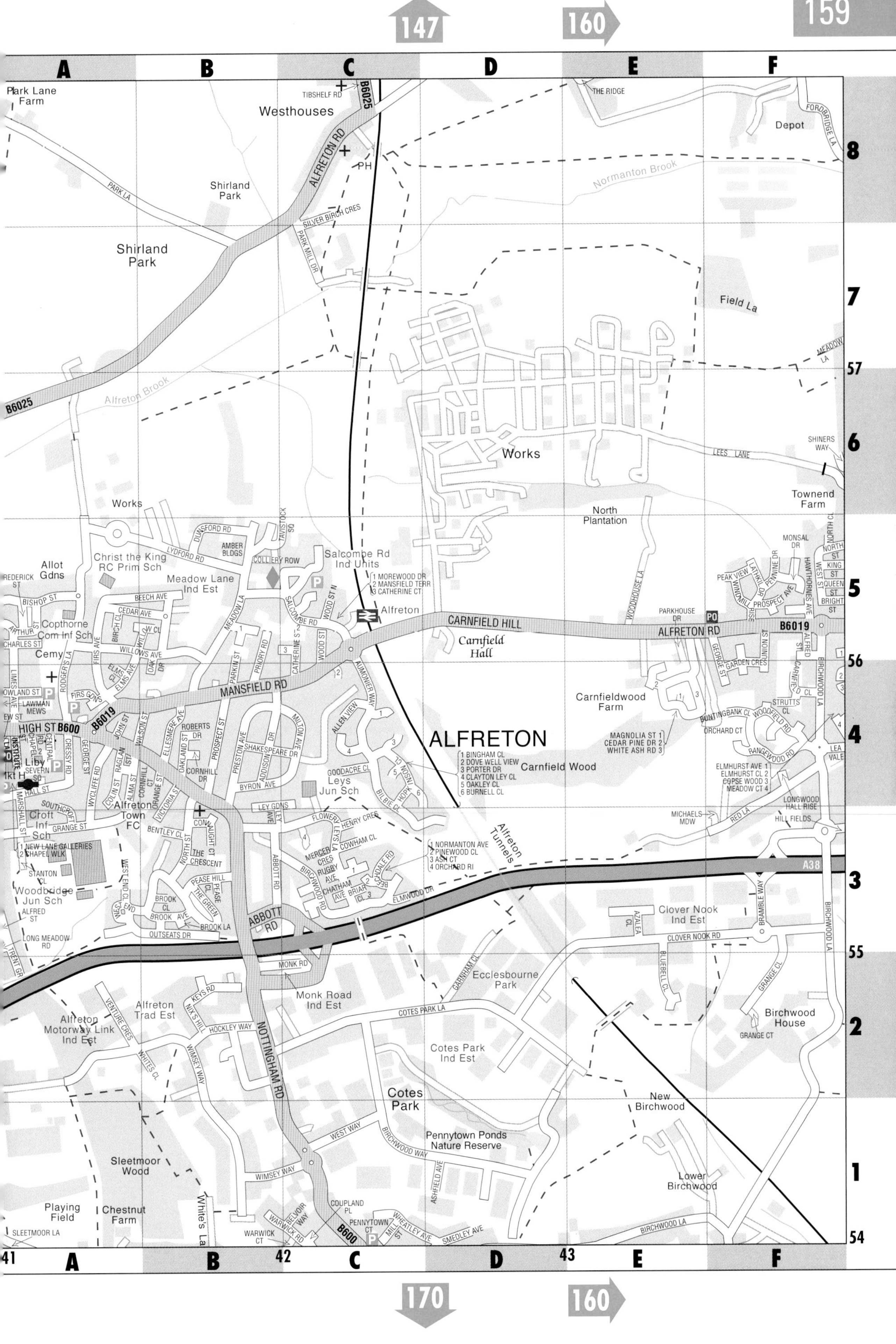

A   B   C   D   E   F

Park Lane Farm

TIBSHELF RD

B6025

Westhouses

PH

ALFRETON RD

THE RIDGE

Depot

8

Shirland Park

PARK LA

SILVER BIRCH CRES

PARK MILL DR

Normanton Brook

Shirland Park

7

Field La

MEADOW LA

B6025

57

Alfreton Brook

SHINERS WAY

LEES LANE

6

Works

Townend Farm

Works

North Plantation

MONSAL DR

NORTH KING ST

Christ the King RC Prim Sch

DUNSFORD RD

LYDFORD RD

AMBER BLDGS

TAVISTOCK SQ

COLLIERY ROW

Salcombe Rd Ind Units

1 MOREWOOD DR
2 MANSFIELD TERR
3 CATHERINE CT

WOODHOUSE LA

PEAK VIEW

WINDMILL HILL

ATKIN RD

PINE DR

PENNINE DR

HAWTHORNES AVE

NORTH ST

QUEEN ST

BRIGHT ST

5

Allot Gdns

FREDERICK

BISHOP ST

MEADOW LANE IND EST

BEECH AVE

CEDAR AVE

BIRCH CL

W CL

WILLOWS AVE

MEADOW LA

PRIORY RD

PARK ST

CATHERINE ST

WOOD ST N

WOOD ST

Alfreton

CARNFIELD HILL

PARKHOUSE DR

ALFRETON RD

B6019

PO

GEORGE ST

GARDEN CRES

UNION ST

GRANFIELD

BIRCHWOOD LA

ALFRED

5

Copthorne Com Inf Sch

CHARLES ST

ARTHUR

Cemy

FIRS AVE

ELMS AVE

ELMS GDNS

FIRS GDNS

Carnfield Hall

56

LIMES

ROWLAND ST

LAWMAN MEWS

P

P

B6019

MANSFIELD RD

JOHN ST

WILSON ST

ROBERTS DR

OAKLAND ST

ELLESMERE AVE

PRESTON AVE

PROSPECT ST

MILTON AVE

Carnfieldwood Farm

Carnfield Wood

STRUTTS

WOODFIELD RD

56

HIGH ST

B600

INSTITUTE

Libv

P

CRESSY RD

RODGERS LA

GEORGE ST

WYCLIFFE RD

COURT ST

RAGLAN ST

ALMAS ST

CORNHILL

VICTORIA ST

ORANGE ST

CORNHILL DR

SHAKESPEARE DR

BYRON AVE

Leys Jun Sch

GOODACRE CL

ALLEN VIEW

AUMONIER WAY

WILSON CL

ALFRETON

1 BINGHAM CL
2 DOVE WELL VIEW
3 PORTER DR
4 CLAYTON LEY CL
5 OAKLEY CL
6 BURNELL CL

MAGNOLIA ST 1
CEDAR PINE DR 2
WHITE ASH RD 3

BUNTINGBANK CL

ORCHARD CT

RANGEWOOD RD

ELMHURST AVE 1
ELMHURST CL 2
COPSE WOOD 3
MEADOW CT 4

LEA VALE

4

Croft Inf Sch

Alfreton Town FC

GRANGE ST

BENTLEY CT

NORTH STREET

CONNAUGHT CT

LEY GDNS

LEYS AVE

FLOWERY LEYS LA

HENRY CRES

COWHAM CL

Alfreton Tunnels

MICHAELS MDW

RED LA

Longwood Hall Rise

HILL FIELDS

4

1 NEW LANE GALLERIES
2 CHAPEL WLK

STANTON CL

Woodbridge Jun Sch

ALFRED ST

THE CRESCENT

PEASE HILL

THE GREEN

PEASE

BROOK CL

MERCER CRES

RUGBY AVE

CHATHAM AVE

BIRCHWOOD LA

ELMWOOD CL

HALL RD

1 NORMANTON AVE
2 PINEWOOD CL
3 ASH CT
4 ORCHARD RI

3

LONG MEADOW RD

TRENT GR

WEST ST

BROOK AVE

OUTSEATS DR

ABBOTT RD

MONK RD

A38

55

Alfreton Motorway Link Ind Est

VENTURE CRES

NIX'S HILL

KEYS RD

HOCKLEY WAY

WHITES CL

WIMSEY WAY

Alfreton Trad Est

Monk Road Ind Est

COTES PARK LA

GARDEN CL

Ecclesbourne Park

Clover Nook Ind Est

CLOVER NOOK RD

AZALEA CL

BLUEBELL CL

GRANGE CL

Birchwood House

GRANGE CT

BIRCHWOOD LA

2

NOTTINGHAM RD

Cotes Park Ind Est

Cotes Park

New Birchwood

1

Sleetmoor Wood

Playing Field

Chestnut Farm

WEST WAY

WIMSEY WAY

BIRCHWOOD WAY

ASHFIELD AVE

COUPLAND PL

WARWICK WAY

BELVOIR WAY

B600

PENNYTOWN

WHEATLEY AVE

SMEDLEY AVE

Pennytown Ponds Nature Reserve

Lower Birchwood

BIRCHWOOD LA

54

159
148

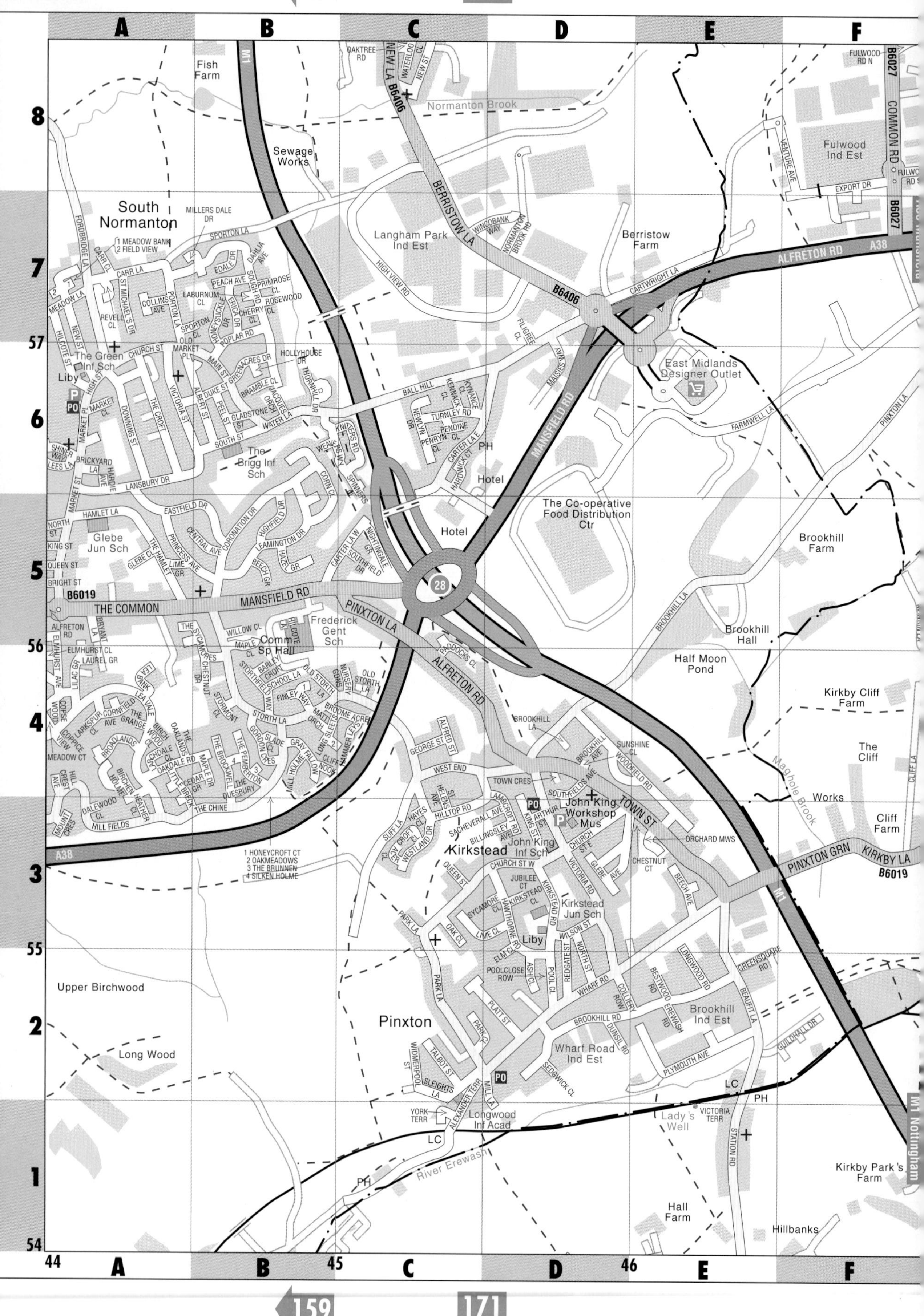
A
B
C
D
E
F
8
7
57
6
5
56
4
3
55
2
1
54
44
45
46
Fish Farm
M1
Sewage Works
Normanton Brook
NEW LA
B6406
Fulwood Ind Est
COMMON RD
B6027
EXPORT DR
VENTURE AVE
South Normanton
MILLERS DALE DR
SPORTON LA
Langham Park Ind Est
BERRISTOW LA
Berristow Farm
ALFRETON RD
A38
CARTWRIGHT LA
HIGH VIEW RD
East Midlands Designer Outlet
MANSFIELD RD
FARMWELL LA
PINXTON LA
The Green Inf Sch
Liby
PO
P
The Brigg Inf Sch
BALL HILL
PH
Hotel
The Co-operative Food Distribution Ctr
Brookhill Farm
Glebe Jun Sch
B6019
THE COMMON
28
Frederick Gent Sch
Comm Sp Hall
BROOKHILL LA
Brookhill Hall
Half Moon Pond
Kirkby Cliff Farm
The Cliff
Magholе Brook
Works
Cliff Farm
TOWN ST
John King Workshop Mus
Kirkstead
John King Inf Sch
Kirkstead Jun Sch
ORCHARD MWS
PINXTON GRN
KIRKBY LA
1 HONEYCROFT CT
2 OAKMEADOWS
3 THE BRUINNEN
4 SILKEN HOLME
Upper Birchwood
Long Wood
Pinxton
Brookhill Ind Est
Wharf Road Ind Est
Longwood Inf Acad
LC
River Erewash
Lady's Well
STATION RD
Hall Farm
Hillbanks
Kirkby Park's Farm
M1 Nottingham

159
171

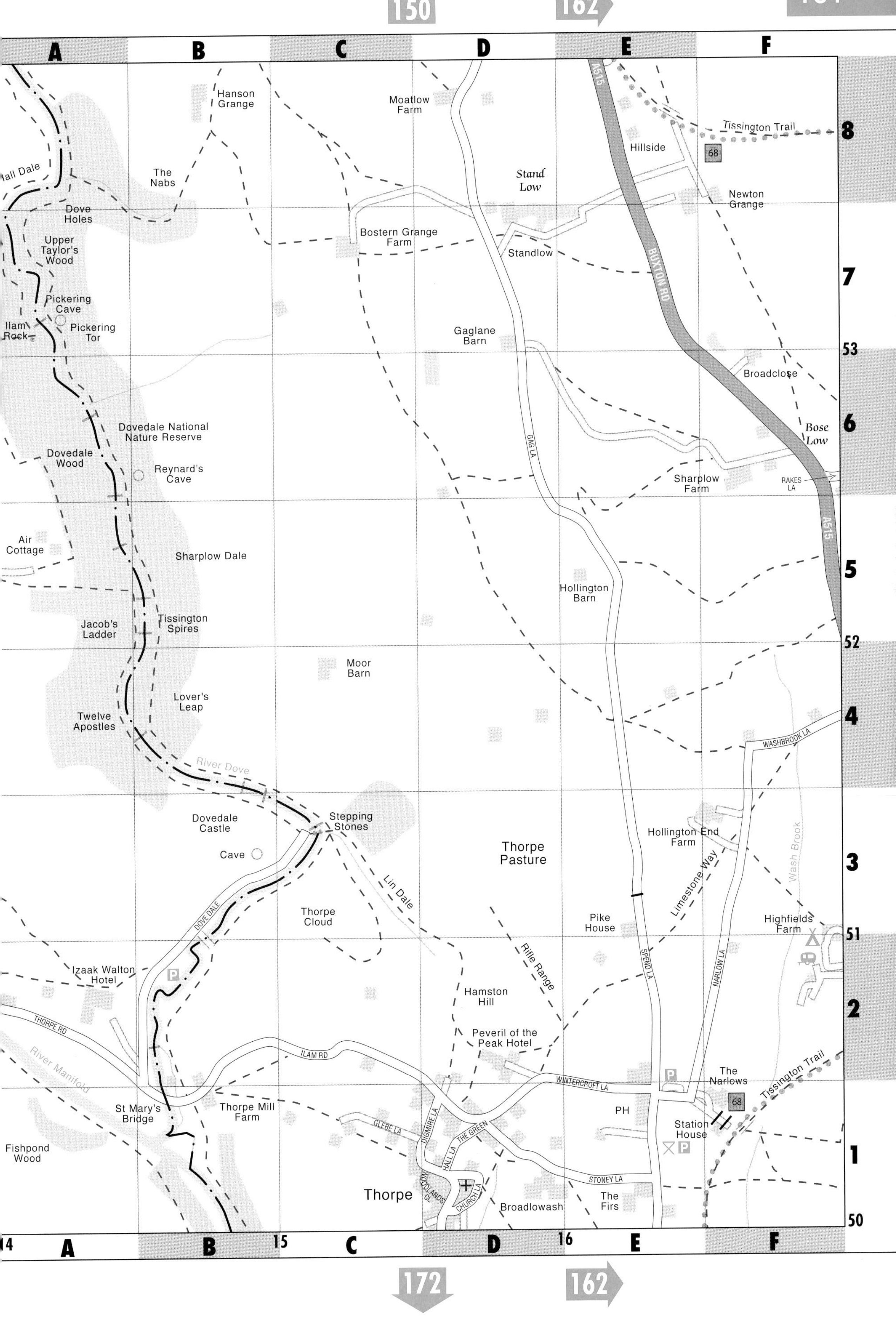

150
162

A **B** **C** **D** **E** **F**

8 **7** **53** **6** **5** **52** **4** **3** **51** **2** **1** **50**

Tissington Trail

Hillside

Newton Grange

Hanson Grange

Moatlow Farm

Stand Low

The Nabs

Bostern Grange Farm

Standlow

Broadclose

Dove Holes

Upper Taylor's Wood

Gaglane Barn

Bose Low

Pickering Cave

Pickering Tor

Ilam Rock

Dovedale National Nature Reserve

Sharplow Farm

RAKES LA

Dovedale Wood

Reynard's Cave

Air Cottage

Hollington Barn

Sharplow Dale

Jacob's Ladder

Tissington Spires

Moor Barn

Lover's Leap

Twelve Apostles

River Dove

Dovedale Castle

Stepping Stones

Thorpe Pasture

Washbrook La

Wash Brook

Cave

Hollington End Farm

Limestone Way

Highfields Farm

Thorpe Cloud

Lin Dale

Pike House

Izaak Walton Hotel

Hamston Hill

Rifle Range

SPEND LA

NARLOW LA

Thorpe Rd

River Manifold

Peveril of the Peak Hotel

The Narlows

WINTERCROFT LA

ILAM RD

PH

St Mary's Bridge

Thorpe Mill Farm

GLEBE LA

DIGMIRE LA

HALL LA

THE GREEN

Station House

Fishpond Wood

WOODLANDS CL

CHURCH LA

STONEY LA

The Firs

Tissington Trail

Thorpe

Broadlowash

DOVE DALE

GAG LA

BUXTON RD

A515

68

68

172
162

A **B** **C** **D** **E** **F**

4 15 16

	A	B	C	D	E	F

8

The Thorns

Crakelow Farm

Crake Low

Shaw's Farm

Limestone Way

Bradbourne Rd

PHS LA

7

Rushycliffe Barn

68

Sitterlow Farm

53

White Meadow

Hunger Hill

High Flats

FLATS LA

Bletch Brook

6

RAKES LA

CHAPEL LA

Tissington

Gorsehill Farm

Town Head Farm

THE ST

Wibben Hill

5

Tissington Hall

THE FOOT

THE GREEN

Bent Farm

Ford

THE AVENUE

P

BENT LA

Lea Cottage Farm

547

B505

52

WASHBROOK LA

DARFIELD LA

Keepers Cottage

Lea Hall

4

PH

Mill Pond Plantation

Square Plantation

Horsley Farm

A515 BUXTON RD

68

Darfield Plantation

Bradbourne Brook

3

Bassett Wood Farm

Tissington Wood Farm

Choughriddins

ASHBOURNE RD

51

Brookwood Farm

2

Bentley Hall

Woodeaves Farm

Woodside

Lees Farm

BRADBOURNE RD

The Priory

1

Firs Farm

Fenny Bentley

Cherry Orchard Farm

Woodeaves Mill

Ravenscliffe

Fitzherbert CE Prim Sch

Bentley Brook

ASHBOURNE CL

Bentley Old Hall

A515

PH

Riddings Park

50

B5056

17	A	B	18	C	D	19	E	F

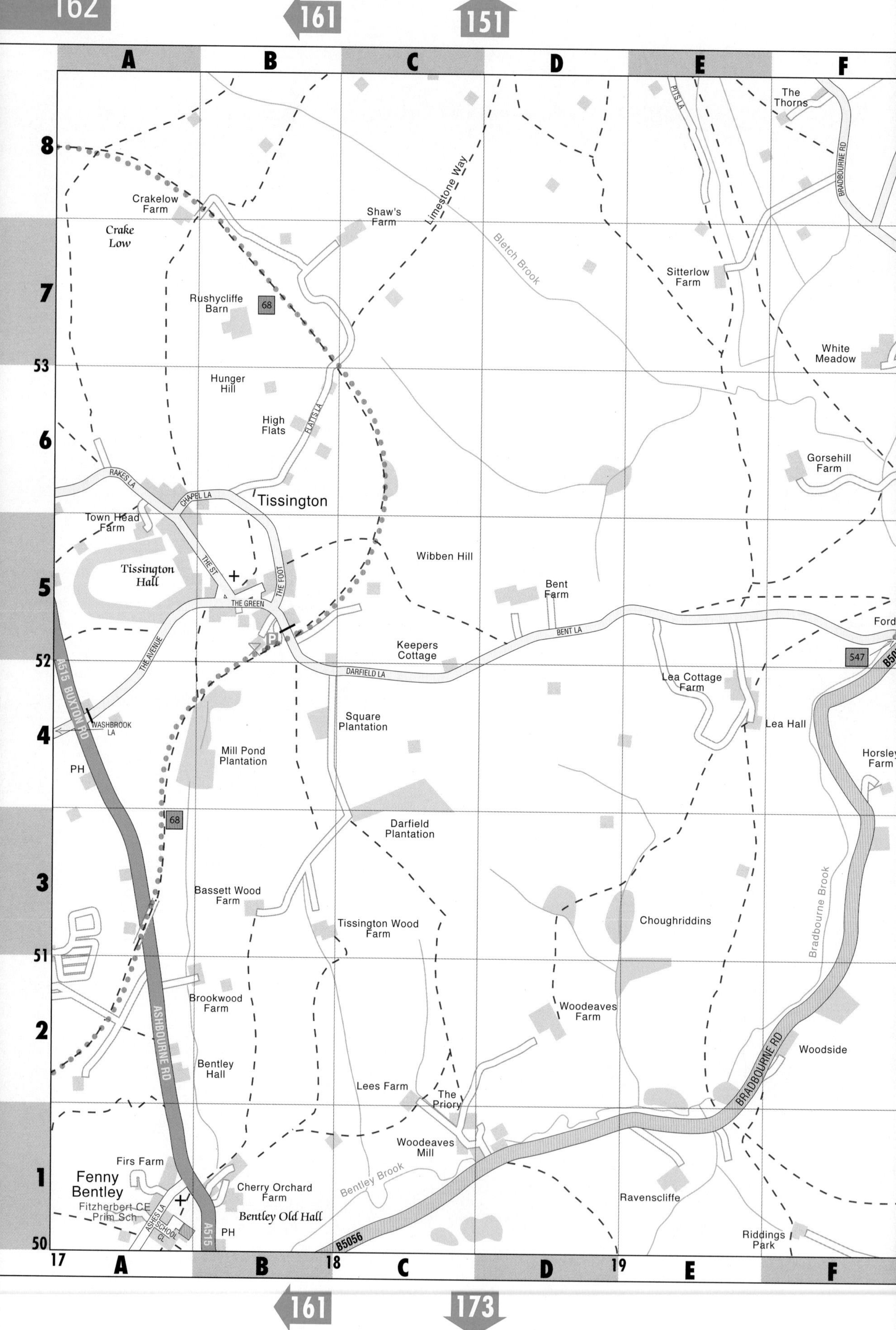

152
164

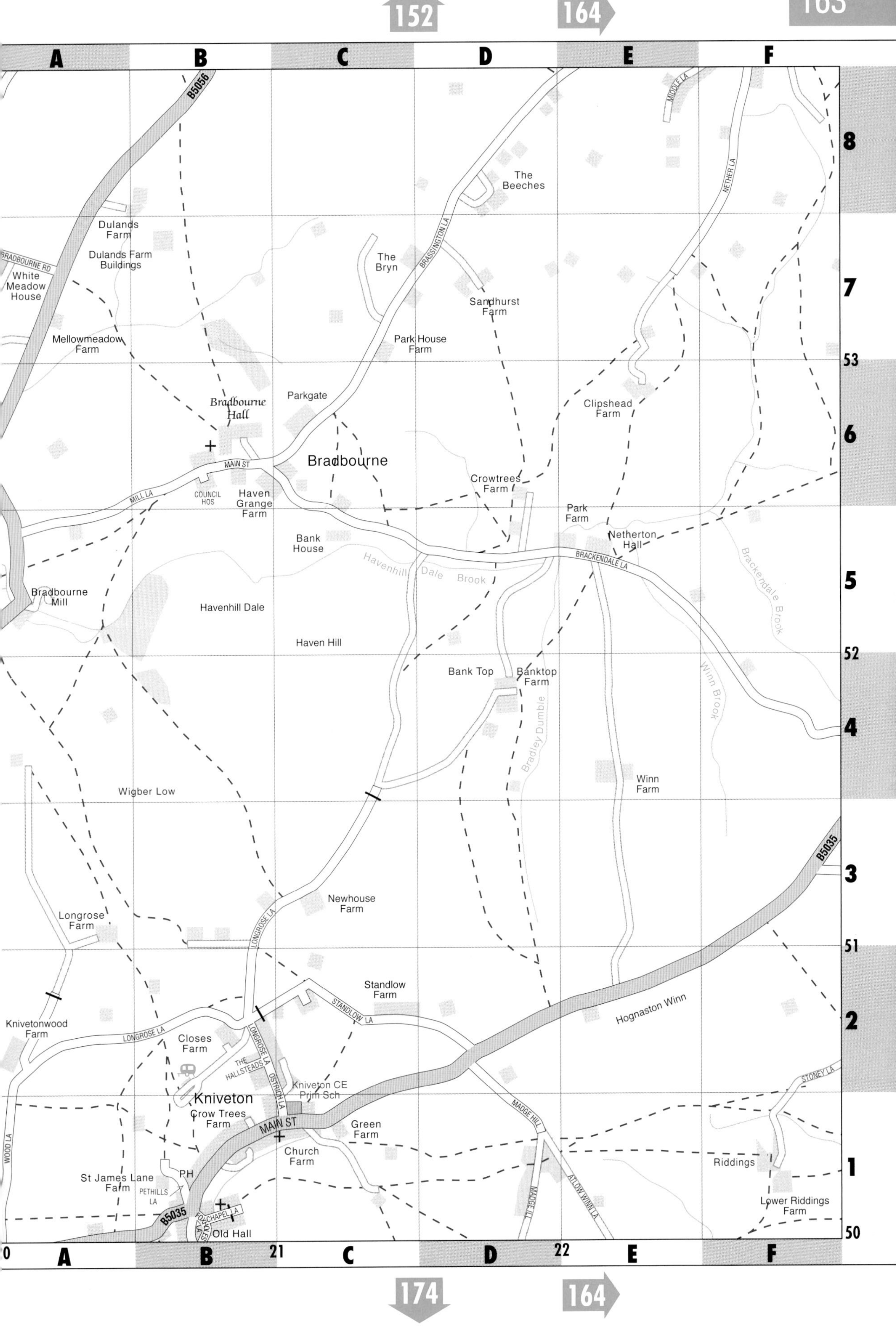
A
B
C
D
E
F
B5056
MIDDLE LA
8
The Beeches
NETHER LA
Dulands Farm
BRADBOURNE RD
White Meadow House
Dulands Farm Buildings
The Bryn
BRASSINGTON LA
7
Sandhurst Farm
Mellowmeadow Farm
Park House Farm
53
Bradbourne Hall
Parkgate
Clipshead Farm
6
Bradbourne
MAIN ST
MILL LA
COUNCIL HOS
Haven Grange Farm
Crowtrees Farm
Park Farm
Netherton Hall
Bank House
Havenhill Dale Brook
BRACKENDALE LA
Brackendale Brook
5
Bradbourne Mill
Havenhill Dale
Haven Hill
52
Bank Top
Banktop Farm
Winn Brook
Bradley Dumble
4
Wigber Low
Winn Farm
B5035
3
Newhouse Farm
Longrose Farm
LONGROSE LA
51
Standlow Farm
STANDLOW LA
Hognaston Winn
2
Knivetonwood Farm
LONGROSE LA
Closes Farm
THE HALLSTEADS
OSTRICH LA
Kniveton CE Prim Sch
STONEY LA
Kniveton
Crow Trees Farm
MAIN ST
Green Farm
MADGE HILL
WOOD LA
Church Farm
1
Riddings
St James Lane Farm
PH
PETHILLS LA
MADGE HILL
ALLOW WINN LA
Lower Riddings Farm
B5035
CHAPEL LA
FOXHOLES LA
Old Hall
50
0
21
22

174
164

163
153

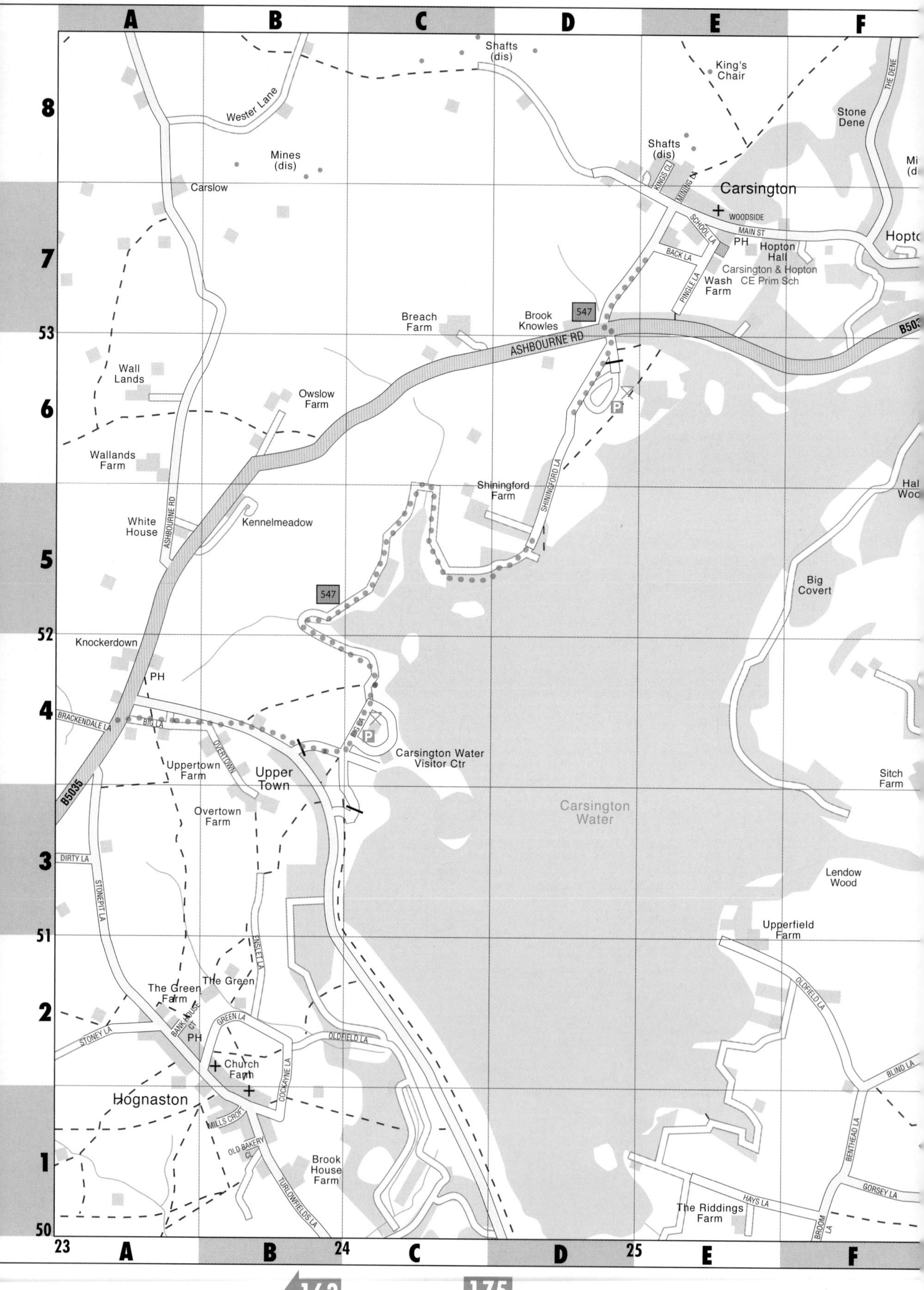
A
B
C
D
E
F
Shafts (dis)
King's Chair
Wester Lane
Stone Dene
THE DENE
Mines (dis)
Shafts (dis)
KINGS CL
MINING LA
Carsington
Carslow
WOODSIDE
SCHOOL LA
MAIN ST
PH
Hopton Hall
BACK LA
Carsington & Hopton CE Prim Sch
Wash Farm
PINGLE LA
Breach Farm
Brook Knowles
547
ASHBOURNE RD
B5035
Wall Lands
Owslow Farm
Wallands Farm
Shiningford Farm
SHININGFORD LA
White House
ASHBOURNE RD
Kennelmeadow
547
Big Covert
Knockerdown
PH
BRACKENDALE LA
BIG LA
OVERTOWN
Uppertown Farm
Upper Town
Carsington Water Visitor Ctr
Sitch Farm
B5035
Overtown Farm
Carsington Water
DIRTY LA
STONEPIT LA
Lendow Wood
Upperfield Farm
ENSLET LA
The Green
The Green Farm
BANK HOUSE CT
PH
GREEN LA
STONEY LA
OLDFIELD LA
OLDFIELD LA
Church Farm
COCKAYNE LA
Hognaston
BLIND LA
MILLS CROFT
OLD BAKERY CL
BENTHEAD LA
Brook House Farm
TURLOWFIELDS LA
GORSEY LA
HAYS LA
The Riddings Farm
BROOM LA
8
7
53
6
5
52
4
3
51
2
1
50
23
24
25

163
175

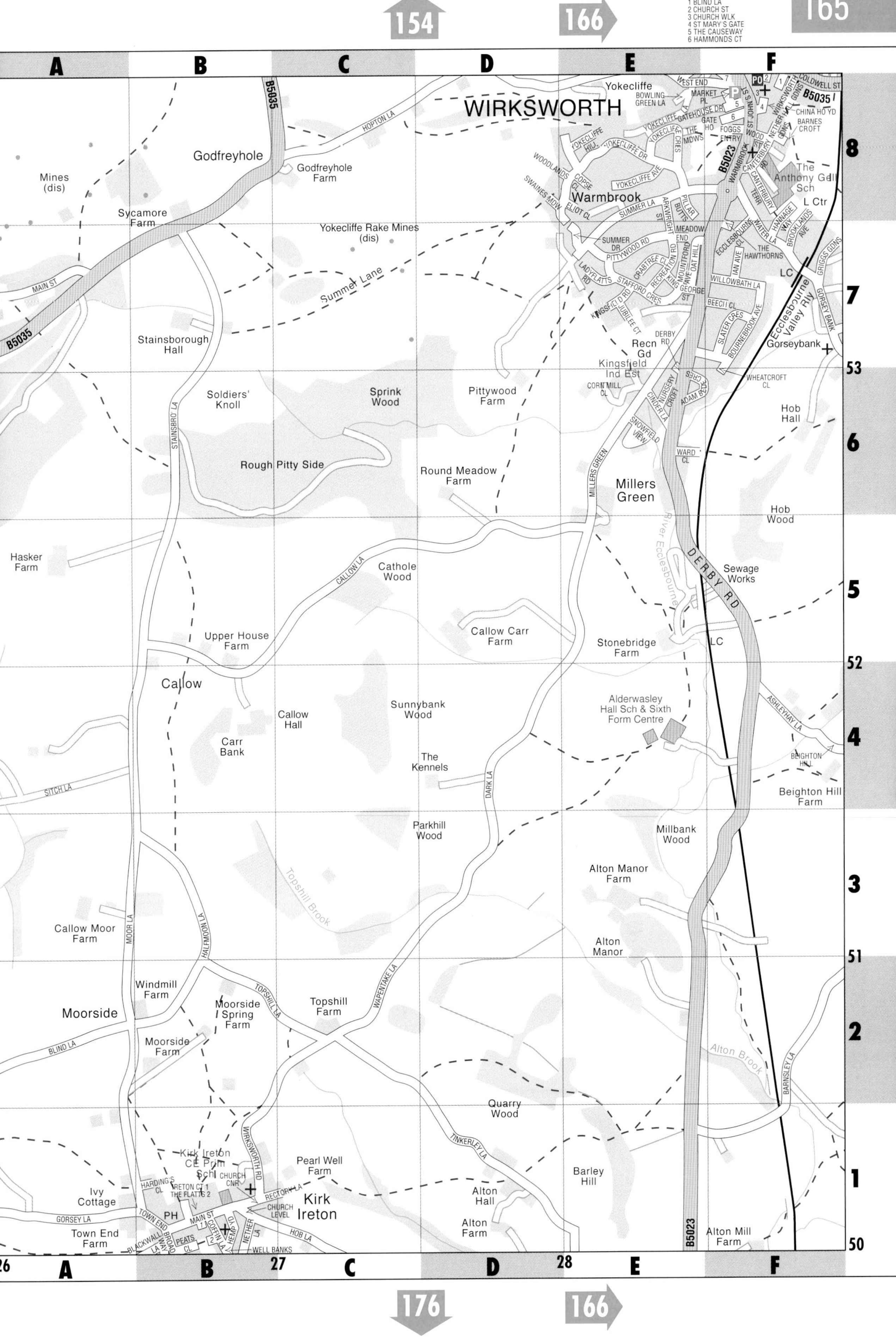

165 155

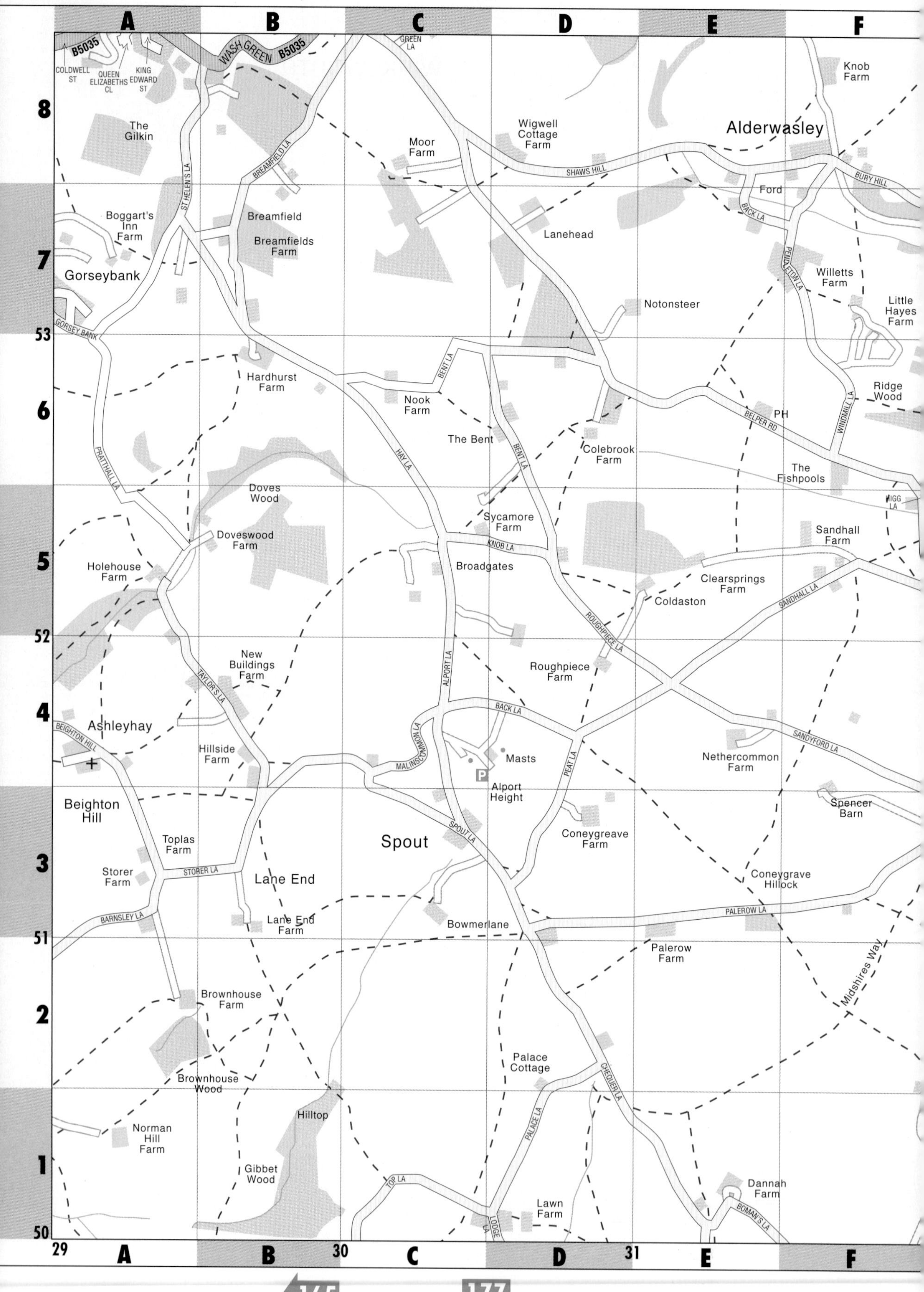
A
B
C
D
E
F
8
7
53
6
5
52
4
3
51
2
1
50
29
30
31
B5035
WASH GREEN B5035
GREEN LA
COLDWELL ST
QUEEN ELIZABETHS CL
KING EDWARD ST
Knob Farm
The Gilkin
Moor Farm
Wigwell Cottage Farm
Alderwasley
ST HELEN'S LA
BREAMFIELD LA
SHAWS HILL
BURY HILL
Ford
BACK LA
Boggart's Inn Farm
Breamfield
Breamfields Farm
Lanehead
Gorseybank
PENDLETON LA
Willetts Farm
Notonsteer
Little Hayes Farm
GORSEY BANK
BENT LA
Hardhurst Farm
Nook Farm
Ridge Wood
PH
BELPER RD
WINDMILL LA
The Bent
HAY LA
BENT LA
Colebrook Farm
PRATTHALL LA
The Fishpools
Doves Wood
NIGG LA
Sycamore Farm
Doveswood Farm
Sandhall Farm
KNOB LA
Holehouse Farm
Broadgates
Clearsprings Farm
Coldaston
SANDHALL LA
ROUGHPIECE LA
New Buildings Farm
ALPORT LA
Roughpiece Farm
TAYLOR'S LA
BACK LA
Ashleyhay
BEIGHTON HILL
MALINSCOMMON LA
Hillside Farm
Masts
PEAT LA
Nethercommon Farm
SANDYFORD LA
Alport Height
Beighton Hill
Spencer Barn
SPOUT LA
Toplas Farm
Coneygreave Farm
Spout
Storer Farm
STORER LA
Lane End
Coneygrave Hillock
BARNSLEY LA
Lane End Farm
Bowmerlane
PALEROW LA
Palerow Farm
Midshires Way
Brownhouse Farm
Palace Cottage
Brownhouse Wood
CHEQUER LA
Hilltop
Norman Hill Farm
PALACE LA
Gibbet Wood
TOP LA
Dannah Farm
Lawn Farm
BOMAN'S LA
LODGE LA

165 177

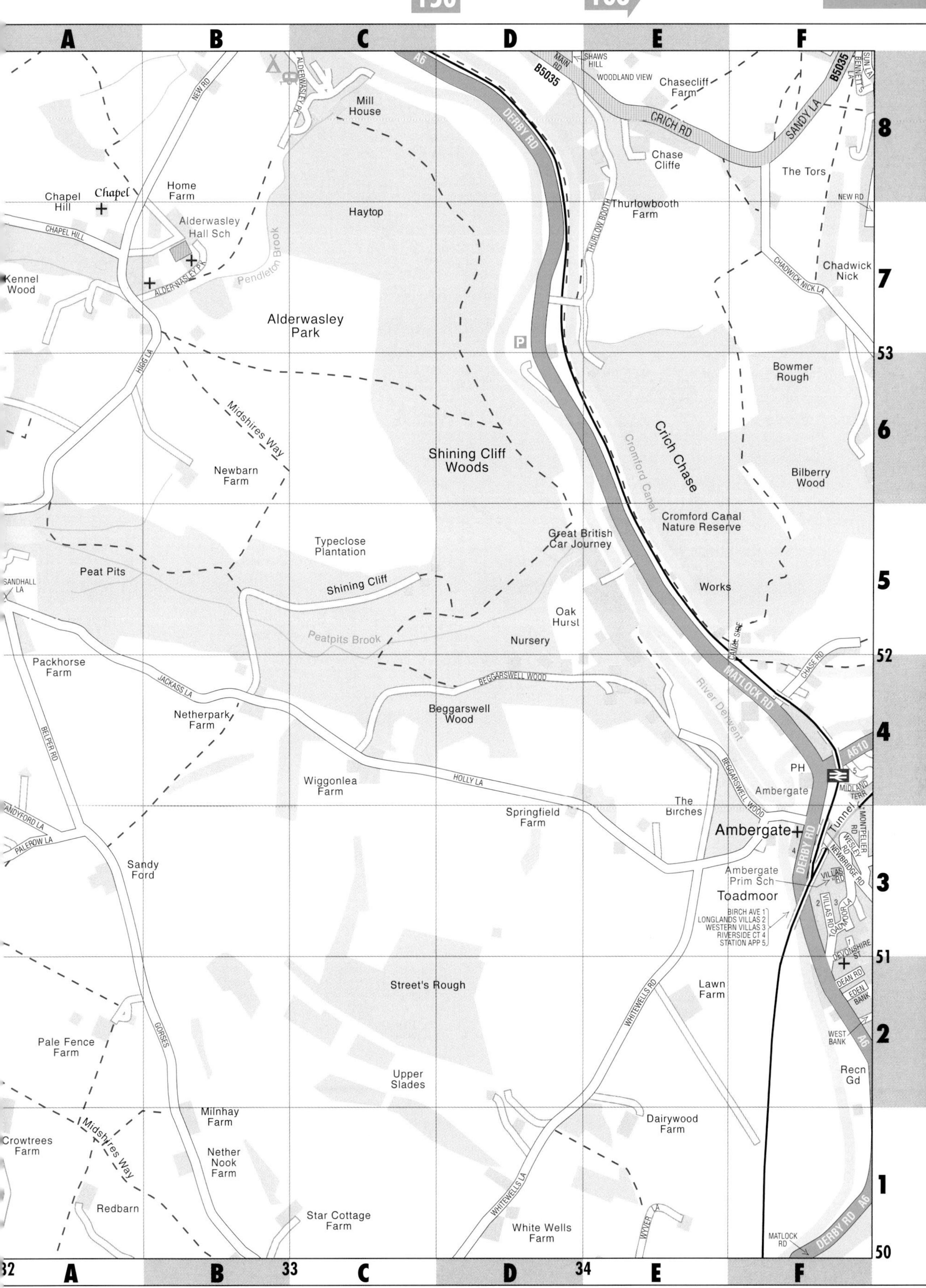
156
168
Mill House
Chasecliff Farm
Chase Cliffe
The Tors
Chapel Hill
Home Farm
Alderwasley Hall Sch
Haytop
Thurlowbooth Farm
Kennel Wood
Chadwick Nick
Alderwasley Park
Pendleton Brook
Bowmer Rough
Midshires Way
Newbarn Farm
Shining Cliff Woods
Crich Chase
Cromford Canal
Bilberry Wood
Typeclose Plantation
Great British Car Journey
Cromford Canal Nature Reserve
Peat Pits
Shining Cliff
Oak Hurst
Works
Peatpits Brook
Nursery
Packhorse Farm
Netherpark Farm
Beggarswell Wood
River Derwent
Wiggonlea Farm
Springfield Farm
The Birches
Ambergate
Toadmoor
Ambergate Prim Sch
BIRCH AVE 1
LONGLANDS VILLAS 2
WESTERN VILLAS 3
RIVERSIDE CT 4
STATION APP 5
Sandy Ford
Street's Rough
Lawn Farm
Pale Fence Farm
Upper Slades
Recn Gd
Milnhay Farm
Dairywood Farm
Crowtrees Farm
Nether Nook Farm
Redbarn
Star Cottage Farm
White Wells Farm
178
168

167
157

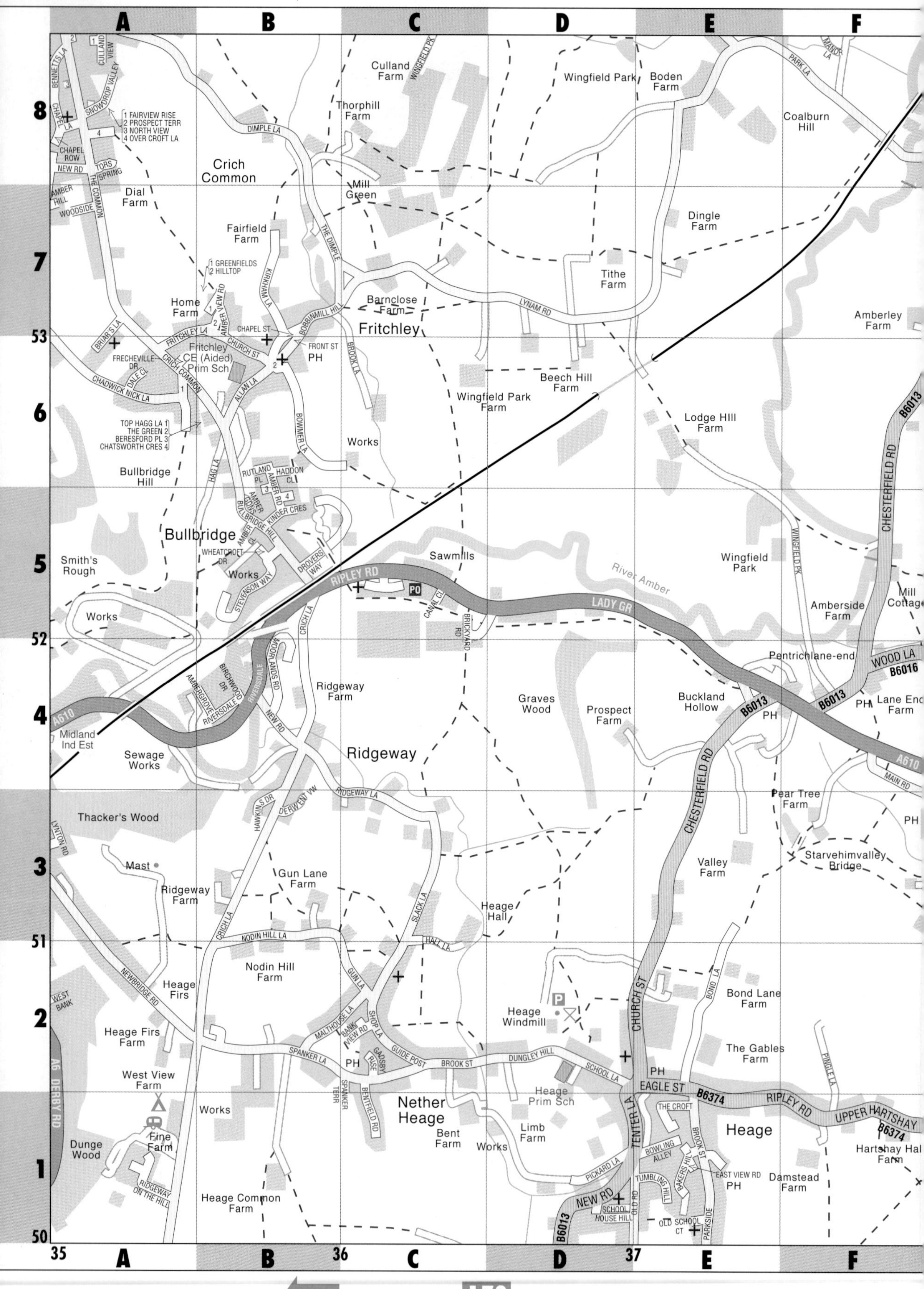
A
B
C
D
E
F
8
7
53
6
5
52
4
3
51
2
1
50
35
36
37
Culland Farm
Thorphill Farm
Wingfield Park
Boden Farm
Coalburn Hill
Crich Common
Mill Green
Dial Farm
Dingle Farm
Fairfield Farm
Tithe Farm
Home Farm
Barnclose Farm
Fritchley
Amberley Farm
Fritchley CE (Aided) Prim Sch
PH
Beech Hill Farm
Wingfield Park Farm
Lodge Hill Farm
Works
Bullbridge Hill
Bullbridge
Smith's Rough
Sawmills
Wingfield Park
River Amber
Amberside Farm
Mill Cottage
Ridgeway Farm
Pentrichlane-end
Graves Wood
Prospect Farm
Buckland Hollow
Lane End Farm
Midland Ind Est
Sewage Works
Ridgeway
Pear Tree Farm
Thacker's Wood
Mast
Starvehimvalley Bridge
Valley Farm
Gun Lane Farm
Heage Hall
Nodin Hill Farm
Bond Lane Farm
Heage Firs
Heage Windmill
The Gables Farm
Heage Firs Farm
West View Farm
Nether Heage
Heage Prim Sch
Heage
Bent Farm
Limb Farm
Hartshay Hall Farm
Damstead Farm
Dunge Wood
Fine Farm
Heage Common Farm
1 FAIRVIEW RISE
2 PROSPECT TERR
3 NORTH VIEW
4 OVER CROFT LA
1 GREENFIELDS
2 HILLTOP
TOP HAGG LA 1
THE GREEN 2
BERESFORD PL 3
CHATSWORTH CRES 4
DIMPLE LA
LYNAM RD
PARK LA
MANOR LA
THE DIMPLE
KIRKHAM LA
BOBBINMILL HILL
CHAPEL ST
FRONT ST
BROOK LA
BOWMER LA
CHURCH ST
FRITCHLEY LA
CRICH COMMON
CHADWICK NICK LA
FRECHEVILLE DR
DALE CL
BRIAR'S LA
ALLAN LA
HAG LA
RUTLAND PL
HADDON CL
AMBER RD
KINDER CRES
BULLBRIDGE HILL
WHEATCROFT DR
STEVENSON WAY
DROVERS WAY
RIPLEY RD
PO
CANAL CL
BRICKYARD RD
LADY GR
CRICH LA
WOODLANDS RD
BIRCHWOOD DR
RIVERSDALE
AMBERGROVE
NEW RD
A610
RIDGEWAY LA
DERWENT VW
HAWKINS DR
WINGFIELD PK
CHESTERFIELD RD
B6013
B6016
WOOD LA
MAIN RD
LYNTON RD
SLACK LA
NODIN HILL LA
HALL LA
GUN LA
NEWBRIDGE RD
MALTHOUSE LA
SHOP LA
SPANKER LA
GUIDE POST
BROOK ST
DUNGLEY HILL
SCHOOL LA
CHURCH ST
EAGLE ST
B6374
RIPLEY RD
UPPER HARTSHAY
BOND LA
PINGLE LA
SPANKER TERR
BENTFIELD RD
GADSBY RISE
TENTER LA
THE CROFT
BOWLING ALLEY
TUMBLING HILL
BAKERS HILL
EAST VIEW RD
PARKSIDE
OLD SCHOOL CT
SCHOOL HOUSE HILL
OLD RD
PICKARD LA
A6 DERBY RD
WEST BANK
RIDGEWAY ON THE HILL
BENNETTS LA
CULLAND VIEW
SNOWDROP VALLEY
CHAPEL LA
CHAPEL ROW
NEW RD
TORS SPRING
AMBER HILL
WOODSIDE
THE COMMON

167
179

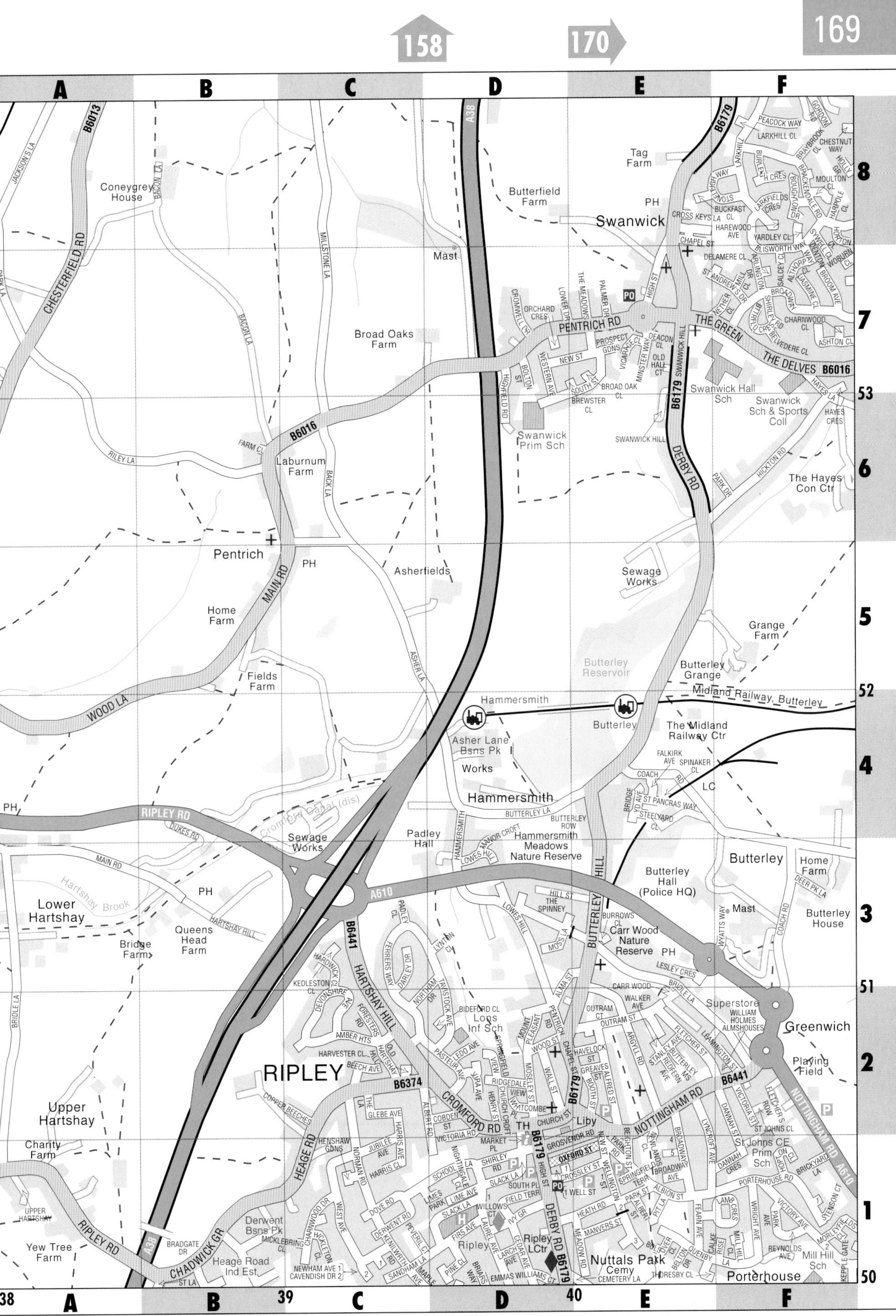

A B C D E F

8
7
53
6
5
52
4
3
51
2
1
50

180
170

38 39 40

A B C D E F

D1
1 THE WILLOWS

E1
1 LOWER MILL
2 MANVERS AVE
3 CLUMBER CL
4 BROADWAY CT
5 BROADWAY DR

F1
1 ASHOVER CL
2 BALLACRAINE DR

169

159

C8
1 Somercotes
Inf Sch

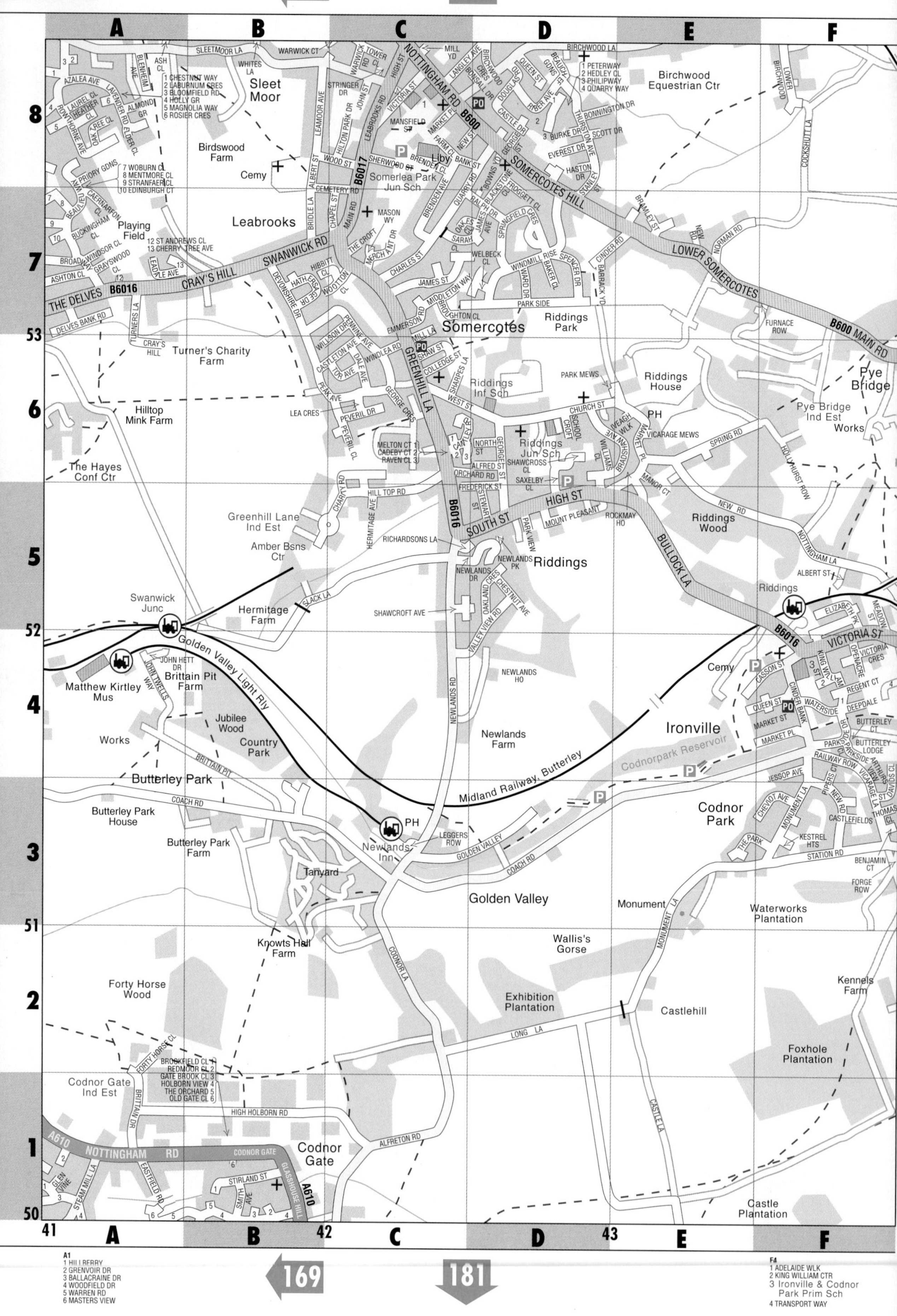

160

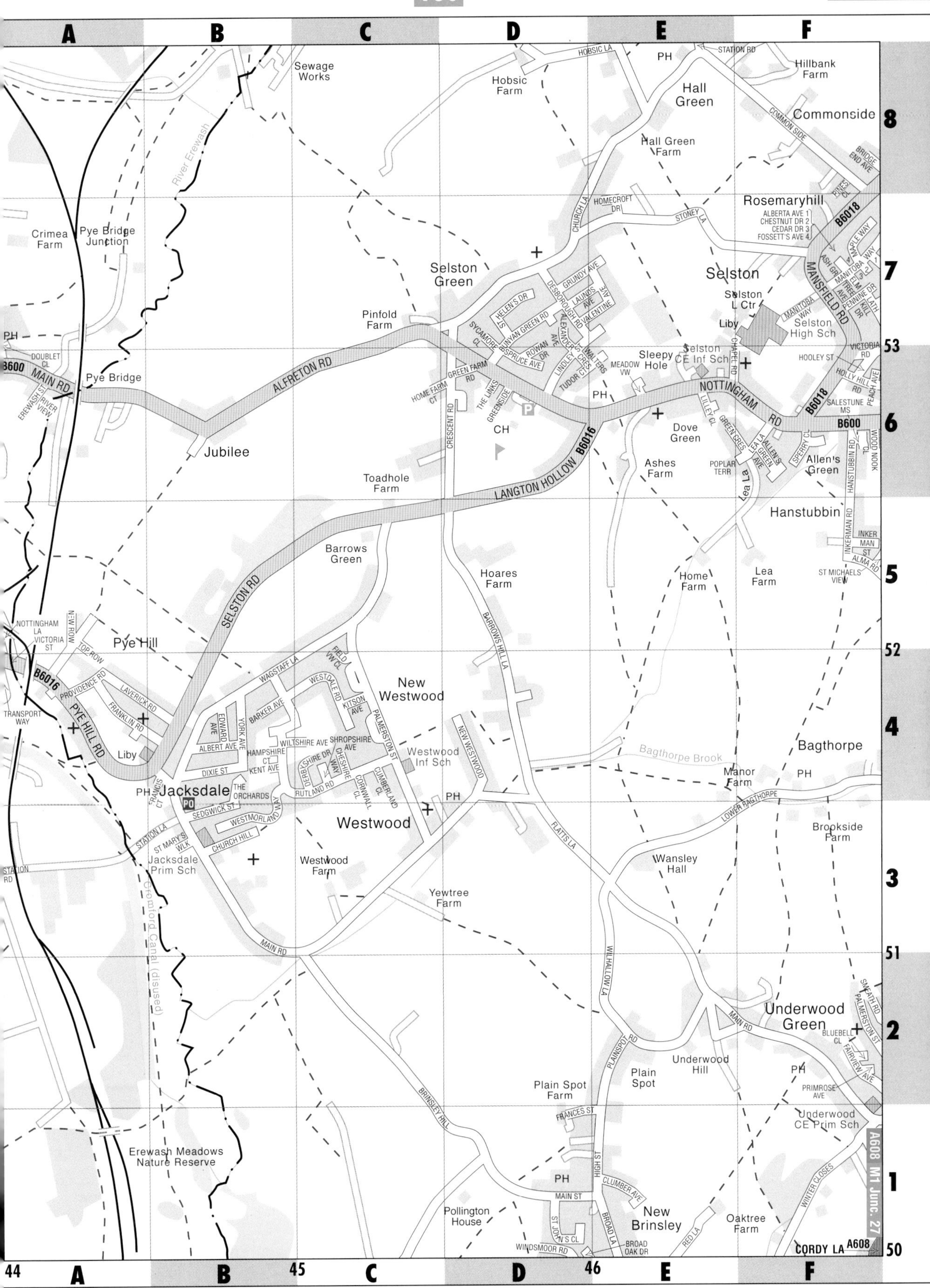
A
B
C
D
E
F
Sewage Works
Hobsic Farm
HOBSIC LA
PH
STATION RD
Hillbank Farm
Hall Green
Commonside
COMMON SIDE
River Erewash
Hall Green Farm
BRIDGE END AVE
8
HOMECROFT DR
CHURCH LA
STONEY LA
Rosemaryhill
ALBERTA AVE 1
CHESTNUT DR 2
CEDAR DR 3
FOSSETT'S AVE 4
B6018
MAPLE WAY
Crimea Farm
Pye Bridge Junction
Selston Green
GRUNDY AVE
Selston
MANSFIELD RD
7
Pinfold Farm
HELEN'S DR
DESBOROUGH RD
LAUNDS AVE
VALENTINE AVE
Selston L Ctr
Selston High Sch
MANITOBA WAY
PENNINE DR
Liby
PH
DOUBLET CL
B600
MAIN RD
Pye Bridge
ALFRETON RD
SYCAMORE CL
BUNYAN GREEN RD
ALEXANDER ST
ROWAN DR
SPRUCE AVE
LINDLEY ST
TUDOR CT
WALTERS CRES
MEADOW VW
Sleepy Hole
Selston CE Inf Sch
CHAPEL RD
VICTORIA RD
53
HOOLEY ST
HOLLY HILL RD
PEACH AVE
ERIWASH ST
RIVER VIEW
HOME FARM CT
GREEN FARM RD
THE LINKS
GREENSIDE
CRESCENT RD
P
CH
PH
NOTTINGHAM RD
B6018
SALESTUNE MS
B600
6
Dove Green
LILLEY CL
GREEN CRES
LEA LA
ALLEN'S GREEN AVE
SPERRY CL
Allen's Green
WOOD NOOK CL
HANSTUBBIN RD
Jubilee
B6016
Ashes Farm
POPLAR TERR
Toadhole Farm
LANGTON HOLLOW
Lea La
Hanstubbin
INKERMAN RD
INKERMAN ST
ALMA RD
Barrows Green
Hoares Farm
Home Farm
Lea Farm
ST MICHAELS VIEW
5
SELSTON RD
NOTTINGHAM LA
VICTORIA ST
NEW ROW
TOP ROW
Pye Hill
BARROWS HILL LA
52
B6016
PROVIDENCE RD
LAVERICK RD
FRANKLIN RD
WAGSTAFF LA
FIELD VW CL
WESTDALE RD
New Westwood
TRANSPORT WAY
PYE HILL RD
EDWARD AVE
YORK AVE
BARKER AVE
KITSON AVE
PALMERSTON ST
NEW WESTWOOD
4
Bagthorpe
ALBERT AVE
WILTSHIRE AVE
SHROPSHIRE AVE
Westwood Inf Sch
Bagthorpe Brook
Liby
HAMPSHIRE CT
KENT AVE
DERBYSHIRE DR
CHESHIRE WAY
Manor Farm
PH
DIXIE ST
PH
Jacksdale
THE ORCHARDS
RUTLAND RD
CORNWALL CL
CUMBERLAND CL
PH
FRANCIS CT
PO
SEDGWICK ST
WESTMORLAND WAY
Westwood
LOWER BAGTHORPE
STATION LA
ST MARY'S WLK
CHURCH HILL
FLATTS LA
Brookside Farm
STATION RD
Jacksdale Prim Sch
Westwood Farm
Wansley Hall
3
Cromford Canal (disused)
Yewtree Farm
MAIN RD
WILHALLOW LA
51
SMEATH RD
PALMERSTON ST
Underwood Green
MAIN RD
BLUEBELL CL
2
PLAINSPOT RD
Underwood Hill
FAIRVIEW AVE
Plain Spot
PH
Plain Spot Farm
PRIMROSE AVE
BRINSLEY HILL
FRANCES ST
Underwood CE Prim Sch
A608 M1 Junc. 27
Erewash Meadows Nature Reserve
HIGH ST
PH
CLUMBER AVE
1
MAIN ST
New Brinsley
Oaktree Farm
WINTER CLOSES
Pollington House
ST JOHN'S CL
BROAD LA
RED LA
WINDSMOOR RD
BROAD OAK DR
CORDY LA
A608
50
44
A
B
45
C
D
46
E
F

182

161

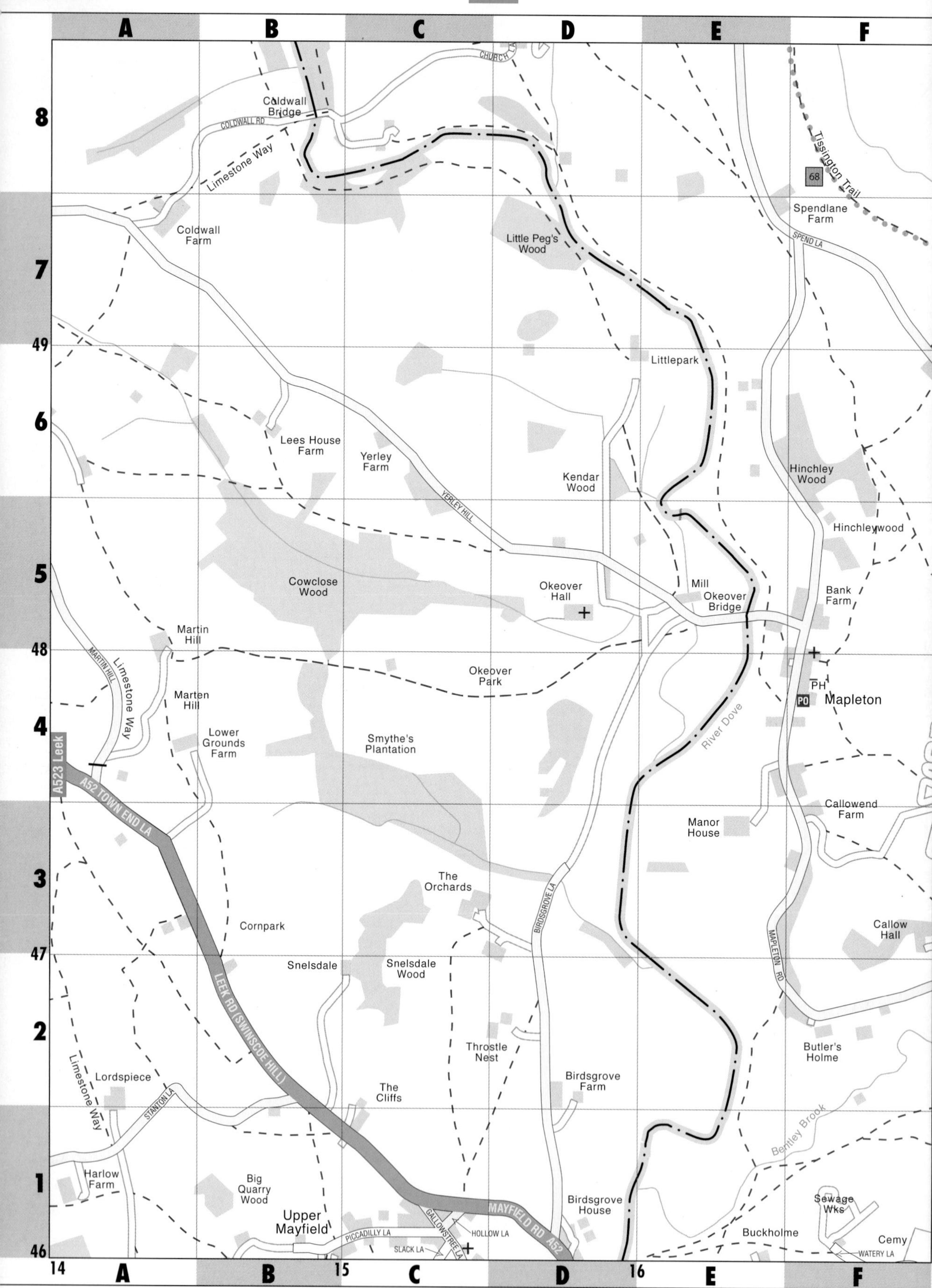

A
B
C
D
E
F
8
7
49
6
5
48
4
3
47
2
1
46
14
15
16
Coldwall Bridge
COLDWALL RD
CHURCH LA
Limestone Way
Tissington Trail
68
Spendlane Farm
SPEND LA
Coldwall Farm
Little Peg's Wood
Littlepark
Lees House Farm
Yerley Farm
Kendar Wood
Hinchley Wood
YERLEY HILL
Hinchleywood
Cowclose Wood
Okeover Hall
Mill
Okeover Bridge
Bank Farm
Martin Hill
MARTIN HILL
Limestone Way
Okeover Park
Marten Hill
PH
PO
Mapleton
Lower Grounds Farm
Smythe's Plantation
River Dove
A523 Leek
A52 TOWN END LA
Callowend Farm
Manor House
The Orchards
Cornpark
BIRDSGROVE LA
MAPLETON RD
Callow Hall
Snelsdale
Snelsdale Wood
LEEK RD (SWINSCOE HILL)
Throstle Nest
Butler's Holme
Limestone Way
Lordspiece
Birdsgrove Farm
The Cliffs
STANTON LA
Bentley Brook
Harlow Farm
Big Quarry Wood
MAYFIELD RD A52
Birdsgrove House
Sewage Wks
Upper Mayfield
PICCADILLY LA
GALLOWSTREE LA
HOLLOW LA
SLACK LA
Buckholme
Cemy
WATERY LA

184

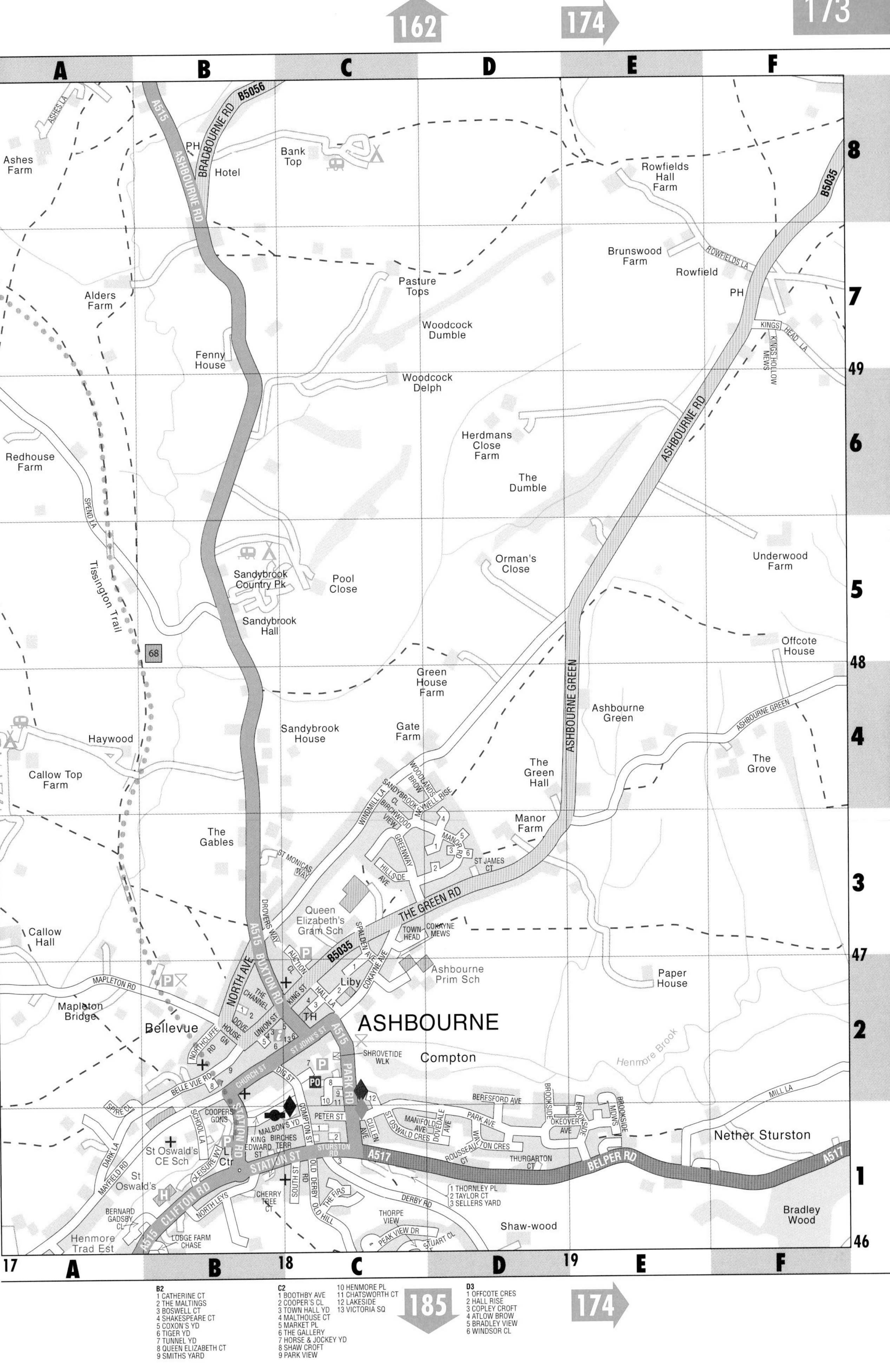

B2
1 CATHERINE CT
2 THE MALTINGS
3 BOSWELL CT
4 SHAKESPEARE CT
5 COXON'S YD
6 TIGER YD
7 TUNNEL YD
8 QUEEN ELIZABETH CT
9 SMITHS YARD

C2
1 BOOTHBY AVE
2 COOPER'S CL
3 TOWN HALL YD
4 MALTHOUSE CT
5 MARKET PL
6 THE GALLERY
7 HORSE & JOCKEY YD
8 SHAW CROFT
9 PARK VIEW
10 HENMORE PL
11 CHATSWORTH CT
12 LAKESIDE
13 VICTORIA SQ

D3
1 OFFCOTE CRES
2 HALL RISE
3 COPLEY CROFT
4 ATLOW BROW
5 BRADLEY VIEW
6 WINDSOR CL

173
163

A B C D E F

8
7
49
6
5
48
4
3
47
2
1
46

WOOD LA
MAIN ST
B5035
ASHBOURNE RD
Brookhouse Farm
Madge Hill
ATLOW WINN LA
Parkside Brook
Atlow Winn
Breck Farm
MADGE HILL
Shaws
WINN LA
Pethills
KINGSHEAD LA
Kniveton Brook
Atlowmoat Farm
Foxhole Farm
FOXHOLES LA
Woodhead
Green Farm
Upper Hallfields
Whitehouse Farm
Offcote Grange
ASHBOURNE GREEN
KNIVETON LA
AGNES MEADOW LA
Agnes Meadow
Annies Meadow House
Parkfields Farm
The Rough
Ridge La
Henmoor Brook
Ox Close
Agnesmeadow Bridge
Corley Farm
Dayfield Brook
Sturston Mill
Tomlinson Carr
Sturston Hall
CORLEY LA
MILL LA
Bradley Pastures
BRADLEY CORNER
A517
Bradley Lodge
New House Farm
BELPER RD
A517
Bradley Smithy
Bradley Wood
Shepherd's Folly
YELDERSLEY LA
YEW TREE LA
Bradley Moor
Bull Hill
Airfield (dis)
Bradley Hall

20 A B 21 C D 22 E F

173
186

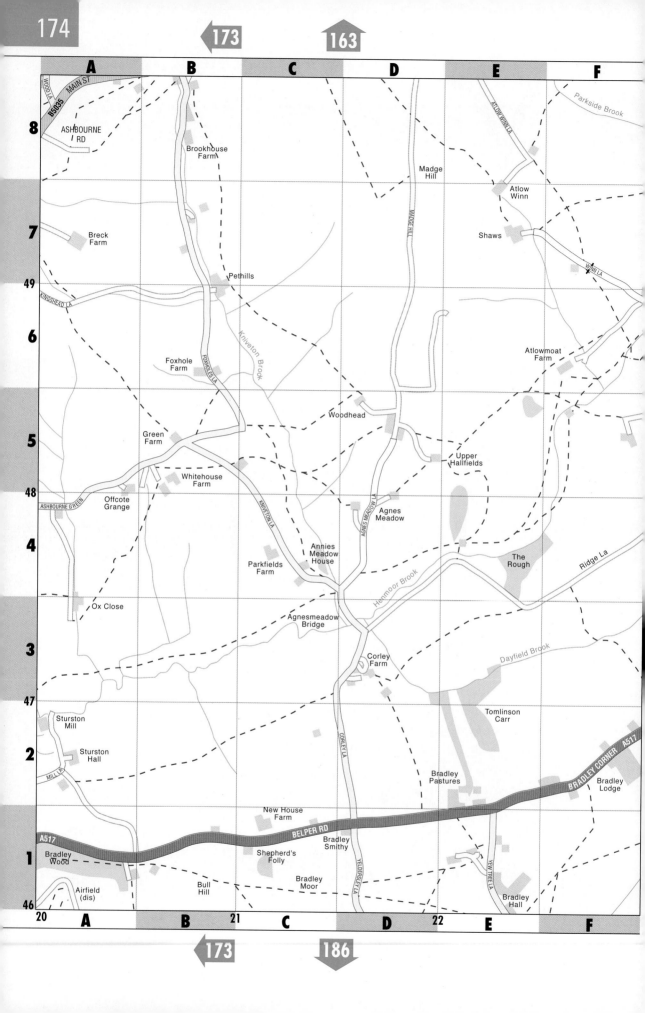

164 176

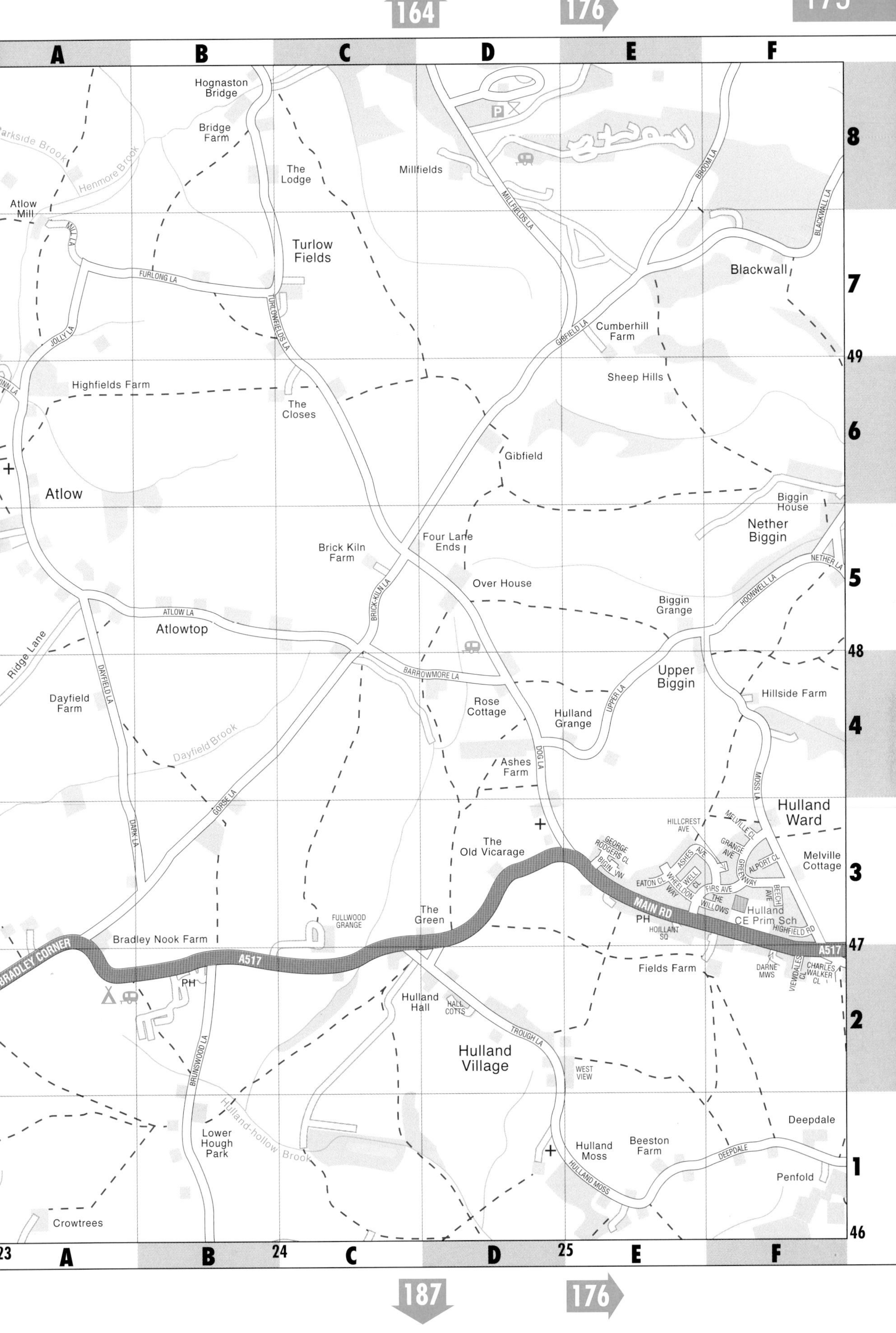
A B C D E F
8 7 6 5 4 3 2 1
49 48 47 46
23 24 25
Hognaston Bridge
Bridge Farm
The Lodge
Millfields
Atlow Mill
Henmore Brook
Parkside Brook
MILL LA
MILLFIELDS LA
BROOM LA
BLACKWALL LA
Turlow Fields
FURLONG LA
TURLOWFIELDS LA
JOLLY LA
Blackwall
Cumberhill Farm
GIBFIELD LA
Sheep Hills
Highfields Farm
The Closes
Gibfield
Atlow
Biggin House
Nether Biggin
Four Lane Ends
Brick Kiln Farm
Over House
NETHER LA
HOONWELL LA
BRICK-KILN LA
Biggin Grange
ATLOW LA
Atlowtop
Ridge Lane
BARROWMORE LA
Upper Biggin
Hillside Farm
Dayfield Farm
DAYFIELD LA
Rose Cottage
Hulland Grange
UPPER LA
Dayfield Brook
Ashes Farm
DOG LA
MOSS LA
GORSE LA
Hulland Ward
DARK LA
HILLCREST AVE
MELVILLE CL
The Old Vicarage
Melville Cottage
GEORGE RODGERS CL
BIGIN VW
ASHES AVE
GRANGE AVE
ALPORT CL
GREENWAY
EATON CL
WHEELDON WAY
WELL CL
FIRS AVE
BEECH AVE
THE WILLOWS
Hulland CE Prim Sch
MAIN RD
HIGHFIELD RD
FULLWOOD GRANGE
The Green
PH
HOILLANT SQ
Bradley Nook Farm
BRADLEY CORNER
A517
Fields Farm
DARNE MWS
VIEWDALES CL
CHARLES WALKER CL
PH
Hulland Hall
HALL COTTS
TROUGH LA
Hulland Village
BRUNSWOOD LA
WEST VIEW
Hulland-hollow Brook
Deepdale
Lower Hough Park
Hulland Moss
Beeston Farm
DEEPDALE
HULLAND MOSS
Penfold
Crowtrees

187 176

175 165

A B C D E F

8

BLACKWALL LA
BROAD WAY
NETHER LA
BANKS
WELL
TOP LONS
BOTTOM LONS
Addcrofts
HOB LA
TIMBERLEY LA
WOOD LA
B5023
Field Farm
FIELD LA
Winneyhill
JEBB'S LA
Ecclesbourne Valley Railway

7
Bennywall Wood
The Mountain
BROAD WAY
Bullhill
Idridgehay Green
JOHNSON LA
THE GN
Holm Brook
CLIFFASH LA

49
Bennywall Brook
Biggin Head Farm
Rakestones Farm
GORSES
CLIFFASH LA
WIRKSWORTH RD
PH
LC
ROOD LA

6
Idridgehay
Hays Farm
Southsitch House
Idridgeha
B502
Carr Wood

5
Biggin
HOONWELL LA
Ford
Mill
Cherry Orchard
MAG LA
WINDLEY LA
BIGGINMILL LA
ECCLESBOURNE LA

48
Nether Biggin
NETHER LA
Hillside Farm
Ireton Wood

4
Millington Green
Redhouse Farm
Lanehead Farm
Hall
Iretonwood Farm
BULLHILL LA
NEW RD
Brook Farm
White House Farm
Mount Pleasant

3
BIGGIN LA
Stock-a-Sitch
Biggin Old Hall
Toad Holes Farm
Sherbourne Brook
Bull Hill
OLD LA
HILLCLIFF LA

Springhill Farm
Lumber Lane Farm
LUMBER LA

47
A517
PH
Massey's Barn

2
ELMS VUE WY
CROSSWAYS LA
Crossways Farm
BELPER RD
Cross o' th' hands
ASHBOURNE RD
A517

Magfield
SMITH-HALL LA
WATERLAGG LA
Waterlagg Cottage
CROSS O THE HANDS
Beechhill Farm

1
Derbyhill Farm
INTAKES LA

46
Moneyhills

26 A B 27 C D 28 E F

175 188

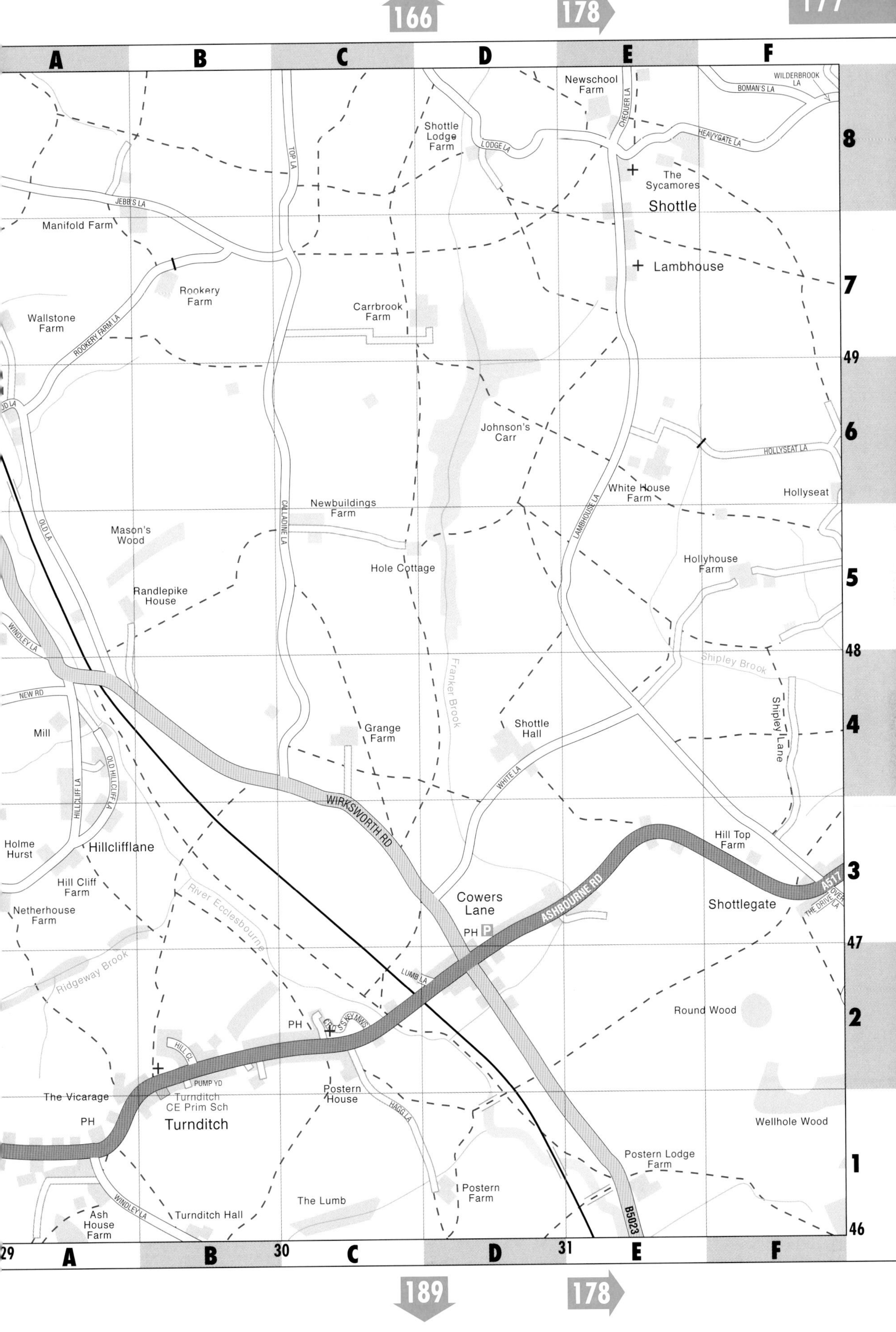

166
178
189
178

A B C D E F

8 7 49 6 5 48 4 3 47 2 1 46

Newschool Farm

WILDERBROOK LA

BOMAN'S LA

HEAVYGATE LA

CHEQUER LA

Shottle Lodge Farm

LODGE LA

TOP LA

The Sycamores

Shottle

Lambhouse

Manifold Farm

JEBB'S LA

Rookery Farm

Wallstone Farm

ROOKERY FARM LA

Carrbrook Farm

HOLLYSEAT LA

Hollyseat

White House Farm

LAMBHOUSE LA

Johnson's Carr

OLD LA

Mason's Wood

CALDONE LA

Newbuildings Farm

Hole Cottage

Hollyhouse Farm

Randlepike House

Shipley Brook

WINDLEY LA

Franker Brook

Shipley Lane

NEW RD

Grange Farm

Shottle Hall

Mill

WHITE LA

HILLCLIFF LA

OLD HILLCLIFF LA

WIRKSWORTH RD

Hill Top Farm

A517

Holme Hurst

Hillclifflane

Cowers Lane

THE DRIVE

OVER LA

Hill Cliff Farm

River Ecclesbourne

PH P

ASHBOURNE RD

Shottlegate

Netherhouse Farm

LUMB LA

Ridgeway Brook

Round Wood

PH

CROSS KEY MWS

HILL CL

PUMP YD

Postern House

HAGG LA

Wellhole Wood

The Vicarage

PH

Turnditch CE Prim Sch

Turnditch

Postern Lodge Farm

B5023

WINDLEY LA

Turnditch Hall

The Lumb

Postern Farm

Ash House Farm

29 30 31

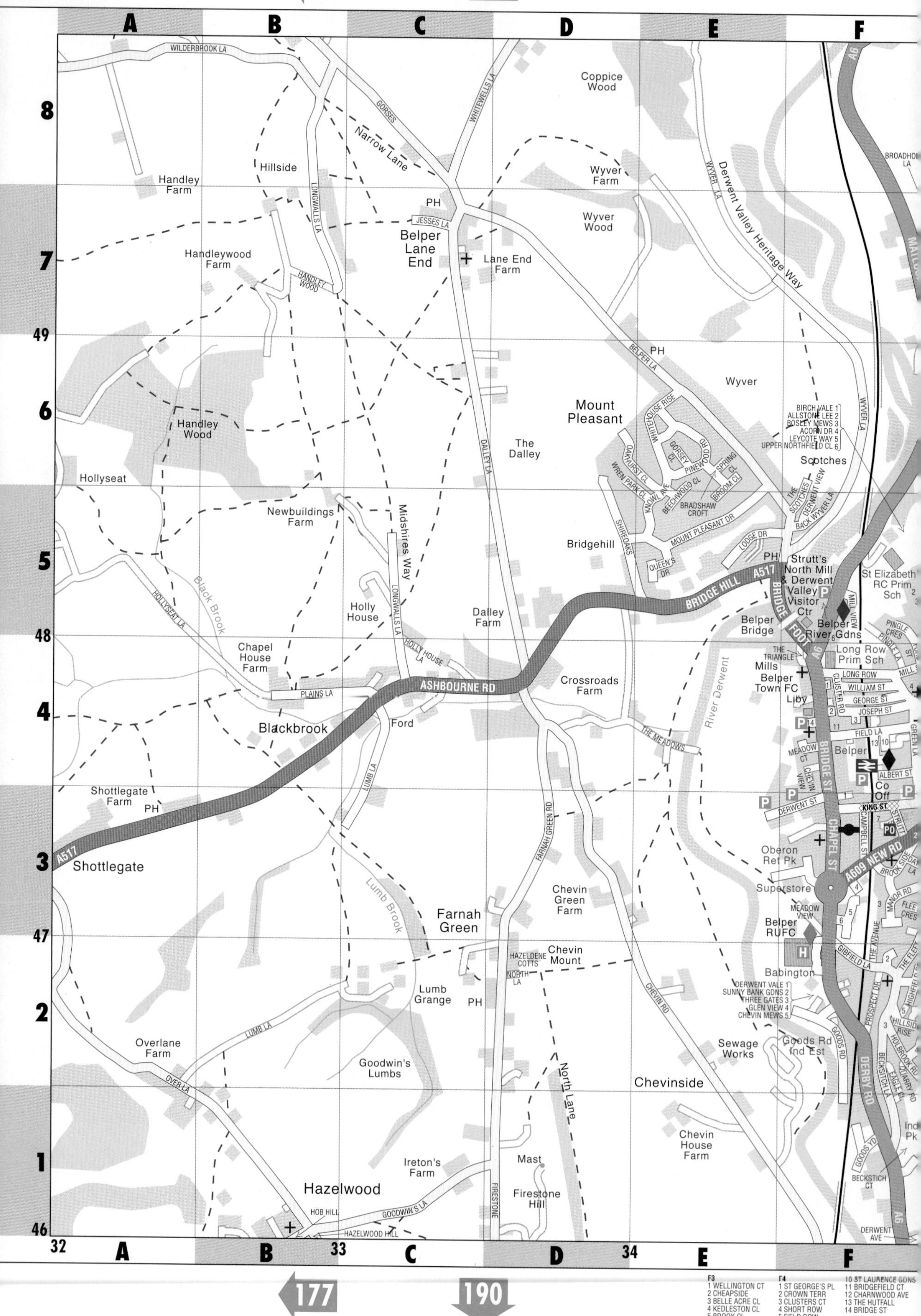

F3
1 WELLINGTON CT
2 CHEAPSIDE
3 BELLE ACRE CL
4 KEDLESTON CL
5 BROOK CL
6 LEIGHTON WAY
7 MIDLAND VIEW

F4
1 ST GEORGE'S PL
2 CROWN TERR
3 CLUSTERS CT
4 SHORT ROW
5 FIELD ROW
6 THE ORCHARD
7 CHURCH WLK
8 ST PETER'S CL
9 CHURCH LA

10 ST LAURENCE GDNS
11 BRIDGEFIELD CT
12 CHARNWOOD AVE
13 THE HUTFALL
14 BRIDGE ST

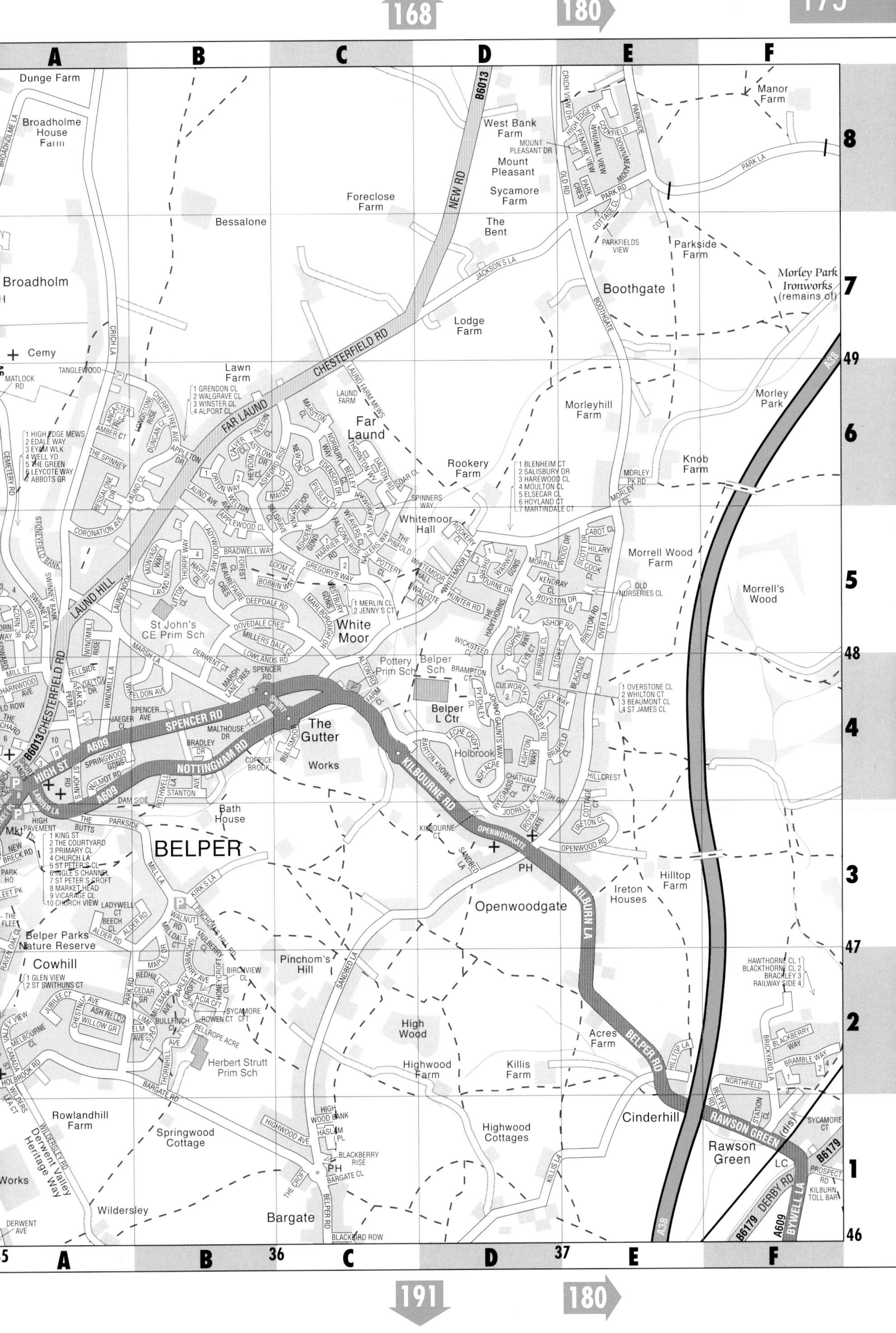
168
180
191
180
BELPER
Dunge Farm
Broadholme House Farm
Broadholm
Cemy
Bessalone
Foreclose Farm
West Bank Farm
Mount Pleasant
Sycamore Farm
The Bent
Manor Farm
Parkside Farm
Morley Park Ironworks (remains of)
Boothgate
Lodge Farm
Lawn Farm
Far Laund
Morleyhill Farm
Morley Park
Knob Farm
Rookery Farm
Whitemoor Hall
Morrell Wood Farm
Morrell's Wood
White Moor
St John's CE Prim Sch
Pottery Prim Sch
Belper Sch
Belper L Ctr
Holbrook
The Gutter
Works
Bath House
Openwoodgate
Ireton Houses
Hilltop Farm
Belper Parks Nature Reserve
Cowhill
Pinchom's Hill
High Wood
Highwood Farm
Killis Farm
Acres Farm
Herbert Strutt Prim Sch
Rowlandhill Farm
Springwood Cottage
Highwood Cottages
Cinderhill
Rawson Green
Wildersley
Bargate
Derwent Valley Heritage Way
Works
CHESTERFIELD RD
FAR LAUND
LAUND HILL
NEW RD
B6013
A38
A609
B6179
SPENCER RD
NOTTINGHAM RD
HIGH ST
KILBOURNE RD
KILBURN LA
BELPER RD
RAWSON GREEN (dis)
BYWELL LA
DERBY RD
BOOTHGATE
PARK LA
JACKSON'S LA
CRICH LA
SANDBED LA
BARGATE RD
HOLBROOK RD
A
B
C
D
E
F
8
7
6
5
4
3
2
1
49
48
47
46
36
37

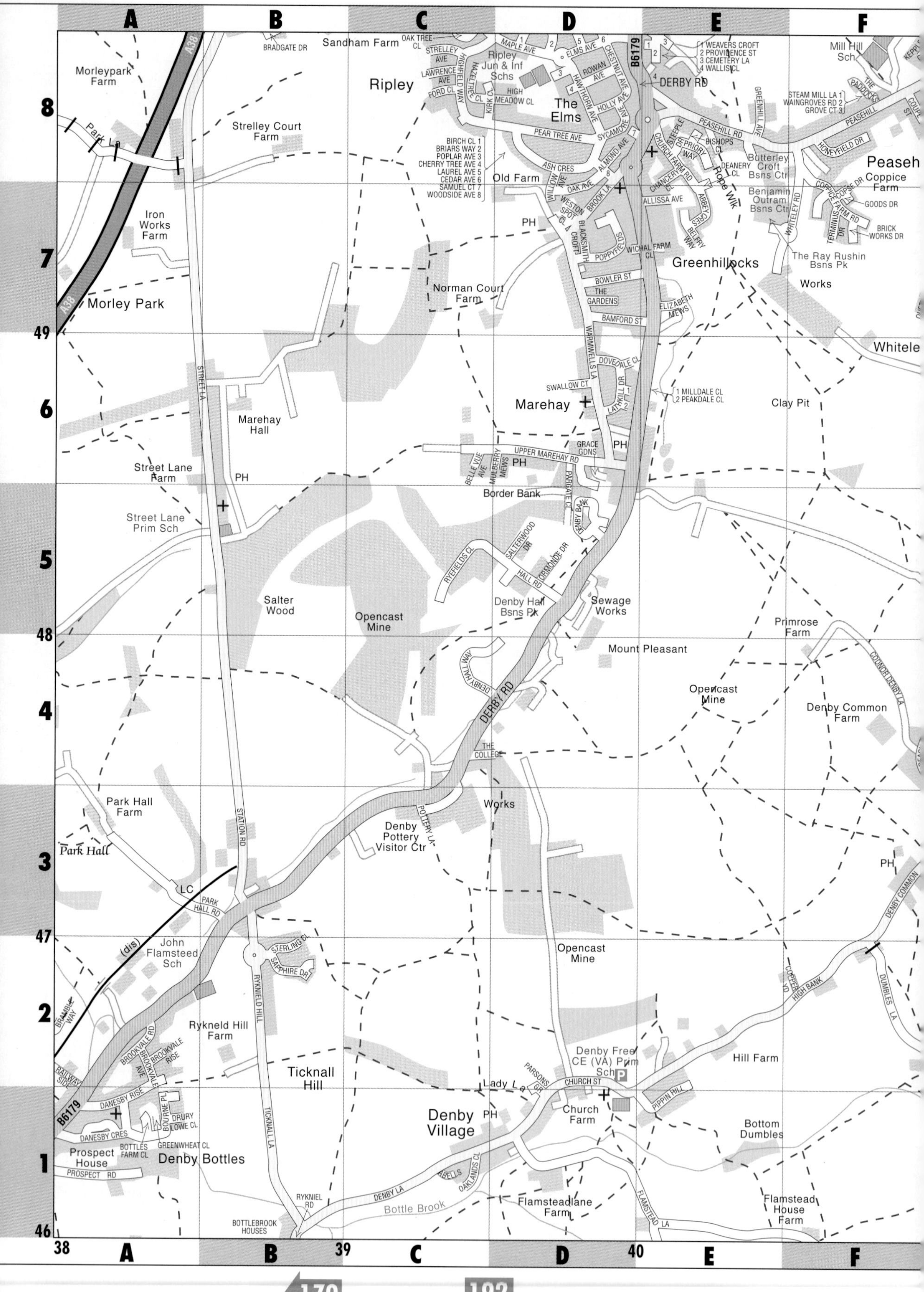
179
169
A
B
C
D
E
F
Morleypark Farm
Sandham Farm
Ripley
Ripley Jun & Inf Schs
The Elms
DERBY RD
Mill Hill Sch
Strelley Court Farm
Old Farm
Butterley Croft Bsns Ctr
Benjamin Outram Bsns Ctr
Peaseh
Coppice Farm
Iron Works Farm
Greenhillocks
The Ray Rushin Bsns Pk
Works
Morley Park
Norman Court Farm
Whitele
Marehay
Clay Pit
Marehay Hall
Street Lane Farm
Border Bank
Street Lane Prim Sch
Salter Wood
Opencast Mine
Denby Hall Bsns Pk
Sewage Works
Primrose Farm
Mount Pleasant
Opencast Mine
Denby Common Farm
DERBY RD
Park Hall Farm
Park Hall
Works
Denby Pottery Visitor Ctr
John Flamsted Sch
Opencast Mine
Rykneld Hill Farm
Ticknall Hill
Denby Free CE (VA) Prim Sch
Hill Farm
Denby Village
Church Farm
Bottom Dumbles
Prospect House
Denby Bottles
Bottle Brook
Flamsteadlane Farm
Flamstead House Farm
STREET LA
STATION RD
RYKNIELD HILL
TICKNALL LA
DENBY LA
FLAMSTEAD LA
HIGH BANK
DENBY COMMON
CODNOR DENBY LA
DUMBLES LA
CHURCH ST
PIPPIN HILL
POTTERY LA
PARK HALL RD
PROSPECT RD
DANESBY CRES
DANESBY RISE
BROOKVALE RD
B6179
A38
8
7
6
5
4
3
2
1
49
48
47
46
38
39
40
192

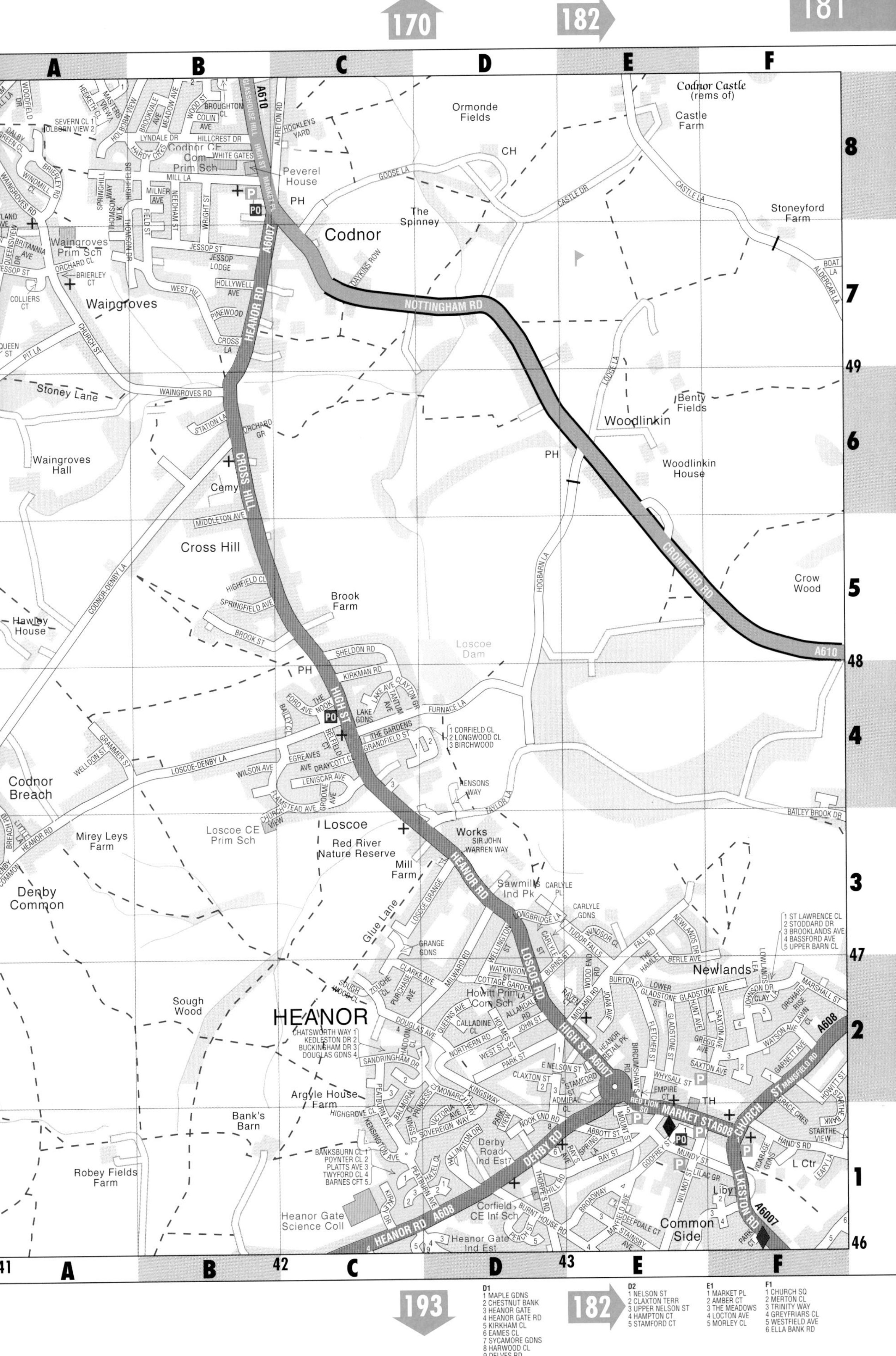
170
182
A
B
C
D
E
F
8
7
49
6
5
48
4
3
47
2
1
46
41
42
43
Codnor Castle
(rems of)
Castle
Farm
Ormonde
Fields
CH
Peverel
House
PH
Codnor
The
Spinney
Stoneyford
Farm
CASTLE LA
CASTLE DR
GOOSE LA
BOAT
LA
ALDERCAR LA
DAYKINS ROW
NOTTINGHAM RD
A610
GLASSHOUSE HILL
ALFRETON RD
HOCKLEYS
YARD
HIGH ST
MARKET PL
A6007
HEANOR RD
BROUGHTON
CL
COLIN
AVE
HILLCREST DR
LYNDALE DR
HARDY CRES
WOOD ST
MEADOW AVE
BROOKVALE
AVE
HOLBORN VIEW
HESKETH CL
MASTERS
VIEW
SEVERN CL 1
HOLBORN VIEW 2
WOODFIELD
DR
DALBY
GREEN CL
WINDMILL
CL
BRIERLEY
RD
WAINGROVES RD
Codnor CE
Com
Prim Sch
WHITE GATES
MILL LA
SPRINGHILL
THOMSON WAY
HIGHFIELDS
THOMSON DR
MILNER
AVE
FIELD ST
NEEDHAM ST
WRIGHT ST
JESSOP ST
JESSOP
LODGE
HOLLYWELL
AVE
WEST HILL
PINEWOOD
CROSS
LA
PO
P
Waingroves
Prim Sch
BRITANNIA
AVE
QUEENSVIEW
DR
JESSOP ST
ORCHARD CL
BRIERLEY
CT
COLLIERS
CT
Waingroves
CHURCH ST
QUEEN
ST
PIT LA
Stoney Lane
WAINGROVES RD
STATION LA
ORCHARD
GR
Waingroves
Hall
Cemy
CROSS HILL
MIDDLETON AVE
Cross Hill
HIGHFIELD CL
SPRINGFIELD AVE
BROOK ST
CODNOR-DENBY LA
Hawley
House
Brook
Farm
Woodlinkin
Benty
Fields
Woodlinkin
House
LODGE LA
PH
CROMFORD RD
HOGBARN LA
Crow
Wood
Loscoe
Dam
A610
SHELDON RD
KIRKMAN RD
PH
HIGH ST
FORD AVE
THE
NOOK
BAILEY CT
LAKE AVE
CLAYTON GR
FANTUM
AVE
LAKE
GDNS
FURNACE LA
THE GARDENS
GRANDFIELD ST
BELFIELD
CT
1 CORFIELD CL
2 LONGWOOD CL
3 BIRCHWOOD
EGREAVES
AVE
DRAYCOTT CL
LENISCAR AVE
GROOME
AVE
WILSON AVE
FLAMSTEAD AVE
CHURCH VIEW
LOSCOE-DENBY LA
GRAMMER ST
WELLDON ST
Codnor
Breach
RENSONS
WAY
TAYLOR LA
BAILEY BROOK DR
Loscoe
Loscoe CE
Prim Sch
Mirey Leys
Farm
Red River
Nature Reserve
Works
SIR JOHN
WARREN WAY
Mill
Farm
HEANOR RD
Denby
Common
Sawmills
Ind Pk
CARLYLE
PL
CARLYLE
GDNS
1 ST LAWRENCE CL
2 STODDARD DR
3 BROOKLANDS AVE
4 BASSFORD AVE
5 UPPER BARN CL
Glue Lane
LOSCOE GRANGE
GRANGE
GDNS
LONGBRIDGE LA
LOSCOE RD
CARLYLE
ST
BURNS ST
TUDOR FALLS
WINDSOR CL
FALL RD
NEWLANDS DR
THE
HAMLET
BERLE AVE
Newlands
LOWLANDS
LEA
MARSHALL ST
WELLINGTON
ST
WATKINSON
ST
COTTAGE GARDEN
MILWARD RD
CLARKE AVE
ZOUCHE
CL
PURCHASE
AVE
SOUGH
WOOD CL
Sough
Wood
Howitt Prim
Com Sch
QUEENS AVE
CALLADINE
CL
HOLMES ST
ALLANDALE
RD
JOHN ST
RAVEN
CT
MIDLAND RD
WOOD END
RD
JOAN AVE
BURTON ST
LOWER
GLADSTONE ST
GLADSTONE AVE
HUNT AVE
SAXTON AVE
JOHNSON DR
CLAY LA
ORCHARD
RISE
LAWN
CL
WATSON AVE
A608
HEANOR
DOUGLAS AVE
CHATSWORTH WAY 1
KEDLESTON DR 2
BUCKINGHAM DR 3
DOUGLAS GDNS 4
HADDON CL
SANDRINGHAM DR
NORTHERN RD
WEST ST
PARK ST
HIGH ST. A6007
HEANOR
RETAIL PK
BIRCUMSHAW'S
RD
FLETCHER ST
GLADSTONE ST
GREGG
AVE
SAXTON AVE
GARNETT AVE
MANSFIELD RD
HOWITT ST
STARTHE
BANK
GRACE CRES
E NELSON ST
CLAXTON ST
STAMFORD
ST
ADMIRAL
CL
WHYSALL ST
EMPIRE
CT
TH
Argyle House
Farm
PEATBURN AVE
BALMORAL
PRINCESS CL
MONARCH WAY
KINGSWAY
HIGHGROVE CL
KENSINGTON
KINGS CT
VICTORIA
AVE
SOVEREIGN WAY
PARK
VIEW
NOOK END RD
RED LION
SQ
MARKET ST
A608
CHURCH ST
STARTHE
VIEW
HAND'S RD
VICARAGE
GDNS
L Ctr
LEAFY LA
Bank's
Barn
BANKSBURN CL 1
POYNTER CL 2
PLATTS AVE 3
TWYFORD CL 4
BARNES CFT 5
HALLINGTON DR
HAZEL CL
Derby
Road
Ind Est
DERBY RD
RAYS
AVE
SPRING
LA
ABBOTT ST
RAY ST
MOUNT ST
GODFREY ST
MUNDY ST
LILAC GR
WILMOT ST
Liby
ILKESTON RD
A6007
Robey Fields
Farm
Heanor Gate
Science Coll
KIRKE DR
HEANOR RD
A608
Corfield
CE Inf Sch
BURNT HOUSE RD
THORPE'S RD
BROADWAY
MAYFIELD AVE
DEEPDALE CT
STAINSBY
AVE
Common
Side
PARK
CT
Heanor Gate
Ind Est
PEACH ST
193
182
D1
1 MAPLE GDNS
2 CHESTNUT BANK
3 HEANOR GATE
4 HEANOR GATE RD
5 KIRKHAM CL
6 EAMES CL
7 SYCAMORE GDNS
8 HARWOOD CL
9 DELVES RD
D2
1 NELSON ST
2 CLAXTON TERR
3 UPPER NELSON ST
4 HAMPTON CT
5 STAMFORD CT
E1
1 MARKET PL
2 AMBER CT
3 THE MEADOWS
4 LOCTON AVE
5 MORLEY CL
F1
1 CHURCH SQ
2 MERTON CL
3 TRINITY WAY
4 GREYFRIARS CL
5 WESTFIELD AVE
6 ELLA BANK RD

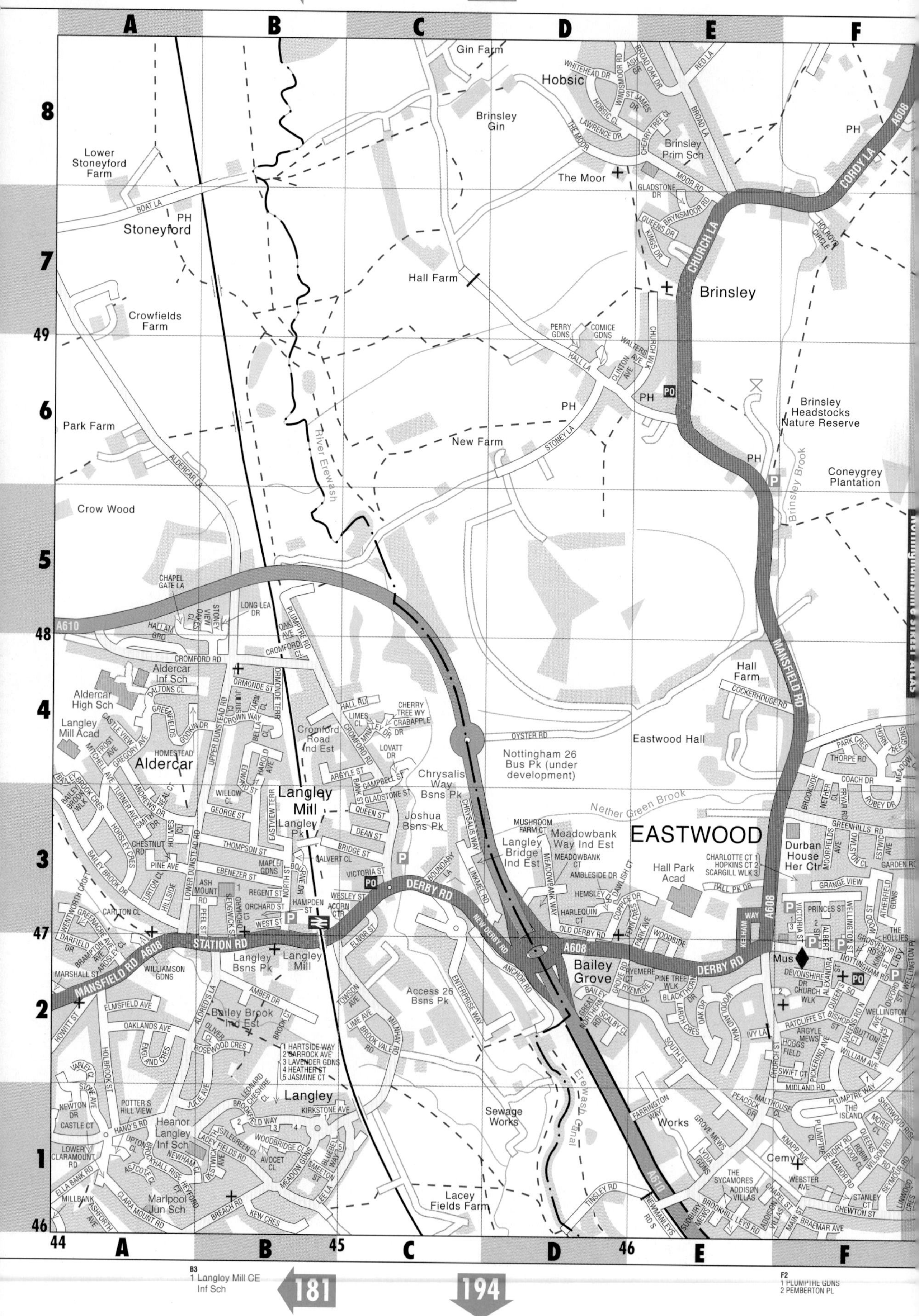

B3
1 Langloy Mill CE
Inf Sch

F2
1 PLUMPTRE GDNS
2 PEMBERTON PL

184

A B C D E F

Staffordshire STREET ATLAS

Stanton
Tinsell Wood
TINSELL LA
MARSH LA
WELLCROFT GRANGE
SALLYFIELD LA
ORDLEY LA
HONEYWALL LA
Boldershaw
Eldergreave Cottage
FIELD LA
Marsh Brook
Smithy Moor Farm
BANKERWALL LA
Wildhay
Wildhay Brook
WILDHAY LA
WILLRIDDING LA
Griff Wood
Ray Wood
Rangemoor Wood
Motcarn Sprink
Stanton Wood
WILDHAY LA
HALL LA
Rangemoor Brook
Gold's Wood
Dydon
The Home Farm
Michael's Lane
RANGEMOOR LA
Far Wood
Ousley Wood
Wooton Hall Farm
Lee Wood
Ashfield Farm
OUSLEY LA
The Hutts Farm
Limestone Way
MICHAEL'S LA
NORTHWOOD LA
Calwichbank Farm
Cliff Bridge
B5032
WOOTTON RD
Northwood Farm
CALWICH BANK
Cockley
The Boxes
STANTON LA
Upper Ellastone
CHURCH LA
Colwich Home Farm
The Grove
WATERY LA
BACK LA
Sandford Brook
PO
PORTAWAY LA
Calwich Park
Calwich Abbey
PH
Tit Brook
Portobello Bridge
Ellastone
MARLPIT LA
Hare Park
SIDES LA
River Dove
Knaveholm
B5033
MILL LA
LITTLEFIELD LA
Lower Ellastone
DOVE ST
MAIN RD
NORBURY HOLLOW
LLL Plantation
Norbury
ROUGHLOW LA
Norbury Hall
Mill House
MILL LA
Hope Wood
LID LA
GREEN LA
B5033
B5032

8
7
45
6
5
44
4
3
43
2
1
42

11 A B 12 C D 13 E F

197
184

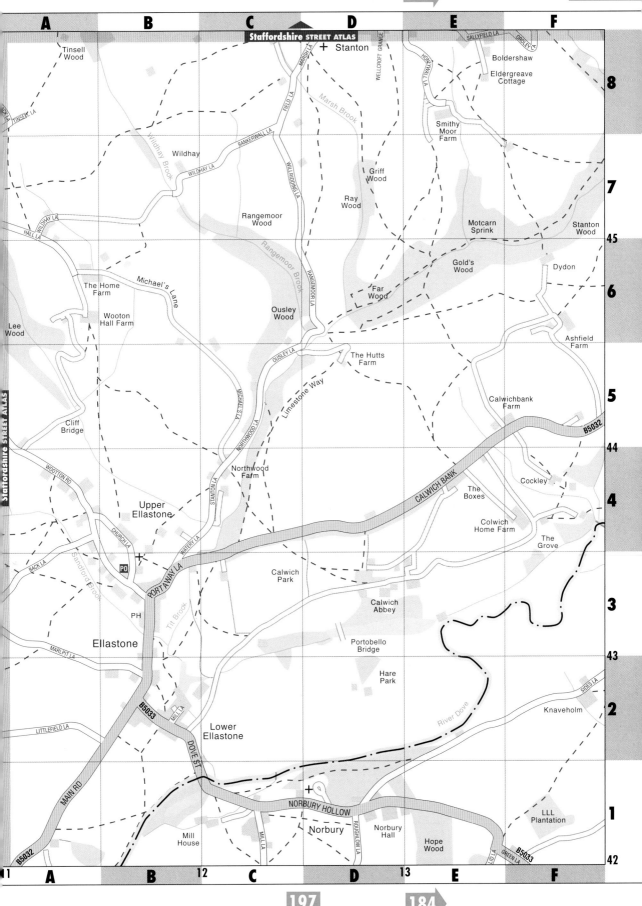

183
172

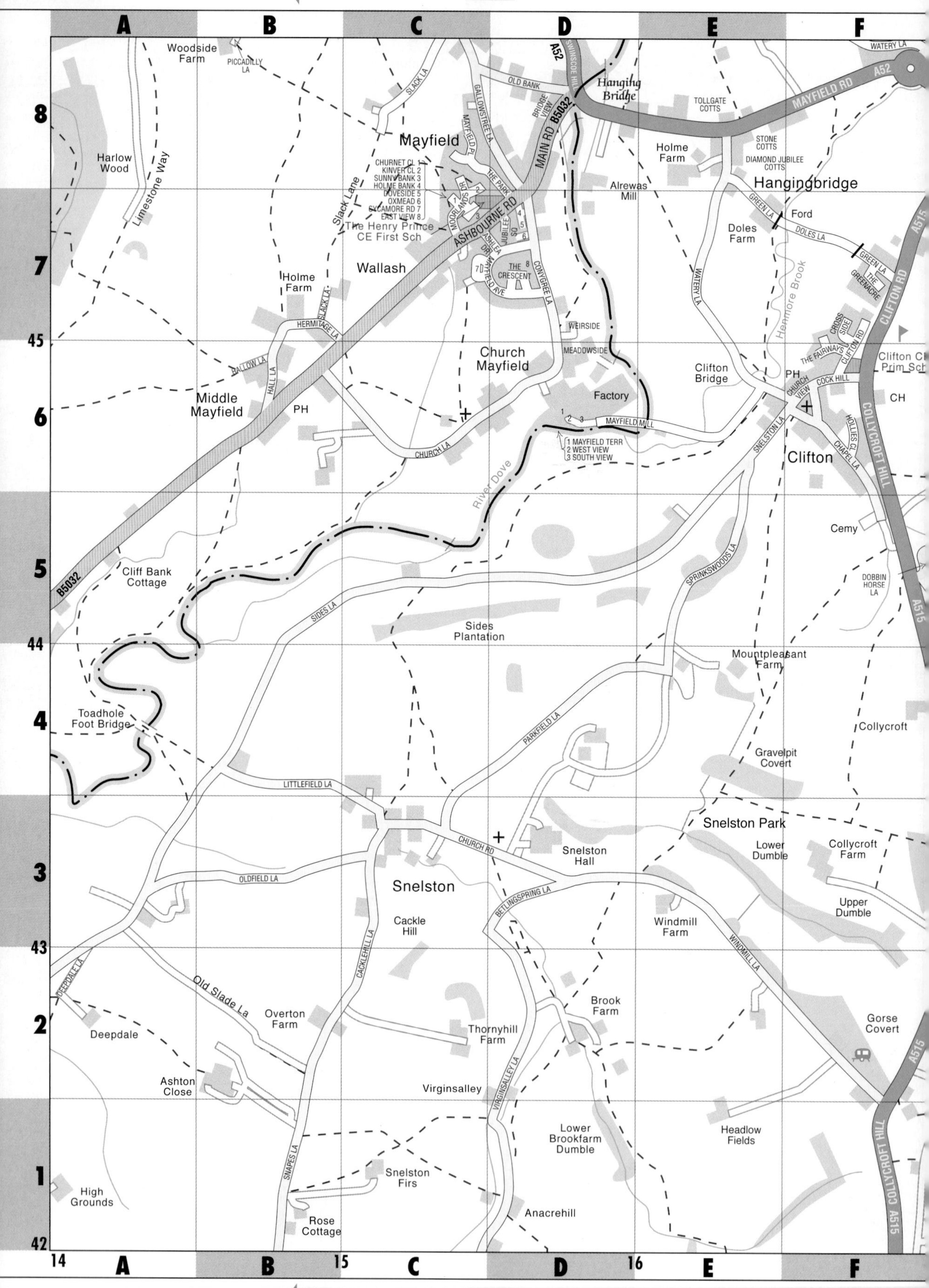
Woodside Farm
Mayfield
Hanging Bridge
Hangingbridge
Holme Farm
Alrewas Mill
Doles Farm
Harlow Wood
Limestone Way
Slack Lane
The Henry Prince CE First Sch
Wallash
Church Mayfield
Middle Mayfield
Factory
Clifton Bridge
Clifton
Clifton CE Prim Sch
Cemy
Cliff Bank Cottage
Sides Plantation
Mountpleasant Farm
Toadhole Foot Bridge
Collycroft
Gravelpit Covert
Snelston Park
Snelston Hall
Lower Dumble
Collycroft Farm
Upper Dumble
Snelston
Cackle Hill
Windmill Farm
Overton Farm
Brook Farm
Thornyhill Farm
Deepdale
Gorse Covert
Ashton Close
Virginsalley
Lower Brookfarm Dumble
Headlow Fields
Snelston Firs
High Grounds
Rose Cottage
Anacrehill
River Dove
Henmore Brook
ASHBOURNE RD
MAIN RD
MAYFIELD RD
CLIFTON RD
COLLYCROFT HILL
SIDES LA
SPRINKSWOODS LA
PARKFIELD LA
LITTLEFIELD LA
CHURCH RD
OLDFIELD LA
BETLINGSPRING LA
WINDMILL LA
CACKLEHILL LA
Old Slade La
SNAPES LA
VIRGINSALLEY LA
DEEPDALE LA
WATERY LA
DOLES LA
GREEN LA
CHURCH LA
HALL LA
HALLOW LA
HERMITAGE LA
SLACK LA
1 MAYFIELD TERR
2 WEST VIEW
3 SOUTH VIEW
CHURNET CL 1
KINVER CL 2
SUNNY BANK 3
HOLME BANK 4
DOVESIDE 5
OXMEAD 6
SYCAMORE RD 7
EAST VIEW 8
TOLLGATE COTTS
STONE COTTS
DIAMOND JUBILEE COTTS
DOBBIN HORSE LA
A52
A515
B5032

183
198

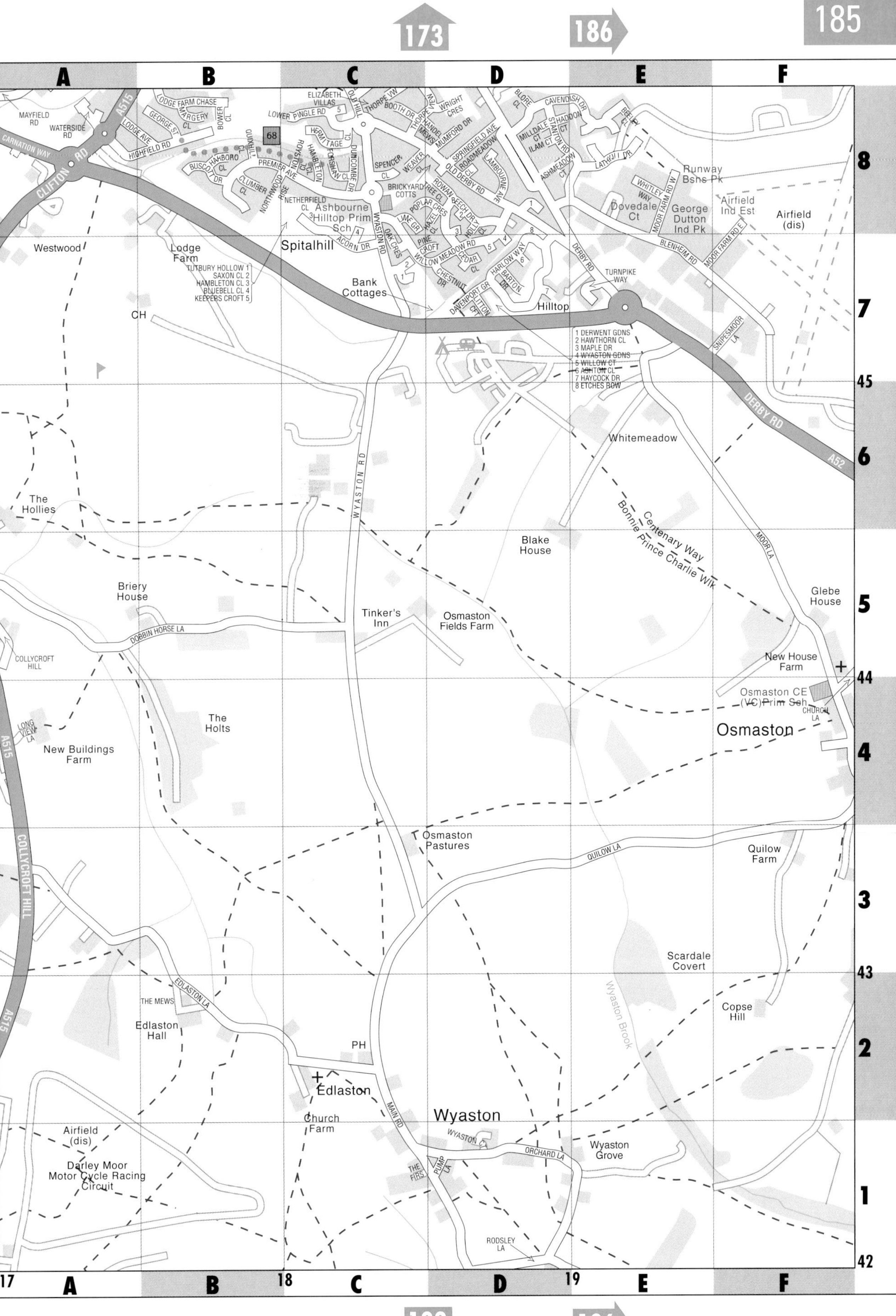

A B C D E F

8

7

45

6

5

44

4

43

3

2

1

42

MAYFIELD RD
WATERSIDE RD
CARNATION WAY
CLIFTON RD
A515
Westwood
LODGE FARM CHASE
GEORGE ST
MARGERY CL
GEORGE AVE
HIGHFIELD RD
BOWER CL
LOWER PINGLE RD
ELIZABETH VILLAS
THORPE VW
BOOTH DR
OLD HILL
HERMITAGE
HENMORE CL
DUNCOMBE DR
WRIGHT CRES
BRIDGE CT
CAVENDISH DR
SHADDON CT
MILLDALE CT
STANTON CT
ILAM CT
Runway Bshs Pk
WHITLEY WAY
Dovedale Ct
George Dutton Ind Pk
Airfield Ind Est
Airfield (dis)

Lodge Farm
TUTBURY HOLLOW 1
SAXON CL 2
HAMBLETON CL 3
BLUEBELL CL 4
KEEPERS CROFT 5
Spitalhill
Ashbourne
Hilltop Prim Sch
ACORN DR
OAK CRES
PINE CROFT
POPLAR CRES
WYASTON RD
WILLOW MEADOW RD
Bank Cottages
CHESTNUT DR
HARLOW DR
BARTON DR
DAVENPORT GR
GRATTON CT
Hilltop
TURNPIKE WAY
DERBY RD
BLENHEIM RD
MOOR FARM RD W
MOOR FARM RD E
SNIPESMOOR LA
CH

1 DERWENT GDNS
2 HAWTHORN CL
3 MAPLE DR
4 WYASTON GDNS
5 WILLOW CT
6 ASHTON CL
7 HAYCOCK DR
8 ETCHES BOW

Whitemeadow
DERBY RD
A52
MOOR LA

The Hollies
Briery House
DOBBIN HORSE LA
Tinker's Inn
Osmaston Fields Farm
Blake House
Centenary Way
Bonnie Prince Charlie Wlk
Glebe House

COLLYCROFT HILL
LONG VIEW LA
New Buildings Farm
The Holts
New House Farm
Osmaston CE (VC) Prim Sch
CHURCH LA
Osmaston

A515
COLLYCROFT HILL
Osmaston Pastures
QUILOW LA
Quilow Farm

THE MEWS
EDLASTON LA
Edlaston Hall
PH
Scardale Covert
Copse Hill
WYASTON BROOK

Edlaston
Church Farm
MAIN RD
Wyaston
WYASTON
ORCHARD LA
Wyaston Grove
THE FIRS
PUMP LA
Airfield (dis)
Darley Moor Motor Cycle Racing Circuit
RODSLEY LA

185
174

A B C D E F
8 7 45 6 5 44 4 3 43 2 1 42
20 21 22
Bradley Moor
Park Farm
Hole in the Wall
Lady's Pond
Bradley
Moorend
Bradley CE Prim Sch
Brook Farm
HADLEY LA
PINFOLD LA
YEW TREE LA
Lady Hole House
Ladyhole Farm
MILLDAM LA
LADY HOLE LA
Firs Farm
Knoll Lodge
Old Hall Farm
DOGKENNEL LA
Airfield (disused)
YELDERSLEY LA
A52
War Farm
Bradley Brook
Home Stead Farm
DERBY DR
Yeldersley Home Farm
CHURCH LA
Yeldersley Hall
Boat House
ROUGH LA
Yeldersley Hollies
Hazelwell Farm
PH
PO
Osmaston
Ian's Oak
The Hollies Farm
MOOR LA
QUILOW LA
The Mount
Madge La
Shirley Bridge
The Rookery
Home Farm
SHIRLEY COMMON
Oak Covert
Bonnie Prince Charlie Wlk
East Deer Park
Shirleycommon Farm
Corner Farm
Osmaston Park
Centenary Way
Shirley Common
PAINTER'S LA
BRICK KILN LA
Ednaston Home Farm
Shirleypark Farm
Shirley Park
The Vicarage
PARK LA
Wyaston Brook
HALL LA
Shirley House

185
200

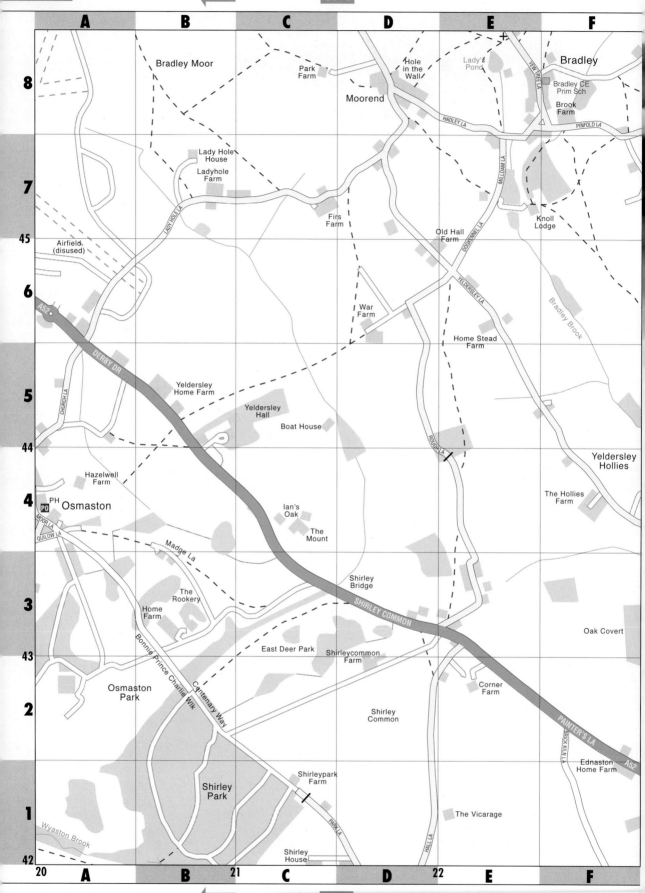

175
188

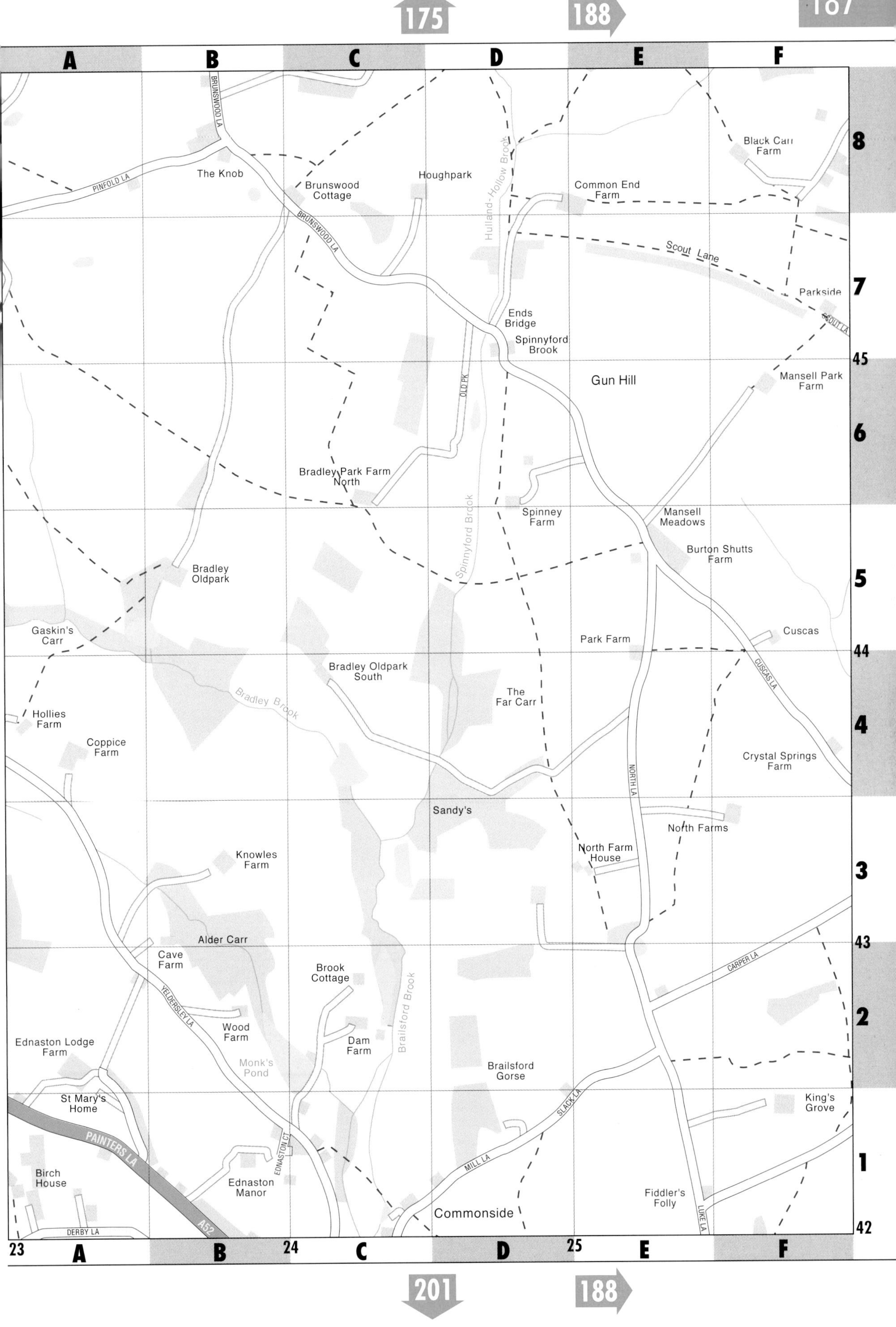
A
B
C
D
E
F
8
7
6
5
4
3
2
1
45
44
43
42
23
24
25
BRUNSWOOD LA
PINFOLD LA
The Knob
Brunswood Cottage
Houghpark
Hulland-Hollow Brook
Common End Farm
Black Carr Farm
Scout Lane
Parkside
SCOUT LA
Ends Bridge
Spinnyford Brook
OLD PK
Gun Hill
Mansell Park Farm
Bradley Park Farm North
Spinney Farm
Spinnyford Brook
Mansell Meadows
Burton Shutts Farm
Bradley Oldpark
Gaskin's Carr
Park Farm
Cuscas
CUSCAS LA
Bradley Oldpark South
Bradley Brook
The Far Carr
Hollies Farm
Coppice Farm
Crystal Springs Farm
NORTH LA
Sandy's
North Farms
Knowles Farm
North Farm House
Alder Carr
CARPER LA
Cave Farm
Brook Cottage
YELDERSLEY LA
Wood Farm
Dam Farm
Brailsford Brook
Ednaston Lodge Farm
Monk's Pond
Brailsford Gorse
St Mary's Home
SLACK LA
King's Grove
PAINTERS LA
EDNASTON CT
MILL LA
Birch House
Ednaston Manor
Fiddler's Folly
Commonside
A52
DERBY LA
LUKE LA

201
188

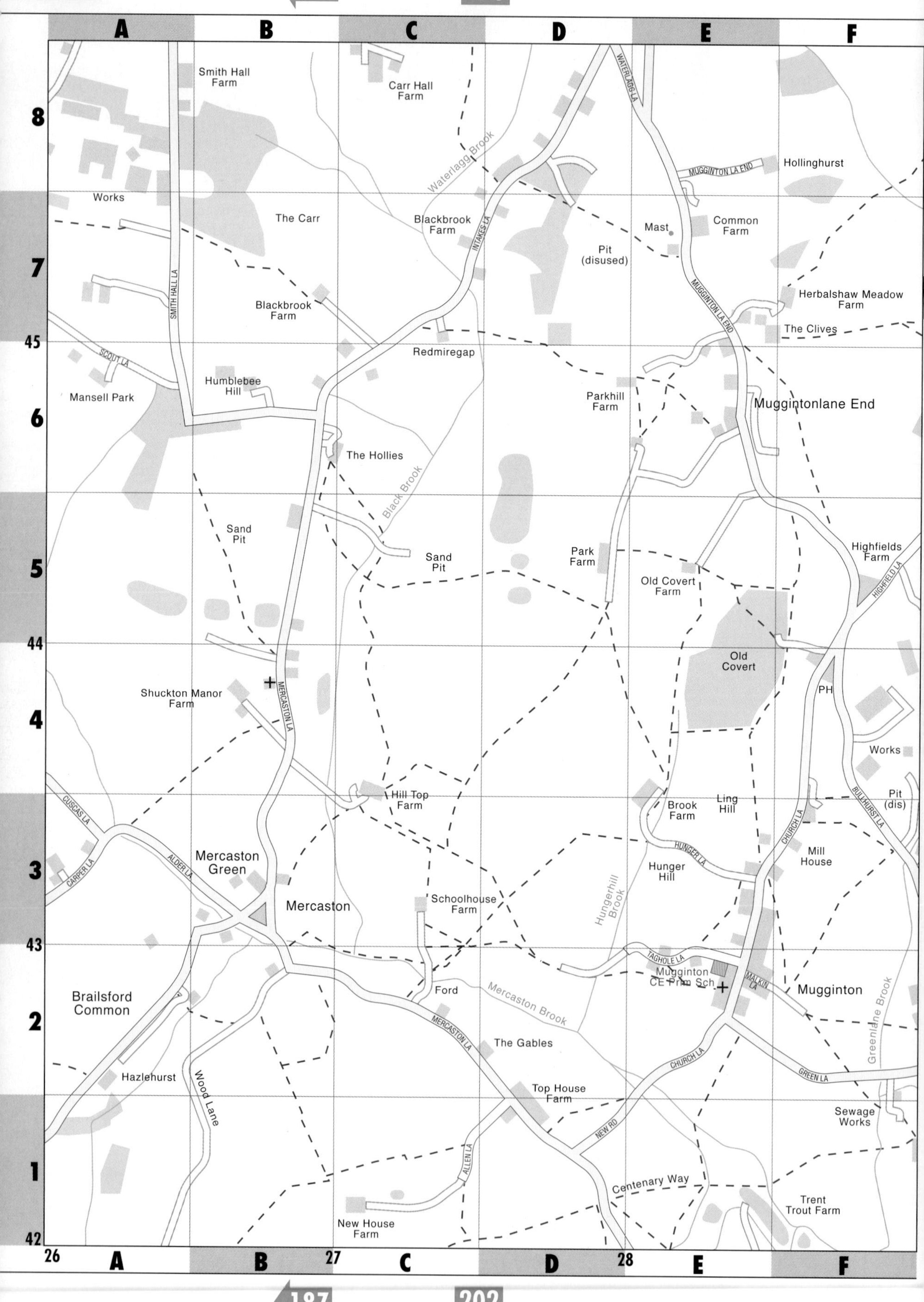

A B C D E F

8

7

45

6

5

44

4

3

43

2

1

42

26 27 28

A B C D E F

Smith Hall Farm

Carr Hall Farm

Works

The Carr

Blackbrook Farm

Waterlagg Brook

INTAKES LA

Pit (disused)

Mast

MUGGINTON LA END

Hollinghurst

Common Farm

Herbalshaw Meadow Farm

The Clives

Blackbrook Farm

Redmiregap

SMITH HALL LA

SCOUT LA

Mansell Park

Humblebee Hill

The Hollies

Black Brook

Parkhill Farm

MUGGINTON LA END

Mugginton lane End

Sand Pit

Sand Pit

Park Farm

Old Covert Farm

Highfields Farm

HIGHFIELD LA

Shuckton Manor Farm

MERCASTON LA

Old Covert

PH

Works

Pit (dis)

BILLHURST LA

Hill Top Farm

Brook Farm

Ling Hill

HUNGER LA

CHURCH LA

Mill House

CUSCAS LA

CARPER LA

ALDER LA

Mercaston Green

Mercaston

Schoolhouse Farm

Hungerhill Brook

Hunger Hill

Brailsford Common

Wood Lane

Ford

MERCASTON LA

Mercaston Brook

The Gables

TAGHOLE LA

Mugginton CE Prim Sch

MALKIN LA

Mugginton

Greenlane Brook

Hazlehurst

Top House Farm

ALLEN LA

NEW RD

CHURCH LA

GREEN LA

Sewage Works

Centenary Way

Trent Trout Farm

New House Farm

177
190

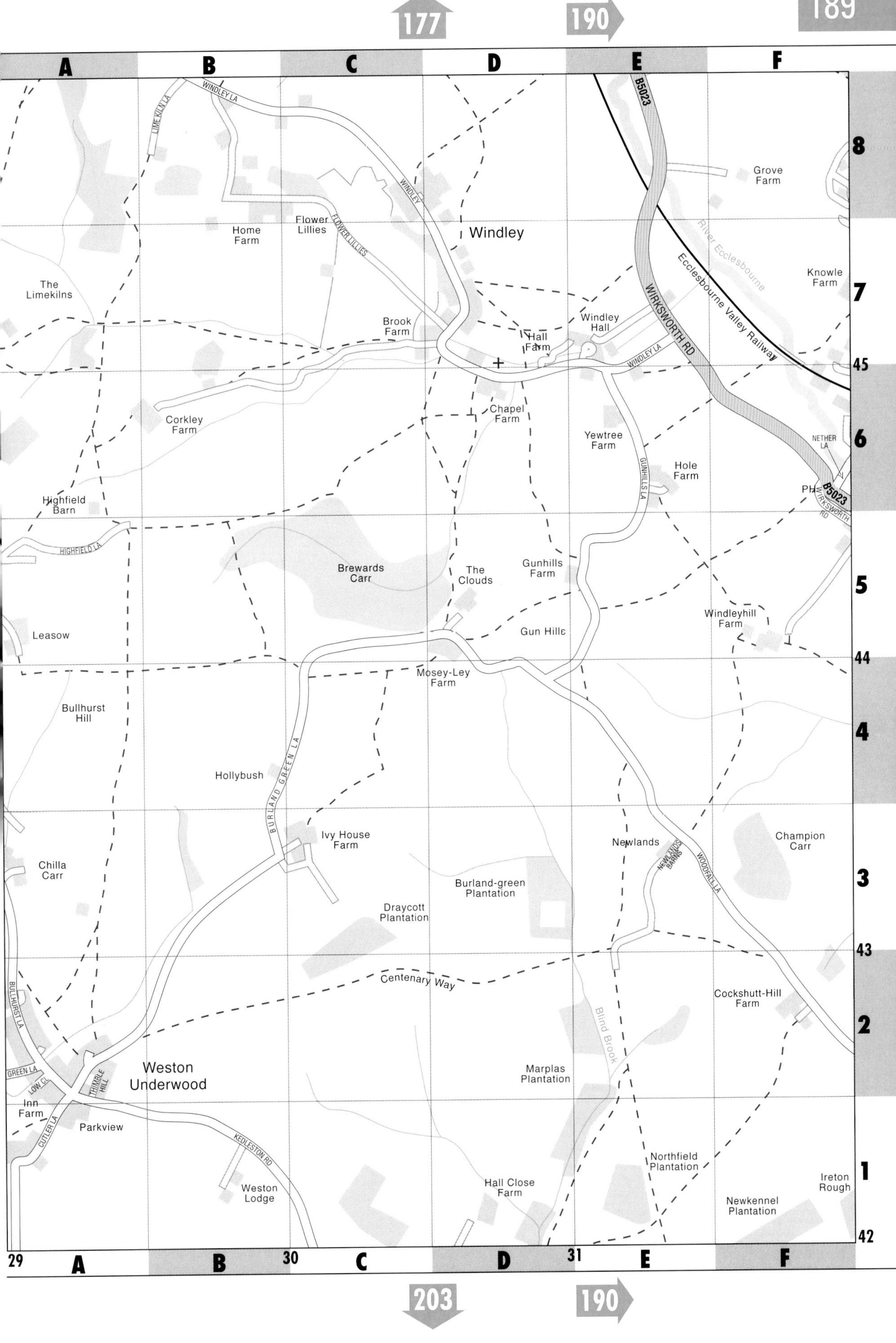
A
B
C
D
E
F
WINDLEY LA
LIME KILN LA
B5023
Grove Farm
Home Farm
Flower Lillies
FLOWER LILLIES
WINDLEY
Windley
River Ecclesbourne
Ecclesbourne Valley Railway
Knowle Farm
The Limekilns
Brook Farm
Windley Hall
Hall Farm
WIRKSWORTH RD
WINDLEY LA
Chapel Farm
Corkley Farm
Yewtree Farm
NETHER LA
Hole Farm
GUNHILLS LA
PH
B5023
WIRKSWORTH RD
Highfield Barn
HIGHFIELD LA
Brewards Carr
The Clouds
Gunhills Farm
Windleyhill Farm
Leasow
Gun Hill
Mosey-Ley Farm
Bullhurst Hill
Hollybush
BURLAND GREEN LA
Ivy House Farm
Newlands
NEWLANDS BARNS
WOODFALL LA
Champion Carr
Chilla Carr
Burland-green Plantation
Draycott Plantation
Centenary Way
Cockshutt-Hill Farm
BULLHURST LA
Blind Brook
Weston Underwood
GREEN LA
LOW CL
THIMBLE HILL
Marplas Plantation
Inn Farm
CUTLER LA
Parkview
KEDLESTON RD
Northfield Plantation
Ireton Rough
Hall Close Farm
Weston Lodge
Newkennel Plantation
8
7
45
6
5
44
4
3
43
2
1
42
29
30
31

203
190

189 178

A B C D E F

8

Hillside Farm
The Knowle
Hazelwood
The Firs Farm
HOB HILL
HAZELWOOD HILL
Mount Farm
SPRING HOLLOW
FIRESTONE
Quarry (dis)
Wallstones Farm House
NORTH LANE
Swainsley Farm
Chevinend
FULLERS CL 1
MILLERS WAY 2
River Derwent
DERBY RD
SHAW LA
HOPPING HILL
FOUNDRY
LITTLE FALLOWS

7

NETHER LA
PRIMROSE COTTS
Hazelwood Hall Farm
Bradshaw House
Courthouse Farm
NORTH LA
JACKSONS LA
BANK BLDGS
MORRELLS LA
SUNNY HILL GDNS 1
DERBY RD 2
Milford Prim Sch
CHEVIN ALLEY
WOOD LA
SUNNY HILL
RIVER VIEW
A6

45

Midshires Way
Milford Tunnel
Milford House
WOODRIDGE

6

B5023
Lapwing Farm
Spring Hill
HAZELWOOD RD
RICHMOND LA
The Oaks
WHARF BK
ASH TREE CL
CHEVIN VALE
CH
MOSCOW FARM CT
Moscow Farm
DERBY RD

5

Windley Meadows
Brook House
River Ecclesbourne
Centenary Way
NETHER CL
HAZELMEAD
CHEVIN RD
CHADFIELD RD
GOLF LA
Cemy
FIR BANK
AVENUE RD
LIME AVE
MAGDALA COTTS
River Derwent
CASTLE ORCH
CASTLE ORCH
MILFORD RD

44

WIRKSWORTH RD
Meadow Farm
SEFTON WAY
CEDAR CL
NB MILL BOURN
WILLIAM CL
CORNHILL
ECCLESBOURNE MDWS
PHILIPS CT
THE PASTURES
CASTLE HILL
CASTLE VIEW
1 ST ALKMUNDS WAY
2 MAYFAIR CT
3 ORCHARD COTTS
4 TAMWORTH CT
5 DE FERRERS CT
6 THE PARK
7 CURZON CT
8 EYES CT
9 William Gilbert CE Endowed Prim Sch

4

Duffield Meadows
THE CROFT
HOLLOWAY RD
CHAMPION
KING ST
VICARAGE LA
ST ALKMUND'S
9
TAMWORTH TERR
STATION APPR
SHOTTLE RD
Duffield
DUFFIELD CT
Duffield

3

Spring Carr
FERRERS CRS
FAIRLAWNS
TAIRLAWNS
Farnah House Farm
MEADOW VALE
Broom Park
MEADOWS CROFT 1
BROOM CL 2
SPRINGFIELD DR 3
HAZEL GR 4
OLD MILL CL 5
Duffield Mdws Prim Sch
Park Rd
HILL VIEW
OLD HALL AVE
The Ecclesbourne Sch
CROWN ST
SNAKE LA
DUCK ISLAND
ECCLESBOURNE CT
MOYLAND ST
PO
DUFFIELD
VILLAGE CT
ECCLESBOURNE AVE
WILTRA GR
Duffield
Liby
DUFFIELD
TOWN ST
LODGE CL
OAK CL
Duffield Millennium Meadow Nature Reserve
Centenary Way
DONALD HAWLEY WAY
CHURCH DR
CHURCH HILL

43

CUMBERHILLS RD
THE LIMES
CUMBERHILLS RD
CANTERBURY CL
CURZON LA
CAVENDISH CL
DEVONSHIRE DR
NEW ZEALAND LA
ROCKLAND PL
GILBERT CRES
MARSDEN CL 1
SCARSDALE RD 2
MELBOURY CT
ST RONAN'S AVE
CHESTNUT CL
MAKENEY RD
CHURCH WLK
CHURCH

2

Champion Farm
CUMBERHILLS GRANGE
Cumberhills Farm
BROADWAY
HALL FARM RD
BROADWAY
EATON CT
CHURCH VIEW
B5023

Centenary Way
Park Leys
WOODALL LA
CUMBERHILLS RD
Celadon
DERBY RD

1

Cumberhill Farm
SUNLIGHT
HAZLEY CROFT

42

BEECH AVE
Flaxholme
FLAXHOLME AVE
A6

32 A B 33 C D 34 E F

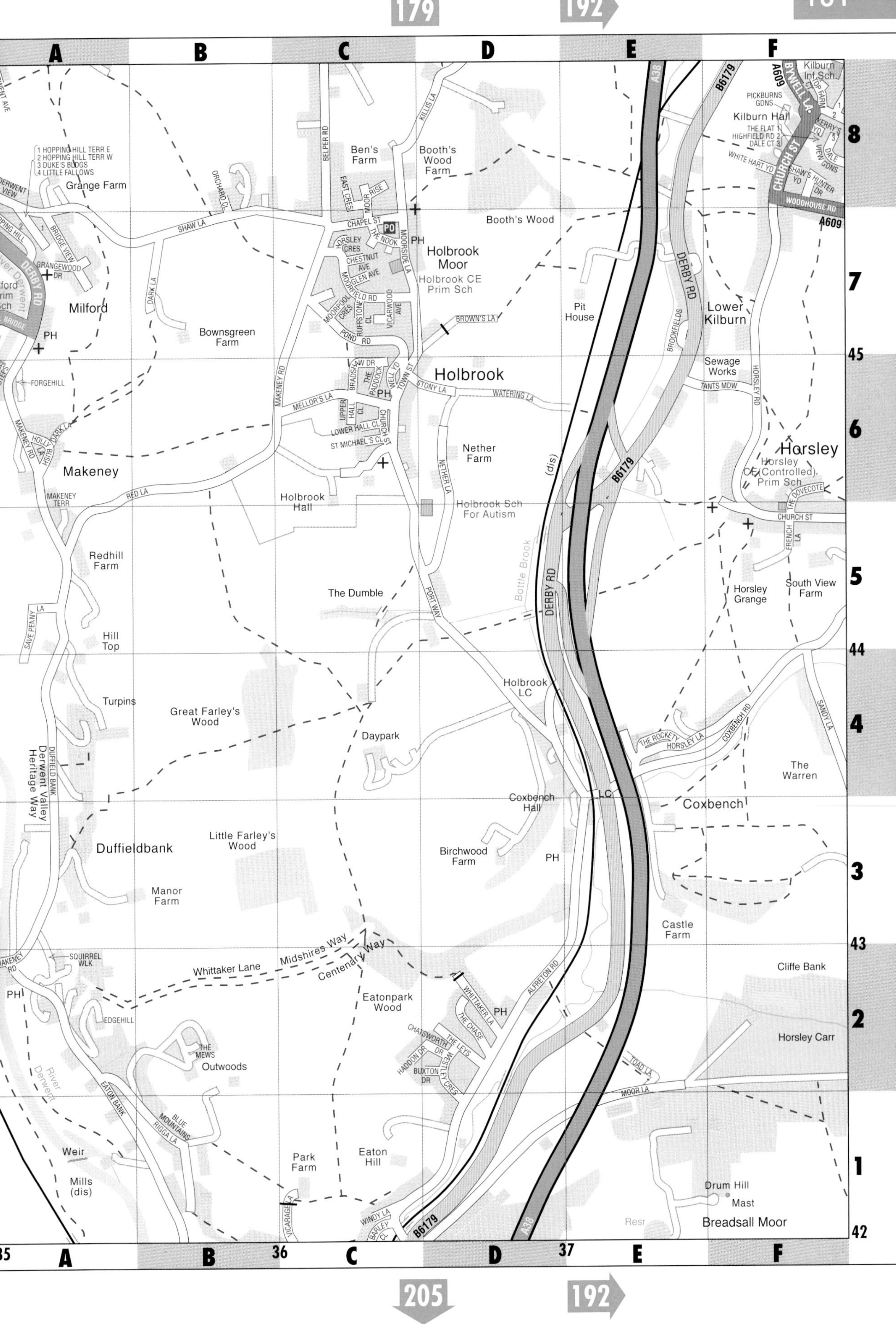
179
192
A
B
C
D
E
F
Kilburn Inf Sch
Kilburn Hall
Ben's Farm
Booth's Wood Farm
Grange Farm
Booth's Wood
Holbrook Moor
Holbrook CE Prim Sch
Milford
Bownsgreen Farm
Pit House
Lower Kilburn
Sewage Works
Holbrook
Horsley
Horsley CE (Controlled) Prim Sch
Makeney
Nether Farm
Holbrook Hall
Holbrook Sch For Autism
Redhill Farm
The Dumble
Horsley Grange
South View Farm
Hill Top
Holbrook LC
Turpins
Great Farley's Wood
Daypark
The Warren
Derwent Valley Heritage Way
Coxbench Hall
Coxbench
Duffieldbank
Little Farley's Wood
Birchwood Farm
Manor Farm
Castle Farm
Cliffe Bank
Midshires Way
Whittaker Lane
Centenary Way
Eatonpark Wood
Horsley Carr
Outwoods
Weir
Mills (dis)
Park Farm
Eaton Hill
Drum Hill
Mast
Resr
Breadsall Moor
A38
B6179
A609
DERBY RD
SHAW LA
RED LA
MAKENEY RD
DUFFIELD BANK
ALFRETON RD
MOOR LA
TOAD LA
PORT WAY
NETHER LA
WATERING LA
STONY LA
HORSLEY RD
CHURCH ST
WOODHOUSE RD
COXBENCH RD
HORSLEY LA
SANDY LA
1 HOPPING HILL TERR E
2 HOPPING HILL TERR W
3 DUKE'S BLDGS
4 LITTLE FALLOWS
8
7
45
6
5
44
4
3
43
2
1
42
35
36
37
205
192

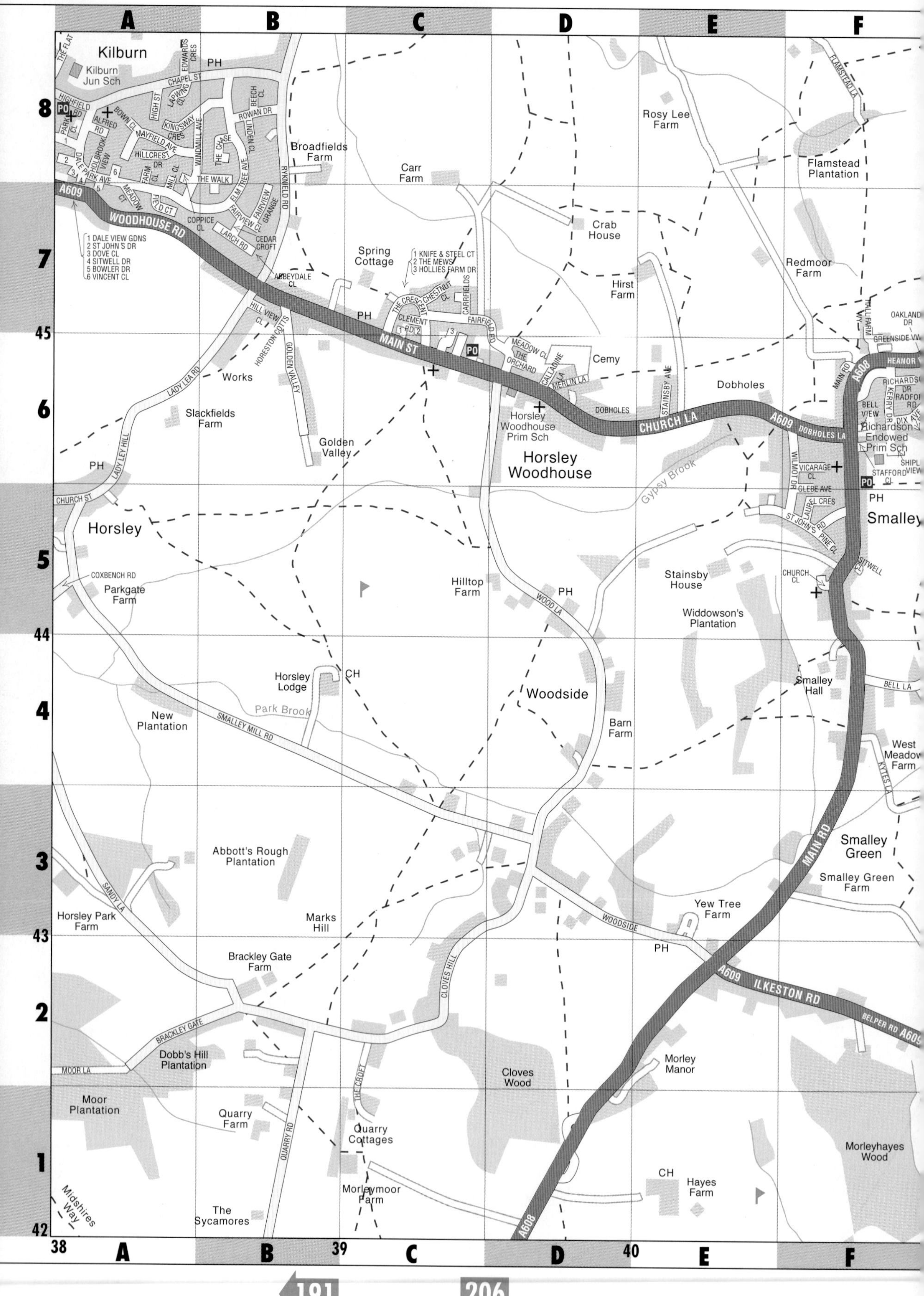

A B C D E F

8

Kilburn

Kilburn Jun Sch

The Flat
Highfield
PO
Alfred Rd
Park Cl
Bown Cl
Mayfield Ave
Hillcrest Dr
Brook View
Dale Park Ave
Chapel St
Lapwing Cl
High St
Kings-way Cres
Meadow Ct
Fld Ct
Mill Cl
Farm
The Chase
Windmill Ave
Lincoln Ct
The Walk
Elm Tree Ave
Rowan Dr
Beech Cl
Rykneld Rd

PH

Broadfields Farm

Carr Farm

Rosy Lee Farm

Flamstead La

Flamstead Plantation

7

A609
Woodhouse Rd
Coppice Cl
Cedar Croft
Larch Rd
Abbeydale Cl

1 Dale View Gdns
2 St John S Dr
3 Dove Cl
4 Sitwell Dr
5 Bowler Dr
6 Vincent Cl

Spring Cottage

1 Knife & Steel Ct
2 The Mews
3 Hollies Farm Dr

Crab House

Redmoor Farm

Oakland Dr
Greenside Vw
Hall Farm Wy
A608

45

Hill View Cl
Horeston Cotts
Golden Valley
Works

Main St
The Cres
Clement Rd
Chestnut Cl
Carrfields
Fairfield Rd
PH
PO
3

Meadow Cl
The Orchard
Merlin La
Callarine

Cemy

Hirst Farm

Stainsby Ave
Dobholes

A609
Dobholes La

Heanor
Richards Dr
Bell View
Dix Av
Richardson
Kerry Dr
Radford Rd
Endowed Prim Sch
Shipl
Stafford Cl
Shipl View

6

Lady Lea Rd
Slackfields Farm

Golden Valley

Horsley Woodhouse Prim Sch

Horsley Woodhouse

Church La

Dobholes

Wilmot Dr
Vicarage Cl
Glebe Ave
Laurel Cres
Pine Cl
St John's Rd

PO
PH
Sitwell

Smalley

PH
Lady Ley Hill
Church St
Horsley
Coxbench Rd
Parkgate Farm

Gypsy Brook

Stainsby House

Church Cl

5

Hilltop Farm

Wood La
PH

Widdowson's Plantation

44

Horsley Lodge
CH

Woodside

Smalley Hall

Bell La

4

New Plantation
Smalley Mill Rd
Park Brook

Barn Farm

West Meadow Farm
Kytes La

3

Sandy La
Horsley Park Farm

Abbott's Rough Plantation

Marks Hill

Cloves Hill

Woodside
PH

Yew Tree Farm

Smalley Green

Smalley Green Farm

Main Rd

43

Brackley Gate Farm

Woodside

A609
Ilkeston Rd

2

Brackley Gate
Moor La
Dobb's Hill Plantation

The Croft

Cloves Wood

Morley Manor

Belper Rd A609

1

Moor Plantation

Quarry Farm
Quarry Rd
Quarry Cottages

Morleymoor Farm

A608

CH
Hayes Farm

Morleyhayes Wood

42

Midshires Way
The Sycamores

38 A B 39 C D 40 E F

181
194

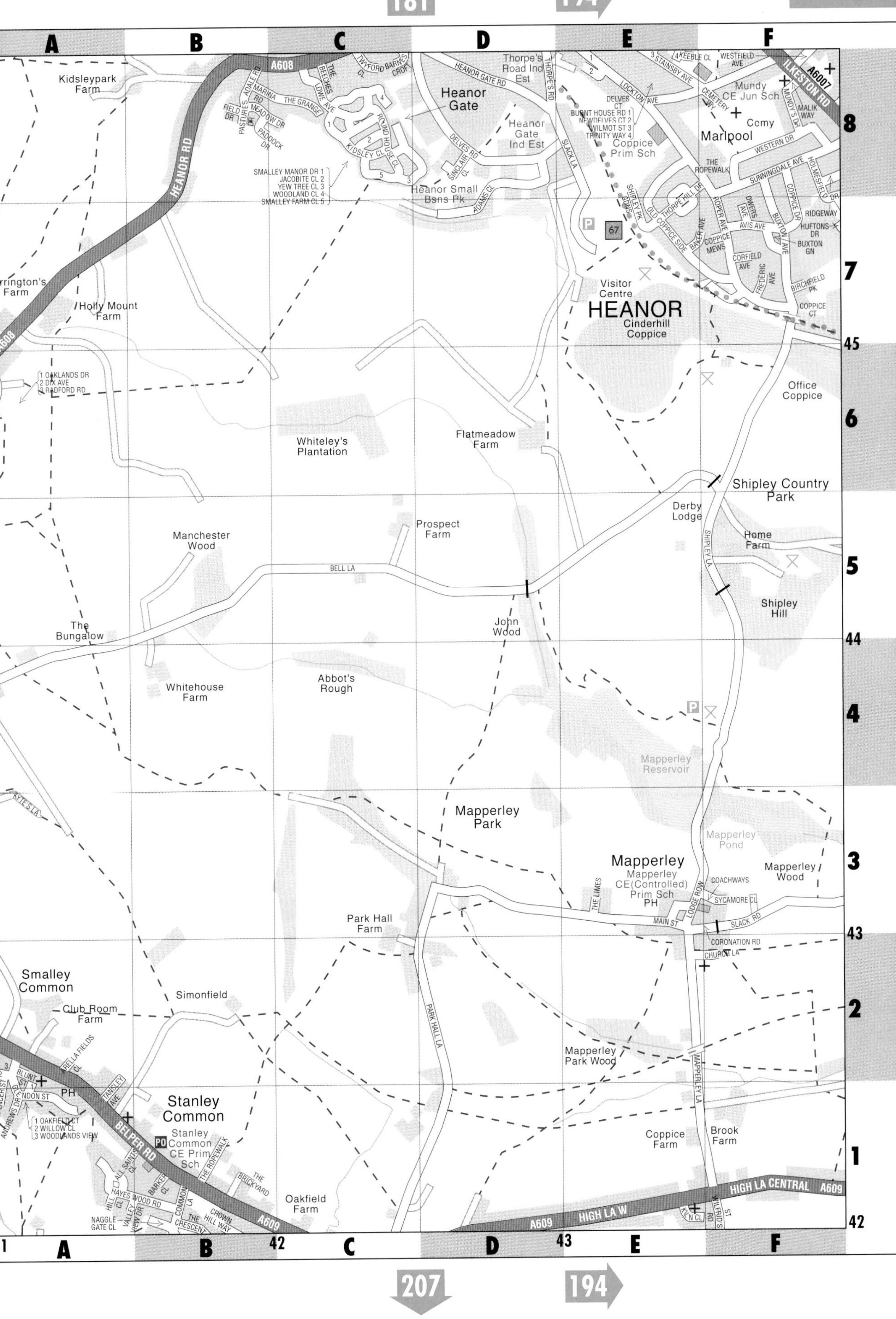
A
B
C
D
E
F
Kidsleypark Farm
A608
HEANOR RD
Heanor Gate
Thorpe's Road Ind Est
HEANOR GATE RD
THORPE'S RD
Heanor Gate Ind Est
Heanor Small Bsns Pk
SMALLEY MANOR DR 1
JACOBITE CL 2
YEW TREE CL 3
WOODLAND CL 4
SMALLEY FARM CL 5
THE GRANGE
KIDSLEY CL
ROUND HOUSE CL
LOWE AVE
THE BEECHES
TWYFORD CL
BARNES CROFT
ADALE RD
MARINA RD
MEADOW DR
PADDOCK DR
PASTURES
FIELD DR
DELVES RD
SINCLAIR CL
ADAMS CL
SLACK LA
LOCKTON AVE
STAINSBY AVE
KEEBLE CL
WESTFIELD AVE
DELVES CT
BURNT HOUSE RD 1
NEWDELVES CT 2
WILMOT ST 3
TRINITY WAY 4
Coppice Prim Sch
Mundy CE Jun Sch
Cemy
Marlpool
CEMETERY WAY
MUNDY'S DR
MALIK WAY
ILKESTON RD
A6007
WESTERN DR
THE ROPEWALK
SUNNINGDALE AVE
HOLMESFIELD DR
RIDGEWAY
HUFTONS DR
BUXTON GN
THORPE HILL DR
SHIPLEY PK
OLD COPPICE SIDE
ROPER AVE
OWERS AVE
COPPICE DR
AVIS AVE
BUXTON AVE
BAKER AVE
COPPICE MEWS
CORFIELD AVE
FREDERIC AVE
BIRCHFIELD PK
COPPICE CT
67
Visitor Centre
HEANOR
Cinderhill Coppice
Arrington's Farm
Holly Mount Farm
1 OAKLANDS DR
2 DIX AVE
3 RADFORD RD
Office Coppice
Whiteley's Plantation
Flatmeadow Farm
Shipley Country Park
Derby Lodge
Prospect Farm
Manchester Wood
BELL LA
Home Farm
SHIPLEY LA
Shipley Hill
The Bungalow
John Wood
Whitehouse Farm
Abbot's Rough
Mapperley Reservoir
KYTES LA
Mapperley Park
Mapperley Pond
Mapperley
Mapperley CE(Controlled) Prim Sch
PH
THE LIMES
LODGE ROW
COACHWAYS
SYCAMORE CL
Mapperley Wood
MAIN ST
SLACK RD
CORONATION RD
CHURCH LA
Park Hall Farm
PARK HALL LA
Smalley Common
Simonfield
Club Room Farm
ARELLA FIELDS CL
BLUNT ST
TANSLEY AVE
Stanley Common
Stanley Common CE Prim Sch
PO
1 OAKFIELD CT
2 WILLOW CL
3 WOODLANDS VIEW
BELPER RD
ALL SAINTS CT
BARKER CL
HAYES WOOD RD
HILL CL
VALLEY VIEW DR
NAGGLE GATE CL
COMMON
THE CRESCENT
CROWN HILL WAY
THE ROPEWALK
THE BRICKYARD
A609
Oakfield Farm
Mapperley Park Wood
MAPPERLEY LA
Coppice Farm
Brook Farm
HIGH LA W
HIGH LA CENTRAL
WILFRID'S RD
ST
8
7
45
6
5
44
4
3
43
2
1
42
41
42
43

207
194

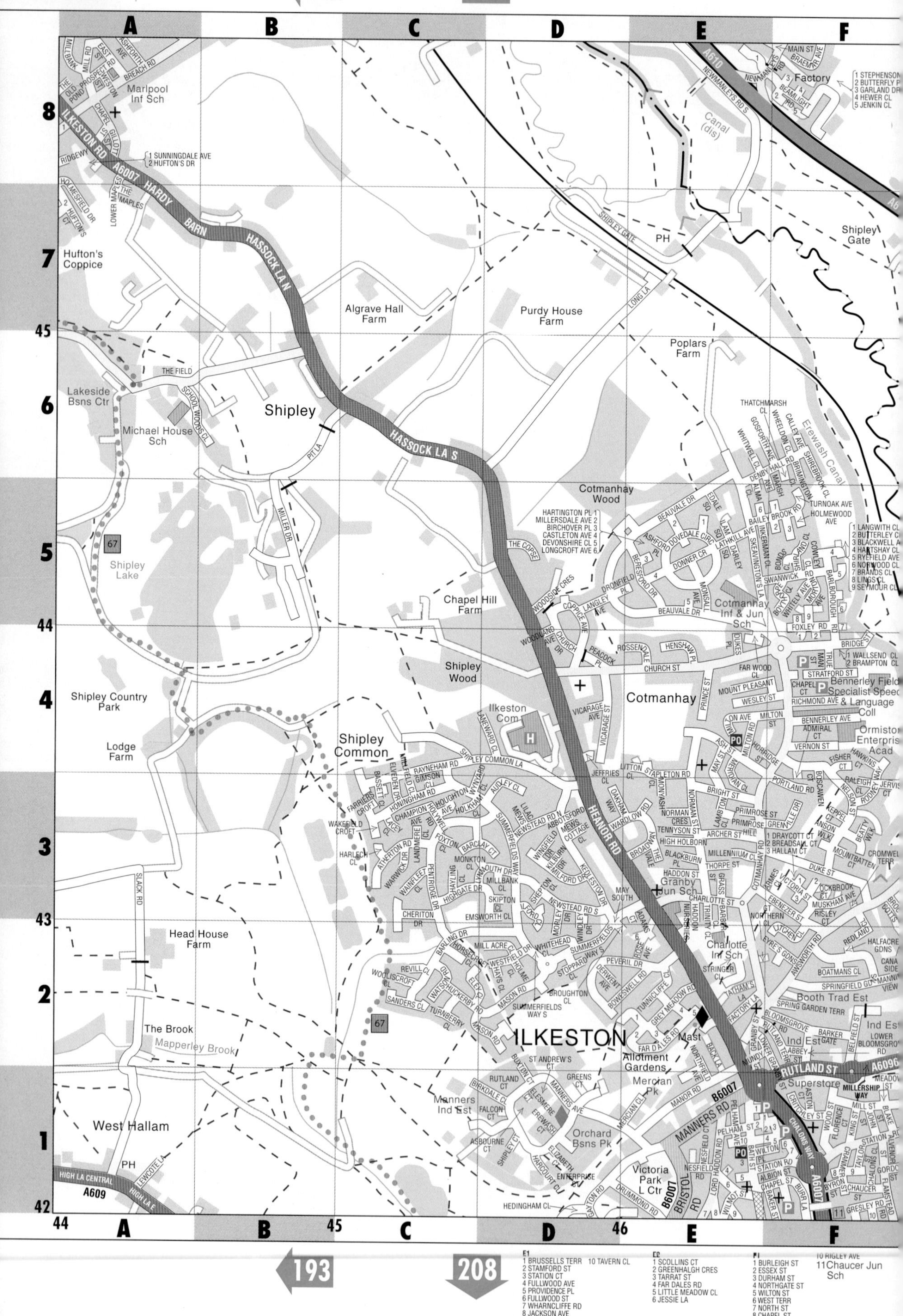

A   B   C   D   E   F

8

7

45

6

5

44

4

3

43

2

1

42

Ilkeston Rd
Marlpool Inf Sch

1 Sunningdale Ave
2 Hufton's Dr

Hufton's
Coppice

Lakeside
Bsns Ctr

Michael House
Sch

Shipley

Algrave Hall
Farm

Purdy House
Farm

Shipley Gate

Canal (dis)

Factory

1 Stephenson
2 Butterfly Cl
3 Garland Dr
4 Hewer Cl
5 Jenkin Cl

Shipley Gate

Poplars
Farm

Erewash Canal

Cotmanhay
Wood

Chapel Hill
Farm

Shipley
Wood

Shipley Lake
67

Shipley Country
Park

Lodge
Farm

Shipley Common

Ilkeston Com

Cotmanhay

Cotmanhay
Inf & Jun
Sch

Bennerley Fields
Specialist Speed

Ormiston
Enterprise
Acad

Head House
Farm

67

Granby
Jun Sch

ILKESTON

Mapperley Brook
The Brook

Manners
Ind Est

Orchard
Bsns Pk

Victoria
Park
L Ctr

West Hallam

High La Central
A609

Iron La E

Allotment
Gardens

Merctan
Pk

Rutland St

Superstore

Millership
Way

Booth Trad Est

44   A   B   45   C   D   46   E   F

E1
1 BRUSSELLS TERR
2 STAMFORD ST
3 STATION CT
4 FULLWOOD AVE
5 PROVIDENCE PL
6 FULLWOOD ST
7 WHARNCLIFFE RD
8 JACKSON AVE
9 GREGORY ST

10 TAVERN CL

E2
1 SCOLLINS CT
2 GREENHALGH CRES
3 TARRAT ST
4 FAR DALES RD
5 LITTLE MEADOW CL
6 JESSIE LA

F1
1 BURLEIGH ST
2 ESSEX ST
3 DURHAM ST
4 NORTHGATE ST
5 WILTON ST
6 WEST TERR
7 NORTH ST
8 CHAPEL ST
9 LOWER CHAPEL ST

10 RIGLEY AVE
11 Chaucer Jun
Sch

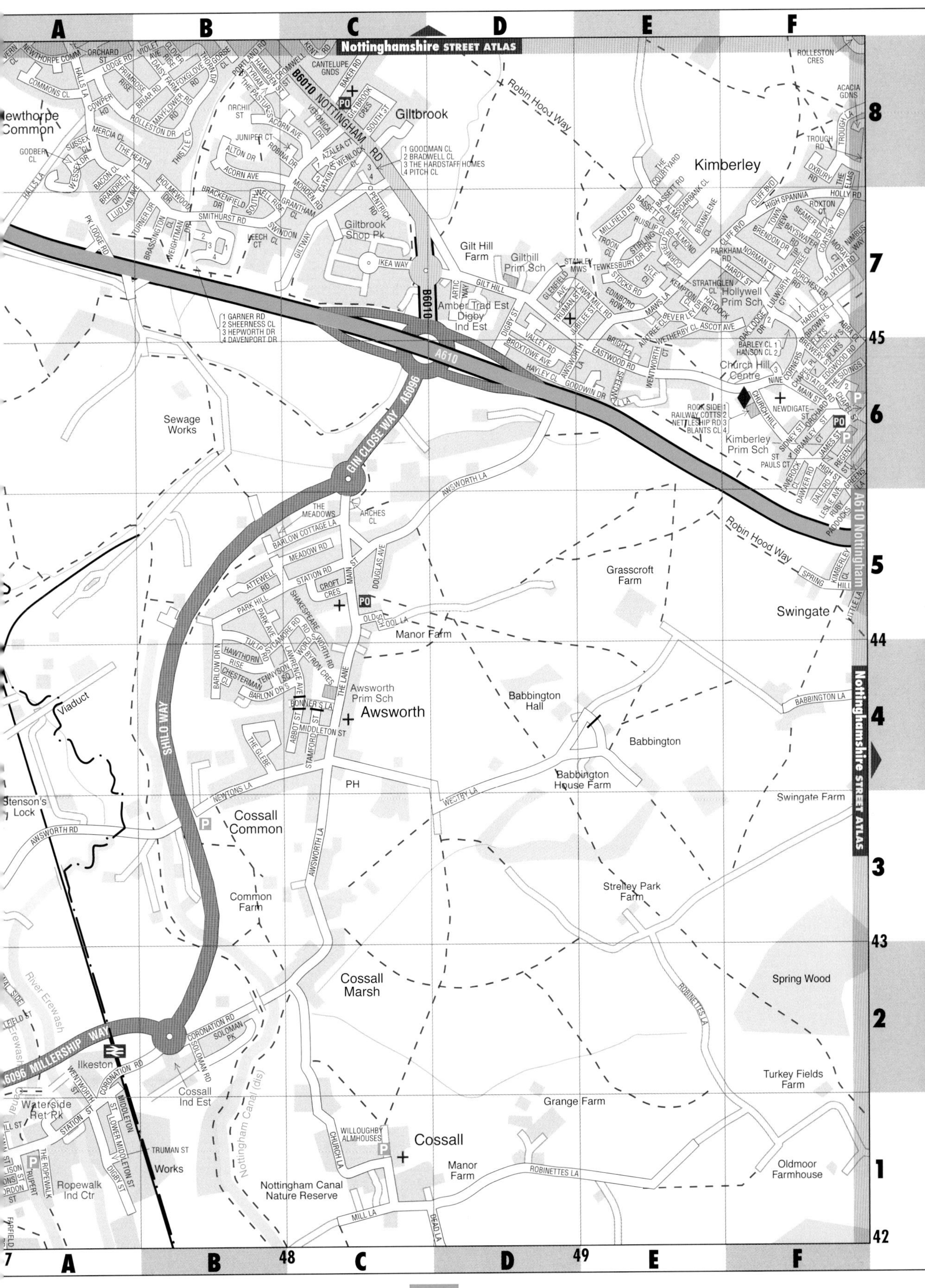
Nottinghamshire STREET ATLAS
A
B
C
D
E
F
8
7
45
6
5
44
4
3
43
2
1
42
48
49
Newthorpe Common
Giltbrook
Kimberley
Robin Hood Way
B6010 NOTTINGHAM RD
Giltbrook Shop Pk
IKEA WAY
Gilt Hill Farm
Gilthill Prim Sch
Hollywell Prim Sch
Amber Trad Est
Digby Ind Est
A610
A6096
GIN CLOSE WAY
Church Hill Centre
Kimberley Prim Sch
Sewage Works
1 GOODMAN CL
2 BRADWELL CL
3 THE HARDSTAFF HOMES
4 PITCH CL
1 GARNER RD
2 SHEERNESS CL
3 HEPWORTH DR
4 DAVENPORT DR
ROCK SIDE 1
RAILWAY COTTS 2
NETTLESHIP RD 3
BLANTS CL 4
A610 Nottingham
Grasscroft Farm
Swingate
AWSWORTH LA
THE MEADOWS
ARCHES CL
BARLOW COTTAGE LA
MEADOW RD
STATION RD
CROFT CRES
MAIN ST
DOUGLAS AVE
Manor Farm
Awsworth Prim Sch
Awsworth
Babbington Hall
Babbington
Babbington House Farm
BABBINGTON LA
Swingate Farm
SHILO WAY
Viaduct
Stenson's Lock
NEWTONS LA
WECTRY LA
PH
Cossall Common
AWSWORTH RD
Common Farm
Strelley Park Farm
Cossall Marsh
Spring Wood
ROBINETTES LA
River Erewash
A6096 MILLERSHIP WAY
Ilkeston
CORONATION RD
SOLOMAN PK
Cossall Ind Est
Nottingham Canal (dis)
Turkey Fields Farm
Waterside Ret Pk
Grange Farm
Cossall
WILLOUGHBY ALMHOUSES
CHURCH LA
Manor Farm
Oldmoor Farmhouse
TRUMAN ST
Works
Ropewalk Ind Ctr
Nottingham Canal Nature Reserve
MILL LA
DEAD LA

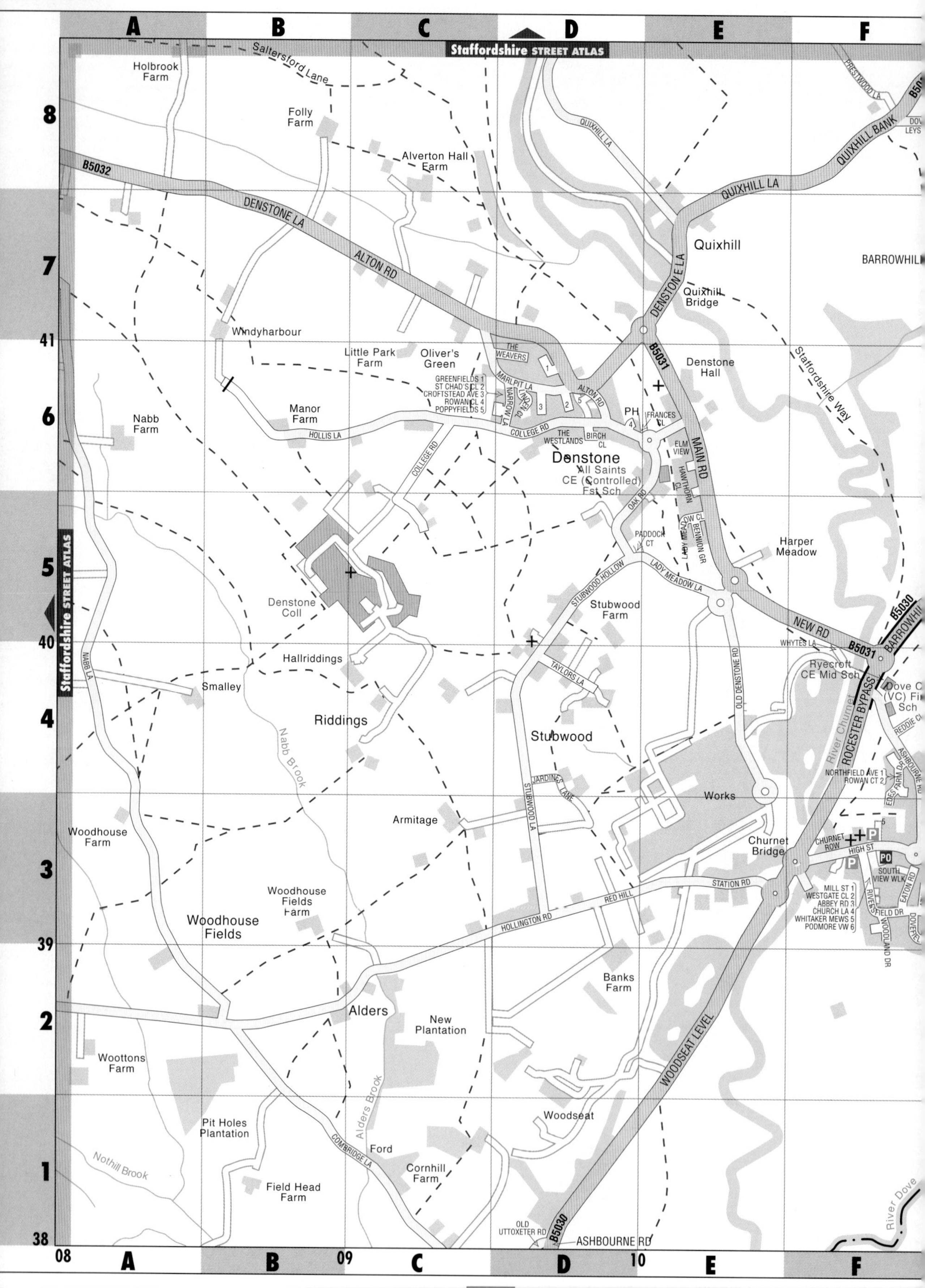
Staffordshire STREET ATLAS
Holbrook Farm
Saltersford Lane
Folly Farm
Alverton Hall Farm
B5032
DENSTONE LA
ALTON RD
Windyharbour
Little Park Farm
Oliver's Green
THE WEAVERS
GREENFIELDS 1
ST CHAD'S CL 2
CROFTSTEAD AVE 3
ROWAN CL 4
POPPYFIELDS 5
MARLPIT LA
NARROW LA
Manor Farm
HOLLIS LA
COLLEGE RD
THE WESTLANDS
BIRCH CL
Denstone
All Saints CE (Controlled) Fst Sch
PH
FRANCES CL
ELM VIEW
HAWTHORN CL
MAIN RD
B5031
OAK RD
PADDOCK CT
LADY MEADOW CL
BENNION GR
Nabb Farm
Denstone Coll
Hallriddings
Smalley
Riddings
Nabb Brook
NABB LA
STUBWOOD HOLLOW
LADY MEADOW LA
Stubwood Farm
TAYLORS LA
Stubwood
JARDINE LANE
STUBWOOD LA
Armitage
Woodhouse Farm
Woodhouse Fields Farm
Woodhouse Fields
HOLLINGTON RD
RED HILL
STATION RD
Alders
New Plantation
Woottons Farm
Pit Holes Plantation
Alders Brook
Ford
COMBRIDGE LA
Cornhill Farm
Field Head Farm
Nothill Brook
Woodseat
Banks Farm
WOODSEAT LEVEL
B5030
OLD UTTOXETER RD
ASHBOURNE RD
QUIXHILL LA
Quixhill
Quixhill Bridge
DENSTON E LA
QUIXHILL BANK
PRESTWOOD LA
DOVE LEYS
BARROWHILL
Denstone Hall
Staffordshire Way
Harper Meadow
NEW RD
WHYTES LA
Ryecroft CE Mid Sch
OLD DENSTONE RD
Works
River Churnet
ROCESTER BYPASS
Dove C (VC) Fi Sch
REDDIE CL
ASHBOURNE RD
NORTHFIELD AVE 1
ROWAN CT 2
FARM DR
EDGE
Churnet Bridge
CHURNET ROW
HIGH ST
PO
SOUTH VIEW WLK
EATON RD
MILL ST 1
WESTGATE CL 2
ABBEY RD 3
CHURCH LA 4
WHITAKER MEWS 5
PODMORE VW 6
RIVERSFIELD DR
WOODLAND DR
DOVEFIELD
River Dove
A B C D E F
8 7 41 6 5 40 4 3 39 2 1 38
08 09 10

183
198
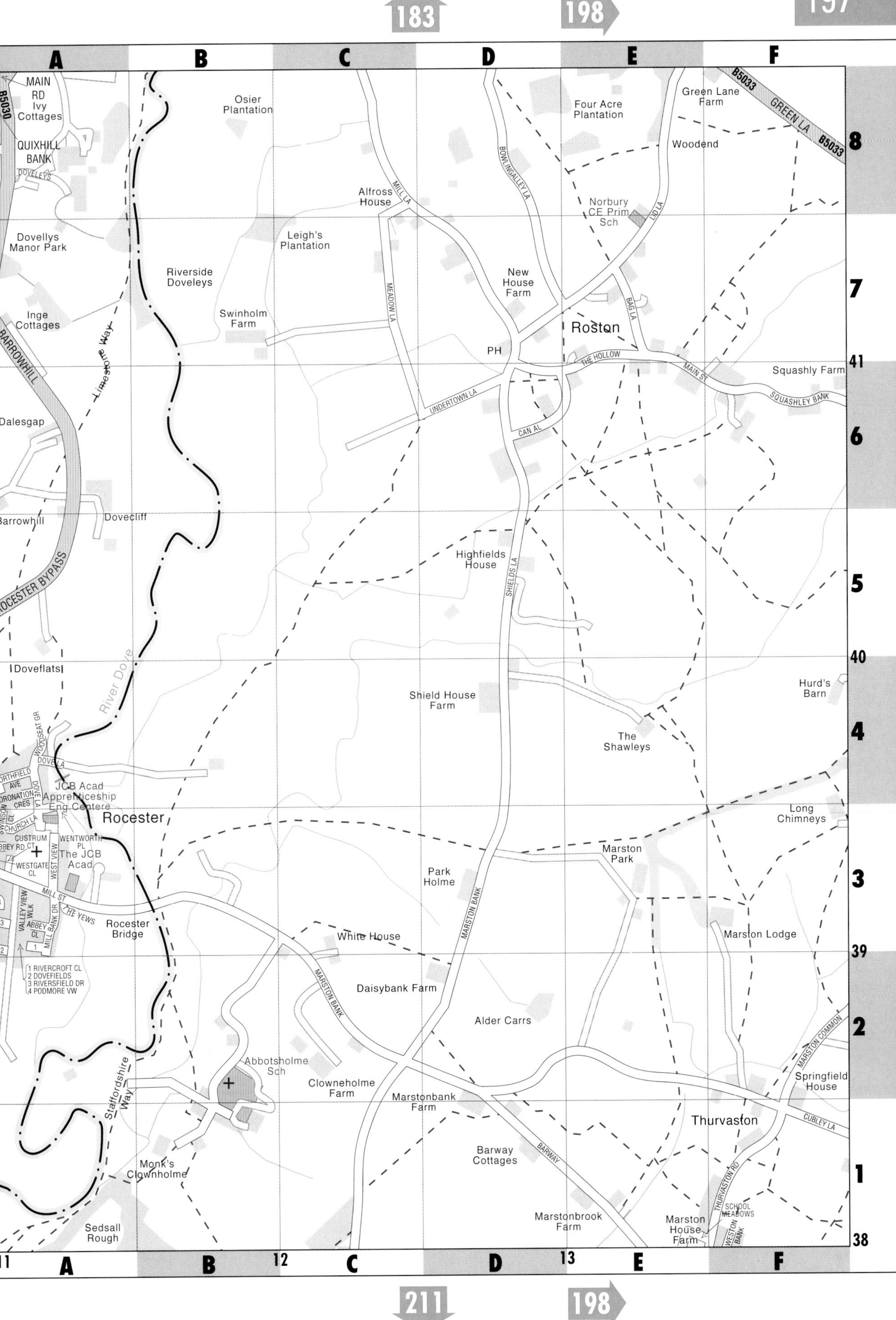
A
B
C
D
E
F
MAIN RD
Ivy Cottages
B5030
QUIXHILL BANK
DOVELEYS
Osier Plantation
Four Acre Plantation
Green Lane Farm
B5033
GREEN LA
Woodend
8
Alfross House
MILL LA
BOWLINGALLEY LA
Norbury CE Prim Sch
LID LA
Dovellys Manor Park
Leigh's Plantation
Riverside Doveleys
New House Farm
7
MEADOW LA
BAG LA
Inge Cottages
Swinholm Farm
Roston
BARROWHILL
Limestone Way
PH
THE HOLLOW
41
Squashly Farm
MAIN ST
SQUASHLEY BANK
UNDERTOWN LA
Dalesgap
CAN AL
6
Barrowhill
Dovecliff
ROCESTER BYPASS
Highfields House
SHIELDS LA
5
River Dove
40
Doveflats
Shield House Farm
Hurd's Barn
WOODSEAT GR
4
The Shawleys
DOVE LA
NORTHFIELD AVE
JCB Acad Apprenticeship Eng Centre
CORONATION CRES
Rocester
Long Chimneys
SWINSON CL
CHURCH LA
CUSTRUM
WENTWORTH PL
ABBEY RD CT
The JCB Acad
WESTGATE CL
WEST VIEW
Marston Park
3
Park Holme
MILL ST
VALLEY VIEW WLK
MILL BANK DR
THE YEWS
ABBEY CL
Rocester Bridge
White House
MARSTON BANK
Marston Lodge
39
1 RIVERCROFT CL
2 DOVEFIELDS
3 RIVERSFIELD DR
4 PODMORE VW
Daisybank Farm
Alder Carrs
2
MARSTON COMMON
Abbotsholme Sch
Staffordshire Way
Clowneholme Farm
Marstonbank Farm
Springfield House
Thurvaston
CUBLEY LA
Barway Cottages
BARWAY
Monk's Clownholme
1
THURVASTON RD
SCHOOL MEADOWS
Sedsall Rough
Marstonbrook Farm
Marston House Farm
WESTON BANK
38
11
12
13
211
198

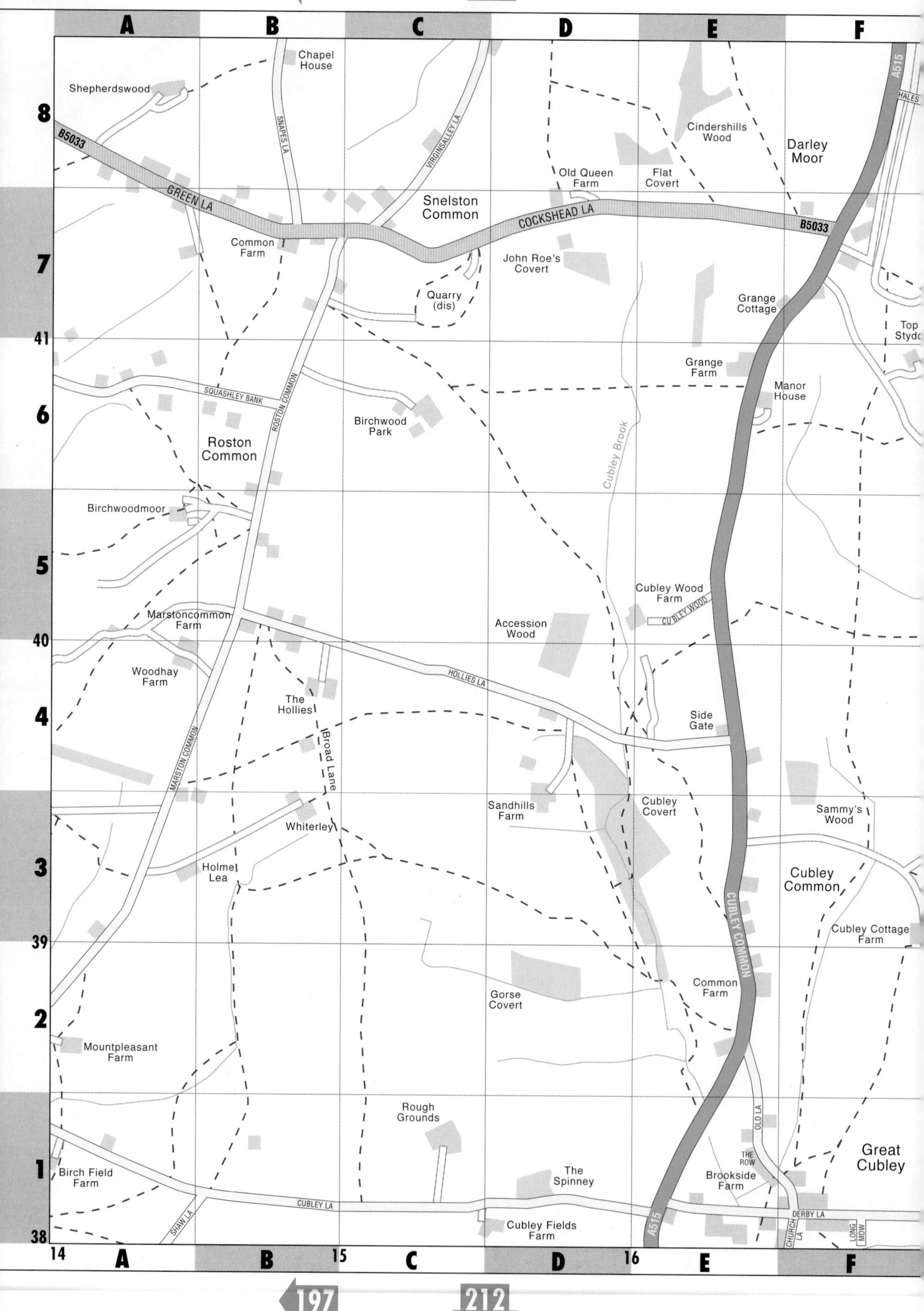

197
184

A B C D E F

8

Shepherdswood

Chapel
House

B5033

GREEN LA

SNAPES LA

VIRGINSALLEY LA

Snelston
Common

Old Queen
Farm

Flat
Covert

Cindershills
Wood

Darley
Moor

A515

TO HALES

COCKSHEAD LA

B5033

7

Common
Farm

Quarry
(dis)

John Roe's
Covert

Grange
Cottage

Top
Stydo

41

Squashley Bank

ROSTON COMMON

Grange
Farm

Manor
House

Cubley Brook

6

Roston
Common

Birchwood
Park

Birchwoodmoor

5

Cubley Wood
Farm

CUBLEY WOOD

Marstoncommon
Farm

Accession
Wood

40

MARSTON COMMON

Woodhay
Farm

The
Hollies

HOLLIES LA

Side
Gate

4

Broad Lane

Whiterley

Holme
Lea

Sandhills
Farm

Cubley
Covert

Sammy's
Wood

Cubley
Common

CUBLEY COMMON

Cubley Cottage
Farm

3

39

Mountpleasant
Farm

Gorse
Covert

Common
Farm

2

Rough
Grounds

OLD LA

THE
ROW

Great
Cubley

1

Birch Field
Farm

The
Spinney

Brookside
Farm

SHAW LA

CUBLEY LA

A515

Cubley Fields
Farm

DERBY LA

CHURCH LA

LONG MDW

38

14   A   B   15   C   D   16   E   F

197
212

185
200

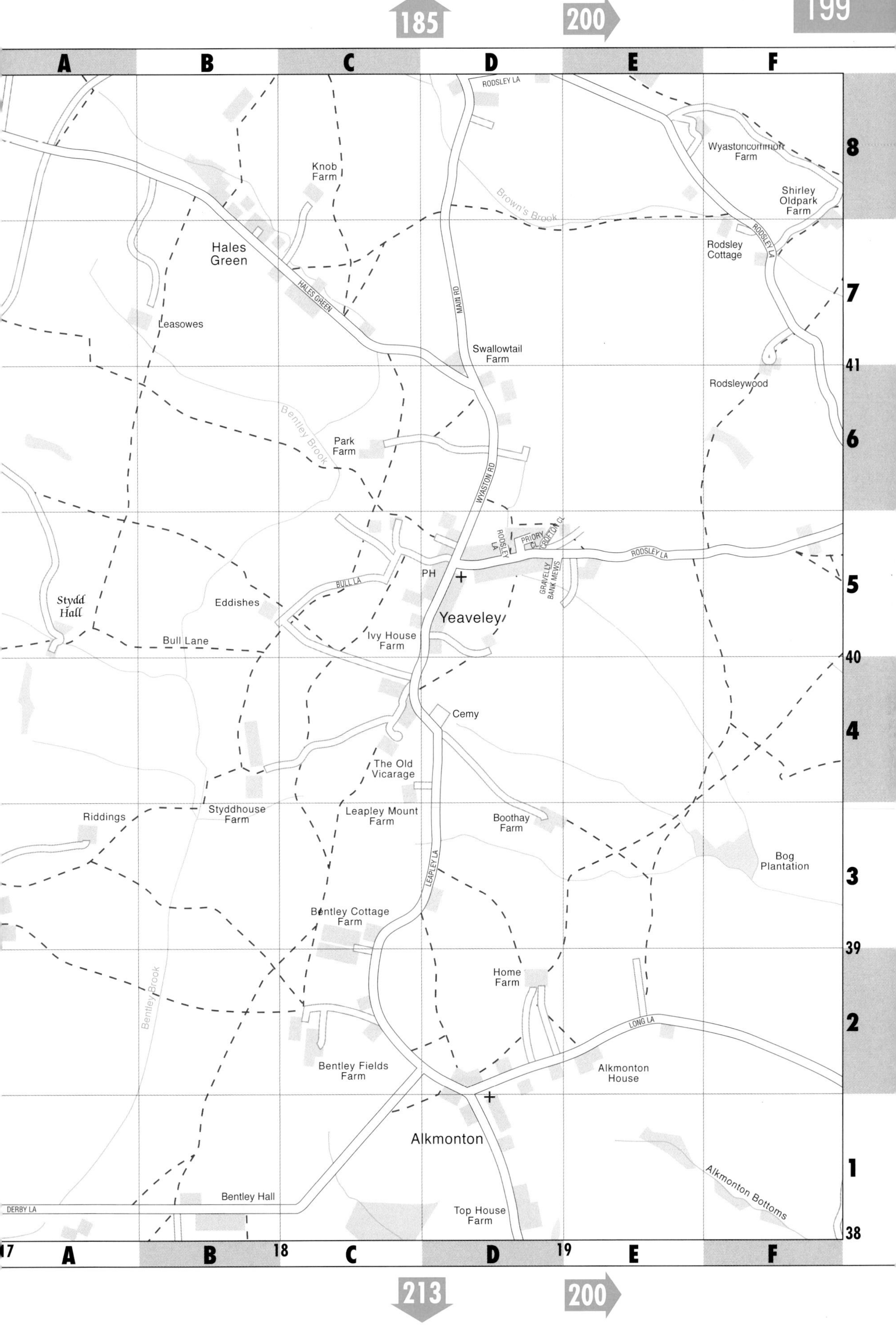
A
B
C
D
E
F
RODSLEY LA
Wyastoncommon Farm
Shirley Oldpark Farm
Knob Farm
Brown's Brook
8
Hales Green
HALES GREEN
MAIN RD
RODSLEY LA
Rodsley Cottage
7
Leasowes
Swallowtail Farm
41
Rodsleywood
Bentley Brook
Park Farm
6
WYASTON RD
RODSLEY LA
PRIORY CL
CROFTON CL
RODSLEY LA
GRAVELLY BANK MEWS
PH
BULL LA
5
Stydd Hall
Eddishes
Yeaveley
Ivy House Farm
Bull Lane
40
Cemy
4
The Old Vicarage
Riddings
Styddhouse Farm
Leapley Mount Farm
Boothay Farm
LEAPLEY LA
Bog Plantation
3
Bentley Cottage Farm
39
Home Farm
Bentley Brook
LONG LA
2
Bentley Fields Farm
Alkmonton House
Alkmonton
1
Alkmonton Bottoms
DERBY LA
Bentley Hall
Top House Farm
38
17
18
19

213
200

199
186

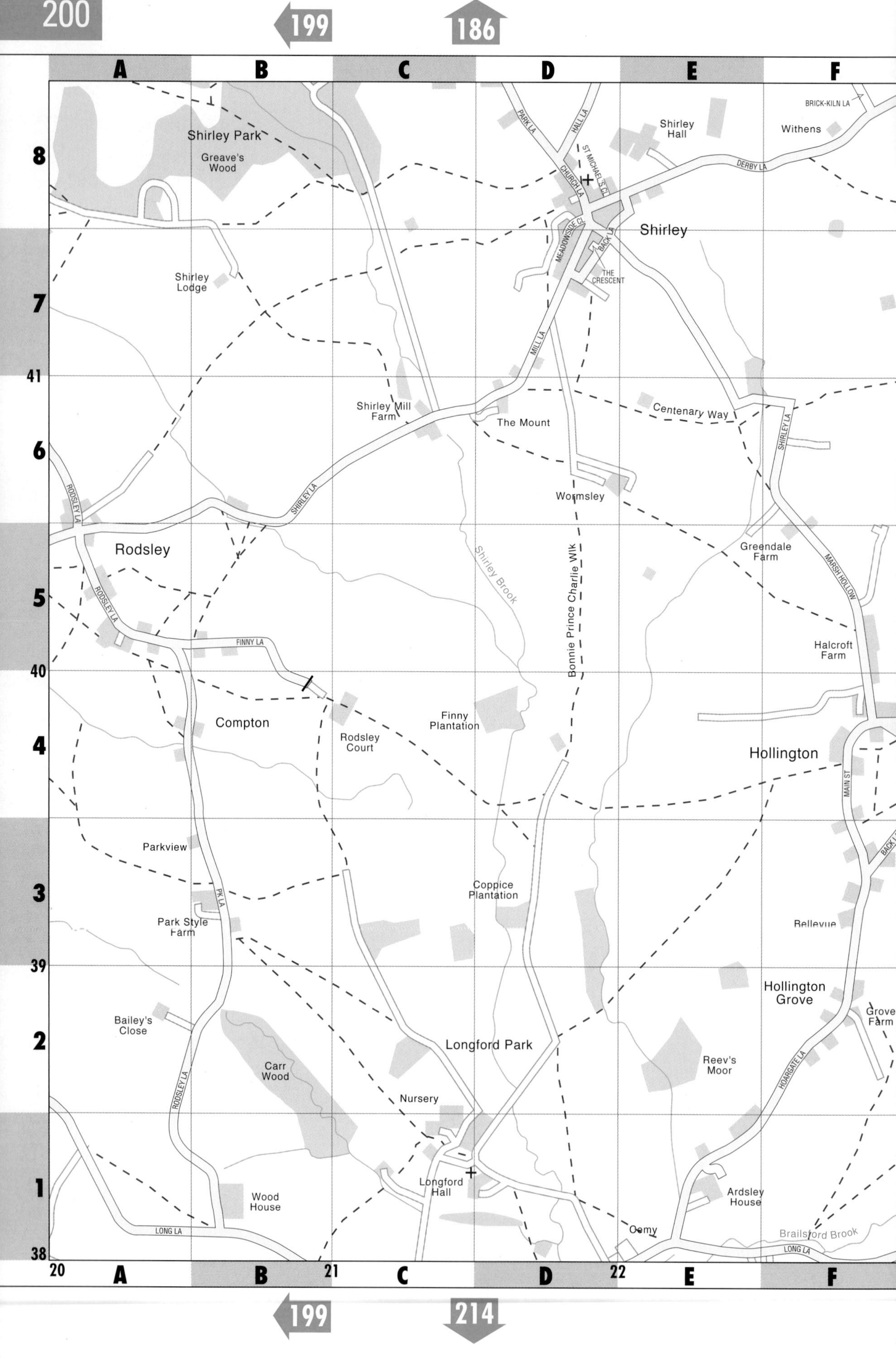
A
B
C
D
E
F
8
7
41
6
5
40
4
3
39
2
1
38
20
21
22
Shirley Park
Greave's Wood
Shirley Lodge
PARK LA
HALL LA
ST MICHAEL'S CL
CHURCH LA
MEADOWSIDE CL
BACK LA
THE CRESCENT
Shirley Hall
Shirley
BRICK-KILN LA
Withens
DERBY LA
MILL LA
Shirley Mill Farm
The Mount
Centenary Way
SHIRLEY LA
Wormsley
RODSLEY LA
Rodsley
Shirley Brook
Bonnie Prince Charlie Wlk
Greendale Farm
MARSH HOLLOW
Halcroft Farm
FINNY LA
Compton
Rodsley Court
Finny Plantation
Hollington
MAIN ST
Parkview
BACK LA
Coppice Plantation
PK LA
Park Style Farm
Bellevue
Hollington Grove
Bailey's Close
Grove Farm
Longford Park
Carr Wood
Reev's Moor
HOARGATE LA
Nursery
Longford Hall
Ardsley House
Wood House
LONG LA
Cemy
Brailsford Brook
LONG LA

199
214

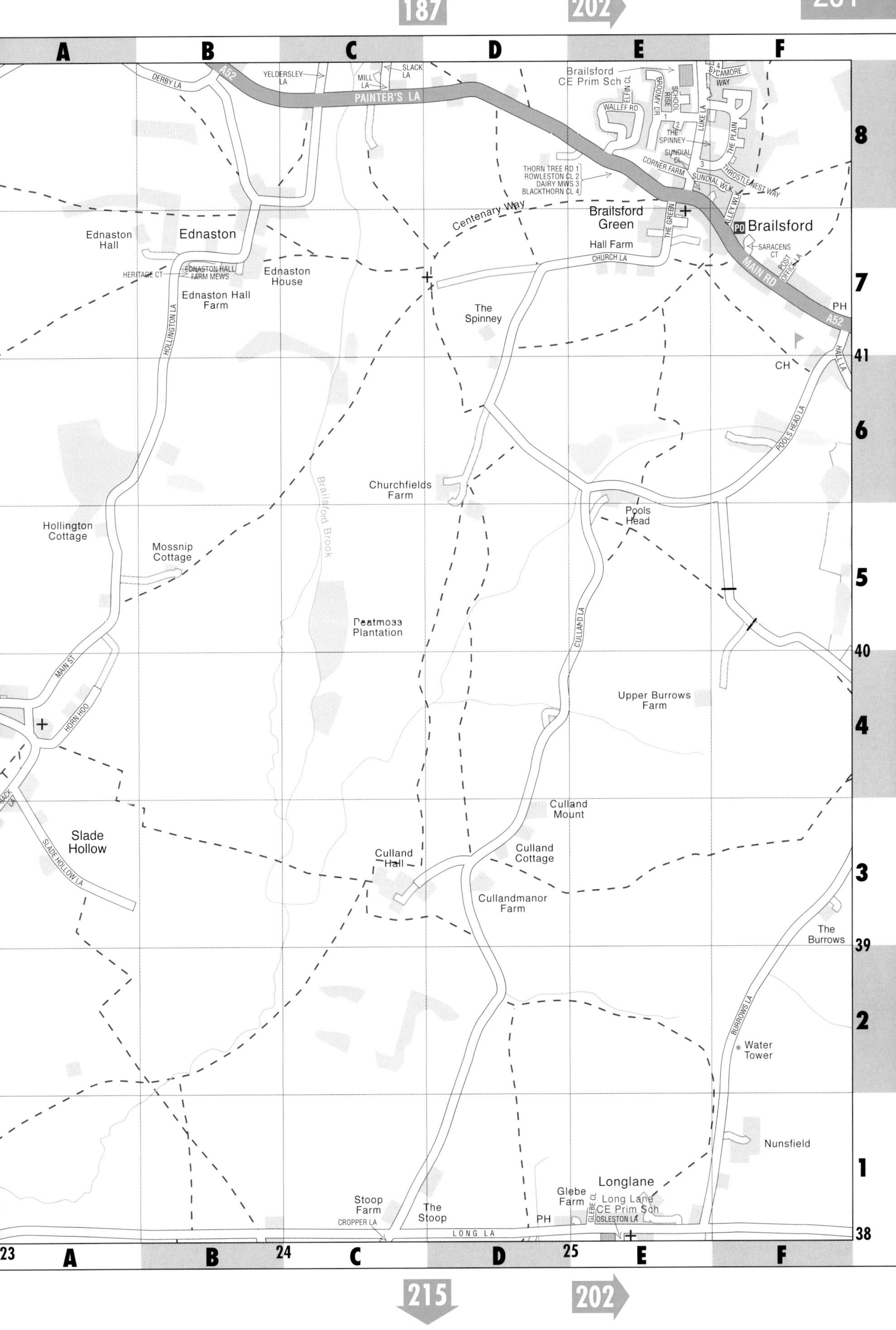

A   B   C   D   E   F

DERBY LA

A52

YELDERSLEY LA

MILL LA

SLACK LA

PAINTER'S LA

Brailsford
CE Prim Sch

SCHOOL CL

ELFIN CL

WALLFF RD

BROOK CL

RISE

LUKE LA

CAMORE
WAY

THE PLAIN

THE
SPINNEY

SUNDIAL
CL

THROSTLE NEST WAY

8

THORN TREE RD 1
ROWLESTON CL 2
DAIRY MWS 3
BLACKTHORN CL 4

Centenary Way

CORNER FARM

SUNDIAL WLK

Ednaston
Hall

Ednaston

Brailsford
Green

THE GREEN

PO

Brailsford

Hall Farm

CHURCH LA

SARACENS
CT
POST
OFFICE LA

HERITAGE CT

Ednaston Hall
FARM MEWS

Ednaston
House

7

Ednaston Hall
Farm

The
Spinney

PH

A52

HOLLINGTON LA

CH

HALL LA

41

6

POOLS HEAD LA

Churchfields
Farm

Pools
Head

Hollington
Cottage

Mossnip
Cottage

Brailsford Brook

CULLAND LA

5

Peatmoss
Plantation

40

MAIN ST

HORN HOO

Upper Burrows
Farm

4

SLADE HOLLOW LA

Slade
Hollow

Culland
Mount

Culland Cottage

Culland
Hall

Cullandmanor
Farm

The
Burrows

3

39

BURROWS LA

2

Water
Tower

Nunsfield

Stoop
Farm

CROPPER LA

The
Stoop

PH

Longlane

Glebe
Farm

GLEBE CL

Long Lane
CE Prim Sch

OSLESTON LA

1

LONG LA

38

23   A   B   24   C   D   25   E   F

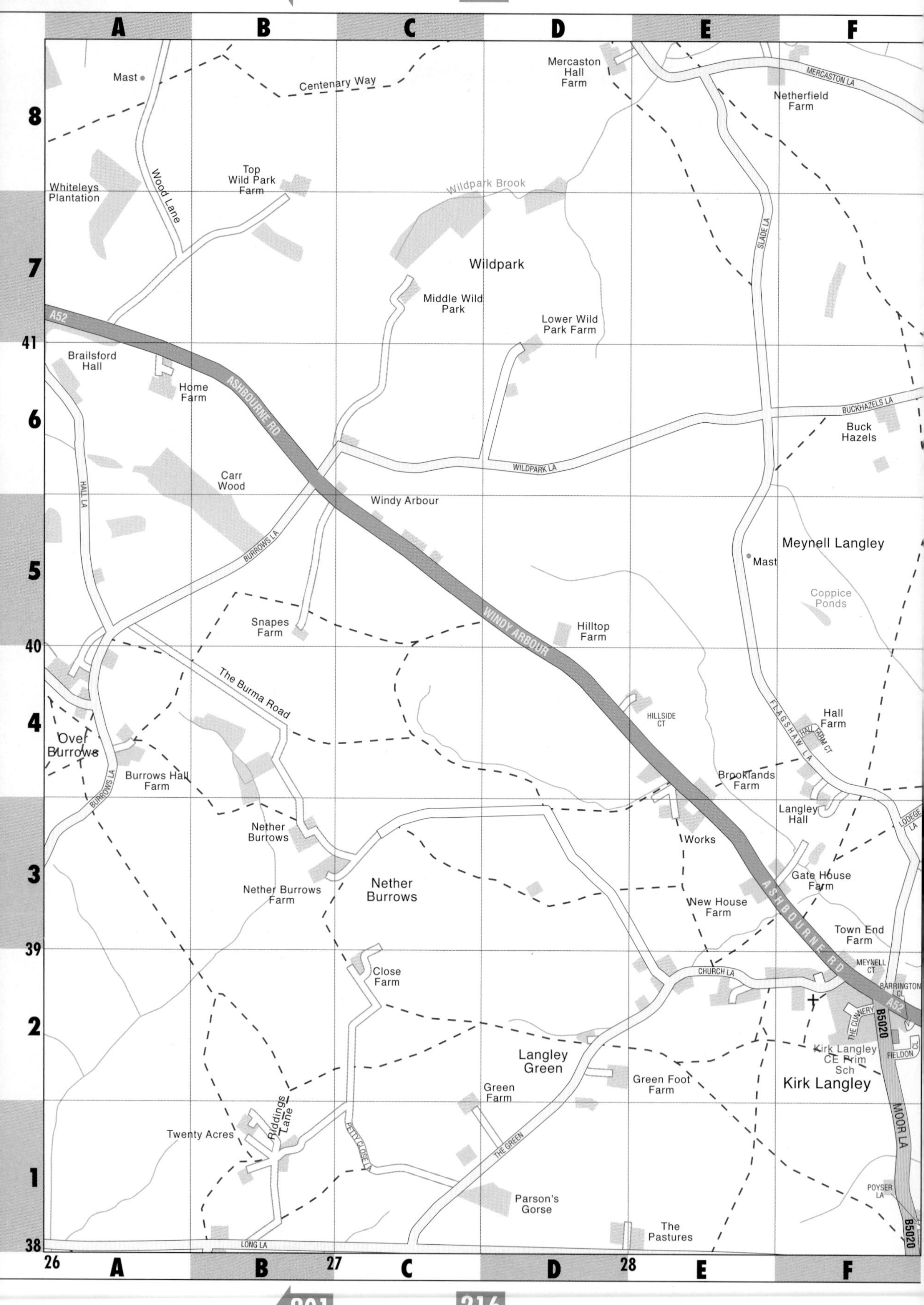

A B C D E F

8

Mast

Centenary Way

Mercaston
Hall
Farm

Netherfield
Farm

MERCASTON LA

Whiteleys
Plantation

Top
Wild Park
Farm

Wildpark Brook

Wood Lane

7

Wildpark

SLADE LA

A52

41

Middle Wild
Park

Lower Wild
Park Farm

Brailsford
Hall

Home
Farm

ASHBOURNE RD

BUCKHAZELS LA

Buck
Hazels

6

HALL LA

Carr
Wood

WILDPARK LA

Windy Arbour

Meynell Langley

Mast

Coppice
Ponds

5

BURROWS LA

WINDY ARBOUR

40

Snapes
Farm

Hilltop
Farm

FLAGSHAW LA

Hall
Farm

KENT FARM CT

The Burma Road

HILLSIDE
CT

Brooklands
Farm

4

Over
Burrows

Langley
Hall

LODGE LA

Burrows Hall
Farm

BURROWS LA

Nether
Burrows

Works

Gate House
Farm

ASHBOURNE RD

3

Nether Burrows
Farm

Nether
Burrows

New House
Farm

Town End
Farm

MEYNELL
CT

BARRINGTON CL

39

Close
Farm

CHURCH LA

+

THE DEANERY

B5020

A52

2

Langley
Green

Green Foot
Farm

Kirk Langley
CE Prim
Sch

FIELDON

Riddings
Lane

Green
Farm

Kirk Langley

Twenty Acres

PETTY CLOSE

THE GREEN

MOOR LA

1

Parson's
Gorse

POYSER
LA

B5020

38

LONG LA

The
Pastures

26 A 27 B C 27 D 28 E F

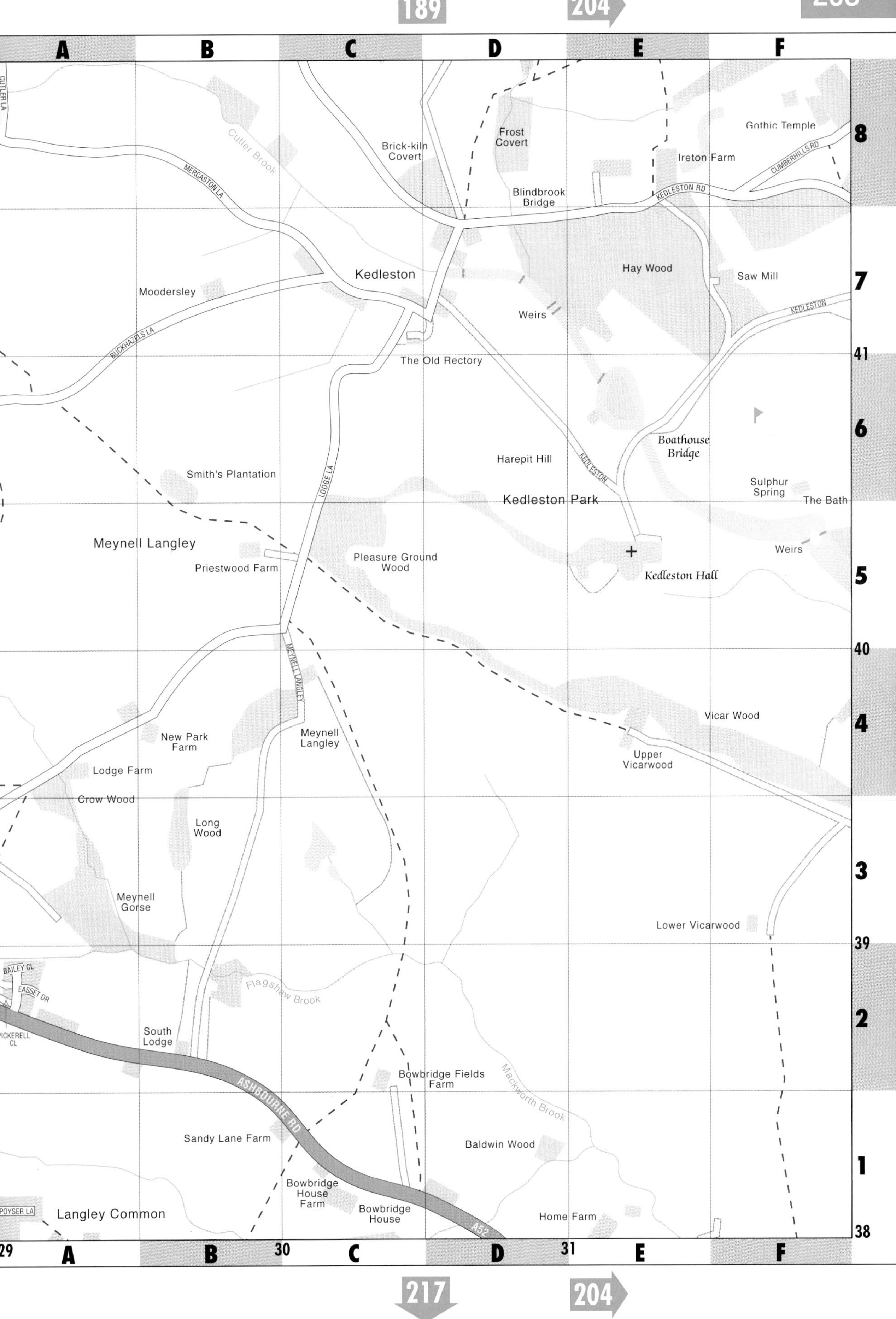

A   **B**   **C**   **D**   **E**   **F**

CUTLER LA

Cutler Brook

MERCASTON LA

Brick-kiln Covert

Frost Covert

Gothic Temple

8

Blindbrook Bridge

Ireton Farm

KEDLESTON RD

CUMBERHILLS RD

Kedleston

Hay Wood

Saw Mill

KEDLESTON

7

Moodersley

Weirs

41

BUCKHAZELS LA

The Old Rectory

6

Boathouse Bridge

Harepit Hill

KEDLESTON

Smith's Plantation

LODGE LA

Kedleston Park

Sulphur Spring

The Bath

Meynell Langley

Pleasure Ground Wood

Kedleston Hall

Weirs

5

Priestwood Farm

MEYNELL LANGLEY

+

40

New Park Farm

Meynell Langley

Vicar Wood

4

Lodge Farm

Upper Vicarwood

Crow Wood

Long Wood

Meynell Gorse

3

Lower Vicarwood

39

BAILEY CL

EASSET DR

Flagshaw Brook

PICKERELL CL

South Lodge

Bowbridge Fields Farm

Mackworth Brook

2

Sandy Lane Farm

ASHBOURNE RD

Baldwin Wood

1

POYSER LA

Langley Common

Bowbridge House Farm

Bowbridge House

A52

Home Farm

38

29   **A**   **B**   30   **C**   **D**   31   **E**   **F**

203
190

A B C D E F

8
7
41
6
5
40
4
3
39
2
1
38

Mast
Park Nook Farm
Quarndon Hill
Burley Meadows
Burleywood Farmhouse
Burley Wood
Park Nook Wood
Park Nook
Bunker's Hill
Quarndon Common
Burley Grange
The Curzon CE Prim Sch
Quarndon
CH
Water Tower
CH
Big Wood
Allestree Hall
Hotel
Cannon Hill
PH
Allestree Park Nature Reserve
Bottom Covert
Woodlands Sch
Portway Inf & Jun Schs
Allestree
Walter Evans CE (Aided) Prim Sch
Liby
Markeaton Brook
Lawn Prim Sch
St Benedict RC Sch & Performing Arts Coll
St Mary's Cath Prim Sch
Markeaton Stones
Osierbed Wood
Markeaton House
Univ of Derby
Darley Grove

CUMBERHILLS RD
BEECH AVE
THE COMMON
INN LA
KEDLESTON
KEDLESTON RD
COACH DR
SULLEYS FIELD
MONTPELIER
BISHOPTHORPE GRO
BURLEY DR
BURLEY LA
BURLEY HILL
DERBY RD
A6
WOODLANDS LA
BARN CL
CHURCH RD
OLD VICARAGE LA
OLD CHURCH CL
BROOK CL
MAPLE GR
IMPERIAL CT
WOODLANDS RD
WEST BANK RD
ELM GR
TAMAR AVE
FIRS CRES
LABURNUM CRES
ST MAWES CL
CHARLESTOWN DR
LISKEARD DR
ST AGNES AVE
ACRESVIEW CL
MIDFIELD CL
CHARTERSTONE LA
PINGLE
RIDDINGS
CHANDRES CT
FOXES WLK
LADYCROFT PADDOCK
CORNHILL
PARK LA
LIME CROFT
POPLARS
SIDDALS LA
ST EDMUND'S CL
PARK VIEW CL
ROBIN CROFT RD
CHURCH WLK
GISBORNE CRES
KINGS CROFT
SHORT AVE
MAIN AVE
POPLAR NOOK
THE PADDOCK
CRABTREE CL
CURZON CL
BANCROFT DR
SHEROSIDE CL
BLENHEIM DR
BLENHEIM PAR
THORN CL
ASH CL
OAK CL
LOCKWOOD RD
RYDAL CL
MULBERRIES
ASKERFIELD AVE
RAVENSDALE RD
COBTHORN DR
ASHBROOK CL
WOODSTOCK CL
KINGSLEY RD
BIRCHES RD
LARCH CL
SYCAMORE AVE
HOLLIES RD
HARDWICK AVE
THIRLMERE AVE
BUTTERMERE DR
PARK WOOD CL
DEVONSHIRE AVE
ST GEORGE'S HO
ST GEORGE'S DRUM CL
ST GEORGE'S CL
BASLOW DR
ABBEY HILL
A38
ROBERT ADAM RD
ORANGERY DR
CRABTREE HILL
QUARN DR
HAREWOOD RD
WELWYN AVE
ALTON CL
BEAUREPER AVE
LEA CL
NESS WLK
PORTREATH DR
RANNOCH CL
WINDERMERE CRES
TAY WLK
CALDER CL
CAVENDISH AVE
BARDEN DR
CHATSWORTH CRES
WELBECK GR
SCARSDALE AVE
HADDON DR
HADDON CL
ALLESTREE LA
CLIFTON RD
ST JOHN'S CL
CADGWITH DR
PENTEWEN CL
FRIARS CL
THATCH CL
THE CLOSE
SOMME RD
NETHERWOOD CT
ROSEMOUNT CT
MEMORIAL RD
POPPYFIELDS MDW
MEYNELL CT
MENIN RD
QUARNDON HT
ST NICHOLAS CL
QUARNDON VIEW
THE ORCHARDS
FAIRWAY CL
ABBEY HILL RD
BRIARSGATE
OAKOVER DR
FERRERS WAY
BIRCHOVER WAY
CAUSEWAY
BANK SIDE
THE RISE
HARPSWELL CL
TRESILIAN CL
FOXLANDS AVE
BRAITHWELL DR
FINNINGLEY DR
PLOUGH GATE
CANONS WLK
WILLOW CL
ABBEY DR
DARLEY DR
LENS RD
YPRES RD
BELLINGHAM CT
OTTERBURN DR
LAMBLEY DR
STOODLEY PIKE GDNS
WIDDYBANK CL
RIBBLESDALE CL
LAWN AVE
FAIRWAY CRES
BEELEY CL
LILAC WAY
ASHOVER RD
PARK FARM CTR
PARK FARM DR
WHITEWAY
MELBOURNE CL
NORBURY CL
WEST CL
EAST CL
FARNWAY
NEWLYN DR
MISTERTON CL
SLACK LA
THE CREST
ALSTONFIELD DR
QUEENSWAY
SONGBIRD CL
DUFFIELD RD
LAVENDER ROW
COPPICE CL
MILE ASH LA
HASKEYS CL
NETHER PARK DR
OSIERS CL
COPPICE END RD
KEDLESTON RD
AMBER RD
THE GREEN
LONGFORD CL
DOVEDALE RISE
KEDLESTON CL
HULLAND VIEW
JACKSDALE CL
FINDERN CL
EDALE CL
CARSINGTON CRES
THORPELANDS DR
CARSINGTON MEWS
WESSINGTON MEWS
WYASTON CL
BERRY PARK CL
LANSCOMBE PARK RD
MARCHINGTON CL
HIGHFIELDS PK
HIGHFIELDS PK DR
CATHERINE McAULEY HO
BENDAN GDNS
BEECHWOOD PK
BEECHWOOD DR
VICARWOOD AVE
WINDLEY CRES
DARLEY PARK RD
DARLEY PARK DR
MARKEATON LA

32 33 34

203
218

D2
1 CARSINGTON HO
2 NORBURY CT
3 KEDLESTON CT

F2
1 WICKERSLEY CL
2 MALTBY CL
3 ST HUGH'S CL
4 ST MATTHEW'S WLK
5 ABBEYCROFT LA

F3
1 BIRCHOVER HO
2 CHURCH LA N
3 TUDOR CT
4 CHURCH LA
5 DEVONSHIRE CT
6 DUFFIELD RD

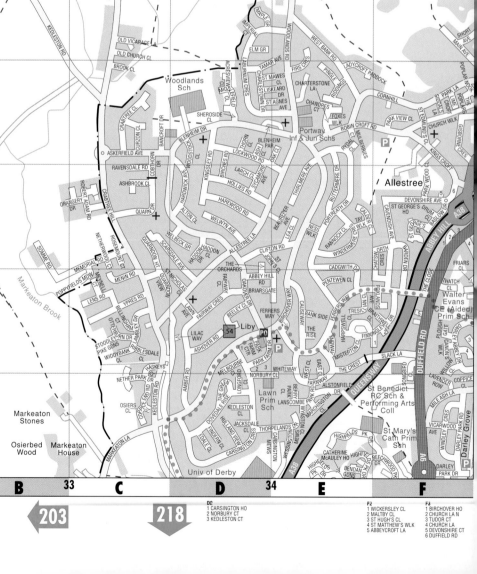

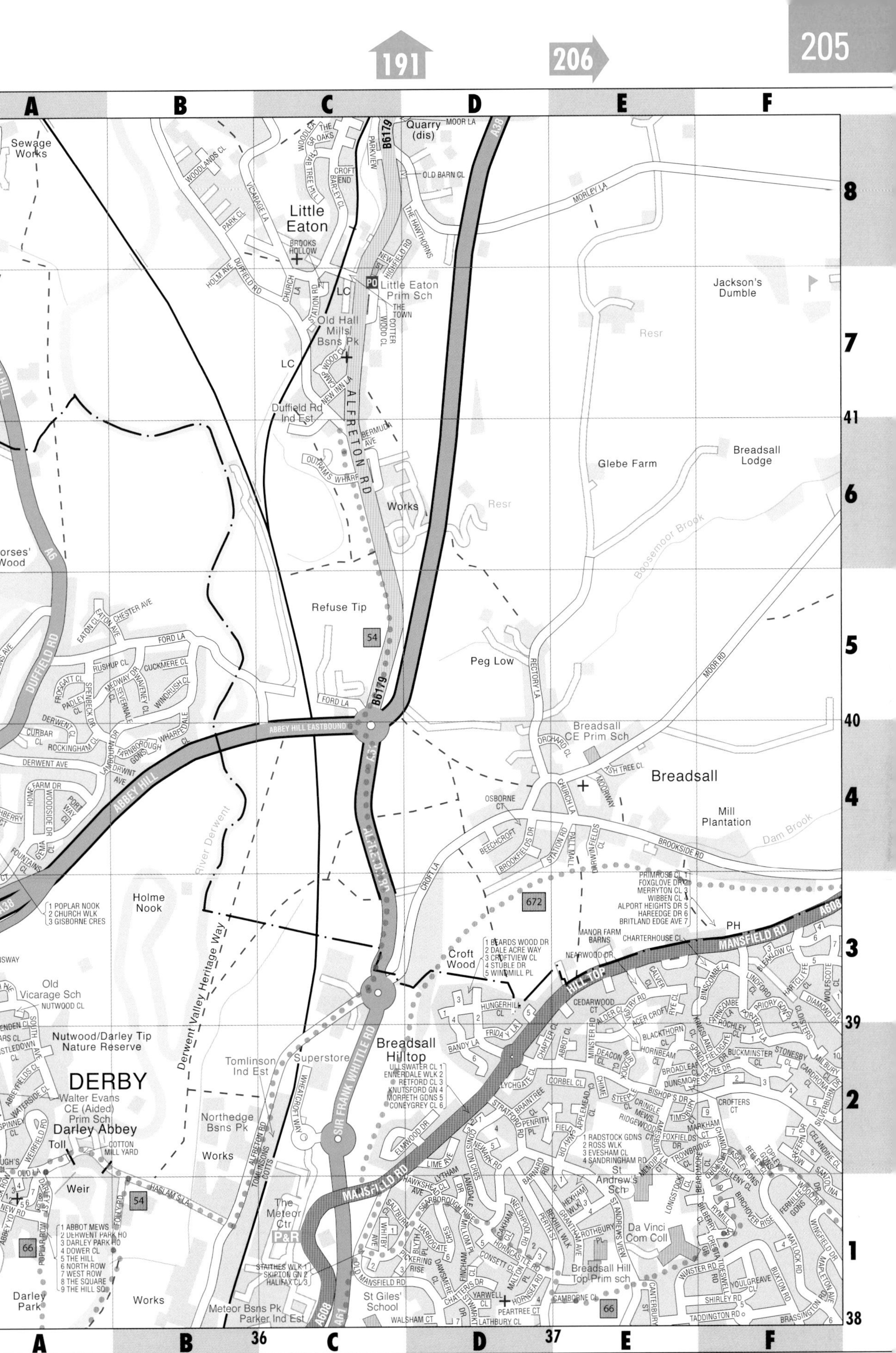

D1
1 KENDAL WLK
2 LEDBURY PL
3 MALVERN WAY
4 FILEY WLK
5 SEASCALE CL
6 REDCAR GDNS
7 WOODHURST CL

F1
1 INGLEDEW CL
2 HEATHERMEAD CL
3 BEAMWOOD CL
4 TANSLEY RISE
5 WOLLATON RD N
6 CHELMORTON PL

F2
1 CARDINAL CL
2 SEDGEBROOK CL
3 SOMERBY WAY
4 GARTHORPE CT
5 TWEEDS MUIR CL
6 PYKESTONE CL
7 HOUGHTON CT
8 RUTHERFORD RISE
9 PADDOCK CROFT
10 EMERALD CL

205
192

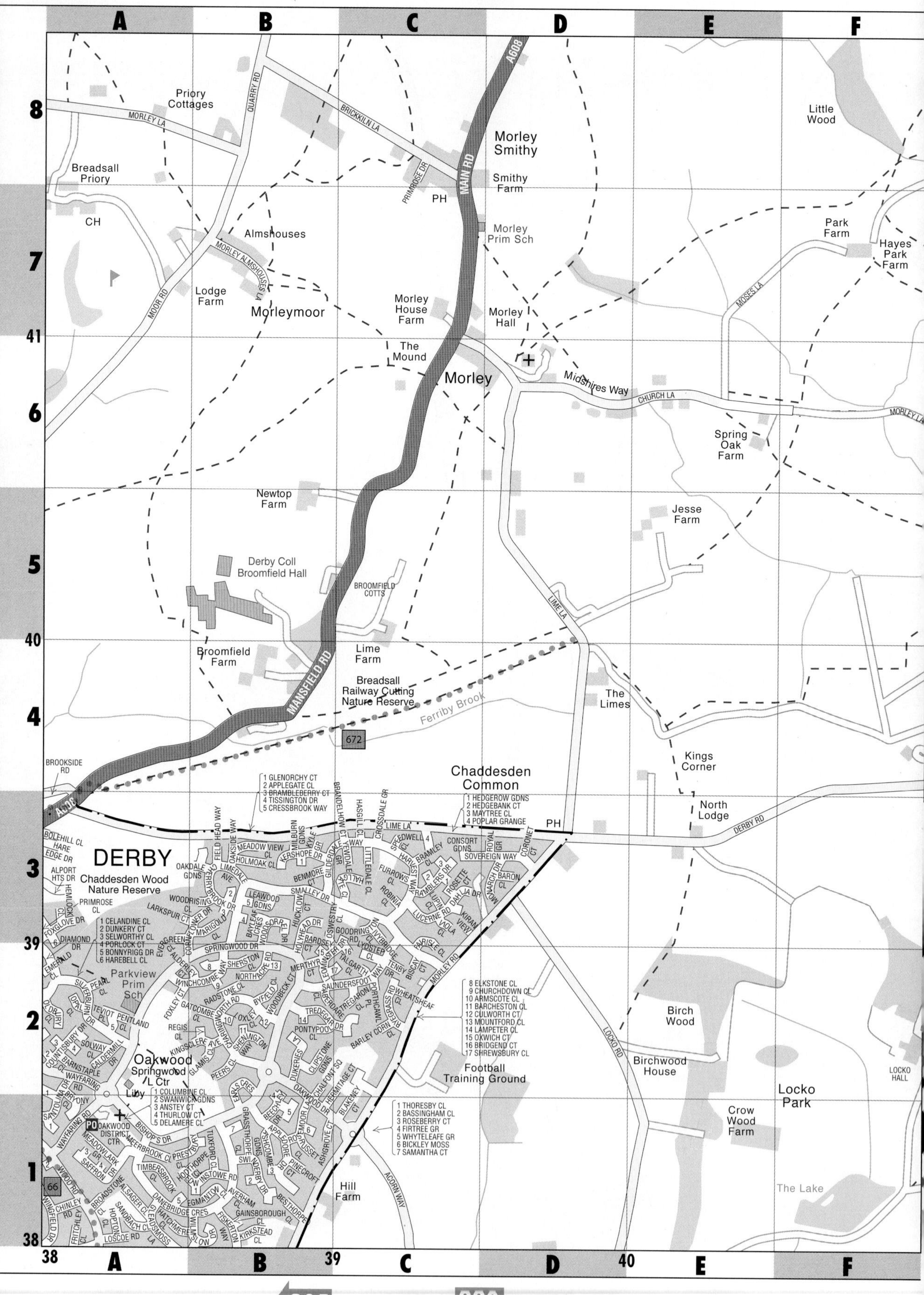
A
B
C
D
E
F
8
7
41
6
5
40
4
3
39
2
1
38
A608
MORLEY LA
Priory Cottages
QUARRY RD
BRICKKILN LA
Little Wood
Morley Smithy
Breadsall Priory
MAIN RD
Smithy Farm
PRIMROSE DR
PH
CH
Almshouses
Morley Prim Sch
Park Farm
Hayes Park Farm
MORLEY ALMSHOUSES LA
MOOR RD
Lodge Farm
Morleymoor
Morley House Farm
Morley Hall
MOSES LA
The Mound
Morley
Midshires Way
CHURCH LA
MORLEY LA
Spring Oak Farm
Newtop Farm
Jesse Farm
Derby Coll Broomfield Hall
BROOMFIELD COTTS
LIME LA
Broomfield Farm
Lime Farm
MANSFIELD RD
Breadsall Railway Cutting Nature Reserve
The Limes
Ferriby Brook
672
Kings Corner
BROOKSIDE RD
Chaddesden Common
North Lodge
DERBY RD
PH
DERBY
Chaddesden Wood Nature Reserve
Parkview Prim Sch
Oakwood
Springwood L Ctr
Football Training Ground
Birch Wood
Birchwood House
Locko Park
LOCKO HALL
Crow Wood Farm
LOCKO RD
Hill Farm
ACORN WAY
The Lake
Oakwood District Ctr
66
1 GLENORCHY CT
2 APPLEGATE CL
3 BRAMBLEBERRY CT
4 TISSINGTON DR
5 CRESSBROOK WAY
1 HEDGEROW GDNS
2 HEDGEBANK CT
3 MAYTREE CL
4 POPLAR GRANGE
1 CELANDINE CL
2 DUNKERY CT
3 SELWORTHY CL
4 PORLOCK CT
5 BONNYRIGG DR
6 HAREBELL CL
8 ELKSTONE CL
9 CHURCHDOWN CL
10 ARMSCOTE CL
11 BARCHESTON CL
12 CULWORTH CT
13 MOUNTFORD CL
14 LAMPETER CL
15 OXWICH CT
16 BRIDGEND CT
17 SHREWSBURY CL
1 COLUMBINE CL
2 SWANWICK GDNS
3 ANSTEY CT
4 THURLOW CT
5 DELAMERE CL
1 THORESBY CL
2 BASSINGHAM CL
3 ROSEBERRY CT
4 FIRTREE GR
5 WHYTELEAFE GR
6 BICKLEY MOSS
7 SAMANTHA CT
38
39
40

205
220

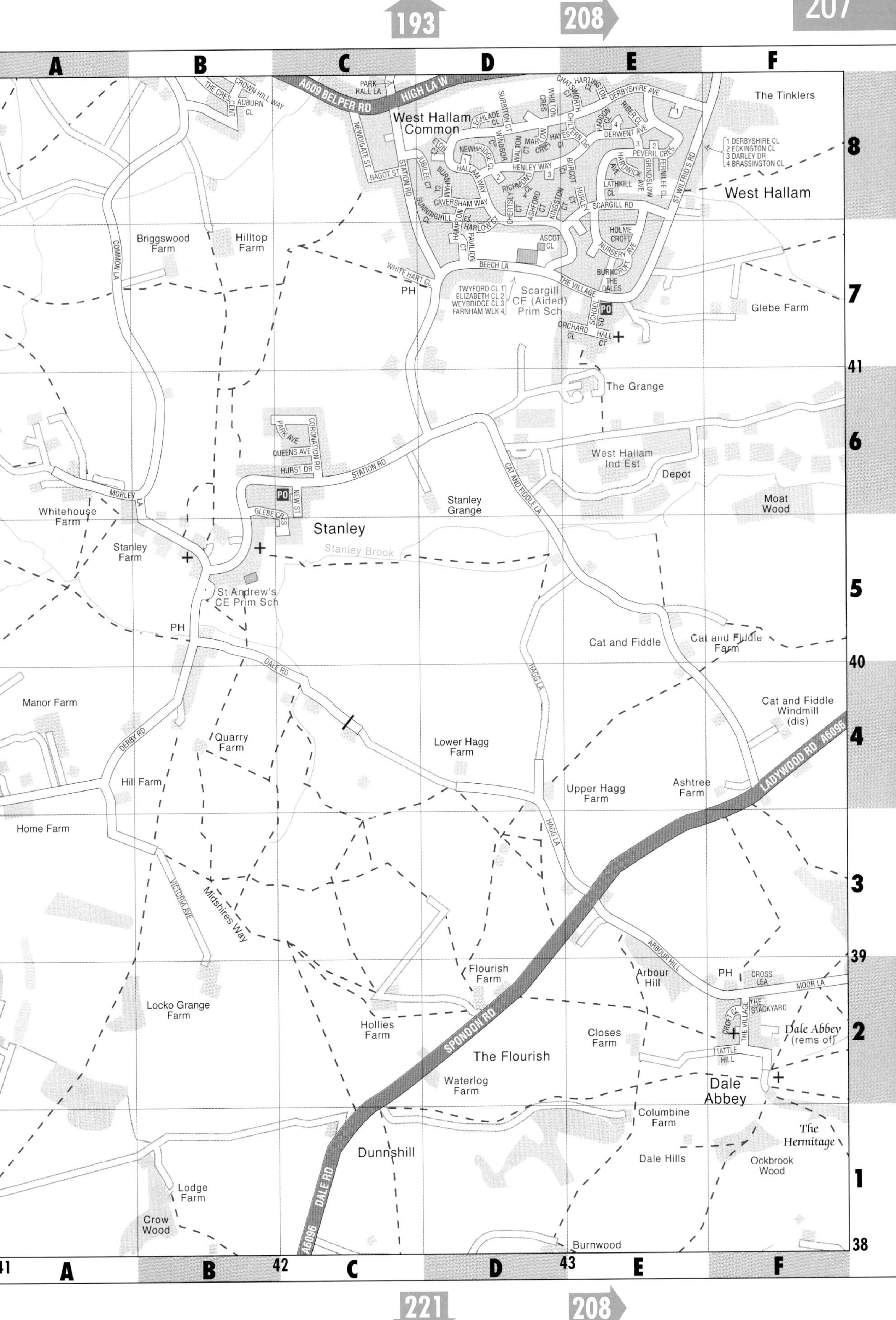
193
208
A
B
C
D
E
F
A609 BELPER RD
HIGH LA W
PARK HALL LA
West Hallam Common
West Hallam
The Tinklers
1 DERBYSHIRE CL
2 ECKINGTON CL
3 DARLEY DR
4 BRASSINGTON CL
Briggswood Farm
Hilltop Farm
COMMON LA
WHITE HART CL
PH
BEECH LA
THE VILLAGE
TWYFORD CL 1
ELIZABETH CL 2
WEYBRIDGE CL 3
FARNHAM WLK 4
Scargill CE (Aided) Prim Sch
PO
ORCHARD CL
HALL CT
Glebe Farm
The Grange
West Hallam Ind Est
Depot
Moat Wood
PARK AVE
QUEENS AVE
CORONATION RD
HURST DR
STATION RD
NEW ST
GLEBE CRES
MORLEY LA
Whitehouse Farm
Stanley Farm
Stanley
Stanley Brook
Stanley Grange
CAT AND FIDDLE LA
St Andrew's CE Prim Sch
PH
DALE RD
Cat and Fiddle
Cat and Fiddle Farm
Manor Farm
DERBY RD
Quarry Farm
HAGG LA
Lower Hagg Farm
Cat and Fiddle Windmill (dis)
LADYWOOD RD A6096
Hill Farm
Upper Hagg Farm
Ashtree Farm
Home Farm
VICTORIA AVE
Midshires Way
ARBOUR HILL
Flourish Farm
Arbour Hill
PH
CROSS LEA
MOOR LA
THE STACKYARD
Locko Grange Farm
Hollies Farm
SPONDON RD
Closes Farm
Dale Abbey (rems of)
The Flourish
TATTLE HILL
Waterlog Farm
Dale Abbey
Columbine Farm
The Hermitage
Dunnshill
Dale Hills
Ockbrook Wood
Lodge Farm
DALE RD
A6096
Crow Wood
Burnwood
41
42
43
38
39
40
41
1
2
3
4
5
6
7
8
221
208

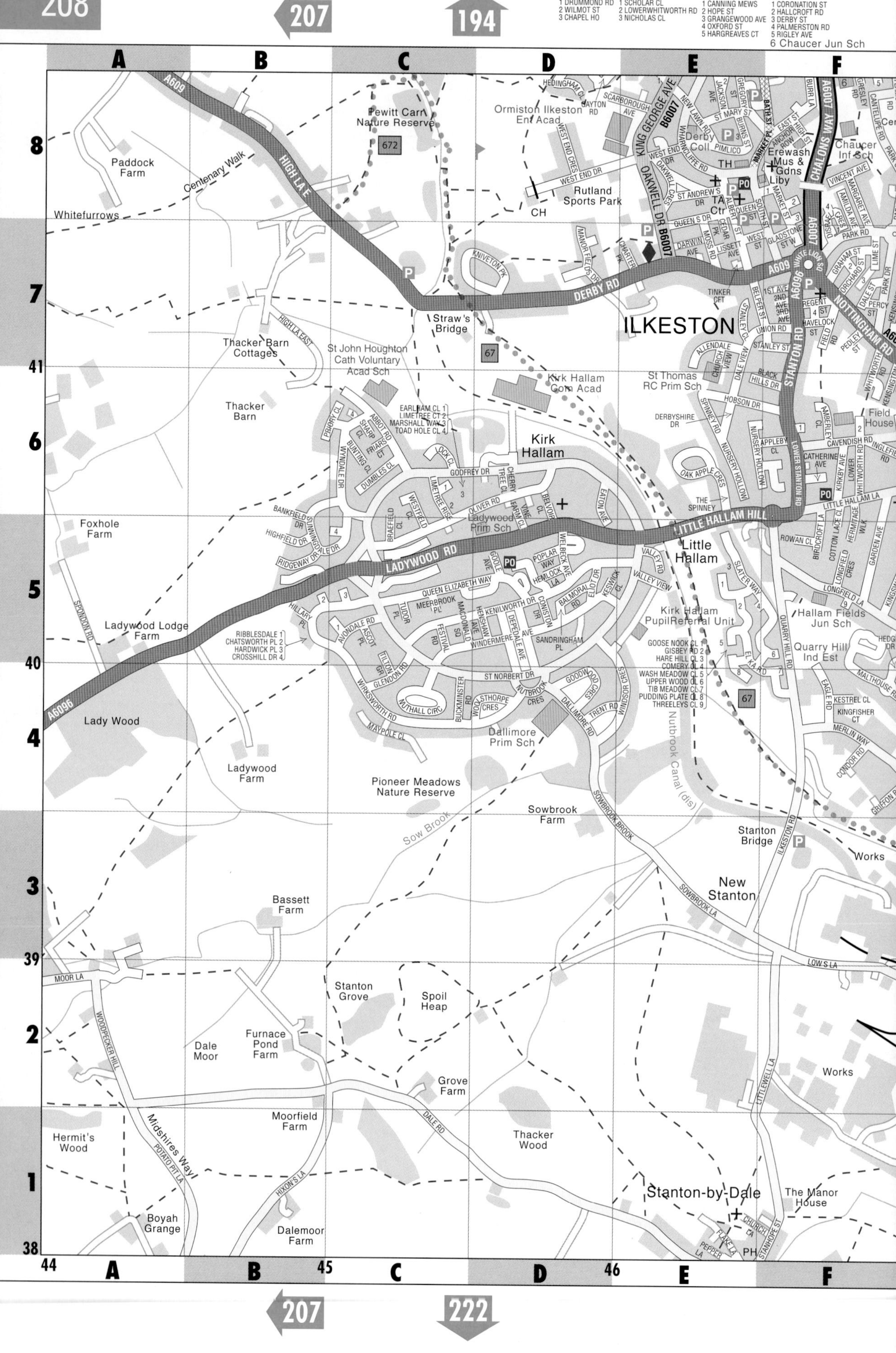

195

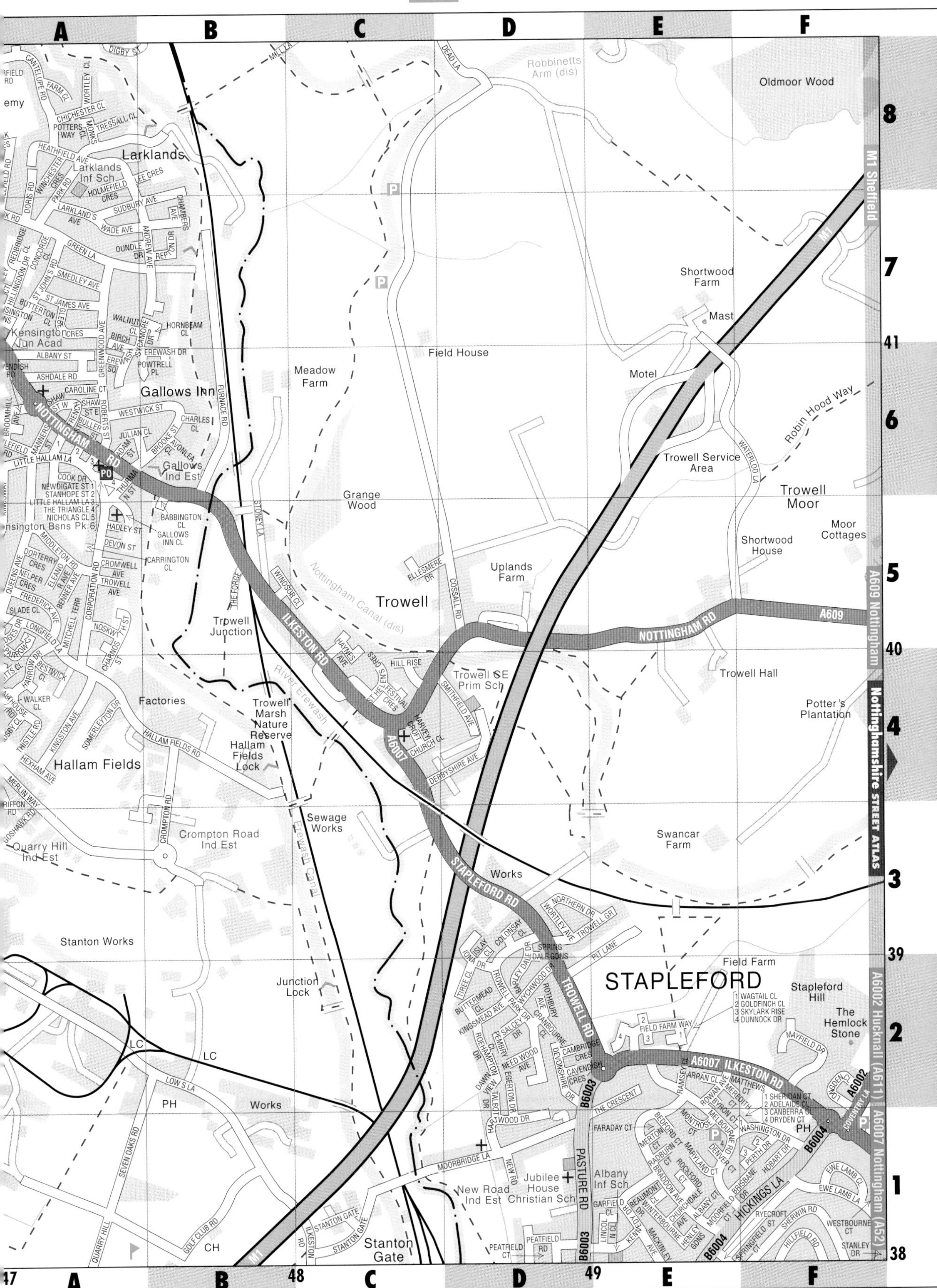
A
B
C
D
E
F
8
7
41
6
5
40
4
3
39
2
1
38
47
48
49
Larklands
Larklands Inf Sch
Kensington Jun Acad
Gallows Inn
Gallows Ind Est
Kensington Bsns Pk
Robbinetts Arm (dis)
Oldmoor Wood
Shortwood Farm
Mast
Field House
Meadow Farm
Motel
Robin Hood Way
Trowell Service Area
Trowell Moor
Moor Cottages
Shortwood House
Grange Wood
Uplands Farm
Trowell
Nottingham Canal (dis)
Trowell Junction
Trowell CE Prim Sch
Trowell Hall
Potter's Plantation
Factories
Trowell Marsh Nature Reserve
Hallam Fields Lock
Hallam Fields
River Erewash
Sewage Works
Crompton Road Ind Est
Quarry Hill Ind Est
Swancar Farm
Works
Stanton Works
STAPLEFORD
Field Farm
Stapleford Hill
The Hemlock Stone
Junction Lock
Erewash Canal
LC
PH
CH
Works
New Road Ind Est
Jubilee House Christian Sch
Albany Inf Sch
Stanton Gate
NOTTINGHAM RD
ILKESTON RD
STAPLEFORD RD
TROWELL RD
A6007 ILKESTON RD
A609
M1
M1 Sheffield
A609 Nottingham
Nottinghamshire STREET ATLAS
A6002 Hucknall (A611)
A6007 Nottingham (A52)
1 WAGTAIL CL
2 GOLDFINCH CL
3 SKYLARK RISE
4 DUNNOCK DR
1 SHERIDAN CT
2 ADELAIDE CL
3 CANBERRA CL
4 DRYDEN CT
NEWDIGATE ST 1
STANHOPE ST 2
LITTLE HALLAM LA 3
THE TRIANGLE 4
NICHOLAS CL 5
Kensington Bsns Pk 6

223

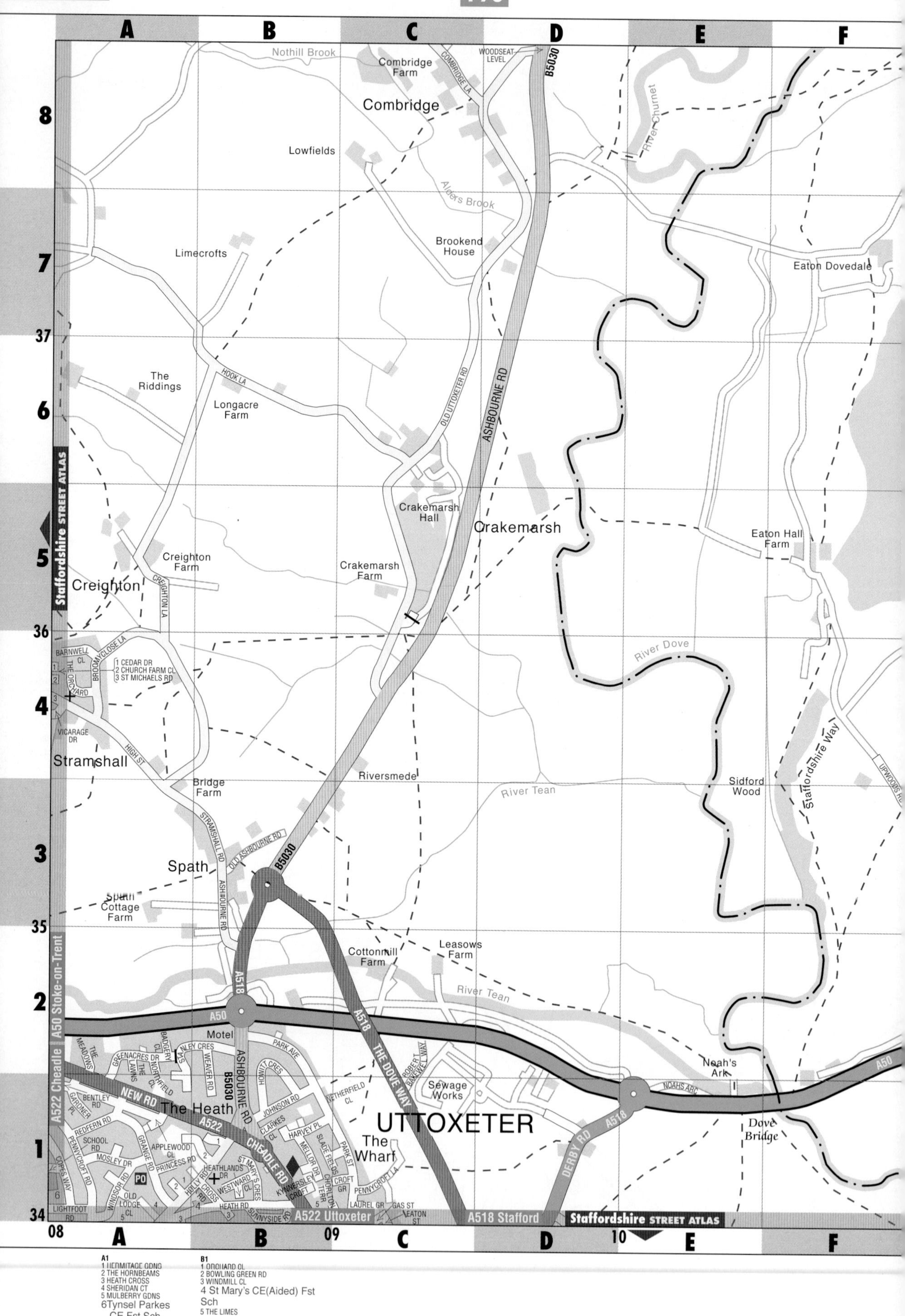

A1
1 HERMITAGE GDNS
2 THE HORNBEAMS
3 HEATH CROSS
4 SHERIDAN CT
5 MULBERRY GDNS
6 Tynsel Parkes
CE Fst Sch

B1
1 ORCHARD CL
2 BOWLING GREEN RD
3 WINDMILL CL
4 St Mary's CE(Aided) Fst
Sch
5 THE LIMES

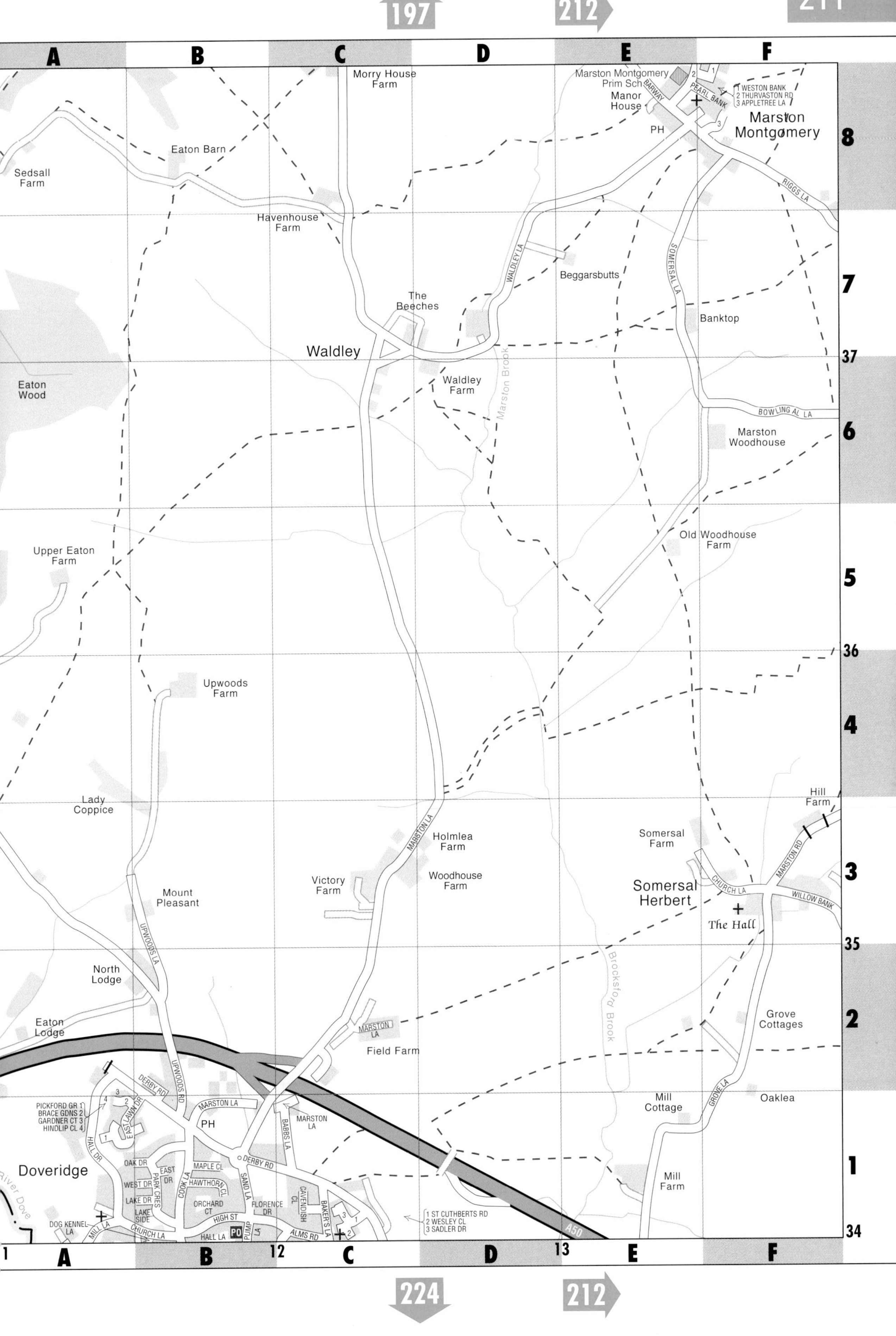

197
212
224
212

Morry House Farm

Marston Montgomery Prim Sch
Manor House
PH

1 WESTON BANK
2 THURVASTON RD
3 APPLETREE LA

Marston Montgomery

Eaton Barn

Havenhouse Farm

Beggarsbutts

The Beeches

Waldley

Banktop

Waldley Farm

Marston Woodhouse

Sedsall Farm

Eaton Wood

Upper Eaton Farm

Old Woodhouse Farm

Upwoods Farm

Lady Coppice

Hill Farm

Holmlea Farm

Somersal Farm

Victory Farm

Woodhouse Farm

Somersal Herbert

The Hall

Mount Pleasant

North Lodge

Grove Cottages

Eaton Lodge

Marston LA

Field Farm

Mill Cottage

Oaklea

PICKFORD GR 1
BRACE GDNS 2
GARDNER CT 3
HINDLIP CL 4

Mill Farm

Doveridge

PH

Marston LA

1 ST CUTHBERTS RD
2 WESLEY CL
3 SADLER DR

DOG KENNEL LA

OAK DR
WEST DR
LAKE DR
LAKE SIDE
ORCHARD CT
MAPLE CL
HAWTHORN CL
HIGH ST
FLORENCE DR
CAVENDISH CL
ALMS RD

River Dove

HALL DR
MILL LA
CHURCH LA
HALL LA
DERBY RD
UPWOODS LA
BABBS LA
SAND LA
BAKER'S LA
PARK CRES
COOK LA

MARSTON LA
MARSTON BROOK
WALDLEY LA
BARWAY
PEARL BANK
SOMERSAL LA
RIGGS LA
BOWLING AL LA
MARSTON RD
CHURCH LA
WILLOW BANK
GROVE LA
BROCKSFORD BROOK
A50

211
198
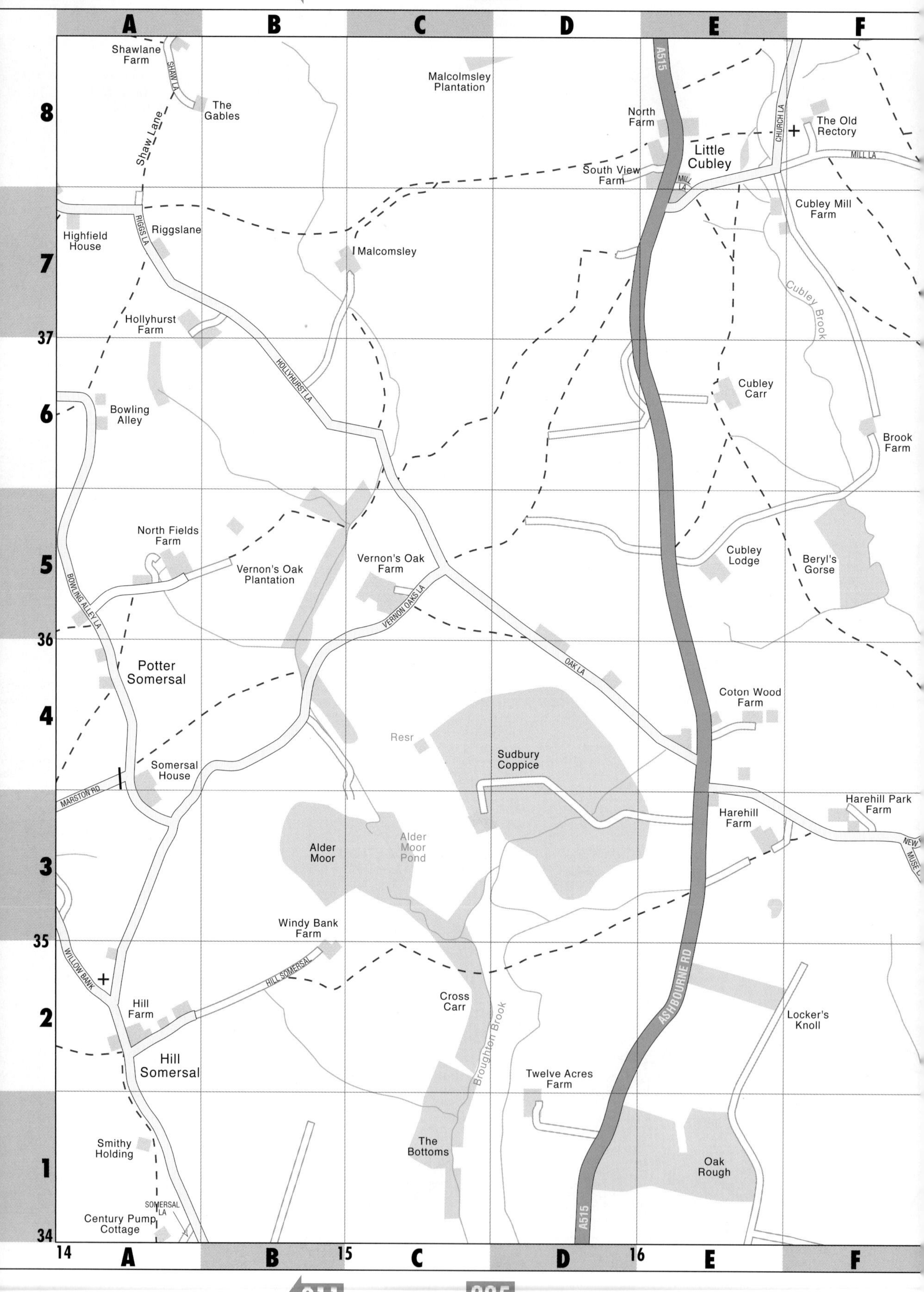
Shawlane Farm
SHAW LA
The Gables
Shaw Lane
Malcolmsley Plantation
A515
North Farm
Little Cubley
South View Farm
MILL LA
CHURCH LA
The Old Rectory
MILL LA
Cubley Mill Farm
Highfield House
RIGGS LA
Riggslane
Malcomsley
Cubley Brook
Hollyhurst Farm
HOLLYHURST LA
Bowling Alley
Cubley Carr
Brook Farm
North Fields Farm
Vernon's Oak Plantation
Vernon's Oak Farm
VERNON OAKS LA
BOWLING ALLEY LA
Cubley Lodge
Beryl's Gorse
Potter Somersal
OAK LA
Coton Wood Farm
Resr
Sudbury Coppice
Somersal House
MARSTON RD
Harehill Farm
Harehill Park Farm
NEW MUSE LA
Alder Moor
Alder Moor Pond
Windy Bank Farm
WILLOW BANK
HILL SOMERSAL
Cross Carr
Broughton Brook
ASHBOURNE RD
Locker's Knoll
Hill Farm
Hill Somersal
Twelve Acres Farm
Smithy Holding
The Bottoms
Oak Rough
SOMERSAL LA
Century Pump Cottage
A515
A B C D E F
8 7 37 6 5 36 4 3 35 2 1 34
14 15 16
211
225

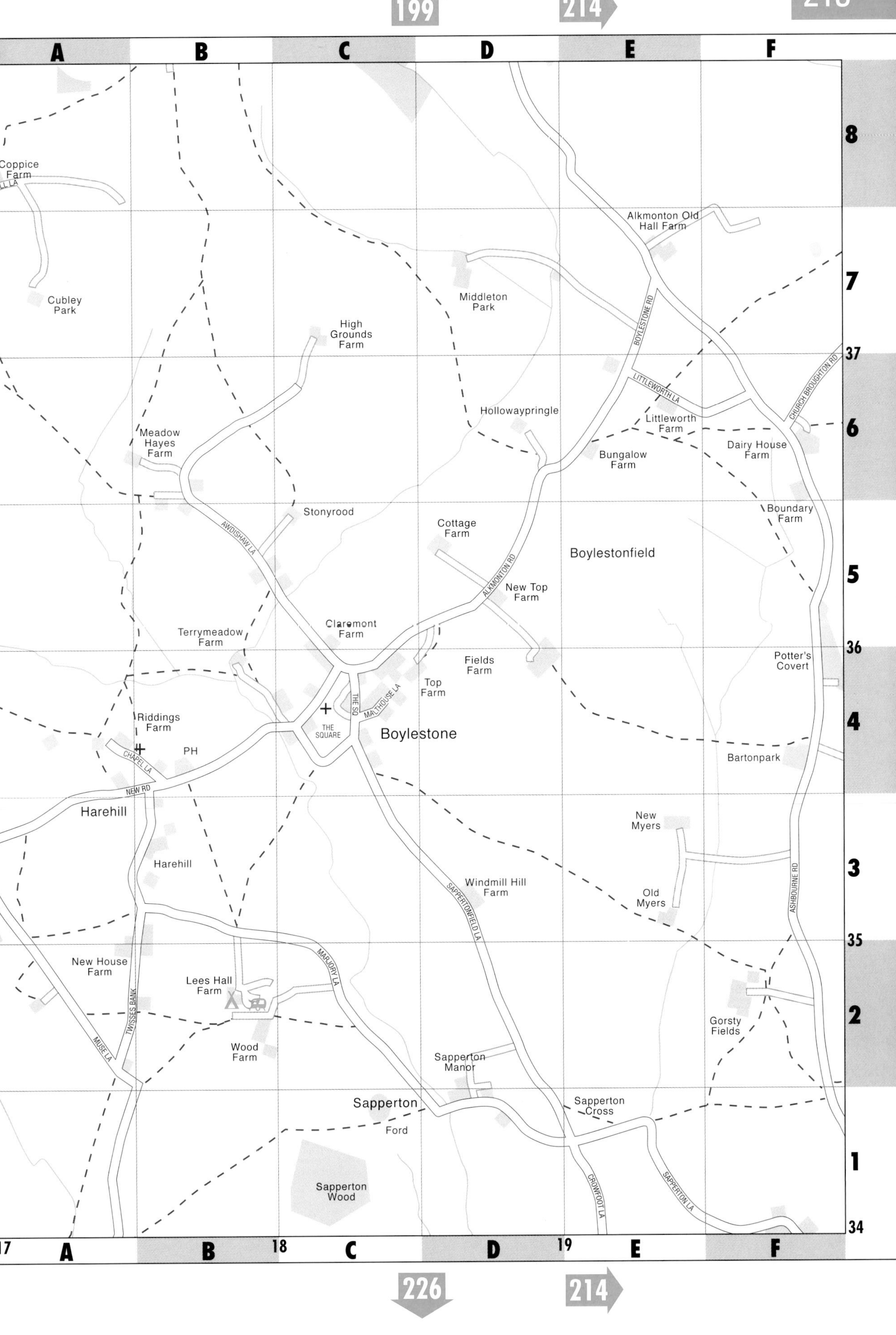

A   **B**   **C**   **D**   **E**   **F**

Coppice Farm

Cubley Park

High Grounds Farm

Middleton Park

Alkmonton Old Hall Farm

Meadow Hayes Farm

Hollowaypringle

Littleworth Farm

Dairy House Farm

BOYLESTONE RD

LITTLEWORTH LA

CHURCH BROUGHTON RD

Stonyrood

Cottage Farm

Bungalow Farm

Boylestonfield

Boundary Farm

AWDISHAW LA

ALKMONTON RD

Terrymeadow Farm

Claremont Farm

New Top Farm

Fields Farm

Potter's Covert

THE SQ

MALTHOUSE LA

Top Farm

Riddings Farm

PH

THE SQUARE

Boylestone

Bartonpark

CHAPEL LA

New Myers

ASHBOURNE RD

NEW RD

Harehill

Harehill

Windmill Hill Farm

Old Myers

SAPPERTONFIELD LA

New House Farm

Lees Hall Farm

MARJORY LA

Gorsty Fields

TWISSES BANK

MUSE LA

Wood Farm

Sapperton Manor

Sapperton

Sapperton Cross

Sapperton Wood

Ford

CROWFOOT LA

SAPPERTON LA

A   **B**   **C**   **D**   **E**   **F**

8   7   37   6   5   36   4   3   35   2   1   34

17   18   19

A B C D E F

8

Alder
Carr

Silverhill
Farm

Long La

Longford
Oaks

Longford
CE VC
Prim Sch

Main St

PH

Ostrich
Farm

Long La

The
Grange

Longford

7

Church Broughton Rd

Newlands
Farm

Woodseats

Sepycoe La

Bupton
Farm

Bonnie Prince Charlie Wlk

Longford La

37

Brookfield
Farm

Marsh
Farm

Thurvaston La

Heathy
Close

West
Mammerton

Fourwinds

6

East
Mammerton

Hill Top
Farm

Lower
Thurvaston

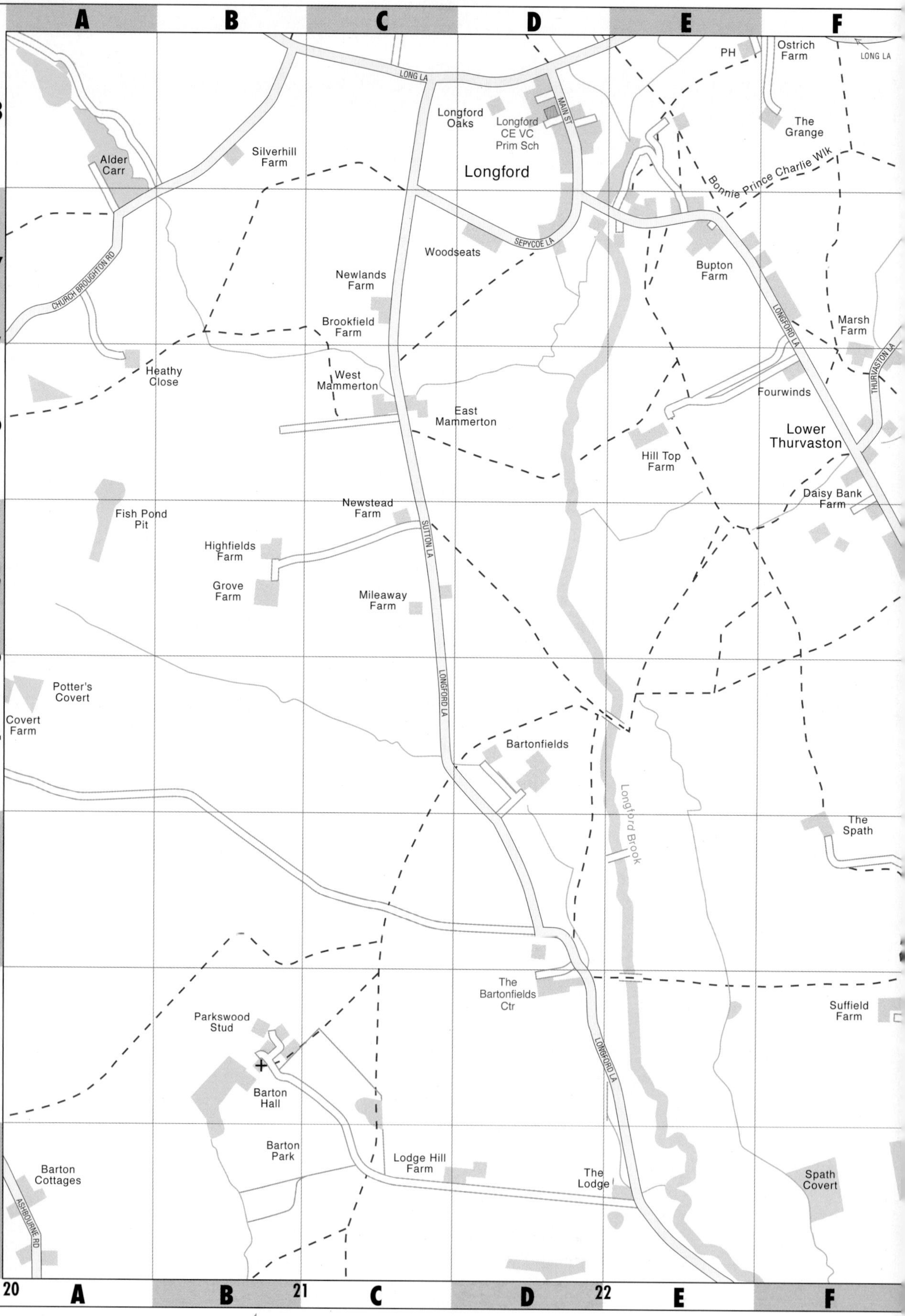

Fish Pond
Pit

Newstead
Farm

Sutton La

Daisy Bank
Farm

5

Highfields
Farm

Grove
Farm

Mileaway
Farm

36

Potter's
Covert

Longford La

4

Covert
Farm

Bartonfields

The
Spath

Longford Brook

3

35

Parkswood
Stud

The
Bartonfields
Ctr

Longford La

Suffield
Farm

2

Barton
Hall

Barton
Park

Lodge Hill
Farm

The
Lodge

Spath
Covert

1

Barton
Cottages

Ashbourne Rd

34

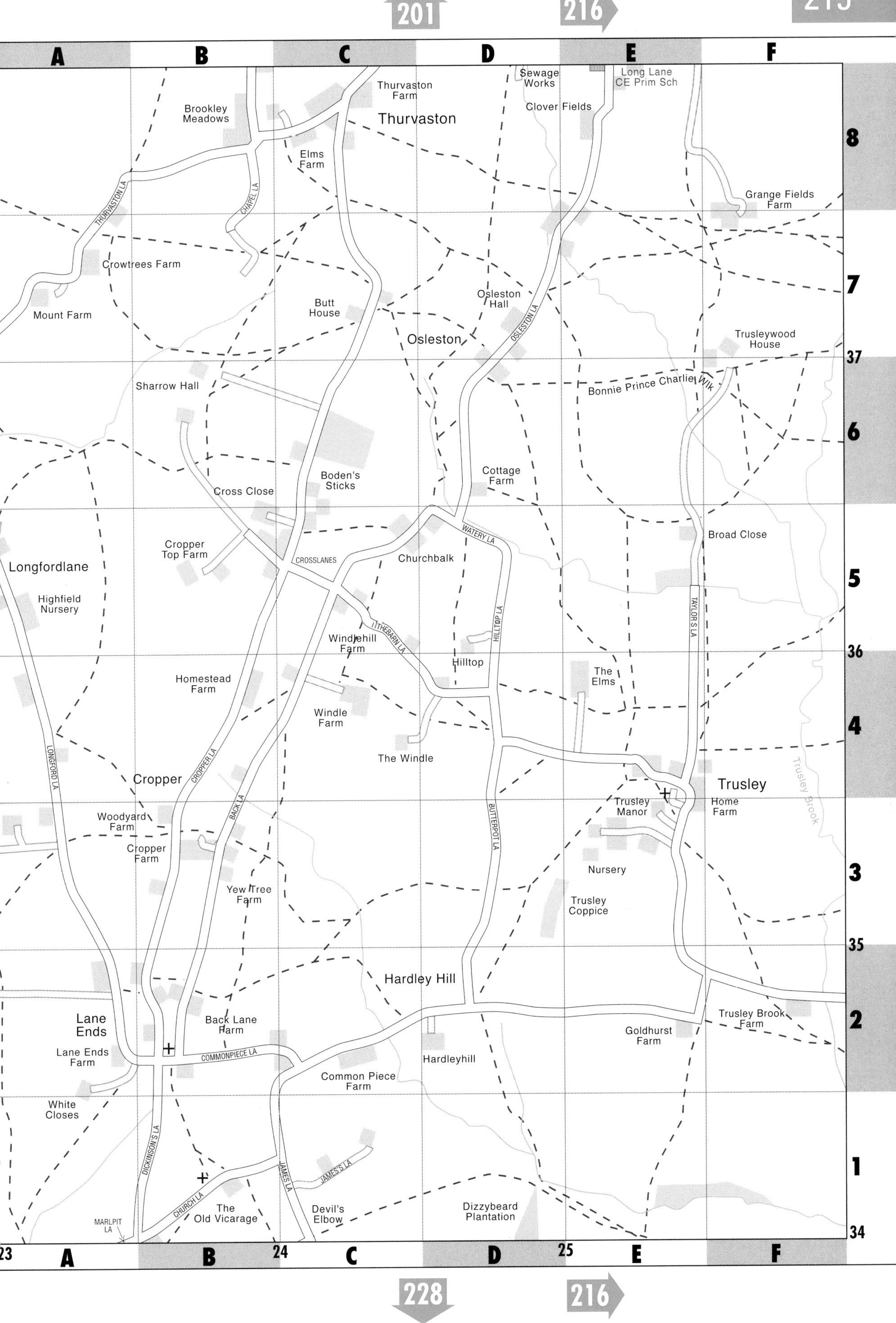

Thurvaston

Brookley Meadows

Thurvaston Farm

Elms Farm

Sewage Works

Long Lane CE Prim Sch

Clover Fields

Grange Fields Farm

Crowtrees Farm

Mount Farm

Butt House

Osleston Hall

Osleston

Trusleywood House

Bonnie Prince Charlie Wlk

Sharrow Hall

Boden's Sticks

Cottage Farm

Broad Close

Cross Close

Cropper Top Farm

CROSSLANES

Churchbalk

WATERY LA

Longfordlane

Highfield Nursery

Windlehill Farm

ITTHEBARN LA

Hilltop

HILLTOP LA

The Elms

Homestead Farm

Windle Farm

The Windle

Cropper

Woodyard Farm

CROPPER LA

BACK LA

Trusley

Trusley Manor

Home Farm

Cropper Farm

Yew Tree Farm

BUTTERPOT LA

Nursery

Trusley Coppice

Hardley Hill

Lane Ends

Back Lane Farm

COMMONPIECE LA

Hardleyhill

Goldhurst Farm

Trusley Brook Farm

Lane Ends Farm

White Closes

DICKINSON'S LA

Common Piece Farm

JAMES LA

JAMES LA

Devil's Elbow

Dizzybeard Plantation

MARLPIT LA

CHURCH LA

The Old Vicarage

LONGFORD LA

THURVASTON LA

CHAPEL LA

OSLESTON LA

TAYLOR'S LA

Trusley Brook

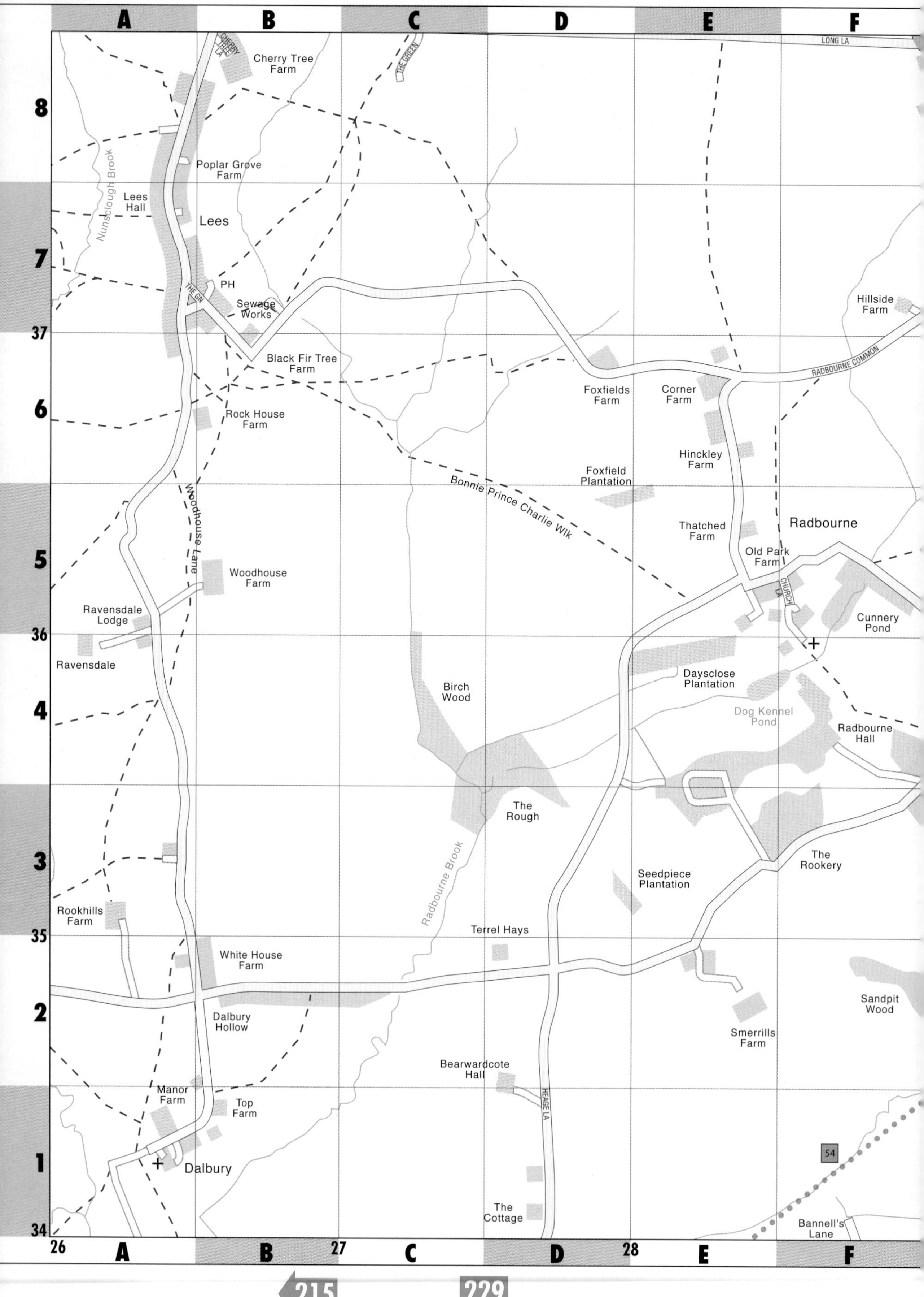

A   B   C   D   E   F

Long La

8

Cherry Tree Farm

Poplar Grove Farm

Nunslough Brook

Lees Hall

Lees

7

THE GN

PH

Sewage Works

Hillside Farm

37

Black Fir Tree Farm

Radbourne Common

6

Rock House Farm

Foxfields Farm

Corner Farm

Foxfield Plantation

Hinckley Farm

Bonnie Prince Charlie Wlk

Woodhouse Lane

Thatched Farm

Radbourne

5

Woodhouse Farm

Old Park Farm

CHURCH LA

Ravensdale Lodge

Cunnery Pond

36

Ravensdale

Daysclose Plantation

Dog Kennel Pond

Radbourne Hall

4

Birch Wood

The Rough

The Rookery

3

Radbourne Brook

Seedpiece Plantation

Rookhills Farm

35

Terrel Hays

White House Farm

Sandpit Wood

2

Dalbury Hollow

Smerrills Farm

Bearwardcote Hall

HEAGE LA

Manor Farm

Top Farm

54

1

Dalbury

Bannell's Lane

The Cottage

34

26   A   B   27   C   D   28   E   F

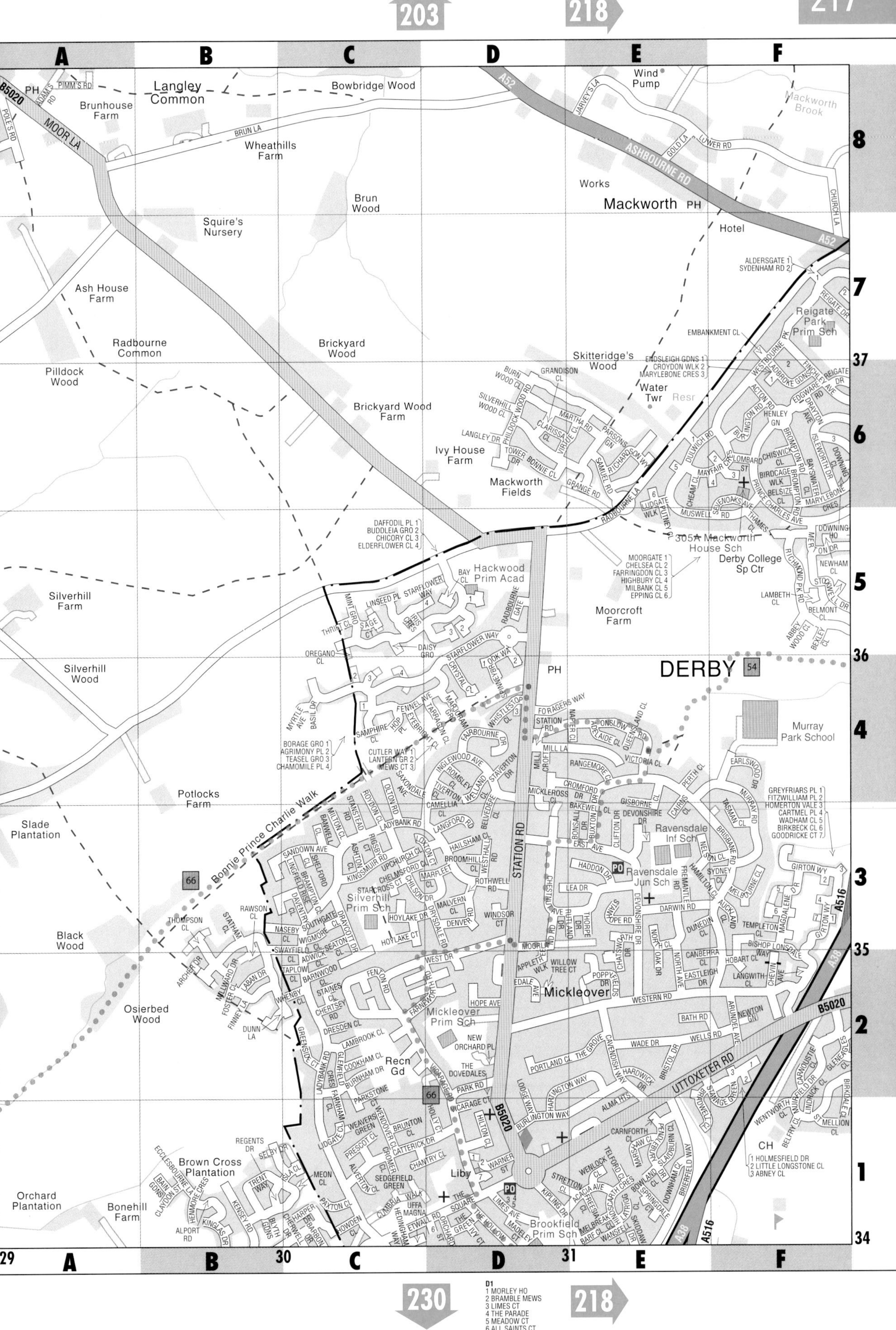

A B C D E F

8
7
37
6
5
36
4
35
3
2
1
34

A B C 30 D E 31 F

B5020
PH
PIMM'S RD
ADAM'S RD
POLE RD
MOOR LA

Brunhouse Farm
Wheathills Farm
Squire's Nursery
Brun Wood
BRUN LA

Langley Common
Bowbridge Wood

Ash House Farm
Radbourne Common
Brickyard Wood
Brickyard Wood Farm
BRICKYARD WOOD

Pilldock Wood

Silverhill Farm
Silverhill Wood

Slade Plantation

Potlocks Farm
Black Wood
Osierbed Wood

Bonnie Prince Charlie Walk

THOMPSON CL
ARCHER DR
MILLWARD DR
FOSTER CL
FINNEY LA
CABAN CL
DUNN LA

Brown Cross Plantation
Orchard Plantation
Bonehill Farm

ECCLESBOURNE DR
GLENDON RD
CLANDON DR
GUNSTON CL
BLYTH GDNS
ALPORT RD
KINGS CL
TRENT WAY
REGENTS DR
SELBY CL
HARPER
CRANFIELD
CAMBRAE
BLYTH GDNS

LANGLEY DR
TOWER DR
BONNIE CL
GRANGE RD
RADBOURNE LA
SAMUEL RD
RICHARDSON DR
PILLDOCK WOOD CL
SILVERHILL WOOD CL
CLARISSA CL
MARTHA RD
GRANDISON CL
BURN WOOD DR

Ivy House Farm
Mackworth Fields
Mackworth House Sch

DAFFODIL PL 1
BUDDLEIA GRO 2
CHICORY CL 3
ELDERFLOWER CL 4

Hackwood Prim Acad

LINSEED PL
STARFLOWER WAY
THRIFT
SAGE CT
MINT GRO
OREGANO CL
DAISY GRO
STARFLOWER WAY
CRYSTAL CL
MYRTLE AVE
BASIL DR
FENNEL AVE
SAMPHIRE CL
ELDERBERRY
MARJORAM
OAK WAY
RADBOURNE GATE

BORAGE GRO 1
AGRIMONY PL 2
TEASEL GRO 3
CHAMOMILE PL 4

CUTLER WAY 1
LANTERN GR 2
MEWS CT 3

STANSTED
MILTON CL
BANWELL
ROXTON CL
UPCHURCH
KINGSMUIR RD
SANDOWN
SHEFFORD
BRAMERTON
OXENDON
CHELMSFORD CL
MARFLEET
SAXONDALE AVE
INGLEWOOD AVE
ROWSLEY
OVERTON
SILVERTON
WELLAND
FARBOURNE
CAMELLIA
LANGFORD
BROOMHILL
ROTHWELL
HAILSHAM CL

Silverhill Prim Sch

RAWSON CL
SINTHAN CL
NASEBY CL
SOUTHGATE
VALENTINE
WIGMORE CL
SEATON CL
ADWICK
ARCHER DR
TAPLOW CL
BARNWOOD
STAINES
CHERTSEY RD
FEN CL
WHENBY
DRESDEN CL
LAMBROOK CL
GREENSIDE
GLENEAGLES
GLOOKHAM CL
FARNHAM
BURNHAM DR
PARKSTONE
WEAVERS GREEN
PRESCOT CL
CATTERICK DR
CHANTRY CL
WARNER ST
HILTON CL
HOLLY CL
VICARAGE CT

MEON CL
ALPERTON
LIDGATE
BRUNTON CL
SEDGEFIELD GREEN
HENINGHAM
CAMBRIA WALK
PAXTON CL
ETWALL

HOYLAKE DR
HOYLAKE CT
MALVERN CL
DENVER
WINDSOR CT
WEST DR
HOPE AVE
MICKLEOVER
APPLETREE
WILLOW TREE CT
MOORL LA
EDALE
PENDEDALE
NEW ORCHARD PL
THE DOVEDALES
PARK RD
BURLINGTON WAY

Mickleover Prim Sch

STATION RD
B5020
LODGE LANE
WENTWORTH WAY
KIPLING DR
STRETTON CL
WE
THE SQUARE
THE GREEN
IVY CT
LIMES AVE
PO

Mickleover
Recn Gd
66

Liby

Brookfield Prim Sch

A52
ASHBOURNE RD
LOWER RD
GOLD LA
JARVEY S LA

Wind Pump
Works
Mackworth PH
Hotel

MACKWORTH
CHURCH LA
A52

ALDERSGATE 1
SYDENHAM RD 2
EMBANKMENT CL

Reigate Park Prim Sch

REIGATE DR
REIGATE AVE
EDGWARE RD
DRAYTON AVE
WESTBOURNE PK
LADBROKE GDNS
ACTON RD
HENLEY GN
BROMPTON AVE
BROMPTON CL
BURLINGTON PK
DULWICH RD
CHISWICK
LOMBARD ST
MAYFAIR
BIRDCAGE WLK
BELSIZE CL
MARYLEBONE CRES
BAYSWATER
ISWORTH CL
DOWNING
MARY EBONE
CHEAM CL
LUDGATE WLK
MUSWELL
SIENOAKS AVE
THAMES CL
CHARLES AVE
DOWNING HO
NEWHAM CL
STOCKWELL DR
RICHMOND CL
ABBEY WOOD CL
BEXLEY CL
BELMONT
LAMBETH CL
ON DR

Skitteridge's Wood
Water Twr
Resr
BURN WOOD CL DE
SILVERHILL WOOD CL
PARSONS
SAMEL RD

Moorcroft Farm

MOORGATE 1
CHELSEA CL 2
FARRINGDON CL 3
HIGHBURY CL 4
MILBANK CL 5
EPPING CL 6

305A Mackworth
Derby College Sp Ctr

PH
DERBY 54
36

STATION RD
FORAGERS WAY
WHISTLESTOP
NAPIER CL
ONSLOW CL
ADELAIDE AVE
QUEENSLAND CL
STATION RD
MILL LA
RANGEMORE DR
CROMFORD DR
MICKLEROSS
BAKEWELL CL
BOLSOVER
CLIFTON CL
VICTORIA CL
TEETH CL
CAIRNS
GISBORNE CL
DEVONSHIRE DR
EAST AVE
NORTH AVE
HADDON CL
CHESTNUT AVE
LEA DR
HOPE RD
THORPE
RUTLAND
DARWIN RD
CANBERRA
EASTLEIGH
HOBART CL
LANGWITH
CHEVIN
WESTERN AVE
BATH RD
WADE DR
WELLS RD
PORTLAND CL
THE GROVE
CAVENDISH WAY
HARTINGTON WAY
ALMA HTS
BRISTOL RD
HARDWICK
CARNFORTH
WENLOCK CL
TELFORD CL
MACAULAY
SCARCLIFFE CL
WANSFELL CL
MELBOURNE
AUCKLAND
TEMPLETON
BISHOP LONSDALE WAY
DUNEDIN
SYDNEY
GIRTON WY
EARLSWOOD DR
TASMAN CL
BRISBANE RD
MURRAY CL
HAMILTON CL
NELSON CL

Murray Park School

Ravensdale Inf Sch
Ravensdale Jun Sch
PO

GREYFRIARS PL 1
FITZWILLIAM PL 2
HOMERTON VALE 3
CARTMEL PL 4
WADHAM CL 5
BIRKBECK CL 6
GOODRICKE CT 7

A516
UTTOXETER RD
B5020
A516
A38
SWADALE CL
KEDLESTON CL
WARWICK CL
NEWLYN DR
STORAGE RD
STANHOPE
ARUNDEL AVE
NEWTON GN
WESTERN AVE
HOLMESFIELD DR
LITTLE LONGSTONE CL
ABNEY CL

CH
1 HOLMESFIELD DR
2 LITTLE LONGSTONE CL
3 ABNEY CL

D1
1 MORLEY HO
2 BRAMBLE MEWS
3 LIMES CT
4 THE PARADE
5 MEADOW CT
6 ALL SAINTS CT
7 HOLLY END RD

← 217   ↑ 204

E5
1 WENTWORTH HO
2 ALEXANDRA MILLS
3 ROWLEYS MILL
4 THE LANGTON

F7
1 KING'S MEAD HO
2 STRUTT'S PARK HO
3 BELPER RD
4 MILFORD ST

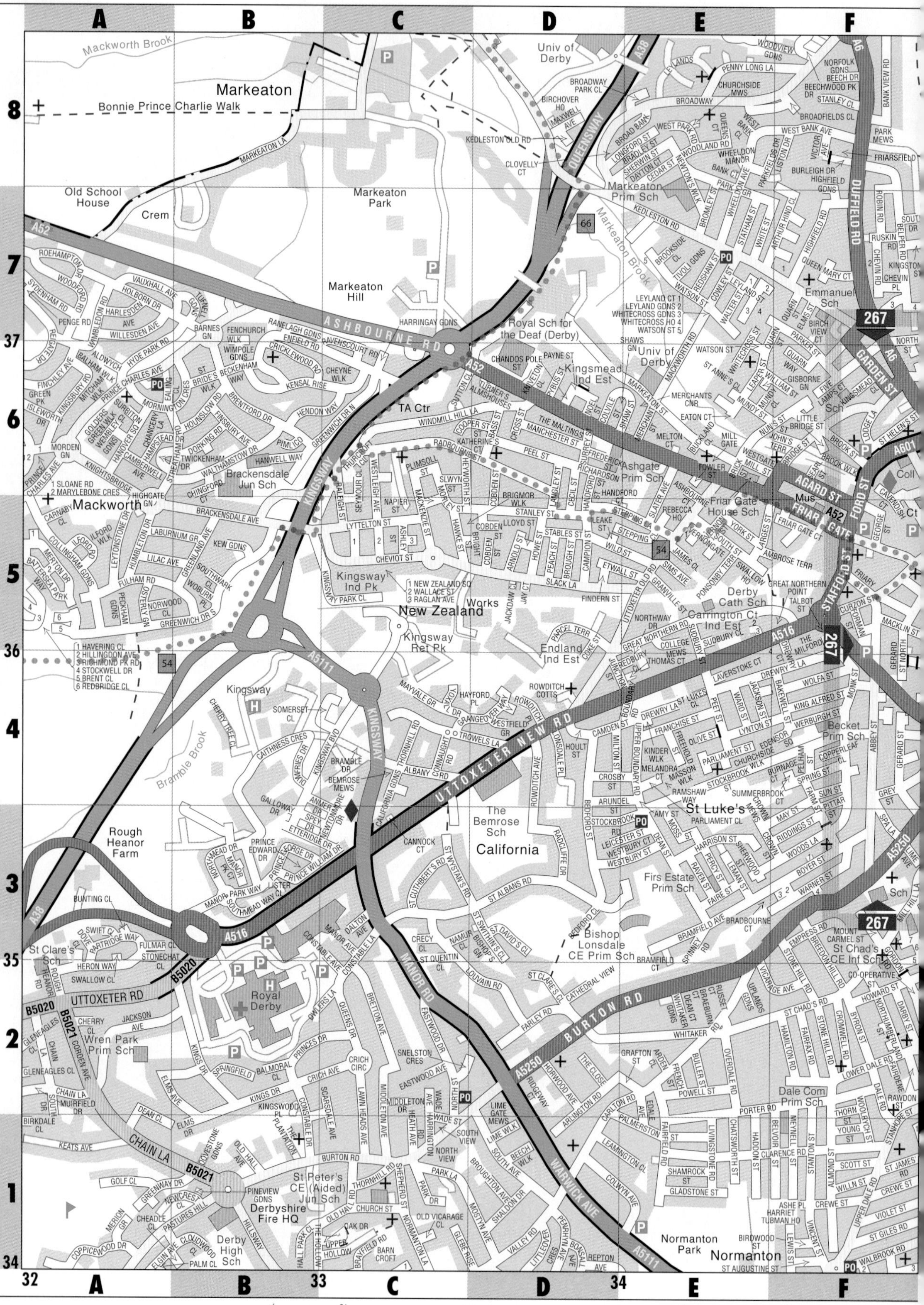

(Map of Derby area — Markeaton, Mackworth, New Zealand, California, St Luke's, Normanton, Uttoxeter Rd, Burton Rd, Ashbourne Rd.)

1 HAVERING CL
2 HILLINGDON AVE
3 RUISLIP PK RD
4 STOCKWELL DR
5 BRENT CT
6 REDBRIDGE CL

1 NEW ZEALAND SQ
2 WALLACE ST
3 RAGLAN AVE

C1
1 BEECHWOOD CRES

E3
1 VALE MILL
2 LORNE ST
3 APPLEBY CT
4 ARGYLE ST
5 UPPER BAINBRIGGE ST
6 TEMPLE ST
7 WESTERN RD

F8
1 HAGTINOG GT
2 DUNCAN RD
3 SUTHERLAND ST

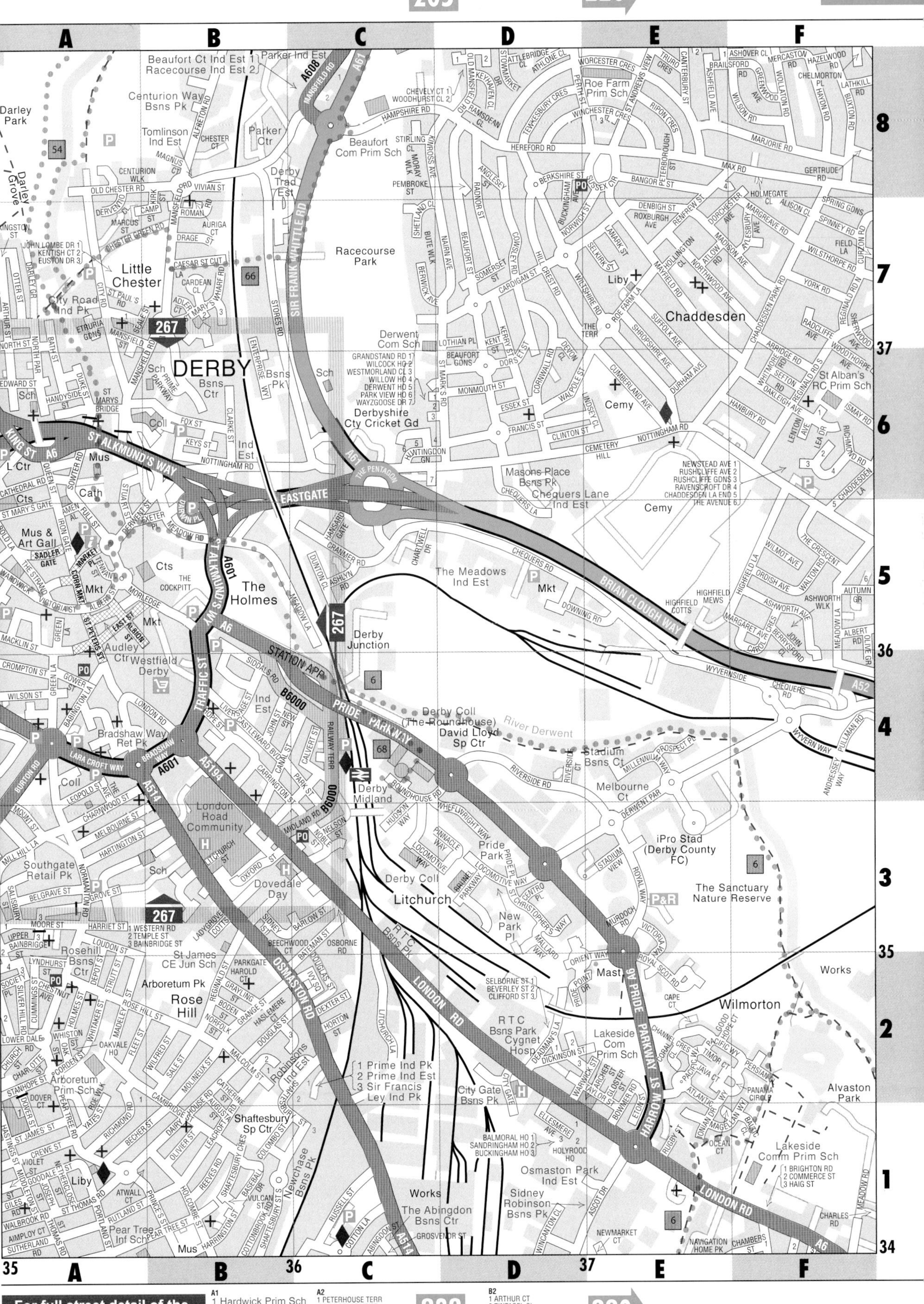

205

220

219

E8
1 ASHOVER RD
2 TADDINGTON CL
3 RINGWOOD CL
4 LIVERPOOL ST

For full street detail of the highlighted area see page 267.

A1
1 HARDWICK PRIM SCH

A2
1 PETERHOUSE TERR
2 CO-OPERATIVE ST
3 INDUSTRIAL ST
4 PROVIDENT ST

B2
1 ARTHUR CT
2 TINTAGEL CL
3 ALEXANDRA GDNS

219
206

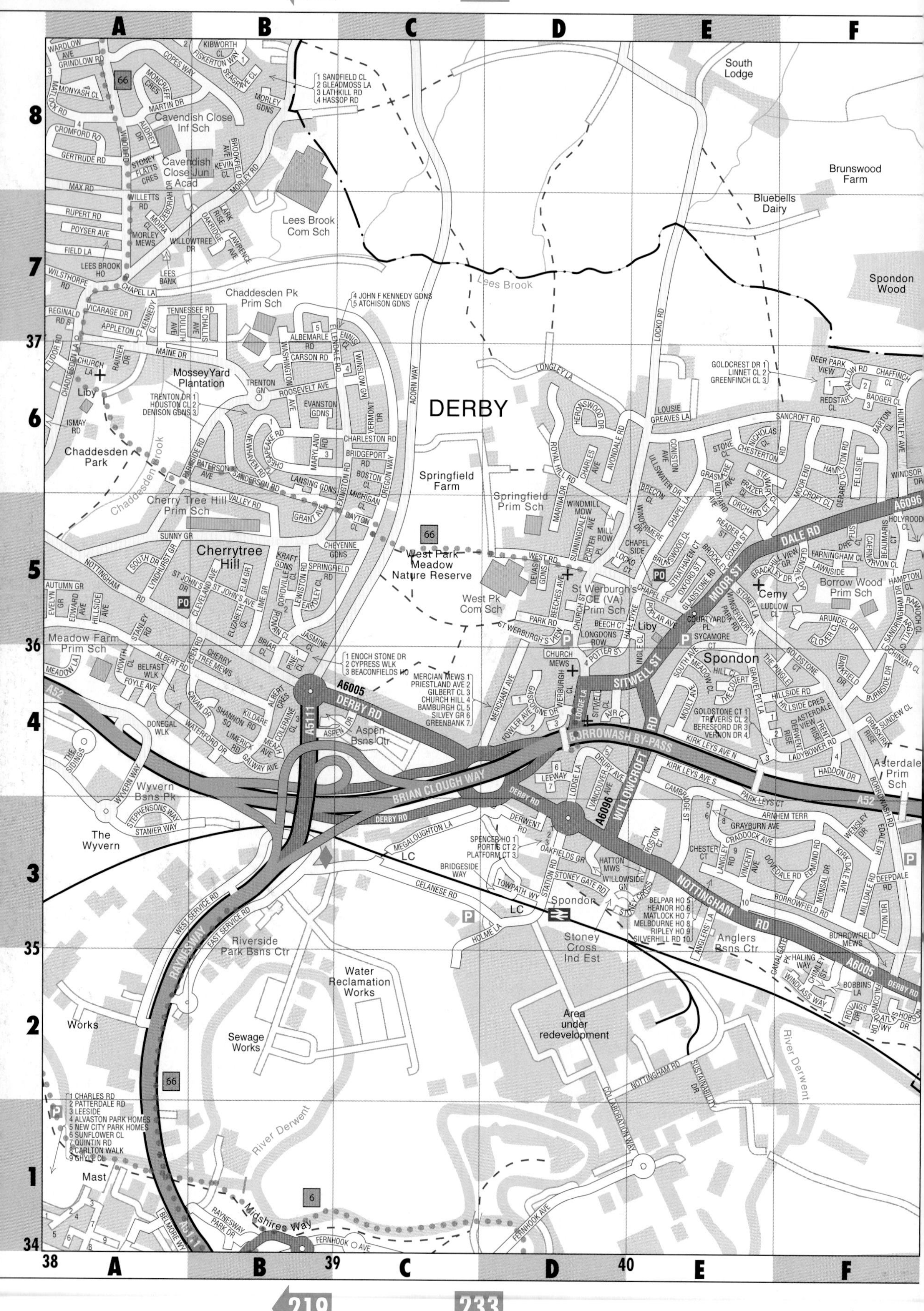
A
B
C
D
E
F
8
7
37
6
5
36
4
3
35
2
1
34
38
39
40
DERBY
South Lodge
Brunswood Farm
Bluebells Dairy
Spondon Wood
Lees Brook
Lees Brook Com Sch
Cavendish Close Inf Sch
Cavendish Close Jun Acad
Chaddesden Pk Prim Sch
MosseyYard Plantation
Chaddesden Park
Chaddesden Brook
Cherry Tree Hill Prim Sch
Cherrytree Hill
Meadow Farm Prim Sch
Springfield Farm
Springfield Prim Sch
West Park Meadow Nature Reserve
West Pk Com Sch
St Werburgh's CE (VA) Prim Sch
Spondon
Borrow Wood Prim Sch
Asterdale Prim Sch
Cemy
Liby
Aspen Bsns Ctr
Wyvern Bsns Pk
The Wyvern
Riverside Park Bsns Ctr
Water Reclamation Works
Sewage Works
Works
Stoney Cross Ind Est
Anglers Bsns Ctr
Area under redevelopment
River Derwent
Midshires Way
Mast
A52
A6005
A5111
A6096
DERBY RD
BRIAN CLOUGH WAY
BORROWASH BY-PASS
NOTTINGHAM RD
RAYNESWAY
ACORN WAY
LOCKO RD
DALE RD
MOOR ST
SITWELL ST
WILLOWCROFT RD
CELANESE RD
NOTTINGHAM RD
COLLABORATION WAY
SUSTAINABILITY DR
FERNHOOK AVE
1 SANDFIELD CL
2 GLEADMOSS LA
3 LATHKILL RD
4 HASSOP RD
4 JOHN F KENNEDY GDNS
5 ATCHISON GDNS
TRENTON DR 1
HOUSTON CL 2
DENISON GDNS 3
1 ENOCH STONE DR
2 CYPRESS WLK
3 BEACONFIELDS HO
MERCIAN MEWS 1
PRIESTLAND AVE 2
GILBERT CL 3
CHURCH HILL 4
BAMBURGH CL 5
SILVEY GR 6
GREENBANK 7
GOLDCREST DR 1
LINNET CL 2
GREENFINCH CL 3
GOLDSTONE CT 1
TREVERIS CL 2
BERESFORD DR 3
VERNON DR 4
SPENCER HO 1
PORTIS CT 2
PLATFORM CT 3
BELPAR HO 5
HEANOR HO 6
MATLOCK HO 7
MELBOURNE HO 8
RIPLEY HO 9
SILVERHILL RD 10
1 CHARLES RD
2 PATTERDALE RD
3 LEESIDE
4 ALVASTON PARK HOMES
5 NEW CITY PARK HOMES
6 SUNFLOWER CL
7 QUINTIN RD
8 CARLTON WALK
9 GHYLL CL

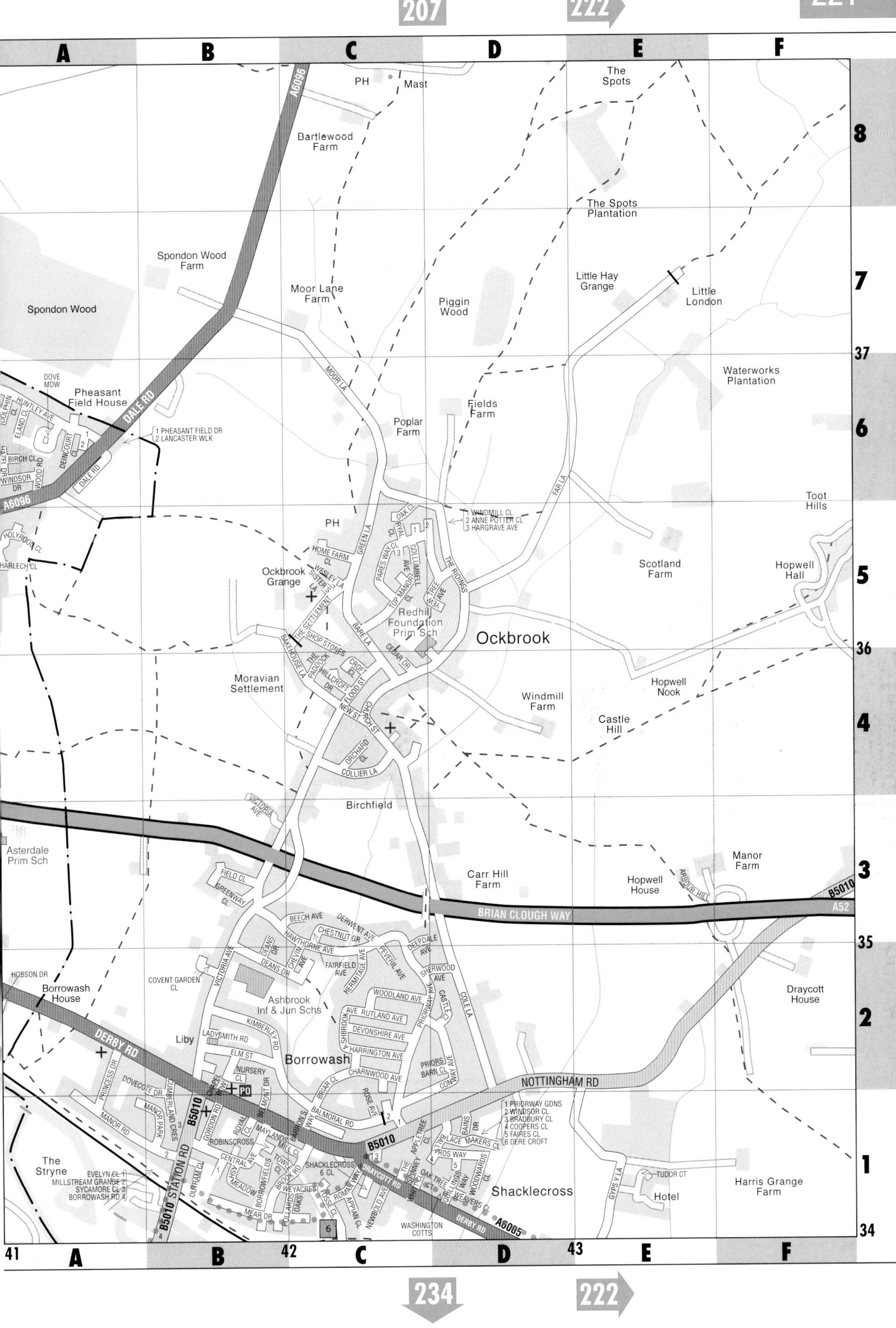

A B C D E F

8
7
37
6
5
36
4
3
35
2
1
34

The Spots
PH Mast
Bartlewood Farm
Spondon Wood Farm
Moor Lane Farm
The Spots Plantation
Piggin Wood
Little Hay Grange
Little London
Spondon Wood
Waterworks Plantation

DOVE MDW
Pheasant Field House
1 PHEASANT FIELD DR
2 LANCASTER WLK
Poplar Farm
Fields Farm
Toot Hills

HOLYROOD CL
HARLECH CL
PH
HOME FARM
Ockbrook Grange
1 WINDMILL CL
2 ANNE POTTER CL
3 HARGRAVE AVE
Scotland Farm
Hopwell Hall

Redhill Foundation Prim Sch
Ockbrook

Moravian Settlement
THE SHOP STONES
Windmill Farm
Hopwell Nook

NEW ST CHURCH ST
ORCHARD CL
COLLIER LA
Castle Hill
Hopwell Nook

Birchfield
VICTORIA AVE

Asterdale Prim Sch
Carr Hill Farm
Hopwell House
Manor Farm

BRIAN CLOUGH WAY
A52
B5010

35
FIELD CL
GREENWAY CL
BEECH AVE DERWENT AVE
CHESTNUT GR
HAWTHORNE AVE
DEEPDALE AVE
Draycott House

HOBSON DR
COVENT GARDEN CL
DEANS DR
FAIRFIELD AVE
WOODLAND AVE
Borrowash House

DERBY RD
Liby
Ashbrook Inf & Jun Schs
RUTLAND AVE
DEVONSHIRE AVE
Borrowash
HARRINGTON AVE

LADYSMITH RD
ELM ST
NURSERY CL
Charnwood AVE
PO
1 PRIORWAY GDNS
2 WINDSOR CL
3 BRADBURY CL
4 COOPERS CL
5 FAIRES CL
6 DERE CROFT

NOTTINGHAM RD
LACE MAKERS CL

The Stryne
EVELYN CL 1
MILLSTREAM GRANGE 2
SYCAMORE CL 3
BORROWASH RD 4
Shacklecross
Harris Grange Farm
TUDOR CT
Hotel

41 A 42 B C 43 D E F

34

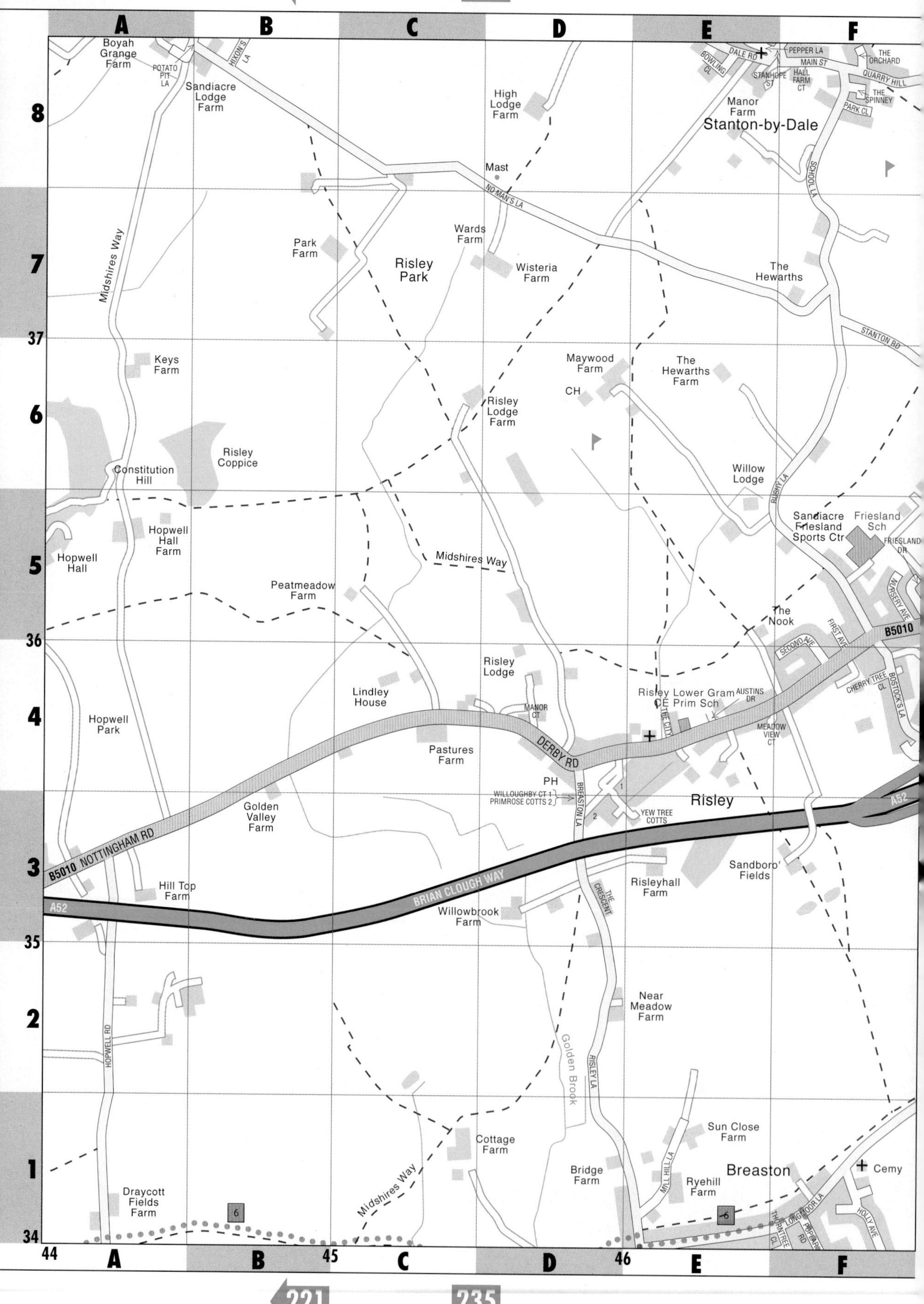
221
208
Boyah Grange Farm
Sandiacre Lodge Farm
High Lodge Farm
Manor Farm
Stanton-by-Dale
Mast
NO MAN'S LA
Park Farm
Risley Park
Wards Farm
Wisteria Farm
The Hewarths
Midshires Way
Keys Farm
Maywood Farm
The Hewarths Farm
CH
Risley Lodge Farm
Risley Coppice
Constitution Hill
Willow Lodge
Hopwell Hall Farm
Hopwell Hall
Sandiacre Friesland Sports Ctr
Friesland Sch
Peatmeadow Farm
The Nook
B5010
Risley Lodge
Lindley House
Hopwell Park
Risley Lower Gram CE Prim Sch
DERBY RD
Pastures Farm
PH
WILLOUGHBY CT
PRIMROSE COTTS
YEW TREE COTTS
Risley
A52
Golden Valley Farm
B5010 NOTTINGHAM RD
BRIAN CLOUGH WAY
Sandboro' Fields
Risleyhall Farm
Hill Top Farm
Willowbrook Farm
Near Meadow Farm
Golden Brook
HOPWELL RD
RISLEY LA
Sun Close Farm
Cottage Farm
Bridge Farm
Breaston
Ryehill Farm
Cemy
Draycott Fields Farm
221
235

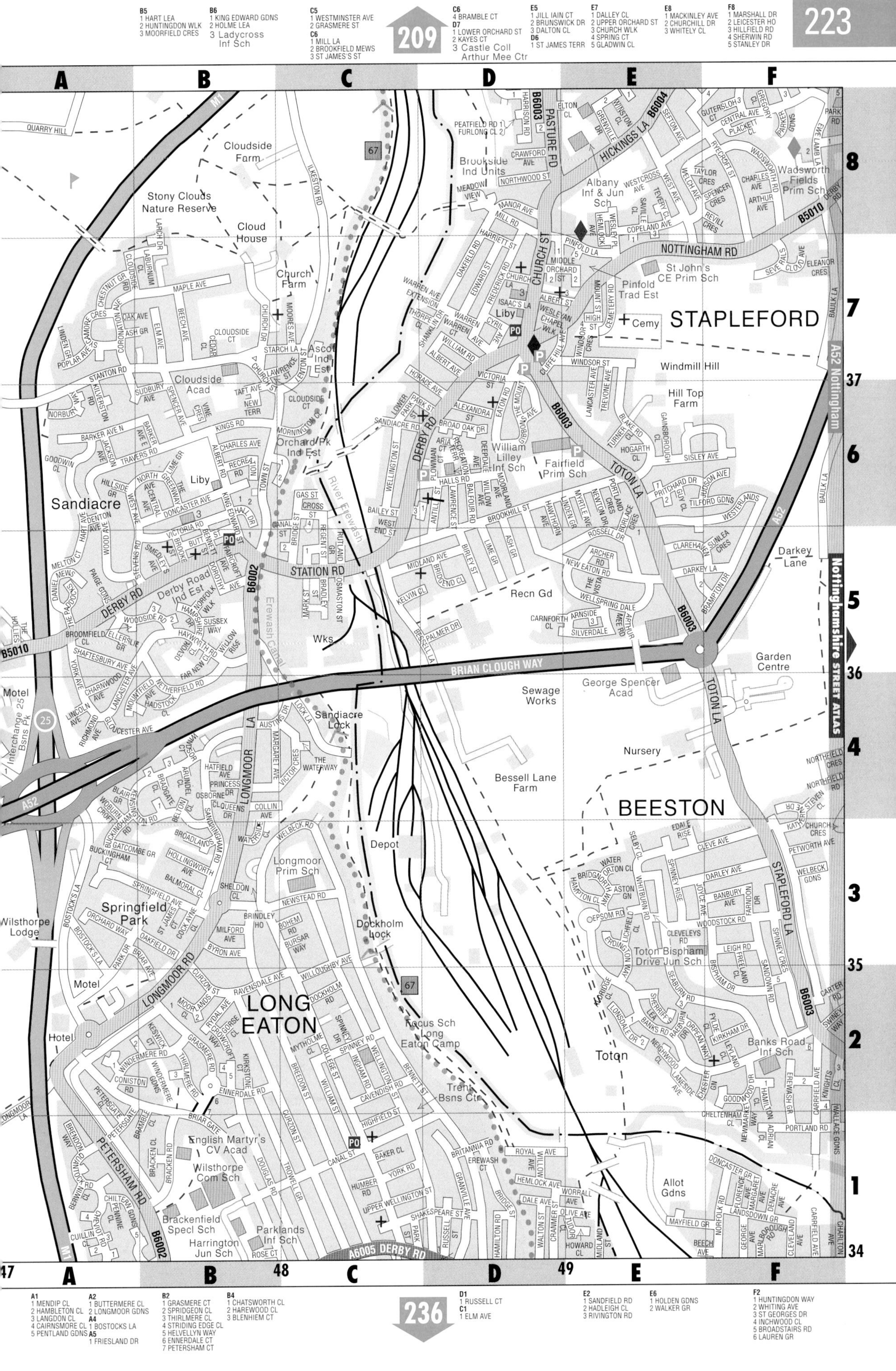
223
B5
1 HART LEA
2 HUNTINGDON WLK
3 MOORFIELD CRES
B6
1 KING EDWARD GDNS
2 HOLME LEA
3 Ladycross Inf Sch
C5
1 WESTMINSTER AVE
2 GRASMERE ST
C6
1 MILL LA
2 BROOKFIELD MEWS
3 ST JAMES'S ST
209
C6
4 BRAMBLE CT
D7
1 LOWER ORCHARD ST
2 KAYES CT
3 Castle Coll Arthur Mee Ctr
E5
1 JILL IAIN CT
2 BRUNSWICK DR
3 DALTON CL
D6
1 ST JAMES TERR
E7
1 DALLEY CL
2 UPPER ORCHARD ST
3 CHURCH WLK
4 SPRING CT
5 GLADWIN CL
E8
1 MACKINLEY AVE
2 CHURCHILL DR
3 WHITELY CL
F8
1 MARSHALL DR
2 LEICESTER HO
3 HILLFIELD RD
4 SHERWIN RD
5 STANLEY DR
STAPLEFORD
Sandiacre
LONG EATON
BEESTON
Toton
Nottinghamshire STREET ATLAS
A52 Nottingham
BRIAN CLOUGH WAY
NOTTINGHAM RD
Cloudside Farm
Stony Clouds Nature Reserve
Cloud House
Church Farm
Cloudside Acad
Orchard Pk Ind Est
Derby Road Ind Est
Brookside Ind Units
Albany Inf & Jun Sch
Wadsworth Fields Prim Sch
St John's CE Prim Sch
Pinfold Trad Est
Windmill Hill
Hill Top Farm
William Lilley Inf Sch
Fairfield Prim Sch
Recn Gd
Sewage Works
George Spencer Acad
Garden Centre
Darkey Lane
Sandiacre Lock
Nursery
Bessell Lane Farm
Depot
Longmoor Prim Sch
Springfield Park
Wilsthorpe Lodge
Dockholm Lock
Toton Bispham Drive Jun Sch
Focus Sch Long Eaton Camp
Trent Bsns Ctr
Banks Road Inf Sch
English Martyr's CV Acad
Wilsthorpe Com Sch
Brackenfield Specl Sch
Harrington Jun Sch
Parklands Inf Sch
Allot Gdns
Motel
Hotel
Interchange 25 Bsns Pk
River Erewash
Erewash Canal
A6005 DERBY RD
A
B
C
D
E
F
47
48
49
34
35
36
37
A1
1 MENDIP CL
2 HAMBLETON CL
3 LANGDON CL
4 CAIRNSMORE CL
5 PENTLAND GDNS
A2
1 BUTTERMERE CL
2 LONGMOOR GDNS
A4
1 BOSTOCKS LA
A5
1 FRIESLAND DR
B2
1 GRASMERE CT
2 SPRIDGEON CL
3 THIRLMERE CL
4 STRIDING EDGE CL
5 HELVELLYN WAY
6 ENNERDALE CT
7 PETERSHAM CT
B4
1 CHATSWORTH CL
2 HAREWOOD CL
3 BLENHEIM CT
236
D1
1 RUSSELL CT
C1
1 ELM AVE
E2
1 SANDFIELD RD
2 HADLEIGH CL
3 RIVINGTON RD
E6
1 HOLDEN GDNS
2 WALKER GR
F2
1 HUNTINGDON WAY
2 WHITING AVE
3 ST GEORGES DR
4 INCHWOOD CL
5 BROADSTAIRS RD
6 LAUREN GR

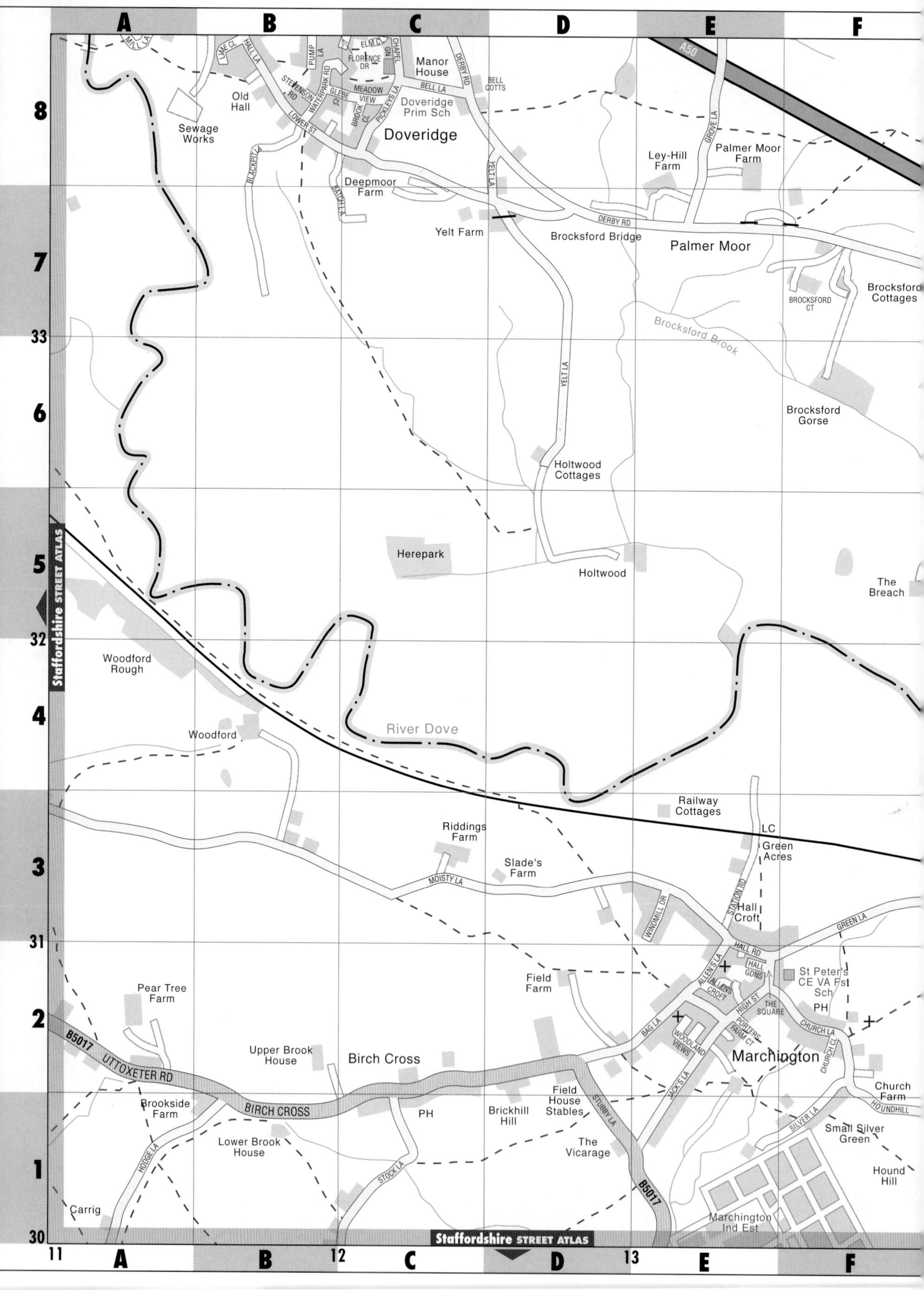

Staffordshire STREET ATLAS

A **B** **C** **D** **E** **F**

8

33

7

6

5

32

4

3

31

2

1

30

11 **A** **B** 12 **C** **D** 13 **E** **F**

Doveridge

Old Hall

Sewage Works

Deepmoor Farm

Manor House

Yelt Farm

Brocksford Bridge

Palmer Moor

Ley-Hill Farm

Palmer Moor Farm

Brocksford Cottages

BROCKSFORD CT

Brocksford Brook

Brocksford Gorse

Holtwood Cottages

Herepark

Holtwood

The Breach

Woodford Rough

Woodford

River Dove

Railway Cottages

LC

Green Acres

Riddings Farm

Slade's Farm

MOISTY LA

Hall Croft

Pear Tree Farm

Field Farm

St Peter's CE VA Fst Sch

PH

Upper Brook House

Birch Cross

Marchington

B5017

UTTOXETER RD

Brookside Farm

BIRCH CROSS

PH

Brickhill Hill

Field House Stables

The Vicarage

Church Farm

Lower Brook House

STOCK LA

B5017

Small Silver Green

Hound Hill

Carrig

Marchington Ind Est

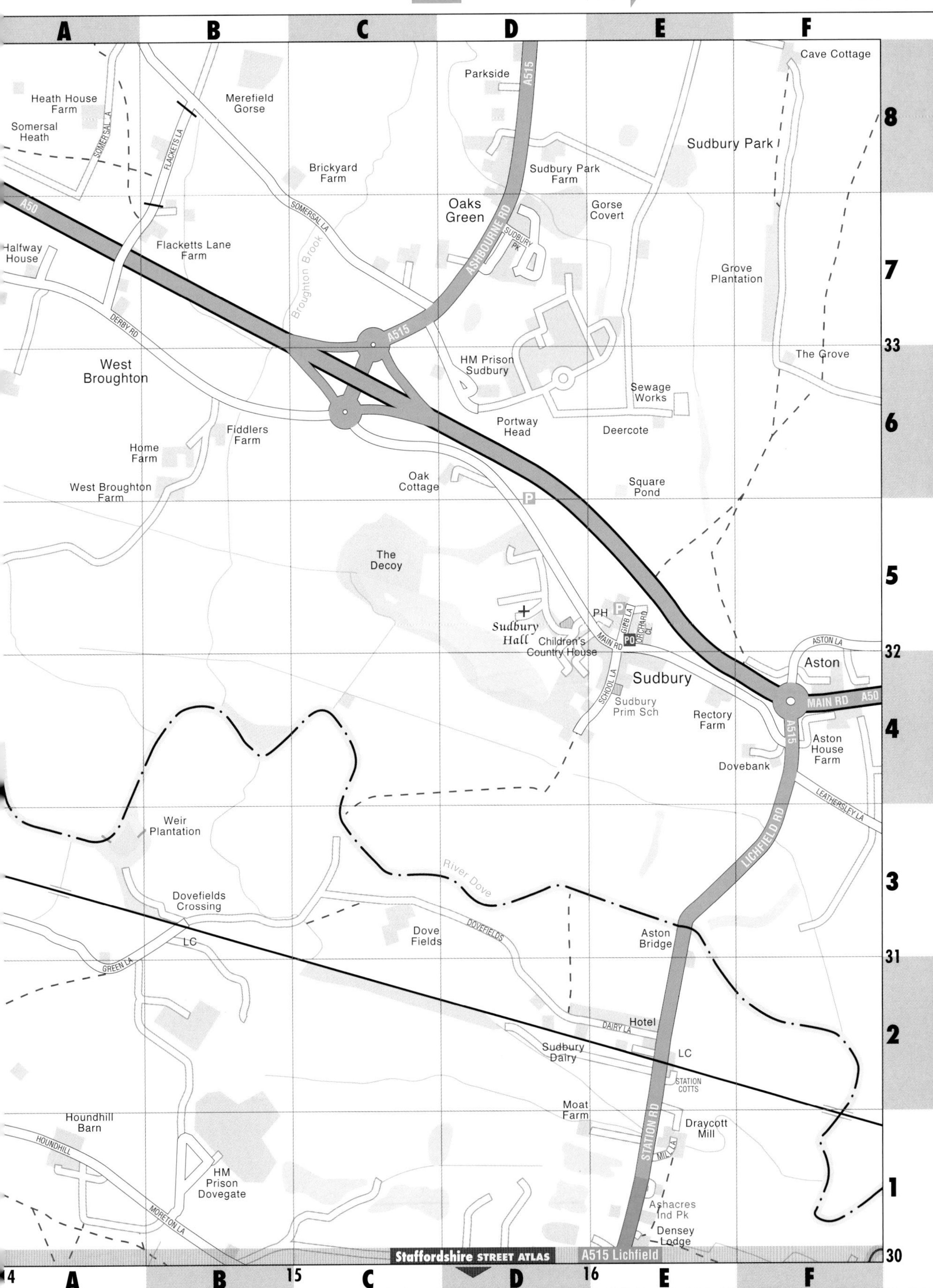

8 Heath House Farm
Somersal Heath
Merefield Gorse
Brickyard Farm
Parkside
Sudbury Park

7 Halfway House
A50
Flacketts Lane Farm
SOMERSAL LA
Oaks Green
Sudbury Park Farm
ASHBOURNE RD
Gorse Covert
Grove Plantation
Cave Cottage

33 West Broughton
DERBY RD
Broughton Brook
A515
HM Prison Sudbury
The Grove

6 Home Farm
Fiddlers Farm
Portway Head
Deercote
Sewage Works

West Broughton Farm
Oak Cottage
Square Pond

5 The Decoy
PH
P
Sudbury Hall
Children's Country House
MAIN RD
ORCHARD CL
GLEBE LA
PO

32 Aston
ASTON LA
Sudbury
MAIN RD
Aston
A50

4 SCHOOL LA
Sudbury Prim Sch
Rectory Farm
Dovebank
A515
Aston House Farm
LEATHERSLEY LA

Weir Plantation

3 Dovefields Crossing
LC
River Dove
Dove Fields
DOVEFIELDS
Aston Bridge
LICHFIELD RD

31 GREEN LA

2 Hotel
DAIRY LA
Sudbury Dairy
LC
STATION COTTS
STATION RD

Houndhill Barn
HOUNDHILL
Moat Farm
Draycott Mill
MILL LA

1 HM Prison Dovegate
MORETON LA
Ashacres Ind Pk
Densey Lodge

225
213

A B C D E F

8
7
33
6
5
32
4
3
31
2
1
30

Mackley House
Fox Hole
Sapperton Brook
The Homestead
SAPPERTON
Foston Mill Farm
Crowfoot Farm
CROWFOOT LA
Dale Brook
MUSE LA
Muselane Farm
MILL LA
Cotefield Farm
WOODHOUSE LA
Dalebrook
Ford
ASTON LA
Aston Heath
Broomhill Farm
Foston Brook
Conygree Wood
Aston Heath Farm
Haylane Farm
BREACH LA
Sailor's Holme
COPLOW LA
HAY LA
Rough Wood
Breach Gorse
ASTON LA
Home Farm
WOODYARD LA
Lawn House
ASTON LA
MAIN RD
HOME FARM DR
Foston
Roundhouse Gall
A50
UTTOXETER RD
FOSTON CL
UTTOXETER RD
Tomlinson Bsns Pk
WOODLAND DR
HM Prison Foston Hall
Maidensley Farm
A50
UTTOXETER RD
Dale Brook
Lemon's Holme
Fishpond Plantation
Puddingbag Covert
Roundabout Covert
Cote House
Leathersley Farm
The Churchleys
LEATHERSLEY LA
BROOM'S LA
WATERY LA
Sweet Holme
Scropton
River Dove
Ivy House Farm
MAIN ST
PH
Brookside Farm
SCROPTON RD
LC
BROOK LA
Brookhouse Farm
MILL LA
CHAPEL LA
LC
River Dove

17 A B 18 C D 19 E F

225
238

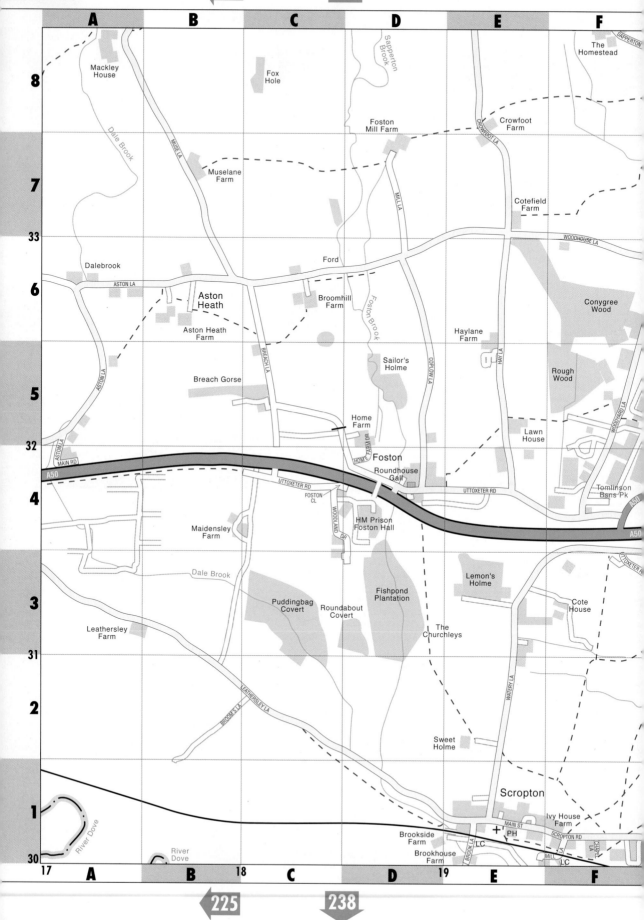

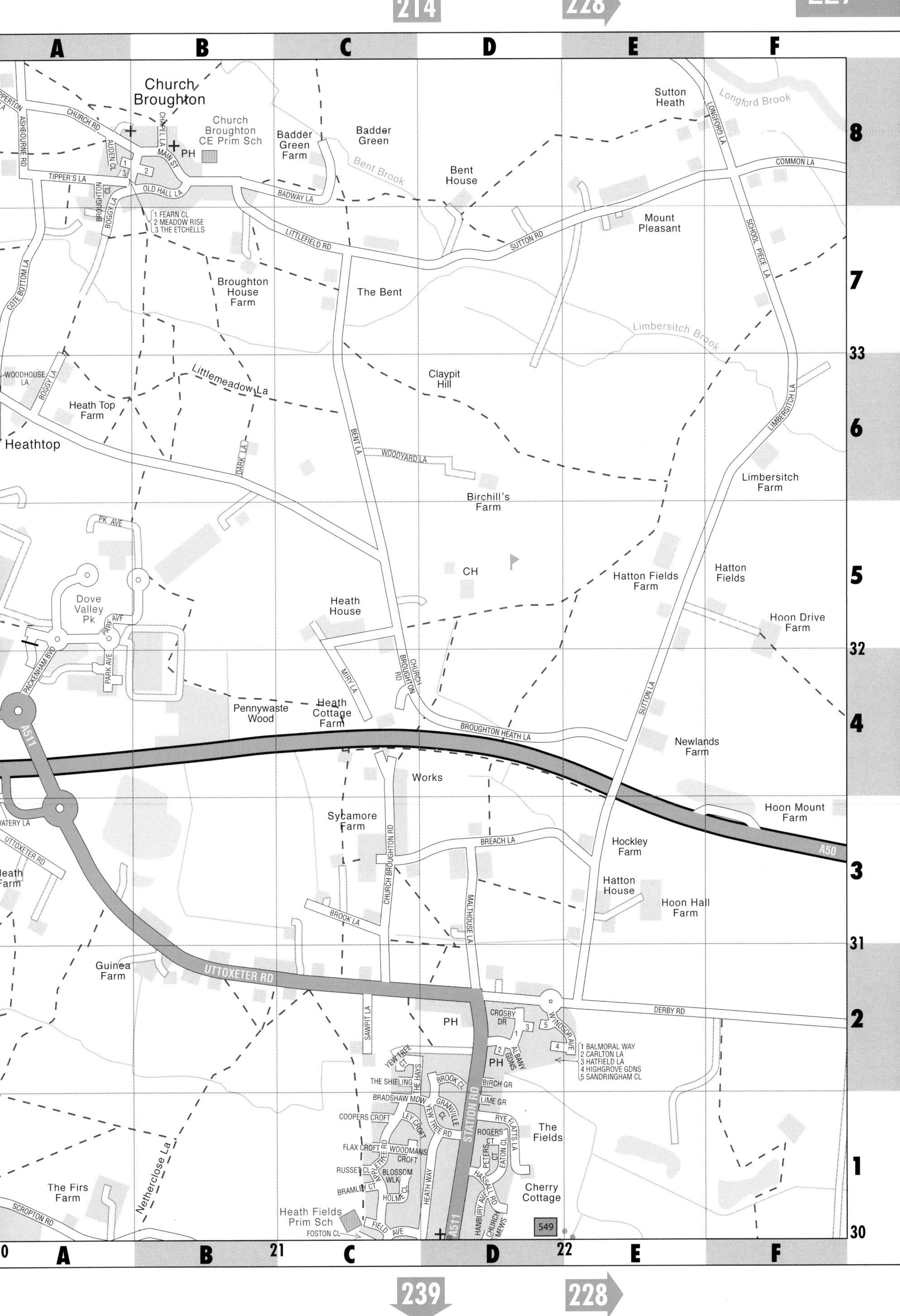

214
228
239
228

A   B   C   D   E   F

8
7
33
6
5
32
4
3
31
2
1
30

Church
Broughton

CHURCH RD
ASHBOURNE RD
PIPPERTON LA
AUDEN CL
CHAPEL LA
MAIN ST
PH
Church
Broughton
CE Prim Sch
Badder
Green
Farm
Badder
Green
Bent Brook
Bent
House
Sutton
Heath
Longford Brook
COMMON LA

TIPPER'S LA
BROUGHTON CL
BOGGY LA
OLD HALL LA
BADWAY LA
LITTLEFIELD RD
1 FEARN CL
2 MEADOW RISE
3 THE ETCHELLS
2
3
SUTTON RD
Mount
Pleasant
SCHOOL PIECE LA
LONGFORD LA

COTE BOTTOM LA
Broughton
House
Farm
The Bent
Limbersitch Brook

WOODHOUSE LA
BOGGY LA
Littlemeadow La
Claypit
Hill

Heath Top
Farm
Heathtop
DARK LA
BENT LA
WOODYARD LA
Birchill's
Farm
Limbersitch
Farm
LIMBERSITCH LA

PK AVE
PARK AVE
Dove
Valley
Pk
Heath
House
CH
Hatton Fields
Farm
Hatton
Fields
Hoon Drive
Farm

PACKENHAM BVD
PARK AVE
MIRY LA
CHURCH BROUGHTON RD
Pennywaste
Wood
Heath
Cottage
Farm
BROUGHTON HEATH LA
SUTTON LA
Newlands
Farm

A511
WATERY LA
UTTOXETER RD
Works
Sycamore
Farm
BREACH LA
Hockley
Farm
Hatton
House
Hoon Mount
Farm
A50

Heath
Farm
BROOK LA
CHURCH BROUGHTON RD
MALTHOUSE LA
Hatton
Hall
Farm

Guinea
Farm
UTTOXETER RD
SAWPIT LA
PH
CROSBY DR
WINDSCAPE
DERBY RD
1 BALMORAL WAY
2 CARLTON LA
3 HATFIELD LA
4 HIGHGROVE GDNS
5 SANDRINGHAM CL
3
5
4
2

Netherclose La
YEW TREE CT
THE SHIELING
BRADSHAW MDW
COOPERS CROFT
STATION RD
BROOK CL
THE HAYS
GRANVILLE CL
YEW TREE RD
LEY CROFT
ALBANY GDNS
PH
BIRCH GR
LIME GR
RYE FLATS LA
The
Fields
Rogers
PETERS CT
EATON CL
HANSALL RD

The Firs
Farm
SCROPTON RD
FLAX CROFT
RUSSET CL
BRAMLEY CT
WOODMANS CROFT
BLOSSOM WLK
HOLME CL
HEATH WAY
FIELD AVE
HANBURY AV
CHURCH RD
Cherry
Cottage
CHURCH MEWS
549
Heath Fields
Prim Sch
FOSTON CL
A511

0   21   22

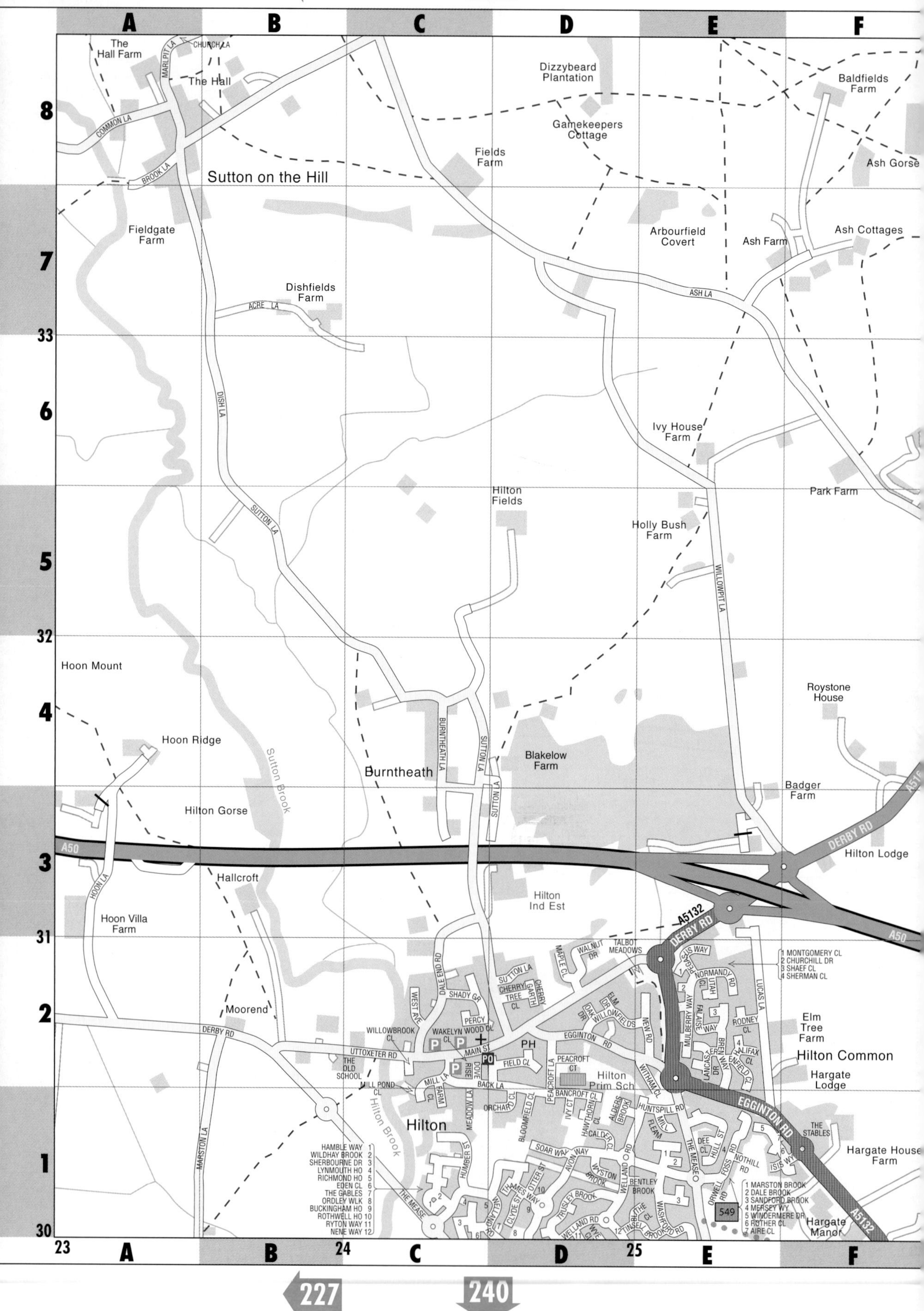

Map grid references (columns A–F, rows 1–8, 30–33):

Column A–B area:
- The Hall Farm
- The Hall
- MARPIT LA
- CHURCH LA
- COMMON LA
- BROOK LA
- Sutton on the Hill
- Fieldgate Farm
- DISH LA
- ACRE LA
- Dishfields Farm
- SUTTON LA
- Hoon Mount
- Hoon Ridge
- Sutton Brook
- Hilton Gorse
- Hallcroft
- HOON LA
- Hoon Villa Farm
- Moorend
- DERBY RD
- MARSTON LA
- Hilton Brook
- Hilton
- UTTOXETER RD
- THE OLD SCHOOL
- MILL POND CL
- WILLOWBROOK CL
- WEST LA
- DALE END RD
- WAKELYN CL
- SHADY GR
- MILL CL
- FARM CL
- MEADOW LA
- THE MEASE
- HUMBER ST
- SOAR WAY
- ORCHARD

Column C–D area:
- Dizzybeard Plantation
- Gamekeepers Cottage
- Fields Farm
- Arbourfield Covert
- ASH LA
- Hilton Fields
- Ivy House Farm
- Holly Bush Farm
- WILLOWPIT LA
- Blakelow Farm
- BURNTHEATH LA
- SUTTON LA
- Burntheath
- Hilton Ind Est
- TALBOT MEADOWS
- WALNUT DR
- MAPLE CL
- CHERRY TREE CL
- CHERRY GARTH
- ELM CL
- OAK CL
- WILLOWFIELDS
- EGGINTON RD
- NEW RD
- PEACROFT LA
- PEACROFT CT
- Hilton Prim Sch
- BANCROFT CL
- BLOOMFIELD CL
- BACK LA
- FIELD CL
- PERCY WOOD CL
- MAIN ST
- RISE
- SUTTON LA
- PH
- PO
- HAWTHORN
- ALDERS BROOK
- CALDER CL
- AVON WAY
- WESTON WAY
- CLYDE ST
- OTTER ST
- JAMES WAY
- TRUSLEY BROOK
- WELLAND RD
- TINSLEY BROOK
- Bentley Brook
- WASHFORD RD

Column E–F area:
- Baldfields Farm
- Ash Gorse
- Ash Cottages
- Ash Farm
- Park Farm
- Royst one House
- Badger Farm
- DERBY RD
- Hilton Lodge
- A50
- A5132
- ISIS WAY
- NORMANDY RD
- UTAH
- FALAISE WAY
- MULBERRY WAY
- RODNEY CL
- LUCAS LA
- BRENTNAL WAY
- SHERMAN WAY
- LANCASTER RD
- ALIFAX
- Elm Tree Farm
- Hilton Common
- Hargate Lodge
- HUNTSPILL RD
- THE MEASE
- DEE CL
- NOTHILL RD
- FOSS RD
- ORWELL CL
- ISIS WAY
- THE STABLES
- Hargate House Farm
- EGGINTON RD
- A5132
- Hargate Manor
- 549

1 MONTGOMERY CL
2 CHURCHILL DR
3 SHAEF CL
4 SHERMAN CL

1 MARSTON BROOK
2 DALE BROOK
3 SANDFORD BROOK
4 MERSEY WY
5 WINDERMERE DR
6 ROTHER CL
7 AIRE CL

1 HAMBLE WAY
2 WILDHAY BROOK
3 SHERBOURNE DR
4 LYNMOUTH HO
5 RICHMOND HO
6 EDEN CL
7 THE GABLES
8 ORDLEY WLK
9 BUCKINGHAM HO
10 ROTHWELL HO
11 RYTON WAY
12 NENE WAY

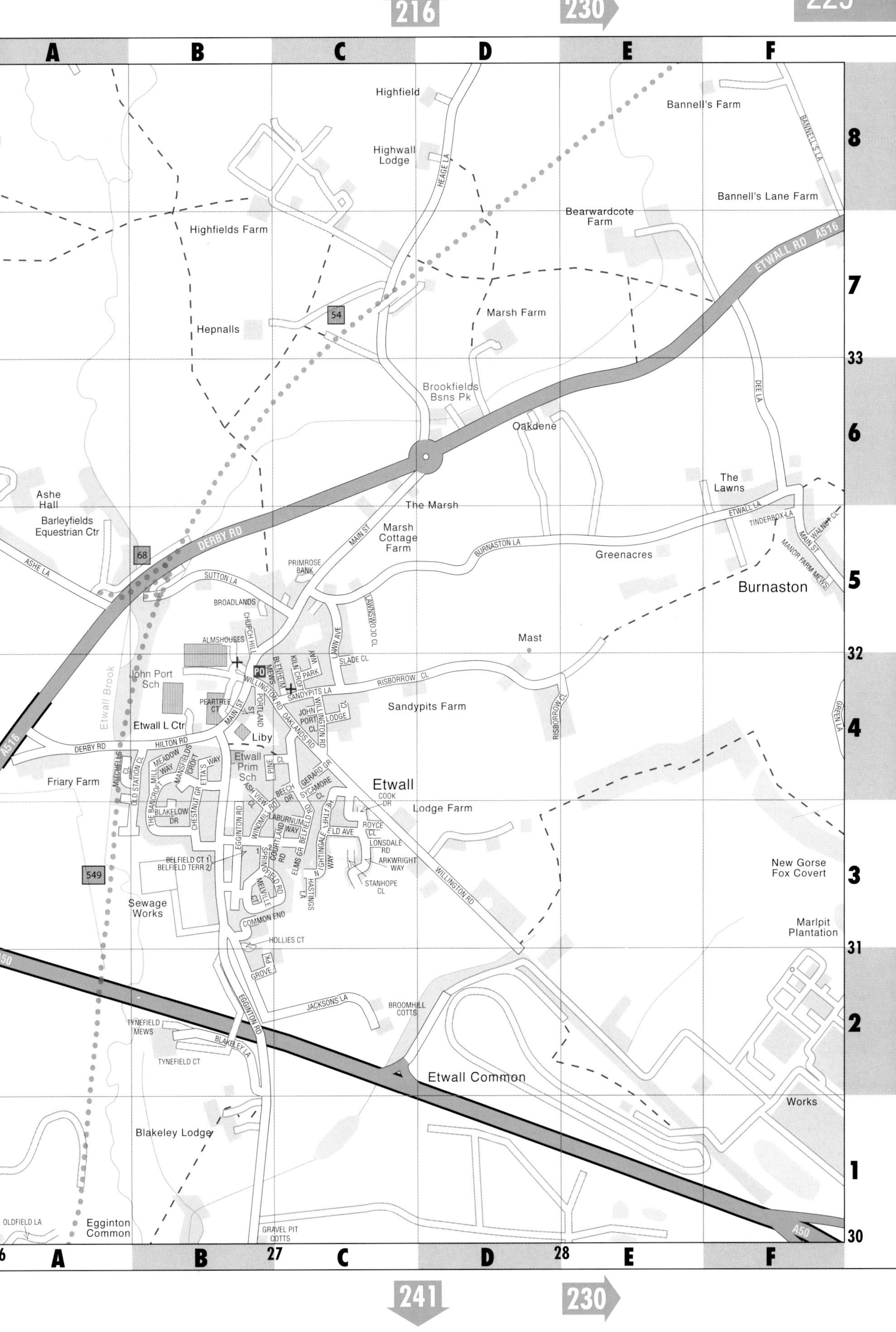

A B C D E F

8

Highfield

Bannell's Farm

Highwall
Lodge

Bannell's Lane Farm

Bearwardcote
Farm

7

Highfields Farm

ETWALL RD A516

Hepnalls

54

33

Marsh Farm

Brookfields
Bsns Pk

6

Oakdene

DEE LA

The
Lawns

Ashe
Hall

The Marsh

ETWALL LA

Barleyfields
Equestrian Ctr

DERBY RD

Marsh
Cottage
Farm

Burnaston

TINDERBOX LA

MANOR FARM MEWS

MAIN ST

DUALING CL

ASHE LA

68

SUTTON LA

PRIMROSE
BANK

BURNASTON LA

Greenacres

5

BROADLANDS

MAIN ST

Burnaston

GREEN LA

A516

Etwall Brook

ALMSHOUSES

CHURCH HILL

LAWN AVE

Mast

32

John Port
Sch

PO

KILN CROFT

PARK

BLETHEM

SANDYPITS LA

SLADE CL

RISBORROW CL

RISBORROW CL

Sandypits Farm

4

Etwall L Ctr

PEARTREE
CT

WILLINGTON RD

PORTLAND

MAIN ST

JOHN
PORT
CL

LODGE

CL

DERBY RD

HILTON RD

Liby

OAKLANDS RD

Etwall
Prim
Sch

Friary Farm

OLD STATION CL

MEADOW
WAY

MANSFIELDS

ETTA'S
WAY

ASH VIEW RD

GERARD GR

SYCAMORE

COOK
DR

Etwall

Lodge Farm

New Gorse
Fox Covert

549

THE BANCROFT

MILL
WAY

BLAKELOW
DR

CHESTNUT GR

EGGINTON RD

BEECH
DR

NIGHTINGALE
CL

FIELD AVE

ROYCE
CL

LONSDALE
RD

ARKWRIGHT
WAY

WILLINGTON RD

Marlpit
Plantation

3

LABURNUM
WAY

ELMS GR

SPRINGFIELD RD

MELVILLE
CL

HASTINGS
LA

STANHOPE
CL

31

Belfield Ct 1
Belfield Terr 2

Sewage
Works

COMMON END

HOLLIES CT

GROVE

Works

2

A450

TYNEFIELD
MEWS

BLAKELEY LA

EGGINTON RD

JACKSONS LA

BROOMHILL
COTTS

Etwall Common

TYNEFIELD CT

1

Blakeley Lodge

OLDFIELD LA

Egginton
Common

GRAVEL PIT
COTTS

A50

30

229
217

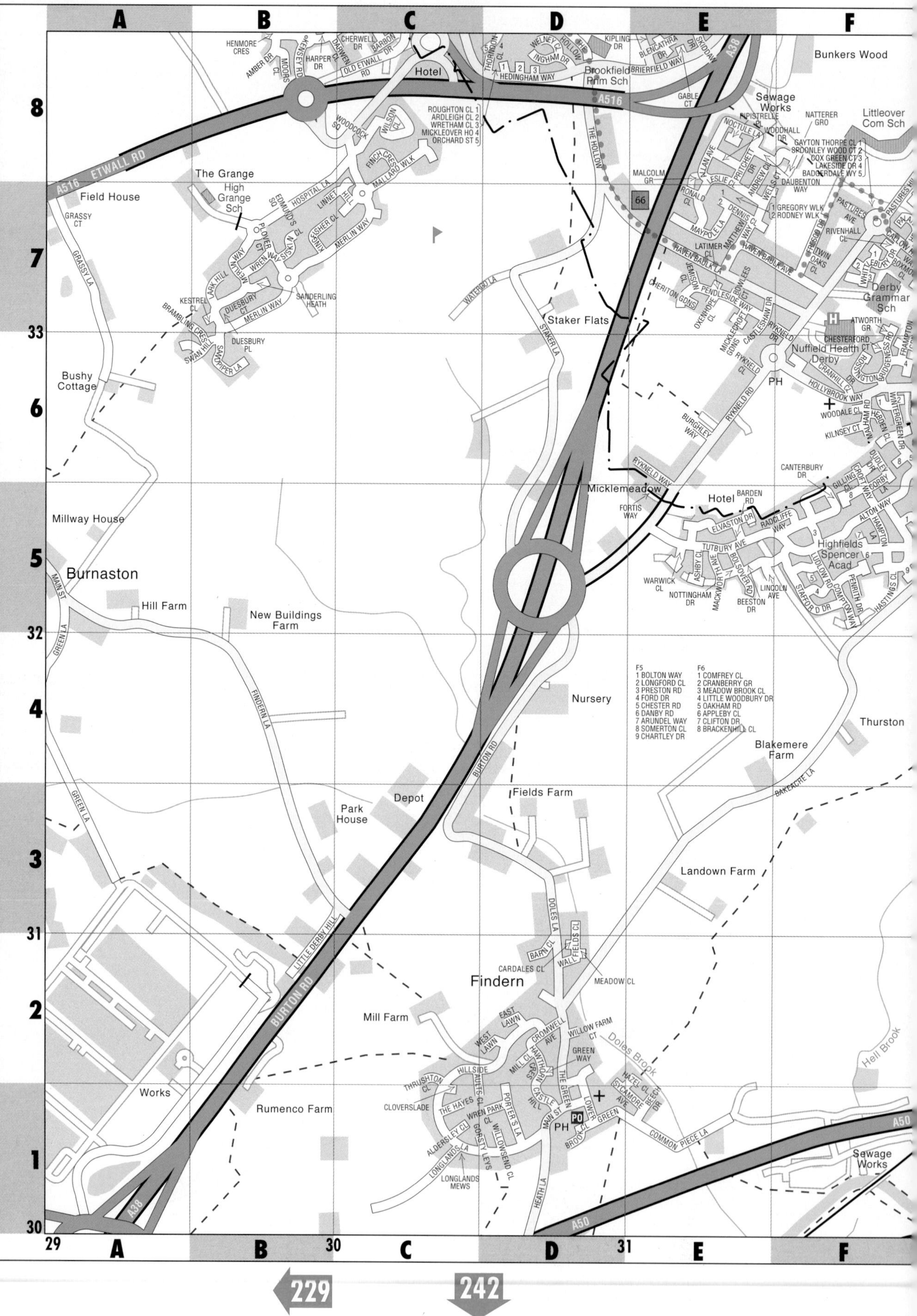
A
B
C
D
E
F
8
7
33
6
5
32
4
3
31
2
1
30
29
30
31
Bunkers Wood
Sewage Works
Littleover Com Sch
Hotel
Brookfield Prim Sch
A516
ETWALL RD
A38
The Grange
High Grange Sch
Field House
GRASSY CT
GRASSY LA
HOSPITAL LA
MERLIN WAY
KESTREL CL
BRAMBLING CRES
SWAN HILL
SANDPIPER LA
DUESBURY PL
DUESBURY CT
SANDERLING HEATH
LARK HILL
WREN WAY
PLOVER CT
EDMUNDS SQ
LINNET HILL
KINGFISHER CL
SISKIN CL
FINCH CRES
MALLARD WLK
WOODCOCK SQ
WILSON CL
OLD ETWALL RD
HENMORE CRES
AMBER DR
MOORS CL
HARPER CL
CHERWELL DR
DARWEN CL
BARBON CL
THORNDON CL
WELNEY CL
INGHAM DR
HEDINGHAM WAY
KIPLING DR
BLENCATHRA DR
BRIERFIELD WAY
SKIDDAW DR
GABLE CT
ROUGHTON CL 1
ARDLEIGH CL 2
WRETHAM CL 3
MICKLEOVER HO 4
ORCHARD ST 5
THE HOLLOW
MALCOLM GR
66
PIPISTRELLE
NOCTULE LA
WOODHALL DR
NATTERER GRO
GAYTON THORPE CL 1
BROADLEY WOOD CT 2
COX GREEN CT 3
LAKESIDE DR 4
BADGERDALE WY 5
DAUBENTON WAY
1 GREGORY WLK
2 RODNEY WLK
RIVENHALL CL
TWIN OAKS CL
PASTURES AVE
Derby Grammar Sch
ATWORTH GR
CHESTERFORD CT
Nuffield Health Derby
HOLLYBROOK WAY
WOODALE CL
KILNSEY CT
PH
RYKNELD RD
RYKNELD WAY
BURGHLEY WAY
HAVEN BAULK LA
HAVEN BAULK AVE
PENDLESIDE WAY
CHERITON GDNS
OXENHOPE CL
MICKLECROFT GDNS
CASTLESHAW DR
Staker Flats
STAKER LA
WATERLOO LA
Micklemeadow
FORTIS WAY
Hotel
BARDEN RD
CANTERBURY DR
ELVASTON DR
RADCLIFFE WAY
TUTBURY AVE
ALTON WAY
Highfields Spencer Acad
ASHBY CL
WARWICK CL
NOTTINGHAM DR
MACKWORTH AVE
BOLSOVER RD
BEESTON DR
LINCOLN AVE
LUDLOW RD
STAFFORD DR
COMPTON WAY
PENRITH DR
HASTINGS CL
Millway House
Bushy Cottage
Burnaston
MAIN ST
GREEN LA
Hill Farm
New Buildings Farm
FINDERN LA
F5
1 BOLTON WAY
2 LONGFORD CL
3 PRESTON RD
4 FORD DR
5 CHESTER RD
6 DANBY RD
7 ARUNDEL WAY
8 SOMERTON CL
9 CHARTLEY DR
F6
1 COMFREY CL
2 CRANBERRY GR
3 MEADOW BROOK CL
4 LITTLE WOODBURY DR
5 OAKHAM RD
6 APPLEBY CL
7 CLIFTON DR
8 BRACKENHILL CL
Nursery
Thurston
Blakemere Farm
BAKEACRE LA
BURTON RD
Fields Farm
Depot
Park House
Landown Farm
DOLES LA
BARN CL
FIELDS CL
WALL CL
CARDALES CL
MEADOW CL
Findern
Mill Farm
LITTLE DERBY HILL
EAST LAWN
WEST LAWN
CROMWELL AVE
WILLOW FARM CT
GREEN WAY
Doles Brook
Hell Brook
HAZEL CL
SYCAMORE AVE
BEECH DR
HILLSIDE
THRUSHTON CL
CLOVERSLADE
THE HAYES
WREN PARK CL
PORTER'S LA
CASTLE HILL
THE GREEN
MAIN ST
LOWER GREEN
BROOK CL
PO
PH
COMMON PIECE LA
ALDERSLEY CL
LONGLANDS LA
LONGLANDS MEWS
GORSTY LEYS
WILLOWSEND CL
HEATH LA
A50
Sewage Works
Works
Rumenco Farm

229
242

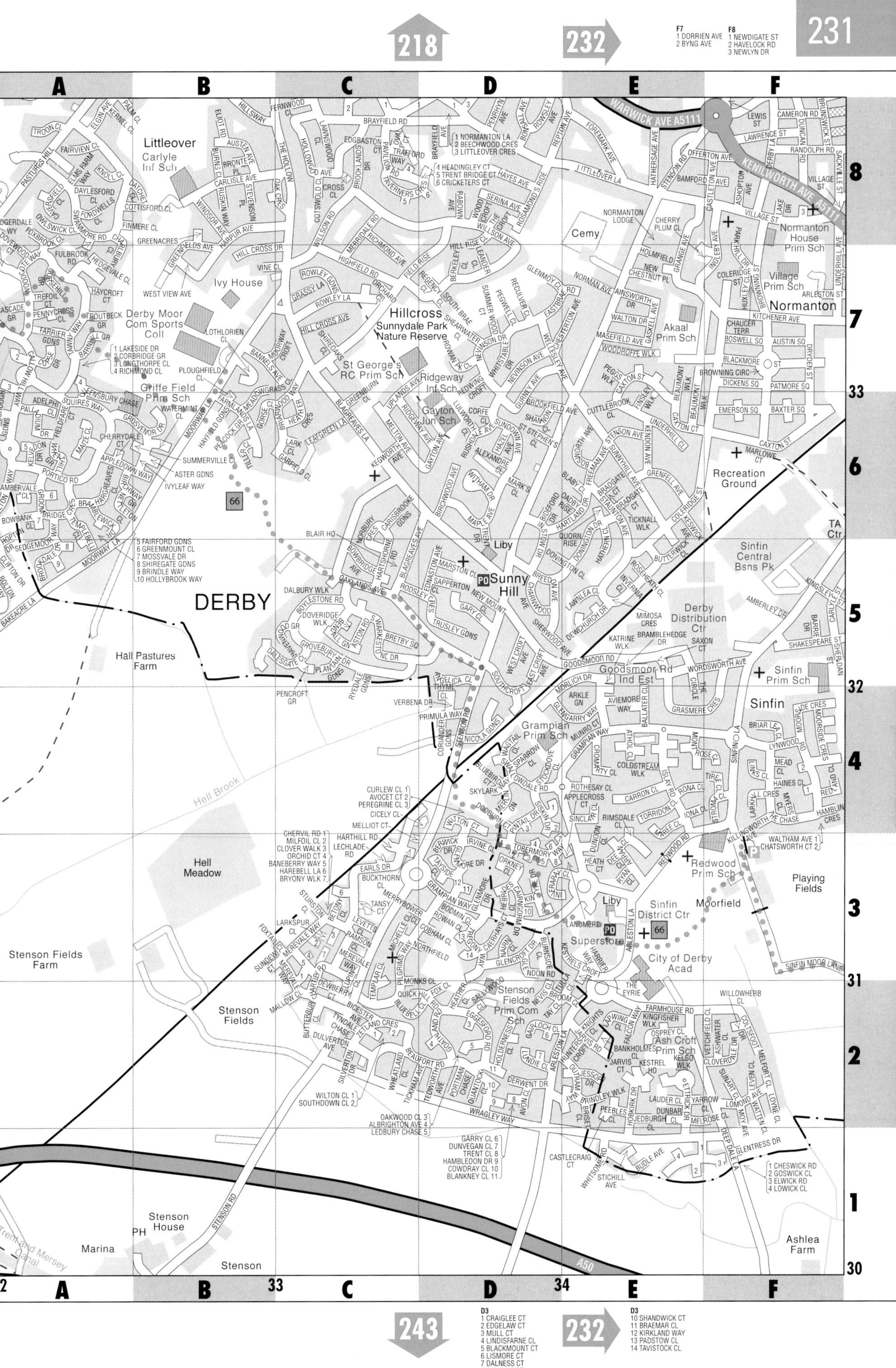

231
219

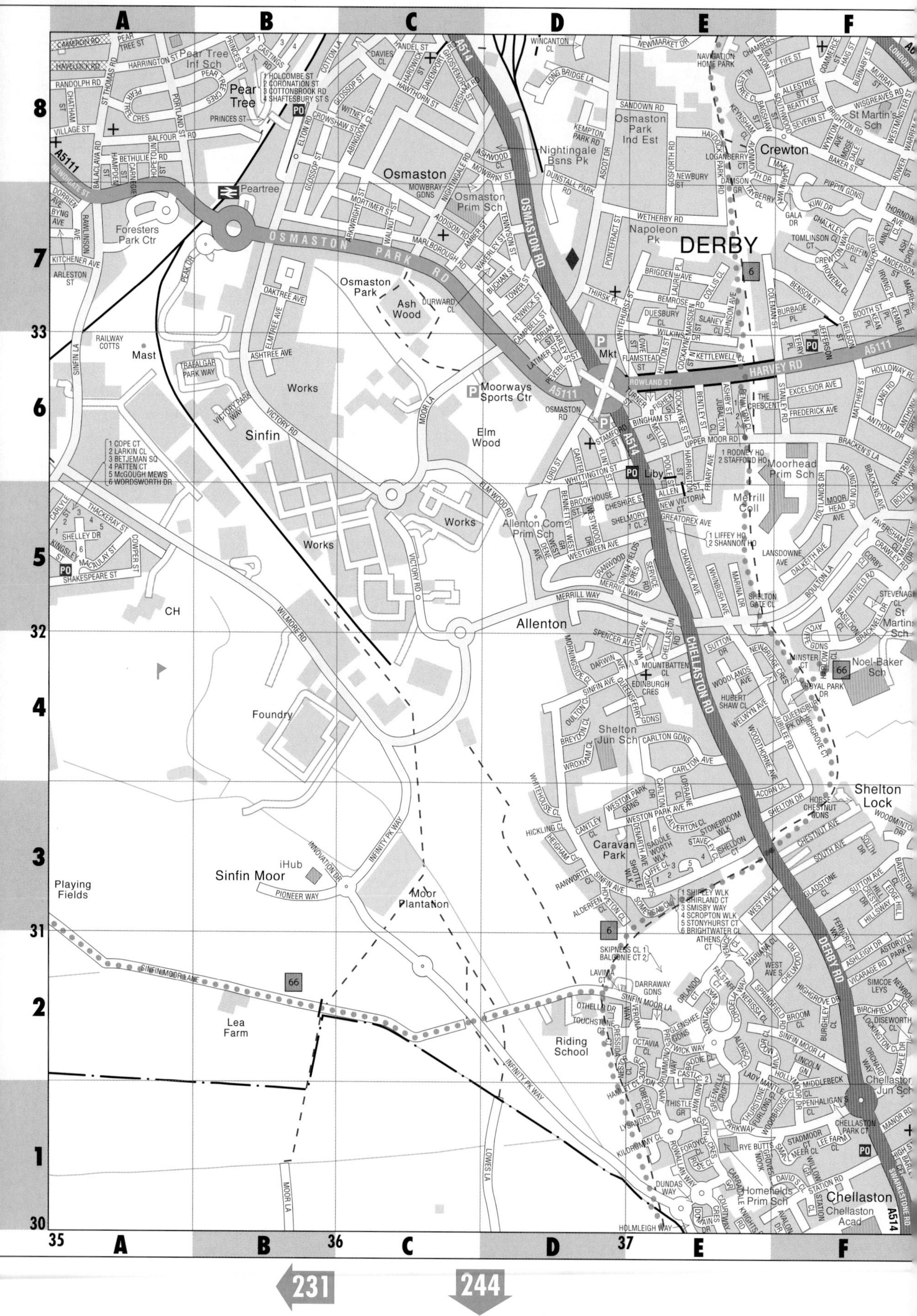
A
B
C
D
E
F
8
7
33
6
5
32
4
3
31
2
1
30
35
36
37
DERBY
Osmaston
Pear Tree
Peartree
Pear Tree Inf Sch
Foresters Park Ctr
OSMASTON PARK RD
OSMASTON RD
A5111
A514
Osmaston Park
Ash Wood
Osmaston Prim Sch
Nightingale Bsns Pk
Osmaston Park Ind Est
Napoleon Pk
Crewton
St Martin's Sch
Railway Cotts
Mast
Works
Sinfin
Moorways Sports Ctr
Elm Wood
Mkt
Liby
HARVEY RD
Moorhead Prim Sch
Merrill Coll
Allenton Com Prim Sch
Allenton
MERRILL WAY
CHELLASTON RD
Noel-Baker Sch
St Martins Sch
Shelton Jun Sch
Shelton Lock
Caravan Park
Foundry
CH
Sinfin Moor
iHub
Moor Plantation
Playing Fields
SINFIN MOOR LANE
Lea Farm
Riding School
INFINITY PK WAY
MOOR LA
LOWES LA
DERBY RD
Chellaston Jun Sch
Homefields Prim Sch
Chellaston
Chellaston Acad
66
6

231
244

220
234

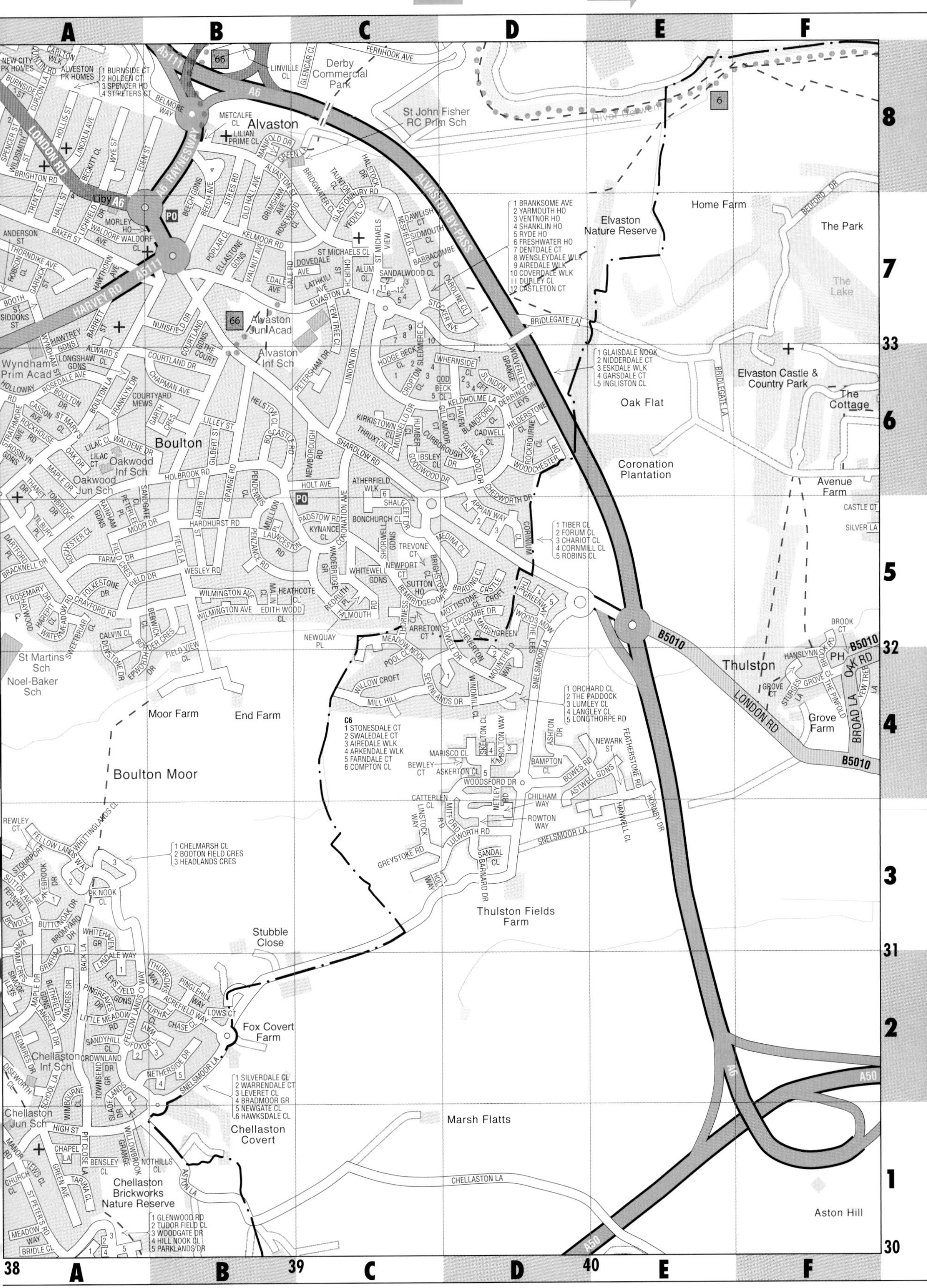
A
B
C
D
E
F
8
7
33
6
5
32
4
3
31
2
1
30
38
39
40
Alvaston
Derby Commercial Park
St John Fisher RC Prim Sch
River Derwent
Elvaston Nature Reserve
Home Farm
The Park
The Lake
Elvaston Castle & Country Park
Oak Flat
The Cottage
Coronation Plantation
Avenue Farm
Thulston
Grove Farm
Boulton
Wyndham Prim Acad
Oakwood Inf Sch
Oakwood Jun Sch
Alvaston Jun Acad
Alvaston Inf Sch
St Martins Sch
Noel-Baker Sch
Moor Farm
End Farm
Boulton Moor
Thulston Fields Farm
Stubble Close
Fox Covert Farm
Chellaston Inf Sch
Chellaston Jun Sch
Chellaston Covert
Chellaston Brickworks Nature Reserve
Marsh Flatts
Aston Hill
ALVASTON BY-PASS
A6 RAYNESWAY
LONDON RD
HARVEY RD
A5111
A6
A50
B5010
SNELSMOOR LA
CHELLASTON LA
BRIDLEGATE LA
HOLT AVE
HOLBROOK RD
SHARDLOW RD
1 BRANKSOME AVE
2 YARMOUTH HO
3 VENTNOR HO
4 SHANKLIN HO
5 RYDE HO
6 FRESHWATER HO
7 DENTDALE CT
8 WENSLEYDALE WLK
9 AIREDALE WLK
10 COVERDALE WLK
11 DURLEY CL
12 CASTLETON CT
1 GLAISDALE NOOK
2 NIDDERDALE CT
3 ESKDALE WLK
4 GARSDALE CT
5 INGLISTON CL
1 TIBER CL
2 FORUM CL
3 CHARIOT CL
4 CORNMILL CL
5 ROBINS CL
1 ORCHARD CL
2 THE PADDOCK
3 LUMLEY CL
4 LANGLEY CL
5 LONGTHORPE RD
C6
1 STONESDALE CT
2 SWALEDALE CT
3 AIREDALE WLK
4 ARKENDALE WLK
5 FARNDALE CT
6 COMPTON CL
1 CHELMARSH CL
2 BOOTON FIELD CRES
3 HEADLANDS CRES
1 SILVERDALE CL
2 WARRENDALE CT
3 LEVERET CL
4 BRADMOOR GR
5 NEWGATE CL
6 HAWKSDALE CL
1 GLENWOOD RD
2 TUDOR FIELD CL
3 WOODGATE DR
4 HILL NOOK CL
5 PARKLANDS DR
1 BURNSIDE CT
2 HOLDEN CT
3 SPENCER HO
4 ST PETERS CT

245
234

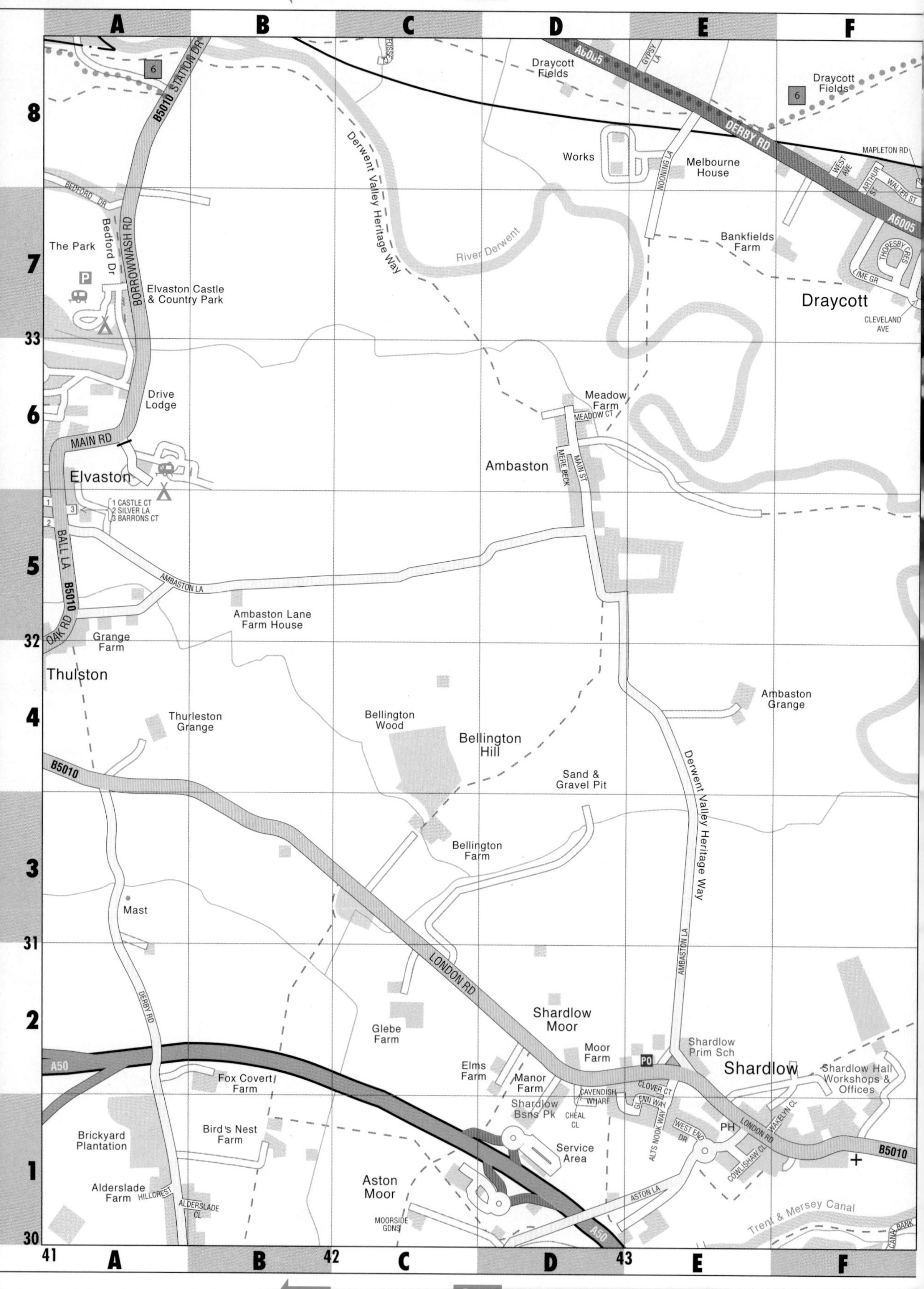

A   B   C   D   E   F

8

7

33

6

5

32

4

31

2

1

30

41   A   B   42   C   D   43   E   F

B5010 STATION DR

6

Draycott Fields

DERBY RD
A6005

Draycott Fields

6

MAPLETON RD

Works

Melbourne House

WOODNING LA
GYPSY LA

WEST AVE
ARTHUR ST
WALTER ST

A6005

BEDFORD DR

Bedford Dr

BORROWWASH RD

The Park

P

Elvaston Castle & Country Park

River Derwent

Bankfields Farm

THORESBY CRES
LIME GR

Draycott

CLEVELAND AVE

Drive Lodge

Derwent Valley Heritage Way

Meadow Farm
MEADOW CT

MAIN RD

Elvaston

MERE BECK

MAIN ST

Ambaston

1 CASTLE CT
2 SILVER LA
3 BARRONS CT

BALL LA
OAK RD
B5010

AMBASTON LA

5

Ambaston Lane Farm House

Grange Farm

Thulston

Ambaston Grange

B5010

Thurleston Grange

Bellington Wood

Bellington Hill

Sand & Gravel Pit

Derwent Valley Heritage Way

DERBY RD

Mast

Bellington Farm

AMBASTON LA

LONDON RD

Shardlow Moor

A50

Glebe Farm

Elms Farm

Moor Farm

Shardlow Prim Sch

PO

Shardlow

Shardlow Hall Workshops & Offices

Fox Covert Farm

Manor Farm

CAVENDISH WHARF

Shardlow Bsns Pk

CHEAL CL

CLOVER CT
FINN WAY

PH
LONDON RD
MAXELYN CL

B5010

Brickyard Plantation

Bird's Nest Farm

ALTS NOOK WAY
WEST END DR

COWLISHAW CL

Aldersade Farm
HILLCREST
ALDERSLADE CL

Aston Moor

Service Area

ASTON LA

A50

Trent & Mersey Canal

CANAL BANK

MOORSIDE GDNS

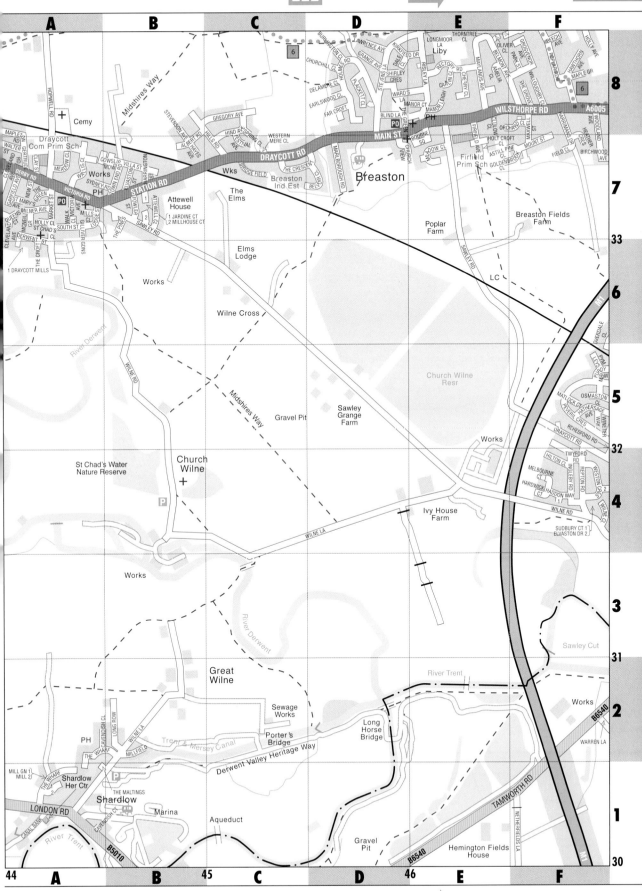
222
236

A B C D E F

Midshires Way
HOPWELL RD
Cemy
Draycott
Com Prim Sch
MAPLETON RD
WALTER ST
GERTRUDE RD
CLAY ST
CLEVELAND AVE
DERBY RD
NEW ST
GARFIELD AVE
ST MARY'S
THE GREEN
QUEENS CT
MILNER AVE
HOLLY CL
MARKET ST
WALK
VICTORIA RD
VICTORIA AVE
SOUTH ST
ST CHAD'S CL
MCNEIL GR
DERWENT ST
THE CROFT
1 DRAYCOTT MILLS
MEADOW CL
Works
COWSLIP MDW
SYDNEY RD
TOWN END RD
ELVASTON ST
VILLA ST
HARRINGTON ST
STATION RD
PO
PH
MILLS CL
LODGE ST
GILLIVER GDNS
THE PINES
FOWLER ST
ATTEWELL CL
SAWLEY RD
Attewell House
1 JARDINE CT
2 MILLHOUSE CT
STEVENSON AVE
ALBERT RD
HAYES AVE
HILLS RD
GREGORY AVE
HIND AVE
SPRING CL
FESTIVAL AVE
WESTERN MERE CL
DRAYCOTT RD
Wks
BRIDGE FIELD
THE CRESCENT
Breaston Ind Est
BELVOIR CL
The Elms
Elms Lodge
Works
Wilne Cross
BURLINGTON CL
LAWRENCE AVE
GRANGE AVE
KIRKFIELD DR
DALE CL
CHURCHILL CL
HOLME RD
DELAMERE CL
EARLSWOOD CL
FAR CROFT
PLACKETT CL
STEPHENS LA
SHIRLEY CRES
WARD'S LA
BLIND LA
MANOR CT
MANOR LEIGH
MAIN ST
THE GREEN
CHURCH VIEW
BOURNE SQ
MEADOW CL
MARLBOROUGH RD
Breaston
LONGMOOR LA
Liby
RISLEY LA
THORNTREE CL
RECTORY RD
CARRION CL
CHERRY CL
MAYLANDS AVE
AMELIA CL
BELMONT AVE
OLIVER CL
PARK ST
GROSVENOR AVE
THE GROVE
WILLOUGHBY CL
BEECH AVE
POPLAR RD
HAWTHORN AVE
MAPLE GR
HOLLY AVE
WILSTHORPE RD
A6005
FIRFIELD AVE
WILLOW CL
HOLT CROFT CL
ORCHARD CL
MAXWELL ST
ASTILL PINE CL
GOLDENBROOK CL
MOUNT ST
HARRIMANS DR
HEATHER CRES
WOODLAND AVE
FIELD CL
BIRCHWOOD AVE
Firfield Prim Sch
Poplar Farm
Breaston Fields Farm
SAWLEY RD
LC
M1
OVERDALE CL
River Derwent
WILNE RD
Midshires Way
Gravel Pit
Sawley Grange Farm
Church Wilne Resr
PYM LEYS
PURDY MDW
OSMASTON CL
MATLOCK CT
HATHERSAGE AVE
PEVERIL CRES
WINSTER WAY
RISHESFORD RD
DRAYCOTT RD
Works
TWYFORD RD
HILTON CL
MELBOURNE CT
INGLEBY RD
REPTON RD
WESTON CRES
HARDWICK CT
HADDON WAY
WILNE CL
WILNE RD
SUDBURY CT 1
ELVASTON DR 2
St Chad's Water Nature Reserve
Church Wilne
P
Ivy House Farm
WILNE LA
Works
River Derwent
Sawley Cut
Great Wilne
River Trent
Sewage Works
Works
B6540
WARREN LA
PH
CAVENDISH CL
LONG ROW
WILNE LA
THE WHARF
MILLFIELD
Trent & Mersey Canal
Porter's Bridge
Long Horse Bridge
Derwent Valley Heritage Way
MILL GN 1
MILL 2
THE WHARF
Shardlow Her Ctr
THE MALTINGS
Shardlow
Marina
LONDON RD
CANAL BANK
River Trent
CAVENDISH CT
B5010
Aqueduct
Gravel Pit
B6540
TAMWORTH RD
NETHERFIELDS LA
Hemington Fields House

8 7 33 6 5 32 4 3 31 2 1 30

44 A B 45 C D 46 E F

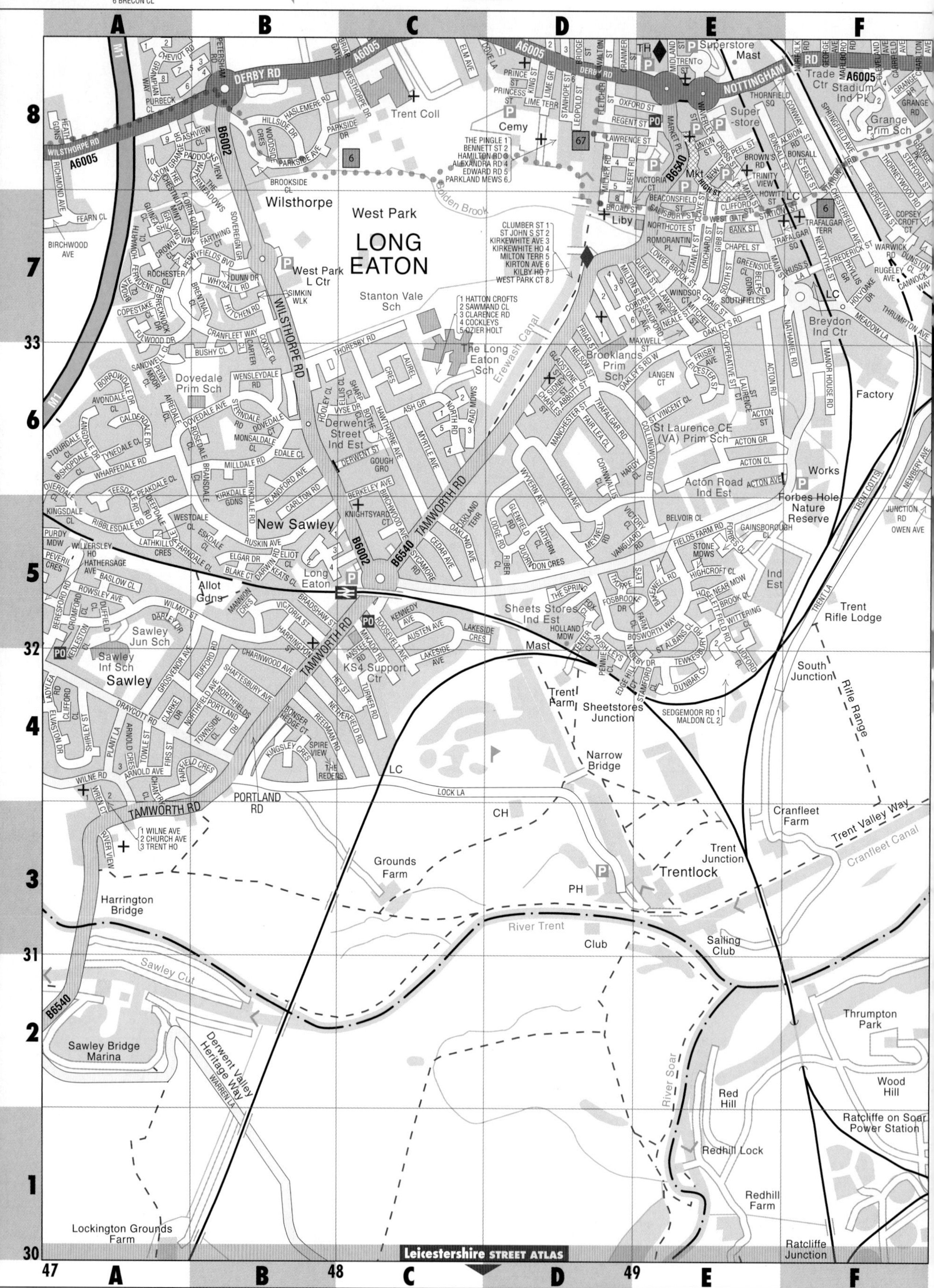

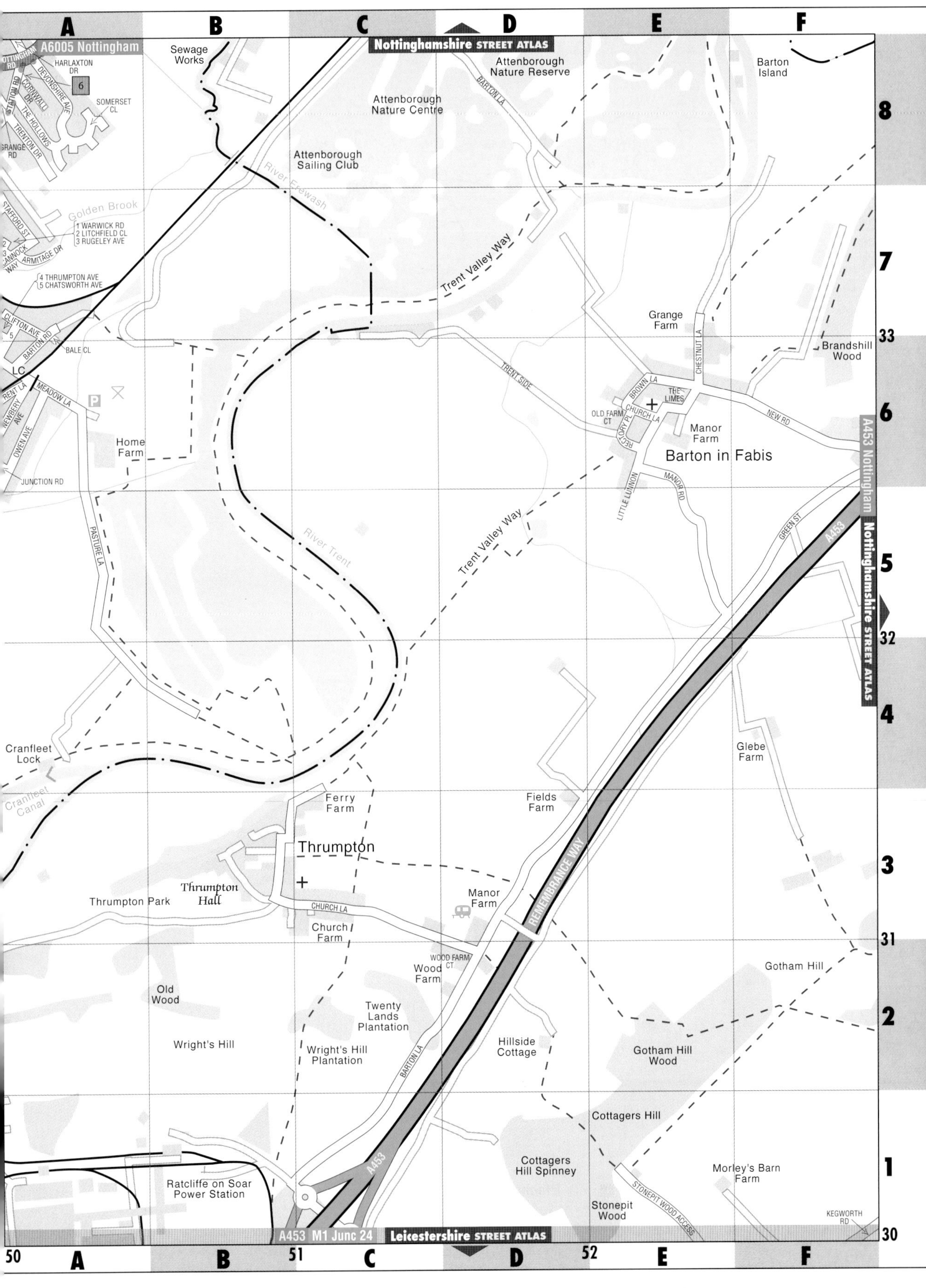

A B C D E F

8
7
33
6

Barton in Fabis

5
32
4

3
31
2
1
30

50 A 51 B C 52 D E F

Nottinghamshire STREET ATLAS

A6005 Nottingham
HARLAXTON DR
DEVONSHIRE AVE
CORNWALL
SOMERSET CL
GRANGE RD
STAFFORD ST
Golden Brook
1 WARWICK RD
2 LITCHFIELD CL
3 RUGELEY AVE
ARMITAGE DR
4 THRUMPTON AVE
5 CHATSWORTH AVE
CLIFTON AVE
BARTON RD
BALE CL
LC
TRENT LA
MEADOW LA
NEWBERY AVE
OWEN AVE
JUNCTION RD
Home Farm
PASTURE LA

Sewage Works
Attenborough Nature Centre
Attenborough Nature Reserve
Barton Island
Attenborough Sailing Club
River Erewash
Trent Valley Way
TRENT SIDE
Grange Farm
CHESTNUT LA
Brandshill Wood
BROWN LA
CHURCH LA
THE LIMES
OLD FARM CT
RECTORY PL
Manor Farm
NEW RD
LITTLE LONDON
MANOR RD
A453 Nottingham
GREEN ST
A453
River Trent
Trent Valley Way

Cranfleet Lock
Cranfleet Canal
Glebe Farm

Ferry Farm
Fields Farm
REMEMBRANCE WAY
Thrumpton
Thrumpton Hall
Thrumpton Park
CHURCH LA
Church Farm
Manor Farm
Gotham Hill
Old Wood
WOOD FARM CT
Wood Farm
Twenty Lands Plantation
Wright's Hill
Wright's Hill Plantation
BARTON LA
Hillside Cottage
Gotham Hill Wood
Cottagers Hill
A453
Ratcliffe on Soar Power Station
Cottagers Hill Spinney
STONEPIT WOOD ACCESS
Morley's Barn Farm
Stonepit Wood
KEGWORTH RD

Nottinghamshire STREET ATLAS

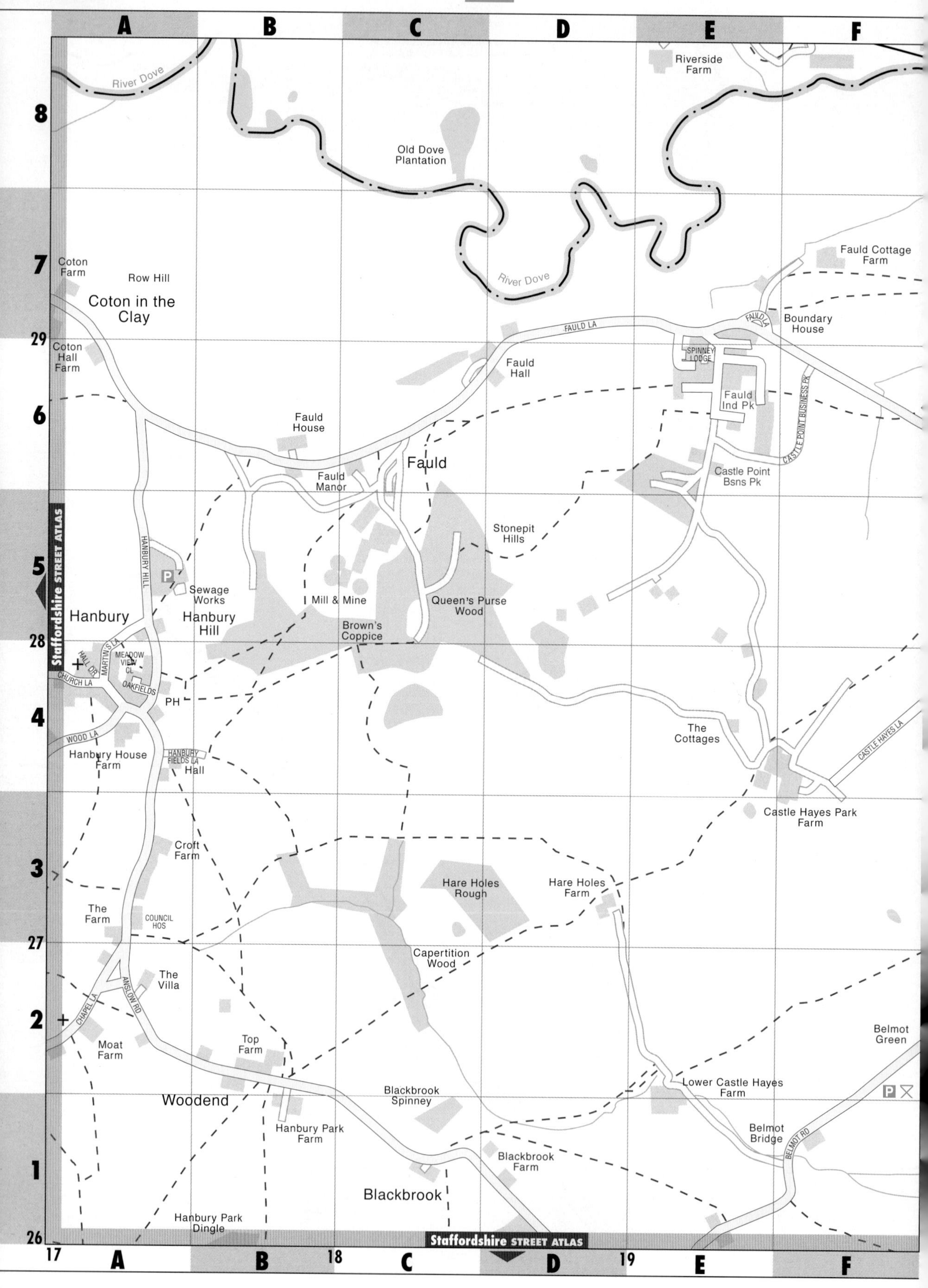

River Dove

8

Old Dove
Plantation

Riverside
Farm

River Dove

Fauld Cottage
Farm

7

Coton
Farm

Row Hill

Boundary
House

Coton in the
Clay

FAULD LA

FAULD LA

29

Coton
Hall
Farm

Fauld
Hall

Spinney
Lodge

6

Fauld
House

Fauld
Ind Pk

CASTLE POINT BUSINESS PK

Fauld

Fauld
Manor

Castle Point
Bsns Pk

Stonepit
Hills

5

HANBURY HILL

P

Sewage
Works

Mill & Mine

Queen's Purse
Wood

Hanbury
Hill

28

Hanbury

Brown's
Coppice

MARTINS LA

HALL DR

MEADOW
VIEW
CL

OAKFIELDS

CHURCH LA

PH

4

WOOD LA

The
Cottages

Hanbury House
Farm

HANBURY
FIELDS LA

Hall

CASTLE HAYES LA

Croft
Farm

Castle Hayes Park
Farm

3

The
Farm

COUNCIL
HOS

Hare Holes
Rough

Hare Holes
Farm

27

Capertition
Wood

The
Villa

ANSLOW RD

CHAPEL LA

2

Belmot
Green

Moat
Farm

Top
Farm

P ✕

Blackbrook
Spinney

Lower Castle Hayes
Farm

Woodend

Hanbury Park
Farm

Belmot
Bridge

BELMOT RD

1

Blackbrook
Farm

Blackbrook

26

Hanbury Park
Dingle

17   A   B   18   C   D   19   E   F

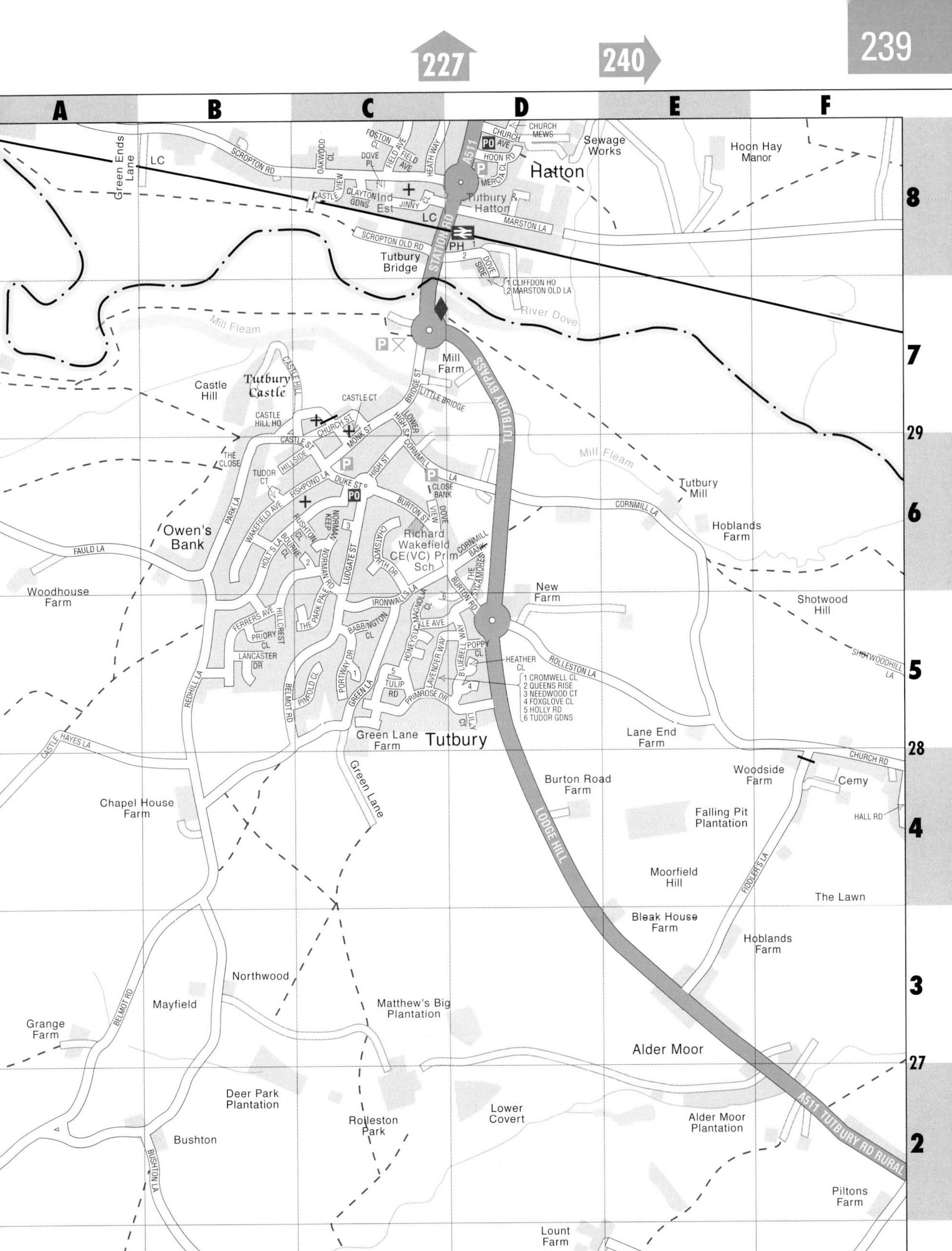

Green Ends Lane
LC

SCROPTON RD
FOSTON CL
OAKWOOD CL
FIELD AVE
DOVE PL
HEATH WAY
CHURCH AVE
CHURCH MEWS
PO
HOON RD
A511
MERCIA CL
Sewage Works
Hoon Hay Manor

Hatton

CASTLE VIEW
CLAYTON GDNS
NI
JINNY
Tutbury & Hatton Ind Est
LC

MARSTON LA

8

SCROPTON OLD RD
STATION RD
PH
1 CLIFFDON HO
2 MARSTON OLD LA
DOVE SIDE

Tutbury Bridge

River Dove

7

Mill Fleam

Castle Hill
Tutbury Castle

CASTLE HILL
P

Mill Farm

BRIDGE ST
LITTLE BRIDGE
MILL ST

TUTBURY BYPASS

29

CASTLE CT
CASTLE HILL HO
THE CLOSE
CASTLE HILL
CASTLE ST
CHURCH ST
MONK ST
HILLSIDE
HIGH ST
LOWER
CORNMILL

Mill Fleam

Tutbury Mill

TUDOR CT
PARK LA
FISHPOND LA
DUKE ST
P
PO
CLOSE BANK
LA
DOVE
CORNMILL LA
Hoblands Farm

6

FAULD LA
Owen's Bank
WAKEFIELD AVE
HOLT ST LA
KEEP
NEWMAN
NORMAN
BURTON
CHADSWORTH ST
LUDGATE ST
Richard Wakefield CE(VC) Prim Sch
BURTON RD
CORNMILL BANK
THE SYCAMORES

Shotwood Hill

Woodhouse Farm

THE PARK
PARK PALE
IRONWALLS LA

New Farm

SHOTWOODHILL LA

REDHILL LA
TERRERS AVE
PRIORY CL
HILLCREST
LANCASTER DR
HONEYSUCKLE
MAGNOLIA
CL
CLE AVE
BABBINGTON CL
POPPY CL
HEATHER CL
ROLLESTON LA

5

BELMOT RD
PINFOLD CL
PORTWAY DR
GREEN LA
TULIP RD
LAVENDER WAY
PRIMROSE DR
1 BLUEBELL WAY
1 CROMWELL CL
2 QUEENS RISE
3 NEEDWOOD CT
4 FOXGLOVE CL
5 HOLLY RD
6 TUDOR GDNS

Lane End Farm

28

Green Lane Farm
Tutbury

Burton Road Farm

Woodside Farm
Cemy
CHURCH RD

HALL RD

Chapel House Farm

Green Lane

Falling Pit Plantation

FIDDLERS LA

4

CASTLE
HAYES LA

LODGE HILL

Moorfield Hill

The Lawn

Grange Farm

Northwood

Mayfield

Matthew's Big Plantation

Bleak House Farm

Hoblands Farm

3

BELMOT RD

Deer Park Plantation

Rolleston Park

Lower Covert

Alder Moor

A511 TUTBURY RD RURAL

27

Bushton

BUSHTON LA

Alder Moor Plantation

Piltons Farm

2

Bushton Bridge

Whitestone Lane

Lount Farm

Lane

LOUNT LA

Newgatefield

The Bungalow

LONGHEDGE LA

1

26

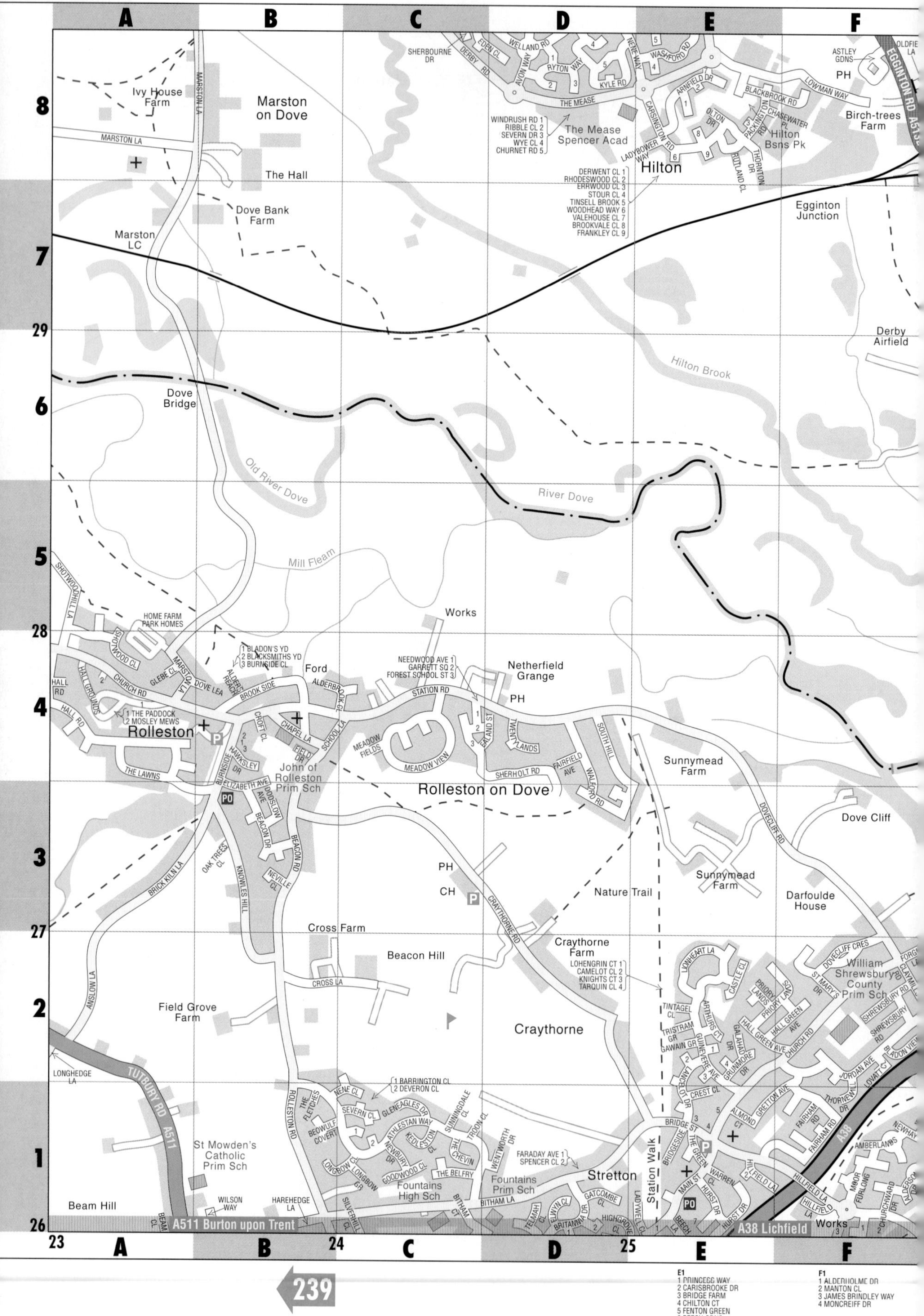

E1
1 PRINCESS WAY
2 CARISBROOKE DR
3 BRIDGE FARM
4 CHILTON CT
5 FENTON GREEN
6 BEECH GDNS

F1
1 ALDERHOLME DR
2 MANTON CL
3 JAMES BRINDLEY WAY
4 MONCREIFF DR

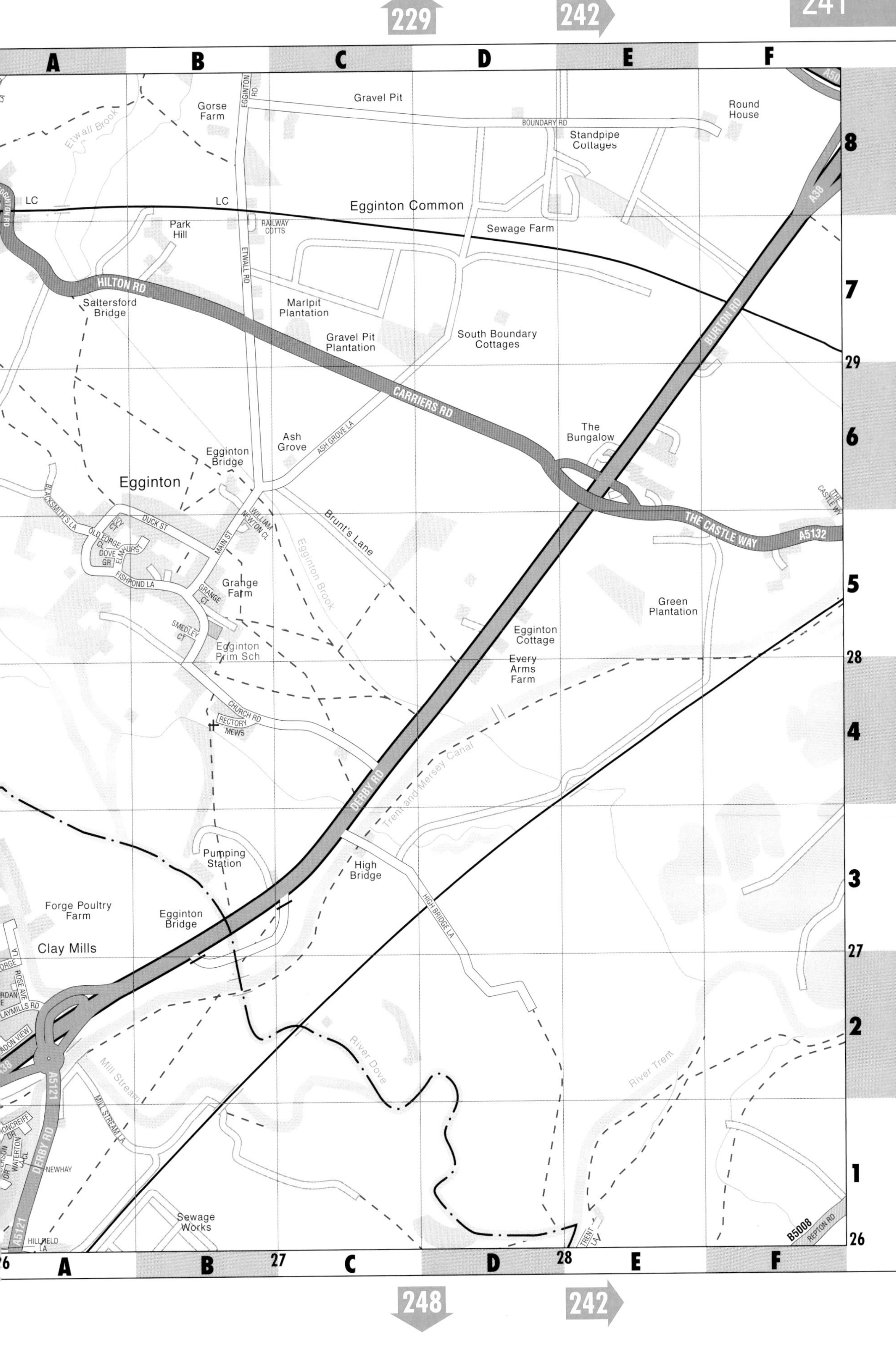

229
242
248
242

A B C D E F

8
7
29
6
5
28
4
3
27
2
1
26

Gorse Farm
Gravel Pit
BOUNDARY RD
Standpipe Cottages
Round House

EGGINTON RD

ELWALL RD

A38

LC
LC
Egginton Common
Sewage Farm
RAILWAY COTTS
Park Hill

HILTON RD
Saltersford Bridge
Marlpit Plantation

BURTON RD

Gravel Pit Plantation
South Boundary Cottages

CARRIERS RD

Ash Grove
Egginton Bridge

Egginton

ASH GROVE LA

The Bungalow

THE CASTLE WAY A5132

THE CASTLE WAY

BLACKSMITHS LA
OLD FORGE CL
CKY CL
DOVE GR
EL MURS
DUCK ST
MAIN ST
WILLIAM NEWTON CL
Brunt's Lane
FISHPOND LA
Egginton Brook

Green Plantation

GRANGE CT
Grange Farm
SMEDLEY CT
Egginton Prim Sch
CHURCH RD
RECTORY MEWS

Egginton Cottage
Every Arms Farm

DERBY RD

Trent and Mersey Canal

Forge Poultry Farm
Pumping Station
Egginton Bridge

Clay Mills

High Bridge

HIGH BRIDGE LA

A38

A5121
DERBY RD
FORGE
ROSEDALE
RDAM E
LAYMILLS RD
ADON VIEW
Mill Stream
MILL STREAM LA

River Dove

River Trent

MONCREFF DR
WATERTON CL
NEWHAY

Sewage Works

HILLFIELD LA

B5008
REPTON RD
TRENT LA

A5121

6   27   28

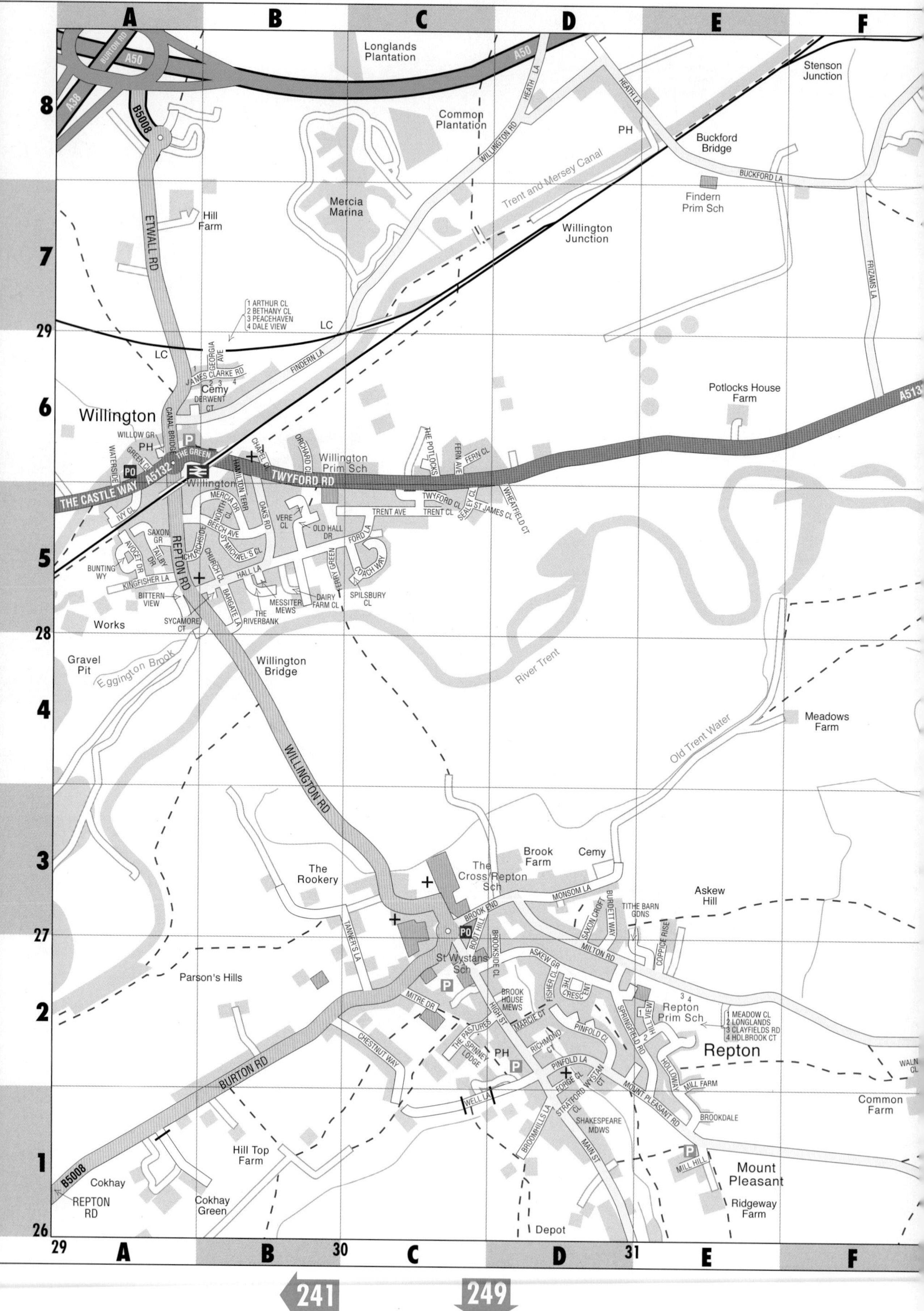

241
230
A B C D E F
Longlands Plantation
Stenson Junction
Common Plantation
Buckford Bridge
Mercia Marina
Hill Farm
Findern Prim Sch
Willington Junction
Trent and Mersey Canal
1 ARTHUR CL
2 BETHANY CL
3 PEACEHAVEN
4 DALE VIEW
Potlocks House Farm
Willington
Willington Prim Sch
TWYFORD RD
THE CASTLE WAY
Works
Gravel Pit
Eggington Brook
Willington Bridge
River Trent
Old Trent Water
Meadows Farm
WILLINGTON RD
The Rookery
Brook Farm
Cemy
The Cross/Repton Sch
Askew Hill
St Wystans Sch
Parson's Hills
Repton Prim Sch
1 MEADOW CL
2 LONGLANDS
3 CLAYFIELDS RD
4 HOLBROOK CT
Repton
BURTON RD
Common Farm
Hill Top Farm
Mount Pleasant
Cokhay
Cokhay Green
REPTON RD
Ridgeway Farm
Depot
29 30 31
241
249

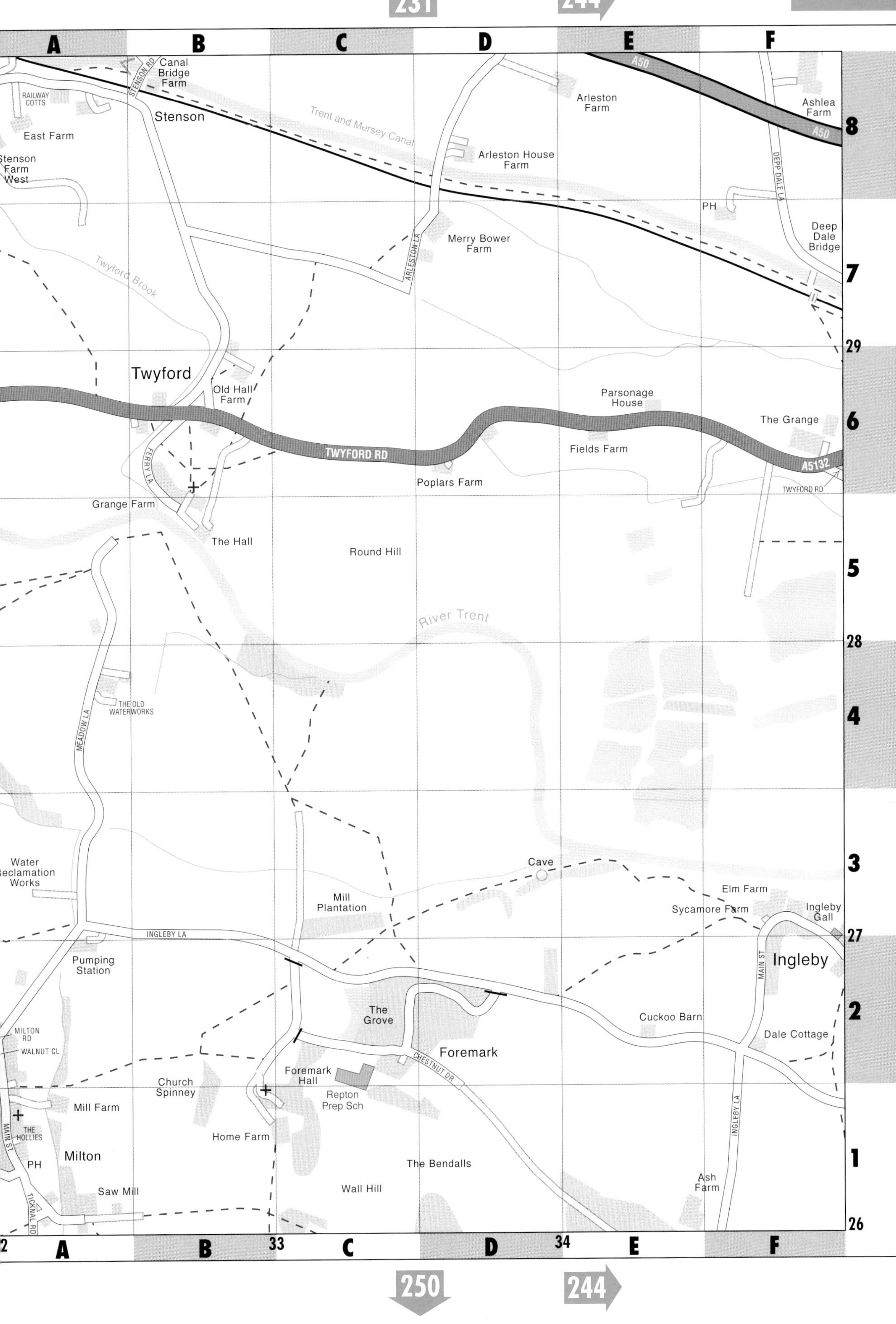

231
244

A   B   C   D   E   F

RAILWAY COTTS

Canal Bridge Farm

Stenson

East Farm

Stenson Farm West

Arleston Farm

A50

Ashlea Farm

A50

Arleston House Farm

PH

Depp Dale Bridge

DEPP DALE LA

8

Trent and Mersey Canal

Twyford Brook

Merry Bower Farm

ARLESTON LA

7

29

Twyford

Old Hall Farm

Parsonage House

The Grange

6

TWYFORD RD

Fields Farm

FERRY LA

Poplars Farm

A5132

TWYFORD RD

Grange Farm

The Hall

Round Hill

5

28

River Trent

MEADOW LA

THE OLD WATERWORKS

4

Water Reclamation Works

Mill Plantation

Cave

3

Elm Farm

Sycamore Farm

Ingleby Gall

INGLEBY LA

27

Pumping Station

Ingleby

MAIN ST

MILTON RD

WALNUT CL

The Grove

Cuckoo Barn

Dale Cottage

2

CHESTNUT DR

Foremark

Mill Farm

Church Spinney

Foremark Hall

Repton Prep Sch

INGLEBY LA

Home Farm

THE HOLLIES

Milton

PH

MAIN ST

The Bendalls

Ash Farm

1

Saw Mill

Wall Hill

TUCKNAL RD

26

2   A   B   33   C   D   34   E   F

250
244

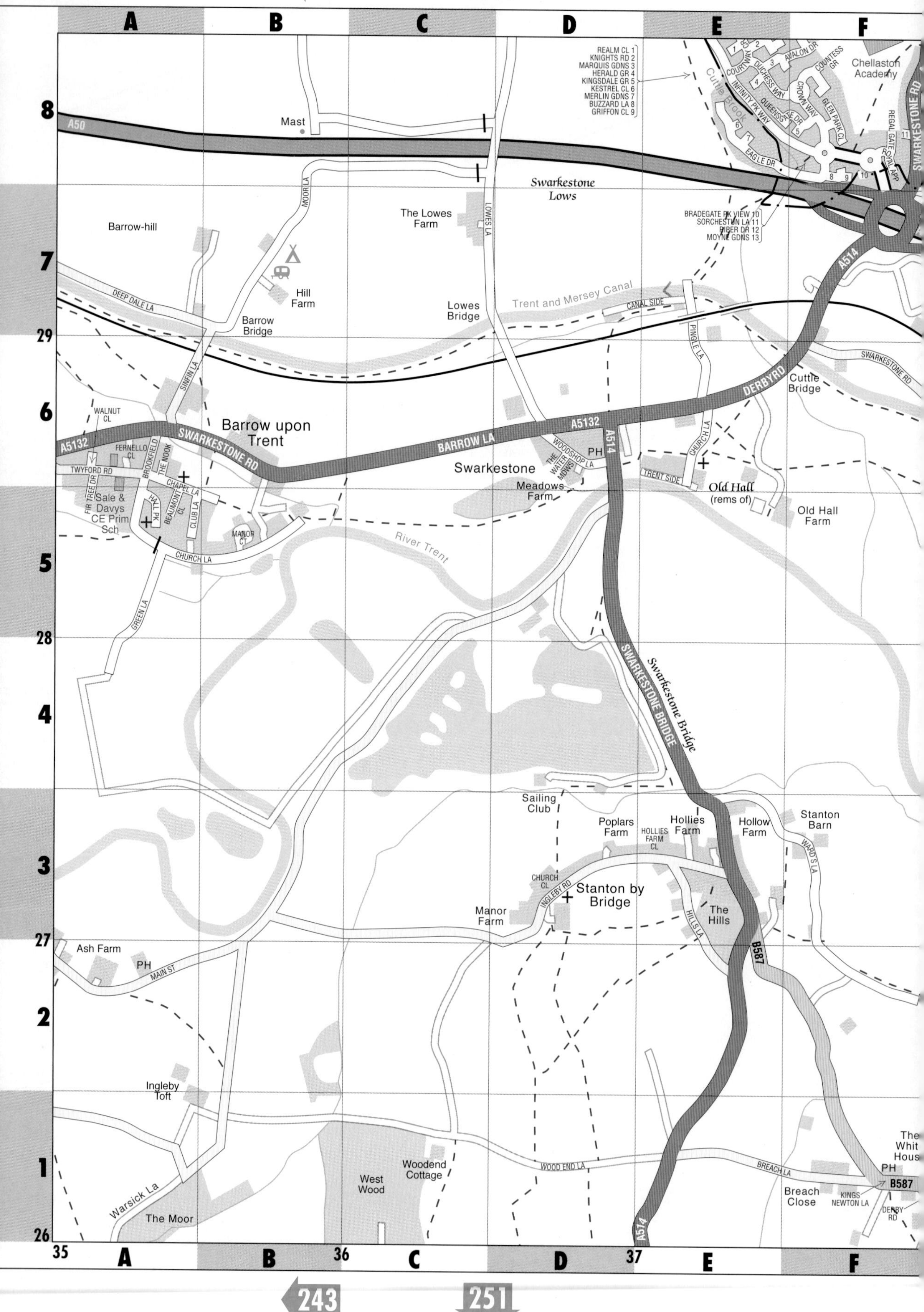

A   B   C   D   E   F

REALM CL 1
KNIGHTS RD 2
MARQUIS GDNS 3
HERALD GR 4
KINGSDALE GR 5
KESTREL CL 6
MERLIN GDNS 7
BUZZARD LA 8
GRIFFON CL 9

Chellaston Academy

SWARKESTONE RD

8

A50

Mast

Swarkestone Lows

BRADEGATE PK VIEW 10
SORCHESTON LA 11
PIBER DR 12
MOYNE GDNS 13

A514

Barrow-hill

The Lowes Farm

7

MOOR LA

Hill Farm

LOWES LA

DEEP DALE LA

Barrow Bridge

Lowes Bridge

Trent and Mersey Canal

CANAL SIDE

29

SINFIN LA

PINGLE LA

SWARKESTONE RD

Cuttle Bridge

DERBY RD

6

WALNUT CL

Barrow upon Trent

A5132

BARROW LA

A5132

A514

CHURCH LA

FERNELLO CL

BROOKFIELD

THE NOOK

SWARKESTONE RD

Swarkestone

THE WATERS MDWS

WOODSHOP LA

PH

TWYFORD RD

FIR TREE DR

HALL PK

BEAUMONT CL

CHAPEL LA

CLUB LA

Meadows Farm

Old Hall
(rems of)

TRENT SIDE

Old Hall Farm

Sale & Davys CE Prim Sch

MANOR CT

5

GREEN LA

CHURCH LA

River Trent

28

4

SWARKESTONE BRIDGE

Sailing Club

Poplars Farm

Hollies Farm

Hollow Farm

Stanton Barn

3

HOLLIES FARM CL

WARD'S LA

CHURCH CL

Manor Farm

INGLEBY RD

Stanton by Bridge

The Hills

HILL'S LA

B587

27

Ash Farm

PH

MAIN ST

2

Ingleby Toft

The Whit Hous PH

1

Warsick La

West Wood

Woodend Cottage

WOOD END LA

BREACH LA

B587

DERBY RD

Breach Close

KINGS NEWTON LA

The Moor

26

35   A   B   36   C   D   37   E   F

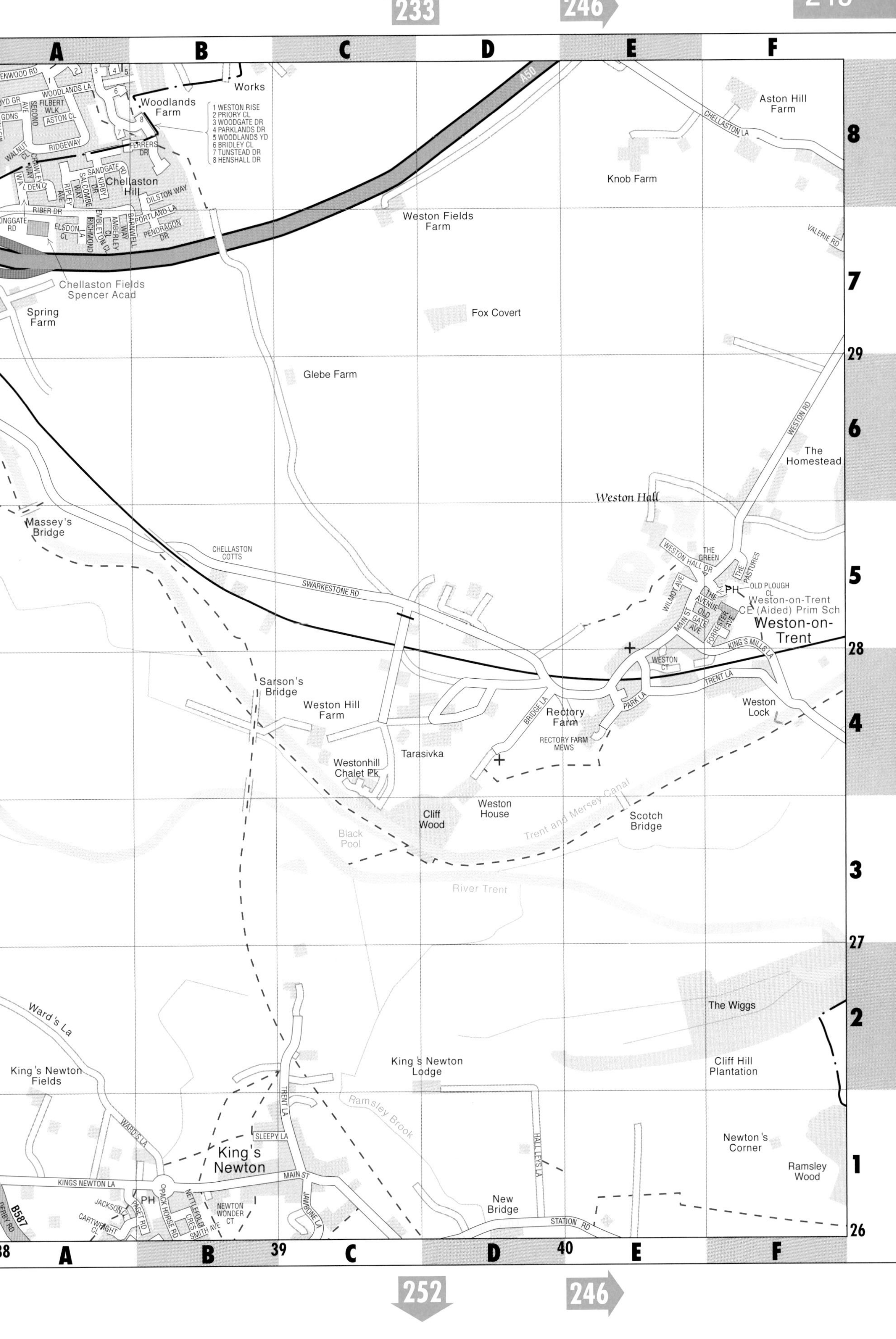

233
246
A
B
C
D
E
F
Woodlands Farm
Works
1 WESTON RISE
2 PRIORY CL
3 WOODGATE DR
4 PARKLANDS DR
5 WOODLANDS YD
6 BRIDLEY CL
7 TUNSTEAD DR
8 HENSHALL DR
Chellaston Hill
Chellaston Fields Spencer Acad
Spring Farm
A50
Weston Fields Farm
Aston Hill Farm
CHELLASTON LA
Knob Farm
VALERIE RD
Fox Covert
Glebe Farm
WESTON RD
The Homestead
Weston Hall
Massey's Bridge
CHELLASTON COTTS
SWARKESTONE RD
WESTON HALL DR
THE GREEN
THE PASTURES
OLD PLOUGH CL
PH
Weston-on-Trent CE (Aided) Prim Sch
Weston-on-Trent
WILMOT AVE
MAIN ST
THE AVENUE
OLD GATE AVE
FORRESTER AVE
KING'S MILLS LA
WESTON CT
TRENT LA
PARK LA
BRIDGE LA
Sarson's Bridge
Weston Hill Farm
Rectory Farm
RECTORY FARM MEWS
Weston Lock
Tarasivka
Westonhill Chalet Pk
Cliff Wood
Weston House
Trent and Mersey Canal
Scotch Bridge
Black Pool
River Trent
The Wiggs
Ward's La
King's Newton Fields
King's Newton Lodge
Cliff Hill Plantation
Ramsley Brook
TRENT LA
WARD'S LA
SLEEPY LA
King's Newton
HALLEYS LA
Newton's Corner
Ramsley Wood
KINGS NEWTON LA
MAIN ST
PH
JACKSON CL
CARTWRIGHT CL
OPACK HORSE RD
NETTLEFOLD CRES
SMITH AVE
NEWTON WONDER CT
JAMBONE LA
New Bridge
STATION RD
B587
DERBY RD
8
7
29
6
5
28
4
3
27
2
1
26
38
39
40
252
246

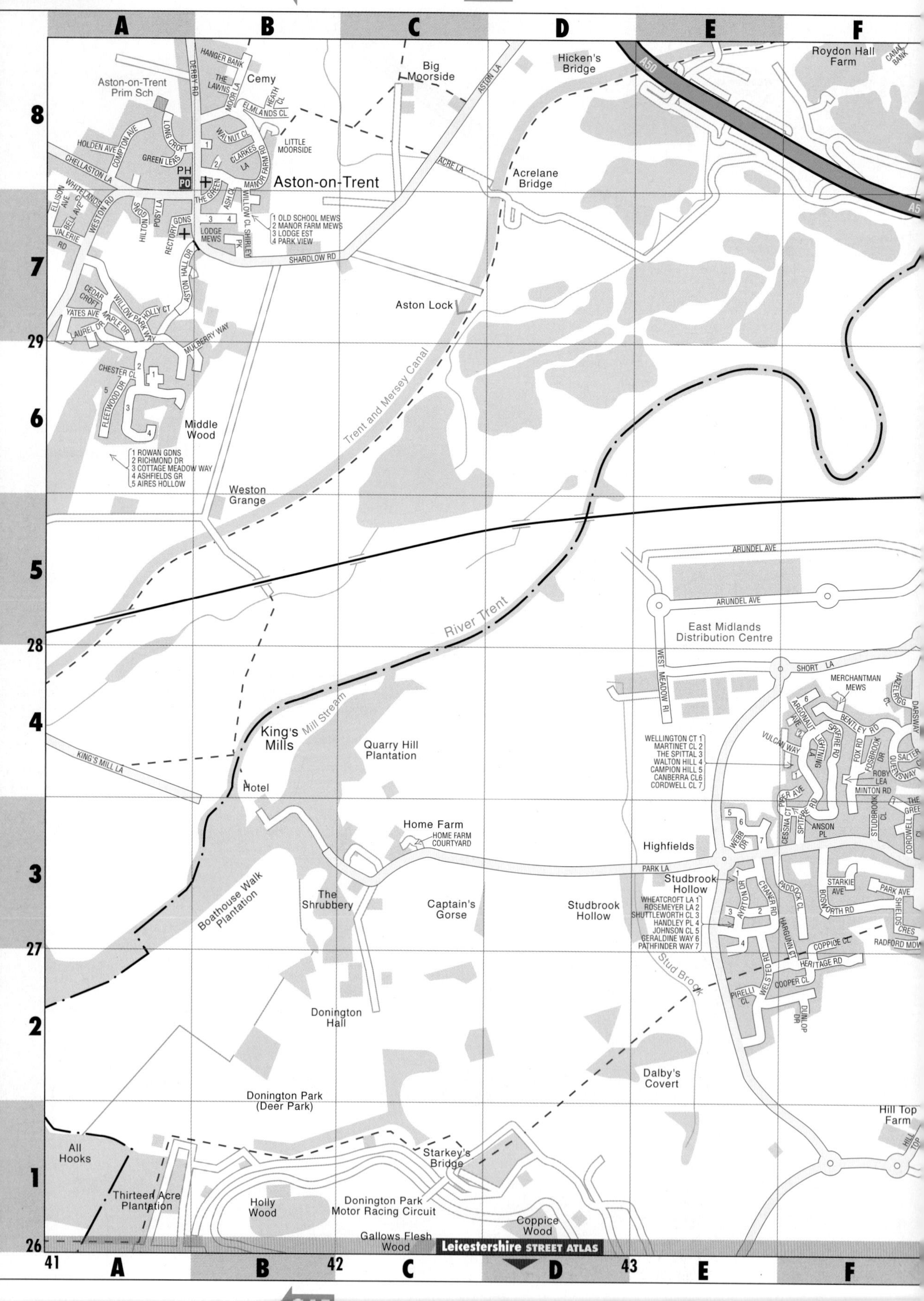
Aston-on-Trent
Aston-on-Trent Prim Sch
Cemy
Big Moorside
Hicken's Bridge
Roydon Hall Farm
LITTLE MOORSIDE
Acrelane Bridge
1 OLD SCHOOL MEWS
2 MANOR FARM MEWS
3 LODGE EST
4 PARK VIEW
SHARDLOW RD
Aston Lock
Trent and Mersey Canal
Middle Wood
1 ROWAN GDNS
2 RICHMOND DR
3 COTTAGE MEADOW WAY
4 ASHFIELDS GR
5 AIRES HOLLOW
Weston Grange
River Trent
ARUNDEL AVE
East Midlands Distribution Centre
WEST MEADOW RD
SHORT LA
MERCHANTMAN MEWS
WELLINGTON CT 1
MARTINET CL 2
THE SPITTAL 3
WALTON HILL 4
CAMPION HILL 5
CANBERRA CL 6
CORDWELL CL 7
King's Mills
Mill Stream
Quarry Hill Plantation
KING'S MILL LA
Hotel
Home Farm
HOME FARM COURTYARD
Highfields
PARK LA
Studbrook Hollow
WHEATCROFT LA 1
ROSEMEYER LA 2
SHUTTLEWORTH CL 3
HANDLEY PL 4
JOHNSON CL 5
GERALDINE WAY 6
PATHFINDER WAY 7
Boathouse Walk Plantation
The Shrubbery
Captain's Gorse
Studbrook Hollow
Stud Brook
Donington Hall
Dalby's Covert
Donington Park (Deer Park)
Hill Top Farm
All Hooks
Starkey's Bridge
Thirteen Acre Plantation
Holly Wood
Donington Park Motor Racing Circuit
Coppice Wood
Gallows Flesh Wood
A50
A
B
C
D
E
F
8
7
29
6
5
28
4
3
27
2
1
26
41
42
43

235

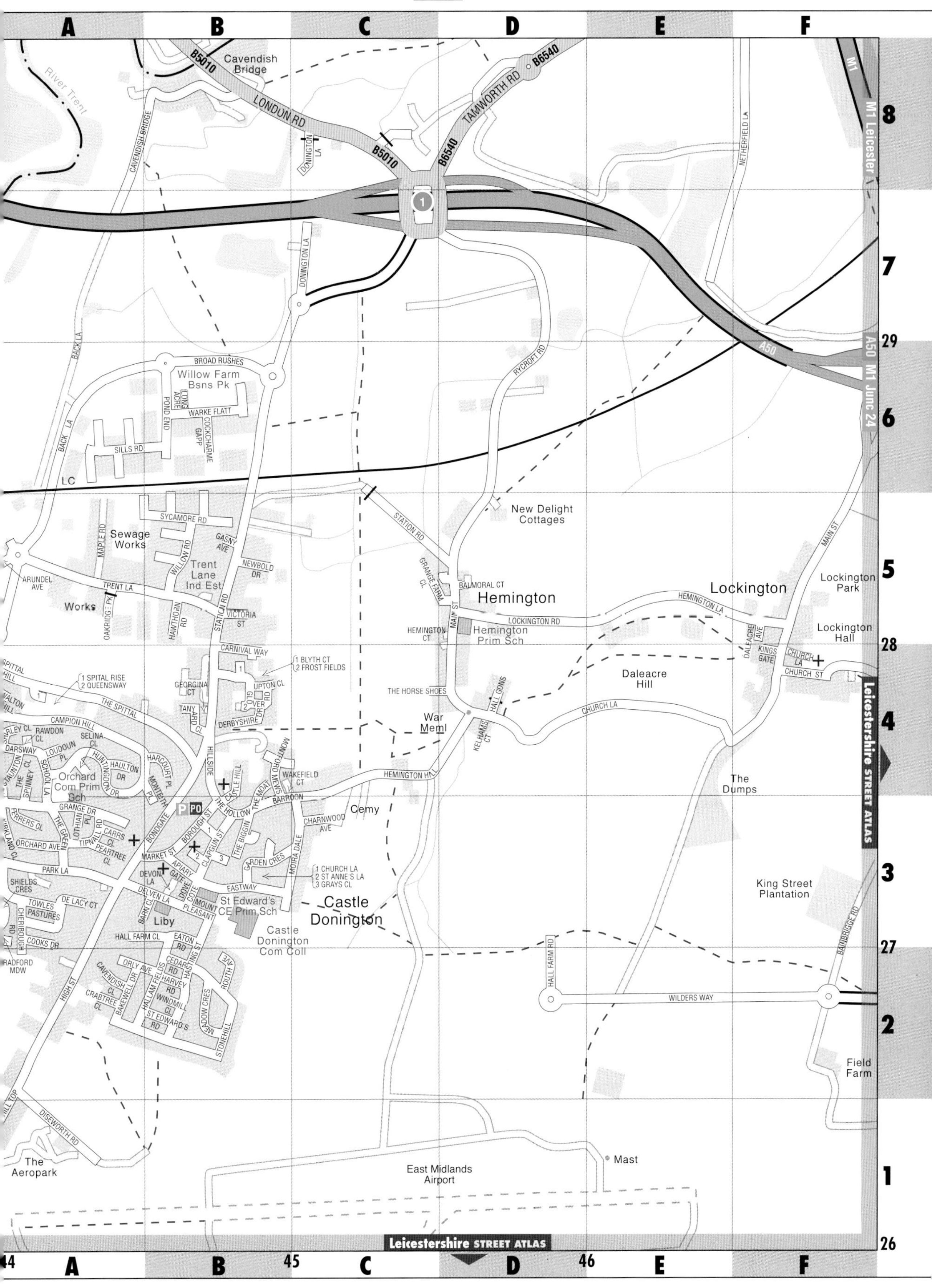

Cavendish Bridge
River Trent
B5010
LONDON RD
B6540
TAMWORTH RD
CAVENDISH BRIDGE
DONINGTON LA
NETHERFIELD LA
M1
M1 Leicester
A50
M1 Junc 24
BACK LA
BROAD RUSHES
Willow Farm Bsns Pk
LONG ACRE
POND END
WARKE FLATT
COCKCHARME GAPP
SILLS RD
RYCROFT RD
LC
SYCAMORE RD
STATION RD
New Delight Cottages
Sewage Works
MAPLE RD
WILLOW RD
GASNY AVE
Trent Lane Ind Est
NEWBOLD DR
ARUNDEL AVE
TRENT LA
Works
OAKRIDGE PK
HAWTHORN RD
STATION RD
VICTORIA ST
GRANGE FARM CL
BALMORAL CT
Hemington
MAIN ST
HEMINGTON CT
LOCKINGTON RD
Hemington Prim Sch
HEMINGTON LA
Lockington
Lockington Park
Lockington Hall
MAIN ST
DALEACRE AVE
KINGS GATE
CHURCH LA
CHURCH ST
Daleacre Hill
CARNIVAL WAY
1 BLYTH CT
2 FROST FIELDS
1 SPITAL RISE
2 QUEENSWAY
SPITTAL HILL
WALTON HILL
THE SPITTAL
GEORGINA CT
UPTON CL
CLOVER DR
TANYARD CL
DERBYSHIRE LA
THE HORSE SHOES
HALL GDNS
KELHAMS CT
CHURCH LA
War Meml
CAMPION HILL
RAWDON CL
SELINA CL
DARSWAY
LOUDOUN PL
HUNTINGDON DR
HAULTON DR
HARCOURT PL
MONTEITH PL
HILLSIDE
CASTLE HILL
MONTFORD MEWS
WAKEFIELD CT
HEMINGTON HILL
The Dumps
STAINTON
THE SPINNEY
SCHOOL LA
Orchard Com Prim Sch
GRANGE DR
LOTHIAN PL
THE GREEN
FERRERS CL
PARKLAND DR
ORCHARD AVE
TIPNALL RD
CARRS CL
PEARTREE CL
BONDGATE
THE HOLLOW
BOROUGH ST
THE MOAT
BARROON
Cemy
CHARNWOOD AVE
THE BIGGIN
CLAPGUN ST
MARKET ST
GARDEN CRES
MOIRA DALE
1 CHURCH LA
2 ST ANNE'S LA
3 GRAYS CL
PARK LA
APIARY GATE
DEVON LA
DOVE COTE
EASTWAY
SHIELDS CRES
DE LACY CT
DELVEN LA
BARN CL
MOUNT PLEASANT
St Edward's CE Prim Sch
Castle Donington
King Street Plantation
TOWLES PASTURES
Liby
Castle Donington Com Coll
CHERIBOUGH RD
COOKS DR
HALL FARM CL
EATON RD
RADFORD MDW
ORLY AVE
CEDAR RD
HASTINGS ST
ROUTH AVE
HALL FARM RD
BAINBRIDGE RD
CAVENDISH CL
BAKEWELL DR
HALLAM FIELDS RD
HARVEY RD
WINDMILL CL
MEADOW CRES
WILDERS WAY
HIGH ST
CRABTREE CL
ST EDWARD'S RD
STONEHILL
Field Farm
HILL TOP
DISEWORTH RD
The Aeropark
Mast
East Midlands Airport
Leicestershire STREET ATLAS

A B C D E F
8 7 29 6 5 28 4 3 27 2 1 26
44 45 46

241

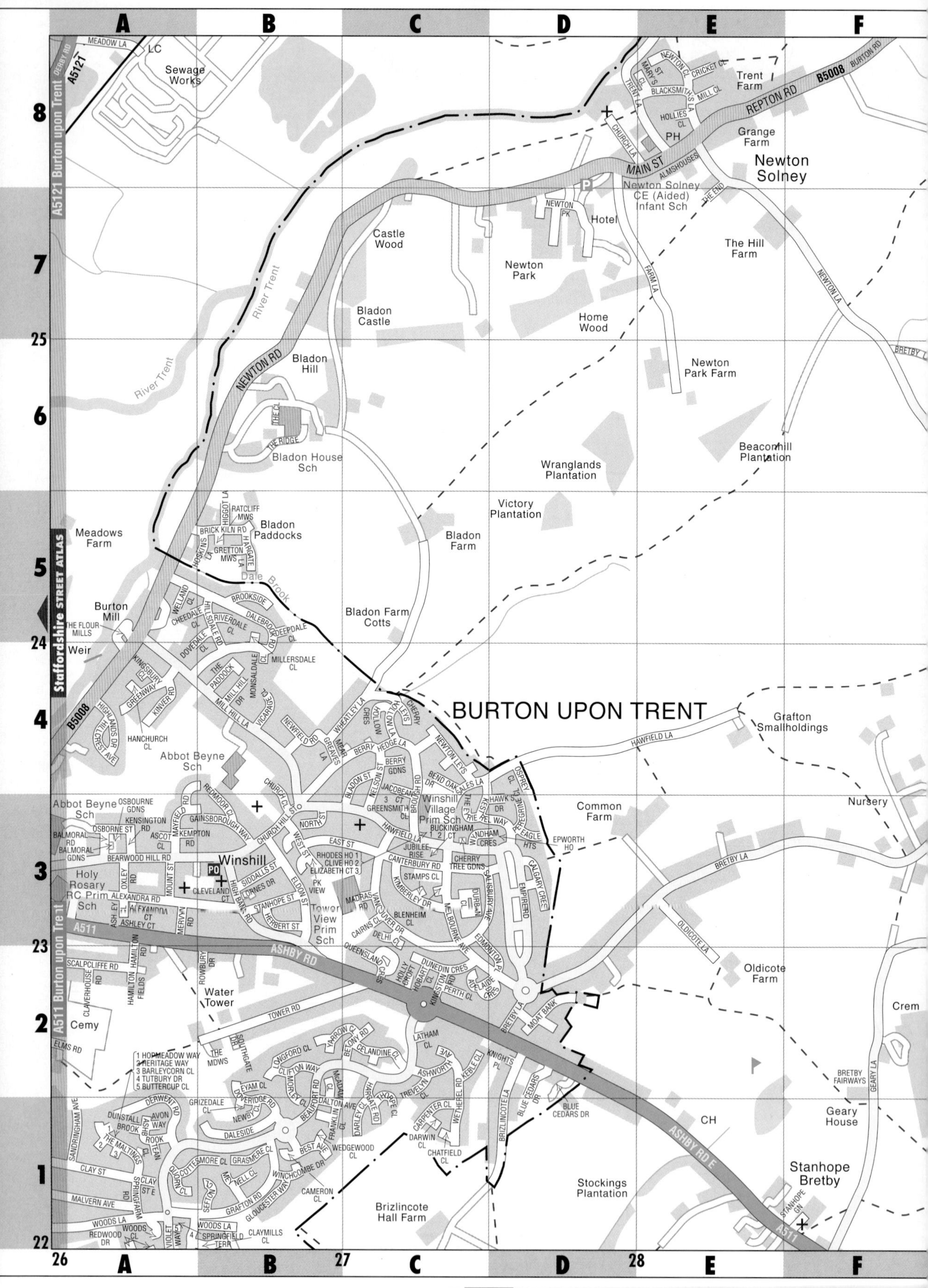
A
B
C
D
E
F
8
7
25
6
5
24
4
3
23
2
1
22
26
27
28
Staffordshire STREET ATLAS
A5121 Burton upon Trent
A511 Burton upon Trent
MEADOW LA
LC
DERBY RD
A5121
Sewage Works
River Trent
NEWTON RD
Castle Wood
Bladon Castle
Bladon Hill
THE CL
THE RIDGE
Bladon House Sch
Meadows Farm
RATCLIFF MWS
HIGGOTT LA
BRICK KILN RD
Bladon Paddocks
HOSKINS LA
GRETTON MWS
HARGATE LA
Dale Brook
Burton Mill
THE FLOUR MILLS
Weir
B5008
WELLAND CL
BROOKSIDE
CHEEDALE CL
RIVERDALE CL
HILLSDALE RD
DALEBROOK RD
DEEPDALE CL
DOVEDALE CL
MILLERSDALE CL
THE PADDOCK
MONSALDALE CL
MILL HILL DR
MILL HILL LA
VICARAGE CL
KINGSBURY CL
GREENWAY
KINVER RD
HIGHLANDS DR
HILLCREST AVE
HANCHURCH CL
Abbot Beyne Sch
NEWFIELD RD
GREAVES LA
MEAR LA
WHEATLEY LA
HOLLOW CRES
HOLLOW LA
CHERRY LEYS
BERRY HEDGE LA
BERRY GDNS
NEWTON LEYS
BEND OAK DR
SALES LA
OSPREY CL
HAWK DR
KESTREL WAY
PEREGRINE
EAGLE HTS
EPWORTH HO
REDMOOR CL
GAINSBOROUGH WAY
CHURCH CL
CHURCH HILL ST
NORTH ST
WEST ST
BLADON ST
NELSON ST
BROUGH RD
JACOBEAN CT
GREENSMITH CL
Winshill Village Prim Sch
HAWFIELD LA
EAST ST
BUCKINGHAM CT
WYNDHAM CRES
JUBILEE RISE
CANTERBURY RD
CHERRY TREE GDNS
RHODES HO 1
CLIVE HO 2
ELIZABETH CT 3
PK VIEW
STAMPS CL
KIMBERLEY DR
DURBAN CL
SALISBURY AVE
EMPIRE RD
CALGARY CRES
Abbot Beyne Sch
OSBOURNE GDNS
KENSINGTON RD
MAYFIELD RD
OSBORNE ST
ASCOT CL
KEMPTON RD
BALMORAL RD
BALMORAL GDNS
BEARWOOD HILL RD
Winshill
PO
Holy Rosary RC Prim Sch
OXLEY RD
MOUNT ST
CLEVELAND CT
HIGH BANK RD
SIDDALLS ST
ORNES DR
STANHOPE ST
HERBERT ST
ELDON ST
Tower View Prim Sch
MADRAS RD
VANCOUVER DR
BLENHEIM CL
MELBOURNE AVE
CAIRNS CL
DELHI CL
QUEENSLAND CRES
ALEXANDRA RD
ASHLEY CT
MERVYN RD
A511
ASHBY RD
HOLLY CROFT
HOBART CL
DUNEDIN CRES
KINGSTON RD
PERTH CL
ADELAIDE CRES
EDMONTON PL
BRETBY LA
MOAT BANK
SCALPCLIFFE RD
CLAYHOUSE RD
HAMILTON FIELDS
HAMILTON RD
ROWBURY DR
Water Tower
TOWER RD
Cemy
ELMS RD
1 HOPMEADOW WAY
2 HERITAGE WAY
3 BARLEYCORN CL
4 TUTBURY DR
5 BUTTERCUP CL
THE MDWS
SOUTHGATE DR
LONGFORD CL
YARROW CL
BELONY RD
CELANDINE CL
LATHAM CL
ASHWORTH AVE
KEBLE CL
KNIGHTS PL
CLIFTON WAY
MORLEY CL
BEAUFORT RD
McADAM CL
DALTON AVE
HARGATE RD
HOPE CL
TREVELYN CL
WETHERELL RD
BRIZLINCOTE LA
BLUE CEDARS DR
EYAM CL
DOVERIDGE RD
GRIZEDALE CL
NEWBY CL
SANDRINGHAM AVE
DERWENT RD
AVON WAY
DUNSTALL BROOK
ASHBROOK
TEAN
DALESIDE
FRANKLIN RD
DARLEY CL
CARPENTER CL
DARWIN CL
CHATFIELD CL
THE MALTINGS
CLAY ST
BEST AVE
WEDGEWOOD CL
CLAY ST E
QUORN CL
COTTESMORE CL
GRASMERE CL
MEYNELL CL
WINCHCOMBE DR
CAMERON CL
MALVERN AVE
SPRINGFARM RD
SEFTON CL
GRAFTON RD
GLOUCESTER WAY
WOODS LA
REDWOOD DR
WOODS CL
VIOLET WAY
SPRINGFIELD TERR
CLAYMILLS CL
Brizlincote Hall Farm
NEWTON CL
ST MARY'S CL
TRENT LA
CRICKET CL
BLACKSMITHS LA
MILL CL
HOLLIES CL
Trent Farm
BURTON RD
B5008
REPTON RD
PH
CHURCH LA
MAIN ST
ALMSHOUSES
Grange Farm
Newton Solney
P
Newton Solney CE (Aided) Infant Sch
THE END
NEWTON PK
Hotel
The Hill Farm
Newton Park
FARM LA
NEWTON LA
Home Wood
Newton Park Farm
BRETBY LA
Beaconhill Plantation
Wranglands Plantation
Victory Plantation
Bladon Farm
Bladon Farm Cotts
BURTON UPON TRENT
Grafton Smallholdings
HAWFIELD LA
Common Farm
Nursery
BRETBY LA
OLDICOTE LA
Oldicote Farm
Crem
BRETBY FAIRWAYS
GEARY LA
Geary House
CH
ASHBY RD E
Stockings Plantation
Stanhope Bretby
STANHOPE GN
A511

255

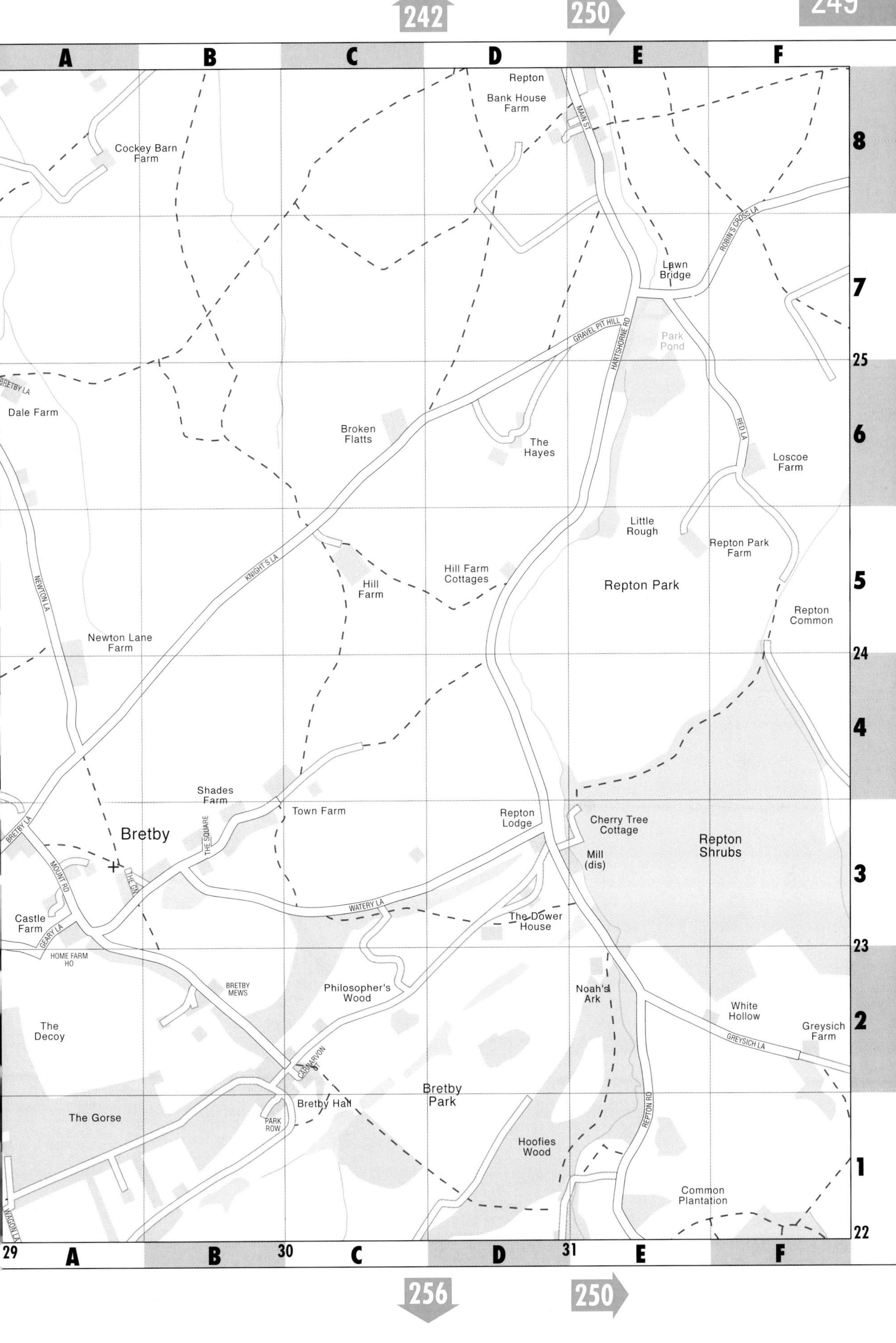

A B C D E F

Repton
Bank House
Farm

MAIN ST

Cockey Barn
Farm

Lawn
Bridge

ROBIN'S CROSS LA

BRETBY LA

Dale Farm

GRAVEL PIT HILL

HARTSHORNE RD

Park
Pond

Broken
Flatts

The
Hayes

RED LA

Loscoe
Farm

KNIGHT'S LA

Little
Rough

Repton Park
Farm

NEWTON LA

Hill Farm
Cottages

Hill
Farm

Repton Park

Repton
Common

Newton Lane
Farm

24

Shades
Farm

Town Farm

Repton
Lodge

Cherry Tree
Cottage

Repton
Shrubs

BRETBY LA

Bretby

THE SQUARE

THE GN

Mill
(dis)

MOUNT RD

Castle
Farm

GEARY LA

WATERY LA

The Dower
House

23

HOME FARM
HO

BRETBY
MEWS

Philosopher's
Wood

Noah's
Ark

White
Hollow

Greysich
Farm

The
Decoy

GREYSICH LA

CAERNARVON

Bretby
Park

REPTON RD

The Gorse

PARK
ROW

Bretby Hall

Hoofies
Wood

WRAGG LA

Common
Plantation

249
243

A   B   C   D   E   F

8

ROBIN'S CROSS LA

Bendalls
Clump

Heath
Wood

Warsick Lane

Seven Spouts
Farm

7

INGLEBY LA

Orangehill
Bridge

The Bendalls
Farmhouse

Knowle Hill
Farm

25

TICKNALL RD

Orange Hill

Brookdale Farm

SPUR'S BOTTOM

6

Dove Cote
Hill

Repton
Common

Tower

P

REPTON RD

5

P

24

Foremark Reservoir

The Grange

BURTON RD

A514

Sailing
Club

NARROW LA

4

HIGH ST

Fairview Farm

THE GREEN

The Scaddows

3

SCADDOWS LA

Repton
Shrubs

Repton
Bog

Bondwood
Farm

Foremark Park
Farm

Basfords Hill
Farm

Mast

23

ASHBY RD

Carver's
Rocks

The
Scaddows

Pottery
House

Hartshorn
Bog

2

Top Farm
House

STAUNTON LA

DERBY RD

GREYSICH LA

BROOK ST

1

TICKNALL RD

A514

COAL LA

Smith's
Gorse

B5006

Gravelpit Hill

THE BUILDINGS
FARM

22

32   A   B   33   C   D   34   E   F

249
257

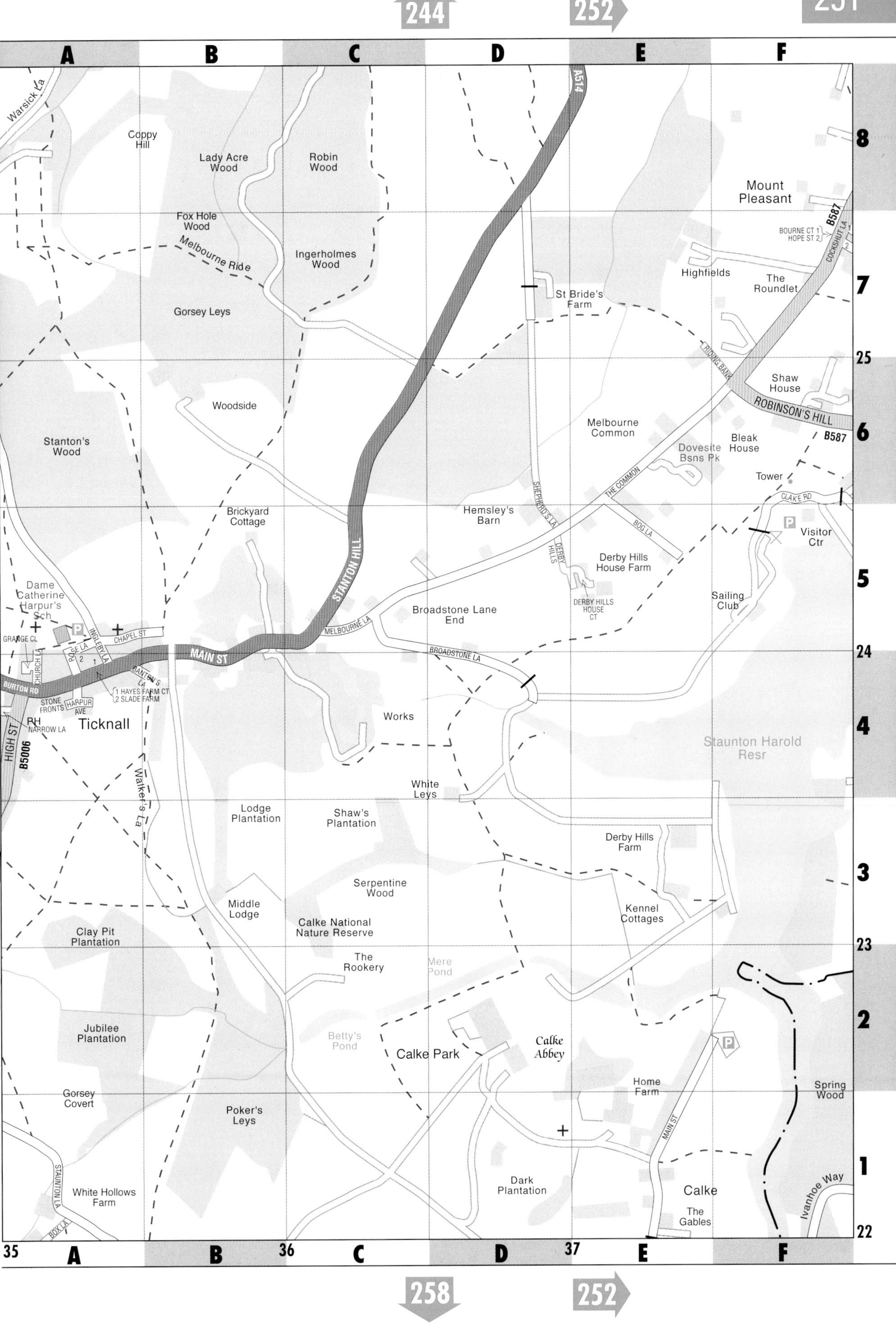

A   B   C   D   E   F

Warsick La
Coppy Hill
Lady Acre Wood
Robin Wood
Mount Pleasant
8

Fox Hole Wood
Melbourne Ride
Ingerholmes Wood
BOURNE CT 1
HOPE ST 2
B587
CROSHILL LA

Gorsey Leys
St Bride's Farm
Highfields
The Roundlet
7

25
THONG BANK

Woodside
Melbourne Common
Shaw House
ROBINSON'S HILL
6

Stanton's Wood
Dovesite Bsns Pk
Bleak House
B587

THE COMMON
Tower
CLAKE RD

Brickyard Cottage
Hemsley's Barn
SHEPHERD'S LA
BOG LA
P
Visitor Ctr

STANTON HILL
DERBY HILLS
Derby Hills House Farm
5

Dame Catherine Harpur's Sch
GRANGE CL
P
CHAPEL ST
MELBOURNE LA
Broadstone Lane End
DERBY HILLS HOUSE CT
Sailing Club

ROSE LA
INGLEBY LA
MAIN ST
BROADSTONE LA
24

BURTON RD
STONE FRONTS
HARPUR AVE
1 HAYES FARM CT
2 SLADE FARM
Works
Staunton Harold Resr
4

PH
NARROW LA
Ticknall
B5006
HIGH ST

White Leys

Walker's La
Lodge Plantation
Shaw's Plantation
Derby Hills Farm
3

Clay Pit Plantation
Middle Lodge
Serpentine Wood
Calke National Nature Reserve
Kennel Cottages

23

The Rookery
Mere Pond
2

Jubilee Plantation
Betty's Pond
Calke Park
Calke Abbey
P
Spring Wood

Gorsey Covert
Poker's Leys
Home Farm
MAIN ST
Calke
1

STAUNTON LA
BOX LA
White Hollows Farm
Dark Plantation
The Gables
22

35   A   B   36   C   D   37   E   F

252

A8
1 LOAKE CT
2 THE CROFT
3 REDWAY CROFT
4 LAMPAD CL

251

245

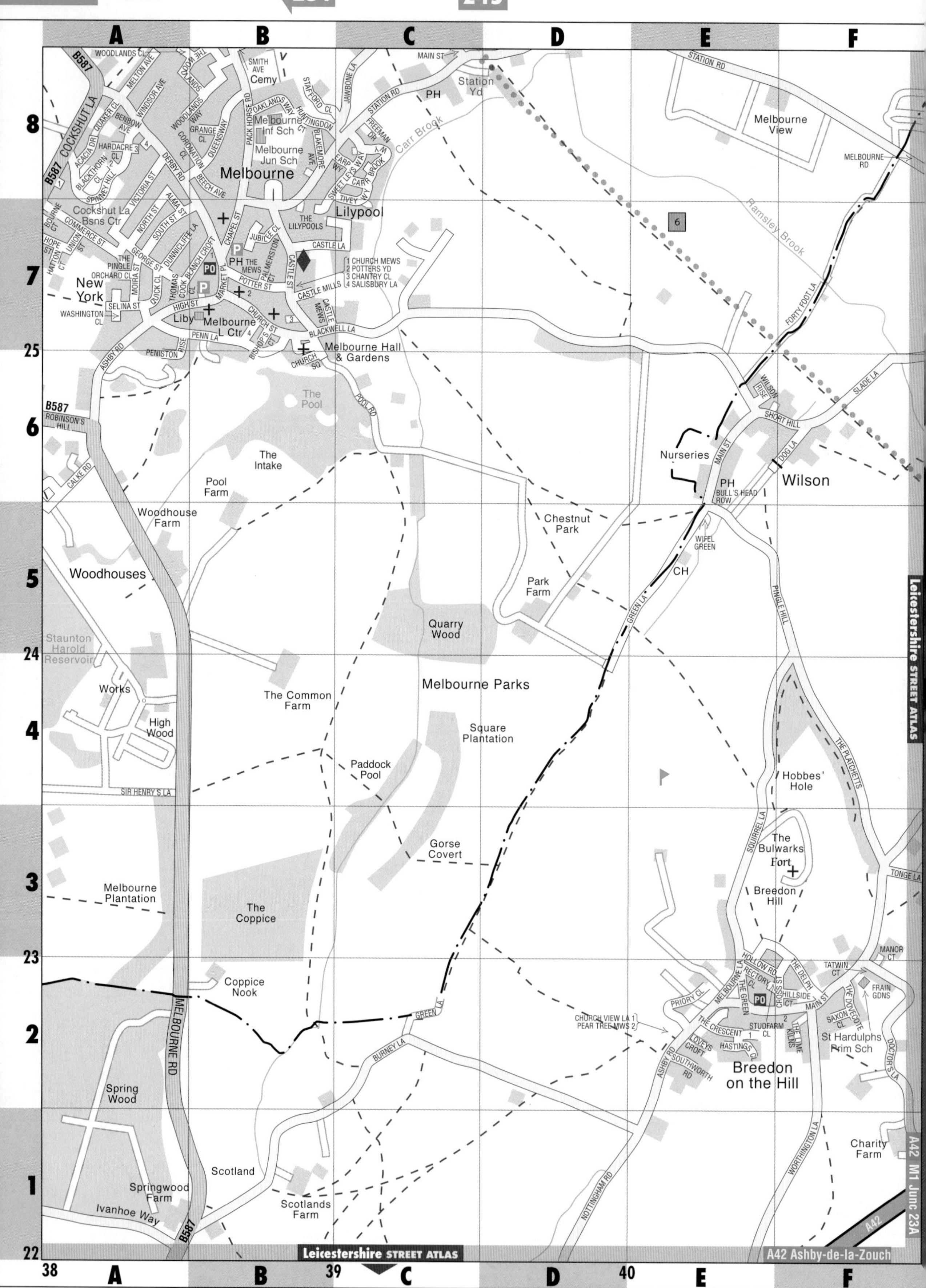

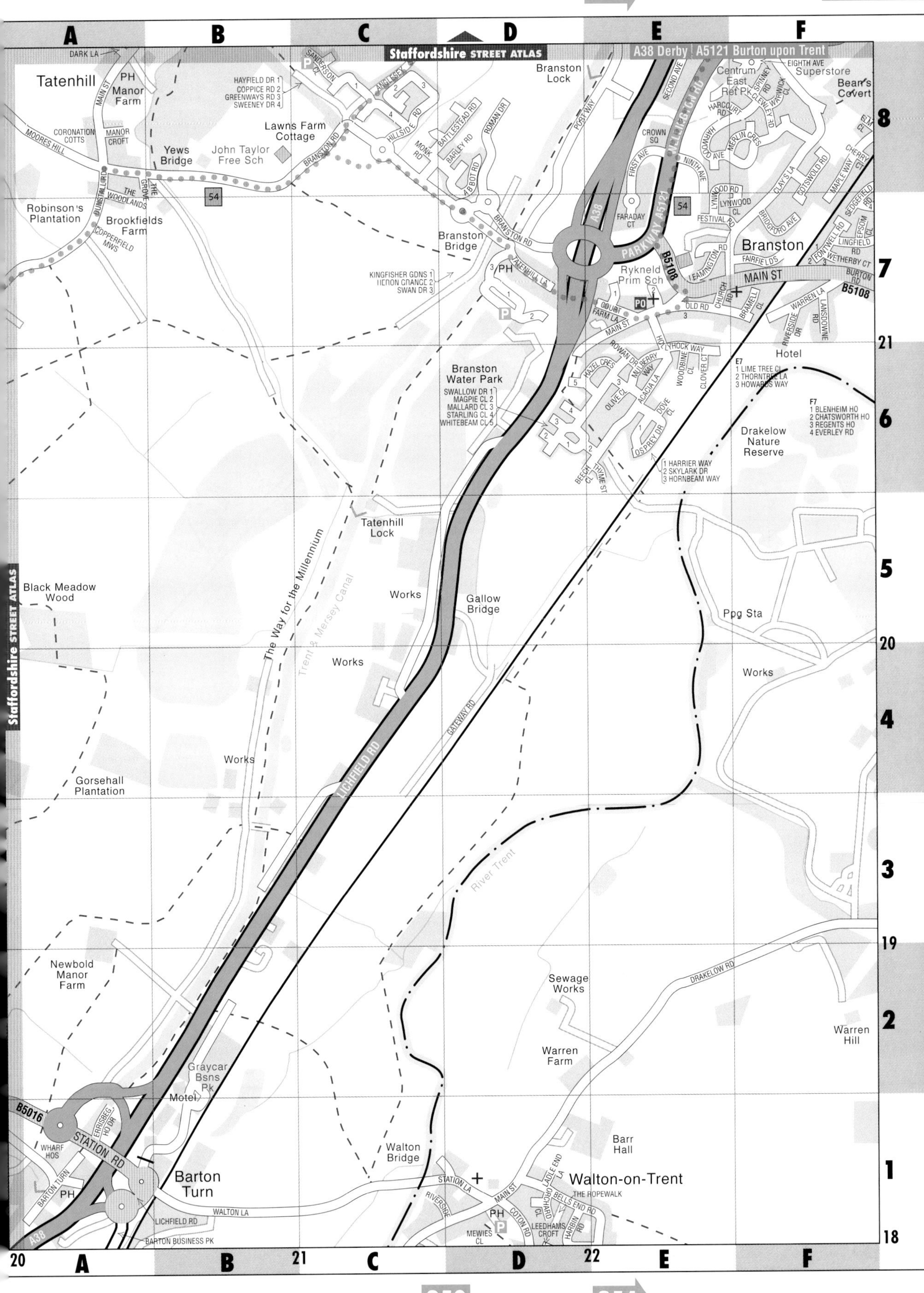

Staffordshire STREET ATLAS

A38 Derby | A5121 Burton upon Trent

Tatenhill

PH
Manor
Farm

MOORES HILL

DARK LA

CORONATION
COTTS

MANOR
CROFT

Yews
Bridge

John Taylor
Free Sch

HAYFIELD DR 1
COPPICE RD 2
GREENWAYS RD 3
SWEENEY DR 4

Lawns Farm
Cottage

Branston
Lock

Centrum
East
Ref Pk

EIGHTH AVE
Superstore

Bean's
Covert

Robinson's
Plantation

Brookfields
Farm

THE
WOODLANDS

COPPERFIELD
MWS

54

CROWN
SQ

Branston

Branston
Bridge

BRANSTON RD

FARADAY
CT

54

KINGFISHER GDNS 1
HERON GRANGE 2
SWAN DR 3

3 PH

P

Rykneld
Prim Sch

PO

Old Rd

MAIN ST

B5108

21

**Branston
Water Park**

SWALLOW DR 1
MAGPIE CL 2
MALLARD CL 3
STARLING CL 4
WHITEBEAM CL 5

Hotel

E7
1 LIME TREE CL
2 THORNTREE LA
3 HOWARDS WAY

F7
1 BLENHEIM HO
2 CHATSWORTH HO
3 REGENTS HO
4 EVERLEY RD

6

Drakelow
Nature
Reserve

1 HARRIER WAY
2 SKYLARK DR
3 HORNBEAM WAY

Black Meadow
Wood

Tatenhill
Lock

The Way for the Millennium

Trent & Mersey Canal

Works

Works

Gallow
Bridge

Ppg Sta

5

20

Works

LICHFIELD RD

GATEWAY RD

Works

4

Gorsehall
Plantation

Works

River Trent

3

Newbold
Manor
Farm

19

DRAKELOW RD

Sewage
Works

Warren
Hill

2

Warren
Farm

Graycar
Bsns
Pk

Motel

B5016

ERRIBECC HO

STATION RD

WHARF HOS

Walton
Bridge

Barr
Hall

Walton-on-Trent

THE ROPEWALK

1

Barton
Turn

PH

A38

BARTON TURN

LICHFIELD RD

WALTON LA

BARTON BUSINESS PK

STATION LA

RIVERSIDE

MAIN ST

PH

P

MEWIES
CL

LEEDHAMS
CROFT

18

253

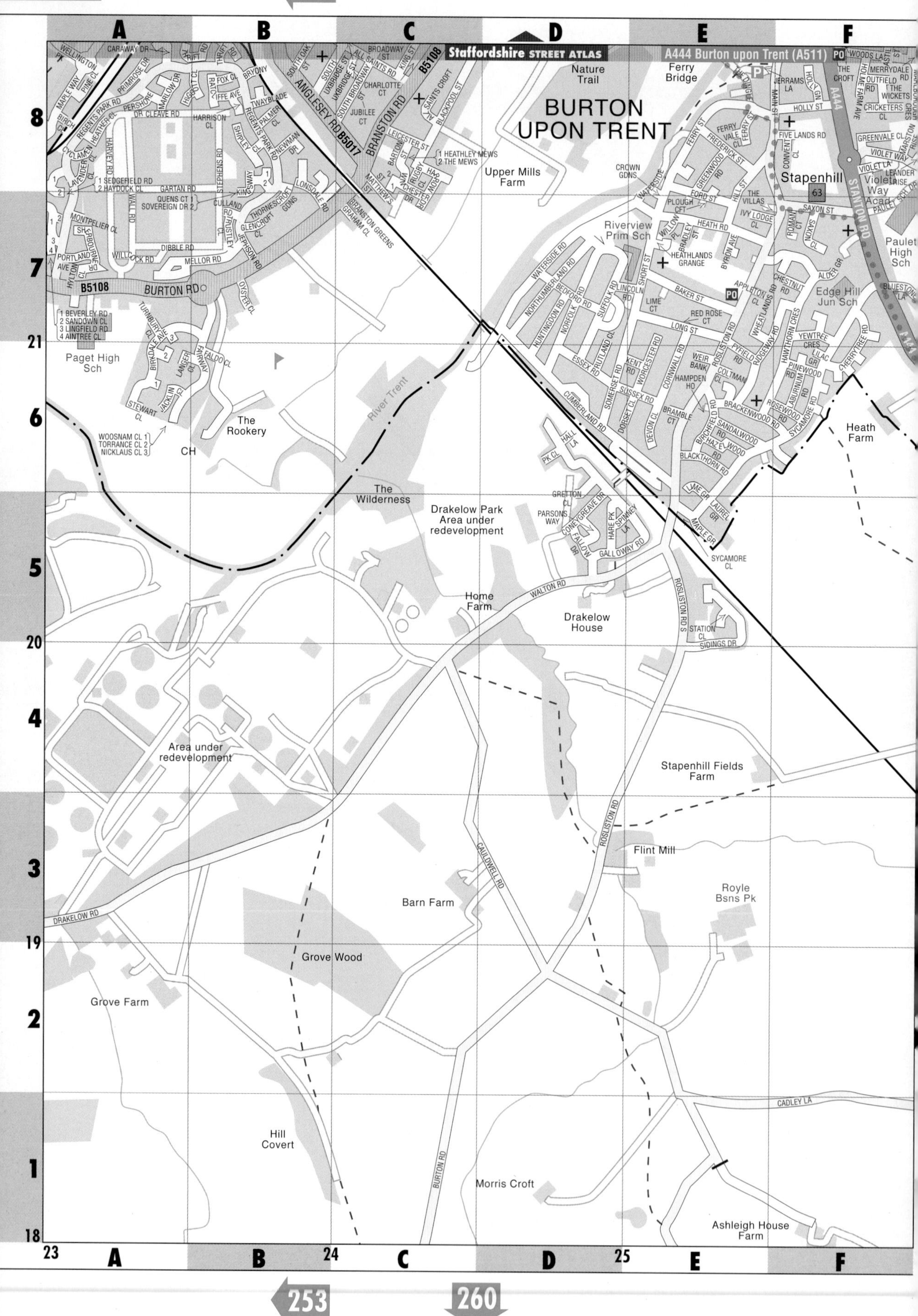
A
B
C
D
E
F
Staffordshire STREET ATLAS
A444 Burton upon Trent (A511)
8
7
21
6
5
20
4
3
19
2
1
18
23
24
25
BURTON UPON TRENT
Nature Trail
Ferry Bridge
Upper Mills Farm
Stapenhill
Riverview Prim Sch
Edge Hill Jun Sch
Paulet High Sch
Violet Way Acad
Heath Farm
Paget High Sch
The Rookery
CH
River Trent
The Wilderness
Drakelow Park Area under redevelopment
Home Farm
Drakelow House
Area under redevelopment
Stapenhill Fields Farm
Flint Mill
Royle Bsns Pk
Barn Farm
Grove Wood
Grove Farm
Hill Covert
Morris Croft
Ashleigh House Farm
B5108
BURTON RD
B5017
ANGLESEY RD
BRANSTON RD
WALTON RD
ROSLISTON RD S
ROSLISTON RD
CAULDWELL RD
DRAKELOW RD
BURTON RD
CADLEY LA
STANTON RD
A444
WATERSIDE RD
NORTHUMBERLAND RD
HUNTINGDON RD
BEDFORD RD
NORFOLK RD
SUFFOLK RD
RUTLAND CL
ESSEX RD
CUMBERLAND RD
SOMERSET RD
DORSET CL
SUSSEX RD
KENT RD
WORCESTER RD
DEVON CL
CORNWALL RD
BRAMBLE CT
HAMPDEN HO
WEIR BANK
BIRCHFIELD RD
SANDALWOOD RD
HAZELWOOD RD
BLACKTHORN RD
LIME GR
LAUREL GR
MAPLE GR
SYCAMORE CL
STATION CL
SIDINGS DR
GALLOWAY RD
FALLOW DR
CONEYGREAVE DR
HARE PK
SPINNEY LA
GRETTON CL
PARSONS WAY
PK CL
HALL LA
HEATHLANDS GRANGE
BAKER ST
LONG ST
RED ROSE CT
LIME CT
LINCOLN RD
SHORT ST
BRADLEY ST
WILLOW PL
HEATH RD
PLOUGH CFT
FORD ST
GREENWOOD RD
FERRY VALE CL
FREDERICK ST
FERRY ST
HILL ST
BYRON AVE
THE VILLAS
IVY LODGE CL
APPLETON CL
WHEATLANDS RD
RIDGEWAY RD
PYFIELD RD
COLTMAN CL
HAWTHORN CRES
CHESTNUT RD
ALDER GR
YEWTREE CRES
LILAC GR
PINEWOOD RD
LABURNUM RD
ROSEWOOD RD
SYCAMORE RD
BRACKENWOOD RD
CHERRYTREE RD
ROMAN CT
SAXON ST
SAXONS CL
CONVENT CL
FIVE LANDS RD
HOLLY ST
JERRAMS LA
MAIN ST
THE CROFT
HOLME FARM AVE
OUTFIELD RD
THE WICKETS
CRICKETERS CL
MERRYDALE RD
GREENVALE CL
VIOLET WAY
VIOLET LA
LEANDER RISE
BLUESTONE LA
CROWN GDNS
WATERSIDE
WELLINGTON PK
CARAWAY DR
MAPLE WAY
PINE CL
PRIMROSE DR
REGENTS PARK RD
HEATHER CL
BIRCH
CYCLAMEN
LAVENDER
HARVEY RD
PERSHORE
MARLOW DR
HIGGOTT CL
FOX CL
BRYONY
TWAYBLADE
DR CLEAVE RD
HARRISON CL
SHIPLEY CL
PALMER CL
NEWMAN DR
1 SEDGEFIELD RD
2 HAYDOCK CL
GARTAN RD
QUENS CT 1
SOVEREIGN DR 2
STEPHENS RD
KINGSWAY
WALL RD
CULLAND RD
THORNESCROFT GDNS
GLENCROFT CL
LONSDALE RD
BRANSTON GREENS
GRAHAM CL
MONTPELIER CL
PORTLAND AVE
HYLTON CL
DIBBLE RD
WILLCOCK RD
MELLOR RD
JEPHSON RD
OYSTER CL
1 BEVERLEY RD
2 SANDOWN CL
3 LINGFIELD RD
4 AINTREE CL
TURNBURY CL
BIRKDALE AVE
LANGER CL
FAIRWAY
FALDO CL
JACKLIN CL
STEWART CL
WOOSNAM CL 1
TORRANCE CL 2
NICKLAUS CL 3
SOUTH OAK ST
UXBRIDGE ST
SOUTH BROADWAY ST
ALL SAINTS RD
BROADWAY ST
KING ST
CHARLOTTE CT
JUBILEE CT
ALL SAINTS CROFT
BLACKPOOL ST
LEICESTER ST
BARTON ST
RUGBY CL
1 HEATHLEY MEWS
2 THE MEWS
ST MATTHEW'S ST
WINCHESTER DR
PO
63

253
260

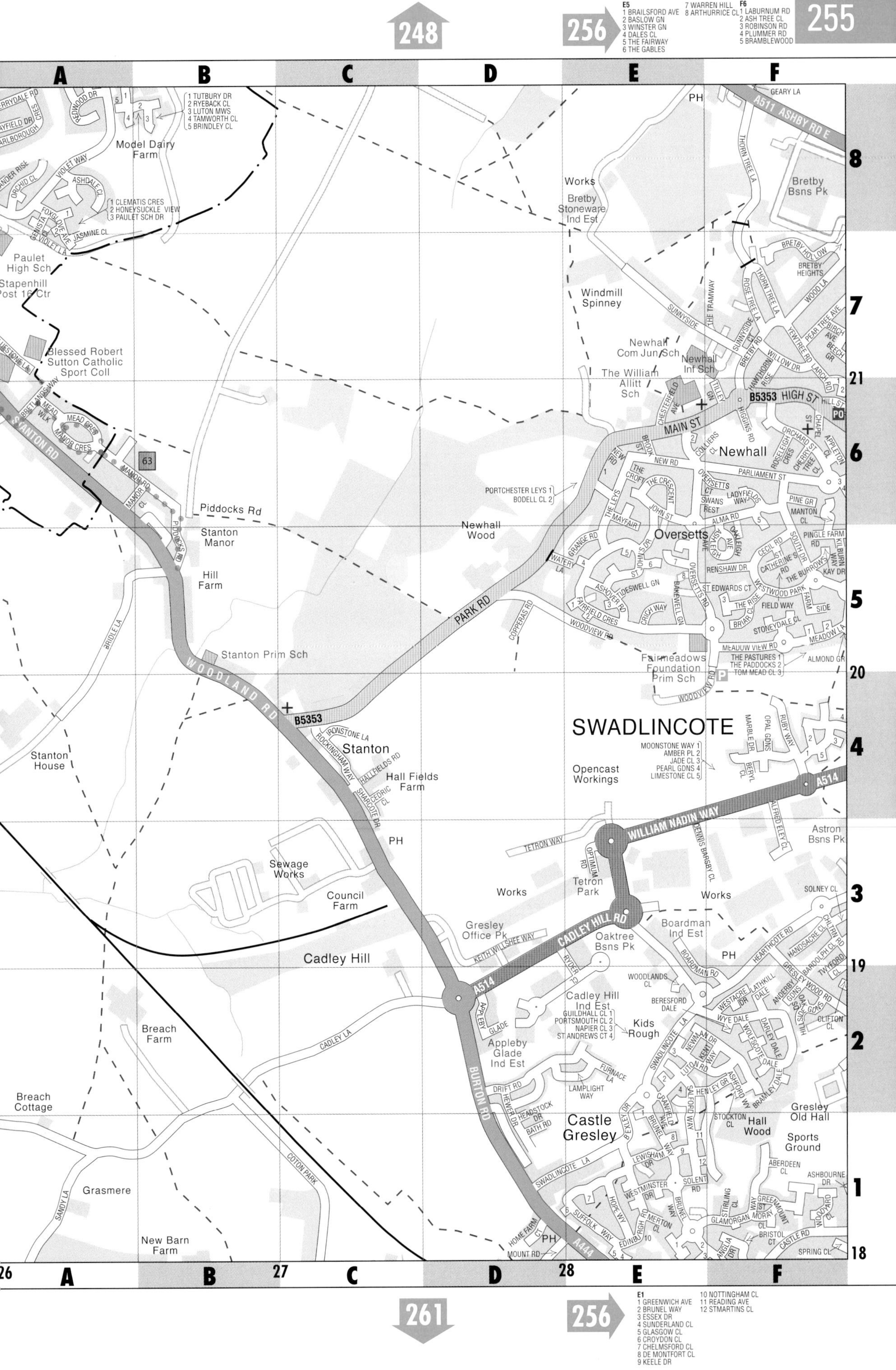
Model Dairy Farm
Paulet High Sch
Stapenhill Post 16 Ctr
Blessed Robert Sutton Catholic Sport Coll
Stanton Manor
Hill Farm
Piddocks Rd
Stanton Prim Sch
Stanton
Hall Fields Farm
Stanton House
Sewage Works
Council Farm
Cadley Hill
Breach Farm
Breach Cottage
Grasmere
New Barn Farm
Newhall Wood
Works
Bretby Stoneware Ind Est
Windmill Spinney
Newhall Com Jun Sch
Newhall Inf Sch
The William Allitt Sch
Newhall
Oversetts
Bretby Bsns Pk
Fairmeadows Foundation Prim Sch
SWADLINCOTE
Opencast Workings
Tetron Park
Gresley Office Pk
Oaktree Bsns Pk
Boardman Ind Est
Astron Bsns Pk
Cadley Hill Ind Est
Appleby Glade Ind Est
Kids Rough
Castle Gresley
Hall Wood
Gresley Old Hall
Sports Ground
WOODLAND RD
PARK RD
B5353
MAIN ST
HIGH ST
A511 ASHBY RD E
WILLIAM NADIN WAY
CADLEY HILL RD
A514
BURTON RD
A444
STANTON RD
CADLEY LA
SWADLINCOTE LA
1 TUTBURY DR
2 RYEBACK CL
3 LUTON MWS
4 TAMWORTH CL
5 BRINDLEY CL
1 CLEMATIS CRES
2 HONEYSUCKLE VIEW
3 PAULET SCH DR
PORTCHESTER LEYS 1
BODELL CL 2
MOONSTONE WAY 1
AMBER PL 2
JADE CL 3
PEARL GDNS 4
LIMESTONE CL 5
THE PASTURES 1
THE PADDOCKS 2
TOM MEAD CL 3
GUILDHALL CL 1
PORTSMOUTH CL 2
NAPIER CL 3
ST ANDREWS CT 4

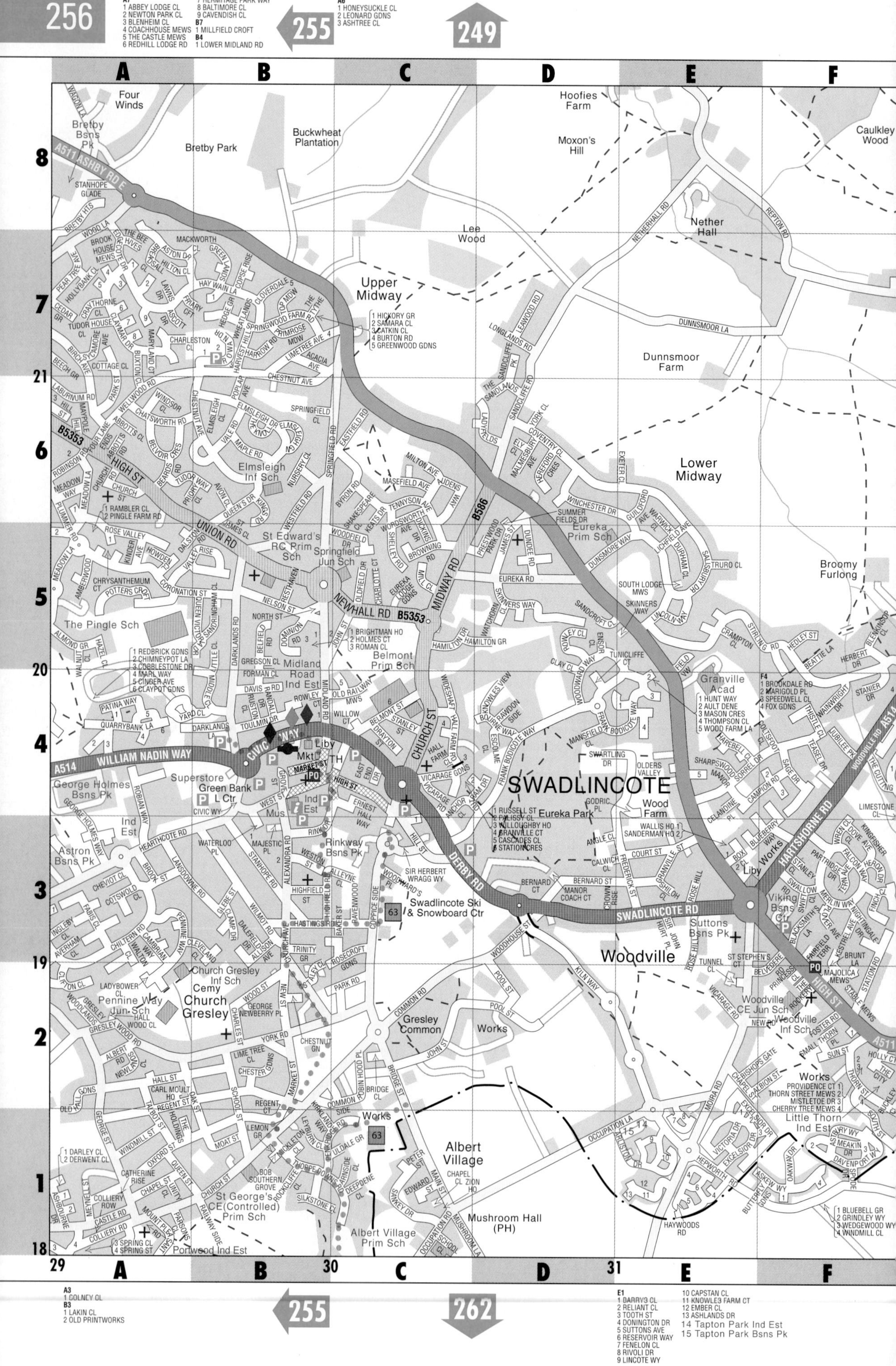

256

A7
1 ABBEY LODGE CL
2 NEWTON PARK CL
3 BLENHEIM CL
4 COACHHOUSE MEWS
5 THE CASTLE MEWS
6 REDHILL LODGE RD

7 HERMITAGE PARK WAY
8 BALTIMORE CL
9 CAVENDISH CL
B7
1 MILLFIELD CROFT
B4
1 LOWER MIDLAND RD

A6
1 HONEYSUCKLE CL
2 LEONARD GDNS
3 ASHTREE CL

255   249

A3
1 GOLNEY CL
B3
1 LAKIN CL
2 OLD PRINTWORKS

255   262

E1
1 DARRYS CL
2 RELIANT CL
3 TOOTH CL
4 DONINGTON DR
5 SUTTONS AVE
6 RESERVOIR WAY
7 FENELON CL
8 RIVOLI DR
9 LINCOTE WY

10 CAPSTAN CL
11 KNOWLES FARM CT
12 EMBER CL
13 ASHLANDS DR
14 Tapton Park Ind Est
15 Tapton Park Bsns Pk

250
258

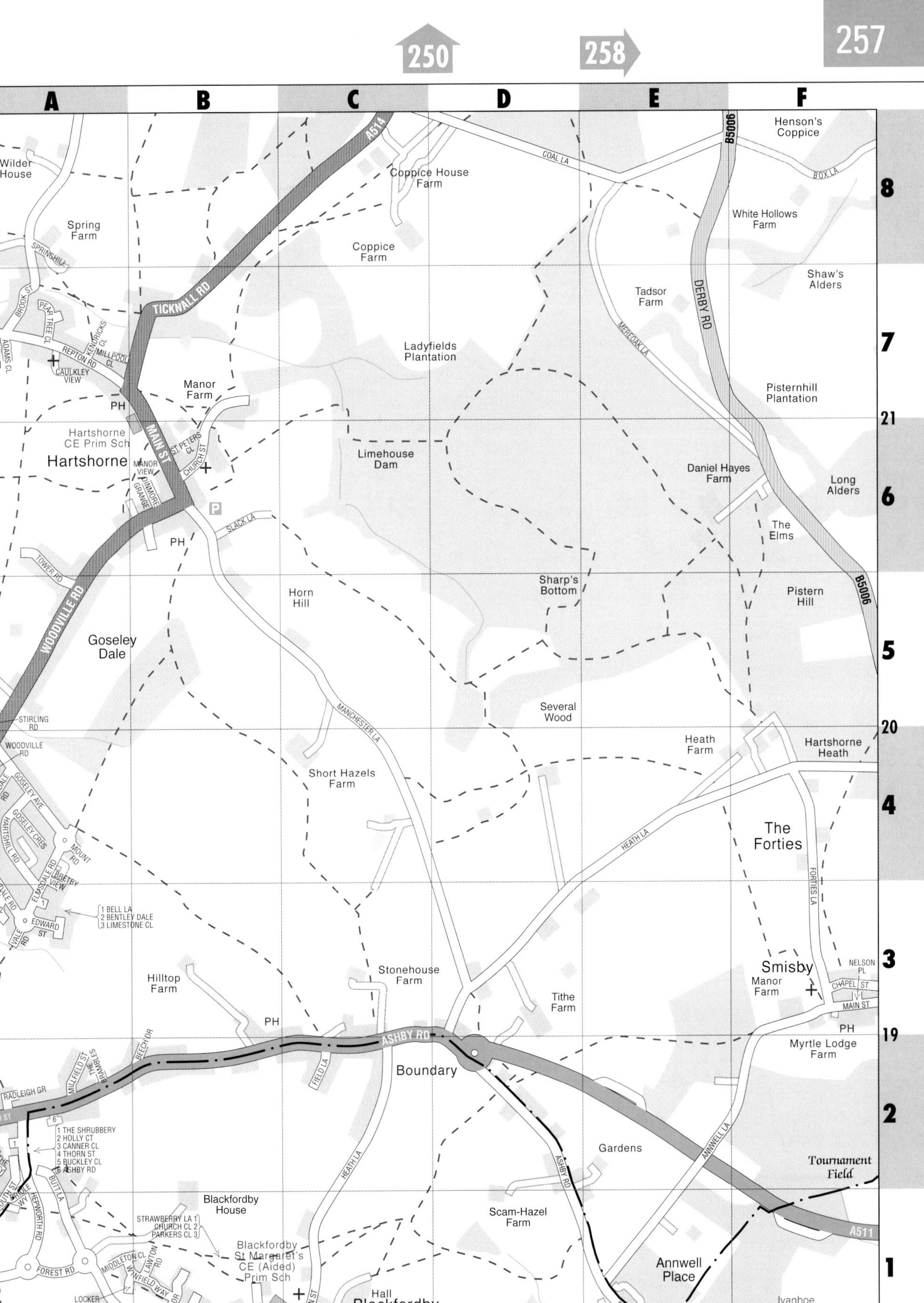
Henson's Coppice
Wilder House
Coppice House Farm
Spring Farm
Coppice Farm
White Hollows Farm
Shaw's Alders
Tadsor Farm
Ladyfields Plantation
Manor Farm
Pisternhill Plantation
Hartshorne CE Prim Sch
Hartshorne
Limehouse Dam
Daniel Hayes Farm
Long Alders
The Elms
Sharp's Bottom
Horn Hill
Pistern Hill
Goseley Dale
Several Wood
Heath Farm
Hartshorne Heath
Short Hazels Farm
The Forties
Smisby
Manor Farm
Stonehouse Farm
Hilltop Farm
Tithe Farm
Myrtle Lodge Farm
Boundary
Gardens
Tournament Field
Blackfordby House
Scam-Hazel Farm
Blackfordby St Margaret's CE (Aided) Prim Sch
Annwell Place
Hall
Blackfordby
Ivanhoe Ind Est
Holywell Farm
Works
1 BELL LA
2 BENTLEY DALE
3 LIMESTONE CL
1 THE SHRUBBERY
2 HOLLY CT
3 CANNER CL
4 THORN ST
5 BUCKLEY CL
6 ASHBY RD
STRAWBERRY LA 1
CHURCH CL 2
PARKERS CL 3
Leicestershire STREET ATLAS

258

257
251

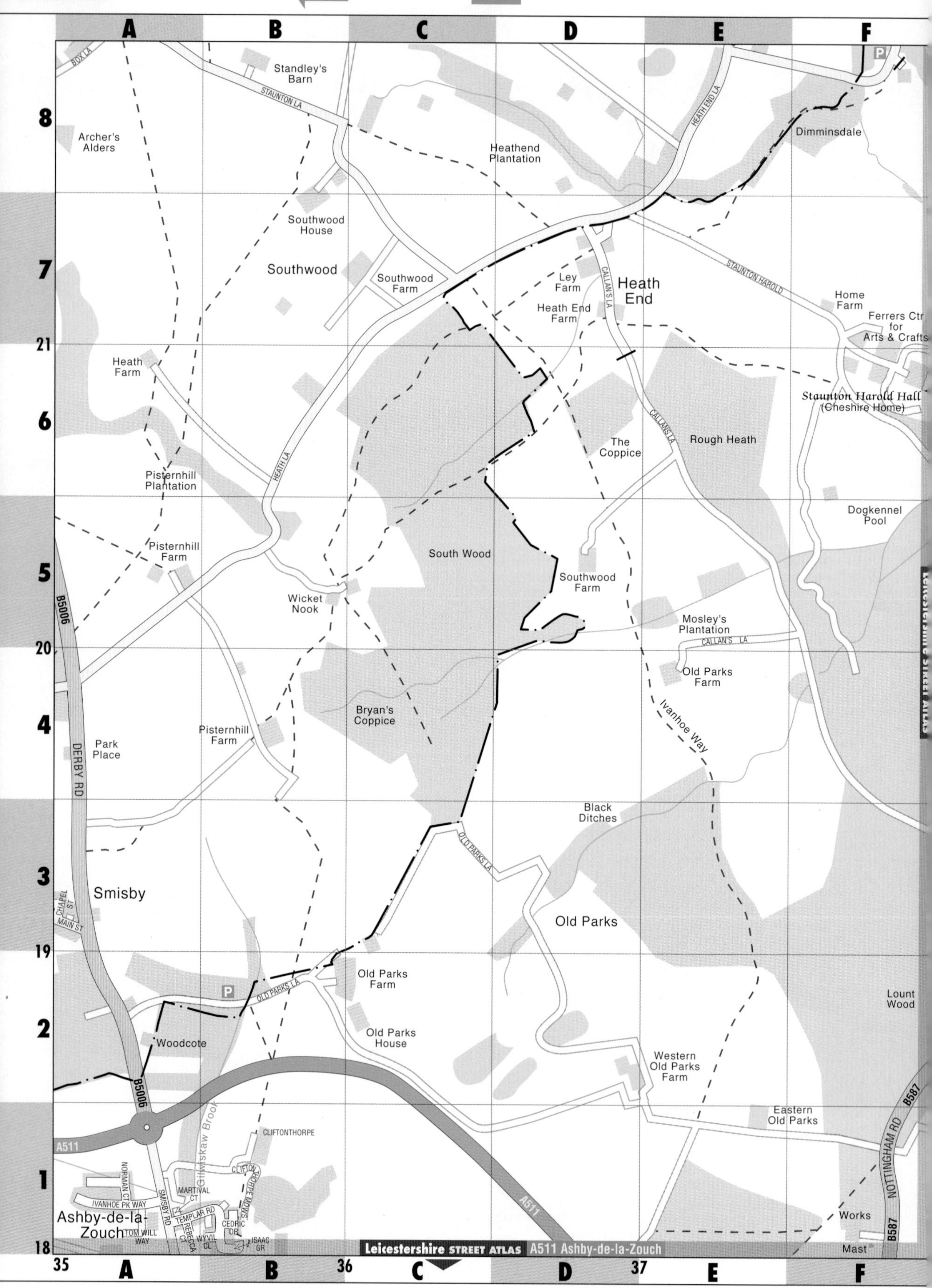
A
B
C
D
E
F
8
7
21
6
5
20
4
3
19
2
1
18
35
36
37
BOX LA
Standley's Barn
STAUNTON LA
Archer's Alders
Heathend Plantation
HEATH END LA
Dimminsdale
Southwood House
Southwood
Southwood Farm
Ley Farm
Heath End Farm
CALLAN'S LA
Heath End
STAUNTON HAROLD
Home Farm
Ferrers Ctr for Arts & Crafts
Heath Farm
Staunton Harold Hall (Cheshire Home)
CALLAN'S LA
The Coppice
Rough Heath
HEATH LA
Pisternhill Plantation
Dogkennel Pool
Pisternhill Farm
South Wood
Southwood Farm
B5006
Wicket Nook
Mosley's Plantation
CALLAN'S LA
Old Parks Farm
Ivanhoe Way
Bryan's Coppice
Pisternhill Farm
Park Place
DERBY RD
Black Ditches
OLD PARKS LA
Smisby
CHAPEL ST
MAIN ST
Old Parks
Old Parks Farm
OLD PARKS LA
P
Lount Wood
Old Parks House
Woodcote
Western Old Parks Farm
B5006
Eastern Old Parks
B587
NOTTINGHAM RD
Gilwiskaw Brook
CLIFTONTHORPE
A511
NORMAN CT
CLIFTONTHORPE MEWS
MARTIVAL CT
IVANHOE PK WAY
SMISBY RD
TEMPLAR RD
Ashby-de-la-Zouch
TOM WILL WAY
REBECCA CT
WYVIL CL
CEDRIC DR
ISAAC GR
A511
Works
B587
Mast

257

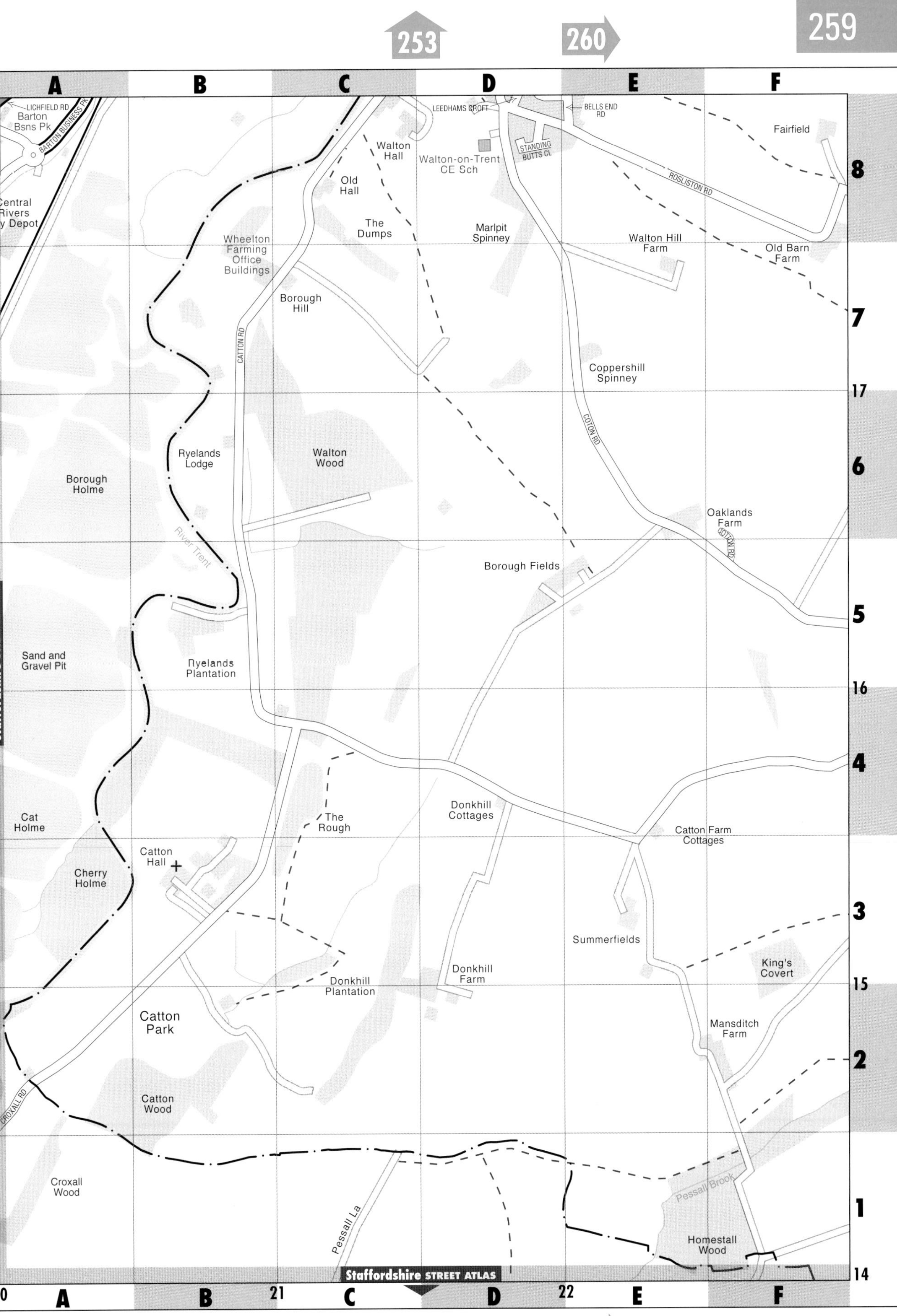

A B C D E F

LICHFIELD RD
Barton
Bsns Pk
Central
Rivers
ly Depot

Walton Hall
Old Hall
The Dumps
Wheelton
Farming
Office
Buildings
Borough
Hill
CATTON RD
Ryelands
Lodge
Walton
Wood
Borough
Holme
River Trent
Sand and
Gravel Pit
Ryelands
Plantation
Cat
Holme
Cherry
Holme
Catton
Hall
The
Rough
Catton
Park
Catton
Wood
CROXALL RD
Croxall
Wood
Pessall La

LEEDHAMS CROFT
Walton-on-Trent
CE Sch
STANDING
BUTTS CL
Marlpit
Spinney
BELLS END
RD
Fairfield
ROSLISTON RD
Walton Hill
Farm
Old Barn
Farm
Coppershill
Spinney
COTON RD
Oaklands
Farm
COTON RD
Borough Fields
Donkhill
Cottages
Catton Farm
Cottages
Summerfields
King's
Covert
Donkhill
Farm
Donkhill
Plantation
Mansditch
Farm
Pessall Brook
Homestall
Wood

	A	B	C	D	E	F

8

ROSLISTON RD

Corner Farm

Nursery

Walton Lane Farm

Rosliston Forestry Ctr

Priory Farm

SANDY LA

Fox Covert

Caldwell

Calves Croft Farm

MAIN ST

7

Moonraker

CHURCH LA

Pegasus Sch

Manor Farm

17

COPPICE VIEW

THE CHASE

BURTON RD

PH

Rosliston CE Prim Sch

Rosliston

Caldwell Covert

6

HOLDON CROFT

PO

CAULDWELL RD

THE GLEBE

VICARAGE WLK

YEW TREE RD

YEW TREE GDNS

MAIN ST

NEW ST

STRAWBERRY LA

Blakenhall Farm

5

CATON LA

KNIGHTWOOD CL

LINTON RD

COTON RD

Field House Farm

COTTON LA

Beehive Farm

16

P

Lads Grave

Longfurlong Farm

P

4

Coton in the Elms

BURTON RD

Pessall Brook

P

Overfields Farm

CHURCH CROFT

OAK TREE CL

Church Farm

ELMS RD

CHAPMANS CROFT

Coton in the Elms CE Prim Sch

GLEBE CL

ELMS LA

3

GREENACRE PK

CHURCH ST

NEW RD

MAIN ST

CHAPEL ST

COTON LA

PH

CROFT FLATS LA

MILL ST

COALPIT LA

MILL GREEN CL

15

Pessall Brook

Malt House Farm

2

P

LULLINGTON RD

Raddle Farm Wood

GRANCEWOOD

Pessall Brook

Church Flatts Farm

1

The Crosses

Grafton House

LITTLE LIVERPOOL

COTON RD

14

255
262

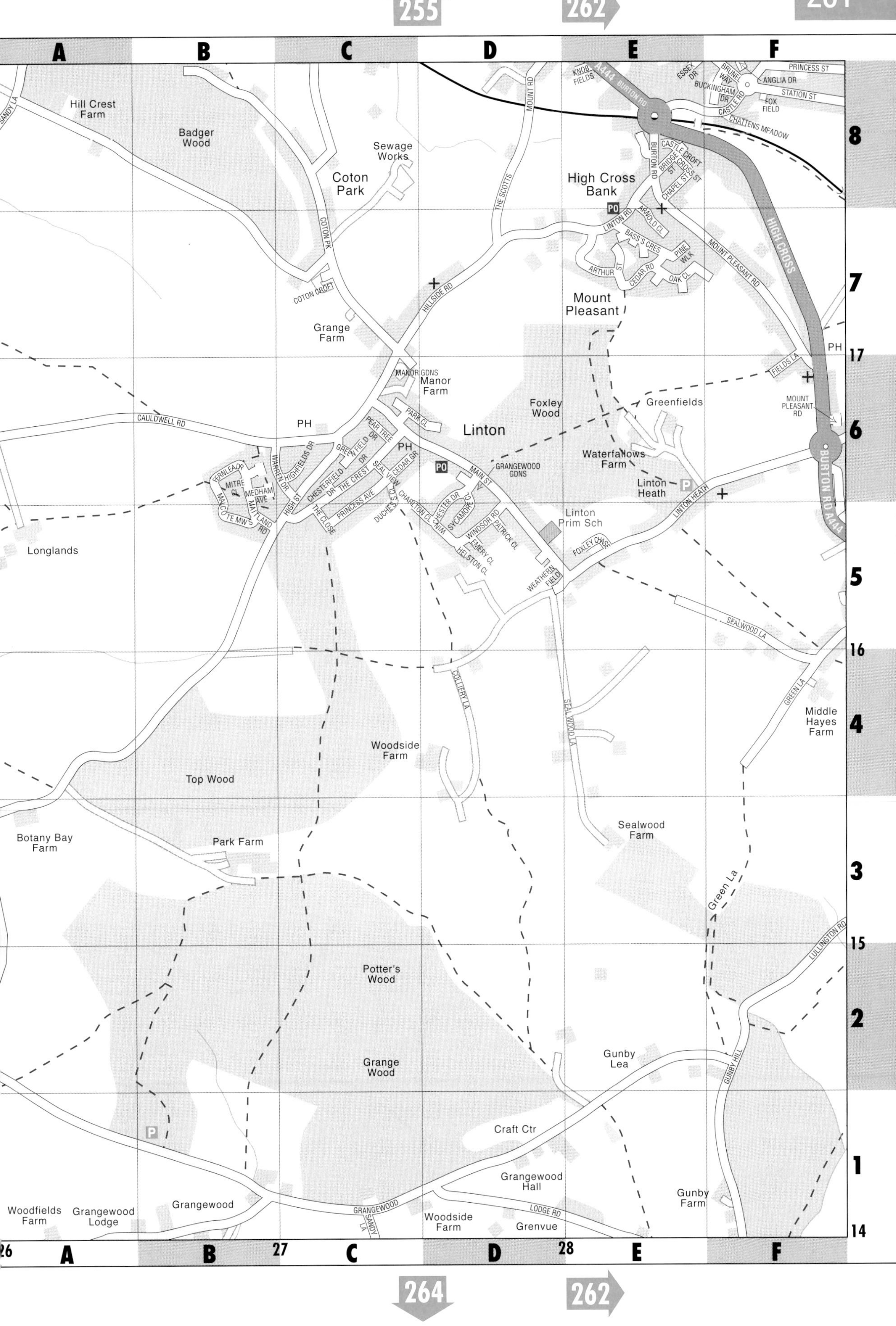
A
B
C
D
E
F
Hill Crest Farm
Badger Wood
Sewage Works
Coton Park
High Cross Bank
Mount Pleasant
Grange Farm
Manor Farm
Foxley Wood
Greenfields
Linton
Waterfallows Farm
Linton Heath
Linton Prim Sch
Longlands
Middle Hayes Farm
Woodside Farm
Top Wood
Botany Bay Farm
Park Farm
Sealwood Farm
Potter's Wood
Grange Wood
Gunby Lea
Craft Ctr
Grangewood Hall
Gunby Farm
Woodfields Farm
Grangewood Lodge
Grangewood
Woodside Farm
Grenvue
SANDY LA
COTON PK
COTON CROFT
MOUNT RD
THE SCOTTS
HILLSIDE RD
BURTON RD
A444
KNOB FIELDS
ESSEX DR
BRUNEL WAY
BUCKINGHAM DR
PRINCESS ST
ANGLIA DR
STATION ST
FOX FIELD
CASTLE RD
CHATTENS MEADOW
CASTLE CROFT
BRIDGE ST
CROSS ST
CHAPEL ST
LINTON RD
ARNOLD CL
BASS'S CRES
PINE WLK
ARTHUR ST
CEDAR RD
OAK CL
MOUNT PLEASANT RD
HIGH CROSS
FIELDS LA
MOUNT PLEASANT RD
BURTON RD A444
MANOR GDNS
PARK CL
PEAR TREE DR
GREENFIELD DR
CAULDWELL RD
HIGHFIELDS DR
WARREN DR
HIGH ST
CHESTERFIELD DR
THE CREST
SEAL VIEW
CEDAR GR
PRINCESS AVE
THE CLOSE
DUCHESS ST
CHARLTON CL
WINCHESTER DR
SYCAMORE CL
WINDSOR RD
PATRICK CL
EMERY CL
HELSTON CL
MAIN ST
GRANGEWOOD GDNS
FERNLEA CL
MITRE CL
MEDHAM AVE
MALCOTE MWS
MAITLAND RD
WEATHERN FIELD
FOXLEY CHASE
LINTON HEATH
SEALWOOD LA
GREEN LA
COLLIERY LA
SEAL WOOD LA
Green La
LULLINGTON RD
GUNBY HILL
GRANGEWOOD
SANDY LA
LODGE RD
PO
PH
P
8
7
17
6
5
16
4
3
15
2
1
14
26
27
28

264
262

261
256

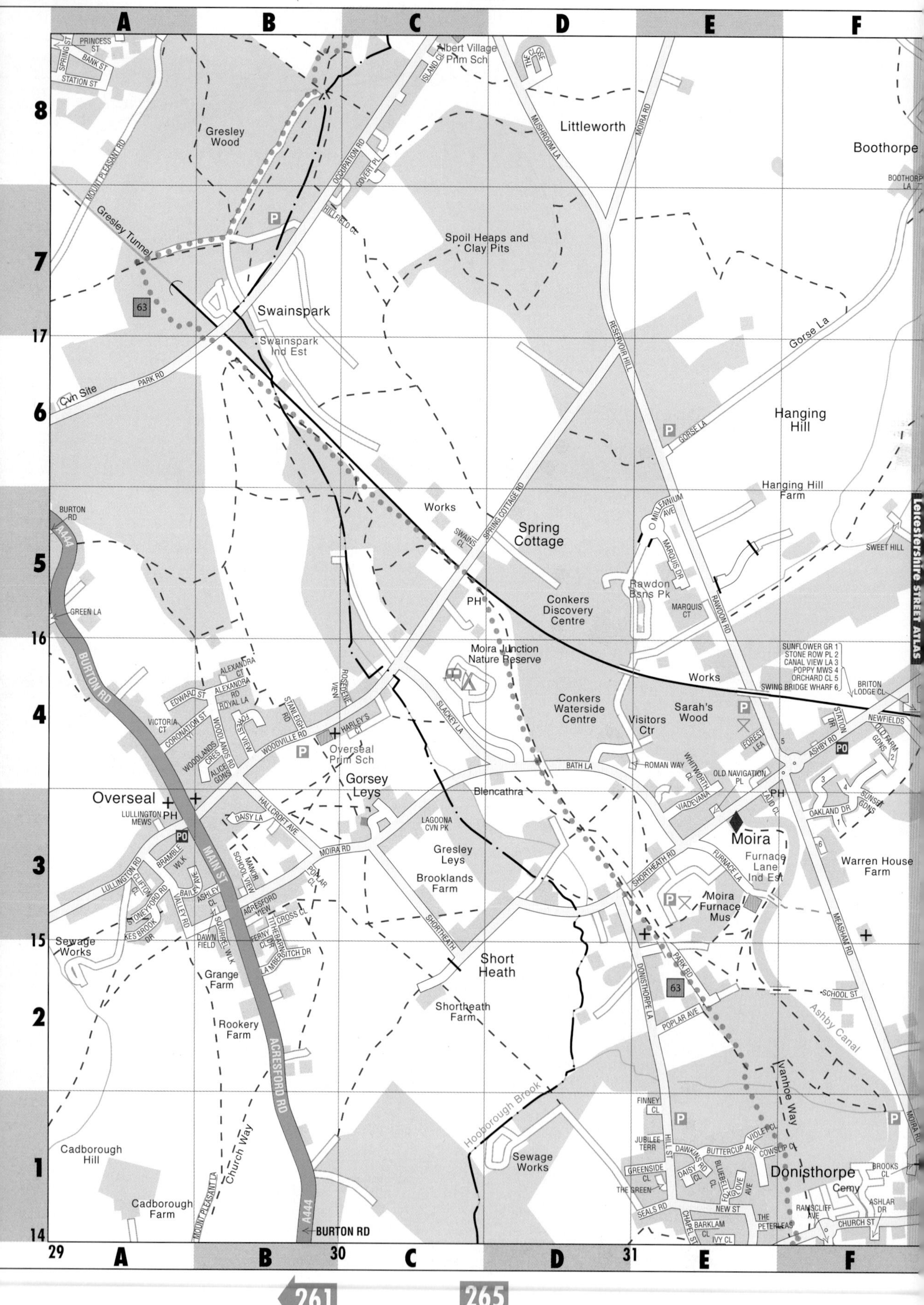
A
B
C
D
E
F
8
7
17
6
5
16
4
3
15
2
1
14
29
30
31
Gresley Wood
Littleworth
Boothorpe
Albert Village Prim Sch
Gresley Tunnel
Spoil Heaps and Clay Pits
Swainspark
Swainspark Ind Est
Cvn Site
PARK RD
Gorse La
Hanging Hill
Hanging Hill Farm
Works
Spring Cottage
Conkers Discovery Centre
Rawdon Bsns Pk
Moira Junction Nature Reserve
Works
SUNFLOWER GR 1
STONE ROW PL 2
CANAL VIEW LA 3
POPPY MWS 4
ORCHARD CL 5
SWING BRIDGE WHARF 6
BRITON LODGE CL
Conkers Waterside Centre
Visitors Ctr
Sarah's Wood
Overseal
Overseal Prim Sch
Gorsey Leys
Blencathra
LAGOONA CVN PK
Gresley Leys
Brooklands Farm
Moira
Furnace Lane Ind Est
Moira Furnace Mus
Warren House Farm
Sewage Works
Grange Farm
Rookery Farm
Short Heath
Shortheath Farm
Hooborough Brook
Ashby Canal
Vanhoe Way
Cadborough Hill
Cadborough Farm
Church Way
Sewage Works
Donisthorpe
Cemy
BURTON RD
MAIN ST
ACRESFORD RD
MOIRA RD
WOODVILLE RD
SPRING COTTAGE RD
RESERVOIR HILL
RAWDON RD
MEASHAM RD
BATH LA
SHORTHEATH RD
DONISTHORPE LA
HILL ST
NEW ST
CHURCH ST
A444
BURTON RD

261
265

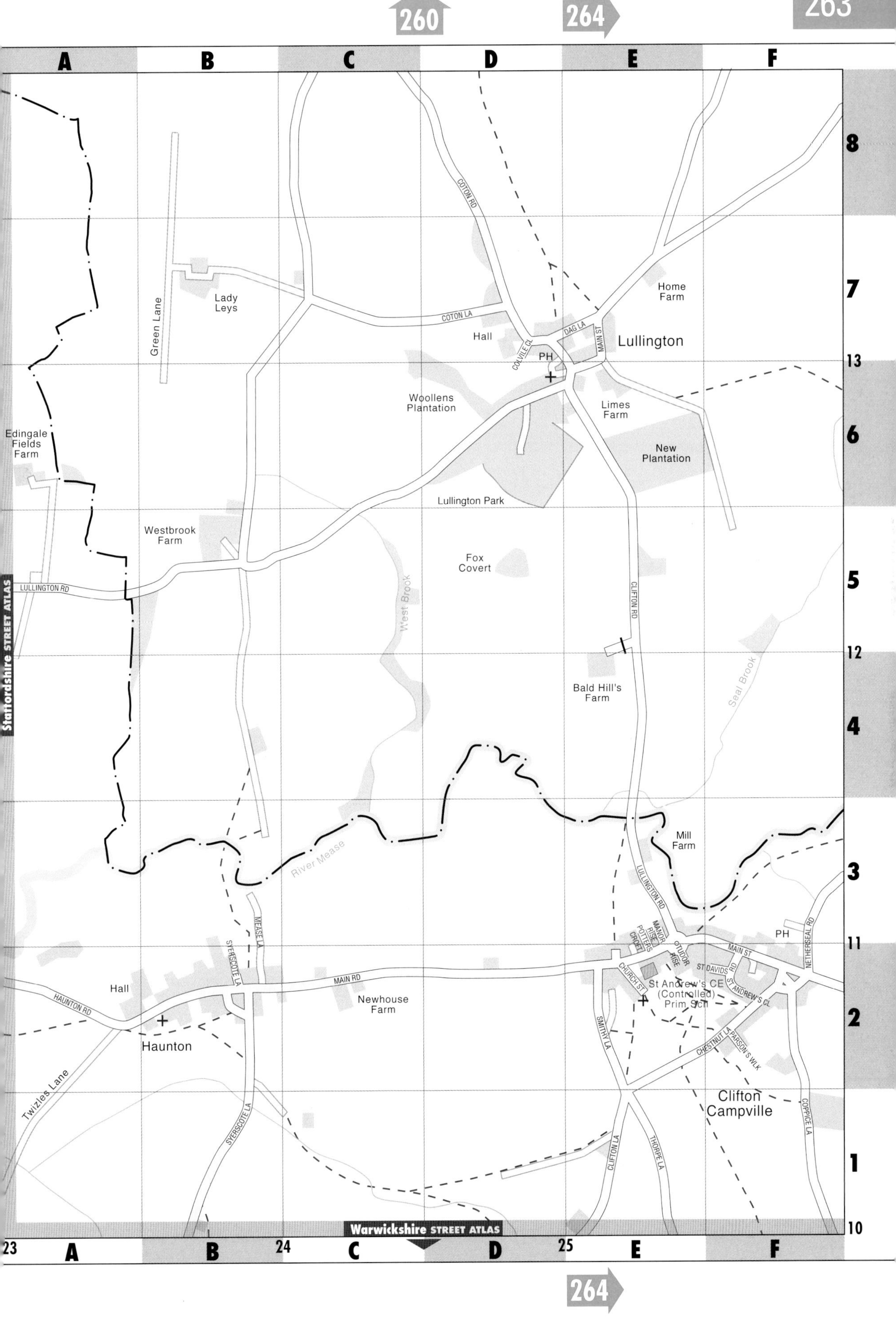

Home Farm

Lullington

Lady Leys

Green Lane

Hall

Woollens Plantation

Limes Farm

New Plantation

Edingale Fields Farm

Lullington Park

Fox Covert

CLIFTON RD

West Brook

Seal Brook

Westbrook Farm

LULLINGTON RD

Bald Hill's Farm

Mill Farm

River Mease

LULLINGTON RD

PH

MEASE LA

SYERSCOTE LA

MANOR RISE

POTTERS CROFT

OUTWOODS RISE

MAIN ST

ST DAVIDS RD

ST ANDREW'S CL

HAUNTON RD

Hall

MAIN RD

Newhouse Farm

CHURCH ST

St Andrew's CE (Controlled) Prim Sch

NETHERSEAL RD

Haunton

Twizles Lane

SYERSCOTE LA

SMITH LA

CLIFTON LA

THORPE LA

CHESTNUT LA

PARSON'S WLK

COPPICE LA

Clifton Campville

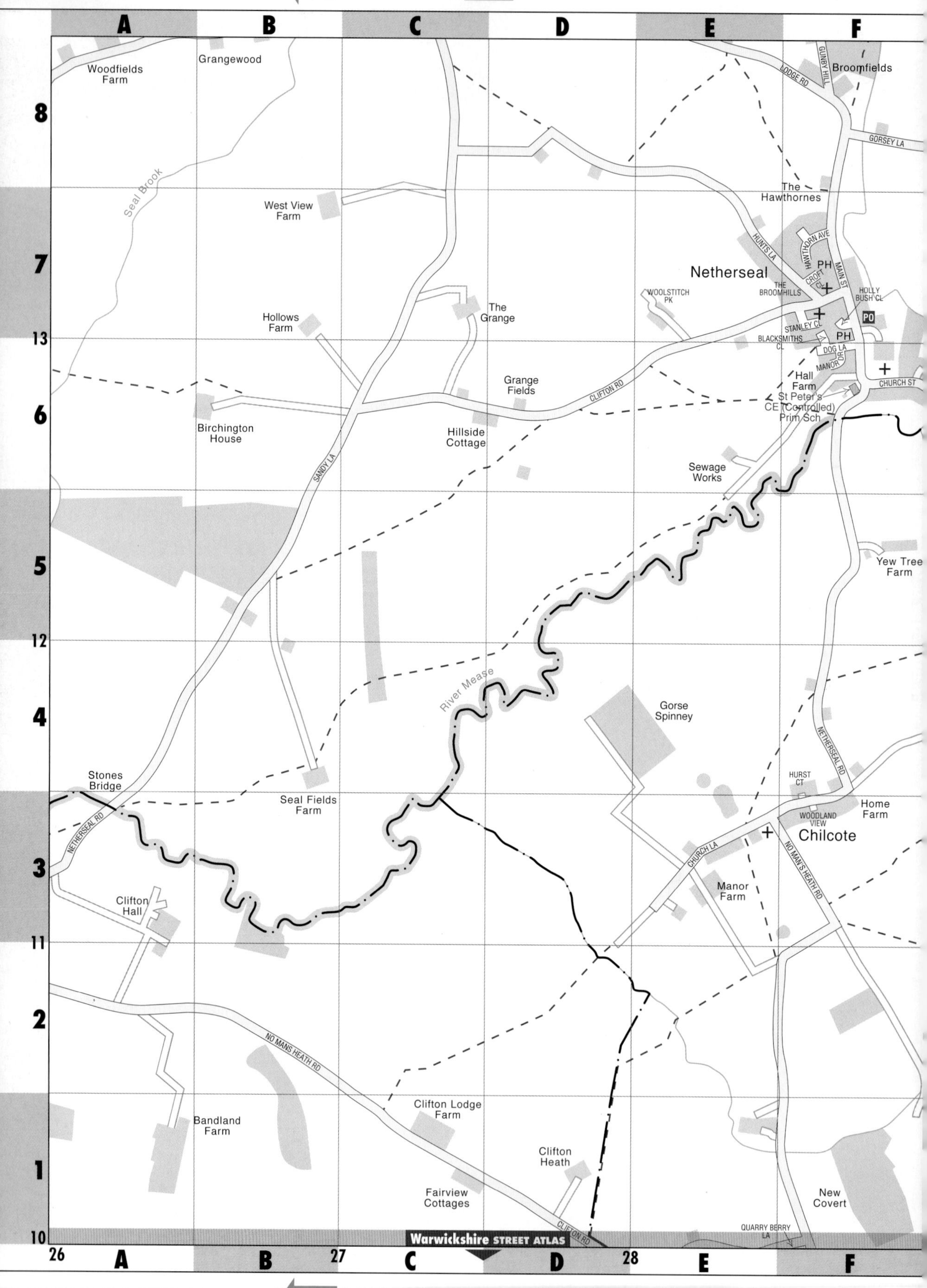

A   B   C   D   E   F

8

7

13

6

5

12

4

3

11

2

1

10

Woodfields Farm

Grangewood

West View Farm

Seal Brook

Hollows Farm

Birchington House

Sandy La

Stones Bridge

Netherseal Rd

Clifton Hall

Seal Fields Farm

River Mease

Bandland Farm

No Mans Heath Rd

Clifton Lodge Farm

Fairview Cottages

Clifton Heath

Clifton Rd

The Grange

Grange Fields

Hillside Cottage

Sewage Works

Clifton Rd

Gorse Spinney

Church La

Manor Farm

Broomfields

Lodge Rd

Gunby Hill

Gorsey La

The Hawthornes

Netherseal

Hunts La

Hawthorn Ave

The Croft

Woolstitch Pk

The Broomhills

PH

Stanley Cl

Blacksmiths Cl

Dog La

Manor Ct

Main St

PH

Holly Bush Cl

PO

Church St

Hall Farm

St Peter's CE (Controlled) Prim Sch

Yew Tree Farm

Netherseal Rd

Hurst Ct

Woodland View

Home Farm

Chilcote

No Mans Heath Rd

New Covert

Quarry Berry La

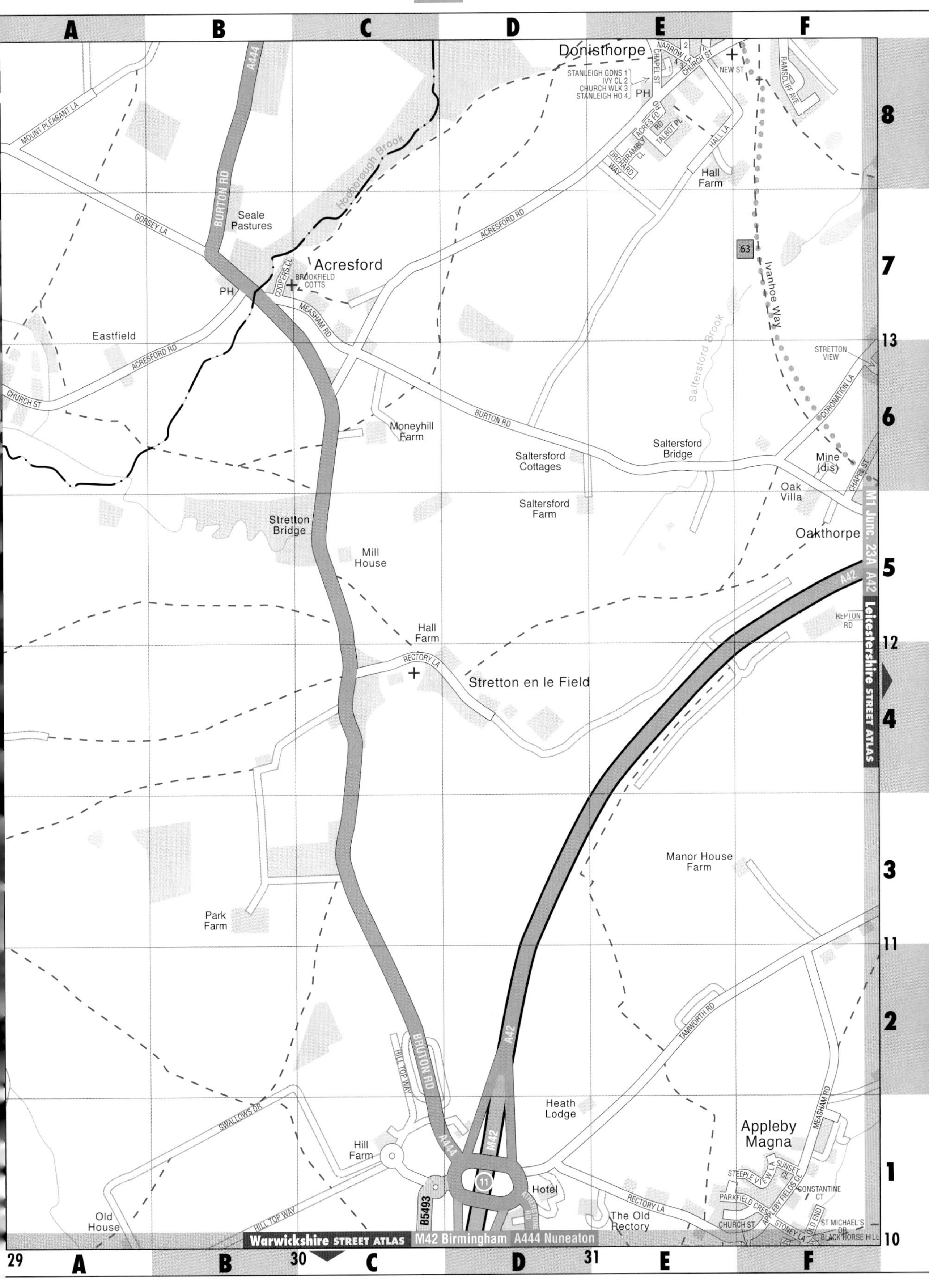

A B C D E F

8
7
13
6
5
12
4
3
11
2
1
10

Donisthorpe

STANLEIGH GDNS 1
IVY CL 2
CHURCH WLK 3
STANLEIGH HO 4

NARROW LA
CHAPEL ST
CHURCH ST
NEW ST

PH

Acresford RD
ACRES
CL

ASSEMBLY
CL

ORCHARD
WAY

TALBOT PL

HALL LA

Hall
Farm

63

Ivanhoe Way

Saltersford Brook

STRETTON
VIEW

CORONATION LA

Mine
(dis)

Oak
Villa

Oakthorpe

M1 Junc. 23A A42 Leicestershire STREET ATLAS

REPTON
RD

Acresford

BROOKFIELD
COTTS

COUPERS CL

PH

MEASHAM RD

BURTON RD

A444

GORSEY LA

MOUNT PLEASANT LA

Seale
Pastures

Hodorough Brook

Eastfield

Acresford RD

CHURCH ST

Burton RD

Moneyhill
Farm

Saltersford
Cottages

Saltersford
Farm

Saltersford
Bridge

Stretton
Bridge

Mill
House

Hall
Farm

RECTORY LA

Stretton en le Field

Park
Farm

A42

BRUTON RD

HILL TOP WAY

SWALLOWS DR

Hill
Farm

Old
House

B5493

HILL TOP WAY

A444

M42

11

Hotel

Heath
Lodge

ATHERSTONE RD

Manor House
Farm

TAMWORTH RD

A42

MEASHAM RD

Appleby
Magna

STEEPLE VIEW LA
SUNSET
CL

CONSTANTINE
CT

PARKFIELD CRES

STEEPLE VIEW LA

RUGBY FIELDS DR

OLD END

STONEY LA

ST MICHAEL'S
DR

BLACK HORSE HILL

CHURCH ST

RECTORY LA

The Old
Rectory

Warwickshire STREET ATLAS M42 Birmingham A444 Nuneaton

29 A B 30 C D 31 E F 10

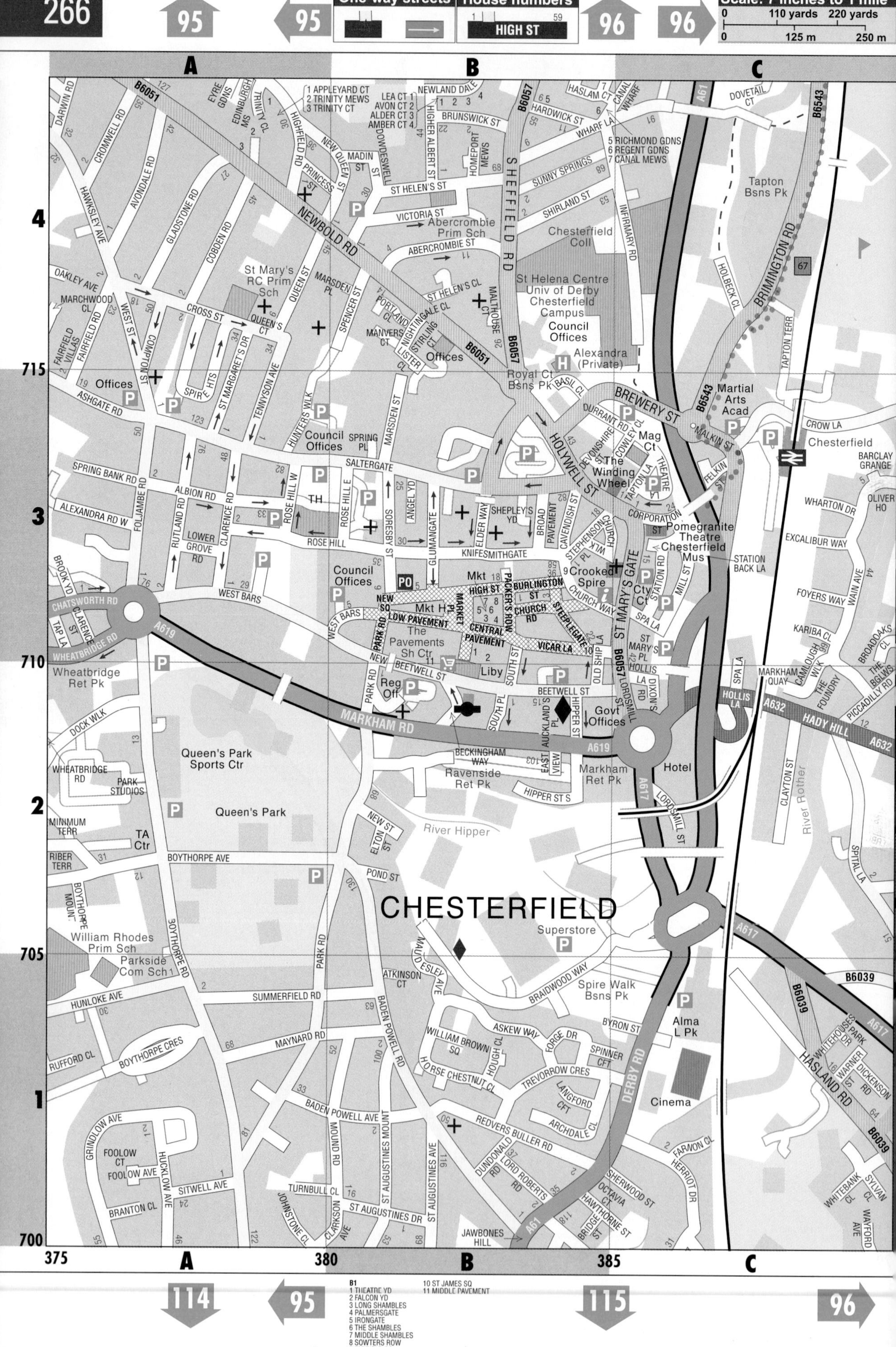

266
95
95
One-way streets
House numbers
HIGH ST
96
96
Scale: 7 inches to 1 mile
110 yards
220 yards
125 m
250 m
A
B
C
4
3
2
1
715
710
705
700
375
380
385
CHESTERFIELD
B6051
NEWBOLD RD
SHEFFIELD RD
B6057
A61
B6543
BRIMINGTON RD
Tapton Bsns Pk
DOVETAIL CT
HASLAM CT
CANAL WHARF
HARDWICK ST
WHARF LA
5 RICHMOND GDNS
6 REGENT GDNS
7 CANAL MEWS
SUNNY SPRINGS
SHIRLAND ST
INFIRMARY RD
Chesterfield Coll
St Helena Centre
Univ of Derby
Chesterfield Campus
Council Offices
Alexandra (Private)
Royal Ct Bsns Pk
BASIL CL
BREWERY ST
Martial Arts Acad
CROW LA
Chesterfield
BARCLAY GRANGE
OLIVER HO
WHARTON DR
EXCALIBUR WAY
STATION BACK LA
FOYERS WAY
WAIN AVE
KARIBA CL
BROADOAKS
CAMLOUGH WLK
THE FOUNDRY
THE BGLWS
PICCADILLY RD
MARKHAM QUAY
HOLLIS LA
A632
HADY HILL
1 APPLEYARD CT
2 TRINITY MEWS
3 TRINITY CT
LEA CT
AVON CT
ALDER CT
AMBER CT
NEWLAND DALE
BRUNSWICK ST
HIGHER ALBERT ST
HOMEPORT MEWS
DOWDESWELL ST
MADIN ST
ST HELEN'S ST
VICTORIA ST
Abercrombie Prim Sch
ABERCROMBIE ST
ST HELEN'S CL
MALTHOUSE CT
NIGHTINGALE CL
PORTLAND CL
STIRLING CT
LISTER CL
MANVERS CT
Offices
DARWIN RD
CROMWELL RD
AVONDALE RD
GLADSTONE RD
COBDEN RD
EYRE GDNS
EDINBURGH MS
TRINITY CL
HIGHFIELD RD
NEW QUEEN ST
PRINCESS ST
HAWKSLEY AVE
OAKLEY AVE
MARCHWOOD CL
FAIRFIELD VILLAS
FAIRFIELD RD
WEST ST
COMPTON ST
CROSS ST
St Mary's RC Prim Sch
QUEEN'S CT
QUEEN ST
MARSDEN PL
SPENCER ST
ST MARGARET'S DR
TENNYSON AVE
SPIRE HTS
ASHGATE RD
HUNTERS WLK
Council Offices
SPRING PL
MARSDEN ST
SALTERGATE
SPRING BANK RD
ALBION RD
ALEXANDRA RD W
FOLJAMBE RD
RUTLAND RD
CLARENCE RD
LOWER GROVE RD
ROSE HILL W
TH
ROSE HILL E
ROSE HILL
SORESBY ST
ANGEL YD
GLUMANGATE
ELDER WAY
SHEPLEY'S YD
BROAD PAVEMENT
CAVENDISH ST
HOLYWELL ST
DURRANT RD
DEVONSHIRE CL
COWLEY CL
Mag Ct
THEATRE LA
TAPTON LA
The Winding Wheel
CORPORATION ST
Pomegranite Theatre
Chesterfield Mus
STATION RD
MILL ST
MALKIN ST
FELKIN ST
TAPTON TERR
HOLBECK CL
KNIFESMITHGATE
STEPHENSON PL
CHURCH WLK
Crooked Spire
CHURCH WAY
Cty Ct
ST MARY'S GATE
SPA LA
ST MARY'S PL
HOLLIS LA
DIXON'S RD
WEST BARS
BROOK YD
CHATSWORTH RD
CLARENCE ST
TAP LA
WHEATBRIDGE RD
A619
Council Offices
PO
NEW SQ
Mkt Hl
MARKET PL
PACKER'S ROW
HIGH ST
BURLINGTON ST
CHURCH RD
STEEPLEGATE
LOW PAVEMENT
CENTRAL PAVEMENT
VICAR LA
The Pavements Sh Ctr
NEW BEETWELL ST
Liby
SOUTH ST
OLD SHIP LA
LORDSMILL ST
PARK RD
Reg Off
BEETWELL ST
SOUTH PL
EAST AUCKLAND'S PL
HIPPER ST
Govt Offices
MARKHAM RD
Wheatbridge Ret Pk
DOCK WLK
Queen's Park Sports Ctr
WHEATBRIDGE RD
PARK STUDIOS
Queen's Park
MINIMUM TERR
TA Ctr
RIBER TERR
BOYTHORPE AVE
BECKINGHAM WAY
Ravenside Ret Pk
VIEW
Markham Ret Pk
HIPPER ST S
Hotel
A617
River Hipper
NEW ST
ELTON ST
POND ST
CLAYTON ST
River Rother
SPITAL LA
BOYTHORPE MOUNT
William Rhodes Prim Sch
Parkside Com Sch
BOYTHORPE RD
PARK RD
Superstore
MAUD ESLEY AVE
ATKINSON CT
BRAIDWOOD WAY
Spire Walk Bsns Pk
B6039
HUNLOKE AVE
SUMMERFIELD RD
BADEN POWELL RD
ASKEW WAY
BYRON ST
Alma L Pk
MAYNARD RD
WILLIAM BROWN SQ
HOUGH CL
FORGE DR
SPINNER CFT
BOYTHORPE CRES
RUFFORD CL
HORSE CHESTNUT CL
TREVORROW CRES
DERBY RD
LANGFORD CFT
Cinema
HASLAND RD
WHITEHOUSES PARK DR
WARNER ST
DICKENSON RD
BADEN POWELL AVE
GRINDLOW AVE
FOOLOW CT
FOOLOW AVE
HUCKLOW AVE
MOUND RD
ST AUGUSTINES MOUNT
REDVERS BULLER RD
ARCHDALE CL
FARNON CL
HERRIOT DR
SITWELL AVE
BRANTON CL
TURNBULL CL
JOHNSTONE CL
CLARKSON AVE
ST AUGUSTINES DR
ST AUGUSTINES AVE
DUNDONALD RD
LORD ROBERTS RD
SHERWOOD ST
OCTAVIA CT
HAWTHORNE ST
BRIDGE ST
JAWBONES HILL
WHITEBANK CL
SYLVAN CL
WAYFORD AVE
114
95
115
96
B1
1 THEATRE YD
2 FALCON YD
3 LONG SHAMBLES
4 PALMERSGATE
5 IRONGATE
6 THE SHAMBLES
7 MIDDLE SHAMBLES
8 SOWTERS ROW
9 RYKNELD SQ
10 ST JAMES SQ
11 MIDDLE PAVEMENT

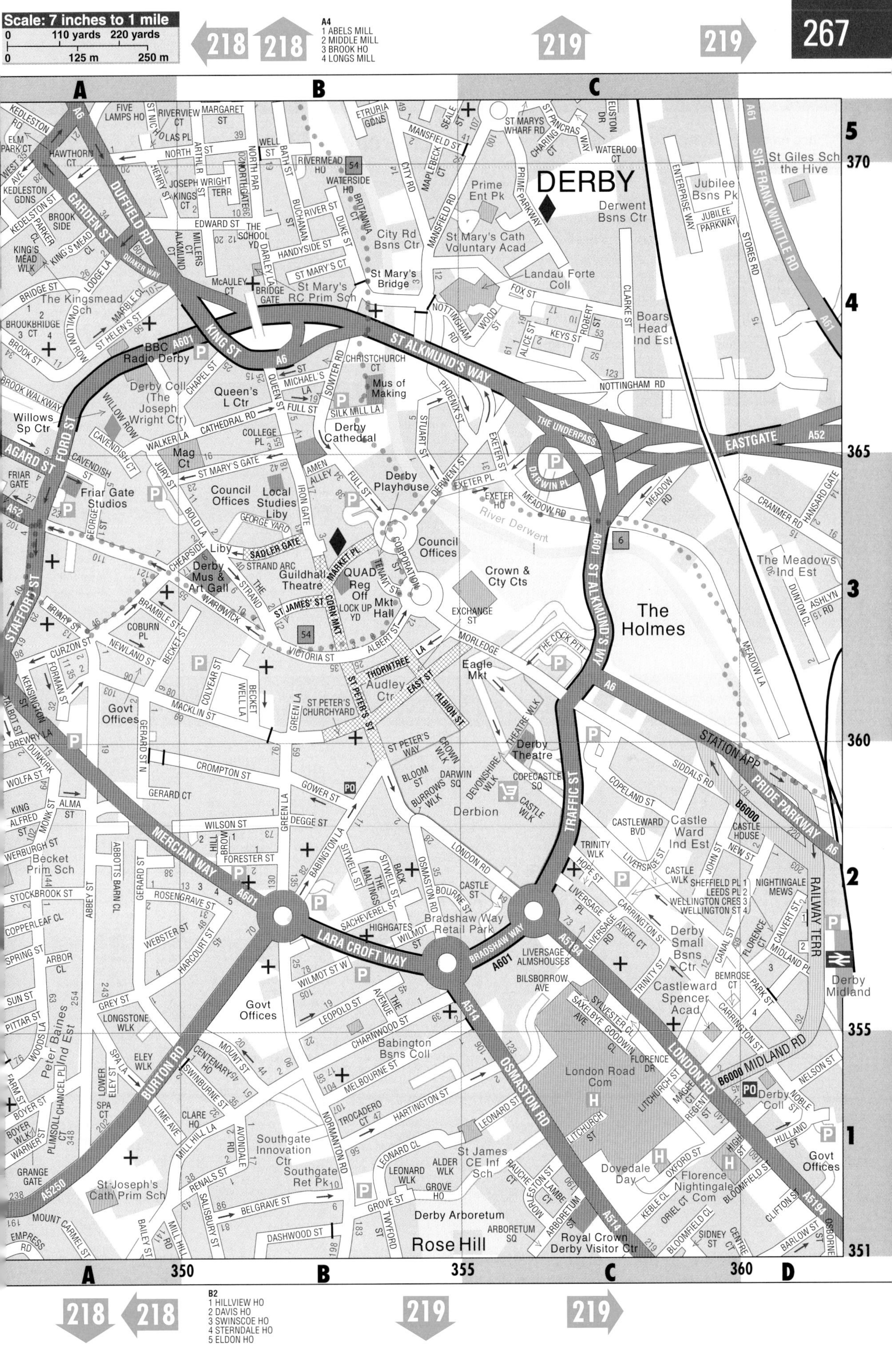

Scale: 7 inches to 1 mile
0
110 yards
220 yards
0
125 m
250 m
218
218
A4
1 ABELS MILL
2 MIDDLE MILL
3 BROOK HO
4 LONGS MILL
219
219
267
A
B
C
5
4
3
2
1
370
365
360
355
351
350
355
360
D
DERBY
KEDLESTON RD
ELM PARK CT
WEST AVE
KEDLESTON GDNS
KEDLESTON ST
FIVE LAMPS HO
RIVERVIEW CT
MARGARET ST
NORTH ST
HAWTHORN CT
HENRY ST
JOSEPH WRIGHT TERR
KINGS CT
NORTHGATE
NORTH PAR
WELL ST
BATH ST
RIVERMEAD HO
WATERSIDE HO
BRITANNIA CT
ETRURIA GDNS
MANSFIELD ST
SEALE ST
MAPLEBECK CT
CITY RD
ST MARYS WHARF RD
ST PANCRAS WAY
CHARING CROSS CT
EUSTON DR
WATERLOO CT
PRIME PARKWAY
Prime Ent Pk
Derwent Bsns Ctr
ENTERPRISE WAY
Jubilee Bsns Pk
JUBILEE PARKWAY
St Giles Sch the Hive
SIR FRANK WHITTLE RD
STORES RD
A61
A6
GARDEN ST
DUFFIELD RD
QUAKER WAY
BROOK SIDE
PARKER CL
KING'S MEAD CL
KING'S MEAD WLK
LODGE LA
EDWARD ST
THE SCHOOL YD
ALKMUND CT
MILLERS CT
DARLEY LA
BUCHANAN ST
RIVER ST
DUKE ST
HANDYSIDE ST
ST MARY'S CT
City Rd Bsns Ctr
MANSFIELD RD
St Mary's Cath Voluntary Acad
Landau Forte Coll
St Mary's Bridge
St Mary's RC Prim Sch
McAULEY CT
BRIDGE GATE
BRIDGE ST
The Kingsmead Sch
BROOKBRIDGE CT
BROOK ST
WILLOW ROW
MARBLE CL
ST HELEN'S ST
BBC Radio Derby
A601
KING ST
CHAPEL ST
Queen's L Ctr
QUEEN ST
ST MICHAEL'S LA
SOWTER RD
CHRISTCHURCH CT
Mus of Making
SILK MILL LA
ST ALKMUND'S WAY
NOTTINGHAM RD
WOOD ST
FOX ST
ALICE ST
KEYS ST
ROBERT ST
CLARKE ST
Boars Head Ind Est
BROOK WALKWAY
Willows Sp Ctr
FORD ST
Derby Coll (The Joseph Wright Ctr)
CATHEDRAL RD
FULL ST
COLLEGE PL
Derby Cathedral
PHOENIX ST
STUART ST
THE UNDERPASS
EASTGATE
A52
AGARD ST
FRIAR GATE
CAVENDISH ST
CAVENDISH CT
WALKER LA
Mag Ct
JURY ST
ST MARY'S GATE
Council Offices
Local Studies Liby
AMEN ALLEY
IRON GATE
Derby Playhouse
DERWENT ST
EXETER PL
EXETER ST
EXETER HO
DARWIN PL
MEADOW RD
River Derwent
MEADOW RD
CRANMER RD
HANSARD GATE
Friar Gate Studios
GEORGE ST
BOLD LA
GEORGE YARD
SADLER GATE
Liby
Council Offices
CORPORATION ST
Crown & Cty Cts
The Meadows Ind Est
DUNTON CL
ASHLYN RD
CHEAPSIDE
STRAND ARC
Derby Mus & Art Gall
THE STRAND
WARDWICK
Guildhall Theatre
MARKET PL
QUAD
Reg Off
TENANT ST
Mkt Hall
LOCK UP YD
ST JAMES' ST
CORN MKT
EXCHANGE ST
The Holmes
MEADOW LA
STAFFORD ST
FRIARY ST
BRAMBLE ST
COBURN PL
BECKET ST
NEWLAND ST
CURZON ST
FORMAN ST
KENSINGTON ST
VICTORIA ST
ALBERT ST
MORLEDGE
THE COCK PITT
THORNTREE LA
EAST ST
ALBION ST
Audley Ctr
Eagle Mkt
COLYEAR ST
BECKET WELL LA
Govt Offices
MACKLIN ST
GREEN LA
ST PETER'S CHURCHYARD
ST PETER'S ST
THEATRE WLK
TALBOT ST
DREWRY LA
DUNKIRK
WOLFA ST
KING ALFRED ST
ALMA ST
MONK ST
GERARD ST N
CROMPTON ST
GERARD CT
ST PETER'S WAY
CROWN WLK
BLOOM ST
DARWIN SQ
DEVONSHIRE WLK
Derby Theatre
COPECASTLE SQ
CASTLE WLK
TRAFFIC ST
STATION APP
SIDDALS RD
PRIDE PARKWAY
COPELAND ST
GOWER ST
PO
BURROWS WLK
Derbion
MERCIAN WAY
WILSON ST
HILL BROW
DEGGE ST
FORESTER ST
BABINGTON LA
SITWELL ST
THE MALTINGS
BACK SITWELL ST
OSMASTON RD
LONDON RD
CASTLE ST
BOURNE ST
CASTLEWARD BVD
Castle Ward Ind Est
B6000
CASTLE HOUSE
NEW ST
JOHN ST
TRINITY WLK
HOPE ST
LIVERSAGE ST
CASTLE WLK
SHEFFIELD PL 1
LEEDS PL 2
WELLINGTON CRES 3
WELLINGTON ST 4
NIGHTINGALE MEWS
RAILWAY TERR
WERBURGH ST
Becket Prim Sch
ABBOTTS BARN CL
GERARD ST
ROSENGRAVE ST
STOCKBROOK ST
ABBEY ST
COPPERLEAF CL
WEBSTER ST
HARCOURT ST
SACHEVEREL ST
HIGHGATES
WILMOT ST
Bradshaw Way Retail Park
BRADSHAW WAY
LIVERSAGE PL
LIVERSAGE RD
ANGEL CT
CARRINGTON ST
Derby Small Bsns Ctr
CANAL ST
FLORENCE CT
MIDLAND PL
CALVERT ST
SPRING ST
ARBOR CL
LARA CROFT WAY
WILMOT ST W
LIVERSAGE ALMSHOUSES
BILSBORROW AVE
TRINITY ST
BEMROSE CT
PARK ST
Castleward Spencer Acad
Derby Midland
SUN ST
PITTAR ST
Peter Baines Ind Est
WOODS LA
GREY ST
LONGSTONE WLK
Govt Offices
LEOPOLD ST
THE AVENUE
CHARNWOOD ST
A514
SAXELBYE AVE
SYLVESTER CL
GOODWIN CL
FLORENCE DR
A5194
MIDLAND RD
NELSON ST
ELEY WLK
SPA LA
MOUNT ST
CENTENARY HO
SWINBURNE ST
Babington Bsns Coll
MELBOURNE ST
London Road Com
LITCHURCH ST
MAGEE CT
REGENT ST
PO
Derby Coll
NOBLE ST
FARM ST
BOYER ST
CHANCEL PL
PLIMSOLL ST
LOWER ELEY ST
SPA CT
BURTON RD
LIME AVE
CLARE HO
TROCADERO CT
HARTINGTON ST
LEONARD ST
HULLAND ST
BOYER WLK
WARNER ST
MILL HILL LA
AVONDALE RD
Southgate Innovation Ctr
NORMANTON RD
LEONARD CL
St James CE Inf Sch
LITCHURCH ST
OXFORD ST
HIGH ST
Govt Offices
GRANGE GATE
St Joseph's Cath Prim Sch
A5250
RENALS ST
SALISBURY ST
Southgate Ret Pk
LEONARD WLK
ALDER WLK
GROVE HO
RAUCHE CT
MORLESTON ST
LAMBE CT
Dovedale Day
KEBLE CL
Florence Nightingale Com
ORIEL CT
BLOOMFIELD ST
CLIFTON ST
MOUNT CARMEL ST
EMPRESS RD
BAILEY ST
MILL HILL
BELGRAVE ST
DASHWOOD ST
GROVE ST
TWYFORD ST
Derby Arboretum
ARBORETUM SQ
ARBORETUM ST
Royal Crown Derby Visitor Ctr
Rose Hill
BLOOMFIELD CL
SIDNEY ST
CENTRE ST
BARLOW ST
OSBORNE
A
B
C
B2
1 HILLVIEW HO
2 DAVIS HO
3 SWINSCOE HO
4 STERNDALE HO
5 ELDON HO
218
218
219
219

Index

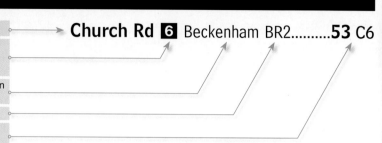

Place name May be abbreviated on the map

Location number Present when a number indicates the place's position in a crowded area of mapping

Locality, town or village Shown when more than one place has the same name

Postcode district District for the indexed place

Page and grid square Page number and grid reference for the standard mapping

Church Rd **6** Beckenham BR2..........**53** C6

Cities, towns and villages are listed in CAPITAL LETTERS

Public and commercial buildings are highlighted in magenta   **Places of interest** are highlighted in blue with a star ★

Abbreviations used in the index

Acad	**Academy**	Comm	**Common**	Gd	**Ground**	L	**Leisure**
App	**Approach**	Cott	**Cottage**	Gdn	**Garden**	La	**Lane**
Arc	**Arcade**	Cres	**Crescent**	Gn	**Green**	Liby	**Library**
Ave	**Avenue**	Cswy	**Causeway**	Gr	**Grove**	Mdw	**Meadow**
Bglw	**Bungalow**	Ct	**Court**	H	**Hall**	Meml	**Memorial**
Bldg	**Building**	Ctr	**Centre**	Ho	**House**	Mkt	**Market**
Bsns, Bus	**Business**	Ctry	**Country**	Hospl	**Hospital**	Mus	**Museum**
Bvd	**Boulevard**	Cty	**County**	HQ	**Headquarters**	Orch	**Orchard**
Cath	**Cathedral**	Dr	**Drive**	Hts	**Heights**	Pal	**Palace**
Cir	**Circus**	Dro	**Drove**	Ind	**Industrial**	Par	**Parade**
Cl	**Close**	Ed	**Education**	Inst	**Institute**	Pas	**Passage**
Cnr	**Corner**	Emb	**Embankment**	Int	**International**	Pk	**Park**
Coll	**College**	Est	**Estate**	Intc	**Interchange**	Pl	**Place**
Com	**Community**	Ex	**Exhibition**	Junc	**Junction**	Prec	**Precinct**

Prom	**Promenade**
Rd	**Road**
Recn	**Recreation**
Ret	**Retail**
Sh	**Shopping**
Sq	**Square**
St	**Street**
Sta	**Station**
Terr	**Terrace**
TH	**Town Hall**
Univ	**University**
Wk, Wlk	**Walk**
Wr	**Water**
Yd	**Yard**

Index of towns, villages, streets, hospitals, industrial estates, railway stations, schools, shopping centres, universities and places of interest

1st–Ald

1st Ave DE7........208 F7
2nd Ave DE7........208 F7
3rd Ave DE7........208 F7

A

Abba Cl NG16........195 F7
Abbey Brook Ct **1**
S8............56 E8
Abbey Brook Dr S8...56 E8
Abbey Cl ST14....197 A3
Abbey Cres DE5....180 E7
Abbey Croft
Chesterfield S40......95 A3
Renishaw S21.......79 C8
Abbeycroft Lane **5**
DE22............204 F2
Abbeydale Cl DE56 . 192 B7
Abbeydale Ct S17.....56 A7
Abbeydale Industrial
Hamlet ★ S7.......56 B8
ABBEYDALE PARK ..55 F6
Abbeydale Park Cres
S17............55 F6
Abbeydale Park Rise
S17............55 F6
Abbeydale Rd S7....43 A8
Abbeydale Road S
S17............56 A7
Abbeyfields Cl
DE22............205 A2
Abbey Gdns SK14.....9 A3
Abbey Hill
Breadsall DE21......205 C4
Derby DE21, DE22 ...205 B4
Derby DE22.......204 F3
Abbeyhill Cl S42......95 A4
Abbey Hill Rd DE22 . 204 D2
Abbey La DE22....205 A1
Abbey Lodge Cl **1**
DE11............256 A7
Abbey Pl S21.......79 C8
Abbey St
Derby DE1, DE22 . 267 A2
Ilkeston DE7.......208 C6
Abbey View Dr S8....43 A3
Abbey View Hts **3**
S8............43 A3
Abbey View Rd S8....43 A3

[column 2]

Abbey Wood Cl DE3 .217 F5
Abbey Yd DE22 .....205 A1
Abbot Beyne Sch
DE15............248 A3
Abbot Cl DE21 .....205 E2
Abbot Mews DE22 . 205 A1
Abbot Rd
Branston DE14......253 D8
Ilkeston DE7.......208 C6
Abbots Croft NG19... 135 E1
Abbotsford Mews
DE7............194 D3
Abbots Gr DE56.....179 A5
Abbotsholme Sch
ST14............197 B2
Abbott Rd
Alfreton DE55......159 B3
Mansfield NG19 .....135 D1
Abbotts Barn Cl
DE22............267 A2
Abbotts Cl DE11 .....256 A6
Abbotts Rd DE11.....256 A6
Abbott St
Awsworth NG16......195 C4
Heanor DE75.......181 E1
Long Eaton NG10 ....236 D6
Abel La DE4 ....142 C2
Abells DE5 ....180 C1
Abels Mill **1** DE1. .267 A4
Abercrombie Prim Sch
Chesterfield S41......96 A5
Chesterfield S41......266 B4
Abercrombie St
S41............266 B4
Aberdare Cl DE21... 206 B2
Aberdeen Close
DE11............255 F1
Abingdon Bsns Ctr The
DE24............219 C1
Abingdon St DE24 . 232 C8
ABNEY............51 F4
Abney Cl
Chesterfield S40......95 D6
Derby DE3 ....217 F2
Sheffield S14 ....43 C6
Abney Dr S14.......43 C6
Abney Grange SK17...51 E2
Abney Rd S14......43 C6
Acacia Ave
Brimington S43......97 A8
Derby DE3 ....217 E1
Swadlincote DE11....256 B7
Acacia Cres S21......60 B5

[column 3]

Acacia Croft DE56... 179 B2
Acacia Ct NG19.....136 E1
Acacia Dr
Melbourne DE73.....252 A8
Pilsley S45 ....132 B3
Acacia Gdns NG16...195 F8
Acacia La
Branston DE14......253 E6
Branston DE14.......256 E6
Access 26 Bsns Pk
NG16............182 C3
Acer Cl
Killamarsh S21.......60 C5
Pinxton NG16.......160 C3
Acer Croft DE21 ... 205 E3
Acorn Cl DE24......232 E3
Acorn Ctr NG16.....182 C3
Acorn Dr
Ashbourne DE6......185 C8
Belper DE56.......179 A5
Clay Cross S45......131 B3
Acorn Ridge
Chesterfield S40......114 B7
Matlock DE4 ....143 B6
Shirebrook NG20 ....119 D5
Acorn Terr SK22......33 B6
Acorn Way
Belper DE56.......179 A5
Derby DE21 ....220 C6
Acreage La NG20 .....119 F2
Acre Ct **5** SK13 .....17 C7
Acre La
Aston-on-Trent
DE72............246 D7
Sutton on the Hill DE6. .228 B7
ACRESFORD 265 C7
Acres Ford Ed DE12. 265 E8
Acresford Rd
Donisthorpe DE12 ...265 D6
Netherseal DE12.....265 B6
Overseal DE12......262 B2
Acresford View
DE12............262 B3
Acres Rd S45......132 B3
Acre St **4** SK13 .....17 C7
Acres The S45......132 B4
Acresview Cl DE22...204 D4
Acres View Cl S41.....95 F7
Acton Ave NG10 ....236 E6
Acton Cl NG10.....236 E6
Acton Ct **1** S43 .....78 B3

[column 4]

Acton Gr NG10 .....236 E6
Acton Rd
Derby DE22 ....217 F6
Long Eaton NG10 ....236 E6
Acton Road Ind Est
NG10............236 E6
Acton St NG10.....236 E6
Adale Rd DE7.......193 B8
Adam Bede Cres
DE4............165 F6
Adams Cl DE75.....193 D7
Adams Close DE11...257 A7
Adams Ct DE7 .....194 E3
Adam's Rd DE6......217 A8
Adam St DE7 ....209 A6
Adastral Ave S12 .....44 A2
Adderley Pl SK13 ......9 F1
Adderley Rd SK13 ......9 F1
Addison Dr DE55 ... 159 B4
Addison Rd
Derby DE24 ....232 C7
Stonebroom DE55 ...146 F3
Addison Sq DE4 ....155 A5
Addison St DE55.....148 A7
Addison Villas
NG16............182 E1
Adelaide Cl
Derby DE3 ....217 E4
Stapleford NG9......209 F1
Adelaide Cres DE15. 248 C2
Adelaide Wlk **1**
NG16............170 F4
Adelphi Cl DE23 .... 231 A6
Adelphi Way S43 .....97 E8
Adin Ave S44.........98 F6
Adler Ct **1** S41 .....219 B7
Adlington Ave S42. . 115 C2
Adlington La S32......72 C8
Admiral Cl DE75.....181 D2
Admiral Court DE7...194 F4
Adrian Cl NG9.......223 F1
Adrian St DE24 .....232 D6
Adwick Cl DE3......217 C2
Aeropark The ★
DE74............247 A1
Agard St DE1.......267 A4
Agnesmeadow La
DE6............174 D4
Agricultural Bsns Ctr
DE45............109 E5
Agricultural Way
DE45............109 E5
Agrimony Pl **2** DE3 217 C4

[column 5]

Aimploy Ct DE23....219 A1
Ainley Cl DE24......232 F7
Ainsworth Dr DE23 . 231 E7
Aintree Ave S21......59 B3
Aintree Cl
Burton upon Trent
DE14............254 A7
Kimberley NG16.....195 E7
Aire Cl **7** DE65 ....228 E1
Airedale Cl NG10 ... 236 A6
Airedale Wlk **3**
DE24............233 C6
Aires Hollow **5**
DE72............246 A6
Airfield Industrial Est
DE6............185 E7
Akaal Prim Sch
DE23............231 E7
Akley Bank Cl S17 ....55 F5
Alabaster La DE4 ....155 A6
Alandale Ave NG20 . 119 F5
Albany Cl S41.......136 C1
Albany Ct NG9.......209 E1
Albany Dr NG19 .....136 C1
Albany Gdns DE65 . 227 D2
Albany Inf & Jun Schs
NG9............223 E8
Albany Inf Sch NG9. .209 E1
Albany Pl NG19 .....136 C1
Albany Rd DE22 ....218 C4
Albany St DE7 .....209 A6
Albemarle Rd DE21. .220 B7
Alberta Ave NG16... 171 F7
Albert Ave
Chesterfield S43......77 D3
Jacksdale NG16......171 B4
Stapleford NG9......223 D7
Albert Cres DE21 ... 220 B4
Albert Ct SK17.......85 C6
Albert Rd
Breaston DE72......235 B7
Chesterfield S43......77 D3
Derby DE21 ....220 A4
Long Eaton NG10 ...236 D8
Ripley DE5 ....169 C2
Sandiacre NG10 ...223 B6
Sheffield, Heeley S8. .43 A6
Swadlincote DE11 ...256 A2
Albert St N **30** S41...95 F8
Albert Sq NG19 ....136 C1
Albert St
Belper DE56.......178 F4
Derby DE1 ....267 B3

[column 6]

Albert St continued
Eastwood NG16......182 F3
Eckington S21.......59 D2
Glossop SK13.......10 A5
Ilkeston DE7.......208 E8
Ironville NG16.......170 F5
Mansfield Woodhouse
NG19............136 C4
Ripley DE5 ....169 E1
Somercotes DE55....170 B8
South Normanton
DE55............160 B6
Stapleford NG9......223 D7
ALBERT VILLAGE...256 C1
Albert Village Prim Sch
DE11............256 C1
Albine Rd NG20.....119 E6
Albion Mill SK14......9 C5
Albion Rd
Chesterfield S40......266 C1
Long Eaton NG10 ...236 F8
New Mills SK22......33 B6
Albion St
Derby DE1 ....219 A5
Derby DE1 ....267 B3
Ilkeston DE7.......194 F1
Mansfield NG19 ....135 F1
Ripley DE5 ....169 E1
Woodville DE11......256 E6
Albrighton Ave
DE24............231 D2
Aldam Cl S17........55 E4
Aldam Croft S17......55 E4
Aldam Rd S17.......55 E4
Aldam Way S17......55 E4
Alder Brook SK23....34 E2
Alderbrook Cl DE13. 240 B4
ALDERCAR.......182 A4
Aldercar High Sch
NG16............182 A4
Aldercar Inf Sch
NG16............182 A4
Aldercar La NG16... 182 A6
Alder Cl
Derby DE21 ....205 E3
Glossop SK13 ....9 F4
Mansfield NG19 .....136 E1
Shirebrook NG20 ...119 D5
Alder Com High Sch
SK14............15 A4
Alder Ct S41........266 B4
Alderfen Cl DE24 ... 232 D3

Alder Gdns S43 ... 78 A1
Alder Gr
Burton upon Trent DE15 ... 254 F7
Buxton SK17 ... 85 A8
Mansfield Woodhouse NG19 ... 136 B5
Alder Grove SK23 ... 47 A6
Alderholme Dr 1 DE13 ... 240 F1
Alder La DE6 ... 188 A3
Alderley Ct DE21 ... 206 A2
Alderney Rd 3 S8 ... 43 A7
Aldern Way DE45 ... 109 F7
Alder Rd
Belper DE56 ... 179 A3
Dronfield S18 ... 57 A3
Alder Rise SK23 ... 45 D8
ALDERS ... 196 C2
Alders Ave SK23 ... 34 E1
Alders Brook DE65 ... 228 D1
Alders Field DE4 ... 144 A3
Aldersgate
Derby DE22 ... 217 F7
New Mills SK22 ... 33 B8
Alders La
Chinley SK23 ... 34 E2
Tansley DE4 ... 144 A3
Alderslade Cl DE72 ... 234 B1
Aldersley Cl DE65 ... 230 C1
Alders Meadow SK23 ... 34 E2
Alderson Dr DE13 ... 240 F1
Alderson Pl S2 ... 43 A8
Alderson Rd S2 ... 43 A8
Alderson Road N S2 ... 43 A8
Alders Rd SK12 ... 32 A7
Alders Reach DE13 ... 240 B4
Alders The S42 ... 113 D7
ALDERWASLEY ... 166 E8
Alderwasley Hall Sch DE56 ... 167 B7
Alderwasley Hall Sch and Sixth Form Centre DE4 ... 165 E4
Alderwasley Pk
Alderwasley DE4 ... 167 B7
Alderwasley DE4 ... 167 C8
Whatstandwell DE56 ... 156 C1
Alder Way
Clowne S43 ... 80 D2
Creswell S80 ... 81 E2
Shirebrook NG20 ... 119 D4
Alder Wlk DE23 ... 267 B1
Aldred Cl S21 ... 60 E8
Aldred's La DE75, NG16 ... 182 B2
Aldridge Cl NG9 ... 223 E2
ALDWARK
152 F7
DE4 ... 153 B7
Aldwark Rd SK17 ... 85 C6
Aldwych DE22 ... 218 A6
Alexander Ave NG16 ... 171 D7
Alexander Rd SK17 ... 47 F1
Alexander Terr NG16 ... 160 C1
Alexandra Ave NG19 ... 136 B5
Alexandra Ct
Burton upon Trent DE15 ... 248 A3
Overseal DE12 ... 262 B4
Alexandra Gdns 3 DE23 ... 219 B2
Alexandra Mills 2 DE1 ... 218 E5
Alexandra Private Hospl S41 ... 266 B4
Alexandra Rd
Burton upon Trent DE15 ... 248 A3
Buxton SK17 ... 85 C5
Dronfield S18 ... 57 B2
Long Eaton NG10 ... 236 D8
Overseal DE12 ... 262 B4
Sheffield S2 ... 43 B7
Swadlincote DE11 ... 256 B3
Alexandra Road E S41 ... 96 C1
Alexandra Road W S40 ... 266 A3
Alexandra St
Eastwood NG16 ... 182 F2
Stapleford NG9 ... 223 D6
Alexandre Cl DE23 ... 231 D6
Alford Cl S40 ... 95 C3
Alfred Eley Cl DE11 ... 255 F4
Alfred Rd DE56 ... 192 A8
Alfred St
Alfreton DE55 ... 158 F3
Pinxton NG16 ... 160 C4
Ripley DE5 ... 169 E2
Somercotes DE55 ... 170 D6
South Normanton DE55 ... 159 F5
ALFRETON ... 159 C4
Alfreton L Ctr DE55 ... 158 F4
Alfreton Motorway Link Ind Est DE55 ... 159 A2
Alfreton Rd
Blackwell DE55 ... 147 E2
Breadsall DE21 ... 205 B2
Codnor DE5 ... 170 C1
Holbrook DE21 ... 191 D2
Little Eaton DE21 ... 205 C6
Matlock DE4 ... 143 E4
Pinxton NG16 ... 160 C4
Alfreton Rd *continued*
Selston DE55, NG16 ... 171 C6
Shirland DE55 ... 158 F6
Tibshelf DE55 ... 147 D4
Alfreton Sta DE55 ... 159 C5
Alfreton Trad Est DE55 ... 159 B2
Algar Cl S2 ... 43 E7
Algar Cres S2 ... 43 F7
Algar Dr S2 ... 43 E7
Algar Pl S2 ... 43 E7
Algar Rd S2 ... 43 E7
Alice Gdns DE12 ... 262 B4
Alicehead Rd S45 ... 113 B2
Alice St DE1 ... 267 C4
Alice's View S42 ... 132 A8
Alice Way S18 ... 76 E5
Alison Cl DE21 ... 219 F7
ALKMONTON ... 199 D1
Alkmonton Rd DE6 ... 213 D5
Alkmund Ct DE1 ... 267 B4
Allan Ave DE23 ... 230 E8
Allandale Rd DE75 ... 181 D2
Allan La DE56 ... 168 B6
Allcroft St NG19 ... 136 C4
Allenby Cl S8 ... 56 E7
Allenby Dr S8 ... 56 E7
Allendale DE7 ... 208 E7
Allendale Rd S42 ... 114 F3
Allendale Way NG19 ... 136 E1
Allen Hill DE4 ... 143 B6
Allen La
Ashover DE4 ... 144 C6
Weston Underwood DE6 ... 188 C1
Allens Croft ST14 ... 224 E2
Allen's Green Ave NG16 ... 171 F6
Allen's La ST14 ... 224 E2
Allen St DE24 ... 232 E5
ALLENTON ... 232 D5
Allenton Com Prim Sch DE24 ... 232 D5
Allen View DE55 ... 159 C4
ALLESTREE ... 204 F3
Allestree Cl DE24 ... 232 E8
Allestree Dr S18 ... 56 C1
Allestree La DE22 ... 204 D3
Allestree Park Nature Reserve* DE22 ... 204 F5
Allestree St DE24 ... 232 F8
Alley The DE4 ... 154 D4
Alley Wlk DE6 ... 201 F7
Allison Ave DE11 ... 256 B3
Allison Gdns DE7 ... 195 A1
Allissa Ave DE5 ... 180 E7
Allpits Rd S44 ... 96 F3
Allport Terr S43 ... 78 B4
All Saints CE(Controlled) Fst Sch ST14 ... 196 E6
All Saints' CE Inf Sch DE4 ... 143 B6
All Saints CE Jun Sch DE4 ... 143 A7
All Saints CE Prim Sch SK6 ... 23 A5
All Saints' CE VA Prim Sch DE45 ... 125 C5
All Saints Cl DE7 ... 193 B1
All Saints Croft DE14 ... 254 C8
All Saints Ct 6 DE3 ... 217 D1
All Saints RC Prim Sch SK13 ... 10 D2
All Saints Rd DE14 ... 254 C8
All Saints' Rd DE4 ... 143 B6
Allsops Pl S41 ... 95 F8
Allstone Lee DE56 ... 178 F5
Alma Cl NE7 ... 194 E5
Alma Cres S18 ... 57 A3
Alma Hill NG16 ... 195 E7
Alma Hts DE3 ... 217 E1
Alma L Pk* S40 ... 266 C1
Alma Rd
North Wingfield S42 ... 132 A8
Selston NG16 ... 171 F5
Swadlincote DE11 ... 255 F6
Tideswell SK17 ... 69 C5
Alma Sq SK17 ... 85 D8
Alma St
Alfreton DE55 ... 159 A4
Buxton SK17 ... 85 D8
Derby DE22 ... 267 A2
Melbourne DE73 ... 252 A7
North Wingfield S42 ... 131 E6
Ripley DE5 ... 169 D3
Alma Street W S40 ... 95 E2
Almond Ave
Barlborough S43 ... 80 A6
Ripley DE5 ... 180 D8
Shirebrook NG20 ... 119 E5
Almond Cl
Calow S44 ... 97 A3
Kimberley NG16 ... 195 E7
Almond Cres S43 ... 79 C4
Almond Ct DE13 ... 240 E1
Almond Dr S21 ... 60 C5
Almond Gr
Swadlincote DE11 ... 256 A5
Swanwick DE55 ... 170 A8
Almond Pl 4 S40 ... 96 E7
Almond Rise NG19 ... 136 E1
Almond St DE23 ... 218 F1
Almshouses
Etwall DE65 ... 229 B5
Newton Solney DE15 ... 248 E8
Alms Rd DE6 ... 211 C1
Alnwick Dr S12 ... 44 C5
Alnwick Rd S12 ... 44 B5
Along The Bottom
Alstonefield DE6 ... 150 A3
Milldale DE6 ... 149 F2
Alonso Cl DE73 ... 232 E2
Alpha Rd SK23 ... 34 E2
Alpine Gr S43 ... 97 A8
Alport Ave
Buxton SK17 ... 85 D7
Sheffield S12 ... 44 E5
Alport Cl
Belper DE56 ... 179 B5
Hulland Ward DE6 ... 175 F3
Alport Dr S12 ... 44 E5
Alport Gr
3 Gamesley SK13 ... 9 E2
Sheffield S12 ... 44 E5
Alport Heights Dr DE21 ... 205 F3
Alport La
Alport DE45 ... 125 E6
Spout DE4, DE56 ... 166 C4
Stanton in Peak DE45 ... 126 B6
Youlgreave DE45 ... 125 C6
Alport Lea 2 SK13 ... 9 E2
Alport Pl S12 ... 44 E4
Alport Rd S12 ... 44 E5
Alport Rise S18 ... 56 D2
Alport Terr DE55 ... 147 C1
Alport Way 1 SK13 ... 9 E2
Alsager Cl DE21 ... 206 A1
Alsfeld Way SK22 ... 33 A8
ALSOP EN LE DALE ... 150 E3
Alsop La DE4 ... 156 C2
Alsop Moor Cotts DE6 ... 150 E5
Alsop Pl SK17 ... 85 E7
Alsop Way SK17 ... 85 E7
ALSTONEFIELD ... 149 D4
Alstonfield Dr DE22 ... 204 E1
Alstonfield Rd SK17 ... 149 A8
Alston Rd SK23 ... 47 B5
Althorp Cl DE55 ... 169 F7
ALTON ... 130 C5
Alton Cl
Chesterfield S40 ... 114 B8
Derby DE22 ... 204 D3
Dronfield S18 ... 75 D8
Alton Dr NG16 ... 195 B8
Alton Hill S42 ... 130 C5
Alton La S45 ... 130 C4
Alton Rd
Belper DE56 ... 179 C4
Denstone ST14 ... 196 C7
Denstone ST14 ... 196 D6
Alton Rise DE4 ... 142 F7
Alton Way
Derby DE23 ... 230 F5
Derby DE23 ... 231 A6
Alts Nook Way DE72 ... 234 E1
Alum Chine Cl S41 ... 115 C8
Alum Cl DE24 ... 233 C7
ALVASTON ... 233 B8
Alvaston By-Pass DE24 ... 233 D7
Alvaston Inf Sch DE24 ... 233 C7
Alvaston Jun Acad DE24 ... 233 C7
Alvaston Park Homes DE24 ... 220 A1
Alvaston Pk* DE24 ... 219 F2
Alvaston St DE24 ... 233 B8
Alvenor St DE7 ... 194 F1
Alverton Cl DE3 ... 217 C1
Alveston Pk Homes DE24 ... 233 A8
Alward's Cl DE24 ... 233 A6
AMBASTON ... 234 D6
Ambaston La
Elvaston DE72 ... 234 A5
Shardlow DE72 ... 234 E2
Amber Bldgs DE55 ... 159 B5
Amber Bsns Ctr DE55 ... 170 B5
Amber Cl
Bullbridge DE56 ... 168 B5
Shirland DE55 ... 146 D1
Amber Cres S40 ... 95 C1
Amber Croft S43 ... 97 C7
Amber Ct
Belper DE56 ... 179 A6
Chesterfield S41 ... 266 B4
2 Heanor DE75 ... 181 E1
Amberdene DE4 ... 143 D6
Amber Dr
Derby DE3 ... 230 B8
Heanor NG16 ... 182 B2
AMBERGATE ... 167 F3
Ambergate Prim Sch DE56 ... 167 F3
Ambergate Sta DE56 ... 167 F4
Amber Gdns DE56 ... 168 B5
Amber Gr DE55 ... 158 F2
Amber Green DE55 ... 158 B6
Ambergrove DE56 ... 168 B4
Amber Hill DE4 ... 168 A7
Amber Hts DE5 ... 169 C2
Amber La S45 ... 129 D3
Amberlands DE13 ... 240 F1
Amberley Cl DE7 ... 208 F6
Amberley Dr
Buxton SK17 ... 85 C5
Derby DE24 ... 231 F5
Amber Pl
Clay Cross S45 ... 131 A4
2 Swadlincote DE11 ... 255 F4
Amber Rd
Bullbridge DE56 ... 168 B6
Derby DE22 ... 204 D1
Amber St DE24 ... 232 C7
Amber Terr DE55 ... 158 B6
Amber Trad Est NG16 ... 195 D7
Ambervale Cl DE23 ... 231 A6
Amber View Rd DE56 ... 168 B7
Amberwood DE11 ... 256 A5
Ambleside Cl
Chesterfield S41 ... 95 C7
Sheffield S20 ... 59 E6
Ambleside Dr
Bolsover S44 ... 98 F1
Eastwood NG16 ... 182 D3
Ambrose Terr DE1 ... 218 E5
Amelia Close DE72 ... 235 E8
Amen Alley DE1 ... 267 B3
Amesbury Cl S41 ... 95 E7
Amesbury La DE21 ... 205 E2
Ameycroft La DE4 ... 143 A8
Amilda Ave DE7 ... 208 F8
Amy St DE22 ... 218 E4
Anchor Ave SK23 ... 47 C6
Anchor Cl DE11 ... 256 C4
Anchor Fold SK23 ... 47 D6
Anchor Rd NG16 ... 182 D2
Anchor Row DE7 ... 208 F8
Anchor Sq DE45 ... 109 D6
Anderby Gdns DE11 ... 255 F2
Anderson Cl S43 ... 77 E3
Anderson St
Derby DE24 ... 232 F7
Derby DE24 ... 233 A7
Andressey Way DE21 ... 219 F4
Andrew Ave DE7 ... 209 B7
Andrew Cl DE23 ... 230 E8
Andrew La SK6 ... 32 A8
Andrews Dr
Langley Mill NG16 ... 182 A3
Stanley Common DE7 ... 193 A1
Andrew St SK6 ... 15 A2
Andwell La S10 ... 42 F6
Angel Ct DE1 ... 267 C2
Angelica Cl DE23 ... 231 D5
Angel Yd S40 ... 266 B3
Angerford Ave S8 ... 43 A4
Angle Cl DE11 ... 256 D3
Anglers Bsns Ctr DE21 ... 220 E3
Anglers' La DE21 ... 220 E3
Anglesey Rd
Burton upon Trent DE14 ... 254 B8
Dronfield S18 ... 76 A8
Anglesey St
Burton upon Trent DE14 ... 253 C8
Derby DE21 ... 219 D8
Angleton Ave S2 ... 44 C8
Angleton Cl S2 ... 44 C8
Angleton Gdns S2 ... 44 C8
Angleton Gn S2 ... 44 C8
Angleton Mews S2 ... 44 C8
Anglia Dr DE11 ... 255 F1
Anglo Cl S17 ... 55 D6
Ankerbold Rd S42 ... 131 D8
Anmer Dr DE22 ... 218 B4
Annabelle Ct SK17 ... 85 D7
Anncroft Rd SK17 ... 84 D5
Anne Potter Cl DE72 ... 221 D5
Annesley Cl
Chesterfield S41 ... 115 C8
Sheffield S8 ... 56 F7
Annesley Rd S8 ... 56 F7
Anns Grove Prim Sch 7 S2 ... 43 A7
Anns Rd S2 ... 43 A7
Anns Road N S2 ... 43 B7
Ann St S80 ... 81 E1
Annwell La LE65 ... 257 E2
ANNWELL PLACE ... 257 E1
Anslow La DE13 ... 240 A2
Anslow Rd DE13 ... 238 B2
Anson Place DE74 ... 246 F3
Anson Wlk DE7 ... 194 F3
Anstee Rd NG10 ... 236 C5
Anstey Ct DE21 ... 206 A1
Antcliff Gdns S45 ... 132 B4
Anthony Bek Com Prim Sch NG19 ... 134 F6
Anthony Cres DE24 ... 232 F6
Anthony Dr DE24 ... 232 F6
Anthony Gell Sch The DE4 ... 165 F8
Antill St NG9 ... 223 D6
Anvil Gro NG19 ... 136 D4
Apiary Gate DE74 ... 247 B3
APPERKNOWLE ... 58 A1
Appian Cl DE72 ... 221 C1
Appian Way
Clay Cross S45 ... 131 B2
Derby DE24 ... 233 D5
Appleby Cl
6 Derby DE23 ... 230 F6
Ilkeston DE7 ... 208 F6
Appleby Fields Cl DE12 ... 265 F1
Appleby Glade DE11 ... 255 D2
Appleby Glade Ind Est DE11 ... 255 D2
APPLEBY MAGNA ... 265 F1
Appleby Rd NG19 ... 134 F6
Applecroft Cl S44 ... 118 B1
Applecross Ct DE24 ... 231 E3
Appledore Ct 2 S41 ... 95 F8
Appledore Dr DE21 ... 206 B1
Appledown Way DE23 ... 231 A6
Applegarth Cl S12 ... 44 A6
Applegarth Dr S12 ... 44 A6
Applegate Cl DE21 ... 206 B3
Applemead Cl DE21 ... 205 F2
Apple St SK14 ... 15 C7
Appleton Cl
Burton upon Trent DE15 ... 254 E7
Derby DE21 ... 220 A7
Swadlincote DE11 ... 255 F6
Appleton Dr
Belper DE56 ... 179 B6
Glossop SK13 ... 17 F8
Appletree Cl DE72 ... 221 C1
Apple Tree Cl S45 ... 131 F5
Appletree Dr S18 ... 57 A1
Appletree La 3 DE6 ... 211 F8
Appletree Rd
Bolsover S44 ... 80 B1
Hatton DE65 ... 227 C1
Apple Tree Rd SK22 ... 24 B1
Appletree Wlk DE3 ... 217 D2
Applewood Cl
Belper DE56 ... 179 B5
Uttoxeter ST14 ... 210 A1
Appleyard Ct S41 ... 266 A4
Arbor Cl DE22 ... 267 A2
Arboretum Prim Sch DE23 ... 219 A2
Arboretum Sq DE23 ... 267 C1
Arboretum St DE23 ... 267 C1
Arbor Gr SK17 ... 84 F7
Arbor Low (Henge)* DE45 ... 123 E4
Arbour Cl S41 ... 115 D6
Arbour Hill
Borrowash DE72 ... 221 E3
Dale Abbey DE7 ... 207 E3
ARBOURTHORNE ... 43 E8
Arbourthorne Com Prim Sch S2 ... 43 D6
Arbourthorne Cotts S2 ... 43 D8
ARBOURTHORNE ESTATE ... 43 E6
Arbourthorne Rd S2 ... 43 E6
Arcadia Ave NG20 ... 119 E5
Archdale Cl
Chesterfield S40 ... 266 B1
Sheffield S2 ... 44 B8
Archdale Rd S2 ... 44 A8
Archer Dr DE3 ... 217 B2
Archer Rd NG9 ... 223 E5
Archer St
Derby DE24 ... 219 E2
Ilkeston DE7 ... 194 E3
Arches Close NG16 ... 195 C5
Arden Cl
Chesterfield S40 ... 95 C5
Derby DE23 ... 218 E2
Glossop SK13 ... 17 A8
Arden Est SK22 ... 33 D7
Arden St SK22 ... 33 C7
Ardleigh Cl DE3 ... 230 D8
Ardsley Cl
Heanor DE75 ... 182 A2
Sheffield S20 ... 44 F2
Ardsley Dr S20 ... 44 F2
Ardsley Gr S20 ... 44 F2
Ardsley Rd S40 ... 95 B3
Arella Fields Cl DE7 ... 193 A2
Argonaut Avenue DE74 ... 246 F4
Argyle Cl
Market Warsop NG20 ... 120 F4
Sheffield S8 ... 43 B5
Argyle Mews NG16 ... 182 F2
Argyle Rd S8 ... 43 B5
Argyle St
Derby DE22 ... 218 F3
Langley Mill NG16 ... 182 C4
Argyll Cl DE21 ... 220 F5
Argyll Rd DE5 ... 169 E2
Aria Ct NG9 ... 223 D6
Arkendale Wlk 4 DE24 ... 233 C6
Arkle Gn DE24 ... 231 E4
Arklow Cl S41 ... 115 B8
Arkwright Ave DE56 ... 179 C6
Arkwright Cl DE4 ... 127 C3
Arkwright Dr SK6 ... 23 A6
Arkwright Gdns DE4 ... 155 A6
Arkwright Mill SK17 ... 89 A6
Arkwright Prim Sch S44 ... 97 D3
Arkwright Rd SK6 ... 23 A6
Arkwright's Cromford Mill* DE4 ... 155 B7
Arkwright St
Derby DE24 ... 232 C7
Wirksworth DE4 ... 165 E8
ARKWRIGHT TOWN ... 97 D3
Arkwright Way DE65 ... 229 C3
Arleston La
Derby DE24 ... 231 D2
Twyford DE73 ... 243 C7
Arleston St DE23 ... 231 F7
Arlington Ave NG19 ... 136 E4
Arlington Dr
Derby DE24 ... 232 F6
Swanwick DE55 ... 169 F7
Arlington Rd DE23 ... 218 D2
Arliston Dr DE11 ... 256 E1
Armes Cl DE7 ... 194 F3
Armitage Dr NG10 ... 237 A7
Armscote Cl DE21 ... 206 B2
Arms Park Dr S20 ... 59 F6
Armytage Ind Est S41 ... 77 A1
Arnfield Dr DE65 ... 240 E8
Arnfield Independent Sch SK13 ... 9 E7
Arnfield La SK13 ... 9 F8
Arnhem Terr DE21 ... 220 F3
Arnold Ave
Long Eaton NG10 ... 236 A4
Sheffield S12 ... 44 B1
Arnold Cl DE11 ... 261 E7
Arnold Cres NG10 ... 236 A4
Arnold St DE22 ... 218 D5
Arnside NG9 ... 223 E5
Arnside Cl
Chesterfield S41 ... 76 D1
Swadlincote DE11 ... 256 C1
Arran Cl
Derby DE24 ... 231 E3
Stapleford NG9 ... 209 E2
Arran Ct DE55 ... 147 F6
Arreton Ct DE24 ... 233 C5
Arridge Rd DE21 ... 219 F6
Arrowscroft Ct SK14 ... 9 D5
Arrowscroft Way SK14 ... 9 D4
Arthington Blgs S2 ... 43 A6
Arthington St S8 ... 43 A6
Arthur Ave NG9 ... 223 F8
Arthur Cl 1 DE65 ... 242 A6
Arthur Ct 1 DE23 ... 219 B2
Arthur Hind Cl DE22 ... 218 F7
Arthur Mee Rd NG9 ... 223 E5
Arthurrice Cl 8 DE11 ... 255 E5
Arthurs Ct DE13 ... 240 E2
Arthur Short Cl S80 ... 82 A6
Arthur St
Alfreton DE55 ... 159 A5
Derby DE1 ... 267 B5
Draycott DE72 ... 234 F8
Linton DE11 ... 261 E7
Pinxton NG16 ... 160 D3
Arthurs View NG16 ... 170 F4
Artic Way NG16 ... 195 D7
Artisan View S8 ... 43 A6
Arun Dale NG19 ... 136 D2
Arundel Ave
Castle Donington DE72 ... 246 E5
Castle Donington DE74 ... 246 E5
Castle Donington DE74 ... 247 A5
Derby DE3 ... 217 F2
Arundel Cl
23 Chesterfield S41 ... 95 F8
Dronfield S18 ... 56 D1
Sandiacre NG10 ... 223 B4
Arundel Ct 6 S43 ... 78 E2
Arundel Dr DE21 ... 220 F5
Arundel Grange SK13 ... 17 A8
Arundel St
Derby DE22 ... 218 D4
Glossop SK13 ... 10 C1
Arundel Way 7 DE23 ... 230 F5
Asbourne Ct DE7 ... 194 D1
Ascot Ave NG16 ... 195 E7
Ascot Cl
Burton upon Trent DE15 ... 248 A3
West Hallam DE7 ... 207 D7
Ascot Dr DE24 ... 232 D8
Ascot Ind Est NG10 ... 223 C7
Ascot Pl DE7 ... 208 C5
Ascott Dr DE11 ... 256 A7
Ash Acre DE56 ... 179 D4
Ashacres Ind Pk DE6 ... 225 E1
Ashberry Ct DE22 ... 205 A4
ASHBOURNE ... 173 C2
Ashbourne Ave S45 ... 131 A5
Ashbourne Cl 4 S40 ... 95 A5
Ashbourne Ct
Derby DE22 ... 218 E6
3 Glossop SK13 ... 17 F8
Ashbourne Dr DE11 ... 256 A1
Ashbourne Green
Ashbourne DE6 ... 173 D4
Ashbourne DE6 ... 173 F4
Ashbourne DE6 ... 174 A4
Ashbourne Hilltop Prim Sch DE6 ... 185 C8
Ashbourne La
Chapel-en-le-Frith SK23 ... 47 D5
Wetton DE6 ... 149 A2
Ashbourne L Ctr DE6 ... 173 B1

Ashbourne Prim Sch DE6 173 C2
Ashbourne Rd
Alstonefield DE6 149 B3
Ashbourne DE6 173 E6
Belper DE56 178 C4
Brailsford DE6 202 B6
Buxton SK17 85 C5
Buxton SK17 85 D4
Carsington DE4 164 D6
Carsington DE6 164 A5
Church Broughton DE65 213 F3
Crakemarsh ST14 210 D6
Derby DE22 218 C7
Fenny Bentley DE6 162 A2
Fenny Bentley DE6 173 B8
Kirk Langley DE6 202 D4
Kniveton DE6 174 A8
Mackworth DE22 217 E8
Mayfield DE6 184 C7
Moneyash DE45 122 F7
Parsley Hay DE45 123 B4
Rocester ST14 196 D1
Rocester ST14 196 F4
Shottle DE56 177 D3
Sudbury DE6 212 E2
Sudbury DE6 225 D7
Turnditch DE56 176 F1
Uttoxeter ST14 210 B1
Ashbourne St NG20 119 F4
Ashbrook DE15 248 A1
Ashbrook Ave DE72 221 C2
Ashbrook Cl DE22 204 C3
Ashbrook Inf Sch DE72 221 B2
Ashbrook Jun Sch DE72 221 B2
Ashbury Dr S8 43 C2
Ashbury La S8 43 C2
Ashby Ave NG19 136 D5
Ashby Cl DE3 230 E5
ASHBY-DE-LA-ZOUCH 258 A1
Ashby La DE11 257 C1
Ashby Rd
Blackfordby DE11, LE65 257 D2
Boundary DE11 257 D2
Breedon on the Hill DE73 252 E2
Burton upon Trent DE15 248 B2
Melbourne DE73 252 A6
Moira DE12 262 F4
Woodville DE11 257 B1
Ashby Road E DE15 248 E1
Ashby St DE24 232 E6
Ash Cl
Aston-on-Trent DE72 246 B7
Barlborough S43 80 B6
Derby DE22 204 D4
Killamarsh S21 60 C5
Mottram in Longdendale SK14 9 A4
Pinxton NG16 160 D2
Somercotes DE55 170 A8
Ashcombe Gdns DE21 206 B1
Ash Cres
Eckington S21 59 B1
Mansfield Woodhouse NG19 136 E2
Ripley DE5 180 D8
Ashcroft Cl DE24 232 F7
Ashcroft Ct S41 77 B3
Ashcroft Dr S41 77 B2
Ash Croft Prim Sch DE24 231 E2
Ash Ct DE55 159 C3
Ashdale Cl DE15 255 A8
Ashdale Rd DE7 209 A6
Ashdene Gdns DE56 179 C5
Ashdown Dr S40 95 D1
Ashe La DE65 229 A5
Ashe Pl DE23 218 F1
Asher La DE5 169 C5
Asher Lane Bsns Pk DE5 169 D4
Ashes Ave DE6 175 F3
Ashes La
Fenny Bentley DE6 162 A1
Fenny Bentley DE6 173 A8
Glossop SK13 10 B2
Ashes The SK13 10 B2
Ashfield Ave
Derby DE21 219 E8
Somercotes DE55 159 D1
Ashfield Cl S12 43 F4
Ashfield Dr S12 43 F4
Ashfield Gr SK6 15 B1
Ashfield Rd
Chapel-en-le-Frith SK23 47 D6
Chesterfield S41 115 D8
Glossop SK13 9 F3
Ash Fields DE56 179 A2
Ashfields Gr 4 DE72 246 A6
Ashford Ave S42 132 A7
Ashford Cl S18 75 D8
Ashford Ct
Chesterfield S41 96 A5
West Hallam DE7 207 D8
Ashford Dr SK17 85 E2
Ashford Gn 2 SK13 9 E1
ASHFORD IN THE WATER 108 E7
Ashford La DE45 89 D2
Ashford Mews SK13 9 E1
Ashford Pl DE7 194 E5
Ashford Rd
Bakewell DE45 109 A7
Bakewell DE45 109 B7
Dronfield S18 75 D8
Ashford Rd The DE45 108 F8
Ashford Rise DE56 179 C6
Ashford Way DE11 255 F2
Ashforth Ave DE75 194 A8
Ashfurlong Cl S17 55 F7
Ashfurlong Dr S17 55 F7
Ashfurlong Pk S17 55 F7
Ashfurlong Rd S17 55 F7
ASHGATE
Chesterfield 95 D4
Old Brampton 94 F4
Ashgate Ave S40 95 C3
Ashgate Croft Sch S40 95 C4
Ashgate Ct 4 S40 95 C4
Ashgate Prim Sch DE22 218 D6
Ashgate Rd
Chesterfield S40 94 F4
Chesterfield S40 95 C4
Ashgate Valley Rd S40 95 D4
Ash Gr
Brinsley NG16 182 D8
Chinley SK23 34 E1
Long Eaton NG10 236 C6
Mastin Moor S43 79 B4
Sandiacre NG10 223 A7
Selston NG16 171 F7
Shirebrook NG20 119 E5
Stapleford NG9 223 D5
Tupton S42 131 D8
Ashgrove Ct DE21 206 B1
Ash Grove La DE65 241 C6
Ashiver Rd S45 145 C8
Ash La
Chesterfield S21 77 D8
Sutton on the Hill DE6, DE65 228 E7
Unstone S18 57 F3
Ashland Rd S21 59 E3
Ashlands Dr 13 DE11 256 E1
Ashlar Dr DE12 262 F1
Ashlea Dr DE6 184 D7
Ashlea Gn S43 81 A4
Ashlea Wlk S43 81 A5
Ashleigh Ave
Glossop SK13 10 B2
Sheffield S12 43 F5
Swadlincote DE11 255 F5
Ashleigh Cl S41 77 B3
Ashleigh Croft S12 43 F5
Ashleigh Ct S21 59 C1
Ashleigh Dr
Chellaston DE73 232 F2
Sheffield S12 43 F5
Ashleigh Pl S12 43 F5
Ashleigh Rd S43 80 B7
Ashley Cl
Killamarsh S21 60 D6
Overseal DE12 262 B3
Tansley DE4 144 A4
Ashley Ct DE15 248 A3
ASHLEYHAY 166 A4
Ashleyhay La DE4 165 F4
Ashley La S21 60 D6
Ashley St DE22 218 C5
Ashlyn Rd DE21 219 C5
Ashmeadow DE72 221 B1
Ashmeadow Ct DE6 185 D8
Ashmore Ave S21 59 B2
Ash Mount Rd NG16 182 B3
Ash Mws S21 59 C2
Ashop Rd DE56 179 D5
ASHOPTON 30 E2
Ashopton Ave DE23 231 F8
Ashopton Dr S33 40 B4
Ashopton Rd
Bamford S33 31 A1
Bamford S33 40 A6
Chesterfield S41 95 C6
ASHOVER 129 F3
Ashover Cl
Derby DE21 219 F8
Harpur Hill SK17 85 D2
1 Ripley DE5 169 F1
ASHOVER HAY 145 B5
Ashover Hay S45 145 B6
Ashover New Rd DE55, S45 145 E8
Ashover Prim Sch S45 129 F3
Ashover Rd
Alton S45 130 E5
Ashover S45 129 E4
Brackenfield DE55 146 B7
Derby DE22 204 D2
1 Derby, Chaddesden DE21 219 E8
Staveley S43 97 C6
Swadlincote DE11 255 E5
Tupton S42 131 D7
Woolley Moor S45 145 F7
Ashover View DE55 147 C1
Ash St
Buxton SK17 85 B6
Ilkeston DE7 194 E4
Sheffield, Mosborough S20 59 C8
Ash Terr SK17 85 C8
Ashton Cl
6 Ashbourne DE6 185 D7
Chesterfield S40 114 C8
Derby DE3 217 C3
Killamarsh S21 60 C6
Swanwick DE55 170 A7
Ashton Dr DE24 233 D4
Ashton Gdns
Clay Cross S42 131 B6
1 Glossop SK13 17 C7
Ashton Rd S45 131 E4
Ashton St SK13 17 C7
Ashton Way DE56 179 D4
Ashtree Ave DE24 232 B6
Ashtree Cl
5 Matlock DE4 143 A7
3 Swadlincote DE11 256 A6
Ash Tree Cl
Breadsall DE21 205 E4
Chesterfield S40 95 C3
Duffield DE56 190 E5
2 Swadlincote DE11 255 F6
Ash Tree Cres NG19 136 C5
Ash Tree Rd S43 80 E2
Ashurst Cl S40 94 F5
Ash Vale S40 95 B3
Ashview Cl NG10 236 A8
Ash View Cl DE65 229 B3
Ashwater Cl DE24 231 F2
Ashwell Ave NG19 136 E5
Ashwood SK13 16 F8
Ashwood Cl
Buxton SK17 85 C7
Derby DE24 232 D8
Mansfield Woodhouse NG19 136 E5
Ashwood Rd
Buxton SK17 66 E1
Disley SK12 32 D6
Ashworth Ave
Burton upon Trent DE15 248 C2
Derby DE21 219 F5
Ashworth Dr NG19 136 E4
Ashworth La SK14 9 A3
Ashworth Wlk DE21 219 F5
Askerfield Ave DE22 204 C4
Asker La DE4 143 D6
Askerton Cl DE24 233 D4
Askew Gr DE65 242 D2
Askew Way
Chesterfield S40 266 B1
Woodville DE11 256 F1
Asline Rd S2 43 A8
Aspen Bsns Ctr DE21 220 B4
Aspen Cl
Buxton SK17 66 B1
Killamarsh S21 60 C6
Aspen Ct 1 NG19 136 E1
Aspen Dr DE21 220 C4
Aspen Rd S21 59 B1
Aspen Rise DE55 146 D1
Aspenshaw SK22 24 E4
Aspenshaw Rd SK22 24 E3
Aspen Way SK6 32 A7
Aspley Cl S40 95 E5
Astbury Way DE11 256 F1
Astcote Cl DE75 182 A1
Astell Way SK23 47 B7
Asterdale Prim Sch
Derby DE21 220 F3
Derby DE21 221 A3
Asterdale View DE21 220 F4
Aster Gdns DE23 231 B6
Aster Rd NG20 119 D2
Astil St DE15 254 F8
Astley Gdns DE65 240 F8
Astlow Dr DE56 179 B6
ASTON
Hope 39 C4
Sudbury 225 F4
Aston Cl
Chellaston DE73 245 A8
Dronfield S18 57 C3
Aston Ct S43 78 F2
Aston Dr DE11 256 A7
Aston Gn NG9 223 E3
Aston Hall Dr DE72 246 A7
ASTON HEATH 226 B6
Aston Hill DE4 140 D2
Aston La
Aston DE6 225 F5
Chellaston DE73 233 B1
Hope S33 39 C4
Oaker DE4 142 D7
Shardlow DE72 234 E1
Sudbury DE6 226 A5
Wensley DE4 142 D7
ASTON-ON-TRENT 246 B8
Aston-on-Trent Prim Sch DE72 246 A8
Aston Rd DE23 231 C5
Astorville Park Rd DE73 232 F2
Astron Bsns Pk DE11 256 A3
Astwell Gdns DE24 233 C4
ASTWITH 133 A5
Astwith Cl S44 116 F1
Astwith La
Astwith S44, S45 133 B5
Astwith S45 132 F5
Atchison Gdns DE21 220 B7
Athens Ct DE73 232 E2
Atherfield Gdns NG16 182 F3
Atherfield Wlk DE24 233 C5
Atherstone Rd DE12 265 D1
Atherton Ave SK14 9 A4
Atherton Cl S2 43 F6
Atherton Gr SK14 9 A4
Atherton Rd
Ilkeston DE7 194 C3
Sheffield S2 43 F6
Athlestan Way DE13 240 C1
Athlone Cl DE21 219 D8
Athol Cl
Chesterfield S40 114 B8
Derby DE24 231 E4
Atkin Pl S2 43 A8
Atkinson Ct S40 266 B1
Atkinson Mews S21 59 C3
Atkins Way ST14 196 F3
Atlantic Cres 1 S8 56 E6
Atlantic Dr S8 56 E6
Atlantic Way
Derby DE24 219 E2
Sheffield S8 56 E6
Atlantic Wlk S8 56 E6
Atlas Way DE21 220 F2
ATLOW 175 A6
Atlow Brow 4 DE6 173 D3
Atlow Cl S40 95 B5
Atlow La DE6 175 A5
Atlow Rd DE21 219 E7
ATLOWTOP 175 B5
Atlow Winn La DE6 163 E1
Attenborough Nature Centre NG10 237 C8
Attenborough Nature Reserve* NG9 237 D8
Attewell Cl DE72 235 B7
Attewell Rd NG16 195 B5
Attlebridge Cl DE21 219 D8
Attlee Rd S43 97 B7
Atwall Ct DE23 219 A1
Atworth Gr DE23 230 F7
Auburn Cl DE7 207 B8
Auckland Cl DE3 217 F3
Auckland Dr S20 59 E5
Auckland Pl DE56 190 E2
Auckland Rise S20 59 E6
Auckland's Pl S40 266 B2
Auckland Way S20 59 E6
Auction Cl DE6 173 C2
Auden Cl DE65 227 A8
Audens Way DE11 256 C6
Audley Cl DE7 194 D3
Audley Ctr DE1 267 B3
Audrey Cotts S32 71 C6
Audrey Cres NG19 136 C5
Audrey Dr DE21 220 A8
Audrey Rd S13 44 C7
Aughton Cl S13 44 D7
Aughton Cres S13 44 D7
Aughton Dr S13 44 C8
Augusta St DE23 219 B2
Ault Dene DE11 256 E4
AULT HUCKNALL 133 F7
Ault Hucknall La
Glapwell S44 134 A7
North Wingfield S44 131 F7
Aults Cl DE65 230 C1
Aumonier Way DE55 159 C4
Auriga Ct DE1 219 B7
Austen Ave
Derby DE23 231 B8
Long Eaton NG10 236 C5
Austin Dr DE72 222 E4
Austins Dr NG10 223 B4
Austin Sq DE23 231 F7
Austin St NG20 120 A4
Autumn Gr DE21 219 F5
Avalon Dr DE73 244 F8
Avenue 1 S41 115 B8
Avenue 2 S41 115 B8
Avenue 3 S41 115 B8
Avenue 4 S41 115 B8
Avenue 5 S41 115 B8
Avenue 6 S41 115 B8
Avenue 7 S41 115 B8
Avenue 8 S41 115 B8
Avenue Cl S32 72 A3
Avenue Rd
Chesterfield S41 96 A8
Duffield DE56 190 E5
Avenue The
Bakewell DE45 109 D5
Belper DE56 178 F2
Chapel-en-le-Frith SK23 46 E2
Derby DE1 267 B2
Derby, Chaddesden DE21 219 F5
Dronfield S18 57 B2
Glossop SK13 10 A4
Northwood DE4 127 B6
Spinkhill S21 60 D2
Stoney Middleton S32 72 A3
Tissington DE6 162 A5
Weston-on-Trent DE72 245 E5
Averham Cl
Derby DE21 206 B1
Swadlincote DE11 256 A3
Ave The
Derby DE1 219 A4
Wingerworth S42 115 C4
Aviemore Cl S43 77 E4
Aviemore Way DE24 231 E4
Avis Ave DE75 193 F7
Avocet Cl DE75 182 B1
Avocet Ct DE24 231 D4
Avocet Drive DE65 242 A5
Avocet Pl NG20 120 D5
Avon Cl
Derby DE24 231 D2
Dronfield S18 57 B3
Swadlincote DE11 256 B6
Avon Ct S41 266 B4
Avondale Cl NG10 236 A6
Avondale Rd
Bolsover S44 118 A8
Chesterfield S40 266 A4
Derby DE23 267 B1
Derby, Spondon DE21 220 D6
Ilkeston DE7 208 C5
Staveley S43 97 D7
Avonlea Cl DE7 209 B6
Avonmouth Dr DE24 232 E8
Avonside Cl S43 78 B3
Avon St DE24 232 E8
Avon Way
Burton upon Trent DE15 248 A1
Hilton DE65 228 D1
Awdishaw La DE6 213 B5
AWSWORTH 195 C4
Awsworth La
Cossall NG16 195 C3
Kimberley NG16 195 D6
Awsworth Prim Sch NG16 195 C4
Awsworth Rd DE7 194 F2
Aycliffe Gdns DE24 232 F4
Aylesbury Ave DE21 219 F7
Aylesbury Way NG19 136 E2
Aylward Cl S2 43 F7
Aylward Rd S2 43 F7
Ayncourt Rd S42 132 B7
Ayr Cl DE21 220 D4
Ayrton Dr DE74 246 E3
Ayton Cl 6 S2 44 A7
Azalea Ave DE55 170 A8
Azalea Cl DE55 159 E3
Azalea Ct NG16 195 C8
Azure Dr S42 132 C8

B

Babbacombe Cl DE24 233 C7
Babbacombe Ct 5 S41 95 F8
Babbington Cl DE13 239 C5
Babbington Close DE7 209 B5
Babbington La NG16 195 F4
Babbington St DE55 148 A6
Babbs La DE6 211 C1
Babington Bsns Coll DE1 267 B1
Babington Cl
Sheffield S2 43 F7
10 Sheffield S2 44 A7
Babington Ct
Sheffield S2 43 F7
9 Sheffield S2 44 A7
Babington Hospl DE56 178 F2
Babington La DE1 267 B2
Bacchus Way DE55 147 B5
Back Bridge St SK22 24 C1
Back Croft S45 131 E2
Back Eccles La SK23 46 C8
Backhill La DE6 151 F3
Back Jodrell St SK22 33 B7
Back La
Alderwasley DE56 166 E7
Alstonefield DE6 149 E3
Biggin SK17 138 D1
Brackenfield DE55 146 A1
Calow S44 116 B8
Castle Donington DE74 247 A6
Chellaston DE73 233 A2
Darley Dale DE4 127 F4
Eckington S21 59 B3
Ellastone DE6 183 A3
Elton DE4 140 E6
Glapwell S44 118 B1
Glossop SK13 16 D6
Hathersage S32 53 A7
Hilton DE65 228 D2
Hollington DE6 200 F3
Hollington DE6 201 A3
Ilkeston DE7 194 E2
Mottram in Longdendale SK14 9 A4
New Totley S17 55 E4
Palterton S44 118 B5
Pilsley S45 132 C2
Ripley DE5 169 C6
Shirley DE6 200 D7
Spout DE4 166 D4
Stonebroom DE55 146 F5
Back La *continued*
Sutton in Ashfield NG17 148 F4
Thorpe Salvin S80 63 B6
Thurvaston DE6 215 B3
Tibshelf DE55 147 F6
Unstone S18 57 F1
Wessington DE55 157 F8
Whatstandwell DE4 156 D1
Wootton DE6 183 A8
Youlgreave DE45 125 A6
Back Mellor Rd SK22 24 C1
BACKMOOR 43 C2
Back Moor SK14 9 A4
Backmoor Cres S8 43 C2
Backmoor Rd S8 43 D2
Back Oth Cross
Flash SK17 102 E2
Flash SK17 103 A3
Back Rd S18 57 F1
Back Rowarth
New Mills SK13 16 F1
Rowarth SK13 24 F8
Back School La DE4 127 E2
Back Sitwell St DE1 267 B2
Back South St S43 77 D3
Back St
Castleton S33 38 C2
Castleton S33 38 C3
Back Union Rd 3 SK22 33 C7
Back Wyver La DE56 178 F5
Bacon Cl NG16 195 A8
Bacon La DE5 169 B6
Bacons La S40 115 A8
Baden Powell Ave S40 266 B1
Baden Powell Rd S40 266 B2
Badger Cl
Chesterfield S40 114 B7
Derby DE21 220 F6
Badgerdale Way DE23 231 A7
Badger La
Ashover S45 145 C8
Woolley Moor S45 145 D8
Badgers Way SK13 17 B7
Badgery Cl ST14 210 A2
Badway La DE65 227 C8
Bage Hill S42 113 E6
Baggaley Cres NG19 136 B1
Bag La
Marchington ST14 224 E2
Roston DE6 197 E7
Bagot St DE7 207 C8
BAGSHAW 47 F7
Bagshawe Ave SK23 46 F6
Bagshaw Hill DE45 109 D6
Bagshaw La SK17 48 B6
Bagshaw's Rd S12 44 B6
Bagshaw St
Derby DE24 232 E8
Pleasley NG19 135 B4
BAGTHORPE 171 F4
Bagthorpe La S42 94 A3
Bailey Ave DE12 262 A3
Bailey Brook Cres
Aldercar NG16 182 A4
Langley Mill NG16 182 A3
Bailey Brook Dr NG16 182 A3
Bailey Brook Ind Est NG16 182 B2
Bailey Brook Rd NE7 194 F5
Bailey Brook Wlk NG16 182 A3
Bailey Cl
Heanor DE75 181 C4
Kirk Langley DE6 203 A2
Bailey Dr S21 60 E8
Bailey Gr SK17 85 E8
BAILEY GROVE 182 D2
Bailey Grove Rd NG16 182 D2
Baileys Mill DE4 143 D4
Bailey St
Derby DE23 267 A1
Stapleford NG9 223 C6
Bainbridge Rd S44 98 F1
Bainbridge St DE23 219 A3
Bainbrigge Rd DE74 247 F3
Baines Wood Cl S41 95 C8
Bains Gdns DE3 217 B1
Bain St DE72 221 D1
Bakeacre La DE65 230 E3
Bakehouse La DE72 221 C5
Bakehurst Cl SK22 33 C7
Baker Ave DE75 193 F7
Baker Cl
Long Eaton NG10 223 C1
Somercotes DE55 170 D7
Baker Cres S42 115 B3
Baker Dr S21 60 C6
Baker Pl S42 115 B3
Baker Rd
Eastwood NG16 195 C8
Mansfield Woodhouse NG19 136 C6
Wingerworth S42 115 B3
Bakers Hill DE56 168 E1
Bakers La DE4 156 A8
Baker's La
Cromford DE4 155 A5
Doveridge DE6 211 C1

Baker St
  Burton upon Trent DE15 254 E7
  Creswell S80 81 E2
  Derby DE24 232 F8
  Ilkeston DE7 194 F1
  Swadlincote DE11 256 C3
BAKESTONE MOOR 81 E5
Bakestone Moor S80 81 F5
BAKEWELL 109 C5
Bakewell Bank 39 SK13 9 D1
Bakewell CE Inf Sch DE45 109 D6
Bakewell Cl
  Derby DE3 217 E3
  40 Gamesley SK13 9 D1
Bakewell Ct SK17 85 D7
Bakewell Dr DE74 247 A2
Bakewell Fold 37 SK13 9 D1
Bakewell Gdns 41 SK13 9 D1
Bakewell Gn
  35 Gamesley SK13 9 D1
  Swadlincote DE11 255 F5
Bakewell Gr 38 SK13 9 D1
Bakewell Lea 34 SK13 9 D1
Bakewell Meth Jun Sch DE45 109 D4
Bakewell Mews 36 SK13 9 D1
Bakewell Rd
  Baslow DE45 91 E4
  Buxton SK17 85 C7
  Congreave DE45 126 C8
  Darley Dale DE4 142 F7
  Foolow SK32 70 E5
  King Sterndale SK17 86 C5
  Long Eaton NG10 236 E5
  Matlock DE4 143 A5
  Over Haddon DE45 109 B2
  Staveley S43 97 C5
Bakewell St DE22 218 F4
Bakewell Station Ind Est DE45 109 E7
Bakewell Wlk 44 SK13 9 D1
Bakwell Rd DE45 90 E2
Balaclava Rd DE23 232 A8
Bale Cl NG10 237 A6
Balfour Rd
  Derby DE23 232 A8
  Stapleford NG9 223 D6
Balgonie Ct DE73 232 E2
Balham Wlk DE22 218 A6
Balkham La
  Mansfield NG20 119 A2
  Stony Houghton NG19 118 F2
  Stony Houghton NG20 119 B2
Ballacraine Dr
  2 Ripley DE5 169 F1
  3 Ripley DE5 170 A1
Ballards Way DE72 221 D1
Ballater Cl
  Derby DE24 231 E4
  Mansfield NG19 135 E2
Balleny Cl DE21 205 F2
Ball Hill DE55 160 C6
BALLIDON 152 A2
Ballidon Cl 1 S41 95 C6
Ballidon Moor DE6 152 C4
Ball La DE72 234 A5
Ball Ridge La SK17 121 E3
Balmoak La S41 96 C5
Balmoral Cl
  Derby DE23 218 B2
  Heanor DE75 181 C1
  Mansfield Woodhouse NG19 136 E5
  Sandiacre NG10 223 B3
Balmoral Cres
  Dronfield S18 56 D2
  Sheffield S10 42 F8
Balmoral Ct DE74 247 D5
Balmoral Dr NG19 135 E2
Balmoral Gdns DE15 248 A3
Balmoral Rd
  Borrowash DE72 221 C1
  Burton upon Trent DE15 248 A3
  Ilkeston DE7 208 D5
Balmoral Way
  Chesterfield S43 77 E4
  1 Hatton DE65 227 D2
Baltic Cl DE24 219 F1
Baltimore Cl 8 DE11 256 A7
Bamburgh Cl DE21 220 D4
BAMFORD 40 B4
Bamford Ave
  Derby DE23 231 F8
  North Wingfield S42 131 F7
Bamford Fold 3 SK13 9 E1
Bamford Gn 4 SK13 9 E1
Bamford Ho S33 40 B3
Bamford La SK13 9 E1
Bamford Mews SK13 9 E1
Bamford Mills S33 40 B3
Bamford Prim Sch S33 40 B4
Bamford Rd S43 97 C5
Bamford St
  Chesterfield S43 77 D4
  Newton DE55 148 A3
  Ripley DE5 180 D7
Bamford Sta S33 40 B1
Bampton Cl DE24 233 D4
Banbury Ave NG9 223 F3
Banchory Cl NG19 135 E2
Bancroft Cl DE65 228 D1
Bancroft Dr DE22 204 C4
Bancroft The DE65 229 B3
Bandy La DE21 205 D2
Baneberry Way DE24 231 C3
Bangor St DE21 219 E8
Bank Bldgs DE56 190 F7
Bankbottom SK13 10 A5
Bank Cl
  Bolsover S44 99 A3
  Creswell S80 100 D8
  Shirebrook NG20 119 F4
  Tibshelf DE55 147 F5
Bank Ct DE22 218 E8
Bankerwall La DE6 183 C7
Bankfield Dr
  Derby DE21 220 F4
  Ilkeston DE7 208 B6
Bankgate SK14 16 A8
Bank Gdns DE4 143 B6
Bankhall SK23 47 A4
Bankholmes Cl DE24 231 E2
Bank House Ct DE6 164 A2
Bank La SK13 10 A7
Bank Rd
  Chesterfield S41 96 A6
  Matlock DE4 143 C5
Bank Row SK13 10 A7
Banksburn Cl DE75 181 C1
Bankside DE45 125 B5
Bank Side
  Derby DE22 204 E2
  Hartington SK17 137 D6
Bankside Cl SK6 15 C1
Banks Rd NG9 223 E2
Banks Road Inf Sch NG9 223 F2
Bank St
  Brimington S43 96 D8
  Broadbottom SK14 16 A8
  Chesterfield S40 95 E3
  Glossop SK13 17 D8
  Hadfield SK13 10 A5
  Hayfield SK22 25 D3
  Langley Mill NG16 182 C3
  Long Eaton NG10 236 E7
  Somercotes DE55 170 C8
  Swadlincote DE11 262 A8
BANKS THE 23 E3
Bankswood Cl SK13 10 A4
Bank Terr SK13 10 A5
Bank The
  Bonsall DE4 142 C1
  Glossop SK13 17 D8
  Hayfield SK22 25 B4
  Stoney Middleton S32 71 F4
BANK TOP 53 A8
Bank Top DE4 141 A5
Bank Top La S30 72 C8
Bank Vale Rd SK22 25 C3
Bank View SK17 69 B5
Bank View Rd
  Derby DE22 218 F8
  Nether Heage DE56 168 C2
Bankwood Cl S14 43 D5
Bank Wood Cl S40 95 B7
Bankwood Com Prim Sch S14 43 D5
BANKWOOD GATE 16 C8
Bankwood Rd S14 43 D5
Bannels Ave DE23 231 B7
Banton's La DE73 251 A4
Banwell Cl DE3 217 C3
BARBER BOOTH 37 A6
Barber Cl DE7 194 E3
Barber's La S21 60 D7
Barbers Row S21 79 D7
Barber St SK13 10 B5
Barbon Cl S40 95 E5
Barbon Dr
  Derby DE3 217 C1
  Derby DE3 230 C8
Barcheston Cl DE21 206 B2
Barclay Ct DE7 194 D3
Barclay Grange S41 266 C3
Bar Croft 3 S40 95 C6
Barden Dr DE22 204 F3
Barden Rd DE3 230 E5
Bardolph Cl DE11 255 F3
Bardsey Ct DE21 206 B3
Bare Jarnett Road SK17 88 B1
Bare La DE72 221 C5
Barf Cl DE3 217 E1
BARGATE 179 C1
Bargate S33 38 C2
Bargate Cl DE56 179 C1
Bargate La DE65 242 B5
Bargate Rd DE56 179 B1
Barholme Cl S41 95 B7
Barker Ave NG16 171 B4
Barker Avenue E NG10 223 B6
Barker Avenue N NG10 223 A6
Barker Cl DE7 193 B1
Barker Fold S40 95 D3
Barker Gate DE7 194 F2
Barker La S40 95 D3
Barker St NG17 148 F4
Barklam Cl DE12 262 E1
BARLBOROUGH 80 B7
BARLBOROUGH COMMON 80 B5
Barlborough Hall Sch S43 61 B1
Barlborough Hospital S43 80 B5
Barlborough Prim Sch SK43 80 B7
Barlborough Rd
  Clowne S43 80 D5
  Ilkeston DE7 194 F5
Barley Cft DE73 232 F1
Barley Cl
  Kimberley NG16 195 F7
  Little Eaton DE21 205 C8
Barleycorn Cl DE15 248 A1
Barley Corn Cl DE21 206 C2
Barleycroft SK13 9 F4
Barley Croft
  Belper DE56 179 B2
  South Normanton DE55 160 B4
Barley Dale Dr NG9 209 D2
Barley La S42 95 A5
Barley Mews
  Dronfield S18 56 B2
  Mansfield Woodhouse NG19 136 E6
Barley Rd DE14 253 D8
Barley Way DE4 143 D6
Barling Dr DE7 194 C2
BARLOW 75 E2
Barlow CE Prim Sch S18 75 E3
Barlow Cottage La NG16 195 C5
Barlow Drive N NG16 195 B4
Barlow Drive S NG16 195 B4
Barlow Grange La S18 93 F8
Barlow Lees La S18 75 F7
Barlow Rd
  Chapel-en-le-Frith SK23 47 C6
  Cutthorpe S18, S42 94 F8
  Staveley S43 78 E1
Barlow St DE1, DE23 267 D1
Barlow View S18 76 B7
Barlow Wood Dr SK6 23 B3
Barmote Croft DE4 154 F1
Barms Way SK17 66 D1
Barnard Ave S18 57 D3
Barnard Rd DE21 205 D2
Barn Cl
  Castle Donington DE74 247 B3
  Chesterfield S41 95 D6
  Findern DE65 230 D2
  Glossop SK13 17 D7
  Matlock DE4 143 A6
  3 Nottingham NG10 236 C5
  Quarndon DE22 204 C6
Barn Croft DE23 218 C1
Barnes Ave S18 56 E2
Barnes Croft
  Heanor DE75 181 C1
  Wirksworth DE4 165 F8
Barnes Gn DE22 218 B7
Barnes La
  Dronfield S17 56 C4
  Dronfield S18 56 C3
  Youlgreave DE45 125 C5
Barnes Rd S41 96 E1
Barnetts Way S45 132 C3
Barnfield Cl
  Holmewood S42 132 E8
  1 Staveley S43 78 E2
Barnfield Dr S32 52 F7
Barnfields S32 52 F7
Barnfield Wlk S43 78 E2
Barn Furlong DE45 90 A4
Barnham Cl S40 114 B8
Barnhill Gr DE23 231 A7
Barn La DE4 127 A7
Barnsfold Ct SK22 25 D3
Barnsley La DE4, DE56 165 F2
Barnstaple Cl DE21 206 A2
Barnstaple Ct 3 S41 95 F8
Barns The S42 115 B4
Barnwell Cl ST14 210 A4
Barnwell La DE4 155 A5
Barnwood Cl DE3 217 C2
Baron Cl DE21 206 D3
Barrack Rd S18 58 A1
Barrack View S18 58 A1
Barrack Yd DE55 170 D7
Barratt Rd S21 59 D2
Bar Rd
  Baslow DE45 91 F6
  Curbar S32 72 F2
Barrett St DE24 233 A7
Barrie Dr DE24 231 F5
Barringer Rd NG19 136 D1
Barrington Cl
  Burton upon Trent DE13 240 C1
  Kirk Langley DE6 202 F2
Barrons Ct DE72 234 A5
Barron's Way DE72 221 C1
Barroon DE74 247 B3
Barrowhill ST14 197 A7
BARROW HILL 78 B4
Barrow Hill ST14 196 F5
Barrow Hill Prim Sch S43 78 B3
Barrow Hill Roundhouse Rly Ctr* S43 78 A4
Barrow La DE73 244 C6
Barrowmore La DE6 175 D4
Barrows Hill La NG16 171 D5
Barrow St S43 78 F2
Barrowstones La DE45 123 B8
BARROW UPON TRENT 244 B6
Barry Rd S43 96 F4
Barrys Cl 1 DE11 256 E1
Barson Gr SK17 85 E2
Bartle Ave S12 43 F4
Bartle Dr S12 43 F4
Bartle Rd S12 43 F4
Bartle Way S12 43 F4
Barton Bsns Pk DE13 259 A8
Barton Business Pk
  Barton-under-Needwood DE13 259 A8
  Walton-On-Trent DE14 253 A1
Barton Cl DE21 220 F6
Barton Cres S40 95 A6
Barton Dr DE6 185 D7
Bartonfields Ctr The DE65 214 D2
Barton Hill DE4 126 C1
Barton Hill Croft DE45 126 C1
BARTON IN FABIS 237 E6
Barton Knowle DE56 179 D4
Barton La
  Broxtowe NG9 237 D8
  Thrumpton NG11 237 C2
Barton Rd
  Long Eaton NG10 237 A6
  Sheffield S8 43 A6
Barton St
  Burton upon Trent DE14 254 C8
  Clowne S43 80 F4
BARTON TURN 253 B1
Barton Turn DE13 253 A1
Barway DE6 211 E8
Baseball Drive DE23 219 B1
Basegreen Ave S12 44 B3
Basegreen Cl S12 44 C3
Basegreen Cres S12 44 B3
Basegreen Dr S12 44 C3
Basegreen Pl S12 44 B3
Basegreen Rd S12 44 C3
Basegreen Way S12 44 C3
Basil Cl
  Chesterfield S41 96 A3
  Chesterfield S41 266 B3
Basildon Cl DE24 232 F5
Basil Dr DE3 217 C4
Basingwerke Ct SK22 25 D3
BASLOW 91 F5
Baslow Cl
  22 Gamesley SK13 9 E1
  Long Eaton NG10 236 A5
Baslow Ct 14 S40 95 D5
Baslow Dr DE22 204 F3
Baslow Fold 21 SK13 9 E1
Baslow Gn
  23 Gamesley SK13 9 E1
  2 Swadlincote DE11 255 E5
Baslow Gr SK17 85 E6
Baslow Mews SK13 9 E1
Baslow Rd
  Ashford in the Water DE45 89 F1
  Bakewell DE45 109 D7
  Baslow DE45 92 E4
  Curbar S32 72 D1
  Holymoorside S42 94 C1
  Sheffield S17 55 C4
  Wadshelf S42 93 A3
Baslow Way 24 SK13 9 E1
BASSETT 42 E5
Bassettbarn La S42 130 B5
Bassett Cl
  Ilkeston DE7 194 C3
  Kimberley NG16 195 E7
Bassett Hill NG20 119 E7
Bassett La S10 42 E6
Bassett Rd NG16 195 E7
Bassett The NG20 119 E6
Bassford Ave DE75 181 F2
Bassingham Cl DE21 206 B1
Bassledene Ct 2 S2 44 A8
Bassledene Rd S2 44 A8
Bass's Cres DE11 261 E7
Bass St DE22 218 D6
Batch La DE6 224 B7
Bateman Cl S43 77 D4
Bateman St DE23 219 C3
Batemill Rd SK22 24 D2
BATEMOOR 57 A5
Batemoor Cl S8 57 A6
Batemoor Dr S8 57 A6
Batemoor Pl S8 57 A6
Batemoor Rd S8 57 A5
Batemoor Wlk S8 57 A6
Bate Wood Ave S43 97 B5
BATHAM GATE 66 F4
Batham Gate
  Bradwell SK17 50 B4
  Peak Forest SK17 48 F1
  Peak Forest SK17 49 A1
Batham Gate Rd SK17 67 B6
Batham Rd S33 51 A8
Bath La
  Ashover S45 129 F6
  Moira DE12 262 D4
  Shirebrook NG19 120 C2
Bath Rd
  Buxton SK17 85 B6
  Castle Gresley DE11 255 D1
  Derby DE3 217 E2
Bath St
  Bakewell DE45 109 D6
  Derby DE1 267 B5
  Ilkeston DE7 194 E1
Bathurst Rd S44 117 F8
Bathurst Terr NG20 100 F2
Batley La NG19 134 E4
Baton Mount 6 S43 81 E2
Battersea Park Way DE22 218 A5
Battlestead Rd DE14 253 D8
Batt St 9 S8 43 A8
Baulk La
  Beeston NG9 223 F7
  Hathersage S32 41 A1
  Hathersage S32 53 A8
Baverstock Cl DE73 232 F3
Baxter Hill NG19 134 F3
Baxter Sq DE23 231 F6
Bay Cl DE3 217 D5
Baycliff Dr S40 95 C3
Bay Ct S21 60 C5
Bayleaf Cres DE21 206 B3
Baysdale Croft S20 59 D7
Baysdale Dr NG19 136 F1
Bayswater Cl DE22 217 F6
Bayswater Rd NG16 195 F7
Bazley Rd S2 43 F6
Beackden Cl DE56 179 E4
Beacomfold SK6 15 B3
Beacom La SK14 15 C6
Beacon Dr DE13 240 B3
Beaconfields Ho DE21 220 B4
Beacon Hill Way S41 115 C7
Beacon Rd DE13 240 B3
Beaconsfield St NG10 236 E7
Beam Cl DE13 240 A1
Beamlight Rd DE7 194 F8
Beamwood Cl 3 DE21 205 F1
Beard Cres SK22 33 D8
Beardmore Cl DE21 205 F2
Beards Rd DE11 256 A6
Beards Wood Dr DE21 205 D3
Bearwood Hill Rd DE15 248 A3
Beatrix Dr SK13 9 E3
Beattie La DE11 256 F5
Beatty St DE24 232 F8
Beatty Wlk DE7 194 F3
BEAUCHIEF 56 D8
Beauchief Abbey La S8 56 C8
Beauchief Abbey (rems of)* S8 56 C8
Beauchief Dr S17 56 C7
Beauchief Gdns DE55 170 D8
Beaufit La NG16 160 E2
Beaufort Com Prim Sch DE21 219 C8
Beaufort Court Ind Est DE21 219 C8
Beaufort Rd
  Burton upon Trent DE15 248 B1
  Derby DE24 231 D2
Beaufort St DE21 219 D7
Beaulieu Way DE55 170 A7
Beaumaris Ct DE21 220 F5
Beaumont Cl
  Barrow upon Trent DE73 244 A5
  Belper DE56 179 D4
  Stapleford NG9 209 E1
Beaumont Dr SK17 47 F1
Beaumont Wlk DE23 231 E6
Beaurepaire Cres DE56 179 B5
Beaureper Ave DE22 204 E3
Beauvale Dr DE7 194 E5
Becher St DE23 219 A1
Beck Cl S44 99 C2
Beckenham Way DE22 218 B6
Becket Ave S8 56 D6
Becket Cres S8 56 E6
Becket Prim Sch DE22 218 F4
Becket Rd S8 56 E6
Becket St DE1 267 A3
Beckets Wood SK23 47 A4
Beckett Ave NG19 135 E1
Becket Well La DE1 267 B3
Becket Wlk S8 56 E6
Beckingham Way S40 266 B2
Beckitt Cl DE24 233 A8
Becksitch La DE56 178 F2
Beckstitch Ct DE56 178 F1
Bedehouse La DE4 155 A6
Bedford Cl DE22 218 D3
Bedford Ct NG9 209 E1
Bedford Dr DE72 233 F7
Bedford Rd DE15 254 D7
Bedford St DE22 218 D3
Bedgrave Cl S21 60 F8
Beech Ave
  Alfreton DE55 159 B5
  Borrowash DE72 221 C3
  Breaston DE72 235 F8
  Creswell S80 81 F1
  Derby DE24 233 B7
  Glossop SK13 17 A8
  Hulland Ward DE6 175 F3
  Long Eaton NG10 223 E1
  Melbourne DE73 252 B8
  New Mills SK22 24 D1
  Pinxton NG16 160 E3
  Quarndon DE22 204 B8
  Ripley DE5 169 C2
  Sandiacre NG10 223 B7
  Willington DE65 242 B5
Beech Cl
  Belper DE56 179 A3
  Branston DE14 256 E6
  Kilburn DE56 192 B8
  Wirksworth DE4 165 F7
Beech Cres
  Eckington S21 59 B1
  Glapwell S44 134 B8
  Killamarsh S21 60 D5
  Mansfield Woodhouse NG19 136 E2
Beechcroft DE21 205 D4
Beech Ct
  Derby DE21 220 D5
  Mansfield Woodhouse NG19 136 B5
Beechdale Cl S40 95 D5
Beechdale Rd
  Alfreton DE55 159 C3
  Mansfield NG19 136 F2
Beech Dr
  Arkwright Town S44 97 D3
  Ashbourne DE6 185 D8
  Derby DE22 218 F8
  Etwall DE65 229 C4
  Findern DE65 230 E1
  Woodville DE11 257 B2
Beeches Ave DE21 220 D5
Beeches Bank S2 43 C8
Beeches Dr S2 43 C8
Beeches Hollow S2 43 C8
Beeches The
  Baslow DE45 91 E5
  Crich DE4 156 F1
  Heanor DE75 193 C8
  Matlock DE4 143 A6
Beechfield Rd SK13 9 F3
Beech Gdns
  Derby DE24 233 B7
  6 Stretton DE13 240 E1
Beech Gr
  Long Duckmanton S44 98 A4
  South Normanton DE55 160 B5
  Swadlincote DE11 255 F7
Beech Hill Ave NG19 135 F1
Beech Hill Cres NG19 135 F1
Beech Hill Dr NG19 135 F1
Beech Hill Sch NG19 135 F1
Beech La
  Burton upon Trent DE13 240 E1
  Dove Holes SK17 66 E8
  West Hallam DE7 207 D7
Beechley Dr DE21 206 B1
Beech Rd SK23 45 E7
Beech Rise SK23 45 C5
Beech St S43 78 A1
Beech Tree Ave NG19 136 B5
Beech Tree Dr S43 80 F2
Beech View Drive SK17 85 C5
Beech Way
  Clay Cross S45 131 E2
  Dronfield S18 57 A3
Beech Wlk
  Cromford DE4 155 A6
  Derby DE23 218 D1
Beechwood SK13 16 F7
Beechwood Cl DE56 178 E5
Beechwood Cres
  1 Derby DE23 218 C1
  Derby DE23 231 C8
Beechwood Ct DE23 219 B3
Beechwood Dr SK6 23 A6
Beechwood Park Dr DE22 204 F1
Beechwood Rd S18 56 F1
Beehive Rd S40 95 D2
Bee Hives The DE11 256 A7
BEELEY 111 B4

Beeley Cl
Ashbourne DE6......**185** E8
Belper DE56.... **179** C6
Creswell S80......**81** D1
Derby DE22 ...... **204** D2
Derby, Oakwood
DE21............**205** F2
North Wingfield S42..**132** A7
Staveley S43..........**97** C6
Beeley Hill Top DE4. **111** A5
Beeley La DE4....... **112** B3
Beeley View S40.... **114** B7
Beeley Way S43 ......**97** C5
Beelow Cl SK17.......**47** C2
Bee Low Rd SK17.....**85** D2
BEESTON..........**223** E4
Beeston Cl S18......**56** C2
Beeston Dr DE3 ....**230** E5
Beet La SK23.........**35** B3
Beetwell St S40 ....**266** B2
Beggarswell Wood
DE56..............**167** D4
Beggarway La DE45...**90** B5
Beighton Fields S21 ..**79** D7
Beighton Hill
Ashleyhay DE4......**165** F4
Ashleyhay DE6......**166** A4
Beighton St DE5.....**169** E1
Bek Cl NG19.........**134** F7
Beldon Cl S2.........**43** D7
Beldon Court S2.......**43** D7
Beldon Pl S2.........**43** D7
Beldon Rd S2.........**43** D7
Belfast Wlk DE21.....**220** A4
Belfield Ct
Etwall DE65.........**229** B3
Heanor DE75........**181** C4
Belfield Gdns NG10...**236** E7
Belfield Ind Est DE7 .**194** F2
Belfield Rd
Etwall DE65.........**229** C3
Swadlincote DE11....**256** B5
Belfield St
Ilkeston DE7.........**194** F2
Ilkeston DE7.........**195** A2
Belfield Terr DE65 ...**229** B3
Belfit Dr
Wingerworth S42.....**114** F2
Wingerworth S42.....**115** A2
Belf Moor Cl S80 .....**82** A5
Belfry Cl DE3.........**217** F1
Belfry The DE13.....**240** C1
Belfry Way DE5......**180** E7
Belgrade Ave SK23 ....**34** E1
Belgrave Cl DE56 ....**179** C5
Belgrave Sq S2........**43** A8
Belgrave St DE23 ....**267** B1
Belklane Dr S21.......**60** E7
Bella Cl NG16........**182** B4
Belland La
Ashover S45.........**113** D2
Holymoorside S45 ...**113** D4
Bell Ave DE72.......**246** A7
Bell Cotts DE6 ......**224** C8
Belle Acre Cl 3
DE56..............**178** F3
BELLEVUE...........**173** B2
Belle Vue Ave DE5...**180** C6
Belle Vue Cl S43......**96** D8
Belle Vue Rd DE6.....**173** B2
Bellhouse La S43.......**78** F3
Bell House La S43......**78** F3
Bellhouse View S43 ..**78** F3
Bellingham Ct DE22 .**204** C2
Bell La
Bonsall DE4 ....**142** C1
Doveridge DE6.......**224** C8
Hartshorne DE11....**257** A3
Heanor DE7, DE75 ...**193** C5
Bellott La SK23 ......**46** E2
Bellrope Acre DE56..**179** B2
Bells End Rd DE12 ...**253** D1
Bellsfield Cl S80......**82** A5
Bell View DE7 ......**192** F6
Belmont Ave DE72...**235** E8
Belmont Cl DE3 .....**217** F5
Belmont Dr
Borrowash DE72 ....**221** B1
Marple SK6..........**15** B1
Staveley S43.........**78** F2
Belmont Prim Sch
DE11..............**256** C4
Belmont St DE11 ....**256** C4
Belmont Terr 1
SK17..............**85** B7
Belmore Way
Alvaston DE24 ......**233** B8
Derby DE21..........**220** A1
Belmot Rd DE13.....**239** B4
Belpar Ho DE21.....**220** E3
BELPER..........**179** B3
Belper La DE56......**178** E6
BELPER LANE END ..**178** C7
Belper L Ctr DE56 ...**179** D2
Belper Parks Nature
Reserve* DE56...**179** A3
Belper Rd
Alderwasley DE4 ....**166** C6
Alderwasley DE56....**167** A4
Ashbourne DE6......**173** C1
Ashbourne DE6......**174** C1
9 Derby DE22......**218** F7
Holbrook DE56....**191** C8
Hulland Ward DE6...**176** D2

Belper Rd continued
Kilburn DE56........**179** E2
Morley DE7.........**192** F2
Shirland DE55.......**146** C2
Stanley Common DE7..**193** B1
West Hallam DE7....**207** C8
Belper Sch DE56 ....**179** D4
Belper St DE7 ......**208** F7
Belper Sta DE56.....**178** F4
BELPH.............**82** C4
Belsize Cl DE22.....**217** F6
Belton Cl
Dronfield S18........**56** C1
Sandiacre NG10 .....**223** B4
Belton Dr DE5 ......**169** E1
Belvedere Ave S40 ..**114** E8
Belvedere Cl
Chesterfield S40......**114** A8
Derby DE3 ....**217** D3
Swanwick DE55......**169** F7
Belvedere Rd DE11 ..**256** F2
Belvedere Terr 1
SK17...............**85** B6
Belvoir Cl
Breaston DE72......**235** D7
Ilkeston DE7........**208** D6
Long Eaton NG10 ...**236** E5
Belvoir Cres DE11 ...**256** A6
Belvoir St DE23......**218** F1
Belvoir Way DE55...**159** C1
Bembridge Dr DE24..**233** C5
Bemrose Ct DE1.....**267** C2
Bemrose Gate S33....**40** A6
Bemrose Mews
DE22..............**218** D4
Bemrose Rd DE24 ...**232** E7
Bemrose Sch The
DE22..............**218** D4
Benbow Ave DE73 ...**252** A8
Benches La SK6 ......**15** E3
Bench Rd SK17.......**85** D8
Bendall Gn DE23.....**231** C5
Bendan Gdns DE22 ..**204** E1
Bend Oak Dr DE15 ..**248** C4
Benjamin Ct NG16...**170** F3
Benjamin Outram Bsns
Ctr DE5 ....**180** E7
Benmore Ct DE21....**206** B3
Benner Ave DE7 .....**209** A5
Bennerley Ave DE7 ..**194** F4
Bennerley Fields
Specialist Speech &
Language Coll DE7 **194** F4
Bennetsitch Rd
SK11..............**102** C3
Bennetts La
Crich DE4..........**167** F8
Crich DE4..........**168** A8
Bennett St
Buxton SK17.........**85** C6
Derby DE24 ....**232** E6
Hollingworth SK14.....**9** D5
Long Eaton NG10 ...**223** C2
Sandiacre NG10 .....**223** B5
Bennimoor Way
S40...............**114** E8
Bennington Wlk
NG19 ....**136** E4
Bennion Gr ST14 ....**196** E5
Bennison Gdns
S45...............**131** D3
Bensley Cl DE73 .....**233** A1
Benson St DE24......**232** F7
Bentfield Rd DE56 ...**168** C1
Bentham Rd S40.....**95** E5
Benthead La DE6....**164** F1
Bentinck Dr S43......**81** A4
Bentinck Rd S44......**98** F7
Bentinck St S80 .....**82** C6
Bentink Cl S80.......**81** C1
Bent La
Ashleyhay DE4 ......**166** C6
Church Broughton
DE65..............**227** C6
Darley Dale DE4 ....**127** D6
Matlock DE4........**143** A4
Matlock DE4........**143** B7
Spout DE4, DE56....**166** C6
Staveley S43.........**79** A3
Tissington DE6 .....**162** D5
Bentley Bridge Cotts
DE4...............**143** E7
Bentley Bridge Rd
DE4...............**143** E7
Bentley Brook
Hilton DE65 ....**228** D1
Matlock DE4........**143** D4
Bentley Cl
Alfreton DE55.......**159** B3
Matlock DE4........**143** A4
Bentley Dale DE11...**257** A3
Bentley Rd
Castle Donington
DE74..............**246** F4
Uttoxeter ST14......**210** A2
Bentley St DE24 .....**232** E6
Benton Dr SK6 ......**23** C8
Bents Cres S18.......**57** C3
Bentside Rd SK12....**32** D5
Bents La S18.........**57** C3
Bent The S32.........**72** E3
Beowulf Covert
DE13..............**240** B1
Beresford Ave
Ashbourne DE6......**173** D2
Chapel-en-le-Frith
SK23..............**47** C6
Beresford Cl S45.....**131** D2

Beresford Dale
DE11..............**255** F2
Beresford Dr
Derby DE21.........**220** E4
Ilkeston DE7........**194** E5
Beresford La
Alstonefield DE6.....**149** D4
Alstonefield SK17....**137** C2
Ashover DE55........**145** D7
Beresford Pl DE56...**168** B6
Beresford Rd
Chapel-en-le-Frith
SK23..............**47** C6
Long Eaton NG10 ...**236** A5
Mansfield Woodhouse
NG19 ....**136** C6
Beresford Way S41...**76** D2
Berkeley Ave NG10 .**236** C6
Berkeley Cl DE23....**231** D7
Berkley Ct SK23......**45** D6
Berkshire St DE21 ..**219** D8
Berle Ave DE75.....**181** E2
Bermuda Ave DE21..**205** C6
Bernard Ave NG19...**136** B5
Bernard Cl S43.......**96** C8
Bernard Ct DE11....**256** D3
Bernard Gadsby Cl
DE6...............**173** A1
Bernard St
Glossop SK13.........**10** C1
Swadlincote DE11....**256** D3
Bernard Walker Ct
SK6...............**15** B2
Berners Cl S2........**43** E6
Berners Dr S2........**43** E6
Berners Pl S2........**43** E6
Berners Rd S2........**43** E6
Berridge La S45.....**145** B4
Berrisford Ave S21....**59** D2
Berristow La DE55...**160** C7
Berry Ave S21........**59** C3
Berry Gdns DE15....**248** C4
Berry Hedge La
DE15..............**248** C4
Berry Park Cl DE22..**204** E1
Berry St S42........**131** E6
Berrystorth Cl S14....**43** E5
Bertrand Ave S45....**131** D3
Berwick Ave
Chesterfield S40.....**114** C7
Derby DE21.........**219** C7
Berwick Cl DE24 ....**233** B5
Berwick Ct S40......**114** C7
Berwick Dr DE24 ...**231** D3
Berwick Rd SK17.....**85** C4
Berwin Cl NG10.....**223** A1
Berwyn Cl S40.......**95** C5
Beryl Cl DE21.......**255** F4
Besom La S32........**53** A8
Bessalone Dr DE56 ..**179** A6
Bessell La NG9 .....**223** D5
Bessie La S33.........**51** B6
Best Ave DE15.......**248** B1
Besthill Cotts SK14...**16** B8
Besthorpe Cl DE21...**206** B1
Bestwick Ave DE75 ..**182** B1
Bestwood Dr S45....**131** C3
Bestwood Pk S45.....**131** C3
Bestwood Rd NG16 ..**160** E2
Bethany Cl 2 DE65 .**242** B6
Bethel Terr S81.......**63** E7
Bethulie Rd DE23....**232** A4
Betjeman Sq DE24...**232** A5
Betlingspring La
DE6...............**184** D3
Betony Cl S21........**60** B5
Betony Close DE24...**231** C3
Betony Rd DE15.....**248** C2
Betty La DE45.......**108** F8
Bevan Cl DE55......**146** E1
Bevan Dr S43.........**97** B7
Bevan Rd S45.......**131** D2
Bevan St DE55......**146** E1
Beverley Dr NG16...**195** F4
Beverley Rd
4 Branston DE14...**253** F7
Burton upon Trent
DE14..............**254** A7
Beverleys Rd S8......**43** A4
Beverley St DE24 ....**219** D2
Bevin Pl S42........**132** A7
Bewdley Cl DE73 ....**233** A3
Bewley Ct DE24.....**233** D4
Bexhill Wlk DE21 ...**205** E1
Bexley Cl
Derby DE3 ....**217** F5
Glossop SK13.........**10** C3
Bexley Dr DE11......**255** E1
BIBBINGTON.......**66** F7
Bicester Ave DE24...**231** C2
Bickley Moss DE21..**206** B1
Bideford Cl DE5 .....**169** D2
Bideford Ct 25 S41...**95** F8
Bideford Dr DE23....**231** D6
Bidston Cl DE4......**143** C7
Bidworth La SK13......**9** C1
BIGGIN
Hartington **138** C4
Hulland Ward.......**176** A5
Biggin CE Prim Sch
SK17..............**138** D3
Biggin Cl S45........**131** D1
Biggin La
Alfreton DE55.......**133** A1
Hulland Ward DE6...**176** B3
Bigginmill La DE6 ...**176** C5
Biggin The DE74.....**247** B3

Bigin View DE6......**175** E3
Big La
Hognaston DE6......**164** A4
Hognaston DE6......**164** C4
Bilberry Cl DE21.....**205** F1
Bilberry Dr NG20 ...**119** D2
Bilbie Cl DE55......**159** C4
Bilby La S43.........**77** E1
Billam St S21........**59** B3
Billingsley Ave
NG16 ....**160** D3
Bilsborrow Ave DE1 .**267** C2
Bingham Cl DE55....**159** C4
Bingham St DE24 ...**232** E6
Bings Rd SK23........**45** F8
Bingswood Ave
SK23..............**45** E8
Bingswood Ind Est
SK23..............**45** E8
Bingswood Rd SK23 ..**45** E7
Bingswood Trading Est
SK23..............**45** E8
Binscombe La DE21..**205** F3
Birch Ave
Ambergate DE56....**167** F3
Ilkeston DE7........**209** A7
Swadlincote DE11 ...**256** A4
Birch Cl
Alfreton DE55.......**159** A5
Burton upon Trent
DE14..............**254** A8
Buxton SK17.........**66** B1
Denstone ST14......**196** D6
Derby DE21.........**221** A6
Grassmoor S42......**115** F3
Killamarsh S21.......**60** C5
Ripley DE5.........**180** D8
Wessington DE55....**157** E8
BIRCH CROSS......**224** C4
Birch Cross ST14 ...**224** B1
Birchenbooth Rd
SK11..............**102** C4
Birchen Cl
Chesterfield S40......**95** C5
Dronfield S18........**56** D1
Birchen Holme
DE55..............**160** A4
Birches Ave DE55...**157** F5
Birches Brook
South Wingfield
DE55..............**157** F5
South Wingfield DE55 .**158** A5
Birches Fold S18......**57** C4
Birches La
Dronfield S18........**57** C4
South Wingfield DE55 .**158** A5
Birches Rd DE22....**204** D4
Birches Terr DE6 ....**173** B1
Birches The SK22.....**25** C2
Birch Farm Ave S8....**57** A8
Birchfield Cl DE73 ..**232** F2
Birchfield Pk DE75..**193** F7
Birchfield Rd DE15 .**254** E6
Birch Gn SK13........**10** C1
Birch Gr
Hatton DE65........**227** D2
Shirebrook NG20 ...**119** D5
Birch Hall Cl S42.....**132** B2
Birch Holt Gr S18.....**76** E5
Birch House Way
S18...............**57** C1
Birchills The S80.....**81** C1
Birchitt Cl S17.......**56** C5
Birchitt Ct S17.......**56** C5
Birchitt Pl S17.......**56** C5
Birchitt Rd S17.......**56** C5
Birchitt View S18.....**57** A3
Birch Kiln Croft S43 ..**96** F7
Birch La S43.........**78** A1
Birchlands NG19....**136** F1
Birchlands Dr S21.....**60** D5
BIRCHOVER........**126** B1
Birchover Ct S41.....**95** C5
Birchover Edge DE4 .**141** B8
Birchover Ho
1 Derby, Allestree
DE22.............**204** F3
Derby, Markeaton
DE22..............**218** D8
Birchover La DE4.....**141** B7
Birchover Pl DE7 ....**194** E5
Birchover Rd DE4....**126** C3
Birchover Rise
DE21..............**205** F1
Birchover Way
DE22..............**204** E2
Birch Rd S80.........**82** C6
Birch Rise S45.......**131** E3
Birchside Ave SK13....**10** B2
Birch St NG20 ......**120** F6
BIRCH VALE.........**25** B2
Birch Vale DE56.....**178** F5
Birch Vale Ind Est
SK22..............**25** A2
Birchvale Rd S12 ....**44** D3
Birch Vale Terr SK22..**24** F3
Birchview Cl DE6....**179** B2
Birch View Ct DE1...**218** F7
Birchway Gr DE23 ..**231** A6
Birchwood
Heanor DE75 ....**181** C4
Heanor DE75 ....**181** B4
Birchwood Ave
Derby DE23 ....**231** D6
Long Eaton, Breaston
NG10 ....**236** A7
Long Eaton, New Sawley
NG10 ....**236** C5
Bitham Ct DE13......**240** C1

Birchwood Cl
7 Sheffield S20.......**59** E8
South Normanton
DE55..............**160** A4
Birchwood Cres
Chesterfield S40......**114** F7
Somercotes DE55....**170** D8
Birchwood Croft S20 .**59** E8
Birchwood Ct S40....**114** F7
Birchwood Dr DE56. **168** B4
Birchwood Gdns 6
S20...............**59** E8
Birchwood Gr S20....**59** E8
Birchwood La DE55 .**159** C3
Birchwood Rd
Alfreton DE55.......**159** C3
Eckington S21........**58** D4
Birchwood Rise 5
S20...............**59** E8
Birchwood View
Ashbourne DE6......**173** C3
Sheffield S20.........**59** E8
Birchwood Way
16 Sheffield S20.....**59** E8
Somercotes DE55....**159** C1
Bircumshaw's Rd
DE75..............**181** E2
Birdcage Wlk DE22 .**217** F6
Birdcroft La DE7.....**208** F5
BIRDHOLME.......**115** A7
Birdholme Cres
S40...............**115** A8
Birding St NG19 ....**136** B1
Birdsgrove La
Ashbourne DE6......**172** D3
Mayfield DE6 ....**172** D4
Bird St S43..........**78** F2
Birdwood St DE23 ..**218** F1
Birkbeck Close DE3..**217** F3
Birkdale Ave DE14..**254** A6
Birkdale Cl
Derby DE3 ....**218** A2
Ilkeston DE7........**194** D1
Birkdale Dr S40 .....**114** D8
Birk Hill Inf Sch S21 ..**59** B2
Birkin Ave S42 .....**115** C1
Birkin La
Grassmoor S42......**115** C4
Holmewood S42......**116** A3
Wingerworth S40,
S42...............**114** C1
Birkin Lane W S42...**115** F2
Birkinstyle Ave
DE55..............**146** F3
Birkinstyle La DE55 .**146** E3
Birkland Ave NG19 ..**136** D3
Birks Cl S80.........**82** D6
BIRLEY...........**93** F7
Birley Acad The S12..**44** D2
Birley Brook Dr S40 ..**95** B7
Birley Croft S41......**95** B7
BIRLEYHAY.........**58** D5
Birley La
Bamford S32 ....**40** F2
Hathersage S32......**41** B3
Sheffield S12.........**44** A3
Birley Moor Ave S12..**44** E3
Birley Moor Cl S12...**44** E3
Birley Moor Cres S12 .**44** E2
Birley Moor Pl S12 ...**44** E2
Birley Moor Rd S12...**44** E2
Birley Moor Way S12..**44** E3
Birley Prim Acad
S12...............**44** D3
Birley Rd
Birley S18............**93** E6
Birley S18...........**93** E7
Birley School Mews
S13...............**44** E5
Birley Spa Com Prim Sch
S12...............**44** E3
Birley Spa La S12.....**44** F3
Birley Vale Ave S12...**44** C5
Birley Vale Cl S12 ...**44** C4
Birley Wood Dr S12...**44** C5
Birstall Cl S41........**95** C7
Biscay Ct DE21 .....**206** C2
Bishopdale Cl NG10..**236** A6
Bishopdale Dr S20....**59** A8
Bishopdale Rise S20..**59** A8
Bishop Lonsdale CE Prim
Sch DE22...........**218** D2
Bishop Lonsdale Way
DE3...............**217** F3
Bishop Purslove CE
Pirmary Sch SK17...**69** C4
Bishops Cl DE5 .....**180** E8
Bishopscourt Rd S8 ..**43** A5
Bishops Ct
Melbourne DE73.....**252** B7
Sheffield S8..........**43** B5
Bishop's Ct DE73 ...**252** B7
Bishop's Dr DE21 ...**205** E2
Bishops Gate DE11 ..**256** E2
Bishop's Gn DE22....**218** D3
Bishop's House (Mus)★
S8...............**43** A4
Bishop's La SK17.....**84** C7
Bishop St
Alfreton DE55.......**159** A5
Eastwood NG16.....**182** F2
Bishopthorpe Gro
DE22..............**204** D7
Bispham Dr NG9.....**223** F2
Bitham Ct DE13.....**240** C1

Bitham La DE13 ....**240** D1
Bittern View DE65 ..**242** A5
Blaby Cl DE23.......**231** E6
Blacka Moor Cres
S17...............**55** C6
Blacka Moor Rd S17..**55** C6
Blacka Moor View
S17...............**55** C6
Blackbanks
Chesterfield S44......**80** A1
Stanfree S44.........**99** B8
Blackberry Cl S43 ....**80** D4
Blackberry Flats S20..**59** E7
Blackberry Rise
DE56..............**179** C1
Blackberry Way
5 Brimington S40....**96** E7
Kilburn DE56.......**179** F2
Blackbird Row
DE56..............**179** C1
BLACKBROOK
Belper............**178** B4
Chapel-en-le-Frith...**47** E6
Tutbury............**253** B2
Blackbrook La SK23 ..**47** E6
Blackbrook Rd
DE65..............**240** E8
Blackburn Pl DE7....**194** E3
Blackcliff Field Cl
S80...............**82** A5
Blackdown Ave S40..**95** B5
Blackedge Cl SK17....**47** F2
BLACKFORDBY.....**257** C1
Blackfordby St
Margaret's CE (Aided)
Prim Sch DE11.....**257** B1
Black Harry La S32...**71** B2
Black Hills Dr DE7 ..**208** F6
Black La SK17.......**105** C2
Blackmore St DE23..**231** F7
Blackmount Ct 5
DE24..............**231** D3
Blackpit La DE6.....**224** B8
Blackpool St DE14...**254** C8
Black Rock★ DE4...**155** F6
Blackrocks Ave DE4 .**142** F7
Blackshale Road
NG19 ....**136** B2
Blackshaw Clough
SK13..............**10** E3
Blackshaw Rd SK13...**10** E2
Blacksmith Croft
DE5...............**180** D7
Blacksmith La S44....**97** A3
Blacksmiths Cl
Glapwell S44 ......**118** C1
Netherseal DE12....**264** F7
Blacksmith's La
Egginton DE65 .....**241** A6
Newton Solney DE15 .**248** E8
Woodville DE11 ....**256** F3
Blacksmiths Yd
Darley Dale DE4 ....**127** E2
Rolleston DE13......**240** B4
Blacksmith Way
NG20 ....**119** F2
Blackstock Cl S14....**43** D2
Blackstock Cres S14..**43** D2
Blackstock Rd S14....**43** D2
Blackstone Cl DE55..**170** D2
Blackstone Dr S81....**63** F8
Blackthorn Cl
4 Brailsford DE6 ...**201** E8
Chesterfield S41....**115** D8
Derby DE21.........**205** C2
Melbourne DE73.....**252** A8
Blackthorn Dr NG16 **182** E2
Blackthorne Cl
DE56..............**179** C7
Blackthorn Rd DE15 **254** E6
Black Tor Rd DE4....**154** D8
BLACKWALL.......**175** F7
Blackwall La DE6 ...**176** A4
Blackthorn Cl
DE56..............**179** C7
BLACKWELL
Sutton in Ashfield...**147** F1
Taddington.........**87** D5
Blackwell Ave DE7...**194** F4
Blackwell Com Prim Sch
DE55..............**147** F1
Blackwell Dale SK17..**87** C6
Blackwell La
Melbourne DE73....**252** B4
Monyash DE45 .....**107** B8
Blackwell Mill Cotts
SK17..............**87** A6
Blackwell Rd NG17 ..**148** C3
Bladon House Sch
DE15..............**248** B6
Bladon St DE15.....**248** C4
Bladon View DE13 ..**241** A2
Blagdon Cl DE4.....**127** C3
Blagreaves Ave
DE23..............**231** C5
Blagreaves La DE23..**231** C6
Blair Gr NG10.......**223** B4
Blair Ho DE23......**231** C5
Blakebrook Dr
DE73..............**233** A3
Blake Ct NG10......**236** B5
Blakeley La DE65....**229** B2
Blakelow Dr DE65 ..**229** B3
Blakelow La DE4 ...**142** A3
Blakemere La DE4...**141** F7
Blakemore Ave
DE73..............**252** B8
Blakeney Ct
Derby DE21 ....**206** C1

Bla–Bra 273

Blakeney Ct *continued*
3 Mansfield Woodhouse NG19 136 E4
Blake Rd NG9 223 E6
Blake St
Ilkeston DE7 194 F1
Mansfield Woodhouse NG19 136 B2
Blanch Croft DE73 252 B7
Blandford Ave NG10 236 B6
Blandford Cl DE24 233 D6
Blandford Dr S41 95 E7
Blankney Cl DE24 231 D2
Blants Cl NG16 195 F6
Blay Ct S43 77 D4
Bleaklow Cl DE21 205 F3
Bleaklow Wlk 29 SK13 9 E1
Blencathra Dr DE3 230 E8
Blenheim Ave DE55 170 A8
Blenheim Cl
Burton upon Trent DE15 248 C3
4 Glossop SK13 10 A5
Mansfield NG19 136 D1
3 Swadlincote DE11 256 A7
Blenheim Ct DE56 179 D5
Blenheim Dr DE22 204 D4
Blenheim Ho 1 DE14 253 F7
Blenheim Mews DE65 229 C4
Blenheim Par DE22 204 D4
Blenheim Pl NG17 148 E3
Blenheim Rd DE6 185 E7
Blenheim Ct 3 NG10 223 B4
Blenkinsop Cl DE11 256 F5
Blessed Robert Sutton Catholic Voluntary Acad DE15 255 A7
Blind La
Bolsover S44 98 F3
Breaston DE72 235 D8
Darley Dale DE4 127 F1
Kirk Ireton DE6 165 A2
1 Wirksworth DE4 165 F8
Blisworth Way DE55 169 F8
Blithe Cl DE65 228 E1
Blithfield Gdns DE73 233 A2
Bloomery Cl DE55 158 E3
Bloomery Way S45 131 E3
Bloomfield Cl
Derby DE1 267 C1
Hilton DE65 228 D1
Bloomfield Rd DE55 170 A8
Bloomfield St DE1 267 D1
Bloomsgrove Rd DE7 194 F2
Bloom St DE1 267 B2
Blore Cl DE6 185 D8
Blossom Cres S12 44 B3
Blossom Wlk DE65 227 C1
Bluebank Lane S44 99 A5
Bluebank View S43 77 D3
Blue Barn La NG20 101 C3
Bluebell Cl
4 Ashbourne DE6 185 C8
Barlborough S43 80 B6
Derby DE24 231 D2
Donisthorpe DE12 262 E1
Hayfield SK22 25 C3
Shirebrook NG20 119 D3
Somercotes DE55 159 E2
Underwood Green NG16 171 F2
Blue Bell Cl S43 97 B5
Bluebell Croft DE4 143 B3
Bluebell Dairy* DE21 220 F7
Bluebell Grove DE11 256 F1
Bluebell Hill DE55 146 C4
Bluebell Pl NG19 136 F4
Bluebell Way
Heanor DE75 182 B1
Tutbury DE13 239 D5
Bluebell Wlk S80 81 E3
Blueberry Cl S43 97 B5
Blueberry Ct S42 116 C1
Blueberry Way DE11 256 F3
Bluebird Ct DE24 231 D4
Blue Cedars Dr DE15 248 D2
Blue John Cavern* S33 37 E3
Blue Lodge Cl S43 97 B5
Blue Mountains DE56 191 B1
Blue Ridge Cl S17 55 E7
Bluestone La DE15 255 A7
Blundestone La DE4 156 A2
Blunt Ave S43 79 C4
Blunt St DE7 193 A2
Blyth Cl
Chesterfield S40 114 B8
Mansfield NG19 135 D1
Blyth Ct DE74 247 B4
Blythe Ct NG19 135 D1
Blyth Gdns DE3 217 B1
Blyth Pl DE21 205 D1
Boam La DE4 142 F8
Boardman Ind Est DE11 255 E3
Boardman Rd DE11 255 E2
Boarfold La
Chisworth SK13 15 F5
Chisworth SK6 15 E5
Boars Head Ind Est DE1 267 C4
Boarslack La
Litton SK17 69 F2
Tideswell SK17 69 E2
Boarstones La SK17 85 E8
Boat La NG16 182 A7
Boatmans Cl DE7 194 F2
Bobbin Mill SK17 89 A6
Bobbinmill Hill DE56 168 B7
Bobbin Mill La S40 95 D2
Bobbins La DE21 220 F2
Bobbin Way DE56 179 C5
Bob Southern Grove DE11 256 B1
Bochum Parkway S8 57 C8
Bocking La S8 56 E8
Bocking Rise S8 56 E8
Bodell Cl 2 DE11 255 E6
Boden Cl DE4 142 E8
Boden St DE23 219 B2
Bodmin Cl DE24 231 D3
Bodmin Way 3 S40 95 C5
Boggard La SK13 16 D6
Boggard Rd SK6 24 A4
Boggy La
Bradwell S33 51 B6
Church Broughton, Heathtop DE65 227 A6
Bog La DE73 251 E5
Bohem Rd NG10 223 C3
Boiley La S21 60 C4
Boland Rd S8 56 D5
Bolden Terr DE55 147 C1
Bold La DE1 267 B3
BOLEHILL
Calow 97 B1
Sheffield 43 A2
Wirksworth 155 A2
BOLE HILL
Ashover S42 130 D8
Barlow S18 75 C2
Bole Hill
Bakewell DE45 109 A4
Sheffield S8 43 A2
Bolehill Cl DE21 206 A3
Bole Hill Cotts S44 97 A1
Bolehill Croft DE4 155 A3
Bolehill Ct 3 S40 95 D5
Bolehill La
Eckington S21 58 F2
Northedge S42 130 C7
Northedge S45 130 C8
Wingerworth S42 114 D1
Bolehill Rd DE4 155 A3
BOLSOVER 99 B3
Bolsover Bsns Pk S44 98 E2
Bolsover Castle* S44 99 A2
Bolsover CE Jun Sch S44 99 B2
Bolsover Cl DE5 169 E1
Bolsover Hill S44 99 A2
Bolsover Hospl S44 99 C2
Bolsover Inf Sch S44 99 B2
Bolsover Rd
Derby DE3 230 E5
Glapwell S44 118 C1
Mastin Moor S43 79 D2
Shuttlewood S44 98 F6
Bolsover Sch The S44 99 C1
Bolton St DE55 169 D7
Bolton Way
1 Derby DE23 230 F5
Derby DE23 231 A5
Boman's La DE56 177 F8
Bonchurch Cl DE24 233 C5
Bond Cl NG19 136 C7
Bonden SK23 35 E1
Bondfield Rd S43 97 C7
Bondgate DE74 247 B3
Bondhay La S80 62 C2
Bond La DE56 168 E2
Bonds Cl DE7 194 F5
Bond St S43 97 C8
Bonington Rise SK6 23 B8
Bonner's La NG16 195 C4
Bonnie Cl DE3 217 D6
Bonnington Dr DE55 170 D8
Bonnyrigg Dr DE21 206 A2
BONSALL 142 E1
Bonsall Ave DE23 231 D8
Bonsall Bank SK13 9 E2
Bonsall CE (Aided) Prim Sch DE4 142 E1
Bonsall Cl SK13 9 E2
Bonsall Ct
2 Chesterfield S41 95 D7
Long Eaton NG10 236 F8
BONSALL DALE 142 D1
Bonsall Dr
Derby DE3 217 E3
Somercotes DE55 170 D8
Bonsall Fold SK13 9 E2
Bonsall La
Alfreton DE55 158 F4
Winster DE4 141 C4
Bonsallmoor La DE4 141 E3
Bonsall St NG10 236 E8
Bonser Cres NG17 148 E2
Bonser Hedge Ct NG10 236 B4
Booker Cl S43 97 C6
Booth Ave NG19 135 A5
Boothbright Cres NG19 135 D2
Boothby Ave 1 DE6 173 C2
Booth Cres NG19 135 D2
Booth Dr DE6 185 C8
BOOTHGATE 179 E7
Boothgate DE56 179 E7
Boot Hill DE65 242 C3
BOOTHORPE 262 F8
Boothorpe La DE11 262 F8
Booth's Ct 1 SK13 10 D1
Booth St
Derby DE24 232 F7
Hollingworth SK14 9 C5
Mansfield Woodhouse NG19 136 B3
Ripley DE5 169 E2
Booth Trad Est NE7 194 F2
Booton Field Cres 2 DE73 233 A3
Boots Yd NG17 148 F3
Borage Gro 1 DE3 217 C4
Border Cl S43 80 F3
Border Cres DE24 233 B5
Border La S80 80 F2
Border Rd NG20 120 A4
Borlace Cres NG9 223 E6
Borough St DE74 247 B3
BORROWASH 221 C2
Borrowash By-pass DE72 221 C3
Borrowash Rd
4 Borrowash DE72 221 A1
Derby DE21 220 F4
Borrowdale Ave 3 S20 59 E6
Borrowdale Cl 2 S20 59 E6
Borrowdale Dr
Long Eaton NG10 236 A6
Sheffield S20 59 E6
Borrowdale Rd S20 59 E6
Borrowfield Rd DE21 220 F3
Borrowfields DE72 221 B1
Borrowwash Rd DE72 234 A7
Borrow Wood Prim Sch DE21 220 F5
Boscastle Rd DE24 233 B6
Boscawen Ct NE7 194 F4
Boscowan Ct DE7 194 F4
Bosley Mews DE56 178 F5
Bostock Rd SK14 16 A8
Bostocks La 1 NG10 223 A4
Bostock's La
Long Eaton NG10 223 A3
Risley NG10, DE72 222 F4
Boston Cl DE21 220 C6
Boswell Ct 3 DE6 173 B2
Boswell Sq DE23 231 F7
Bosworth Ave DE23 231 E6
Bosworth Rd DE74 246 F3
Bosworth Way NG10 236 E5
Botany Bsns Pk SK23 45 D6
Botany Mews SK23 45 E6
Bothe Cl NG10 236 C6
Bottlebrook Houses DE5 180 B1
Bottles Farm Cl DE5 180 A1
Bottomhill Rd
Tideswell SK17 69 E1
Upperdale SK17 89 C4
Bottom Lons DE6 176 B8
Bottom of Moor SK17 121 A3
Bottom Rd S42 114 E1
Bottom Row NG19 135 E7
Bottom Row Main Rd S42 93 F2
Boughton Dr DE55 169 F8
Boughton La S43 80 D4
Boulevard The SK14 9 D4
BOULTON 233 B6
Boulton Cl S40 95 A5
Boulton Dr DE24 233 A6
Boulton La
Derby DE24 233 A6
Derby, Allenton DE24 232 F5
BOUNDARY 257 C2
Boundary Cl
Shirebrook NG20 119 E6
Staveley S43 79 A3
Boundary Gdns DE55 147 F5
Boundary La NG16 182 C3
Boundary Rd
Derby DE22 218 E4
Egginton DE65 241 D8
Boundary Wlk NG20 100 F1
Bournebrook Ave DE4 165 F7
Bourne Cl
Brimington S43 96 E8
Tutbury DE13 239 B6
Bourne Dr NG16 182 B3
Bourne Mill Cl S43 80 B6
Bourne Pl DE5 180 A1
Bourne Sq DE72 235 E7
Bourne St DE1 267 B2
Bourne Way DE11 256 D4
Bowbank Cl DE23 231 A6
Bowbridge Ave DE23 231 C5
Bowden Cl SK22 25 C3
Bowden Cres SK22 33 D8
Bowden Ct S43 80 F7
BOWDEN HEAD 35 D1
Bowden Hey Rd SK23 47 C7
Bowden La
Chapel-en-le-Frith SK23 47 C7
Chapel-en-le-Frith SK23 47 D8
Hope S33 39 A4
Bowden Rd SK13 10 C3
Bowdon Ave S43 80 A6
Bower Close DE6 185 B8
Bower Dr DE4 156 F1
Bower Farm Rd S41 77 B2
Bower St DE24 232 F8
Bowes Rd DE24 233 D4
Boweswell Rd DE7 194 E2
Bowland Cl DE3 217 E1
Bowland Dr S40 114 B7
Bowland Rd SK13 17 A8
Bowlees Ct DE23 230 E7
Bowler Dr DE56 192 A7
Bowler La
Darley Dale DE4 143 B8
Farley DE4 128 A1
Matlock DE4 143 B8
Bowler Rd DE4 127 C3
Bowler St DE5 180 D7
Bowling Al La DE6 211 E7
Bowling Alley DE56 168 E1
Bowlingalley La DE6 197 D8
Bowling Alley La DE6 212 A5
Bowling Cl DE7 222 E8
Bowling Gn DE4 153 A1
Bowling Green La
Chapel-en-le-Frith SK23 47 B6
Wirksworth DE4 154 E1
Wirksworth DE4 165 E8
Bowling Green Rd 2 ST14 210 B1
Bowman Cl S12 43 F2
Bowmer La DE56 168 B6
Bowmer Rd DE24 219 E1
Bown Cl DE56 192 A8
Bowness Cl
Chesterfield S41 95 D7
Dronfield S18 56 E1
Bowness Rd S41 95 D7
Bowns Hill DE4 157 A1
Bowns Yd DE55 170 D8
BOWSHAW 56 F4
Bowshaw S18 56 F4
Bowshaw Ave S8 57 A5
Bowshaw Cl S8 57 A5
Bowshaw View S8 57 A5
Bow St NG19 136 E4
Bowstonegate Rd SK12 32 E1
Box Cl DE11 256 E3
Box La
Ticknall DE7 257 F8
Ticknall DE73 251 A1
Ticknall DE73 258 A8
Boxmoor Cl DE23 230 F7
Boyd Gr DE73 245 A8
Boyer St DE22 267 A1
Boyer Wlk DE22 267 A1
BOYLESTONE 213 C4
Boylestone Rd
Alkmonton DE6 213 E7
Derby DE23 231 C5
BOYLESTONFIELD 213 E5
BOYTHORPE 95 E1
Boythorpe Ave S40 266 A2
Boythorpe Bsns Units S40 95 E2
Boythorpe Cl DE7 194 F5
Boythorpe Cres S40 266 A1
Boythorpe Mount S40 266 A2
Boythorpe Rd S40 266 A2
Boythorpe Rise S40 95 E2
Brabyns Brow SK6 23 A7
Brabyns Prep Sch SK6 23 A7
Brace Gdns 2 DE6 211 A1
Bracken Ave S44 116 F1
Bracken Cl
Hollingworth SK14 9 D6
Long Eaton NG10 223 B1
Marple SK6 23 C7
Brackendale Ave S45 131 E2
Brackendale Cl S43 96 D7
Brackendale La DE6 163 E5
Brackendale Rd DE55 169 F8
BRACKENFIELD 145 D2
Brackenfield Ave NG19 136 E4
Brackenfield Close S42 115 F2
Brackenfield Dr NG16 195 B7
Brackenfield Gr S12 44 D3
Brackenfield La
Brackenfield DE55 145 D1
Brackenfield La *continued*
Wessington DE55 157 D8
Brackenfield Specl Sch NG10 223 B1
Brackenfield View DE55 145 D1
Brackenhill Cl 8 DE23 230 F6
Bracken La DE4 156 B5
Bracken Rd
Long Eaton NG10 223 B1
Shirebrook NG20 119 D3
Brackens Ave DE24 232 F5
Brackensdale Ave DE22 218 B5
Brackensdale Jun Sch DE22 218 B6
Brackens La S43 80 B6
Bracken's La DE24 232 F6
Bracken Way SK13 17 F7
Brackenwood Rd DE15 254 E6
Brackley DE56 179 F2
Brackley Dr DE21 220 E5
Brackley Gate DE7 192 A2
Brackmills Cl 7 NG19 136 E1
Bracknell Dr DE24 232 F5
BRADBOURNE 163 C6
Bradbourne Cl S43 97 C8
Bradbourne Ct DE22 218 E3
Bradbourne La DE6 152 E1
Bradbourne Rd
Bradbourne DE6 163 A7
Fenny Bentley DE6 162 E2
Fenny Bentley DE6 173 B8
Parwich DE6 162 F8
Bradbury Cl
Borrowash DE72 221 C1
Chesterfield S40 95 E3
Bradbury Dr S42 114 E4
Bradbury Pl S40 95 E3
Bradbury St S8 43 A6
Braddon Ave NG9 209 E1
Bradford Ct S81 63 F8
Bradford Rd DE45 125 C5
Bradgate Cl NG10 223 B4
Bradgate Croft S41 115 C7
Bradgate Ct DE23 231 E6
Bradgate Dr
Ripley DE5 169 B1
Ripley DE5 180 B8
Bradgate Pk View 10 DE73 244 F8
Brading Cl DE24 233 D5
BRADLEY 186 F8
Bradley CE Prim Sch DE6 186 F8
Bradley Cl
Birchover DE4 126 B1
6 Brimington S43 96 E8
Bradley Corner
Bradley DE6 174 F2
Bradley DE6 175 A2
Bradley Dr DE56 179 B4
Bradley La
Barlow S18 75 C4
Pilsley DE45 91 B3
Bradley St
Burton upon Trent DE15 254 E7
Derby DE22 218 E8
Sandiacre NG10 223 C5
Bradley View 5 DE6 173 D3
Bradley Way S43 96 E7
Bradmoor Gr DE73 233 B2
Bradshaw Ave DE55 170 E6
Bradshaw Cres SK6 23 A7
Bradshaw Croft DE56 178 E6
Bradshaw Dr DE56 191 C6
Bradshaw La
Old Brampton S42 93 E2
Stoney Middleton S32 70 E8
Tunstead Milton SK23 46 D5
Bradshaw Mdw DE65 227 C1
Bradshaw Rd
Marple SK6 23 A7
Staveley S43 97 B6
Bradshaw St NG10 236 B5
Bradshaw Way DE1 267 C2
Bradshaw Way Ret Pk DE1 267 B2
BRADWAY 56 C5
BRADWAY BANK 56 A6
Bradway Cl S17 56 B5
Bradway Dr S17 56 B5
Bradway Grange Rd S17 56 C5
Bradway Prim Sch S17 56 B5
Bradway Rd
Sheffield, Bradway S17 56 B5
Sheffield, Lower Bradway S17 56 C6
BRADWELL 51 B7
Bradwell CE Inf Sch S33 51 B7
Bradwell Cl
Derby DE3 217 E1
Dronfield S18 56 C1
Eastwood NG16 195 C8
Bradwell Ct 4 S40 95 D5
Bradwell Fold 10 SK13 9 E1
Bradwell Gr S45 131 D2
Bradwell Head Rd S33 51 A8
BRADWELL HILLS 51 B6
Bradwell Jun Sch S33 51 A7
Bradwell Lea 12 SK13 9 E1
Bradwell Pl S43 97 C7
Bradwell St 1 S2 43 B6
Bradwell Terr 11 SK13 9 E1
Bradwell Way DE56 179 B5
Braeburn Ct DE23 218 E2
Braefield Cl DE7 208 C5
Braemar Ave NG16 182 F1
Braemar Cl
Chesterfield S43 77 D4
11 Derby DE24 231 D3
Brafield Cl DE56 179 D4
Braidwood Way
Chesterfield S40 96 A1
Chesterfield S41 266 B1
BRAILSFORD 201 F7
Brailsford Ave
4 Gamesley SK13 9 E2
1 Swadlincote DE11 255 E5
Brailsford CE Prim Sch DE6 201 E7
Brailsford Cl 7 SK13 9 E2
Brailsford Gdns 8 SK13 9 E2
Brailsford Gn 5 SK13 9 E2
Brailsford Mews 6 SK13 9 E2
Brailsford Rd DE21 219 F8
Braintree Cl DE21 205 D2
Braithwell Cl DE22 204 F2
Bramah Edge Ct SK13 9 F7
Bramall Ct S2 43 A8
Bramall La S2 43 A8
Bramble Bank SK13 17 E8
Brambleberry Ct DE21 206 B3
Bramble Cl
Holmewood S44 116 F1
Long Eaton NG10 223 B2
Shirebrook NG20 119 E6
South Normanton DE55 160 B6
Bramble Ct
Burton upon Trent DE15 254 E6
4 Nottingham NG10 223 C6
Bramble Dr DE22 218 C4
Bramblehedge Dr DE23 231 E5
Bramble Mews 2 DE3 217 D1
Bramble St DE1 267 A3
Brambles The DE11 257 B1
Bramble Way
Denby Bottles DE56 180 A2
Kilburn DE56 179 F2
South Normanton DE55 159 F3
Bramblewick Dr DE23 231 A6
Bramble Wlk DE12 262 A3
Bramblewood 5 DE11 255 F6
Brambling Cres DE3 230 B6
Brambling Ct S41 96 C2
Brambly Cl DE12 265 E8
Bramell Cl DE14 253 F7
Bramfield Ave DE22 218 E3
Bramfield Ct DE22 218 E4
Bramham Rd SK6 23 A4
BRAMLEY 58 F3
Bramley Ave S13 44 F8
Bramley Cl
Derby DE21 206 C3
Sheffield S20 59 C7
Staveley S43 97 B5
Bramley Ct
Hatton DE65 227 C1
Kimberley NG16 195 F6
Bramley Dale DE11 255 F2
Bramley Hall Rd S13 44 F8
Bramley La
Baslow DE45 91 C7
Sheffield S13 44 F8
Bramley Mews S21 59 D3
Bramleymoor La S21 58 E1
Bramley New Pk S21 58 F3
Bramley Park Cl S13 44 F8
Bramley Pk S21 58 F3
Bramley Pk Rd S13 44 F8
Bramley Rd
Bramley-Vale S44 117 E1
Eckington S21 58 E1
4 Nottingham NG10 236 B5
Bramley St DE55 170 E7
BRAMLEY-VALE 117 E1
Bramley Vale Prim Sch S44 117 E1
Bramley View S21 58 F3
Bramlyn Cl S43 80 D5
Bramlyn Ct S43 80 D5
BRAMPTON 95 D2
Brampton Ave DE75 182 A2
Brampton Cl
Derby DE3 217 C3
Ilkeston DE7 194 F4
Brampton Ct
Belper DE56 179 D4

Brampton Ct *continued*
Chesterfield S40 . . . . 95 C2
Brampton Dr NG9 . . . 223 F5
Brampton House Mews
S40 . . . . 95 D3
Brampton Prim Sch
S40 . . . . 95 E3
Bramshill Rise S40 . . . 95 D1
Branch La S45 . . . . 132 F5
Brancliffe La S81 . . . . . 63 F8
Brandelhow Ct
DE21 . . . . 206 C3
Brandene Cl S44 . . . . . . 97 A3
Brandreth Dr NG16 . 195 A8
Brands Cl DE7 . . . . 194 F5
Brandside Ave SK17 . . 85 E1
Branklene Cl NG16 . 195 E7
Branksome Ave
DE24 . . . . 233 C7
Branksome Chine Ave
S41 . . . . 115 C8
Bransdale Ave
NG19 . . . . 136 E1
Bransdale Cl NG10 . . 236 B6
BRANSTON 253 F7
Branston Greens
DE16 . . . . 254 C7
Branston Rd
Branston DE14 . . . . . . 253 D7
Burton upon Trent
DE14 . . . . 254 C8
Tatenhill DE13, DE14 . 253 C8
Branton Cl S40 . . . . . 266 A1
BRASSINGTON 153 A1
Brassington Cl
Eastwood NG16 . . . . . . 195 B7
West Hallam DE7 . . . . . 207 E8
Youlgreave DE45 . . . . 125 C5
Brassington Cres
SK13 . . . . 9 D1
Brassington Ct [4]
NG19 . . . . 136 E4
Brassington La
Bradbourne DE4 . . . . . 163 D7
Brassington DE6 . . . . . . 152 E1
Clay Cross S42, S45 . . 131 C6
Wirksworth DE4 . . . . . 154 D1
Brassington Prim Sch
DE4 . . . . 153 A1
Brassington Rd
DE21 . . . . 205 F1
Brassington St S45 . 131 D4
Braybrook Cl DE55 . . . 169 F8
Brayfield Ave DE23 . 231 D8
Brayfield Rd DE23 . . 231 C8
Breach La
Barrow upon Trent
DE73 . . . . 244 E1
Hatton DE65 . . . . 227 D3
Scropton DE6 . . . . 226 C5
Breach Rd
Denby DE5 . . . . 181 A4
Heanor DE75 . . . . 194 A8
BREADSALL 205 E4
Breadsall CE Prim Sch
DE21 . . . . 205 E4
Breadsall Cl DE11 . . . 256 A7
Breadsall Ct DE7 . . . . 194 F3
BREADSALL
HILLTOP 205 D2
Breadsall Hill Top Prim
Sch DE21 . . . . 205 E1
Breadsall Rly Cutting
Nature Reserve*
DE7 . . . . 206 C4
Breamfield La
Washgreen DE4 . . . . . 155 C1
Wirksworth DE4 . . . . . 166 B8
Brearley Ave S43 . . . . . 77 D3
Brearley Ct S41 . . . . . . 77 B3
Brearley Hall S41 . . . . 77 C4
Brearley St S41 . . . . . . 77 C3
Brearley Wetland Nature
Reserve* S41 . . . . . . 77 C2
BREASTON 235 D7
Breaston Ind Est
DE72 . . . . 235 C7
Breaston La DE72 . . . 222 D3
Brechin Ct NG19 . . . . 136 B6
Breckbank NG19 . . . . 136 E1
BRECK END 35 C1
Breck La S21, S43 . . . . 78 C6
Breckland Rd S40,
S42 . . . . 114 B8
Brecknock Dr NG10. 236 A7
Brecon Cl
Chesterfield S40 . . . . 95 C5
Derby DE21 . . . . 220 E6
[6] Long Eaton NG10 . . 236 A8
Bredon Cl [7] NG10 . . 236 A8
Breedon Ave DE23 . . 231 D5
Breedon Hill Rd
DE23 . . . . 218 F3
BREEDON ON THE
HILL 252 E2
Breedon St NG10 . . . 223 C2
Brenden Ave DE55 . . . 170 C7
Brenden Cl DE55 . . . . 170 C8
Brendon Ave S40 . . . . . 95 C4
Brendon Cl SK13 . . . . . 17 A8
Brendon Ct [3] S40 . . . . 95 C4
Brendon Dr NG16 . . . . 195 F7
Brendon Way NG10 . 223 A1
Brent Cl
Chesterfield S40 . . . . 95 D5

Brent Cl *continued*
[5] Derby DE22 . . . . . . 218 A5
Brentford Dr DE22 . . 218 B6
Brentnall Cl NG10 . . 236 B7
Brentwood Ave S33 . . . 40 B3
Brentwood Rd S33 . . . . 40 B3
Bren Way DE65 . . . . . 228 E2
BRETBY 249 A3
Bretby Bsns Pk
DE15 . . . . 255 F8
Bretby Fairways
DE15 . . . . 248 F2
Bretby Heights
DE11 . . . . 255 F7
Bretby Hollow DE11 . 255 F7
Bretby Hts DE11 . . . . 256 A8
Bretby La
Bretby DE15 . . . . 248 E3
Burton upon Trent
DE15 . . . . 248 D2
Burton upon Trent
DE15 . . . . 248 F6
Newton Solney DE15 . 249 A6
Bretby Rd
Chesterfield S40 . . . . 95 A6
Swadlincote DE11 . . . . 255 F7
Bretby Sq DE23 . . . . . 231 C5
Bretby Stoneware Ind
Est DE11 . . . . 255 E8
Bretby View DE11 . . . 257 A4
Bretlands Way
DE15 . . . . 255 A6
BRETTON 71 A8
Bretton Ave
Bolsover S44 . . . . 99 C2
Derby DE23 . . . . 218 C2
Bretton Cl S40 . . . . 95 A5
Bretton Gr S12 . . . . 44 D3
Bretton Rd DE56 . . . . 179 E5
Brewery St
Chesterfield S41 . . . . . 266 C3
Kimberley NG16 . . . . . . 195 F6
Brewster Cl DE55 . . . 169 E7
Breydon Cl DE24 . . . . 232 D4
Breydon Ind Ctr
NG10 . . . . 236 F7
Brian Clough Way
Derby DE21 . . . . 220 C4
Risley DE72 . . . . 222 C3
Stapleford NG9 . . . . . . 223 D5
Briar Ave NG10 . . . . . 223 A3
Briar Briggs Rd S44 . . . 98 F3
Briar Cl
Alfreton DE55 . . . . 159 C3
Borrowash DE72 . . . . . 221 C2
[6] Buxton SK17 . . . . 85 C8
Chesterfield S41 . . . . 95 E5
Derby DE21 . . . . 220 B5
Shirebrook NG20 . . . . . 119 E2
Swadlincote DE11 . . . . 255 F5
Briardene Cl S40 . . . . . 94 F5
Briarfield Ave S12 . . . . 44 A3
Briarfield Cres S12 . . . 44 A2
Briarfield Rd S12 . . . . . 44 A3
Briar Gate NG10 . . . . 223 B1
Briargrove Rd SK22 . . . 24 C4
Briar Lea Cl DE24 . . . 231 F4
Briar Rd NG16 . . . . . . 195 B8
Briars Cl S21 . . . . 60 D5
Briarsgate DE22 . . . . 204 D2
Briar's La DE4 . . . . . . 168 A7
Briars Way DE5 . . . . . 180 D8
Briarthorn Cl SK6 . . . . 23 A3
Briar View S43 . . . . 96 E7
Briarwood Cres SK6 . . 23 A3
Briarwood Way
DE23 . . . . 231 C6
Brickbridge Rd SK6 . . . 23 A5
Brickbridge Rd South
SK6 . . . . 23 A5
Brickfields Cl DE4 . . . 155 A4
Brickfield St SK13 . . . . 10 B5
Brickhouse La S17 . . . 55 C8
BRICK HOUSES 55 D8
Brickhouse Yd S40 . . . 95 E3
Brick Kiln Dr S40 . . . 115 C8
Brickkiln La DE7 . . . . 206 C8
Brick-kiln La
Brailsford DE6 . . . . 186 F1
Hulland Ward DE6 . . . 175 C5
Brick Kiln La
Rolleston DE13 . . . . . . 240 A3
Washgreen DE4 . . . . . . 155 A1
Brick Kiln Rd DE15 . . 248 B5
Brick Row DE22 . . . . . 205 A1
Brick St DE1 . . . . 218 E6
Brick Works Dr DE5 . 180 F7
Brickyard Cotts
DE6 . . . . 185 D8
Brickyard La
Cuckney NG20 . . . . 101 F5
Kilburn DE56 . . . . 179 F2
Ripley DE5 . . . . 169 F1
South Normanton
DE55 . . . . 160 A6
Brickyard Rd DE56 . . 168 C5
Brickyard The DE7 . . 193 B1
Bricky Cl S43 . . . . 80 D5
Bridge Bank Cl [6]
S40 . . . . 95 D6
Bridge Cl
Swadlincote DE11 . . . 256 C2
Whitwell S80 . . . . 82 A5
Bridge End Ave
NG16 . . . . 171 F8
Bridge Farm [3]
DE13 . . . . 240 E1
BRIDGEFIELD 17 B7

Bridgefield [4] SK13 . . . 17 B8
Bridge Field DE72 . . 235 C7
Bridgefield Ct
[1] Belper DE56 . . . . . . 178 F4
Dove Holes SK17 . . . . . . 47 E1
Bridge Foot DE56 . . . . 178 F5
Bridge Gate DE1 . . . . . 267 B4
Bridge Hill DE56 . . . . 178 E5
Bridgeholme SK23 . . . . 47 A8
BRIDGEHOLM
GREEN 47 A8
Bridgeholm Mill
SK23 . . . . 47 A8
BRIDGEMONT 33 E2
Bridgemont SK23 . . . . . 33 E1
Bridgend Cl NG9 . . . . 223 D5
Bridgend Ct DE21 . . . 206 C2
Bridgeness Rd DE23 . 230 F6
Bridgeport Rd DE21 220 C6
Bridge St Ind Est
S45 . . . . 131 C4
Bridgeside DE13 . . . . 240 E1
Bridgeside Way
DE21 . . . . 220 D3
Bridge St
Bakewell DE45 . . . . . . 109 D6
Belper DE56 . . . . 178 F4
Bradwell S33 . . . . 51 A7
Burton upon Trent, Stretton
DE13 . . . . 240 E1
Buxton SK17 . . . . 85 C8
Chesterfield S40 . . . . . 266 B1
Clay Cross S45 . . . . . . 131 C3
Derby DE1 . . . . 267 A4
Ilkeston DE7 . . . . 194 F4
Killamarsh S21 . . . . 60 D6
Langley Mill NG16 . . . . 182 C3
Linton DE11 . . . . 261 E8
Long Eaton NG10 . . . . 223 D1
New Mills SK22 . . . . 24 C1
Pilsley S45 . . . . 132 C2
Sandiacre NG10 . . . . . . 223 C5
Swadlincote DE11 . . . . 256 C2
Tupton S42 . . . . 115 D1
Tutbury DE13 . . . . 239 C7
Whaley Bridge SK23 . . . 45 E7
Bridge The DE56 . . . . 191 A7
Bridge View
Belper DE56 . . . . 191 A7
Mayfield DE6 . . . . 184 D8
Bridgewater St S42 . 115 C1
Bridgeway SK23 . . . . . . 47 B4
Bridge Way S41 . . . . . . 76 D3
Bridge Yd Ave DE5 . . 169 E4
Bridgford Ave DE14 . . 253 F7
Bridgnorth Way
NG9 . . . . 223 E3
Bridgwater Cl DE24 . 233 C7
Bridle Cl DE73 . . . . . . 233 A1
Bridlegate La
Derby DE24 . . . . 233 D7
Elvaston DE24 . . . . 233 E6
Bridle La
Ripley, Greenwich
DE5 . . . . 169 E2
Ripley, Lower Hartshay DE5,
DE56 . . . . 169 A2
Somercotes DE55 . . . . . 170 B7
Swadlincote DE15 . . . . 255 A5
Bridle Rd
Bolsover S44 . . . . 80 B1
Staveley S43 . . . . 79 B2
Bridle Stile S20 . . . . . . 59 C7
Bridle Stile Cl S20 . . . . 59 C7
Bridle Stile Gdns S20 59 B7
Bridleway SK22 . . . . . . 24 D1
Bridleway The
NG19 . . . . 136 F1
Brierfield Way DE3 . 230 E8
Brierley Cl S43 . . . . 78 E1
BRIERLEY GREEN 34 B2
Brierley Pk SK23 . . . . . 34 B1
Brierley Rd
Ripley DE5 . . . . 181 A8
Stonebroom DE55 . . . . 146 F3
Unstone Green S18 . . . . 76 E6
Brierlow Bar
Chelmorton SK17 . . . . . 105 B8
Sterndale Moor SK17 . . 105 E5
Brierlow Rd
Brierlow Bar SK17 . . . 105 A8
Harpur Hill SK17 . . . . . . 85 F1
Brigden Ave DE24 . . . 232 E7
Brigg Inf Sch The
DE55 . . . . 160 B6
Brighstone Cl
DE24 . . . . 233 C5
BRIGHTGATE 142 B4
Brightman Ho DE11 . 256 B5
Bright Mdw S20 . . . . . . 60 A5
Brighton Rd DE24 . . . 232 F8
Bright Sq NG19 . . . . . 135 D2
Bright St
Derby DE22 . . . . 218 D5
Ilkeston DE7 . . . . 194 E3
Kimberley NG16 . . . . . . 195 E6
North Wingfield S42 . . 131 F6
South Normanton
DE55 . . . . 159 F5
Brightwater Cl
DE24 . . . . 232 E3
Brigmor Wlk DE22 . . . 218 C5
BRIMINGTON 96 F7
Brimington Cl NE7 . . . 194 F6
BRIMINGTON
COMMON 96 F5
Brimington Ct [6]
NG19 . . . . 136 E4

Brimington Jun Sch
S43 . . . . 96 D8
Brimington Manor Inf
Sch S43 . . . . 96 F5
Brimington Rd S41 . . . 96 B5
Brimington Road N
S41 . . . . 96 B8
Brimmesfield Cl S2 . . . 43 F7
Brimmesfield Dr S2 . . 43 E8
Brimmesfield Rd S2 . . 43 E7
Brincliffe Cl S40 . . . . . 95 B1
Brindle Way DE23 . . . 231 A5
Brindley Cl
Derby DE72 . . . . 245 B8
Sheffield S8 . . . . 43 A4
Brindley Cres S8 . . . . . 43 A4
Brindley Ct S21 . . . . . . 60 C6
Brindley Ho
Chesterfield S41 . . . . 96 B6
Long Eaton NG10 . . . . 223 B3
Brindley Rd [6] S41 . . . 96 A6
Brindley Way S43 . . . . 78 F2
Brindley Wlk DE24 . . 231 E2
BRINDWOODGATE . . . 75 D5
Brinkburn Cl S17 . . . . . 55 F6
Brinkburn Ct S17 . . . . . 55 F6
Brinkburn Dr S17 . . . . 55 F6
Brinkburn Vale Rd
S17 . . . . 55 F6
Brinks Road S33 . . . . . 39 A7
BRINSLEY 182 E7
Brinsley Headstocks
Nature Reserve*
NG16 . . . . 182 F6
Brinsley Hill NG16 . . 171 C2
Brinsley Prim Sch
NG16 . . . . 182 E8
Brisbane Cl NG19 . . . 136 C6
Brisbane Dr NG9 . . . . 209 F1
Brisbane Rd DE3 . . . . 217 F3
Briset Cl DE24 . . . . . . 231 E2
Bristol Ct DE11 . . . . . 255 F1
Bristol Dr DE3 . . . . . . 217 E2
Bristol Rd DE7 . . . . . . 194 E1
Britannia Ave DE5 . . 181 A7
Britannia Ct DE1 . . . . 267 B4
Britannia Dr DE13 . . . 240 D1
Britannia Mills Trading
Est SK23 . . . . 33 F1
Britannia Rd
Chesterfield S40 . . . . . 115 B7
Long Eaton NG10 . . . . 223 D1
Britannia Trad Est
SK23 . . . . 33 F1
Britland Edge Ave
DE21 . . . . 205 F3
Briton Lodge Cl
DE12 . . . . 262 F4
Brittain Dr DE5 . . . . . 170 A1
Brittain Pit DE5 . . . . . 170 B4
Brittain Pit Farm*
DE5 . . . . 170 A4
Brixham Ct [8] S41 . . . . 95 F8
Brizlincote La DE15 . 248 D1
Broadacre Way [3]
DE55 . . . . 148 B7
Broad Bank DE22 . . . 218 E8
BROADBOTTOM 16 A8
Broadbottom Prim Sch
SK14 . . . . 15 F8
Broadbottom Rd SK14 . 9 A3
Broadbottom Sta
SK14 . . . . 16 A8
Broadfield Rd S2 . . . . . 43 A7
Broadfields Cl DE22 . 218 F8
Broadgorse Cl S40 . . . 114 F7
Broadhey View SK22 . . 24 B1
BROADHOLM 179 A7
Broadholme La
DE56 . . . . 179 A8
Broad La
Brinsley NG16 . . . . 182 E8
Creswell S80 . . . . 82 D6
Elvaston DE72 . . . . 233 F4
Broadlands
Etwall DE65 . . . . 229 B5
Sandiacre NG10 . . . . . . 223 B3
South Normanton
DE55 . . . . 160 A4
Broadleaf Cl DE21 . . 205 E2
Broadley Rd S13 . . . . . 44 C7
Broadleys S45 . . . . . . 131 C3
Broadmeadow DE4 . 127 C3
Broad Oak Cl DE55 . . 169 E7
Broad Oak Dr
Brinsley NG16 . . . . 182 E8
New Brinsley NG16 . . . 171 D1
Stapleford NG9 . . . . . . 223 D6
Broadoaks Cl S41 . . . 266 C3
Broad Pavement
S40 . . . . 266 B3
Broad Pl S80 . . . . 82 C6
Broad Rushes DE74 . 247 B6
Broad St NG10 . . . . . . 236 D7
Broadstairs Rd [5]
NG9 . . . . 223 F2
Broadstone Cl DE21 206 A1
Broadstone La
DE73 . . . . 251 D4
Broadway
Derby DE22 . . . . 218 E8
Duffield DE56 . . . . 190 E2
Heanor DE75 . . . . 181 E1
Ilkeston DE7 . . . . 194 E3
Ripley DE5 . . . . 169 E1
Swanwick DE55 . . . . . . 169 F7
Broad Way
Kirk Ireton DE6 . . . . . . 176 B8

Broad Way *continued*
Kirk Ireton DE6 . . . . . . 176 C7
Broadway Ave DE5 . . 169 E1
Broadway Ct [4]
DE5 . . . . 169 E1
Broadway Dr [5]
DE5 . . . . 169 E1
Broadway La SK17 . . . . 87 F5
Broadway Lane SK17 . 88 A5
Broadway Park Cl
DE22 . . . . 218 E8
Broadway St DE14 . . 254 C8
Broad Wlk
Buxton SK17 . . . . 85 B7
Darley Dale DE4 . . . . . 127 C3
Brockhall Rise
DE75 . . . . 182 A1
Brockhill Ct [3] S43 . . . 96 F8
Brockholes
Glossop SK13 . . . . 16 F8
Glossop SK13 . . . . 17 A8
BROCKHURST 129 C6
Brockhurst La S45 . . . 129 C6
Brocklehurst Ave S8 . . 57 C8
Brocklehurst Ct S40 . . 95 D2
Brocklehurst Piece
S40 . . . . 95 D2
Brockley DE21 . . . . . . 220 E5
Brockley Ave S44 . . . . . 98 F6
Brockley La SK17 . . . . . 69 C3
Brockley Prim and Inf
Sch S44 . . . . 98 F7
Brocksford Ct DE6 . . . 224 F7
Brockway Cl S45 . . . 131 D2
BROCKWELL 95 E4
Brockwell Ct [5] S41 . . 95 D6
Brockwell Inf Sch
S40 . . . . 95 D4
Brockwell Jun Sch
S40 . . . . 95 D4
Brockwell La
Chesterfield S40 . . . . 95 E4
Cutthorpe S42 . . . . 94 F7
Cutthorpe S42 . . . . 95 A7
Brockwell Pl S40 . . . . . 95 E4
Brockwell Terr S40 . . . 95 E4
Brockwell The DE55 160 B4
Brodie Cl DE73 . . . . . 232 E2
Brome Head Way
S41 . . . . 95 D7
Bromley Ct DE7 . . . . . 209 A7
Bromley St DE22 . . . . 218 E7
Brompton Rd DE22 . . 217 F6
Bromyard Dr DE73 . . . 233 A3
Bronte Cl NG10 . . . . . 236 A7
Bronte Pl DE23 . . . . . 231 B8
Bronte St DE55 . . . . . 146 C5
Brook Ave DE55 . . . . . 159 B3
Brookbank Ave S40 . . . 95 D4
Brookbank Rd S43 . . . . 80 F4
Brook Bldgs S33 . . . . . . 51 A7
BROOK BOTTOM 23 F1
Brook Bottom Rd
SK22 . . . . 33 A8
Brookbridge Ct
DE1 . . . . 267 A4
Brook Cl
Alfreton DE55 . . . . 159 B3
[5] Belper DE56 . . . . . . 178 F3
Doveridge DE6 . . . . 224 C8
Findern DE65 . . . . 230 D1
Hatton DE65 . . . . 227 D2
Holymoorside S42 . . . . 113 D7
Long Eaton NG10 . . . . 236 E5
Quarndon DE22 . . . . . . 204 C4
Brook Cotts DE7 . . . . . 194 F3
Brook Ct
Elvaston DE72 . . . . 233 F4
Heanor NG16 . . . . 182 B2
Sheffield S8 . . . . 43 A5
Brookdale DE65 . . . . . 242 E1
Brookdale Ave SK6 . . . 23 A4
Brookdale Dr DE23 . . 231 A5
Brookdale Rd
Hartshorne DE11 . . . . . 257 A4
Swadlincote DE11 . . . . 256 F4
Brooke Dr S43 . . . . 96 F5
Brook End DE65 . . . . . 242 D3
Brooke St
Ilkeston DE7 . . . . 209 B6
Sandiacre NG10 . . . . . . 223 B5
Tibshelf DE55 . . . . 148 A6
BROOKFIELD 9 E3
Brookfield DE73 . . . . . 244 A6
Brookfield Ave
Chesterfield S40 . . . . 95 A2
Derby, Chaddesden
DE21 . . . . 220 B8
Derby, Littleover
DE23 . . . . 231 D6
Brookfield Cl
Codnor DE5 . . . . 170 B1
[1] Grassmoor S41 . . . . 115 F2
Brookfield Com Sch
S40 . . . . 95 A2
Brookfield Cotts
Acresford DE12 . . . . . . 265 C7
Bakewell DE45 . . . . 109 E8
Brookfield Cres
NG20 . . . . 119 E5
Brookfield Ind Est
Glossop SK13 . . . . 9 E3
Tansley DE4 . . . . 143 F4
Brookfield La DE45 . . 109 E8
Brookfield Mews [2]
NG10 . . . . 223 C6
Brookfield Mobile Home
Pk S42 . . . . 130 F5
Brookfield Pk S42 . . . 130 F5

Brookfield Prim Sch
Derby DE3 . . . . 217 D1
Derby DE3 . . . . 230 D8
Shirebrook NG20 . . . . . 119 F5
Brookfield Rd
Bolsover S44 . . . . 99 A1
Bolsover S44 . . . . 118 A8
Brookfields
Calver S32 . . . . 72 C1
Horsley DE56 . . . . 191 E7
Brookfields Bsns Pk
DE65 . . . . 229 D6
Brookfields Dr
DE21 . . . . 205 D4
Brookfield View Dr
S40 . . . . 95 B3
Brookfield Way
Heanor DE75 . . . . 182 B1
Tansley DE4 . . . . 143 F4
Brook Fold SK23 . . . . . . 47 C7
Brookhill S43 . . . . 80 F4
Brookhill Ave NG16 . 160 D4
Brookhill Ind Est
NG16 . . . . 160 E2
Brookhill La
Pinxton NG16 . . . . 160 D4
Pinxton NG16 . . . . 160 E5
Brookhill Leys Rd
NG16 . . . . 182 E1
Brookhill Rd NG16 . . 160 D2
Brookhill St NG9 . . . 223 D6
Brook Ho [3] DE1 . . . . 267 A4
Brookhouse Ct
Hayfield SK22 . . . . 25 D3
Whaley Thorns NG20 . 101 A1
Brook House Dr
SK17 . . . . 66 E3
Brook House Mews
Repton DE65 . . . . 242 D2
Swadlincote DE11 . . . . 256 A7
Brookhouse St
DE24 . . . . 232 D5
Brook La
Alfreton DE55 . . . . 159 B3
Clowne S43 . . . . 80 F4
Crich DE56 . . . . 168 C6
Hatton DE65 . . . . 227 C3
Ripley DE5 . . . . 180 D7
Scropton DE65 . . . . 226 E1
Sutton on the Hill
DE6 . . . . 228 A8
Brooklands SK17 . . . . . 85 C8
Brooklands Ave
Chapel-en-le-Frith
SK23 . . . . 47 D6
Heanor DE75 . . . . 181 F2
Wirksworth DE4 . . . . . 165 F7
Brooklands Bank
DE45 . . . . 109 E6
Brooklands Dr
Derby DE23 . . . . 231 C8
Glossop SK13 . . . . 17 B7
Brooklands Prim Sch
NG10 . . . . 236 D6
Brooklands Rd SK23 . . 47 D6
Brook Lea DE4 . . . . . . 143 C4
Brookleton DE45 . . . . 125 C5
Brooklime Dr S40 . . . 115 D2
Brooklyn Dr S40 . . . . . 95 D4
Brooklyn Pl [2] S8 . . . . 43 A5
Brooklyn Rd [5] S8 . . . . 43 A5
Brook Mdw SK13 . . . . . 10 E1
Brook Park East Road
NG20 . . . . 120 A2
Brook Rd
Borrowash DE72 . . . . . 221 B1
Elvaston DE72 . . . . 233 F4
Sheffield S8 . . . . 43 A5
Brooks Cl DE12 . . . . . . 262 F1
Brooks Hollow
DE21 . . . . 205 C7
BROOKSIDE 94 F2
Brookside
Ashbourne DE6 . . . . . . 173 D1
Beeley DE4 . . . . 111 B3
Bradwell S33 . . . . 51 A7
Burton upon Trent
DE15 . . . . 248 B5
Buxworth SK23 . . . . 46 A8
Derby DE1 . . . . 267 A4
Eastwood NG16 . . . . . . 182 F4
Glossop SK13 . . . . 17 B8
New Mills SK22 . . . . 24 E7
Whaley Bridge SK23 . . . 34 A1
Brook Side
Bakewell DE45 . . . . . . 109 D6
Belper DE56 . . . . 178 F3
Rolleston DE13 . . . . . . 240 B4
Brookside Ave
NG19 . . . . 136 C5
Brookside Bar S40 . . . . 94 F1
Brookside Cl
Derby DE1 . . . . 218 E7
Glossop SK13 . . . . 9 F4
Long Eaton NG10 . . . . 236 B8
Repton DE65 . . . . 242 D2
Brookside Glen
Chesterfield S40 . . . . 94 F1
Chesterfield S40 . . . . 95 A1
Brookside Gr SK17 . . . 84 D5
Brookside Ind Units
NG9 . . . . 223 D8
Brookside Meadows
DE6 . . . . 173 E1
Brookside Rd
Breadsall DE21 . . . . . . 205 E4
Chapel-en-le-Frith
SK23 . . . . 47 B5

Brookside Way NG17 148 F1
Brooks Rd S43 78 B4
Brook St
Clay Cross S45 131 A4
Derby DE1 267 A4
Glossop SK13 10 C1
Hartshorne DE11 250 A1
Hartshorne DE11 257 A7
Heage DE56 168 E1
Heanor DE75 181 B5
Nether Heage DE56 168 C2
Renishaw S21 79 C8
Swadlincote DE11 256 A3
Swadlincote, Newhall DE11 255 E6
Brook Vale S40 95 E2
Brookvale Ave
Codnor DE5 181 B8
Denby Village DE5 180 A2
Brookvale Cl 8 DE65 240 E8
Brook Vale Cl S18 75 D3
Brookvale Rd DE5 180 A2
Brook Vale Rd NG16 182 C2
Brookvale Rise DE5 180 A2
Brookview Ct S18 57 A3
Brook Walkway DE1 267 A4
Brook Wlk DE4 143 C4
Brook Yd S40 266 A3
Broom Ave
Pilsley S45 132 C2
Swanwick DE55 169 F7
Broombank Pk S41 76 D3
Broombank Rd S41 76 C3
Broom Bsns Pk S41 76 D3
Broom Cl
Belper DE56 178 E6
Chellaston DE73 232 F2
Chesterfield S41 95 D7
Derby, Sinfin DE73 231 E2
Duffield DE56 190 D3
Broom Dr S42 115 E2
Broome Acre DE55 160 C4
Broomfield Ave S41 115 D7
Broomfield Cl NG10 223 A5
Broomfield Cotts DE7 206 C5
Broom Gdns S43 96 F7
Broomhall Court S21 59 C3
Broomhill Ave DE7 209 A6
Broomhill Cl
Derby DE3 217 D3
Eckington S21 59 B3
Broomhill Cotts DE65 229 C2
Broomhill Ct S41 76 F2
Broomhill Rd S41 76 F2
Broomhills La DE65 242 D1
Broomhills The DE12 264 F7
Broom La DE6 175 E7
Broom's La DE6 226 B2
Broomyclose La ST14 210 A4
Broomy Dr DE6 201 E8
Brosscroft SK13 10 A6
Brosscroft Cl
Glossop SK13 10 A6
Hadfield SK13 10 A6
Brosscroft Village SK13 10 A6
BROUGH 39 D2
Brougham Ave NG19 135 D2
Brough La S33 51 C7
Brough Rd DE15 248 C3
Brough St DE22 218 D5
Broughton Ave DE23 218 D1
Broughton Cl
Church Broughton DE65 227 A8
Ilkeston DE7 194 D2
Somercotes DE55 170 C7
Broughton Close DE5 181 B8
Broughton Heath La DE65 227 D4
Broughton Rd S41 95 D7
Brow Cres S20 59 F7
Brown Ave NG19 136 B4
Brown Edge Close SK17 66 C1
Brown Edge Rd SK17 66 C2
Brownhill La HD9 3 B8
Brownhills La S42 130 C4
Brown Hills La S10 42 E8
Browning Cir DE23 231 F7
Browning Ct S40 95 B3
Browning Rd DE11 256 C5
Browning St DE23 231 F7
Brown La
Ashover S45 145 B8
Barton in Fabis NG11 237 E6
Dronfield S18 57 C3
Flash SK17 103 B3
Brownlow Rd NG19 135 F1
Brown's Flats NG16 195 F6
Brown's La DE56 191 D7
Brown's Rd NG10 236 E8
Broxtowe Ave NG16 195 D6
Brunel Parkway DE24 219 D3
Brunel Way
2 Castle Gresley DE11 255 E1
Church Gresley DE11 261 F8
Brun La DE6, DE22 217 B8
Brunnen The DE55 160 B4
Brunner Ave NG20 119 F3
Brunnister La DE6 149 D2
Brunswick Dr 2 NG9 223 E5
Brunswick St
Chesterfield S41 266 B4
Derby DE23 231 F8
Pilsley S45 132 C1
Brunswood Cl DE21 220 E5
Brunswood Ho DE4 143 B2
Brunswood La
Bradley DE6 187 B8
Bradley DE6 187 C7
Hulland Ward DE6 175 B2
Brunswood Rd DE4 143 B1
Brunt La DE11 256 F3
Brunton Cl DE3 217 C1
Brunts Sch The NG19 136 C1
Brushes SK15 4 A3
Brushes Rd SK15 4 A3
BRUSHES THE 76 F3
BRUSHFIELD 88 D4
Brushfield Gr S12 44 D4
Brushfield Rd S40 94 F5
Brussels Terr 1 DE7 194 E1
Bryant La DE55 160 A5
Bryn Lea S41 96 C2
Brynsmoor Rd NG16 182 E7
Bryony DE14 254 B8
Bryony Cl
Derby DE21 206 A1
Killamarsh S21 60 B6
Bryony Way NG19 136 F4
Bryony Wlk 7 DE24 231 C3
BUBNELL 91 D6
Bubnell Ct 15 S40 95 D5
Bubnell Rd
Baslow DE45 91 D6
Dronfield S18 56 E2
Buchanan St DE1 267 B4
Buchan St DE24 232 D7
Buckdale La DE4 141 A6
Buckden Cl S40 95 D4
Buckfast Cl DE55 169 E8
Buckford La DE65, DE73 242 E8
Buckhazels La
Kedleston DE6 202 F6
Mackworth DE6, DE22 203 B7
Buckingham Ave DE21 219 D8
Buckingham Cl
2 Dronfield S18 56 D2
Mansfield Woodhouse NG19 136 E5
Swanwick DE55 170 A7
Buckingham Ct
Burton upon Trent DE15 248 C3
Sandiacre NG10 223 A3
Buckingham Dr
Church Gresley DE11 261 F8
Heanor DE75 181 C2
Buckingham Ho DE65 228 D1
Buckingham Rd NG10 223 A4
Buckland Cl DE1 218 E6
Buckland Ct 18 S41 95 F8
Buckland Gr SK14 15 A8
Buckleather La S18 74 C1
Buckley Cl
Woodville DE11 256 F2
Woodville DE11 257 B1
Buckley Dr DE4 143 D7
Buckminster Cl DE21 205 F2
Buckminster Rd DE7 208 C4
Buckthorn Cl
Derby DE24 231 C3
Hillstown S44 118 D8
Buckthorn Dr
Bolsover S44 99 D1
Hillstown S44 118 D8
Buck Wood View S14 43 D5
Buddleia Gro 2 DE3 217 D5
Budget La S44 118 E6
Budle Ave DE23 231 E1
Bullace Ct 3 NG19 136 E1
BULLBRIDGE 168 B5
Bullbridge Hill DE56 168 B5
Buller St
Derby DE23 218 E2
Ilkeston DE7 209 A6
BULL FARM 135 C2
Bullfinch Cl DE56 179 B2
Bullhill La DE56 176 E3
Bullhurst La DE6 188 F4
Bulling La DE4 156 F1
Bullivant Ave S80 100 C8
Bull La
Matlock DE4 143 D6
Yeaveley DE6 199 C5
Bull Mews Cotts DE4 143 C5
Bullock Cl NG19 136 B5
Bullock La NG16, DE55 170 E5
Bullpit La DE56 205 A8
Bull's Head Row DE73 252 E6
Bullsmoor DE56 179 C4
Bulltor Lane SK17 88 B5
Bumpmill La DE55 146 B1
Bun Alley DE45 91 C3
Bungalows The
Chesterfield, Brampton S40 95 D3
Chesterfield, Hady S41 266 C2
1 Chesterfield, Newbold S41 95 E7
1 Chesterfield, Whittington Moor S41 96 A8
Clowne S43 81 A4
Elton DE4 140 D6
Killamarsh S21 60 C6
New Mills SK22 24 D1
Stonebroom DE55 146 E3
Bunkers Hill S21 60 E6
Bunker's Hill S80 62 D8
Buntingbank Cl DE55 159 F4
Bunting Cl
Chesterfield S42 95 B1
Derby DE3 218 A3
Ilkeston DE7 208 C6
Sheffield S8 43 B2
Buntingfield La S45 129 B7
Bunting Ho S41 77 A3
Bunting Nook S8 43 B1
Bunting Way DE65 242 A5
Bunyan Cres DE55 146 F3
Bunyan Green Rd NG16 171 D7
BURBAGE 84 E6
Burbage Bank SK13 9 E2
Burbage Cl
Belper DE56 179 D5
Dronfield S18 56 D2
Burbage Ct 8 S40 95 D5
Burbage Gr
Gamesley SK13 9 E2
Sheffield S12 44 D5
Burbage Heights SK17 84 B3
Burbage Pl DE24 232 F7
Burbage Prim Sch SK17 84 F6
Burbage Rd S43 97 D8
Burbage Way
Buxton SK17 84 F6
Gamesley SK13 9 E2
Burch Pl S32 71 E6
Burcot Cl DE7 207 E8
Burdekin Cl SK23 47 C6
Burdett Way DE65 242 D3
Burdock Cl DE21 205 E2
Burgess Cl S41 115 D7
Burghley Cl DE73 232 F2
Burghley Way DE23 230 E6
Burke Dr DE55 170 D8
Burkitt Dr S43 79 B3
Burland Green La DE6 189 B4
Burleigh Cres DE55 169 F8
Burleigh Dr DE22 218 F8
Burleigh St 1 DE7 194 F1
Burley Cl S40 115 A7
Burley Dr DE22 204 E7
Burley Hill
Allestree DE22 204 F7
Duffield DE22 205 A7
Burley La DE22 204 E7
Burlington Ave NG20 119 F6
Burlington Cl
Breaston DE72 235 D8
Sheffield S17 55 E7
Burlington Dr NG19 135 F2
Burlington Glen S17 55 E7
Burlington Gr S17 55 E7
Burlington Rd
Buxton SK17 85 A7
Derby DE22 217 F6
Sheffield S17 55 E7
Burlington St S40 266 B3
Burlington Way DE3 217 D1
Burlow Ave SK17 85 C3
Burlow Rd SK17 85 D2
Burma Rd S45 113 F1
Burnaby St DE24 232 F8
Burnage Ct DE22 218 F4
BURNASTON 229 F5
Burnaston Cl S18 56 C1
Burnaston Ct 2 NG19 136 E4
Burnaston La DE65 229 D5
Burnbridge Rd S41 77 C3
Burncroft DE7 207 E7
Burnell Cl DE55 159 C4
Burnell St S43 96 F8
Burnett La DE4 143 A8
Burney La DE73 252 C2
Burnham Cl DE7 207 D8
Burnham Dr DE3 217 C2
Burns Ave NG19 136 C2
Burns Cl
Chesterfield S40 114 F7
Derby DE23 231 B8
Burns Dr
Dronfield S18 76 C8
Grassmoor S42 115 E3
Burnshaw St DE55 146 C5
Burnside
Glossop SK13 9 F4
Rolleston DE13 240 B4
Burnside Ave
Chapel-en-le-Frith SK23 47 C7
Sheffield S8 43 A5
Shirland DE55 146 D1
Burnside Cl DE24 231 D3
Burnside Close DE13 240 B4
Burnside Ct DE24 233 A8
Burnside Dr
Derby DE21 220 F4
Mansfield NG19 135 E2
Burnside St DE24 233 A8
Burns St
Heanor DE75 181 D2
Ilkeston DE7 208 E8
BURNTHEATH 228 C4
Burntheath La DE65 228 C4
Burnt House Rd
Heanor DE75 181 D1
1 Heanor DE75 193 E8
Burnt Oaks Cl NG19 136 D3
Burn Wood Cl DE3 217 D6
Burre Cl DE45 109 E6
BURRFIELDS 47 C6
Burrfields Rd SK23 47 B6
Burr La DE7 194 F1
Burrowfield Mews DE21 220 F2
Burrows Cl DE5 169 E4
Burrows La
Brailsford DE6 201 F2
Middleton DE4 154 D5
Over Burrows DE6 202 B5
Burrows The DE11 255 F5
Burrows Wlk DE1 267 B2
Burrs Wood Croft S41 95 B7
Bursar Way NG10 223 C3
Bursdon Cl S41 77 A1
Burton Close Dr DE45 109 E4
Burton Close Mews DE45 109 D4
Burton Edge DE45 109 D4
Burton Rd
Ashby-de-la-Zouch LE65 257 E1
Burnaston DE65 230 B2
Burton upon Trent DE14 254 B7
Castle Gresley DE11 255 D2
Coton in the Elms DE12 260 D3
Derby DE23 218 C1
Findern DE3 230 D4
Findern DE65 230 B2
Oakthorpe DE12 265 D6
Overseal DE11 262 B1
Overseal DE12 262 A4
Overseal DE12 262 A5
Repton DE15, DE65 242 B2
Rosliston DE12 260 C6
Rosliston DE16 254 C1
4 Swadlincote DE11 256 B7
Swadlincote DE11 256 D6
Ticknall DE73 250 F4
Willington DE65 241 F7
Burton St
Heanor DE75 181 E2
Tutbury DE13 239 C6
Wingerworth S42 115 C2
BURTON UPON TRENT 254 D8
Burwell Cl SK13 17 A8
Burwell Ct NG19 136 E4
Bury Hill DE4 166 F8
Buscott Dr DE6 185 B8
Bushey Wood Gr S17 55 D7
Bushey Wood Rd S17 55 E6
Bushton La DE13 239 B2
Bushy Cl NG10 236 B6
Business Pk The NG19 135 D6
Buskeyfield La NG20 101 F4
Butcher's La DE4 127 F4
Bute St SK13 10 E3
Bute Wlk DE21 219 C7
Butler Cres NG19 135 D2
Butler Way S21 60 C6
Butterbur Close DE24 231 C2
Buttercup Ave DE12 262 E1
Buttercup Cl
5 Burton upon Trent DE15 248 A1
Glossop SK13 17 E8
Butterfield Cres DE55 169 F7
Butterfield La DE55 145 E1
Butterfly Gardens DE11 256 F1
Butterfly Pl 2 DE7 194 F8
Butterhall Cl S80 82 A5
BUTTERLEY
Ripley 169 F3
Tansley 144 F5
Butterley Cl NE7 194 F6
Butterley Croft Bsns Ctr DE5 180 E8
Butterley Ct NG16 170 F4
Butterley Hill DE5 169 E3
Butterley La
Ashover DE4, S45 144 E5
Ripley DE5 169 D4
Butterley Lodge NG16 170 F4
Butterley Mews DE5 169 E2
Butterley Row DE5 169 E4
Butterley Sta★ DE5 169 E4
Buttermead Cl NG9 209 D2
Buttermere Cl
Chesterfield S41 95 D7
1 Long Eaton NG10 223 A2
Buttermere Ct NG19 136 D3
Buttermere Dr
Derby DE22 204 E3
Dronfield S18 56 E1
Buttermilk La S44 98 D4
Butterpot La DE6 215 D3
Butterton Cl DE7 209 A7
Butterton Dr 6 S40 95 A5
Butterwick Cl
Derby DE23 231 E5
Forest Town NG19 136 F1
Butt Hill S80 81 F6
Butt Hill Cl S80 81 F6
Butt La
Blackfordby DE11 257 A1
Mansfield Woodhouse NG19 136 C2
Buttonoak Dr DE73 233 A3
Butts Cl DE7 209 A4
Butts Dr DE4 143 D4
Butts Hill S17 55 D4
Butts Rd
Ashover S45 129 F3
Bakewell DE45 109 D5
Darley Dale DE4 127 B3
Great Longstone DE45 89 F4
Butt St NG10 223 B5
Butts Terr DE45 109 D5
Butts The DE56 179 A3
Butts View DE45 109 D5
BUXTON 85 A7
Buxton and Leek Coll SK17 85 D3
Buxton Ave DE75 193 F7
Buxton Baths 9 SK17 85 B8
Buxton Cl
17 Gamesley SK13 9 E2
Swadlincote DE11 256 A7
Buxton Com Sch SK17 85 A6
Buxton Ct DE7 194 D1
Buxton Ctry Pk★ SK17 84 E6
Buxton Dr
Derby DE3 217 E3
Little Eaton DE21 191 D2
Buxton Gn DE75 193 F7
Buxton Hospl SK17 85 C5
Buxton Inf Sch SK17 85 C7
Buxton Jun Sch SK17 85 B6
Buxton Mews SK13 9 E2
Buxton Mus & Art Gall★ 17 SK17 85 B7
Buxton New Rd SK11 83 A6
Buxton Old Rd SK12 32 E4
Buxton Opera House★ SK17 85 B7
Buxton Raceway★ SK17 104 B7
Buxton Rd
Alsop en le Dale DE6 150 D1
Alstonefield DE6 149 B5
Ashbourne DE6 173 B2
Ashford in the Water DE45 108 E8
Bakewell DE45 109 B7
Bridgemont SK23 33 E2
Castleton S33 38 B2
Chapel-en-le-Frith SK17, SK23 47 E5
Chinley SK23 34 F2
Derby DE21 219 F8
Dove Holes SK17 66 F8
Earl Sterndale SK17 105 A2
Flash SK17 102 D1
Hartington upper Quarter SK11 83 F2
Hartington upper Quarter SK17 103 C6
High Lane SK12 32 A6
Horwich End, New Horwich SK23 45 E6
Longnor SK17 121 B7
Mansfield NG19 135 D1
New Mills SK22, SK23 33 C4
New Smithy SK23 35 A1
Tideswell SK17 69 C3
Tissington DE6 161 E7
Tissington DE6 162 A4
Whaley Bridge SK23 33 E1
Buxton Road W SK12 32 B5
Buxton Spa Swimming Pool SK17 85 A7
Buxton Sta SK17 85 B8
Buxton Terr SK14 9 D5
Buxton Wlk 9 SK13 9 E1
BUXWORTH 34 A1
Buxworth Prim Sch SK23 34 A1
Buzzard La 8 DE73 244 F8
Byeways La DE4 154 C8
Byfield Cl DE21 206 B2
Byng Ave 2 DE23 231 F7
Byron Ave
Alfreton DE55 159 B4
Burton upon Trent DE15 254 E7
Long Eaton NG10 223 B3
Mansfield Woodhouse NG19 136 C2
Byron Cl
Dronfield S18 76 C7
Grassmoor S42 115 E3
Byron Cres NG16 195 C4
Byron Ct NG9 209 E2
Byron Gr DE55 146 F3
Byron Lodge SK17 85 C6
Byron Rd
Chesterfield S40 115 A8
Swadlincote DE11 256 C6
Byron St
Buxton SK17 85 C6
Chesterfield S40 266 C1
Derby DE23 218 F2
Ilkeston DE7 194 F1
Shirebrook NG20 119 E4
Shirland DE55 146 C1
Bywell La DE56 179 F1

C

Cabot Cl DE56 179 E5
Cacklehill La DE6 184 C2
Cadeby Ct DE55 170 C6
Cadgwith Dr DE22 204 E3
Cadley Hill Ind Est DE11 255 E2
Cadley Hill Rd DE11 255 E3
Cadley La
Castle Gresley DE11 255 C2
Cauldwell DE16 254 F1
Cadman Ct S20 59 D6
Cadman Rd S12 44 C6
Cadman St S20 59 D6
Cadwell Cl DE24 233 D6
Caerhays Ct DE24 231 D3
Caernarfon Cl DE55 170 A7
Caernarvon Cl
Chesterfield S40 95 C1
Derby DE21 220 F5
Caernarvon Rd S18 76 B8
Caesar St DE1 219 B7
Cairn Dr
Buxton SK17 85 D4
Chesterfield S43 77 D4
Cairngorm Cl S43 77 D4
Cairngorm Dr DE24 231 D3
Cairns Cl
Burton upon Trent DE15 248 C3
Derby DE3 217 E3
Cairnsmore Cl 4 NG10 223 A1
Caithness Cres DE22 218 B4
Caldene Terr SK23 45 E7
Calder Cl
Derby DE22 204 E3
Hilton DE65 228 D1
Calderdale Dr NG10 236 A6
Caldermill Dr DE21 206 A2
Caldey Rd S18 76 A8
CALDWELL 260 E7
Cale Rd SK22 33 D8
Calesdale Cl SK17 85 B5
Calf Croft S80 82 A5
Calgary Cres DE15 248 D3
Calico Cres SK15 4 A6
Calico Drive SK6 23 C2
Calico La SK23 33 D4
CALIFORNIA 218 D3
California Gdns DE22 218 C4
California La S43 80 A7
CALKE 251 E1
Calke Abbey★ LE65 251 D2
Calke Ave NG17 148 E2
Calke National Nature Reserve★ DE73 251 C3
Calke Rd DE73 252 A6
Calke Rise DE5 169 F1
Calladine Cl DE75 181 D2
Calladine La
Horsley Woodhouse DE7 192 D6
Shottle DE56 177 C5
Callan's La
Ashby-de-la-Zouch LE65 258 E5
Heath End LE65 258 D7
Calley Ave NE7 194 F6
Callin Low DE45 124 C5
CALLOW 165 B4
Callow Dr S14 43 D5
Callow Hill Way DE23 231 A7
Callow La DE4, DE6 165 C5
Callow Mount S14 43 D5
Callow Pl S14 43 D5
Callow Rd S14 43 C5

Callywhite Ind Est S18 57 C1
Callywhite La S18 57 C1
CALOW 96 F1
Calow Brook Dr S41 115 E8
Calow CE Prim Sch S44 96 F3
Calow Cl SK13 9 E2
Calow Gn SK13 9 E2
CALOW GREEN 116 A8
Calow La
Calow S41, S44 96 F1
Chesterfield S41 115 E8
Calow Lane Ind Est S41 115 E8
Calstock Cl S40 95 A4
CALTON LEES 110 F5
Calton View DE45 109 D5
CALVER 72 C2
Calver Ave S42 132 A7
Calver Bank 8 SK13 9 D2
Calver Bridge S32 72 D2
Calver Cl
Belper DE56 179 B6
Derby DE21 205 E3
10 Gamesley SK13 9 E2
Calver Cres S43 97 D8
Calver Fold 6 SK13 9 D2
Calver Mews SK13 9 E2
Calver Mill La S32 72 D2
Calver Pl 7 SK13 9 D2
Calver Rd DE45 91 D6
CALVER SOUGH 72 C2
Calver St NG19 136 E4
Calvert Cl NG16 182 B3
Calverton Cl DE24 232 E3
Calvert St
Derby DE1 219 B4
Derby DE1 267 D2
Calvin Cl DE24 233 A5
Calwich Bank ST14 183 E4
Calwich Cl DE11 256 D3
Camberwell Ave DE22 218 A6
Camberwell Ct 10 S43 78 B3
Camborne Cl DE21 205 E1
Cambrian Cl 1 S40 95 D6
Cambrian Way DE11 256 A3
Cambria Rd NG19 135 C4
Cambridge Cres
Bramley-Vale S44 117 E1
Stapleford NG9 209 D2
Cambridge Ct 13 S8 43 B6
Cambridge Lodge 14 S8 43 B6
Cambridge Rd
1 Brimington S43 96 F8
Sheffield S8 43 B6
Cambridge St
Blackwell DE55 147 E1
Derby, Rose Hill DE23 219 B2
Derby, Spondon DE21 220 E3
Camdale Rise S12 44 F1
Camdale View S12 44 F1
Camden St DE22 218 D4
Camellia Cl DE3 217 D3
Camelot Cl DE13 240 E2
Camelot Ct NG19 135 D1
Cameron Cl DE15 248 B1
Cameron Rd DE23 231 F8
Camerory Way S43 77 D5
Cam Height S32 41 F2
Camlough Wlk S41 266 C2
Camms Cl S21 59 D4
Campbell Ct S43 77 D4
Campbell Dr S43 78 B4
Campbell St
Belper DE56 178 F3
Derby DE24 232 D7
Langley Mill NG16 182 C4
Camphil La SK17 51 E2
Campion Cl
Shirebrook NG20 119 D3
Wingerworth S42 115 A1
Campion Dr S21 60 C6
Campion Hill
5 Castle Donington DE74 246 F4
Castle Donington DE74 247 A4
Campion Rd DE11 256 F4
Campion St DE22 218 D5
Campsie Ct 8 DE24 231 D3
Camp St DE1 219 B7
Camp Wood Cl DE21 205 C7
Canada St DE56 179 A2
Canal Bank DE72 235 A1
Canal Bridge
Killamarsh S21 60 D6
Willington DE65 242 A6
Canal Cl DE56 168 C5
Canalgate Pk DE21 220 F3
Can Alley DE6 197 D6
Canal Mews S41 266 B4
Canalside S21 60 B1
Canal Side
Ambergate DE56 167 F5
Ilkeston DE7 194 F2
Ilkeston DE7 195 A2
Swarkestone DE73 244 E7
Canal Side *continued*
Whaley Bridge SK23 33 F1
Canalside Cres S40 96 C7
Canal St
Derby DE1 267 C2
Ilkeston DE7 195 A1
Long Eaton NG10 223 C1
Marple SK6 23 A6
Sandiacre NG10 223 C6
Whaley Bridge SK23 45 E8
Canal View La DE12 262 F3
Canal Wharf S41 96 B5
Canberra Cl
6 Castle Donington DE74 246 F4
Derby DE3 217 E2
Stapleford NG9 209 F1
Candlemass Ct NG19 136 D2
CANHOLES 84 E5
Cannell Cl S45 131 B4
Canner Cl DE11 257 A2
Canning Mews 1 DE7 208 F7
Cannock Ct DE22 218 C3
Cannock Way NG10 237 A7
Cannon Fields S32 52 F8
Cannon St SK14 9 C5
Canon's Wlk DE22 204 F2
Cantelupe Gdns NG16 195 C7
Cantelupe Rd DE7 209 A8
Canterbury Cl
Chesterfield S40 115 A8
Duffield DE56 190 E3
Mansfield Woodhouse NG19 136 C5
Canterbury Dr DE23 230 F5
Canterbury Pl SK23 47 A5
Canterbury Rd
Burton upon Trent DE15 248 C3
Sheffield S8 43 B5
Wirksworth DE4 165 F8
Canterbury St DE21 219 E8
Canterbury Terr DE4 165 F8
Cantley Cl DE24 232 D3
Cantley Rd DE55 170 C6
Cantrell Cl S43 96 D8
Canyon Mdw S43 81 E2
Cape Court DE24 219 E2
Capel Rise S43 96 D8
Capstan Cl
Swadlincote DE11 256 E1
10 Woodville DE11 256 E1
Capthorne Cl S40 94 F5
Caraway Dr
Burton upon Trent DE14 254 A8
Shirebrook NG20 119 D2
Cardale Rd NG19 135 C4
Cardales Cl DE65 230 D2
Cardean Cl DE1 219 B7
Carder Gn SK17 121 B6
Cardigan St DE21 219 D7
Cardinal Cl 1 DE21 205 F2
Cardinshaw Rd DE4 143 E8
Cardlemere La SK17 138 F2
Cardrona Cl DE21 205 F2
Cardwell Ave S13 44 F7
Cardwell Dr S13 44 F7
Carfield Ave S8 43 B5
Carfield La S8 43 C5
Carfield Pl S8 43 B5
Carfield Prim Sch S8 43 B5
Carisbrooke Dr 2 DE13 240 E1
Carisbrooke Gdns DE23 231 C6
Carlin Cl DE72 235 E8
Carlin St S13 44 E6
Carlisle Ave DE23 231 B8
Carlisle Cl S41 76 E3
Carlisle Gr SK17 85 A8
Carlisle Rd SK17 84 F8
Carl Moult Ho DE11 256 A2
Carlton Ave
Derby DE24 232 E4
Northwood DE4 127 A6
Carlton Cl
Clay Cross S45 131 D2
Heanor DE75 182 A3
Sheffield S20 59 C6
Carlton Dr DE24 232 E3
Carlton Gdns DE24 232 E4
Carlton La 2 DE65 227 D2
Carlton Mews S2 43 E7
Carlton Rd
Chesterfield S40 115 A6
Derby DE23 218 E2
Long Eaton NG10 236 B5
Carlton St NG19 136 C1
Carlton Walk DE24 220 A1
Carlton Wlk DE24 233 A8
Carlyle Gdns DE75 181 E3
Carlyle Inf Sch DE23 231 B8
Carlyle Pl DE75 181 D3
Carlyle Rd
Stonebroom DE55 146 F3
Stretton DE55 147 A3
Carlyle St
Derby DE24 231 F5
Heanor DE75 181 D3
Carlyon Gdns S40 114 F8
Carnaby Cl DE22 218 A5
Carnarvon Ct DE15 249 C2
Carnarvon Rd NG17 148 F2
Carnation Rd NG20 119 C3
Carnation Way DE6 185 A8
Carnegie St DE23 232 A8
Carnfield Cl DE55 159 F4
Carnfield Hall* DE55 159 D5
Carnfield Hill DE55 159 D5
Carnforth Cl
Derby DE3 217 E1
Stapleford NG9 223 D5
Carnival Way DE74 247 B4
Carnoustie Ave S40 114 C8
Carnoustie Cl DE3 217 F2
Carnworth Dr S45 131 C5
Carol Cres DE21 219 F5
Caroline Cl DE24 233 D7
Caroline Ct
Hope S33 38 F4
Ilkeston DE7 209 A6
Carpenter Ave
Mansfield NG19 135 D2
Mastin Moor S43 79 B3
Carpenter Cl DE15 248 C2
Carpenter Croft S12 44 C6
Carpenter Gdns S12 44 C6
Carpenter Mews S12 44 C6
Carper La DE6 187 F2
Carradale Gr DE73 232 E1
Carr Bank SK13 17 E8
Carr Brook Cl SK23 45 E5
Carr Brook Way DE73 252 C8
Carr Brow SK6 32 A7
Carr Cl DE55 160 A7
Car Rd S18 74 B6
Carr Farm Close SK13 17 E8
Carrfield Ave
Beeston NG9 223 F2
Long Eaton NG10 223 F1
Carrfield Ct 1 S8 43 B6
Carrfield Dr S8 43 B6
Carrfield La S8 43 B6
Carrfield Rd S8 43 B6
Carrfields DE7 192 C7
Carrfield St S8 43 B6
Carrhouse La SK14 9 C4
Carriage Dr The SK13 9 F5
Carriers Mdw SK23 47 B7
Carriers Rd DE65 241 D6
Carrington Cl NG9 209 A5
Carrington Court Ind Est DE1 218 E5
Carrington St
Derby DE1 219 B4
Derby DE1 267 C2
Carr La
Brackenfield DE55 145 D3
Crich DE4 156 E2
Dronfield S18 56 C2
Hollinsclough SK17 104 E1
Longnor SK17 121 A8
Matlock DE4 143 E2
Scarcliffe S44 117 F7
South Normanton DE55 160 A7
Stalybridge SK15 4 A7
Thornhill S33 39 F5
Wingerworth S42 115 C2
Carr Lane Mews S18 56 D2
Carrock Ave DE75 182 B1
Carron Cl DE24 231 E4
Carr Rd SK17 84 D5
Carrs Cl DE74 247 A3
CARR VALE 117 F8
Carr Vale Rd S44 98 F1
Carr Wood DE5 169 E2
Carrwood Ind Est S41 76 C4
Carr Wood Nature Reserve* DE5 169 E3
Carrwood Rd
Chesterfield S41 76 C4
Renishaw S21 79 B8
CARSINGTON 164 E7
Carsington Cl S40 95 B5
Carsington Cres DE22 204 D1
Carsington Ct 3 NG19 136 E3
Carsington Ho 1 DE22 204 D2
Carsington & Hopton CE Prim Sch DE4 164 E7
Carsington Mews DE22 204 E1
Carsington Rd DE65 240 E8
Carsington Water Visitor Ctr* DE6 164 C4
Carson Croft DE4 143 C6
Carson Mount S12 44 B3
Carson Rd DE21 220 B6
Carter Cl NG10 236 B6
Carter Grange 11 S8 43 B6
Carterhall La S12 44 C2
Carterhall Rd S12 44 B2
Carter La
Shirebrook NG20 119 E4
Shirebrook, Warsop Vale NG20 120 C4
Carter Lane E DE55 160 C6
Carter Lane W
Shirebrook NG20 119 D4
South Normanton DE55 160 C5
Carter Pl S8 43 B6
Carter Rd
Beeston NG9 223 F2
Sheffield S8 43 A6
Carter St DE24 232 D6
CARTLEDGE 75 B7
Cartledge La S18 75 A7
Cartmel Cl S18 56 E1
Cartmel Cres S41 95 E8
Cartmel Place DE3 217 F3
Cart Rd DE55 157 F4
Cartworth Moor Rd HD9 3 E8
Cartwrightcl DE73 245 A1
Cartwright La DE55 160 E7
Cartwright St S81 63 F7
Car Vale Dr S13 44 C8
Car Vale View S13 44 C8
Carver Cl S26 61 E6
Carver Way S26 61 E6
Cary Gr S2 43 F8
Cary Rd
Eckington S21 59 B3
Sheffield S2 44 A8
Cascade Gr DE23 231 A7
Cascades Cl 5 DE11 256 C4
Caspian Close NG19 136 F2
Casson Ave DE24 233 A6
Casson Dr S26 61 E7
Casson St NG16 170 F4
Castings Rd DE23 232 B8
Castlebeck Ave S2 44 C8
Castlebeck Dr S2 44 C8
Castle Cl
Bakewell DE45 109 E6
Borrowash DE72 221 D2
Stretton DE13 240 E2
Castle Coll Arthur Mee Ctr 3 NG9 223 D7
Castlecraig Ct DE24 231 E2
Castle Croft
Derby DE24 233 D5
Linton DE11 261 E8
Castle Ct
Eastwood NG16 182 A1
Elvaston DE72 234 A5
Glossop SK13 10 A4
Tutbury DE13 239 C7
Castledale Croft S2 44 B8
Castledale Gr S2 44 C8
Castledale Pl S2 44 B8
CASTLE DONINGTON 247 C3
Castle Donington Com Coll DE74 247 B3
Castle Dr
Bakewell DE45 109 E7
Codnor NG16 181 E8
Somercotes DE55 170 D8
Castle Edge Rd
New Mills SK22 24 B2
Stockport SK6 24 A7
Castle Farm S81 62 E7
Castlefields NG16 170 F3
Castlegate La SK17, DE45 89 C5
Castle Gn S44 118 B7
CASTLE GRESLEY 255 E1
Castle Hayes La DE13 239 A5
Castle Hill
Castle Donington DE74 247 B4
Duffield DE56 190 E4
Eckington S21 59 D4
Findern DE65 230 D1
Glossop SK13 10 E2
Holmesfield Common S17 74 F8
Tutbury DE13 239 B7
Castle Hill Cl S21 59 D4
Castle Hill Ho DE13 239 B7
Castle Ho DE1 267 D2
Castle Ind Est S44 98 E2
Castle La
Bolsover S44 99 A1
Ironville NG16 170 E1
Melbourne DE73 252 B7
Castleland Way DE73 232 E2
Castle Mews
Mansfield Woodhouse NG19 136 B3
Melbourne DE73 252 B7
Castle Mews The 5 DE11 256 A7
Castle Mills DE73 252 B7
Castle Mount Cres DE45 109 D7
Castle Mount Way DE45 109 E7
Castle Orch DE56 190 E4
Castle Point Bsns Pk DE13 238 E6
Castle Point Business Pk DE13 238 F6
Castle Rd DE11 255 F1
Castlerigg Way 1 S18 56 E1
Castle Row S17 56 B6
Castlerow Cl S17 56 B6
Castlerow Dr S17 56 B6
Castlerow View S17 56 B6
Castleshaw Dr DE23 230 E7
Castle St
Bakewell DE45 109 D6
Bolsover S44 99 A2
Castleton S33 38 B2
Castle St *continued*
Derby DE1 267 C2
Glossop SK13 10 A4
Mansfield Woodhouse NG19 136 B3
Melbourne DE73 252 B7
Tutbury DE13 239 C6
CASTLETON 38 C2
Castleton Ave
Derby DE23 231 F8
Ilkeston DE7 194 E5
Somercotes DE55 170 C6
Castleton Bank 27 SK13 9 E1
Castleton CE Prim Sch S33 38 C2
Castleton Cl NG19 136 C4
Castleton Cres SK13 9 E1
Castleton Ct 12 DE24 233 C7
Castleton Gn 26 SK13 9 E1
Castleton Gr
28 Gamesley SK13 9 E1
Staveley S43 97 B5
Castleton Rd
Hathersage S32 52 E8
Hope S33 38 E3
Castleton Terr 25 SK13 9 E1
Castleton Visitor Ctr* S33 38 B2
Castle View
Aldercar NG16 182 A4
Duffield DE56 190 E4
Eckington S21 59 D3
Hatton DE65 239 C7
Palterton S44 118 B6
Castle View Dr DE4 155 C6
Castle View Prim Sch DE4 143 D5
Castleward Bvd
Derby DE1 219 B4
Derby DE1 267 C2
Castle Ward Ind Est DE1 267 C2
Castleward Spencer Acad DE1 267 C2
Castle Way The DE65 241 F5
Castle Wlk DE1 267 C2
Cat and Fiddle La DE7 207 E5
Catchford View S40 95 B7
Catcliff Cl DE45 109 D4
Catcliff Cotts DE45 109 D5
Cat & Fiddle Windmill The* DE7 207 F4
Cathedral Rd DE1 267 B4
Cathedral View DE22 218 D2
Catherine Ave
Ilkeston DE7 208 F6
Mansfield Woodhouse NG19 136 C3
Catherine Ct
Alfreton DE55 159 C5
1 Ashbourne DE6 173 B2
Chesterfield S40 95 E3
Catherine McAuley Ho DE22 204 E1
Catherine Rise DE11 256 A1
Catherine St
Alfreton DE55 159 C4
Chesterfield S40 95 E3
Derby DE23 219 B2
Cath of All Saints, Derby* DE1 267 B4
Catkin Cl 3 DE11 256 B7
Catkin Dr NG16 195 C8
Cat La S2, S8 43 C5
Cator Rd NG19 135 D3
Catterick Dr DE3 217 C1
Catterlen Cl DE24 233 C4
Catterwood Dr SK6 15 B2
Catton La DE12 260 B5
Catton Rd DE13 259 B7
Caudor Way 1 DE4 143 A5
Caudwell Cl S42 131 D8
Caudwell's Mill & Craft Ctr* DE4 126 F8
Cauldon Dr S40 95 A5
Cauldwell Rd
Caldwell DE12 261 B6
Drakelow DE16 254 D3
Caulfield Cl S41 76 D1
Caulkley View DE11 257 A7
Causeway DE22 204 E2
Causeway Gdns S17 55 D8
Causeway Glade
Sheffield S17 55 C8
Sheffield S17 55 D8
CAUSEWAY HEAD 55 C8
Causeway Head Rd S17 55 D8
Causeway Ho S45 129 D4
Causeway La
Crich DE4 156 F5
Matlock DE4 143 C5
Causeway The
Ashover S45 129 D4
Eyam S32 71 E5
Sheffield S17 55 D7
5 Wirksworth DE4 165 F8
Cavan Dr DE21 220 B4
Cavell Dr S45 131 E2
Cavendish Ave
Buxton SK17 84 F6
Cavendish Ave *continued*
Derby DE22 204 F3
Sheffield, Abbeydale Park S17 55 F7
CAVENDISH BRIDGE DE72 247 A8
Cavendish Cir 6 SK17 85 B8
Cavendish Cl
Castle Donington DE74 247 A2
Creswell S80 81 D1
Doveridge DE6 211 C1
Duffield DE56 190 D2
Holmewood S42 116 E1
Shardlow DE72 235 B2
9 Swadlincote DE11 256 A7
Cavendish Close Inf Sch DE21 220 A8
Cavendish Close Jun Acad DE21 220 B8
Cavendish Cotts DE4 154 F2
Cavendish Cres NG9 209 D2
Cavendish Ct
Chesterfield S41 96 A5
Derby DE1 267 A4
Shardlow DE72 235 A1
Cavendish Dr
Ashbourne DE6 185 D8
Clowne S43 81 A4
Ripley DE5 169 C1
Cavendish Flats DE45 110 E8
Cavendish Hospl The SK17 85 A8
Cavendish Jun Sch S41 95 F8
Cavendish Pl S43 78 B3
Cavendish Rd
Bolsover S44 99 B1
Ilkeston DE7 208 F6
Long Eaton NG10 223 C2
Matlock DE4 143 C7
Cavendish Rise S18 75 F8
Cavendish Sq S21 77 D8
Cavendish St
Chesterfield S40 266 B3
Derby DE1 267 A3
Langwith NG20 119 F8
Mansfield Woodhouse NG19 136 A3
Staveley S43 97 D8
Cavendish Street N S41 77 A2
Cavendish Way DE3 217 E2
Cavendish Wharf DE72 234 D2
Cavendish Wlk S44 99 A2
Caversfield Cl DE23 231 A8
Caversham Way DE7 207 D8
Cavill Rd S8 43 A3
Cawdor Rd S2 43 F6
Caxterway La SK17 86 E3
Caxton Cl S43 77 D3
Caxton Ct DE23 231 E6
Caxton St DE23 231 E7
Caythorpe Ct 4 NG19 136 E3
Ceal The SK6 15 B2
Cecil Ave S18 57 A2
Cecil Rd
Dronfield S18 57 A2
Swadlincote DE11 255 F5
Cecil St DE22 218 D6
Cedar Ave
Alfreton DE55 159 A5
Chesterfield S40 95 D5
Long Eaton NG10 236 E5
Mansfield Woodhouse NG19 136 C5
Ripley DE5 169 D1
Cedar Cl
Ashbourne DE6 185 D7
Duffield DE56 190 D4
Eckington S21 59 B2
Glapwell S44 118 B1
Glossop SK13 10 B2
Killamarsh S21 60 C5
Sandiacre NG10 223 B7
Shirebrook NG20 119 E6
Cedar Croft
Aston-on-Trent DE72 246 A7
Kilburn DE56 192 B7
Cedar Dr
Ockbrook DE72 221 C4
Selston NG16 171 F7
Uttoxeter ST14 210 A4
Cedar Gr
Belper DE56 179 B2
Linton DE12 261 C6
South Normanton DE55 160 B4
Swadlincote DE11 256 A7
Cedar Park Dr S44 99 C2
Cedar Pine Dr DE55 159 E4
Cedar Pk DE7 208 E7
Cedar Rd
Castle Donington DE74 247 B2
Linton DE11 261 E7
Cedar St
Brimington S43 78 A1
Derby DE22 218 E8
Hollingwood S43 97 A8

Cedar St continued
Shirland DE55 146 C5
Cedarwood Ct DE21 205 E2
Cedric Cl DE15 255 C4
Cedric Drive LE66 258 B1
Celandine Cl
Burton upon Trent DE15 248 C2
Derby DE21 206 A2
Celandine Ct S17 56 A5
Celandine Gdns S17 56 A5
Celandine Pl DE11 256 E4
Celanese Rd DE21 220 C3
Cemetery Hill DE21 219 F6
Cemetery La
Ripley DE5 169 E1
3 Ripley DE5 180 E8
Staveley S43 78 E1
Wirksworth DE4 154 F1
Cemetery Rd
Belper DE56 179 A5
Chesterfield S41 96 C2
Clay Cross S45 131 E2
Dronfield S18 76 B8
Glossop SK13 10 C4
Somercotes DE55 170 C7
Stapleford NG9 223 E7
Cemetery Terr S43 96 E7
Cemetery Way DE75 193 F8
Centenary Ho DE1 267 B1
Centenary Rd NG19 135 F1
Central Area L Ctr DE4 143 A6
Central Ave
Borrowash DE72 221 B1
Chesterfield S40 95 E2
Creswell S80 100 D8
Sandiacre NG10 223 B6
South Normanton DE55 160 B5
Stapleford NG9 223 F8
Central Cl
Shirebrook NG20 119 E3
Unstone Green S18 76 E6
Central Dr
Blackwell DE55 147 E1
Buxton SK17 85 D5
Calow S44 96 F3
3 Chesterfield S41 96 C1
Shirebrook NG20 119 E3
Wingerworth S42 114 F3
Central Pavement S40 266 B3
Central Rd DE55 159 A4
Central St
Chesterfield S41 96 C1
Holmewood S42 132 E8
Central Store 6 SK13 10 C1
Central Wlk S43 96 D7
Centre Ct DE1 267 C1
Centre St S44 117 D1
Centro Pl DE24 219 D3
Centrum East Ret Pk DE14 253 F8
Centurion Way Bsns Pk DE21 219 B8
Century Way S43 80 F7
Cessna Court DE74 246 F3
CHADDESDEN 219 E7
Chaddesden Cl S18 56 C1
Chaddesden La DE21 220 A6
Chaddesden Lane End DE21 219 F6
Chaddesden Park Prim Sch DE21 220 B7
Chaddesden Park Rd DE21 219 F7
Chaddesden Wood Nature Reserve* DE21 206 A3
Chadfield Rd DE56 190 E5
Chadwell Cl S41 115 C7
Chadwick Ave DE24 232 E5
Chadwick Ct S43 78 D1
Chadwick Gr DE5 169 B1
Chadwick Hill
Elton DE4 140 F7
Elton DE4 141 A6
Chadwick Nick La
Crich DE4 167 F7
Fritchley DE4 168 A6
Chadwick Rd S13 44 C7
Chadwick St SK13 17 B8
Chaffinch Cl DE21 220 F6
Chain La DE3 218 A2
Chalfont Sq DE21 206 B2
Chalkley Cl DE24 232 F7
Challands Cl 1 S41 115 C8
Challands Way S41 115 C8
Challis Ave DE21 220 B7
Challoner Gn S20 59 E8
Challoner Way S20 59 E8
Chalons Cl DE7 194 F1
Chalons Way DE7 208 F8
Chambers Ave DE7 209 B7
Chambers Ct SK14 9 A3
Chambers St DE24 219 F1
Chamomile Pl 4 DE3 217 C4
Champion Ave DE7 194 C3
Champion Hill DE56 190 E4
Chancel Pl DE22 267 A1
Chancery Cl DE5 180 E7
Chancery La DE22 218 A4
Chancet Wood Cl S8 56 F8
Chancet Wood Dr S8 56 F8
Chancet Wood Rd 1 S8 56 F8
Chancet Wood Rise S8 56 F8
Chancet Wood View S8 56 F8
Chander Hill La S42 113 C8
Chandlers Ford DE21 205 F2
Chandos Cres S21 60 D6
Chandos Pole St DE22 218 D6
Chandres Ct DE22 204 E4
Chaneyfield Way S40 95 B7
Channel Cres DE24 219 E2
Channel The DE6 173 B2
Chanterelle Walk S43 80 D2
Chantrey Ave S41 96 A6
Chantrey Rd S8 43 A3
Chantry Cl
Derby DE3 217 C1
Disley SK12 32 E5
Long Eaton NG10 236 A4
Melbourne DE73 252 B7
Chantry Ct SK17 69 C4
Chantry Fold SK12 32 E6
Chantry La SK17 69 D4
Chantry Rd SK12 32 E6
Chapel Brow
Broadbottom SK13 16 E6
Glossop SK13 10 A7
Chapel By-Pass
Bridgemont SK23 33 F1
Buxworth SK23 46 A8
Chapel-en-le-Frith SK23 47 D7
Whaley Bridge SK23 45 F8
Whitehough SK23 46 D8
Chapel Cl
Blackwell DE55 147 F1
Clowne S43 80 E4
Moira DE11 256 C1
Willington DE65 242 B6
Youlgreave DE45 125 B5
Chapel Croft
Elton DE4 140 E6
Middleton DE4 154 D5
Chapel Ct DE7 194 F4
CHAPEL-EN-LE-FRITH 47 B6
Chapel-en-le-Frith CE VC Prim Sch SK23 47 C6
Chapel-en-le-Frith High Sch SK23 47 A5
Chapel-en-le-Frith Sta SK23 47 B3
Chapel Gate
Chapel-en-le-Frith 36 D3
Chapel Gate La NG16 182 A5
Chapel Gn DE6 224 C8
Chapel Hill
Alderwasley DE4 167 A7
Ashover S45 129 F4
Beeley DE4 111 B4
Cromford DE4 155 A7
Chapel Ho 3 DE7 208 E8
Chapel Houses SK6 23 A5
Chapel La
Apperknowle S18 58 A1
Bakewell DE45 109 D5
Barrow upon Trent DE73 244 A6
Boylestone DE6 213 B4
Chellaston DE73 233 A1
Church Broughton DE65 227 B8
Clifton DE6 184 F6
Crich DE4 168 A8
Derby, Chaddesden DE21 220 A7
Derby, Spondon DE21 220 E5
Glossop SK13 9 F5
Hanbury DE13 238 A2
Holloway DE4 156 B5
Kniveton DE6 163 B1
Middleton DE4 154 D5
Rolleston DE13 240 B4
Scropton DE65 226 F1
Sheffield, Hillfoot S17 55 D4
Taddington SK17 88 B3
Thurvaston DE6 215 B8
Tissington DE6 162 B6
Wirksworth DE4 154 F1
Chapel Lane E S41 115 D7
Chapel Lane W S40 95 C2
Chapel Lofts SK13 10 B5
CHAPEL MILTON 47 B8
Chapel Mws 8 DE4 116 E1
Chapel Pl NG16 195 F6
Chapel Rd
Bolsover S44 98 F1
Grassmoor S42 115 F3
Hayfield SK22 25 D2
Horwich End SK23 45 E5
Selston NG16 171 E6
Chapel Row
Borrowash DE72 221 B2
Crich DE4 168 A8
Chapel Side DE21 220 E5
Chapel St
Alfreton DE55 159 A4
Belper DE56 178 F3
Brimington S43 96 F8
Buxton SK17 85 B7
3 Chesterfield S41 96 A8
Chapel St continued
Coton in the Elms DE12 260 D3
Derby DE1 267 B4
Derby, Spondon DE21 220 E5
Donisthorpe DE12 265 E8
Donisthorpe, Oakthorpe DE12 265 F6
Duffield DE56 190 F3
Eastwood NG16 182 F1
Fritchley DE56 168 B6
Glossop SK13 10 C1
Hayfield SK22 25 D2
Heanor DE75 194 A8
Holbrook DE56 191 C7
8 Ilkeston DE7 194 F1
Kilburn DE56 192 A8
Kimberley NG16 195 F6
Linton DE11 261 E8
Long Eaton NG10 236 E7
Longnor SK17 121 B6
Melbourne DE73 252 B7
Monyash DE45 107 B2
Monyash SK17 107 B4
New Houghton NG19 135 A7
New Mills SK22 33 B6
New Mills, Rowarth SK22 24 E7
Ripley DE5 169 D2
Sheffield S20 59 C6
Smisby LE65 257 F3
Somercotes DE55 170 C7
Stonebroom DE55 147 A4
Swadlincote, Church Gresley DE11 256 A1
Swadlincote, Newhall DE11 255 F6
Swanwick DE55 169 E8
Ticknall DE73 251 A5
Whaley Bridge SK23 45 E8
Whaley Thorns NG20 101 A3
Woodville DE11 256 F2
Chapel Way S42 115 D1
Chapel Wlk
Alfreton DE55 159 A4
Curbar S32 72 E2
Chapel Yd
Dronfield S18 57 A2
Harthill S26 61 E6
South Wingfield DE55 157 E3
Chapman Ave DE24 233 B6
Chapman La S42 115 F3
Chapmans Croft DE12 260 D3
Chapter Cl DE21 205 D2
Chardin Ave SK6 23 C8
Charing Ct DE1 267 C5
Charingworth Rd DE21 206 B2
Chariot Cl DE24 233 D5
Charity Rd DE55 170 C5
Charlbury Cl DE23 231 A8
Charles Ashmore Rd S8 57 A8
Charles Ave
Derby DE21 220 D6
Sandiacre NG10 223 B6
Stapleford NG9 223 F8
Charles Cl DE7 209 B6
Charles La SK13 10 E3
Charles Rd DE24 220 A1
Charles St
Alfreton DE55 159 A5
4 Buxton SK17 85 C8
Chesterfield S40 95 E3
Glossop SK13 10 C1
Long Eaton NG10 236 D6
Mansfield NG19 136 A1
Somercotes DE55 170 C7
Swadlincote DE11 256 B2
Charleston Cl DE11 256 A7
Charleston Rd DE21 220 C6
CHARLESTOWN 17 C6
Charlestown SK13 17 C6
Charlestown Dr DE22 204 D4
Charlestown Rd SK13 17 C7
Charlestown View SK13 16 C6
Charles Walker Cl DE6 175 F2
CHARLESWORTH 16 C6
Charlesworth Cl SK23 33 D3
Charlesworth Cres SK23 33 D3
Charlesworth Ct 1 NG19 136 E3
Charlesworth Gdns S44 117 E8
Charlesworth Rd SK23 33 D3
Charlesworth Sch SK13 16 D6
Charlesworth Sch (Infant Sch) SK13 16 C6
Charlesworth St S44 117 E8
Charley La SK23 47 A8
Charlotte Ct
Burton upon Trent DE14 254 C8
Eastwood NG16 182 F3
Sheffield S2 43 B8
Swadlincote DE11 256 C5
Charlotte Inf Sch DE7 194 E2
Charlotte La S33 51 A7
Charlotte Rd S2 43 B8
Charlotte St
Derby DE23 219 A2
Ilkeston DE7 194 E3
Charlton Ave NG10 223 F1
Charlton Cl DE12 261 D5
Charnock Ave S12 44 B2
Charnock Cres S12 44 A3
Charnock Dale Rd S12 44 B2
Charnock Dr S12 44 B3
Charnock Gr S12 44 B2
Charnock Hall Prim Sch S12 44 B2
Charnock Hall Rd S12 44 A2
Charnock View Rd S12 44 B2
Charnock Wood Rd S12 44 B1
Charnos Street DE7 209 A4
Charnwood Ave
12 Belper DE56 178 F4
Belper DE56 179 A4
Borrowash DE72 221 C2
Castle Donington DE74 247 C3
Derby DE23 231 D5
Long Eaton NG10 236 B4
Sandiacre NG10 223 A4
Charnwood Cl DE55 169 F7
Charnwood Cres DE55 148 B3
Charnwood Dr DE5 169 C1
Charnwood Gr NG19 136 B5
Charnwood St DE1 267 B2
Charter Cl S44 134 B8
Charterhouse Cl DE21 205 F3
Charter Pk DE7 208 E7
Charterstone La DE22 204 E4
Chartley Dr 9 DE23 230 F5
Chartley Road DE24 231 C2
Chartwell Ave S42 114 D5
Chartwell Dr DE21 219 C5
Chase Cl DE73 233 B2
Chasecliff Cl S40 95 D5
Chase Rd DE56 167 F4
Chase The
Derby DE24 231 F4
Kilburn DE56 192 B8
Little Eaton DE21 191 D2
Rosliston DE12 260 C6
Chase View DE4 156 F1
Chasewater Pl DE65 240 E8
Chatfield Cl DE15 248 C1
Chatham Ave DE55 159 C3
Chatham Ct DE56 179 D4
Chatham St DE23 232 A8
Chatsworth Ave
Chesterfield S40 95 C2
Clowne S43 80 F4
Crich DE4 156 F1
Darley Dale DE4 142 F7
Long Eaton NG10 237 A6
Shirebrook NG20 119 E6
Chatsworth Bsns Pk S40 95 E2
Chatsworth Cl
Alfreton DE55 158 F3
Bolsover S44 99 C2
1 Sandiacre NG10 223 B4
Chatsworth Cres
Bullbridge DE56 168 B5
Derby DE22 204 F3
Chatsworth Ct
11 Ashbourne DE6 173 C2
2 Chesterfield S40 95 C2
Derby DE24 231 F4
Staveley S43 97 D8
West Hallam DE7 207 E8
Chatsworth Dr
Derby DE3 217 E3
Little Eaton DE21 191 D2
North Wingfield S42 131 F6
Tutbury DE13 239 C6
Chatsworth Farm Shop* DE45 91 C2
Chatsworth Ho* DE45 92 A1
Chatsworth Ho 2 DE14 253 F7
Chatsworth Lodge SK17 85 A8
Chatsworth Park Ave S12 44 A5
Chatsworth Park Dr S12 44 A5
Chatsworth Park Gr S12 44 A5
Chatsworth Park Rd S12 44 A5
Chatsworth Park Rise S12 44 A5
Chatsworth Pl
Dronfield S18 56 D2
Ilkeston DE7 208 B5
Chatsworth Rd
Buxton SK17 85 E7
Creswell S80 81 C1
Pilsley DE45 91 D1
Rowsley DE4 111 A2
Sheffield S17 55 F6
Swadlincote DE11 256 A6
Chatsworth St
Derby DE23 218 E1
Tibshelf DE55 148 A6
Chatsworth Tech Pk 8 S41 96 A8
Chatsworth View S32 72 E1
Chatsworth Way DE75 181 C2
Chattens Meadow DE11 261 F8
Chatteris Dr DE21 205 D1
Chatterton La
Marple SK6 24 A8
Mellor SK6 24 B8
Chaucer Dr S18 76 C7
Chaucer Inf Sch DE7 208 F8
Chaucer Jun Sch
11 Ilkeston DE7 194 F1
Ilkeston DE7 208 D8
Chaucer Rd S41 95 F8
Chaucer St DE7 194 F1
Chaucer Terr DE23 231 F7
Chavery Close S44 97 D2
Chavery Rd S45 131 E4
Chaworth Cl 3 DE55 158 E2
Cheadle Cl DE23 218 B1
Cheadle Rd ST14 210 B1
Cheal Cl DE72 234 D2
Cheam Cl DE22 217 E6
Cheapside
2 Belper DE56 178 F3
Derby DE1 267 B3
Chedworth Dr DE24 233 D6
Cheedale SK17 85 D7
Cheedale Ave S40 95 D6
Cheedale Cl
Burton upon Trent DE15 248 B5
Chesterfield S40 95 D6
Cheetham Ave S18 76 E5
CHELLASTON 233 A1
Chellaston Acad DE73 232 F1
Chellaston Academy DE73 244 F8
Chellaston Brickworks Nature Reserve* DE73 233 A1
Chellaston Cotts DE72 245 B5
Chellaston Fields Spencer Acad DE72 245 A7
Chellaston Inf Sch DE73 233 A2
Chellaston Jun Sch
Chellaston DE73 232 F1
Derby DE24 233 A1
Chellaston La DE72, DE73 233 D1
Chellaston Park Ct DE73 232 F1
Chellaston Rd DE24 232 E4
Chelmarsh Cl
Chellaston DE73 233 A3
1 Derby DE73 233 A3
CHELMORTON 87 B1
Chelmorton Cl NG19 136 E3
Chelmorton Pl
6 Derby DE21 205 F1
Derby DE21 219 F8
Chelmsford Cl DE3 217 C3
Chelmsford Close 7 DE11 255 E1
Chelmsford Way 6 S43 78 B3
Chelsea Cl DE22 217 F6
Cheltenham Cl NG9 223 F2
Chelwood Rd DE73 232 F2
Chendre Cl SK22 25 C3
Chepstow Cl S40 114 F8
Chepstow Gdns S42 114 F7
Chequer La DE56 166 D2
Chequers La DE21 219 D6
Chequers Lane Ind Est DE21 219 D6
Chequers Rd
Derby DE21 219 D5
Derby DE21 219 F4
Cheribough Rd DE74 247 A3
Cheriton Cl NG19 135 E1
Cheriton Ct 13 S41 95 F8
Cheriton Dr DE7 194 C3
Cheriton Gdns DE23 230 E7
Cherry Bank Rd S8 43 A3
Cherrybrook Dr DE21 206 B3
Cherry Cl
Ashford in the Water DE45 108 F8
Breaston DE72 235 E8
Derby DE3 218 A2
Shirebrook NG20 119 E6
South Normanton DE55 160 B7
Cherry Ct DE14 253 F8
Cherrydale Ct DE23 231 A6
Cherry Garth DE65 228 D2
Cherry Gro SK13 10 C3
Cherry Leys DE15 248 C4
Cherry Plum Cl DE23 231 E7
Cherry St S2 43 A8
Cherry Street S S2 43 A8
Cherry Tree Ave
Belper DE56 179 B6
Ripley DE5 180 D8
Shireoaks S81 63 F7
Swanwick DE55 170 A7
Cherry Tree Cl
Bolsover S44 99 C1
Brinsley NG16 182 E8
Clowne S43 80 E3
Derby DE22 218 B4
Hilton DE65 228 D2
Ilkeston DE7 208 D6
Mansfield Woodhouse NG19 136 B4
Risley DE72 222 F4
Swadlincote DE11 255 F6
Cherry Tree Ct
Ashbourne DE6 173 B1
Chapel-en-le-Frith SK23 47 A6
Cherry Tree Dr
Buxton SK17 66 D1
Creswell S80 81 D2
Killamarsh S21 60 D5
Long Duckmanton S44 98 A4
Cherry Tree Gdns DE15 248 C3
Cherry Tree Gr
Mastin Moor S43 79 C3
North Wingfield S42 131 F5
CHERRYTREE HILL 220 B5
Cherry Tree Hill Prim Sch DE21 220 B5
Cherry Tree La DE6 216 B8
Cherry Tree Mews
Derby DE21 220 B4
Woodville DE11 256 F2
Cherrytree Rd DE15 254 F6
Cherry Tree Sq SK17 69 C3
Cherry Tree Way NG16 182 C4
Chertpit La SK17, DE45 89 D6
Chertsey Cl S40 114 F8
Chertsey Ct DE7 207 D8
Chertsey Rd DE3 217 C2
Chervil Road DE24 231 C3
Cherwell Cl 1 S43 96 E8
Cherwell Dr
Derby DE3 217 C1
Derby DE3 230 C8
Cheryls Bank SK13 16 B8
Chesapeake Rd DE21 220 B6
Chesham Cl
Glossop SK13 10 B5
Hadfield SK13 10 B5
Cheshire St DE24 232 E5
Cheshire Way NG16 171 C4
Chess Burrow NG19 136 D2
Chessel Cl S8 43 A4
Chester Ave DE22 205 B5
Chester Cl DE72 246 A6
Chester Ct
Derby, Little Chester DE21 219 B8
Derby, Spondon DE21 220 E3
Eckington S21 59 B2
CHESTERFIELD 266 B2
Chesterfield Ave
Chesterfield S43 77 E3
Long Eaton NG10 236 F7
Swadlincote DE11 255 E6
Chesterfield Coll S41 266 B4
Chesterfield Coll Automotive Ctr S41 96 A6
Chesterfield Coll (Tapton House Campus) S41 96 C5
Chesterfield Dr DE12 261 C6
Chesterfield Mus* S41 266 C3
Chesterfield Rd
Alfreton DE55 158 F5
Astwith S45 132 E5
Barlborough S43 79 F5
Barlborough S43 80 A5
Baslow DE45 92 C5
Beeley DE4 111 B3
Beeley DE4 112 A4
Belper DE56 179 A4
Belper DE56 179 C6
Bolsover S44 98 E2
Bramley-Vale S44 117 D2
Brimington, Middlecroft S43 97 B8
Brimington, Tapton S41, S43 96 D7
Calow S41, S44 96 E2
Calow S44 97 C2
Darfoulds S80 63 E1
Darley Dale DE4 111 E1
Darley Dale DE4 127 D2
Dronfield S18 57 B1
Eckington S21 59 B2
Farley DE4 128 F1
Fritchley DE5 168 F5
Grassmoor S42 115 F1
Heage DE56 168 E3
Holmewood S42 116 C2
Long Duckmanton S44 98 C3
Matlock DE4 143 D7

Chesterfield Rd continued
New Houghton NG19 . .134 F7
North Wingfield S42. . . 132 A8
Oakerthorpe DE55 . . . .158 B2
Pentrich DE5 . . . . 169 A7
Pilsley DE55, S45 . . . . 133 A1
Pleasley NG19 . . . . . . 135 A6
Rowsley DE4. . . . . 111 A1
5 Sheffield S8. . . . . . .43 A6
Shirland DE55. . . . . . 146 C3
Shirland DE55. . . . . . 146 E1
Shuttlewood S44 . . . . . .98 E5
Sutton in Ashfield
  NG17. . . . . .148 E4
Chesterfield Road N
NG19 . . . . 135 D3
Chesterfield Road S
S8. . . . . .57 A6
Chesterfield Royal Hospl
S44. . . . . .96 A7
Chesterfield Small Bsns
Ctr S41. . . . . .96 A7
Chesterfield Sta
S41. . . . . 266 C3
Chesterfield Trade Ctr
S41. . . . . .96 A6
Chesterfield Trad Est
S41. . . . . .76 C3
Chesterford Ct
DE23. . . . . .230 F6
Chester Gdns DE11 . 256 B2
Chester Gn NG9 . . . . 223 F2
Chester Green Rd
DE1. . . . . 219 A7
Chester Ho S40. . . . . .95 E3
Chesterman Cl
NG16 . . . . 195 B4
Chester Rd 5 DE23. .230 F5
Chester St
Chesterfield S40. . . . . .95 E3
Mansfield NG19 . . . . . 135 E1
Chesterton Ave
DE23. . . . . .231 E7
Chesterton Cl S43 . . . .96 F3
Chesterton Rd DE21 220 E6
Chestnut Ave
Belper DE56 . . . . . . 179 A2
Chellaston DE73. . . . .232 F3
Derby DE3 . . . . .217 D3
Derby, Rose Hill
  DE23. . . . . 219 A2
Eckington S21. . . . . . .59 B2
Glapwell S44 . . . . . . 118 C1
Holbrook DE56 . . . . 191 C7
Killamarsh S21 . . . . .60 C5
Repton DE65 . . . . . .243 D2
Ripley DE5 . . . . 180 D8
Somercotes DE55. . . . 170 D5
Swadlincote DE11 . . .256 B6
Chestnut Bank 2
DE75. . . . . .181 D1
Chestnut Centre Otter,
  Owl & Wildlife Pk★
  SK23. . . . . .47 E8
Chestnut Cl
Buxton SK17. . . . . . . .66 B1
Dronfield S18 . . . . . . .76 C8
Duffield DE56 . . . . . 190 A4
Horsley Woodhouse
  DE7. . . . . 192 C7
New Mills SK22. . . . . .24 E1
Chestnut Cotts DE6. 151 D1
Chestnut Ct
Cromford DE4. . . . . . 155 A6
Pinxton NG16 . . . . . .160 E3
Chestnut Dr
Ashbourne DE6. . . . . 185 D7
Barlborough S43 . . . . .80 A6
Clowne S43. . . . . .80 D4
Creswell S80 . . . . . . .81 D2
Selston NG16 . . . . . 171 F7
Shirebrook NG20 . . . 119 D4
South Normanton
  DE55. . . . . .160 B4
Chestnut Drive S43. . .78 A1
Chestnut Gdn DE11 . . 256 B2
Chestnut Gr
Borrowash DE72 . . . .221 C3
Etwall DE65 . . . . . . .229 B3
Mansfield Woodhouse
  NG19 . . . . 136 B5
Sandiacre NG10. . . . . 223 A7
Tibshelf DE55. . . . . . 147 F5
Chestnut La
Barton in Fabis
  NG11. . . . . .237 E6
Clifton Campville B79. .263 F2
Chestnut Rd
Burton upon Trent
  DE15. . . . . .254 F7
Langley Mill NG16. . . .182 A3
Chestnuts The
NG10 . . . . 236 A8
Chestnut Way
Repton DE65. . . . . . .242 C2
Swanwick DE55 . . . . 170 A8
Cheswick Rd 1
DE23. . . . . .231 E1
Chevely Ct DE21 . . . 219 D8
Cheverton Cl DE24. .233 D5
Chevin Alley DE56 .190 F7
Chevin Ave
Borrowash DE72 . . . 221 C2
Derby DE3 . . . . .217 D2
Chevin Bank DE56 190 D6

Chevin Mews DE56 .178 F2
Chevin Pl DE1 . . . . . .218 F7
Chevin Rd
Belper, Chevinside
  DE56. . . . . .178 E2
Belper, Milford DE56 . .190 F8
Derby DE1 . . . . .218 F7
Duffield DE56. . . . . . 190 E5
CHEVINSIDE 178 E2
Chevin The DE13 . . 240 C1
Chevin Vale DE56. . 190 E5
Chevin View DE56 . .178 F4
Cheviot Ave NG16 . .170 F3
Cheviot Cl DE11 . . . 256 A3
Cheviot Rd NG10 . . 223 A1
Cheviot St DE22 . . . 218 C5
Cheviot Way 1 S40 .95 C5
CHEW. 16 A5
Chew Rd SK15. . . . . . .5 C8
Chewton St NG16. . . .182 F1
Cheyenne Gdns
DE21. . . . . 220 C5
Cheyne Wlk DE21 . . 218 C6
Chichester Cl DE7 . 209 A8
Chicory Cl 3 DE3 . 217 D5
Chigwell Way 2 S43 .78 B3
CHILCOTE. 264 F3
Children's Country
  House at Sudbury,
  The★ DE6. . . . . . . .225 D5
Chilham Way DE24 . 233 D4
Chilson Dr DE3 . . . . 217 C3
Chiltern Cl
Chesterfield S40. . . . .95 C4
Grassmoor S42 . . . . 115 F3
Chiltern Ct 2 S40 . .95 C4
Chiltern Dr DE7 . . . 207 E8
Chiltern Gdns NG10. 223 A1
Chiltern Rd DE11 . . 256 A3
Chilton Cres NG19 . 136 C6
Chilton Ct 4 DE13. . 240 E1
Chime Cl DE21 . . . . 205 C2
Chimley St DE21. . . 220 F2
Chimneypot La
DE11. . . . . 256 A4
China House Yd
DE4. . . . . 165 F8
Chine The DE55 . . . 160 B3
Chingford Ct DE22. .218 B6
CHINLEY. 34 F1
CHINLEY HEAD 34 F5
Chinley Lodge SK23 . .34 E2
Chinley Prim Sch
SK23. . . . . .34 F1
Chinley Rd DE21 . . . 206 A1
Chinley Sta SK23 . . . .34 D2
Chippinghouse Rd
S2. . . . . .43 A7
Chiswick Cl DE22 . .217 F6
Chiswick Ct 13 S43 . .78 B3
CHISWORTH 16 B5
Chisworth Ct 2
NG19 . . . . 136 E5
Chiverton Cl S18 . . . .57 A2
Chorlton Terr ST14 . 210 B1
Christ Church CE Prim
Sch S41. . . . . .96 A5
Christchurch Ct
DE1. . . . . .267 B4
Christ the King RC Prim
Sch DE55. . . . . .159 A5
Chrysalis Way NG16 182 D3
Chrysalis Way Bsns Pk
NG16 . . . . 182 C4
Chrysanthemum Ct
DE11. . . . . 256 A5
CHUNAL. 17 D4
Chunal SK13. . . . . . . .16 C4
Chunal La SK13. . . . . .17 D5
Chunal Lane Flats
SK13. . . . . .17 C6
Church Al DE45. . . . 109 D5
Church Alley DE45. . 109 D5
Church Ave
Buxton SK17. . . . . . . .67 B5
Clay Cross S45. . . . . 131 E2
Hatton DE65 . . . . . . 239 D8
Long Eaton NG10 . . . 236 A4
Swadlincote DE11 . . .256 B8
Tideswell SK17. . . . . .69 C4
Church Bank
Hathersage S32. . . . . .41 B1
Hathersage S32. . . . . .53 A8
Whaley Bridge SK23. . .45 D7
Church Broughton CE
Prim Sch DE65. . . . 227 B8
CHURCH BROUGHTON,
HEATHTOP. 227 A6
Church Broughton Rd
Alkmonton DE6. . . . . .213 F6
Alkmonton DE6. . . . . .214 A7
Hatton DE65. . . . . . . 227 C3
Church Brow
Chapel-en-le-Frith
  SK23. . . . . .47 B6
Mottram in Longdendale
  SK14. . . . . .9 A3
Church Cl
Barrow upon Trent
  DE73. . . . . 244 C3
Blackfordby DE11. . . .257 B1
Blackwell DE55. . . . . 147 C1
Burton upon Trent
  DE15. . . . . .248 B3
Chellaston DE73. . . . .233 A1
Clowne S43. . . . . .80 F3

Church Cl continued
Glossop SK13. . . . . . .10 E2
Marchington ST14. . . . 224 F2
North Wingfield S45. . 132 A5
Peak Forest SK17 . . . .49 A3
Renishaw S21. . . . . . .79 B8
Smalley DE7. . . . . . . 192 F5
Staveley S43. . . . . . . .97 C7
Trowell NG9 . . . . 209 C4
Willington DE65 . . . . . 242 B5
Wingerworth S42. . . . 115 A4
Church Cnr DE21 . . . 165 B1
Church Cres NG9 . . .223 F3
Church Croft
Coton in the Elms
  DE12. . . . . 260 C3
Ripley DE5 . . . . .169 D2
Church Ct NG20 . . . . 119 E3
Churchdale Ave
NG9 . . . . 209 E1
Churchdale Mews
S12. . . . . .44 D4
Churchdale Rd S12. .44 D4
Churchdown Cl
DE21. . . . . 206 B2
Church Dr
Duffield DE56. . . . . . 190 F2
Ilkeston DE7. . . . . . . 194 D4
Sandiacre NG10. . . . . 223 B7
Shirebrook NG20 . . . . 119 E3
Church Farm Cl
ST14. . . . . 210 A4
Church Farm La
SK17. . . . . .88 A3
Church Farm Mews
S42. . . . . 116 B3
Church Farm Rd
DE5. . . . . 180 E8
Churchfields S80 . . .81 E1
Church Fold S33 . . . .16 C7
Church Gdns NG19 . 136 C3
CHURCH GRESLEY . . 256 B2
Church Gresley Inf Sch
DE11. . . . . .256 B2
Church Hill
Derby DE21 . . . . . . 220 D4
Etwall DE65 . . . . . . .229 B5
Jacksdale NG16 . . . . .171 B3
Kimberley NG16 . . . . 195 F6
Mansfield Woodhouse
  NG19 . . . . 136 C3
Newton DE55 . . . . . . 148 A1
Church Hill Ave
NG19 . . . . 136 C3
Church Hill Centre
NG16 . . . . 195 F6
Church Hill St DE15. 248 B3
Church Hole Cl 2
S43. . . . . .81 E2
Churchill Ave DE4 . 154 D5
Churchill Cl DE72. . 235 D8
Churchill Dr
Hilton DE65 . . . . . . 228 C2
2 Stapleford NG9. . .223 E8
Church La
Bakewell DE45. . . . . 109 D6
Barrow upon Trent
  DE73. . . . . 244 A5
Barton in Fabis NG11. .237 E6
Baslow DE45 . . . . . . .91 E5
Beeley DE4. . . . . 111 A4
Belper DE56. . . . . . . 179 A4
Brackenfield DE55 . . . 145 D2
Brailsford DE6 . . . . . 201 E7
Bramley-Vale S44. . . . .117 F2
Brinsley NG16 . . . . . .182 E7
Breadsall DE21. . . . . 205 E4
Brinsley NG16 . . . . . .182 E7
Buxton SK17. . . . . . . .86 B7
Caldwell DE12 . . . . . 260 E7
Calow S44. . . . . .97 A3
Castle Donington
  DE74. . . . . 247 B3
Chapel-en-le-Frith
  SK23. . . . . .47 B6
Chelmorton SK17 . . . .106 B8
Chesterfield S40. . . . .266 B3
Chilcote DE12. . . . . . 264 E3
Clowne S43. . . . . .80 F3
Cossall NG16 . . . . . . 195 C1
Cubley DE6. . . . . 198 F1
Cubley DE6. . . . . 212 E8
4 Derby DE22. . . . .204 F3
Derby, Chaddesden
  DE21. . . . . 220 A6
Derby, Darley Abbey
  DE22. . . . . 205 A2
Doveridge DE6. . . . . .211 B1
Eckington S12. . . . . . .58 E7
Ellastone DE6. . . . . . 183 B4
Great Longstone DE45. .90 A4
Hanbury DE13. . . . . . 238 A4
Heath S44. . . . . .117 B3
Heath, Stockley S44. . 117 D3
Hemington DE74. . . . 247 E4
Holmewood S42. . . . .116 B3
Horsley Woodhouse
  DE7. . . . . 192 C6
Killamarsh S21. . . . . .60 E6
Kirk Langley DE6. . . . 202 E2
Little Eaton DE21 . . . 205 C7
Litton SK17. . . . . .69 F3
Lockington DE74. . . . .247 F4
Mackworth DE22 . . . .217 F7
Mapperley DE7 . . . . .193 F2
Marchington ST14 . . .224 F2
Marple SK6. . . . . .23 A5
Mayfield DE6 . . . . . . 184 C6
Monyash DE45 . . . . . 107 C1

Church La continued
Morley DE7. . . . . 206 E6
Mugginton DE6. . . . . 188 F3
New Mills SK22. . . . . .33 C8
North Wingfield S42. . .131 F5
Osmaston DE6 . . . . . 186 A5
Peak Forest SK17 . . . .49 A3
Pleasley NG19 . . . . . 135 A5
Rocester ST14 . . . . . 197 A3
Rowsley DE4. . . . . . . 110 E1
Selston NG16 . . . . . . 171 D7
Sheffield, Townhead
  S17. . . . . .55 D6
Sheldon DE45. . . . . . 108 B6
Shirley DE6 . . . . 200 D8
Somersal Herbert
  DE6. . . . . .211 D3
South Wingfield DE55. 157 F4
Stanton-by-Dale DE7 . 208 F1
Stapleford NG9. . . . . .223 D7
Stonebroom DE55 . . . 146 F5
Sutton on the Hill DE6. 215 B1
Sutton On The Hill
  DE6. . . . . 228 A8
Swarkestone DE73.. . 244 E6
Thorpe DE6. . . . . 161 D1
Thrumpton NG11 . . . . 237 C3
Ticknall DE73 . . . . . . 251 A4
Tideswell SK17. . . . . .69 D4
Trusley DE6. . . . . . . 215 F5
Weston Underwood
  DE6. . . . . 188 E2
Churchland Ave
S42. . . . . 132 D8
Church Lane N
Chesterfield S41. . . . . .77 A3
2 Derby DE22. . . . .204 F3
Church Level DE6. . . 165 B1
CHURCH
MAYFIELD. 184 D6
Church Mdw SK17. . . .85 D4
Church Mdws
Calow S44. . . . . .96 F3
North Wingfield S42. . .131 F5
Churchmead NG17. . 148 F3
Church Mews
Derby DE21 . . . . . . 220 D4
Hatton DE65. . . . . . . 227 D1
Killamarsh S21. . . . . .60 E7
Melbourne DE73. . . . .252 B7
Sheffield S20. . . . . . . .59 D7
Church Rd
Branston DE14. . . . . . 253 E7
Burton upon Trent
  DE13. . . . . 240 F2
Church Broughton
  DE65. . . . . 227 A8
Darley Dale DE4. . . . .127 B2
Egginton DE65. . . . . . 241 B4
Hollingworth SK14. . . .9 D4
Marple SK6. . . . . .23 E6
New Mills SK22. . . . . .33 C7
Quarndon DE22 . . . . . 204 C5
Rolleston DE13. . . . . .239 F4
Rolleston DE13. . . . . .240 A4
Shuttlewood S44 . . . . .99 A6
Shuttlewood, Stanfree
  S44. . . . . .99 B8
Snelston DE6 . . . . . . 184 C3
Swadlincote DE11 . . .256 A6
Church Rise DE55 . 146 C4
Churchside
Grassmoor S41 . . . . 115 D5
Scarcliffe S44. . . . . . 118 C6
Willington DE65 . . . . . 242 A5
Church Side
Calow S44. . . . . .96 F3
Sutton in Ashfield
  NG17. . . . . .148 F3
Churchside La S45. 115 D6
Churchside Mws
DE22. . . . . 218 E8
Churchside Wlk
DE22. . . . . 218 E4
Church Sq
1 Heanor DE75. . . .181 F1
Melbourne DE73. . . . .252 B6
Church St
Alfreton DE55. . . . . . 158 F4
Alstonefield DE6. . . . 149 E3
Appleby Magna DE12. .265 F1
Ashbourne DE6. . . . . .173 B2
Ashford in the Water
  DE45. . . . . 108 F8
Ashover S45. . . . . . . 129 F3
Barlborough S43 . . . . .80 B7
Baslow DE45. . . . . . . .91 E5
Belper DE56. . . . . . . 179 A3
Bolsover S44. . . . . . . .99 A1
Bonsall DE4 . . . . . . .142 E1
Bradwell S33 . . . . . . .51 A7
Brassington DE4. . . . 153 A1
Brimington S43. . . . . .96 E8
Buxton SK17. . . . . . . .85 B6
Calow S44. . . . . .96 F3
Clifton Campville B79. .263 F2
Clowne S43. . . . . .80 E3
Coton in the Elms
  DE12. . . . . 260 C3
Creswell S80 . . . . . . .81 F1
Denby Village DE5 . . . 180 D1
Derby DE1 . . . . 218 C1
Derby, Alvaston DE24. 233 C7
Derby, Rose Hill
  DE23. . . . . 219 A2
Derby, Spondon DE21. 220 D5

Church St continued
Donisthorpe DE12 . . .262 F1
Dronfield S18 . . . . . . .57 A1
Eastwood NG16 . . . . .182 F2
Eckington S21. . . . . . .59 E4
Eyam S32. . . . . .71 D5
Fritchley DE56 . . . . . 168 B6
Glossop SK13. . . . . . . .10 D2
Hadfield SK13. . . . . . . .10 A4
Hartington SK17 . . . . . 137 D5
Hartshorne DE11 . . . . 257 B6
Hayfield SK22. . . . . . . .25 D2
Heage DE56. . . . . 168 E2
Holbrook DE56 . . . . . 191 C6
Holloway DE4. . . . . . . 156 A6
Horsley DE21. . . . . . . 191 F5
Ilkeston DE7. . . . . 194 E4
Kilburn DE56. . . . . 191 F8
Lockington DE74. . . . . 247 F4
Longnor SK17. . . . . . . 121 B6
Mansfield Woodhouse
  NG19 . . . . 136 C3
Marple SK6. . . . . .23 A5
Matlock DE4. . . . . 143 C4
Melbourne DE73. . . . . 252 B7
Monyash DE45 . . . . . . 107 C2
Monyash DE45 . . . . . . 108 A2
Nethersea! DE12 . . . . . 264 F6
Ockbrook DE72. . . . . . 221 C4
Pilsley S45 . . . . 132 C1
Pleasley NG19 . . . . . . 135 B4
Ripley DE5 . . . . 169 D2
Ripley, Waingroves
  DE5. . . . . .181 A7
Sandiacre NG10. . . . . . 223 B7
Shirland DE55. . . . . . . 146 D2
Somercotes DE55. . . . . 170 D6
South Normanton
  DE55. . . . . 160 A6
Stapleford NG9. . . . . . . 223 D7
Staveley S43. . . . . .78 E2
Swadlincote DE11 . . . . 256 B1
Swadlincote, Lower Medway
  DE11. . . . . 256 C4
Swadlincote, Newhall
  DE11. . . . . 256 A6
Tansley DE4. . . . . 144 A4
Tideswell SK17. . . . . . .69 C4
Tintwistle SK13 . . . . . . .10 A7
Tintwistle SK14 . . . . .9 F7
Tutbury DE13 . . . . 239 C7
Unstone S18. . . . . .76 E7
Wessington DE55. . . . . 157 E8
Whaley Thorns NG20 . . 101 A2
2 Wirksworth DE4 . . . . 165 F8
Youlgreave DE45 . . . . . 125 C5
Church Street E
NG16 . . . . 160 D3
Church Street Mews
S33. . . . . .51 A7
Church Street N S41. .77 A3
Church Street S
Chesterfield S40. . . . . 115 A7
Glossop SK13. . . . . . . .10 E2
Church Street W
Chesterfield S40. . . . . .95 C2
Pinxton NG16 . . . . 160 D3
Church Terr SK13. . . .10 D2
CHURCHTOWN. 127 B2
CHURCH TOWN 60 E6
Church View
Alfreton DE55. . . . . . . 147 F1
Barlborough S43 . . . . . .80 A7
Belper DE56. . . . . 179 A4
Blackwell DE55. . . . . . 147 F1
Breaston DE72. . . . . . . 235 D7
Chesterfield S40. . . . . .95 C2
Clay Cross S45. . . . . . . 131 F3
Clifton DE6 . . . . 184 F6
Clowne S43. . . . . .80 F3
Duffield DE56. . . . . . . 190 E2
Glapwell S44 . . . . 134 B8
Heanor DE75. . . . . . . .181 B4
Ilkeston DE7. . . . . 208 E7
Killamarsh S21. . . . . . .60 E7
Mottram in Longdendale
  SK14. . . . . .9 A3
New Houghton NG19 . . 134 F7
New Mills SK22. . . . . . . .33 C8
Church View Cl
DE55. . . . . 146 E3
Church View Cotts
SK17. . . . . .84 E6
Church View Dr
Baslow DE45. . . . . . . .91 E4
Tupton S42. . . . . .131 E7
Church View La
DE73. . . . . 252 E2
Churchward Dr
DE13. . . . . 240 F1
Church Way S40. . . 266 B3
Church Wlk
7 Belper DE56. . . . . 178 F4
Brinsley NG16 . . . . . . 182 E6
Chesterfield S40. . . . . 266 B3
Derby DE22. . . . . 204 F4
Donisthorpe DE12 . . . 265 E8
Eastwood NG16 . . . . . 182 F2
Glossop SK13. . . . . . . .10 E2
Parwich DE6 . . . . 151 D1
3 Stapleford NG9. . . 223 D7
3 Wirksworth DE4 . . 165 F8
Churnet Cl DE6. . . . . 184 C7
Churnet Rd DE65 . . . 240 D8
Churnet Row ST14 . . . 196 F3

Churston Rd S40. . . . . . . .95 D3
Cicely Cl DE23 . . . . . 231 D4
Cinder Ave DE11. . . .256 A4
Cinder Bank NG16. . . 170 F4
CINDERHILL. 179 E1
Cinder Hill S81. . . . . .63 D7
Cinderhill La S8 . . . . . .57 C8
Cinder La
Killamarsh S21. . . . . .60 F7
Wirksworth DE4. . . . .165 E6
Cinder Rd DE55. . . . 170 D7
Circle Cl S2 . . . . .44 B8
Circle The
Derby DE24 . . . . .231 E5
Mansfield Woodhouse
  NG19 . . . . .136 B4
Sheffield S2 . . . . .43 F8
Circuit Drive NG10. .236 F8
Circular Dr S21. . . . . . . .79 B8
Circular Rd
Chesterfield S40. . . . .115 B8
Staveley S43. . . . . . . .78 D1
City Gate DE24 . . . . 219 D2
City Gate Bsns Pk
DE24. . . . . 219 D2
City of Derby Acad
DE24. . . . . 231 E3
City Rd
Derby DE1 . . . . 219 A7
Sheffield S12, S2. . . . . .43 F8
City Rd Bsns Ctr
DE1. . . . . 267 B4
City Road Ind Pk
DE1. . . . . 219 A7
City The
Blackfordby DE11. . . .257 A2
Risley DE72. . . . . . . .222 E4
Woodville DE11 . . . . . 256 F2
Civic Ctr S18. . . . . . . .57 A1
Civic Way DE11. . . . 256 B4
Clake Rd DE73. . . . . .251 F6
Clamp Dr DE11. . . . .256 B7
Clapgun St DE74. . . .247 B3
Clara Mount Rd
DE75. . . . . 182 A1
Clarehaven NG9. . . . 223 E5
Clare Ho DE11. . . . . . 267 B1
Claremont Cl 15
NG19 . . . . 136 E4
Clarence Ind Trad Est
S41. . . . . .96 B8
Clarence Rd
Chesterfield S40. . . . . 266 A3
Derby DE23 . . . . .218 F1
Long Eaton NG10 . . . . 236 C6
Clarence St
Chesterfield S40. . . . . 266 A3
Stonebroom DE55 . . . . 147 B4
Clarence Terr DE4. . .143 A1
Clarence Villas DE4. 143 B2
Clarendon Rd S43 . . . .97 C7
Clarke Ave DE75. . . .181 C2
Clarke Dr NG10. . . . . 236 A4
Clarkes Cl ST14. . . . .210 B1
Clarkes La DE72 . . . . 246 B8
Clarke St DE1. . . . . . 267 C4
Clarkson Ave S40. . . 266 B1
Clark Way
3 Grassmoor S41. . .115 F2
Grassmoor S42 . . . . . 116 A2
Clatterway DE4. . . . . 154 E8
Claverhouse Rd
DE15. . . . . 248 A2
Claxton St DE75 . . . . 181 D2
Claxton Terr 2
DE75. . . . . 181 D2
Clay Cl DE11. . . . . . . 256 D5
CLAY CROSS. 131 B4
Clay Cross Com Hospl
S45. . . . . 131 B4
Clay Cross Countryside
Ctr★ S45. . . . . 131 C3
Claydon St DE3. . . . . 217 D1
Claye St NG10 . . . . . 236 E7
Clayfields Rd 3
DE65. . . . . 242 C2
Clay Fields View
S45. . . . . 131 B2
Clayholes Rd SK23. . . .45 B4
Clay La
Clay Cross S45 . . . . . . 131 B2
Heanor DE75. . . . . . . .181 F2
Claylands Cl SK14 . . . . . .9 D4
Claylands Gr S80 . . . . .81 E5
Claylands Pl S80. . . . . . .81 E5
Claylands Rd S80. . . . . .81 E5
Claymar Dr DE11. . . .256 A7
CLAY MILLS. 241 A3
Claymills Cl DE15. . . 248 B1
Claymills Rd DE13 . . 241 A2
Claypit La S42. . . . . . . 112 F8
Clay Pit Way S43 . . . . .80 C6
Claypot Gdns DE11 . . 256 A4
Clay's La DE14. . . . . .253 F6
Clayson Gn S81. . . . . . .63 D8
Clay St
Burton upon Trent
  DE15. . . . . 248 A1
Draycott DE72 . . . . . . 235 A7
Shirland DE55. . . . . . 146 E1
Clay Street E DE15. . 248 A1
Clayton Cl DE55. . . . . 146 F5
Clayton Gardens
DE65. . . . . 239 E6
Clayton Gr DE75. . . .181 C4
Clayton Ley Cl DE55. 159 C4
Clayton St S41. . . . . . 266 C2
Cleave Rd DE14. . . . . 254 A8

Clegg Hill Dr NG17 148 E4
Clematis Cres DE15 255 A8
Clement La SK17/S33 50 C6
Clement Rd
Horsley Woodhouse DE7 192 C7
Marple SK6 23 C7
Cleve Ave
Beeston NG9 223 F3
Darley Dale DE4 142 F7
Cleveland Ave
Derby DE21 220 B5
Draycott DE72 235 A7
Long Eaton NG10 223 F1
Cleveland Cl DE11 256 B3
Cleveland Ct DE15 248 B3
Cleveland Rd DE55 146 F3
Cleveland Way S40 95 C5
Cleveleys Rd NG9 223 E3
Clewley Rd DE14 253 F8
Cliffash La DE56 176 E6
Cliff Bottom S32 71 F4
Cliff Bvd NG16 195 F7
Cliff Coll S32 91 D8
Cliffdon Ho DE65 239 D8
Cliffefield Rd S8 43 A5
Cliffe Field Rd S8 43 A4
Cliffe Hill Ave NG9 223 D7
Cliffe La
Hathersage S32 52 F8
Tideswell SK17 69 C4
Cliffe Rd SK13 17 D8
Cliffe View Rd S8 43 A5
Cliffe Wlk The SK17 69 C4
Cliff Hill S43 80 D3
Cliff La
Alport DE45 125 F3
Curbar S32 72 E1
Elton DE45 140 D8
Kirkby-in-Ashfield NG16 160 F4
Cliff Nook DE55 160 B4
Clifford Cl
Chesterfield S40 95 B2
Long Eaton NG10 236 A4
Clifford St
Derby DE24 219 D2
Long Eaton NG10 236 F7
Cliff Rd SK17 85 D8
CLIFTON 184 F6
Clifton Ave
Barlborough S43 80 A7
Long Eaton NG10 237 A7
CLIFTON CAMPVILLE 263 F1
Clifton CE Prim Sch DE6 184 F6
Clifton Cl
Overseal DE12 262 A3
Swadlincote DE11 256 A2
Clifton Ct S17 56 B3
Clifton Dr
Buxton SK17 85 C4
7 Derby DE23 230 F6
Derby DE23 231 A5
Derby DE3 217 E3
Clifton La B79 263 E1
Clifton Rd
Ashbourne DE6 185 A8
Buxton SK17 85 C7
Clifton Campville B79 264 D1
Derby DE22 204 D3
Lullington DE12 263 E5
Matlock Bath DE4 155 A8
Netherseal DE12 264 D6
Clifton St
Chesterfield S40 95 E3
Derby DE1 267 D1
Cliftonthorpe LE65 258 B1
Clifton Thorpe Mdws LE65 258 B1
Clifton Way DE15 248 B2
Clinthill La S80 81 E7
Clinton Ave NG16 182 D6
Clinton St DE21 219 D6
Clipstone Gdns DE21 206 B2
Clive Ho DE15 248 C3
Clock Tower Bsns Ctr The S43 78 B2
Clodhall La
Baslow DE45 73 C1
Baslow DE45 92 E8
Curbar S32 72 F2
Old Brampton S42 93 B5
Cloisters Ct DE21 205 F2
Cloonmore Croft S8 43 C1
Cloonmore Dr S8 43 C1
Close Bank DE13 239 C6
Close The
Derby, Allestree DE22 204 F2
Derby, Normanton Park DE23 218 D2
Great Longstone DE45 89 F4
Linton DE12 261 C5
Marple SK6 15 B1
Matlock DE4 143 B6
Moira DE11 262 D8
Newton Solney DE15 248 B6
Shirebrook NG20 119 F5
Tutbury DE13 239 B6
Cloud Ave NG9 223 F7
Cloudside Acad NG10 223 B7
Cloudside Ct NG10 223 B7
Cloudside Rd NG10 223 A7
Cloudwood Cl DE23 218 B1
Clough Ave SK6 23 C6
Clough Bank S2 43 B8
Cloughfield Cl SK23 45 D8
Clough La
Disley SK12 32 D7
Hayfield SK22 25 C5
Sheffield S10 42 F5
Wensley DE4 141 D8
Clough Mill SK22 25 C5
Cloughside SK12 32 E6
Clough Side SK6 23 C7
Clough St SK17 85 B7
Clough The
Bamford S33 40 C4
Chesterfield S41 96 E1
Clovelly Ct DE22 218 D8
Clover Cl DE21 220 F5
Clover Ct
Branston DE14 253 E6
Shardlow DE72 234 E2
Sheffield S8 43 C2
Tibshelf DE55 148 B7
Cloverdale DE11 256 B7
Cloverdale Dr DE24 231 F2
Clover La SK17 85 D4
Clover Nook Ind Est DE55 159 E3
Clover Nook Rd DE55 159 E3
Clover Rise NG16 195 B8
Cloverslade DE65 230 C1
Clover Walk DE24 231 C3
Clover Way NG19 136 F4
Cloves Hill DE7 192 C2
CLOWNE 80 D3
Clowne Jun & Inf Schs S43 80 E3
Clowne Rd
Barlborough S43 80 C6
Shuttlewood S44 99 A8
Club La DE73 244 A5
Clubmill Terr S40 95 E4
Club Row S32 71 E6
Clulow Cl DE72 235 E8
Clumber Ave NG16 171 E1
Clumber Cl
Ashbourne DE6 185 B8
Clowne S43 80 F4
3 Ripley DE5 169 E1
Clumber Ct NG19 135 E2
Clumber Dr NG19 135 E2
Clumber Pl S43 97 C6
Clumber St NG10 236 D7
Clun Ct NG19 136 D2
Clune St S43 81 A5
Cluster Rd DE56 178 F4
Clusters Ct 3 DE56 178 F4
Clyde St DE65 228 D1
Coach Dr
Eastwood NG16 182 F4
Quarndon DE22 204 D7
Coachhouse Mews 4 DE11 256 A7
Coachmans La SK23 33 D3
Coach Rd
Hollingworth SK14 9 C5
Ironville DE55 170 D3
Ripley DE5 169 E4
Ripley DE5 170 B3
Shireoaks S81 63 F6
Coach Way DE65 242 C5
Coachways DE7 193 F3
COAL ASTON 57 B4
Coalburn Cres DE4 157 A1
Coal La DE11, DE73 257 D8
Coalpit La
Coton in the Elms DE12 260 E3
Youlgreave DE45 125 C6
Coarses View SK23 47 C7
Coasthill DE4 156 F1
Coatestown La SK17 104 B1
Coatsby Rd NG16 195 F7
Cobblersnook La DE4 151 D8
Cobblestone Dr DE11 256 A4
Cobden Edge SK6 23 F4
Cobden Pl NG19 135 E2
Cobden Rd
Chesterfield S40 266 A4
Matlock DE4 143 C6
Cobden St
Derby DE22 218 D5
Long Eaton NG10 236 E7
Ripley DE5 169 D2
Cobham Cl DE24 231 D3
Cobnar Ave S8 43 A2
Cobnar Dr
Chesterfield S41 95 D8
Sheffield S8 43 A2
Cobnar Rd S8 43 A2
Cobnar Wood Cl S18 76 B3
Cobnar Wood Close Ind Est S41 76 B3
Cobthorn Dr DE22 204 C3
Coburn Pl DE1 267 A3
COCK ALLEY 97 A1
Cock Ayne Cl NG10 223 B3
Cockayne La DE6 164 B2
Cockayne Street N DE24 232 E6
Cockayne Street S DE24 232 E6
Cock Brow SK14 15 C7
Cockcharme Gapp DE74 247 B6
Cockerhouse Rd NG16 182 E4
Cock Hill
Baslow DE45 91 F5
Clifton DE6 184 F6
Cockleys NG10 236 C6
Cock Pitt The DE1 267 C3
Cockshead La
Holmewood DE4 116 E3
Snelston DE6 198 D7
Cockshut La
Melbourne DE73 251 F7
Whaley Thorns NG20 101 A4
Cockshut Lane Bsns Ctr DE73 252 A7
Cockshutt Ave S8 56 D8
Cockshutt Dr S8 56 D8
Cockshutt La DE55 170 F8
Cockshutt Rd S8 56 D8
COCKYARD 46 E4
Cod Beck Cl DE24 233 D6
Coddington La
Crich DE4 156 E2
Whatstandwell DE4 156 D1
CODNOR 181 C7
CODNOR BREACH 181 A4
Codnor CE Com Prim Sch DE5 181 B8
Codnor Denby La DE5 180 F4
Codnor-Denby La DE5 181 A5
CODNOR GATE 170 B1
Codnor Gate DE5 170 B1
Codnor Gate Ind Est DE5 170 A1
Codnor La DE5 170 C2
CODNOR PARK 170 E3
Coffin La DE6 165 B1
Coggers La S32 52 F8
Coisley Hill S13 44 F6
Cokayne Ave DE6 173 C2
Cokayne Mews DE6 173 C3
Cokefield Terr DE55 148 C1
Coke St DE22 218 D5
COLDEATON 150 B6
Cold Eaton DE6 150 C6
Coldharbour La S45 145 A4
Cold Side
Bradfield S33 21 F8
Bradfield S33 22 A8
Glossop S33 14 F3
Coldstream Wlk DE24 231 E4
Coldwall Rd DE6 172 B8
Coldwell End DE45 125 A5
Coldwell St DE4 165 F8
Cole La DE72 221 D3
Coleman St DE24 232 E7
Coleraine Cl DE21 220 B4
Coleridge St
Derby, Littleover DE23 231 E6
Derby, Normanton DE23 231 F7
Colin Ave DE5 181 B8
Colin St DE55 159 A4
Collaboration Way DE21 220 D1
Collage Rd S21 60 D2
Colledge St DE55 170 C6
College Ave S43 78 D1
College Dr SK17 85 D3
College Mews DE1 218 E5
College Rd
Buxton SK17 85 A6
Denstone ST14 196 C6
Spinkhill S21 60 D2
College Side NG18 136 C1
College St NG10 223 C2
College The DE5 180 C4
College View S43 80 E3
College Way SK17 85 B5
Collier Ave NG19 136 B5
Collier La DE72 221 C4
Colliers Cl DE11 255 E6
Colliers Ct DE5 181 A7
Collier St SK13 17 C8
Colliers Trek S43 80 C5
Colliers Way S45 131 B4
Colliery Cl S43 78 F1
Colliery Ct S42 116 C1
Colliery Drive S21 60 D5
Colliery La DE12 261 D4
Colliery Rd
Blackwell DE55 147 F1
Creswell S43 81 E1
Creswell S80 100 E8
Swadlincote DE11 256 A1
Colliery Row
Alfreton DE55 159 B5
Pinxton NG16 160 D2
Swadlincote DE11 256 A1
Collin Ave NG10 223 B4
Collingham Gdns DE22 218 A5
Collingham Rd NG19 135 D1
Collingwood Cres DE4 143 A6
Collingwood Rd NG10 236 E6
Collins Ave DE55 160 A7
Collins Yd S18 57 B1
Collis Cl DE24 232 E7
Collishaw Cl 6 S41 96 C1
Collumbell Ave DE72 221 C5
Collycroft Hill
Clifton DE6 184 F6
Snelston DE6 184 F1
Wyaston DE6 185 A3
Wyaston DE6 185 A5
Colne Cl NG19 136 D2
Colombo St DE23 219 B1
Colonade The NG20 119 E2
Colonel Wright Cl DE45 109 C5
Colonnade The 3 SK17 85 B8
Colonsay Cl NG9 209 D3
COLSHAW 103 E4
Colshaw La SK17 103 E4
Coltman Cl DE16 254 E6
Colton Cl S41 76 E1
Coltsfoot Cl DE11 256 F4
Coltsfoot Dr DE24 231 F2
Coltsworth La S43 80 E8
Columbell Way DE4 127 D2
Columbia St NG17 148 F3
Columbine Cl DE21 206 A1
Colver Rd S2 43 A8
Colvile Cl DE12 263 D7
Colvile St DE22 218 D6
Colwell Dr DE24 233 D5
Colwick Cl NG19 135 E1
Colwick Way S8 43 B2
Colwyn Ave DE23 218 D1
Colyear St DE1 267 B3
COMBRIDGE 210 C8
Combridge La
Alders ST14 196 B1
Combridge ST14 210 C8
COMBS 46 E1
Combs Bank 53 SK13 9 D2
Combs Cl SK22 33 A8
Combs Fold 51 SK13 9 D2
Combs Gdns 2 SK13 9 D1
Combs Gr 49 SK13 9 D2
Combs Inf Sch SK23 46 E1
Combs Lea 1 SK13 9 D1
Combs Mews 48 SK13 9 D2
Combs Rd SK23 46 E3
Combs Terr 50 SK13 9 D2
Combs Way 52 SK13 9 D2
Comery Cl 4 DE7 208 E5
Comfrey Cl 1 DE23 230 F6
Comice Gdns NG16 182 D6
Comley Cres S41 76 D2
Commerce St
Derby DE24 232 F8
Melbourne DE73 252 A7
Commercial Rd
Grindleford S32 72 C8
Tideswell SK17 69 C4
COMMON END 132 F7
Common End DE65 229 B3
Common La
Chelmorton SK17 87 A1
Cutthorpe S42 94 E8
King Sterndale SK17 86 A1
Mansfield NG19 135 F5
Mansfield Woodhouse NG19 136 A4
Newgate S18 75 E1
Shirebrook NG20 119 C2
Shirebrook NG20 119 C4
Shirland DE55 146 C3
Stanley DE7 207 A7
Sutton on the Hill DE6 228 A8
Commonpiece La DE6 215 B2
Common Piece La DE65 230 E1
Commonpiece Rd S45 131 C3
Common Rd
Harthill S26 62 B5
Sutton in Ashfield NG17 148 F2
Swadlincote DE11 256 C2
Thorpe Salvin S80 62 F6
Commons Cl NG16 195 A8
COMMONSIDE
Brailsford 187 D1
Selston 171 F8
Sutton in Ashfield 148 F2
COMMON SIDE
Barlow 75 D3
Heanor 181 E1
Common Side
Selston NG16 171 F8
Swadlincote DE11 256 C2
Commonside Rd S18 75 D2
Common The
Crich DE4 168 A7
Holmesfield Common S17 74 E8
Melbourne DE73 251 E5
Quarndon DE22 204 C8
South Normanton DE55 160 A5
Common Wood DE4 143 B3
Compass Cres S41 77 C3
COMPSTALL 15 A3
Compstall Mills Ests SK6 15 B2
Compstall Rd
Compstall SK6 15 A3
Marple SK6 15 A2
COMPTON 173 D2
Compton Ave DE72 246 A8
Compton Cl 6 DE24 233 C6
Compton Dr S80 81 D1
Compton Gr SK17 85 B6
Compton Rd SK17 85 B6
Compton St
Ashbourne DE6 173 C2
Chesterfield S40 266 A4
Holmewood S42 116 E1
Langwith NG20 119 F8
Compton Way DE23 230 F5
Com Side Croft S12 43 F5
Conalan Ave S17 56 B5
Concert Pl 6 SK17 85 B7
Concorde Cl DE7 209 A7
Concorde Way NG19 135 E3
Condliff Rd SK17 69 B5
Condor Rd DE7 208 F4
Conduit Rd S44 118 B8
Conduit Road S44 99 A1
Conduit St
Glossop SK13 9 F7
Tintwistle SK13 9 F7
Coneygreave Dr DE16 254 D5
Coney Green Bsns Ctr S45 131 E4
Coney Green Networking Ctr S45 131 E4
Coney Green Rd S45 131 E4
Coneygrey Cl DE21 205 D2
CONGREAVE 126 D7
Congreave La DE45 126 D7
Coniston Ave DE21 220 E6
Coniston Cl NG19 136 F4
Coniston Cres DE21 205 D2
Coniston Dr
Clay Cross S45 131 B2
Ilkeston DE7 208 D5
Coniston Rd
Chesterfield S41 95 E8
Dronfield S18 56 E1
Long Eaton NG10 223 A2
Coniston Way S41 95 E8
Conjoint La SK17 69 E4
Conkers Discovery Ctr DE12 262 D5
Conkers Waterside Ctr DE12 262 D4
Conksbury Ave DE45 125 C6
Conksbury La DE45 125 C6
Connaught Ct DE55 159 B3
Connaught Rd DE22 218 C4
Connelly Ct S40 95 E3
Consett Cl DE21 205 D1
Consort Gdns DE21 206 C3
Constable Ave DE23 218 C2
Constable Cl
3 Dronfield S18 56 E1
Sheffield S14 43 E2
Constable Dr
Derby DE23 218 B1
Marple SK6 23 B8
Sheffield S14 43 D2
Constable La DE23 218 C3
Constable Pl S14 43 E2
Constable Rd S14 43 D2
Constable Way S14 43 D2
Constantine Ct DE12 265 F1
Convent Ct DE15 254 F8
Conway Ave DE72 221 D2
Conway Rd NG10 236 F8
Conway St NG10 236 F8
Conygree La DE6 184 D7
Cook Cl DE56 179 E5
Cook Dr
Etwall DE65 229 C3
Ilkeston DE7 209 A6
Cooke & Beard Homes S8 43 B5
Cooke Cl
Clay Cross S42 131 B6
Long Eaton NG10 236 B7
Cookfield DE56 179 E8
Cookham Cl DE3 217 C2
Cook La DE6 211 B1
Cooks Dr DE74 247 A3
Coole Well Cl S43 97 D8
Coombes La SK13 16 C5
Coombes View SK14 15 F8
Coombsdale La
Calver S32 72 A2
Stoney Middleton DE45 71 C1
Coombs La S32 90 F8
Coombs Rd DE45 109 F5
Co-operative St
Derby DE23 218 F2
Disley SK12 32 D6
Long Eaton NG10 236 E6
Cooper Cl DE74 246 F2
Coopers Cl
Acresford DE12 265 B7
Borrowash DE72 221 D1
Cooper's Cl 2 DE6 173 C2
Coopers Croft DE65 227 C1
Coopers Gdns DE6 173 B1
Cooper St
Derby DE22 218 D6
Glossop SK13 10 B1
Copecastle Sq DE1 267 C2
Cope Ct DE24 232 A5
Copeland Ave NG9 223 E8
Copeland St DE1 267 C2
Copenhagen Rd S45 131 E4
Copestake Cl NG10 236 A7
Copes Way
Derby DE21 220 A8
Uttoxeter ST14 210 A1
Copley Croft 3 DE6 173 D3
COPLOW DALE 50 E3
Coplow Dale SK17 50 F3
Coplow La DE65 226 D5
Copperas Rd DE11 255 D5
Copper Beech Dr SK13 9 E1
Copper Beeches DE5 169 C2
Copperfield Mws DE14 253 A7
Copperleaf Cl DE22 267 A2
Copper Yd DE5 180 F2
Coppice Ave
High Lane SK12 32 A6
Ilkeston DE7 194 D5
Coppice Brook DE56 179 B4
Coppice Cl
Castle Donington DE74 246 F3
Chesterfield S41 115 D6
Derby DE22 204 F1
High Lane SK12 32 A6
Kilburn DE56 192 A7
Coppice Ct DE75 193 F7
Coppice Dr
Eastwood NG16 182 D3
Heanor DE75 193 F7
Coppice End Rd DE22 204 C1
Coppice Farm Rd DE5 180 F7
Coppice La
Clifton Campville B79 263 F1
High Lane SK12 32 A5
Coppice Mews DE75 193 F7
Coppice Prim Sch DE75 193 E8
Coppice Rd DE14 253 C8
Coppice Rise DE65 242 E2
Coppice Side DE11 256 C3
Coppice The
Horwich End SK23 45 F5
Shirebrook NG20 119 D3
Coppice View DE55 160 A4
Coppicewood Dr DE23 218 A1
Copse Cl DE4 165 E8
Copse Dr DE5 180 F7
Copse Gr DE23 231 A7
Copse Rise DE11 256 B7
Copseside Cl 10 NG10 236 A8
Copse The
Ilkeston DE7 194 D5
Marple SK6 23 C8
Copsewood DE55 160 A4
Copsey Croft Ct NG10 236 F7
Copthorne Com Inf Sch DE55 159 A5
Copthorne Dr 4 DE55 158 E2
Copthurst Rd HD9 3 E7
Coral Cl DE24 219 E2
Coral Way S45 131 D4
Corbar Grange SK17 85 A8
Corbar Rd SK17 66 B1
Corbar Woods La SK17 66 A1
Corbel Cl DE21 205 E2
Corbridge Gr DE23 231 A7
CORBRIGGS 115 F5
Corby Cl DE24 232 F5
Corby La DE23 230 F6
Cordelia Way DE73 232 E2
Corden Ave DE3 218 A2
Corden St DE23 219 A2
Cordville Cl DE21 220 B5
CORDWELL 74 E6
Cordwell Ave S41 95 C8
Cordwell Cl
Castle Donington DE74 246 F3
7 Castle Donington DE74 246 F4
Staveley S43 97 D8
Cordwell La S18 74 E5
Cordy La
Brinsley NG16 182 F8
New Brinsley NG16 171 F1
Selston NG16 182 F8
Corfe Cl DE23 231 D6
Corfield Ave DE75 193 F7
Corfield CE Inf Sch DE75 181 D1
Corfield Cl DE75 181 D4
Coriander Gdns DE23 231 D4
Corinium Cl DE24 233 D5
Corker Rd S12 44 A6
Corks La SK12 32 E5
Corley La DE6 174 D2
Cornbrook DE45 108 F7
Corn Cl DE55 160 B6

Cornel Ct [4] NG19 . . 136 E1
Corner Farm DE6 . . . 201 E8
Corner Pin Cl [7] S43 . 78 F2
Cornfield Ave DE55 . 160 A4
Cornfield Cl [1] S42 . . 95 A5
Cornfield Rd NG16 . . 195 E7
Cornflower Dr DE21 206 B3
Cornhill DE22 . . . . 204 F4
Cornhill Cl DE56 . . . . 190 D4
Cornhill Dr DE55 . . . . 159 B4
Cornmill Bank
DE13 . . . . 239 D6
Cornmill Cl
Bolsover S44 . . . . 99 B2
Calver S32 . . . . 72 C1
Derby DE72 . . . . 233 D5
Corn Mill Cl DE4 . . . . 165 E6
Cornmill Ho SK13 . . . . . 10 D1
Cornmill La DE13 . . . 239 E6
Corn Mill Terr DE4 . . 143 E7
Corn Mkt DE1 . . . . . . 267 B3
Corn St SK13 . . . . 10 D1
Cornstone Ave [1]
DE55 . . . . 148 B7
Cornwall Ave
Brimington S43 . . . . 96 F8
Buxton SK17 . . . . 85 E7
Cornwall Cl
[4] Brimington S43 . . . . . 96 F8
Westwood NG16 . . . . 171 C4
Cornwall Dr
Brimington S43 . . . . 96 F8
Grassmoor S42 . . . . . . 115 F3
Long Eaton NG10 . . . . 237 A8
Cornwallis Cl NG10 . 236 D6
Cornwall Rd
Burton upon Trent
DE15 . . . . 254 E6
Derby DE21 . . . . 219 D6
Shireoaks S81 . . . . 63 F7
Coronation Ave
Belper DE56 . . . . 179 A5
Derby DE24 . . . . 233 C5
New Houghton NG19 . . 134 F7
Sandiacre NG10 . . . . . 223 A7
Coronation Cl DE73 . 252 B8
Coronation Cotts
DE13 . . . . 253 A8
Coronation Cres
ST14 . . . . 197 A4
Coronation Dr
Shirebrook NG20 . . . . . 119 F2
South Normanton
DE55 . . . . 160 B5
Coronation La
DE12 . . . . 265 F6
Coronation Rd
Brimington S43 . . . . 96 E8
Cossall DE7, NG16 . . . 195 A2
Mapperley DE7 . . . . 193 F3
Stanley DE7 . . . . 207 C6
Coronation St
Derby DE23 . . . . 232 B8
[1] Ilkeston DE7 . . . . . . 208 F8
Overseal DE12 . . . . . . 262 A4
Swadlincote DE11 . . . . 256 A5
Whitwell S80 . . . . 82 A6
Coronet Ct DE21 . . . . 206 D3
Corporation Rd
DE7 . . . . 209 A5
Corporation St
Chesterfield S41 . . . . . 266 C3
Derby DE1 . . . . 267 B3
Corve Way S40 . . . . 94 F5
COSSALL 195 C1
COSSALL COMMON 195 B3
Cossall Ind Est DE7 . . 195 B2
COSSALL MARSH . . 195 C2
Cossall Rd NG9 . . . . . 209 D5
Cote Bottom La
DE65 . . . . 227 A7
COTE GREEN 15 C1
Cote Green La SK6 . . . . 15 B1
Cote Green Rd SK6 . . . 15 C1
Cote Hilloc DE4 . . . . 127 A6
Cote La SK22 . . . . 25 D3
COTES PARK 159 C2
Cotes Park Ind Est
DE55 . . . . 159 D2
Cotes Park La DE55 . 159 C2
Cotgrave Rd NG19 . . . 135 F2
Cotman Dr SK6 . . . . 23 C8
COTMANHAY 194 E4
Cotmanhay Inf & Jun Sch DE7 . . . . 194 E5
Cotmanhay Rd DE7 . . 194 F3
Coton Cl NG19 . . . . . . 136 E4
COTON IN THE CLAY 238 A7
COTON IN THE ELMS 260 C4
Coton in the Elms CE Prim Sch DE12 . . . . 260 D3
Coton La
Coton in the Elms
DE12 . . . . 260 F3
Lullington DE12 . . . . . 263 D7
Rosliston DE12 . . . . . . 260 D5
COTON PARK 261 C8
Coton Pk DE12 . . . . . 255 C1
Coton Rd
Coton in the Elms
DE12 . . . . 260 C1
Lullington DE12 . . . . . 263 D8
Coton Rd *continued*
Walton-on-Trent
DE12 . . . . 259 E6
Walton upon Trent
DE12 . . . . 259 F5
Cotswold Cl
[2] Chesterfield S40 . . . . 95 C5
Derby DE23 . . . . 231 C8
Glossop SK13 . . . . 17 A8
[4] Long Eaton NG10 . . . 236 B8
Swadlincote DE11 . . . 256 A3
Cotswold Dr S42 . . . 115 E3
Cotswold Rd DE14 . . . 253 F8
Cottage Cl
Heage DE56 . . . . 179 E8
Ilkeston DE7 . . . . 194 D3
Poolsbrook S43 . . . . 98 A7
Swadlincote DE11 . . . 256 A7
Cottage Ct DE56 . . . . 179 E3
Cottage Garden La
DE75 . . . . 181 D2
Cottage La SK13 . . . . 9 E2
Cottage Meadow Way [3]
DE72 . . . . 246 A6
Cottages The SK23 . . . 47 B6
Cottam Cres SK6 . . . . . 23 B7
Cottam Dr S43 . . . . 80 C6
Cotterdale Cl NG19 . 136 E1
Cotterhill La S43 . . . . . 96 E7
Cotter Wood Cl
DE21 . . . . 205 C7
Cottesmore Cl DE15 248 B1
Cottesmore Rd
DE15 . . . . 248 A1
Cottisford Cl DE23 . . 231 A8
Cottonbrook Rd
DE23 . . . . 232 B8
Cotton Cl SK23 . . . . 45 E5
Cotton La DE24 . . . . . 219 C1
Cotton Lace Cl DE7 . . 208 F6
Cotton Mill Hill S42 . 113 E7
Cotton Mill Yard
DE21 . . . . 205 A2
Cotton St S44 . . . . 99 A1
Cotts The SK17 . . . . 86 D5
Council Hos
Bradbourne DE6 . . . . . 163 B6
Hanbury DE13 . . . . . . 238 A3
Countess Gr DE73 . . . 244 F8
Counting House Rd
SK12 . . . . 32 E5
Countisbury Dr
DE21 . . . . 206 A2
County Est The
NG17 . . . . 148 E2
Coupe La S42, S45 . . 131 A5
Coupe St DE5 . . . . 180 F8
Coupland Cl S41 . . . . . . 77 C4
Coupland Pl DE55 . . 159 C1
Court Farm La DE14 253 E7
Court La DE45 . . . . . . 108 E8
Courtland Dr DE24 . . 233 B6
Courtland Gdns
DE24 . . . . 233 B7
Courtland Rd DE65 . 229 C3
Courtney Way DE56 . 179 D5
Court Pl S43 . . . . 97 C8
Court St DE11 . . . . . . 256 E3
Court The DE24 . . . . . 233 B6
Court View S43 . . . . 80 E3
Courtway Cres
DE73 . . . . 244 E8
Courtyard Mews
DE24 . . . . 233 A6
Courtyard Pl DE21 . . 220 E5
Courtyard The
Bakewell DE45 . . . . . . 109 D6
Belper DE56 . . . . 179 A4
Darley Dale DE4 . . . . . 127 C3
Hollingworth SK14 . . . . . . 9 D5
Kimberley NG16 . . . . . . 195 E8
Covent Garden Close
DE72 . . . . 221 B2
Coventry Cl DE11 . . . 256 D6
Coventry La NG9 . . . . 209 F2
Coverdale Wlk
DE24 . . . . 233 C7
Covert Pl DE11 . . . . . 262 C8
Covert The DE21 . . . . 220 E4
Cowbrook Ave SK13 . . 10 F1
Cowbrook Ct SK13 . . . . 10 F1
Cowburn Dr SK22 . . . . . 24 C1
Cowdale Cotts SK17 . . 86 A4
Cowdray Cl DE24 . . . 231 D2
COWERS LANE 177 D3
Cowham Cl DE55 . . . 159 C3
COWHILL 179 A2
Cow La
Brimington S43 . . . . 77 E1
Hyde SK14 . . . . 9 D6
COWLEY 75 D7
COWLEY BAR 75 B8
Cowley Bottom S18 . . . 75 E8
Cowley Cl
Chesterfield S41 . . . . . 266 C3
Ilkeston DE7 . . . . 194 F5
Cowley Gdns S20 . . . . . 59 E8
Cowley La S18 . . . . 75 D7
Cowley St DE22 . . . . . 218 E7
Cowlishall Dr S45 . . 131 B7
Cowlishaw Cl DE72 . 234 E1
Cowlow La SK17,
SK23 . . . . 47 C2
Cowper Rd NG16 . . . 195 A8
Cowper St DE24 . . . . 232 A5
Cowpingle La S43 . . . . 77 E1
Cowsell Dr S45 . . . . . 131 E2
Cowsley Rd DE21 . . . 219 D7
Cowslip Cl DE12 . . . . 262 E1
Cowslip Mdw DE72 . 235 B7
COXBENCH 191 F3
Coxbench Rd DE21 . . 191 F4
Cox Green Ct DE23 . . 230 F7
Coxon St DE21 . . . . . . 220 E5
Coxon's Yd [5] DE6 . . 173 B2
Cox's La NG19 . . . . . . 136 B5
Crabapple Dr NG16 . 182 C4
Crabtree Ave SK12 . . . . 32 E5
Crabtree Cl
Castle Donington
DE74 . . . . 247 A2
Clay Cross S45 . . . . 131 E3
Derby DE22 . . . . 204 C4
Wirksworth DE4 . . . . . 165 E7
Crabtree Ct SK12 . . . . . 32 D6
Crabtree Hill DE22 . . 204 C3
Crab Tree Hill DE21 . 205 C8
Cracken Cl SK23 . . . . . . 34 D2
Cracroft La S44 . . . . . 118 F6
Craddock Ave DE21 . 220 E3
Craddock Mews S2 . . . 43 E7
Cradock Rd S2 . . . . 43 F7
Crafty Flats La DE12 . 260 F3
Cragdale Gr S20 . . . . . . 59 D7
Cragg La DE55 . . . . . . 148 A2
Craggon Dr S43 . . . . . . 77 D4
Craggs Dr S43 . . . . 80 E3
Craggs Rd S44 . . . . 99 A2
Crag Hall La SK11 . . 102 A5
Craglands Gr S40 . . . . . 95 A5
Crags Bsns Pk S80 . . 100 E8
Cragside Cl S41 . . . . . . 96 C3
Crags Rd
Belph S80 . . . . 82 B3
Creswell S43 . . . . 81 F1
Creswell S80 . . . . 82 A1
Crags View S80 . . . . 81 F1
Craig Dr SK23 . . . . 45 E6
Craiglee Ct [1] DE24 . 231 D3
Craig St NG10 . . . . . . 236 E7
CRAKEMARSH 210 D5
Crampton Cl DE11 . . 256 E5
Cranberry Gr [2]
DE23 . . . . 230 F6
Cranborne Rd S41 . . . . 95 E7
Cranbourne Cl NG9 . 209 D2
Cranbrook Ct NG19 . 136 C6
Craner Rd DE74 . . . . 246 E3
Cranfield Ave DE11 . 255 E2
Cranfleet Way NG10 236 B7
Cranhill Cl DE23 . . . . 230 F6
Cranleigh Rd S43 . . . . . 79 B3
Cranmer Gr NG19 . . . 135 D3
Cranmer Rd DE21 . . . 267 D3
Cranmer St
Ilkeston DE7 . . . . 194 F1
Long Eaton NG10 . . . . 223 D1
Cranwood Cl DE24 . . 232 D5
Cratcliff View DE4 . . 126 A1
Craven Rd S41 . . . . 95 F5
Crawford Ave NG9 . . 223 D8
Crawford Rd S8 . . . . . . 43 A4
Crawley Rd DE24 . . . 232 F5
Crawley Way DE72 . . 245 A8
Crawshaw Ave S8 . . . . 56 D8
Crawshaw Gr S8 . . . . . 56 D8
Crawshaw Mews S18 . 56 C1
Crayford Rd DE24 . . . 233 A5
Cray's Hill
Swanwick DE55 . . . . . 170 A6
Swanwick DE55 . . . . . 170 B7
CRAYTHORNE 240 D2
Craythorne Cl DE11 . 256 A7
Craythorne Rd
DE13 . . . . 240 D3
Creamery La DE6 . . . 151 D1
Crecy Cl DE22 . . . . . . 218 C3
CREIGHTON 210 A5
Creighton La ST14 . . 210 A5
Cres S26 . . . . 61 E5
Crescent S26 . . . . 61 E5
Crescent Dr SK23 . . . . . 33 D2
Crescent Prim Sch
NG19 . . . . 135 D2
Crescent Rd
Ashover S42 . . . . 113 D7
Selston NG16 . . . . 171 D6
Crescent Row SK22 . . . 25 A2
Crescent The
Alfreton DE55 . . . . 159 B3
Barlborough S43 . . . . . . 80 C6
Bradwell S33 . . . . 51 A8
Breaston DE72 . . . . . . 235 C7
Breedon on the Hill
DE73 . . . . 252 E2
Brimington S43 . . . . 96 C7
Buxton SK17 . . . . 85 B8
Chapel-en-le-Frith
SK23 . . . . 47 C7
Clay Cross S45 . . . . . . 131 C2
Derby, Boulton DE24 . . 232 E6
Derby, Chaddesden
DE21 . . . . 219 F5
Holmesfield S18 . . . . 75 A8
Holymoorside S42 . . . 113 D8
Hope S33 . . . . 39 A4
Horsley Woodhouse
DE7 . . . . 192 C7
Mayfield DE6 . . . . 184 D7
New Mills SK22 . . . . 33 B8
Repton DE65 . . . . 242 D2
Risley DE72 . . . . 222 D3
Sheffield S17 . . . . 55 E5
Shirebrook NG20 . . . . . 119 E6
Shirley DE6 . . . . 200 D7
Stanley DE7 . . . . 207 B8
Crescent The *continued*
Stapleford NG9 . . . . . . 209 E2
Swadlincote DE11 . . . . 255 E6
CRESSBROOK 89 A6
Cressbrook Ave
S42 . . . . 132 B7
Cressbrook Way
DE21 . . . . 206 B3
Cressida Ct DE73 . . . 232 D2
Cresswell Ave SK22 . . . 33 C8
Cresswellpart La S33 . 50 E7
Cresswell St SK22 . . . . 33 C8
Cressy Rd DE55 . . . . . 159 A4
Cresta Gr DE21 . . . . . 205 F1
Crest Cl DE13 . . . . . . 240 E1
Crest The
Derby DE22 . . . . 204 E2
Linton DE12 . . . . 261 C6
CRESWELL 81 F2
Creswell Bsns Pk
S80 . . . . 100 E8
Creswell CE (Controlled) Inf Sch S80 . . . . 81 E1
Creswell Crags★
S80 . . . . 82 A1
Creswell Ct [12]
NG19 . . . . 136 E4
Creswell Jun Sch
S80 . . . . 81 E1
Creswell L Ctr S80 . . . . 81 F1
Creswell Rd
Clowne S43 . . . . 80 F4
Cuckney NG20 . . . . . . 101 E3
Creswell Sta S80 . . . . . 81 E1
Creswick Cl S40 . . . . 114 B8
Crewe St DE23 . . . . . . 218 F1
CREWTON 232 F8
Crewton Way DE24 . . 232 F7
CRICH 156 F1
Crich Ave DE23 . . . . . 218 C2
Crich Carr CE Prim Sch
DE4 . . . . 156 C1
Crich CE Inf Sch
DE4 . . . . 156 F1
Crich Cir DE23 . . . . . . 218 C2
CRICH COMMON . . . 168 B8
Crich Common
DE56 . . . . 168 A6
Crich Jun Sch DE4 . . 157 A1
Crich La
Belper DE56 . . . . 179 A7
Ridgeway DE56 . . . . . . 168 B3
Crich Pl
Buxton SK17 . . . . 85 E7
North Wingfield S42 . . . 131 F6
Crich Rd
Crich DE4 . . . . 167 E8
Staveley S43 . . . . 97 C7
Crich Tramway Village★
DE4 . . . . 156 E2
Crich View
Bolsover S44 . . . . 118 B8
Newton DE55 . . . . 148 A4
Crich View Dr DE56 . 179 E8
Crich Way DE11 . . . . 255 E5
Cricket Cl DE15 . . . . . 248 E8
Cricketers Cl DE15 . . . 254 F8
Cricketers Ct DE23 . . 231 D8
Cricket View S43 . . . . . 80 E2
Cricklewood Ct [7]
S43 . . . . 78 B3
Cricklewood Rd
DE22 . . . . 218 B6
Crimbles La DE45 . . . 125 B5
Cringle Mews DE21 . 205 E2
Cripton La S45 . . . . . 129 E5
Crispin Cl S12 . . . . 44 A4
Crispin Dr S12 . . . . 44 A4
Crispin Gdns S12 . . . . . 44 A4
Crispin Rd [3] S12 . . . . 44 A4
CRIST 46 B8
Critchley St DE7 . . . . 194 F1
Critch's Flats NG16 . . 195 F6
Croft Ave DE6 . . . . . . 151 D1
Croft Cl
Dale Abbey DE7 . . . . . . 207 F2
Derby DE21 . . . . 220 F5
Netherseal DE12 . . . . . 264 F7
Ockbrook DE72 . . . . . . 221 C4
Pinxton NG16 . . . . 160 C3
Rolleston DE13 . . . . . . 240 B4
Croft Cres NG16 . . . . 195 C5
Croft Ct NG17 . . . . 148 F4
Croft End DE21 . . . . . 205 C8
Crofters Cl S21 . . . . 60 C4
Crofters Ct DE21 . . . . 205 E2
Croft Gr ST14 . . . . 210 C1
Croft House Way S44 98 F1
Croft Inf Sch DE55 . . 159 A3
Croft La DE21 . . . . 205 D3
Croft Lea S18 . . . . 56 C2
Croft Manor SK13 . . . . 10 E1
Croft Meadow DE4 . 154 C5
Crofton Cl
Dronfield S18 . . . . 56 F1
Yeaveley DE6 . . . . 199 D5
Crofton Rise S18 . . . . . 56 F1
Croft Pk SK13 . . . . 10 D1
Croft Rd
Great Longstone
DE45 . . . . 90 A4
Sheffield, Intake S12 . . . 44 B5
Croftstead Ave
ST14 . . . . 196 D6
Crofts The S32 . . . . 53 A8
Croft The
Bamford S33 . . . . 40 B3
Belper DE56 . . . . 179 C1
Croft The *continued*
Burton upon Trent
DE15 . . . . 254 F8
Derby DE23 . . . . 231 D8
Draycott DE72 . . . . . . 235 A6
Duffield DE56 . . . . 190 D4
Glossop SK13 . . . . 10 A6
Heage DE56 . . . . 168 E1
[2] Melbourne DE73 . . 252 A8
Morley DE7 . . . . 192 C2
Mottram in Longdendale
SK14 . . . . 9 A4
Shirebrook NG20 . . . . . 119 F3
Shirland DE55 . . . . 146 D2
Somercotes DE55 . . . . 170 C7
South Normanton
DE55 . . . . 160 A6
Swadlincote DE11 . . . . 255 E6
Taddington SK17 . . . . . . 88 A3
Croft View
Clowne S43 . . . . 80 F3
Staveley S43 . . . . 97 C6
Croftview Cl DE21 . . 205 D3
Croft Way DE23 . . . . . 230 F6
Croft Wlk S80 . . . . 82 A6
Cromarty Cl DE24 . . . 231 E4
Cromarty Rise S18 . . . 56 D2
Cromdale Ave S43 . . . . 77 D4
Cromer Cl DE3 . . . . . . 217 C1
CROMFORD 155 A6
Cromford Bank [21]
SK13 . . . . 9 D2
Cromford Canal Nature Reserve★ DE56 . . . . . 167 E5
Cromford CE Prim Sch
DE4 . . . . 155 B6
Cromford Cl
Aldercar NG16 . . . . 182 B4
[22] Gamesley SK13 . . . . . 9 D2
Long Eaton NG10 . . . . 236 A5
North Wingfield S42 . . . 132 B7
Cromford Ct
[4] Chesterfield S41 . . . . 95 D7
Horwich End SK23 . . . . . 45 E6
Cromford Dr
Derby DE3 . . . . 217 E4
Staveley S43 . . . . 97 C8
Cromford Fold [23]
SK13 . . . . 9 D2
Cromford Gn [20] SK13 . . 9 D2
Cromford Gr [18] SK13 . . 9 D2
Cromford La SK17 . . . 85 E7
Cromford Lea [19] SK13 . 9 D2
Cromford Mews
SK23 . . . . 45 E5
Cromford Pl
Buxton SK17 . . . . 85 E7
[24] Gamesley SK13 . . . . . 9 D2
Cromford Rd
Aldercar NG16 . . . . 182 B4
Clay Cross S45 . . . . . . 131 A5
Crich DE4 . . . . 156 F2
Derby DE21 . . . . 220 A8
Heanor NG16 . . . . 181 E5
Ripley DE5 . . . . 169 C2
Wirksworth DE4 . . . . . . 154 F1
Cromford Road Ind Est
NG16 . . . . 182 B4
Cromford Sta DE4 . . 155 C7
Cromford Way [17]
SK13 . . . . 9 D2
Cromford Wharf★
DE4 . . . . 155 C7
Crompton Cl DE4 . . . 127 E1
Crompton Rd
Ilkeston DE7 . . . . 209 B4
Mansfield NG19 . . . . . 135 D3
Staveley S43 . . . . 78 F2
Crompton Road Ind Est
DE7 . . . . 209 B3
Crompton St
Derby DE1 . . . . 267 B2
New Houghton NG19 . . 134 F8
Cromwell Ave
Blackwell DE55 . . . . . . 147 E1
Chapel-en-le-Frith
SK23 . . . . 47 A5
Findern DE65 . . . . 230 D2
Ilkeston DE7 . . . . 209 A5
Cromwell Cl DE13 . . 239 C5
Cromwell Dr DE55 . . 169 D7
Cromwell Rd
Bolsover S44 . . . . 118 B8
Chesterfield S40 . . . . . 266 A4
Derby DE23 . . . . 218 F2
Cromwell St NG16 . . 195 C8
Cromwell Terr DE7 . . 194 F3
Crooked Spire (St Mary & All Saints Church)★
S40 . . . . 266 B3
Crookes Ave
[1] Mansfield Woodhouse
NG19 . . . . 136 C3
Pleasley NG19 . . . . 135 A5
Crook Stile DE4 . . . . 143 A7
CROPPER 215 B4
Cropper La
Sutton on the Hill
DE6 . . . . 215 B4
Thurvaston DE6 . . . . . 201 C1
Cropston Cl S41 . . . . 115 C7
Cropton Cl DE24 . . . . 233 C6
Crosby Dr DE65 . . . . . 227 D2
Crosby St DE22 . . . . . 218 D4
Cross Chantrey Rd
S8 . . . . 43 A3
Cross Cl
Derby DE23 . . . . 231 C8
Cross Cl *continued*
Overseal DE12 . . . . 262 B3
Cross Cliffe SK13 . . . . . 17 E8
Crossdale Gr DE21 . . 206 C3
Crossfield Gr SK6 . . . . . 15 B1
Crossgate La SK13 . . . . . 9 F7
Crossgreen Cotts
DE4 . . . . 142 B8
Crosshill DE5 . . . . 181 B6
CROSS HILL 181 B5
Crosshill Dr DE7 . . . . 208 C5
Crossings Ave SK23 . . . 47 A6
Crossings Mdw SK23 . 47 A6
Crossings Rd SK23 . . . . 46 F6
Cross Key Mws
DE56 . . . . 177 C2
Cross Keys La DE55 . 169 E7
Cross Keys Row
SK23 . . . . 47 B8
Cross La
Calver S32 . . . . 72 B2
Codnor DE5 . . . . 181 B7
Dronfield S18 . . . . 57 C5
Dronfield, Coal Aston
S18 . . . . 57 C3
Dronfield, Quoit Green
S18 . . . . 57 B1
Flagg SK17 . . . . 106 E7
Ible DE4 . . . . 153 E7
Monyash DE45 . . . . 107 B2
Rolleston DE13 . . . . 240 B2
Sheffield S17 . . . . 55 C8
Shirland DE55 . . . . 158 E8
Sutton in Ashfield
NG17 . . . . 148 F2
Wessington DE55 . . . . . 157 F8
Crossland Dr S12 . . . . . 44 A3
Crossland Pl S12 . . . . . 44 A4
Crossland Rd S32 . . . . . 53 A7
Crosslands Cl SK13 . . . 17 D8
Crossland Villas S32 . . 53 A7
Crosslanes DE6 . . . . . 215 C5
Cross Lanes DE4 . . . . 144 C1
Cross Lea DE7 . . . . . . 207 F2
Crossley St DE5 . . . . . 169 E2
Cross London St S43 . 77 D3
Crosslow La DE6 . . . 150 E5
Cross Myrtle Rd S2 . . . 43 B7
CROSS O' THE HANDS
DE56 . . . . 176 E1
Cross Park Rd [1] S8 . . 43 A5
Cross Rd ST14 . . . . . . 210 B1
Cross/Repton Sch The
DE65 . . . . 242 C3
Cross Rise SK13 . . . . . . 17 E8
Crossroads Bsns Pk
S43 . . . . 80 E4
Cross Side DE6 . . . . . . 184 F7
Cross St
Bolsover S44 . . . . 118 C8
Breedon on the Hill
DE73 . . . . 252 F2
Brimington S43 . . . . 96 E8
[8] Broadbottom SK14 . . 16 A8
Buxton SK17 . . . . 85 D8
Castleton S33 . . . . 38 B2
Chapel-en-le-Frith
SK23 . . . . 47 B6
Chesterfield S40 . . . . . 266 A4
Clay Cross S45 . . . . 131 C3
Derby DE22 . . . . 218 D6
Glossop SK13 . . . . 10 C1
Grassmoor S42 . . . . . . 115 F3
Hadfield SK13 . . . . 10 A5
Hollingworth SK14 . . . . . . 9 D4
Killamarsh S21 . . . . 60 F7
Linton DE11 . . . . 261 E8
Long Eaton NG10 . . . . 236 E8
Mansfield Woodhouse
NG19 . . . . 136 B2
New Mills SK22 . . . . 33 C8
North Wingfield S42 . . . 131 E6
Sandiacre NG10 . . . . . . 223 C6
Cross The
[1] Glossop SK13 . . . . . . 10 A5
Great Longstone DE45 . . 89 F4
Crossways La DE6 . . 176 B2
Cross Wellington St
S43 . . . . 77 D3
Crow Croft Rd S45 . . 132 C2
Crowcroft Way
NG10 . . . . 223 B2
CROWDEN 6 E3
Crowden Dr SK13 . . . . 10 B5
CROWDICOTE 121 E7
Crowdicote Rd
SK17 . . . . 105 D1
Crowestones SK17 . . . 85 C6
Crowfoot La DE65 . . 226 E8
Crow Hill
Palterton S44 . . . . 118 A5
Pleasley NG19 . . . . 135 B5
Crowhill La DE45 . . . 109 A6
Crow Hill La NG19 . . 136 B2
Crow Hill Rd HD9 . . . . . 3 B8
CROWHOLE 75 D4
Crow La
Brackenfield DE55 . . . 146 A6
Chesterfield S41 . . . . . . 96 C3
Unstone S18 . . . . 76 F7
Crown Cl
Chesterfield S43 . . . . . . 77 D3
Long Eaton NG10 . . . . 236 A7
Crown Gdns DE16 . . 254 E8
Crown Hill Way
Stanley Common
DE7 . . . . 193 B1
West Hallam DE7 . . . . . 207 B8

Crown La S18 ... 58 A1
Crownland Dr DE73. 233 A2
Crown Mews DE22 ... 218 E3
Crown Rd S41 ... 96 A5
Crown Rise DE11 ... 256 D3
Crown Sq
Branston DE14 ... 253 E8
Matlock DE4 ... 143 B5
Crown St
Clowne S43 ... 80 E3
Derby DE22 ... 218 E3
Duffield DE56 ... 190 E4
Marple SK6 ... 23 A3
Crown Terr 2 DE56 ... 178 F4
Crown Way
Aldercar NG16 ... 182 B4
Chellaston DE73 ... 244 F8
Crown Wlk DE1 ... 267 B2
Crown Yd DE4 ... 154 F1
Crowshaw St DE24 ... 232 B8
Crowstones Rd DE4. 127 B3
Crowther Pl 7 S7 ... 43 A8
Croxall Rd DE12 ... 259 A2
Croxton Ct 5 NG19. 136 E3
Croydon Close 6
DE11 ... 255 E1
Croydon Wlk DE22 ... 217 F6
Cruck Cl S18 ... 56 E2
Crystal Cl DE3 ... 217 D4
Cubley Common
DE6 ... 198 E3
Cubley La DE6 ... 198 B1
Cubley Wood DE6 ... 198 E5
Cuckmere Cl DE22 ... 205 B5
CUCKNEY ... 101 F3
Cuckoostone La
DE4 ... 128 F2
Cuillin Cl NG10 ... 223 A1
Cullabine Ct S2 ... 44 A7
Cullabine Rd S2 ... 44 A7
Culland La DE6 ... 201 E5
Culland Rd DE14 ... 254 B7
Culland View DE4 ... 168 A8
Cullen Ave DE6 ... 173 C1
Cullumbell La S45 ... 129 A7
Culworth Cl DE56 ... 179 D4
Culworth Ct DE21 ... 206 B2
Cumberhills Grange
DE56 ... 190 D2
Cumberhills Rd
Duffield DE22, DE56 ... 190 C1
Duffield DE56 ... 190 D3
Quarndon DE22 ... 204 A8
Weston Underwood
DE22 ... 203 F8
Cumberland Ave
Derby DE21 ... 219 E6
Market Warsop NG20 ... 120 F5
Cumberland Cl
Buxton SK17 ... 85 D4
Westwood NG16 ... 171 C4
Cumberland Cres
DE72 ... 221 B2
Cumberland Dr
Chesterfield S41 ... 76 D1
Chesterfield S41 ... 95 C8
Cumberland Rd
Burton upon Trent
DE15 ... 254 D6
Wildboarclough SK11. 102 A8
Cumbria Wlk DE3 ... 217 C1
Cummings St DE23 ... 219 A2
Cundy Rd S44 ... 99 A3
Cunliffe St S18 ... 57 C4
Cunnery La DE4 ... 144 B3
Cunnery The DE6 ... 202 F2
Cunningham Pl
DE45 ... 109 D6
Cupola Pk DE4 ... 156 B2
CURBAR ... 72 E2
Curbar Cl
Little Eaton DE22 ... 205 A4
North Wingfield S42 ... 132 A7
Curbar Curve S43 ... 97 C6
Curbar La S32 ... 72 D2
Curbar Prim Sch S32 72 D1
Curborough Dr
DE24 ... 233 D6
Curlew Ave
Eckington S21 ... 59 B3
Harpur Hill SK17 ... 85 D2
Curlew Cl DE24 ... 231 D4
Curlew Way SK13 ... 16 F8
Curtis Gr SK13 ... 10 A3
Curzon Ave S18 ... 75 F8
Curzon CE Prim Sch The
DE22 ... 204 D6
Curzon Cl
Derby DE22 ... 204 C4
Killamarsh S21 ... 60 D6
Curzon Ct DE56 ... 190 E3
Curzon La
Derby DE24 ... 233 A8
Duffield DE56 ... 190 D3
Curzon Rd
Buxton SK17 ... 85 C7
Derby DE21 ... 219 F7
Curzon St
Derby DE1 ... 267 A3
Long Eaton NG10 ... 223 B2
Curzon Terr SK17 ... 88 D7
Cuscas La DE6 ... 187 F4
Custrum Ct ST14 ... 197 A3
Cut La DE1, DE21 ... 219 B7
Cutler Cl S21 ... 60 B7
Cutler La
Weston Underwood
DE22 ... 203 A8
Cutler La *continued*
Weston Underwood
DE6 ... 189 A1
Cutlers Ct 12 S2 ... 43 C8
Cutler Way DE3 ... 217 D4
Cuttholme Cl S40 ... 95 B4
Cuttholme Rd S40 ... 95 C4
Cuttholme Way 1
S40 ... 95 C4
Cutthorn Rd SK11 ... 102 C5
CUTTHORPE ... 94 F7
Cutthorpe Grange
S40 ... 95 A7
CUTTHORPE GREEN . 94 F7
Cutthorpe Prim Sch
S42 ... 94 D7
Cutthorpe Rd
Chesterfield S40 ... 95 A8
Cutthorpe S18 ... 94 F7
Cutting The DE11 ... 256 F4
Cuttlebrook Cl
DE23 ... 231 E6
Cyclamen Cl DE14 ... 254 A8
Cygnet Fold NG19 ... 136 C4
Cygnet Hosp DE24 ... 219 D2
Cypress Ave
Clay Cross S45 ... 131 B3
Sheffield S8 ... 43 C1
Cypress Cl S21 ... 60 C5
Cypress Way SK6 ... 32 A7
Cypress Wlk DE21 ... 220 B5
Cyprus Rd S8 ... 43 A5
Cyril Ave NG9 ... 223 D7

D

Dade Ave S43 ... 97 C6
Daffodil Pl 1 DE3 ... 217 D5
Dag La DE12 ... 263 E7
Dagnall Gdns DE45 . 109 D5
Dagnall Terr DE45 ... 109 D5
Dagnam Cl S2 ... 43 F6
Dagnam Cres S2 ... 43 F6
Dagnam Dr S2 ... 43 F7
Dagnam Pl S2 ... 43 F6
Dagnam Rd S2 ... 43 F7
Dahlia Ave DE55 ... 160 B7
Dahlia Dr DE21 ... 206 C3
Dairy Farm Cl DE65. 242 B5
Dairyfield Dr S80 ... 101 E8
Dairy House Rd
DE23 ... 219 B1
Dairy La ST14 ... 225 E2
Dairy Mws 3 DE6 ... 201 E8
Daisy Cl
Donisthorpe DE12 ... 262 E1
Shirebrook NG20 ... 119 D2
Daisy Farm Rd
NG16 ... 195 B8
Daisy Gro DE3 ... 217 C5
Daisy La DE12 ... 262 B3
Daisymere La SK17 ... 67 A2
Dakeyne Cl DE4 ... 127 F1
Dakin Ave SK17 ... 85 D8
Dakin Ct SK17 ... 66 E1
DALBURY ... 216 B1
Dalbury Rd S18 ... 56 C1
Dalbury Wlk DE23 ... 231 C5
Dalby Green Cl
DE5 ... 181 A8
DALE ABBEY ... 207 F2
Daleacre Ave DE74 ... 247 F5
Dale Acre Way
DE21 ... 205 D3
Dale Ave
Long Eaton NG10 ... 223 D1
Newton DE55 ... 148 A3
Somercotes DE55 ... 170 C6
DALEBANK ... 145 C8
Dale Bank Cres S43 ... 77 D3
Dalebank La S45 ... 145 B8
Dale Bottom DE6 ... 149 D2
Dale Brook DE65 ... 228 E1
Dalebrook Rd DE15. 248 B5
Dale Cl
Breaston DE72 ... 235 D8
Fritchley DE56 ... 168 A6
Langwith NG20 ... 119 E8
Matlock DE4 ... 154 D8
Staveley S43 ... 97 C8
Stonebroom DE55 ... 147 B4
Whaley Thorns NG20 ... 100 F1
Dale Com Prim Sch
DE23 ... 218 F2
Dale Cres
Hathersage S32 ... 53 B8
Tupton S42 ... 115 C1
Dale Ct DE56 ... 191 F8
DALE END ... 140 C7
Dale End
Biggin SK17 ... 138 B4
Brassington DE4 ... 153 A1
Wirksworth DE4 ... 154 F1
Dale End Rd DE65 ... 228 C2
Dalefield Dr DE11 ... 256 B3
Dalehead Ct S32 ... 71 E5
Dale Head Rd
Dove head SK17 ... 103 E8
Hartington upper Quarter
SK17 ... 84 D1
Hartington upper Quarter
SK17 ... 104 A8
Dale Hill DE55 ... 158 B5
Dale La
Buxton SK17 ... 85 E8
Glapwell S44 ... 134 D7
Dale Park Ave DE56. 192 A8
Dale Rd
Buxton, Higher Buxton
SK17 ... 85 C7
Buxton, Peak Dale
SK17 ... 67 B7
Derby DE21 ... 221 A6
Derby DE21, DE72 ... 221 A6
Derby, Alvaston DE24 ... 233 B7
Derby, Normanton
DE23 ... 218 F2
Dronfield S18 ... 76 B8
Killamarsh S21 ... 60 E6
Kimberley NG16 ... 195 F6
Matlock Bath DE4 ... 143 B3
Middleton DE45 ... 124 F3
New Mills SK22 ... 33 C7
Over Haddon DE45 ... 109 A1
Stanley DE7 ... 207 C4
Stanton-by-Dale DE7 . 208 C1
Thurvaston DE7 ... 201 C1
Tupton S42 ... 115 C1
Dale Rd North DE4 ... 116 C3
Dale Road N DE4 ... 127 A5
Dale Road S DE4 ... 127 D1
Dales Cl 4 DE11 ... 255 E5
Dalesfield DE4 ... 143 A6
Dalesgate Cl DE23 ... 231 C5
Daleside DE15 ... 248 B1
Dale Side SK17 ... 85 B7
Dale St
Ilkeston DE7 ... 208 F7
Mansfield NG19 ... 136 B1
Dales The DE7 ... 207 E7
Dalestorth Ave
NG19 ... 135 D1
Dale Terr SK17 ... 85 B6
Dale The
Bonsall DE4 ... 142 D1
Hathersage S32 ... 53 B8
North Wingfield SK17 ... 131 F5
Stoney Middleton S32 ... 71 E4
Wirksworth DE4 ... 154 E1
Dale View
Earl Sterndale SK17 ... 105 B3
Ilkeston DE7 ... 208 E7
Litton SK17 ... 69 E3
Mottram in Longdendale
SK14 ... 9 A3
Shirland DE55 ... 146 C4
4 Willington DE65 ... 242 B6
Dale View Cl S45 ... 132 B3
Dale View Gdns
DE56 ... 191 F8
Dale View Rd S45 ... 132 B4
Dale View Terr SK17 . 89 A6
Dalewood Cl
Chesterfield S41 ... 96 E1
South Normanton
DE55 ... 160 A3
Dalkeith Ave DE24 ... 232 F5
Dalley Cl 1 NG9 ... 223 E7
Dalley La DE56 ... 178 C6
Dallimore Prim Sch
DE7 ... 208 D4
Dallimore Rd DE7 ... 208 D4
Dalness Ct 7 DE24 . 231 D3
Dalston Rd DE11 ... 256 A5
Dalton Ave
Burton upon Trent
DE15 ... 248 B1
Derby DE22 ... 218 C3
Dalton Cl 3 NG9 ... 223 E5
Dalton Dr DE56 ... 179 A4
Dalton Road DE56 ... 179 C6
Daltons Cl NG16 ... 182 A4
Dalvey Way S43 ... 77 D5
Dam Cl DE55 ... 158 E3
Dame Catherine Harpur's
Sch DE73 ... 251 A5
Dam La
Alsop en le Dale
DE6 ... 150 E3
Shirland DE55 ... 146 F1
Damon Cl S45 ... 132 C1
Damon Dr S43 ... 96 F8
Damsbrook Dr S43 ... 80 E3
Damsbrook La
Bolsover S80 ... 99 D8
Clowne S43 ... 80 D1
Dam Side DE56 ... 179 A4
Damside La SK17 ... 49 A3
Damson Croft S43 ... 78 A2
Damson Gr DE24 ... 232 E8
Damstead Pk Ave
DE55 ... 158 E3
Danbury Cl S42 ... 115 E3
Danby Ave S41 ... 77 B2
Danby Rd 6 DE23 ... 230 F5
DANEBANK ... 32 E5
Dane Bank Dr SK12 ... 32 D6
Danebridge Cres
DE21 ... 206 A1
Dane Gr SK17 ... 85 C4
Dane Hill Cl SK12 ... 32 D5
Danesby Cres DE5 ... 180 A1
Danesby Rise DE5 ... 180 A1
DANESMOOR ... 131 E3
Danesmoor Ind Est
S45 ... 131 F2
Danesway SK23 ... 47 B6
Danewood Gdns S13 ... 44 C8
Daniel Mews NG10 ... 223 A5
Dannah Cres DE5 ... 169 F1
Dannah St DE5 ... 169 F2
Darby St DE23 ... 218 F2
Darcy Rd S21 ... 59 C3
Daresbury Cl S2 ... 43 D6
Daresbury Dr S2 ... 43 D6
Daresbury Pl S2 ... 43 D6
Daresbury Rd S2 ... 43 D6
Daresbury View S2 ... 43 D6
Darfield Ave S20 ... 44 F2
Darfield Cl S20 ... 44 F2
Darfield Dr DE75 ... 182 A2
Darfield La DE6 ... 162 C4
DARFOULDS ... 63 F1
Darkey La NG9 ... 223 E5
Dark La
Ashbourne DE6 ... 173 A1
Ashover DE55 ... 145 C6
Bradley DE6 ... 175 B3
Calow S44 ... 96 F2
Chesterfield S44 ... 96 E4
Church Broughton
DE65 ... 227 B6
Crich DE4 ... 156 F5
Cromford DE4 ... 154 F4
Holbrook DE56 ... 191 B7
North Wingfield S42 ... 132 B7
Pilsley S45 ... 132 D2
Tatenhill DE13 ... 253 A8
Tideswell SK17 ... 69 C3
Wirksworth DE4,
DE56 ... 165 D3
Youlgreave DE45 ... 125 D7
Darklands La DE11 ... 256 A4
Darklands Rd DE11 . 256 B5
DARLEY ABBEY ... 205 A2
Darley Abbey Dr
DE22 ... 204 F2
Darley Ave
Beeston NG9 ... 223 F3
Darley Dale DE4 ... 127 C3
North Wingfield S42 ... 132 B7
DARLEY BRIDGE ... 142 C8
Darley Churchtown CE
Prim Sch DE4 ... 127 B3
Darley Cl
Burton upon Trent
DE15 ... 248 C1
Harthill S26 ... 61 E6
Staveley S43 ... 78 E1
Swadlincote DE11 ... 256 A1
DARLEY DALE ... 127 C2
Darley Dale DE11 ... 255 F2
Darley Dale Prim Sch
DE4 ... 127 E2
Darley Dale Sta★
DE4 ... 127 C2
Darley Dr
Long Eaton NG10 ... 236 A5
Ripley DE5 ... 169 C3
West Hallam DE7 ... 207 E8
Darley Gr
Buxton SK17 ... 85 D6
Derby DE1 ... 219 A7
DARLEY HILLSIDE ... 127 D4
Darley House Est
DE4 ... 142 E8
Darley La DE1 ... 267 B4
Darley Lodge Dr
DE4 ... 142 E8
Darley Moor Motor Cycle
Racing Circuit
DE6 ... 185 A1
Darley Park★ DE22 . 205 A1
Darley Park Dr
DE22 ... 204 F1
Darley Park Ho
DE22 ... 205 A1
Darley Park Rd
DE22 ... 204 F1
Darley Rd
Ashover S45 ... 113 B2
Ashover S45 ... 128 D8
Ashover SE45 ... 112 E1
Darley Sq DE7 ... 194 E5
Darley St DE22 ... 205 A1
Darley Way
Buxton SK17 ... 85 E7
North Wingfield S42 ... 132 B7
Darne Mws DE6 ... 175 F2
Darnley Dr S2 ... 44 A8
Darraway Gdns
DE73 ... 232 D2
Darsway DE74 ... 246 F4
Dartford Pl DE24 ... 233 A5
Dartmouth Ct 20
S41 ... 95 F8
Dartnall Cl SK12 ... 32 A6
Darwen Cl DE3 ... 230 C8
Darwent Rd S41 ... 96 C6
Darwin Ave
Buxton SK17 ... 85 C7
Chesterfield S40 ... 95 E5
Derby DE24 ... 232 D4
Ilkeston DE7 ... 208 E7
Darwin Cl DE15 ... 248 C1
Darwin Fields Close
DE21 ... 205 E4
Darwin Forest Ctry
Patk★ DE4 ... 128 C7
Darwin Pl DE1 ... 267 C3
Darwin Rd
Chesterfield S40 ... 266 A4
Derby DE3 ... 217 E3
Long Eaton NG10 ... 236 B5
Darwin Sq DE1 ... 267 B2
Darwood La S44 ... 118 B8
Dashwood St DE23 . 267 B1
Datchet Cl DE23 ... 231 A8
Daubenton Way
DE3 ... 230 E8
Daveham Ave SK17 ... 85 C6
Davenport Dr NG16. 195 B7
Davenport Gr DE6 ... 185 D7
Davenport Rd
Derby DE24 ... 232 C8
Tupton S42 ... 131 C8
Davenport Way
DE11 ... 256 F1
Daventry Cl DE3 ... 217 C3
Davey Ct S44 ... 98 F3
Davian Way S40 ... 114 E8
David Lloyd Sp Ctr
DE24 ... 219 D4
David Nieper Acad
DE55 ... 159 A3
David's Cl DE73 ... 232 F1
Davids Dr S42 ... 114 F4
Davies Close DE24 ... 232 C8
Da Vinci Com Coll
DE21 ... 205 E1
Davis Ho 2 DE1 ... 267 B2
Davis Rd DE11 ... 256 B4
Davy Gro S20 ... 60 A6
Dawber La S21 ... 60 F7
Dawgates La NG19 ... 134 F2
Dawkins Rd DE12 ... 262 E1
Dawlish Ct
4 Chesterfield S41 ... 95 F8
Derby DE24 ... 233 C7
Eastwood NG16 ... 182 D3
Dawn Field DE12 ... 262 B3
Dawn View NG9 ... 209 D2
Dawsmere Cl DE21 . 205 D1
Dawver Rd NG16 ... 195 F6
Dayfield La DE6 ... 175 A4
Day Gr SK14 ... 9 A3
Daykins Row DE5 ... 181 C7
Daylesford Cl DE23 . 231 A8
Days La DE56 ... 178 F3
Days Mill Cl DE4 ... 143 A6
Dayton Cl DE21 ... 220 C5
Dayton Ct DE22 ... 218 E8
Deacon Cl
Derby DE21 ... 205 E2
Swanwick DE55 ... 169 E7
Deacon Ct SK23 ... 47 A5
Dead La NG16 ... 195 D1
Deadman's La DE24. 219 D2
Deakon Dr S18 ... 57 B3
Deamon St DE55 ... 147 E1
Dean Cl DE23 ... 218 A2
Dean Ct DE23 ... 218 E2
Deanery Close DE5 . 180 E7
Deanhead Dr S20 ... 44 F2
Dean Rd DE56 ... 167 F2
Deans Cl S40 ... 96 D7
Deans Dr DE72 ... 221 B2
Deansgate NG19 ... 135 A5
Dean St
Derby DE22 ... 218 E3
Langley Mill NG16 ... 182 C3
Debdale La NG19 ... 136 A2
Debdale Way NG19 . 136 B2
Deben Cl S40 ... 114 C8
Deben Down NG19 ... 136 D3
Deborah Dr DE21 ... 220 A7
Dee Cl
Derby DE24 ... 231 E3
Derby DE65 ... 228 E1
Dee La DE65 ... 229 F6
Deep Carr La DE4 ... 143 D4
Deepdale
Hulland Ward DE6 ... 175 F1
Ironville NG16 ... 170 F4
Deepdale Ave
Borrowash DE72 ... 221 C3
Stapleford NG9 ... 223 D6
Deepdale Bsns Pk
DE45 ... 109 B6
Deepdale Cl
Burton upon Trent
DE15 ... 248 B5
Staveley S43 ... 78 E3
Deepdale Ct DE75 ... 181 E1
Deepdale La DE6 ... 184 A2
Deep Dale La
Barrow upon Trent
DE73 ... 243 F7
Barrow upon Trent
DE73 ... 244 A7
Derby DE24, DE73 ... 231 F1
Deepdale Rd
Belper DE56 ... 179 B5
Bolsover S44 ... 98 F3
Derby DE21 ... 220 F3
Long Eaton NG10 ... 236 A5
Mansfield NG19 ... 136 E1
Deepdene Cl DE11 ... 256 C1
Deep La
Hardstoft S44, S45 ... 133 B3
Sheen SK17 ... 121 F3
Sheen SK17 ... 122 B1
DEEP PIT ... 43 F8
Deepsick La S44 ... 97 C1
Deepwell Ave S20 ... 59 F6
Deepwell Bank S20 ... 59 F6
Deepwell Ct S20 ... 59 F6
Deepwell Dr S20 ... 60 A6
Deepwell Mews
Killamarsh S20 ... 60 A6
Sheffield S20 ... 60 A6
Deepwell View S20 ... 59 F6
Deerlands Rd
Chesterfield S40 ... 95 B3
Wingerworth S42 ... 114 F2
Deerleap La S42 ... 130 D3
Deerpark Cres S42 ... 114 F3
Deer Park Prim Sch
S42 ... 114 F3
Deer Park View
DE21 ... 220 F6
Deer Pk La DE5 ... 169 F3
De Ferrers Ct DE56 . 190 E3
Degge St DE1 ... 267 B2
Dein Court NG17 ... 148 E4
Deincourt Cl DE21 ... 221 A6
Deincourt Cres S42 ... 131 F8
Deira Dr S17 ... 55 E6
De Lacy Ct DE74 ... 247 A3
Delamere Cl
Breaston DE72 ... 235 D8
Derby DE21 ... 206 A1
Swanwick DE55 ... 169 F7
Delf St S2 ... 43 B7
Delhi Cl DE15 ... 248 C3
Dell The
Chesterfield S40 ... 95 B3
Horwich End SK23 ... 45 F5
Delph Bank S40 ... 114 E8
Delph Cl S32 ... 71 D6
Delph The DE73 ... 252 F2
Delven La DE74 ... 247 B3
Delves Bank Rd
DE55 ... 170 A7
Delves Cl S40 ... 95 D1
Delves Ct DE75 ... 193 E8
Delves Rd
9 Heanor DE75 ... 181 D1
Heanor DE75 ... 193 D8
Killamarsh S21 ... 60 C6
Delves The DE55 ... 169 F7
De Montfort Close 8
DE11 ... 255 E1
Denacre Ave NG10 ... 223 F1
Denacre La DE4 ... 127 F3
Denarth Ave DE24 ... 232 E3
Denbigh St DE21 ... 219 E7
Denby Bank DE5 ... 180 D5
DENBY BOTTLES ... 180 A1
Denby Cl S42 ... 115 B4
Denby Comm DE5 ... 180 F3
DENBY COMMON ... 181 A3
Denby Free CE (VA)
Prim Sch DE5 ... 180 D1
Denby Hall Bsns Pk
DE5 ... 180 D5
Denby Hall Rd NE7 ... 194 F6
Denby Hall Way
DE5 ... 180 C4
Denby La DE5, DE56 . 180 C1
Denby Pottery Visitor
Ctr★ DE5 ... 180 C3
Denby Rd S43 ... 97 C7
DENBY VILLAGE ... 180 C1
Denefield Cl SK6 ... 15 B1
Dene Fields Ct DE4 . 143 C5
Dene The
Hopton DE4 ... 153 F1
Hopton DE4 ... 154 A1
Hopton DE4 ... 164 F8
Denham St S45 ... 131 D3
Denison Gdns
DE21 ... 220 B6
Denman Cres S32 ... 72 A3
Denmark Rd S2 ... 43 B6
Dennis Barsby Cl
DE11 ... 255 E3
Dennis Cl DE23 ... 230 E7
Dennor Dr NG19 ... 136 E5
Denson Cl 4 S2 ... 43 B6
DENSTONE ... 196 D6
Denstone Coll ST14 . 196 B5
Denstone Dr DE24 ... 233 A4
Denstone La
Denstone ST14 ... 196 C7
Denstone ST14 ... 196 E7
Dentdale Ct DE24 ... 233 C7
Dent La S12 ... 44 F2
Denton Ave NG10 ... 223 A6
Denton Cl NG19 ... 136 E1
Denton Way DE55 ... 169 F7
Denver Ct NG9 ... 209 E1
Denver Rd DE3 ... 217 D3
Depedale Ave DE7 ... 208 D5
De Peverel Ct DE55. 146 D2
Depot St DE23 ... 219 A2
DERBY ... 267 C4
Derby Arboretum★
DE23 ... 267 B1
Derby Cath★ DE1 ... 267 B3
Derby Cathedral Sch
DE1 ... 218 E5
Derby Coll Broomfield
Hall DE7 ... 206 B5
Derby Coll (Ilkeston
Campus) DE7 ... 208 E8
Derby Coll Sp Ctr
DE22 ... 217 F5
Derby Coll (The Joseph
Wright Ctr) DE1 ... 267 A4
Derby Coll (The
Quantum Ctr) DE1 267 D1
Derby Coll (The
Roundhouse)
DE24 ... 219 C4
Derby Commercial Pk
Derby DE21 ... 220 D2
Derby DE24 ... 233 E8
Derby Distribution Ctr
DE24 ... 231 E5
Derby Dr DE6 ... 186 A5
Derby Gram Sch
DE23 ... 230 F7
Derby High Sch
DE23 ... 218 B1
Derby Hills DE73 ... 251 E6

Derby Hills House Ct DE73 251 E5
Derby Knoll SK23 33 F1
Derby La
Brailsford DE6 201 B8
Derby DE23 231 F8
Great Cubley DE6 198 F1
Monyash DE45 123 C7
Shirley DE6 200 E8
Derby Midland Sta DE1 219 C4
Derby Moor Com Sports Coll DE23 231 B7
Derby Mus & Art Gall★ DE1 267 B3
Derby Pl S2 43 C6
Derbyrd DE73 244 E6
Derby Rd
Alfreton DE55 158 F3
Ambergate DE56 167 F3
Ashbourne DE6 185 E7
Ashbourne DE6 185 F6
Aston-on-Trent DE72 234 A2
Borrowash DE21, DE72 221 A2
Burton upon Trent DE13 241 A1
Chellaston DE73 232 F2
Clay Cross S45, S42 131 C5
Crich DE4 167 D8
Cromford DE4 155 C6
Dale Abbey DE7, DE21 206 E3
Derby, Spondon DE21 220 C3
Doveridge DE6 211 B1
Doveridge DE6 224 D7
Draycott DE72 234 E8
Duffield DE56 190 F6
Duffield, Flaxholme DE56 190 F1
Eastwood NG16 182 E2
Egginton DE65 241 C4
Etwall DE65 229 A4
Hatton DE65 227 E2
Heanor DE75 181 D1
Hilton DE65 228 E3
Hilton DE65 228 F3
Hilton DE65 240 C8
Horsley DE21, DE56 191 D5
Ilkeston DE7 208 D7
Kilburn DE56 179 F1
Langley Mill NG16 182 C3
Long Eaton NG10 236 B8
Lower Kilburn DE56 191 E7
Marston on Dove DE65 228 B2
Melbourne DE73 244 F1
Melbourne DE73 252 A8
2 Milford DE56 190 F7
New Mills SK22 24 D1
Ripley DE5 180 C3
Ripley DE5 180 E8
Risley DE72 222 D4
Sandiacre NG10 223 A5
Smisby LE65 258 A4
Stanley DE7 207 B4
Stapleford NG9 223 D6
Swadlincote DE11 256 C3
Swanwick DE5, DE55 169 E5
Ticknall DE11, DE73 257 F7
Uttoxeter ST14 210 D1
West Broughton DE6 225 A7
Whatstandwell DE4 156 B2
Wingerworth S42 115 A6
Wirksworth DE4 165 E6
Derby Road Ind Est
Clay Cross S45 131 B5
Heanor DE75 181 D1
Sandiacre NG10 223 B5
Derbyshire Ave
Trowell NG9 209 D4
West Hallam DE7 207 E8
Derbyshire Cl DE7 207 E8
Derbyshire Craft Ctr★ S32 72 D2
Derbyshire Cty Cricket Gd DE21 219 C6
Derbyshire Dales National Nature Reserve★ SK17 89 A8
Derbyshire Dr
Castle Donington DE74 247 B4
Ilkeston DE7 208 E6
Westwood NG16 171 C4
Derbyshire Flying Ctr★ S33 51 A7
Derbyshire La S8 43 A3
Derbyshire Level SK13 17 F6
Derby Small Bsns Ctr
Derby DE1 267 C2
Derby, Pear Tree DE23 219 B1
Derby St
Glossop SK13 17 C8
3 Ilkeston DE7 208 F8
Sheffield S2 43 C6
Derby Terr S2 43 C6
Derby Theatre★ DE1 267 B2
Derby Trad Est DE21 219 B8
Dere Croft 6 DE72 221 C6
Derrington Leys DE24 233 D6
Derventio Cl DE1 219 A7
DERWENT 30 C6
Derwent Ave
Belper DE56 179 A1
Borrowash DE72 221 C3
Darley Dale DE4 127 C4
Derby DE72 205 A4
Grindleford S32 72 C8
Ilkeston DE7 194 D2
West Hallam DE7 207 E8
Derwent Bsns Ctr DE1 267 C4
Derwent Bsns Pk DE5 169 B1
Derwent Cl
Derby DE22 205 A4
Dronfield S18 57 B3
Glossop SK13 17 F8
Grindleford S32 72 C8
1 Hilton DE65 240 E8
Swadlincote DE11 256 A1
Derwent Com Sch DE21 219 C7
Derwent Cres S41 95 D7
Derwent Ct
Belper DE56 179 B4
5 Sheffield S17 56 A5
Willington DE65 242 B6
Derwent Dr
Baslow DE45 91 D6
Chinley SK23 34 E1
Derby DE24 231 D2
Tibshelf DE55 147 F6
Derwent Gdns DE6 185 D8
Derwent Gr DE55 158 F2
Derwent Ho DE21 219 C6
Derwent La
Derwent S33 30 B7
Derwent S33 30 C6
Hathersage S32 52 F8
Northwood DE4 127 A6
Derwent Par DE21, DE24 219 E3
Derwent Park Ho DE22 205 A1
Derwent Pl S45 131 A5
Derwent Rd
Burton upon Trent DE15 248 A2
Buxton SK17 85 C6
Derby DE21 220 D3
Dronfield S18 57 B3
Ripley DE5 169 C1
Derwent Rise DE21 220 F4
Derwentside Ind Pk DE56 178 F1
Derwent Sq SK23 34 E1
Derwent St
Belper DE56 178 F3
Derby DE1 267 C4
Draycott DE72 235 A7
Long Eaton NG10 236 C6
Derwent Street Ind Est NG10 236 C6
Derwent Terr DE4 143 A7
Derwent Vale DE56 178 F2
Derwent Valley Visitor Ctr★ DE56 178 F5
Derwent View
Baslow DE45 91 E6
Belper, Milford DE56 191 A8
Belper, Mount Pleasant DE56 178 F5
Darley Dale DE4 127 B3
Mastin Moor S43 79 C3
Ridgeway DE56 168 B3
Derwent Way
Matlock DE4 143 A5
Whatstandwell DE4 156 B3
Desborough Rd NG16 171 D7
De Sutton Pl S26 61 E5
DETHICK 156 B8
Dethick La DE4 144 D1
Dethick Way S42 132 B7
Devas Gdns DE21 220 D5
Deveron Cl DE13 240 C1
Deveron Rd S20 59 F7
Devizes Cl S40 114 F8
Devon Cl
Burton upon Trent DE15 254 E6
Grassmoor S42 115 F2
Sandiacre NG10 223 B5
Devon Dr S43 96 F8
Devon La DE74 247 B3
Devon Park View S43 96 F8
Devonshire Ave
Borrowash DE72 221 C2
Darley Dale DE4 142 F7
Derby DE22 204 F3
Long Eaton NG10 237 A8
Ripley DE5 169 C2
Devonshire Avenue E S41 115 C8
Devonshire Avenue N S43 77 E3
Devonshire Bsns Ctr S43 78 B2
Devonshire Cl
Chesterfield S41 95 F8
Dronfield S18 75 F8
Ilkeston DE7 194 E5
Sheffield S17 55 F6
2 Staveley S43 78 E2
Devonshire Cotts S44 118 E6
Devonshire Ct
Brimington S43 96 D7
5 Derby DE22 204 F3
Devonshire Dr
Chinley SK23 34 E2
Creswell S80 81 C1
Derby DE3 217 E3
Duffield DE56 190 D2
Eastwood NG16 182 F2
Langwith NG20 119 F8
Rowsley DE4 110 F1
Sheffield S17 55 E7
Somercotes DE55 170 B7
Stapleford NG9 209 D2
Devonshire Drive DE55 148 A3
Devonshire Glen S17 55 F6
Devonshire Gr S17 55 E6
Devonshire Pk S43 96 E8
Devonshire Rd
Buxton SK17 85 B8
Sheffield S17 55 F6
Devonshire Rd E 3 S41 115 C8
Devonshire Road E S41 115 C8
Devonshire Road N S43 77 D3
Devonshire Sq DE4 111 A3
Devonshire St
Ambergate DE56 167 F3
Brimington S43 96 E8
Chesterfield S41 266 B3
New Houghton NG19 135 A7
3 Staveley S43 78 E2
Devonshire Terr
Holmewood S42 116 E1
Matlock Bath DE4 143 A2
Devonshire Terrace Rd S17 55 D7
Devonshire Villas 28 S41 95 F8
Devonshire Way S43 81 A4
Devonshire Wlk DE1 267 C2
Devon St DE7 209 A5
De Warren Pl S26 61 F5
Dewberry Court DE24 231 C2
Dewchurch Dr DE23 231 E5
Dewint Ave SK6 23 B8
Dewley Way S45 131 D5
Dew Pond La SK17 85 E8
Dewsnap La SK14 9 A6
Dewy La DE4, DE55 144 F1
Dexter St DE23 219 C2
DH Lawrence Birthplace Mus★ NG16 182 F2
Dialstone S33 51 A7
Diamond Ct DE45 109 D5
Diamond Dr DE21 205 F3
Diamond Jubilee Cotts DE6 184 E8
Dibble Rd DE14 254 A7
Dickens Dr
Holmewood S42 116 D1
Swadlincote DE11 256 C5
Dickenson Rd S41 266 C1
Dickens Sq DE23 231 F7
Dickinson's La DE6 215 B1
Dickinson St DE24 219 D2
Dicklant La S45 145 B8
Didcot Cl S40 114 F8
Didsbury Terr SK22 25 E2
Digby Ct 4 NG19 136 C3
Digby Ind Est NG16 195 D7
Digby St
Cossall DE7 195 A1
Ilkeston DE7 209 A8
Kimberley NG16 195 D7
Diglands Ave SK22 24 D1
Diglands Cl SK22 24 D1
Diglee Rd SK23 33 C3
Digmire La DE6 161 D1
Dig St
Ashbourne DE6 173 B2
Hartington SK17 137 D6
Dilston Way DE72 245 A8
DIMPLE 143 A6
Dimple Cres DE4 143 B5
Dimple La DE56 168 B8
Dimple Rd DE4 143 A6
Dimple Road Bsns Ctr DE4 143 B6
Dimple The DE56 168 B7
Dingle Cl SK13 17 A8
Dingle La S41, S44 96 E1
Dingle The DE15 254 E8
Dingley Cl NG19 136 E5
Dinmore Grange DE11 257 B6
Dinnington La DE55 157 C6
Dinting CE Prim Sch SK13 10 A1
Dinting CE VA Prim Sch
Glossop SK13 10 A4
Glossop SK14 9 F1
Dinting La SK13 10 A1
Dinting Lane Trad Est SK13 10 A1
Dinting Lodge Ind Est SK13 9 F2
Dinting Rd SK13 10 B2
Dinting Sta SK13 10 A2
Dinting Vale SK13 10 A1
Dinting Vale Bsns Pk SK13 9 F2
Dirty La
Castleton S33 38 A3
Great Hucklow SK17 70 B8
Hognaston DE6 164 A3
Stockport SK6 15 F2
Discovery Way S41 77 A1
Diseworth Cl DE73 232 F2
Diseworth Rd DE74 247 A1
Dish La DE6 228 B6
Dishwell La S26 61 E6
DISLEY 32 C5
Disley Prim Sch SK12 32 D6
Disley Sta SK12 32 C6
Disraeli Cres DE7 208 F8
Ditch Cotts SK17 105 F8
Ditch The
Chelmorton SK17 105 F8
Chelmorton SK17 106 A8
Division Rd NG20 119 E4
Division St S43 97 C8
Dix Ave
Smalley DE7 192 F6
2 Smalley DE7 193 A6
Dixie St NG16 171 B4
Dixon Croft S43 77 D4
Dixon Ct S41 77 B3
Dixon's Rd S41 266 C2
Dobbinhorse La DE6 185 B5
Dobbin La S18 75 C6
Dobbs Cl S21 60 C6
Dobholes DE7 192 D6
Dobholes La DE7 192 F6
Dobroyd Ave S2 44 A7
Dobson Pl S43 97 B6
Dockholm Rd NG10 223 C2
Dock Wlk S40 266 A2
Doctor La S26 61 F5
Doctor's La DE73 252 F2
Dodburn Ct DE24 231 D4
Dodgewell Cl DE55 147 F1
Dodslow Ave DE13 240 B3
Doe Hill La DE55 147 D5
DOEHOLE 145 A2
Doehole La
Ashover DE4, DE55 144 F3
Brackenfield DE55 145 A2
Doe La S12 58 C5
DOE LEA 117 D1
Doe Lea Nature Reserve★ S44 117 D2
Doghole La DE4 154 C4
Dogkennel La DE6 186 E7
Dog Kennel La DE6 211 B1
Dog La
Hulland Ward DE6 175 D4
Netherseal DE12 264 F6
Stonebroom DE55 146 E2
Wilson DE73 252 E6
Dokindale Rd SK17 88 B2
Dolby Rd SK17 85 D2
Doles La
Clifton DE6 184 F7
Findern DE65 230 D3
Whitwell S80 82 B7
Dolly La
Chinley SK23 34 A2
Furness Vale SK23 33 F3
Dolly Wood Cl SK23 34 B1
Dolphin Cl DE21 221 A6
Domain Dr DE73 232 E1
Dominion Rd DE11 256 B5
Dominoe Gr S12 44 D5
Donald Hawley Way DE56 190 F3
Doncaster Ave NG10 223 B6
Doncaster Gr NG10 223 F1
Donegal Wlk DE21 220 A4
Donington Cl DE23 231 E5
Donington Dr
Derby DE23 231 E5
4 Woodville DE11 256 E1
Donington La DE72, DE74 247 C7
Donington Park Motor Racing Circuit★ DE74 246 C1
DONISTHORPE 262 F1
Donisthorpe La DE12 262 E2
Donkey La S32 72 C2
Donner Cres DE7 194 E5
Dorchester Ave DE21 219 F7
Dorchester Rd NG16 195 F7
DORE 55 E7
Dore Cl S17 56 A7
Dore Ct S17 56 A7
Dore Hall Croft S17 55 D7
Dore La S32 53 A7
Dore Lodge Gardens S17 55 F7
Dore Prim Sch S17 55 D6
Dore Rd S17 55 E8
Dore & Totley Sta S17 56 A7
Doris Rd DE7 209 A7
Dorking Rd DE22 218 B6
Dormy Cl NG19 136 E5
Dorothy Ave
Mansfield Woodhouse NG19 136 C1
Sandiacre NG10 223 B5
Dorothy Dr NG19 136 F1
Dorothy Vale S40 95 C4
Dorrien Ave DE23 232 A7
Dorset Ave 2 S43 96 F8
Dorset Cl
Brimington S43 77 F1
Burton upon Trent DE15 254 E6
Buxton SK17 85 D4
Dorset Dr S43 96 F8
Dorset St DE21 219 D6
Dorterry Cres DE7 209 A5
Dotterel Place NG20 120 D4
Doublet Close DE55 171 A6
Double Villas DE55 146 F3
Douglas Ave
Awsworth NG16 195 C5
Heanor DE75 181 C2
Douglas Gdns DE75 181 C2
Douglas Rd
Chesterfield S41 96 C6
Long Eaton NG10 223 B1
Somercotes DE55 170 D8
Douglas St
Derby DE23 219 B2
Derby DE23 219 C2
Douse Croft La S10 42 F6
Dove Bank SK6 24 A6
Dove Bk SK6 23 F6
Dove CE Academy ST14 196 F4
Dove Cl
Branston DE14 253 E6
Branston DE14 256 E6
Derby DE3 218 A3
Kilburn DE56 192 A8
Woodville DE11 256 F3
Dovecliff Cres DE13 240 F2
Dovecliff Rd DE13 240 E3
Dovecote DE74 247 B3
Dovecote Dr DE72 221 B2
Dovecote Rd SK6 23 C2
Dovecotes S45 129 F3
Dovecote The
Breedon on the Hill DE73 252 F2
Horsley DE21 191 F6
Dove Dale★ DE6 161 B3
Dovedale Ave
Ashbourne DE6 173 D1
Derby DE24 233 C7
Long Eaton NG10 236 B6
Staveley S43 97 B5
Dovedale Circ DE7 194 E5
Dovedale Cl
Burton upon Trent DE15 248 B5
Ripley DE5 180 D6
Dovedale Cres
Belper DE56 179 B5
Buxton SK17 84 F6
Dovedale Ct DE6 185 E8
Dovedale Ct
4 Chesterfield S41 95 E7
1 Glossop SK13 10 F1
Long Eaton NG10 236 B6
Dovedale Day Hospl DE1 267 C1
Dovedale National Nature Reserve★ DE6 161 A6
Dovedale Prim Sch NG10 236 B6
Dovedale Rd DE21 220 F3
Dovedale Rise DE22 204 D1
Dovedales The DE3 217 D2
Dovefields
Draycott in the Clay ST14 225 D3
Rocester ST14 196 F3
Dove Fst Sch ST14 197 A3
Dove Gr DE65 241 A5
DOVE HEAD 103 D6
Dovehead and Three Shires Head
Flash SK17 102 F4
Flash SK17 103 A5
DOVE HOLES 47 E2
Dove Holes CE Prim Sch SK17 47 F1
Dove Holes Sta SK17 47 E1
Dove House Gn DE6 173 B2
Dove La
Long Eaton NG10 236 C8
Rocester ST14 197 A4
Dove Lea DE13 240 B4
Doveleys ST14 197 A8
Dove Leys La ST14 196 F8
Dove Meadow DE21 221 A6
Dove Pl DE65 239 C8
Dover Ct DE23 219 A2
Dove Rd DE5 169 C1
DOVERIDGE 211 A1
Dove Ridge SK17 121 C6
Doveridge Cl S41 77 A2
Doveridge Gr SK17 85 E6
Doveridge Prim Sch DE6 224 C8
Doveridge Rd DE15 248 B1
Doveridge Wlk DE23 231 C5
Dove Rise DE65 228 C1
Dover St
Creswell S80 81 E1
Derby DE23 219 A1
Doveside DE6 184 D7
Dove Side DE65 239 D8
Dovesite Bsns Pk DE73 251 E6
Dove St DE6 183 B2
Dovestone Gdns DE23 218 B1
Dovetail Ct S41 266 C4
Dove Valley Pk DE65 227 A5
Dove View DE13 239 C6
Dove Way The ST14 210 C2
Dove Well View DE55 159 C4
Dovewood Ct DE23 231 A7
Dowcarr La S26 61 C5
Dowdeswell St S41 266 B4
Dower Cl DE22 205 A1
Dowie Way DE4 156 F2
Downham Cl DE3 217 E1
Downing Cl DE22 217 F6
Downing Ho DE22 217 F6
Downing Rd
Derby DE21 219 D5
Sheffield S8 56 E8
Downing Row S32 52 F8
Downing St DE55 160 A6
Downings The S26 61 F5
Downlands S43 96 D7
Downlee Cl SK23 46 F5
Downmeadow DE56 179 E8
Downs The NG19 136 F1
Dowry La SK23 45 D5
Drabbles Rd DE4 143 A6
Drage St DE1 219 B7
Drake Ave S43 98 A8
Drakelow Nature Reserve★ DE14 253 F6
Drakelow Rd
Walton-On-Trent DE12 256 E2
Walton-on-Trent DE16 254 A3
Walton upon Trent DE12 253 E2
Drake Terr S43 96 C8
DRAYCOTT 234 F7
Draycott Cl DE75 181 C4
Draycott Com Prim Sch DE72 235 A7
Draycott Ct DE7 194 F3
Draycott Dr DE3 217 C3
Draycott Mills DE72 235 A7
Draycott Pl S18 75 D8
Draycott Rd
Borrowash DE72 221 C1
Breaston DE72 235 C7
Long Eaton NG10 236 A4
North Wingfield S42 131 F7
Drayton Ave
Derby DE22 217 F6
Mansfield NG19 135 D1
Drayton St DE11 256 C4
Dresden Cl DE3 217 C2
Drewry Ct DE1 218 F5
Drewry La DE22 218 F4
Dreyfus Cl DE21 220 F5
Drift Road DE11 255 D2
Drive The DE56 177 F3
DRONFIELD 56 E2
Dronfield Bypass S41 76 F2
Dronfield Henry Fanshawe Sch The S18 57 B2
Dronfield Inf Sch S18 57 A1
Dronfield Jun Sch S18 57 A1
Dronfield Pl DE7 194 E5
Dronfield Rd S21 59 B2
Dronfield Sp Ctr S18 57 A1
Dronfield Sta S18 57 A1
Drovers Way
Ashbourne DE6 173 B3
Bullbridge DE56 168 B5
Drovers Wlk 3 SK13 10 D1
Drum Cl DE22 204 F3
Drummond Rd DE7 194 E1
Drummond Way DE73 232 E2
Drury Ave DE21 220 D4
Drury La
Biggin SK17 138 C2
Dronfield S18 57 C3
Sheffield S17 55 D7
Drury Lowe Cl DE5 180 A1
Dryden Ave S40 115 A8
Dryden Ct NG9 209 E1
Dryden St DE23 231 F7
Dryhurst Dr SK12 32 D6
Dryhurst La SK12 32 D6
Drysdale Rd DE3 217 D3
Dry Stone Edge Rd SK17 103 A6
Dry Stones Edge Rd SK17 102 F7
Duchess St
Creswell S80 81 F1
Whitwell S80 82 A6
Duchess Way DE73 244 E8
Duck Island DE56 190 E4
DUCKMANTON 98 A5
Duckmanton Prim Sch
Duckmanton S43 97 F6
Duckmanton S44 98 A5
Duckmanton Rd S44 98 A5
Duck Row DE45 91 C3
Ducksett La S21 59 E2
Duck St DE65 241 B5
Duddy Road SK12 32 E6

Dudley Dr DE23......230 F6
Dudwood La DE4....140 F7
Duesbury Cl DE24...232 E7
Duesbury Ct DE3....230 B7
Duesbury Pl DE3....230 B7
Duesbury The DE55..160 B4
Duewell Ct **9** S43....78 B3
DUFFIELD..........190 F3
DUFFIELDBANK....191 A3
Duffield Bank DE56..191 A4
Duffield Cl NG10....236 A5
Duffield Ct DE56....190 F3
Duffield Meadows Prim
 Sch DE56..........190 D3
Duffield Millennium
 Mdw Nature Reserve★
 DE56..............190 F3
Duffield Rd
 6 Derby DE22....204 F3
 Derby DE22........205 A5
Duffield Rd Ind Est
 DE21..............205 C7
Duffield Sta DE56...190 F4
Duke Dr DE45......126 D2
Duke Field DE4.....154 D5
Duke of Norfolk CE Prim
 Sch SK13...........10 D1
Duke of Norfolk's Prim
 Sch SK13...........10 A1
Dukeries Ct S43.....80 F3
Dukeries La DE21....206 B2
Duke's Bldgs DE56..191 A7
Dukes Cl S42........116 E1
Dukes Dr
 Ashford in the Water
 DE45..............108 F8
 Chesterfield S41.....95 E6
 Curbar S32..........72 C2
Duke's Dr
 Buxton SK17........85 C5
 Glapwell S44.......134 A7
Duke's Dr The DE45 108 E8
Dukes Fold SK13.....17 B7
Dukes Pl DE7.......194 E4
Dukes Rd DE5......169 B4
Dukes St SK13.......17 C8
Duke St
 Buxton SK17........84 E6
 Chesterfield S41.....96 A8
 Clowne S43.........81 A4
 Creswell S80........81 F1
 Derby DE1.........267 B4
 Ilkeston DE7.......194 F3
 Middleton DE4.....154 D5
 Sheffield S20........59 D6
 South Normanton
 DE55..............160 B6
 Staveley S43.........78 E2
 Tutbury DE13......239 C6
 Whitwell S80........82 A6
Duluth Ave DE21....220 A7
Dulverton Ave
 DE24..............231 C2
Dulwich Cl **11** S43....78 B3
Dulwich Rd DE22...217 E6
Dumb Hall La S80....63 B2
Dumbles Cl DE7.....208 C6
Dumbles La S45.....180 F2
Dumbles Rd S44......98 F1
Dumbleton Rd S21....60 E5
Dumble Wood Grange
 S41................95 C7
Dumfries Dr DE22..218 B4
Dunbar Cl
 Derby DE24........231 E2
 Nottingham NG10...236 E4
Dunbar Close NG10..236 E4
Duncan Cl DE56.....179 B6
Duncan Rd
 2 Derby DE23......218 F8
 Derby DE23........231 F8
Duncombe Dr DE6...185 C8
Dundas Way DE73...232 E1
Dundee Dr NG19.....136 B6
Dundee Rd DE11....256 D5
Dundonald Rd S40...266 B1
Dunedin Cl DE3.....217 E3
Dunedin Cres DE15..248 C2
Dunedin Glen S20....59 E6
Dunedin Gr S20......59 E6
Dunge Rd SK23......45 A2
Dungley Hill SK23....58 D2
Dungreave Ave DE4..127 A5
Dunkery Ct DE21....206 A2
Dunkirk DE22.......267 A2
Dunlop Dr DE7.....246 F2
Dunlow La S32.......71 C5
Dunn Brigg NG19...136 D2
Dunn Dr NG10......236 B7
Dunne La SK13.......10 E2
Dunnicliffe La DE73..252 A7
Dunn La DE3........217 B2
Dunnock Dr **4** NG9..209 E2
DUNNSHILL........207 C1
Dunnsmoor La
 DE11..............256 E7
Dunoon Cl DE24....231 E3
Dunsa La DE45.......91 D1
Dunsford Rd DE55..159 B5
Dunshill Wlk S45...131 E4
Dunsil Cl NG19......136 B1
Dunsil Ct NG19......136 B1
Dunsil Rd
 7 Mansfield NG19..136 B1
 Pinxton NG16......160 D2
Dunsley Mdws Nature
 Reserve★ DE4.....154 E7
Dunsmore Dr DE21..205 F2

Dunsmore Way
 DE11..............256 D5
Dunstall Brook
 DE15..............248 A1
Dunstall Park Rd
 DE24..............232 D8
Dunstall Rd DE13...253 A7
Dunston Cl NG10...236 F7
Dunston Ct S41......76 F1
Dunston La S41......95 D8
Dunston Pl S41......76 F1
Dunston Prim Sch
 S41................95 D8
Dunston Rd S41......76 D2
Dunston Tech Pk
 S41................76 E1
Dunston Trad Est
 S41................76 E2
Dunston Way S41....76 F1
Dunton Cl DE21....267 D3
Dunvegan Ave S45..131 E2
Dunvegan Ct DE24..211 B1
Duper La S32........51 E5
Durban Cl DE15.....248 C3
Durham Ave
 Chesterfield S43.....77 D3
 Derby DE21.......219 E6
 Grassmoor S42.....115 F2
Durham Cl
 Chesterfield S43.....77 D3
 Mansfield Woodhouse
 NG19..............136 D4
Durham St **8** DE7..194 F1
Durley Chine Dr
 S41................115 C8
Durley Cl DE24.....233 C7
Durlstone Cl S12.....44 A5
Durlstone Cres S12..44 A5
Durlstone Dr
 Sheffield S12.......43 F5
 Sheffield S12.......44 A5
Durlstone Gr S12.....44 A5
Durrant Rd S41.....266 B3
Durvale Ct S17.......55 E6
Durward Cl DE24...232 C7
Dyche Cl S8.........57 B6
Dyche Dr S8.........57 B6
Dyche La S8, S18.....57 B5
Dyche Pl S8.........57 B6
Dyche Rd S8.........57 B6
Dye House La SK22...33 C8
Dykes Cl S44.........99 A2
Dyke Vale Rd S12....44 F5
Dymond Gr S42.....115 F3
Dystelegh Rd SK12..32 D6

E

Each Well La DE55..158 F3
Eades Fold S33.......38 C3
Eagle Cl DE56.......178 F2
Eagle Dr DE73......244 E8
Eagle Hts DE15.....248 D3
Eagle Par SK17.......85 B7
Eagle Rd DE7......208 F4
Eagle St
 4 Buxton SK17.....85 B7
 Heage DE56........168 E2
Eagle Terr
 Birchover DE4.....126 B1
 Wensley DE4.......142 A7
EAGLE TOR........126 A2
Eagle Way NG19....136 E2
Ealand St DE13.....240 D4
Ealing Cl DE22.....218 B6
Ealing Ct **3** S43.....78 B3
Eames Cl **6** DE75...181 D1
Eardley Cl DE21....220 B5
Earlham Ct DE7....208 C6
Earls Cres DE21....206 B2
Earls Drive DE24....231 C3
EARL STERNDALE..105 C3
Earl Sterndale CE Prim
 Sch SK17..........105 C3
Earl Sway **5** SK13...17 B8
Earlswood Cl DE72..235 D8
Earlswood Dr DE3..217 F4
Earnshaw St SK14....9 D4
Earp Way DE73....252 C8
Easedale Cl S40......94 F5
Easset Dr DE6......203 A2
East Ave
 Derby DE3.........217 E3
 Stanfree S44........80 B1
East Bank Pl S2......43 D6
East Bank Rd S2.....43 D6
East Bank Way S2....43 D6
Eastbrae Rd DE21...219 A3
East Brook Cl SK23...47 C6
East Cl DE22........204 E2
Eastcliffe Ct S2......43 C8
East Cres
 Holbrook DE56.....191 C8
 Long Duckmanton S44..98 A6
East Croft Ave DE23 231 D5
Eastcroft Cl S20......59 F8
Eastcroft Dr S20......59 F8
Eastcroft Glen S20...59 F8
Eastcroft View S20...59 F7
East Dr DE6........211 B1
East End DE4......140 F7
East End Dr DE11...256 C4

Eastern Ave
 Bolsover S44.......118 B8
 Sheffield S2........43 D6
Eastern Cres S2......43 D6
Eastern Dr S2.......43 D7
Eastern Wlk S2......43 D7
Eastfield Dr DE55...160 A5
Eastfield Rd
 Dronfield S18.......76 C8
 Ripley DE5........180 E6
 Swadlincote DE11..256 C6
Eastgate DE21......267 D4
East Glade Ave S12..44 E3
East Glade Cl S12....44 E3
East Glade Cres S12..44 E4
East Glade Dell S12..44 E4
East Glade Pl S12....44 E3
East Glade Rd S12...44 E3
East Glade Sq S12...44 E3
East Glade Way S12..44 E4
East Lawn DE65....230 D2
East Lawn Dr S40...230 D2
Eastleigh Ct S41....115 D8
Eastleigh Dr
 Derby DE3.........217 E2
 Mansfield Woodhouse
 NG19..............136 B6
East Midlands Airport
 DE74..............247 C1
East Midlands Designer
 Outlet (Sh Ctr)
 DE55..............160 E6
East Midlands
 Distribution Ctr
 DE74..............246 E5
EASTMOOR.........93 D4
Eastmoor Rd S43.....96 F4
East Nelson St
 DE75..............181 D2
East Par S80.........82 A5
East Rd S2..........43 B7
East Service Rd
 DE21..............220 B3
Eastside Cl S41......96 B8
Eastside Rd S41......96 B8
Eastsides La SK17....69 F2
East St
 Bramley-Vale S44...117 D1
 Burton upon Trent
 DE15..............248 C3
 Clay Cross S45....131 D4
 Clowne S43.........81 A5
 Creswell S80........81 D1
 Derby DE1.........267 B3
 Heanor DE75......194 A8
 Ilkeston DE7.......208 F8
 Long Eaton NG10..236 F8
 Renishaw S21.......79 B8
 Scarcliffe S44......118 E6
 Warsop Vale NG20..120 D5
East Vale SK6........23 A5
East View
 Chesterfield S40...266 B2
 Hillstown S44.......118 B7
 Mayfield DE6......184 D7
 Shirebrook NG20...119 F6
 Whaley Thorns NG20.101 A3
East View Ave S21....59 C2
East View Ind Est
 NG20..............119 F6
East View Rd DE56..168 E1
Eastview Terr
 NG16..............182 B3
Eastway DE74......247 B3
EASTWOOD.........182 E3
Eastwood Ave DE23.218 C2
Eastwood Cl S41....115 D8
Eastwood Cotts S32..53 B8
Eastwood Dr
 Calow S44..........97 B2
 Derby DE23........218 C2
Eastwood Grange Sch
 S45................130 B4
Eastwood La S45....130 B2
Eastwood Park
 Apartments S41...115 C7
Eastwood Park Dr
 S41................115 D8
Eastwood Rd NG16..195 E6
Eather Ave NG19...136 C4
Eaton Ave
 Derby DE22........205 B5
 Ilkeston DE7.......208 D6
Eaton Bank DE56...191 A1
Eaton Cl
 Derby DE22........205 A5
 Hatton DE65.......227 D1
 Hulland Ward DE6..175 E3
Eaton Ct
 Baslow DE45........91 F5
 Derby DE1.........218 E6
 Duffield DE56......190 E2
Eaton Dr DE45.......91 F5
Eaton Fold S32......71 F3
Eaton Grange Dr
 NG10..............236 A8
Eaton Hill DE45......91 F5
Eaton La S45.......129 B5
Eaton Pl DE45.......91 F5
Eaton Rd
 Castle Donington
 DE74..............247 B3
 Rocester ST14.....196 F3
Eatons Rd NG9.....223 D6
Eaton St S14.......210 C1
Eaves Ave SK23......47 C5
Eaves Knoll Rd SK22..33 B8
Ebenezer Brow SK13..10 B7

Ebenezer St
 Glossop SK13........17 D7
 Ilkeston DE7.......194 F3
 Langley Mill NG16..182 B3
Ecclesbourne Ave
 DE56..............190 F3
Ecclesbourne Cl
 Duffield DE56......190 E3
 Wirksworth DE4...165 F7
Ecclesbourne Cotts
 DE4..............154 F2
Ecclesbourne Ct
 DE56..............190 E3
Ecclesbourne Dr
 Buxton SK17........84 F6
 Buxton SK17........85 A6
Ecclesbourne La
 Derby DE3.........217 B1
 Idridgehay DE56...176 F5
Ecclesbourne Mdws
 DE56..............190 D4
Ecclesbourne Pk
 DE55..............159 D2
Ecclesbourne Sch The
 DE56..............190 D3
Ecclesbourne Valley
 Rly★ DE4.........154 F2
Eccles Cl
 Hope S33...........39 A4
 Whaley Bridge SK23..45 D8
ECCLES FOLD.......46 C8
Eccles Fold SK23.....47 A6
Eccles La S33.........51 A8
Eccles Rd
 Chapel-en-le-Frith, Higher
 Crossings SK23.....47 A6
 Chapel-en-le-Frith, Hilltop
 SK23...............46 C7
Eccles Terr SK23.....46 B8
ECKINGTON..........59 C4
Eckington Bsns Ctr
 S21................59 E4
Eckington Camm's
 Endowed CE Prim Sch
 S21................59 D4
Eckington Cl DE7...207 E8
Eckington Hall S20...59 D5
Eckington Jun Sch
 S21................59 D3
Eckington Mews S20 59 D5
Eckington Rd
 Chesterfield S43.....77 D5
 Dronfield S18.......57 D4
 Sheffield S20........59 F8
 Staveley S43.........78 F4
Eckington Sch S21...59 A3
Eckington Swimming
 Pool S21............59 D3
Eckington Way S20...59 F8
EDALE..............37 C8
Edale Ave
 Derby DE23........218 A8
 Derby, Alvaston DE24..233 B7
 Derby, Markeaton
 DE3...............217 D2
Edale Bank SK13.....9 C4
Edale CE Prim Sch
 S33................37 C8
Edale Cl
 Derby DE22........204 D1
 Gamesley SK13......9 C4
 Long Eaton NG10..236 B6
Edale Cres SK13......9 E1
Edale Ct **3** S41......95 E1
Edale Dr
 Derby DE22........220 F3
 South Normanton
 DE55..............160 B7
 Wingerworth S42...115 B4
EDALE END..........29 C2
Edale Fold SK13......9 C4
Edale Gr SK17........85 E7
Edale Mews SK17....85 E7
Edale Mill S33.......37 E7
Edale Rd
 Hayfield SK22.......26 A2
 Hayfield SK22.......35 B8
 Hope S33...........38 F7
 Mastin Moor S43....79 C4
Edale Rise NG9.....223 E3
Edale Sq SK17.......85 E7
Edale Sta S33........37 C7
Edale Way DE56....179 A5
Eden Bank DE56....167 F2
Eden Cl DE65.......240 C8
Edenhall Rd S2.......43 F7
Eden Low NG19....136 E3
Eden Rd DE21......220 B4
Edensor Ave SK17....85 E7
Edensor Cl S42......131 F6
Edensor Ct S43.......97 C8
Edensor Dr DE56...179 C6
Edensor Sq DE22...218 F4
Eden St
 Derby DE24........233 A8
 Wingerworth S42...114 C3
Edes Farm Dr ST14..196 F4
Edgbaston Ct S43...231 C8
Edgecote Dr DE11..256 A7
Edgefold Rd DE4...143 B5
Edgehill DE56......191 A4
Edge Hill DE73.....232 F3
Edge Hill Ct NG10..236 D4
Edgehill Gr NG19...136 C3
Edge Hill Jun Sch
 DE15..............254 F7

Edge La S33.........51 B6
Edgelaw Ct **2** DE24 231 D5
Edge Mount View
 S32................72 E2
Edge Rd
 Eyam S32...........71 E7
 Eyam Moor S32.....52 E1
 Matlock DE4.......143 B6
EDGETOP..........103 F1
Edge Top Rd
 Longnor SK17......121 D7
 Moseley SK17......103 F2
Edge View S32.......72 B3
Edge View Cl S32....72 C7
Edge View Dr DE45...90 A4
Edgware Rd DE22...217 F6
Edgwood Rd NG16..195 F6
Edinboro Row NG16 195 E7
Edinburgh Cres
 DE24..............232 A8
Edinburgh Ct
 Chesterfield S42...114 E4
 Swanwick DE55....170 A7
Edinburgh Mews
 S41................266 A4
Edinburgh Mws S40..95 F5
Edinburgh Rd
 Chesterfield S41.....95 F5
 Wingerworth S42...114 E4
Edinburgh Road
 DE11..............255 E1
Edith Wood Cl DE24 233 B5
EDLASTON..........185 C2
Edlaston La DE6....185 B2
Edmonton Pl DE15..248 D2
Edmund Ave S17.....56 D6
Edmund Cl S17......56 D6
Edmund Dr S17......56 D6
Edmund Rd
 Derby DE21........220 F1
 Sheffield S2........43 B8
Edmund's Sq S2.....230 B7
Edmund St S41.......95 F8
Ednaston Ave DE23.231 D5
Ednaston Hall Farm
 Mews DE6.........201 B7
Edson Way S43.......81 F5
Edward Ave
 Derby DE21........220 A5
 Jacksdale NG16....171 B4
Edward Rd NG10...236 D8
Edwards Cres DE56.192 A8
Edward St
 Aldercar NG16.....182 B4
 Belper DE56.......179 A4
 Derby DE1.........267 B4
 Eckington S21.......59 D3
 Glossop SK13.......10 C1
 Hartshorne DE11..257 A3
 Marple SK6.........15 B1
 Moira DE11.........256 C1
 Overseal DE12.....262 A4
 Stapleford NG9....223 D7
 Staveley S43........97 C8
Edward Wlk S42....115 D1
Edwin Ave S40......114 D8
Edwin Rd S2.........43 C6
Edwinstowe Rd
 DE21..............206 B1
Egerton Dr NG9....209 D2
Egerton Rd S18......57 B2
Eggesford Rd DE24.231 D2
Eggington Rd
 Etwall DE65.......229 B3
 Hilton DE65.......240 F8
EGGINTON.........241 B6
Eggington Prim Sch
 DE65..............241 B6
Egginton Rd
 Etwall DE65.......229 B2
 Hilton DE65.......228 D2
Egmanton Cl DE21..206 B1
Egreaves Ave DE75..181 C4
EGSTOW..........131 D5
Egstow Pl S45......131 D4
Egstow St S45......131 D4
Ehlinger Ave SK13...10 A5
Eider Cl NG20......119 D3
Eighth Ave DE14....253 F8
Eland Cl DE21......221 A6
Eland Rd NG20......119 F5
Elder Cl DE55......170 A8
Elder Ct S21.........60 C5
Elderflower Cl **4**
 DE3...............217 D5
Elder Way S40......266 B3
Eldon Cl SK23........47 C6
Eldon Ho **5** DE1....267 B2
Eldon La SK17........49 B5
Eldon St
 Burton upon Trent
 DE15..............248 B3
 Clay Cross S45....131 C4
Eleanor Ave DE7...209 A5
Eleanor Cres NG9..223 F7
Elesmere Ct DE7...194 D1
Eley Cl DE7.........194 D1
Eley Way SK23.......47 B4
Eley Wlk DE1.......267 A1
Elfin Cl DE6.........201 E8
Elgar Dr NG10......236 B8
Elgin Ave DE23.....218 A1
Elgin Cl S40........114 C7
Eliot Cl
 Calow S43...........96 F5
 Long Eaton NG10..236 D4
Eliot Dr DE7........208 D5

Dud-Elm 283

Eliot Rd DE23......231 B8
Elizabeth Ave
 Buxton SK17........85 D7
 Disley SK12.........32 D5
 Rolleston DE13....240 B3
Elizabeth Cl
 Derby DE21........220 B5
 West Hallam DE7..207 D8
Elizabeth Ct
 Baslow DE45........91 F5
 Burton upon Trent
 DE15..............248 C3
 Ilkeston DE7.......194 D1
Elizabeth Mews
 DE5...............180 E7
Elizabeth Pk NG16..170 F5
Elizabeth Villas DE6 185 C8
Elka Rd DE7.........208 E5
Elkstone Cl DE21...206 B2
Elkstone Rd S40......95 A5
Ella Bank Rd DE75..182 A1
ELLASTONE........183 B3
Ellastone Gdns
 DE24..............233 B7
Ellendale Rd DE21..220 B7
Ellerscroft SK22......24 E1
Ellerslie Gr NG10...223 A5
Ellesmere Ave
 Alfreton DE55.....159 B4
 Derby DE24........219 D1
Ellesmere Dr NG9...209 C5
Ellesmere Rd NG19.136 F1
Elliott Ave S33.......51 A8
Elliott Dr S43........97 C6
Ellis Cl NG10.......236 C6
Ellison Ave DE72...246 A7
Ellison Cl S14.........9 D5
Ellisons Rd S21......60 F8
Ellison St SK13.......10 D1
Elma La S80........101 D6
Elm Ave
 Belper DE56.......179 B2
 Darley Dale DE4..142 F7
 1 Long Eaton NG10..223 C1
 Long Eaton NG10..236 C8
 Sandiacre NG10...223 B7
Elm Cl
 Bolsover S44........99 C1
 Branston DE14....253 F8
 Chesterfield S41.....95 F8
 Doveridge DE6....224 C8
 Killamarsh S21......60 C5
 Mottram in Longdendale
 SK14...............9 A4
 Pinxton NG16.....160 D3
Elm Cres S20........59 C8
Elm Dr
 Hilton DE65.......228 D2
 Killamarsh S21......60 C5
Elmfield SK23........47 A5
Elm Gr
 Clay Cross S45....131 D3
 Derby DE22........204 D5
 Derby, Cherrytree Hill
 DE21..............220 B5
 Glossop SK13.......10 C2
Elmhurst DE65.....241 A5
Elmhurst Ave DE55.160 A4
Elmhurst Cl DE55...160 A4
Elmhurst Rd NG19..136 F1
Elmlands Cl DE72...246 B8
Elm Lodge Farm Cl
 S41................95 F7
Elm Park Ct DE1....267 B4
Elm Rd
 Eckington S21.......59 C2
 Pilsley S45.........132 C1
Elms Ave
 Alfreton DE55.....159 A4
 Derby DE23........218 B2
 Ripley DE5.........180 D8
Elms Cl DE55.......159 A4
Elmsdale Rd DE11..257 A4
Elms Dr DE23.......218 B1
Elms Farm Way
 DE23..............231 A8
Elmsfield Ave DE75.182 A2
Elms Gr DE65.......229 C3
Elmslea Ave DE12..260 D3
Elmsleigh Cl DE11..256 B6
Elmsleigh Dr DE11..256 B6
Elmsleigh Gr DE11..256 B6
Elmsleigh Inf Sch
 DE11..............256 B6
Elms Rd
 Burton upon Trent
 DE15..............248 A1
 Coton in the Elms
 DE12..............260 D3
Elms St DE1.........218 F7
Elm St
 Borrowash DE72...221 B2
 Brimington S43......97 A8
 Holmewood S42...116 B4
ELMS THE..........180 D8
Elms The NG16.....195 F7
Elms View DE6.....176 A2
ELMTON...........100 A7
Elmton Cl
 Clowne S43.........80 F3
 Creswell S80.......100 D8
Elmton La S44........99 C3
Elmton Park Mews
 S80................99 E5
Elmton Rd S80.......81 E1

Elmton View S80 81 D2
Elmton Way S80 100 E8
Elmtree Ave
Derby DE24 232 B7
Selston NG16 171 F7
Elm Tree Ave
Kilburn DE56 192 B7
Mansfield Woodhouse NG19 136 A4
Shirebrook NG20 119 D4
Shirland DE55 146 C1
Elmtree Cl S81 63 F7
Elm Tree Cl S44 118 B5
Elm Tree Cres S18 57 A3
Elm Tree Dr S42 114 F4
Elm Tree Ho S12 44 A6
Elm Tree Row DE55 148 A5
Elm View ST14 196 E6
Elm Wlk S45 132 C1
Elmwood Dr
Alfreton DE55 159 C3
Derby DE21 205 D2
Sheffield S20 59 D6
Elm Wood Rd DE24 232 D5
Elnor Ave SK23 45 E5
Elnor La SK23 45 F4
Elnor St NG16 182 C3
Elsdon Cl DE72 245 A8
Elsecar Cl DE56 179 D5
Elstead La DE11 257 B1
Elston Cl NG19 135 D1
Elstree Dr S12 44 B4
Elstree Rd S12 44 B4
ELTON 140 E6
Elton Bank 6 SK13 9 D1
Elton CE Prim Sch DE4 140 E6
Elton Cl
8 Gamesley SK13 9 D1
North Wingfield S42 132 A5
Stapleford NG9 223 D8
Elton Gr SK17 85 E6
Elton Lea 7 SK13 9 D1
Elton Pl 9 SK13 9 D1
Elton Rd
Derby DE24 232 B8
Winster DE4 141 B6
Elton St
Chesterfield S40 96 A2
Chesterfield S40 266 B2
Elton View S43 97 D8
ELVASTON 234 A6
Elvaston Castle & Ctry Pk★ DE21 233 F6
Elvaston Cl S18 56 B1
Elvaston Dr
Derby DE3 230 E5
Long Eaton NG10 236 A4
Elvaston La DE24 233 C7
Elvaston Nature Reserve★ DE24 233 E7
Elvaston Rd S42 131 F6
Elvaston St DE72 235 B7
Elvaston Way S13 44 B7
Elveden Dr DE7 194 C3
Elvin Way S42 131 C8
Elwick Rd 3 DE23 231 F1
Elwood Rd S17 56 C6
Elwyn Cl DE13 240 D1
Ely Cl
Mansfield Woodhouse NG19 136 D4
Swadlincote DE11 256 D6
Elyn Ave S42 132 B7
Elysee Gdns SK17 85 C3
Embankment Cl DE22 217 F7
Embankment Close NG20 119 E3
Ember Cl 12 DE11 256 E1
Ember La DE4 142 E1
Embleton Way DE72 245 A8
Embridge Cswy SK10 64 B5
Emerald Cl
10 Derby DE21 205 F2
Derby DE21 206 A2
Mansfield NG19 135 F1
Emerald Dr S40 115 E6
Emerson Sq DE23 231 F6
Emery Cl DE12 261 D5
Emes Dr S42 115 B2
Emes Pl S42 115 B2
Emes Rd S42 115 B2
Emmanuel Sch DE22 218 F7
Emmas Williams Ct DE5 169 D1
Emmerson Rd DE55 170 C7
Emmet Field Cl S40 114 F8
EMMETT CARR 79 C7
Emmett Carr Cl S21 79 C7
Emmett Carr Dr S21 79 C8
Emmett Carr La S21 79 C8
Empire Ct DE75 181 E2
Empire Rd DE15 248 D3
Empress Rd DE23 267 A1
Emsworth Cl DE7 194 D3
Endland Ind Est DE1 218 D5
Endowood Rd S40 114 A8
Endsleigh Gdns DE22 217 F6
End The DE15 248 E8
Enfield Cl DE65 228 E2
Enfield Rd
Chesterfield S41 96 A5
Derby DE22 218 B6
England Cres DE75 182 A2
English Martyrs' Catholic Voluntary Acad NG10 223 B1
Ennerdale Ave 4 S20 59 E6
Ennerdale Cl S18 56 E1
Ennerdale Cres S41 95 C8
Ennerdale Ct 6 NG10 223 B2
Ennerdale Dr S20 59 E6
Ennerdale Rd NG10 223 B2
Ennerdale Wlk DE21 205 D2
Ennis Cl DE21 220 C7
Enoch Stone Dr DE21 220 B4
Enslet La DE6 164 B2
Ensor Cl DE11 256 D5
Ensor Way SK22 33 C7
Enterprise Cl NG19 135 E2
Enterprise Ct S80 81 E1
Enterprise Ct DE7 194 D1
Enterprise Dr S42 116 D1
Enterprise Rd NG19 135 E3
Enterprise Way
Derby DE21 267 C4
Duckmanton S44 98 B4
Langley Mill NG16 182 C2
Mansfield NG19 135 E2
Sheffield S20 60 B8
Epping Cl DE22 217 E6
Epsom Cl DE14 253 F7
Epsom Rd NG9 223 E3
Epworth Dr DE24 233 A4
Epworth Ho DE15 248 D3
Erdington Way NG9 223 E3
Erewash Ct
Ilkeston DE7 194 D1
Long Eaton NG10 223 D1
Erewash Dr DE7 209 B6
Erewash Gr NG9 223 F2
Erewash Mus & Gdns★ DE7 208 F8
Erewash Rd NG16 160 E2
Erewash Sq DE7 209 A6
Erewash St DE55 171 A6
Erica Dr DE55 160 B7
Erin Rd
Poolsbrook S43, S44 98 B7
Staveley S43 78 F1
Ernest Hall Way DE11 256 C4
Ernocroft La SK6 15 E2
Ernocroft Rd SK6 15 B1
Errington Ave S2 43 E6
Errington Cl S2 43 E6
Errington Cres S2 43 E6
Errington Rd
Chesterfield S40 114 D8
Sheffield S2 43 E6
Errington Way S2 43 E7
Errisbeg House Dr DE14 253 A1
Errwood Ave SK17 85 A6
Errwood Cl 3 DE65 240 E8
Errwood Forest Walks★ SK17 64 E2
Erskine Cres S2 43 C7
Erskine Rd S2 43 C7
Erskine St SK6 15 B3
Erskine View S2 43 C7
Escolme Cl DE11 256 D4
Eskdale Cl
Bolsover S44 98 F1
Chesterfield S41 76 D1
Dronfield S18 56 E1
Long Eaton NG10 236 B5
Eskdale Wlk DE24 233 D6
Essendine Cres S8 43 B3
Essex Dr 8 DE11 255 E1
Essex Rd DE15 254 D6
Essex St
Derby DE21 219 D6
2 Ilkeston DE7 194 F1
Estwic Ave NG16 182 F3
Etchells The DE65 227 A8
Etches Row 8 DE6 185 D7
Etherow Brow 6 SK14 16 A8
Etherow Ctry Pk★ SK6 15 C3
Etherow Ctry Pk Visitor Ctr★ SK6 15 B2
Etherown Country Pk SK6 15 C3
Etherow Way SK13 9 E5
Eton Ct DE7 207 D8
Eton St DE24 219 E1
Etruria Gdns DE1 267 B5
Etta's Way DE65 229 B4
Etteridge Dr DE22 218 B3
Ettrick Cl 4 S40 95 C5
Ettrick Dr DE24 231 E2
ETWALL 229 C3
Etwall Cl S40 95 A6
ETWALL COMMON 229 D2
Etwall La DE65 229 F5
Etwall L Ctr DE65 229 B4
Etwall Prim Sch DE65 229 B4
Etwall Rd
Burnaston DE3 229 F7
Derby DE3 217 C1
Etwall Rd *continued*
Derby DE3 230 A8
Egginton DE65 241 B7
Willington DE65 242 A7
Etwall St DE22 218 E5
Eureka Lodge Gdns DE11 256 C5
Eureka Prim Sch DE11 256 D5
Eureka Rd DE11 256 D5
Euston Dr DE1 219 B7
Euston Wlk NG19 136 C7
Evans Ave DE22 205 A5
Evans Cl S33 51 A7
Evanston Gdns DE21 220 B6
Evelyn Cl DE72 221 B1
Evelyn Devonshire Cotts S45 132 F2
Evelyn Gr DE21 220 A5
Everard Ave S17 56 A5
Everard Dr S17 56 A5
Everard Glade 3 S17 56 A5
Everest Dr DE55 170 D8
Everett Cl S43 96 E7
Evergreen Cl DE21 206 A3
Everley Rd 4 DE14 256 F7
Evershill Cl DE55 146 F5
Evershill La DE55 146 F6
Eversleigh Rise DE4 142 B8
Everton St NG19 135 E1
Evesham Ave SK13 10 A5
Evesham Cl DE21 205 E1
Ewart La DE55 158 F3
Ewe Dale La DE6 149 A3
Ewe Lamb Cl NG9 209 F1
Ewe Lamb La NG9 209 F1
Excalibur Way
Chesterfield S40 96 B3
Chesterfield S41 266 C3
Excalibur Wlk NG19 135 D1
Excelsior Ave DE24 232 F6
Excelsior Dr DE11 256 E1
Exchange St DE1 267 B3
Exe Fold NG19 136 D2
Exeter Cl DE11 256 E6
Exeter Ct 19 S41 95 F8
Exeter Ho DE1 267 C3
Exeter Pl
Derby DE1 219 B5
Derby DE1 267 C3
Exeter St DE1 267 C4
Exford Ct NG19 136 C6
Exlowmere La DE4 140 F5
Explore Way S80 63 D1
Export Dr NG17 160 F8
EYAM 71 D6
Eyam CE (Controlled) Prim Sch S32 71 D5
Eyam Cl
Burton upon Trent DE15 248 B2
15 Gamesley SK13 9 D2
North Wingfield S42 132 A8
Eyam Fold 29 SK13 9 D2
Eyam Gdns 28 SK13 9 D2
Eyam Gn 16 SK13 9 D2
Eyam Gr 14 SK13 9 D2
Eyam Hall★ S32 71 D5
Eyam La SK13 9 E2
Eyam Lea SK13 9 E2
Eyam Mews SK13 9 E2
Eyam Moor Stone Circle★ S32 52 F3
Eyam Mus★ S32 71 D6
Eyam Wlk DE56 179 A5
Eyam Woodlands S32 72 C7
Eyebright Cl DE3 217 C4
Eyes Ct DE56 190 E3
Eyre Cres S2 43 D8
Eyre Gdns S40 266 A4
Eyre's Gdns DE7 194 F2
Eyre St
Clay Cross S45 131 C3
Creswell S80 81 D1
Eyre Street E S41 115 C8
Eyrie The
Burton upon Trent DE15 248 C3
Derby DE24 231 E3

F

Fabis Cl DE11 256 A3
Fabric View S42 132 D8
Factory La DE7 194 E2
Factory St S40 95 D2
Fairbourne Dr DE3 217 D4
Fairburn Croft Cres S43 80 B6
Faircroft Ave NG10 223 B5
Fairdene DE23 218 F2
Faires Cl DE72 221 D1
Faire St DE22 218 E3
Fairfax Dr S2 44 B8
Fairfax Rd
Derby DE23 218 F2
Sheffield S2 44 B8
Fairfax Rise
Sheffield S13 44 B8
Sheffield S2 44 B8
FAIRFIELD 85 D8
Fairfield Ave
Borrowash DE72 221 C3
Hilcote DE55 148 C1
Fairfield Ave *continued*
Rolleston DE13 240 D4
Stonebroom DE55 147 B4
Fairfield CE Controlled Jun Sch SK17 85 E7
Fairfield Cl
Brimington S43 96 D8
Whaley Thorns NG20 101 A2
Fairfield Cres
Long Eaton NG10 236 B4
Swadlincote DE11 255 E5
Fairfield Ct S42 94 F4
Fairfield Dr
Chesterfield S42 94 F4
Chesterfield S42 95 A4
North Wingfield S42 132 A6
Fairfield Inf Sch SK17 85 E8
Fairfield Prim Sch NG9 223 D6
Fairfield Rd
Bolsover S44 118 A8
Buxton SK17 85 C8
Chesterfield S40 266 A4
Derby DE23 218 E1
Horsley Woodhouse DE7 192 C7
Fairfields
Branston DE14 253 F7
Branston DE14 256 F7
Fairfield Terr DE11 256 F3
Fairfield Villas S40 266 A4
Fairford Cl S40 114 F7
Fairford Gdns DE23 231 A6
Fairham Rd DE13 240 F1
Fairholme Dr NG19 135 E1
Fairholmes DE4 143 D5
Fairisle Cl DE21 206 C3
Fairlawns DE56 190 D3
Fair Lea Cl NG10 236 D6
Fairleigh S2 44 A8
Fairmeadows Foundation Prim Sch DE11 255 E5
Fair View S40 95 E4
Fairview Ave NG16 171 F2
Fairview Cl
Derby DE23 231 A8
Kilburn DE56 192 B7
Fairview Grange DE56 192 B7
Fairview Rd S18 57 A3
Fairview Rise DE4 168 A8
Fairway DE14 254 B6
Fairway Cl DE22 204 D2
Fairway Cres DE22 204 D2
Fairways Cl SK13 10 F1
Fairways The
Clay Cross S45 131 E3
Clifton DE6 184 F6
Mansfield Woodhouse NG19 136 D6
Fairway The 5 DE11 255 E5
Fairwinds Cl S18 57 A1
Fairwood Dr DE24 233 D6
Fairy Bank Cres SK22 25 D3
Fairy Bank Rd SK22 25 D3
Falaise Way DE65 228 E2
Falcon Cl SK22 33 D8
Falcon Ct DE7 194 D1
Falcon Rd S18 57 C3
Falcon Rise S18 57 D3
Falconside Dr DE21 220 F2
Falcons Rise DE56 179 C5
Falcon Way
Derby DE24 231 E2
Woodville DE11 256 F3
Falcon Yd S40 266 B3
Faldo Cl DE14 254 B6
Falkirk Ave DE5 169 E4
Falkland Rise S18 76 A8
FALLGATE S45 130 B1
Fallgate S45 145 A8
Fallow Dr DE16 254 D5
Fallowfield S43 80 D2
Fallowfield Rd S43 77 D3
Fallow Rd DE21 220 F6
Fall Rd DE75 181 E3
Falmouth Rd DE24 233 C5
Fal Paddock NG19 136 D2
Falstaff Ct DE73 232 E2
Fanny Ave S21 60 E5
Fan Rd S43 78 F1
Fan Road Ind Est S43 78 F2
Fanshaw Ave S21 59 C2
Fanshaw Bank S18 57 A1
Fanshaw Cl S21 59 C2
Fanshaw Dr S21 59 C2
Fanshawe Gate La S17, S18 55 E1
Fanshaw Rd
Dronfield S18 57 B2
Eckington S21 59 C2
Fanshaw Way S21 59 C2
Faraday Ave DE13 240 D1
Faraday Ct
Branston DE14 253 E7
Stapleford NG9 209 E1
Far Clay Gr S81 63 F7
Far Croft DE72 235 D8
Far Cross DE4 143 C7
Far Dales Road DE7 194 E2
Farfield Rd DE7 209 A8
Far Green DE4 143 B6
Far Hill S33 51 A7
Farish Pl 5 S2 43 B6
Far La
Barlow S18 75 B3
Ockbrook DE72 221 D6
FAR LAUND 179 C6
Far Laund DE56 179 B6
FARLEY 128 B1
Farley Hill DE4 143 A8
Farley La DE4 128 B3
Farley Rd DE23 218 D2
Farlow Rd S18 56 E2
Farm Cl
Belper DE56 179 C4
Chesterfield S40 114 F6
Dronfield S18 57 B4
Hilton DE65 228 C1
Ilkeston DE7 209 A8
Kilburn DE56 192 A8
Long Eaton NG10 236 E5
Ripley DE5 169 B6
Sheffield S12 44 A2
Somercotes DE55 170 C8
Whaley Thorns NG20 101 A2
Farm Cres S20 59 C6
Farm Croft Rd NG19 136 C6
Farm Dr DE24 233 A5
Farmfields Cl S44 98 E3
Farmhouse Rd DE24 231 E2
Farmhouse Way
5 Grassmoor S41 115 F2
Grassmoor S42 116 A2
Farmilo Cres NG19 135 E1
Farmilo Prim Sch NG19 135 C4
Farm La
Hardstoft S45 132 F3
High Lane SK12 32 A6
Matlock DE4 143 C7
Newton Solney DE15 248 E7
Farmlands La DE23 231 B6
Farm Lane S21 59 C3
Farm Side DE11 255 F5
Farm St DE22 267 A1
Farmstead Cl S14 43 D5
Farm View S42 131 D8
Farmway NG19 136 C2
Farmwell La DE55 160 E6
Farm Wlk S20 59 C7
FARNAH GREEN 178 C3
Farnah Green Rd DE56 178 D3
Farnborough Gdns DE22 205 B4
Farncombe La DE21 205 F3
Farndale Ave S40 114 B8
Farndale Cl NG10 236 A5
Farndale Ct 5 DE24 233 C6
Farndale Rd
Chesterfield S43 78 E4
Staveley S43 78 E4
Farndon Dr NG9 223 F3
Far New Cl NG10 223 B5
Farneworth Rd DE3 217 D2
Farnham Cl DE3 217 C1
Farnham Wlk DE7 207 D8
Farningham Cl DE21 220 F5
Farnon Cl S40 266 C1
Farnsley La S32 71 B4
Farnsworth Ct 5 S41 115 C8
Farnsworth Dr S45 131 C5
Farnsworth Gr NG17 148 F3
Farnsworth La S45 131 C5
Farnsworth St S41 115 C8
Farnway DE22 204 E1
Farrendale Cl NG19 136 D1
Farrier Gdns DE23 231 A7
Farriers Croft DE7 194 C3
Farriers Way S21 60 D5
Farringdon Cl DE22 217 F6
Farrington Way NG16 182 E1
Farthing Ct NG10 236 B7
Farwater Cl S18 76 A8
Farwater La S18 56 F1
Far Wood Cl DE7 194 E4
Far Woodseats La SK13 15 F5
FAULD 238 C6
Fauld Ind Pk DE13 238 E6
Fauld La
Tutbury DE13 239 A6
Tutbury, Fauld DE13 238 D7
Fauvel Pl SK13 10 C1
Fauvel Rd SK13 10 C2
Faversham Cl DE24 232 F5
Fawfield Head SK17 121 A3
Fawn Cl S42 114 F3
Fay Gdns SK13 9 E4
Faywood Dr SK6 23 A6
Fearn Ave DE5 169 E1
Fearn Cl
Church Broughton DE65 227 B8
Long Eaton DE72 236 A7
Featherbed La
Bolsover S44 99 A5
Darfoulds S80 63 F1
Featherstone Rd DE24 233 E4
Feld La
Holmewood S42 116 C1
Holmewood S42 132 C8
Felkin St S41 266 C3
Fellbrigg Rd S2 43 D7
Fellow Lands Way
Chellaston DE73 233 A2
Derby DE73 233 A3
Fellside
Belper DE56 179 A4
Derby DE21 220 F6
Fellview Cl S32 53 A7
Felton Ave NG19 136 C6
Fenchurch Wlk DE22 218 B7
Fen Cl DE55 148 A3
Fenelon Cl 7 DE11 256 E1
Fenland Way S40 114 E8
Fennel Ave DE3 217 C4
Fennel St DE45 108 E8
FENNY BENTLEY 162 A1
Fenton Ave DE11 257 B1
Fenton Drive S12 44 F4
Fenton Green 5 DE13 240 E1
Fenton Rd DE3 217 C2
Fenton St S21 59 B2
Fenwick St DE24 232 D7
Ferguson Ave NG19 136 B4
Fern Ave
Staveley S43 97 D8
Willington DE65 242 C6
Fernbank S33 51 A7
Fern Bank SK23 47 C7
Fern Bank Ave DE55 147 E1
Fernbank Dr S21 59 B3
Fern Cl
Eckington S21 59 B3
Holmewood S44 116 F1
Shirebrook NG20 119 E6
Willington DE65 242 C6
Fern Cres NG16 182 D3
Ferncroft Ave S20 59 C7
Ferncroft Wlk DE73 232 F2
Ferndale Ave SK17 67 C4
Ferndale Cl S18 57 D3
Ferndale Rd
Buxton SK17 67 C4
Dronfield S18 57 D3
Ferndale Rise S18 57 D3
Ferndene Dr NG10 236 A7
Ferndown Dr 5 DE55 148 B7
Fernello Cl DE73 244 A6
Ferneydale Ave SK17 85 C4
Fernhill SK6 23 B6
Fernhill Cl SK13 10 D3
Fernhill Ct DE73 233 A3
Fernhook Ave DE21 220 D1
Fernhook Avenue
Alvaston DE24 233 C8
Derby DE21 220 B1
FERNILEE 45 E1
Fernilee Cl
New Mills SK22 24 C1
West Hallam DE7 207 E8
Fernilee Cotts SK23 45 E1
Fernilee Gdns DE21 205 F1
Fern Lea
Hollingworth SK14 9 D6
Shirland DE55 146 D3
Fernlea Cl SK13 9 E4
Fernlea Dr DE11 261 B6
Fernleigh Rise NG19 136 D1
Fern Rd SK17 85 B5
Fern Royd S32 53 A7
Fern Sq S32 71 D6
Fern View Cl S12 44 F3
Fern View Gr S12 44 F3
Fernway SK17 85 C4
Fern Way S21 59 B3
Fernwood SK6 23 C7
Fernwood Cl
Chesterfield S41 115 E7
Derby DE23 231 C8
Shirland DE55 146 D3
Ferny Cl DE12 262 B3
Ferrers Ave DE13 239 B5
Ferrers Cl DE74 247 A3
Ferrers Cres DE56 190 D3
Ferrers Ctr for Arts & Crafts★ LE65 258 F7
Ferrers Way
Derby DE22 204 D2
Derby DE22 204 E2
Ripley DE5 169 C3
Ferry Gn DE65 242 B5
Ferry La DE73 243 B6
Ferry Mdws 1 S8 43 A2
Ferry St DE15 254 E8
Ferry Vale Cl DE15 254 E8
Festival Ave DE72 235 C7
Festival Crescent DE7 209 C4
Festival Rd
Branston DE14 253 E7
Ilkeston DE7 208 C5
Fiddlers Elbow
Hathersage S11 53 D7
Hathersage S32 41 F1
Fiddler's La DE13 239 F4
Fiddle St SK17 85 C3
Fidlers Cl S33 40 B3
Fidlers Well S33 40 B4
Field Ave
Hatton DE65 239 C8
Renishaw S21 79 B8
Field Cl
Borrowash DE72 221 B3
Breaston DE72 235 F7

Field Cl *continued*
Dronfield S18 ....56 C2
Hilton DE65 .... 228 D2
Mansfield Woodhouse NG19 .... 136 D5
Field Cres DE24 .... 233 A5
Field Ct
Chesterfield S43.......77 D4
Kilburn DE56........ 192 A7
Field Dr
Derby DE24 .... 233 A5
Rolleston DE13....... 240 A3
Shirebrook NG20 .....119 E2
Field Drive DE7...... 193 B8
Fielden Ave NG19... 135 D2
Field End DE4 ...... 153 A1
Fieldfare Ct DE23... 231 A6
Fieldfare Ho S41 .....77 B3
Field Farm Way NG9 .... 209 E2
Fieldgate Dr DE21 ...205 F2
Field Head SK13......16 D7
Fieldhead La HD9......2 F8
Fieldhead Rd S8......43 A7
Fieldhead Way S41 ...95 C6
Field Head Way DE21.............. 206 B3
Field House DE7 ....208 F6
Field House La SK6...23 A6
Fielding's Rd S80.....81 F1
Field La
Belper DE56.........178 F4
Blackfordby DE11.... 257 C2
Derby DE21 ....219 F7
Derby, Boulton DE24...233 B5
Derby, Chaddesden DE21............. 220 A7
Glapwell NG19, S44 .. 134 C6
Killamarsh S20.........60 B6
Killamarsh S21.........60 B5
Kirk Ireton DE6.......176 B8
Mayfield DE6 .... 183 C8
Fieldon Cl DE6 ...... 202 F2
Field Rd DE7 ....208 F7
Field Rise DE23...... 231 C7
Field Row 5 DE56...178 F4
Fields Cres SK14.......9 D6
Fields Farm Rd NG10 .... 236 E5
Fields Gr SK14.........9 D5
Fieldside Cl S43 .....80 A6
Fields La DE11.......261 F6
Field St DE5........ 181 B8
Fields The
Crich DE4 ....156 E2
Middleton DE4 ...... 154 D4
Fieldsway Dr DE21.. 205 E2
Field Terr DE5....... 169 D1
Field The DE75 ..... 194 A6
Field View
Chesterfield S40..... 115 A7
Clowne S43...........80 F3
Shuttlewood S44 ......98 F6
South Normanton DE55............. 160 A7
Swadlincote DE11 ....256 E5
Field View Cl
Derby DE24 ....233 B5
Westwood NG16 .... 171 C4
Fieldview Pl S41......95 C6
Field Way DE11.......255 F5
Fife St DE24.........232 F8
Filbert Wlk DE73 .... 245 A8
Filey Wlk 4 DE21 .. 205 D1
Filigree Close DE55............. 160 D7
Fincham Cl DE21 ... 205 D1
Finch Cl DE11 ....256 F3
Finch Cres DE3....... 230 C8
Finchley Ave DE22...217 F6
FINDERN 230 D2
Findern Cl
Belper DE56.........179 B6
Derby DE22 .... 204 D1
Findern La
Burnaston DE65......230 B4
Willington DE65 ......242 B6
Findern Prim Sch DE65................242 E8
Findern St DE22 .... 218 D5
Finley Way DE55.... 160 B4
Finmere Cl DE23.... 231 A8
Finney Cl DE12 ..... 262 E1
Finney La DE3 ...... 217 B2
Finningley Dr DE22 . 204 F2
Finny La DE6 .... 200 B5
Finsbury Ave DE22.. 218 B6
Finsley Wlk DE23 ... 231 E6
Fir Bank DE56 ...... 190 D5
Firbeck La S80 ....63 A1
Fir Cl NG20......... 119 E6
Firestone DE56..... 178 D1
Firfield Ave DE72 ... 235 E8
Firfield Prim Sch DE72................235 E7
Fir Pl S21 ....60 C5
Fir Rd S21............59 C2
Firs Ave
Alfreton DE55....... 159 A5
Hulland Ward DE6 ....175 F3
Ripley DE5 .... 169 D1
Firs Cres DE22...... 204 E4
Firs Estate Prim Sch DE22................218 E3
Firs Gdns DE55 ..... 159 A4
Firs Par DE4........ 143 C5
Firs St NG10........ 236 A4
Fir St S43 ....78 B1
First Ave
Branston DE14.......253 E7
Risley NG10 ....222 F5
Firs The
Ashbourne DE6...... 173 C1
Wyaston DE6 .... 185 C1
Firth Ct S43 ....77 D4
Firthwood Ave S18 ....57 D3
Firthwood Cl S18......57 D3
Firthwood Rd S18 ....57 D3
Fir Tree Ave DE55 .. 146 C4
Fir Tree Dr DE73.... 244 A6
Firtree Gr DE21..... 206 B2
Firvale S26...........61 E5
Firvale Rd S40...... 114 B8
Fisher Cl
Chesterfield S40......114 F7
Repton DE65........ 242 D2
Fisher Ct DE7........194 F4
Fisher La DE56 ..... 190 E4
Fishers Bridge SK22 . 25 D2
Fisher St DE24...... 232 E6
Fishes La S45 ...... 131 A3
Fishpond La
Egginton DE65 ...... 241 A5
Tutbury DE13 .... 239 C6
Fishponds Cl S42... 115 A3
Fishponds Rd S13 ....44 C7
Fishponds Road W S13................44 C7
Fishponds View S13 ..44 B7
Fiskerton Way DE21 206 B1
Fitzalan St SK13 ......10 C1
Fitzherbert CE Prim Sch DE6............... 162 A1
Fitzhubert Rd
8 Sheffield S2........44 A7
Sheffield S2 ....44 A8
Fitzroy Rd S2.........43 B6
Fitzwilliam Dr NG19 .136 F2
Fitzwilliam Place DE3................217 F3
Five Lamps Ct DE1...218 F6
Five Lamps Ho DE1 . 267 A5
Five Lands Rd DE15..254 F8
Five Trees Ave S17 ...56 A6
Five Trees Cl S17.....56 A6
Five Trees Dr S17 ....56 A6
Flackets La
Sudbury DE6.........225 B7
Sudbury DE6.........225 B8
FLAGG..............106 F6
Flagg La SK17 ....106 F7
Flagshaw La DE6 ...202 F4
Flake La DE7 ...... 208 E1
Flamstead Ave DE75............. 181 C4
Flamstead La
Denby Village DE5 ....180 E1
Smalley DE5.........192 F8
Flamstead Rd DE7 ...194 F1
Flamstead St DE24.. 232 E6
Flamsteed Cres S41 ..96 A6
Flanders Cl 2 NG19 ....135 F1
FLASH............. 103 A3
Flash CE Prim Sch SK17...............103 B3
Flash La
Beeley DE4..........112 B2
Darley Dale DE4 .... 128 A7
Flat La SK17........ 106 B8
Flat The DE56 ....191 F8
Flatts La
Tissington DE6.......162 B6
Westwood NG16 .... 171 D3
Flatts The DE6...... 165 B1
Flax Croft DE65..... 227 C1
FLAXHOLME 190 F1
Flaxholme Ave DE56...............190 F1
Flaxpiece Rd S45.... 131 D3
Fleet Cres DE56 .....178 F3
Fleet Pk DE56 ..... 179 A3
Fleet St DE23...... 219 A2
Fleet The DE56 ......178 F2
Fleetwood Dr DE72 . 246 A6
Fletcher Ave S18 .....57 A1
Fletcher's Row DE5..169 F2
Fletcher St
Heanor DE75 ....181 E2
Long Eaton NG10 .... 236 D8
Ripley DE5 ....169 E2
Fletches The DE13.. 240 B1
Fleury Cl S14.........43 E4
Fleury Cres S14 ......43 E4
Fleury Pl S14.........43 E4
Fleury Rd S14 ....43 E4
Fleury Rise S14.......43 E4
Flint Ave NG19 ......136 F1
Flint La DE4 .... 142 B8
Flintson Ave S43 .....77 D4
Flint St DE24 .... 232 D6
Flint Way SK17 ....85 E2
Flixton Rd NG16 .....195 F7
Flood St DE72 ...... 221 C4
Florence Ave NG10 ..223 F1
Florence Cl
Chesterfield S40......114 F6
Pleasley NG19 ....134 F4
Florence Ct
Derby DE1 .... 267 D2
Ilkeston DE7.........194 F1
Florence Dr
Derby DE1 .... 267 C2
Doveridge DE6 ...... 224 C8
Florence Gladwin Cl DE4................ 141 C6
Florence Rd
Clay Cross S45 ....131 E4
Wingerworth S42.....114 E4
Florence Way SK14....9 D5
Florin Gdns NG10... 236 B7
FLOURISH THE..... 207 D2
Flour Mills The DE15............. 248 A5
Flower Lillies DE56 . 189 C7
Flowery Leys La DE55............. 159 C3
Fly Hill DE45........ 109 D6
Focus Sch Long Eaton Campus NG10 ..... 223 C2
Foggs Entry DE4.....165 F8
Foggs Hill DE4 ..... 127 C4
Fold End La SK17 ... 121 B6
Folds Head S32.......72 C2
Folds La
Calver S32 ....72 B2
Horwich End SK23 .....45 F3
Folds Yd DE4........156 F2
Fold The S32.........71 F4
Foljambe Ave S40 .. 114 D8
Foljambe Rd
Brimington S43........96 E8
Chesterfield S40..... 266 A3
Folkestone Dr DE24. 233 A5
Folly Rd DE22 ...... 205 B1
Fontwell Rd DE14....253 F7
FOOLOW 70 E6
Foolow Ave S40 .... 266 A1
Foolow Ct S40...... 266 A1
Foolow Rd
Eyam S32 ....71 B7
Foolow SK17..........70 F6
Foot The DE6....... 162 B5
Foragers Way DE3.. 217 D4
Forbes Cl NG10..... 236 E5
Forbes Hole Nature Reserve★ NG10 ....236 F5
FORD................58 E5
Ford Ave DE75...... 181 C4
Fordbridge La DE55 160 A7
Ford Cl
Dronfield S18 ....56 F1
Ripley DE5 .... 180 C8
Ford Dr 4 DE23.....230 F5
Ford Gr SK14..........9 A4
Ford La
Breadsall DE21...... 205 C5
Derby DE22 ....205 B5
Eckington S12, S21.....58 E5
Willington DE65 ..... 242 C5
Ford Rd S21..........58 E4
Ford St
Belper DE56.........178 F4
Burton upon Trent DE15...............254 E7
Derby DE1 .... 267 A4
Tupton S42 .... 131 D8
Ford Way SK14 ....9 A4
Fordwells Cl DE23 .. 231 A8
Fordyce Cl DE73.... 232 E1
FOREMARK 243 D2
Foremark Ave DE23. 231 E8
Forest Ave SK17 .....85 C6
Forest Cl DE56...... 179 B5
Forest Ct S43.........80 B6
Forest Dr S45 ...... 132 C2
Foresters Park Ctr DE23................ 232 A7
Foresters Rd DE5 ... 169 C2
Forester St DE1 .... 267 B2
Foresters Way SK23 ..47 C7
Forest La SK17 ....50 C2
Forest Lea DE12 .... 262 E4
Forest Rd DE11 ..... 257 A1
Forest School St DE13................ 240 C4
Forest View DE12... 262 B4
Forge Cl DE65...... 242 D2
Forge Dr S40....... 266 B1
Forgehill DE56 ..... 191 A6
Forge La
Burton upon Trent DE13............. 241 A2
Killamarsh S21........60 B7
Pleasley NG19 ....135 B8
Forge Rd
Chinley SK23..........34 E1
Whaley Bridge SK23....45 F7
Forge Row NG16 ....170 F3
Forge Steps DE56... 191 A6
Forge Terr SK23 ......34 E1
Forge The
Dronfield S18 ....57 A1
Trowell NG9 ....209 B5
Forman Cl DE11 .... 256 B4
Forman St DE1, DE22................ 267 A3
Forrester Ave DE72..245 F5
Forrester's La S18....57 C4
Forshaw Cl DE6 .... 185 C8
Forster Cl DE4...... 157 A1
Forth Ave S18 ....56 D2
Forties La LE65 ......257 F3
FORTIES THE 257 F4
Fortis Way DE3..... 230 E5
Forty Foot La DE73 ..252 F7
Forty Horse Cl DE5 . 170 A2
Forum Cl DE24 ..... 233 D5
Fosbrook Dr DE74 ..246 F4
Fosbrooke Dr NG10. 236 D5
Fosse Cl
Borrowash DE72 .... 221 C1
Borrowash DE72 .... 234 C8
Fossett's Ave NG16 ..171 F7
Foss Rd DE65....... 228 E1
Foster Cl DE3....... 217 B2
Foster Rd DE11......256 F2
FOSTON 226 D4
Foston Cl
Hatton DE65........ 227 C1
Hatton DE65........ 239 C8
Foston Dr S40 ....95 B5
Foundry Cl SK13......10 C1
Foundry Ct 1 SK22...33 C7
Foundry La
Belper DE56.........190 F8
Horwich End SK23 .....45 F5
Foundry St S41........96 A8
Foundry Street Ind Est 7 S41 ....96 A8
Foundry The S41 ... 266 C2
Fountains Cl DE22.. 205 A4
Fountains High Sch DE13.............. 240 C1
Fountains Prim Sch DE13.............. 240 D1
Fountain Sq
Disley SK12 ....32 D6
Youlgreave DE45 .....125 B5
Fountain St
Buxton SK17..........85 B7
Tideswell SK17........69 C4
FOURLANE ENDS.... 158 C4
Four Lane Ends
Darley Dale DE4 ..... 127 C1
Swadlincote DE11 ... 256 A6
Four Lanes SK14.......9 A4
Fowler Ave DE21 ... 220 D4
Fowler St
Chesterfield S41.......76 F2
Derby DE22 ....218 E6
Draycott DE72 ....235 B7
Foxbrook Cl
Chesterfield S42.......94 F5
Derby DE23 .... 231 A8
Foxbrook Ct S40.... 114 B8
Foxbrook Dr S40 ... 114 B8
Fox Cl
Burton upon Trent DE14...............254 B8
Derby DE24 .... 231 D2
Long Eaton NG10 .... 236 D5
Foxcote Way S40 ... 114 B8
Fox Croft
Greenhill S8 ....56 F7
Tibshelf DE55........147 F5
Foxcroft Chase S21................60 C6
Foxcroft Dr S21 ......60 C5
Foxcroft Gr S21 ......60 C6
Foxdale Ave S12.......44 B5
Foxdell Way DE73 .. 233 A2
Foxes Wlk DE22 .... 204 E4
Foxes Yd SK17........66 D1
Fox Field DE11 ......261 F8
Foxfield Close S12....44 F2
Foxfields Dr DE21 .. 205 E2
Fox Gdns DE11 ......256 F4
Foxglove Ave
Burton upon Trent DE15............. 255 A8
Donisthorpe DE12 ....262 E1
Foxglove Cl
Bolsover S44 ....99 D1
Calow S44............97 A3
4 Tutbury DE13..... 239 D5
Foxglove Dr
Bolsover S44 ....99 D1
Derby DE21 .... 205 F3
Derby DE21 .... 206 A3
Foxglove Gr NG19 ...136 F4
Foxglove Rd NG16.. 195 B8
FOX GREEN.........100 F8
Foxhall La S10........42 F6
Fox Hill S44 ....118 F7
Foxholes DE6....... 163 B1
Foxholes La
Kniveton DE6 ....174 B6
Tansley DE4 .... 144 A7
Fox Hollies The DE55............. 146 D2
Fox La
Baslow DE45 ....73 E1
Creswell S80 .... 100 D8
Creswell S80 ....100 E8
Holmesfield S18.......74 B5
Sheffield, Base Green S12................44 C3
Sheffield, Lower Bradway S17.................56 D6
Foxlands Ave DE22 ..204 F2
Fox Lane Ct S12 ......44 C4
Fox Lane View S12 ...44 C4
Foxlea SK13..........16 F8
Foxley Chase DE11 .. 261 E5
Foxley Ct DE21 .... 206 A2
Foxley Oaks S41......77 B1
Foxley Rd DE7.......194 F5
Fox Low Ave SK17 ....85 C4
Foxpark View DE55 . 147 E5
Fox Rd
Castle Donington DE74...............246 F4
Whitwell S80 ....82 A6
Fox St DE1 .... 267 C4
Foxstone Cl S43 ......97 D8
Foxstone Way S21.....59 C2
Foxtail Cl DE24 .... 231 C3
Foxton Cl DE7 ...... 194 C3
Foxwood Ave S12 ....44 B6
Foxwood Cl
Chesterfield S41..... 115 D6
Foxwood Cl *continued*
Chesterfield, Sheepbridge S41.................76 F1
Foxwood Dr S12......44 B6
Foxwood Gr S12......44 B5
Foxwood Ind Pk S41..76 F1
Foxwood Rd
Chesterfield S41.......76 F2
Sheffield S12 ....44 B6
Foxwood View S41 ....76 F1
Foxwood Way S41....76 E2
Foyers Way
Chesterfield S40.......96 B3
Chesterfield S41..... 266 C3
Foyle Ave DE21 .... 220 A4
Frain Gdns DE73.....252 F2
Framlingham Pl S2....43 D7
Framlingham Rd S2 ..43 D7
Frampton Gdns DE23...............230 F6
Frances Cl ST14 .... 196 E6
Frances Dr S42..... 114 E4
Frances St NG16..... 171 D1
Franchise St DE22 .. 218 E4
Francis Cl S43........96 D7
Francis Ct NG16 .... 171 B4
Francis St DE21..... 219 D6
Frank Bodicote Way DE11.............. 256 D4
Frankley Cl 9 DE65 240 E8
Franklin Ave S80 .....81 F5
Franklin Cl DE15..... 248 B1
Franklin Cres S80 .....81 F5
Franklin Rd NG16... 171 A4
Franklyn Dr
Derby DE24 .... 233 A6
Staveley S43..........78 F3
Franklyn Rd S40......95 E4
Frankwright Dr S2....43 C8
Frazer Cl DE21 ..... 220 E6
Frecheville Dr DE56 168 A6
Frecheville St S43 ....78 D1
Frederic Ave DE75...193 F7
Frederick Ave
Derby DE24 ....232 F6
Ilkeston DE7........ 209 A5
Frederick Gent Sch DE55...............160 B5
Frederick Rd NG9 .. 223 D7
Frederick St
Alfreton DE55....... 159 A5
Burton upon Trent DE15...............254 E8
Derby DE22 .... 218 D6
Grassmoor S42 ....115 E3
Long Eaton NG10 .....236 F7
Somercotes DE55.... 170 D5
Woodville DE11 ......256 E3
FREEBIRCH 93 D6
Freebirch View S40...95 B7
Freeby Ave NG19 ... 136 D5
Freehold St DE22 ... 218 E4
Freeland Cl NG9......223 F3
Freeman Ave DE23 . 231 E6
Freeman Dr DE73... 252 C8
Freesia Cl DE3...... 217 E1
Freetown SK13 ....17 C8
Fremantle Rd DE3 .. 217 E3
French La DE21......191 F5
French St
Derby DE23 ....218 E2
Ilkeston DE7........ 209 A6
French Terr NG20 ... 101 A2
Fresco Dr DE23......230 F7
Fresh Ct SK13 ....16 F7
Freshfield Cl SK6......15 B1
Freshfields Donkey Village★ SK17.......48 D2
Freshwater Ho DE24.............. 233 C7
Freshwaters S42 ... 116 D1
Fretson Cl S2 ....44 A8
Fretson Gn S2........44 A8
Fretson Rd S2........44 A8
Fretson Rd S S2 ......44 A8
Freydon Way S44.....97 A3
Friar Gate DE1 ......218 F5
Friar Gate Ct DE1....218 F5
Friar Gate House Sch DE1................218 E6
Friar Gate Studios DE1............... 267 A3
Friar Gr SK17.........85 C6
Friars Cl DE22 ..... 205 A2
Friars Ct DE7 ...... 208 C6
Friarsfield DE22 .....218 F8
Friar St NG10....... 236 D7
Friary Ave DE24 .... 232 E6
Friary Croft DE11 ... 256 A7
Friary St DE1 .... 267 A3
Friday La DE21 ..... 205 D2
FRIDEN............ 139 A6
Friden Cotts SK17 .. 139 A6
Friden Rd
Middleton DE45 ..... 124 C3
Newhaven SK17......139 B8
Youlgreave DE45 .... 125 A5
Friesland Dr
Sandiacre NG10......222 F5
1 Sandiacre NG10 ... 223 A5
Friesland Sch NG10 .222 F5
Frinton Cl S40.......114 F7
Frisby Ave NG10.... 236 E6
FRITCHLEY 168 C7
Fritchley CE (Aided) Prim Sch DE56.....168 B6
Fritchley Cl DE21 ... 206 A1
Fritchley La DE56... 168 A7
Frith Cl S12 ....44 B5
Frithhall La S42 ......94 C2
Frith Knoll Rd SK23...47 D7
Frith Rd S12..........44 B5
Frith View SK23 ......47 A5
Frithwood Dr S18 ....57 C2
Frithwood La
Creswell S80 ....100 F7
Creswell S80 .... 101 A8
Elmton S80......... 100 D7
Frizams La DE73....242 F7
FROGGATT 72 C5
Froggatt Cl
Derby DE22 .... 205 A5
Staveley S43..........97 C6
Froggatt Edge S32....72 D6
Froggatt La S32 ......72 C5
Froggatt Rd S32......72 C3
Froggett Cl DE55 ... 170 D7
Front St DE56 ...... 168 B6
Front Terr DE55 ......145 F4
Frood Cl SK23........47 C7
Frost Ave NG16..... 182 A4
Frost Fields DE74... 247 B4
Fryar Rd NG16.......182 F4
Fulbrook Rd DE23 .. 231 A8
Fulford Cl S40...... 114 C8
Fulham Rd DE22.... 218 A5
Fuller Dr S41.........96 C6
Fullers Cl
Belper DE56.........190 F8
Milford DE56 ....190 F8
Fulleylove Ct S44.....99 B1
Full St DE1 .... 267 B3
Fullwood Ave 4 DE7................ 194 E1
Fullwood Grange DE6............... 175 C3
Fullwood Ind Est NG17 ....148 F1
Fullwood St 6 DE7. 194 E1
Fullwood Stile La S33................38 F6
Fulmar Cl
Derby DE3 .... 218 A3
Mansfield NG19 ......136 E1
Fulwood Dr NG10... 236 A7
Fulwood Head Rd S10.................42 D7
Fulwood Ind Est NG17 ....160 F8
Fulwood La S10, S11 ..42 E5
Fulwood Rd N NG17 .160 F8
Fulwood Road N NG17 ....148 F1
Fulwood Road S NG17 ....160 F8
Furlong Cl NG9..... 223 D8
Furlong La
Alstonefield DE6..... 149 C4
Atlow DE6...........175 B7
Castleton S33.........38 C3
Furnace Cl S42..... 115 E2
Furnace Hillock Way S41................ 115 E5
Furnace Hill Rd S45................ 131 D5
Furnace La
Barlow S18...........75 F3
Brimington S40.......96 F6
Castle Gresley DE11...255 E2
Heanor DE75 .... 181 D4
Moira DE12..........262 E3
Furnace Lane Ind Est DE12...............262 E3
Furnace Rd DE7 .... 209 B6
Furnace Row DE55 ..170 F7
Furnall Ave DE45 .....90 A3
Furness Cl 2 SK13 ...17 F8
Furness Lodge Cl SK23................33 D4
FURNESS VALE 33 C3
Furness Vale Bsns Ctr SK23................33 D4
Furness Vale Prim Sch SK23................33 D3
Furness Vale Sta SK23................33 D4
Furniss Ave S17 ......55 D6
Furniss Mews S17....55 E6
Furrows Cl DE21.... 206 C3
Fyfield Rd DE15 .... 254 E6
Fylde Cl NG9 ....223 F2

G

Gable Ct DE3....... 230 E8
Gables Cl S42 ...... 132 D8
Gables The
Hilton DE65 .... 228 D1
6 Swadlincote DE11..255 E5
Gadley Cl
Buxton SK17..........84 F7
Buxton SK17..........84 F8
Gadley La SK17 ....84 F8
Gadsby Cl DE7...... 209 A4
Gadsby Rise DE56 .. 168 C2
Gag La DE6........ 161 D6
Gainsborough Ave SK6..................23 B8
Gainsborough Cl
Derby DE21 ....206 B1
Long Eaton NG10 .....236 E5
Stapleford NG9.......223 E6

Gainsborough Rd S18 … 75 E8
Gainsborough Way DE15 … 248 B3
Gairloch Cl DE24 … 231 D2
Gala Dr DE24 … 232 F7
Galahad Dr DE13 … 240 E2
Gallery La S42 … 113 D7
Gallery The 6 DE6 … 173 C2
Galloway Dr DE22 … 218 B3
Galloway Rd DE16 … 254 D5
Gallows Ind Est DE7 209 B6
GALLOWS INN … 209 B6
Gallows Inn Cl DE7 … 209 A5
Gallowstree La DE6 … 184 C8
Galway Ave DE21 … 220 B4
Gambols La SK17 … 103 D5
GAMESLEY … 9 D1
Gamesley Com Prim Sch SK13 … 9 E2
Gamesley Fold SK13 … 16 D8
Gander La S43 … 80 B5
Gang La S44 … 118 E5
Gannow Cl S21 … 60 F7
Gapsick La S43, S80 … 81 B5
Garden Ave
Ilkeston DE7 … 208 F5
New Houghton NG19 … 134 F7
Renishaw S21 … 79 B7
Shirebrook NG20 … 119 E4
Garden Cl
Chesterfield S43 … 77 D3
Whitwell S43 … 81 F5
Garden Cres
Castle Donington DE74 … 247 B3
South Normanton DE55 … 159 F4
Gardeners Ct
Bolsover S44 … 99 A2
Mansfield Woodhouse NG19 … 136 C3
Garden Rd NG16 … 182 F3
Garden St
7 Broadbottom SK14 … 16 A8
Derby DE1 … 267 A4
Gardens The
Heanor DE75 … 181 C4
Ripley DE5 … 180 D7
Gardner Ct 3 DE6 … 211 A2
Gardner Pl ST14 … 210 A1
Gardom Cl S18 … 56 D1
Garfield Ave DE72 … 235 A7
Garfield Cl
Derby DE23 … 231 C6
Stapleford NG9 … 209 E1
Garland Cl S20 … 59 E7
Garland Croft S20 … 59 E7
Garland Dr 3 DE7 … 194 F8
Garland Mount 15 S20 … 59 E8
Garland Way S20 … 59 E7
Garner La DE4, DE55 … 157 D2
Garner Rd NG16 … 195 B7
Garnett Ave DE75 … 181 F2
Garnham Cl DE55 … 159 D2
Garrett Gn S45 … 131 E3
Garrett La S45 … 131 D2
Garrett Sq DE13 … 240 C4
Garrick St DE24 … 233 A7
Garrison Rd SK22 … 24 F2
Garry Cl DE24 … 231 D2
Garsdale Ct DE24 … 233 D6
Gartan Rd DE14 … 254 A8
Garth Cres DE24 … 233 B6
Garthorpe Ct 4 DE21 … 205 F2
Garth Rd SK6 … 23 A6
Garth Way S18 … 56 F1
Garth Way Cl S18 … 56 F1
Garton Mill Dr DE4 … 143 E7
Gartrice Gdns S20 … 60 A5
Gartrice Gr S20 … 60 A5
Gary Cl DE23 … 231 D5
Gascoigne Dr DE21 … 220 D4
Gashouse La S20, S21 … 59 D5
Gaskell Ave DE23 … 231 E7
Gasny Ave DE74 … 247 B5
Gas St
Hollingworth SK14 … 9 D5
Sandiacre NG10 … 223 C6
Uttoxeter ST14 … 210 C1
Gatcombe Cl
Burton upon Trent DE13 … 240 D1
Derby DE21 … 206 B2
Gatcombe Gr NG10 … 223 A3
Gate Brook Cl DE5 … 170 B1
Gatefield Cl S41 … 95 C7
Gateham Hallow SK17 … 149 A7
Gate Ho DE4 … 165 F8
Gate Ho The S32 … 72 D2
Gatehouse Dr DE4 … 165 F8
Gatehouse La S32 … 40 E3
Gateland La S18 … 75 E5
Gates The
Taddington SK17 … 88 C2
Taddington SK17 … 107 D8
Gateway Ct DE4 … 143 A6
Gauledge La SK17 … 121 B6
Gaunt Cl
Killamarsh S21 … 60 C6
Gaunt Cl *continued*
Sheffield S14 … 43 D3
Gaunt Dr S14 … 43 D3
Gaunt Pl S14 … 43 D4
Gaunt Rd S14 … 43 D3
Gaunt Way S14 … 43 D3
Gawain Gr DE13 … 240 E2
Gawsworth Cl SK13 … 10 A5
Gayton Ave DE23 … 231 D6
Gayton Jun Sch DE23 … 231 D6
Gayton Rd NE7 … 194 D1
Gayton Thorpe Cl DE23 … 230 F7
Geary La DE15 … 248 F2
Geer La S12 … 58 D5
Gelderd Pl S18 … 76 A8
Gema Cl DE22 … 205 A4
Genista Cl DE15 … 255 A8
GENTSHILL … 131 E2
Gentshill Ave S45 … 131 E2
George Ave NG10 … 223 F1
George Cl S40 … 96 C7
George Cres DE55 … 170 C6
George Dutton Ind Pk DE6 … 185 E8
George Holmes Bsns Pk DE11 … 256 A4
George Holmes Way DE11 … 256 A3
George Inn Ct S80 … 81 F6
George Newberry Pl DE11 … 256 B2
George Percival Pl S45 … 131 A4
George Rd
Alstonefield DE6 … 149 E4
Matlock DE4 … 143 C6
George Rodgers Cl DE6 … 175 E3
George Spencer Acad NG9 … 223 E5
George St
Alfreton DE55 … 159 A4
Ashbourne DE6 … 185 B8
Belper DE56 … 178 F4
Brimington S43 … 96 E8
7 Buxton SK17 … 85 B8
Chesterfield S41 … 76 F2
Compstall SK6 … 15 B2
Derby DE1 … 218 F5
Derby DE1 … 267 A3
Glossop SK13 … 17 C8
Langley Mill NG16 … 182 B3
Mansfield Woodhouse NG19 … 136 D3
Melbourne DE73 … 252 A7
North Wingfield S42 … 131 E7
Pinxton NG16 … 160 C4
Somercotes DE55 … 170 D8
Somercotes, Riddings DE55 … 170 D6
South Normanton DE55 … 159 F5
Swadlincote DE11 … 256 A1
Whaley Bridge SK23 … 45 E7
Whaley Thorns NG20 … 101 A2
George Yard DE1 … 267 B3
Georgia Ave DE65 … 242 B6
Georgina Ct DE74 … 247 B4
Geraldine Way 6 DE74 … 246 E3
Gerard Cl
Chesterfield S40 … 95 C1
Derby DE21 … 220 F6
15 Sheffield S8 … 43 B6
Gerard Ct DE1 … 267 A2
Gerard Gr DE65 … 229 C4
Gerard St N DE1 … 267 A2
Gerard St North DE1 … 218 F5
Gerard St
Derby DE1 … 267 A2
Sheffield S8 … 43 B6
Gertrude Rd
Derby DE21 … 219 F8
Derby DE21 … 220 A8
Draycott DE72 … 235 A7
Gervase Ave S8 … 56 E6
Gervase Dr S8 … 56 E6
Gervase Pl S8 … 56 E6
Gervase Rd S8 … 56 E6
Gervase Wlk 2 S8 … 56 E6
Ghyll Cl DE24 … 220 A1
Gibb Ct S43 … 77 D4
Gibb La
Marple SK6 … 23 E5
Sudbury DE6 … 225 E5
Gibbons Ave NG9 … 223 D6
Gibbons Dr S14 … 43 E2
Gibbons Way S14 … 43 E2
Gibbons Wlk S14 … 43 E2
Gibb St NG10 … 236 E7
Gibfield La
Belper DE56 … 178 F2
Kirk Ireton DE6 … 175 F7
Gifford Rd S8 … 43 A7
Gilbert Ave S40 … 114 D8
Gilbert Cl DE21 … 220 D4
Gilbert Cres DE56 … 190 E2
Gilbert St DE24 … 233 B6
Gilderdale Way DE21 … 206 B3
Gildwells La NG20 … 119 B7
Gillamoor Ct DE24 … 233 D6
Gilleyfield Ave S17 … 55 E7
Gilling Cl
Derby DE23 … 230 F5
Gilling Cl *continued*
Derby DE23 … 230 F6
Gilliver Gdns DE72 … 235 A7
Gill La DE4 … 127 C4
Gillott St DE75 … 194 A8
Gill's La S42 … 115 E2
Gilmour Way S2 … 43 F8
GILTBROOK … 195 C8
Giltbrook Cres NG16 … 195 C8
Giltbrook Shopping Pk NG16 … 195 C7
Gilt Hill NG16 … 195 D7
Gilthill Prim Sch NG16 … 195 D7
Giltway NG16 … 195 C7
Gimson Cl DE7 … 194 C3
Gin Close Way NG16 … 195 C6
Gin La
Ashover S45 … 144 F8
Ravensnest S45 … 144 F7
Gipsyhill La S80 … 81 B8
Gipsy La
Alstonefield DE6 … 149 F4
Apperknowle S18 … 58 A1
Chesterfield S41 … 77 B1
Market Warsop NG20 … 120 F6
Gird La SK6 … 15 E1
Girdon Cl SK17 … 84 F6
Girton Way DE3 … 217 F3
Gisbey Rd 2 DE7 … 208 E5
Gisborne Cl DE3 … 217 E3
Gisborne Cres DE22 … 204 F4
Gisborne Gn DE1 … 218 E6
Gisbourne Cl S43 … 78 F1
Gisbourne Dr SK23 … 47 B5
Gittos La S42 … 115 C2
Glade Cl S40 … 95 E5
Glade Croft S12 … 44 A4
Glade Lea S12 … 44 A4
Glade The
Buxton SK17 … 85 A8
Chesterfield S40 … 95 D3
Hayfield SK22 … 25 C3
Gladstone Ave
Blackwell DE55 … 147 E1
Heanor DE75 … 181 F2
Gladstone Cl
Chellaston DE73 … 232 F3
Glossop SK13 … 17 D8
Gladstone Dr NG16 … 182 E7
Gladstone Rd
Alfreton DE55 … 158 F3
Chesterfield S40 … 266 A4
Derby DE21 … 220 E5
Gladstone St W DE7 … 208 F7
Gladstone St
Derby DE23 … 218 E1
Glossop SK13 … 17 D8
Hadfield SK13 … 10 A4
Heanor DE75 … 181 E2
Langley Mill NG16 … 182 C3
Long Eaton NG10 … 236 D6
Mansfield Woodhouse NG19 … 136 C2
South Normanton DE55 … 160 B6
Gladstone Terr NG19 … 136 C2
Gladwin Cl 5 NG9 … 223 E7
Gladwin Gdns S40 … 114 D8
Gladwins Mark SE45 … 112 E2
Glaisdale Nook DE24 … 233 D6
Glamis Cl DE21 … 206 B2
Glamorgan Way DE11 … 255 F1
GLAPWELL … 134 C8
Glapwell La S44 … 118 B2
Glasgow Close 5 DE11 … 255 E1
GLASSHOUSE COMMON … 77 D5
Glasshouse Hill DE5 181 B8
Glasshouse La S43 … 77 D4
Glastonbury Cl NG19 … 136 D4
Glastonbury Rd DE24 … 233 C7
Glaven Cl NG19 … 136 D2
Gleadless Ave S12 … 44 A4
Gleadless Bank S12 … 43 F4
Gleadless Comm S12 … 44 A5
Gleadless Ct S2 … 43 B6
Gleadless Dr S12 … 43 F4
Gleadless Mount S12 … 44 A3
Gleadless Prim Sch S12 … 44 B5
Gleadless Rd
Sheffield S12, S14, S2 … 43 D5
Sheffield S14 … 43 D5
Gleadless Rise
Sheffield S12 … 43 F5
1 Sheffield, Gleadless Townend S12 … 44 A3
GLEADLESS VALLEY … 43 E3
Gleadless Valley Nature Reserve* S8 … 43 C4
Gleadless View
Sheffield S12 … 43 F5
2 Sheffield, Gleadless Townend S12 … 44 A3
Gleadsmoss La DE21 … 206 A1
Glebe Ave
Great Longstone DE45 … 90 A3
Harthill S26 … 61 E7
Pinxton NG16 … 160 D3
Ripley DE5 … 169 C2
Smalley DE7 … 192 F6
Glebe Cl
Bonsall DE4 … 142 E1
Coton in the Elms DE12 … 260 C3
Doveridge DE6 … 224 B8
Holmewood S42 … 132 D8
Rolleston DE13 … 240 A4
South Normanton DE55 … 160 A5
Thurvaston DE6 … 201 E1
Glebe Cres
Ilkeston DE7 … 209 A7
Stanley DE7 … 207 B6
Glebe Ct DE45 … 90 A3
Glebe Farm Cl S26 … 61 E7
Glebe Field Cl DE4 … 156 F1
Glebe Gdns S42 … 131 F5
Glebe Jun Sch DE55 … 160 A5
Glebe La DE6 … 161 C1
Glebe Pk S32 … 71 D5
Glebe Rd SK17 … 85 D8
Glebe Rise DE23 … 218 D1
Glebe St DE11 … 256 B3
Glebe The
Awsworth NG16 … 195 B4
Chesterfield S41 … 77 A2
Rosliston DE12 … 260 C6
Glebe View
Barlborough S43 … 80 B6
5 Forest Town NG19 … 136 E1
Glebe Way The S41 … 77 A2
Gledhill Cl S18 … 57 A1
Glen Ave DE56 … 191 C7
Glenavon Cl S43 … 77 D5
Glenbrook Hill SK13 … 10 C2
Glencar Cl DE24 … 233 C8
Glen Cl DE55 … 148 A3
Glencoe Way S40 … 95 B4
Glencroft Cl DE14 … 254 B7
Glencroft Dr DE24 … 231 D3
Glendale Dr DE21 … 220 F5
Glendevon Way DE73 … 232 E2
Glendon Rd
Derby DE24 … 231 D3
Ilkeston DE7 … 208 C4
Glendon St DE7 … 193 A1
Gleneagles Cl
Chesterfield S40 … 114 C8
Derby DE3 … 217 F2
Gleneagles Dr DE13 240 C1
Glenfield Ave NG16 … 195 D7
Glenfield Cres
Chesterfield S41 … 96 A7
Derby DE3 … 217 C2
Glenfield Rd NG10 … 236 D5
Glengarry Way DE24 … 231 E4
Glenholme Dr S13 … 44 E7
Glenholme Pl S13 … 44 F7
Glenholme Rd S13 … 44 F7
Glenholme Way S13 … 44 E7
Glenmoor Rd SK17 … 66 D1
Glenmore Cl S43 … 97 B5
Glenmore Croft S12 … 44 C6
Glenmore Dr DE24 … 231 D3
Glenmoy Cl DE23 … 231 D7
Glenn Way DE72 … 234 E1
Glenorchy Ct DE21 … 206 B3
Glen Park Cl DE73 … 244 F8
Glen Rd DE4 … 156 D1
Glenshee Gdns DE73 … 232 E2
Glenthorn Cl S81 … 63 F7
Glenthorne Cl S40 … 95 C2
Glentress Dr DE23 … 231 E1
Glen Vale S18 … 56 D1
Glen View DE56 … 178 F2
Glen View Rd S8 … 56 E8
Glen Vine DE5 … 170 A1
Glenwood Rd DE73 … 245 A8
Glinton Ave DE55 … 147 E1
GLOSSOP … 10 B2
Glossop Brook Bsns Pk SK13 … 10 B1
Glossop Brook Rd SK13 … 10 B1
Glossop Brook View SK13 … 16 C8
Glossop Central Sta SK13 … 10 C1
Glossopdale Sch
Glossop SK13 … 9 F4
Glossop SK13 … 10 A4
Glossop L Ctr SK13 … 10 D1
Glossop Pool SK13 … 10 C2
Glossop Rd
Broadbottom SK13 … 16 D7
Gamesley SK13 … 9 E1
Hayfield SK22 … 25 C6
Marple SK6 … 15 D3
Glossop's Croft S41 … 77 B2
Glossop St DE24 … 232 B8
Gloster St DE24 … 219 E2
Gloucester Ave
Chesterfield S41 … 95 F5
Sandiacre NG10 … 223 A4
Gloucester Rd S41 … 95 F5
Gloucester Way
Burton upon Trent DE15 … 248 B1
4 Glossop SK13 … 17 F8
Glover Rd
Castle Donington DE74 … 247 B4
Sheffield, Highfield S8 … 43 A7
Sheffield, Totley Rise S17 … 55 F5
Gloves La
Alfreton DE55 … 147 E2
Blackwell DE55 … 147 D2
Glumangate S40 … 266 B3
Gn The DE56 … 176 E7
Go Ape!* SK17 … 84 F6
Goathland Rd DE24 … 231 D2
Goatscliffe Cotts S32 … 72 C7
Goatscliff Farm La S32 … 72 B7
Godber Cl NG16 … 195 A8
Goddard La
Glossop SK13 … 10 A6
New Mills SK22 … 24 E7
Goddard Rd SK13 … 10 A4
Godfrey Dr DE7 … 208 D6
GODFREYHOLE … 165 B8
Godfrey St DE75 … 181 E1
Godkin Dr NG16 … 182 A4
Godric Pl DE11 … 256 D4
Godward Rd SK22 … 33 B8
Gold Cl DE4 … 142 B8
Goldcrest Dr DE21 … 220 F6
Goldcrest Ho S41 … 77 B3
Goldcrest Road NG19 … 136 F2
GOLDEN VALLEY … 170 D3
Golden Valley
Horsley Woodhouse DE7 … 192 B6
Somercotes DE55 … 170 D3
Golden Valley Light Rly* DE5 … 170 B4
Golders Green Wlk DE22 … 218 A6
Goldfinch Cl 2 NG9 … 209 E2
Goldhill DE4 … 144 A4
Golding Ho DE4 … 143 C6
Gold La DE22 … 217 E8
Goldsitch Moss La SK17 … 102 F1
Goldstone Ct DE21 … 220 E4
Golf Cl DE23 … 218 A1
Golf Club Rd DE7 … 209 B1
Golf La DE56 … 190 E5
Golf Terr SK17 … 66 D1
Golling Gate
Hollinsclough SK17 … 103 F3
Hollinsclough SK17 … 104 A3
Gomersal La S18 … 57 A1
Goodacre Cl DE55 … 159 C4
Goodale St DE23 … 219 A1
Good Hope Ct DE24 … 219 E2
Goodman Cl
Chapel-en-le-Frith SK23 … 47 B7
Eastwood NG16 … 195 C8
Goodman Ct S44 … 97 A3
Goodricke Ct 7 DE3 … 217 F3
Goodrington Rd DE21 … 206 C3
Goods Dr DE5 … 180 F7
Goodsmoor Rd DE23, DE24 … 231 E5
Goodsmoor Rd Ind Est DE24 … 231 E5
Goods Rd DE56 … 178 F2
Goods Road Ind Est DE56 … 178 F2
Goods Yd DE56 … 178 F1
Goodwin Cl
Crich DE4 … 157 A1
Derby DE1 … 267 C1
Sandiacre NG10 … 223 A6
Goodwin Dr NG16 … 195 E6
Goodwin Rd 6 S8 … 43 A6
Goodwin's La DE56 … 178 C1
Goodwood Cl DE13 … 240 C1
Goodwood Cres DE7 … 208 D4
Goodwood Dr
Beeston NG9 … 223 F2
Derby DE24 … 233 C6
Gooker La DE55 … 158 F3
Goole Ave DE7 … 208 D5
GOOSEGREEN … 146 D3
Goose Green La DE55 … 146 D3
Goose Green View DE45 … 91 F5
Goosehill S33 … 38 B2
Goose La DE5 … 181 C8
Goose Nook Cl 1 DE7 … 208 E5
Gordon Ave 2 S8 … 43 A2
Gordon Cres DE55 … 160 B4
Gordondale Rd NG19 … 136 B1
Gordon Rd
Borrowash DE72 … 221 B1
Derby DE23 … 218 F3
Swanwick DE55 … 158 F1
Swanwick DE55 … 169 F8
Tideswell SK17 … 69 C3
Gordon St DE7 … 195 A1
Gordon Works 12 S2 … 43 A6
Gore La S33 … 51 A8
Gorman Cl S41 … 95 E8
Gorse Bank S44 … 116 F2
Gorsebank La DE45 … 91 F7
Gorse Cl
Derby DE23 … 231 B6
Eastwood NG16 … 195 B8
Long Eaton NG10 … 223 B2
Gorse Dr S21 … 60 D5
Gorsehill Gr DE23 … 231 A7
Gorse La
Bradley DE6 … 175 B3
Moira DE12 … 262 E6
Sheffield S10 … 42 F7
Gorse Ridge Dr DE45 … 91 E6
Gorses
Alderwasley DE56 … 167 B2
Alderwasley DE56 … 178 C8
Idridgehay DE6 … 176 D5
Gorse Valley Rd S41 … 115 E7
Gorse Valley Way S41 … 115 E7
Gorse Way SK13 … 17 F7
GORSEYBANK … 166 A7
Gorsey Bank DE4 … 165 F7
Gorsey Brigg S18 … 56 D1
Gorseybrigg Prim Sch S18 … 56 D1
Gorsey Brow SK14 … 9 A1
Gorsey Cl DE56 … 178 E6
Gorsey Intakes SK14 … 16 A8
Gorsey La
Kirk Ireton DE6 … 165 A1
Netherseal DE12 … 265 A7
GORSEY LEYS … 262 C4
Gorsty Leys DE65 … 230 D1
Gosber Rd S21 … 59 E3
Gosber St S21 … 59 D3
Goseley Ave DE11 … 257 A4
Goseley Cres DE11 … 257 A4
Gosforth Ave NE7 … 194 E6
Gosforth Cl S18 … 56 F1
Gosforth Cres 3 S18 … 56 F1
Gosforth Dr S18 … 75 D8
Gosforth Gn S18 … 56 F1
Gosforth La S18 … 56 F1
Gosforth Rd DE24 … 232 E8
GOSFORTH VALLEY … 56 E2
Goshawk Rd DE7 … 209 A3
Goswick Cl 2 DE23 … 231 E1
GOTHAM … 139 D1
Gough Gro NG10 … 236 C6
Gower Cres S40 … 95 C5
Gower St
Derby DE1 … 219 A4
Derby DE1 … 267 B2
GOWHOLE … 33 E4
Goyt Forest Walks* SK11 … 83 E7
Goytlands SK17 … 84 F6
Goyt Pl SK23 … 45 E7
Goyt Rd
Disley SK12 … 32 D5
Horwich End SK23 … 45 E6
New Mills SK22 … 33 D6
Goytside SK23 … 33 C5
Goyt Side Rd S40 … 95 E2
Goyt's La SK17 … 65 A3
Goyts Moss Rd SK11 … 83 C4
Goyt Valley Ind Est SK23 … 33 D4
Goyt Valley Walks* SK17 … 64 E4
Goyt View SK22 … 33 B6
Grace Cres DE75 … 181 F2
Grace Gdns DE5 … 180 D6
Gradbach Mill La SK11 … 102 B1
Grafham Cl DE73 … 233 A2
Grafton Rd DE15 … 248 B1
Grafton St DE23 … 218 E2
Grafton Terr DE4 … 127 A5
Graham Cl DE14 … 254 C7
Graham Dr SK12 … 32 C6
Graham St DE7 … 208 F7
Grammer St DE5 … 181 A4
Grampian Cres S40 … 95 B4
Grampian Prim Sch DE24 … 231 D4
Grampian Way
Derby DE24 … 231 E4
Long Eaton NG10 … 236 A8
Granary Cl S40 … 95 A8
Granby Ave SK23 … 34 E1
Granby Cl S45 … 132 C2
Granby Croft DE45 … 109 D5
Granby Jun Sch DE7 … 194 E3
Granby Rd
Bakewell DE45 … 109 D5
Bradwell S33 … 50 F7
Buxton SK17 … 85 D7
Granby St DE7 … 194 E2
Grandfield St DE75 … 181 C4
Grandison Cl DE3 … 217 D6
Grandstand Rd DE21 … 219 C6
Grange Ave
Breaston DE72 … 235 D8
Chapel-en-le-Frith SK23 … 47 B5
Derby DE23 … 231 E7
Dronfield S18 … 56 E1
Hulland Ward DE6 … 175 F3
Grange Cl
Melbourne DE73 … 252 B8
Somercotes DE55 … 159 F2

Grange Cl *continued*
Ticknall DE73 251 A4
Grange Ct
Egginton DE65 241 B5
South Normanton
DE55 159 F2
Grange Dale DE4 153 C8
Grange Dr
Castle Donington
DE74 247 A3
Long Eaton NG10 236 F8
Grange Farm Cl
DE74 247 D5
Grange Gate DE22 267 A1
Grange Gdns DE75 181 C3
Grange La
Barlow S18 75 B1
Darley Dale DE4 127 F1
Ible DE4 153 D7
GRANGEMILL 153 D8
Grangemill Pl S43 97 C8
Grangeover Way
DE22 218 D4
Grange Park Ave
Calow S43 96 F4
Chapel-en-le-Frith
SK23 47 B5
Grange Park Rd
SK23 47 B5
Grange Pk NG10 236 F8
Grange Prim Sch
NG10 236 F8
Grange Rd
Buxton SK17 85 C7
Derby DE24 233 B6
Derby DE3 217 E6
Long Eaton NG10 236 F8
Long Eaton NG10 237 A8
Pilsley S45 132 C2
Swadlincote DE11 255 E5
Uttoxeter ST14 210 A1
Grange Road S SK14 15 A8
Grange St
1 Alfreton DE55 158 F3
Alfreton DE55 159 A3
Derby DE23 219 B2
Grange The
Brimington S43 96 D8
Chesterfield S42 94 F4
Chesterfield S42 95 A4
Smalley DE75 193 C8
South Normanton
DE55 160 A4
Grange View NG16 182 F3
Grange Wlk S42 115 E2
Grangewood
Coton in the Elms
DE12 260 F2
Grangewood DE12 261 C1
Grangewood Ave 3
DE7 208 F7
Grangewood Ct S40 114 F7
Grangewood Dr
DE56 191 A7
Grangewood Gdns
DE12 261 D6
Grangewood Rd
S40 114 F7
Gransden Way S40 114 C8
Grant Ave DE21 220 B5
Grantham Ave
DE21 205 E1
Grantham Cl NG16 195 C7
Granville Acad
DE11 256 E4
Granville Ave NG10 223 D1
Granville Cl
Chesterfield S41 115 D8
Duffield DE56 190 E3
Hatton DE65 227 D1
Granville Ct DE11 256 C4
Granville Sports Coll
DE11 256 E4
Granville St
Derby DE1 218 E5
Woodville DE11 256 E3
Graphite Way
Glossop SK13 9 F6
Hollingworth SK13 9 F6
Grasmere Ave
Clay Cross S45 131 B3
Derby DE21 220 E6
Grasmere Cl
Burton upon Trent
DE15 248 B1
Chesterfield S41 95 D7
Grasmere Cres
DE24 231 E4
Grasmere Ct 1
NG10 223 B2
Grasmere Rd
Dronfield S18 56 D1
Long Eaton NG10 223 B2
Grasmere St 2
NG10 223 C5
Grasscroft Cl 3 S40 95 D6
Grasscroft Mobile Home
Pk S43 77 D5
Grassdale View S12 44 F3
GRASSHILL 115 E4
GRASSMOOR 115 F3
Grassmoor Cl S12 43 F5
Grassmoor Cres SK13 9 D2
Grassmoor Ctry Pk* S42,
S41 116 A4
Grassmoor Prim Sch
S42 115 F2
Grass St DE7 194 E3
Grassthorpe Cl
DE21 206 B1
Grassthorpe Rd S12 44 B4
Grassy Ct DE3 230 A7
Grassy La DE65 230 A7
Gratton Ct S43 78 F3
Gratton La
Ashbourne DE6 149 E5
Dale End DE45 140 C7
Elton DE45 140 C7
Gravelly Bank Mews
DE6 199 D5
Gravel Pit Cotts
DE65 229 B1
Gravel Pit Hill DE65 249 E7
Gravel Pit La DE21 220 E4
Graves Park Animal
Farm* S8 43 B1
Graves Tennis & L Ctr
S8 57 B7
Graves Trust Homes
Sheffield, Common Side
S12 44 A5
Sheffield, Greenhill S8 56 F8
Sheffield, Little Norton
S8 57 A8
Grayburn Ave DE21 220 E3
Graycar Bsns Pk
DE13 253 B2
Gray Fallow DE55 160 B4
Grayling St DE23 219 B2
Grays Cl
Castle Donington
DE74 247 B3
Crich DE4 157 A1
Grayshott Wlk S40 114 F8
Gray St
Clowne S43 80 F4
Sheffield, Mosborough
S20 59 C7
Grayston Ct SK6 23 B7
Grayswood Cl DE55 170 A7
Great British Car
Journey* DE56 167 E5
Great Common Cl
S43 80 B6
Great Croft S18 56 D2
GREAT CUBLEY 198 F1
GREAT HUCKLOW 70 B8
Great Hucklow CE Prim
Sch SK17 51 B1
GREAT LONGSTONE 90 B4
Great Northern Cl
DE7 194 E2
Great Northern Cotts
NG19 135 A5
Great Northern Point
DE22 218 F4
Great Northern Rd
Derby DE1 218 F5
Eastwood NG16 182 D2
Greatorex Ave DE24 232 E5
GREAT WILNE 235 C2
Greaves Close S44 98 B3
Greaves La DE45 108 F8
Greaves St
Ripley DE5 169 E2
Shirland DE55 146 E1
Greave Way S43 96 C8
Greenacre Ave
DE75 182 A3
Greenacre Cl S12 43 F5
Greenacre Pk DE12 260 C3
Greenacres DE23 231 B8
Greenacres Cl S18 76 C7
Greenacres Dr
South Normanton
DE55 160 B6
Uttoxeter ST14 210 A2
Greenacre The DE6 184 F7
Greenacre Way S12 43 F5
Green Ave DE73 233 A1
Greenaway Dr S44 118 A8
Greenaway La DE4 127 E1
Greenbank
Derby DE21 220 D4
Hollingworth SK13 9 F5
Green Bank SK13 16 F7
Greenbank Dr S40 95 C4
Green Bank L Ctr
DE11 256 B4
Greenbank Rd SK6 15 B1
Greenburn Cl DE23 231 C6
Green Chase S21 59 C3
Green Cl
Curbar S32 72 E2
Matlock DE4 143 B6
Newton DE55 148 A3
Renishaw S21 60 B1
Renishaw S21 79 B8
Staveley S43 97 C6
Unstone Green S18 76 E6
Willington DE65 242 A6
Green Cowden
DE45 108 F4
Green Cres NG16 171 E6
Green Cross S18 57 B2
Greendale Ave S42 113 E8
Greendale Ct S18 57 B2
Greendale Sh Ctr
S18 57 B2
Greendale The
DE55 157 D8
GREEN FAIRFIELD 67 C2
Green Farm Cl S40 95 C6
Green Farm Rd
NG16 171 D6
Greenfield Ave S80 82 C6
Greenfield Cl
New Mills SK22 33 A8
Sheffield S8 56 F7
Greenfield Dr
Linton DE12 261 C6
Sheffield S8 56 F7
Greenfield Ho SK13 10 A6
Greenfield La S45 145 A7
Greenfield Rd S8 56 F7
Greenfields
Aldercar NG16 182 A4
Denstone ST14 196 D6
Eckington S21 59 C3
Fritchley DE56 168 B7
Greenfields Ave
DE23 231 B8
Greenfield St SK13 10 A6
Greenfinch Cl DE21 220 F6
Greengate Cl S40 95 C2
Green Glen S40 95 C2
Greenhalgh Crescent 2
DE7 194 E2
Greenhall Rd S21 59 C3
Greenhead S33 40 B4
Greenhead Cres
SK17 138 C2
Greenhead Pk S33 40 B4
GREENHILL 56 F7
Green Hill DE4 154 E1
Greenhill Ave
Ripley DE5 180 E8
Sheffield S8 56 F8
Greenhill La DE55 170 C6
Greenhill Lane Ind Est
DE55 170 B5
Greenhill Main Rd
S8 56 F7
GREENHILLOCKS 180 E7
Greenhill Parkway
S8 56 D6
Greenhill Prim Sch
S8 56 E7
Greenhills DE45 109 B7
Green Hills DE45 109 B7
Greenhills Rd NG16 182 F3
Greenhill Wlk SK12 32 D6
Greenholme Pk
NG19 136 E6
Greenhouse La S10 42 F5
Green Inf Sch The
DE55 160 A6
Green La
Alsop en le Dale
DE6 150 C2
Bakewell DE45 108 C3
Barrow upon Trent
DE73 244 A5
Belper DE56 178 F4
Bonsall DE4 153 F8
Breedon on the Hill
DE73 252 C2
Burnaston DE65 230 A4
Buxton SK17 85 A6
Buxton, Water Swallows
SK17 67 C2
Chelmorton SK17 106 D8
Chesterfield S41 96 D4
Chinley SK23 34 E2
Clifton DE6 184 F7
Compstall SK14 15 B8
Creswell S80 82 C5
Cutthorpe S42 94 E7
Darley Dale DE4 127 B3
Derby DE1 219 A5
Derby DE1 267 B2
Derby DE1 267 B3
Derby, Alvaston DE24 233 C8
Dethick S45 144 C1
Disley SK12 32 D4
Dronfield S18 57 B2
Earl Sterndale SK17 105 C1
Flagg SK17 106 D7
Glossop SK13 16 F8
Glossop, Brookfield
SK13 9 F4
Hognaston DE6 164 B2
Hollingworth SK14 9 D6
Ilkeston DE7 209 A7
Killamarsh S21 60 C3
Mansfield NG19 135 A2
Marchington ST14 225 A2
Ockbrook DE72 221 C5
Overseal DE12 261 F4
Overseal DE12 262 A5
Pilsley S45 132 C3
Pleasley S44 134 D8
Roston DE6 197 F8
Shirebrook NG19,
NG20 119 C2
Tansley DE4 144 A5
Tupton S42 115 D1
Tutbury DE13 239 C5
Washgreen DE4 155 C1
Weston Underwood
DE6 188 F2
Wilson DE73 252 E5
Greenland Ave
DE22 218 B5
Greenland Cl S42 132 A7
Green Lands DE11 256 B7
Green Lea S18 56 C2
Green Leas DE72 246 A8
Greenlow DE6 150 D5
Greenmount Cl
DE23 231 A6
Greenmount St
DE11 255 F1
Green Oak Ave S17 55 E4
Green Oak Cres S17 55 E4
Green Oak Dr S17 55 E4
Green Oak Gr S17 55 E4
Green Oak Rd S17 55 E4
Green Park Ave SK23 47 C6
Green Pastures S17 55 E7
Green Pk DE22 218 A6
Green Rd The DE6 173 C3
Greens Ct DE7 194 D1
Greenshall La SK12 32 F5
Greenshank Rd
NG20 120 D4
GREENSIDE 58 C3
Greenside NG16 171 D6
Greenside Ave S41 96 A7
Greenside Cl
Barlborough S43 80 C4
Donisthorpe DE12 262 E1
Long Eaton NG10 236 E7
Greenside Ct DE3 217 C2
Greenside View
DE7 192 F6
Greens La NG16 195 F6
Greensmith Cl
DE15 248 C3
Greensquare Rd
NG16 160 E2
Green St
Barton in Fabis
NG11 237 F5
Chesterfield S41 77 A2
Green The
Alfreton DE55 159 B3
Alstonefield DE6 149 E4
Aston-on-Trent DE72 246 B8
Bamford S33 40 B4
Belper DE56 179 A5
Birchover DE4 126 B1
Brackenfield DE55 145 D2
Bradwell S33 51 B6
Brailsford DE6 201 E7
Breedon on the Hill
DE73 252 E2
Bretby DE15 249 A3
Burton upon Trent
DE13 240 E1
Castle Donington
DE74 247 A3
Chesterfield S41 115 D7
Clowne S43 80 E4
Crich DE4 156 D1
Curbar S32 72 E2
Derby DE22 204 D1
Derby, Markeaton
DE3 217 D1
Donisthorpe DE12 262 E1
Draycott DE72 235 A7
Elmton S80 100 B7
Findern DE65 230 D1
Fritchley DE56 168 B6
Froggatt S32 72 D5
Glapwell S44 134 B8
Glossop SK13 17 A7
Hardstoft S45 133 A3
Kirk Langley DE6 202 C1
Lees DE6 216 A7
Lees DE6 216 C8
Litton SK17 69 E3
Mansfield Woodhouse
NG19 136 A5
Marple SK6 23 A3
Matlock DE4 154 D5
Middleton DE4 154 D5
North Wingfield S42 132 A7
Sheffield S17 55 D4
Stanton in Peak DE4 126 C5
Sutton in Ashfield
NG17 148 F1
Swanwick DE55 169 E7
Thorpe DE6 161 C1
Ticknall DE73 250 F3
Tissington DE6 162 B5
Wessington DE55 157 E8
Weston-on-Trent
DE72 245 F5
Willington DE65 242 A6
Greenvale Cl DE15 254 F8
Greenview DE4 153 A1
Greenville Croft
DE73 232 E1
Green Water Mdw
SK14 9 D5
Greenway
Ashbourne DE6 173 C3
Brassington DE4 153 A1
Burton upon Trent
DE15 248 A4
Hulland Ward DE6 175 F3
Whitwell S80 81 F6
Wingerworth S42 115 C2
Green Way DE65 230 D2
Greenway Cl
Borrowash DE72 221 B3
Derby DE72 221 B3
Greenway Croft
DE4 154 F1
Greenway Dr DE23 218 A1
Greenways S40 114 C8
Greenways Rd DE14 253 C8
Greenway The
Derby DE72 233 D5
Sandiacre NG10 223 B6
Sheffield S8 56 F8
Greenwheat Cl DE5 180 A1
GREENWICH 169 F2
Greenwich Ave 1
DE11 255 E1
Greenwich Ct 12 S43 78 B3
Greenwich Drive N
DE22 218 C6
Greenwich Drive S
DE22 218 B5
Greenwood Ave
Derby DE21 219 F8
Ilkeston DE7 209 A7
Mansfield Woodhouse
NG19 136 B4
Sutton in Ashfield
NG17 148 F2
Greenwood Gdns 5
DE11 256 B7
Greenwood Rd
DE15 254 E8
Greenwood View 7
S43 81 E2
Greer La S44 118 D1
Gregg Ave DE75 181 F2
Greggs Ave SK23 46 F5
Gregory Ave
Aldercar NG16 182 A4
Breaston DE72 235 C8
Gregory Cl
Brimington S43 96 D8
Stapleford NG9 223 F8
Gregory Croft SK17 88 B2
Gregory Ct 10 S8 43 B6
Gregory La S43 77 D1
Gregory Rd S8 43 A6
Gregory St DE7 208 E8
Gregorys Way DE56 179 C5
Gregory Wlk DE23 230 E7
Gregson Cl DE11 256 B5
Grendon Cl DE56 179 B6
Grenfell Ave DE23 231 E6
Grenville Dr
Ilkeston DE7 194 F3
Stapleford NG9 223 E8
Grenvoir Dr 2 DE5 170 A1
Gresham Rd DE24 232 C8
Gresley Office Pk
DE11 255 D3
Gresley Rd
Ilkeston DE7 194 F1
Sheffield S8 56 E5
Gresley Wlk S8 56 E5
Gresley Woodlands
DE11 256 A2
Gresley Wood Rd
Swadlincote DE11 255 F2
Woodville DE11 256 A2
Gressingham Cl
NG19 136 F2
Gretton Ave DE13 240 E1
Gretton Cl DE16 254 D6
Gretton Mws DE15 248 B5
Gretton Rd SK17 85 D8
Greyfriars Cl 4
DE75 181 F1
Greyfriars Place
DE3 217 F3
Grey Meadow Road
DE7 194 E2
Greysich La
Bretby DE11 250 A1
Bretby DE65 249 F2
Grey St DE22 267 A2
Greystoke Rd DE75 233 C3
Greystones Ct S26 61 D6
Griffe Field Prim Sch
DE23 231 A6
GRIFFE GRANGE 153 D4
Griffin Cl
Derby DE24 232 F7
New Mills SK22 33 D6
Staveley S43 97 E8
Griffon Cl 9 DE73 244 F8
Griffon Rd DE7 208 F4
Griggs Gdns DE4 165 F7
Grimshaw Ave DE24 233 B7
Grinders Well La
S45 130 C7
GRINDLEFORD 72 C7
Grindleford Gdns 16
SK13 9 E2
Grindleford Gr 13
SK13 9 E2
Grindleford Lea 14
SK13 9 E2
Grindleford Prim Sch
S32 72 C8
Grindleford Rd S32 72 C4
Grindleford Sta S32 53 D2
Grindleford Wlk 15
SK13 9 E2
Grindley Way DE11 256 F1
GRINDLOW
70 C8
Great Hucklow SK17 70 C7
Grindlow Ave S40 266 A1
Grindlow Cl S14 43 C6
Grindlow Dr S14 43 C6
Grindlow Rd DE21 220 A8
Grindon Cl S40 95 C5
GRINDSBROOK
BOOTH 37 C8
Grindslow Ave DE7 207 E8
Grin Low
Ashford in the Water
DE45 108 B4
Ashford in the Water
SK17 107 F4
Grinlow Cl SK17 85 C3
Grin Low Rd SK17 85 B3
Grinton Wlk S40 114 F8
Grisedale Road E
DE45 90 A4
Grisedale Road W
DE45 90 A4
Grisedale Wlk S18 56 E1
Gritstone Rd DE4 143 D7
Grizedale Cl DE15 248 B1
Groombridge Cres
DE23 231 A6
Groome Ave DE75 181 C4
Grosvenor Ave
Breaston DE72 235 F8
Long Eaton NG10 236 A4
Grosvenor Cl 3
NG19 136 B3
Grosvenor Dr DE23 231 A6
Grosvenor Rd
Eastwood NG16 182 F2
Marple SK6 23 A7
Ripley DE5 169 D2
Grosvenor St
Derby DE24 219 C1
Derby DE24 232 C8
Grove Ave S17 55 D5
Grovebury Dr DE23 231 C5
Grove Cl DE72 233 F4
Grove Cotts
2 Holmewood DE4 116 E1
Pleasley NG19 135 B4
Grove Ct
Elvaston DE72 233 F4
Ripley DE5 180 F8
Grove Farm Cl S43 96 E7
Grove Gdns S43 96 F5
Grove Ho DE23 267 B1
Grove House Ct S17 55 E5
Grove La
Buxton SK17 85 C6
Darley Dale DE4 127 E1
Old Brampton S42 94 B4
Somersal Herbert
DE6 211 F2
Grove Mews NG16 182 E1
Grove Par 2 SK17 85 B8
Grove Pk DE65 229 B2
Grove Pl DE45 125 B5
Grove Rd
Calow S43 96 E5
Chesterfield S41 96 A7
Sheffield, Totley Brook
S17 55 F5
Groves Nook DE73 232 E1
Grove St
Chesterfield S41 115 C8
Derby DE1 219 A3
Derby DE23 267 B1
Mansfield Woodhouse
NG19 136 B3
New Mills SK22 33 B7
Swadlincote DE11 256 B4
Grove The
Breaston DE72 235 F8
Derby DE3 217 E2
Glossop SK13 9 F4
Poolsbrook S43 98 A8
Sheffield, Hillfoot S17 55 D5
Tatenhill DE13 253 A8
Grove Way
Calow S43 96 F5
Mansfield Woodhouse
NG19 136 B3
Grundy Ave NG16 171 D7
Grundy Nook S80 82 A5
Grundy Rd S45 131 C3
Grunmore Dr DE13 240 E2
Guernsey Rd S2 43 A7
Guide Post DE56 168 C2
Guildford Ave
Chesterfield S40 114 D8
Mansfield Woodhouse
NG19 136 C6
Sheffield S2 43 D8
Swadlincote DE11 256 E6
Guildford Cl S45 131 E3
Guildford La S45 131 E3
Guildford Rise S2 43 E8
Guildford View S2 43 E7
Guildford Wlk S2 43 E8
Guildhall Cl DE11 255 E2
Guildhall Dr NG16 160 F2
Guildhall Theatre*
DE1 267 B3
Guinea Cl NG10 236 A7
Guinevere Ave
DE13 240 E2
Gulliver's Kingdom*
DE4 155 A8
Gunby Hill DE12 261 F2
Gunhills La DE56 189 E6
Gun La DE56 168 C2
Gun Rd SK6 16 C2
Gurney Ave DE23 231 D6
Gutersloh Ct NG9 223 F8
GUTTER THE 179 C4
Guy Cl NG9 223 E6
Gypsy La
Creswell S80 81 E1
Draycott DE72 221 E1

H

Hackney Grange
DE4 142 F7
Hackney La
Barlow S18 75 E2
Barlow S18 75 F1

Hackney Rd DE4 ... 143 A7
Hackthorn Rd 4 S8 ... 43 A3
Hackwood Prim Acad DE22 ... 217 D5
Haddon Ave S43 ... 81 A4
Haddon Cl
Alfreton DE55 ... 158 F3
Bullbridge DE56 ... 168 B6
Chesterfield S40 ... 95 C1
Derby DE22 ... 204 D3
Dronfield S18 ... 57 B2
Heanor DE75 ... 181 C2
West Hallam DE7 ... 207 E8
Haddon Ct DE6 ... 185 D8
Haddon Dr
Bakewell DE45 ... 109 E4
Derby DE22 ... 204 D3
Derby, Markeaton DE3 ... 217 E3
Derby, Spondon DE21 ... 220 F4
Little Eaton DE21 ... 191 C2
Haddon Gn 31 SK13 ... 9 D2
Haddon Hall★ DE45 ... 110 B1
Haddon Ho DE45 ... 109 E3
Haddon Lea 32 SK13 ... 9 D2
Haddon Mews 30 SK13 ... 9 D2
Haddon Nurseries DE7 ... 194 E3
Haddon Pl
Shirebrook NG20 ... 119 E6
Staveley S43 ... 97 D8
Haddon Rd
Bakewell DE45 ... 109 F3
Buxton SK17 ... 85 D8
Haddon Park DE4 ... 110 A1
North Wingfield S42 ... 132 A8
Haddon St
Derby DE23 ... 218 E1
Ilkeston DE7 ... 194 E3
Tibshelf DE55 ... 148 A6
Haddon Way NG10 ... 235 F4
Hade La SK17 ... 106 E7
Hades La SK17 ... 88 B3
HADFIELD ... 10 B5
Hadfield Dr SK23 ... 34 F1
Hadfield Etherow Ind Est SK13 ... 9 E5
Hadfield Ind Est SK13 ... 9 F6
Hadfield Inf Sch SK13 ... 9 F5
Hadfield Pl SK13 ... 17 C8
Hadfield Rd
Glossop SK13 ... 9 F4
Hadfield SK13 ... 10 A5
Hadfields Ave SK14 ... 9 D5
Hadfield Sq 1 SK13 ... 17 C8
Hadfield St SK13 ... 17 C8
Hadfield Sta SK13 ... 10 A5
Hadleigh Cl 2 NG9 ... 223 E2
Hadley La DE6 ... 186 E8
Hadley St DE7 ... 209 A5
Hadstock Cl NG10 ... 223 B4
HADY ... 96 D2
Hady Cres S41 ... 96 C3
Hady Hill S41 ... 96 C2
Hady La S41 ... 96 E1
Hady Prim Sch S41 ... 96 D2
Haeking La S42 ... 131 B8
Hag Bank La SK12 ... 32 D7
Hagg Bank La SK12 ... 32 C8
Hagg La
Dale Abbey DE7 ... 207 D4
Turnditch DE56 ... 177 C1
Hag La DE56 ... 168 B6
Hague Ave S21 ... 79 B8
HAGUE BAR ... 32 F8
Hague Bar Prim Sch SK22 ... 32 E8
Hague Bar Rd SK22 ... 33 A7
Hague Fold SK6 ... 23 F1
Hague Fold Rd SK22 ... 32 F8
Hague La S21, S43 ... 79 B6
Hague Rd SK14 ... 16 A8
Hague St
Charlesworth SK13 ... 16 D6
Glossop SK13 ... 17 D7
Haig Hill Farm Hamlet S42 ... 115 E1
Haigh Memorial Homes S8 ... 57 A7
Haigh Moor Cl S13 ... 44 F8
Haigh Moor Rd S13 ... 44 F8
Haig St DE24 ... 232 F8
Hailsham Cl DE3 ... 217 D3
Haines Cl DE24 ... 231 F4
Halcyon App S42 ... 115 C2
Halcyon Cl S12 ... 44 F3
Haldane Cres S44 ... 98 F2
HALES GREEN ... 199 B7
Hales Green DE6 ... 199 C7
Halesworth Cl S40 ... 114 B8
Half Acre Gardens DE7 ... 194 F2
Half Acre La
Dronfield S18 ... 57 D1
Dronfield S18 ... 76 D8
Half Croft S43 ... 96 F7
Halfmoon La DE6 ... 165 B3
HALFWAY ... 59 F7
Halfway Cl S20 ... 59 F7
Halfway Ctr S20 ... 59 E7
Halfway Dr S20 ... 59 E7
Halfway Gdns S20 ... 59 E7
Halfway Jun Sch S20 ... 59 E6
Halfway Nursery Inf Sch S20 ... 59 F7
Halifax Cl
Derby DE21 ... 205 C1
Hilton DE65 ... 228 E2
Haling Way DE21 ... 220 F2
Hallam Ct
Dronfield S18 ... 76 A8
Ilkeston DE7 ... 194 F3
HALLAM FIELDS ... 209 A4
Hallam Fields DE74 ... 247 B2
Hallam Fields Jun Sch DE7 ... 208 F5
Hallam Fields Rd DE7 ... 209 B4
Hallam Grove NG16 ... 182 A5
HALLAM MOORS ... 41 E8
Hallamway NG19 ... 136 C1
Hallam Way
Langley Mill NG16 ... 182 C3
West Hallam DE7 ... 207 D8
Hall Bank
Buxton SK17 ... 85 B7
Hartington SK17 ... 137 E5
Hall Cl
Cutthorpe S42 ... 94 E8
Dronfield S18 ... 56 C2
Mottram in Longdendale SK14 ... 9 A5
Hallcliff La S42 ... 93 F1
Hall Cotts DE6 ... 175 D2
Hallcroft DE4 ... 154 C5
Hallcroft Ave DE12 ... 262 B3
Hallcroft Rd 2 DE7 ... 208 F8
Hall Ct DE7 ... 207 E7
Halldale La DE4 ... 127 E3
Hall Dale View DE4 ... 127 D3
Hall Dr
Doveridge DE6 ... 211 A1
Hanbury DE13 ... 238 A4
Mottram in Longdendale SK14 ... 9 A5
Sandiacre NG10 ... 223 B6
Sutton Scarsdale S44 ... 116 F6
Sutton Scarsdale S44 ... 117 A6
Hall Dyke DE21 ... 220 D5
Hall End La DE45 ... 108 F8
Hall Farm
Holmewood S42 ... 132 D8
Mansfield Woodhouse NG19 ... 136 C6
Hall Farm Cl
Castle Donington DE74 ... 247 B3
Chesterfield S41 ... 115 D7
Swadlincote DE11 ... 256 C4
Whaley Bridge SK23 ... 33 D1
Whaley Bridge SK23 ... 45 D8
Hall Farm Ct
Kirk Langley DE6 ... 202 F4
Stanton-by-Dale DE7 ... 222 F8
Hall Farm Gdns S42 ... 132 D8
Hall Farm Rd
Castle Donington DE74 ... 247 D2
Duffield DE56 ... 190 E2
Swadlincote DE11 ... 256 C4
Hall Farm Way DE7 ... 192 F6
Hallfield Cl S42 ... 115 A4
Hallfieldgate La DE55 ... 146 D1
Hallfield Rd DE55 ... 148 A3
Hallfields Rd DE15 ... 255 C4
Hallfields Rise DE55 ... 146 C1
Hallflash La S44 ... 116 A8
Hall Gardens DE56 ... 190 E3
Hallgate Cl DE21 ... 206 C3
Hallgate La S45 ... 132 B2
Hall Gate View S33 ... 51 A8
Hall Gdns
Hemington DE74 ... 247 D4
Marchington ST14 ... 224 E2
HALL GREEN ... 171 E8
Hall Green Ave DE13 ... 240 F2
Hall Grounds DE13 ... 240 A4
HALLHILL ... 46 F7
Hallicar La DE4 ... 154 D5
Hallington Dr DE75 ... 181 D1
Hall La
Ashbourne DE6 ... 173 C2
Brailsford DE6 ... 202 A6
Brinsley NG16 ... 182 D6
Burton upon Trent DE16 ... 254 D6
Donisthorpe DE12 ... 265 E8
Doveridge DE6 ... 211 B1
Doveridge DE6 ... 224 B8
Litton SK17 ... 69 E3
Mayfield DE6 ... 183 A7
Mayfield DE6 ... 184 B6
Nether Heage DE56 ... 168 C3
Newton DE55 ... 148 A3
Shirley DE6 ... 200 D8
Staveley S43 ... 78 D3
Thorpe DE6 ... 161 D1
Willington DE65 ... 242 B5
Hall Leys La DE73 ... 245 D1
Hall Meadow Croft S20 ... 59 F5
Hall Meadow Dr S20 ... 59 F5
Hall Meadow Gr S20 ... 59 F5
Hall Meadow Rd SK13 ... 10 D2
Hallmoor Rd DE4 ... 127 C4
HALLOWES ... 76 C8
Hallowes Ct
Dronfield S18 ... 57 B1
Dronfield S18 ... 76 B8
Hallowes Dr S18 ... 76 B8
Hallowes La S18 ... 76 B8
Hallowes Rise S18 ... 76 C8
Hallow La DE6 ... 184 B6
Hall Park Acad NG16 ... 182 E3
Hall Park Cl DE23 ... 218 B1
Hall Pk DE73 ... 244 A5
Hall Pk Dr NG16 ... 182 E3
Hall Rd
Aldercar NG16 ... 182 C4
Brimington S43 ... 96 E7
Marchington ST14 ... 224 E2
Marehay DE5 ... 180 D5
Rolleston DE13 ... 239 F4
Hall Rise
2 Ashbourne DE6 ... 173 D3
Darley Dale DE4 ... 127 D3
Hall's Ct SK13 ... 10 C1
Hallside Ct S20 ... 59 D6
Halls La NG16 ... 195 A8
Halls Rd NG9 ... 223 D6
Hall's Row 1 S40 ... 95 D2
Hall St
Alfreton DE55 ... 159 A4
Derby DE24 ... 233 A7
New Mills SK22 ... 33 B8
Swadlincote DE11 ... 256 A2
Hallsteads SK17 ... 47 F1
Hallsteads Cl SK17 ... 47 F1
Hallsteads The DE6 ... 163 B2
Hallsworth Bridge SK14 ... 9 E4
Hall Terr S45 ... 131 D3
Hall The
Glossop SK13 ... 17 A7
Middleton DE4 ... 154 D5
Hall View S41 ... 95 E6
Hall Wlk S42 ... 115 D1
Hall Wood Cl DE11 ... 256 A2
Hallworth Wlk S21 ... 58 E2
Hallyburton Cl S2 ... 43 C6
Hallyburton Dr S2 ... 43 C6
Hallyburton Rd S2 ... 43 C6
Halstead Cl NG19 ... 136 F2
Halstock Dr DE24 ... 233 C8
Halton Cl S41 ... 76 E1
Hamble Cl NG19 ... 136 D3
Hambledon Cl S40 ... 95 C5
Hambledon Dr DE24 ... 231 D2
Hambleton Ave S42 ... 131 F6
Hambleton Cl
Ashbourne DE6 ... 185 C8
2 Long Eaton NG10 ... 223 A1
Hambleton Rise NG19 ... 136 F1
Hamble Way DE65 ... 228 C1
Hamblin Cres DE24 ... 231 F4
Hamill Ct S42 ... 131 F7
Hamilton Cl
Beeston NG9 ... 223 F2
Derby DE3 ... 217 F3
Hamilton Dr
Market Warsop NG20 ... 120 F4
Swadlincote DE11 ... 256 C5
Hamilton Fields DE15 ... 248 A2
Hamilton Gr DE11 ... 256 D5
Hamilton Rd
Burton upon Trent DE15 ... 248 A2
Derby DE23 ... 218 F2
Derby, Spondon DE21 ... 220 F6
Long Eaton NG10 ... 223 D1
Hamilton Terr DE65 ... 242 B6
Hamlet Ct DE73 ... 232 E1
Hamlet La DE55 ... 160 A5
Hamlet The
Heanor DE75 ... 181 E3
South Normanton DE55 ... 160 A5
Hammer Leys DE55 ... 160 C4
HAMMERSMITH ... 169 D4
Hammersmith DE5 ... 169 D4
Hammersmith Meadows Nature Reserve★ DE5 ... 169 D3
Hammersmith Sta★ DE5 ... 169 D4
Hammonds Ct 6 DE4 ... 165 F8
Hampden Ho DE15 ... 254 E6
Hampden St
Derby DE23 ... 232 A8
Eastwood NG16 ... 195 B8
Langley Mill NG16 ... 182 B3
Hampshire Cl SK13 ... 17 F8
Hampshire Ct NG16 ... 171 B4
Hampshire Dr NG10 ... 223 B5
Hampshire Rd DE21 ... 219 C8
Hampstead Dr DE22 ... 218 A6
Hampton Cl
Beeston NG9 ... 223 E3
Derby DE21 ... 220 F5
West Hallam DE7 ... 207 D8
Hampton Ct 4 DE75 ... 181 D2
Hampton La DE23 ... 230 F5
Hampton St S41 ... 115 D7
HANBURY ... 238 A5
Hanbury Ave DE65 ... 227 D1
Hanbury Cl
Chesterfield S40 ... 95 A5
Dronfield S18 ... 56 F1
Hanbury Fields La DE13 ... 238 A4
Hanbury Hill DE13 ... 238 A5
Hanbury Rd DE21 ... 219 F6
Hanchurch Cl DE15 ... 248 A4
Handby Ct S41 ... 115 D7
Handby St S41 ... 115 D8
Handel Mews DE6 ... 185 D8
Handel St DE24 ... 232 C8
Handford Ct DE22 ... 218 D6
Handford St DE22 ... 218 D5
HANDLEY
145 F8
S45 ... 130 F1
Handley Ct S43 ... 77 D4
Handley La
Ashover S45 ... 145 F8
Clay Cross S45 ... 131 A1
Monyash SK17 ... 107 B2
Pilsley DE45 ... 91 B1
Handley Pl 4 DE74 ... 246 E3
Handley Rd
Chesterfield S43 ... 77 D5
Chesterfield S43 ... 77 D6
Handley Wood DE56 ... 178 B7
Handsacre Cl DE11 ... 255 F3
Hand's Rd DE75 ... 182 A1
Handyside St
Derby DE1 ... 219 A6
Derby DE1 ... 267 B4
Hangar Hill S80 ... 82 A6
Hanger Bank DE72 ... 246 B8
HANGINGBRIDGE ... 184 F8
Hangthwaite Cl S13 ... 44 B7
Hanley Cl SK12 ... 32 D5
Hannage Way DE4 ... 165 F7
Hannah Bowman Way DE45 ... 125 C6
Hanover Sq DE22 ... 218 A6
Hansard Gate DE21 ... 267 D3
Hanslynn DE72 ... 233 F4
Hanson Cl NG16 ... 195 F7
Hanston Ct S43 ... 77 D4
HANSTUBBIN ... 171 F5
Hanstubbin Rd NG16 ... 171 F6
Hanwell Cl DE72 ... 233 E3
Hanwell Way DE22 ... 218 B6
Harbin Rd DE12 ... 253 D1
Harboro Cl DE6 ... 185 B8
Harby Ave NG19 ... 136 D5
Harcourt Cl
Chesterfield S41 ... 115 C7
Ilkeston DE7 ... 194 D1
Harcourt Pl DE74 ... 247 B4
Harcourt Rd DE14 ... 253 F8
Harcourt St DE1 ... 267 B2
Hardacre Cl DE73 ... 252 A8
Hardcastle Mews SK23 ... 47 B6
HARDHURST ... 76 E6
Hardhurst Rd
Derby DE24 ... 233 B5
Unstone Green S18 ... 76 E6
Hardie Ave DE55 ... 160 A6
Hardie Pl S43 ... 97 D8
Hardie St S21 ... 59 D3
Harding's Cl DE6 ... 165 B1
Harding's La SK17 ... 138 A5
Hard La S26 ... 61 E8
HARDLEY HILL ... 215 C2
Hard Meadow La S45 ... 130 B2
Hardstaff Homes The
Eastwood NG16 ... 195 C8
Mansfield Woodhouse NG19 ... 136 B3
HARDSTOFT ... 133 A3
Hardstoft Rd S45 ... 132 E2
Hardwick Ave
Chesterfield S43 ... 77 D3
Derby DE22 ... 204 D3
Glapwell S44 ... 134 B8
Shirebrook NG20 ... 119 E4
West Hallam DE7 ... 207 E8
Hardwick Cl
Blackwell DE55 ... 147 D1
Clowne S43 ... 81 A4
Dronfield S18 ... 57 C2
Holmewood S42 ... 132 E8
Ripley DE5 ... 169 C3
Hardwick Ct
Heath S44 ... 117 B2
Holmewood S42 ... 132 E8
Long Eaton NG10 ... 235 F4
South Normanton DE55 ... 160 C6
5 Staveley S43 ... 78 E2
Hardwick Dr
Arkwright Town S44 ... 97 D2
Arkwright Town S44 ... 97 D3
Derby DE3 ... 217 E2
Hardwick Gdns 5 SK17 ... 85 B7
Hardwick Hall Dr S44 ... 131 D4
Hardwick Hall & Park★ S44 ... 133 E4
Hardwick La S45 ... 129 D6
Hardwick Mount SK17 ... 85 C7
Hardwick Old Hall★ S44 ... 133 E4
Hardwick Park Farm★ NG17 ... 134 A3
Hardwick Pl DE7 ... 208 C5
Hardwick Prim Sch 1 DE23 ... 219 A1
Hardwick Rd SK17 ... 85 D4
Hardwick Square E SK17 ... 85 C7
Hardwick Square N SK17 ... 85 C7
Hardwick Square S SK17 ... 85 B7
Hardwick Square W SK17 ... 85 B7
Hardwick St
Buxton SK17 ... 85 B8
Chesterfield S41 ... 266 B4
Derby DE24 ... 232 C8
Langwith NG20 ... 119 F8
Shirebrook NG20 ... 120 A4
Tibshelf DE55 ... 148 A7
Hardwick's Yd S40 ... 95 E2
Hardwick View Cl NG19 ... 134 F7
Hardwick View Rd S42 ... 132 F8
Hardy Barn DE75 ... 194 A7
Hardybarn La SK17 ... 67 B2
Hardy Cl
Kimberley NG16 ... 195 F7
Long Eaton NG10 ... 236 D6
Hardy Cres DE5 ... 181 B8
Hardy La SK17 ... 69 C4
Hardy St
Alfreton DE55 ... 158 F5
Kimberley NG16 ... 195 F7
Harebell Cl
Derby DE21 ... 206 A3
Swadlincote DE11 ... 256 E4
Harebell Dr NG20 ... 119 D2
Harebell La 6 DE24 ... 231 C3
Hareedge Dr DE21 ... 205 F3
Hare Edge Dr DE21 ... 206 A3
Harehedge La DE13 ... 240 B1
HAREHILL ... 213 A3
Hare Hill Cl 3 DE7 ... 208 E5
Harehill Cres S42 ... 114 D4
Harehill Ct S40 ... 114 F7
Harehill Rd S40 ... 114 F7
Harepit Cl DE24 ... 233 A5
Hare Pk DE16 ... 254 D5
Harewood SK14 ... 16 A8
Harewood Ave DE55 ... 169 F8
Harewood Cl
Belper DE56 ... 179 D5
2 Sandiacre NG10 ... 223 B4
Harewood Cres S42 ... 131 B6
Harewood Lo SK14 ... 16 A8
Harewood Rd
Beeley DE4 ... 112 B4
Derby DE22 ... 204 D3
Holymoorside S42 ... 112 F5
Holymoorside S42 ... 113 C5
Hargate Hill La SK13 ... 16 E7
Hargate La DE15 ... 248 B5
Hargate Rd
Burton upon Trent DE15 ... 248 C1
Buxton SK17 ... 84 F6
HARGATEWALL ... 68 B3
Hargrave Ave DE72 ... 221 C5
Hargreaves Cl DE23 ... 231 A6
Hargreaves Ct 5 DE7 ... 208 F7
Hargunn Ct DE74 ... 246 F2
Harlaxton Dr NG10 ... 237 A8
Harlech Cl
Derby DE21 ... 221 A5
Ilkeston DE7 ... 194 C3
Harlequin Ct NG16 ... 182 D3
Harlesden Ave DE22 ... 218 A7
HARLESTHORPE ... 80 E5
Harlesthorpe Ave S43 ... 80 F5
Harlesthorpe La S43 ... 80 E5
Harley's Ct DE12 ... 262 C4
Harlow Cl
Derby DE24 ... 232 F4
Mansfield Woodhouse NG19 ... 136 C6
Harlow Ct DE7 ... 207 D7
Harlow Way DE6 ... 185 D7
Harold Ave NG16 ... 182 B4
Harold Ct DE23 ... 219 B2
Harper Dr
Derby DE3 ... 217 C1
Derby DE3 ... 230 B8
Harper Hill S45 ... 113 F4
Harperhill Cl S40 ... 114 F7
Harper Way S44 ... 98 B3
Harpole Cl DE55 ... 169 F8
Harport Dr S45 ... 131 E2
Harpswell Cl DE22 ... 204 E2
Harpur Ave
Derby DE23 ... 231 B8
Ticknall DE73 ... 251 A4
Harpur Crewe Cotts DE6 ... 149 D3
HARPUR HILL ... 85 C3
Harpur Hill Bsns Pk SK17 ... 85 B2
Harpur Hill Prim Sch SK17 ... 85 C4
Harpur Hill Rd SK17 ... 85 C4
Harrier Rd DE56 ... 179 C5
Harrier Way DE24 ... 231 E3
Harriet St DE23 ... 219 A3
Harriett St NG9 ... 223 D7
Harriet Tubman Ho DE23 ... 218 F1
Harrimans Dr DE72 ... 235 F8
Harringay Gdns DE22 ... 218 C6
Harrington Ave DE72 ... 221 C2
Harrington Jun Sch NG10 ... 223 B1
Harrington Rd
Derby DE23 ... 218 C1
10 Sheffield S2 ... 43 A8
Harrington St
Derby, Allenton DE24 ... 232 E6
Derby, Normanton DE23 ... 232 A8
Draycott DE72 ... 235 B7
Long Eaton NG10 ... 236 B5
Harris Ave DE5 ... 169 C2
Harris Cl DE5 ... 169 C1
Harrison Cl DE14 ... 254 B8
Harrison Dr DE4 ... 154 F1
Harrison La
Sheffield S10 ... 42 F7
Tibshelf DE55 ... 147 F6
Harrison Rd NG9 ... 223 D8
Harrison St DE22 ... 218 E3
Harrison Way DE4 ... 127 A6
Harris Rd SK17 ... 85 C3
Harris Way S45 ... 131 C4
Harrogate Cres DE21 ... 205 D1
Harrop La S10 ... 42 F6
Harrots La SK17 ... 137 D6
Harrow Dr
Burton upon Trent DE14 ... 254 C8
Ilkeston DE7 ... 209 A4
Harrow Rd DE11 ... 256 B7
Harrow St DE24 ... 219 E1
Harryfields SK14 ... 9 A1
Hart Ave NG10 ... 223 A6
Hartcliffe Cl DE21 ... 205 F3
Hartfield Cl S41 ... 115 B7
Hartford Cl S8 ... 43 A3
Hartford Rd S8 ... 43 A3
HARTHILL ... 61 F6
Harthill Field Rd S26 ... 62 A3
Harthill La S43 ... 61 E1
Harthill Prim Sch S26 ... 61 E5
Harthill Rd
Derby DE24 ... 231 C3
Sheffield S13 ... 44 B7
Thorpe Salvin S80 ... 62 D7
HARTINGTON ... 137 D5
Hartington Ave SK17 ... 85 E7
Hartington CE Prim Sch SK17 ... 137 D5
Hartington Cl DE7 ... 207 E8
Hartington Ct
Clowne S43 ... 81 A4
Dronfield S18 ... 57 B2
Hartington Dr
Chinley SK23 ... 34 E1
Creswell S80 ... 81 C1
Hartington Gdns 11 SK17 ... 85 B7
Hartington Ind Est S43 ... 78 E4
Hartington Pl DE7 ... 194 E5
Hartington Rd
Buxton SK17 ... 85 B7
Chesterfield S41 ... 96 C2
Dronfield S18 ... 57 B2
Hartington St
Derby DE1, DE23 ... 267 B1
Langwith NG20 ... 119 F8
Hartington View S43 ... 78 F4
Hartington Way DE3 ... 217 D2
Hartland Ct 21 S41 ... 95 F8
Hartland Dr DE23 ... 231 E6
Hartland Way S41 ... 77 A1
Hart Lea 1 NG10 ... 223 B5
Hartley St S2 ... 43 A7
Hartopp Ave S2 ... 43 C6
Hartopp Cl S2 ... 43 C6
Hartopp Dr S2 ... 43 D6
Hartopp Rd S2 ... 43 D6
Hartshay Cl DE7 ... 194 F5
Hartshay Hill DE5 ... 169 C2
Hartshill Rd DE11 ... 257 A4
HARTSHORNE ... 257 A6
Hartshorne CE Prim Sch DE11 ... 257 B6
Hartshorne Rd
Derby DE23 ... 231 C5
Repton DE65 ... 249 E7
Woodville DE11 ... 256 F3
Hartside Cl 16 S40 ... 95 D5
Hartside Gdns 1 NG10 ... 236 A8
Hartside Way DE75 ... 182 B1
Hartwood Dr NG9 ... 209 D1
Harvester Cl DE5 ... 169 C2
Harvester Way S43 ... 80 D2
Harvest Hill DE11 ... 256 B7
Harvest Way
Chesterfield S40 ... 94 F5
2 Chesterfield S42 ... 95 A5
Derby DE21 ... 206 C3
Harvey Clough Mews S8 ... 43 B3

Harvey Clough Rd S8 43 B3
Harvey Croft NG9 209 C4
Harvey Ct S44 98 F2
Harvey Pl ST14 210 B1
Harvey Rd
Burton upon Trent DE14 254 A8
Castle Donington DE74 247 B2
Chesterfield S41 96 E2
Derby DE24 232 E6
Harwich Rd S2 43 F8
Harwood Ave DE14 253 F8
Harwood Cl
8 Heanor DE75 181 D1
Sheffield S2 43 A8
Harwood St 2 S2 43 A8
Hasgill Cl DE21 206 C3
Haskeys Cl DE22 204 C2
Haslam Cres S8 56 E6
Haslam Ct
Bolsover S44 98 F2
Chesterfield S41 266 B4
Haslam Pl DE56 179 C1
Haslam's La DE21, DE22 205 B1
HASLAND 115 D7
HASLAND GREEN 115 C7
Hasland Hall Com Sch S41 115 D7
Hasland Inf Sch S41 115 C8
Hasland Jun Sch S41 115 D7
Hasland La S44 97 C1
Hasland Rd S41 115 C8
Haslemere Ct DE23 219 B2
Haslemere Rd NG10 236 B8
Haslin Rd SK17 85 D2
Hassall Rd DE65 227 D1
Hassock Lane N DE75 194 B7
Hassock Lane S DE7, DE75 194 C6
Hassocky La S44, S42 116 B6
HASSOP 90 F5
Hassop Cl
Buxton SK17 85 D6
Chesterfield S41 95 C6
Dronfield S18 57 C2
Hassop Rd
Calver S32 72 B1
Derby DE21 220 A8
Hassop DE45 90 D1
Hassop DE45 90 E4
Staveley S43 78 F3
Hastilar Cl S2 44 B8
Hastilar Rd S2 44 B8
Hastilar Road S S13 44 C7
Hastings Cl
Breedon on the Hill DE73 252 E2
Chesterfield S41 95 D6
Derby DE23 230 F5
Hastings La DE65 229 C3
Hastings Rd
Buxton SK17 85 C4
Swadlincote DE11 256 B3
Hastings St
1 Derby DE23 218 F8
Derby DE23 219 A1
Hasting St DE74 247 B2
Haston Dr DE55 170 D8
Hatchmere Cl DE21 206 A1
Hatfield Ave NG10 223 B4
Hatfield La 3 DE65 227 D2
Hatfield Rd DE24 232 F5
Hathaway Cl S42 131 B6
Hathern Cl
Calow S43 96 F4
Derby DE23 231 E5
Long Eaton NG10 236 D5
HATHERSAGE 53 B7
Hathersage Ave
Derby DE23 231 E8
Long Eaton NG10 235 F5
Hathersage Cres SK13 9 E2
Hathersage Dr
Glossop SK13 17 F8
Somercotes DE55 170 B7
Hathersage Pk S32 53 A7
Hathersage Rd
Bamford S32, S33 40 B1
Grindleford S32 72 C8
Sheffield S11, S17 54 D6
Hathersage St Michael's CE (Aided) Prim Sch S32 53 A8
Hathersage Sta S32 53 A7
HATTON 239 D8
Hatton Cl S18 75 D8
Hatton Crofts NG10 236 C6
Hatton Ct DE73 252 A7
Hatton Dr S40 95 B5
Hatton Mws DE21 220 E3
Haulton Dr DE74 247 A4
HAUNTON 263 B2
Haunton Rd B79 263 A2
Havelock Rd DE23 232 A8
Havelock St
Ilkeston DE7 208 F7
Ripley DE5 169 E2
Haven Baulk Ave DE23 230 E7
Haven Baulk La DE23 230 E7
Haven Ct DE24 233 D6
Havenwood Gr DE23 231 C5
Havercroft Terr S21 60 B7
Havering Close DE22 218 A5
Hawfield La DE15 248 E4
Hawke Brook Cl S44 99 B3
Hawke St DE22 218 C5
Hawk Green Rd SK6 23 A3
Hawkhill Rd S32 71 D6
Hawkinge Ho 13 S41 95 D5
Hawking La
Stainsby S44 133 A7
Stainsby Common S44 132 F7
Hawkins Ct DE7 194 F4
Hawkins Dr DE56 168 B3
Hawk Rd SK22 33 E8
Hawksdale Cl DE73 233 A2
Hawk's Dr DE15 248 D3
Hawkshead Ave
Derby DE21 205 D1
Dronfield S18 56 E1
Hawkshead Fold SK13 10 E3
Hawkshead Rd SK13 10 E3
Hawksley Ave S40 95 E4
Hawksley Dr
Darley Dale DE4 127 B4
Rolleston DE13 240 B4
Hawksway S21 59 B3
Hawleys Cl DE4 143 E6
Hawley St S18 58 A1
Hawthorn Ave
Breaston DE72 235 F8
Derby DE24 233 A7
Mastin Moor S43 79 C4
Netherseal DE12 264 F7
Ripley DE5 180 D8
Stapleford NG9 223 D6
Hawthorn Bank
Glossop SK13 9 F4
New Mills SK22 33 B6
Hawthorn Cl
Ashbourne DE6 185 D8
Chinley SK23 34 E1
Clowne S43 80 D4
Denstone ST14 196 E6
Disley SK12 32 E6
Doveridge DE6 211 B1
Hilton DE65 228 D1
Hope S33 39 A4
Mansfield Woodhouse NG19 136 E5
Hawthorn Cres
Burton upon Trent DE15 254 F7
Findern DE65 230 D2
Hawthorn Ct DE1 267 A5
Hawthorn Dr DE4 155 A6
Hawthorne Ave
Borrowash DE72 221 C2
Creswell S80 81 E2
Dronfield S18 57 A3
Glapwell S44 134 B8
Long Eaton NG10 236 C6
Shirebrook NG20 119 D4
Shirland DE55 146 C5
Tibshelf DE55 148 B8
Hawthorne Cl
Ashover DE55 145 D8
Barlborough S43 80 A6
Kilburn DE56 179 F2
Killamarsh S21 60 D5
Hawthorne Rd
Barlborough S43 80 A6
Pinxton NG16 160 D3
Hawthornes Ave DE55 159 F5
Hawthorne St S40 266 C1
Hawthorn Gr SK14 9 D6
Hawthorn Hill S43 78 F6
Hawthorn Rd
Castle Donington DE74 247 B5
Chapel-en-le-Frith SK23 47 B4
Eckington S21 59 B2
Hawthorn Rise
Awsworth NG16 195 B4
Swadlincote DE11 255 F7
Hawthorn St DE24 232 C8
Hawthorns The
Belper DE56 179 D5
Little Eaton DE21 205 D8
Wirksworth DE4 165 F7
Hawthorn Way S42 94 F5
Hawton Cl NG19 135 F1
Hawtrey Gdns DE24 233 A7
Haxby Cl S13 44 E6
Haxby Pl S13 44 E6
Haxby St S13 44 E6
Haybrook Ct S17 55 E5
Haycock Dr 7 DE6 185 D7
Haycroft Cl NG19 136 E5
Haycroft Ct DE23 231 A7
Haycroft Gdns S43 79 B4
Hayden Ct 1 SK13 10 C1
Haydn Fold SK13 16 D7
Haydn Rd DE21 219 F8
Haydock Cl
Burton upon Trent DE14 254 A7
Kimberley NG16 195 E7
Haydock Park Rd DE24 232 E8
Hayes Ave
Breaston DE72 235 B7
Hayes Ave *continued*
Derby DE23 231 D8
Hayes Cl
Pinxton NG16 160 C3
West Hallam DE7 207 E8
Hayes Conf Ctr The DE55 170 A6
Hayes Cres DE55 169 F7
Hayes Ct S20 59 E6
Hayes Dr S20 59 E6
Hayes Farm Ct DE73 251 A4
Hayes La
Grassmoor S40 115 F4
Swanwick DE55 169 F7
Hayes The DE65 230 C1
Hayes Wood Rd DE7 193 A1
HAYFIELD 25 C2
Hayfield Cl
Belper DE56 179 B5
Dronfield S18 56 D1
Staveley S43 78 F3
Wingerworth S42 114 F3
Hayfield Cres S12 44 D3
Hayfield Dr
Branston DE14 253 C8
Sheffield S12 44 D3
Hayfield Gdns DE23 231 B6
Hayfield Pl S12 44 D3
Hayfield Prim Sch SK22 25 C3
Hayfield Rd
Chapel-en-le-Frith SK23 47 B8
Chinley SK23 35 A3
New Mills SK22 24 E1
New Mills SK22 33 D8
Hayfield Road E SK23 47 C6
Hayfield View S21 59 C3
Hayfield Visitor Ctr★ SK22 25 C2
Hayford Pl DE22 218 D4
Hayford Way S43 78 E1
Hay La
Ashover S45 145 B7
Holymoorside S45 113 D5
Scropton DE65 226 E5
Spout DE4 166 C5
Haylee La SK23 46 D1
Hayley Cl NG16 195 D6
Hayley Croft DE56 190 F1
Hayling Cl DE7 194 C3
Hayman Cl 3 NG19 136 C3
Haymans Cnr 5 NG19 136 C3
Haynes Ave NG9 209 C5
Hays Cl DE7 194 D2
Haysden La 3 S8 43 A2
Hays La DE6 164 E1
Hays The DE65 227 C2
Hay The S45 145 B6
Hay Wain La DE11 256 B7
Haywards Cl SK13 10 C3
Haywood Cl DE24 233 A5
Haywoods Rd DE11 256 E1
Hayworth Rd NG10 223 B5
Hazel Ave
Derby DE23 231 D6
Killamarsh S21 60 C5
Pilsley S45 132 B3
Hazelbadge Cres S12 44 E3
Hazelby Rd S80 100 F8
Hazel Cl
Ashbourne DE6 185 D8
Dronfield S18 76 B8
Findern DE65 230 E2
Heanor DE75 181 D1
Swadlincote DE11 256 A5
Hazel Cres
Branston DE14 253 E6
Branston DE14 256 E6
Shirebrook NG20 119 D4
Hazel Croft S17 55 C8
Hazel Ct
Dronfield S18 76 B8
Matlock DE4 143 D5
Hazel Dene DE4 143 D5
Hazeldene Cl DE56 190 E5
Hazeldene Cotts DE56 178 D2
Hazel Dr
Chesterfield S40 114 E8
Derby DE21 221 A6
Wingerworth S42 115 B3
HAZELFORD 53 A5
Hazel Gr
Calver S32 72 C2
Duffield DE56 190 E3
Mansfield Woodhouse NG19 136 B5
Mastin Moor S43 79 C4
Matlock DE4 143 D5
South Normanton DE55 160 B5
Hazelhurst S41 115 D6
Hazelhurst Ave S41 96 A5
Hazelhurst La S41 96 A5
Hazelmererd S80 100 B8
Hazelmere Rd S80 81 D2
Hazel Rd S21 59 C2
Hazelrigg Cl DE74 246 F4
Hazeltree Cl DE5 180 C8
HAZELWOOD 190 A8
Hazelwood Cl
5 Dronfield S18 56 C1
1 Glossop SK13 10 A6
Hazelwood Cl *continued*
6 Tibshelf DE55 148 B7
Hazelwood Hill
Hazelwood DE56 178 B1
Hazelwood DE56 190 C8
Hazelwood Rd
Burton upon Trent DE15 254 E6
Derby DE21 219 F8
Duffield DE56 190 D5
Hazlebarrow Cl S8 57 C6
Hazlebarrow Cres S8 57 C7
Hazlebarrow Ct S8 57 B7
Hazlebarrow Dr S8 57 B7
Hazlebarrow Gr S8 57 C7
Hazlebarrow Rd S8 57 B7
Hazlehurst Ave S41 96 B5
Hazlehurst La
Chesterfield S41 96 B5
Eckington S8 57 F8
Hazlewood Dr S43 80 B6
Headingley Ct DE23 231 C8
Headland Cl S43 96 E7
Headland Rd S43 96 E7
Headlands Cres 3 DE73 233 A3
Headstock Drive DE11 255 D1
HEAGE 168 E1
Heage La DE65 229 D8
Heage Prim Sch DE56 168 D2
Heage Rd DE5 169 C1
Heage Road Ind Est DE5 169 B1
Heage Windmill★ DE56 168 D2
Healaugh Way S40 115 B8
Heale St S43 80 E3
HEANOR 181 C2
HEANOR GATE 193 C8
Heanor Gate 3 DE75 181 D1
Heanor Gate Ind Est DE75 193 D8
Heanor Gate Rd DE75 193 D8
Heanor Gate Science Coll DE75 181 C1
Heanor Ho DE21 220 E3
Heanor Langley Inf Sch 1 NG16 182 B3
Heanor Rd
Denby DE5 181 A3
Heanor, Heanor Gate DE75 181 D1
Ilkeston DE7 194 D3
Smalley DE7, DE75 193 B7
Heanor Retail Pk DE75 181 E2
Heanor Small Bsns Ctr DE75 193 D8
Hearthcote Rd DE11 256 A3
HEARTHSTONE 143 D1
Hearthstone La DE4 143 D1
HEATH 117 B2
Heath Ave
Derby DE23 218 C1
Killamarsh S21 60 D5
Heath Cl DE72 246 B8
Heath Common S44 117 B2
HEATHCOTE
138 B5
SK17 138 B5
Heathcote Cl DE24 233 C5
Heathcote Dr S41 115 E8
Heathcote Ho S41 96 B6
Heath Cross 3 ST14 210 A1
Heath Ct
Chesterfield S40 115 A8
Derby DE24 231 E3
HEATH END 258 D7
Heath End La DE73 258 E8
Heather Ave S44 116 F1
Heather Bank Cl 2 SK13 17 A7
Heather Cl
Burton upon Trent DE14 254 A8
Calow S44 97 A3
Derby DE24 231 D2
Glossop SK13 10 C3
South Normanton DE55 160 A3
Swanwick DE55 170 A8
Heather Close DE13 239 D5
Heather Cres
Breaston DE72 235 F7
Derby DE23 231 C6
Heather Ct DE75 182 B1
Heather Falls SK22 33 B8
Heather Gdns S41 115 E7
Heather Gr SK14 9 D6
Heather La S32 53 A6
Heather Lea Ave S17 55 C7
Heather Lea Pl S17 55 C7
Heatherley Dr NG19 136 E1
Heatherley Prim Sch NG19 136 E1
Heathermead Cl 2 DE21 205 F1
Heathers Edge S32 53 A6
Heather Vale S41 115 E7
Heather Vale Cl S41 115 E7
Heather Vale Rd S41 115 D7
Heather Way
Holymoorside S42 113 D7
Shirebrook NG20 119 D2
Heathfield DE4 143 C7
Heathfield Ave
Chesterfield S40 95 D3
Etwall DE65 229 C3
Ilkeston DE7 209 A8
Heathfield Cl
Dronfield S18 75 F8
Wingerworth S42 115 B4
Heathfield Gdns
Buxton SK17 85 A8
Tibshelf DE55 148 A7
Heathfield Nook Rd SK17 85 E2
Heathfield Rd S12 44 D4
Heath Fields Prim Sch DE65 227 C1
Heath Gdns DE72 236 A8
Heath Gr SK17 85 C6
Heath La
Blackfordby DE11 257 C2
Findern DE65 242 D8
Hartshorne DE11 257 E4
Smisby LE65 258 B6
Heathlands Dr ST14 210 B1
Heathlands Grange DE15 254 E7
Heath Lane SK23 46 F5
Heathley Mews DE14 254 C8
Heath Park Rd SK17 85 C6
Heath Prim Sch S44 116 F1
Heath Rd
Burton upon Trent DE15 254 E7
Glossop SK13 10 D2
Holmewood S44 116 E1
Holmewood, Williamthorpe S42 132 E8
Ripley DE5 169 E1
Uttoxeter ST14 210 B1
Heath St SK17 85 B6
HEATH THE 210 A1
Heath The
Eastwood NG16 195 A8
Glossop SK13 10 C3
HEATHTOP 227 A6
Heath View SK17 85 E1
Heath Way DE65 227 D1
Heathy Dales SK17 69 B2
Heaton Cl S18 56 D1
Heaton Ct 4 S40 95 C2
Heaton Pl SK17 85 E8
Heaton St S40 95 C2
Heavygate La DE56 177 F8
Hebden Cl DE23 230 F6
Hebden Dr SK13 17 F8
Hebrides Cl DE24 231 D3
Heddon Bar NG19 136 E3
Hedgebank Ct DE21 206 C3
Hedge Gr DE11 256 B7
Hedgerow Gdns DE21 206 C3
Hedges Dr DE7 209 A5
Hedgevale Cl DE23 231 A7
Hedingham Cl NE7 194 D1
Hedingham Way DE3 230 D8
Hedley Cl DE55 170 D8
Hedley Dr S43 96 D8
Hedley St DE11 256 F5
HEELEY 43 B6
Heeley Arches S2 43 A7
Heeley Bank Rd S2 43 B7
Heeley City Farm★ S2 43 B7
Heeley Gn S2 43 B6
Heigham Cl DE24 232 D3
Heights of Abraham The★ DE4 143 A2
Heild End SK11 102 A2
Helmsley Ave S20 59 E7
Helmsley Cl S41 95 C7
Helmton Dr S8 43 A2
Helmton Rd S8 43 A2
Helpston Cl DE55 147 C1
Helston Cl
Chesterfield S41 115 B8
Derby DE24 233 B6
Linton DE12 261 D5
Helvellyn Way 5 NG10 223 B2
Heming Ave S45 132 C2
HEMINGTON 247 D5
Hemington Ct DE74 247 C5
Hemington Hill DE74 247 C4
Hemington La DE74 247 E5
Hemington Prim Sch DE74 247 D5
Hemlock Ave
Long Eaton NG10 223 D1
Stapleford NG9 223 E8
Hemlock Cl DE21 206 A3
Hemlock La DE7 208 D5
Hemlock Stone The★ NG9 209 F2
HEMMING GREEN 94 B4
Hemper Gr S8 56 D7
Hemper La S8 56 D7
Hemp Yd DE6 165 B1
Hemsley Dr NG16 182 D3
HEMSWORTH 43 D3
Hemsworth Rd S8, S14 43 C2
Henderson Cl S45 131 E5
Hendon Way DE22 218 B6
Henley Ave S8 57 C8
Henley Gdns NG9 209 E1
Henley Gn DE22 217 F6
Henley Grove DE11 255 F2
Henley Way DE7 207 D8
HENMOOR 131 A4
Henmore Cres
Derby DE3 217 B1
Derby DE3 230 B8
Henmore Pl 10 DE6 173 C2
Henmore Trad Est DE6 173 A1
Hennymoor Cl S80 82 A5
Hennymoor La S80 82 C2
Henry Ave
Mansfield Woodhouse NG19 136 B5
Matlock DE4 143 C6
Henry Bradley Inf Sch S43 96 F8
Henry Cres DE55 159 C3
Henry St
Chesterfield S41 96 B8
Derby DE1 267 A4
Eckington S21 59 D3
Glossop SK13 10 C1
Grassmoor S42 115 E3
Ripley DE5 169 D2
Henshall Dr DE72 245 B8
Henshall Ho S41 96 B6
Henshaw Ave DE7 208 D5
Henshaw Gardens DE5 169 C1
Henshaw Pl DE7 194 E4
HEPTHORNE LANE 131 E6
Hepworth Dr NG16 195 B7
Hepworth Rd DE11 256 E1
Herald Gr DE73 244 E8
Herbert Dr DE11 256 F5
Herbert St DE15 248 B3
Herbert Strutt Prim Sch DE56 179 B2
Herb Garden at Hardstoft The★ S45 132 E3
HERDINGS 43 F3
Herdings Ct S12 44 A3
Herdings Rd S12 44 A3
Herdings View
Sheffield S12 43 F3
Sheffield S12 44 A3
Hereford Ave NG19 136 D5
Hereford Cl SK17 85 C4
Hereford Cres DE11 256 D6
Hereford Dr S43 96 F8
Hereford Rd
Buxton SK17 85 C4
Derby DE21 219 D8
Hereward's Rd S14 43 D1
Herewood Cl NG20 119 F4
Heritage Ct DE6 201 B7
Heritage Dr S43 80 D5
Heritage High Sch S43 80 D4
Heritage Rd DE74 246 F2
Heritage St S43 81 E2
Heritage Way DE15 248 A1
Hermitage Ave
Borrowash DE72 221 C2
Somercotes DE55 170 C5
Hermitage Cl DE6 185 C8
Hermitage Ct DE21 206 B1
Hermitage Gdns 1 ST14 210 A1
Hermitage La DE6 184 B6
Hermitage Park Way 7 DE11 256 A7
Hermitage Wlk DE7 208 F6
Hernstone La SK17 49 B2
Heron Cl SK13 17 F8
Heron Dr DE11 256 F3
Heron Grange DE14 253 D7
Heron Rd S43 98 A8
Heronswood Dr DE21 220 D6
Heron View SK13 16 F8
Heron Way
Derby DE3 218 A2
Mansfield NG19 135 C1
Herriot Dr S40 266 C1
Hesketh Cl DE5 181 A8
Hessey St S13 44 F6
Hetton Drive S45 131 D4
Hewer Cl 4 DE7 194 F8
Hewer Ct S20 60 A6
Hewer Drive DE11 255 D2
Hewers Holt S43 80 B6
Hewett St NG20 120 D5
Hewitt Pl S26 61 E5
Hexham Ave DE7 209 A4
Hexham Wlk DE21 205 E1
Heyden Bank 26 SK13 9 D2
Heyden Fold 27 SK13 9 D2
Heyden Terr 25 SK13 9 D2
Heydon Cl DE56 179 B6
Heyford Ct DE75 182 A1
Heysbank Rd SK12 32 D5
Hey St NG10 236 C4
Heywood St S43 96 E8
Heywood View S43 80 C6

Heywood Villas [5] S43 96 E8
Heyworth Rd SK23 47 C6
Heyworth St DE22 218 D6
Hibbert St SK22 33 B6
Hibbitt Cl DE55 170 B7
Hickings La NG9 223 E8
Hickingwood La S43 81 A5
Hickinwood Cres S43 80 F5
Hickleton Cl DE5 169 C1
Hickleton La S2 44 A7
Hickling Cl
Derby DE24 232 D3
[1] Nottingham NG10 236 B5
Hickory Gr [1] DE11 256 B7
Hickton Rd DE55 169 F6
HIDEBANK 33 C8
Hide La SK17 137 E7
Hides Gn S44 99 A2
HIGGENHOLES 109 D8
Higger La S32 52 F8
Higgins Rd DE11 255 F6
Higg La
Alderwasley DE4 166 F5
Alderwasley DE56 167 A6
Higgot La DE15 248 B5
Higgott Cl DE14 254 B8
HIGHAM 146 C3
Higham La
Compstall SK14 15 A7
Stonebroom DE55 146 E4
Highashes La S45 113 E1
Highbank SK13 9 F7
High Bank DE5 180 F2
Highbank Rd SK13 17 F7
High Bank Rd DE15 248 B3
High Bridge La
DE15 241 D3
Highbury Cl DE22 217 F6
Highbury Grove S40 95 F5
Highbury Rd S41 95 F5
High Cliffe S32 71 D7
Highcliffe Ave
NG20 119 D4
Highcroft Cl NG10 236 E5
High Cross
Hartington SK17 137 F5
Linton DE11 261 F7
HIGH CROSS BANK 261 E8
High Ct [1] DE4 143 C6
Highdale Fold [6]
S18 57 A1
High Edge Dr DE56 179 E8
High Edge Mews
DE56 179 A5
Higher Albert St
S41 266 B4
Higher Barn Rd SK13 9 F4
HIGHER
BIBBINGTON 67 A6
HIGHER BUXTON 85 C6
HIGHER CHISWORTH
SK13 16 B4
Higher Cliffe SK6 23 D2
HIGHER CROSSINGS 46 F6
HIGHER DINTING 10 A2
Higher Dinting SK13 10 A2
HIGHER DISLEY 32 E5
HIGHER GAMESLEY 16 D8
Higher Hallsteads
SK17 47 F3
Higher La SK12 32 E1
Higher Noon Sun
SK22 24 F2
Higher Sq SK13 10 A7
HIGHFIELD 43 A8
Highfield DE45 108 E8
Highfield Ave
Chesterfield S41 95 E6
Dove Holes SK17 47 E1
Mansfield NG19 136 B1
Shirebrook NG20 119 D6
Highfield Cl
Bakewell DE45 109 C5
Heanor DE75 181 B5
Mansfield NG19 136 B1
High Field Cl S44 118 A5
Highfield Cotts
Alfreton DE55 158 D3
Derby DE21 219 E5
Highfield Ct SK14 9 A4
Highfield Dr
Bakewell DE45 109 C5
Ilkeston DE7 208 B5
Matlock DE4 143 D6
South Normanton
DE55 160 B5
Highfield Gdns
Derby DE22 218 F7
Hollingworth SK14 9 D5
Highfield Hall Prim Sch
S41 95 F6
Highfield La
Chesterfield S41 95 E6
Clay Cross SK17 131 F3
Derby DE21 219 F5
Hartington SK17 137 F5
Weston Underwood
DE6 188 F5
Highfield Mews
DE21 219 E5
Highfield Pl S2 43 A8
Highfield Rd
Ashbourne DE6 185 B8
Belper DE56 178 F2

Highfield Rd *continued*
Bolsover S44 99 A1
Chesterfield S41 266 A4
Derby DE22 218 F7
Derby, Littleover
DE23 231 C7
Glossop SK13 17 D8
Hayfield SK22 25 D3
Hulland Ward DE6 175 F3
Kilburn DE56 191 F8
Little Eaton DE21 205 C8
Marple SK6 23 B6
Swadlincote DE11 256 B3
Swanwick DE55 169 D7
HIGHFIELDS 132 C7
Highfields
Buxton SK17 67 B5
Clowne S43 80 D2
Codnor DE5 181 B8
Highfields Cl [5]
DE55 158 E3
Highfields Cres S18 76 A8
Highfields Dr
Holmewood S42 132 D8
Linton DE12 261 C6
Highfields Lower Sch
DE4 143 C3
Highfields Park Dr
DE22 204 E1
Highfields Rd S18 76 A8
Highfields Sch DE4 143 E7
Highfields Spencer Acad
DE23 230 E3
Highfield St
Long Eaton NG10 223 C2
Swadlincote DE11 256 B3
Highfields Way S42 132 D8
Highfield Terr
Chesterfield S41 95 F5
New Mills SK22 33 D8
Highfield View Rd
S41 95 F5
Highfield Way DE5 180 C8
HIGHGATE 25 D1
Highgate Cl S43 77 D3
Highgate Dr
Dronfield S18 76 C7
Ilkeston DE7 194 D3
Highgate Gn DE22 218 A5
Highgate La S18 76 C7
Highgate Rd SK22 25 E1
Highgates DE1 267 B2
High Gr
Belper DE56 179 D4
Mansfield NG19 136 E1
High Grange Sch
DE3 230 B7
Highgrove Cl
Burton upon Trent
DE13 240 C1
[6] Chesterfield S41 96 A8
Heanor DE75 181 C1
Highgrove Ct DE24 232 F4
Highgrove Dr DE73 232 F2
Highgrove Gdns [4]
DE65 227 D2
High Hazel Ct S45 131 D4
High Hazel Dr NG19 136 B1
High Hazels Cl S45 131 E4
High Hazels Rd S43 80 B5
High Hazels Wlk
S45 131 E4
High Hill Rd
New Mills SK22 24 D1
New Mills SK22 33 D8
High Holbeck S80 101 C7
High Holborn DE7 194 E3
High Holborn Rd
DE5 170 B1
High La
Broadbottom SK13 16 E7
Eckington S12 44 E1
Holloway, Dethick Common
DE4 144 E2
Holloway, Upper Holloway
DE4 156 D6
Holymoorside S42 113 E5
Sheffield S12 58 F8
Wigley S42 93 F4
High La East DE7 208 B7
Highland Cl
Buxton SK17 85 C5
Mansfield Woodhouse
NG19 136 D3
Highland Rd
Chesterfield S43 77 D4
Chesterfield S43 77 D5
Highlands Dr DE15 248 A4
Highlands Pl S41 76 F1
HIGH LANE 32 A8
High Lane Central
DE7 193 F1
High Lane E DE7 208 B8
High Lane W DE7 193 E1
High Lea Rd SK22 33 A8
High Leys Rd S43 80 E2
Highlightley La S18 75 C5
HIGH LOW 52 E5
Highlow Cl S40 95 C5
High Mdws SK13 17 B7
High Meadow Cl
DE5 180 D8
High Pavement
DE56 179 A3
High Peak Rd SK17 85 C3
High Peak School
SK12 32 E1
High Rd DE55 157 F4

High Ridge
Mansfield NG19 136 F2
Matlock DE4 143 C7
High Spannia NG16 195 F7
High St
Alfreton DE55 158 F4
Alfreton DE55 159 A4
Apperknowle S18 58 A1
Barlborough S43 80 A7
Belper DE56 179 A4
Bolsover S44 99 A1
Bonsall DE4 142 D1
Brimington S43 96 F7
Brinsley NG16 171 E1
Buxton SK17 85 B7
Calver S32 72 B2
Castle Donington
DE74 247 A2
Chapel-en-le-Frith
SK23 47 B6
Chellaston DE73 233 A1
Chesterfield S41, S43 77 D4
Chesterfield, Stonegravels
S40 266 B3
Clay Cross S45 131 C3
Clowne S43 80 D3
Codnor DE5 181 B8
Derby DE1 267 C1
Doveridge DE6 211 B1
Dronfield S18 57 A1
Eckington S21 59 D3
Ilkeston DE7 208 F8
Kilburn DE56 192 A8
Killamarsh S21 60 D6
Kimberley NG16 195 F6
Linton DE12 261 C6
Long Eaton NG10 236 E8
Longnor SK17 121 C6
Mansfield Woodhouse
NG19 136 C3
Marchington ST14 224 E2
Melbourne DE73 252 A7
New Mills SK22 33 C8
Pilsley DE45 91 C3
Pleasley NG19 135 B5
Repton DE65 242 D2
Ripley DE5 169 D1
Rocester ST14 196 F3
Sheffield, Dore S17 55 D7
Sheffield, Mosborough
S20 59 D7
Somercotes DE55 170 C8
Somercotes, Riddings
DE55 170 D5
South Normanton
DE55 160 A6
Stapleford NG9 223 E7
Staveley S43 78 E2
Stonebroom DE55 147 A4
Stoney Middleton S32 71 F3
Stramshall ST14 210 A4
Swadlincote, Church Gresley
DE11 256 C3
Swadlincote, Newhall
DE11 256 A6
Swanwick DE55 169 F7
Tibshelf DE55 148 A7
Ticknall DE73 251 A4
Tideswell SK17 69 C4
Tutbury DE13 239 C6
Whitwell S80 81 F6
Woodville DE11 256 F2
Highstairs La DE55 146 C8
Highstones Gdns
SK13 10 F2
Highstool La SK17 106 B6
High Street E SK13 10 D1
High Street Mews
S20 59 C7
High Street W SK13 10 B1
High Tor* DE4 143 B3
High Tor Rd DE4 143 B2
High Trees S17 55 D7
Highview SK13 17 A7
High View Cl S41 96 D2
High View Rd DE55 160 C7
Highway La DE6 151 F2
High Withins La
DE6 149 A3
Highwood Ave
DE56 179 C1
High Wood Bank
DE56 179 C1
Highwood Cl SK13 17 B8
High Wood Fold SK6 23 C8
Highwood La S80 81 D5
Highwood Pl S21 59 C3
High Wood Way
S43 80 C5
Hilary Cl DE56 179 E5
HILCOTE 148 C1
Hilcote La DE55 148 B1
Hilcote St DE55 160 A6
Hilderstone Cl
DE24 233 D6
Hillary Pl DE7 208 B5
Hillberry [1] DE5 170 A1
Hillberry Rise S40 114 F6
Hill Brow DE1 267 B2
Hill Cl
Derby DE21 220 E4
Stanley Common DE7 193 A1
Turnditch DE56 177 B2
Hillcliff La
Hulland Ward DE56 176 F2
Turnditch DE56 177 A3
HILLCLIFFLANE 177 A3
Hill Cotts DE45 125 B5

Hillcrest
Aston-on-Trent
DE72 234 A1
Belper DE56 179 E4
Blackwell DE55 147 E1
[2] Matlock DE4 143 A7
Tutbury DE13 239 B5
Hill Crest
Crich DE4 157 A1
Shirebrook NG20 119 D3
Hillcrest Ave
Burton upon Trent
DE15 248 A4
Hulland Ward DE6 175 F3
South Normanton
DE55 160 A4
Hill Crest Ave DE55 157 E8
Hillcrest Close S44 98 F6
Hill Crest Cotts DE4 142 F8
Hillcrest Dr
Codnor DE5 181 B8
Kilburn DE56 192 A8
Hillcreste Dr DE73 232 F3
Hillcrest Gr S43 78 F4
Hillcrest Rd S41 115 D7
Hill Crest Rd DE21 219 D7
Hill Crest Rise S26 61 F5
Hillcroft Dr DE72 221 C4
HILLCROSS 231 C7
Hill Cross DE45 108 F8
Hill Cross Ave DE23 231 C7
Hill Cross Dr DE23 231 B7
Hill Dr SK23 45 D8
Hillend SK14 9 A1
Hillend La SK14 9 A1
Hillfield Cl DE11 262 B7
Hillfield La DE13 240 F1
Hillfield Rd NG9 209 F1
Hill Fields DE55 160 A3
HILLFOOT 55 D5
Hillfoot Ct S17 55 D4
Hillfoot Rd S17 55 D5
Hill Gr S43 78 B4
Hill Green Cl DE12 260 D3
Hill Head S33 51 A7
Hill Head Dr SK17 85 E1
Hillhead La SK17 85 E1
Hillhouses La S42 114 E3
Hillingdon Avenue
DE22 218 A5
Hillingdon Dr DE7 209 A7
Hill La
Hathersage S32 52 F8
Holymoorside S42 113 D6
Hillman Dr S43 97 C7
Hillmoor St NG19 135 C3
Hillmorton DE45 108 F7
Hill Nook Cl DE73 233 A1
Hillock The S32 72 E2
Hill Pond Ave SK22 24 D1
Hill Rd
Ashover S45 129 F4
Heanor DE75 181 D1
Hill Rise NG9 209 C4
Hill Rise Cl DE23 231 D8
HILLS AND HOLES 120 E5
Hillsdale Rd DE15 248 B5
Hillside
Ashover S45 130 A4
Brassington DE4 152 F1
Buxton SK17 85 D3
Castle Donington
DE74 247 B4
Chinley SK23 47 B8
Curbar S32 72 E2
Findern DE65 230 C2
Holloway DE4 156 A6
Langley Mill NG16 182 A3
Middleton DE4 154 D4
Sheffield S20 59 C7
Tutbury DE13 239 C6
Whitwell S80 81 F5
Hillside Ave
Ashbourne DE6 173 C3
Derby DE21 220 A5
Dronfield S18 76 A8
Hillside Cl
Disley SK12 32 E6
Glossop SK13 9 E3
Whitwell S80 81 F5
Hillside Cotts S32 53 B7
Hillside Cres DE21 220 F4
Hillside Ct
Breedon on the Hill
DE73 252 F2
Kirk Langley DE6 202 E4
Hillside Dr
Chesterfield S40 95 D1
Long Eaton NG10 236 B8
Mastin Moor S43 79 C3
Hillside Gdns
[4] Matlock DE4 143 A7
Swadlincote DE11 255 F2
Hillside Gr
Marple SK6 15 B1
Sandiacre NG10 223 A6
Hillside Green S26 61 E5
Hillside La DE6 152 F1
Hillside Pk
Alfreton DE55 158 B4
South Wingfield DE55 158 B4
Hillside Rd
Branston DE14 253 C8
Derby DE21 220 F4
Linton DE12 261 D7
Hillside Rise DE56 178 F2
Hillside View SK22 33 A8
Hills La DE73 244 E3

Hillsmede [2] DE55 147 F6
HILL SOMERSAL 212 A2
Hill Sq The DE22 205 A1
Hills Rd DE72 235 C7
Hill St
Burton upon Trent
DE15 254 E8
Clay Cross S45 131 C3
Donisthorpe DE12 262 E1
Ripley DE5 169 D3
Sheffield S2 43 A8
Swadlincote DE11 255 F6
Swadlincote, Church Gresley
DE11 256 C3
Wingerworth S42 115 C4
HILLS THE 51 A6
Hills The S33 51 A6
HILLSTOWN 118 C8
Hillstown Bsns Ctr
S44 118 B7
Hillsview Ct NG19 135 A5
Hillsway
Chellaston DE73 232 F3
Derby DE23 218 B1
Shirebrook NG20 119 D3
Hill The
Cromford DE4 155 A5
Derby DE22 205 A1
Glapwell S44 118 A1
HILLTOP
Chapel-en-le-Frith 46 B6
Flash 103 B5
Hilltop DE56 168 B7
HILL TOP 76 A7
Hill Top
Bolsover S44 99 A2
Castle Donington
DE74 247 A1
Derby DE21 205 E3
Flash SK17 103 B5
Hilltop Ave NG20 119 E4
Hilltop Cl S44 118 B1
Hilltop Dr [3] DE55 158 F1
Hilltop La
Belper DE56 179 E2
Thurvaston DE6 215 D5
Hilltop Rd
Ashover S45 129 F5
Chesterfield S41 77 B2
Dronfield S18 76 B7
Glossop SK13 10 B3
Pinxton NG16 160 C3
Wingerworth S42 114 D4
Hill Top Rd DE55 170 C5
Hill Top Rise SK23 45 D8
Hilltops View DE4 143 D5
Hilltop Way S18 76 A7
Hill View
Duffield DE56 190 D3
Repton DE65 242 E2
Whaley Bridge SK23 45 C8
Hill View Cl DE7 192 B7
Hillview Ct NG19 136 D4
Hill View Gr DE21 220 E5
Hillview Ho [1] DE1 267 B2
Hill View Rd S43 96 E8
Hillwood Dr SK13 17 F8
HILLYFIELDS 132 B7
HILTON 228 C1
Hilton Bsns Pk
DE65 240 E8
Hilton Cl
Derby DE3 217 D1
Long Eaton NG10 235 F4
Pleasley NG19 135 C3
Swadlincote DE11 256 A7
HILTON COMMON 228 F2
Hilton Gdns DE72 246 A7
Hilton Ind Est DE65 228 D3
Hilton Park Dr
DE55 170 C8
Hilton Prim Sch
DE65 228 D2
Hilton Rd
Disley SK12 32 B7
Egginton DE65 241 B7
Etwall DE65 229 B4
Hinckley Ct DE4 110 F1
Hind Ave DE72 235 C8
Hindersitch La DE4 156 D2
Hindlip Cl [4] DE6 211 A1
HIND LOW 105 B7
Hindscarth Cres
DE3 217 E1
Hinton Gr SK14 15 A8
Hipley Cl S40 95 B6
Hipper St S40 266 B2
Hipper Street S S40 266 B2
Hipper Street W S40 95 E2
Hitchen Road NG10 236 B7
Hixon's La DE7 208 B1
Hoades St S42 131 C8
Hoargate La DE6 200 F2
Hobart Cl
Burton upon Trent
DE15 248 C2
Derby DE3 217 F2
Hobart Dr NG9 209 F1
Hob Hill DE56 190 B8
Hob Hill Mdws SK13 17 D7
Hobhouse Rd NG19 135 D2
Hob Hurst's Ho*
DE45 111 F7
Hobkirk Dr DE24 231 E2
Hob La DE6 176 D8
Hobroyd SK13 16 B7
HOBSIC 182 D8
Hobsic Cl NG16 182 D8

Hobsic La NG16 171 E8
Hobson Dr
Derby DE21 220 F2
Derby DE72 221 A2
Ilkeston DE7 208 E6
Hobson Moor Rd SK14 9 A7
Hockerley Ave SK23 45 D8
Hockerley Cl SK23 45 D8
Hockerley La SK23 45 D8
Hockerley New Rd
SK23 45 D8
HOCKLEY 115 A2
Hockley La
Ashover S45 130 A1
Dalebank S45 145 C8
Wingerworth S42 115 A3
Hockley Rise S42 115 A2
Hockleys Yard DE5 181 C8
Hockley Way DE55 159 B2
Hodder Cl DE4 156 F2
Hodding Rd S80 82 C6
Hodge Beck Cl
DE24 233 C6
Hodge Fold SK14 15 F8
Hodge La
Ashover S45 128 E7
Broadbottom SK14 15 F8
Marchington ST14 224 A1
Uppertown S45 128 F7
Hodmire La S44 133 E7
HODTHORPE 82 C6
Hodthorpe Cl DE21 206 B1
Hodthorpe Prim Sch
S80 82 C5
Hogarth Cl NG9 223 E6
Hogarth Rd SK6 23 B8
Hogarth Rise S18 75 F8
Hogbarn La DE75,
NG16 181 D5
Hoggs Field NG16 182 F2
HOGNASTON 164 A1
Hogshaw Dr SK17 66 C1
Hogshaw Villas Rd
Buxton SK17 66 C1
[1] Buxton SK17 85 C8
Hoillant Sq DE6 175 E3
Holbeach Dr S40 114 E8
HOLBECK 101 C7
Holbeck Ave S44 99 C2
Holbeck Cl S41 266 C4
Holbeck La S80 101 D8
Holbeck St S80 81 D1
HOLBECK
WOODHOUSE 101 E7
Holbein Cl S18 75 F8
Holborn Dr DE22 218 A7
Holborn View DE5 170 B1
HOLBROOK
Belper 191 D6
Sheffield 60 A8
Holbrook Ave
North Wingfield S42 132 A7
Sheffield S20 60 A8
Holbrook CE Prim Sch
DE56 191 C7
Holbrook Cl
Chesterfield S40 114 C8
Pleasley NG19 135 A5
Holbrook Ct [4]
DE65 242 E2
Holbrook Dr S13 44 B6
Holbrook Gn S20 60 A8
Holbrook Ind Est
S20 60 A8
HOLBROOK MOOR 191 D7
Holbrook Pl S43 97 C6
Holbrook Rd
Belper DE56 178 F2
Derby DE24 233 B6
Sheffield S13 44 B7
Holbrook Sch For Autism
DE56 191 D5
Holbrook St DE75 182 A2
Holbrook View
DE56 192 A8
Holbrook Way S42 132 A7
Holburn Ave S18 57 A2
Holcombe St DE23 219 B1
Holden Ave DE72 246 A8
Holden Ct DE24 233 A8
Holden Gdns [1]
NG9 223 E6
Holderness Cl DE24 231 D2
Holdings The DE11 256 A1
Holdon Croft DE12 260 C6
HOLEHOUSE 16 C5
HOLESTONE 144 C8
Holestone Gate Rd
S45 129 D1
Holker Ave SK17 85 C8
Holker Rd SK17 85 C7
Holkham Cl DE7 194 C3
Holland Cl DE55 146 F5
Holland Mdw NG10 236 D5
Holland Pl [8] S2 43 A8
Holland Rd
Chesterfield S41 76 F2
Sheffield S2 43 A8
Hollbank Cotts
DE55 158 B3
Hollens Way
Chesterfield S40 95 A5
Woodnook S40 94 F5
Hollies Cl
Clifton DE6 184 F6
Dronfield S18 76 C8
Newton Solney DE15 248 E8
Hollies Ct DE65 229 B3

Hollies Dr SK6...23 A5
Hollies Farm Cl DE73...244 E3
Hollies Farm Drive DE7...192 C7
Hollies La DE6...198 C4
Hollies Rd DE22...204 D3
Hollies The
Eastwood NG16...182 F2
Repton DE65...243 A1
Sandiacre NG10...223 A5
Shirebrook NG20...119 E2
Hollin Bank Rd S32...41 B4
Hollin Cl S41...95 C8
Hollincross La SK13...17 C8
Hollindale Dr S12...44 C5
Hollin Dr SK23...47 B5
HOLLINGTON...200 F4
Hollington Cl DE21...219 E7
Hollington La DE6...201 B7
Hollington Rd ST14...196 D3
Hollingwood Cres S43...78 A1
Hollingwood Prim Sch S43...78 A1
HOLLINGWORTH...9 C6
Hollingworth Ave NG10...223 B3
Hollingworth Prim Sch SK14...9 C5
Hollinhey Terr SK14...9 C5
Hollin Hill Rd S43...81 A3
HOLLINS 94 A4
Wigley S42...93 F4
Hollins Ave SK17...85 B7
Hollins Bank 41 SK13...9 D2
Hollins Cl 40 SK13...9 D2
HOLLINSCLOUGH...104 C1
Hollinsclough CE VA Prim Sch SK17...104 D2
Hollinsclough Rake
Hollinsclough SK17...103 F3
Hollinsclough SK17...104 B2
Hollinsend Ave S12...44 C5
Hollinsend Pl S12...44 C5
Hollinsend Rd S12...44 B5
Hollins Fold 43 SK13...9 D2
Hollins Gdns 46 SK13...9 D2
Hollins Gr 42 SK13...9 D2
HOLLINS GREEN...130 E3
Hollins Ind Pk SK13...10 B5
Hollins La
Chapel-en-le-Frith SK23...46 C2
Crich DE4...157 A4
Marple SK6...23 C8
Hollins Mews 44 SK13...9 D2
Hollinsmoor Rd SK6, SK22...24 D7
Hollins Mount SK6...23 B8
Hollins Spring Ave S18...76 A8
Hollins Spring Rd S18...76 A8
Hollins St SK17...85 B7
Hollins The DE4...156 A6
Hollins Way 45 SK13...9 D2
Hollins Wood Cl DE4...156 A5
HOLLIN WOOD...34 B1
Hollinwood La SK6...23 B2
Hollinwood Rd SK12...32 D6
Hollis La
Chesterfield S40...96 B2
Chesterfield S41...266 C2
Denstone ST14...196 B6
Hollis St DE24...233 A8
Holllins Ave 47 SK13...9 D2
HOLLOWAY...156 B5
Holloway DE65...242 E2
Holloway Rd
Derby DE24...232 F6
Duffield DE56...190 E4
Hollow Cres DE15...248 C4
Hollowford Ctr S33...38 C4
Hollowford Rd S33...38 B4
Hollow Gate
Bradwell S33...51 A7
Froggatt S32...72 C5
Hollow La
Burton upon Trent DE15...248 C4
Mayfield DE6...172 C1
Sheffield, Mosborough S20...59 D6
Hollowood Ave DE23...231 C8
Hollow O'the Moor SK17...87 E4
Hollow Rd DE73...252 E2
Hollows The NG10...237 A8
Hollow The
Bamford S33...40 B3
Castle Donington DE74...247 B4
Derby, Littleover DE23...231 C8
Derby, Markeaton DE3...230 D8
Holloway DE4...156 B5
Roston DE6...197 E7
Holly Ave
Breaston DE72...222 F1
Creswell S80...81 D2
Ripley DE5...180 D8
Hollybank S12...44 B6
Holly Bank
Glossop SK13...17 E8
Hollingworth SK14...9 D5
Hollybank Ave S12...44 C6
Hollybank Cl
Sheffield S12...44 D6
Swadlincote DE11...256 A7
Holly Bank Cl
New Houghton NG19...135 A6
South Wingfield DE55...158 B3
Hollybank Cres S12...44 C6
Holly Bank Ct DE4...156 F1
Hollybank Dr S12...44 D6
Hollybank Rd S12...44 C6
Hollybank Way S12...44 D6
Hollybrook Way DE23...230 F6
Holly Brook Way DE23...230 F6
Holly Bush Cl DE12...264 F7
Holly Bush La DE56...191 A6
Holly Cl
Ashbourne DE6...185 D8
Chesterfield S41...77 A3
Draycott DE72...235 A7
Killamarsh S21...60 C5
Holly Croft DE15...248 C2
Holly Ct
Aston-on-Trent DE72...246 A7
3 Chesterfield S40...95 C2
Derby DE3...217 D1
2 Mansfield NG19...136 E1
Woodville DE11...256 F2
Holly End Rd 7 DE3...217 D1
Holly Gdns S12...44 C6
Holly Gn DE15...254 F8
Holly Gr
Sheffield S12...44 C6
Swanwick DE55...169 F8
Holly Hill Rd NG16...171 F6
Hollyhock Drive NG19...135 F1
Hollyhock Way DE14...253 E6
Hollyhouse Dr DE55...160 B6
Holly House La DE56...178 C4
Holly House Sch S41...77 A3
Hollyhurst La DE6...212 B6
Hollyhurst Row DE55...170 F6
Holly La
Alderwasley DE56...167 D4
Glossop SK13...10 C3
Tansley DE4...144 A4
Hollymoor Dr DE73...232 F2
Holly Mount 2 SK13...10 D1
Holly Rd
Kimberley NG16...195 F7
Mansfield NG19...136 F2
5 Tutbury DE13...239 C5
Uttoxeter ST14...210 B1
Hollyseat La
Blackbrook DE56...178 A5
Shottle DE56...177 F6
Holly St DE15...254 F8
Hollythorpe Cl S41...115 D8
Hollythorpe Cres S8...43 A4
Hollythorpe Rd S8...43 B4
Hollywell Ave DE5...181 B7
Hollywell Prim Sch NG16...195 F7
Hollywood Rd SK6...23 F8
Holm Ave DE21...205 B7
Holm Cl S18...56 D2
HOLME...2 F8
Holme Bank DE6...184 D7
Holmebank Cl S40...95 E4
Holmebank E S40...95 E4
Holmebank View S40...95 E4
Holmebank W S40...95 E4
Holmebrook Ct S40...95 D4
Holmebrook View S41...95 C6
Holme Cl
Hatton DE65...227 C1
Holloway DE4...156 A5
Ilkeston DE7...194 D2
Holme Croft DE7...207 E7
Holme Ct DE45...109 D5
Holme Farm Ave DE15...254 F8
Holmefield Cres DE7...209 A8
Holmefield Rd S80...82 A6
Holmegate Close DE21...219 F8
Holme Hall Cres S40...95 B5
Holme Hall Prim Sch S40...95 B5
Holme La
Bakewell DE45...109 D7
Derby DE21...220 C3
Holme Lea 2 NG10...223 B6
Holme Mdws S21...60 D5
Holme Park Ave S41...95 C7
Holme Rd
Chesterfield S41...96 A6
Matlock Bath DE4...143 B1
Holmes Cl NG16...182 A3
Holmes Ct DE11...256 B5
HOLMESDALE...57 C2
Holmesdale Cl S18...57 C3
Holmesdale Inf Sch S18...57 C2
Holmesdale Rd S18...57 C3
HOLMESFIELD...75 A8
Holmesfield Cl DE4...144 A5
HOLMESFIELD COMMON...74 E8
Holmesfield Dr
Derby DE3...217 F2
Shipley DE75...194 A8
Holmesfield Rd S18...56 B1
Holmes Rd DE72...235 D8
Holmes St
Derby DE23...219 A2
Heanor DE75...181 D2
HOLMEWOOD...116 E1
Holmewood Ave NE7...194 F5
Holmewood Bsns Pk S42...116 C2
Holmewood Dr NG16...195 B8
Holmewood Ind Est S42...132 F8
Holmewood Ind Pk S42...116 D1
Holme Woods La HD9...2 F6
Holmfield
Buxton SK17...84 E6
Derby DE23...231 E7
HOLMGATE...130 E4
Holmgate Prim Sch S45...131 A4
Holmgate Rd
Clay Cross S45...131 A4
Clay Cross S45...131 C3
Holm La DE55...158 A4
Holmley Bank S18...57 A3
HOLMLEY COMMON...57 A3
Holmley La S18...57 A3
Holmoak Cl DE21...206 B3
Holmshaw Dr S13...44 E8
Holmshaw Gr S13...44 E8
Holmwood Terr 2 SK17...85 C8
Holroyd Circle NG16...182 F7
Holt Ave DE24...233 C6
Holt Croft Cl DE72...235 E7
Holt Dr DE4...142 F7
Holt La
Lea DE4...156 B7
Matlock DE4...143 B5
Holtlands Dr DE24...232 F5
Holt Rd DE4...127 F1
Holt's La
Tutbury DE13...239 B6
Tutbury DE13...239 C6
Holt Way DE76...233 C3
Holyhead Dr DE21...206 B3
Holymoor Rd S42...113 E8
HOLYMOORSIDE...113 D8
Holyoake Ave S13...44 E8
Holyoake Dr NG10...236 F7
Holyrood Cl DE21...221 A5
Holyrood Ho DE24...219 D1
Holy Rosary RC Prim Sch DE15...248 A3
Holywell DE45...109 D4
Holywell La DE45...125 B5
Holywell Rd DE7...194 C3
Holywell St S41...266 B3
Homecroft Dr NG16...171 E7
Home Farm Cl DE72...221 C5
Home Farm Cotts SK17...105 C2
Home Farm Courtyard DE74...246 C3
Home Farm Ct
Castle Gresley DE11...255 D1
Selston NG16...171 C6
Home Farm Dr
Derby DE22...205 A4
Foston DE65...226 D4
Home Farm Ho DE15...249 A3
Home Farm Park Homes DE13...240 A5
Homefields Prim Sch DE73...232 E1
Home La DE55...145 C2
Homemoss Ho SK17...85 A8
Homeport Mews S41...266 B4
Homer Dr SK6...23 B8
Homerton Vale DE3...217 F3
Homestead NG16...182 A4
Homestead Rd SK12...32 C6
Homestead Way SK23...47 C5
Honeycroft Cl DE56...179 B2
Honeycroft Ct DE55...160 B4
Honeyfield Dr DE5...180 F8
Honey Pot Cl 4 NG10...236 F8
Honeysuckle Avenue DE13...239 C5
Honeysuckle Cl 1 DE11...256 A6
Honeysuckle Dr DE55...160 B7
Honeysuckle Pl SK13...10 C3
Honeysuckle Road S41...115 E7
Honeysuckle View DE15...255 A8
Honeywall La DE6...183 E8
Honingham Rd DE7...194 C3
Honiton Ct 11 S41...95 F8
Hoodcroft La S43...80 A4
Hook La ST14...210 B6
Hoole St S41...115 D8
Hooley Cl NG10...236 B6
Hooley St NG16...171 F6
Hoon La DE65...228 A3
Hoon Rd DE65...239 D8
Hoonwell La DE6...175 F5
HOPE
Alstonefield...149 D3
Castleton...38 F4
Hope Ave DE3...217 D2
HOPEDALE...149 C2
Hopedale Head DE6...149 C2
Hopedale Rd S12...44 D4
Hopefield Ave S12...44 D4
Hope Prim Sch S33...39 A4
Hope Rd
Edale S33...29 B1
Edale S33...38 A8
Hope S33...39 D2
Hope St
Chesterfield S40...95 E3
Derby DE1...219 B4
Derby DE1...267 C2
Glossop SK13...10 E2
2 Ilkeston DE7...208 F7
Melbourne DE73...252 A7
Hope Sta S33...39 C3
Hope Terr DE4...143 B2
Hopetoun St DE23...232 A8
Hope Valley Coll S33...38 F3
Hope Way DE11...255 E1
Hopewell Rd DE4...143 C6
Hop Inge The S26...61 F5
Hopkins Ct
Eastwood NG16...182 F3
5 Holmewood DE4...116 E1
Hopkinson Cl DE55...159 C4
Hopmeadow Way DE15...248 A1
Hopping Hill DE56...190 F8
Hopping Hill Terrace E DE56...191 A7
Hopping Hill Terrace W DE56...191 A7
Hopping La DE45...125 B3
Hop Pl DE3...217 C4
HOPTON...164 F7
Hopton Cl
Derby DE21...206 A1
Ripley DE5...169 F1
Hopton Dr DE23...231 A5
Hopton La
Wirksworth DE4...154 D1
Wirksworth DE4...165 C8
Hoptonwood Cl DE4...154 D4
Hopton Wood Way SK17...85 E2
Hopwell Rd DE72...222 A2
Horace Ave NG9...223 D6
Hordern Cl SK13...10 A4
Horderns La SK23...47 B5
Horderns Park Rd SK23...47 B5
Horderns Rd SK23...47 A5
Horeston Cotts DE7...192 B7
Hornbeam Cl
Brimington S43...78 A2
Derby DE21...205 E2
Ilkeston DE7...209 B7
Hornbeam Dr S42...115 B5
Hornbeam La S42...115 B4
Hornbeams The 2 ST14...210 A1
Hornby Dr DE72...233 E3
Horncastle Rd DE21...205 D1
Horner Rd 1 S7...43 A7
Horn Hoo DE6...201 A4
Hornscroft Rd S44...99 A1
Hornsea Rd DE21...205 D1
Hornthorpe Rd S21...59 C2
Horridge St DE7...194 F4
Horse Chestnut Cl S40...266 B1
Horse Chestnut Gdns DE73...232 F3
Horsecroft Cl DE7...194 C2
Horse Croft La DE4...141 C6
Horsedale DE4...142 C1
Horse Fair Ave SK23...47 A6
Horsehead La S44...99 C2
Horse & Jockey Yd 7 DE6...173 C2
Horse Mill La SK17...87 F4
Horseshoe Ave SK17...47 F1
Horse Shoes The DE74...247 D4
Horsewood Rd S40...114 B8
HORSLEY...191 F6
Horsley CE (Controlled) Prim Sch DE21...191 F5
Horsley Cl S40...95 A5
Horsley Cres
Holbrook DE56...191 C7
Langley Mill NG16...182 A3
HORSLEYGATE...74 E6
Horsleygate La S18...74 E7
Horsleygate Rd S17, S18...74 B7
Horsley La DE21...191 E4
Horsley Rd DE21, DE56...191 F6
HORSLEY WOODHOUSE...192 D6
Horsley Woodhouse Prim Sch DE7...192 D6
Horson Moor Rd SK14...4 C1
Horton Cl
Sheffield S20...59 E7
Swanwick DE55...169 F8
Horton Dr S20...59 E7
Horton St DE23...219 C2
HORWICH END...45 D5
Horwood Ave DE23...218 D2
Hoselett Field Rd NG10...236 E5
Hoskins La DE15...248 B5
Hospital La DE3...230 B7
Houfton Cres S44...98 F3
Houfton Rd S44...98 F3
Hough Cl S40...266 B1
Houghton Ave DE7...194 C3
Houghton Cl SK22...25 C2
Houghton Ct 7 DE21...205 F2
Houldsworth Cres S44...98 F2
Houldsworth Dr S41...96 E2
Hoult St DE22...218 D4
Houndhill ST14...224 F1
Hound hill ST14...225 A1
Houndkirk Rd S11, S17...42 F2
Hounslow Rd DE22...218 B6
Housley Rd SK32...70 E5
Houston Cl DE21...220 B6
Hoveton Cl DE24...232 D3
Howard Cl
Glossop SK13...10 B2
11 Long Eaton NG10...223 E1
Howard Dr
Chesterfield S41...77 A2
North Wingfield S42...131 F5
Howards Mdw SK13...17 B7
Howard St
Derby DE23...218 F2
Glossop SK13...10 C1
Howards Way
3 Branston DE14...253 E7
3 Branston DE14...256 E7
Howarth Cl NG10...236 A7
Howden Cl
Derby DE3...217 C1
Staveley S43...78 F2
Swadlincote DE11...256 A5
Howden Rd SK22...24 C1
Howe Grove S45...131 E5
Howells Pl S43...79 B3
Howe St DE22...218 D5
Howitt Cres ST14...210 B2
Howitt Prim Com Sch DE75...181 D2
Howitt St
Heanor DE75...181 F2
Long Eaton NG10...236 E7
How La S33...38 C3
Howth Cl DE21...220 A4
Hoylake Ave S40...114 C7
Hoylake Cl NG19...136 E6
Hoylake Ct DE3...217 C3
Hoylake Dr DE3...217 C3
Hoyland Ct DE56...179 E5
Hoyle Ct DE45...109 D5
Hubert Shaw Cl DE24...232 E4
Huckerby Rd DE7...194 C2
Hucklow Ave
Chesterfield S40...266 A1
North Wingfield S42...132 A8
Staveley S43...97 D7
Hucklow Bank 36 SK13...9 D2
Hucklow Cl 35 SK13...9 D2
Hucklow Ct DE21...206 B3
Hucklow Fold 34 SK13...9 D2
Hucklow Lanes 33 SK13...9 D2
Hucknall Ave S40...95 C4
Hudson Cl S26...61 E7
Hudson Mount S44...118 B8
Hudson Pl
Darley Dale DE4...142 E8
7 Holmewood DE4...116 E1
Hudson Way DE24...219 C3
Hufton's Ct DE75...194 A7
Huftons Dr DE75...193 F7
Hufton's Dr DE75...194 A7
Hugh La S33...51 A7
Hugh St SK13...10 B1
Hulford Dr S41...76 D2
Hulland CE Prim Sch DE6...175 F3
Hulland Moss DE6...175 E1
Hulland St DE1...267 D1
Hulland View DE22...204 D1
HULLAND VILLAGE...175 D2
HULLAND WARD...175 F3
Hull St DE65...228 E1
Humber Cl
Derby DE24...233 C6
9 Sheffield S2...43 C8
Humber Rd NG10...223 C1
Humber St DE65...228 C1
Humbleton Dr DE22...218 A5
Humphrey Gate SK17...88 A2
Humphrey Rd S8...56 E8
HUNDALL...77 B7
Hundall Ct 4 S40...95 D6
Hundall La
Chesterfield S41...77 A4
Hundall La *continued*
Unstone S18...77 A7
Hungerhill Cl DE21...205 D3
Hungerhill La S42, S45...113 B4
Hunger La DE6...188 E3
Hungry La
Bradwell S33...51 A6
Hathersage S32...53 B8
Hunloke Ave S40...95 E1
Hunloke Cres S40...95 E1
HUNLOKE ESTATE...115 C2
Hunloke Park Prim Sch S42...115 A4
Hunloke Rd S42...132 E8
Hunloke View S42...115 B4
Hunsdon Rd S21...59 C3
Hunstone Ave S8...57 A7
Hunt Ave DE75...181 E2
Hunter Dr DE56...191 F8
Hunter Pk S18...57 C1
Hunter Rd DE56...179 D5
Hunters Chase NG19...136 B2
Hunters Croft DE24...231 E2
Hunters Green Cl SK23...34 E1
Hunters La SK13...16 F8
Hunter's La S13...44 C6
Hunters Wlk S41...266 A3
Huntingdon Ave S44...99 B1
Huntingdon Ct DE73...252 B8
Huntingdon Dr DE74...247 A4
Huntingdon Gn DE21...219 C6
Huntingdon Rd DE15...254 D7
Huntingdon Way 1 NG9...223 F2
Huntingdon Wlk 2 NG10...223 B5
Hunt La S45...145 B8
Huntley Ave DE21...220 F5
Huntley Cl S43...97 B8
Hunts La DE12...264 E8
Huntsman Rd S43...78 F2
Huntspill Rd DE65...228 E1
Hunts Row DE55...157 E3
Hunt Way DE11...256 E4
Hurdlow Gn 10 SK13...9 D1
Hurdlow Lea 11 SK13...9 D1
Hurdlow Mews SK13...9 D1
Hurdlow Way 12 SK13...9 D1
Hurds Hollow DE4...143 A6
Hurker Rise DE4...143 C7
Hurl Dr S12...43 F5
Hurley Ct DE7...207 E8
HURL FIELD...43 E5
Hurlfield Ct S12...44 A6
Hurlfield Dr S12...43 F6
Hurlfield Rd S12...43 F5
Hurrier Pl S20...60 A6
Hurstbrook Cl SK13...10 F1
Hurst Cl SK13...10 E1
Hurstclough La S32, S33...40 D2
Hurst Cres SK13...17 E8
Hurst Ct DE12...264 F4
Hurst Dr
Burton upon Trent DE13...240 E1
Stanley DE7...207 C6
Hurst La DE55...146 A5
Hurst Lea Rd SK22...33 C7
Hurst Mills Ind Est 6 SK13...10 F1
Hurst Rd SK13...10 F1
Hurst Rise DE4...143 D5
Huss's La NG10...236 F7
Hutchings Cres S43...80 D5
Hutfall The 13 DE56...178 F4
HUTHWAITE...148 E3
Huthwaite All Saints CE (Aided) Inf Sch NG17...148 F2
Huthwaite La DE55...148 C2
Hut La
Ashover S45...129 E6
Killamarsh S21...60 F4
Hutmoor Butts SK17...107 A3
Hutton St DE24...232 E6
Huxley Cl DE23...231 F7
Hyde Bank Ct SK22...33 C7
Hyde Bank Rd SK22...33 C8
Hyde Park Rd DE22...218 A6
Hyde Rd SK14...9 A4
Hydro Cl DE45...91 F6
Hylton Cl DE14...254 A7
Hyndley Rd S44...98 F3

I

Ian Ave DE4...165 F7
Ians Way S40...95 C4
Ibbotsons Croft S32...53 A8
Ibbotsons Farm Cotts S32...53 A8
IBLE...153 E7
Ibsley Cl DE24...233 C6
Ida's Rd S21...59 D4
IDRIDGEHAY...176 F6

IDRIDGEHAY GREEN ... 176 E7
Idridgehay Sta★ DE56 ... 176 F6
Ihub DE24 ... 232 B3
Ikea Way NG16 ... 195 C7
Ilam Cl S43 ... 97 C6
Ilam Ct DE6 ... 185 D8
Ilam Moor La DE6 ... 149 D1
Ilam Rd DE6 ... 161 C2
Ilam Sq DE7 ... 194 E5
Ilford Cl DE7 ... 194 D3
Ilford Ct S43 ... 77 D4
Ilford Rd DE22 ... 218 A5
Ilford Wlk DE22 ... 218 A5
Ilfracombe Ct 1 S41 ... 95 F8
Ilion St NG19 ... 135 F2
ILKESTON ... 208 E7
Ilkeston Com Hospl DE7 ... 194 D4
Ilkeston Rd
  Heanor DE75 ... 193 F8
  Sandiacre DE7, NG10 ... 223 C8
  Smalley DE7 ... 192 F2
  Stanton-by-Dale DE7 ... 208 F3
  Stapleford NG9 ... 209 F2
  Trowell NG9 ... 209 C5
Ilkeston Stn DE7 ... 195 A2
Immaculate Conception RC Prim Sch S21 ... 60 C2
Immingham Grove S43 ... 78 D1
Imperial Ct DE22 ... 204 D5
Imperial Rd DE4 ... 143 B5
Inby Cl S42 ... 132 A7
Inchwood Cl 4 NG9 ... 223 F2
Independent Hill DE55 ... 158 F3
Industrial St 3 DE23 ... 219 A2
Infinity Park Way DE24 ... 232 C3
Infinity Pk Way
  Chellaston DE73 ... 244 E8
  Derby DE73 ... 232 D2
Infirmary Rd S41 ... 266 C4
Ingham Dr DE3 ... 230 D8
Ingham Rd NG10 ... 223 C2
Ingleborough Gdns 8 NG10 ... 236 A8
INGLEBY ... 243 F2
Ingleby Ave DE23 ... 231 F7
Ingleby Cl
  Dronfield S18 ... 56 C1
  Swadlincote DE11 ... 256 A3
Ingleby Gall★ DE73 ... 243 F3
Ingleby La
  Ingleby DE65 ... 243 F1
  Repton DE65 ... 243 B3
  Ticknall DE65 ... 250 F7
  Ticknall DE73 ... 251 A5
Ingleby Rd
  Barrow upon Trent DE73 ... 244 D3
  Long Eaton NG10 ... 235 F4
Ingle Cl DE21 ... 220 E5
Ingledew Cl 1 DE21 ... 205 F1
Inglefield Rd DE7 ... 209 A6
Ingleton Rd S41 ... 115 B7
Inglewood Ave DE3 ... 217 D4
Ingliston Cl DE24 ... 233 D6
INGMANTHORPE ... 94 C7
Inkerman Cl NE7 ... 194 E5
Inkerman Cotts S40 ... 95 C3
Inkerman Rd NG16 ... 171 F5
Inkerman St NG16 ... 171 F5
INKERSALL ... 97 D7
Inkersall Dr S20 ... 59 E8
INKERSALL GREEN ... 97 D6
Inkersall Green Rd S43 ... 97 C7
Inkersall Prim Sch S43 ... 97 C7
Inkersall Rd S43 ... 97 E7
Inn La DE22 ... 204 B7
Innovation Dr DE24 ... 232 B3
Inns La DE55 ... 157 E4
Institute La DE55 ... 159 A4
Instow Dr DE23 ... 231 D6
Intake Ind Est S44 ... 98 E3
Intake La
  Bakewell DE45 ... 109 E3
  Cromford DE4 ... 155 B6
  Holloway DE4 ... 155 E4
Intake Prim Sch S12 ... 44 C6
Intake Rd S44 ... 98 E3
Intakes La
  Hulland Ward DE56 ... 176 D1
  Hulland Ward DE56 ... 188 C7
Interchange 25 Bsns Pk NG10 ... 223 A4
Invaders Close NG10 ... 236 F8
Inveraray Cl DE24 ... 231 D3
Invernia Cl DE23 ... 231 E5
Iona Cl
  Derby DE24 ... 231 E4
  Tibshelf DE55 ... 147 F5
Iona Dr NG9 ... 209 D2
Ionian Dr DE24 ... 219 E1
iPro Stad (Derby County FC)★ DE24 ... 219 E3
Ireland Cl S43 ... 78 F1
Ireland Ind Est S43 ... 78 F1
Ireland St S43 ... 78 F2
Ireland Trad Est S43 ... 78 F1
Ireton Cl DE56 ... 179 E3
Ireton Ct DE6 ... 165 B1
IRETON WOOD ... 176 D4
Iris Cres DE3 ... 217 C5
Iron Cliff Rd S44 ... 98 F3
Irongate S40 ... 266 B3
Iron Gate DE1 ... 267 B3
Ironside Cl S14 ... 43 D3
Ironside Pl S14 ... 43 E3
Ironside Rd S14 ... 43 E3
Ironside Wlk S14 ... 43 D2
Ironstone La DE15 ... 255 C4
IRONVILLE ... 170 E4
Ironville & Codnor Park Prim Sch NG16 ... 170 F4
Ironwalls La DE13 ... 239 C5
Irvine Cl DE24 ... 231 D3
Irving Pl DE24 ... 232 F7
Isaac Grove LE66 ... 258 B1
Isaac's La NG9 ... 223 D7
Isis Way DE65 ... 228 F1
Isla Cl DE3 ... 217 C1
Island Cl DE11 ... 262 C8
Island The
  Castleton S33 ... 38 B2
  Eastwood NG16 ... 182 F1
Islay Cl NG9 ... 209 D3
Islay Rd DE24 ... 231 E4
Isleworth Dr DE22 ... 217 F6
Islington La
  Elton DE4 ... 140 F6
  Winster DE4 ... 141 A5
Ismay Rd DE21 ... 219 F6
Ivan Brook Cl 4 S18 ... 56 C1
Ivanhoe Cl S42 ... 115 D1
Ivanhoe Ct 3 S41 ... 96 A6
Ivanhoe Ind Est LE65 ... 257 F1
Ivanhoe Pk Way LE65 ... 258 A1
Iveagh Wlk DE55 ... 170 E5
Ivel Cres S81 ... 63 F8
Ivonbrook Cl DE4 ... 142 B8
Ivybridge Cl DE21 ... 206 C3
Ivy Cl
  Chesterfield S41 ... 77 A2
  Donisthorpe DE12 ... 262 E1
  Willington DE65 ... 242 A5
Ivycroft SK13 ... 9 E4
Ivy Ct
  Derby DE3 ... 217 D1
  Egginton DE65 ... 241 A5
  Hilton DE65 ... 228 D1
  Sheffield S8 ... 43 C2
Ivy Farm Cl S43 ... 80 E3
Ivy Gr DE5 ... 169 D1
Ivy House DE23 ... 231 B7
Ivy La
  Eastwood NG16 ... 182 E2
  Elton DE4 ... 140 E6
Ivyleaf Way DE23 ... 231 B6
Ivy Lodge Cl DE15 ... 254 E7
Ivy Side Cl S21 ... 60 D6
Ivy Side Gdns S21 ... 60 D6
Ivy Spring Cl S42 ... 115 B4
Ivy Spring Close S42 ... 115 B4
Ivy Sq DE23 ... 219 C2
Ivywood Gdns S44 ... 98 A5

J

Jackass La DE56 ... 167 B4
Jackdaw Cl DE22 ... 218 D5
Jacklin Cl DE14 ... 254 A6
JACKSDALE ... 171 B4
Jacksdale Cl DE22 ... 204 D1
Jacksdale Prim Sch NG16 ... 171 B3
Jack's La ST14 ... 224 E2
Jackson Ave
  Derby DE3 ... 218 A2
  Ilkeston DE7 ... 208 E8
  Sandiacre NG10 ... 223 A6
  Tupton S42 ... 131 C8
  Whitwell S43 ... 81 F5
Jackson Cl DE73 ... 245 A1
Jackson Rd
  Clay Cross S45 ... 131 E3
  Matlock DE4 ... 143 B6
Jacksons Edge Rd SK12 ... 32 B6
Jacksons La
  Belper DE56 ... 190 E7
  Etwall DE65 ... 229 C2
Jackson's La
  Heage DE56 ... 179 D7
  Ripley DE5 ... 169 A8
Jacksons Ley DE4 ... 154 E3
Jackson St
  Derby DE22 ... 218 E4
  Glossop SK13 ... 17 C7
  Glossop, Padfield SK13 ... 10 C5
  Mottram in Longdendale SK14 ... 9 A3
Jackson Tor Rd DE4 ... 143 B6
Jackys La S26 ... 61 E6
Jacobean Ct DE15 ... 248 C4
Jacobite Cl 2 DE75 ... 193 C8
Jacques Orch DE55 ... 160 B6
Jade Cl 3 DE11 ... 255 F4
Jaeger Cl DE56 ... 179 A4
Jaggers La DE4 ... 128 E5
Jagger's La S32 ... 52 E8
Jago Ave S43 ... 81 A4
James Andrew Cl S8 ... 56 F7
James Andrew Cres S8 ... 56 E7
James Andrew Croft S8 ... 56 F7
James Ave DE55 ... 170 D7
James Brindley Way
  Burton upon Trent DE13 ... 240 F1
  3 Stretton DE13 ... 240 F1
James Cl DE1 ... 218 E5
James Clarke Rd DE65 ... 242 B6
James's La DE6 ... 215 C1
James's La DE65 ... 215 C1
James St
  Chesterfield S41 ... 96 A6
  7 Glossop SK13 ... 17 C8
  Kimberley NG16 ... 195 F6
  Somercotes DE55 ... 170 C7
  Swadlincote DE11 ... 256 D5
James Walton Ct S20 ... 59 F7
James Walton Dr S20 ... 59 F7
James Walton Pl S20 ... 59 F7
James Walton View S20 ... 59 F7
Jane La SK23 ... 34 B1
Jankyns Croft SK12 ... 32 E5
Jap La DE45 ... 110 E8
Jardine Ct DE72 ... 235 B7
Jardines La ST14 ... 196 D4
Jarnett The SK17 ... 107 B8
Jarvey's La DE22 ... 217 E8
Jarvis Ct DE24 ... 231 E2
Jarvis Rd DE24 ... 231 E2
Jasmin Cl NG20 ... 119 D6
Jasmine Cl
  Burton upon Trent DE15 ... 255 A8
  Derby DE21 ... 220 B5
  Swanwick DE55 ... 169 F7
Jasmine Ct DE75 ... 182 B1
Jasmine Dr DE55 ... 148 B7
Jasper Ave S40 ... 115 E7
Jaspers La DE4 ... 153 A1
Jaunty Ave S12 ... 44 C4
Jaunty Cl S12 ... 44 B3
Jaunty Cres S12 ... 44 C4
Jaunty Dr S12 ... 44 B3
Jaunty La S12 ... 44 B4
Jaunty Mount S12 ... 44 C3
Jaunty Pl S12 ... 44 B3
Jaunty Rd S12 ... 44 C3
Jaunty View S12 ... 44 C3
Jaunty Way S12 ... 44 B4
Java Ct DE24 ... 219 E2
Jawbone La DE73 ... 252 C8
Jaw Bones Hill S40 ... 115 A8
Jay Ct DE22 ... 218 D5
JCB Acad The ST14 ... 197 A3
Jebb Gdns S40 ... 95 C2
Jebb's La
  Idridgehay DE56 ... 176 F8
  Shottle DE56 ... 177 B8
Jedburgh Cl DE24 ... 231 E2
Jefferson Pl DE24 ... 232 F7
Jeffery St 6 S2 ... 43 B6
Jeffrey La S33 ... 51 A6
Jeffries Ave DE4 ... 156 F1
Jeffries Close DE7 ... 194 D4
Jeffries La DE4 ... 156 F1
Jellicoe St NG20 ... 101 A2
Jemison Cl DE23 ... 230 E7
Jenkin Cl 5 DE7 ... 194 F8
Jennison St NG19 ... 136 A1
Jenny's Ct DE56 ... 179 C5
Jephson Rd DE14 ... 254 B7
Jepson Rd S41 ... 115 C7
Jermyn Ave S12 ... 44 F4
Jermyn Cl S12 ... 44 F3
Jermyn Cres S12 ... 44 F4
Jermyn Dr S12 ... 44 F3
Jermyn Way S12 ... 44 F3
Jerram's La DE16 ... 254 E8
Jersey Rd S2 ... 43 A7
Jervis Ct DE7 ... 194 F3
Jervis Pl S43 ... 97 B6
Jesop Dr DE24 ... 231 E2
Jesses La DE56 ... 178 C7
Jessie La DE7 ... 194 E2
Jessop Ave NG16 ... 170 F4
Jessop Lodge DE5 ... 181 B7
Jessop St DE5 ... 181 B7
Jetting St
  Ashover S45 ... 129 F1
  Ashover S45 ... 130 A1
Jill Iain Ct 1 NG9 ... 223 E5
Jinny Cl DE65 ... 239 C8
Joan Ave DE75 ... 181 E2
Joan La S33 ... 40 C3
Jodrell Ave DE56 ... 179 D3
Jodrell Mdw SK23 ... 45 E8
Jodrell Rd SK23 ... 45 D8
Jodrell St SK22 ... 33 B7
Joes La SK17 ... 104 B2
John Bank La DE45 ... 108 F7
John Berrysford Cl DE21 ... 219 F5
John Dalton St SK13 ... 9 E5
John Davies Prim Sch NG17 ... 148 F4
John Davies Workshops NG17 ... 148 F3
John Eaton's Almshouses S8 ... 43 B2
John F Kennedy Gdns DE21 ... 220 C6
John Flamsteed Sch DE5 ... 180 B2
John Hett Dr DE5 ... 170 A4
John Kennedy Rd SK14 ... 9 A3
John King Inf Sch NG16 ... 160 D3
John King Workshop Mus★ NG16 ... 160 D3
John Lombe Dr DE1 ... 219 A7
Johnnygate La S18 ... 75 A4
John of Rolleston Prim Sch DE13 ... 240 B4
John O'Gaunts Way DE56 ... 179 D4
Johno Wood Cl 1 DE55 ... 158 E3
John Port Cl DE65 ... 229 C4
John Port Sch DE65 ... 229 B4
Johnson Ave DE24 ... 232 E7
Johnson Cl 5 DE74 ... 246 E3
Johnson Dr DE75 ... 181 F2
Johnson La
  Idridgehay DE56 ... 176 E7
  Monyash DE45 ... 107 F6
Johnson Rd ST14 ... 210 B1
Johnson St SK23 ... 45 E8
Johnson Way SK23 ... 47 D6
John St
  Alfreton DE55 ... 159 A4
  Brimington S43 ... 96 E8
  Chesterfield S40 ... 95 E3
  Clay Cross S45 ... 131 D4
  Clowne S43 ... 80 D3
  Compstall SK6 ... 15 B3
  Creswell S80 ... 81 E1
  Derby DE1 ... 267 C2
  Eckington S21 ... 59 D3
  Glossop SK13 ... 17 C8
  Heanor DE75 ... 181 D2
  Ilkeston DE7 ... 194 F1
  Marple SK6 ... 23 A5
  Matlock DE4 ... 143 B6
  North Wingfield S42 ... 131 F7
  Somercotes DE55 ... 170 C8
  Swadlincote DE11 ... 255 E6
  Swadlincote, Albert Village DE11 ... 256 C2
  Swadlincote, Lower Medway DE11 ... 256 C5
Johnstone Cl S40 ... 266 A1
John Taylor Free Sch DE13 ... 256 B8
John Turner Rd DE4 ... 127 C3
John Twells Way DE5 ... 170 A4
John Walton Cl SK13 ... 16 C7
Jolly La DE6 ... 175 A7
Jones St SK13 ... 10 A5
Jordan Ave DE13 ... 240 F2
Jordan St SK13 ... 10 E1
JORDANTHORPE ... 57 B7
Jordanthorpe Ctr S8 ... 57 B6
Jordanthorpe Gn S8 ... 57 C6
Jordanthorpe Parkway S8 ... 57 C6
Jordanthorpe View S8 ... 57 C7
Joseph Fletcher Dr S42 ... 114 F2
Joseph Roe Dr DE4 ... 157 A1
Joseph St
  Belper DE56 ... 178 F4
  Derby DE23 ... 219 A1
  Eckington S21 ... 59 D3
  Marple SK6 ... 23 A6
Joseph Stone Court S20 ... 59 D7
Joseph Wright Terr DE1 ... 267 B4
Joshua Bsns Pk NG16 ... 182 C3
Joules Croft DE4 ... 140 E7
Joyce Ave NG9 ... 223 F3
Jubalton Cl DE24 ... 232 E6
JUBILEE ... 171 B6
Jubilee Ave DE5 ... 169 C1
Jubilee Bsns Pk DE21 ... 267 C4
Jubilee Cl DE73 ... 252 B7
Jubilee Cotts S44 ... 97 A1
Jubilee Cres
  Clowne S43 ... 81 A4
  Killamarsh S21 ... 60 E7
  Whitwell S80 ... 81 E5
Jubilee Ct
  Belper DE56 ... 179 A2
  Burton upon Trent DE16 ... 254 C8
  Pinxton NG16 ... 160 D3
  Shirebrook NG20 ... 119 F2
  West Hallam DE7 ... 207 D8
  Wirksworth DE4 ... 165 E7
Jubilee Gdns
  New Mills SK22 ... 33 C7
  Whitwell S80 ... 81 F5
Jubilee Parkway DE21 ... 267 C4
Jubilee Pk DE11 ... 256 F4
Jubilee Pl S80 ... 81 F5
Jubilee Rd
  Chapel-en-le-Frith SK23 ... 47 B5
  Derby DE24 ... 232 F4
  Whitwell S80 ... 81 F5
Jubilee Rise DE15 ... 248 C3
Jubilee Sq DE6 ... 184 D7
Jubilee St
  Kimberley NG16 ... 195 E7
  New Mills SK22 ... 33 C7
Jubilee Terr DE12 ... 262 E1
Judd Cl S20 ... 60 A6
Judson Ave NG9 ... 223 F6
Judy Hill DE4 ... 127 F1
Julia Cres DE55 ... 146 F3
Julian Cl DE7 ... 209 B6
Julie Ave DE75 ... 182 B1
Julius Cl NG16 ... 182 B4
Jumble Rd S17 ... 42 F1
Junction Rd NG10 ... 237 A6
Junction St DE1 ... 218 E4
Juniper Cl S43 ... 78 A2
Juniper Ct NG16 ... 195 C8
Juniper Rise S21 ... 60 C5
Jura Ave DE5 ... 169 D2
Jury St DE1 ... 267 A3

K

Kariba Cl
  Chesterfield S40 ... 96 B3
  Chesterfield S41 ... 266 C3
Katherine Dr NG9 ... 223 F4
Katrine Wlk DE24 ... 231 E5
Kay Dr DE11 ... 255 F5
Kayes Ct 2 NG9 ... 223 D7
Kean Pl DE24 ... 232 F7
Kearsley Rd S2 ... 43 A8
Keats Ave DE23 ... 218 A1
Keats Cl NG10 ... 236 B5
Keats Dr DE11 ... 256 C6
Keats Rd
  Chesterfield S41 ... 95 F8
  Stonebroom DE55 ... 146 F3
Keats Way S42 ... 115 E4
Keats Wlk DE55 ... 146 F3
Keble Cl
  Burton upon Trent DE15 ... 248 C2
  Derby DE1 ... 267 C1
Kedelston st DE1 ... 267 A4
KEDLESTON 203 C7
  DE22 ... 203 F7
Kedleston DE22 ... 204 A7
Kedleston Cl
  4 Belper DE56 ... 178 F3
  Burton upon Trent DE13 ... 240 C1
  Chesterfield S41 ... 95 C6
  Derby DE22 ... 204 D1
  Long Eaton NG10 ... 236 A5
  Ripley DE5 ... 169 C3
Kedleston Ct
  3 Derby DE22 ... 204 D2
  4 Staveley S43 ... 78 E2
  Tibshelf DE55 ... 148 B6
Kedleston Dr
  Heanor DE75 ... 181 C2
  Ilkeston DE7 ... 194 D3
Kedlestone Cl NG17 ... 148 F2
Kedleston Gdns DE1 ... 267 A4
Kedleston Hall★ DE22 ... 203 E5
Kedleston Old Rd DE22 ... 218 D8
Kedleston Rd
  Buxton SK17 ... 85 C7
  Derby DE22 ... 218 E7
  Quarndon DE22 ... 204 B5
  Weston Underwood DE2 ... 189 B1
  Weston Underwood DE22 ... 203 E8
Kedleston St DE1 ... 267 A4
Keeble Cl DE75 ... 193 E8
Keele Dr 9 DE11 ... 255 E1
Keeling La DE4 ... 126 B1
Keeling Terr DE4 ... 126 B1
Keepers Corner Rd NG19 ... 118 E1
Keepers Croft 5 DE6 ... 185 C8
Keepers La S18 ... 75 E3
Kegworth Ave DE23 ... 231 C6
Kegworth Rd NG11 ... 237 F1
Keilder Ct S40 ... 95 D1
Keith Willshee Way DE11 ... 255 D3
Kelburn Ave S40 ... 95 C1
Keldeston Cl S41 ... 95 C6
Keldholme La DE24 ... 233 D6
Kelgate S20 ... 59 D6
Kelhams Court DE74 ... 247 D4
Kelham Way NG16 ... 182 E3
Kelmoor Rd DE24 ... 233 B7
Kelsons Ave SK17 ... 85 D5
Kelso Wlk DE24 ... 231 E2
KELSTEDGE ... 129 D4
Kelstedge La S45 ... 129 D5
Kelvedon Dr DE23 ... 231 A6
Kelvin Cl NG9 ... 223 C5
Kemble Pl DE24 ... 232 F7
Kemp Cl S21 ... 60 C6
Kemp Rd SK6 ... 23 C7
Kempton Cl NG16 ... 195 E7
Kempton Park Rd DE24 ... 232 D8
Kempton Rd DE15 ... 248 A3
Kendal Cl SK17 ... 85 C4
Kendal Dr S18 ... 56 E1
Kendal Rd S41 ... 95 E8
Kendal Wlk 1 DE21 ... 205 D1
Kendon Ave DE23 ... 231 E6
Kendray Cl DE56 ... 179 D5
Kendricks Cl DE11 ... 257 A7
Kenilworth Ave DE23 ... 231 F8
Kenilworth Ct 4 S41 ... 96 A6
Kenilworth Dr DE7 ... 208 D5
Kenilworth Rd DE5 ... 169 C1
Kenmere Cl S45 ... 131 D2
Kennack Cl DE55 ... 160 C6
Kennedy Ave
  Long Eaton NG10 ... 236 C5
  Mansfield Woodhouse NG19 ... 136 D4
Kennedy Cl DE21 ... 220 A7
Kennedy Ct 1 DE4 ... 116 E1
Kennedy Dr NG9 ... 209 E1
Kennet Paddock NG19 ... 136 D3
Kennett Gr SK17 ... 84 E6
Kennet Vale S40 ... 95 D5
Kenninghall Cl S2 ... 43 D7
Kenninghall Dr S2 ... 43 D7
Kenninghall Rd S2 ... 43 D7
Kenninghall View S2 ... 43 D7
Kenning Pl S45 ... 131 C5
Kenning St S45 ... 131 C3
Kensal Rise DE22 ... 218 B6
Kensey Rd
  Derby DE3 ... 217 B1
  Derby DE3 ... 230 B8
Kensington Ave DE75 ... 181 C1
Kensington Bsns Pk DE7 ... 209 A6
Kensington Chase S10 ... 42 F8
Kensington Cl NG19 ... 136 E5
Kensington Ct S10 ... 42 F8
Kensington Dr S10 ... 42 F8
Kensington Gdns DE7 ... 208 F7
Kensington Gr SK13 ... 17 A8
Kensington Jun Acad DE7 ... 209 A7
Kensington Pk S10 ... 42 F8
Kensington Rd
  Burton upon Trent DE15 ... 248 A3
  Sandiacre NG10 ... 223 A4
Kensington St
  Derby DE1 ... 267 A3
  Ilkeston DE7 ... 208 F6
Kent Ave NG16 ... 171 B4
Kent Cl S41 ... 95 F5
Kent Grange 12 S8 ... 43 B6
Kent House Cl S12 ... 58 E8
Kentish Ct DE1 ... 219 B7
Kentmere Cl S18 ... 56 E1
Kentmere Way
  Staveley S43 ... 78 C1
  Staveley S43 ... 97 C8
Kent Rd
  Burton upon Trent DE15 ... 254 E6
  Eastwood NG16 ... 195 C8
  Glossop SK13 ... 10 D1
  Sheffield S8 ... 43 B6
Kent's Bank Rd SK17 ... 85 C6
Kent St
  Chesterfield S41 ... 115 C8
  Derby DE21 ... 219 D7
Kent Way DE11 ... 255 E2
Kenwell Dr S17 ... 56 B5
Kenyon Rd S41 ... 96 E1
Keppel Ct DE7 ... 194 F3
Kepple Gate DE5 ... 180 F8
Kernel Cl DE23 ... 231 A8
Kernel Dr NG20 ... 119 D2
Kernel Way NG20 ... 119 D2
Kerry Dr DE7 ... 192 F6
Kerry St DE21 ... 219 D7
Kerry's Yd DE56 ... 191 F8
Kershaw St SK13 ... 17 C8
Kershope Dr DE21 ... 206 B3
Kerwin Cl S17 ... 55 C8
Kerwin Dr S17 ... 55 C8
Kerwin Rd S17 ... 55 C8
Kesbrook Dr DE12 ... 262 A3
Kestrel Ave DE11 ... 256 F3
Kestrel Cl
  Bolsover S44 ... 98 F3
  Burnaston DE3 ... 230 B7
  Ilkeston DE7 ... 208 F4
  Killamarsh S21 ... 60 B7
  Marple SK6 ... 23 A3
  6 Swarkestone DE73 ... 244 E8
  Tibshelf DE55 ... 147 E5
Kestrel Ct S42 ... 116 C1
Kestrel Dr S21 ... 59 B3
Kestrel Ho DE24 ... 231 E2
Kestrel Hts NG16 ... 170 F3
Kestrel Road S42 ... 115 F1
Kestrels Croft DE24 ... 231 F3
Kestrel View SK13 ... 16 F8
Kestrel Way DE15 ... 248 D3
Keswick Ave DE23 ... 231 E6

Keswick Cl
Bolsover S44 98 F1
Ilkeston DE7 208 D5
Keswick Ct NG10 223 B2
Keswick Dr
Chesterfield S41 95 C8
Chesterfield S41 95 D8
Keswick Pl S18 56 D1
Kettlewell Cl DE24 232 E6
Ketton Ave S8 43 B3
Kevin Cl DE21 220 B8
Kew Cres
Heanor DE75 182 B1
Sheffield S12 44 A2
Kew Gdns DE22 218 B5
Keyhaven Cl DE21 219 D8
Keynsham Cl DE24 232 E8
Keys Rd DE55 159 B2
Keys St DE1 267 C4
Kibworth Cl
Chesterfield S41 115 C7
Derby DE21 220 B8
Kidd La SK17 104 B1
Kidd Rd SK13 17 E6
Kidsley Cl
7 Chesterfield S40 95 A5
Smalley DE75 193 C8
Kilbourne Ct DE56 179 D3
Kilbourne Rd DE56 179 C4
KILBURN 192 A8
Kilburn Dr DE7 194 D3
Kilburn Inf Sch
DE56 191 F8
Kilburn Jun Sch
DE56 192 A8
Kilburn La DE56 179 E3
Kilburn Rd S18 56 C1
Kilburn Toll Bar
DE56 179 F1
Kilburn Way DE11 255 F5
Kilby Ho NG10 236 E7
Kildale Gdns S20 59 D7
Kildare Rd DE21 220 B4
Kildonan Gr S12 44 C3
Kildrummy Cl DE73 232 E1
KILLAMARSH 60 E6
Killamarsh Inf Sch
S21 60 E7
Killamarsh Jun Sch
S21 60 E7
Killamarsh La S21,
S26 61 B6
Killamarsh Sp Ctr
S21 60 D7
Killingworth Ave
DE24 231 F4
Killis La
Belper DE56 179 D1
Holbrook DE56 191 D8
Kilmory Fold SK13 10 E3
Kiln Bent Rd HD9 3 A6
Kiln Cl
Dove Holes SK17 47 F2
West Hallam DE7 193 E1
Kiln Croft DE65 229 C4
Kiln Hill S18 57 C3
Kiln La
Glossop SK13 10 A5
Harpur Hill SK17 85 B2
Parwich DE6 151 D2
Kilnsey Ct DE23 230 F6
Kiln Way
Swadlincote DE11 256 D2
Swadlincote DE11 256 D3
Kilverston Rd NG10 223 A6
Kilvington Ave S13 44 B7
Kilvington Cres S13 44 B7
Kilvington Rd S13 44 B7
KIMBERLEY 195 F8
Kimberley Cl NG16 195 E6
Kimberley Dr DE15 248 C3
Kimberley Prim Sch
NG16 195 F6
Kimberley Rd DE72 221 B2
Kimbolton Way
DE24 233 D4
Kinder Ave DE11 256 A5
Kinder Cl SK13 17 A8
Kinder Cres DE56 168 B5
Kinder Dr SK6 23 A6
Kinder Gr SK17 85 A6
Kinderlee Way SK13 16 B5
Kinder Rd
Hayfield SK22 25 E2
Staveley S43 97 B6
Kinder Row SK22 25 F2
Kinder View SK22 33 C7
Kinder View Cl SK22 33 A6
Kinder Way SK17 85 E7
Kinder Wlk DE22 218 E4
King Alfred St DE22 267 A2
King Charles Ct SK13 17 D7
King Cup Cl SK13 17 E8
King Ecgbert Rd S17 55 E5
King Ecgbert Sch
S17 55 D6
King Edward Ave
SK13 10 D1
King Edward Gdns 1
NG10 223 B6
King Edward St
Ashbourne DE6 173 B1
Sandiacre NG10 223 B6
Shirebrook NG20 119 F4
1 Washgreen DE4 155 A1
Wirksworth DE4 166 A8
Kingfisher Ave
DE11 256 F3
Kingfisher Cl DE3 230 B7
Kingfisher Ct
Bolsover S44 98 F3
Ilkeston DE7 208 F4
Kingfisher Gdns
DE14 253 D7
Kingfisher Ho S41 77 B3
Kingfisher La DE65 242 A5
Kingfisher Mews
SK6 23 A6
Kingfisher Rd NG19 135 D1
Kingfisher View S43 80 E4
Kingfisher Way SK13 16 F8
Kingfisher Wlk
DE24 231 E2
King George Ave
DE7 208 E8
King George St
Wessington DE55 145 E1
Wessington DE55 157 E8
Wirksworth DE4 165 E7
Kinglas Dr DE3 217 B1
Kingsbury Cl DE15 248 A4
Kingsbury Rd DE22 218 A6
Kings Cl
Carsington DE4 164 E8
Clowne S43 80 F3
Creswell S80 81 F1
Heanor DE75 181 C1
King's Cl SK17 85 D8
Kingsclere Ave
DE21 206 B2
Kingsclere Wlk S40 114 F8
Kings Coppice S17 55 D6
Kings Croft DE22 204 F4
Kingscroft Cl S17 55 E8
Kings Ct
Derby DE1 267 B4
5 Glossop SK13 17 C8
Kingsdale Cl NG10 236 A5
Kingsdale Gr DE73 244 F8
Kings Dr
Brinsley NG16 182 E7
Derby DE3, DE23 218 B2
Kingsfield Ind Est
DE4 165 E6
Kingsfield Rd DE4 165 E7
Kingsgate S32 72 C2
Kings Gate DE74 247 F4
Kingsgate Rd DE72 245 B8
Kingshead La DE6 174 A6
Kings Head La DE6 173 F7
Kings Hill DE4 153 A2
Kings Hollow Mews
DE6 173 F7
Kingsland Cl DE21 205 F2
Kingsley Ave
Chesterfield S40 114 F8
Mansfield Woodhouse
NG19 136 D5
Kingsley Cl NG19 136 D4
Kingsley Cres
Long Eaton NG10 236 B4
Stonebroom DE55 146 F3
Kingsley Ct NG19 136 D5
Kingsley Rd DE22 204 D4
Kingsley St DE24 231 F5
Kingsmead Ave
NG9 209 D2
King's Mead Cl DE1 267 A4
King's Mead Ho 1
DE22 218 F7
Kingsmead Ind Est
DE22 218 D6
Kingsmead Sch The
DE1 267 A4
King's Mead Wlk
DE1 267 A4
Kingsmede Ave S40 95 D1
Kings Mews S21 59 E3
King's Mill La DE72 245 F5
King's Mills La DE72 245 F5
Kingsmoor Fields
SK13 10 D3
Kingsmoor Rd SK13 10 D2
Kingsmuir Rd DE3 217 C3
KING'S NEWTON 245 B1
Kings Newton La
DE73 244 F1
Kings Rd
Sandiacre NG10 223 B6
Swadlincote DE11 256 B6
King's Rd SK17 85 D8
King St
Alfreton DE55 158 F4
Ashbourne DE6 173 C2
Bakewell DE45 109 D5
Belper DE56 178 F3
Brimington S43 77 F1
Broadbottom SK14 16 A8
Burton upon Trent
DE14 254 C8
Clay Cross S45 131 C3
Clowne S43 80 E3
Creswell S80 81 F1
Creswell, Hodthorpe
S80 82 C6
Derby DE1 267 B4
Duffield DE56 190 E4
Eastwood NG16 182 F2
Glossop SK13 17 C8
Hollingworth SK14 9 D5
Ilkeston DE7 194 F1
Long Eaton NG10 236 D8
Mansfield Woodhouse
NG19 136 D2
Middleton DE4 154 D5
Pinxton NG16 160 D3
King St *continued*
Shirebrook NG20 120 D5
South Normanton
DE55 159 F5
Tibshelf DE55 148 A7
Youlgreave DE45 125 B5
KING STERNDALE 86 C5
Kingsthorpe Cl 6
NG19 136 E1
Kingston Ave DE7 209 A4
Kingston Ct
3 Barrow Hill S43 78 B3
West Hallam DE7 207 D8
Kingston Rd DE15 248 C2
Kingston St DE1 218 F7
King Street N S41 96 A7
King Street S S40 115 A7
Kingsway
Burton upon Trent
DE14 254 B8
Derby DE22 218 B5
Heanor DE75 181 D2
Ilkeston DE7 209 A5
Kings Way S80 82 C6
Kingsway Bvd DE22 218 B4
Kingsway Cres
DE56 192 A8
Kingsway Hospital
DE3 218 B4
Kingsway Ind Pk
DE22 218 C5
Kingsway Park Cl
DE22 218 C5
Kingsway Ret Pk
DE22 218 C5
Kingswood Ave
DE56 179 C6
Kingswood Cl
Chesterfield S41 95 C8
Chesterfield S41 95 D8
Kingswood Pl DE23 218 B2
King William Ctr 2
NG16 170 F4
King William St
NG16 170 F4
Kinnaird Gdns SK17 85 A7
Kinross Ave DE21 219 C8
Kintyre Dr DE24 231 D3
Kinver Cl DE6 184 C8
Kinver Rd DE15 248 A4
Kipling Cl S18 76 C8
Kipling Dr DE3 217 D1
Kipling Rd S41 95 F8
Kiran View DE21 206 C3
Kirby Cl S41 115 C7
Kirby La DE4 142 B7
Kirkby Ave
Ilkeston DE7 208 F6
Sheffield S12 44 A4
Kirkby Dr S12 44 A4
Kirkby La NG16 160 F3
Kirkby Rd S12 44 A4
Kirkby View S12 44 A4
Kirkby Way S12 44 A3
Kirk Cl DE5 180 C8
Kirkcroft Ave S21 60 D7
Kirkcroft Dr S21 60 D6
Kirkcroft La S21 60 D6
Kirk Dale Ave DE21 220 F3
Kirkdale Cl S40 115 B8
Kirkdale Gdns NG10 236 B6
Kirkdale Rd NG10 236 B6
Kirkewhite Ave
NG10 236 D7
Kirkewhite Ho
NG10 236 D7
Kirkfield Dr DE72 235 D8
KIRK HALLAM 208 D6
Kirk Hallam Com Acad
DE7 208 D6
Kirk Hallam Pupil
Referral Unit DE7 208 E5
Kirkham Cl 5 DE75 181 D1
Kirkham Dr NG9 223 F2
Kirkham La DE56 168 B7
KIRK IRETON 165 C1
Kirk Ireton CE Prim Sch
DE6 165 B1
Kirkistown Cl DE24 233 C6
Kirkland Cl DE74 247 A3
Kirkland Way
12 Derby DE24 231 D3
Swadlincote DE11 256 B1
KIRK LANGLEY 202 F2
Kirk Langley CE Prim
Sch DE6 202 F2
Kirkley Dr DE75 181 C1
Kirk Leys Avenue N
DE21 220 E4
Kirk Leys Avenue S
DE21 220 E4
Kirkman Rd DE75 181 C4
Kirk's La DE56 179 B3
Kirk St DE1 219 B8
KIRKSTEAD 160 D3
Kirkstead Cl
Derby DE21 206 B1
Pinxton NG16 160 D3
Kirkstead Jun Sch
NG16 160 D3
Kirkstead Rd NG16 160 D3
Kirkstone Ave DE75 182 B1
Kirkstone Ct NG10 223 B2
Kirkstone Rd
Buxton SK17 85 D3
Chesterfield S41 95 D8
Kirton Ave NG10 236 D7
Kishfield La SK23 45 A6
Kissingate L Ctr
NG20 119 E4
Kitchener Ave DE23 231 F7
Kitchener Terr
NG20 101 A2
Kitchen Wood La
S18 75 C8
Kitson Ave NG16 171 C4
Kiwi Dr DE24 232 F7
Knabb Rd DE4 127 F3
Knabhall La DE4 144 C5
Knapp Ave NG16 182 F1
Knarr Rd SK17 102 C5
Knifesmithgate S40 266 B3
Knife & Steel Ct
DE7 192 C7
Knighton Cl S41 115 B7
Knighton Ct S42 131 E6
Knighton St S42 131 E6
Knightsbridge DE22 218 A6
Knights Cl
Beeston NG9 223 F2
Derby DE24 231 E2
Knights Ct DE13 240 E2
Knight's La DE15 249 B5
Knights Pl DE15 248 D2
Knights Rd
Chellaston DE73 244 E8
Mansfield NG19 135 D1
Knightsyard Ct
NG10 236 C5
Knightwake Rd SK22 33 A8
Knightwood DE12 260 D5
Knitters Road DE55 160 C6
KNIVETON 163 B1
Kniveton CE Prim Sch
DE6 163 C1
Kniveton Close
DE22 218 D6
Kniveton La DE6 174 C4
Kniveton Pk DE7 208 C7
Knob Fields DE11 261 E8
Knob La DE4 166 D5
Knoll Cl DE23 231 A8
Knoll St SK22 33 B8
Knoll The
Chesterfield S40 94 F2
Dronfield S18 57 D3
Shirebrook NG20 119 D3
Swadlincote DE11 256 B6
Tansley DE4 144 A5
KNOTBURY 102 F5
Knotbury Edge La
SK17 102 F5
Knotcross Rd S45 145 B6
Knowl Ave DE56 178 E5
Knowle Ave SK23 47 B5
Knowle Gn S17 55 C7
Knowle Rd SK6 23 C6
Knowles Cl SK17 85 E8
Knowles Cres SK17 85 E8
Knowles Farm Ct 11
DE11 256 E1
Knowles Hill DE13 240 B3
Knowles Ind Est
SK23 33 D3
Knowleston Pl DE4 143 C4
Knowles View
DE11 256 D4
Knowle Top S20 59 E7
Knowsley Hill SK17 121 F4
Knutsford Gn DE21 205 D2
Kraft Gdns DE21 220 B5
Kye La S26 61 E6
Kyle Cl S21 60 B1
Kyle Gr DE21 206 B3
Kyle Rd DE65 240 D8
Kynance Cl
Derby DE24 233 C5
South Normanton
DE55 160 C6
Kynnersley Croft
ST14 210 B1
Kytes La DE7 192 F3
Kyte's La DE7 193 A3

L

Laban Dr DE3 217 B2
Laburnum Ave
NG20 119 E5
Laburnum Cl
Bolsover S44 99 C1
Creswell S80 81 F1
Darley Dale DE4 127 B3
Sandiacre NG10 223 B7
South Normanton
DE55 160 B7
Laburnum Cres
Derby DE22 204 D4
Swanwick DE55 170 A8
Laburnum Ct S44 97 A3
Laburnum Gr
Derby DE22 218 B5
Killamarsh S21 60 C5
Mansfield Woodhouse
NG19 136 A4
Laburnum Rd
Burton upon Trent
DE15 254 F6
Swadlincote DE11 256 A6
Laburnum St
Brimington S43 78 B1
Hollingwood S43 97 B8
Laburnum Way
DE65 229 C3
Laceby Ct NG19 136 E4
Lace Makers Cl
DE72 221 D1
Lacey Cl DE7 194 C3
Lacey Fields Rd
DE75 182 B1
Ladbroke Gdns
DE22 217 F6
Ladies Spring Ct S17 56 A7
Ladies Spring Dr S17 56 A7
Ladies Spring Gr S17 56 A7
Ladle End La DE12 253 D1
LADMANLOW 84 E4
Ladybank Rd
Derby DE3 217 C2
Sheffield S20 59 D6
Lady Bank View S21 59 D4
Ladybower Cl DE11 256 A2
Ladybower Ct
Glossop SK13 10 C1
4 Sheffield S17 56 A5
Ladybower Dr S32 53 A7
Ladybower La S43 97 D8
Ladybower Rd DE21 220 F4
Ladybower Way
DE65 240 E8
Ladycroft SK17 66 C1
Ladycroft Paddock
DE22 204 E4
Ladycross Inf Sch 3
NG10 223 B6
Lady Field Rd S80 62 D8
Ladyfields DE11 256 D6
Ladyfields Way
DE11 255 F6
Ladyflatts Rd DE4 165 E7
Ladygrove
Bullbridge DE56 168 D5
Sawmills DE56 168 D5
Ladygrove Cotts
DE23 219 B3
Ladygrove Rd DE4 127 E2
Lady Hole La DE6 186 B7
Lady Ida's Dr
Eckington S21 59 C4
Sheffield S20, S21 59 C5
Ladylea Rd NG10 236 A4
Lady Lea Rd DE21,
DE7 192 A6
Lady Ley Hill DE21 192 A6
Lady Manners Sch
DE45 109 C4
Lady Mantle Cl
DE73 232 E2
Lady Meadow Cl
ST14 196 E5
Lady Meadow La
ST14 196 E5
Ladypit Rd SK23 33 E4
Ladysmith Rd DE72 221 B2
Ladythorn Ave SK6 23 A5
Ladywell Cl DE13 240 E1
Ladywell Ct DE56 179 A3
Ladywood Ave DE56 179 B5
Ladywood Dr S41 95 C7
Ladywood Prim Sch
DE7 208 D5
Ladywood Rd DE7 208 C5
Lake Ave DE75 181 C4
Lake Dr
Derby DE23 231 F8
Doveridge DE6 211 B1
Lake Gdns DE75 181 C4
Lake Lands S42 114 F2
Lakeside
12 Ashbourne DE6 173 C2
Bakewell DE45 109 B7
Wingerworth S42 114 F2
Lake Side
Doveridge DE6 211 A1
Glossop SK13 10 A6
Lakeside Bsns Ctr
DE75 194 A6
Lakeside Cl S41 77 C4
Lakeside Community
Prim Sch 219 F1
Lakeside Com Prim Sch
DE24 219 E2
Lakeside Cres NG10 236 D5
Lakeside Dr DE23 231 A7
Lakeside Inf Sch
NG10 236 C5
Lakes Rd SK6 23 B6
Lake View SK23 33 D4
Lake View Ave S40 95 C5
Lakin Cl 1 DE11 256 B3
Lamb Cres DE5 169 F1
Lambcroft Rd NG16 160 D3
Lambe Ct DE23 267 C1
Lambersitch Dr
DE12 262 B2
Lambeth Cl DE3 217 F5
Lambgates SK13 10 A5
Lambgates La SK13 10 A5
Lamb Hill Cl S13 44 D7
LAMBHOUSE 177 E7
Lambhouse La
DE56 177 E5
Lambley Dr DE22 204 C2
Lambourn Ct DE22 205 A3
Lambourn Dr DE22 205 B4
Lambourne Ave
DE6 185 D8
Lambpart La SK17/
S33 50 D5
Lambrook Cl DE3 217 C2
Lambton Cl DE7 194 E3
Lampad Cl 4 DE73 252 A8
Lampeter Cl DE21 206 B2
Lamplight Way
DE11 255 E2
Lanark St DE21 219 E7
Lancaster Ave
Sandiacre NG10 223 A4
Stapleford NG9 223 E7
Lancaster Dr
Hilton DE65 228 E2
Tutbury DE13 239 B5
Lancaster Rd S41 95 E8
Lancaster Rise
DE56 179 A6
Lancaster St S44 117 F1
Lancaster Wlk DE21 221 A6
Lancelot Cl S40 114 D8
Lancelot Dr DE13 240 E2
Lancelot Way NG19 135 D1
Lancing Rd S2 43 A8
Landau Forte Coll
DE1 267 C4
Lander La DE56 179 A4
Landmere DE24 231 E3
Landmere Cl DE7 194 C3
Landon Cl S40 114 B7
Landsdowne Ave S41 95 E6
Landsdown Gr
NG10 223 F1
Landseer Cl
4 Dronfield S18 56 E1
Sheffield S14 43 D2
Landseer Dr
Marple SK6 23 B7
Sheffield S14 43 E2
Landseer Pl S14 43 E2
Landseer Wlk S14 43 E2
LANE 2 E8
LANE ENDS
Disley 32 E4
Marple 15 D1
Sutton on the Hill 215 A2
LANE HEAD 69 E5
Lane Head
Longnor SK17 121 B7
Stoney Middleton S32 71 C3
Tideswell SK17 69 D5
Lane Head Gn S33 37 C7
Lanehead Rd
Birch Vale SK22 25 B7
Horwich End SK23 45 C5
Lane Head Rd S17 55 C4
Lanesend Cotts SK23 46 A8
Laneside Ave NG9 223 E2
Laneside Cl SK23 47 A5
Laneside Rd
New Mills SK22 33 E7
New Mills, Rowarth
SK22 24 E6
Lanes The DE4 155 A3
Lane The
Awsworth NG16 195 C4
Brimington S43 77 F1
Ripley DE5 169 C2
Spinkhill S21 60 D1
Stanton in Peak DE4 126 C5
Laneward Cl DE7 194 D4
Langdale Cl S40 94 F5
Langdale Dr
Derby DE21 205 D1
Dronfield S18 57 A3
Long Eaton NG10 236 A6
Langdale Sq S43 96 D8
Langdon Cl 3
NG10 223 A1
Langen Ct NG10 236 E6
Langer Cl DE14 254 B6
Langerfield Ave
S40 115 A7
Langer La
Wingerworth S40,
S42 114 E5
Wingerworth S42 114 E3
Langford Croft S40 266 B1
Langford Rd DE3 217 D3
Langham Park Ind Est
DE55 160 C7
Langhurst Ct S40 95 D4
Langhurst Rd S40 95 D4
LANGLEY 182 B1
Langley Ave
Ilkeston DE7 194 D5
Somercotes DE55 170 C8
Langley Bridge Ind Est
NG16 182 C3
Langley Bsns Pk
NG16 182 B2
Langley Cl
3 Chesterfield S40 95 A5
Mansfield NG19 135 E1
Langley Close DE24 233 D4
LANGLEY
COMMON 217 B8
Langley Ct SK13 10 A5
Langley Dr
Derby DE3 217 D6
Glossop SK13 17 F8
LANGLEY GREEN 202 D2
Langley Inf Sch
DE75 182 A1
LANGLEY MILL 182 B3
Langley Mill Acad
NG16 182 A4
Langley Mill CE Inf Sch
NG16 182 B3
Langley Mill Sta
NG16 182 B3

Langley Pk NG16 182 B3
Langley Rd DE21 220 E3
Langley St DE22 218 D6
Lang Rd DE24 232 F6
Langsett Ave 13 SK13 9 D1
Langsett Dr DE73 233 A2
Langsett Gn 15 SK13 9 D1
Langsett Gr 14 SK13 9 D1
Langsett La SK13 9 D2
Langsett Lea 25 SK13 9 D1
Langsett Terr 24 SK13 9 D1
Langstone Ave S44 99 C1
Langton Hollow
NG16 171 D6
Langton The 4
DE22 218 E5
Langtree Ave S41 77 A1
LANGWITH 119 F8
Langwith Bassett Comm Prim Sch NG20 119 E7
Langwith Cl
Derby DE3 217 F2
Ilkeston NE7 194 F5
Langwith Dr NG20 100 F1
LANGWITH JUNCTION 119 D6
Langwith Lodge Dr NG20 101 B2
Langwith Maltings NG20 119 F8
Langwith Rd
Bolsover S44 118 C8
Cuckney NG20 101 E1
Scarcliffe S44 118 F7
Shirebrook NG20 119 F5
Langwith-Whaley Thorns Sta NG20 100 F2
Lansbury Ave
Mastin Moor S43 79 B4
Pilsley S45 132 C1
Lansbury Ct S21 59 D3
Lansbury Dr DE55 160 A6
Lansbury Rd S21 59 D2
Lanscombe Park Rd DE22 204 E1
Lansdowne Ave DE24 232 F5
Lansdowne Rd
Branston DE14 253 F7
Brimington S43 96 D7
Buxton SK17 66 B1
Swadlincote DE11 256 A3
Lansing Gdns DE21 220 B6
Lantern Gr DE3 217 D4
Lantern Pike View SK22 25 A2
Lantern View SK22 24 B1
Lant La DE4 144 B8
Lapwing Cl
Belper DE56 192 A8
Derby DE24 231 E2
Lara Croft Way DE1 219 A4
Lara Croft Wy DE1 267 B2
Larch Ave
Killamarsh S21 60 C5
Mansfield Woodhouse NG19 136 B5
Ripley DE5 169 D1
Shirebrook NG20 119 D4
Larch Cl DE22 204 D3
Larch Cres NG16 182 E2
Larchdale Cl DE55 160 A4
Larch Dr NG10 223 B7
Larch Rd
Eckington S21 59 B2
Kilburn DE56 192 B7
Swadlincote DE11 255 F6
Larch Way
Chesterfield S40 95 D5
Glossop SK13 17 F8
Larges St DE1 218 E5
Lark Cl
Derby DE23 231 C6
3 Mansfield NG19 135 F1
Larkfields Cres DE55 169 F8
Larkhill DE55 169 F8
Lark Hill DE3 230 B7
Larkhill Cl DE55 169 F8
Lark Hill Cotts SK22 33 A8
Larkhill Cres DE24 231 F4
Larkin Cl DE24 232 A5
LARKLANDS 209 B8
Larkland's Ave DE7 209 A7
Larklands Inf Sch DE7 209 A8
Lark Rise DE21 220 B7
Larkspur Cl
Derby DE24 231 C3
Mansfield NG19 136 D2
South Normanton DE55 160 A4
Larkspur Ct DE21 206 A3
Larkstone La DE6 149 A1
Larpit Gn S80 82 A5
Lascelles Rd SK17 85 B8
Lashley Gdns DE21 205 F2
Latham Cl DE15 248 C2
Lathbury Cl DE21 205 D1
Lathkil Dr DE55 159 F5
Lathkil Gr
Buxton SK17 85 D7
Tibshelf DE55 147 F6
Lathkill Ave
Derby DE24 233 C7
Lathkill Ave *continued*
Ilkeston DE7 194 E5
Staveley S43 97 C6
Lathkill Cl
Sheffield S13 44 C7
West Hallam DE7 207 E8
Lathkill Ct S42 132 A7
Lathkill Dale DE11 255 F2
Lathkilldale Cres NG10 236 A5
Lathkill Dr
Ashbourne DE6 185 E8
Ripley DE5 180 D6
Selston NG16 171 F7
Lathkill Gr S45 131 D1
Lathkill La DE4 156 C2
Lathkill Rd
Derby DE21 219 F8
Sheffield S13 44 C7
Latimer Cl DE23 230 E7
Latimer St DE24 232 D6
Latrigg Cl DE3 217 E1
Laud Cl DE12 262 E3
Lauder Cl DE24 231 E2
Launceston Rd DE24 233 B5
Laund Ave DE56 179 B6
Laund Cl DE56 179 A6
Laund Farm DE56 179 C6
Laund Farm Mews DE56 179 C6
Laund Hill DE56 179 A5
Laund Nook DE56 179 A5
Launds Ave NG16 171 D7
Laurel Ave
Arkwright Town S44 97 D3
Mansfield Woodhouse NG19 136 F1
Ripley DE5 169 D1
Laurel Cl
Eckington S21 59 C2
Shirebrook NG20 119 D6
Swanwick DE55 170 A8
Laurel Cres
Brimington S43 78 A1
Long Eaton NG10 236 C6
Smalley DE7 192 F5
Laurel Dr
Aston-on-Trent DE72 246 A7
Killamarsh S21 60 C5
Laurel Garth Cl S41 77 B3
Laurel Gr
Burton upon Trent DE15 254 E5
South Normanton DE55 160 A4
Laurel Grove ST14 210 C1
Laurence Cl S41 77 A2
Lauren Gr 6 NG10 223 F1
Laurie Pl DE24 232 E7
Lavant Ct 3 S43 96 E8
Lavender Cl
Burton upon Trent DE14 254 A8
Shirebrook NG20 119 D3
Tibshelf DE55 148 B7
Lavender Gdns DE75 182 B1
Lavender Rd DE55 170 A8
Lavender Row DE22 204 F1
Lavender Way DE13 239 C5
Lavender Wlk DE55 157 F5
Laverdene Ave S17 55 F5
Laverdene Cl S17 55 E4
Laverdene Dr S17 55 F4
Laverdene Rd S17 55 E4
Laverdene Way S17 55 F4
Laver Dr S41 95 B6
Laverick Rd NG16 171 A4
Laverock Cl NG16 195 F6
Laverstoke Ct DE22 218 E4
Lavinia Ct DE73 232 D2
Lawman Gdns DE55 158 F4
Lawman Mews DE55 159 A4
Lawn Ave
Derby DE22 204 D2
Etwall DE65 229 C5
Lawn Cl DE75 181 F2
Lawnfold SK13 9 E4
Lawn Heads Ave DE23 218 C2
Lawn La DE45 126 B6
Lawnlea Cl DE23 231 E5
Lawn Mill Rd NG16 195 E7
Lawn Prim Sch DE22 204 D1
Lawns Dr DE11 256 A7
Lawnside DE21 220 F5
Lawns La DE45 125 F5
Lawns The
Aston-on-Trent DE72 246 B8
Rolleston DE13 240 A4
Uttoxeter ST14 210 A2
Lawnswood Cl DE23 231 C8
Lawnswood Close DE65 229 C5
Lawn The S18 57 B2
Lawn Villas S44 97 A2
Lawrence Ave
Awsworth NG16 195 C4
Breaston DE72 235 D8
Derby DE21 220 B7
Eastwood NG16 182 F2
Holmewood S42 116 D1
Lawrence Ave *continued*
Mansfield Woodhouse NG19 136 B4
Ripley DE5 180 C8
Lawrence Dr NG16 182 D8
Lawrence St
Derby DE23 231 F8
Long Eaton NG10 236 D8
Sandiacre NG10 223 B7
Stapleford NG9 223 D6
Lawson Ave NG10 236 E7
Lawson Cl S44 99 D1
Lawson Rd S44 99 D1
Lawton Rd DE11 257 B1
Laxfield Cl S40 114 C8
Layton Dr S41 77 B1
LCPL Steven Bagshaw Ave SK14 9 F6
LEA 156 B7
Lea Bank DE55 160 A4
LEA BRIDGE 156 A6
Leabrook Rd S18 56 C1
LEABROOKS 170 B7
Leabrooks Ave NG19 136 D5
Leabrooks Rd DE55 170 C8
Lea Cl DE22 204 E3
Lea Cres DE55 170 C6
Leacroft Rd
Derby DE23 219 B1
Winster DE4 141 C6
Lea Ct S41 266 B4
Leadale Ave DE55 170 A7
Leadale Cres NG19 136 E5
Leadbeater Dr S12 44 A5
Leadbeater Rd
Sheffield S12 43 F5
Sheffield S12 44 A4
Leaden Knowle SK23 34 C1
Leadhill Rd S40 95 A4
LEADMILL 53 B5
Lea Dr
Derby, Chaddesden DE21 219 F6
Derby, Markeaton DE3 217 E3
Leafenden Cl DE22 205 A3
Leafgreen La DE23 231 C6
Leafield Rd SK12 32 C6
Leafy La DE75 181 F1
Lea Gardens* DE4 156 A7
Leaholme Est S44 98 D2
Leake St DE22 218 D5
Lea La
Matlock DE4 156 C2
Selston NG16 171 F6
LEAM 53 A3
Lea Main Rd DE4 156 B8
Leam Glen NG19 136 D2
Leamington Cl DE23 218 D1
Leamington Dr DE55 160 B5
Leamington Rd DE14 253 E7
Leamington St DE5 169 F2
Leamoor Ave DE55 170 B8
Lea Moor Rd DE4 156 E8
Leander Cl DE23 231 D7
Leander Ct 5 S43 78 F2
Leander Rise DE15 255 A8
Leantown SK13 16 D6
Lean Town SK13 17 D6
Leaper St DE1 218 E6
Leapley La DE6 199 D3
Lea Prim Sch DE4 156 A7
Lea Rd
Cromford DE4 155 D6
Dronfield S18 57 A1
Hayfield SK22 25 C3
Lea DE4 156 A7
Leas Ave NG19 135 A5
Leashaw DE4 156 C4
Leashaw Rd DE4 156 C3
Leas Park Jun Sch NG19 136 C4
Leas Rd NG19 136 D4
Lea St SK22 33 B8
Leathersley La DE6, DE65 226 C2
Lea Vale DE55 160 A4
Leaway The NG20 119 D3
Lea Wood Croft DE4 156 A5
Leawood Gdns DE21 206 B3
Leawood Pump Ho* DE4 155 F4
Leawood Rd DE11 256 D7
Leche Croft DE56 179 D4
Lechlade Cl DE7 207 D8
Lechlade Rd DE24 231 C3
Ledbury Chase DE24 231 D2
Ledbury Pl 2 DE21 205 D1
Leden Cl SK17 85 D4
Ledo Ave DE5 169 D2
Leebangs Rd SK14 16 A8
Leech Ct NG16 195 B7
Lee Cres DE7 209 B8
Lee Dale SK17 85 C3
Leedhams Croft DE12 259 D8
Leeds Pl DE1 267 D2
Leeds Rd S81 63 F7
Lee Farm Cl DE73 232 F1
Leefield Rd SK23 47 B5
LEE HEAD 16 C6
Lee Head SK13 16 C5
Leek Rd
Buxton SK17 84 E5
Longnor SK17 121 B6
Mayfield DE6 172 B2
Lee La DE75 182 B1
Leeming La NG19, NG20 136 E7
Leeming Lane N NG19 136 E5
Leeming Lane S NG19 136 C2
Leeming Pk NG19 136 C3
Lee Mount SK13 17 C7
Leen Valley Dr NG20 119 D3
Lee Rd S41 96 E2
LEES 216 B7
Lees Bank DE21 220 A7
Lees Brook Com Sch DE21 220 B8
Lees Brook Ho DE21 220 A7
Lees Hall Ave S8 43 B5
Lees Hall Pl S8 43 B5
Lees Hall Rd S8 43 B4
Lees House Ct S8 43 A4
Leeside DE24 220 A1
Lees La DE55 159 F6
Lees Mill 4 SK22 33 C7
Lees Nook S8 43 A4
Lees Rd DE4 126 E3
Lees Row SK13 10 C5
Lees The DE72 233 D5
Leeswood Cl S41 95 D8
Lee Vale Dr SK13 16 D7
Leeway DE21 220 D4
Leggers Row DE55 170 C3
Legh Rd SK12 32 A6
Leicester Dr SK13 17 F8
Leicester Ho 2 NG9 223 F8
Leicester St
Burton upon Trent DE14 254 C8
Derby DE22 218 E3
Long Eaton NG10 236 E6
Leigh Rd NG9 223 F3
Leighton Dr
Marple SK6 23 C8
Sheffield S14 43 F3
Leighton Pl S14 43 F3
Leighton Rd
Sheffield S12 44 A3
Sheffield S14 43 E4
Leighton View S14 43 E5
Leighton Way 6 DE56 178 F3
Leigh Way S42 131 F7
Leisure La SK17 137 E5
Leisure Way DE6 173 B1
Leman St DE22 218 E3
Lemon Gr DE11 256 B1
Lemont Rd S17 55 E4
Leniscar Ave DE75 181 C4
Lens Rd DE22 204 C2
Lenthall Inf Sch S18 57 B3
Lenton Ave DE21 219 F6
Lenton St NG10 223 C7
Leominster Dr DE21 206 B2
Leonard Cheshire Cl DE75 182 B1
Leonard Cl
Derby DE23 267 B1
Sheffield S2 44 A7
Leonard Gdns 2 DE11 256 A6
Leonard St DE1 267 C1
Leonard Wlk DE23 267 B1
Leopold St
Derby DE1 267 B2
Long Eaton NG10 236 D8
Lesley Cres DE5 169 E3
Leslie Ave NG16 195 F6
Leslie Cl DE23 230 E8
Lesser La
Buxton SK17 85 F8
Chapel-en-le-Frith SK23 65 D7
Level La SK17 84 D5
Leven Cl DE24 231 F2
Levens Way S41 95 E8
Leveret Cl DE73 233 B2
Levetts Close DE24 231 C3
Lewcote La DE7 194 A1
Lewisham Drive DE11 255 E1
Lewis Rd S13 44 C7
Lewis St DE23 218 F1
Lewiston Rd DE21 220 B5
Lexington Rd DE21 220 C6
Ley Ave DE55 159 B3
Leyburn Cl
Chesterfield S40 95 E5
Swadlincote DE11 256 B1
Leycote Way DE56 178 F5
Ley Croft
Hatton DE65 227 C1
Mansfield Woodhouse NG19 136 D5
Leyfield Rd S17 55 D7
Leygate View SK22 33 B8
Ley Gdns DE55 159 B4
Ley La
Mansfield Woodhouse NG19 136 D4
Marple SK6 23 D8
Leyland Cl
Beeston NG9 223 F2
Bolsover S44 99 D1
Leyland Ct DE1 218 E7
Leyland Dr S44 99 D1
Leyland Gdns DE1 218 E7
Leylands DE22 218 E8
Leylands Cottages SK14 15 F8
Leylands La SK14 15 F7
Leyland St DE1 218 E7
LEYS 154 A8
Leys Ct DE56 179 D4
Leys Field Gdns DE73 233 A2
Leys Jun Sch DE55 159 C4
Leys La DE4 154 B7
Leys The
Little Eaton DE21 191 D2
Swadlincote DE11 255 E6
Leyton Ct S43 77 D4
Leytonstone Dr DE22 218 A5
Liberty 4 NG19 135 F1
Lichfield Ave DE11 256 E5
Lichfield Cl NG9 223 E3
Lichfield Dr DE24 233 A7
Lichfield Rd
Branston DE13, DE14 253 C4
Chesterfield S40 114 D8
Sudbury ST14 225 F3
Walton-On-Trent DE14 253 A1
Lichford Rd S2 43 C6
Lickpenny La
Ashover DE4 144 E4
Tansley S45 144 D5
Lidgate Cl DE3 217 C1
Lid La
Ashover S45 129 A6
Roston DE6 197 E7
Lifes Rd SK17 138 C3
Liffey Ho DE24 232 E5
Liffs Rd DE6, SK17 150 C7
Light Alders La SK12 32 A6
Light Alders Lodge SK12 32 A6
Lightfoot Rd ST14 210 A1
Lightning Lane DE74 246 F4
LIGHTWOOD
Eckington 58 F2
Sheffield 57 F8
Lightwood Ave 3 SK17 85 C8
Lightwood La
Chesterfield S21 77 E8
Eckington S8 43 F1
Eckington, Middle Handley S21 58 E1
Lightwood Rd
Buxton SK17 66 B1
Eckington S21 58 E2
Lilac Ave DE22 218 A5
Lilac Cl
Derby DE24 233 A6
Holmewood S44 116 F2
Lilac Ct DE24 233 A6
Lilac Gr
Bolsover S44 99 C1
Burton upon Trent DE15 254 F6
Church Warsop NG20 120 F7
Glapwell S44 134 B8
Heanor DE75 181 E1
Shirebrook NG20 119 E5
South Normanton DE55 160 A4
Lilac Mews DE7 194 D3
Lilac St
Brimington S43 78 B1
Staveley S43 97 A8
Lilac Way
Derby DE22 204 D2
Shirland DE55 146 D1
Lilian Prime Cl DE24 233 B8
Lilley Cl NG16 171 E6
Lilley St DE24 233 B6
Lilly Ct DE13 239 D5
Lillymede Cl S40 114 F6
Lilybank Cl DE4 143 C5
Lilybank Ct 6 DE4 143 C6
LILYPOOL 252 B7
Lilypools The DE73 252 B7
Lilystreet Farmway 2 DE55 158 F1
Lilywood Cl S44 97 B3
Limbersitch La DE65 227 F6
Limb La S17 55 D8
Lime Ave
Derby DE1 267 A1
Derby, Breadsall Hilltop DE21 205 D2
Duffield DE56 190 E5
Langley Mill NG16 182 C2
New Mills SK22 24 D1
Ripley DE5 169 D1
Staveley S43 78 E1
Lime Cl
Calow S44 97 A3
Doveridge DE6 224 B8
Pinxton NG16 160 D3
Lime Cres
Belper DE56 179 B2
Church Warsop NG20 120 F7
Lime Croft DE22 204 F4
Limecroft View S42 115 B3
Lime Ct DE15 254 E7
Limedale Ave DE21 206 B3
Lime Gate Mews DE23 218 D2
Lime Gr
Ashbourne DE6 185 C8
Burton upon Trent DE15 254 E5
Darley Dale DE4 127 C3
Derby DE21 220 B5
Draycott DE72 234 F7
Hatton DE65 227 D1
Long Eaton NG10 236 D8
Sandiacre NG10 223 B6
South Normanton DE55 160 A5
Stapleford NG9 223 D5
Lime Grove Ave DE4 143 C5
Lime Grove Wlk DE4 143 B5
Limehouse La S26 61 E7
LIMEKILN FIELD 99 A3
Limekiln Fields Rd S44 99 A3
Lime Kiln La
Marple SK6 23 A5
Turnditch DE56 189 B8
Wensley DE4 142 B8
Lime Kilns The DE73 252 F2
Limekiln Way
Barlborough S43 80 C6
Shireoaks S81 63 F7
Lime Kiln Way SK17 85 D2
Lime La
Derby DE21 206 C3
Morley DE7, DE21 206 D5
Lime Rd S21 59 B2
Limerick Rd DE21 220 B4
Limers Rake SK17 104 D1
Limes Ave
Derby DE3 217 D1
Whaley Thorns NG20 101 A2
Limes Cl NG16 182 C4
Limes Cl The DE4 143 C5
Limes Cres NG20 119 D5
Limes Ct 3 DE3 217 D1
Limes Pk DE5 169 C1
Lime St DE7 208 F7
Limes The
Barton in Fabis NG11 237 E6
Duffield DE56 190 D3
Mapperley DE7 193 E3
5 Uttoxeter ST14 210 B1
Limestone Cft 2 DE4 143 A5
Limestone Cl
Hartshorne DE11 257 A4
5 Swadlincote DE11 255 F4
Swadlincote DE11 256 F4
Limestone Ct SK17 47 F2
Limestone Terr NG19 136 B4
Lime Terr NG10 236 D8
Limetree Ave DE11 256 B7
Lime Tree Ave
Darley Dale DE4 127 B3
Glapwell S44 134 B8
Killamarsh S21 60 C5
Mansfield Woodhouse NG19 136 A5
Lime Tree Bsns Pk DE4 143 C4
Limetree Cl S43 96 F5
Lime Tree Cl
1 Branston DE14 253 E7
1 Branston DE14 256 E7
Swadlincote DE11 256 B2
3 Tibshelf DE55 147 F6
Limetree Ct DE7 208 C6
Lime Tree Gr
Arkwright Town S44 97 D3
Clay Cross S45 131 E2
Lime Tree Pk SK17 85 D6
Lime Tree Rd DE4 143 C5
Limetree Rise DE7 208 C6
Lime Wlk
Clay Cross S45 131 E5
Derby DE23 218 D1
Linacre Ave S45 131 D2
Linacre Rd S40, S42 95 A5
Linacre Reservoirs* S42 94 B5
Linacres Dr DE73 233 A2
Linacre Way SK13 17 F7
Linbery Cl DE55 158 B4
Lincoln Ave
Derby DE24 233 A8
Derby DE3 230 E5
Sandiacre NG10 223 A4
Lincoln Cl
Stapleford NG9 209 E1
Tibshelf DE55 148 A6
Lincoln Dr NG19 136 D4
Lincoln Gn DE73 232 F2
Lincoln Rd DE15 254 D7
Lincoln St
Alfreton DE55 158 F3
Chesterfield S40 115 A8
Tibshelf DE55 148 A6
Lincoln Way
6 Glossop SK13 17 F8
North Wingfield S42 131 F6
Swadlincote DE11 256 E5

Lincote Way 9
DE11 256 E1
Lindale Rd S41 76 E1
Lindale Way DE73 233 A2
Linden Ave
Chesterfield S40 95 B1
Clay Cross S45 131 D2
Dronfield S18 57 B3
Linden Cl
Denstone ST14 196 D6
Kilburn DE56 192 B8
Linden Ct S45 131 D2
Linden Dr S41 115 D6
Linden Gr
Matlock DE4 143 C5
Sandiacre NG10 223 A7
Shirebrook NG20 119 F4
Stapleford NG9 223 E6
Linden Park Gr S40 95 D3
Linden Rd S80 81 E2
Linden St
Mansfield NG19 136 A1
Shirebrook NG20 119 F4
Shirebrook NG20 120 A4
Linden Way SK6 32 A7
Lindford Cl DE21 205 F3
Lindisfarne Cl 4
DE24 231 D3
Lindisfarne Ct S40 95 D1
Lindisfarne Rd S18 76 B8
Lindley St NG16 171 D6
Lindon Dr DE24 233 C6
Lindrick Cl
Derby DE3 217 F1
Mansfield Woodhouse
NG19 136 D6
Lindrick Gdns S40 114 C8
Lindrick Way S43 80 B5
Lindsey Cl DE21 219 E6
Lindup Rd S17 56 E2
Lindway La
Brackenfield DE55 145 B1
Dethick DE55 144 F1
Linear View S43 80 F4
Lingfield Rd DE14 253 F7
Lingfield Rise DE3 217 C3
Lingfoot Ave S8 57 B6
Lingfoot Cl S8 57 B6
Lingfoot Cres S8 57 C6
Lingfoot Dr S8 57 C6
Lingfoot Pl S8 57 B6
Lingfoot Wlk S8 57 C6
Ling La S44 118 C4
Linglongs Ave SK23 45 C5
Linglongs Rd SK23 45 C5
Ling Rd S40 114 D8
Lings Cl DE7 194 F5
Lings Cres S42 132 A8
Lingwell Croft Ave
S21 59 D2
Linkmel Rd NG16 182 C3
Links Cl DE24 231 F4
Links Rd
Chapel-en-le-Frith
SK23 46 F5
Dronfield S18 76 B8
Links The NG16 171 D6
Links View SK17 66 D1
Linley La S12, S13 44 E5
Linnet Cl DE21 220 F6
Linnet Hill DE3 230 C7
Linnet Ho S41 77 A3
Linnet Way S43 81 E1
Linscott Cl S41 95 D7
Linshaws Rd HD9 3 E5
Linstock Way DE74 233 C3
LINTON 261 D6
Linton Heath DE12 261 E6
Linton Prim Sch
DE12 261 D5
Linton Rd
Chesterfield S40 114 C8
Linton DE11 261 E7
Rosliston DE12 260 E5
Linwood Cres NG16 182 F1
Linwood Ct NG19 136 E4
Lionheart La DE13 240 E2
Lipp Ave S21 60 C7
Liskeard Dr DE22 204 D4
Lismore Ct 6 DE24 231 D3
Lismore Gr SK17 85 A7
Lismore Pk SK17 85 A7
Lismore Rd
Buxton SK17 85 A7
Sheffield S8 43 B5
Lisset Cl DE55 158 B3
Lissett Ave DE7 208 E7
Lister Ave S12 44 B3
Lister Cl
Chesterfield S41 266 B4
Derby DE3 218 B3
Sheffield S12 44 B3
Lister Cres S12 44 B3
Lister Dr S12 44 B3
Lister Pl S12 44 B3
Lister Way S12 44 B3
Liston Dr DE22 218 F8
Litchen Cl DE7 194 F2
Litchfield Cl NG10 237 A7
LITCHURCH 219 C3
Litchurch La DE24 219 C2
Litchurch St DE1 267 C1
Little Acre NG19 136 E5
LITTLE BOLEHILL 155 B2
Little Bolehill DE4 155 A2
Little Breck DE55 160 A4
Little Bridge DE13 239 C7
Little Bridge St DE1 218 F6
Little Brind Rd S40 95 B7
Littlebrook Cl SK13 10 A4
LITTLE CHESTER 219 A7
Little Cl DE11 256 B5
LITTLE CUBLEY 212 E8
Littledale Cl DE21 206 C3
Little Debdale La
NG19 135 F1
Little Derby Hill
DE3 230 B2
LITTLE EATON 205 C8
Little Eaton Prim Sch
DE21 205 C7
Little Edge S32 71 C6
Little Fallows
Belper DE56 190 F7
4 Milford DE56 191 A7
Little Fen DE55 147 F5
Littlefield La
Ellastone DE6 183 A2
Snelston DE6 184 B4
Littlefield Rd DE65 227 C7
Littlefields SK14 9 A4
LITTLE HALLAM 208 E5
Little Hallam Hill
DE7 208 E6
Little Hallam La
DE7 209 A6
LITTLE HAYFIELD 25 B5
LITTLE HUCKLOW 50 E2
Little La
Ashford in the Water
DE45 89 E1
Bradwell S33 51 A7
Heanor DE5 181 A3
Kimberley NG16 195 F5
Litton SK17 69 E3
Pleasley NG19 135 B5
Sheffield, Woodthorpe
Estate S12 44 B6
Shirebrook NG20 119 D3
Sutton in Ashfield
NG17 148 E2
Thorpe Salvin S80 63 B6
Little Liverpool
DE12 260 C1
Little London DE4 156 A6
LITTLE LONGSTONE 89 E4
Little Longstone Cl
DE3 217 F2
Little Lunnon NG11 237 E6
LITTLE MATLOCK 135 F7
Little Meadow Close 5
DE7 194 E2
Little Meadow Rd
DE73 233 A2
LITTLEMOOR 130 C3
Littlemoor
Chesterfield S41 95 D7
Eckington S21 59 E4
Littlemoor Bsns Ctr
S21 59 E4
Littlemoor Cres S41 95 D7
Littlemoor Ct 3
SK13 17 C8
Littlemoor Ctr 2
S41 95 E7
Littlemoor La
Matlock Bath DE4 143 F1
Newton DE55 148 B4
Littlemoor Rd SK14 9 A2
Little Moorside
DE72 246 B8
Little Morton Rd S42,
S45 132 A5
LITTLE NORTON 57 A8
Little Norton Ave S8 57 A8
Little Norton Dr S8 57 A8
Little Norton La S8 57 A8
Little Norton Way S8 57 A7
LITTLEOVER 231 B8
Littleover Com Sch
DE23 230 F8
Littleover Cres
DE23 218 D1
Littleover La DE23 231 E8
Little Thorn Ind Est
DE11 256 F2
Littlewell La DE7 208 F2
Little Woodbury Dr 4
DE23 230 F6
Little Wood Dr S12 44 A3
Littlewood La
Mansfield Woodhouse
NG19 136 A6
Pleasley Vale NG19 135 F8
Shirebrook NG20 119 F1
Little Wood La S26,
S80 62 D4
Little Wood Rd S12 44 A3
LITTLEWORTH 262 D8
Littleworth La DE6 213 E6
LITTON 69 F3
Litton Bank SK13 9 E1
Litton CE Prim Sch
SK17 69 E3
Litton Cft DE6 185 D7
Litton Cl
Belper DE56 179 B5
Ilkeston DE7 194 E4
Staveley S43 97 C8
Litton Ct 6 S40 95 D5
Litton Dale
Litton SK17 69 D2
Tideswell SK17 69 D2
Litton Dr DE21 220 F3
Litton Fold 16 SK13 9 E1
Litton Gdns 17 SK13 9 E1
Litton Mews SK13 9 E1
LITTON MILL 88 E7
Litton Rd
Buxton SK17 85 E7
Mansfield Woodhouse
NG19 136 E4
Littonslack SK17 88 E7
Litton Slack SK17 88 E8
Liverpool St 4
DE21 219 E8
Liversage Almshouses
DE1 267 C2
Liversage Pl DE1 267 C2
Liversage Rd DE1 267 C2
Liversage St DE1 267 C2
Livingstone Rd
DE23 218 E1
Lloyd St DE22 218 D5
Loadshead La S42 112 D8
Loads Rd
Holymoorside S42 113 B7
Holymoorside S42 113 D7
Loake Ct 1 DE73 252 A8
Lochinvar Cl DE21 220 F4
Lock Cl DE7 208 C6
Locker Smith La
DE11 257 A1
LOCKINGTON 247 F5
Lockington Cl DE73 232 F2
Lockington Rd
DE74 247 D5
Lock La
Long Eaton NG10 236 C4
Sandiacre NG10 223 C4
Locko Ct DE21 220 D5
Lockoford La
Chesterfield, Stonegravels
S41 96 A6
Chesterfield, Tapton
S41 96 C6
Lockoford Rd S41 96 A5
Locko Hall DE7 206 F2
Locko La S45 132 E3
Locko Rd
Derby DE21 220 E7
Morley DE21 206 D2
Pilsley S45 132 C4
Lockside SK6 23 A6
Lockton Ave DE75 193 E8
Lock Up Yd DE1 267 B3
Lockwood Rd DE22 204 D4
Locomotive Way
DE24 219 C3
Lodege La DE6 202 F3
Lode La DE6 149 F4
Lodes La SK17 67 C7
Lodes View SK17 47 F2
Lodge Ave DE6 185 B8
Lodge Bank SK13 10 A6
Lodge Cl
Calow S43 97 A4
Duffield DE56 190 E3
Etwall DE65 229 C4
Lodge Ct SK14 9 A4
Lodge Dr
Belper DE56 178 E5
Wingerworth S42 115 A4
Lodge Est DE72 246 B7
Lodge Farm Chase
DE6 185 B8
Lodge Farm Cl S40 114 C7
Lodge Hill
Rolleston DE13 239 E3
Tutbury DE13 239 D4
Lodge La
Alstonefield DE6 149 B3
Derby DE1 267 A4
Derby, Spondon DE21 220 D4
Heanor NG16 181 E6
Mackworth DE6,
DE22 203 C5
Shottle DE56 177 D8
Lodge Mews DE72 246 B7
Lodge Moor Rd S10 42 F8
Lodge Pl S43 97 C6
Lodge Rd
Eastwood NG16 195 A8
Long Eaton NG10 236 D5
Netherseal DE12 261 D1
Lodge Row DE7 193 E3
Lodge St DE72 235 A7
Lodge The
Glossop SK13 10 A6
Tideswell SK17 69 C3
Lodge Way DE3 217 D1
Lodge Wlk S43 97 C6
Loganberry Ct DE24 232 E8
Lohengrin Ct DE13 240 E2
Lomas Cotts SK17 69 E3
Lombard St DE22 217 F6
Lomond Ave DE24 231 F2
London Ho DE45 109 D5
London Rd
Buxton SK17 85 C6
Castle Donington
DE72 247 B8
Derby DE23, DE24 219 D2
Derby DE24 219 E1
Derby DE24 233 F4
Shardlow DE72 234 C2
Shardlow DE72 234 E1
Sheffield, Heeley S2 43 A6
Sheffield, Highfield S2 43 A8
London Road Com Hospl
DE1 267 C1
London Road S S2 43 A7
London St S43 77 D3
Long Acre DE74 247 B6
Longacre Rd S18 76 A7
Long Acre View S20 60 A8
Long Acre Way S20 60 A8
Longbourne Ct
NG19 136 F2
Longbow Cl DE13 240 C1
Longbow Gr DE13 240 C1
Longbridge La
Buxton SK17 67 B4
Heanor DE75 181 D3
Long Bridge La
DE24 232 D8
Long Causeway
Bamford S32 40 F5
Hallam Moors S10 41 F8
Soughley S10 42 A8
LONGCLIFFE 152 F4
Longcliff Wlk 2 S41 95 C6
Longclough Dr SK13 17 A8
Longcourse La S44 98 A2
Long Croft DE72 246 A8
Longcroft Ave
Dronfield S18 56 C2
Ilkeston NE7 194 E5
Longcroft Cl S42 131 D8
Longcroft Cres S18 56 C2
Longcroft Ct S40 114 F7
Longcroft Rd S18 56 C2
Longcroft View S80 82 A6
Longdale NG19 136 E1
Longdale Dr SK14 9 A3
Longdale Gdns SK14 9 A3
Longden Cl NG9 209 F2
Longdendale Com
Language Coll SK14 9 C5
Longdons Row
DE21 220 D5
LONG
DUCKMANTON 98 A3
LONG EATON 236 C7
Long Eaton Sch The
NG10 236 C6
Long Eaton Sta
NG10 236 C5
Long Eaton Trade Ctr
NG10 236 F8
Longedge Gr S42 115 B3
Longedge La S42 114 F3
Longedge Rise S42 115 A3
Longfield Cres DE7 208 F5
Long Field Grange
S41 95 C6
Longfield La DE7 208 F5
LONGFORD 214 D8
Longford CE VC Prim
Sch DE6 214 D8
Longford Cl
Burton upon Trent
DE15 248 B2
Derby DE22 204 D1
2 Derby DE23 230 F5
Sheffield S17 56 A5
Longford Cres S17 56 A5
Longford Dr S17 55 F4
Longford La
Church Broughton
DE65 214 D2
Church Broughton
DE65 227 F8
Longford DE6 214 F7
Longford DE6, DE65 214 C4
Sutton on the Hill
DE6 215 A4
LONGFORDLANE 215 A5
Longford Rd S17 56 A4
Longford Spinney
S17 55 F4
Longford St DE22 218 E8
Long Gallery DE4 110 E6
Longhedge La
Burton upon Trent
DE13 239 F1
Pleasley NG19 134 E5
Long Hill
Darley Dale DE4 127 C4
Whaley Bridge SK17,
SK23 65 C5
Longhurst La
1 Marple SK7 24 C7
Marple Bridge SK6 23 D7
Stockport SK6 23 D3
Longhurst View S80 81 F5
Long La
Alkmonton DE6 199 E2
Alkmonton DE6 200 A1
Alstonefield DE6 149 B5
Ashover S42 130 A6
Broadbottom SK13 16 C7
Chapel-en-le-Frith
SK23 47 B4
Chapel-en-le-Frith, Combs
SK23 46 C3
Chesterfield S21 77 C7
Cressbrook SK17 89 B7
Disley SK12 32 E4
Holloway DE4 156 B6
Killamarsh S21 60 F6
Kirk Langley DE6 202 B1
Longford DE6 214 C8
Shipley DE75 194 E7
Shirebrook NG20 119 E3
Taddington SK17 87 E5
Thurvaston DE6 201 D1
Wardlow SK17 70 E2
Longlands S44 99 B2
Longlands Dr SK22 33 B8
Longlands La
DE65 230 C1
Longlands Mews
DE65 230 C1
Longlands Rd
New Mills SK22 33 B8
Swadlincote DE11 256 D7
Longlands Villas
DE56 167 F3
Long Lane CE Prim Sch
DE6 201 E1
Long Lea Dr NG16 182 B5
Longley La DE21 220 D6
Longlieve Gdns S45 132 B2
Longload La DE4 154 E5
Long Mdw
Great Cubley DE6 198 F1
Mansfield Woodhouse
NG19 136 D5
Longmeade Dr SK23 47 B4
Long Meadow La
SK17 69 E1
Long Meadow Rd
DE55 158 F3
Longmoor Gdns 2
NG10 223 A2
Longmoor La
Breaston DE72 222 E1
Breaston DE72 235 E8
Sandiacre NG10 223 B4
Longmoor Prim Sch
NG10 223 C3
Longmoor Rd
Glossop SK13 17 A7
Long Eaton NG10 223 B2
LONGNOR 121 A6
Longnor Craft Ctr★
SK17 121 B7
Longnor Gn 38 SK13 9 D2
Longnor Mews 39
SK13 9 D2
Longnor Way 37 SK13 9 D2
Long Rake DE45 123 D4
Longreave La DE45 90 C4
Longridge La SK17 66 F7
Longrose La
Kniveton DE6 163 B2
Kniveton DE6 163 B3
Long Row
Belper DE56 178 F4
Shardlow DE72 235 B2
Long Row Prim Sch
DE56 178 F4
Long Shambles S40 266 B3
Longshaw Cl
North Wingfield S42 131 F6
Staveley S43 97 D8
Longshaw Ct 10 S40 95 D5
Longshaw Estate & Ctry
Pk★ S11 54 A3
Longshaw Estate Trail★
S11 54 A4
Longshaw Estate Visitor
Ctr★ S11 54 A4
Longshaw Gdns
DE24 233 A6
Longshaw Lodge
S11 54 A4
Longside Rd
Disley SK12 32 F4
Holymoorside S42 112 E6
Long Sleets DE55 160 B4
Longs Mill 4 DE1 267 A4
Longson Rd SK23 47 C6
Long St DE15 254 E7
Longster La NG20,
NG19 120 C3
Longstock Cl DE21 205 E1
Longstone Bsns Pk
DE45 90 A4
Longstone CE Prim Sch
DE45 89 F4
Longstone Cres S12 44 D4
Longstone La DE45 89 F2
Longstone Rise
DE56 179 B6
Longstone Wlk DE1 267 A2
Longthorpe Cl DE23 231 A7
Longthorpe Road
DE24 233 D4
Long View La DE6 185 A4
Longwalls La DE56 178 C5
Longway Bank DE4 156 A2
Longwood Cl DE75 181 D4
Longwood Hall Rise
DE55 159 F4
Longwood Inf Acad
NG16 160 C2
Longwood Rd NG16 160 E2
Lonsdale Dr NG9 223 E2
Lonsdale Gr DE4 142 F7
Lonsdale Pl DE22 218 D4
Lonsdale Rd
Burton upon Trent
DE14 254 B8
Pilsley S45 132 B2
Lons Inf Sch DE5 169 D2
Loom Cl DE56 179 C5
Loosemore Dr S12 43 F5
Lord Haddon Rd
DE7 194 E1
Lord Roberts Rd
S40 266 B1
Lords Cl S44 99 A1
Lordsmill St S41 266 C2
Lord St
Derby DE24 232 D6
Glossop SK13 10 D1
Hollingworth SK14 9 D4
Lorne Cl S18 56 D2
Lornes Dr DE15 248 B3
Lorne St DE22 218 F3
Lorraine Cl DE24 232 E3
LOSCOE 181 C3
Loscoe CE Prim Sch
DE75 181 B3
Loscoe Ct 2 S40 95 D5
Loscoe-Denby La DE5,
DE75 181 B4
Loscoe Grange
DE75 181 D3
Loscoe Rd
Derby DE21 206 A1
Heanor DE75 181 D2
Losehill Hall Study
Centre★ S33 38 C4
Lose Hill La S33 38 F6
Losk Cnr S44 118 D2
Losk La
Palterton S44, NG19 118 C3
Scarcliffe NG20 119 A2
Lothian Pl
Castle Donington
DE74 247 A3
Derby DE21 219 D7
Lothlorien Cl DE23 231 B7
Loudon St DE23 219 A3
Loudoun Pl DE74 247 A4
Loundes Rd S18 76 E6
Loundes Wood Ave
S41 95 C8
LOUNDSLEY GREEN 95 B6
Loundsley Green Rd
S40 95 C5
Lount La DE13 239 E1
Lousie Greaves La
DE21 220 E6
Louvain Rd DE22,
DE23 218 D2
Louwil Ave NG19 136 E5
Lovatt Cl DE13 240 F2
Lovatt Dr NG16 182 C4
Love La
Flash SK11 102 C1
Stonebroom DE55 147 C4
Loveys Croft DE73 252 E2
Lowburn Rd S13 44 C7
Low Cl DE6 189 A2
Low Comm S21 79 D7
Lowcroft SK17 66 C2
Lowe Avenue DE7 193 C8
LOWEDGES 57 A6
Lowedges Cl S8 56 E6
Lowedges Cres S8 56 F6
Lowedges Dr S8 56 F6
Lowedges Jun Academy
SK13 56 F6
Lowedges Pl S8 57 A6
Lowedges Prim Sch
S8 56 E6
Lowedges Rd S8 56 E6
Lower Al S44 97 A1
Lower Bagthorpe
NG16 171 F3
Lower Bank SK13 17 D8
Lower Bank Cl SK13 9 F3
Lower Barn Rd SK13 9 E4
Lower Birchwood
DE55 170 F8
Lower Bloomsgrove Rd
DE7 194 F2
LOWER BRADWAY 56 C6
Lower Brook St
NG10 236 E7
Lower Burch Pl S32 71 E5
Lower Chapel St
9 Ilkeston DE7 194 F1
Stonebroom DE55 147 B4
Lower Clara Mount Rd
DE75 182 A1
Lower Cliffe SK22 23 D3
LOWER CROSSINGS 46 F6
Lower Dale Rd
DE23 218 F2
LOWER DINTING 10 B1
Lower Dr DE55 169 D7
Lower Dunstead Rd
Aldercar NG16 182 B3
Langley Mill NG16 182 A3
Lower Eaves View
SK23 47 C5
Lower Eley St DE1 267 A1
LOWER
ELLASTONE 183 C2
Lower Fold SK6 23 B8
Lower Gladstone St
DE75 181 E2
Lower Gn DE65 230 D1
Lower Granby St
DE7 194 F2
Lower Greenshall La
SK12 32 F6
Lower Grove Rd
S40 266 A3
Lower Hague SK22 32 E8
Lower Hall Cl DE56 191 C6
Lower Hardwick St 1
SK17 85 B8
LOWER
HARTSHAY 169 A3
Lower Higham Visitor
Ctr★ SK14 15 A8
Lower High St DE13 239 C7
LOWER KILBURN 191 F7
Lower La SK23 34 D1

Lowerlea SK12 32 C6
Lower Macclesfield Rd
Horwich End SK23 45 D6
Horwich End SK23 45 E6
Lower Mantle Cl
S45 131 D4
Lower Maples DE75 194 A8
Lower Market St
SK14 16 B8
Lower Meadows Prim Sch S8 57 A5
Lower Middleton St
DE7 195 A1
Lower Midland Rd 1
DE11 256 B4
LOWER MIDWAY 256 E6
Lower Mill 1 DE5 169 E1
Lower Orchard St 1
NG9 223 D7
Lower Park St NG9 223 C6
LOWER PILSLEY 132 B3
Lower Pingle Rd
DE6 185 C8
Lower Rd DE22 217 F8
Lower Rock St 2
SK22 33 C7
Lower Smithy La
SK17 88 A3
Lower Somercotes
DE55 170 E7
Lower Sq SK13 10 A7
Lower St DE6 224 B8
Lower Stanton Rd
DE7 208 F6
Lower Strines Rd
SK6 23 A5
Lower Terrace Rd
SK17 69 B5
LOWER THURVASTON 214 F6
Lowerwhitworth Rd 2
DE7 208 F6
Lower Whitworth Rd
DE7 208 F6
Lower Wood SK17 89 A7
Lower Wood Cotts
SK17 89 A7
Lowes Hill DE5 169 D3
Lowes La DE73 244 C7
Lowe St DE24 232 E6
LOWFIELD 43 B8
Lowfield SK14 16 A8
Lowfield Ave S12 58 E8
Lowfield Com Prim Sch 8 S2 43 A7
Lowfield Ct 4 S2 43 A7
Lowfields S43 79 A2
LOWGATES 78 F3
Lowgates S43 79 A2
Lowick Cl 4 DE23 231 E1
Lowlands Lea DE75 181 F2
Lowlands Rd DE56 179 B4
Low Lea Rd SK6 23 B6
Low Leas DE4 156 A8
LOW LEIGHTON 33 D8
Low Leighton Rd
SK22 33 D8
Lowman Way DE65 240 F8
Low Mdw SK23 45 D8
Low Mdw Row S81 63 E7
Low Meadows DE45 91 E6
Low Pavement S40 266 B3
Lowry Ct SK14 9 A4
Lowry Dr
Dronfield S18 56 F1
Marple SK6 23 B8
Lows Ct DE73 233 B2
Lowside S32 72 B2
Lowside Cl S32 72 B2
Low's La DE7 209 B2
Loxley Cl
Chesterfield S40 95 B3
Derby DE21 206 B2
Loxley La S80 82 A5
Loxton Ct DE3 217 D3
Loyne Cl DE24 231 F2
Lucas La DE65 228 E2
Lucas Rd S41 95 E5
Lucas Terr SK22 25 C3
Lucas Works S18 57 A2
Luccombe Dr DE24 233 D5
Lucerne Rd DE21 206 C3
Ludborough Wlk 14
NG19 136 E4
Ludburn La SK17 121 C1
Ludford Cl NG10 236 E4
Ludgate St DE13 239 C6
Ludgate Wlk DE22 217 E6
Ludham Cl S41 95 F7
Ludham Gdns S41 95 F7
Ludlam Ave NG16 195 A8
Ludlam Ho S2 43 E6
Ludlow Cl DE21 220 F5
Ludlow Rd DE23 230 F5
Ludworth Prim Sch
SK6 23 B8
Luke La DE6 201 E8
LULLINGTON 263 E7
Lullington Mews
DE12 262 A3
Lullington Rd
Clifton Campville B79 263 E3
Coton in the Elms DE12 260 C2
Edingale DE12 263 A5
Lullington Rd *continued*
Overseal DE12 262 A3
Lulworth Cl DE23 231 D6
Lulworth Ct NG16 195 F7
Lulworth Rd DE72 233 D3
Lumber La DE6 176 D2
Lumb La
Belper DE56 178 C4
Cowers Lane DE56 177 D2
Hazelwood DE56 178 B2
Northwood DE4 127 B6
Lumb The SK14 9 A6
Lumford Cotts
DE45 109 D7
Lumley Close DE24 233 D4
LUMSDALE 143 E6
Lumsdale DE4 143 E6
Lumsdale Cres DE4 143 D5
Lumsdale Rd
Matlock DE4 143 D4
Staveley S43 97 C8
Lumsdale Terr DE4 143 E7
Lum's Hill Rise DE4 143 D6
Luna Croft
Sheffield S12 43 F2
Sheffield S12 44 A3
Lunch Lane SK17 88 F8
Lundie Cl DE24 231 D2
Lundy Rd S18 76 B8
Lune Mdw NG19 136 E3
Lupin Cl
Derby DE21 206 C3
Derby DE24 231 C3
Shirebrook NG20 119 D3
Lupin Way S44 97 A3
Lupton Cres S8 56 F6
Lupton Dr S8 56 F6
Lupton Rd S8 56 F6
Lupton Wlk S8 57 A6
Luton Rd DE11 255 E2
Lutyens Court S40 94 F2
Lychgate Cl DE21 205 D2
Lydden Cl S43 96 E8
Lydford Ave S41 77 B1
Lydford Rd DE55 159 B5
LYDGATE 74 D8
Lydgate S32 71 E5
Lydgate Cotts S33 40 A6
Lydgate Dr S42 114 E3
Lydgate La S33 40 A6
Lydia Gdns NG16 182 E1
Lydstep Cl DE21 206 C2
Lyle Cl NG16 195 E7
Lymefield SK14 16 A8
Lymefield Terr SK14 16 B7
Lymefield Visitor Ctr*
SK14 16 B8
Lyme Park* SK12 32 B1
Lyme Park Ctry Pk*
SK12 32 B2
Lyme Pk
Chinley SK23 34 E2
Disley SK12 32 B2
Lyme Rd SK12 32 A6
Lymewood Dr SK12 32 C6
Lynam Rd DE55,
DE56 168 D7
Lyncroft Ave DE5 169 E1
Lyndale Dr DE5 181 B8
Lynden Ave NG10 236 D5
Lyndhurst Gr DE21 220 A5
Lyndhurst St DE23 219 A2
Lyne Ave SK13 17 A8
Lynholmes Rd DE4 143 D5
Lynholmes Rise
DE4 143 D5
Lynmouth Dr DE7 194 D3
Lynmouth Ho DE65 228 C1
Lynne Cl SK13 17 F8
Lynton Cl DE5 169 D3
Lynton Ct 10 S41 95 F8
Lynton Rd DE56 168 A3
Lynton St DE22 218 E4
Lynwood Cl
Branston DE14 253 F7
1 Dronfield S18 56 D1
Lynwood Rd
Branston DE14 253 E8
Derby DE24 231 F4
Lysander Dr DE73 232 E1
Lytham Cl DE21 205 D1
Lyttelton St DE22 218 C5

M

M1 Commerce Pk
S44 98 B4
Macaulay St DE24 232 A5
Macclesfield Main Rd
SK17 84 D5
Macclesfield Old Rd
SK17 84 D6
Macclesfield Rd
Buxton SK17 85 A6
Horwich End SK23 45 D6
Macdonald Cl S42 115 F3
Macdonald Sq DE7 208 D5
Machins Ct S18 57 A2
Mackenzie St DE22 218 C5
Mackinley Ave NG9 209 E1
Macklin St DE1 267 B3
MACKWORTH 217 E8
Mackworth Ave
DE3 230 E5
Mackworth Cl
5 Sheffield S2 44 A7
Swadlincote DE11 256 B7
Mackworth Rd DE1,
DE22 218 E6
Macmillan Mews S40 95 B3
Macnair Ct SK6 23 A5
Macnair Mews SK6 23 A5
Macready Pl DE24 232 F7
Maddock La DE4 153 A1
Madehurst Gdns S2 43 B7
Madehurst Rd S2 43 B7
Madehurst Rise S2 43 B7
Madehurst View S2 43 B7
Madeley Ct DE3 217 D1
Madeley St DE23 219 A2
Madin Dr S43 97 B6
Madin St
Chesterfield S41 266 B4
Tupton S42 131 D8
Madison Ave DE21 219 F7
Madras Rd DE15 248 C3
Magdala Cotts DE56 190 E5
Magdalene Drive
DE3 217 F3
Magee Ct DE1 267 C1
Magellan Way DE24 219 E1
Mag La
Creswell NG20 100 D5
Idridgehay DE56 176 D5
Magnolia Close
DE13 239 C5
Magnolia St DE55 159 E4
Magnolia Way DE55 170 A8
Magnus Ct DE21 219 B8
Magpie Way S40 95 D6
Maguire Ave SK13 10 A6
Maiden Rd NG20 119 D2
Maidstone Dr DE24 232 F5
Maidwell Cl DE56 179 C6
Main Ave
Derby DE22 204 F5
Sheffield S17 55 E4
Main Bright Rd 8
NG19 136 B1
Main Bright Wlk
NG19 136 B1
Main Dr S42 114 E2
Maine Dr DE21 220 A6
Main Rd
Abney S32 51 E3
Abney S33 52 A4
Bamford S33 40 B3
Barlow S18 75 E2
Bradwell S33 51 A8
Brailsford DE6 201 F7
Chesterfield, Ashgate S42 94 F4
Chesterfield, West Handley S21 77 D7
Cressbrook SK17 89 C7
Crich DE4 156 D1
Cutthorpe S42 94 E8
Darley Bridge DE4 142 B8
Denstone ST14 196 E6
Denstone ST14 197 A8
Earl Sterndale SK17 105 C2
Eckington, Lightwood S21 58 F3
Eckington, Ridgeway S12 58 E8
Ellastone ST14 183 A1
Elmton S80 100 A7
Elvaston DE72 234 A6
Eyam S32 71 C6
Flagg SK17 106 E6
Foolow SK17 70 D6
Great Hucklow SK17 70 B8
Grindleford S32 72 C7
Hathersage S32 53 A8
Haunton B79 263 C2
Heath S44 117 B2
Holmesfield S18 75 A8
Hulland Ward DE6 175 E3
Jacksdale NG16 171 B3
Lea DE4 156 B8
Little Hucklow SK17 50 F2
Lower Hartshay DE5 168 F4
Marsh Lane S21 58 E4
Mayfield DE6 184 D8
Morley Smithy DE21 206 C8
Nell Croft S11 54 A5
Renishaw S21 79 B8
Ripley DE5 169 A3
Ripley, Pentrich DE5 169 C5
Shirland DE55 146 D1
Smalley DE7 192 F3
Somercotes, Leabrooks DE55 170 C7
Somercotes, Pye Bridge DE55 170 F6
Stanton in Drive DE4 126 C5
Stonebroom DE55 147 A5
Sudbury DE6 225 F4
Sudbury, Aston DE6 226 A4
Taddington SK17 88 A3
Underwood Green NG16 171 F2
Unstone S18 76 E7
Upper Padley S32 53 F4
Wadshelf S42 93 E4
Wardlow SK17 70 C1
Wensley DE4 127 C1
Wensley DE4 142 A7
Whaley Thorns NG20 101 A1
Winster DE4 141 E6
Wyaston DE6 185 C2
Yeaveley DE6 199 D7
Main St
Awsworth NG16 195 C5
Biggin SK17 138 C3
Main St *continued*
Blackfordby DE11 257 C1
Bolsover S44 98 F1
Bolsover S44 117 F8
Bradbourne DE6 163 B6
Branston DE14 253 F7
Breaston DE72 235 D8
Breedon on the Hill DE73 252 F2
Brinsley NG16 171 D1
Burnaston DE65 229 F5
Burton upon Trent, Stapenhill DE15 254 E8
Burton upon Trent, Stretton DE13 240 E1
Caldwell DE12 260 F7
Calke LE65 251 E1
Calver S32 72 C1
Carsington DE4 164 E7
Chelmorton SK17 106 A8
Church Broughton DE65 227 B8
Clifton Campville B79 263 F2
Coton in the Elms DE12 260 D3
Eastwood NG16 182 F1
Edensor DE4 110 D8
Egginton DE65 241 B5
Elton DE4 140 E6
Elvaston DE72 234 D6
Etwall DE65 229 B4
Etwall DE65 229 C5
Findern DE65 230 D1
Great Longstone DE45 90 A4
Hartshorne DE11 257 B6
Hemington DE74 247 D5
Hilton DE65 228 C2
Hollington DE6 200 F4
Hollington DE6 201 A4
Hopton DE4 165 A7
Horsley Woodhouse DE7 192 C6
Ingleby DE65 243 F2
Ingleby DE73 244 A2
Kimberley NG16 195 F6
King's Newton DE73 245 C1
Kirk Ireton DE6 165 B1
Kniveton DE6 163 B1
Kniveton DE6 174 A8
Linton DE12 261 D6
Little Longstone DE45 89 D4
Lockington DE74 247 F5
Long Eaton NG10 236 E7
Longford DE6 214 D8
Lullington DE12 263 E7
Mapperley DE7 193 E3
Middleton DE4 154 D4
Moira DE11 256 C1
Netherseal DE12 264 F7
Newton DE55 148 A4
Newton Solney DE15 248 E8
Over Haddon DE45 109 A1
Overseal DE12 262 B3
Palterton S44 118 A5
Repton DE65 242 D1
Rosliston DE12 260 D6
Roston DE6 197 E6
Scarcliffe S44 118 E6
Scropton DE65 226 E1
Sheldon DE45 108 A6
Sheldon DE45 108 B6
Shirebrook NG20 119 E3
Smisby LE65 257 F3
South Normanton DE55 160 B6
Stanton-by-Dale DE7 222 F8
Sutton in Ashfield NG17 148 F3
Swadlincote DE11 255 E6
Tatenhill DE13 253 A8
Ticknall DE73 251 B4
Ticknall, Milton DE65 243 A1
Walton-on-Trent DE12 253 D1
Weston-on-Trent DE72 245 E5
Whaley Thorns ND20 100 F2
Whaley Thorns NG20 101 A2
Wilson DE73 252 E6
Winster DE4 141 C6
Youlgrave DE45 125 B5
Mais Cl DE4 144 A5
Maisies Way DE55 160 D6
Maitland DE11 261 B6
Maize Cl DE23 231 A6
Majestic Place
DE11 256 B3
Majolica Mews
DE11 256 F2
MAKENEY 191 A6
Makeney Rd
Belper DE56 191 A6
Duffield DE56 190 F2
Holbrook DE56 191 C6
Makeney Terr DE56 191 A6
Malbon's Yd DE6 173 C1
MALCOFF 35 E2
Malcolm Gr DE23 230 E8
Malcolm St DE23 219 B2
Malcote Mws DE11 261 B6
Maldon Close NG10 236 E5
Malham Cl S40 95 D5
Malham Gdns S20 59 D7
Malham Gr S20 59 E7
Malham Rd DE23 230 F6
Malia Rd S41 96 C6
Malik Way DE75 193 F8
Malin Cl DE24 233 B5
Malinder Cl S21 60 D6
Malinscommon La
DE56 166 C4
Malkin La DE6 188 E2
Malkin St S41 266 C3
Mallard Cl NG20 119 E3
Mallard Ct
Mansfield NG19 136 A2
6 Staveley S43 78 F2
Mallard Dr S21 60 B7
Mallard Way DE24 219 D3
Mallard Wlk DE3 230 C8
Mallatratt Pl NG19 136 B4
Mallory Cl S41 76 E3
Mallow Close DE24 231 C2
Mall The S45 131 C3
Malmesbury Ave
DE11 256 D6
Malpas Rd DE4 143 B6
Malson Way S41 95 F6
Maltby Ave DE55 146 E5
Maltby Cl 2 DE22 204 F2
Malthouse Cl
Eastwood NG16 182 F1
Wirksworth DE4 154 F3
Malthouse Ct
4 Ashbourne DE6 173 C2
Chesterfield S41 266 B4
Malthouse Drive
DE56 179 B4
Malthouse La
Ashover S45 129 F3
Boylestone DE6 213 C4
Froggatt S32 72 C5
Hatton DE65 227 D3
Nether Heage DE56 168 B2
Wingerworth S42 114 C3
Malthouse Mws
DE4 157 F4
Malthouse Rd
Ilkeston DE7 208 F4
Whitwell S80 82 A6
Malt House Yard
S44 118 E6
Maltings The
2 Ashbourne DE6 173 B2
Burton upon Trent DE15 248 A1
Derby DE1 267 B2
Derby DE22 218 D6
Shardlow DE72 235 B1
Malton Pl DE21 205 D1
Malton Wlk S40 114 F7
Malvern Ave DE15 248 A1
Malvern Cl DE3 217 D3
Malvern Gdns
5 Long Eaton NG10 236 A8
Matlock DE4 143 B6
Malvern Rd S40 95 E4
Malvern Rise SK13 10 A5
Malvern Way 3
DE21 205 D1
Manchester La
DE11 257 C5
Manchester Rd
Buxton SK17 65 F1
Chapel-en-le-Frith SK23 46 E5
Glossop SK13, SK14 9 E7
Tideswell SK17 50 A1
Tideswell SK17 69 B5
Manchester St
Derby DE22 218 D6
Long Eaton NG10 236 D6
Mandalay Rd NG19 135 B4
Mandarin Close
NG19 136 E2
Mandarin Way DE24 232 F8
Manifold Ave
Ashbourne DE6 173 D1
Staveley S43 97 D8
Manifold Dr DE24 233 B8
Manitoba Way
NG16 171 F7
Manknell Rd S41 96 A8
Manners Ave DE7 194 D1
Manners Cl SK23 34 D2
Manners Ind Est
DE7 194 C1
Manners Rd DE7 194 E1
Manners St DE7 209 A6
Manning View DE7 194 F2
Mannion Cres NG10 236 B5
Manor DE4 157 E3
Manor Ave
Brimington S43 96 F7
Derby DE23 218 C3
Stapleford NG9 223 D8
Manor Bglws 4 S18 56 F1
Manor Cl
Brassington DE4 153 A1
Chesterfield S44 80 B1
Newton DE55 148 A3
Pilsley S45 132 D1
Swadlincote DE15 255 A6
Manor Coach Ct
DE11 256 D3
Manor Court Rd S44 98 F3
Manor Cres
Burton upon Trent DE15 255 A6
Chesterfield S40 95 D3
Dronfield S18 56 F1
Manor Croft
Hepthorne Lane S42 131 F5
Ripley DE5 169 D3
Tatenhill DE13 253 A8
Manor Ct
Barrow upon Trent DE73 244 B5
Breaston DE72 235 E8
Breedon on the Hill DE73 252 F3
Clowne S43 80 F3
Risley DE72 222 D4
Somercotes DE55 170 E5
South Wingfield DE55 157 E3
Manor Dr
Brimington S43 96 F7
Chesterfield S40 95 D3
Netherseal DE12 264 F6
Manor Farm S45 132 D1
Manor Farm Barns
DE21 205 E3
Manor Farm Cotts
DE45 89 E4
Manor Farm Ct
Killamarsh S21 60 D5
Whitwell S80 81 F6
Manor Farm Mews
Aston-on-Trent DE72 246 B8
Burnaston DE65 229 F5
Long Duckmanton S44 98 A3
Manor Farm Rd
DE72 246 B8
Manor Fields Dr
DE7 208 D7
Manor Gdns DE11 261 C6
Manor Gr S43 80 A6
Manor House Court
S41 96 A5
Manor House Rd
NG10 236 F6
Manor La
Fritchley DE55 168 F8
South Wingfield DE55 157 F1
Manorleigh DE72 235 E8
Manor Leigh DE72 235 E8
Manor Mws 6
NG19 136 C3
Manor Park Ct
DE22 218 B3
Manor Park Rd SK13 10 E1
Manor Park View
SK13 10 E2
Manor Park Way
DE3 218 B3
Manor Pk DE72 221 B1
Manor Rd
Ashbourne DE6 173 D3
Barlborough S43 80 A7
Barton in Fabis NG11 237 E6
Belper DE56 178 F3
Borrowash DE72 221 A1
Calow S43 96 F6
Chellaston DE73 232 F1
Chesterfield S40 95 C3
Derby DE23 218 C2
Derby DE73 233 A1
Eastwood NG16 182 F1
Harthill S26 61 F8
Horwich End SK23 45 E5
Ilkeston DE7 194 E1
Killamarsh S21 60 E5
Mansfield Woodhouse NG19 136 A4
South Wingfield DE55 157 F3
Swadlincote DE15 255 B6
Manor Rise B79 263 E3
Manor School View
DE12 262 B3
Manor Sch The
NG19 136 C5
Manor St SK13 10 D1
Manor View
Hartshorne DE11 257 B6
Sheffield S20 59 E7
Manse Ave S80 100 D8
Manse Cl
Creswell S43 81 D1
Creswell S80 100 D8
Mansfeldt Cres S41 95 E6
Mansfeldt Rd S41 95 E6
MANSFIELD 135 F2
Mansfield Cl DE11 256 D4
Mansfield Dr S12 44 C6
Mansfield Rd
Alfreton DE55 159 B4
Bramley-Vale S44 117 E1
Brinsley NG16 182 F4
Chesterfield S41 115 F6
Clowne S43 80 E2
Creswell S80 81 F1
Creswell S80 100 F8
Creswell S80 101 A8
Derby DE1 219 A6
Derby DE1, DE21 267 B4
Eastwood NG16 182 F4
Glapwell NG19, S44 134 C8
Heanor DE75 182 A2
Heath S44 117 A3
Holmewood S42 116 C3
Killamarsh S21 60 F6
Mansfield Woodhouse NG19 136 C2
Morley DE21 206 B4
Palterton S44 118 B6
Scarcliffe S44 118 E5
Sclston NG16 171 F7
Sheffield S12 44 B6
Shirebrook NG20 120 F1
South Normanton DE55 160 D6
Spion Kop NG19 136 F8

Mansfield Rd *continued*
Tibshelf DE55 148 B7
Whitwell S80 82 F7
Mansfields Croft DE65 229 B4
Mansfield St
Derby DE1 267 B5
Somercotes DE55 170 C8
Mansfield Terr DE55 159 C5
Mansfield View S12 44 B6
MANSFIELD WOODHOUSE 136 E2
Mansfield Woodhouse Sta NG19 136 A3
Manton Cl
2 Burton upon Trent DE13 240 F1
Swadlincote DE11 255 F6
Manvers Ave 2 DE5 169 E1
Manvers Ct
Chesterfield S41 266 B4
Shirebrook NG20 120 A4
Manvers Rd S44 97 A4
Manvers St
Mansfield Woodhouse NG19 136 A3
Ripley DE5 169 E1
Shirebrook NG20 120 A4
Manystones La
Brassington DE4 153 B3
Middleton DE4 154 B2
Maple Ave
Derby DE23 231 D6
Disley SK12 33 A6
Ripley DE5 180 C8
Sandiacre NG10 223 B7
Maplebeck Ct DE1 267 B5
Maple Cl
Alfreton DE55 160 B5
Doveridge DE6 211 B1
Hilton DE65 228 D2
Mansfield NG19 136 E1
Maple Dr
Ashbourne DE6 185 D7
Aston-on-Trent DE72 246 A7
Belper DE56 179 B2
Chellaston DE73 233 A2
Creswell S80 81 E2
Derby, Boulton DE24 233 A6
Killamarsh S21 60 C5
South Normanton DE55 160 B4
Maple Gdns
1 Heanor DE75 181 D1
Langley Mill NG16 182 B3
Maple Gr
Breaston DE72 235 F8
Burton upon Trent DE15 254 E5
Derby DE22 204 D5
Glapwell S44 134 B8
Maple Rd
Castle Donington DE74 247 A5
Swadlincote DE11 256 B6
Maple St S43 97 B8
Maples The DE75 194 A7
Mapletoft Ave NG19 136 A5
MAPLETON 172 F4
Mapleton Ave DE21 205 F1
Mapleton Rd
Ashbourne DE6 173 A2
Draycott DE72 235 A8
Maple View DE4 143 C3
Maple Way
Branston DE14 253 F8
Burton upon Trent DE14 254 A8
Selston NG16 171 F7
MAPPERLEY 193 E3
Mapperley CE (Controlled) Prim Sch DE7 193 E3
Mapperley La DE7 193 E2
Mapperley Rd S18 56 C1
Marble Cl DE1 267 A4
Marble Ct SK17 85 E2
Marble Dr DE11 255 F4
MARCHINGTON 224 E2
Marchington Cl DE22 204 E1
Marchwood Cl S40 95 E4
Marcie Ct DE65 242 D2
Marcus St DE1 219 A7
Mardale Cl S41 76 E1
Maree Cl DE24 231 E4
MAREHAY 180 D6
Marfleet Cl DE3 217 D3
Margaret Ave
Derby DE21 219 F5
Ilkeston DE7 208 F8
Long Eaton NG10 223 F1
Sandiacre NG10 223 B4
Margaret St DE1 267 B5
Margery Cl DE6 185 B8
Margreave Rd DE21 219 F7
Mariana Cl DE73 232 E2
Marigold Cl DE21 206 B3
Marigold Pl DE11 256 F4
Marina Dr
Derby, Allenton DE24 232 E5
Derby, Spondon DE21 220 D5
Shireoaks S81 63 F6
Marina Rd DE7 193 B8
Marine Dr S41 96 C3
Marion Ct SK17 85 C6
Marisco Cl DE24 233 D4
Marjoram Gro DE3 217 D4
Marjorie Rd DE21 219 F8
Marjory La DE6, DE65 213 C2
MARKEATON 218 B8
Markeaton La
Derby DE22 204 C1
Derby DE22 218 B8
Markeaton Pk★ DE22 218 C7
Markeaton Prim Sch DE22 218 E7
Markeaton St DE22 218 E6
Market Arc 2 SK13 10 C1
Market Cl
Hope S33 39 A4
Shirebrook NG20 119 F3
South Normanton DE55 160 A6
Market Head DE56 179 A3
Market Pl
Alfreton DE55 158 F4
5 Ashbourne DE6 173 C2
Belper DE56 179 A3
Bolsover S44 99 A1
7 Buxton SK17 85 B7
Castleton S33 38 C2
Chapel-en-le-Frith SK23 47 B6
8 Charlesworth SK13 16 C8
Chesterfield S40 266 B3
Codnor DE5 181 B8
Compstall SK6 15 A2
Crich DE4 156 F1
Cromford DE4 155 A6
Cromford DE4 155 B6
Derby DE1 219 A5
Derby DE1 267 B3
Hartington SK17 137 D5
1 Heanor DE5 181 E1
Ilkeston DE7 208 E8
Ironville NG16 170 F4
Long Eaton NG10 236 E8
Longnor SK17 121 B6
Mansfield Woodhouse NG19 136 C3
Melbourne DE73 252 B7
Mottram in Longdendale SK14 9 A3
Ripley DE5 169 D1
Shirebrook NG20 119 F4
Somercotes DE55 170 C8
Somercotes, Riddings DE55 170 E6
South Normanton DE55 160 A6
South Wingfield DE4 157 F4
Staveley S43 78 E2
Sutton in Ashfield NG17 148 F3
Tideswell SK17 69 C4
Wirksworth DE4 165 F8
Market Sq SK17 69 C4
Market St
Bakewell DE45 109 D6
Broadbottom SK14 16 A8
Buxton SK17 85 B7
Castle Donington DE74 247 B3
Chapel-en-le-Frith SK23 47 C6
Clay Cross S45 131 D4
Disley SK12 32 D6
Draycott DE72 235 A7
Eckington S21 59 E3
Glossop SK13 10 C1
Hayfield SK22 25 D3
Heanor DE75 181 E1
Hollingworth SK14 9 D5
Ilkeston DE7 208 F8
Ironville NG16 170 F4
Mottram in Longdendale SK14 9 A4
New Mills SK22 33 B7
Shirebrook NG20 119 F4
South Normanton DE55 160 A5
Staveley S43 78 E2
Sutton in Ashfield NG17 148 F3
Swadlincote DE11 256 B4
Whaley Bridge SK23 33 E1
Whaley Bridge SK23 45 E7
Market View 15 SK17 85 B7
Markham Cres S43 78 F2
Markham Ct
Derby DE21 205 F2
Duckmanton S44 98 A5
Markham La S44 98 B4
Markham Quay S41 266 C2
Markham Rd
Chesterfield S40 266 B2
Long Duckmanton S44 98 B5
Markham Ret Pk S40 266 B2
Markham Rise S45 131 B4
Markham Vale Environment Ctr S44 98 B4
Markhma La S44 98 B6
Markland Ave S43 81 A4
Markland Cres S43 81 A4
Markland La S80, S43 81 A2
Markland View S80 81 D3
Mark's Cl DE23 231 D6
Mark St NG10 223 C5
Marlborough Cres DE15 255 A8
Marlborough Dr DE56 179 C5
Marlborough Rd
Breaston DE72 235 D7
Buxton SK17 85 B8
Derby DE24 232 C7
Long Eaton NG10 223 F1
Mansfield NG19 135 F1
Marlow Brow SK13 10 A4
Marlow Cres DE7 207 D8
Marlow Dr DE14 254 A8
Marlowe Ct DE23 231 F6
Marlow St
5 Buxton SK17 85 C8
5 Glossop SK13 10 A5
Marlpit La
Bolsover S44 99 C3
Denstone ST14 196 D6
Ellastone DE6 183 A3
Sutton on the Hill DE6 228 A8
MARLPOOL 193 F8
Marlpool Inf Sch DE75 194 A8
Marlpool Jun Sch DE75 182 A1
Marl Way DE11 256 A4
MARPLE 23 A5
Marple Rd SK13 16 B5
MARPLERIDGE 23 A2
Marples Ave NG19 136 E5
Marple Sta SK6 23 A7
Marquis Ct DE12 262 E5
Marquis Dr DE12 262 E5
Marquis Gdns DE73 244 E8
Marriott SK23 34 E1
Marrison Dr S21 60 C6
Marsden Cl DE56 190 E3
Marsden Pl
2 Chesterfield S40 95 D2
Chesterfield S41 266 B4
Marsden Row S33 40 B4
Marsden St
Chesterfield S40 266 B3
Derby DE24 232 E7
Glossop SK13 10 A4
Marsden Wood Grove S45 131 E7
Marshall Dr 1 NG9 223 F8
Marshall St
Alfreton DE55 159 A3
Heanor DE75 181 F2
Marshall Way DE7 208 C6
Marsham Dr SK6 23 A5
Marsh Ave
Dronfield S18 57 B3
Hope S33 38 F4
Ilkeston NE7 194 E6
Marshaw Cl DE3 217 E1
Marsh Cl S20 59 C6
Marshes The S33 38 E4
Marshfield Gr S43 79 A2
Marsh Green SK23 47 B4
Marshgreen Cl DE24 233 D5
Marsh Green La S45 129 F4
Marsh Hall La SK23 46 F5
Marsh Hollow DE6 200 F5
Marsh La
Belper DE56 179 B5
Mayfield DE6 183 D8
New Mills SK22, SK23 33 D6
MARSH LANE 58 F3
Marsh Lane Cres DE56 179 B4
Marsh Lane Prim Sch S21 58 E3
Marsh Lane Trad Est SK22 33 D7
Marsh View S21 59 B2
Marsh Way SK23 46 F5
Marston SK17 106 B7
Marston Bank
Marston Montgomery DE6 197 C2
Marston Montgomery DE6 197 D3
Marston Brook DE65 228 E1
Marston Cl
Belper DE56 179 C6
Derby DE23 231 D5
Dronfield S18 75 D8
Marston Common
Marston Montgomery DE6 197 F2
Marston Montgomery DE6 198 A4
Marstone Cres S17 55 F5
Marston La
Doveridge DE6 211 B1
Doveridge DE6 211 C2
Hatton DE65 239 D8
Marston on Dove DE65 228 B1
Marston on Dove DE65 240 A8
Rolleston DE13 240 A4
MARSTON MONTGOMERY 211 F8
Marston Montgomery Prim Sch DE6 211 E8
Marston Old La DE65 239 D8
MARSTON ON DOVE 240 B8
Marston Rd
Somersal Herbert DE6 211 F3
Somersal Herbert DE6 212 A3
Marston Rise DE15 254 F8
Martha Rd DE3 217 E6
Martin Ct S21 59 C3
Martindale Cl S43 97 C8
Martindale Ct DE56 179 D5
Martin Dr DE21 220 A8
Martinet Close DE74 246 F4
Martin Rise S21 59 C3
MARTINSIDE 47 D3
Martins La S42 131 B8
Martin's La DE13 238 A4
Martival Court LE66 258 A1
Martlet Ave SK12 32 C6
Marx Ct S45 131 C3
Mary Ann St S41 76 E4
Mary Devonshire Cotts DE45 91 C2
Maryland Ct
Stapleford NG9 209 E1
Swadlincote DE11 256 A7
Maryland Rd DE21 220 B6
Marylebone Cres
Derby DE22 218 A6
3 Derby DE3 217 F6
Mary St
Eckington S21 59 D3
Whaley Thorns NG20 101 A2
Mary Swanwick Com Prim Sch S41 77 A3
Masefield Ave
Derby DE23 231 E7
Holmewood S42 116 D1
Holmewood S42 132 C8
Holmewood S42 132 E8
Swadlincote DE11 256 C6
Masefield Rd S13 44 C6
Masefield Way S42 132 E8
Mason Cres
Sheffield S13 44 D6
Swadlincote DE11 256 E4
Mason Gr S13 44 D7
Mason Mills Sh Village DE4 155 A7
Mason Rd DE7 194 D2
Masons Cotts S21 59 A1
Masons Gr SK13 10 A6
Masons Place Bsns Pk DE21 219 D6
Mason St S80 81 F6
Mason Way DE55 170 C7
Masson Cl 12 S40 95 D5
Masson Hill View DE4 142 F7
Masson Mills (Working Textile Mus)★ DE4 155 A7
Masson Rd DE4 143 A2
Masson Shopping Village DE4 155 A7
Masson Terr DE4 144 A5
Masson Wlk DE22 218 E4
Masters View
6 Ripley DE5 170 A1
Ripley DE5 181 A8
Mastin Ave S43 80 D5
MASTIN MOOR 79 D4
Matcham Way SK17 84 E5
MATHERSGRAVE 145 C3
Mathersgrave La DE55 145 B2
Mather's Way S42 115 D1
MATLOCK 143 A5
MATLOCK BANK 143 C5
Matlock Bank 8 SK13 9 E1
MATLOCK BATH 143 C5
Matlock Bath Aquarium★ DE4 143 A1
Matlock Bath Holy Trinity CE Prim Sch DE4 155 A8
Matlock Bath Sta DE4 143 B1
MATLOCK BRIDGE 143 B5
MATLOCK CLIFF 143 D4
Matlock Ct NG10 235 F5
MATLOCK DALE 143 A2
Matlock Dr S43 97 C5
Matlock Farm Park★ DE4 128 D5
Matlock Gdns 5 SK13 9 E1
Matlock Gn DE4 143 C4
MATLOCK GREEN 143 C5
Matlock Ho DE21 220 E3
Matlock La 7 SK13 9 E1
Matlock Parks Nature Reserve★ DE4 143 B3
Matlock Pl 6 SK13 9 E1
Matlock Rd
Ambergate DE56 167 F4
Ashover S42, S45 113 E3
Belper DE56 178 F8
Brackenfield DE55 145 C2
Derby DE21 205 F1
Holymoorside S40, S42 114 B7
Wessington DE55 157 E8
Matlock Riverside Sta★ DE4 143 A6
Matlock St Giles CE (VA) Prim Sch DE4 143 C3
Matlock Spard DE4 142 F5
Matlock Spa Rd DE4 143 A5
Matlock St DE45 109 D5
Matlock Sta DE4 143 B5
Mattersey Ct 4 NG19 136 B1
Matthew Cl SK13 9 F7
Matthew Kirtley Mus★ DE5 170 A4
Matthews Ct NG9 209 E1
Matthews Fold S8 43 C1
Matthews La S8 43 C1
Matthew St DE24 232 F6
Matthew Way DE23 230 E7
Matt Orch DE55 160 B4
Maudesley Ave S41 266 B1
Maugerhay S8 43 C1
Maunleigh NG19 136 E1
Maun Valley Pk Nature Reserve★ NG19 136 E2
Mawfa Ave S14 43 D2
Mawfa Cres S14 43 D2
Mawfa Dr S14 43 D2
Mawfa Rd S14 43 D2
Mawfa Wlk S14 43 D2
Mawkin La NG16 160 F5
Maws La NG16 195 E7
Mawstone La
Youlgrave DE45 125 C4
Youlgreave DE45 125 B3
Maxey Pl S8 43 A6
Max Rd DE21 219 F8
Maxwell Ave DE22 218 D8
Maxwell St DE72 235 F8
May Ave S41 77 C3
Maybank Cl SK23 35 A1
Mayfair DE11 255 E6
Mayfair Cres DE22 217 F6
Mayfair Ct DE56 190 E4
MAYFIELD 184 C8
Mayfield Ave
Heanor DE75 181 E1
Kilburn DE56 192 A8
Mayfield DE6 184 C7
Mayfield Dr
Burton upon Trent DE15 255 A8
North Wingfield S42 131 F6
Stapleford NG9 209 F2
Mayfield Gr NG10 223 E1
Mayfield Mill DE6 184 D6
Mayfield Pl DE6 184 C8
Mayfield Rd
Burton upon Trent DE15 248 A3
Chesterfield S40 95 C2
Derby DE21 219 E7
Marple SK6 15 B1
Mayfield DE6 172 D1
Sheffield S10 42 F7
Mayfield Terr
Hathersage S32 53 A8
Mayfield DE6 184 D6
Mayflower Cl SK13 17 E8
Mayflower Ct
Sheffield S12 44 B6
Shirebrook NG20 119 E4
Mayflower Rd NG16 195 B8
Mayhall Ave NG19 136 A4
Maylands DE72 221 B1
Maylands Ave DE72 235 E8
Maynard Rd
Chesterfield S40 266 A1
Grindleford S32 53 D1
Maynestone Rd SK23 34 E5
Maypole Cl DE7 208 C4
Maypole Hill DE11 256 A6
Maypole La DE23 230 E7
May South DE7 194 D3
May St
Derby DE22 218 F3
Ilkeston DE7 194 E4
Maytree Cl DE21 206 C3
Mayvale Gr DE22 218 C4
McAdam Cl DE15 248 B2
McAuley Ct DE1 267 B4
McDavid Way S44 98 C5
McGough Mews DE24 232 A5
McGregor's Way S40 115 B7
McMahon Ave S43 97 B6
McNeil Gr DE72 235 A7
Mdws The DE4 165 E8
Mead Cl DE24 231 F4
Mead Cres DE15 255 A6
Meadow Ave
Buxton SK17 67 B5
Codnor DE5 181 B8
Meadow Bank
Glossop SK13 16 F7
Hollingworth SK14 9 D6
Mansfield Woodhouse NG19 136 E6
South Normanton DE55 160 A7
Meadowbank Ct NG16 182 D3
Meadowbank Way NG16 182 D3
Meadowbank Way Ind Est NG16 182 D3
Meadow Brook Cl 3 DE23 230 F6
Meadowbrook Ind Est S20 60 A8
Meadowbrook Pk S20 60 A8
Meadow Cl
Barlborough S43 80 C6
Bolsover S44 118 A8
Chesterfield S43 77 D2
Derby DE21 220 E4
Dove Holes SK17 47 E1
Draycott DE72 235 A7
Dronfield S18 57 C4
Eastwood NG16 182 F4
Findern DE65 230 D2
Horsley Woodhouse DE7 192 D6
Repton DE65 242 E2
Stoney Middleton S32 72 B3
Tibshelf DE55 148 B7
Whaley Bridge SK23 45 C8
Meadow Cotts NG19 136 C3
Meadow Cres
Castle Donington DE74 247 B2
Sheffield S20 59 B7
Meadowcroft SK14 9 A4
Meadow Croft S42 132 D8
Meadowcroft Gdns S20 59 E8
Meadowcroft Glade S20 59 E8
Meadowcroft Rise 2 S20 59 E8
Meadow Ct
Belper DE56 178 F4
Chesterfield S43 77 D4
5 Derby DE3 217 D1
Elvaston DE72 234 D6
2 Grassmoor S41 115 F2
Grassmoor S42 116 A2
Kilburn DE56 192 A7
South Normanton DE55 159 F4
Meadow Drive DE7 193 B8
Meadow End DE4 165 E7
Meadow Farm Prim Sch DE21 220 A4
Meadowfield SK23 45 D8
Meadowfield Cl SK13 9 F3
Meadow Fields DE13 240 C4
Meadowgate Pk S21 60 D7
Meadow Gdns DE75 182 B1
Meadow Gr
Newton DE55 148 A3
Sheffield S17 55 E4
Meadowgrass Cl DE23 231 B6
Meadow Grove Rd S17 55 D4
Meadowhead S8 56 F8
Meadow Head Ave S8 56 F8
Meadow Head Cl S8 56 E7
Meadow Head Dr S8 56 F8
Meadow Head Pl S17 56 F8
Meadowhead Sch S8 57 A7
Meadowhill Rd S41 115 D8
Meadow House Way S44 98 C3
Meadow La
Burton upon Trent DE13 248 A8
Derby DE1, DE21 267 D3
Derby, Chaddesden DE21 219 F5
Disley SK12 32 D6
Dove Holes SK17 47 E2
Hilton DE65 228 C1
Long Eaton NG10 236 F7
Newton DE55 159 F7
Repton DE65 243 A4
Roston DE6 197 C7
Shirebrook NG19, NG20 119 D2
Swadlincote DE11 256 A6
Tideswell SK17 69 B2
Meadowlands S44 99 C2
Meadow Lane Ind Est DE55 159 B5
Meadowlark Gr DE21 206 A1
Meadow Nook DE24 233 C5
Meadow Pl DE4 142 F7
Meadow Rd
Awsworth NG16 195 C5
Clay Cross S45 131 A5
Derby DE1 267 C3
Derby, Wilmorton DE21, DE24 219 F1
Ripley DE5 169 E1
Meadow Rise
Brassington DE4 153 A1
Chesterfield S42 94 F4
Church Broughton DE65 227 B8
Glossop SK13 16 F7
Meadows Croft DE56 190 D3
Meadows Dr S43 97 F8
Meadowside
Disley SK12 33 A6
Mayfield DE6 184 D6

Meadowside *continued*
Whaley Bridge SK23 45 D8
Meadowside Cl
Shirley DE6 200 D8
Wingerworth S42 115 B4
Meadows Ind Est The DE21 219 D5
Meadows Rd SK22 25 D2
Meadow St
Ilkeston DE7 194 F1
Ironville NG16 170 F5
New Mills SK22 33 C8
Meadows The
Awsworth NG16 195 C5
Belper DE56 178 E4
Burton upon Trent DE15 248 B2
Chesterfield S42 95 A5
Dove Holes SK17 47 F1
Great Longstone DE45 90 A4
3 Heanor DE75 181 E1
Killamarsh S21 60 D6
Swanwick DE55 169 E7
Uttoxeter ST14 210 A2
Meadows Wlk S43 80 F4
Meadow Vale DE56 190 D3
Meadow View
Belper DE56 178 F3
Bolsover S43 80 F3
Chesterfield S40 114 A8
Darley Dale DE4 142 F7
Doveridge DE6 224 C8
Higham DE55 146 C2
Holmewood S42 132 D8
Rolleston DE13 240 C4
Selston NG16 171 E6
South Wingfield DE55 157 F5
South Wingfield DE55 158 A5
Stapleford NG9 223 D8
Meadow View Cl
Derby DE21 206 B3
Hanbury DE13 238 A4
Meadow View Ct DE72 222 E4
Meadow View Rd
Sheffield S8 56 F8
Swadlincote DE11 255 F5
Meadow Way
Chellaston DE73 233 A1
Swadlincote DE11 256 A6
Meads The S8 57 B8
Mead The S41 115 C8
Meadway Dr S17 55 D7
Meadway The S17 55 D7
Mead Wlk DE15 255 A6
Meakin Drive DE11 256 F1
Meakin St S41 115 D8
Meal Hill Rd HD9 2 F8
Meal St SK22 33 C8
Mear Dr DE72 221 B1
Mear Greaves La DE15 248 B4
Mease La B79 263 B2
Mease Spencer Acad The DE65 240 D8
Mease The
Hilton DE65 228 C1
Hilton DE65 228 E1
Measham Rd
Appleby Magna DE12 265 F1
Donisthorpe DE12 265 D6
Moira DE12 262 F3
Meath Ave DE21 220 B4
Meden Ave NG19 134 F7
Meden Bank NG19 135 B5
Meden Cl NG19 135 B5
Meden Rd NG19 136 D4
Meden Sq NG19 135 B5
Medham Ave DE11 261 B6
Medina Cl DE24 233 D5
Medlock Cl S40 114 B7
Medlock Rd S40 114 C8
Medway Dr DE22 205 B5
Meerbrook Cl DE21 206 A1
Meerbrook Dr DE4 154 F2
Meerbrook Pl DE7 208 C5
MEERSBROOK 43 B5
MEERSBROOK BANK 43 A5
Meersbrook Park Rd S8 43 A5
Meersbrook Rd S8 43 B5
Meersbrook Works 13 S2 43 A6
Meersdale S2 43 C6
Megaloughton La DE21 220 C3
Megdale DE4 143 A6
Melandra Castle Rd SK13 9 D2
Melandra Ct DE22 218 E4
Melandra Rd SK13 9 E3
Melanie Cl SK13 17 A8
Melbourn Cl DE56 190 E3
MELBOURNE 252 B8
Melbourne Ave
Burton upon Trent DE15 248 C3
Dronfield S18 56 B1
Melbourne Cl
Belper DE56 179 A2
Derby DE22 204 D2
Derby, Markeaton DE3 217 F3
Melbourne Ct DE24 219 E4
Melbourne Ct
Long Eaton NG10 235 F4
8 Staveley S43 78 E2
Melbourne Hall & Gdns* DE73 252 C7
Melbourne Ho DE21 220 E3
Melbourne Inf Sch DE73 252 B8
Melbourne Jun Sch DE73 252 B8
Melbourne La
Breedon on the Hill DE73 252 E2
Ticknall DE73 251 C5
Melbourne L Ctr DE73 252 B7
Melbourne Rd
Breedon on the Hill DE73 252 A2
Melbourne DE73 252 F8
Stapleford NG9 209 E1
Melbourne St
Derby DE1 267 B1
Mansfield Woodhouse NG19 136 C6
Melbreak Cl DE3 217 E1
Melfort Cl DE24 231 F2
Melling Cl S40 114 F8
Melling Ct S40 114 F8
Mellington Cl S8 43 C2
Melliot Ct DE23 231 C3
MELLOR 23 D5
Mellor Dr ST14 210 B1
Mellor La
Barlow S18 75 E1
Chapel-en-le-Frith SK23 47 A6
Mellor Prim Sch SK6 23 C6
Mellor Rd
Burton upon Trent DE14 254 B7
New Mills SK6, SK22 24 C3
Mellor's La DE56 191 C6
Mellors Rd NG19 135 D1
Mellor St DE24 232 E6
Mellor Way S40 115 A7
Melrose Cl
Chesterfield S40 95 D3
Derby DE24 231 E2
Melrose Ct 7 S41 96 A6
Melrose Way DE55 158 B4
Meltham La S41 96 B6
Melton Ave
Derby DE23 231 C6
Melbourne DE73 252 A8
Melton Ct
Derby DE22 218 E6
Sandiacre NG10 223 A5
Somercotes DE55 170 C6
Melville Cl DE6 175 F3
Melville Cres S43 96 F4
Melville Ct DE65 229 B3
Melville Dr S2 44 A8
Memorial Croft DE4 154 F3
Memorial Pl SK17 67 C5
Memorial Rd DE22 204 C3
Memorial View DE4 156 F2
Mendip Cl 1 NG10 223 A1
Mendip Cres S40 95 B4
Mendip Ct DE21 205 E2
Menin Rd DE22 204 C2
Mentmore Cl DE55 170 A7
Meon Cl DE3 217 B1
MERCASTON 188 B3
Mercaston Cl S40 95 A5
MERCASTON GREEN 188 B3
Mercaston La
Hulland Ward DE6 188 B4
Mackworth DE6, DE22 203 B8
Mercaston DE6 188 C2
Weston Underwood DE6 202 F8
Mercaston Rd DE21 219 F8
Mercer Cres DE55 159 C3
Merchant Ave DE21 220 D4
Merchant Drive DE55 170 C7
Merchantman Mews DE74 246 F4
Merchants Cnr DE22 218 E6
Merchant St
Derby DE22 218 E6
Shirebrook NG20 120 A4
Mercia Cl
Eastwood NG16 195 A8
Hatton DE65 239 D8
Mercia Dr
Sheffield S17 55 E6
Willington DE65 242 B5
Mercian Cl DE7 194 E1
Mercian Mews DE21 220 D4
Mercian Pk DE7 194 E1
Mercian Wy DE1 267 A2
Mere Beck DE72 234 D6
Meredith Ct NG9 209 E2
Mereoak La DE11, DE73 257 E7
Mereside Gdns SK23 45 D6
Merevale Way DE24 231 C3
Meridian Cl DE7 194 E4
Merion Gr DE23 218 A1
Merlin Ave S44 98 F3
Merlin Cl DE56 179 C5
Merlin Cres DE14 253 F8
Merlin Gdns 7 DE73 244 E8
Merlin Gn DE24 231 D4
Merlin La DE7 192 D6
Merlin Road NG19 136 B2
Merlin Way
Burnaston DE3 230 B7
Ilkeston DE7 208 F4
Woodville DE11 256 F3
Merrial Cl DE45 109 C4
Merrick Cl S40 95 D5
Merridale Rd DE23 231 C8
Merrill Coll DE24 232 E5
Merrill Way DE24 232 D5
Merrybower Cl DE24 231 D3
Merrydale Rd DE15 255 A8
Merryton Cl DE21 205 F3
Mersey Bank Rd SK13 9 F4
Mersey Way
Hilton Common DE65 228 E1
13 Sheffield S2 43 C8
Merthyr Ct DE21 206 B2
Merton Cl 2 DE75 181 F1
Merton Close DE11 255 E1
Merton Ct NG9 209 E1
Merton Drive DE22 217 F5
Mervyn Rd DE15 248 A3
Mesne La DE45 109 E7
Messiter Mews DE65 242 B5
Metcalfe Ave S21 60 C6
Metcalfe Cl DE24 233 B8
Meteor Bsns Pk DE21 205 B1
Meteor Ctr The DE21 205 C1
Methley Cl S12 43 F6
Metro Ave DE55 148 A3
Mettesford DE4 143 D5
Meverill Rd SK17 69 D5
Mevril Rd SK23 45 E5
Mevril Springs Way SK23 45 E5
Mewies Cl DE12 253 D1
Mews Ct DE3 217 D4
Mews The
Burton upon Trent DE14 254 C8
Horsley Woodhouse DE7 192 C7
Little Eaton DE56 191 B2
Melbourne DE73 252 B7
New Mills SK22 33 D8
Wyaston DE6 185 B2
Meynell Cl
Burton upon Trent DE15 248 B1
Chesterfield S40 95 C2
Meynell Ct
Derby DE22 204 C2
Kirk Langley DE6 202 F2
Meynell Langley DE6 203 C4
Meynell Rd NG10 236 D5
Meynell Rise DE6 173 C4
Meynell St
Derby DE23 218 F1
Swadlincote DE11 256 A1
Meynell Way S21 60 C6
Michael Cl S42 115 A5
Michael House Sch DE75 194 A6
Michael's La DE6 183 C5
Michaels Mdw DE55 159 F3
Michaelwood Way S43 98 F6
Michelle Cl DE24 231 C3
Michigan Cl DE21 220 C5
Michlow Cl S33 51 A8
Michlow Dr S33 51 A8
Michlow La S33 51 A8
Micklebring Cl DE5 169 C1
Micklecroft Gdns DE23 230 E7
Mickledon Cl 3 NG10 236 B8
MICKLEOVER 217 E2
Mickleover Ho DE3 230 D8
Mickleover Prim Sch DE3 217 D2
Mickleross Cl DE3 217 D4
Mickleton Cl DE11 256 B1
MICKLEY 56 B3
Mickley Inf Sch DE55 146 C4
Mickley La
Sheffield S17, S18 55 F4
Shirland DE55 146 C5
Middlebeck Cl DE73 232 F2
Middle Cl DE11 256 B4
MIDDLECROFT 97 C7
Middlecroft Rd S43 97 D7
Middlefield Cl
Derby DE22 204 D4
Sheffield S17 55 C7
Middlefield Croft S17 55 C7
Middlegate Field Dr S80 82 A5
MIDDLE HANDLEY 77 F8
Middle Hay Cl S14 43 E4
Middle Hay Pl S14 43 E4
Middle Hay Rise S14 43 E4
Middle Hay View S14 43 E4
Middle La
Clay Cross S45 131 E3
Crich DE4 156 D1
Stanton Lees DE45 126 E3
MIDDLE MAYFIELD 184 B6
Middle Mdw S81 63 E7
Middle Mill 2 DE1 267 A4
Middle Orchard St NG9 223 D7
Middle Ox Cl S20 59 F6
Middle Ox Gdns S20 59 F6
Middle Pavement S40 266 B3
MIDDLEPEAK 154 E3
Middle Rd S42 114 E1
Middle Row SK17 89 A7
Middle Shambles S40 266 B3
Middle St
Bolsover S44 99 A1
Bolsover, Hillstown S44 118 C8
Stanton in Peak DE4 126 C5
MIDDLETON
Wirksworth 154 D4
Youlgrave 124 E3
Middleton Ave
Codnor DE5 181 B6
Derby DE23 218 C2
Middleton Cl DE11 257 A1
Middleton Com Prim Sch DE4 154 D4
Middleton Dale
Foolow SK32 70 F5
Hope Valley S32 71 A5
Middleton Dr
Derby DE23 218 C2
Staveley S43 97 B5
Middleton La S32 71 D3
Middleton Rd
Ilkeston DE7 209 A5
Mansfield Woodhouse NG19 136 C5
Middleton DE4 154 E2
Middleton St
Awsworth NG16 195 C4
Cossall DE7 195 A1
Derby DE23 219 A1
Middleton Top DE4 154 C2
Middleton Top Visitor Ctr* DE4 154 D3
Middleton Way DE55 170 C7
Middletown Mdws S43 80 A6
Midgley La SK11 102 A1
Midhill Cres S2 43 B7
Midhill Rd S2 43 B7
Midland Ave NG9 223 D5
Midland Cotts
Grindleford S32 53 D2
Pleasley NG19 135 A6
Rowsley DE4 110 F1
Midland Ct
Barlborough S43 80 A5
5 Chesterfield S41 115 B7
Midland Ind Est DE56 168 A4
Midland Pl DE1 267 D2
Midland Railway Butterley* DE5 169 F4
Midland Railway Ctr The* DE5 169 E4
Midland Rd
Chapel-en-le-Frith SK23 47 A6
Derby DE1 267 D1
Eastwood NG16 182 F2
Heanor DE75 181 E2
Swadlincote DE11 256 B4
Midland Road Ind Est DE11 256 B4
Midland St NG10 236 E8
Midland Terr
Ambergate DE56 167 F4
Barrow Hill S43 78 B4
Blackwell DE55 147 C1
4 Chesterfield S41 115 B7
New Mills SK22 33 C7
Midland View
7 Belper DE56 178 F3
North Wingfield S42 131 F7
Midland Way S43 80 A5
Midway DE22 204 E2
Midway Ctr S45 131 D4
Midway Rd DE11 256 C5
Mikado Rd NG10 236 C5
Milbank Cl DE22 217 E6
Milburn Gdns DE21 206 B3
Milbury Cl DE21 205 F2
Mile Ash La DE22 204 F1
MILEHILL 115 F5
Milfoil Close DE24 231 C3
MILFORD 191 A7
Milford DE45 109 D6
Milford Ave NG10 223 B3
Milford Cl S42 115 B4
Milford Ct DE45 109 D6
Milford Dr DE7 194 D3
Milford Prim Sch DE56 190 F7
Milford Rd
Duffield DE56 190 E4
Staveley S43 97 C5
Milford St 4 DE1 218 F7
Milford The DE22 218 F5
Milken La S45 130 B4
Milking La S43 80 B3
Milkings La DE45 123 D8
Mill DE72 235 A1
Mill Acre Cl DE7 194 D2
Millash La S80 82 B4
Millbank DE75 194 A8
Millbank Ave DE56 179 B2
Millbank Cl DE7 194 D3
Mill Bank Ct S32 53 A8
Mill Bank Dr ST14 197 A3
Millbridge S33 38 C3
Mill Bridge S33 38 C2
Millbrook SK14 9 D6
Millbrook Ho SK14 9 E6
MILL BROW 23 E8
Mill Brow
2 Broadbottom SK14 16 A8
Marple SK6 23 D8
Mill Brow Rd SK6 23 E8
Mill Cl
Borrowash DE72 221 C1
Findern DE65 230 D2
Kilburn DE56 192 A7
Newton Solney DE15 248 E8
Swadlincote DE11 256 C5
Swanwick DE55 169 F7
Mill Cliff SK17 85 C7
Mill Cres
Whitwell S80 82 A6
Wingerworth S42 115 C3
Mill Croft DE3 217 D4
Millcross La S18 75 E3
Mill Ct
Chinley SK23 34 E1
Glossop SK13 10 C1
MILLDALE 149 F2
Milldale Ave SK17 84 F6
Milldale Cl
Chesterfield S40 95 C5
Ripley DE5 180 D6
Milldale Ct
Ashbourne DE6 185 D8
Belper DE56 179 B3
Milldale Rd
Derby DE21 220 F3
Long Eaton NG10 236 B6
Sheffield S17 55 F5
Milldam La DE6 186 E7
Millennium Ave DE12 262 E5
Millennium Cl DE7 194 E3
Millennium Ct NG19 135 E2
Millennium Way
Chesterfield S41 76 F1
Derby DE24 219 E4
Miller Ave S43 79 C4
Miller Dr DE7 194 B5
Millers Ct DE1 267 B4
MILLER'S DALE 88 A2
Millersdale Ave DE7 194 E5
Millersdale Cl DE15 248 B5
Millers Dale Cl DE56 179 C5
Millersdale Ct 3 SK13 10 F1
Millers Dale Dr DE55 160 A7
Millersdale Way SK17 85 B6
Millers Gn DE4 165 E6
MILLERS GREEN 165 E6
Millership Way
Ilkeston DE7 194 F2
Ilkeston DE7 195 A2
Millers La DE55 145 E2
Millers Vale SK22 33 C8
Millers Way DE56 190 F8
Mill Farm DE65 242 E2
Mill Farm Cl S32 72 C1
Mill Farm Dr 2 DE55 148 B7
Millfield DE72 235 B2
Millfield Cl DE7 194 C3
Millfield Croft 1 DE11 256 B7
Millfield Mobile Home Pk S42 130 F5
Millfield Pk S42 130 F5
Millfield Rd
Ilkeston DE7 209 A7
Kimberley NG16 195 F7
Millfields La DE6 175 D8
Millfield St DE11 257 A2
Mill Fleam DE65 228 E1
Mill Gate DE22 218 E6
Mill Gn
Shardlow DE72 235 A1
Staveley S43 78 E2
Mill Green Way S43 80 E4
Mill Hill
Elvaston DE24 233 C4
Long Duckmanton S44 117 B6
Repton DE65 242 E1
Mill Hill Cl DE5 169 F1
Mill Hill Dr DE15 248 B4
Mill Hill La
Breaston DE72 222 E1
Burton upon Trent DE15 248 B4
Derby DE1, DE23 267 B1
Mill Hill Rd DE23 267 A1
Mill Hill Sch DE5 180 F8
Mill Holme DE55 160 B4
Millhouse Ct DE72 235 B7
MILLINGTON GREEN 176 A4
Mill La
Ashbourne DE6 173 F1
Ashford in the Water DE45 108 F8
Ashover S45 129 C5
Atlow DE6 175 A7
Ault Hucknall S44 133 C8
Barlow S18 75 D4
Belper DE56 179 B3
Bolsover S44 99 A3
Bradbourne DE6 163 B6
Brailsford DE6 201 C8
Castleton S33 38 C3
Chesterfield S40 95 D2
Clay Cross S42, S45 130 F5
Clay Cross S45 131 B2
Codnor DE5 181 B8
Commonside DE6 187 D1
Cossall NG16 195 C1
Cossall NG16 209 C8
Cubley DE6 212 E8
Cubley DE6 212 F8
Cubley DE6 213 A8
Derby DE3 217 D4
Doveridge DE6 211 A1
Dronfield S18 57 B1
Ellastone DE6 183 B2
Eyam S32 71 E5
Grassmoor S42 115 D3
Hartington SK17 137 D5
Heath S44 117 B1
Hilton DE65 228 C2
Holloway DE4 156 A5
Holmesfield S18 74 F5
Holmewood S42 116 B4
Hope Valley S33 40 B3
Longnor SK17 121 B5
Old Bolsover S44 79 F1
Pinxton NG16 160 D1
Renishaw S21 60 A2
Roston DE6 197 D7
1 Sandiacre NG10 223 C6
Scropton DE65 226 F1
Scropton, Foston DE65 226 D7
Sheffield S17 55 F5
Shirley DE6 200 D7
Shuttlewood S44 98 F8
Somercotes DE55 170 C7
Sudbury DE6 225 E1
Sutton in Ashfield NG17 148 F1
Tupton S42 131 C8
Whitwell S80 82 A6
Mill Meadow Way DE65 229 B4
Mill Moor Cl DE73 232 F2
Millom Pl DE21 205 D1
Millpond SK23 34 F1
Mill Pond Ave SK22 24 D1
Millpond Cl DE55 158 E3
Mill Pond Cl
Hilton DE65 228 C2
Strines SK6 23 C2
Mill Pond Cotts DE4 155 A7
Millpool Cl DE11 257 A7
Mill Rd
Cromford DE4 155 B6
Eckington S21 59 E4
Heanor DE75 194 A8
Stapleford NG9 223 D8
Millrise S44 99 A3
Mill Rise S42 115 C3
Mill Row DE21 220 D5
Mills Cl DE72 235 A7
Mills Croft DE6 164 B1
Mills Ct DE4 156 F1
Mill St
Alfreton DE55 159 C1
Bakewell DE45 109 D6
Barlow S18 75 D3
Belper DE56 179 A4
Chesterfield S41 266 C3
Clowne S43 80 E3
Coton in the Elms DE12 260 D3
Derby DE1 218 E6
Glossop SK13 10 D1
Hayfield SK22 25 D3
Ilkeston DE7 194 F1
Rocester ST14 197 A3
Somercotes DE55 170 C8
Stoney Middleton S32 72 A3
Millstone Cl 1 S18 56 D2
Millstone Ct DE4 143 E7
Millstone La
Ashford in the Water DE45 108 F7
Ripley DE5 169 C8
Mill Stream Cl S40 95 C1
Millstream Grange 2 DE72 221 A1
Mill Stream La DE13 241 A1
MILLTHORPE 74 F5
Millthorpe La S18 75 A6
MILLTOWN 145 B8
Milltown
Charlesworth SK13 16 C8
Glossop SK13 10 D1
Mill View DE56 178 F5
Millward Dr DE3 217 B2
Millway NG19 136 D1
Millway La DE6 149 F3
Mill Wlk
Bolsover S44 99 A3
Whitwell S80 82 A6

Mill Wood La S80....82 D4
Mill Yd DE55 ....170 C8
Milnbank Ave SK17...85 D8
Milner Ave
  Codnor DE5 ....181 B8
  Draycott DE72 .....235 A7
Milnhay Rd NG16 ...182 C2
MILTON 243 A1
Milton Ave
  Alfreton DE55.......159 C4
  Ilkeston DE7........194 E4
  Shirland DF55.......146 C4
  Swadlincote DE11 ..256 C6
Milton Cl DE3 ....217 C3
Milton Cres S40 .....115 A7
Milton Ct 12 SK17....85 B7
Milton Pl S43........78 F2
Milton Rd
  Ilkeston DE7........194 E4
  Repton DE65 ....242 D2
Milton St
  Derby DE22 ....218 D4
  Ilkeston DE7........194 E4
  Long Eaton NG10 ...236 D7
Milton Terr NG10 ...236 D7
Milward Rd DE75 ...181 D2
Mimosa Cres DE23 ..231 E5
Miners Hill DE4......153 A1
Minimum Terr S40 ..266 A2
Mining La DE4.......164 E7
Minkley Dr NG16 ...182 C4
Minninglow La
  Ballidon DE4........151 F7
  Ballidon DE4........152 A6
  Parwich DE4........151 F8
Minster Court DE24..232 F4
Minster Rd DE21.....205 E2
Minster Way DE55 ..169 E7
Mint Gr NG10 ....236 A7
Mint Gro DE3.......217 C5
Minton Rd DE74 ....246 F4
Miracle Ct DE45 ....109 D6
Mires La
  Great Longstone
  DE45.............90 B4
  Tideswell SK17.......70 A3
Mires The
  Birchover DE4 ......126 A1
  Great Longstone DE45..90 B3
  Wetton DE6 ....149 A3
Miriam Ave
  Chesterfield S40.....114 A8
  Holymoorside S40 ...113 F8
Miry La DE65 ....227 C4
Miry Mdw SK23......47 B6
Misterton Cl DE22 ..204 E2
Misterton Ct 3
  NG19 ....136 B1
Mistletoe Dr DE11 ..256 F2
Mitcham Wlk DE22 ..218 A6
Mitchell Ave NG16 ..182 A4
Mitchells Cl DE65...229 A4
Mitchell St
  Clowne S43..........80 F4
  Long Eaton NG10 ...236 E7
Mitchell Terr DE7....209 A5
Mitchell Villas S43...77 E3
Mitchell Way S43....77 E3
Mitford Rd DE72.....233 D3
Mitre DE11 ....261 B6
Mitre Dr DE65 ......242 C2
Mizzen Road S43....80 E5
Moat Bank DE15....248 D2
Moat St DE11........256 B1
Moat The DE74 .....247 B4
Model La S80.........100 E8
Model View S80 ....100 E8
Model Village S80 ..100 E8
Model Village Prim Sch
  NG20 ....119 E3
Mods La S18.........75 D3
Moffatt Rd S2........43 B7
MOIRA 262 E3
Moira Cl DE21 ......220 A7
Moira Dale DE74....247 F3
Moira Furnace Mus★
  DE12.............262 E3
Moira Junc Nature
  Reserve★ DE12....262 D4
Moira Rd
  Donisthorpe DE12 ..262 F1
  Moira DE11.........262 E8
  Overseal DE12......262 B3
  Woodville DE11 ....256 E2
Moira St DE73 ......252 A7
Moisty La
  Marchington ST14 ..224 C3
  Stoney Middleton S32..71 B3
Molineux Ave S43 ...78 D1
Molineux St DE23...219 B2
Molloy Pl 11 S8 ......43 A6
Molloy St 10 S8 .....43 A6
Molyneaux Bsns Pk
  DE4..............127 B3
Monarch Dr DE21...206 D3
Monarch Way DE75..181 D2
Moncreiff Dr
  Burton upon Trent
  DE13.............241 A1
  4 Stretton DE13....240 F1
Moncrieff Cres
  DE21.............220 A8
Mondello Dr DE21...220 A8
Moneyash Rd SK17..121 D6
Monk Rd
  Alfreton DE55.......159 B2

Monk Rd continued
  Branston DE14......253 D8
Monk Road Ind Est
  DE55.............159 C2
Monks Cl
  Derby DE24 ....231 C3
  Ilkeston DE7........209 A8
Monksdale La
  Tideswell SK17.......68 F2
  Wheston SK17.......68 F4
Monk's Rd SK13......17 A4
Monk St
  Derby DE22 ....267 A2
  Tutbury DE13 ......239 C7
Monks Way S81 .....63 F7
Monkton St DE7....194 D3
Monkwood Rd S41...95 D8
Monmouth St DE21..219 D6
Monnies End S43.....80 D5
Monsal Ave SK17....85 D7
Monsal Cres
  Staveley S43........97 C6
  Tibshelf DE55......147 F6
Monsaldale Cl
  Burton upon Trent
  DE15.............248 B4
  Long Eaton NG10 ..236 B6
Monsal Dr
  Derby DE21 ....220 F3
  South Normanton
  DE55.............159 F5
Monsal Gr SK17 .....85 D7
MONSAL HEAD
  89 D4
  Little Longstone DE45..89 D3
Monsall Ave DE7 ...194 E5
Monsdale La DE45 ..151 E2
Monsom La DE65 ...242 D3
Montague Way
  DE73.............232 E2
Montagu St SK6......15 B2
Monteith Pl DE74....247 B4
Montford Mews
  DE74.............247 B4
Montgomery Cl
  DE55.............228 E2
Montpelier DE22 ...204 D7
Montpelier Cl DE14..254 D7
Montpelier Gdns 5
  SK17.............85 D8
Montpelier Pl DE14..66 D1
Montpelier Rd DE56..167 F3
Montrose Cl DE24 ..231 E4
Montrose Ct NG9 ...209 E1
Montrose Pl S18......56 D2
Montrose Sq SK6....15 B2
Monument La NG16..170 E3
MONYASH 107 C2
Monyash CE Prim Sch
  DE45.............107 C1
Monyash Cl
  Derby DE21 ....220 A8
  Ilkeston DE7........194 E3
  Staveley S43........97 C7
Monyash Gr 32 SK13..9 D1
Monyash Gr 31 SK13..9 D1
Monyash Lea 33 SK13..9 D1
Monyash Mews 30
  SK13.............9 D1
Monyash Pl 29 SK13..9 D1
Monyash Rd
  Bakewell DE45......109 C5
  Over Haddon DE45...108 D2
  Over Haddon DE45...109 A2
Monyash Way
  Belper DE56 ....179 B5
  Buxton SK17.......85 E7
  1 Gamesley SK13....9 E1
Moonpenny Way S18..57 A1
Moonstone Way
  Chesterfield S40.....115 E7
  1 Swadlincote DE11..255 F4
Mooracre La S44.....99 D1
Moorbridge La NG9..209 D1
Moorbrook La
  Bradwell S33........50 F7
  Bradwell S33........51 A7
Moor Cres S20.......59 C7
Moor Croft DE4......143 E7
Moor Dr DE24 ......233 B5
Moore Cl S42........116 D1
MOOREDGE 144 C5
Mooredge Dr DE4 ..143 D6
Mooredge Rd DE4 ..157 B2
MOOREND
  Bradley.............186 D8
  Marple.............24 A6
Moorend DE4 ......111 C3
Moor End DE21......220 F6
Moor End Rd SK6....24 A5
Moores Ave NG10...223 C7
Moore St DE23 .....219 B2
Moor Farm Ave S20..59 B8
Moor Farm Cl DE55..148 B4
Moor Farm Garth
  S20..............59 C8
Moor Farm Rd S20..59 B8
Moor Farm Road E
  DE6..............185 F7
Moor Farm Road W
  DE6..............185 E8
MOORFIELD SK13....18 B6
Moorfield DE4.......143 C7
Moorfield Ave S44...99 B1
Moorfield Cres 3
  NG10.............223 B5
Moorfield Ct NG9...209 E4

Moorfield La NG20...100 F4
Moorfield Prec SK14...9 D5
Moorfield Rd DE56 .191 C7
Moorfields Ave
  NG16.............182 F3
Moorfield Sq S44.....99 B1
Moorfield St SK14 ...9 D5
Moorfield Terr SK14 ..9 D5
Moor Furlong DE13..240 F1
Moorgate DE22......217 E6
Moorgate Ave NG19..134 F7
Moorgate Cres S18 ..76 B8
MOORHAIGH 135 A3
Moorhaigh Close
  NG19.............134 F7
Moorhaigh La NG19..135 A3
MOORHALL 74 D2
Moorhall DE45 .....109 C5
Moorhay Cl SK14 ...9 D5
Moorhead Ave DE24.232 F5
Moorhead Prim Sch
  DE24.............232 F6
Moorhen Dr S43......98 A8
Moorings The SK12...32 E6
Moor La
  Aston-on-Trent
  DE72.............246 B8
  Barrow upon Trent
  DE73.............244 B8
  Bolsover S44........99 B1
  Bonsall DE4 ....142 B2
  Calow S44..........116 C8
  Dale Abbey DE7 ....207 F2
  Darley Dale DE4 ....127 C4
  Derby DE24 ....232 C6
  Elton DE4 ....140 E5
  Flagg SK17.........106 E4
  Horsley DE7........192 A2
  Kirk Ireton DE6.....165 A3
  Kirk Langley DE6....202 F1
  Little Eaton DE7,....191 E1
  Little Eaton DE21 ..205 D8
  Ockbrook DE72.....221 C6
  Osmaston DE6......185 F5
  Scarcliffe S44.......119 A8
  Taddington SK17....87 E1
  Youlgreave DE45....125 B5
Moorland Ave NG9 .223 D6
Moorland Ctr The★
  S33..............37 C8
Moorland Dr S44....116 F2
Moorland Rd
  Derby DE3 ....217 D3
  Hathersage SK17....53 A7
Moorlands Cl NG10..223 B2
Moorlands Dr DE6...184 C7
Moorlands La
  Bonsall DE4 ....142 B3
  Froggatt S32........72 C5
Moorlands Rd DE56..168 B4
Moorland Terr DE4 .144 A4
Moorland View
  Apperknowle S18....58 A1
  Sheffield S12........44 A2
Moorland View Rd
  S40..............95 C1
Moorlawn Ave S42 .113 E7
Moorpark Ave S40...114 C8
Moorpool Cres
  DE56.............191 C7
Moor Rd
  Ashover S45........129 F3
  Breadsall DE7, DE21..205 F5
  Brinsley NG16......182 E8
  Fawfieldhead SK17..121 A1
  Great Longstone DE45,
  S32..............89 F6
  Great Longstone S32..90 A7
  Great Longstone SK17..89 F8
  Wardlow SK17.......70 E1
Moor Rise DE56 ....191 C8
Moors Cl DE3........230 B8
MOORSIDE 165 A2
Moorside Cl
  Cromford DE4......155 A5
  Glossop SK13.......17 B7
  Sheffield S20........59 C8
Moorside Cres
  DE24.............231 E4
Moorside Gdns
  DE72.............234 C1
Moorside La DE56 ..191 C7
Moorspring Way
  S45..............131 B7
Moor St DE21........220 E5
Moor The
  Brinsley NG16 .....182 D8
  Middleton DE4 .....154 C4
  Tideswell SK17......69 C5
Moorthorpe Gn S20 ..44 F2
Moorthorpe Way
  S20..............44 F2
Moortop Rd S18, S21..58 B1
Moor Valley S20......44 F2
Moorview Cl
  Brimington S43......96 D7
  Wingerworth S42....115 B3
Moorview Ct 2 S17 ..56 B5
Moor View Rd S43...79 A2
Moorway DE21 .....205 E4
Moorway Croft
  DE23.............231 B7
Moorway La DE23 ..231 B6
Moorways Sports Ctr
  DE24.............232 D6
Moorwinstow Croft
  S17..............55 E7
Moorwood La S17 ..55 C1

Moorwoodmoor La
  DE55.............157 D6
Moray Cl DE11......255 F1
Moray Ct NG16 .....195 F7
Moray Pl S18........56 D2
Moray Wlk DE21....219 C8
Mordaunt Rd S2.....43 F6
Morden Gn DE22 ...218 A6
Morden Rd NG16 ...195 C8
Morefern Dr DE21 ..205 F2
Morel Cl NG16......182 F1
Moreton La ST14 ...225 B1
Morewood Dr DE55..159 B5
Morgana Rd NG19 .135 D1
Morland Bank S14...43 E3
Morland Cl S14......43 F3
Morland Dr S14 .....43 F3
Morland Pl S14......43 F3
Morland Rd
  Hayfield SK22.......25 B2
  Sheffield S14........43 F3
Morledge
  Derby DE1 ....267 C3
  Matlock DE4........142 F6
  1 Matlock DE4 .....143 A7
Morleston St DE23..267 C1
MORLEY 206 C6
Morley Almshouses La
  DE7..............206 B7
Morley Ave S40......95 C4
Morley Cl DE56......179 E6
  Burton upon Trent
  DE15.............248 B2
  Dronfield S18.......56 C1
  5 Heanor DE75....181 F1
Morley Dr DE7......194 D3
Morleyfields Cl DE5..169 F1
Morley Gdns DE21 ..220 B8
Morley Ho
  Derby, Alvaston
  DE24.............233 A7
  1 Derby, Markeaton
  DE3..............217 D1
Morley La
  Little Eaton DE7,
  DE21.............205 E8
  Morley DE21........206 F6
  Stanley DE7 ....207 B6
Morley Mews DE21 .220 A7
Morley Pk Rd DE56 .179 E6
Morley Prim Sch
  DE7..............206 C7
Morley Rd DE21 ....220 B8
Morley St
  Derby DE22 ....218 C5
  Glossop SK13.......17 D8
Morlich Dr DE24....231 E5
Morningside Cl
  DE24.............232 D4
Mornington Cl
  NG10.............223 C6
Mornington Cres
  DE22.............218 B6
Mornington Rd S42..132 D8
Mornington Rise
  DE4..............143 C4
Morpeth Gdns
  DE21.............205 D2
Morrells La DE56....190 F7
Morrell Wood Dr
  DE56.............179 D5
Morris Ave S41......95 E5
Morris Dr S41.......95 E5
Mortimer Rd S6......31 E8
Mortimer St DE24 ..232 C7
MORTON 146 F5
Morton Ave
  Clay Cross S45......131 B4
  Ilkeston DE7........194 F5
Morton Gdns S20....59 F6
Morton La S18, S21..58 C1
Morton Mount S20 ..59 F7
Morton Prim Sch
  DE55.............147 A5
Morton Rd
  Pilsley S45 ....147 C8
  Shirland DE55......146 D6
Morton St NG19 ....135 E1
Morven Ave
  Bolsover S44........99 B1
  Mansfield Woodhouse
  NG19.............136 B2
Morven St S80......100 F8
MOSBOROUGH 59 D7
Mosborough Hall Dr
  S20..............59 E6
Mosborough Hall Farm
  S20..............59 B8
Mosborough Moor
  S20..............59 B8
Mosborough Parkway
  S13..............44 F5
Mosborough Pkwy
  S12..............44 F5
Mosborough Prim Sch
  S20..............59 C7
Mosborough Rd S13..44 B7
Moscow Farm Ct
  DE56.............190 F5
Mosedale Cl DE24 ..232 E8
Moseley St DE5......169 D2
Moses La DE7 ......206 E2
Moses View S81......63 F7
Mosley Dr ST14......210 A1
Mosley Mews DE13..240 A4
Mosley Rd SK17.....85 B6
Mossbank Cl SK13 ...9 E4

Moss Beck Ct S21...59 C2
Mossbrook Ct S21...59 E4
Mossbrook Sch S8 ..57 C8
Mosscar Cl NG20...120 C1
Mosscar St NG20...120 F2
Mossdale Ave S20 ...59 C6
Moss Dr S21.........60 D5
Moss Edge Rd HD9...3 C8
Moss House Ct S20 .59 C6
Moss La
  Broadbottom SK14..15 E8
  Hulland Ward DE6 ..175 F4
  Ripley DE5 ....169 D3
Moss Rd
  Ilkeston DE7........208 D7
  Sheffield S17........55 B4
Moss Rise Pl S21....59 C3
Moss St
  Derby DE22 ....218 C3
  Hollingworth SK14 ...9 A5
Moss The SK17.......102 D1
Mossvale Dr DE23 .231 A6
Moss View S20......59 C6
Moss View Rd SK23..47 C5
Moston Wlk S40.....114 E6
Mostyn Ave DE23 ..218 D1
Mottistone Cl DE24..233 D5
Mottram CE Prim Sch
  SK14.............9 A3
Mottram Fold SK14...9 A3
MOTTRAM IN
  LONGDENDALE ...9 B4
Mottram Moor SK14..9 B4
Mottram Old Rd
  SK14.............15 B8
Mottram Rd SK14....16 A1
Moulbourn Dr DE56..190 D4
Mouldridge La DE4 .139 F2
Moult Ave DE21.....220 E4
Moulton Cl
  Belper DE56 ....179 D5
  Swanwick DE55....169 F8
Mound Rd S40......266 C1
Mountbatten Cl
  DE24.............232 E4
Mountbatten Ct
  DE7..............194 F3
Mount Carmel St
  DE23.............267 A1
Mountcastle St S41..95 F8
Mountcastle Wlk S41..95 F8
Mount Cres DE55 ...160 A3
Mountfield Ave
  NG10.............223 A4
Mountfield Way
  DE24.............233 D4
Mountford Ave DE4..165 E7
Mountford Cl DE21 .206 B2
Mountford Croft S17..55 E5
MOUNT PLEASANT
  Belper.............178 D6
  Blackwell 147 E2
  Castle Gresley 261 E7
  Melbourne 251 F8
  Repton............242 E1
Mount Pleasant
  Ashford in the Water
  DE45.............108 F8
  Buxworth SK23......46 A8
  Castle Donington
  DE74.............247 A6
  Cromford DE4......155 A7
  Ilkeston DE7........194 E4
  Ripley DE5 ....169 D2
  Somercotes DE55...170 D5
  Youlgreave DE45 ...125 C5
Mount Pleasant Ct
  S32..............72 C8
Mount Pleasant Dr
  Belper DE56 ....178 E5
  Heage DE56 ....179 E6
Mount Pleasant La
  Netherseal DE12 ..265 A8
  Overseal DE12 ....262 B1
Mount Pleasant Rd
  Castle Gresley DE12..262 A7
  Grindleford S32.....72 C8
  Linton DE11 ....261 E8
  Mount Pleasant DE11..261 F7
  Repton DE65 ....242 E1
Mount Pleaseant
  SK6..............15 B3
Mount Rd
  Bretby DE15 ....249 A3
  Compstall SK14 ....15 A6
  Hartshorne DE11 ..257 A4
  Linton DE11 ....261 D8
Mount St Mary's RC Coll
  S21..............60 C2
Mount St
  Breaston DE72 .....235 F7
  Burton upon Trent
  DE15.............248 A3
  Derby DE1 ....267 B1
  Glossop SK13.......17 C8
  Heanor DE75 ......181 D1
  Mansfield NG19 ....136 A1
  Stapleford NG9.....223 E7
Mount The
  Chesterfield S41......77 A3
  Stapleford NG9.....223 D6
Mount View Ave S8..43 B4
Mount View Gdns S8..43 A3
Mount View Lodge 2
  S8..............43 A3
Mount View Rd S8...43 B3

Mouselow Mews
  ....10 A3
Mowbray Gdns
  DE24.............232 C3
Mowbray St DE24...232 B6
Moy Ave DE24.......231 F2
Moyne Gdns
  Chellaston DE73 ...245 A8
  13 Derby DE73 ....244 F8
MUDD 9 A2
Mudhurst La SK12 ...32 E3
MUGGINTON 188 F2
Mugginton CE Prim Sch
  DE6..............188 E2
MUGGINTONLANE END
  188 E6
  DE56.............188 E7
Muirfield Cl S41.....96 B6
Muirfield Dr
  Derby DE3 ....217 F2
  Derby DE3 ....218 A2
Muirfield Way
  NG19.............136 E6
Mulberries Ct DE22.204 E4
Mulberry Cl
  Belper DE56 ....179 B3
  Wingerworth S42...115 A4
Mulberry Croft
  Brimington S43......78 A1
  Staveley S43........78 A1
Mulberry Gdns 5
  ST14.............210 A1
Mulberry Grove
  S42..............131 C7
Mulberry Mews
  DE5..............180 C6
Mulberry Rd S21....59 B2
Mulberry Way
  Aston-on-Trent
  DE72.............246 A6
  Branston DE14.....253 E6
  Branston DE14.....256 E6
  Hilton DE65 ....228 E2
  Killamarsh S21......60 B5
Mulberry Wlk S45 ..132 C4
Mull Ct 3 DE24 ....231 D3
Mullion Pl DE24....233 B5
Mumford Dr DE6 ..185 D8
Mundella Pl S8......43 A3
Mundella Prim Sch 5
  S8..............43 A3
Mundy CE Jun Sch
  DE75.............193 F8
Mundy Cl DE1 ......218 E6
Mundy's Dr DE75 ...193 F8
Mundy St
  Derby DE1 ....218 E6
  Heanor DE75 ......181 E1
  Ilkeston DE7........194 E2
Munro Cl S21.......60 D6
Munro Ct DE24 ....231 E4
Murdoch Rd DE24 .219 E3
Murrayfield Dr 6
  S20..............59 E6
Murray La S42.......115 C2
Murray Park Sch
  DE3..............217 F4
Murray Rd
  Derby DE3 ....217 F4
  Killamarsh S21......60 E7
Murray St DE24.....232 F4
Musard Pl S21.......78 D1
Musard Way S21....60 C6
Muse La
  Boylestone DE6 ...213 A2
  Church Broughton
  DE6..............226 B7
Museum of Making★
  DE1..............267 B4
Musgrave Ho S33....40 B3
Mushroom Farm Ct
  NG16.............182 D3
Mushroom La
  Albert Village DE11 .256 C1
  Moira DE11.........262 D8
Muskham Ave DE7...194 F3
Muskham Ct 1
  NG19.............136 B1
Mus of Industry &
  History The (Silk Mill
  Mus)★ DE1.......267 B4
Musters St NG20....120 A4
Muswell Rd DE22 ..217 E5
Mycock La
  Flagg SK17.........106 F4
  Flagg SK17.........106 F5
Myers Cl DE24......231 F4
Mynd The NG19 ....136 E6
Myrce Way S17......55 E6
Myrtle Ave
  Derby DE3 ....217 C4
  Long Eaton NG10 ..236 C6
  Stapleford NG9.....223 E6
Myrtle Cl
  Sheffield S2 ....43 C6
  Shirebrook NG20 ..119 D6
Myrtle Cres S2......43 C7
Myrtle Gr S43.......78 A1
Myrtle Rd S2........43 B7
Myrtle Springs S12 .43 F5
Myrtle Springs Dr
  S12..............43 F5
Mytham Bridge S33..40 B1
Mytholme Cl NG10..223 C2

N

Nabb La ST14 196 A4
Naggle Gate Close DE7 193 B1
Nailers Way DE56 179 C5
Nailor La DE4 142 D3
Nairn Ave DE21 219 D7
Nairn Cl DE24 231 D3
Nairn Dr S18 56 D1
Namur Cl DE22 218 C3
Nan Gell's Hill DE4 155 A3
Napier Cl
 Derby DE3 217 E4
 Swadlincote DE11 255 E2
Napier Ct S43 80 B5
Napier St DE22 218 C5
Naples Cres NG19 134 F5
Napoleon Pk DE24 232 E7
Narlow La DE6 161 F2
Narrowdale La
 Alstonefield SK17 149 C7
 Clay Cross SK17 131 D2
Narrowgate La SK17 70 D3
Narrow La
 Denstone ST14 196 D6
 Donisthorpe DE12 265 E8
 Ticknall DE73 250 F4
Narrowleys La S45 129 F3
Naseby Cl DE3 217 C3
Naseby Dr NG10 236 E4
Naseby Rd DE56 179 D4
Nathaniel Rd NG10 236 F7
National Sikh Her Ctr & Holocaust Mus★ DE23 219 B1
National Stone Ctr★ DE4 154 F3
National Tramway Mus★ DE4 156 E2
Natterer Grove DE23 230 F8
Navigation Home Park DE24 232 E8
Navigation Way S18 57 D1
Neal Ct NG16 182 A3
Neale Bank S43 96 D7
Neale St
 Clowne S43 80 F4
 Long Eaton NG10 236 E7
Near Mdw NG10 236 E5
Nearwell Cl SK23 46 F6
Nearwood Dr DE21 205 E3
Needham St DE5 181 B8
Needham Terr DE4 143 A7
Needwood Ave DE13 240 C4
Need Wood Ave NG9 209 D2
Needwood Ct DE13 239 C6
Neighwood Cl NG9 223 E2
Neilson St DE24 232 F7
Nelper Cres DE7 209 A5
Nelson Cl DE3 217 F3
Nelson Pl LE65 257 F3
Nelson St
 Burton upon Trent DE15 248 C4
 Chesterfield S41 96 A6
 Derby DE1 219 C3
 Derby DE1 267 D1
 [1] Heanor DE75 181 D2
 Ilkeston DE7 194 F3
 Long Eaton NG10 236 D6
 Swadlincote DE11 256 B5
Nene Cl DE13 240 C1
Nene Way DE65 240 D8
Nerissa Cl DE73 232 E2
Nesbit St S44 118 B8
Nesfield Cl
 Chesterfield S41 95 D8
 Derby DE24 233 C7
Nesfield Ct DE7 194 E1
Nesfield Rd DE7 194 E1
Ness Wlk DE22 204 E3
Nestor Cl DE73 232 D2
Nether Ave S21 60 C6
NETHER BIGGIN 175 F5
Nether Blindlow La SK17 106 B5
NETHER BOOTH 29 A1
NETHER BURROWS 202 C3
Netherby Manor S17 56 A7
NETHER CHANDERHILL 94 C1
Nether Cl
 Duffield DE56 190 E5
 Eastwood NG16 182 F4
 Swanwick DE55 169 F7
 Wingerworth S42 115 A2
Netherclose St DE23 219 A1
Nether Croft Cl S43 96 E7
Nethercroft La S45 131 E3
Nether Croft Rd S43 96 E7
Netherdene Rd S18 57 A1
Nether End
 Baslow DE45 91 F5
 Baslow DE45 92 A5
Nether Farm Cl S43 96 F5
Netherfield Cl
 Ashbourne DE6 185 C8
Netherfield Cl *continued*
 Staveley S43 79 A2
 Uttoxeter ST14 210 C1
Netherfield Close DE4 143 C4
Netherfield La
 Castle Donington DE72, DE74 247 F8
 Hollins S42 94 A3
 Wadshelf S42 93 F2
Netherfield Rd
 Chapel-en-le-Frith SK23 47 D6
 Chesterfield S40 114 A8
 Long Eaton NG10 236 C4
 Sandiacre NG10 223 B4
Netherfields Cres S18 76 A8
Nether Gdns DE4 165 F8
NETHER GREEN 60 D7
Nethergreen Ave S21 60 D7
Nethergreen Ct S21 60 D7
Nethergreen Gdns S21 60 D7
Netherhall Rd DE11 256 F8
NETHER HANDLEY 77 F7
NETHER HEAGE 168 C1
Nether La
 Brassington DE4 163 F8
 Hazelwood DE56 190 A7
 Holbrook DE56 191 D6
 Kirk Ireton DE6 176 B8
NETHER LANGWITH 101 B1
Netherleigh Ct S40 95 B3
Netherleigh Rd S40 95 B3
Nether Mill Ct [3] DE4 155 A1
Nethermoor Ave S21 60 D7
Nethermoor Cl S21 60 D7
Nethermoor Cotts DE55 147 D5
Nethermoor Dr S21 60 D7
Nethermoor La S21 60 D7
Nethermoor Rd
 Tupton S42 131 C8
 Wingerworth S42 115 A1
NETHER PADLEY 53 E1
Nether Park Dr DE22 204 C1
NETHER PILSLEY 132 D1
NETHERSEAL 264 E7
Netherseal Rd
 Chilcote DE12 264 F4
 Clifton Campville B79 263 F2
 Clifton Campville DE12 264 A3
Netherside S33 51 A7
Netherside Dr DE73 233 B2
Nether Slade Road DE7 194 E2
Nether Springs Rd S44 98 F3
NETHER STURSTON 173 F1
NETHERTHORPE 79 A2
Netherthorpe S43 79 A2
Netherthorpe Airfield S80 63 B5
Netherthorpe Cl
 Killamarsh S21 60 C7
 Staveley S43 78 F2
Netherthorpe La S21 60 C7
Netherthorpe Rd [3] S43 78 F2
Nether Thorpe Rd S80 63 B5
Netherthorpe Sch S43 79 A2
Nether View S44 99 B4
Nether Way DE4 127 C3
Nether Wheel Row S13 44 F5
Netherwood Ct DE22 204 C3
Netley Rd DE24 233 D4
Nettlefold Cres DE73 245 B1
Nettleship Rd NG16 195 F6
Nettleton Cl DE23 231 A6
Nettleton La SK17 85 D3
Nettleworth Inf Sch NG19 136 C4
Networkcentre Barlborough Links S43 80 A5
Neville Cl DE13 240 B3
Nevinson Ave DE23 231 D7
Nevinson Dr DE23 231 D7
Nevis Cl
 Chesterfield S40 95 D4
 Derby DE24 231 D2
Newark [8] S20 59 E8
Newark Rd DE21 205 D2
Newark St DE24 233 E4
New Bank St SK13 10 A5
NEW BARLBOROUGH 80 D5
New Barlborough Cl S43 80 D5
Newbarn Cl NG20 119 D2
New Bath Rd DE4 155 A8
New Beetwell St
 Chesterfield S40 95 F3
 Chesterfield S40 266 B2
Newbery Ave NG10 236 F6
NEWBOLD 95 E6
Newbold Ave
 Borrowash DE72 221 C1
 Chesterfield S41 95 E6
Newbold Back La S40 95 E5
Newbold CE Prim Sch S41 95 E7
Newbold Cl DE73 232 F2
Newbold Ct [1] S41 95 D7
Newbold Dr
 Castle Donington DE74 247 B5
 Chesterfield S41 95 E6
NEWBOLD MOOR 95 F7
Newbold Rd
 Chesterfield S40 95 D6
 Chesterfield S41 95 B7
NEW BOLSOVER 98 F2
New Bolsover S44 98 F1
New Bolsover Prim Sch S44 98 F1
Newborough Rd DE24 233 C6
Newbound La NG17 134 D2
Newboundmill La NG19 135 A4
New Breck Rd DE56 179 A3
New Bridge S32 72 C3
Newbridge Cl DE7 207 D8
Newbridge Cres DE24 232 E4
Newbridge Ct S41 77 A1
Newbridge Dr S43 96 D8
Newbridge La
 Brimington S43 96 D8
 Chesterfield S41 77 B1
Newbridge Rd DE56 168 A2
Newbridge St S41 77 A1
NEW BRIMINGTON 77 F1
NEW BRINSLEY 171 E1
Newburgh Terr S32 72 C2
Newbury Dr DE13 240 C1
Newbury St DE24 232 E8
Newby Cl DE15 248 B1
Newby Rd S41 95 C8
Newcastle St
 Mansfield Woodhouse NG19 136 B3
 Sutton in Ashfield NG17 148 F3
Newchase Bsns Pk DE23 219 C1
New Chestnut Pl DE23 231 E7
New Church St S33 51 A7
New City Park Homes DE24 220 A1
New Cl S32 71 C6
New Cl La DE45 109 B2
New Cotts
 Buxton SK17 84 E4
 Whaley Thorns NG20 101 F3
Newcrest Cl DE23 218 B1
Newdelves Ct [2] DE75 193 E8
New Derby Rd NG16 182 D3
Newdigate St
 Derby DE23 232 A8
 Ilkeston DE7 209 A6
 Kimberley NG16 195 F6
 West Hallam DE7 207 C8
New Eaton Rd NG9 223 E5
Newell Way DE4 127 C3
New England Way NG19 135 C3
New Fall St NG17 148 F3
Newfield Cres S17 55 C7
Newfield Croft S17 55 C8
Newfield Farm Cl S14 43 E5
NEWFIELD GREEN 43 D5
Newfield Green Rd S2 43 D6
Newfield La S17 55 C7
Newfield Pl S17 55 C7
Newfield Rd DE15 248 B4
Newfields DE12 262 F4
Newfield Secondary Sch S8 43 C3
New Gardens DE45 109 D5
NEWGATE 75 D1
 Newgate S18 75 D1
Newgate Cl DE73 233 B2
NEWHALL 255 F6
Newhall Com Jun Sch DE11 255 E6
Newhall Inf Sch DE11 255 F7
Newhall Rd DE11 256 C5
New Hall Rd S40 95 D2
Newham Ave DE5 169 C1
Newham Cl DE75 182 A1
Newham Close DE22 217 F5
NEWHAVEN 138 F5
Newhaven Ave NG19 136 B3
Newhaven Cl S40 95 B1
New Haven Gdns S17 55 E4
Newhaven Rd DE21 220 B6
Newhay
 Burton upon Trent DE13 240 F1
 Stretton DE13 241 A1
New High St SK17 85 D8
Newhill Lane S12 44 F4
Newholme Hospl DE45 109 D7
NEW HORWICH 45 E6
New Horwich Rd SK23 45 E7
NEW HOUGHTON 134 F7
New Houses
 Chesterfield S41 96 C3
 Tideswell SK17 88 E8
New Inn La DE21 205 C7
New La
 Bradwell S33 50 E6
 Hilcote DE55 148 C1
 Over Haddon DE45 109 C1
Newland Dale S41 266 B4
Newland Gdns S41 95 E5
NEWLANDS 181 F2
Newlands Ave
 Chesterfield S40 95 C3
 Sheffield S12 44 A6
Newlands Barns DE22 189 E3
Newlands Cl
 Ripley DE5 169 E2
 Swadlincote DE11 256 A2
Newlands Cres DE55 148 A3
Newlands Dr
 Glossop SK13 9 F4
 Heanor DE75 181 E3
 Sheffield S12 44 A6
 Somercotes DE55 170 D5
Newlands Gr S12 44 B6
Newlands Ho DE55 170 D4
Newlands Inn Sta★ DE55 170 C3
Newlands Pk DE55 170 D5
Newlands Rd
 Sheffield S12 44 A6
 Somercotes DE55 170 C4
Newland St DE1 267 A3
Newlands The DE4 155 A7
New Lane Galleries DE55 159 A4
New Lawn Rd DE7 208 E8
New Linden St NG20 120 A4
New Lumford DE45 109 C7
Newlyn Dr
 [3] Derby DE23 231 F8
 South Normanton DE55 160 C6
Newlyn Pl S8 43 A3
Newman Dr
 Burton upon Trent DE14 254 B8
 Swadlincote DE11 255 E2
Newmanleys Rd NG16 194 F8
Newmanleys Rd (South) NG16 182 E1
Newmanleys Road S NG16 194 E8
NEWMARKET 131 A2
Newmarket Ct DE24 219 E1
Newmarket Dr DE24 232 E8
Newmarket La S45 130 F3
New Market St SK17 85 B6
Newmarket Way NG9 223 F2
New Mill La NG19 136 E3
NEW MILLS 33 D7
New Mills Adult Com Ed Ctr SK22 33 C8
New Mills Central Sta SK22 33 B7
New Mills Her Ctr★ SK22 33 B7
New Mills L Ctr SK22 33 C8
New Mills Newtown Sta SK22 33 B6
New Mills Prim Sch SK22 33 B8
New Mills Rd
 Broadbottom SK13 16 B4
 Hayfield SK22 25 B3
New Mills Sch and Sixth From Ctr [1] SK22 33 C8
New Mount Cl DE23 231 D5
Newness Ct [4] DE4 143 C6
New Orchard Pl DE3 217 D2
New Park Ct SK22 33 D7
New Park Pl DE24 219 D3
Newport Cres NG19 135 E1
Newport Ct DE24 233 C5
Newquay Pl DE24 233 C5
New Queen St S41 266 B4
New Rd
 Alderwasley DE4 167 B8
 Alderwasley DE56 156 B1
 Alfreton DE55 170 E5
 Apperknowle S18 58 A1
 Bamford S33 40 B5
 Barlborough S43 80 B7
 Barton in Fabis NG11 237 F6
 Belper DE56 178 F3
 Boylestone DE6 213 B4
 Bradwell S33 51 A4
 Bradwell, Bradwell Hills S33 51 B6
 Coton in the Elms DE12 260 D3
 Crich DE4 168 A8
 Denstone ST14 196 F5
 Derby DE22 205 A1
New Rd *continued*
 Eyam S32 71 F5
 Fawfieldhead SK17 121 B1
 Flash SK17 102 F1
 Flash SK17 103 A3
 Glossop SK13 9 F7
 Grindleford S32 72 B5
 Heage DE56 179 D8
 Hilton DE65 228 E2
 Hollinsclough SK17 104 D1
 Holmesfield S18 75 A5
 Holymoorside S42 113 D7
 Horwich End SK23 45 E6
 Idridgehay DE56 176 F4
 Ironville NG16 170 F3
 Middleton DE4 154 B5
 Ridgeway DE56 168 B4
 Somercotes DE55 170 E7
 Somercotes NG16, DE55 170 D2
 Stapleford NG9 209 D1
 Swadlincote DE11 255 E6
 Uttoxeter ST14 210 A1
 Weston Underwood DE6 188 D1
 Whaley Bridge SK23 34 A1
 Whaley Bridge, Bridgemont SK23 33 F1
 Wingerworth S42 114 E3
 Wirksworth DE4 155 A3
 Woodville DE11 256 E2
 Youlgreave DE45 125 C5
New Rd (Baslow Rd) DE45 108 F8
New Road Ind Est NG9 209 D1
New Row NG16 171 A5
NEW SAWLEY 236 B5
New School Cl S20 59 C7
New School Ct S20 59 C7
New School Rd S20 59 C7
New Scott St NG20 101 A2
Newshaw La SK13 9 F4
NEW SMITHY 35 A1
New Sq S40 266 B3
New St
 Alfreton DE55 159 A4
 Bakewell DE45 109 D6
 Bolsover S44 99 A3
 [3] Broadbottom SK14 16 A8
 Buxton SK17 67 B5
 Chesterfield S40 266 B2
 Derby DE1 219 B4
 Derby DE1 267 C2
 Donisthorpe DE12 262 E1
 Draycott DE72 235 A7
 Grassmoor S42 115 F3
 Hilcote DE55 160 C8
 Little Eaton DE21 205 C8
 Long Eaton NG10 236 E8
 Matlock DE4 143 C5
 New Mills SK22 33 D7
 Newton DE55 148 A4
 North Wingfield S42 131 F6
 Ockbrook DE72 221 C4
 Pilsley S45 132 D1
 Ripley DE5 169 E1
 Rosliston DE12 260 D6
 Sheffield, Holbrook S20 60 A8
 Shirland DE55 146 C2
 Somercotes DE55 170 C8
 South Normanton DE55 160 A6
 Stanley DE7 207 C6
 Stonebroom DE55 147 A5
 Sutton in Ashfield NG17 148 F3
 Swadlincote DE11 256 B2
 Swanwick DE55 169 E7
 Tupton S45 131 C8
 Whitwell S80 81 E5
NEW STANTON 208 E3
New Station Rd S44 99 B1
Newstead Ave
 Derby DE21 219 F6
 Sheffield S12 44 E3
Newstead Cl
 Dronfield S18 56 C1
 Sheffield S12 44 E3
Newstead Ct SK17 84 F7
Newstead Dr S12 44 E2
Newstead Gr S12 44 E3
Newstead Rd
 Long Eaton NG10 223 C3
 Sheffield S12 44 F3
Newstead Rise S12 44 F2
Newstead Road N DE7 194 D3
Newstead Road S DE7 194 D3
Newstead Terr [3] SK17 85 B6
Newstead Way S12 44 E2
New Street Bus Link S20 60 A8
New Terr
 Pleasley NG19 134 F5
 Sandiacre NG10 223 B6
NEWTHORPE 195 A8
Newthorpe Comm NG16 195 A8
NEWTHORPE COMMON 195 A8
NEWTON 148 B3
Newton Cl
 Belper DE56 179 C6
 Newton Solney DE15 248 E8
Newton Ct [16] S41 95 F8
Newtondale Ave NG19 136 E1
Newton Dr
 Eastwood NG16 182 A1
 Stapleford NG9 223 E6
Newton Gn DE3 217 F2
NEWTON GREEN 148 A4
Newton La
 Bretby DE15 249 A5
 Newton Solney DE15 248 F7
 Tibshelf DE55 147 F6
Newton Leys DE15 248 C4
Newtonmore Dr DE22 218 B3
Newton Park Cl [2] DE11 256 A7
Newton Pk
 Burton upon Trent DE15 248 D7
 Newton Solney DE15 248 D7
Newton Prim Sch DE55 148 A3
Newton Rd
 Burton upon Trent DE15 248 A5
 Tibshelf DE55 147 F4
Newtons Croft Cres S43 80 B6
Newtons La NG16 195 B4
NEWTON SOLNEY 248 E8
Newton Solney CE (Aided) Infant Sch DE15 248 E8
Newton's Wlk DE22 218 E8
Newton Wonder Ct DE73 245 B1
Newtonwood La
 Tibshelf DE55 148 B5
 Tibshelf DE55, NG17 148 C5
NEW TOTLEY 55 E4
NEWTOWN 33 B6
Newtown Prim Sch SK22 33 B6
New Tythe St NG10 236 F7
New Victoria Ct DE24 232 E5
NEW WESTWOOD 171 C4
New Westwood NG16 171 D4
New Whittington Com Prim Sch S43 77 D3
New Whittington Com Prim Sch (Handley Rd Site) S43 77 D4
New Wye St SK17 85 C8
NEW YORK 252 A7
NEW ZEALAND 218 C5
New Zealand La DE56 190 E2
New Zealand Sq DE22 218 C5
Nicholas Cl
 Derby DE21 220 E6
 [3] Ilkeston DE7 208 F6
 [5] Ilkeston DE7 209 A6
Nicholas St S41 115 D7
Nicholson Ct
 [9] Sheffield S8 43 B6
 Tideswell SK17 69 C4
Nicholson Pl [7] S8 43 B6
Nicholson Rd S8 43 A6
Nicholson's Row NG20 119 F3
Nicklaus Cl DE14 254 A7
Nicola Gdns DE23 231 D4
Nicolas Cl SK17 85 E8
Nidderdale Ct DE24 233 D6
Nields Way SK6 23 D4
Nightingale Ave NG19 135 A4
Nightingale Bsns Pk DE24 232 D8
Nightingale Cl
 Chesterfield S41 96 A4
 Chesterfield S41 266 B4
 Clay Cross S45 131 E2
 Holloway DE4 155 F6
 Kelstedge S45 129 D4
 Ripley DE5 169 D1
Nightingale Dr
 Mansfield NG19 135 E1
 Woodville DE11 256 F3
Nightingale Gr DE55 160 C5
Nightingale Mews DE1 267 D2
Nightingale Rd DE24 232 C8
Nightingale Way DE65 229 C3
Nikolas Rd S21 60 B1
Nimbus Way NG16 195 F7
Nine Corners NG16 195 F6
Nine Ladies Stone Circle★ DE4 126 D3
Ninelands Rd S32 53 A7
Ninth Ave
 Branston DE14 253 E8
 Branston DE14 256 E8
NITHEN END 84 F8
Nitticarhill Rd
 Barlborough S26 61 D1
 Barlborough S43 80 C8
Nix's Hill DE55 159 B2
Noahs Arc ST14 210 E1
Noble Rd S42 131 F7
Noble St DE1 267 D1

Noctule La DE3 230 E8
Nodder Rd S13 44 C7
Nodin Hill La DE56 168 B3
Noe La S33 40 A2
Noel-Baker Acad DE24 233 A4
Noel-Baker Sch DE24 232 F4
Noel St DE22 218 D6
No Mans Heath Rd B79 264 B2
No Man's Heath Rd DE12 264 F3
No Man's La DE7, DE27 222 D7
Nook End Rd DE75 181 D1
Nook La S44 97 B3
Nook The
Barrow upon Trent DE73 244 A6
Eyam S32 71 D6
Heanor DE75 181 C4
Holbrook DE56 191 C7
Shirebrook NG20 119 D3
Stoney Middleton S32 72 A4
Nooning La DE72 234 E8
NORBRIGGS 79 C3
Norbriggs Prim Sch S43 79 B3
Norbriggs Rd S43 79 C2
Norburn Dr S21 60 D6
NORBURY 183 D1
Norbury CE Prim Sch DE6 197 E7
Norbury Cl
Chesterfield S40 95 B5
Derby DE22 204 D1
Dronfield S18 56 D1
Norbury Cres DE23 231 C5
Norbury Ct 2 DE22 204 D2
Norbury Hollow DE6 183 D1
Norbury Way
Belper DE56 179 C6
Sandiacre NG10 223 A6
Norfolk Ave S42 115 F2
Norfolk Cl S40 114 B8
Norfolk Com Prim Sch S2 43 D8
Norfolk Ct NG19 136 E5
Norfolk Gdns DE22 218 F8
Norfolk Park Ave S2 43 D8
Norfolk Park Sch S2 44 A8
Norfolk Rd
Burton upon Trent DE15 254 D7
Long Eaton NG10 223 F1
Norfolk Sq 3 SK13 10 C1
Norfolk St
Derby DE23 219 B2
Glossop SK13 10 D1
Norfolk Wlk NG10 223 B5
Norgreave Way S20 59 E7
Norman Ave DE23 231 E7
Norman Cres DE7 194 E3
Norman Ct LE65 258 A1
Normandy Rd DE65 228 E2
Normanhurst Pk DE4 127 E1
Norman Keep DE13 239 C6
Norman Rd
Ripley DE5 169 C1
Somercotes DE55 170 E7
Tutbury DE13 239 C6
Norman St
Ilkeston DE7 194 E3
Kimberley NG16 195 F7
NORMANTON 231 F7
Normanton Ave DE55 159 C3
Normanton Brook Rd DE55 160 D7
Normanton Gr S13 44 F6
Normanton Hill S13 44 D6
Normanton Ho 3 SK17 85 A7
Normanton House Prim Sch DE23 231 F8
Normanton La DE23 231 C8
Normanton Lodge DE23 231 E8
Normanton Rd DE1 267 B1
Normanton Spring Cl S13 44 F6
Normanton Spring Rd S13 44 F5
Northacre Rd DE21 206 B2
Northam Dr DE5 169 C2
North Ave
Ashbourne DE6 173 B2
Derby DE3 217 E2
Derby, Darley Abbey DE22 205 A3
Sandiacre NG10 223 A6
North Brook Rd SK13 9 E4
North Church St DE45 109 D6
North Cl
Derby DE3 217 E3
Glossop SK13 9 F7
South Normanton DE55 159 F5
Unstone Green S18 76 E6
Willington DE65 242 B5
Northcliffe Rd DE6 173 B2
Northcote Ave S2 43 B6
Northcote Rd S2 43 B6
Northcote St NG10 236 E7
Northcote Way S44 117 D1
North Cres
Duckmanton S44 98 A5
Killamarsh S21 60 E8
NORTHEDGE 130 C6
Northedge Bsns Pk DE21 205 B2
Northedge La S42 130 B7
North End DE4 154 F1
Northern Ave S2 43 E7
Northern Comm S18 56 B2
Northern Dr NG9 209 D3
Northern Rd DE75 181 D2
North Farm Cl S26 61 E7
Northfield
Derby DE24 231 D3
Kilburn DE56 179 F2
Shirland DE55 146 D2
Northfield Ave
Ilkeston DE7 194 E1
Long Eaton NG10 236 B4
Mansfield Woodhouse NG19 136 A4
Rocester ST14 197 A4
Northfield Cl ST14 210 A2
Northfield Cres NG9 223 F4
Northfield Jun Sch S18 57 C3
Northfield La
Mansfield Woodhouse NG19 135 F4
Mansfield Woodhouse NG19 136 A5
Mansfield Woodhouse NG19 136 B5
Palterton S44 118 C6
Northfield Pk NG19 136 B5
Northfield Prim Sch NG19 136 B5
Northfield Rd NG9 223 F4
Northfields
Clowne S43 80 F3
Long Eaton NG10 236 B4
Northgate DE1 267 B4
North Gate S44 98 E3
Northgate Ho S21 59 D3
Northgate St 4 DE7 194 F1
North Gr S44 98 A6
North La
Belper DE56 178 D2
Belper, Milford DE56 190 E7
Brailsford DE6 187 E4
Old Brampton S42 94 D4
Northlands
4 Buxton SK17 85 D8
Harthill S26 61 E7
North Leys DE6 173 B1
Northmead Dr DE73 218 B3
Northmoor Cl S43 96 F7
North Moor View S43 96 F7
North Par
Derby DE1 267 B4
Matlock Bath DE4 143 A1
North Rd
Buxton SK17 66 D1
Calow S44 96 F3
Clowne S43 80 E4
Glossop SK13 10 C3
Hayfield SK22 25 D3
Long Eaton NG10 236 C6
North Row DE22 205 A1
Northside S42 115 D1
North Side S42 115 D1
North St
Alfreton DE55 159 B3
Blackwell DE55 147 F2
Bramley-Vale S44 117 D1
Burton upon Trent DE15 248 B3
Clay Cross S45 131 B5
Cromford DE4 155 A6
Derby DE1 267 B5
Derby DE23 218 C2
7 Ilkeston DE7 194 F1
Langley Mill NG16 182 B3
Melbourne DE73 252 A7
North Wingfield S42 131 E6
Pinxton NG16 160 D3
Shirebrook NG20 120 D4
Somercotes DE55 170 D6
South Normanton DE55 159 F5
Swadlincote DE11 256 B5
Whaley Thorns NG20 101 A2
North Terr 1 S41 115 B7
Northumberland Rd DE15 254 D7
Northumberland St DE23 218 F2
North View
Crich DE4 168 A8
Derby DE23 218 C1
North View St S44 98 F1
Northway Dr DE1 218 E4
NORTH WINGFIELD 132 B8
North Wingfield Prim Sch
North Wingfield S42 131 F7
North Wingfield S42 131 F8
North Wingfield Rd S42 115 E3
NORTHWOOD 127 B5
Northwood Ave
Derby DE21 219 E7
Northwood Ave *continued*
Temple Normanton DE4 116 C3
Northwood La
Ellastone DE6 183 C5
Northwood DE4 127 A6
Northwood Rise DE6 185 B8
Northwood St NG9 223 D8
NORTON 57 B8
Norton Ave
Chesterfield S40 114 A8
Sheffield S14 43 E2
Shuttlewood S44 98 F6
Shuttlewood S44 99 A6
Norton Church Glebe S8 43 C1
Norton Church Rd S8 43 B1
Norton Free CE Prim Sch S8 43 C1
Norton Green Cl S8 43 C1
Norton Hall S8 43 B1
Norton Hall Ct S8 43 B1
Norton La S8 43 C1
Norton Lawns S8 43 C1
NORTON LEES 43 A4
Norton Lees Cl S8 43 A3
Norton Lees Cres S8 43 A4
Norton Lees Glade S8 43 A4
Norton Lees La S8 43 A4
Norton Lees Rd S2 43 A3
Norton Lees Sq S8 43 A3
Norton Mews S8 43 C1
Norton Park Ave S8 57 B8
Norton Park Cres S8 57 A8
Norton Park Dr S8 57 A8
Norton Park Rd S8 57 B8
Norton Park View S8 57 B8
NORTON WOODSEATS 43 A2
Norwell Ct 2 NG19 136 B1
Norwich Cl NG19 136 D5
Norwich St DE21 219 D7
NORWOOD 60 F8
Norwood Ave S41 115 E6
Norwood Cl
Chesterfield S41 115 E6
Derby DE22 218 A5
Ilkeston DE7 194 F5
Norwood Cres S21 60 F7
Norwood Ind Est S21 60 E8
Norwood La NG20 100 E5
Norwood Pl S21 60 F7
Noskwith St DE7 209 A5
Nothill Rd DE65 228 E1
Nothills Cl DE73 233 A1
Nottingham 26 Bus Pk (under development) NG16 182 D3
Nottingham Canal Nature Reserve★ DE7, NG16 195 C1
Nottingham Cl
10 Castle Gresley DE11 255 E1
Wingerworth S42 115 B3
Nottingham Dr
Derby DE3 230 E5
Wingerworth S42 115 B3
Nottingham La
Ironville NG16 170 F5
Pye Hill NG16 171 A5
Nottingham Rd
Alfreton DE55 159 B2
Ashby-de-la-Zouch LE65 258 F1
Belper DE56 179 B4
Borrowash DE72 221 D2
Breedon on the Hill DE73 252 D1
Codnor DE5, NG16 181 C8
Derby DE1, DE21 267 C4
Derby DE21 220 E2
Derby, Chaddesden DE21 219 E6
Derby, Spondon DE21 220 E3
Eastwood, Bailey Grove NG16 182 E2
Eastwood, Giltbrook NG16 195 C8
Ilkeston DE7 209 A6
Long Eaton NG10 236 F8
Ripley DE5 169 E2
Selston NG16 171 F6
Stapleford NG9 223 E7
Tansley DE4 144 B4
Trowell NG9 209 E5
Nowill Ct 2 S8 43 A6
Nowill Pl 3 S8 43 A6
Nuffield Health Derby Hospl DE23 230 F6
Nunbrook Gr SK17 85 C8
Nunn Brook Rd NG17 148 E2
Nunn Brook Rise NG17 148 E2
Nunn Cl NG17 148 E1
Nunsfield Dr DE24 233 B7
Nunsfield Rd SK17 66 C1
Nun's St DE1 218 E6
Nursery Ave
Sandiacre NG10 222 F5
West Hallam DE7 207 E7
Nursery Cl
Borrowash DE72 221 B2
4 Glossop SK13 17 C8
Nursery Cl *continued*
Swadlincote DE11 256 B6
Nursery Croft DE4 165 E6
Nursery Dr
Bolsover S44 98 F2
Buxton SK17 66 C2
Nursery Gdns DE55 160 C4
Nursery Hollow DE7 208 E6
Nursery La SK17 84 E6
Nutbrook Cres DE7 208 D4
Nuthall Circ DE7 208 C4
Nuttall Cl DE55 158 F3
Nuttall St DE55 158 F3
Nuttall Terr S44 117 D1
NUTTALS PARK 169 E1
Nutwood Cl DE22 205 A3
Nutwood/Darley Tip Nature Reserve★ DE56 205 A2

O

Oadby Dr S41 115 C7
Oadby Rise DE23 231 E6
Oakamoor Cl S40 95 A5
Oak Apple Cres DE7 208 E6
Oak Ave
Aldercar NG16 182 B5
Disley SK12 33 A6
Ripley DE5 180 D7
Sandiacre NG10 223 A7
Shirebrook NG20 119 D4
Oak Bank SK12 33 A6
Oak Bank Ave S41 77 B2
Oakbank Ct S17 55 E5
Oak Cl
Brimington S43 96 D7
Chapel-en-le-Frith SK23 47 C5
Derby DE22 204 E4
Duffield DE56 190 E2
Killamarsh S21 60 C5
Linton DE11 261 E7
Mottram in Longdendale SK14 9 A4
Ockbrook DE72 221 C5
Pinxton NG16 160 C3
Oak Cres
Ashbourne DE6 185 C7
Derby DE23 231 C8
Wingerworth S42 114 F3
Oakdale Cl S45 131 E2
Oakdale Gdns DE21 206 B3
Oakdale Rd DE55 160 A4
Oakdell S18 57 D3
Oak Dr
Alfreton DE55 159 B4
Derby DE23 218 C1
Derby DE3 217 E2
Derby, Boulton DE24 233 A6
Doveridge DE6 211 B1
Eastwood NG16 182 E2
Hilton DE65 228 D2
Mansfield Woodhouse NG19 136 E2
Oakenthorpe Nature Reserve★ DE55 158 C3
Oaker Terr DE4 142 A7
OAKERTHORPE 158 C3
Oakerthorpe Rd
Bolehill DE4 154 F4
Bolehill DE4 155 B2
Wirksworth DE4 155 B2
Oakes Cl
Langley Mill NG16 182 A5
Somercotes DE55 170 C7
Oakes Park View S14 43 D1
Oakes The S8 43 D1
Oakfield Ave S40 95 B1
Oakfield Ct DE7 193 A2
Oakfield Dr NG10 223 B3
Oakfield Rd
Glossop SK13 9 E3
Stapleford NG9 223 D7
Oakfields DE13 238 A4
Oakfields Gr DE21 220 D3
Oak Grove Gn S17 55 E4
Oakham Cl DE21 205 D1
Oakham Rd 5 DE23 230 F6
Oakham Way DE7 194 E3
Oakhill Rd S18 57 C3
Oakhurst Cl DE56 178 D6
Oak La DE6 212 D4
Oakland Ave
Long Eaton NG10 236 C5
Sutton in Ashfield NG17 148 F2
Oakland Cres DE55 170 D5
Oakland Croft NG17 148 F3
Oakland Dr DE12 262 F3
Oaklands SK22 25 C3
Oaklands Ave
Derby DE23 231 C5
Heanor DE75 182 A2
Marple Bridge SK6 23 C8
Oaklands Cl DE5 180 D1
Oaklands Dr 1 DE7 193 A6
Oaklands Drive DE7 192 F6
Oaklands Rd DE65 229 C4
Oaklands St DE55 159 B4
Oaklands The DE55 160 A4
Oaklands Way DE73 252 B8
Oakland Terr NG10 236 C5
Oaklea SK17 85 C5
Oaklea Way S42 131 B6
Oakleigh Ave
Derby DE21 219 F6
Mansfield Woodhouse NG19 136 E4
Swadlincote DE11 255 F5
Oakley Ave S40 95 E4
Oakley Cl DE55 159 C4
Oakley's Rd NG10 236 E7
Oakley's Road W NG10 236 D6
Oak Lodge Dr NG16 195 F7
Oakmeadows DE55 160 B4
Oakover Dr DE22 204 D2
Oak Rd
Denstone ST14 196 D5
Elvaston DE72 233 F4
Grassmoor S42 115 F3
Matlock DE4 143 C5
Shardlow DE72 234 A5
Sheffield, Gleadless Townend S12 44 A2
Oakridge DE21 220 B7
Oakridge Cl NG19 136 F1
Oakridge Pk DE74 247 A5
Oaks Ave
Creswell S80 100 C8
Hayfield SK22 25 D2
Oaks Barn DE45 109 A2
Oaksedge La
Tansley DE4 143 F6
Tansley DE4 144 A5
Oaksetts Dr S43 82 E2
Oaks Farm La S44 97 A2
OAKS GREEN 225 D7
Oakside Way DE21 206 B3
Oaks La
Ashover S45 129 C5
Cutthorpe S18, S42 94 A8
Oak Sq DE11 255 F2
Oaks Rd DE65 242 B5
Oak St
Brimington S43 78 A1
Derby DE23 219 A2
Glossop SK13 10 C1
Sheffield S20 59 C8
Sheffield, Heeley S8 43 A7
Swadlincote DE11 256 A2
Oakstedge La S45 145 B7
Oaks The
Glossop SK13 17 A7
Little Eaton DE21 205 C8
OAKTHORPE 265 F5
Oaktree Ave DE24 232 B7
Oak Tree Ave S44 134 B8
Oaktree Bsns Pk DE11 255 E3
Oak Tree Cl
Arkwright Town S44 97 D3
Ripley DE5 180 C8
Swanwick DE55 170 A8
Oak Tree Close DE12 260 D4
Oak Tree Cotts S44 97 A1
Oak Tree Cres NG19 136 B4
Oak Tree Ct DE72 221 D1
Oak Tree Gdns DE4 144 A4
Oaktree Rd DE55 160 C8
Oak Tree Rd S43 80 E2
Oak Trees Cl DE13 240 B3
Oakvale Ho DE23 219 A2
Oakview S17 55 E5
Oak View Gardens DE55 146 E5
Oakway Dr DE11 256 F1
Oakwell Cres DE7 208 E8
Oakwell Dr
Crich DE4 156 F1
Ilkeston DE7 208 E8
OAKWOOD 206 A2
Oakwood SK13 16 F8
Oakwood Cl
Derby DE65 231 D2
Hatton DE65 239 C8
Oakwood District Ctr DE21 206 A1
Oakwood Dr
Bolsover S44 98 F3
Darley Dale DE4 142 E8
Derby DE21 206 B2
Oakwood Inf Sch DE24 233 A6
Oakwood Jun Sch DE24 233 A6
Oakwood Rd SK12 32 D6
Oakwood Way S43 79 B4
Oakworth Cl 1 S20 59 E6
Oakworth Dr S20 59 D6
Oakworth Gr S20 59 D6
Oakworth View S20 59 D6
Oat Hill DE4 165 F7
Oats Orch S20 59 D6
Oberon Cl DE73 232 E1
Oberon Ret Pk DE56 178 F3
Occupation Cl S43 80 A6
Occupation La
North Wingfield S42 131 E7
Sheffield, Birley S12 44 F3
Woodville DE11 256 D1
Occupation Rd
Chesterfield S41 95 F8
Moira DE11 262 C8
New Houghton NG19 134 F7
Ocean Ct DE24 219 E1
Ochbrook Ct DE7 194 F3
OCKBROOK 221 D5
Octavia Cl DE73 232 E2
Octavia Ct S40 266 B1
Oddfellows Cotts 16 SK17 85 B7
Oddfellows Rd S32 53 A7
Oddfellows Row S32 53 A7
Oddfellows Terr S32 53 A7
Oddfellow Terr DE45 109 D6
Oddford La DE4 127 D2
Odom Ct S2 43 B6
Odridgehay Sta★ DE56 176 F6
Offcote Cres 1 DE6 173 D3
OFFERTON 52 D7
Offerton Ave DE23 231 F8
Offerton La S33 52 C7
Offridge Cl S43 80 F2
Off Spring Bank SK22 33 C8
Ogden St SK14 16 B8
OGSTON 146 A4
Ogston La DE55 146 B4
Ogston New Rd DE55 145 E4
Okeover Ave DE6 173 D1
OKER 142 D7
Oker Ave DE4 127 B3
Oker Dr DE4 127 B3
Oker La DE4 142 D6
Oker Rd DE4 142 B7
Old Ashbourne Rd ST14 210 B3
Old Bakery Cl
Chesterfield S41 77 A2
Hognaston DE6 164 B1
Old Bakery Way NG18 136 C1
Old Bank DE6 184 D8
Old Barn Cl DE21 205 D8
OLD BRAMPTON 94 D4
Old Brampton Rd DE45 92 D5
Old Brick Works La S41 96 A6
Oldbury Cl DE21 206 A2
Old Buxton Rd SK11 83 A6
Old Chester Rd DE1 219 A8
Old Church Cl DE22 204 C5
Old Coach Rd DE4 143 F4
Old Coalpit La
Chelmorton SK17 86 F1
Chelmorton SK17 105 D8
Old Colliery La S42 132 E8
Old Coppice Side DE75 193 E7
Old Court House Shops 4 SK17 85 B8
Old Cross SK13 10 E2
OLD DAM 49 B4
Old Dam SK17 49 A4
Old Dam La SK17 49 C4
Old Denstone Rd ST14 196 E4
Old Derby Rd
Ashbourne DE6 173 C1
Eastwood NG16 182 D3
Olde Derwent Ave DE4 143 B4
Olde English Rd DE4 143 B4
Old End DE12 265 F1
Olders Valley DE11 256 E4
Old Etwall Rd DE3 230 C8
Old Fall St NG17 148 F3
Old Farm Ct NG11 237 E6
Old Farm Gdns DE12 262 F4
Old Farmhouse The DE45 109 D6
Oldfield Dr DE11 256 C5
Oldfield La
Egginton DE65 241 A8
Hognaston DE6 164 B2
Kirk Ireton DE6 164 F2
Snelston DE6 184 B3
Warrencarr DE45 126 F2
Wensley DE4 142 A8
Old Forge Bsns Pk 5 S2 43 A7
Old Forge Cl DE65 241 A5
Old Gate HD9 2 F7
Old Gate Ave DE72 245 E5
Old Gate Cl 6 DE5 170 B1
OLD GLOSSOP 10 E2
Old Green Close S80 82 A6
Old Hackney La DE4 142 F8
Old Hall Ave
Derby DE23 218 B1
Derby, Alvaston DE24 233 B7
Duffield DE56 190 E3
Old Hall Cl
Darley Dale DE4 127 C3
Glossop SK13 10 D2
Pilsley S45 132 C2
Old Hall Ct DE55 169 E7
Old Hall Dr
Horwich End SK23 45 E4
Willington DE65 242 B5
Old Hall Gdns
Stoney Middleton S32 72 A4
Swadlincote DE11 256 A2
Old Hall Jun Sch S40 95 C2

Old Hall La
Church Broughton DE65 227 B8
Marple SK6 23 C5
Mottram in Longdendale SK14 9 A5
Whitwell S80 81 F6
Old Hall Mews S8 56 F7
Old Hall Mills Bsns Pk DE21 205 C7
Old Hall Rd
Chesterfield S40 95 D3
Derby DE23 218 C1
Old Hall Sq 3 SK13 10 A5
Old Hartshay Hill DE5 169 C2
Oldhay Cl S17 55 D6
Old Hay Gdns S17 55 C6
Old Hay La S17 55 C6
Old Hill
Ashbourne DE6 173 C1
Ashbourne DE6 185 C8
Old Hillcliff La DE56 177 A3
Old House Mus* DE45 109 C6
Old House Rd S40 95 D6
Old Houses S41 96 C3
Oldicote La DE15 248 E3
Oldikes SK17 102 E1
Oldknow Rd SK6 23 A6
Old La
Cubley DE6 198 E1
Derby DE22 205 A2
Idridgehay DE56 176 F3
Sheffield S20 60 A7
Shottle DE56 177 A5
Tintwistle SK13 6 E3
Wirksworth DE4 154 F2
Old Lime Ct DE4 143 C5
Old Lodge Cl ST14 210 A1
Old Longhill Rd SK17 65 B4
Old Manor Rd NG19 136 C3
Old Mansfield Rd DE21 205 C1
Old Market Pl DE55 160 A6
OLD MATLOCK 143 C4
Old Mill Cl
Duffield DE56 190 E3
Mansfield NG19 136 E1
Old Mill Dr S40 95 A8
Old Mill La
Calver S32 72 D2
Mansfield NG19 136 E1
Old Mill Lane Ind Est NG19 136 C1
Old Nurseries Cl DE56 179 E5
Old Nursery Gdns DE4 144 A5
Old Oak Cl DE4 157 A1
Old Orchard DE45 109 A1
Old Park Ave S8 56 D7
Old Park Rd S8 56 D7
Old Parks La LE65 258 C3
Old Peverel Rd S44 98 A5
Old Pheasant Ct S40 95 A2
Old Pit La
Clay Cross S45 131 F3
Smalley DE7 193 A6
Old Pk DE6 187 D6
Old Plough Close DE72 245 F5
Old Pond The DE75 194 A8
Old Porter La DE4 154 F3
Old Post Office Row S33 40 B4
Old Printworks 2 DE11 256 B3
Old Quarry Cl S43 80 C6
Old Railway Mws DE11 256 C4
Old Rd
Branston DE14 253 E7
Buxton SK17, SK23 65 C5
Chesterfield S40 95 C3
Darley Dale DE4 127 C1
Furness Vale SK23 33 D4
Glossop SK13 10 A7
Heage DE56 179 E8
Horwich End, New Horwich SK23 45 E6
Mottram in Longdendale SK14 9 A5
Oldridge Cl S40 95 B6
Old School Cl
Bramley-Vale S44 117 D1
Holymoorside S42 113 D7
Tideswell SK17 69 C4
Old School Close DE4 127 E1
Old School Ct DE56 168 E1
Old School Ho The S42 113 D7
Old School La
Awsworth NG16 195 C5
Chesterfield S44 96 F2
Creswell S43 81 F1
Pleasley NG19 135 A5
Old School Mews DE72 246 B8
Old School The DE65 228 C2
Old Ship La S40 266 B3
Old Smithy Row SK22 33 C7
Old St SK14 16 A8
Old Station Cl
Etwall DE65 229 B4
Rowsley DE4 126 F8
Old Station Yd S43 96 C8
Old Stone La DE4 143 E7
Old Storth La DE55 160 B4
Old Swanwick Colliery Rd DE55 158 F1
Old Tennis Courts The SK17 85 B8
Old Terr NG19 134 F4
OLD TUPTON 131 C7
Old Turnpike Dr DE4 157 A1
Old Uttoxeter Rd
Crakemarsh ST14 210 C6
Rocester ST14 196 D1
Old Vicarage Cl DE23 218 C1
Old Vicarage La DE22 204 C5
Old Vicarage Sch DE22 205 A3
Old Water La NG19 135 D1
Old Waterworks The DE73 243 A4
Oldwell Cl S17 55 D4
OLD WHITTINGTON 77 B1
Old Whittington La S18 76 E6
Old Works La S44 97 B3
Olive Ave
Long Eaton NG10 223 E1
Shirebrook NG20 119 D6
Olive Cl
Branston DE14 253 E6
Branston DE14 256 E6
Olive Cres S12 44 A2
Olive Gdns S41 95 F6
Olive Gr DE21 219 F5
Olive Grove Rd S2 43 B8
Oliver Cl DE75 182 B2
Oliver Close DE72 235 E8
Olive Rd S20 59 D7
Oliver Ho S41 266 C3
Oliver Rd DE7 208 C6
Olive St DE22 218 E4
Olive Terr 1 SK14 16 A8
Olivet Rd S8 43 A3
Olivier St DE23 219 B1
OLLERBROOK BOOTH 37 D8
Ollersett Ave
New Mills SK22 24 D1
New Mills SK22 33 D8
Ollersett Dr SK22 33 D8
Ollersett Ho SK22 33 D8
Ollersett La SK22 24 E1
Olton Dr DE65 240 E8
Olton Rd DE3 217 C4
Olympian Way DE4 127 B4
Onslow Rd DE3 217 E4
Onward Cotts SK17 85 E8
Opal Cl DE21 206 A2
Opal Gdns DE11 255 F4
Opal St S40 115 E6
Openacre NG16 170 F4
OPENWOODGATE 179 D3
Openwoodgate DE56 179 D3
Openwood Rd DE56 179 E3
Optimum Rd DE11 255 E3
Orange Birch Cl S43 80 D2
Orange Cl NG20 119 E6
Orange St DE55 159 B4
Orchard Ave
Castle Donington DE74 247 A3
Whaley Bridge SK23 45 D7
Orchard Bsns Pk DE7 194 D1
Orchard Cl
Barlborough S43 80 A7
Belper DE56 191 B8
Bolsover S44 99 B1
Breadsall DE21 205 D4
Breaston DE72 235 F8
Clowne S43 80 E3
Derby DE23 231 C7
Elvaston DE24 233 D4
Hilton DE65 228 D1
Melbourne DE73 252 A7
Moira DE12 262 F4
Ockbrook DE72 221 C4
Ripley DE5 181 A7
Shirebrook NG20 119 E5
Sudbury DE6 225 E5
1 Uttoxeter ST14 210 B1
Walton-on-Trent DE12 253 D1
West Hallam DE7 207 E7
Willington DE65 242 B6
Orchard Com Prim Sch DE74 247 A3
Orchard Cotts DE56 190 E4
Orchard Cres
Glapwell S44 134 B8
Swanwick DE55 169 D7
Orchard Ct
Derby DE21 220 E5
Doveridge DE6 211 B1
Langley Mill NG16 182 B3
South Normanton DE55 159 F4
Orchard Ct *continued*
Sutton-in-Ashfield NG17 148 E2
Orchard Dr
1 Creswell S43 81 E2
Creswell S80 81 E2
Gamesley SK13 9 E1
Orchard Gr DE5 181 B6
Orchard La DE6 185 D1
Orchard Lee S26 61 E6
Orchard Mews S18 56 E2
Orchard Mws NG16 160 E3
Orchard Park Ind Est NG10 223 C6
Orchard Pl S21 60 D6
Orchard Rd
Compstall SK6 15 B2
Darley Dale DE4 142 E8
Matlock Bath DE4 143 A1
Somercotes DE55 170 C6
Whaley Bridge SK23 45 D7
Orchard Rise
Alfreton DE55 159 C3
Heanor DE75 181 F2
Orchard Sq S18 56 D2
Orchard St
5 Derby DE3 230 D8
Derby, Markeaton DE3 217 D1
Eastwood NG16 195 A8
Ilkeston DE7 208 F7
Kimberley NG16 195 F6
Langley Mill NG16 182 B3
Long Eaton NG10 236 E7
Mansfield NG19 136 B1
Swadlincote DE11 255 F6
Orchards The
Derby DE22 204 D3
Jacksdale NG16 171 B4
Orchards Way S40 95 D1
Orchard The
Belper DE56 179 A4
Chesterfield S43 80 E5
Codnor DE5 170 B1
Disley SK12 32 D6
Horsley Woodhouse DE7 192 D6
Morton DE55 147 A5
Stanton-by-Dale DE7 222 F8
Uttoxeter ST14 210 A4
Youlgreave DE45 125 C5
Orchard View
Bolsover S44 117 F8
Mansfield Woodhouse NG19 136 B3
North Wingfield S45 131 F5
Orchard View Rd S40 95 C4
Orchard Way
Chellaston DE73 232 F2
Clay Cross S45 131 B3
Donisthorpe DE12 265 E8
Sandiacre NG10 223 A3
Orchid Cl
Burton upon Trent DE15 255 A8
Calow S44 97 A3
Orchid Court DE24 231 C3
Orchid Dr SK23 46 F5
Orchid Gr
Pleasley NG19 134 F5
Pleasley NG19 135 A5
Orchid Gro NG20 119 D2
Orchid Way
Shirebrook NG20 119 D3
Wingerworth S40 115 D2
Orchil Street NG16 195 B8
Ordish Ave DE21 219 F5
Ordley La DE6 183 F8
Ordley Wlk DE65 228 D1
Oregano Cl DE3 217 C5
Oregon Way DE21 220 C6
Ore St S45 131 C5
Orford Ave SK12 32 D6
Organ Way SK14 9 D5
Oriel Ct DE1 267 C1
Orient Way DE24 219 E2
Orkney Cl DE24 231 D3
Orlando Ct DE73 232 E2
Orly Ave DE74 247 A2
Ormesby Cl S18 56 C1
Ormiston Enterprise Acad DE7 194 F4
Ormond Cl
Chesterfield S40 114 B7
Sheffield S8 57 B6
Ormond Dr S8 57 B6
Ormonde Dr DE5 180 D5
Ormonde St NG16 182 B4
Ormonde Terr NG16 182 B4
Ormond Rd S8 57 B7
Ormond Way S8 57 B7
Ormsby Rd S41 95 F7
Ormskirk Rise DE21 220 F4
Orpean Way NG9 223 E2
Orpen Dr S14 43 E2
Orpen Ho S8 43 D2
Orpen Way S14 43 E2
Orton Way DE56 179 B6
Orwell Road DE65 228 E1
Orwins Cl 5 S41 95 D7
Osborne Cl NG10 223 B4
Osborne Croft S26 61 F6
Osborne Ct DE21 205 D4
Osborne Pl SK13 10 A5
Osborne Rd DE23 219 C3
Osborne St
Burton upon Trent DE15 248 A3
Derby DE23 267 D1
Osbourne Gdns DE15 248 A3
Oscar Ct S43 77 D3
Osiers Cl DE22 204 C1
OSLESTON 215 D7
Osleston La
Longlane DE6 201 E1
Thurvaston DE6 215 D7
OSMASTON
Ashbourne 185 F4
Derby 232 C8
Osmaston CE (VC) Prim Sch DE6 185 F4
Osmaston Cl NG10 235 F5
Osmaston Park Ind Est DE24 232 E8
Osmaston Park Rd DE23, DE24 232 C7
Osmaston Prim Sch DE24 232 C7
Osmaston Rd
Derby DE23, DE24 219 B2
Derby DE24 232 D6
Osmaston St NG10 223 C5
Osmaton Park Ind Est DE24 219 D1
Osmund Ct S21 59 C3
Osmund Rd S21 59 C3
Osprey Cl
Burton upon Trent DE15 248 D4
Derby DE24 231 E2
Osprey Dr
Branston DE14 253 E6
Branston DE14 256 E6
Osterly Gn DE22 218 A5
Ostrich La DE6 163 B1
Oswestry Cl DE21 206 B3
Othello Dr DE73 232 D2
Otterburn Dr DE22 204 C2
Otterhole Cl SK17 84 F7
Otter St
Derby DE1 219 A7
Hilton DE65 228 D1
Otter Way NG19 135 D1
Oulton Cl DE24 232 D4
Oundle Dr
Ilkeston DE7 209 B7
Mansfield NG19 135 D1
Ousley La DE6 183 C5
Outfield Rd DE15 254 F8
Outgang La
Mansfield Woodhouse NG19 136 D4
Pleasley NG19 135 C6
Out La S42, S44 132 F6
Outlands Rd S33 50 F6
Outram Cl DE72 221 B1
Outram Ct DE5 169 E2
Outram Dr DE11 256 D4
Outram Rd S41 95 F6
Outram St DE5 169 E2
Outrams Wharf DE21 205 C6
Outram Way DE24 231 E2
Outram Wy SK23 34 E1
Outseats Dr DE55 159 B3
Outwood Acad City S13 44 F6
Outwood Acad Newbold S41 95 F6
Oval Ct DE23 231 C8
OVER BURROWS 202 A4
Over Croft La DE4 168 A8
Overcroft Rise S17 55 D4
Overdale DE4 143 D5
Overdale Ave SK17 85 D8
Overdale Cl NG10 236 A6
Overdale Dr SK13 17 B8
Overdale Gdns S17 55 D6
Overdale Rd
Derby DE23 218 E2
New Mills SK12 32 F6
Overdale Rise S17 55 C6
Overend Cl S14 43 D4
Overend Dr S14 43 D4
Overend Rd S14 43 D4
Overend Way S14 43 D4
OVERGREEN 94 B8
OVER HADDON 109 B1
Over Hill Rd SK22, SK23 34 A5
Over La
Baslow DE45 91 E6
Belper DE56 179 E5
Hazelwood DE56 178 A2
Overlees S18 75 D3
OVER LEIGH 45 F6
Overmoor View DE55 148 B7
Over Rd DE45 91 E6
OVERSEAL 262 A3
Overseal Prim Sch DE12 262 B4
OVERSETTS 255 E5
Oversetts Ct DE11 255 F6
Oversetts Rd DE11 255 E5
Overstone Cl DE56 179 D4
Overton Cl S43 78 F3
Overtown DE6 164 B4
OVER WOODHOUSE 98 E3
Owen Ave NG10 237 A6
Owen Falls Ave S41 96 C3
OWEN'S BANK 239 B6
Owers Ave DE75 193 F7
OWLCOTES 117 A4
Owlcotes View S44 118 A8
OWLER BAR 55 B1
Owler Bar Rd S11 54 B4
Owler Car La S18 57 F5
Owlers La DE23 218 C2
Owlers The SK23 45 E6
Owlston Cl NG16 182 F3
Owlswick Cl DE23 231 A8
OWLTHORPE 59 B8
Owlthorpe Ave S20 59 B8
Owlthorpe Cl S20 59 B8
Owlthorpe Dr S20 59 B8
Owlthorpe Gr S20 59 B8
Owlthorpe La S20 59 B8
Owlthorpe Rise S20 59 B8
Oxbury Rd NG16 195 F8
Ox Cl S45 131 D3
Ox Close Ave S17 56 A5
Oxclose Dr 2 S18 56 C1
Oxclose La
Alsop en le Dale DE6 150 C2
Dronfield S18 56 C1
Mansfield NG19 135 D3
Mansfield Woodhouse NG19 136 A3
Oxclose Park Gdns S20 59 F6
Oxclose Park Rd S20 59 F6
Oxclose Park Rise S20 59 F6
Oxclose Park Road N S20 59 F7
Oxclose Park View S20 59 F6
Oxclose Park Way S20 59 F6
Oxcroft Est S44 99 D7
Oxcroft Ind Est S44 99 A8
Oxcroft La
Bolsover S44 99 A2
Bolsover S44 99 B6
Elmton S44 99 E8
Oxcroft View S44 99 B8
Oxcroft Way S43 80 B5
Oxenhope Cl DE23 230 E7
Oxford Cl S43 96 F8
Oxford Rd S43 96 F8
Oxford St
Blackwell DE55 147 E1
Bramley-Vale S44 117 F1
Derby DE1 267 C1
Derby, Spondon DE21 220 E5
Eastwood NG16 182 F2
4 Ilkeston DE7 208 F7
Long Eaton NG10 236 D8
Mansfield Woodhouse NG19 136 C1
Ripley DE5 169 D1
Swadlincote DE11 256 A1
Oxhay Gdns DE4 157 A1
Ox Hill S20 60 A5
Oxley Rd DE15 248 A3
Oxmead DE6 184 D7
Oxpasture La NG20 100 B5
Oxton Rake Rd S18 94 A8
OXTON RAKES 94 B8
Oxwich Ct DE21 206 B2
Oyster Cl DE14 254 B7
Oyster Rd NG16 182 D4
Ozier Holt NG10 236 C6

P

Pacific Way DE24 219 E2
Packenham Bvd DE65 227 A4
Packer's Row S40 266 B3
Pack Horse Rd DE73 252 B8
Packington Rd DE65 240 E8
Packman La S26, S80 62 C6
Paddington Ct S43 78 B4
Paddock Cl
Castle Donington DE74 246 F3
Sheffield S2 43 E6
Wingerworth S42 114 F3
Paddock Cres S2 43 E5
Paddock Croft 9 DE21 205 F2
Paddock Ct ST14 196 E5
Paddock Dr DE75 193 C8
Paddock La SK23 45 F5
Paddocks Cl NG16 160 C4
Paddocks The
Mansfield Woodhouse NG19 136 E5
Pilsley S45 132 C2
Ripley DE5 180 F8
Sandiacre NG10 223 A5
Staveley S43 79 C3
Sutton in Ashfield NG17 148 F2
Swadlincote DE11 255 F5
Paddocks View NG10 236 B8
Paddock The
Alfreton DE55 157 F3
Blackwell DE55 147 F1
Bolsover S44 99 B1
Burton upon Trent DE15 248 B4
Buxton SK17 84 F7
Paddock The *continued*
Elvaston DE24 233 D4
Glossop SK13 9 E5
Holbrook DE56 191 C6
Hollingworth SK14 9 E5
Horwich End SK23 45 F6
Ockbrook DE72 221 C4
Pleasley NG19 135 A5
Rolleston DE13 240 A4
Shirebrook NG20 119 D4
Paddock Way S18 57 B3
PADFIELD 10 C5
Padfield Com Prim Sch SK13 10 B5
Padfield Gate SK13 17 D7
Padfield Main Rd SK13 10 C5
Padley Cl
Derby DE22 205 A5
Ripley DE5 169 C3
Padley Hill S32 53 E1
Padley Rd S32 53 D1
Padley Way S42 131 F5
Padley Wood La S45 147 B8
Padley Wood Rd S45 132 C2
Padstow Cl 13 DE24 231 D3
Padstow Rd DE24 233 C5
Paget High Sch DE14 254 A7
Paget Road DE73 245 A1
Paige Gardens NG10 223 A5
Paignton Ct 15 S41 95 F8
Painters La DE6 187 A1
Painter's La DE6 186 B5
Painters Way
Darley Dale DE4 127 D3
Winster DE4 141 C6
Paisley Cl S43 97 C8
Palace La DE56 166 D1
Palace Rd SK17 85 B8
Palatine Gr DE23 230 F7
Palerow La DE56 166 E3
Palissy Cl DE11 256 D4
Palladium Dr DE23 231 A6
Pall Mall DE21 205 E4
Palm Cl DE23 218 A1
Palmer Cl DE14 254 B8
Palmer Cres 3 S18 57 B1
Palmer Dr
Stapleford NG9 223 D5
Swanwick DE55 169 E7
PALMER MOOR 224 E7
Palmersgate S40 266 B3
Palmerston Ct DE73 252 B7
Palmerston Rd 4 DE7 208 F8
Palmerston St
Derby DE23 218 E1
Underwood Green NG16 171 F2
Westwood NG16 171 C4
PALTERTON 118 A5
Palterton La
Long Duckmanton S44 117 D7
Palterton S44 118 C5
Palterton Prim Sch S44 118 B5
Panama Circle DE24 219 F2
Pankhurst Pl S45 131 C3
Panthers Place S41 96 A5
Parade The
4 Derby DE3 217 D1
Sheffield S12 44 A6
Paradise St SK13 10 A5
Parcel Terr DE22 218 D5
Pares Way DE72 221 C5
Pares Way Cl DE72 221 C5
Pargate Cl DE5 180 D6
Park Ave
Ashbourne DE6 173 D1
Awsworth NG16 195 B5
Castle Donington DE74 246 F3
Darley Dale DE4 127 C3
Dronfield S18 57 B2
Eastwood NG16 182 E3
Furness Vale SK23 33 D3
Glapwell S44 118 C1
Holmesfield S18 75 A8
Ilkeston DE7 208 F8
Mansfield Woodhouse NG19 136 C4
Ripley DE5 169 F1
Scropton DE65 227 A5
Shirebrook NG20 119 E4
Stanley DE7 207 C6
Uttoxeter ST14 210 B2
Park Cl
Burton upon Trent DE16 254 D6
Chesterfield S40 115 A7
Glossop SK13 10 D2
Kilburn DE56 192 A8
Linton DE12 261 C6
Little Eaton DE21 205 B8
Matlock DE4 143 D4
Pinxton NG16 160 C2
Shirland DE55 146 E1
Stanton-by-Dale DE7 222 F8
Park Cotts DE4 127 A5
Park Cres
Chapel-en-le-Frith SK23 47 B5

Park Cres continued
Doveridge DE6 211 B1
Eastwood NG16 182 F4
Furness Vale SK23 10 D3
Glossop SK13 10 B3
Heage DE56 179 E8
Ilkeston DE7 209 A8
Park Ct DE75 181 F1
Park Dene Dr SK13 10 C2
Park Dr
Chesterfield S41 266 C1
Derby DE23 218 C1
Ilkeston DE7 208 F7
Sandiacre NG10 223 A3
Swanwick DE55 169 F6
Park Edge S32 52 F8
Parker Ave S44 96 F3
Parker Cl DE1 267 A4
Parker Ctr DE21 219 B8
Parke Rd SK17 69 C4
Parker Gdns NG9 223 F8
Parker Ind Est DE21 205 B1
Parkers Cl DE11 257 B1
Parkers La S17 55 D8
Parker's La NG19 136 C3
Parker St DE1 218 F7
Park Farm S18 56 C2
Park Farm Ctr DE22 204 D2
Park Farm Dr DE22 204 D2
Park Farm Mews
S21 60 D1
Parkfield Cres DE12 265 F1
Parkfield Ct SK17 85 A7
Parkfield La DE6 184 D4
Parkfield Pl S2 43 A8
Parkfields S43 80 E3
Parkfields Dr DE22 218 E8
Parkfields View
DE56 179 E8
Parkgate
Derby DE23 219 B2
Dronfield S18 57 C2
Parkgate Cl S20 59 A8
Parkgate Croft S20 59 A8
Parkgate Dr S20 59 A8
Parkgate La S21, S43 77 E5
Park Gr DE22 218 E7
Park Grange Croft Sta
S2 43 C8
Park Grange Ct S2 43 C8
Park Grange Dr S2 43 C8
Park Grange Mount
S2 43 C8
Park Grange Rd S2 43 D7
Park Grange Rise S2 43 C8
Park Grange View
S2 43 D8
Park Hall SK17 85 B8
Park Hall Ave S40,
S42 114 B8
Park Hall Cl S40 114 B7
Park Hall Gdns
Chesterfield S40 114 B7
Mansfield Woodhouse
NG19 136 C5
Parkhall La S21 60 D2
Park Hall La
Mapperley DE7 193 D2
West Hallam DE7 207 C8
Park Hall Rd
Denby Village DE5 180 A3
Mansfield Woodhouse
NG19 136 C5
Parkham Rd NG16 195 F7
PARK HEAD 157 C2
Park Head Rd DE4 143 B5
Park Hill
Awsworth NG16 195 B5
Eckington S21 59 E3
Park Hill Cl SK22 24 C1
Park Hill Dr DE23 231 F7
Park Ho DE56 179 A3
Parkhouse Cl S45 131 B4
Parkhouse Dr DE55 159 E5
Park House Prim Sch
S45 132 B4
Parkhouse Rd S42,
S45 132 A4
Parkin St DE55 159 B4
Park Jun & Inf Schs The
NG20 119 E5
Park La
Baslow DE45 91 F5
Baslow DE45 92 A5
Castle Donington
DE74 246 E3
Chesterfield S41 95 F7
Darley Dale DE4 127 D2
Derby, Allestree DE22 204 F4
Derby, Normanton Park
DE23 218 C1
Hayfield SK22 25 D5
Heage DE56 179 F8
Holbeck NG20, S80 101 C6
Over Haddon DE45,
DE4 110 C1
Pinxton NG16 160 C2
Ripley DE5 169 A7
Rodsley DE6 200 B3
Shirland DE55 159 A8
Shirley DE6 200 D8
South Wingfield
DE55 157 D1
Stanton in Peak DE4 126 C5
Tutbury DE13 239 B6
Weston-on-Trent
DE72 245 E4
Parkland Ave SK22 24 C1
Parkland Cres S12 44 E2
Parkland Dr S42 115 A2
Parkland Mews
NG10 236 D8
Parklands Dr DE73 245 A8
Parklands Inf Sch
NG10 223 B1
Park Leys Ct DE21 220 E4
Park Lodge Rd
NG16 195 A7
Park Mews
Derby DE22 218 F8
Mansfield Woodhouse
NG19 136 C4
Somercotes DE55 170 D6
Park Mill Dr DE55 159 C7
Park Nook Cl DE73 233 A3
Park Pale The DE13 239 C5
Park Rd
Ashbourne DE6 173 C2
Bakewell DE45 109 D5
Bakewell DE45 109 F3
Belper DE56 179 A2
Buxton SK17 85 A7
Buxton SK17 85 A8
Chapel-en-le-Frith
SK23 47 B6
Chesterfield S40 266 A2
Derby DE3 217 D2
Derby, Spondon DE21 220 D5
Donisthorpe DE12 262 E2
Duffield DE56 190 D3
Glossop SK13 10 A4
Heage DE56 179 E8
High Lane SK12 32 A6
Holmewood S42 116 E1
Horwich End SK23 45 D6
Ilkeston DE7 208 F7
Mansfield Woodhouse
NG19 136 B3
New Mills SK22 33 C7
Over Haddon DE45 110 B2
Overseal DE11 261 F6
Overseal DE12 262 A6
Ripley DE5 169 E1
Shirebrook NG20 119 E5
Stapleford NG9 223 F8
Swadlincote DE11,
DE15 255 D5
Swadlincote, Church Gresley
DE11 256 C2
Tupton S42 131 C7
Park Rise S18 75 A8
Park Row
Bretby DE15 249 B1
Clay Cross S45 131 D4
Parks Ave DE55 157 F3
Parkside
Belper DE56 179 A3
Buxton SK17 85 A8
Chesterfield S41 96 A7
Heage DE56 179 E8
Renishaw S21 60 B1
Park Side DE55 170 D7
Parkside Ave NG10 236 B8
Parkside Cl NG16 170 F4
Parkside Close S12 44 F2
Parkside Com Sch
S40 266 A1
Parkside Dr
Ironville NG16 170 F4
Long Eaton NG10 236 B8
Parkside La SK6 23 C6
Parkside Mews S12 44 F3
Parkside Rd DE21 220 B6
Parkside Sh Ctr S21 60 D7
Parkside Shopping Ctr
S20 60 D7
Parkside View S40 95 B6
Park Spring Cl 10 S2 43 C8
Park Spring Dr S2 43 C8
Park Spring Grove
S2 43 C8
Park Spring Pl S2 43 C8
Park Spring Way S2 43 C8
Park St
Alfreton DE55 158 F3
Barlborough S43 80 B7
Breaston DE72 235 F8
Chesterfield S40 115 A7
Derby DE1 267 D2
Heanor DE75 181 D2
Long Eaton NG10 223 C1
Mansfield Woodhouse
NG19 136 B3
Ripley DE5 169 E1
Stapleford NG9 223 D6
Swadlincote DE11 256 A6
Uttoxeter ST14 210 C1
Wessington DE55 145 E1
Wessington DE55 157 E8
Parkstone Ct DE3 217 C2
Parkstone Delph S12 44 A2
Park Studios S40 266 A2
Park Terr
Charlesworth SK13 16 C8
Northwood DE4 127 A5
Park The
Bakewell DE45 109 D5
Darley Dale DE4 127 D3
Duffield DE56 190 E3
Ironville NG16 170 E3
Mansfield Woodhouse
NG19 136 C1
Mayfield DE6 184 C8
Parkview DE21 205 C8
Park View
9 Ashbourne DE6 173 C2
Park View continued
Aston-on-Trent DE72 246 B7
Bakewell DE45 109 D5
Barlborough S43 80 B7
Burton upon Trent
DE15 248 B3
Chesterfield S41 115 D7
Clowne S43 80 F5
Hadfield SK14 9 F5
Heanor DE75 181 D1
Northwood DE4 127 A5
Pleasley NG19 135 A5
Somercotes DE55 170 D5
Whaley Thorns NG20 100 F2
Park View Ave S20 59 E7
Park View Cl DE22 204 F4
Park View Ct S8 43 A2
Park View Dr SK23 47 B6
Park View Ho DE21 219 C6
Parkview Prim Sch
DE21 206 A2
Park View Rise SK22 24 C1
Parkville Cl SK17 85 D5
Parkway
Branston DE14 253 E7
Branston DE14 256 E7
Chellaston DE73 232 E1
New Mills SK22 24 C1
Whitwell S80 82 B6
Park Way DE65 229 C4
Parkway Ct S8 56 F7
Parkway The DE4 127 C3
Parkwood Cl 2
DE55 158 E3
Park Wood Close
DE22 204 F3
Parkwood Sch DE55 158 F4
Parliament Cl DE22 218 E4
Parliament St
Derby DE22 218 E4
Swadlincote DE11 255 F6
PARSLEY HAY 123 B4
Parsonage Cl S20 59 D6
Parsonage Croft
DE45 109 C5
Parsonage Gdns SK6 23 A4
Parson House Outdoor
Pursuit Ctr S11 54 B6
Parsons Cl
Hartington SK17 137 D5
Swadlincote DE11 256 A1
Parsons Gate S33 40 A6
Parsons Gn DE3 217 E6
Parsons Gr DE5 180 D2
Parsons La S33 39 D3
Parsons Way DE16 254 D5
Parson's Wlk B79 263 F2
Parthenon Cl NG19 134 F5
Partington Ct 2
SK13 10 F1
Partington Pk SK13 10 C3
Partington Theatre★ 7
SK13 10 C1
Partridge Cl S21 59 B3
Partridge Dr DE11 256 F3
Partridge Way DE3 218 A3
PARWICH 151 E1
Parwich Cl S40 95 A5
Parwich Dale
Hartington Nether Quarter
SK17 150 F8
Parwich DE6 151 B4
Parwich La DE4 151 E7
PARWICH LEES 151 A2
Parwich Prim Sch
DE6 151 D2
Parwich Rd S42 131 F5
Pasteur Ave DE5 169 D2
Pasture Gr S21 59 C3
Pasture La
Brassington DE4 152 D1
Flagg SK17 106 D6
Hilcote DE55 148 C1
Long Eaton NG10 237 A5
Stonebroom DE55 147 A3
Pasture Rd NG9 209 D1
Pastures Ave DE23 230 F7
Pastures Drive DE7 193 B8
Pastures Hill DE23 218 B1
Pastures The
Duffield DE56 190 E4
Eastwood NG16 195 B8
Mansfield Woodhouse
NG19 136 E5
Repton DE65 242 C2
Swadlincote DE11 255 F5
Weston-on-Trent
DE72 245 F5
Patchwork Row
NG20 119 F4
Paterson Ave DE21 220 B6
Pathfinder Way 7
DE74 246 E3
Patina Way DE11 256 A4
Patmore Sq DE23 231 F7
Paton Gr S43 96 D8
Patrick Cl DE12 261 D5
Patten Ct DE24 232 A5
Patterdale Cl 2 S18 56 E1
Patterdale Rd DE24 220 A1
Pattison St S44 98 F6
Paulet High Sch
DE15 254 F7
Paulet Sch Dr DE15 254 F7
Pavements The (Sh Ctr)
S40 266 B3
Pavilion Cl S43 80 E2
Pavilion Ct DE7 207 D7
Pavilion Drive S43 97 E8
Pavilion Gdns NG19 134 F8
Pavilion Gdns The★
SK17 85 B7
Pavilion La SK6 23 C2
Pavilion Mans 3
SK17 85 B7
Pavilion Rd DE23 231 C8
Pavilion Workshops
S42 116 D1
Paxton Cl
Derby DE3 217 C1
Matlock DE4 143 A6
Paxton Ct S14 43 F4
Paxton Pl SK17 84 E5
Paxton Rd S41 96 C5
Payler Cl S2 44 A8
Payne St DE22 218 D6
Peacehaven 3
DE65 242 B6
Peach Ave
Selston NG16 171 F6
South Normanton
DE55 160 B7
Peach St
Derby DE22 218 D5
Heanor DE75 181 D1
Peacock Cl
Glossop SK13 9 E4
Killamarsh S21 60 D6
Peacock Dr NG16 182 E1
Peacock Gr DE23 231 B6
Peacock Pl DE7 194 D4
Peacock Way DE55 169 F8
Peacroft Ct DE65 228 D2
Peacroft La DE65 228 D2
Peafield La NG19 136 F4
Peafield Lane Prim Sch
NG19 136 F3
Peak Ave DE55 170 B6
Peak Cavern★ S33 38 B2
Peak Cavern Rd S33 38 B2
Peak Cl
Belper DE56 179 A4
Pilsley S45 132 C1
PEAK DALE 67 B5
Peakdale Cl
Long Eaton NG10 236 A6
Ripley DE5 180 D6
Peakdale Cres S12 44 E5
Peak Dale Prim Sch
SK17 67 B5
Peakdale Rd
Glossop SK13 9 E3
Marple SK6 23 A4
Peak District Mining
Mus★ DE4 143 A1
Peak Dr DE23, DE24 232 A7
PEAK FOREST 49 B3
Peak Forest CE Prim Sch
SK17 49 A3
Peak Ho SK13 10 A5
Peaklands Pk S32 71 F3
Peakland View DE4 127 C3
PEAKLEY HILL 75 C6
Peaknaze Cl SK13 17 B8
Peak Pl S43 97 D7
Peak Railway★ DE4 143 A5
Peak Rd SK22 33 D8
Peak Sch SK23 34 F2
Peaks The SK23 46 C5
Peak The NG20 119 E3
Peaktor La DE4 126 E7
Peak View
Buxton SK17 105 E6
Clowne S43 80 D5
Glossop SK13 9 F4
South Normanton
DE55 159 F5
Peak View Cl S32 72 B2
Peak View Dr DE6 173 C1
Peak View Rd S40 95 D5
Peak Village Outlet Sh
Ctr DE4 110 F1
Pearce La S42 114 D3
Pearl Bank DE6 211 F8
Pearl Cl DE21 206 A2
Pearl Gdns 4 DE11 255 F4
Pearl Way SK14 9 A2
Pearson Croft S41 95 C6
Pearson Gdns S44 117 E8
Pearson Trad Est
S41 96 B8
PEAR TREE 232 B8
Pear Tree S45 129 F3
Pear Tree Ave
Ripley DE5 180 D8
Swadlincote DE11 255 F7
Wingerworth S42 114 E3
Peartree Cl DE74 247 A3
Pear Tree Cl
Brimington S43 97 A8
Glossop SK13 9 E4
Hartshorne DE11 257 A7
Killamarsh S21 60 C5
Marple SK6 23 B8
Pear Tree Cres
DE23 232 A8
Peartree Ct
Derby DE21 205 D1
Etwall DE65 229 B4
Pear Tree Dr
Linton DE12 261 C6
Shirebrook NG20 119 E6
Pear Tree Inf Sch
Derby DE23 219 A1
Derby DE23 232 B8
Peartree La NG17 134 B1
Pear Tree Mews
DE73 252 F2
Pear Tree Rd
Derby DE23 219 A1
Pilsley S45 132 C1
Peartree Sta DE23 232 B7
Pease Cl
Alfreton DE55 159 B3
Clay Cross S45 131 C5
PEASEHILL 180 F8
Peasehill DE5 180 F8
Pease Hill DE55 159 B3
Peasehill Rd DE5 180 E8
Peaslows La
Bagshaw SK23 47 F6
Sparrowpit SK23 48 A6
Peasunhurst La
Ashover S45 113 A1
Ashover SE45 112 F1
Peatburn Ave DE75 181 C1
Peatfield Ct NG9 209 D1
Peatfield Rd
Killamarsh S21 60 F7
Stapleford NG9 209 D1
Peat La
Chapel-en-le-Frith
SK23 35 F2
Spout DE4, DE56 166 D4
Peats Cl DE6 165 B1
Peckham Gdns
DE22 218 A5
Pedley Ave 4 S20 59 E8
Pedley Dr S20 59 E8
Pedley St DE7 208 F7
Peebles Cl DE24 231 E2
Peel Cres NG19 135 D2
Peel Gdns S18 56 F1
Peel St
Derby DE22 218 D6
Glossop SK13 10 C5
Langley Mill NG16 182 B3
Long Eaton NG10 236 E8
South Normanton
DE55 160 B6
Peeres Rd SK6 23 C1
Peers Cl DE21 206 B2
Peet St DE22 218 E4
Pegasus Ct S44 99 B1
Pegasus Sch DE12 260 F7
Pegasus Way DE65 228 E2
Peggars Cl S43 80 B6
Peggs Wlk DE23 231 E7
Peggy La DE55 146 B6
Pegwell Cl DE23 231 D7
Pelham Ave DE7 194 E1
Pelham St
Derby DE22 218 F4
Ilkeston DE7 194 E1
Pemberton Pl 3
NG16 182 F2
Pemberton The
DE55 160 B4
Pembleton Dr NG19 135 D1
Pembrey Cl NG9 209 D2
Pembroke Cl S40 95 C1
Pembroke Ct S41 95 F7
Pembroke Rd
Dronfield S18 76 A8
Shireoaks S81 63 F7
Pembroke St DE21 219 D8
Penalton Cl DE24 232 E6
Pencroft Gr DE23 231 C5
Pendean Cl DE55 147 E1
Pendennis Cl DE24 233 B6
Pendine Cl DE55 160 C6
Pendlebury Dr DE3 217 E1
Pendleside Way
DE23 230 E7
Pendleton La DE56 166 F7
Pendragon Dr DE72 245 A8
Penfold Way DE55 147 B5
Penge Rd DE22 218 A7
Penhaligan's Cl
DE73 232 F1
Penistone Gdns
S45 131 D2
Peniston Rise DE73 252 A7
Penkridge Rd DE11 256 B1
Pen La S45 131 E3
Penmore Cl S41 115 C8
Penmore Gdns 4
S41 96 C1
Penmore La S41 115 C8
Penmore St S41 115 C8
Penncroft Dr S45 131 D2
Penncroft La S45 131 D3
Pennie Cl NG10 236 D4
Penniment La NG19 135 B2
Pennine Ave DE55 170 C7
Pennine Cl
Long Eaton NG10 223 A1
Mansfield Woodhouse
NG19 136 C4
Newton DE55 148 A3
Sutton in Ashfield
NG17 148 E4
Tibshelf DE55 147 F6
Pennine Dr
Selston NG16 171 F7
South Normanton
DE55 159 F5
Pennine Rd SK13 17 A8
Pennine View
Heage DE56 179 E8
Palterton S44 118 A5
Pennine Way
Chesterfield S40 95 C5
Grassmoor S42 115 F3
Pennine Way continued
Swadlincote DE11 256 A3
Pennine Way Jun Sch
DE11 256 A2
Pennine Wlk S42 115 F3
Penn La DE73 252 B7
Penn Moor Cl NG10 236 A6
Penns Rd S2 43 C6
Penn St DE56 179 A4
Penny Acres Prim Sch
S18 74 F8
Pennycress Cl DE23 231 A7
Pennycroft La ST14 210 C1
Pennycroft Rd ST14 210 A1
Penny Engine La S21 59 E4
Pennyfields Bvd
NG10 236 B7
Penny Gn S80 82 A5
Penny La S17 55 C5
Penny Long La
DE22 218 E8
Pennytown Ct DE55 159 C1
Pennytown Ponds
Nature Reserve★
DE55 159 D1
Pennyunk La DE45 89 E1
Pennywell Dr S42 113 D7
Penrhyn Ave DE23 218 D1
Penrith Dr DE23 230 F5
Penrith Pl DE21 205 D2
Penrose Cres S44 97 D3
Penryn Cl DE55 160 C6
Pentagon The DE21 219 C6
Pentewen Cl DE22 204 E2
Penthorpe Cl S12 44 B6
Pentland Cl
5 Chesterfield S40 95 C5
Derby DE21 206 A2
Pentland Gdns
NG10 223 A1
Pentland Rd S18 56 D1
PENTRICH 169 B5
Pentrich Ct 1 S40 95 D5
Pentrich Rd
Giltbrook NG16 195 C7
Ripley DE5 169 D2
Swanwick DE55 169 D7
Pentridge Dr DE7 194 C3
Penzance Rd DE24 233 B5
Pepper La
Stanton-by-Dale
DE7 208 E1
Stanton-By-Dale DE7 222 E8
Percival Cl SK17 138 D3
Percy St
Derby DE22 218 E3
Ilkeston DE7 208 F7
Percy Wood Cl
DE65 228 C2
Peregrine Cl
Burton upon Trent
DE15 248 D3
Derby DE24 231 D4
Peregrine Way
Harthill S26 61 E5
Tibshelf DE55 147 E5
Periwinkle Road
S42 115 A2
Perlethorpe Ave
NG19 136 A1
Perrydale
Peak Forest SK17 49 A5
Perryfoot SK17 48 F6
PERRYFOOT 48 E7
Perry Gdns NG16 182 D6
Pershore Dr DE14 254 A8
Perth Cl
Burton upon Trent
DE15 248 C2
Derby DE3 217 E4
Mansfield Woodhouse
NG19 136 C5
Perth Dr NG9 209 F1
Perth St DE21 205 D1
Peter Baines Ind Est
DE22 267 A1
Peterborough St
DE21 219 E8
Peterdale Cl S43 96 E8
Peterdale Rd S43 96 E8
Peterhouse Terr 1
DE23 219 A2
Peterleas The DE12 262 E1
Peterlee Pl DE24 233 A5
Peter More Hill S80 81 E4
Peters Ave S45 131 B4
Peters Ct DE65 227 D1
Petersgate NG10 223 A1
Petersgate Cl NG10 223 A2
Petersham Ct 7
NG10 223 B2
Petersham Dr DE24 233 C6
Petersham Rd
NG10 223 A1
Peters St DE11 256 C1
Peter St
Ashbourne DE6 173 C1
Glossop SK13 10 A6
Peterway DE55 170 D8
Pettifor Terr DE55 147 C1
Pettyclose La S41,
S43 96 D5
Petty Close La DE6 202 C1
Petworth Ave NG9 223 F3
Pevensey Ave S41 95 E6

Pevensey Ct S41 ... 95 E7
Peverel House DE5 .. 181 B8
Peveril Ave
Borrowash DE72 ... 221 C2
New Mills SK22 ... 24 C1
Peveril Castle★ S33 .. 38 C2
Peveril Cl
Castleton S33 ... 38 C2
Darley Dale DE4 ... 127 C3
Somercotes DE55 ... 170 C6
Peveril Cres
Long Eaton NG10 ... 235 F5
West Hallam DE7 ... 207 E8
Peveril Ct
1 Glossop SK13 ... 17 F8
Ripley DE5 ... 169 C1
Peveril Dr
Ilkeston DE7 ... 194 D2
Somercotes DE55 ... 170 C6
Peveril Gdns SK12 ... 33 A6
Peveril Ho SK17 ... 85 A6
Peveril Mews SK12 ... 33 A6
Peveril Rd
Bolsover S44 ... 98 F3
Buxton SK17 ... 85 C7
Castleton S33 ... 38 C2
Chesterfield S41 ... 95 F7
Eckington S21 ... 59 E3
Tibshelf DE55 ... 147 F6
Peveril St DE24 ... 232 D6
Pewit Cl S42 ... 132 D8
Pewit La DE55 ... 147 C6
Pewitt Carr Nature Reserve★ DE7 ... 208 C8
Pheasant Field Dr DE21 ... 221 A6
Pheasant Hill NG19. 136 A1
Phildock Wood Rd DE3 ... 217 D6
Philip Howard Rd SK13 ... 17 C8
Philips Croft DE56 .. 190 E4
Philipway DE55 ... 170 D8
Phoenix Ct S12 ... 44 E1
Phoenix Rd S12 ... 44 E1
Phoenix Rise NG19. 135 A5
Phoenix St DE1 ... 267 B4
Phoneix Ri NG19 ... 134 F5
Phyllis Gr NG10 ... 236 F7
Piccadilly Cl NG19 .. 136 C6
Piccadilly La
Mayfield DE6 ... 172 C1
Mayfield DE6 ... 184 B8
Piccadilly Rd S41 ... 96 C3
Pickard Cres S13 ... 44 D8
Pickard Dr S13 ... 44 D8
Pickard La DE56 ... 168 D1
Pickburns Gdns
Belper DE56 ... 191 F8
Kilburn DE56 ... 191 F8
Pickerell Cl DE6 ... 203 A2
Pickering Ave NG16 . 182 F2
Pickering Dr DE11 .. 257 B1
Pickering Rise DE21 ... 205 D1
Pickford Gr 1 DE6 . 211 A1
Pickford Pl SK23 ... 47 B6
Pickford's House (Mus)★ DE1 ... 218 F5
Pickleys La DE6 ... 224 C8
Pickton Cl S40 ... 95 D2
Picory Corner DE45. 126 C7
Pictor Gr SK17 ... 85 D7
Pic Tor La DE4 ... 143 B4
Pictor Rd SK17 ... 85 D7
Piddocks Rd DE15 .. 255 B5
Pighills La S18 ... 57 B4
Pig La DE4 ... 111 B4
Pike Cl
Chesterfield S40 ... 95 B5
Hayfield SK22 ... 25 C3
PIKEHALL ... 139 E3
Pike Hall La DE6 ... 151 E4
Pike's La SK13 ... 17 B8
Pike View Cl SK23 ... 34 E2
Pilgrim Ct S81 ... 63 F7
Pilgrims Way DE24 . 231 C3
PILHOUGH ... 126 E7
Pilhough La DE4 ... 126 C6
Pilhough Rd DE4 ... 126 E5
Pillar Butts DE4 ... 165 E8
PILSLEY
Baslow ... 91 C3
Clay Cross ... 132 D1
Pilsley CE (Aided) Prim Sch DE45 ... 91 C2
Pilsley Cl
Belper DE56 ... 179 C6
Clay Cross S45 ... 131 E3
PILSLEY GREEN ... 147 C8
Pilsley La DE45 ... 91 D3
Pilsley Prim Sch S45 ... 132 C1
Pilsley Rd
Clay Cross S45 ... 131 E3
Lower Pilsley S45 ... 132 A4
Stonebroom DE55 ... 147 B6
Pimlico
Derby DE22 ... 218 B6
Ilkeston DE7 ... 208 E8
Pimm's Rd DE6 ... 217 A8
Pinchom's Hill Rd DE56 ... 179 B3
Pinch The DE6 ... 150 B2
Pindale Ave S43 ... 97 C7
Pindale Rd
Castleton S33 ... 38 D1
Hope S33 ... 38 E1
Pinders La DE6 ... 152 D4
Pine Ave NG16 ... 182 A3
Pine Cl
Burton upon Trent DE14 ... 254 A8
Creswell S80 ... 81 F1
Derby DE21 ... 220 B4
Etwall DE65 ... 229 C4
Killamarsh S21 ... 60 C5
Mansfield Woodhouse NG19 ... 136 C5
Ripley DE5 ... 169 D1
Shirebrook NG20 ... 119 E6
Smalley DE7 ... 192 F5
Pine Croft DE6 ... 185 D7
Pinecroft Ct DE21 .. 206 B1
Pine Gr DE11 ... 255 F6
Pines Cl NG16 ... 171 F7
Pine St S43 ... 97 A8
Pines The DE72 ... 235 B7
Pine Tree Wlk NG16 ... 182 E2
Pine View
Chesterfield S40 ... 95 B3
Clay Cross S45 ... 131 E3
Pineview Gdns DE23 ... 218 B1
Pine Wlk DE11 ... 261 E7
Pinewood DE5 ... 181 B7
Pinewood Cl
Alfreton DE55 ... 159 C3
Shirland DE55 ... 146 D1
Pinewood Dr DE55 .. 146 D2
Pinewood Rd
Belper DE56 ... 178 E6
Burton upon Trent DE15 ... 254 F6
Matlock DE4 ... 143 B7
Pinfold SK13 ... 9 E4
Pinfold Cl
Holymoorside S42 ... 113 E8
Repton DE65 ... 242 D2
Tutbury DE13 ... 239 C5
Pinfold Cres SK17 ... 69 C3
Pinfold Gdns NG19 .. 136 F2
Pinfold Hill S32 ... 72 E2
Pinfold La
Bradley DE6 ... 187 A8
Repton DE65 ... 242 D2
Stapleford NG9 ... 223 E7
Pinfold Rd SK17 ... 69 C3
Pinfold St S21 ... 59 D3
Pinfold The
Belper DE56 ... 179 C5
Elvaston DE72 ... 233 F4
Glapwell S44 ... 118 B1
Middleton DE45 ... 124 E3
Pinfold Trad Est NG9 ... 223 E7
Pinfold View DE45 .. 109 C5
Pingle DE22 ... 204 E4
Pingle Cl S81 ... 63 E7
Pingle Cres DE56 ... 178 F5
Pingle Farm Rd
Swadlincote DE11 ... 255 F5
3 Swadlincote DE11. 256 A5
Pingle Grange S43 ... 96 E7
Pingle Hill DE73 ... 252 F5
Pinglehill Way DE73 ... 233 B2
Pingle La
Belper DE56 ... 178 F5
Carsington DE4 ... 164 E7
Heage DE56 ... 168 F2
Swarkestone DE73 ... 244 E7
Pingle Rd S21 ... 60 E7
Pingle Rise DE4 ... 143 D6
Pingle Sch The DE11 ... 256 A5
Pingle The
Derby DE21 ... 220 F4
Long Eaton NG10 ... 236 D8
Melbourne DE73 ... 252 A7
Sheffield S21 ... 59 D6
Pingot Rd SK22 ... 33 D8
Pingott La SK13 ... 10 A5
Pingreaves Dr DE73 233 A2
Pinhole Pl 3 S43 ... 81 E2
Pinnacle Way DE24. 219 D3
Pintail Dr DE24 ... 231 D4
PINXTON ... 160 C2
Pinxton Gn NG16 ... 160 F3
Pinxton La
Kirkby-in-Ashfield NG17 ... 160 F6
South Normanton DE55 ... 160 C5
Pioneer Meadows Nature Reserve★ DE7 ... 208 C4
Pioneer Way DE24 .. 232 B3
Piper Ave S45 ... 131 E4
Piper Avenue DE74 . 246 F3
Piper Close NG19 ... 136 B2
Piper Gro NG20 ... 119 D2
Piper La S42 ... 94 E3
Piper Rd S44 ... 97 D3
Pipers Ct NG16 ... 170 F3
Piper St NG20 ... 119 D2
Pipeyard La S21 ... 59 C2
Pipistrelle Pl DE3 ... 230 E8
Pippenwell Rd SK17 ... 106 A7
Pippin Gdns DE24 ... 232 F7
Pippin Hill DE5 ... 180 E1
Pipworth La S21 ... 59 F4
Pirelli Cl DE74 ... 246 E2
Pitch Cl S43 ... 80 E2
Pitch Close NG16 ... 195 C8
Pit Close La DE73 ... 233 A1
Pit La
Codnor DE5 ... 181 A7
Crich DE4, DE55 ... 157 B6
Mansfield NG19 ... 135 A5
Pleasley NG19 ... 134 F5
Ripley DE5 ... 169 E1
Sheffield S12 ... 44 A6
Shipley DE75 ... 194 B6
Shirland DE55 ... 158 D8
Stonebroom DE55 ... 147 A5
Pit Lane NG9 ... 209 E3
Pits La
Parwich DE6 ... 151 E1
Parwich DE6 ... 162 E8
Pittar St DE22 ... 267 A2
Pitt Hill NG20 ... 100 F2
Pittlemere La SK17 ... 50 A1
Pitt St S21 ... 59 C2
Pittywood Rd DE4 .. 165 E7
Pk Cres DE4 ... 143 A5
Pk House Ct S45 ... 131 E3
Pk La S44 ... 98 A3
Pk Rd DE45 ... 109 F4
Pk View Mws S8 ... 43 B2
Placket La DE4 ... 141 B6
Plackett Cl
Breaston DE72 ... 235 D8
Stapleford NG9 ... 223 F8
Plains La DE56 ... 178 B4
Plainspot Rd NG16 .. 171 E2
Plain The DE6 ... 201 F8
PLAISTOW ... 156 F6
Plaistow Gn Rd DE4 157 A4
PLAISTOW GREEN ... 156 F4
Plaistow Green Rd
Crich DE4 ... 156 F2
Plaistow Green DE4 ... 156 F4
Plantain Gdns DE23. 231 C5
Plantation Cl
Chesterfield S40 ... 95 A5
Whitwell S80 ... 81 E5
Plantation Rd 7 S8 .. 43 A6
Plantations The 9 NG10 ... 236 A8
Plantation The DE23 ... 218 B1
Plantin Rise S20 ... 59 E7
Plantin The S20 ... 59 E7
Plant La NG10 ... 236 A4
Platchetts The DE73 . 252 F4
Platform Ct DE21 ... 220 D3
Platts Ave DE75 ... 181 C1
Platt St
Glossop SK13 ... 10 B5
Pinxton NG16 ... 160 D2
Platts Yard DE4 ... 157 F4
Pleasant Ave S44 ... 118 B7
Pleasant Cl S12 ... 44 B6
Pleasant Pl S40 ... 95 D3
Pleasant Rd S12 ... 44 B6
Pleasant View SK6 ... 15 B3
PLEASLEY ... 135 B6
PLEASLEYHILL ... 135 C4
Pleasley Hill Way NG19 ... 135 C2
Pleasley Pit and Country Pk★ NG19 ... 134 E6
Pleasley Rd NG17 ... 134 C1
Pleasley Springs NG19 ... 135 B5
Pleasley Vale Nature Reserve★ NG19 ... 135 D7
Pleasley Vale Outdoor Activity Ctr NG19 .. 135 D6
Plimsoll Ct DE22 ... 267 A1
Plimsoll St DE22 ... 218 C6
Plough Croft DE16 .. 254 E7
Ploughfield Cl DE23 231 B6
Plough Gate DE22 ... 204 F2
Plover Ave DE11 ... 256 F3
Plover Cl SK13 ... 17 F8
Plover Ct DE3 ... 230 B7
Plover Way S44 ... 96 F3
Plowman Ct NG9 ... 223 D6
Plowright Cl S14 ... 43 D5
Plowright Dr S14 ... 43 D5
Plowright Mount S14 ... 43 D5
Plowright Way S14 ... 43 D5
Plucksbridge Rd SK6 . 23 B3
Plumbley Hall Mews S20 ... 59 C6
Plumbley Hall Rd S20 ... 59 C6
Plumbley La S20 ... 59 B6
Plumbleywood La S12, S20 ... 58 F6
Plummer Rd DE11 ... 256 A5
Plumptre Cl NG16 ... 182 F1
Plumptre Gdns 2 NG16 ... 182 F2
Plumptre Rd NG16 .. 182 B5
Plumptre Way NG16 . 182 F1
Plymouth Ave NG16. 160 E2
Plymouth Ct 7 S41 ... 95 F8
Pochard Close NG19 ... 136 F2
Pocknedge La S42 .. 113 D8
Podmore View ST14 . 196 F3
Podnor La SK6 ... 24 A6
Poets Cl S42 ... 132 C8
Pole La SK6 ... 24 B4
Pole's Rd DE6 ... 217 A8
Pollards Oaks DE72. 221 C1
Pollard Way 3 DE4. 116 E1
Polly Froggatt La S32 ... 72 B2
Polyfields La S44 ... 118 B8
Pomegranate Rd S40 ... 95 D6
Pomegranate Theatre★ S41 ... 266 C3
Pomeroy Cotts SK17 ... 106 B4
Pond Cotts DE4 ... 143 E6
Pond End DE74 ... 247 B6
Pond La
Tupton S42 ... 131 D8
Wingerworth S42 ... 114 E4
Pond Rd DE56 ... 191 C7
Pond St S40 ... 266 B2
Pondwell Cnr S43 ... 96 F7
Pondwell Dr S43 ... 96 F7
Ponsonby Terr DE1. 218 E5
Pontefract St DE24 . 232 D7
Pontypool Cl DE21 .. 206 B2
Pool Cl
Elvaston DE24 ... 233 C4
Pinxton NG16 ... 160 D2
Poolclose Row NG16 ... 160 D2
Poole's Cavern★ SK17 ... 85 A6
Poole St DE24 ... 232 E6
Pool Rd DE73 ... 252 D6
POOLSBROOK ... 98 A7
Poolsbrook Ave S43 .. 98 A8
Poolsbrook Cres S43 . 98 A8
Pools Brook Ctry Pk★ S43 ... 79 B1
Poolsbrook Rd S44 ... 98 A5
Poolsbrook Sq S43 ... 98 A8
Poolsbrook View S43 ... 98 A8
Pools Head La DE6 .. 201 F6
Pool's La S21 ... 77 C7
Pool St DE11 ... 256 D2
Pope Carr Rd DE4 .. 143 C5
Poplar Ave
Chesterfield S40 ... 95 B2
Derby DE21 ... 220 E5
Moira DE12 ... 262 E2
New Mills SK22 ... 24 D1
Ripley DE5 ... 180 D8
Sandiacre NG10 ... 223 A7
Swadlincote DE11 ... 256 B6
Poplar Cl
Derby DE24 ... 233 B7
Dronfield S18 ... 76 C7
Killamarsh S21 ... 60 C5
Overseal DE12 ... 262 B3
Poplar Cres DE6 ... 185 D8
Poplar Dr
Chesterfield S42 ... 115 C1
Glapwell S44 ... 134 B8
Pleasley NG19 ... 135 B4
Poplar Grange DE21 ... 206 C3
Poplar Grove S45 ... 132 A4
Poplar Heights S44 ... 98 A4
Poplar Nook DE22 ... 204 F4
Poplar Rd
Breaston DE72 ... 235 F8
Eckington S21 ... 59 C2
South Normanton DE55 ... 160 B7
Poplar Row DE22 ... 205 A1
Poplar St 2 NG19 .. 136 C3
Poplars The
Derby DE22 ... 204 F4
Whitwell S80 ... 82 A5
Poplar Terr
Chapel-en-le-Frith SK23 ... 47 B7
Selston NG16 ... 171 E6
Poplar Way
High Lane SK6 ... 32 A7
Ilkeston DE7 ... 208 D5
Poppleton Croft S40 .. 96 F4
Poppy Cl NG20 ... 119 D3
Poppy Close DE13 .. 239 D5
Poppy Cres S40 ... 96 C7
Poppy Ct S42 ... 116 C1
Poppyfields
Clowne S43 ... 80 D2
5 Denstone ST14 ... 196 C6
Ripley DE5 ... 180 D7
Poppy Fields Close DE4 ... 142 F7
Poppyfields Dr DE3. 217 E2
Poppyfields Mdw DE22 ... 204 C2
Poppy Gdns DE55 ... 148 B7
Poppy Mws DE12 ... 262 F4
Porlock Cl 2 NG10. 236 A8
Porlock Ct DE21 ... 206 A2
Portaway La ST14 .. 183 B3
Portchester Leys 1 DE11 ... 255 E6
Porteous Cl DE4 ... 127 D3
Porter Dr DE55 ... 159 C4
Porter Ho 9 S43 ... 78 E2
PORTERHOUSE ... 169 F1
Porterhouse Rd DE5 ... 169 F1
Porter La DE4 ... 154 E3
Porter Pl DE21 ... 220 D5
Porter Rd DE23 ... 218 F2
Porters Farm Ct ST14 ... 224 E2
Porters La DE21 ... 205 F3
Porter's La
Derby DE21 ... 205 F3
Findern DE65 ... 230 D1
Porter St S43 ... 78 E2
Porthcawl Pl DE21 .. 206 C2
Portico Rd DE23 ... 231 A6
Portis Ct DE21 ... 220 D3
Portland Ave
Bolsover S44 ... 99 B1
Burton upon Trent DE14 ... 254 A7
Creswell S80 ... 81 E1
Portland Cl
Chesterfield S41 ... 266 B4
Derby DE3 ... 217 D2
Portland Court Mews NG19 ... 136 C4
Portland Cres
Bolsover S44 ... 99 B1
Mansfield Woodhouse NG19 ... 136 D3
Stapleford NG9 ... 223 E6
Portland Dr NG20 ... 119 F3
Portland Gr SK23 ... 34 E2
Portland Heights DE55 ... 148 E4
Portland La DE72 ... 245 A8
Portland Rd
Beeston NG9 ... 223 F1
Eastwood NG16 ... 195 B8
Ilkeston DE7 ... 194 F3
Long Eaton NG10 ... 236 B4
New Mills SK22 ... 24 D1
Shirebrook NG20 ... 119 F4
Whaley Thorns NG20. 101 A3
Portland Sq DE45 ... 109 D6
Portland St
Clowne S43 ... 81 A4
Derby DE23 ... 232 A8
Etwall DE65 ... 229 B4
Mansfield Woodhouse NG19 ... 136 C3
New Houghton NG19 . 135 A7
Whitwell S80 ... 81 F6
Portland Terr NG20. 101 A2
Portman Chase DE24 ... 231 D2
Porton La DE55 ... 160 A7
Portreath Dr DE22 .. 204 E3
Portsmouth Cl DE11 ... 255 E2
Port Way
Branston DE14 ... 253 D8
Holbrook DE21, DE56. 191 D5
Portway Cl DE22 ... 205 A4
Portway Close S12 ... 44 E5
Portway Dr
Matlock DE4 ... 143 D6
Tutbury DE13 ... 239 C5
Portway Inf Sch DE22 ... 204 E4
Portway Jun Sch DE22 ... 204 E4
Portwood Ind Est DE11 ... 256 A1
Posthill Cl S80 ... 82 A6
Postmans La S42 ... 116 C4
Post Office La DE6 ... 201 F7
Post Office Rd DE6 . 149 E4
Post Office Row SK17 ... 69 E3
Post St SK13 ... 10 B5
Posy La DE72 ... 246 A7
Potato Pit La
Dale Abbey DE7 ... 208 A1
Stanton-by-Dale DE7 . 222 A8
Potlocks The DE65 .. 242 C6
Potter Rd SK13 ... 9 E3
Potters Cl S41 ... 77 C2
Potters Croft
Clifton Campville B79 ... 263 E2
Swadlincote DE11 ... 256 A5
Potters Hill
Crich DE55 ... 157 A5
Plaistow DE4 ... 156 F6
Potter's Hill View NG16 ... 182 A1
Potters La DE4, DE55 ... 157 B5
Potters Nook S81 ... 63 F7
POTTER SOMERSAL ... 212 A4
Potter St
Derby DE21 ... 220 D4
Melbourne DE73 ... 252 B7
Potters Way DE7 ... 209 A8
Potters Yd DE73 ... 252 B7
Pottery Cl DE56 ... 179 C5
Pottery La DE5 ... 180 C3
Pottery Lane E S41 ... 96 B8
Pottery Lane W S41 .. 96 A7
Pottery Prim Sch DE56 ... 179 C4
Poulter Ctry Pk★ NG20 ... 100 E2
Poulter St NG20 ... 100 F1
Pounder La DE4 ... 142 D2
Powell Dr S21 ... 60 C6
Powell St DE23 ... 218 E2
Pown St SK17 ... 137 A6
Powtrell Pl DE7 ... 209 B6
Poynter Cl DE75 ... 181 C1
Poynton Wood Cres S17 ... 56 A6
Poynton Wood Glade S17 ... 56 A6
Poyser Ave DE21 ... 220 A7
Poyser La
Kirk Langley DE6 ... 203 A1
Langley Common DE6. . 202 F1
Pratt Cl NG19 ... 135 D1
PRATTHALL ... 94 B7
Pratthall La DE4 ... 166 A6
Premier Ave DE6 ... 185 B8
Prescot Cl DE3 ... 217 C1
Press La S42 ... 130 D6
Prestbury Cl DE21 .. 206 B1
Preston Ave DE55 ... 159 B4
Preston Rd 3 DE23. . 230 F5
Preston St S8 ... 43 A7
Prestwick Way DE73 ... 232 E2
Prestwold Way S41. 115 C7
Prestwood La ST14 . 196 F8
Prestwood Park Dr DE11 ... 256 D5
Pretoria St S44 ... 98 F6
Pride Park DE24 ... 219 D3
Pride Parkway DE24 ... 219 D3
Pride Pl DE24 ... 219 D3
Pride Point Dr DE24 ... 219 D2
PRIESTCLIFFE ... 87 F5
PRIESTCLIFFE DITCH ... 87 D4
Priestcliffe Lees (Nature Reserve)★ SK17 ... 88 B7
Priestcliffe Rd
Priestcliffe SK17 ... 88 A5
Taddington SK17 ... 87 F4
Priestfield Gdns S41 .. 95 B7
Priest La SK23 ... 45 A6
Priestland Ave DE21 ... 220 D4
Priestley Ave DE55 .. 146 C5
Primary Cl DE56 ... 179 A4
Prime Enterprise Pk DE1 ... 267 C4
Prime Ind Est DE23 . 219 C2
Prime Ind Pk DE23 . 219 C2
Prime Parkway DE1 267 C4
Primrose Ave NG16 .. 171 F2
Primrose Bank DE65 ... 229 C5
Primrose Bsns Pk DE55 ... 147 F1
Primrose Cl
Derby DE21 ... 205 F3
Killamarsh S21 ... 60 E7
South Normanton DE55 ... 160 B7
Primrose Cotts
Hazelwood DE56 ... 190 C7
Risley DE72 ... 222 D3
Primrose Cres 1 SK13 ... 17 B8
Primrose Ct
Hayfield SK22 ... 25 D3
Mansfield Woodhouse NG19 ... 136 F4
Primrose Dr
Burton upon Trent DE14 ... 254 A8
Morley DE7 ... 206 C8
Tutbury DE13 ... 239 C5
Primrose Hill
Blackwell DE55 ... 147 F1
Glossop SK13 ... 17 B8
Ilkeston NE7 ... 194 E3
Primrose La
Glossop SK13 ... 17 B8
Hayfield SK22 ... 25 C5
Killamarsh S21 ... 60 E7
Marple SK6 ... 24 A4
Tideswell SK17 ... 69 C3
Primrose Mdw DE11 ... 256 B7
Primrose Rise NG16 195 B8
Primrose St DE7 ... 194 E3
Primrose Terr 2 SK13 ... 17 B8
Primrose Vale Cotts SK22 ... 25 C4
Primrose Way NG20 . 119 F6
Primula Cl NG20 ... 119 D3
Primula Way DE23 .. 231 D4
Prince Charles Ave DE22 ... 218 A6
Prince Edward Drive DE22 ... 218 B3
Prince Edward Prim Sch S12 ... 44 A7
Prince George Drive DE22 ... 218 B3
Prince of Wales Rd S2 ... 44 B7
Princes Dr DE23 ... 218 B2
Princes Rd SK23 ... 34 E2
Prince's Rd SK17 ... 85 D8
Princess Ave
Linton DE12 ... 261 C5
South Normanton DE55 ... 160 A5
Princess Cl
Heanor DE75 ... 181 D2
Woodville DE11 ... 256 F2
Princess Ct S2 ... 44 B8
Princess Dr
Borrowash DE72 ... 221 A2
Sandiacre NG10 ... 223 B4
Princess Pl S45 ... 131 C2
Princess Rd
Dronfield S18 ... 57 B2
Uttoxeter ST14 ... 210 A1

Princess St
Brimington S43. . . . . . . .96 F8
Chesterfield S40. . . . . 266 A4
Glossop SK13. . . . . .17 C8
Long Eaton NG10 . . . . 236 D8
Swadlincote DE11 . . . .261 F8
Princes St
Derby DE23. . . . . .232 B8
Eastwood NG16 . . . . . .182 F3
Prince's St DE23. . . . .219 B1
Princess Way DE13 . 240 E1
Prince St
Ilkeston DE7. . . . . .194 E4
Long Eaton NG10 . . . 236 D8
Prince William Drive
DE22. . . . . 218 B3
Pringle La S41. . . . . . .76 F4
Printers Brow SK14. . .9 D5
Printers Dr SK15. . . . . .4 A6
Printers Drive SK6. . .23 C2
Printers Fold SK14. . . .9 D5
Printers Pk SK14 . . . . .9 E5
Priors Barn Cl DE72. 221 D2
Priorway Ave DE72 . 221 D2
Priorway Gdns
DE72. . . . . 221 C1
Priory Cl
Breedon on the Hill
DE73. . . . . .252 E2
Chellaston DE73. . . . . 245 A8
Ilkeston DE7. . . . . 208 C6
Swadlincote DE11 . . . 256 A6
Tutbury DE13 . . . . . . .239 B5
Yeaveley DE6 . . . . 199 D5
Priory Ct S26. . . . . . . .61 E5
Priory Gdns
Derby DE21. . . . . 205 F3
Swanwick DE55 . . . . . 170 A8
Priory Lands DE13 . 240 F1
Priory Rd
Alfreton DE55. . . . . . . .159 B5
Eastwood NG16 . . . . . .182 F1
Mansfield Woodhouse
NG19. . . . . .136 B3
Priory Sq NG19 . . . . 136 B3
Priory Way
Newton DE55 . . . . 148 A3
Ripley DE5 . . . . .180 E8
Pritchard Dr NG9 . . 223 E6
Pritchett Dr DE23. . 230 E8
Private Dr S43. . . . . . .78 A1
Privet Cl S44 . . . . .99 D1
**Proact Stad
(Chesterfield FC)**
S40. . . . . .96 A7
Progress Ct DE45. . . 109 D6
Prospect Ave DE55 . .159 F5
Prospect Cotts S43. . .80 E5
Prospect Ct
1 Sheffield S17. . . . . .56 B5
Sutton in Ashfield
NG17. . . . . .148 E1
Prospect Dr
Belper DE56. . . . . .178 F2
Matlock DE4. . . . . 143 A6
Sheffield S17 . . . . .55 F5
Shirebrook NG20 . . . . .119 C3
Prospect Gdns
DE55. . . . . 169 E7
Prospect Ho S43. . . . .78 F1
Prospect Pl
Derby DE24. . . . . 219 E4
Sheffield S17 . . . . .56 A5
Prospect Rd
Chesterfield S41. . . . . .76 F2
Denby Village DE5 . . . 180 A1
Dronfield S18. . . . . . . .57 C3
Heanor DE75 . . . . .194 A8
Pilsley S45 . . . . .132 C1
Sheffield, Bradway Bank
S17. . . . . .56 A5
Sheffield, Lowfield S2. . .43 A7
Prospect St DE55. . . .159 B4
Prospect Terr
Bakewell DE45. . . . . . . 109 C6
Chesterfield S40. . . . . .95 E4
Crich DE4 . . . . .168 A8
Providence Ct DE11. 256 F2
Providence Pl
Alfreton DE55. . . . . . . .158 F3
5 Ilkeston DE7 . . . . . 194 E1
Providence Rd
NG16 . . . . 171 A4
Providence St DE5. . 180 E8
Provident St **4**
DE23. . . . . 219 A2
Pryor Mede S26. . . . . .61 E5
Pryor Nook S26. . . . . .61 E5
Pudding Bag La
S45. . . . . .129 F4
Pudding Plate Cl **8**
DE7. . . . . 208 E5
Puddle Hill
Bonsall DE4 . . . . 142 C1
Slaley DE4 . . . . 154 C8
Pulborough Gdns
DE23. . . . . 231 A6
Pullman Cl S43. . . . . . .78 F3
Pullman Rd DE21. . . .219 F4
Pump Cl DE4 . . . . 143 C3
Pump La
Doveridge DE6 . . . . . . 224 B8
Wyaston DE6 . . . . 185 D1
Pump Yd DE56 . . . . . 177 B2
Punch Bowl Pk SK17. .85 A8
Purbeck Ave S40 . . . . .95 D4
Purbeck Cl
Long Eaton NG10 . . . . 236 A8

Purbeck Cl continued
Mansfield Woodhouse
NG19. . . . . .136 C6
Purchase Ave DE75 . 181 C2
Purdy Mdw NG10 . . . .235 F5
Pursglove Dr SK17. . . .69 D4
Pursglove Rd SK17 . . .69 D4
Putney Cl DE22. . . . . 217 E5
Pybus St DE22. . . . . . 218 D6
PYE BRIDGE. 170 F6
Pye Bridge Ind Est
DE55. . . . . .170 F6
Pyegrove SK13. . . . . . .10 F1
Pyegrove Rd SK13 . . . .10 F1
PYE HILL 171 A5
Pye Hill Rd NG16 . . . 171 A4
Pykestone Cl **6**
DE21. . . . . .205 F2
Pym Chair Rd SK23 . 264 F6
Pym Leys NG10. . . . . .235 F5
Pynot Rd S41. . . . . . . .77 B2
Pytchley Cl DE56 . . . 179 D4

Q

Quad DE1 . . . . .267 B3
Quadrant Mews **5**
SK17. . . . . .85 B8
Quadrant The
Buxton SK17. . . . . .85 B8
Sheffield S17 . . . . .55 E5
Quaker Cl DE73. . . . . .252 D8
Quaker Way DE1 . . . . 267 A4
Quantock Cl DE73. . . .231 D2
Quantock Rd NG10 . 223 A1
Quantock Way S40 . . .95 B5
QUARNDON. 204 D6
Quarndon Hts DE22. 204 C3
Quarndon View
DE22. . . . . 204 C2
Quarn Dr DE22 . . . . . 204 C3
Quarn St
Derby DE1 . . . . .218 E6
Derby DE1 . . . . .218 F7
Quarn Way DE1. . . . . .218 F6
Quarry Bank
Clowne S43. . . . . .80 D4
Matlock DE4 . . . . .143 B7
Quarrybank La
DE11. . . . . 256 A4
Quarry Bank Rd S41 . .96 C2
Quarry Berry La
DE12. . . . . .264 F1
Quarry Cl SK13. . . . . . .10 D1
Quarry Gro S45. . . . . .131 C5
Quarry Hill
Eckington S21. . . . . . . .58 D2
Sheffield S17 . . . . .59 A8
Stanton-by-Dale DE7 . 223 A8
Quarry Hill Ind Est
DE7. . . . . .208 F5
Quarry Hill Rd DE7. . 208 F5
Quarry La
Alton S42 . . . . 130 C5
Brackenfield DE55 . . . 145 D6
Chesterfield S40. . . . . .95 C2
Matlock DE4 . . . . .143 E7
Northedge S42. . . . . . 130 C6
Stonebroom DE55 . . . 146 F3
Quarry Rd
Apperknowle S18. . . . . .58 A1
Belper DE56 . . . . 178 F2
Bolsover S44. . . . . .99 A3
Hayfield SK22. . . . . . . .24 F2
Killamarsh S21. . . . . . .60 C7
Morley DE7 . . . . .192 B1
New Mills SK22. . . . . . .33 D7
Sheffield, Totley Brook
S17. . . . . .55 E5
Somercotes DE55 . . . 170 C2
Whaley Bridge SK23. . .33 D3
Quarry Vale Gr S12. . .44 C4
Quarry Vale Rd S12. . .44 C4
Quarry Way **4**
DE55. . . . . .170 D8
Quartz Dr SK17 . . . . . .85 D2
Queen Anne Ct S14. . .43 E3
Queen Elizabeth Ct
8 Ashbourne DE6. . .173 B2
Sheffield S14 . . . . .43 E3
Queen Elizabeth's Acad
NG19 . . . . 136 A1
Queen Elizabeths Cl
2 Washgreen DE4 . . .155 A1
Wirksworth DE4. . . . . 166 A8
Queen Elizabeths Close
DE4. . . . . 155 A1
**Queen Elizabeth's Gram
Sch** DE6. . . . . .173 C3
Queen Elizabeth Way
DE7. . . . . 208 C5
Queen Mary Ct S2 . . . .44 A7
Queen Mary Cres **1**
S2. . . . . .44 A8
Queen Mary Ct
Derby DE1 . . . . .218 F7
Sheffield S2 . . . . .44 A8
Queen Mary Gr S2. . . .43 F7
Queen Mary Mews
S2. . . . . .44 A7
Queen Mary Rd
Chesterfield S40. . . . . .95 B1
Sheffield S2 . . . . .44 B8
Queen Mary Rise **3**
S2. . . . . .44 A8
Queens Ave
Heanor DE75 . . . . 181 D2

Queens Ave continued
Ilkeston DE7. . . . . 209 A5
Stanley DE7. . . . . 207 C6
Queen's Ave SK17 . . . .85 D8
Queensbury Chase
DE23. . . . . 231 A6
Queensbury Park Drive
DE23. . . . . .232 F4
Queens Cl S80. . . . . . . .82 C5
Queens Ct
Burton upon Trent
DE14. . . . . .254 E8
Buxton SK17. . . . . .85 D8
Creswell S80 . . . . .81 F2
Derby DE22 . . . . .218 E8
Draycott DE72 . . . . . . 235 A7
Queen's Ct
Chesterfield S41. . . . . 266 A4
Marple SK6. . . . . .23 A6
Queens Dr
Brinsley NG16 . . . . . . .182 E7
Derby DE23 . . . . 218 C2
Sandiacre NG10 . . . . . .223 B4
Queen's Dr
Belper DE56 . . . . .178 E5
Glossop SK13 . . . . .10 F1
Ilkeston DE7. . . . . 208 E8
Swadlincote DE11 . . . .256 B6
Queensferry Gdns
DE24. . . . . .232 E4
Queensgate Dr
DE73. . . . . .244 F8
Queens Gdns DE22 . . .43 C8
Queensland Cl DE3 . 217 E4
Queensland Cres
DE15. . . . . .248 C2
Queen's L Ctr DE1. . . 267 B4
Queens Mews S2. . . . .43 C8
Queen's Park Sports Ctr
S40. . . . . .266 A2
Queens Rd
Creswell S80 . . . . .82 C6
Sheffield, Lowfield S2. . .43 B8
Queen's Rd SK17 . . . . .85 D8
Queens Ret Pk S2. . . . .43 B8
Queens Rise DE13 . 239 C6
Queens Road N
NG16 . . . . .182 F2
Queens Road S
NG16 . . . . .182 F1
Queen's Sq NG16 . . . .182 F2
Queens Stables S2 . . .43 C8
Queen St
Belper DE56 . . . . .179 A3
Brimington S43. . . . . . .77 F1
Chesterfield S40. . . . . 266 A4
Clay Cross S45 . . . . . . .131 C3
Creswell S80 . . . . .81 F1
Derby DE1. . . . . .267 B4
Eckington S21. . . . . . . .59 E3
Glossop SK13 . . . . .17 B8
Hadfield SK13. . . . . . . .10 A4
Ilkeston DE7. . . . . 208 E8
Ironville NG16 . . . . . . 170 F4
Langley Mill NG16. . . 182 C3
Long Eaton NG10 . . . .236 E7
Longnor SK17. . . . . . . .121 B6
Marple SK6. . . . . .23 A6
Middleton DE4 . . . . . .154 D5
Pilsley S45 . . . . .132 D1
Pinxton NG16 . . . . . . 160 C3
Ripley DE5 . . . . 181 A7
Sheffield, Mosborough
S20. . . . . .59 C7
Somercotes DE55. . . . 170 D8
South Normanton
DE55. . . . . .159 F5
Staveley S43. . . . . .97 D8
Swadlincote DE11 . . . 256 A1
Tideswell SK17. . . . . . .69 C4
Queen Street Mews
S20. . . . . .59 C7
Queen Street N S41. . .96 A8
Queens View S2. . . . . .43 B8
Queensview Dr DE5. 181 A7
Queensway
Castle Donington
DE74. . . . . .246 F4
Castle Donington
DE74. . . . . .247 A4
Derby DE22 . . . . 204 F2
Holmewood S42. . . . . .116 E1
Holmewood S42. . . . . .132 E8
Melbourne DE73. . . . .252 B8
Pilsley S45 . . . . .132 C1
Stonebroom DE55 . . . 146 F3
Queen's Way S42. . . . 115 D1
Queens Wlk S42. . . . . .115 D1
Queen's Wlk
Tupton S42 . . . . 115 C1
Whaley Thorns NG20 . .101 A1
Queen Victoria Dr
DE11. . . . . 256 B5
Queen Victoria Rd
Sheffield S17 . . . . .55 F5
Tupton S42 . . . . 115 C1
Quenby La S45 . . . . . . 169 E1
Quentin Rd SK23 . . . . .47 C6
Quick Cl DE73. . . . . . .252 A7
Quick Hill Rd DE24. . 232 D1
Quillings Way DE72. 221 D1
Quilow La DE6 . . . . . . 185 E3
Quintin Rd DE4. . . . . 233 A8
QUIXHILL. 196 E7
Quixhill Bank
Denstone ST14. . . . . . .196 E6
Denstone ST14. . . . . . 197 A8
Quixhill Cl DE6 . . . . . 185 B8

Quixhill La ST14 . . . .196 D8
Quoit Gn S18. . . . . .57 B1
QUOIT GREEN. 57 B1
Quorn Cl DE15. . . . . . 248 A1
Quorndon Cres
NG10 . . . . 236 D5
Quorn Dr 5 S40. . . . .95 A5
Quorn Rise DE23 . . . . 231 E6

R

Rabbit La
Eckington S21. . . . . . . .60 A2
Hyde SK14 . . . . .9 A6
Rabown Ave DE23. . . 231 D8
Racecourse Ind Est
DE21. . . . . 219 C8
Racecourse Mount
S41. . . . . .95 F3
Racecourse Park
DE21. . . . . 219 C7
Racecourse Rd S41. . .76 F1
RADBOURNE. 216 F5
Radbourne Comm 4
S18. . . . . .56 D1
Radbourne Common
DE6. . . . . .216 F6
Radbourne Gate
DE3. . . . . 217 D5
Radbourne La DE22. 217 E6
Radbourne St
Derby DE22 . . . . 218 C6
Mansfield Woodhouse
NG19. . . . . .136 E4
Radburn Ct NG9 . . . . 209 E1
Radcliffe Ave DE21 . 219 F7
Radcliffe Dr DE22. . . 218 D3
Radcliffe Way DE23. 230 F5
Radford Mdw
Castle Donington
DE74. . . . . .246 F4
Castle Donington
DE74. . . . . .247 A2
Radford Rd
Smalley DE7 . . . . .192 F6
3 Smalley DE7 . . . . . 193 A6
Radford St DE24. . . . 232 F7
Radleigh Gr DE11. . . 257 A2
Radleigh Grange
DE11. . . . . 257 A2
RADMANTHWAITE . 135 D3
Radmanthwaite La
NG19 . . . . 135 B5
Radmanthwaite Rd
NG19 . . . . 135 D3
Rad Mdws NG10 . . . . 236 C6
Radnor Pl NG19 . . . . 135 C4
Radnor St DE21. . . . . 219 D7
Radstock Gdns
DE21. . . . . 205 E1
Radstone Cl DE21. . . 206 B2
Raeburn Cl S14. . . . . . .43 E2
Raeburn Dr
Beeston NG9 . . . . .223 E2
Marple SK6. . . . . .23 B8
Raeburn Pl S14. . . . . . .43 E3
Raeburn Rd S14 . . . . . .43 E3
Raeburn Way S14 . . . .43 E2
Raglan Ave DE22 . . . 218 C5
Raglan St DE55 . . . . . 159 A4
Railway Ave S80. . . . 100 D8
Railway Cottages
S44. . . . . .98 C2
Railway Cotts
Derby DE24 . . . . 232 A6
Derby, Stenson DE73 . 243 A8
Egginton DE65 . . . . . .241 B7
Holmewood S42. . . . . .116 F1
Kimberley NG16 . . . . .195 F6
Temple Normanton
S41. . . . . 116 A5
Railway Row NG16. . 170 F4
Railway Side
Denby Bottles DE5 . . 180 A2
Rawson Green DE56. . .179 F2
Swadlincote DE11 . . . 256 B1
Railway St
Glossop SK13 . . . . .10 C1
Hadfield SK13. . . . . . . .10 A5
Railway Terr
Buxton SK17. . . . . .85 C8
3 Chesterfield S41. . .115 B7
Derby DE1 . . . . .267 D2
Disley SK12 . . . . .32 D6
Railway View S45. . . . 131 F4
Rainham Gdns
DE24. . . . . 233 A5
Rainier Dr DE21 . . . . 220 A6
Rain's La DE4 . . . . . . 154 C4
Rake Head Rd HD9 . . .2 E7
Rake La DE45. . . . . . . 124 D3
Rakes La DE6. . . . . . . 162 A6
Rakes Rd DE45. . . . . 107 C1
Rakes The
Alstonefield DE6. . . . . 149 D4
Alstonefield DE6. . . . . 149 D5
Rake The DE45 . . . . . 123 B6
Raleigh Cl DE7 . . . . . .194 F3
Raleigh Rd S2. . . . . . . .43 B6
Raleigh St DE22 . . . . 218 C6
Ralley Cl S42 . . . . .132 D8
Ralph Dr DE55. . . . . . 170 D7
Ralph Rd S43. . . . . .79 A2
Ralston Croft S20. . . . .59 E6
Ralston Cl S20 . . . . . . .59 D6
Ralston Gr S20 . . . . . . .59 D6
Ralston Pl S20. . . . . . . .59 D6

Rambler Cl DE11 . . . 256 A5
Ramblers Dr DE21. . 206 C3
Ramcroft S44. . . . . . . 117 D3
Ramper Ave S43. . . . . .80 C2
Ramscliff Ave
Donisthorpe DE12 . . . .262 F1
Donisthorpe DE12 . . . .265 F8
Ramsdean Cl DE21. . 219 D8
Ramsden Cl S43. . . . . .80 E4
Ramsden La HD9. . . . . .3 B7
Ramsden Rd HD9. . . . . .3 C7
Ramsey Ave S40. . . . . .95 D1
Ramsey Cl NG9 . . . . . 209 E2
Ramshaw Cl S41. . . . . .95 C7
Ramshaw Rd S18. . . . .76 E6
Ramshaw Way
DE22. . . . . 218 E4
Ramsley Ct **17** S40. . .95 D5
Ramson Close DE24 . 231 C3
Randal Cres S23. . . . . .45 E5
Randall Pl 1 S2. . . . . .43 A8
Randall St S21. . . . . . .59 B2
Randolph Rd DE23. . 231 F8
Ranelagh Gdns
DE21. . . . . 218 B7
Raneld Mount S40. . 114 C8
Rangemoor La DE6 . 183 D6
Rangemore Cl DE3 . 217 E4
Rangewood Rd
DE55. . . . . .159 F4
Ranmoor Cl S41. . . . . 115 C8
Ranmoor Hill S32. . . . .52 E8
Ranmoor La S32. . . . . .52 E8
Rannoch Cl
Derby DE22 . . . . 204 E3
Derby, Spondon DE21. .220 F5
Ranworth Cl DE24 . . 232 D3
Ratcliffe Ave DE14 . . 254 B8
Ratcliffe Cl S41. . . . . . 115 C7
Ratcliffe La S80. . . . . .82 D6
Ratcliffe St NG16 . . . 182 F3
Ratcliff Mws DE15 . . 248 B5
Rauche Ct DE23 . . . . 267 C1
Raven Ave DE55 . . . . .147 F5
Ravencar Rd S21. . . . . .59 B3
Raven Cl DE55. . . . . . 170 C6
Raven Ct DE75. . . . . . 181 E2
Raven Oak Cl DE56 . 179 A3
Ravens Cl SK13. . . . . . .16 F8
Ravenscourt Rd
DE22. . . . . 218 C6
Ravenscroft Ave S13. .44 E8
Ravenscroft Cl S13 . . .44 E8
Ravenscroft Cres
S13. . . . . .44 E8
Ravenscroft Ct S13. . .44 E8
Ravenscroft Dr
Derby DE21 . . . . .219 F6
Sheffield S13 . . . . .44 E7
Ravenscroft Oval
S13. . . . . .44 E8
Ravenscroft Pl S13. . .44 E8
Ravenscroft Rd S13. .44 E7
Ravenscroft Way S13 .44 E8
Ravensdale Ave
NG10 . . . . 223 B2
Ravensdale Cl S43. . . .97 C5
Ravensdale Cotts
SK17. . . . . .89 A8
**Ravensdale Inf &
Nursery Sch** DE3 . .217 E3
Ravensdale Rd
Derby DE22 . . . . 204 C3
Dronfield S18. . . . . . . .56 D1
Ravenshorn Way S21 .79 C8
Ravenside Ret Pk
S40. . . . . .266 B2
RAVENSNEST. 144 F7
Raven St DE22 . . . . . . 218 E3
Ravenstor Rd DE4 . . .154 F2
Ravenswood Rd S40. .95 A5
Ravensworth Cl **4**
S2. . . . . .44 A7
Ravenwood DE11. . . 256 C3
Rawdon Bsns Pk
DE12. . . . . .262 E5
Rawdon Cl DE74. . . . 247 A4
Rawdon Rd DE12 . . . 262 E5
Rawdon Side DE11. . 256 D4
Rawdon St DE23. . . . 218 F2
Rawlins Ct S18 . . . . . . .57 C4
Rawlinson Ave
DE23. . . . . 232 A7
Rawson Cl DE3 . . . . . 217 B3
Rawson Gn DE56 . . . .179 F1
RAWSON GREEN 179 F1
Rawson Way S2 . . . . . .43 A8
Rayleigh Ave S43. . . . .96 D8
Raymond Way
NG19 . . . . 136 D1
Raynald Rd S2. . . . . . . .44 A8
Rayneham Rd DE7. . .194 C4
Raynesway
Derby DE21 . . . . 220 A2
Derby, Alvaston DE21. .233 B8
Raynesway Park Dr
DE21. . . . . 220 B1
Ray Rushin Bsns Pk The
DE5. . . . . .180 E2
Ray's Ave DE75. . . . . . 181 E1
Ray St DE75 . . . . 181 E1
Reader St DE21. . . . . 220 E5
Reading Ave **11**
DE11. . . . . 255 E1
Realm Cl DE73. . . . . . 244 E8

Rebecca Court
LE66 . . . . .258 A1
Rebecca Ho DE1. . . . 218 E5
Recreation Cl
Blackwell DE55. . . . . . .147 E1
Clowne S43. . . . . .80 E4
Recreation Dr NG20 .119 F2
Recreation Rd
Calow S43. . . . . .96 F5
New Houghton NG19 . 134 F7
Sandiacre NG10 . . . . .223 B6
Shirebrook NG20 . . . . .119 E6
Tideswell SK17. . . . . . .69 C4
Wirksworth DE4. . . . . .165 E7
Recreation St NG10. 236 F7
Recreation Terr
NG9 . . . . .223 D6
Recreation View
NG20 . . . . 119 E6
Rectory Cl
Breedon on the Hill
DE73. . . . . .252 E2
Eckington S21. . . . . . . .59 E4
Long Duckmanton S44 . .98 A3
Rectory Dr S42 . . . . . 114 E4
Rectory Farm Mews
DE72. . . . . 245 E4
Rectory Gdns
Aston-on-Trent
DE72. . . . . .246 A7
Harthill S26 . . . . .61 E6
Killamarsh S21. . . . . . .60 D6
Long Duckmanton S44 . .98 A3
Rectory Gro S44. . . . . .98 A3
Rectory La
Appleby Magna
DE12. . . . . .265 E1
Breadsall DE21. . . . . . 205 D5
Kirk Ireton DE6. . . . . .165 B1
Stretton en le Field
DE12. . . . . .265 D4
Rectory Mews
DE65. . . . . 241 B4
Rectory Pl NG11 . . . . 237 E6
Rectory Rd
Breaston DE72. . . . . . .235 E8
Clowne S43. . . . . .80 E4
Killamarsh S21. . . . . . .60 D5
Langwith NG20. . . . . . .119 D7
Long Duckmanton S44 . .98 A4
Staveley S43. . . . . .78 E2
Reculver Cl DE23 . . . 231 D7
Redacre Cl S44. . . . . . .99 C2
Red Barn Cl DE55 . . 148 B3
Redbarn La DE55 . . . 148 B3
Red Brick Cl DE55 . . .147 A5
Redbrick Gdns
DE11. . . . . 256 A4
Red Brick La DE55 . . .147 A5
Redbridge Cl
6 Derby DE22. . . . . 218 A5
Ilkeston DE7. . . . . 209 A7
Shirebrook NG20 . . . . .119 F2
Redbrook Ave S41. . . 115 B8
Redbrow Hollow
SK6. . . . . .15 A2
Redbury Cl DE1. . . . . 218 E4
Redcar Gdns **6**
DE21. . . . . 205 D1
Reddie Cl ST14 . . . . . .196 F4
Reddish Ave SK23 . . . .45 D6
Reddish La SK23. . . . . .45 D6
Reddish Rd SK23. . . . . .45 D6
Redens The NG10. . . . 236 B4
Redfearn La SK17. . . . 104 B2
Redfern Ave DE5 . . . . 169 E2
Redfern Cl SK13. . . . . .10 A6
Redfern La S14 . . . . . 104 C1
Redfern Rd ST14 . . . . 210 A1
Redfern St S42 . . . . . . 131 C7
Redgap La SK17 . . . . . .86 A8
Redgate SK13 . . . . .10 C4
Redgate St NG16 . . . 160 D2
Redgrove Way S40 . . 114 C8
Red Hill ST14. . . . . . . .196 E3
Redhill Ct DE56. . . . . 179 B2
**Redhill Foundation Prim
Sch** DE72. . . . . .221 C5
Redhill La DE13. . . . . .239 B5
Red Hill La DE4. . . . . 144 D3
Redhill Lodge Rd **6**
DE11. . . . . 256 A7
Redhouse Cl S43 . . . . .77 D4
Redhouse La SK12. . . .32 E7
**Redhouse Stables
Working Carriage
Mus** DE4 . . . . 127 D1
Red La
Belper DE56 . . . . .191 B6
Brinsley NG16 . . . . . . .171 E1
Chesterfield S41. . . . . .77 C1
Chesterfield S41. . . . . .96 B8
Disley SK12 . . . . .32 C5
Repton DE65. . . . . . . .249 F6
South Normanton
DE55. . . . . .159 F3
Redland Cl
Derby DE24 . . . . 231 F4
Ilkeston DE7. . . . . .194 F3
Red Lion Hill DE4. . . 153 A1
Red Lion Row S32 . . . .72 C8
Red Lion Sq DE75. . . 181 E1
Red Lodge SK12 . . . . . .32 A6
Redmires Dr DE73. . 233 A2
Redmires Rd S10. . . . .42 B8

Redmoor Cl
Burton upon Trent DE15 248 B3
Codnor DE5 170 B1
Redmoor La
Disley SK12 33 A4
New Mills SK22 33 B6
Rednall Cl S40 95 A5
Red Pine Cl S43 80 D2
Red River Nature Reserve★ DE75 181 C3
Red Rose Ct DE15 254 E7
Redruth Pl DE24 233 C5
Redshaw St DE1 218 E7
Redstart Cl DE21 220 F6
Redthorn Rd S13 44 F8
Redvers Buller Rd S40 266 B1
Redway SK17 131 A5
Redway Croft [3] DE73 252 A8
Redwing Croft DE23 231 D7
Redwood Ave S21 60 C5
Redwood Cl S43 97 B8
Redwood Dr DE15 255 A8
Redwood Prim Sch DE24 231 F3
Redwood Rd DE24 231 E3
Reedman Rd NG10 236 B4
Reeves Ave S45 132 C1
Reeves Rd DE23 219 B1
Regal Gate DE73 244 F8
Regency Cl
Derby DE23 231 D7
[4] Glossop SK13 10 D1
Regent Ct
Ironville NG16 170 F4
Swadlincote DE11 256 B2
Regent Gdns S41 266 B4
Regents Dr DE3 217 B1
Regents Gn [6] S41 115 F2
Regents Ho [3] DE14 253 F7
Regents Park Rd DE14 254 B8
Regent St
Clowne S43 80 D4
Derby DE1 267 C1
Glossop SK13 10 D1
Glossop, Padfield SK13 10 B5
Ilkeston DE7 208 F7
Kimberley NG16 195 F6
Langley Mill NG16 182 B3
Long Eaton NG10 236 D8
Stapleford NG10 223 C5
Swadlincote DE11 256 B2
Reginald Road N DE21 219 F7
Reginald Road S DE21 219 F6
Reginald St DE23 219 B2
Regis Cl DE21 206 B2
Reigate Dr DE22 218 A7
Reigate Park Prim Sch DE22 217 F7
Reliant Cl [2] DE11 256 E1
Rembrandt Dr S18 56 E1
Remembrance Way
Brimington S40 96 C7
Thrumpton NG11 237 D3
Rempstone Dr S41 115 C7
Renals St DE23 267 B1
Reney Ave
Sheffield S17 56 D6
Sheffield S8 56 D6
Reney Cres S8 56 D6
Reney Dr S8 56 D6
Reney Rd S8 56 E7
Reney Wlk
Sheffield S17 56 D6
Sheffield S8 56 D6
Renfrew St DE21 219 E7
RENISHAW 79 B8
Renishaw Hall & Gdns★ S21 59 F2
Renishaw Pk
Eckington S21 59 F2
Eckington S21 60 A2
Renishaw Prim Sch S21 79 B8
Renishaw Rd S43 79 C4
Renshaw Dr DE11 255 F5
Rensons Way DE75 181 D4
REPTON 242 E2
Repton Ave DE23 218 D1
Repton Cl S40 95 A5
Repton Ct [8] NG19 136 E4
Repton Dr DE7 209 B7
Repton Pl S18 56 C1
Repton Prep Sch DE65 243 C2
Repton Prim Sch DE65 242 E2
Repton Rd
Appleby Magna DE12 265 F5
Hartshorne DE11 256 F8
Long Eaton NG10 235 F4
Newton Solney DE15 241 F1
Newton Solney DE15 248 F8
Repton DE65 242 A1
Ticknall DE73 250 E5
Willington DE65 242 A5
Reservoir Hill DE12 262 D6
Reservoir Hos DE55 146 A5
Reservoir Rd SK23 45 D7
Reservoir Terr S40 95 E4
Reservoir Way [6] DE11 256 E1
Resthaven DE11 256 B5
Retford Cl DE21 205 D2
Revell Close DE55 160 A7
Revill Cl DE7 194 C2
Revill Cres NG9 223 F8
Revolution Ho (Mus)★ S41 77 A2
Rewley Ct DE73 233 A3
Reynard Cres S21 79 B8
Reynards La SK17 137 E4
Reynolds Ave DE5 169 F1
Reynolds Cl S18 75 E8
Reynolds Dr SK6 23 B8
Rhein O' Thorns NG20 120 E5
Rhodes Ave S41 95 F5
Rhodes Cotts S43 80 F4
Rhodes Ho DE15 248 C3
Rhodesia Rd S40 95 C2
Rhodes St SK13 10 B5
Rhodes Top SK13 10 B5
Rhodeswood Ave SK14 9 F6
Rhodeswood Cl [2] DE65 240 E8
Rhodeswood Dr SK13 10 A6
Rhuddlan Pl SK23 34 D1
Ribble Cl DE65 240 D8
Ribblesdale DE7 208 C5
Ribblesdale Cl DE22 204 C2
Ribblesdale Dr S12 44 F1
Ribblesdale Rd NG10 236 A5
RIBER 143 E3
Riber Ave DE55 170 D8
Riber Bank [14] SK13 9 E1
Riber Cl
[20] Gamesley SK13 9 E1
Long Eaton NG10 236 D5
Staveley S43 97 C5
West Hallam DE7 207 E8
Riber Cres S42 131 B5
Riber Ct [11] S40 95 D5
Riber Dr
Derby DE72 245 A8
[12] Derby DE73 244 F8
Riber Fold [18] SK13 9 E1
Riber Gn [19] SK13 9 E1
Riber Rd
Lea DE4 156 A8
Matlock DE4 143 C2
Riber Terr S40 266 A2
Riber View Cl DE4 144 A5
Richard La SK17 69 C3
Richards Ct [2] S2 43 B6
Richardson Dr DE7 192 F6
Richardson Endowed Prim Sch DE7 192 F6
Richardsons La DE55 170 C5
Richardson St DE22 218 D6
Richardson Way DE22 217 E6
Richards Rd S2 43 B6
Richard Wakefield CE (VC) Prim Sch DE13 239 C6
Richmond Ave
Derby DE23 231 C8
Ilkeston DE7 194 F4
Long Eaton DE72 236 A8
Sandiacre NG10 223 A4
Sheffield S13 44 F8
Richmond Cl
Chesterfield S40 114 E8
Derby DE23 231 A7
Glossop SK13 10 A5
West Hallam DE7 207 D8
Richmond Ct
[5] Barrow Hill S43 78 B3
Repton DE65 242 D2
Sheffield S13 44 D7
Richmond Dr
[2] Aston-on-Trent DE72 246 A6
Duffield DE56 190 D5
Mansfield Woodhouse NG19 136 D2
Richmond Farm Mews S13 44 D7
Richmond Gdns S41 266 B4
Richmond Gr S13 44 E8
Richmond Hall Ave S13 44 D8
Richmond Hall Cres S13 44 D7
Richmond Hall Dr S13 44 D8
Richmond Hall Rd S13 44 D8
Richmond Hall Way S13 44 D7
Richmond Hill Ho S13 44 D7
Richmond Hill Rd S13 44 D7
Richmond Ho DE65 228 C1
Richmond La DE72 245 A8
Richmond Pk Rd
[3] Derby DE22 218 A5
Derby DE3 217 F5
Richmond Pk Rd *continued*
Sheffield S13 44 E8
Richmond Pl S13 44 D7
Richmond Rd
Derby, Chaddesden DE21 219 F6
Derby, Rose Hill DE23 219 A1
Sheffield S13 44 D7
Richmond Terr SK6 23 B1
Richworth Rd S13 44 F8
Ricroft Rd SK6 15 B3
RIDDINGS
Denstone 196 B4
Somercotes 170 D5
Riddings DE22 204 E4
Riddings Cl S2 44 A7
Riddings Croft S41 95 C6
Riddings Inf Sch DE55 170 D6
Riddings Jun Sch DE55 170 D6
Riddings La S32 72 D4
Riddings St DE22 218 F3
Riddings Sta★ NG16 170 F5
Ridd Way S42 115 A3
Ridge Ave SK6 23 A4
Ridge Cl SK13 9 E3
Ridge Cres SK6 23 A3
Ridgedale Rd S44 118 A8
Ridgedale View DE5 169 D2
Ridge End Fold SK6 23 A2
Ridgehill Ave S12 44 B5
Ridgehill Gr S12 44 B5
Ridge La
Chapel-en-le-Frith, Combs SK23 46 E1
Marple SK6 23 A2
Ridge Rd
Eckington S21 58 E2
Marple SK6 23 A3
Ridge The
Blackwell DE55 147 E1
Blackwell DE55 159 E8
Marple SK6 23 A2
Marple SK6 23 A3
Newton Solney DE15 248 B6
Ridge Top La SK22 25 C2
RIDGEWAY
Bullbridge 168 C4
Sheffield 58 E8
Ridgeway
Chellaston DE73 245 A8
Clowne S43 80 F2
Clowne S43 81 A3
Dronfield S18 57 D3
Heanor DE75 193 F8
Shirebrook NG20 119 F5
Ridgeway Ave
Bolsover S44 99 C2
Derby DE23 231 D6
Ridgeway Courtyard S12 58 E8
Ridgeway Craft Ctr★ S12 58 E8
Ridgeway Cres S12 44 A6
Ridgeway Ct DE23 218 D2
Ridgeway Dr
Ilkeston DE7 208 B5
Sheffield S12 44 A6
Ridgeway Inf Sch DE23 231 D6
Ridgeway La DE56 168 C4
RIDGEWAY MOOR 58 E7
Ridgeway Moor S12 58 E6
Ridgeway Moor Farm Ct S20 58 E6
Ridgeway On The Hill DE56 168 A1
Ridgeway Prim Sch S12 58 E8
Ridgeway Rd
Burton upon Trent DE15 254 E7
Sheffield S12 44 A5
Ridgeways The SK22 25 D2
Ridgeway W S43 80 E2
Ridgewood Ct DE21 205 E2
Ridgewood Dr DE4 155 C6
Ridgway The SK12 32 C6
Riding Bank DE73 251 F6
Riding Hill Ave NG20 119 D3
Ridings Rd SK13 9 F5
Ridings The
Mansfield NG19 136 F1
Ockbrook DE72 221 D5
Rigga La DE56 191 B1
Riggotts La S42 114 D7
Riggotts Way S42 94 E8
Riggs La
Marston Montgomery DE6 211 F8
Marston Montgomery DE6 212 A7
Rigley Ave [10] DE7 194 F1
Rigsby Ct DE3 217 C3
Riley Ave DE55 157 D8
Riley Back La S32 71 E6
Riley La
Ripley DE5 169 A6
Stoney Middleton S32 71 F5
Stoney Middleton S32 72 A5
Rimsdale Cl DE24 231 E3
Ringer Ct S43 80 E3
Ringer Gdns S43 80 E3
Ringer La
Clowne S43 80 E3
Clowne S43 80 F1
Clowne S80 99 F8
Elmton S80 100 A8
Ringer Way S43 80 E3
RINGINGLOW 42 F4
Ringinglow Rd S10, S11 42 E4
Ring-o-Bells La SK12 32 D6
Ringstone Rise SK23 33 E2
Ringstone Way SK23 45 D8
Ringwood Ave
Chesterfield S41 95 E7
Compstall SK14 15 A8
Staveley S43 97 C8
Ringwood Cl [3] DE21 219 E8
Ringwood Mdws S43 77 F1
Ringwood Rd S43 96 F8
Ringwood View S43 96 F7
Rink Dr DE11 256 B3
Rinkway Bsns Pk DE11 256 B3
RIPLEY 169 C2
Ripley Ave DE72 245 B8
Ripley Ho DE21 220 E3
Ripley Hospl DE5 169 D1
Ripley Inf Sch DE5 180 D8
Ripley Jun Sch DE5 180 D8
Ripley L Ctr DE5 169 D1
Ripley Rd
Bullbridge DE56 168 D5
Heage DE56 169 A1
Ripley DE5 169 B4
Ripon Cres DE21 219 E8
Ripon Gdns SK17 85 D5
Ripple Wlk S40 96 C7
Risborrow Cl DE65 229 D4
RISE END 154 E3
Rise End DE4 154 D3
Rises The SK13 9 F5
Rise The
Derby DE22 204 E2
Horwich End SK23 45 C6
Swadlincote DE11 255 F5
Risings The SK22 24 B1
RISLEY 222 E3
Risley Ct DE7 194 F3
Risley La DE72 222 D2
Risley Lower Gram CE Prim Sch DE72 222 E4
Risley Way S42 115 B4
Rivenhall Cl DE23 230 F7
Riverbank DE4 110 F1
Riverbank The DE65 242 B5
Riverbank Way SK13 17 F7
Rivercroft Cl ST14 197 A3
River Ct S17 56 A7
Riverdale S32 72 C7
Riverdale Cl DE15 248 B5
Rivermead Ho DE1 267 B5
Riversdale DE56 168 B4
Riversfield Dr ST14 196 F3
Riverside
Baslow DE45 91 D6
Walton-on-Trent DE12 253 C1
Riverside Bsns Pk DE45 109 C7
Riverside Cl
Calver S32 72 D1
Glossop SK13 10 D1
Riverside Court SK17 84 F7
Riverside Cres
Bakewell DE45 109 D6
Holymoorside S42 113 E7
Riverside Ct
Ambergate DE56 167 F3
Baslow DE45 91 E6
Calver S32 72 D2
Derby DE24 219 D4
Riverside Dr
Branston DE14 253 F7
Calver S32 72 D1
Riverside Park Bsns Ctr DE21 220 B2
Riverside Rd DE21 219 D4
Riverside Studios S18 57 B1
Riverside Way
Bolsover S44 98 E2
Mansfield Woodhouse NG19 136 D5
River St DE1 267 B4
Riversvale SK17 84 F7
RIVER'S VALE 84 F7
River View
Aldercar DE55 171 A6
Belper DE56 190 F7
Chesterfield S40 115 A8
Long Eaton NG10 236 A3
Longnor SK17 121 B6
Tideswell SK17 88 D7
Riverview Cotts [2] SK13 17 C7
Riverview Court DE1 267 A5
Riverview Prim Sch DE15 254 E7
Rivington Rd [3] NG9 223 E2
Rivoli Dr [8] DE11 256 E1
Roadmeadow Cl DE6 185 D8
Robert Bakewel Way ST14 210 C2
Robert Cl S18 76 E5
Robert Rd S8 57 A7
Roberts Ave NG17 148 F2
Roberts Cl S2 43 D8
Roberts Dr DE55 159 B4
Robertson Rd SK17 85 B6
Robertson's Ave S44 98 A4
Roberts St DE7 209 A6
Robert St DE1 267 C4
Robey Dr NG16 182 F3
Robey Vale S81 63 F8
Robian Way DE11 256 A4
Robina Dr NG16 195 C8
Robin Court S21 60 D7
Robin Croft S40 114 F7
Robincroft Rd S42 114 D4
Robin Croft Rd DE22 204 E4
Robinettes La
Cossall NG16 195 D1
Cossall NG16 195 E2
ROBIN HOOD 92 D5
Robin Hood Cl NG16 182 F1
Robin Hood Pl DE11 256 C2
Robin Hood Prim Sch [1] NG19 136 B3
Robin Hood Rd DE4 156 C2
Robinia Cl DE21 206 C3
Robinlands La S33 38 B4
Robin Rd DE1 218 F7
Robins Cl DE72 233 D5
Robinscross DE72 221 B1
Robin's Cross La DE65 249 F7
Robinson Ct [4] DE4 116 E1
Robinson Ind Est DE23 219 B2
Robinson Rd DE11 256 A6
Robinson's Hill DE73 251 F6
Robinson Way S21 60 C6
Robinwood Lodge [30] SK13 9 E1
Robridding Rd S45 129 A4
Robson Cl DE24 233 A7
Roby Lea DE74 246 F4
ROCESTER 197 A3
Rocester Bypass
Rocester ST14 196 F4
Rocester ST14 197 A5
Rocester Way S42 131 F6
Roche [9] S20 59 E8
Rochester Cl
Derby DE24 233 A5
Long Eaton NG10 236 A7
Rochley Cl DE21 205 F2
Rock Art Cl [4] S43 81 E2
Rock Bank
Buxton SK17 85 C3
Horwich End SK23 45 E6
Rockbourne Cl DE24 233 D6
Rockcliffe Cl DE11 256 B1
Rock Cres S45 131 A5
Rockety The DE21 191 E4
Rockfield Rd SK17 85 D8
Rockford Ct NG9 209 E1
Rockhall Terr SK22 25 E2
Rock Ho DE4 155 B6
Rock House Cl DE55 147 F5
Rockhouse Rd DE24 233 A6
Rockingham [11] S20 59 E8
Rockingham Cl
Chesterfield S40 95 C3
Derby DE22 205 A4
[3] Dronfield S18 56 C1
Rockingham Way DE15 255 C4
Rock La S44 116 E6
Rocklands The NG20 119 E4
Rockley Cl S40 114 F7
Rockley Way NG20 119 E4
Rockmay Ho DE55 170 E6
Rock Mill Bsns Pk S32 71 E4
Rock Mill La SK22 33 B7
Rock Side NG16 195 F6
Rockside Cotts S43 80 E4
Rockside Hall DE4 143 C6
Rockside Hydro DE4 143 C6
Rockside Steps DE4 143 C6
Rockside View DE4 143 C7
Rock Sq S32 71 D6
Rock St SK22 33 C7
Rocks The DE4 144 A5
Rockstone Way NG19 136 B2
Rock Terr
Bakewell DE45 109 D6
Buxton SK17 85 B6
Rock The DE45 109 C6
Rockvale Terr DE4 143 B1
Rockvale Villas DE4 143 B1
Rock View SK17 88 A7
Rodge Croft S41 77 A3
Rodger's La DE55 159 A5
Rodknoll La S42 93 D2
Rod Moor Rd S17, S18 56 B4
Rodney Cl DE65 228 F2
Rodney Ho DE24 232 E6
Rodney Way DE7 194 F3
Rodney Wlk DE23 230 E7
RODSLEY 200 A5
Rodsley Cl
Chesterfield S40 95 B5
Yeaveley DE6 199 D5
Rodsley Cres DE23 231 D5
Rodsley La
Rodsley DE6 199 F7
Rodsley DE6 200 A2
Rodsley DE6 200 A5
Yeaveley DE6 199 E5
Rodwood Ave S43 80 A7
Roebuck Pl SK23 47 B6
Roecar Cl S41 77 B2
Roe Cross Ind Est SK14 9 A5
Roe Cross Rd SK14 9 A5
Roe Farm La DE21 219 E7
Roe Farm Prim Sch DE21 219 E8
Roehampton Dr
Derby DE22 218 A7
Stapleford NG9 209 D2
Roe's Ct DE4 157 A2
Roe's La DE4 157 A1
Roe Wlk DE23 219 A1
Rogers Ave S80 81 D1
Rogers Ct DE65 227 D1
Rolaine Cl NG19 136 C4
ROLLESTON 240 A4
Rolleston Cres NG16 195 F8
Rolleston Dr NG16 195 B8
ROLLESTONE 43 D5
Rolleston La DE13 239 D5
ROLLESTON ON DOVE 240 C3
Rolleston Rd DE13 240 B1
Rollins La SK6 15 A1
Roman Bank NG19 136 D3
Roman Cl [3] DE11 256 C5
Roman Ct DE16 254 F7
Roman Dr DE14 253 D8
Roman Rd DE1 219 B7
Roman Way
Borrowash DE72 221 C1
Moira DE12 262 E4
Romeley Cres S43 80 D3
Romeley La S43 80 D3
Romford Way [4] S43 78 B3
Romney Dr S18 56 E1
Romney Gdns S2 43 B6
Romorantin Pl NG10 236 E7
Romsley Cl DE3 217 D4
Rona Cl DE24 231 E4
Ronald Cl DE23 230 E7
Rood La
Clowne S43 80 E3
Idridgehay DE56 176 F6
Idridgehay DE56 177 A6
Rookery Close DE56 179 D5
Rookery Farm La DE56 177 A7
Rookery The DE11 256 F2
Roosevelt Ave
Derby DE21 220 B6
Long Eaton NG10 236 C5
Roost The S32 53 A6
Roper Ave DE75 193 F7
Roper Hill S10 42 D7
Ropewalk Ind Ctr DE7 195 A1
Ropewalk The
Heanor DE75 193 F8
Ilkeston DE7 195 A1
Stanley Common DE7 193 B1
Walton-on-Trent DE12 253 D1
Rosamond Ave S17 56 A6
Rosamond Cl S17 56 A6
Rosamond Ct S17 56 A5
Rosamond Dr S17 56 A6
Rosamond Glade S17 56 A6
Rosamond Pl S17 56 A6
Rosamond's Ride DE23 231 D8
Rose Ave
Borrowash DE72 221 C1
Burton upon Trent DE13 241 A2
Calow S44 97 A3
Clowne S43 81 A5
Ilkeston DE7 194 E2
Rose Bank Cl SK14 9 D5
Rosebay Gdns SK23 47 B4
Roseberry Ct DE21 206 B1
Rose Cl DE73 232 E1
Rose Cottage Dr NG17 148 F2
Rose Cotts
Bonsall DE4 142 C1
Chesterfield S41 96 C2
Rose Cres S43 79 C4
Rosecroft Gdns DE11 256 C3
Rose Ct
Clay Cross S45 131 A4
Long Eaton NG10 223 B1
Rosedale Ave
Chesterfield S40 115 B8
Derby DE24 233 A6
Rosedale Cl NG10 236 B6
Rosedale View S40 114 D7
Rosedale Way NG19 136 F2
Rosedene View DE12 262 C4

Rose End Ave DE4 155 A6
Rosefinch Way NG19 136 F2
Rose Garth Cl S41 96 C1
Rose Gdns S44 97 D2
Roseheath Cl DE23 231 E5
ROSE HILL 219 B2
Rose Hill
Chesterfield S40 266 B3
Sheffield S20 59 B8
Woodville DE11 256 E3
Rose Hill Ave S20 59 B8
Rosehill Bsns Ctr DE23 219 A2
Rose Hill Cl S20 59 B8
Rosehill Ct S44 99 A1
Rose Hill Dr S20 59 B8
Rose Hill E S40 266 B3
Rose Hill Mews S20 59 B8
Rose Hill St DE23 219 A2
Rose Hill View S20 59 B8
Rose Hill W S40 266 A3
Rose La
Mansfield Woodhouse NG19 136 C3
Ticknall DE73 251 A4
Roseland La NG20 119 C3
Roseleigh Cres DE11 255 F6
Rosemary Ct 1 S8 43 A3
Rosemary Dr DE24 233 A5
ROSEMARYHILL 171 F7
Rosemeyer La 2 DE74 246 E3
Rosemoor La DE21 206 B1
Rosemount Ct DE22 204 C3
Rosengrave St DE1 267 B2
Rose Tree La DE11 255 F7
Rosette Ct DE21 206 C3
Rose Valley DE11 256 A5
Rose Way S21 60 D5
Rosewood SK14 9 D5
Rosewood Ave S44 98 F3
Rosewood Cl
Derby DE24 233 B7
South Normanton DE55 160 B7
Rose Wood Cl S41 95 D8
Rosewood Cres DE75 182 B2
Rosewood Rd DE15 254 F6
Roseybank SK23 34 B1
Rosier Cres DE55 170 A8
Rosling Way S44 97 D2
ROSLISTON 260 D6
Rosliston CE Prim Sch DE12 260 C6
Rosliston Forestry Ctr★ DE12 260 C8
Rosliston Rd
Burton upon Trent DE15 254 D3
Walton-on-Trent DE12 259 E8
Rosliston Road S DE15 254 E5
Roslyn Cres S32 53 A7
Roslyn Rd S32 53 A7
Ross Ct S21 60 D4
Rossell Dr NG9 223 E5
Rossendale DE7 194 E4
Rossendale Cl S40 114 E8
Rosser Ave S12 43 F2
Rossington Dr DE23 230 F6
Rosslyn Gdns DE24 233 A6
Ross Wlk DE21 205 E1
ROSTON 197 E7
Roston Cl 3 S18 56 D1
Roston Common DE6 198 B6
Roston Court DE21 220 E3
Rosyth Cres DE73 232 E1
Rothay Cl S18 75 E8
Rothbourne Croft DE6 151 D2
Rothbury Ave NG9 209 D2
Rothbury Pl DE21 205 E1
Rother Ave S43 96 D8
Rother Cl S40 114 E8
Rother Close DE65 228 E1
Rother Croft S42 131 D8
Rotherham Cl S21 60 F8
Rotherham Rd
Bolsover S44 99 E2
Eckington S20, S21 59 F6
Killamarsh S21 60 F8
New Houghton NG19 134 F7
Pleasley NG19 134 F6
Scarcliffe S44 118 D7
Shirebrook S44, NG19 118 D3
Spinkhill S43 61 D2
Rotherham Road N S20 59 F8
Rotherside Rd S21 59 F4
Rother St S45 132 C2
Rothervale Rd S40 115 A8
Rother Valley Ctry Pk★ S21 60 C8
Rother Valley Way S20 60 B8
Rother Way S41 96 B6
Rother Wlk S45 131 E4
Rotherwood Rd S21 60 E7
Rothesay Cl DE24 231 E4
Rothey Gr S40 94 F5
Rothwell Ho DE65 228 D1
Rothwell La DE56 179 B4
Rothwell Rd DE3 217 D3
Rough Heanor Rd DE3 218 A2
Rough La DE6 186 E4
Roughlow La DE6 183 D1
Roughpiece La DE4 166 D5
Roughton Cl DE3 230 D8
Round Hill Cl SK13 9 F3
Round House Cl DE75 193 C8
Roundhouse Gall★ DE65 226 D4
Roundhouse Rd DE24 219 C4
Round Way SK22 33 D8
Rouse St S45 132 D1
Rousseau Cl DE6 173 D1
Routh Ave DE74 247 B2
Rovings Dr DE21 220 F2
Rowallan Way DE73 232 E1
Rowan Ave
Ripley DE5 180 D8
Stapleford NG9 209 E2
Rowan Cl
Creswell S80 81 E2
Darley Dale DE4 127 B3
Denstone ST14 196 D6
Derby, Cherrytree Hill DE21 220 B5
Derby, Sinfin DE24 231 D3
Ilkeston DE7 208 F5
Mansfield NG19 136 D1
Rowan Croft NG17 148 F4
Rowan Ct ST14 196 F4
Rowan Dr
Branston DE14 253 E6
Branston DE14 256 E6
Kilburn DE56 192 B8
Selston NG16 171 D6
Shirebrook NG20 119 D5
Shirland DE55 146 D1
Swadlincote DE11 256 B7
Wingerworth S42 115 C4
Rowan Gdns 1 DE72 246 A6
Rowan Grove S42 115 C4
Rowan Park Cl DE23 231 D7
Rowan Rd
Clowne S43 80 D2
Eckington S21 59 C1
Mastin Moor S43 79 C3
Rowan Sch The S17 55 E6
Rowan Tree Cl
Ashbourne DE6 185 D8
Killamarsh S21 60 C5
Rowan Tree Dell S17 55 E3
Rowan Tree Rd S21 60 C5
Rowan Wlk SK13 9 E4
ROWARTH 24 E7
Rowarth Ave 13 SK13 9 D2
Rowarth Bank 9 SK13 9 D2
Rowarth Cl 10 SK13 9 D2
Rowarth Dr SK22 33 D7
Rowarth Fold 12 SK13 9 D2
Rowarth Way 11 SK13 9 D2
Rowbury Dr DE15 248 B2
Rowdale Cres S12 44 D5
Rowditch Ave DE22 218 D4
Rowditch Cotts DE1 218 D4
Rowditch Pl DE22 218 D4
Rowena Cl DE24 232 F7
Rowen Ct DE56 179 B2
Rowesley Rd DE4 111 A4
Rowfields La DE6 173 F7
ROWLAND 90 C5
Rowland Ct DE55 158 F4
Rowland Rd 3 S2 43 A8
Rowland St
Alfreton DE55 159 A4
Derby DE24 232 E6
Rowleston Cl 2 DE6 201 E8
Rowley Cl DE11 256 D5
Rowley Ct DE11 256 B4
Rowley Gdns DE23 231 C7
Rowley La DE23 231 C7
Rowleys Mill 3 DE1 218 E5
ROWSLEY 111 A1
Rowsley Ave
Derby DE23 231 D8
Long Eaton NG10 236 A5
Rowsley CE (Controlled) Prim Sch DE4 126 F8
Rowsley Cl SK13 9 E2
Rowsley Cres S43 97 C8
Rowsley Gn SK13 9 E2
Rowsley Gr SK13 9 E2
Rowsley Mews SK13 9 E2
Rowsley South Sta★ DE4 127 A5
Rowsley Wlk SK13 9 E2
Row The
Great Cubley DE6 198 E1
Lea DE4 156 B8
ROWTHORNE 134 C6
Rowthorne Ave DE55 170 A8
Rowthorne La S44 134 B7
Rowthorne Trail Nature Reserve★ NG17 134 D3
Rowton Grange Rd SK23 47 B5
Rowton Way DE72 233 D3
Roxburgh Ave DE21 219 E7
Roxton Ave 2 S8 56 F8
Roxton Ct NG16 195 F7
Royal App DE73 244 F8
Royal Ave NG10 223 D1
Royal Cl DE72 221 B1
Royal Court Bsns Pk S41 266 B3
Royal Croft Dr DE45 91 E6
Royal Crown Derby Visitor Ctr★ DE23 267 C1
Royal Derby Hospl DE23 218 B2
Royale Cl S21 59 E3
Royal Gate DE56 179 D3
Royal Gr DE21 206 D3
Royal Hill Rd DE21 220 D6
Royal La DE12 262 B4
Royal Oak Ct S43 79 D4
Royal Oak Pl DE45 109 D5
Royal Park Drive DE24 232 F4
Royal Rd SK12 32 D5
Royal Sch for the Deaf (Derby) DE22 218 D6
Royal Scot Rd DE24 219 E2
Royal Way DE24 219 E3
Royce Cl DE65 229 C3
Roydon Cl DE3 217 C3
Royle Ave SK13 10 D1
Royle Bsns Pk DE15 254 E3
Royston Cl
Ashbourne DE6 185 C8
Chesterfield S40 114 B7
Royston Dr DE56 179 D5
RTC Bsns Pk DE24 219 D2
Rubens Cl
Dronfield S18 56 F1
Marple SK6 23 C8
Ruby Dr S40 115 E6
Ruby Ho S8 43 B5
Ruby Paddocks NG16 195 F5
Ruby Way DE11 255 F4
Rudyard Ave DE21 220 E6
Rufford Cl S40 95 E1
Rufford Dr NG19 136 E3
Rufford Rd NG10 236 B4
Ruffstone Cl DE56 191 C7
Rugby Ave DE55 159 C3
Rugby Cl DE14 254 C8
Rugby Drive S41 96 A5
Rugby Pk View NG20 120 E4
Rugby St DE24 219 E1
Rugeley Ave NG10 237 A7
Ruislip Cl NG16 195 E7
Runway Bsns Pk DE6 185 E8
Rupert Rd DE21 220 A7
Rupert St
Ilkeston DE7 195 A1
Pilsley S45 132 B3
Rushcliffe Ave DE21 219 F6
Rushcliffe Gdns DE21 219 F6
Rushdale Ave
Derby DE23 231 D6
Sheffield S8 43 B5
Rushdale Mount 4 S8 43 A5
Rushdale Rd S8 43 B5
Rushdale Terr 3 S8 43 A5
Rushen Mount S40 114 F6
Rushes The
Glossop SK13 9 F4
Mansfield Woodhouse NG19 136 D5
Rush La SK6 24 A6
Rushleigh Ct S17 55 D7
Rushley Ave S17 55 D8
Rushley Cl S17 55 D8
Rushley Dr S17 55 D7
Rushley Rd S17 55 D7
Rush Leys NG10 236 D5
Rushmere SK13 17 E8
Rushpool Ave NG19 136 D3
Rushpool Cl NG19 136 F2
Rushton Cl DE13 239 C6
Rushton Dr SK6 23 A5
Rushup Cl DE22 205 A5
Rushup La SK17, SK23 48 D8
Rushycroft SK14 9 A4
Rushy La NG10, DE72 222 E6
Ruskin Ave NG10 236 B5
Ruskin Rd
Derby DE1 218 F7
Mansfield NG19 135 D1
Ruskin Sq S8 43 A6
Ruskin Way DE23 231 B8
Rusk The S43 80 B6
Russell Ct 1 NG10 223 D1
Russell Gdns S42 131 B6
Russell St
Compstall SK6 15 B3
Derby DE24 219 C1
Long Eaton NG10 223 D1
Swadlincote DE11 256 C3
Russet Cl
Derby DE21 206 B1
Hatton DE65 227 C1
Russet Ct DE23 218 E2
Ruston Cl
Chesterfield S40 95 B6
Swadlincote DE11 256 B4
Rutherford Rise 8 DE21 205 F2
Ruthyn Ave S43 80 A7
Rutland Ave
Bolsover S44 99 A1
Borrowash DE72 221 C2
Matlock DE4 143 C6
Ripley DE5 181 A7
Rutland Cl
Burton upon Trent DE15 254 D6
Hilton DE65 240 E8
Rutland Ct
Ilkeston DE7 194 D1
3 Matlock DE4 143 C6
Rutland Dr DE3 217 E3
Rutland Gate Cl 7 DE4 143 C6
Rutland Gr NG10 223 C5
Rutland Mews DE45 109 E6
Rutland Pl DE56 168 B6
Rutland Rd
Chesterfield S40 266 A3
Westwood NG16 171 C4
Rutland Sports Pk DE75 208 D8
Rutland Sq DE45 109 D6
Rutland St
Chesterfield S41 77 A2
Derby DE23 219 A1
Ilkeston DE7 194 F2
Matlock DE4 143 C6
Rutland Terr
Barlow S18 75 E3
Ilkeston DE7 194 F2
Rutland Way SK23 34 D2
Ryal Cl DE72 221 C5
Ryan Cl DE24 231 E3
Rycroft Rd DE74 247 D6
Rydal Ave NG10 223 B2
Rydal Cl
Derby DE22 204 E4
Dronfield S18 56 D1
Rydal Cres S41 95 E8
Rydal Way S45 131 B3
Ryde Ho DE24 233 C7
Ryder Cl DE11 255 E2
Ryder Point Rd DE4 154 A4
Rye Butts DE73 232 E1
Rye Cl DE21 205 E3
Rye Cres S45 131 D3
Ryecroft DE4 127 D2
Ryecroft CE Mid Sch ST14 196 E4
Ryecroft Glen Rd S17 56 A8
Ryecroft St NG9 223 E8
Ryecroft View S17 55 D8
Rye Ct S45 131 D3
Ryedale Gdns DE23 231 C5
Ryefield Ave DE7 194 F5
Ryefields Cl DE5 180 C5
Rye Flatt La S40 95 C2
Rye Flatts La DE65 227 D1
Ryegrass Cl DE56 179 D4
Ryegrass Rd DE21 206 C2
Ryehill Ave S40 95 A2
Ryemere Cl NG16 182 E2
Ryemere Ct NG16 182 E2
Rykneld Cl DE23 230 E6
Rykneld Ct S45 131 C3
Rykneld Dr DE23 230 F7
Rykneld Prim Sch DE14 253 E7
Rykneld Rd DE23 230 E6
Rykneld Rise S42 115 A3
Rykneld Sq S40 266 B3
Rykneld Way DE23 230 E6
Rykniеld Hill DE5 180 B2
Rykniеld Rd DE56, DE7 192 B8
RYLAH 117 F5
Rylah Hill S44 118 A5
Rymill Dr DE21 205 F1
Ryton Way DE65 228 D1

S

Sacheveral La DE4 140 F4
Sacheverall Ave NG16 160 D3
Sacheverel St DE1 267 B2
Sackerville Terr S21 60 B7
Sackville Cl S40 114 B8
Sackville St DE23 231 F8
Saddlers Cl NG19 136 F1
Saddlers Croft S42 131 F7
Saddletree View S43 79 B4
Saddleworth Wlk DE24 232 E3
Sadler Dr 3 DE6 211 C1
Sadler Gate DE1 267 B3
Saffron Dr DE21 206 A1
Saffron St NG19 136 F2
Sage Ct DE3 217 C5
Sage Dr DE11 256 F4
Sage Mews SK23 47 B8
Sail Ct S41 76 E5
St Agnes Ave DE22 204 D4
St Aidan's Ave S2 43 D8
St Aidan's Dr S2 43 E8
St Aidan's Pl S2 43 E8
St Aidan's Rd S2 43 E8
St Aidan's Rise S2 43 E8
St Aidan's Way S2 43 E8
St Albans Cl
Holmewood S42 132 E8
Long Eaton NG10 236 E5
St Alban's RC Prim Sch DE21 219 F6
St Albans Rd DE22 218 D3
St Albans St SK22 33 C8
St Alkmund's Cl DE56 190 E4
St Alkmunds Way DE56 190 E4
St Alkmund's Way DE1 267 B4
St Andrew's CE (Controlled) Prim Sch B79 263 E2
St Andrew's CE Jun Sch
Glossop SK13 9 F4
Glossop SK13 10 A4
St Andrew's CE Methodist (Aided) Prim Sch 5 S18 56 D1
St Andrew's CE Prim Sch DE7 207 B5
St Andrews Cl DE55 170 A7
St Andrew's Cl B79 263 F2
St Andrews Ct
Glossop SK13 10 A4
Swadlincote DE11 255 E2
St Andrew's Ct DE7 194 D1
St Andrew's Dr
Ilkeston DE7 208 E8
Swanwick DE55 169 F7
St Andrews Rise S40 114 C8
St Andrew's Sch DE21 205 E1
St Andrews View DE21 205 E1
St Andrews Wlk SK22 33 D8
St Anne's CE Prim Sch DE45 91 E5
St Anne's Cl
Baslow DE45 91 E5
Derby DE1 218 E6
Staveley S43 97 E8
St Anne's La DE74 247 B3
St Anne's RC Prim Sch SK17 66 B1
St Annes St 4 SK14 16 A8
St Anne's Well★ SK17 85 B8
St Ann's Cl SK23 46 F6
St Anselms Preparatory Sch DE45 109 C6
ST AUGUSTINES 115 B7
St Augustines Ave S40 115 A8
St Augustines Cres S40 115 A8
St Augustines Dr S40 266 B1
St Augustines Mount S40 266 B1
St Augustines Rd S40 115 A8
St Augustines Rise 1 S40 115 A8
St Augustine St DE23 218 F1
St Barnabas Ho 12 S2 43 A8
St Barnabas La 4 S2 43 A8
St Barnabas Rd 5 S2 43 A8
St Bartholomew's CE Controlled Sch SK17 121 B7
St Benedict RC Sch & Performing Arts Coll DE22 204 E1
St Benedicts Ct S2 43 D8
St Bride's Wlk DE22 218 B6
St Catherine's Rd DE11 255 F5
St Chad's CE Inf Sch DE23 218 F2
St Chad's Cl
Denstone ST14 196 D6
Draycott DE72 235 A7
St Chad's Rd DE23 218 F2
St Chad's Water Nature Reserve★ DE72 235 A4
St Chad's Way S41 96 A8
St Charles Cl SK13 9 F5
St Charles's RC Prim Sch SK13 9 E5
St Christopher's Way DE24 219 D3
St Clare's Cl DE22 218 D2
St Clare's Sch DE3 218 A2
St Cuthberts Rd 1 DE6 211 C1
St Cuthbert's Rd DE22 218 C3
St Davids Cl NG16 170 F3
St David's Cl DE22 218 D3
St Davids Rd B79 263 F2
St David's Rise S40 114 D8
St Edmund's Ave NG19 136 C3
St Edmund's CE Prim Sch NG19 136 C3
St Edmund's Cl DE22 204 F4
St Edward's CE Prim Sch DE74 247 B3
St Edwards Ct DE11 255 E5
St Edward's RC Prim Sch DE11 256 B5
St Edward's Rd DE74 247 B2
St Elizabeth Cl S2 43 B8
St Elizabeth's RC Prim Sch DE56 178 F5
St Elphins House 6 DE4 116 E1
St George's CE(Controlled)Prim Sch DE11 256 B1
St George's CE Prim Sch SK22 33 C8
St George's Cl DE22 204 F3
St Georges Dr 3 NG9 223 F2
St George's Ho DE22 204 F3
St George's Pl 1 DE56 178 F4
St George's RC Prim Sch DE23 231 C7
St Georges Rd SK22 33 C8
St Giles CE Prim Sch S21 60 C6
St Giles Cl S40 115 B8
St Giles Rd DE23 218 F1
St Giles' Sch DE21 205 C1
St Giles Sch the Hive DE1 267 D5
St Giles Wlk DE4 143 C4
St Hardulph's Prim Sch DE73 252 F2
St Helena Centre Univ of Derby Chesterfield Campus S41 266 B4
St Helens Ave NG16 160 C4
St Helen's Cl
Chesterfield S41 266 B4
Darley Dale DE4 127 B3
Grindleford S32 72 D8
St Helen's Cres NG9 209 C4
St Helen's Croft S32 72 D8
St Helen's Dr NG16 171 D7
St Helen's La DE4 166 A7
St Helen's St
Chesterfield S41 266 B4
Derby DE1 267 A4
St Hugh's Cl DE22 205 A2
St Ives Dr 4 S8 43 A2
St James Ave DE7 209 A7
St James' CE Inf Sch DE23 267 C1
St James' CE Prim Sch 7 SK13 17 B8
St James Cl
Belper DE56 179 D4
2 Chesterfield S41 96 C1
Glossop SK13 17 C7
Swadlincote DE11 256 B6
Willington DE65 242 C5
St James' Court S8 43 B1
St James Ct
Ashbourne DE6 173 D3
Sandiacre NG10 223 B3
St James' Dr NG16 182 D8
St James Gdns NG19 136 E6
St James' Rd DE23 218 F1
St James's CE Jun Sch DE23 219 B3
St James's Ct SK17 85 C3
St James Sq S40 266 B3
St James' Sq SK22 33 C8
St James's St 3 NG9 223 C6
St James' St
14 Buxton SK17 85 B7
Derby DE1 267 B3
Derby, Rose Hill DE23 219 A1
St James Terr 1 NG9 223 D6
St James' Terr SK17 85 B7
St John Fisher RC Prim Sch DE24 233 C8
St John Houghton Cath Voluntary Acad Sch DE7 208 C6
St John's 4 SK17 85 A7
St John's Ave DE21 220 B5
St John's CE Prim Sch
Belper DE56 179 B5
Ripley DE5 169 F1
Stapleford NG9 223 E7
St Johns Cl
Bamford S33 40 B3
Chesterfield S40 114 B7
Ripley DE5 169 F2
St John's Cl
Brinsley NG16 171 D1
Derby DE22 204 D3
St John's Cres S43 80 F3
St John's Dr
Derby DE21 220 B5
Kilburn DE56 192 A8
Swadlincote DE11 255 E5
St John's Mount S41 95 F8
St Johns Pl S43 78 D1
St Johns Rd
23 Chesterfield S41 95 F8
Staveley S43 78 D1
St John's Rd
Belper DE56 179 A4

St John's Rd *continued*
Buxton SK17 85 A7
Chesterfield S41 95 F8
Dronfield S18 76 E7
Ilkeston DE7 209 A7
Matlock Bath DE4 143 B3
Smalley DE7 192 F5
Tideswell SK17 69 C4
St Johns Road Bsns Ctr
S41 95 F8
St John's St
Long Eaton NG10 236 D7
Wirksworth DE4 165 F8
St John St
Hayfield SK22 25 D2
[7] Middlepeak DE4 154 F1
St John's Terr DE1 218 F6
St Joseph's Cath Prim Sch DE23 267 A1
St Joseph's RC & CE VA Prim Sch S43 97 D8
St Joseph's RC Prim Sch
Matlock DE4 143 D6
Shirebrook NG20 119 F5
St Joseph's St DE4 143 C5
St Katherines Cl
DE4 110 E1
St Katherine's Ct
DE22 218 D6
St Laurence CE (Voluntary Aided) Prim Sch NG10 236 E6
St Laurence Ct
NG10 236 E6
St Laurence Gdns [10]
DE56 178 F4
St Lawrence Ave
S44 118 C8
St Lawrence Cl
DE75 181 F2
St Lawrence Rd S42 131 F6
St Lawrence View
S80 81 F5
St Leonards Dr S41 96 C1
St Leonards Pl
DE55 146 E1
ST LUKE'S 218 E3
St Luke's CE Prim Sch
Glossop SK13 10 C1
Shireoaks S81 63 F7
St Lukes Cl DE22 218 E4
St Lukes Ct [27] S41 95 F8
St Lukes View S81 63 F7
St Margaret's Dr
S40 266 A3
St Margaret's RC Prim Sch SK13 16 D8
St Marks Cl DE4 155 A6
St Mark's Rd
Chesterfield S40 95 E3
Derby DE21 219 D6
St Martins Cl [12]
DE11 255 E1
St Martin's Cl S41 95 D6
St Martins Ct DE55 158 F4
St Martin's Rd SK6 23 A6
St Martins Sch
Derby DE23 232 F5
Derby DE24 233 A4
St Martin's Sch
DE24 232 F8
St Martin's Wlk S80 82 C6
St Mary & All Saints Church (Crooked Spire)* S40 266 B3
St Mary's Ave DE72 235 A7
St Marys Bridge
DE1 219 A6
St Mary's Cath Prim Sch
DE22 204 F1
St Mary's Cath Voluntary Acad DE1 267 C4
St Mary's CE (Aided) Fst Sch [4] ST14 210 B1
St Mary's Cl
Chinley SK23 34 E2
Derby DE24 233 A6
Newton Solney DE15 248 E8
St Mary's Cres ST14 210 B1
St Mary's Ct
Derby DE1 267 B4
Hollingworth SK14 9 C5
St Mary's Dr DE13 240 F2
St Mary's Gate
Chesterfield S41 266 C3
Derby DE1 267 B3
[4] Wirksworth DE4 165 F8
St Mary's Pl S41 266 C3
St Mary's RC High Sch
S41 95 C7
St Mary's RC Prim Sch
Chesterfield S40 266 A4
Derby DE1 267 B4
Glossop SK13 17 D8
Marple SK6 23 B7
New Mills SK22 33 B8
St Mary's Rd
Disley SK12 32 D5
Glossop SK13 17 C8
New Mills SK22 33 B8
St Mary St DE7 208 E8
St Mary's View DE4 142 B7
St Marys Wharf Rd
DE1 219 B7
St Mary's Wlk NG16 171 B3
St Matthew's Cl S21 60 B1
St Matthew's St
DE14 254 C8
St Matthew's Wlk [4]
DE22 204 F2
St Mawes Cl DE22 204 D4
St Mellion Cl DE3 217 F1
St Michaels Cl
Crich DE4 156 F2
Derby DE24 233 C7
St Michael's Cl
Holbrook DE56 191 C6
Shirley DE6 200 D8
Willington DE65 242 B5
St Michael's Dr
Appleby Magna
DE12 265 F1
South Normanton
DE55 160 A7
St Michael's La DE1 267 B4
St Michaels Rd [3]
ST14 210 A4
St Michaels View
Derby DE24 233 C7
Selston NG16 171 F5
St Monicas Way
DE6 173 C3
St Morden's Catholic Primary School
DE13 240 B1
St Nicholas Cl DE22 204 D2
St Nicholas Pl DE1 267 A5
St Norbert Dr DE7 208 D4
St Oswald Cres DE6 173 C1
St Oswald's CE Inf Sch
DE6 173 B1
St Oswald's Hospl
DE6 173 B1
St Pancras Way
Derby DE1 267 C5
Ripley DE5 169 E4
St Pauls Ave S41 115 D6
St Pauls Ct NG16 195 F6
St Paul's Rd DE1 219 A7
St Peter & St Paul Sch
S41 96 D3
St Peter's CE(Aided) Jun Sch DE23 218 C1
St Peter's CE (Controlled) Prim Sch
DE12 264 F6
St Peter's CE VA Fst Sch
ST14 224 F2
St Peter's Churchyard
DE1 267 B3
St Peters Cl
Hartshorne DE11 257 B6
Long Duckmanton S44 98 A4
St Peter's Cl DE56 179 A4
St Peters Croft
DE56 179 A4
St Peters Ct DE24 233 A8
St Peter's Rd
Buxton SK17 66 D1
Chellaston DE73 233 A1
Thorpe Salvin S80 62 E7
St Peter's St
Derby DE1 219 A5
Derby DE1 267 B3
St Peter's Way DE1 267 B2
St Philip Howard Catholic Voluntary Acad [6] SK13 17 B8
St Philip's Dr S41 115 B8
St Quentin Cl
Derby DE22 218 C3
Sheffield S17 56 B5
St Quentin Dr S17 56 B5
St Quentin Mount
S17 56 B5
St Quentin Rise S17 56 B5
St Quentin View S17 56 B5
St Ronan's Ave
DE56 190 E2
St Stephen's Cl
DE23 231 D6
St Stephen's Ct
DE11 256 E3
St Swithin's Cl
DE22 218 D3
St Swithuns Ct
DE56 179 A2
St The DE6 162 B5
St Theresa's RC Prim Sch S2 44 B7
St Thomas Cl DE55 147 E5
St Thomas More Cath Sch Buxton SK17 85 B8
St Thomas of Canterbury RC Prim Sch [5] S8 56 F8
St Thomas RC Prim Sch
DE7 208 E6
St Thomas Rd DE23 219 A1
St Thomas' St S40 95 C2
St Vincent Cl NG10 236 E6
St Werburgh's CE (VA) Prim Sch DE21 220 D5
St Werburghs View
DE55 148 A3
St Werburgh's View
DE21 220 D5
St Wilfrid's Rd
[11] Sheffield S2 43 A8
West Hallam DE7 207 E8
St Wystan's Rd
DE22 218 C3
St Wystans Sch
DE65 242 C2
Salcey Cl DE55 169 F7
Salcey Dr NG9 209 D2
Salcey Sq S40 95 D1
Salcombe Ct [12] S41 95 F8
Salcombe Rd DE55 159 C5
Salcombe Rd Ind Units
DE55 159 C5
Salcombe Way
DE72 245 A8
Sale & Davys CE Prim Sch DE73 244 A6
Sales Ave S42 131 C8
Sales La DE15 248 C4
Sale St DE23 219 B2
Salestune Mews
NG16 171 F6
Salford Way DE11 255 E2
Salisbury Ave
Burton upon Trent
DE15 248 D3
Chesterfield S41 95 E7
Dronfield S18 76 A7
Salisbury Cl NG19 136 D4
Salisbury Cres S41 95 F7
Salisbury Dr
Belper DE56 179 D5
Swadlincote DE11 256 E5
Salisbury Ho SK17 85 C7
Salisbury La DE73 252 B7
Salisbury Rd S18 76 B8
Salisbury St
Derby DE1 219 A3
Derby DE23 267 B1
Glossop SK13 10 A5
Long Eaton NG10 236 E7
Sallyfield La DE6 183 E8
Sallywood Cl DE24 231 D2
Saltburn Cl DE21 205 C1
Salter Cl DE74 246 F4
Saltergate S40 266 B3
Saltergate La S33 40 B2
Salters La
Matlock DE4 142 F3
Matlock DE4 143 A2
Matlock Bath DE4 142 F4
Salvin Cres S43 80 E4
Samantha Ct DE21 206 B1
Samara Cl [2] DE11 256 B7
Samphire Cl DE3 217 C4
Sampson's La NG19 135 B3
Sampsons Yd NG17 148 F3
Samuel Cl S2 43 D7
Samuel Ct DE5 180 D8
Samuel Dr S2 43 D7
Samuel Pl S2 43 D7
Samuel Rd S2 43 D8
Samuel Road DE22 217 E6
Samuel St SK14 9 C4
Samuel Wood Cl
SK13 16 C8
Sancroft Ave DE21 220 E6
Sancroft Rd DE21 220 F6
Sanctuary Nature Reserve The*
DE24 219 E3
Sandal Cl DE72 233 D3
Sandalwood Cl
DE24 233 C7
Sandalwood Rd
DE15 254 E6
Sandbach Cl DE21 206 A1
Sandbed La
Belper DE56 179 C2
Belper DE56 179 D3
Sandby Croft S14 43 E2
Sandby Ct S14 43 E2
Sandby Dr
Marple SK6 23 B8
Sheffield S14 43 E2
Sandcliffe Pk DE11 256 D7
Sandcliffe Rd DE11 256 D6
Sandcroft Cl DE11 256 D5
Sanderling Heath
DE3 230 B7
Sanderling Way
NG19 136 E2
Sanderman Ho
DE11 256 E3
Sanders Cl DE7 194 C2
Sanderson Cl DE14 253 C8
Sanderson Rd DE21 220 B6
Sandfield Cl DE21 220 B8
Sandfield Rd [1]
NG9 223 E2
Sandford Ave NG10 236 E7
Sandford Brook
DE65 228 E1
Sandgate Ave NG19 136 D4
Sandgate Cl DE24 233 A6
Sandgate Rd
Derby DE72 245 A8
Mansfield Woodhouse
NG19 136 D4
Sandhall La
Alderwasley DE56 167 A5
Spout DE56 166 F5
Sandham La DE5 169 C1
Sandhill La
Broadbottom SK6 16 A2
Marple SK6 15 E1
Sandhills Rd S44 99 C1
SANDIACRE 223 A6
Sandiacre Friesland Sp Ctr NG10 222 F5
Sandiacre Rd NG9 223 C6
Sandiway
Chesterfield S40 114 C8
Glossop SK13 17 F7
Sand La DE6 211 B1
Sandlands The
DE11 256 D6
Sandlands Way
NG19 136 F2
Sandown Ave DE3 217 C3
Sandown Cl
Burton upon Trent
DE14 254 A7
Eckington S21 59 B2
Sandown Rd
Beeston NG9 223 F2
Derby DE24 232 E8
Sandpiper La DE3 230 B6
Sandpiper Place
NG20 120 D5
Sandringham Ave
DE15 248 A1
Sandringham Cl
Calow S44 97 A4
[5] Chesterfield S41 96 A8
[5] Hatton DE65 227 D2
Swadlincote DE11 256 B5
Sandringham Ct
[13] Buxton SK17 85 B7
Mansfield Woodhouse
NG19 136 B6
Sandringham Dr
Derby DE21 220 F5
Heanor DE75 181 C2
Mansfield Woodhouse
NG19 136 B6
Sandringham Ho
DE24 219 D1
Sandringham Pl
Ilkeston DE7 208 D5
Sheffield S10 42 F8
Sandringham Rd
Calow S44 97 A4
Derby DE21 205 E1
Mansfield Woodhouse
NG19 136 E5
Sandiacre NG10 223 B4
Sands Cl S14 43 E4
Sandstone Ave
Chesterfield S40 95 B1
Chesterfield S40 114 B8
Sandwell Cl NG10 236 A6
Sandwood Cl DE55 148 A3
Sandybank Cl SK13 9 E4
Sandybrook Cl DE6 173 C4
Sandybrook Country Pk
DE6 173 B5
Sandybrook Hall
DE6 173 B5
Sandy Cl S80 81 F5
Sandycliffe Cl NG19 136 F1
Sandyford La DE56 166 F4
Sandyhill Cl DE73 233 A2
Sandy La
Broadbottom SK13 16 A4
Caldwell DE12 261 A8
Chinley SK23 35 B3
Crich DE4 167 F8
Farley DE4 128 D1
Grangewood DE12 261 C1
Hartington upper Quarter
SK23 65 A3
Hollinsclough SK17 104 A1
Hollinsclough SK17 104 B2
Horsley DE21, DE7 192 A3
Matlock DE4 143 D8
Netherseal DE12 264 B6
Rainow SK17 64 A4
Whitwell S80 81 F5
Sandypits La DE65 229 C4
Sanforth St S41 96 A6
Sankey Dr DE11 256 C1
Santolina Dr DE21 205 F1
SAPPERTON 213 C1
Sapperton Cl DE23 231 D5
Sappertonfield La DE6,
DE65 213 D3
Sapperton La DE65 213 E1
Sapphire Dr DE5 180 B2
Saracens Court DE6 201 F7
Sarah Cl DE55 170 C7
Sark Rd S2 43 A7
Saundby Ave NG19 135 D1
Saundersfoot Way
DE21 206 C2
Savage La S17 55 D7
Save Penny La
DE56 191 A5
Saville Cl NG9 223 E8
Saville House Sch [2]
NG19 136 B3
Savoy The [2] SK17 85 B7
SAWLEY 236 A4
Sawley Inf and Nursery Sch NG10 236 A5
Sawley Jun Sch
Long Eaton NG10 236 A4
Long Eaton NG10 236 A5
Sawley Rd
Breaston DE72 235 E6
Draycott DE72 235 B7
Sawmand Cl NG10 236 C6
Sawmill Mws S41 96 B5
Sawmills Ind Pk
DE75 181 D3
Saw Pit Ind Est
DE55 148 C6
Sawpit La DE65 227 C2
Saw Pit La DE55 148 B5
Saxelby Cl DE55 170 D6
Saxelbye Ave DE1 267 C2
Saxon Ave S17 55 E6
Saxon Cl
[2] Ashbourne DE6 185 C8
Breedon on the Hill
DE73 252 F2
Burton upon Trent
DE15 254 F7
Saxon Close DE6 185 C7
Saxon Croft DE65 242 D3
Saxon Ct DE23 231 E5
Saxondale Ave DE3 217 C4
Saxon Gr DE65 242 A5
Saxon Rd S2 43 A6
Saxon St DE15 254 F7
Saxton Ave DE75 181 F2
Saxton Cl S41 115 C8
Scaddows La DE73 250 E3
Scalby Cl NG16 182 D2
Scaliot Cl SK22 33 B8
Scalpcliffe Rd DE15 248 A2
Scarborough Ave
DE7 208 E8
Scarborough Rise
DE21 205 D1
SCARCLIFFE 118 E6
Scarcliffe Cl DE24 232 E3
Scarcliffe Lanes
NG20 119 C7
Scarcliffe Prim Sch
S44 118 F6
Scarcliffe Terr
NG20 101 A2
Scargill CE (Aided) Prim Sch DE7 207 D7
Scargill Rd DE7 207 E8
Scargill Wlk NG16 182 F3
Scarlet Way NG20 119 D2
Scarsdale Ave
Derby, Allestree
DE22 204 D3
Derby, Littleover
DE23 218 C2
Scarsdale Cl S18 76 B8
Scarsdale Cres S43 96 D7
Scarsdale Cross [1]
S18 57 B1
Scarsdale Pl [8] SK17 85 B7
Scarsdale Rd
[2] Chesterfield S41 96 A8
[2] Dronfield S18 57 B1
Dronfield S18 76 B8
Duffield DE56 190 E3
Scarsdale St S44 117 E8
Scarthin DE4 155 A6
Schofield Ct DE4 110 F1
Scholar Cl [1] DE7 208 F6
School Ave S20 59 F7
School Board La
S40 95 E3
School Cl
Blackwell DE55 147 C1
Darley Dale DE4 127 C3
Fenny Bentley DE6 162 A1
Glossop SK13 9 E5
Moira DE11 256 C1
Newton DE55 148 B3
Sheffield S20 59 F7
Shirland DE55 146 D2
Stonebroom DE55 146 F4
School Croft DE55 170 D6
Schoolfleld Cl S44 99 C1
School House Hill
DE56 168 D1
School La
Arkwright Town S44 97 D3
Ashbourne DE6 173 B1
Baslow DE45 91 E5
Beeley DE4 111 B4
Brackenfield DE55 145 C2
Carsington DE4 164 E7
Castle Donington
DE74 247 A4
Chellaston DE73 233 A2
Compstall SK14 15 B5
Compstall SK6 15 B4
Crich DE4 157 A1
Cuckney NG20 101 F3
Dronfield S18 57 A1
Eckington S21 58 E3
Fawfieldhead SK17 121 A2
Great Hucklow SK17 70 B8
Hassop DE45 90 F5
Hassop DE45 91 A5
Hathersage S32 53 A8
Heage DE56 168 D2
Hope Valley S33 39 A3
Ingmanthorpe S18 94 D7
Mansfield Woodhouse
NG19 136 C3
Old Brampton S42 93 F3
Over Haddon DE45 109 B1
Ripley DE5 169 D1
Rolleston DE13 240 A3
Rowsley DE4 126 F8
Rowsley DE45 126 F8
Sheffield S8 43 C1
Sheffield, Greenhill S8 56 F7
South Normanton
DE55 160 B4
Stanton-by-Dale DE7,
NG10 222 F8
Stanton in Peak DE4 126 C5
Sudbury DE6 225 E4
Taddington SK17 87 F3
School Lane Cl S8 43 C1
School Meadow
DE6 197 E1
School Piece La
DE65 227 F7
School Rd
Buxton SK17 67 B5
Chesterfield S41 96 A7
Matlock DE4 143 D5
Uttoxeter ST14 210 A1
School Rise DE6 201 E8
School Sq DE7 207 E7
School St
Eckington S21 59 D3
Moira DE12 262 F2
Sheffield, Mosborough
S20 59 D7
Swadlincote DE11 256 B2
School View S42 132 A7
School Woods Cl
DE75 194 A6
School Yd The DE1 267 B4
Schooner Dr S41 76 E5
Scollins Court [1]
DE7 194 E2
Scotches The DE56 178 F5
Scotia Cl S2 43 F8
Scotia Dr S2 43 F8
Scotland St S80 81 F6
Scotswood Rd
NG19 136 B6
Scott Cl S42 115 E3
Scott Cres DE55 146 F3
Scott Dr
Belper DE56 179 E5
Marple SK6 23 B8
Somercotes DE55 170 D8
Scott St DE23 218 F1
Scotts The DE11 261 D8
Scotty Brook Cres
SK13 17 E8
Scout La
Hulland Ward DE56 188 A6
Hulland Ward DE6 187 F7
Scowerdons Cl S12 44 F5
Scowerdons Dr S12 44 F5
Scratta La S80 63 C2
Screetham La DE4 112 C1
SCROPTON 226 E1
Scropton Old Rd
DE65 239 C8
Scropton Rd DE65 239 B8
Scropton Wlk DE24 232 E3
Sea Breeze Terr
S13 44 D8
Seaburn Rd NG9 223 E2
Seagrave Ave S12 44 B4
Seagrave Cl DE21 220 B8
Seagrave Cres S12 44 B4
Seagrave Dr
Chesterfield S41 115 C7
Sheffield S12 44 B4
Seagrave Rd S12 44 B4
Seale St DE1 267 B5
Sealey Cl DE65 242 C5
Seals Rd DE12 262 E1
Seal View DE12 261 C6
Sealwood La DE12 261 F5
Seal Wood La DE12 261 E4
Seamer Rd NG16 195 F7
Seanor La S45 132 B4
Searl St DE1 218 F6
Searson Ave S44 99 A1
Searston Ave S42 132 D8
Seascale Cl [5]
DE21 205 D1
Seaton Cl DE3 217 C3
Seaton Ct [9] S41 95 F8
Sebastian Cl SK6 23 B7
Second Ave
Branston DE14 253 E8
Chellaston DE73 245 A8
Risley DE72 222 F5
Sedbergh Cres S41 95 D8
Sedgebrook Cl [2]
DE21 205 F2
Sedgebrook St
NG19 136 E3
Sedgefield Gn DE3 217 C1
Sedgefield Rd
Branston DE14 253 F7
Burton upon Trent
DE14 254 A8
Sedgemoor Cl S40 95 B4
Sedgemoor Rd
NG10 236 E5
Sedgemoor Way
DE23 231 A5
Sedgwick Cl NG16 160 D2
Sedgwick St
Jacksdale NG16 171 B3
Langley Mill NG16 182 B3
Seely La S42 115 C2
Sefton Ave NG9 223 E8
Sefton Cl DE15 248 B1
Sefton Rd DE21 219 F6
Sefton St SK13 17 C8
Sefton Way DE56 190 D4
Selborne St DE24 219 D2
Selby Cl
Beeston NG9 223 E3
Chesterfield S40 114 C8
Selby Dr DE3 217 B1
Selhurst Rd S41 95 F5
Selig Par S12 44 C2
Selina Cl DE74 247 A4
Selina St DE73 252 A7
Selkirk St DE21 219 E7
Sellers Yard [3] DE6 173 C1
Selly Oak Gr S8 57 C6
Selly Oak Rd S8 57 C6
Selmer Ct S43 96 D8
SELSTON 171 E7

Selston CE Inf Sch NG16 171 E6
SELSTON GREEN 171 D7
Selston High Sch NG16 171 F7
Selston L Ctr NG16 171 F7
Selston Rd NG16 171 B5
Selworthy Cl DE21 206 A2
Selwyn St
Bolsover S44 118 C8
Derby DE22 218 C6
Senners La SK17 87 A2
Sepycoe La DE6 214 D7
Serina Ave DE23 231 D8
Serlby Dr S26 61 F5
Serlby La S26 61 F6
Serpentine Wlk S8 57 B8
Service Rd DE24 232 E5
Setcup La S21 59 D2
Sett Cl SK22 33 B8
Settlement Dr S43 80 F7
Settlement The DE72 221 C5
Setts Way S42 115 B4
Sevenlands Dr DE24 233 C4
Sevenoaks Ave DE22 217 F6
Seven Oaks Rd DE7 209 A1
Severals NG9 223 F7
Severnale Cl DE22 205 B5
Severn Cl
Burton upon Trent DE13 240 C1
Ripley DE5 181 A8
Severn Cres S42 132 A5
Severn Dr DE65 240 D8
Severn Sq DE55 159 A4
Severn St DE24 232 F8
Sewell Rd S20 59 F6
Sexton St SK13 9 F7
Seymour Cl
Derby DE22 218 C5
Ilkeston DE7 194 F5
Seymour La S43 79 C1
Seymour Link Rd
Woodthorpe S43 79 C2
Woodthorpe S43 98 C7
Seymour Rd NG16 182 F1
SHACKLECROSS 221 D1
Shacklecross Cl DE72 221 C1
Shady Gr DE65 228 C2
Shaef Cl DE65 228 E2
Shaftesbury Ave
Chesterfield S40 95 D3
Long Eaton NG10 236 B4
Mansfield NG19 135 E2
Sandiacre NG10 223 A5
Shaftesbury Cres DE23 219 B1
Shaftesbury Sp Ctr DE23 219 B1
Shaftesbury St DE23 219 B2
Shaftesbury Street South DE23 219 B1
Shafton Cl S45 131 E4
Shafton Wlk S45 131 E4
Shakespeare Ave
Creswell S80 81 D1
Mansfield Woodhouse NG19 136 B4
Shirland DE55 146 C4
Shakespeare Cl
Clay Cross S42 131 B6
Repton DE65 242 D1
Swadlincote DE11 256 C6
Shakespeare Cres S18 76 C7
Shakespeare Ct 4 DE6 173 B2
Shakespeare Dr DE55 159 B4
Shakespeare Mdws DE65 242 D1
Shakespeare Rd NG16 195 C5
Shakespeare St
Derby DE24 232 A5
Grassmoor S42 115 E3
Holmewood S42 116 D1
Long Eaton NG10 223 D1
Shaldon Dr DE23 218 D1
Shalfleet Dr DE24 233 C5
Shallcross Ave SK23 45 F4
Shallcross Cres
High Peak SK23 45 E4
Horwich End SK23 45 E4
Shallcross Hall Barns SK23 45 E4
Shallcross Mill Rd SK23 45 E5
Shallcross Rd SK23 45 E4
Shambles The S40 266 B3
Shamrock Pl S43 79 C4
Shamrock St DE23 218 E1
Shandwick Ct 10 DE24 231 D3
Shanklin Dr NG9 223 D7
Shanklin Ho DE24 233 C7
Shannon Cl DE23 231 D6
Shannon Ho DE24 232 E5
Shannon Sq DE21 220 B4
Shap Cl 7 S40 95 C5
Sharcote Dr DE15 255 C4
SHARDLOW 234 E2
Shardlow Bsns Pk DE72 234 D1
Shardlow Hall Workshops & Offices DE72 234 F2
Shardlow Her Ctr* DE72 235 A1
Shardlow Prim Sch DE72 234 E2
Shardlow Rd
Aston-on-Trent DE72 246 B7
Derby DE24, DE74 233 C6
Sharley Park Com Prim Sch S45 131 E3
Sharley Pk L Ctr S45 131 D4
Sharman Cl S18 58 A1
Sharman Wlk S18 58 A1
Sharp Cl
Ilkeston DE7 208 C6
Long Eaton NG10 236 C6
Sharpe Ave S8 56 E8
Sharpes Ind Est DE11 256 B4
Sharpes La DE55 170 C6
Sharpe's Pottery Mus* DE11 256 B4
Sharpswood Manor DE11 256 E4
Sharrard Cl S12 44 B5
Sharrard Dr S12 44 B5
Sharrard Gr S12 44 B6
Sharrard Rd S12 44 B5
SHATTON 39 F1
Shatton La
Bamford S33 40 A1
Thornhill S32, S33 51 E7
Shawcroft 8 DE6 173 C2
Shawcroft Ave DE55 170 C5
Shawcross Cl DE55 170 D6
Shawfield Rd SK13 9 F3
Shaw La
Belper DE56 191 B7
Glossop SK13 9 F3
Holloway DE4 156 C8
Marston Montgomery DE6 198 A1
Shaws Gn DE22 218 D6
Shaws Hill
Crich DE4 156 D1
Wirksworth DE4 166 D8
Shaw's Row S40 95 D2
Shaw St
Chesterfield S41 96 A8
Derby DE22 218 E6
Dronfield S18 57 C4
Glossop SK13 17 C8
Holmewood S42 116 D1
Mottram in Longdendale SK14 9 A4
Somercotes DE55 170 C6
Shaw Street E DE7 209 A6
Shaw Street W DE7 209 A6
Shaw's Yd DE56 191 F8
Shaw The SK13 10 A3
Shaw Wood Cl DE55 157 F3
Shawwood Dr DE55 158 A1
Shaw Wood View DE55 157 F3
Sheaf Bank S2 43 A7
Sheaf Bank Bsns Pk S2 43 A7
Sheardhall Ave SK12 32 E5
Sheards Cl S18 56 F1
Sheards Dr S18 56 E1
Sheards Way S18 56 F1
Shearsby Dr NG19 136 F2
Shearwater Cl DE23 231 D7
SHEEN 137 A7
Sheen La
Sheen SK17 121 F2
Sheen SK17 122 A2
SHEEPBRIDGE 76 E2
Sheepbridge Bsns Ctr S41 76 E2
Sheepbridge La S41 76 E2
Sheepcote Hill S21 60 D6
Sheepcote Rd S21 60 C6
Sheephill Rd S17 42 F1
Sheep La DE55 158 C8
Sheeplea La S45 129 E8
Sheepwash La S45 145 B8
Sheerness Cl NG16 195 B7
Sheets Stores Ind Est NG10 236 D5
SHEFFIELD 44 D6
Sheffield Coll The S14 43 B8
Sheffield Inclusion Ctr S2 43 E7
Sheffield Pl DE1 267 D2
Sheffield Rd
Baslow DE45 92 B7
Chapel-en-le-Frith SK23 47 E7
Chesterfield S41 96 A6
Chesterfield S41 96 A7
Creswell S80, S43 81 D3
Dronfield S18 56 F3
Eckington S20, S21 59 E5
Glossop SK13 10 F1
Glossop SK13 11 A1
Hathersage S32 53 A7
Killamarsh S21 60 D7
Nell Croft S11 54 A6
Sheffield Rd *continued*
Owler Bar S17 74 A8
Ramsley Moor S17 73 E4
Renishaw S21, S43 79 D8
Sheepbridge S41 76 E3
Sheffield S20 44 F2
Unstone S18, S41 76 E4
Sheffield Springs Acad S2 43 F6
Sheffield Transport Sports Club S8 56 F7
Shelden Cl 4 SK13 9 D1
Shelden Fold 3 SK13 9 D1
Shelden Mews SK13 9 D1
Shelden Pl 5 SK13 9 D1
SHELDON 108 A6
Sheldon Cl NG10 223 B3
Sheldon Ct DE24 232 E3
Sheldon Gdns DE4 156 F1
Sheldon La
Bakewell DE45 108 E5
Bakewell DE45 109 A5
Sheldon Moor SK17 107 D6
Sheldon Rd
Buxton SK17 85 D7
Chesterfield S40 95 B5
Heanor DE75 181 C5
Shelford Cl DE3 217 C3
Shelford La DE4 156 B7
Shelley Ave NG19 136 B4
Shelley Dr
Derby DE24 232 A5
Dronfield S18 76 C7
Shelley Gr DE55 146 F3
Shelley Rd DE11 256 C5
Shelley St S42 116 D1
Shelmory Cl DE24 232 E5
Shelton Cl NG19 135 E1
Shelton Dr DE24 232 F3
Shelton Gate Cl DE24 232 E5
Shelton Jun Sch DE24 232 D4
SHELTON LOCK 232 F3
Shenington Way DE21 206 B2
Shepherds Cl S21 60 C4
Shepherd's La DE73 251 D6
Shepherd St DE23 218 C1
Shepley St
Charlesworth SK13 11 A2
Chesterfield S40 95 D2
Glossop SK13 10 F2
Hadfield SK13 9 E3
Shepley's Yd S40 266 B3
Shepton Cl DE7 194 D3
Sheraton Way SK17 66 B1
Sherbourne Ave S41 95 E8
Sherbourne Dr
Belper DE56 179 D5
Burton upon Trent DE14 254 A7
Hilton DE65 228 C1
Sherbrooke Rd SK12 32 D6
Sherbrook Gr SK17 85 C5
Sherholt Rd DE13 240 D4
Sheridan Ct
Stapleford NG9 209 F1
4 Uttoxeter ST14 210 A1
Sheridan St DE24 231 F5
Sheriff Dr DE4 143 B6
Sherman Cl DE65 228 E2
Sheroside Cl DE22 204 D4
Sherriff's Lea NG9 223 E2
Sherroside Cl DE22 204 D4
Sherston Cl DE21 206 B2
Sherwin Rd
Stapleford NG9 209 F1
4 Stapleford NG9 223 F8
Sherwin St DE22 218 E8
Sherwood Ave
Borrowash DE72 221 D2
Creswell S80 81 D1
Derby, Chaddesden DE21 219 F7
Derby, Littleover DE23 231 D5
Hope S33 39 A3
Pinxton NG16 160 D3
Shirebrook NG20 119 E4
Sherwood Chase S17 55 E5
Sherwood Copse SK17 69 C4
Sherwood Ct
Bolsover S44 117 F8
Mansfield NG19 136 B2
Sherwood Dr
Crich DE4 157 A1
Shirebrook NG20 119 E3
Sherwood Fold SK13 16 D7
Sherwood Foresters Regiment Meml* DE4 156 E3
Sherwood Hall L Ctr DE4 143 C5
Sherwood Pl 2 S18 56 D1
Sherwood Rd
Buxton SK17 85 C5
Dronfield S18 56 D1
Killamarsh S21 60 E7
Matlock DE4 143 C4
Tideswell SK17 69 C3
Sherwood Rise
Eastwood NG16 182 F1
Mansfield Woodhouse NG19 136 A1
Sherwood St
Bolsover S44 117 F8
Sherwood St *continued*
Chesterfield S40 266 C1
Derby DE22 218 E3
Mansfield Woodhouse NG19 136 B2
Newton DE55 148 B4
Shirland DE55 146 C5
Somercotes DE55 170 C8
Sutton in Ashfield NG17 148 F3
Shetland Cl
Derby DE21 219 C7
Mansfield NG19 136 F1
Shirebrook NG20 119 D2
Shetland Rd
Dronfield S18 76 B8
Tibshelf DE55 147 F5
Shibden Cl S8 43 B2
Shields Cres
Castle Donington DE74 246 F3
Castle Donington DE74 247 A3
Shields La DE6 197 D5
Shieling The DE65 227 C2
Shilling Way NG10 236 A7
Shiloh Cl DE11 256 E3
Shiloh Rd SK22, SK6 24 B6
Shilo Way NG16 195 B4
Shiners Way DE55 159 F6
Shiner Way DE55 160 A6
Shinwell Ave S43 97 B7
SHIPLEY 194 B6
Shipley Cl DE14 254 B8
SHIPLEY COMMON 194 C4
Shipley Common La DE7 194 D4
Shipley Country Park* DE7 194 A4
Shipley Country Park Visitor Ctr* DE75 193 E7
Shipley Ct DE7 194 D1
Shipley Gate DE7 194 D7
Shipley La DE7, DE75 193 F5
Shipley Pk Gdns DE75 193 E7
Shipley View DE7 192 F6
Shipley Wlk DE24 232 E3
Shipman Ct S20 59 D7
Shippen Rural Bsns Ctr The S18 75 E2
Shippon La S32 72 B2
SHIREBROOK 119 F3
Shirebrook Acad NG20 119 D5
Shirebrook Bsns Pk NG20 120 A3
Shirebrook Cl NE7 194 F6
Shirebrook Ct S2 43 A6
Shirebrook Dr SK13 17 E8
Shirebrook Rd S8 43 A6
Shirebrook Sta NG20 120 A4
Shiregate Gdns DE23 231 A5
Shire Hill Hospl SK13 10 E3
Shire La
Holmewood S44 116 F4
Sutton Scarsdale S44 117 A6
SHIREOAKS 63 E6
Shireoaks DE56 178 D5
Shireoaks Cl DE23 231 C7
Shireoaks Comm S81 63 F7
Shireoaks Rd
Dronfield S18 57 C2
Shireoaks S81 63 F6
Shireoaks Row S81 63 E7
Shireoaks Sta S81 63 E7
Shires The NG19 136 F1
Shire Way SK13 10 E3
SHIRLAND 146 D2
Shirland Cl DE7 194 F5
Shirland Ct DE24 232 E3
Shirland Prim Sch DE55 146 D2
Shirland St S41 266 B4
SHIRLEY 200 E8
Shirley Cl
Castle Donington DE74 247 A4
Chesterfield S40 95 B5
Hope S33 39 A4
Shirley Common DE6 186 D3
Shirley Cres DE72 235 D8
Shirley La
Hollington DE6 200 F6
Rodsley DE6 200 B6
Shirley Pk DE72 246 B7
Shirley Rd
Derby DE21 205 F1
Ripley DE5 169 D1
Swanwick DE55 169 F7
Shirley St NG10 236 A4
Shop La DE56 168 C2
Shop Stones DE72 221 C5
Shoreham St S2 43 A8
Short Ave DE22 204 F5
Shortbrook Bank 10 S20 59 E8
Shortbrook Cl S20 59 F8
Shortbrook Com Prim Sch S20 59 E8
Shortbrook Croft 6 S20 59 F8
Shortbrook Dr S20 59 E8
Shortbrook Rd S20 59 E8
Shortbrook Way 13 S20 59 E8
Shortbrook Wlk 12 S20 59 E8
Short Cl S42 113 D7
Shortheath DE12 262 C3
SHORT HEATH 262 D2
Shortheath Rd DE12 262 E3
Short Hill DE73 252 E6
Short La DE74 246 F4
Short Lands DE56 179 A4
Shortlands The DE4 143 B3
Short Row 4 DE56 178 F4
Shorts La S17 55 B6
Short St
Belper DE56 179 B4
Burton upon Trent DE15 254 E7
Shorwell Gdns DE24 233 C5
SHOTTLE 177 E8
SHOTTLEGATE 177 F3
Shottle Wlk DE24 232 E3
Shotwood Cl DE13 240 A4
Shotwoodhill La DE13 240 A5
Shrewsbury Cl DE21 206 C2
Shrewsbury Mws SK13 10 C1
Shrewsbury Rd DE13 240 F2
Shrewsbury St SK13 10 C1
Shrewsbury Terr S17 55 D4
Shropshire Ave
Derby DE21 219 E7
Westwood NG16 171 C4
Shropshire Dr SK13 17 F8
Shrovetide Wlk DE6 173 C2
Shrubbery The DE11 257 A2
Shuckstone La DE4 156 F6
Shudehill Cl SK22 25 D3
Shunters Drift S43 80 B6
SHUTTLEWOOD 98 F7
Shuttlewood Rd S44 99 A4
Shuttleworth Cl 3 DE74 246 E3
Shutts La
Bakewell DE45 109 C3
Bakewell DE45 109 C4
Sicklebrook La S18 57 F4
Sickleholme S33 40 B1
Sidcup Ct S43 78 B4
Siddalls St DE15 248 B3
Siddals La DE22 204 F4
Siddals Rd DE1 267 C2
Siddons St DE24 233 A7
Side End La SK23 45 A2
Sides La DE6 184 B5
Sidings Dr DE16 254 E5
Sidings The
Chinley SK23 34 E2
Derby DE21 220 A4
Kimberley NG16 195 F6
Mansfield NG19 136 A3
Whaley Bridge SK23 45 E8
Sidings Way DE55 147 C1
Siding The S43 80 E4
Sidlaw Cl 6 S40 95 C5
Sidmouth Cl DE24 233 C7
Sidmouth Ct 17 S41 95 F8
Sidney Robinson Bsns Pk DE24 219 D1
Sidney St
Derby DE1 219 B3
Kimberley NG16 195 F6
Long Eaton NG10 236 D6
Siggate S33 38 D1
Signal Way NG19 136 B2
Silken Holme DE55 160 B4
Silk Hill SK23 45 F8
Silk Mill La DE1 267 B4
Silk St SK13 10 E1
Silkstone Cl
Sheffield S12 44 E4
Swadlincote DE11 256 B1
Silkstone Cres S12 44 E4
Silkstone Dr S12 44 D4
Silkstone Pl S12 44 E4
Silkstone Rd S12 44 E4
Sills Rd DE74 247 A6
Silver Birch Cres DE55 159 C8
Silver Birch Way S42 115 B4
Silverburn Dr DE21 206 A2
Silverdale NG9 223 E5
Silverdale Ave NG19 136 B4
Silverdale Cl
Chellaston DE73 233 A2
Chesterfield S41 76 E1
Silverhill Cl DE13 240 C1
Silverhill La NG17 148 F8
Silverhill Prim Sch DE3 217 C3
Silverhill Rd DE21 220 E3
Silver Hill Rd DE23 219 A2
Silverhill Wood Cl DE3 217 D6
Silver La
Elvaston DE72 234 A5
Marchington ST14 224 F1
Silverlands SK17 85 C7
Silverlands Cl SK17 85 C7
Silverlands Pk SK17 85 C7
Silver Mill Rd S2 43 A8
Silver Springs SK14 15 A8
Silverton Dr DE24 231 C2
Silver Well Dr S43 97 D8
Silvey Gr DE21 220 D4
Simcoe Leys DE73 233 A2
Simcrest Ave S21 60 D5
Simkin Walk NG10 236 B7
SIMMONDLEY 17 A7
Simmondley La SK13 17 A8
Simmondley New Rd SK13 17 A7
Simmondley Prim Sch SK13 17 A8
Simmondley Village SK13 16 A7
Simons Cl SK13 17 A7
Simons Wlk SK13 17 A8
Sims Ave DE1 218 E5
Sims Croft S41 77 C3
Sinclair Cl
Derby DE24 231 E4
Heanor DE75 193 D8
SINFIN 231 F4
Sinfin Ave DE24 232 D3
Sinfin Central Bsns Pk DE23, DE24 231 F5
Sinfin District Ctr DE24 231 E3
Sinfin Fields Cres DE24 232 D5
Sinfin La
Barrow upon Trent DE73 244 A6
Derby DE23, DE24 231 F4
Sinfin Moor La
Chellaston DE73 232 E2
Derby DE24 231 F3
Sinfin Prim Sch DE24 231 F5
Sir Francis Ley Ind Pk DE23 219 C1
Sir Frank Whittle Rd DE21 219 C7
Sir Henry's La DE73 252 A4
Sir Herbert Wragg Way DE11 256 C3
Sir John Hurt Pl DE11 256 E3
Sirjohn Warren Way DE75 181 D3
Sir Joseph's La DE4 127 B4
Sir William Hill Rd
Eyam S32 71 C8
Great Hucklow SK17 70 F8
Grindleford S32 53 B1
Sir William Terr S32 72 C8
Siskin Cl DE3 230 B7
Siskin Dr DE24 231 D4
Sisley Ave NG9 223 E6
Sister's La DE72 221 C5
Sitch La
Hayfield SK22 24 F3
Kirk Ireton DE4 165 A4
Wensley DE4 142 D7
Sitwell 14 S20 59 E8
Sitwell Ave S40 266 A1
Sitwell Cl
Derby DE21 220 D4
Smalley DE7 192 F5
Sitwell Dr DE56 192 A8
Sitwell Grange La S45 147 D8
Sitwell Mus* S21 59 F2
Sitwell St
Derby DE1 267 B2
Derby, Spondon DE21 220 E4
Eckington S21 59 C3
Sitwell Villas DE55 146 E5
Skeavington's La DE7 194 E5
Skeldale Dr S40 115 B8
Skellow Cl 2 S2 44 A7
Skelton Cl DE24 233 D4
Skelton Rd S8 43 A5
Skelwith Cl S41 95 D8
Skiddaw Cl 2 S40 95 D6
Skiddaw Dr DE3 217 E1
Skimmer St S42 132 C8
Skinner St S80 81 D2
Skinners Way
Swadlincote DE11 256 D5
Swadlincote DE11 256 E5
Skipness Cl DE73 232 E2
Skipper Dr 7 S41 115 F2
Skipsea Rd S13 44 B7
Skipton Cl DE7 194 D3
Skipton Gn DE21 205 C1
Skye Gdns DE55 147 F5
Skylark Rise 3 NG9 209 E2
Skylark Way DE24 231 D4
Slackey La DE12 262 C4
SLACKHALL 47 F8
Slack La
Ashover S45 129 C2
Brailsford DE6 187 D1
Chesterfield S40 95 B3
Derby, Allestree DE22 204 F2
Derby, New Zealand DE22 218 D5
Hartshorne DE11 257 B6
Heath S44 116 F2
Mayfield DE6 184 C8

Slack La continued
Nether Heage DE56 . . 168 C3
Ripley DE5 . . . . 169 D1
Shipley DE75 . . . . 193 E8
Somercotes DE55. . . . . 170 B5
Wessington DE55 . . . . 157 D8
Slack Rd
Ilkeston DE7 . . . . 194 A3
Mapperley DE7 . . . . . . 193 F3
Slacks Cotts SK17 . . . . 84 E4
Slacks La S42 . . . . 25 C5
Slack's La S45 . . . . 132 C2
Slade Cl
Etwall DE65 . . . . 229 C4
Ilkeston DE7 . . . . 209 A5
South Normanton
DE55 . . . . .160 B4
Slade Farm DE73 . . . 251 A4
Slade Fields ST14 . . . 210 B1
Slade Hollow La
DE6 . . . . 201 A3
Slade La
Weston Underwood
DE6 . . . . .202 E7
Wilson DE73 . . . . .252 F6
Slade Lands Dr
DE73 . . . . 233 A2
Slag La S43 . . . . .77 D6
Slaidburn Cl DE3 . . . 217 E1
SLALEY 154 C7
Slaley La DE4 . . . . 154 C8
Slancote La SK17 . . . . .69 A2
Slaney Cl DE24 . . . . . 232 E2
Slant Cl SK13 . . . . .17 E8
Slant La
Mansfield Woodhouse
NG19 . . . . .136 B4
Shirebrook NG20 . . . . 119 D4
Slatelands Ave SK13 . . 17 B8
Slatelands Rd SK13 . . . 17 B8
Slate Pit Dale S42 . . . 113 E4
Slatepit La S18, S42 . .93 C8
Slater Ave DE24 . . . . . 218 E6
Slater Cres DE4 . . . . . 165 F7
Slater St S45 . . . . 131 D3
Slater Way DE7 . . . . . 208 E5
Slate St S2 . . . . .43 B8
Slayley Hall La S80 . . .80 C4
Slayley View S43 . . . . 80 C5
Slayley View Rd S43 . .80 B6
Slaypit La S80 . . . . . . .62 D6
SLEAT MOOR 170 B8
Sledgegate La DE4 . . 156 B7
Sledmere Cl DE24 . . . 233 C7
Sleepy La DE73 . . . . . 245 C1
Sleetmoor La DE55 . . 170 B8
Sleights La NG16 . . . . 160 C2
Slindon Croft DE24 . . 233 D6
Slipperlow La SK17 . . .87 F2
Sloade La
Eckington S12 . . . . . . .58 D7
Ridgeway S12 . . . . . . .58 D6
Sloane Rd DE22 . . . . . 218 A6
SMALLDALE
Bradwell 50 F8
Peak Dale 67 D7
Smalldale Cotts
SK17 . . . . .67 D7
Smalldale Head Rd
S33 . . . . .50 F7
Smalldale Rd
Buxton SK17 . . . . .67 C4
Sheffield S12 . . . . .44 D4
SMALLEY 192 F5
**SMALLEY
COMMON** 193 A2
Smalley Dr DE21 . . . . 206 B3
Smalley Farm Cl 5
DE75 . . . . 193 C8
SMALLEY GREEN . . . 192 F3
Smalley Manor Dr 1
DE7 . . . . 193 C8
Smalley Manor Drive
DE7 . . . . 193 C8
Smalley Mill Rd DE21,
DE7 . . . . 192 B4
Small Gate NG19 . . . 136 E6
Small Knowle End
Buxton SK17 . . . . .67 C4
Peak Dale SK17 . . . . . .67 D5
Small Meer Cl DE73 . .232 F1
Small Thorn Pl
DE11 . . . . 256 E1
Smeath Rd NG16 . . . . 171 F2
Smeckley Wood Cl
S41 . . . . .76 C3
Smedley Ave
Ilkeston DE7 . . . . 209 A7
Somercotes DE55 . . . . 159 D1
Smedley Ct DE65 . . . . 241 B5
Smedley Pl SK13 . . . . .10 E2
Smedley's Ave
NG10 . . . . 223 A5
Smedley St DE4 . . . . . 143 B6
Smedley Street E
DE4 . . . . 143 C5
Smedley Street W
DE4 . . . . 143 B7
Smeeton St DE75 . . . . 182 B1
Smelter Wood Ave
S13 . . . . .44 E7
Smelter Wood Cl
S13 . . . . .44 E7
Smelter Wood Cres
S13 . . . . .44 E7

Smelter Wood Ct
S13 . . . . .44 E7
Smelter Wood Dr
S13 . . . . .44 E7
Smelter Wood La
S13 . . . . .44 E7
Smelter Wood Pl
S13 . . . . .44 F7
Smelter Wood Rd
S13 . . . . .44 E7
Smelter Wood Rise
S13 . . . . .44 F7
Smelter Wood Way
S13 . . . . .44 E7
Smeltinghouse La
S18 . . . . .75 E3
SMISBY 257 F3
Smisby Rd LE65 . . . . . 258 A1
Smisby Way DE24. . . 232 E3
Smith Ave
Codnor DE5 . . . . 170 B1
King's Newton DE73 . . 245 B1
Staveley S43 . . . . .97 C7
Smithbrook Cl SK23 . .47 C6
Smith Cres S41 . . . . . . .96 D1
Smith Dr NG16 . . . . . 182 A3
SMITHFIELD 47 C6
Smithfield Ave
Chesterfield S41 . . . . . 115 C7
Trowell NG9 . . . . 209 D4
Smithfield Rd S12 . . . .44 A3
Smith-Hall La DE6 . . 176 A1
Smith Hall La DE6 . . 188 A7
Smith La S42 . . . . 115 C2
Smith Rd DE4 . . . . . . 143 B6
Smiths La
Bakewell DE45 . . . . . . 109 E6
Shirland DE55 . . . . 146 C7
Smithson Ave S44 . . . . .99 B1
Smiths Yard 9 DE6. . 173 B1
Smithurst Rd NG16 . . 195 B7
Smithy Ave S45 . . . . . 131 C4
Smithy Brook Fold
SK23 . . . . .47 B7
Smithy Brook Rd
S21 . . . . .79 C8
Smithy Cl
Glossop SK13 . . . . .10 D1
Parwich DE6 . . . . 151 D1
Smithy Croft S18 . . . . .56 D2
Smithy Fold SK13 . . . . .10 D1
SMITHY-HILL 51 A7
Smithy Hill S33 . . . . . .51 A7
Smithy House DE45 . . .91 C2
Smithy Knoll Rd S32 . .72 C2
Smithy La
Clifton Campville
B79 . . . . .263 E2
Marple SK6 . . . . .15 F1
Marple Bridge, SK6 . . .24 A8
Parwich DE6 . . . . 151 D2
Taddington SK17 . . . . . .88 A3
Smithy Mdws S32 . . . .53 A8
SMITHY MOOR 146 B7
Smithy Pl S42 . . . . 115 F2
Smuse La DE4 . . . . . . 143 E4
Snake La DE56 . . . . . . 190 E4
Snake Pass SK13 . . . . . 11 B1
Snake Rd
Bamford S33 . . . . .29 D6
Derwent S33 . . . . .30 B2
High Peak S33 . . . . . . .28 D8
**Snake Woodland Forest
Walk**★ S33 . . . . .19 F3
SNAPE HILL 57 A2
Snape Hill S18 . . . . . . .57 A2
Snapehill Cl S18 . . . . . .57 A3
Snape Hill Cl S18 . . . . .57 A3
Snape Hill Cres S18 . . .57 A2
Snape Hill Dr S18 . . . . .57 B3
Snape Hill Gdns S18 . . .57 B3
Snape Hill La S18 . . . . .57 A2
Snapes La DE6 . . . . . 184 B1
Snelsmoor La
Chellaston DE73 . . . . . .233 B2
Derby DE24 . . . . 233 D4
Derby DE72 . . . . 233 D3
SNELSTON 184 C3
Snelston Cl S18 . . . . . . .56 D1
Snelston Cres DE23. 218 D2
Snelston La DE6 . . . . 184 E6
Snipe Cl S42 . . . . 113 D7
Snipesmoor La DE6. . 185 F7
SNITTERTON 142 D5
Snitterton Rd
Matlock DE4 . . . . 143 A5
Snitterton DE4 . . . . . . 142 D6
Snowberry Ave
DE56 . . . . 179 B3
Snowberry Close
S41 . . . . 115 E7
Snowdon La
Apperknowle S21 . . . . . .58 B2
Unstone S18 . . . . .57 F3
Snowdrop Dr NG19 . .136 F4
Snowdrop Valley
DE4 . . . . 168 A8
Snowfield View
DE4 . . . . 165 E6
Soaper La S18 . . . . . . .57 A2
Soarbank Cl NG16 . . . 195 E7
Soar Cl DE56 . . . . 179 C6
Soar Way DE65 . . . . . 228 D1
Society Pl DE23 . . . . . . 219 A2
Soft Water La S33 . . . .51 A7
Soldier's Croft
DE45 . . . . 107 C2
Solent Rd DE11 . . . . . 255 E1

Solney Cl
Swadlincote DE11 . . . . .255 F3
1 Swadlincote DE11 . 256 A3
Soloman Pk NG16 . . . 195 B2
Soloman Rd DE7 . . . . 195 B2
Solomans Ct SK17 . . . .85 D2
Solomons View SK17 .85 C7
Solway Cl DE21 . . . . . 206 A2
Solway Rise S18 . . . . . .56 D2
Somerby Way 3
DE21 . . . . .205 F2
SOMERCOTES 170 C7
Somercotes Hill
DE55 . . . . 170 C8
Somercotes Inf Sch 1
DE55 . . . . 170 C8
Somercotes Rd S12. . .44 D5
Somerlea Park Jun Sch
DE55 . . . . 170 C8
Somerleyton Dr
DE7 . . . . 209 A4
Somersal Cl DE24 . . . 232 E3
**SOMERSAL
HERBERT** 211 E3
Somersal La
Marston Montgomery
DE6 . . . . .211 F6
Somersal Herbert
DE6 . . . . 212 A1
Sudbury DE6 . . . . 225 C7
Somersall Cl S40 . . . . . .95 A1
Somersall Halldr S40 .95 A1
Somersall La S40 . . . . . .95 A1
Somersall Park Rd
S40 . . . . .95 A1
Somersall Willows
S40 . . . . .95 A1
Somersby Ave S40 . . . 114 B8
Somerset Cl
Buxton SK17 . . . . .85 C4
Derby DE22 . . . . .218 B4
Long Eaton NG10 . . . . 237 A8
Somerset Dr S43 . . . . . .97 A8
Somerset Rd DE15 . . . 254 D6
Somerset St DE21 . . . 219 D7
Somerton Cl 8
DE23 . . . . .230 F5
Somme Rd DE22 . . . . 204 B3
Songbird Cl DE22 . . . .204 F1
SOOKHOLME 120 D2
Sookholme Cl NG20 .119 F3
Sookholme La
NG20 . . . . 120 E3
Sorchestun La 11
DE73 . . . . .244 F8
Soresby St S40 . . . . . . 266 B3
Sorrel Dr DE11 . . . . . . 256 E4
Sough La
Calver S32 . . . . .72 B2
Taddington SK17 . . . . . .87 D2
Wirksworth DE4 . . . . . 154 F2
Wirksworth, Steeple Grange
DE4 . . . . 155 B2
Soughley La S10. . . . . .42 C8
Sough Rd DE55 . . . . . 160 B7
Sough Wood Cl
DE75 . . . . 181 C2
Southall St 9 S8 . . . . .43 A6
Southard's La S80 . . . .62 E5
South Ave
Buxton SK17 . . . . .85 B7
Chellaston DE73 . . . . . .232 F3
Derby DE23 . . . . .218 D1
Derby, Darley Abbey
DE22 . . . . .205 A2
Derby, Spondon DE21 .220 E4
Shirebrook NG20 . . . . 119 D3
Southbourne Ct S17 . .55 D6
South Brae Cl DE73. . 231 D7
South Broadway St
DE14 . . . . 254 C8
Southbrook Cl SK13 . . .9 E4
South Church St
DE45 . . . . 109 D5
South Cl
Glossop SK13 . . . . .9 D5
Unstone Green S18 . . . .76 E6
Southcote Dr S18. . . . .56 D1
South Cres
Bolsover S44 . . . . .99 B1
Duckmanton S44 . . . . . .98 A5
Killamarsh S21 . . . . . . .60 E7
Southcroft
Alfreton DE55 . . . . 159 A3
1 Buxton SK17 . . . . . . .85 A7
Derby DE23 . . . . 231 D4
South Ct S17 . . . . .55 E7
**South Darley CE Prim
Sch** DE4 . . . . .142 B7
Southdown Ave S40 . .95 C5
Southdown Cl DE24. 231 C2
Southdown Close
S44 . . . . 117 D1
South Dr
Chellaston DE73 . . . . . .232 F3
Derby, Cherrytree Hill
DE21 . . . . 220 A5
Derby, Littleover DE3 .218 F7
Swadlincote DE11 . . . . .255 F5
**South East Derbyshire
Coll** DE75 . . . . .181 F1
Southend S42 . . . . 115 F2
South End DE4 . . . . . . 155 A4
South Farm Ave S41. 115 D6
Southfield Cl S80. . . . . .81 C5
Southfield Dr
Dronfield S18 . . . . .76 C8

Southfield Dr continued
South Normanton
DE55. . . . . 160 C5
Southfield Ind Site
S80 . . . . .82 A4
Southfield La S80 . . . . .82 A4
Southfield Mount
S18 . . . . .76 C8
Southfields
Clowne S43 . . . . .80 F3
Long Eaton NG10 . . . . .236 F2
Southfields Ave
NG16 . . . . 160 D4
Southgate S21 . . . . . . .59 E3
Southgate Bglws
S80 . . . . .81 C7
Southgate Cl DE3. . . . 217 C3
Southgate Cres S43 . .80 F5
Southgate Ct S21. . . . .59 E3
Southgate Dr DE15 . . 248 B2
Southgate Innovation Ctr
DE23 . . . . .267 B1
Southgate Ret Pk
DE23 . . . . .267 B1
Southgate Way S43. . .78 B4
South Head Dr SK23 . .47 B7
South Hill
Ashover DE55 . . . . . . .145 F7
Rolleston DE13 . . . . . . 240 D4
Stretton DE55 . . . . . . .146 A7
South Hill La DE55 . . . 145 F6
South Lodge Ct S40 . . .95 B3
South Lodge Mws
DE11 . . . . 256 E5
South Marlow St
SK13 . . . . .10 A4
Southmead Way
DE3 . . . . 218 A3
South Mews 10 SK17. .85 B7
Southmoor Cl S43 . . . .96 F4
**SOUTH
NORMANTON** 160 A7
South Oak St DE14. . . 254 B8
South Par DE4 . . . . 143 A1
South Park Ave
DE4 . . . . 127 C3
South Pl
Chesterfield, Brampton
S40 . . . . .95 D2
Chesterfield, Stonegravels
S40 . . . . 266 B2
Ripley DE5 . . . . 169 D1
South St
Ashbourne DE6 . . . . . . 173 C1
Blackwell DE55 . . . . . . .147 F2
Buxton SK17 . . . . .85 B7
Chesterfield S40 . . . . . 266 B2
Derby DE1 . . . . 218 E5
Draycott DE72 . . . . . . 235 A7
Eastwood, Bailey Grove
NG16 . . . . .182 F2
Eastwood, Giltbrook
NG16 . . . . 195 C8
Ilkeston DE7 . . . . 208 F8
Long Eaton NG10 . . . . .236 E7
Melbourne DE73 . . . . . 252 A7
Pilsley S45 . . . . 132 D1
Sheffield S20 . . . . .59 D6
Somercotes DE55 . . . . 170 D5
South Normanton
DE55 . . . . 160 B6
Swanwick DE55 . . . . . . 169 E7
Woodville DE11 . . . . . . 257 A1
South Street N S43 . . .77 D3
South Terr S18 . . . . .94 C7
South Uxbridge St
DE14 . . . . 254 B8
South View
Bamford S33 . . . . .40 B4
Chesterfield S41 . . . . . . .95 D7
Derby DE23 . . . . 218 C1
Mayfield DE6 . . . . 184 D6
New Mills SK22 . . . . . . .33 B8
Pilsley DE45 . . . . .91 C2
Sheffield S20 . . . . .60 A7
Whitwell S80 . . . . .81 F5
Whitwell S80 . . . . .82 A5
South View Rd SK13 . .17 F7
South View Wlk
ST14 . . . . .196 F3
Southwark Cl DE22 . . 218 B5
Southwell Rise
NG16 . . . . 195 B7
**SOUTH
WINGFIELD** 157 E3
**South Wingfield Prim
Sch** DE55 . . . . .157 F4
SOUTHWOOD 258 B7
Southwood 2 SK17. . .85 A7
Southwood Ave S18 . .76 B7
Southwood Dr S43 . . . .80 F3
Southwood St DE24. .232 F8
Southworth Rd
DE73 . . . . 252 E2
Sovereign Dr DE14 . . 254 B8
Sovereign Gr NG10 . . 236 B7
Sovereign Way
Chapel-en-le-Frith
SK23 . . . . .47 B7
Derby DE21 . . . . 206 D3
Heanor DE75 . . . . 181 D1
Sowbrook Brook
DE7 . . . . 208 D4
Sowbrook La DE7. . . . 208 E3
Sowter Rd DE1 . . . . . . 267 B4
Sowters Row S40. . . . 266 B3
Spa Brook Cl S12 . . . . .44 F4
Spa Brook Dr S12 . . . .44 F5

Spa Croft DE55 . . . . 147 E5
Spa Ct DE1 . . . . 267 A1
Spa La
Chesterfield, Hady
S41 . . . . 266 C2
Derby DE1 . . . . 267 A1
Mansfield Woodhouse
NG19 . . . . .136 F4
Spalden Ave DE6 . . . 173 C3
Spang La NG17 . . . . . 148 E4
Spanker La DE56 . . . 168 B2
Spanker Terr DE56 . . 168 C2
Sparkbottom La
SK23 . . . . .46 C5
Sparrowbusk Cl S43 . .80 B6
Sparrow Cl
Derby DE24 . . . . 231 D4
Ilkeston DE7 . . . . 209 A5
SPARROWPIT 48 B6
SPATH 210 A3
Spa View Ave S12 . . . .44 F3
Spa View Dr S12 . . . . .44 F3
Spa View Pl S12 . . . . . .44 F3
Spa View Rd S12 . . . . .44 F3
Spa View Terr S12 . . . .44 F3
Spa View Way S12. . . .44 F3
Speedway Close
NG10 . . . . 236 F8
Speedwell SK13 . . . . . . .9 F7
Speedwell Cavern★
S33 . . . . .37 F2
Speedwell Cl
Derby DE21 . . . . 206 C3
Glossop SK13 . . . . .9 F7
Woodville DE11 . . . . . .256 F4
Speedwell Ind Est
S43 . . . . .78 F2
Speedwell Inf Sch
S43 . . . . .78 E1
Speedwell La
Kimberley NG16 . . . . . .195 E6
Nottingham NG16 . . . . 195 E6
Speetley View S43. . . .80 B7
Speighthill Cres
S42 . . . . 114 E4
Spenbeck Dr DE22. . . 205 A3
Spencer Ave
Belper DE56 . . . . .179 F4
Derby DE24 . . . . 232 D4
Sandiacre NG10 . . . . . 223 B6
Staveley S43 . . . . .79 B2
Spencer Cl
Ashbourne DE6 . . . . . . 185 C8
Burton upon Trent
DE13 . . . . 240 D1
Spencer Cres NG9 . . . 223 F8
Spencer Dr DE55 . . . . 170 D7
Spencer Gr SK17 . . . . .85 B6
Spencer Ho
Derby, Crewton
DE24 . . . . 233 A4
Derby, Spondon DE21. 220 D3
Spencer Rd
Belper DE56 . . . . .179 B4
Buxton SK17 . . . . .85 B6
Chapel-en-le-Frith
SK23 . . . . .46 F6
Sheffield S20 . . . . .43 A7
Spencer St
Bolsover S44 . . . . 117 F8
Chesterfield S40 . . . . . 266 A4
Derby DE24 . . . . 233 A8
Stanley Common DE7 . 193 A1
Spend La DE6 . . . . 161 E2
Sperry Cl NG16 . . . . . .171 F6
Spey Dr DE22 . . . . 218 B3
Spilsbury Cl DE65. . . 242 C5
Spinaker Close S8. . . 169 E4
Spindle Drive S42 . . . 115 A2
Spindletree Dr
DE21 . . . . .205 F2
SPINKHILL 60 D2
Spinkhill Ave S13 . . . .44 C8
Spinkhill Dr S13 . . . . . .44 D8
Spinkhill La S21 . . . . . .60 B2
Spinkhill Rd
Killamarsh S21 . . . . . . .60 E4
Sheffield S13 . . . . .44 D8
Spinkhill View S21 . . . .60 B1
Spinnaker Road S43. . .80 C5
Spinnerbottom SK22. .24 F2
Spinner Croft
Chesterfield S40 . . . . . . .96 A1
Chesterfield S40 . . . . . 266 B1
Spinners Close
DE55 . . . . 160 C6
Spinners Way DE56 . . 179 C5
Spinneybrook Way
DE3 . . . . 217 D2
Spinney Cl
Derby DE22 . . . . 205 A2
Glossop SK13 . . . . .10 C2
Mansfield Woodhouse
NG19 . . . . .136 E6
Spinney Cres NG9 . . . 223 F3
Spinney Dr NG10 . . . . 223 C2
Spinney Hill DE73. . . 252 A2
Spinney La DE16 . . . . 254 D5
Spinney Lodge
Repton DE65 . . . . 242 C2
Tutbury DE13 . . . . 238 E6
Spinney Rd
Branston DE14 . . . . . . .253 F8
Derby DE22 . . . . 218 E3
Derby, Chaddesden
DE21 . . . . 219 F7
Ilkeston DE7 . . . . 208 E6
Long Eaton NG10 . . . . 223 C2

Spinney Rise NG9 . . 223 E3
Spinney The
Belper DE56 . . . . .179 A6
Borrowash DE72 . . . . 221 C1
Brailsford DE6 . . . . . . .201 E8
Castle Donington
DE74. . . . . 247 A4
Ilkeston DE7 . . . . 208 E6
Ripley DE5 . . . . 169 D3
Sheffield S17 . . . . .55 C7
Shirebrook NG20 . . . . 119 D3
Stanton-by-Dale
NG10 . . . . .222 F8
SPION KOP 120 F2
Spion Pk Mws NG20 .120 F2
Spire Close DE6 . . . . . 173 A1
Spire Heights S41 . . . .96 B2
Spire Hollin SK13 . . . . .10 C2
Spire Hollin Ho SK13 .10 C2
Spire Inf Sch S40. . . . 115 A4
Spire Jun Sch S40. . . 115 A4
Spire La S44 . . . . 118 B6
Spire Valley S45 . . . . 131 D5
Spire View NG10. . . . 236 B4
Spire Walk Bsns Pk
S40 . . . . 266 B1
Spire Wlk S40 . . . . . . .96 B2
SPITAL 96 C1
Spital Brook Cl S41. . .96 C1
Spital Gdns S41 . . . . . .96 C2
SPITALHILL 185 C8
Spital La
Chesterfield S40. . . . . . .96 B2
Chesterfield S41. . . . . . .96 C1
Spital Rise DE74 . . . . 247 A4
SPITEWINTER 113 D1
Spitewinter La S18,
S42 . . . . .93 D8
Spitfire Road DE74 . .246 F3
Spittal DE74 . . . . 247 A4
Spittal Gn S44 . . . . . . 118 A8
Spittal Hill DE74 . . . . 247 A4
Spittal The 3 DE74. .246 F4
Spode Drive DE11 . . . 256 F1
SPONDON 220 E4
Spondon Rd
Dale Abbey DE7 . . . . . 207 D2
Ilkeston DE7 . . . . 208 F5
Spondon Sta DE21. . . 220 D3
Spooner Dr S21 . . . . . .60 C6
Spooner La S32 . . . . . .72 C5
Spoonley Wood Ct
DE23 . . . . .230 F7
Sporton Cl DE55 . . . . 160 A7
Sporton La DE55 . . . . 160 B7
Spotswood Cl S14 . . . .43 E5
Spotswood Dr S14. . . .43 E5
Spotswood Mount
S14 . . . . .43 E4
Spotswood Pl S14 . . . .43 D4
Spotswood Rd S14 . . .43 E5
SPOUT 166 C3
Spout La
Spout DE56 . . . . 166 C3
Tansley DE4 . . . . 144 A4
Spridgeon Cl 2
NG10 . . . . 223 B2
Springbank
Glossop SK13 . . . . .9 F5
Unstone S18 . . . . .76 E8
Spring Bank
Buxton SK17 . . . . .67 C4
Great Longstone DE45. .90 A4
New Mills SK22. . . . . . .33 C8
Springbank Gdns
SK22 . . . . .33 B8
Springbank Prim Sch
Eastwood NG16 . . . . . .182 E2
1 Eastwood NG16 . . .182 E2
Spring Bank Rd
S40 . . . . 266 A3
Spring Cl
Belper DE56 . . . . .178 E6
Breaston DE72 . . . . . . 235 C8
Renishaw S21 . . . . .79 C7
Swadlincote DE11 . . . . 256 A1
Wirksworth DE4 . . . . . 154 F2
Spring Close Dell
S14 . . . . .43 E4
Spring Close Mount
S14 . . . . .43 E4
Spring Close View
S14 . . . . .43 E4
SPRING COTTAGE . . 262 D5
Spring Cottage Rd
DE12 . . . . 262 D5
Spring Ct 4 NG9 . . . 223 F4
Spring Ct Mews SK14. .9 D5
Springdale SK17. . . . . .84 F7
Springdale Ct DE3 . . 217 E1
Spring Dale Gdns
NG9 . . . . 209 D3
Springfarm Rd
DE15 . . . . 248 A1
Springfield
Broadbottom SK13 . . . . .16 C4
Derby DE23 . . . . .218 B2
Springfield Ave
Ashbourne DE6 . . . . . . 185 D8
Chesterfield S40 . . . . . . .95 D3
Heanor DE75 . . . . 181 B5
Long Eaton NG10 . . . . 236 F8
Sandiacre NG10 . . . . . 223 B3
Shirebrook NG20 . . . . 119 C5
Springfield Cl
Bradwell S33 . . . . .51 A7
Clowne S43 . . . . .80 E3
Crich DE4 . . . . 157 A1

Springfield Cl *continued*
Eckington S21 59 C3
Glossop SK13 9 E4
Swadlincote DE11 256 B6
Springfield Cres
Bolsover S44 98 F3
Somercotes DE55 170 D7
Springfield Ct NG9 209 E1
Springfield Dr DE56 190 D3
Springfield Gdns
DE7 194 F2
Springfield Jun Sch
DE11 256 C5
SPRINGFIELD PARK 223 A3
Springfield Prim Sch DE21 220 D5
Springfield Rd
Barlow S18 75 D3
Bradwell S33 51 A8
Chellaston DE73 232 F2
Derby, Cherrytree Hill DE21 220 B5
Etwall DE65 229 B3
Holmewood S42 132 E8
Repton DE65 242 D2
Swadlincote DE11 256 B6
Springfield Rise DE4 143 C6
Springfield Terr
Burton upon Trent DE15 248 A1
Hayfield SK22 25 D2
Ripley DE5 169 E1
Springfield View DE5 169 D2
Spring Gardens DE55 157 D8
Spring Gardens Ctr The SK17 85 B8
Spring Garden Terr DE7 194 F2
Spring Gdns
Buxton SK17 85 C8
Derby DE21 219 F7
Glossop SK13 10 A5
Springhill DE11 257 A8
Spring Hill
Kimberley NG16 195 F5
Mansfield Woodhouse NG19 136 B3
Whitwell S80 82 A6
Springhill Way DE5 181 A8
Spring Hollow DE56 190 C8
Spring House Cl S42 94 F5
Spring La
Elmton S80 99 F6
Heanor DE75 181 E1
Renishaw S21 79 C7
Sheffield S2 43 E8
Shireoaks S80, S81 63 F5
Warsop NG20 120 C6
Spring Mdw 4 DE55 148 B7
Springmeadow SK13 16 D7
Spring Mount SK22 33 C8
Spring Pl S40 266 B3
Spring Rd DE55 170 E6
Spring Rise SK13 16 F7
Springs L Ctr S21 43 F6
Spring St
Broadbottom SK14 16 A8
Derby DE22 267 A2
Glossop SK13 10 B1
Hollingworth SK14 9 C5
Swadlincote DE11 262 A8
Whitwell S80 82 A6
Spring The NG10 236 D5
Spring Vale SK22 24 E3
Springvale Cl S45 131 D2
Springvale Gdns S45 131 E2
Springvale Rd S45 131 D2
Spring Vale Rd
Brimington S43 96 E8
Hayfield SK22 25 E2
Spring Water Ave S12 44 F3
Springwater Cl S12 44 F3
Spring Water Dr
Glossop SK13 9 E3
Sheffield S12 44 F3
Spring Way S2 44 A8
Springwell Com Coll S43 97 D7
Springwell Hill
Middle Handley S21 78 A8
Unstone S21 77 F6
Springwell Park Dr S43 97 C7
Springwell St NG17 148 F2
Springwood SK13 16 F8
Spring Wood Cl S41 95 C8
Springwood Ct S43 77 D4
Springwood Dr
Derby DE21 206 B2
Mansfield Woodhouse NG19 136 C2
Springwood Farm Rd DE11 256 B7
Springwood Gdns DE56 179 A4
Springwood L Ctr DE21 206 A2
Springwood Rd S8 43 A6
Springwood St S42 116 B4
Sprinkswoods La DE6 184 E5
Spruce Ave NG16 171 D6
Spruce Cl S40 95 B2
Spruce Rise S21 60 C5
Spurr St S2 43 B8
Sq The DE4 142 A7
Square The
Boylestone DE6 213 C4
Bretby DE15 249 B3
8 Buxton SK17 85 B8
Clay Cross S45 131 E3
Derby DE3 217 D1
Derby, Darley Abbey DE22 205 A1
Elmton S80 100 A7
Eyam S32 71 E5
Hartington SK17 137 D5
Marchington ST14 224 E2
Middleton DE45 124 F3
Monyash DE45 107 C2
Whitwell S80 81 F6
Squashley Bank
Roston DE6 197 F6
Roston DE6 198 B6
Squires La S33 38 C3
Squires Way DE23 231 A6
Squirrel La DE73 252 E4
Squirrel Wlk
Duffield DE56 191 A2
Overseal DE12 262 B3
Stable Cl DE4 156 B5
Stable Cotts DE4 155 A6
Stable La
Alstonefield DE6 149 B1
Buxton SK17 84 E5
Stable Mews DE11 256 F2
Stables Ct S44 99 C1
Stables La SK17 85 C4
Stables St DE22 218 D5
Stables The DE65 228 F1
Stacey Rd NG19 135 D2
Stackyard The DE7 207 F2
STADEN 85 E5
Staden Bsns Pk SK17 85 E5
Staden La SK17 85 E4
Stadium Bsns Ct DE24 219 E4
Stadium Ind Pk NG10 236 F8
Stadium View DE24 219 E3
Stadmoor Ct DE73 232 F1
Staffa Dr DE55 147 F5
Stafford Cl
Dronfield S18 56 C2
6 Glossop SK13 17 F8
Melbourne DE73 252 B8
Smalley DE7 192 F6
Stafford Cres DE4 165 E7
Stafford Dr DE23 230 F5
Stafford Ho DE24 232 E6
Stafford St
Derby DE1 267 A3
Long Eaton NG10 236 F8
New Mills SK22 24 C1
Staines Cl DE3 217 C2
Stainforth St NG19 136 C2
Stainsbro' La DE4, DE6 165 B6
STAINSBY 133 B7
Stainsby Ave
Heanor DE75 193 E8
Horsley Woodhouse DE7 192 E6
Stainsby Cl S42 132 F8
Stainsby Gr NG17 148 F2
Stainsby Mill* S44 133 D7
Staithes Wlk DE21 205 C1
Staker La DE3 230 D6
Staley Close DE11 256 B2
Staley Dr
Glapwell S44 118 C1
Glapwell S44 134 B8
Stalybridge Ctry Pk* SK15 4 A2
Stalybridge Rd SK14 9 A4
Stamford Cl NG10 236 E4
Stamford Ct 5 DE75 181 D2
Stamford St
Awsworth NG16 195 C4
Derby DE24 232 D6
Heanor DE75 181 E2
2 Ilkeston DE7 194 E1
Stamps Cl DE15 248 C3
Stanage Gn DE3 217 F1
Stanage Rise S12 44 E5
Stanage Way S40 94 F5
Stancliffe Ave DE4 127 C3
Stancliffe View DE4 127 B3
Standall Close S18 56 B3
Standing Butts Cl DE12 259 D8
Standlow La DE6 163 C2
Stand Park Ind Est S41 96 A7
Stand Rd S41 95 F7
Stanedge Rd
Bakewell DE45 109 B6
Bakewell DE45 109 C6
Stanford Rd S18 56 C1
Stanford Way S40 114 B8
STANFREE 99 B8
STANHOPE BRETBY 248 F1
Stanhope Cl DE65 229 C3
Stanhope Glade DE15 256 A8
Stanhope Gn DE15 248 F1
Stanhope Rd
Derby DE3 217 E3
Sheffield S12 44 C5
Swadlincote DE11 256 B3
Stanhope St
Bramley-Vale S44 117 E1
Burton upon Trent DE15 248 B3
Derby DE23 218 F8
Derby DE23 219 A2
Ilkeston DE7 209 A6
Long Eaton NG10 236 D8
Stanton-by-Dale NG10 222 E8
Stanier Ct S41 115 C7
Stanier Dr DE11 256 F4
Stanier Way
Derby DE21 220 A3
Renishaw S21 60 B1
Staniforth Ave S21 59 B3
Stanleigh Gdns DE12 265 E8
Stanleigh Ho DE12 265 E8
Stanleigh Rd DE12 262 B4
STANLEY
Tibshelf 133 D1
West Hallam 207 C5
Stanley Ave
Ripley DE5 169 E2
Staveley S43 97 B7
Stanley Cl
Derby DE22 218 F8
Ilkeston DE7 208 E7
Netherseal DE12 264 F7
Woodville DE11 256 F3
STANLEY COMMON 193 B1
Stanley Common CE Prim Sch DE7 193 B1
Stanley Cres ST14 210 A2
Stanley Ct NG16 182 F1
Stanley Dr
Beeston NG9 209 F1
5 Stapleford NG9 223 F8
Stanley Hall La SK12 32 C6
Stanley La S44, NG17 133 D2
Stanley Mws NG16 195 D7
Stanley Rd
Derby, Allenton DE24 232 F6
Derby, Cherrytree Hill DE21 220 A5
Sheffield S8 43 B5
Stanley St
Chesterfield S41 96 C2
Derby DE22 218 D5
Ilkeston DE7 208 F7
Killamarsh S21 60 D7
Long Eaton NG10 236 E7
Somercotes DE55 170 D8
Swadlincote DE11 256 C4
STANSHOPE 149 D1
Stanshope La DE6 149 C2
Stanstead Rd DE3 217 C3
STANTON
Mayfield 183 D8
Swadlincote 255 C4
Stanton Ave DE56 179 B4
STANTON BY BRIDGE 244 D3
STANTON-BY-DALE 222 E8
Stanton Cl
Alfreton DE55 159 A3
Darley Dale DE4 127 B3
Stanton Cres S12 44 D4
STANTON GATE 209 C1
Stanton Gate DE7 209 C1
Stantonhall La DE4 126 D7
Stanton Hill DE73 251 C5
STANTON IN PEAK 126 C5
Stanton in Peak CE Prim Sch DE4 126 C5
Stanton La
Ellastone DE6 183 C4
Mayfield DE6 172 A2
STANTON LEES 126 F3
Stanton Moor View DE4 142 F7
Stanton Pl NG19 134 F7
Stanton Prim Sch DE15 255 B5
Stanton Rd
Ashbourne DE6 185 D8
Burton upon Trent DE15 254 F7
Ilkeston DE7 208 F7
Sandiacre NG10 223 A7
Stanton St
Derby DE23 218 F1
New Houghton NG19 134 F7
Stanton Vale Sch NG10 236 C7
Stanton View DE45 109 C4
Stanwood Dr S40 114 B8
Stanyforth St SK13 10 A4
STAPENHILL 254 F8
STAPLEFORD 223 C4
Stapleford La NG9 223 F3
Stapleford Rd NG9 209 D3
Stapleton Rd DE7 194 E4
Starch La NG10 223 C7
Starcross Ct DE3 217 C3
Starflower Way DE3 217 D5
STARKHOLMES 143 C2
Starkholmes Rd DE4 143 C2
Starkie Ave DE74 246 F3
Starkie St SK13 10 E3
Starling Rd SK17 85 D2
Starthe Bank DE75 181 F1
Starthe View DE75 181 F1
Starth La DE4 144 A3
Start La SK23 45 B7
Statham Ave S42 131 C8
Statham Cl DE3 217 B3
Statham St DE22 218 E7
Station App
Ambergate DE56 167 F4
Buxton SK17 85 B8
Derby DE1 267 B4
Duffield DE56 190 F4
Hathersage S32 53 A7
Station Back La S41 266 C3
Station Cl
Burton upon Trent DE16 254 E5
Chellaston DE73 232 F1
Kilburn DE56 179 F1
Station Cotts DE6 225 E2
Station Cres 6 DE11 256 C4
Station Ct 3 DE7 194 E1
Station Dr
Elvaston DE72 234 A8
Moira DE12 262 F4
Station Hill NG19 136 B3
Station La
Chesterfield S41, S43 77 C2
Codnor DE5 181 B6
Walton-on-Trent DE12 253 D1
Station La Ind Est S41 77 B2
Station New Rd S42 131 D7
Station Rd
Ashbourne DE6 173 B1
Awsworth NG16 195 C5
Bakewell DE45 109 E6
Bamford S33 40 B2
Barrow Hill S43 78 B3
Bolsover S44 98 F2
Borrowash DE72 221 B1
Breadsall DE21 205 E4
Brimington S43 96 D8
Brimington, Hollingwood S43 78 A2
Burton upon Trent DE13 253 A1
Buxton SK17 85 B7
Castle Donington DE74 247 C5
Chapel-en-le-Frith SK23 47 B6
Chellaston DE73 232 F1
Chesterfield S41 96 A7
Chesterfield S41 266 C3
Chesterfield, Old Whittington S41 77 A1
Chinley SK23 34 D2
Clowne S43 80 E4
Creswell S43 81 E1
Darley Dale DE4 127 C2
Denby Village DE5 180 B3
Derby DE3 217 D3
Derby, Spondon DE21 220 D3
Dove Holes SK17 47 F1
Draycott DE72 235 B7
Draycott in the Clay ST14 225 E1
Duffield DE56 190 F4
Furness Vale SK23 33 D4
Glossop SK13 10 A5
Great Longstone DE45 89 F3
Hathersage S32 53 A7
Hatton DE65 239 D8
Hayfield SK22 25 D2
Hayfield, Birch Vale SK22 25 A2
Hope S33 39 B3
Ilkeston DE7 194 F1
Ironville NG16 170 F3
Killamarsh S21 60 B6
Kimberley NG16 195 F6
Langley Mill NG16 182 B2
Little Eaton DE21 205 C7
Long Eaton NG10 236 F8
Marchington ST14 224 E3
Marple SK6 23 A7
Marple, Strines SK6, SK22 23 D1
Melbourne DE73 252 C8
New Mills SK22 33 B7
North Wingfield S42 131 E6
North Wingfield S45 131 E7
Pilsley S45 132 D1
Renishaw S21 60 A2
Rocester ST14 196 E3
Rolleston DE13 240 C4
Sandiacre NG10 223 C5
Scarcliffe S44 118 F6
Scarcliffe S44 119 A5
Selston NG16 160 E1
Selston NG16 171 F8
Sheffield S20 59 E7
Shirebrook NG20 119 E6
Spinkhill S21 60 D2
Stanley DE7 207 C6
Stonebroom DE55 147 B5
Tibshelf DE55 147 F6
Upper Padley S11 53 E2
Station Rd *continued*
West Hallam DE7 207 C8
Whaley Bridge SK23 34 A1
Whitwell S80 82 A5
8 Wirksworth DE4 154 F1
Woodville DE11 256 F2
Station Road Ind Est S43 80 E4
Station St
Ashbourne DE6 173 B1
Cossall DE7 195 A1
Glossop SK13 10 D1
Long Eaton NG10 236 E7
Mansfield Woodhouse NG19 136 B3
Swadlincote DE11 261 F8
Station View NG20 119 E4
Station Wlk 1 SK17 85 D8
Station Yard SK22 33 A6
Station Yd DE73 252 C8
Staton La
Apperknowle S18 58 A1
Apperknowle S18 77 A8
Staunton Ave DE23 231 E6
Staunton Cl
Castle Donington DE74 247 A4
Chesterfield S40 115 A6
Staunton Harold DE73 258 E7
Staunton Harold Resr Visitor Ctr* DE73 251 F5
Staunton La
DE73 258 B8
Ticknall DE73 251 A1
STAVELEY 78 D1
Staveley Cl DE24 232 E3
Staveley Jun Sch S43 78 E1
Staveley La
Barrow Hill S21, S43 78 A5
Eckington S21 59 E2
Staveley S43 78 E7
Staveley Rd
Chesterfield S43 77 E3
Long Duckmanton S44 97 E4
Poolsbrook S43 98 A8
Sheffield S8 43 A7
Staverton Dr DE3 217 D4
Stead Mews S21 59 D3
Stead St S21 59 D3
Steam Mill La DE5 170 A1
Steele Ave S43 97 B6
Steele Ct SK17 85 A8
Steel La S44 99 B2
Steel's La S44 118 B6
Steelyard Cl DE5 169 E4
Steeping Cl S43 96 E8
Steep La S42 114 A4
Steeple Cl DE21 205 E2
Steeple Dr DE5 180 E8
Steeple End Fold SK22 25 D2
Steeplegate S40 266 B3
STEEPLE GRANGE 155 A3
Steeple Grange
Chesterfield S41 96 D1
Wirksworth DE4 154 F3
Steeple Grange Light Rly* DE4 154 F4
Steep Turnpike DE4 143 C5
Steetley La S80 63 E3
STENSON 243 B8
Stenson Ave DE23 231 E6
Stenson Ct DE5 169 F1
Stenson Fields Prim Com Sch DE24 231 D2
Stenson Rd DE23, DE24 231 D4
Stenton Rd S8 56 F7
Stephenson Cl S45 131 B4
Stephenson Ct S40 95 B2
Stephenson La S45 131 C5
Stephenson Pl
Chesterfield S40 266 B3
Clay Cross S45 131 A4
Stephenson Rd
1 Eastwood DE7 194 E8
Staveley S43 78 E1
Stephensons Way DE21 220 A3
Stephens Rd DE14 254 B8
Stephouses SK6 23 F8
Stepping Cl DE22 218 E5
Stepping La DE22 218 E5
Sterland St S40 95 E3
Sterling Cl DE5 180 B2
Sterndale Cl SK17 69 E3
Sterndale Ho 4 DE1 267 B2
Sterndale La SK17 69 E3
Sterndale Moor SK17 105 E6
Sterndale Rd NG10 236 B6
Sterry Cl S43 80 E2
Stevenage Cl DE24 232 F5
Steven Cl NG9 223 F4
Steven Mangle Close S12 44 E2
Stevens La DE72 235 D8
Stevenson Ave DE72 235 B8
Stevenson Ho S41 96 B6
Stevenson Pl DE23 231 B8
Stevenson Rd DE6 224 B8
Stevenson Way DE56 168 B5
Stevens Rd NG10 223 A5
Steward Gate S33 40 A6
Stewart Cl
Burton upon Trent DE14 254 A6
Derby DE21 220 E6
Stewart St DE55 170 D5
Stichill Ave DE23 231 E1
Stile Croft DE4 154 D5
Stiles Cl SK13 9 E5
Stiles Rd DE24 233 D8
Stillman Cl S41 115 C8
Stinting La
Mansfield NG19 136 E2
Shirebrook NG20 119 D3
Stirland St DE5 170 B1
Stirling Cl
Castle Gresley DE11 255 F1
Derby DE21 219 C8
Stirling Ct S41 266 B4
Stirling Gr NG16 195 E7
Stirling Rd
Swadlincote DE11 256 E5
Woodville DE11 257 A5
Stockbrook Rd DE22 218 D3
Stockbrook St DE22 218 E4
Stockdove Cl DE24 231 D4
Stocker Ave DE24 233 D7
Stock La ST14 224 C1
STOCKLEY 117 E4
Stockley La S44 117 F1
Stockley View S44 118 B8
Stockport Rd
Broadbottom SK14 15 D8
Marple SK6 23 A6
Stocks Brow SK13 10 A7
Stocks Green Ct S17 55 D4
Stocks Green Dr S17 55 D4
Stocks La SK23 45 A4
Stocks Rd NG16 195 E7
Stocks The SK13 10 A7
Stockton Close DE11 255 F2
Stockton Dr SK23 34 E1
Stockwell Ct S40 114 F7
Stockwell Dr
4 Derby DE22 218 A5
Derby DE3 217 F5
Stoddard Dr DE75 181 F2
Stodhart Flats SK23 47 C8
STOKE 72 C6
Stoke Cl DE56 179 E5
Stoke La S32 72 C5
Stollard St S45 131 D4
Stone Ave NG16 182 A1
Stone Bank Ct S18 57 B1
Stonebench La SK17 106 C3
Stone Bench Way SK17 85 E8
Stonebridge La NG20 120 F4
STONEBROOM 146 F4
Stonebroom Ind Est DE55 147 B4
Stonebroom La DE55 147 B5
Stonebroom Prim Sch DE55 147 A4
Stonebroom Wlk DE24 232 E3
Stonechat Cl DE3 218 A3
Stone Cl
Derby DE21 220 E6
Dronfield S18 57 C3
Stonecliff Terr SK17 85 D8
Stone Cotts DE6 184 E8
Stonecroft S80 82 C6
Stonecroft Rd S17 55 F5
Stonedale Cl S20 59 D7
Stone Fronts DE73 251 A4
Stone Gr NG20 101 A1
STONEGRAVELS 96 A5
Stonegravels Croft 7 S20 59 E6
Stonegravels La S41 96 A5
Stonegravels Way S20 59 F6
Stoneheads
Whaley Bridge SK23 33 B1
Whaley Bridge SK23 45 B8
Whaley Bridge SK23 45 C8
Stoneheads Rise SK23 45 D8
Stonehill DE74 247 B2
Stone Hill Rd DE23 218 F2
Stoneholes Dr S45 131 E2
Stone La
Chesterfield S43 77 D4
Sheffield S13 44 F5
Stoneleigh Way DE55 169 F8
Stoneley Cl S12 44 B1
Stoneley Cres S12 44 B1
Stoneley Dell S12 44 B1
Stoneley Dr S12 44 B1
Stonelow
Baslow DE45 92 F4
Wadshelf S42 93 B5
Stonelow Cres S18 57 C2
Stonelow Gn S18 57 B2
Stonelow Jun Sch S18 57 C2
Stonelow Rd S18 57 C2

Stone Mdws NG10 236 E5
Stonepit La DE6 164 A3
Stone Rd S18 57 C3
Stoneridge SK13 9 F5
Stone Row
Chesterfield S40 95 D2
Marple SK6 23 A6
Stone Row Pl DE12 262 F4
Stonerows La S45 145 C6
Stonesby Cl DE21 205 F2
Stonesdale Ct 1 DE24 233 C6
Stones La DE4 156 F1
Stone St S20 59 D7
Stones The S33 38 B2
Stonewell La SK17 137 D5
Stoney Cl DE45 109 D4
Stoneycroft La S42 114 A5
Stoney Cross DE21 220 E3
Stoney Cross Ind Est DE21 220 D3
Stoneydale Cl DE11 255 F5
Stoneyfield Bank DE56 179 A5
Stoney Flatts Cres DE21 220 A8
STONEYFORD 182 A7
Stoneyford Rd DE12 262 A3
Stoney Furlong Rd DE45 91 E6
Stoney Gate Rd DE21 220 D3
Stoney Hill DE4 155 B2
Stoney La
Appleby Magna DE12 265 F1
Ashover S42 130 C3
Brinsley NG16 182 D6
Derby DE21 220 E5
Hognaston DE6 164 A2
Selston NG16 171 E7
Thorpe DE6 161 E1
Trowell NG9 209 B5
Stoneyland Dr SK22 33 B8
STONEY MIDDLETON 72 A4
Stoney Middleton CE Prim Sch S32 71 F3
Stoneyside DE45 125 C5
Stoney View
5 Creswell S43 81 E2
Langley Mill NG16 182 B5
Stoney Way DE4 143 C4
Stoney Wood Dr DE4 156 C1
Stony Clouds Nature Reserve★ NG10 223 B8
STONY HOUGHTON 118 F1
Stonyhurst Ct DE24 232 E3
Stony La DE56 191 D6
Stony Ridge Rd S11 54 C5
Stoodley Pike Gdns DE22 204 C2
Stoops Cl S40 95 D6
Stoppard Cl DE7 194 D2
Storer La DE4 166 B3
Stores Rd DE21 267 D4
Storey Road SK12 32 E6
Storforth La S41 115 B7
Storforth Lane Terr S41 115 C8
Storforth Lane Trad Est S40 115 B8
Stormont Cl DE55 160 B4
Stormont Gr S43 97 C7
Stornoway Cl 9 DE24 231 D3
Storrs Rd S40 95 B2
Storth Bank SK13 16 F7
Storth Brook Ct SK13 16 A7
Storthfield Way DE55 160 B4
Storth La DE55 160 B4
Storth Meadow Rd
Charlesworth SK13 16 A7
Glossop SK13 16 F7
Stort Sq NG19 136 D2
Stour Cl
Brimington S43 96 E8
4 Hilton DE65 240 E8
Stourdale Cl NG10 236 A6
Stourport Dr DE73 233 A3
Stow Ct 6 NG19 136 E3
Stowmarket Dr DE21 219 D8
Stradbroke Ave S13 44 D7
Stradbroke Cl S13 44 E7
Stradbroke Cres S13 44 E7
Stradbroke Dr S13 44 E7
Stradbroke Pl S13 44 E7
Stradbroke Prim Sch S13 44 D7
Stradbroke Rd S13 44 E6
Stradbroke Rise S40 114 C8
Stradbroke Way S13 44 E7
Stradbroke Wlk S13 44 D7
STRAMSHALL 210 A4
Stramshall Rd ST14 210 B3
Strand Arc DE1 267 B3
Strand The DE1 267 B3
Stranfaer Cl DE55 170 A7
Stranraer Cl NG19 136 C6
Stratford Cl DE65 242 D1
Stratford Rd DE21 205 D2
Stratford St DE7 194 F4
Strathallan Cl DE4 127 C4
Strathaven Ct DE21 220 E5
Strathglen Cl NG16 195 E7
Strathmore Ave DE24 233 A6
Stratton Rd S44 99 A2
Strawberry Bank NG17 148 E4
Strawberry La
Blackfordby DE11 257 B1
Rosliston DE12 260 D5
Strawberry Lee La S17 55 B5
Straw La
Clay Cross DE55 146 D8
Shirland DE55 146 D8
Streatham Rd DE22 218 B6
Street Farm Cl S26 61 E6
Streetfield Cres S20 59 D6
Streetfields S20 59 E6
Street La
Ripley DE5 169 B1
Ripley DE5 180 B6
Street Lane Prim Sch DE5 180 B5
Street The SK10, SK17 64 C5
Street The★ SK17 64 E4
Strelley Ave DE5 180 C8
Stretfield Rd S33 39 B1
Strettea La DE55 146 C2
STRETTON
Clay Cross 146 C7
Rolleston on Dove 240 D1
Stretton Cl DE3 217 D1
STRETTON EN LE FIELD 265 D4
Stretton Handley CE Prim Sch DE55 145 D7
STRETTON HILLSIDE 146 B5
Stretton Rd
Clay Cross S45 131 C1
Shirland DE55 146 C8
Stonebroom DE55 146 E5
Tansley DE4 144 C4
Stretton View DE12 265 F6
Striding Edge Cl 4 NG10 223 B2
STRINES 23 C2
Strines Rd
Marple SK6 23 B4
Marpleridge SK6 23 B2
New Mills SK6 32 D8
Strines SK6 23 D1
Strines Sta SK6 23 D1
Stringer Cl DE7 194 E2
Stringer Dr DE55 170 C8
Stroma Cl DE24 231 F4
Strouts Way S2 43 E8
Strutt Close DE55 148 A3
Strutts Cl DE55 159 F4
Strutt's North Mill★ DE56 178 F5
Strutt's Park Ho 2 DE22 218 F7
Strutt St
Belper DE56 178 F3
Derby DE23 219 A2
Stuart Cl
Ashbourne DE6 173 D1
Chesterfield S41 96 C6
Stuart St
Derby DE1 219 A6
Derby DE1 267 B4
Stubben Edge La S45 130 C2
Stubbing Rd S40 114 F7
Stubbins La SK23 34 D2
Stubbins Wood NG20 119 E6
Stubbins Wood La NG20 119 E5
Stubbin Wood Sch NG20 119 F6
Stubby La ST14 224 E1
Stuble Dr DE21 205 D3
Stubley Cl S18 56 E2
Stubley Croft S18 56 D2
Stubley Dr S18 56 E2
Stubley Hollow S18 56 F3
Stubley La S18 56 D2
Stubley Pl S18 56 E2
STUBWOOD 196 D4
Stubwood Hollow ST14 196 D5
Stubwood La ST14 196 D4
Studbrook Cl DE74 246 F3
Studfarm Cl DE73 252 E2
Studios The S40 95 E3
Studland Cl NG19 136 D6
Stunstead La DE4 141 A2
Stupenhill Post 16 Ctr DE15 255 A7
Sturge Croft 3 S2 43 B6
Sturges La DE72 233 F4
Sturston Close DE24 231 C3
Sturston Rd DE6 173 C1
SUDBURY 225 E4
Sudbury Ave
Ilkeston DE7 209 B7
Sandiacre NG10 223 A6
Sudbury Cl
Chesterfield S40 95 B5
Sudbury Cl *continued*
Derby DE1 218 E5
Sudbury Ct NG10 235 F4
Sudbury Dr NG17 148 E2
Sudbury Hall★ DE6 225 D5
Sudbury Mews NG16 182 E1
Sudbury Pk DE6 225 D7
Sudbury Prim Sch DE6 225 E4
Sudbury St DE1 218 E5
Sudhall Cl S41 95 D8
Suff La NG16 160 C3
Suffolk Ave DE21 219 E7
Suffolk Rd DE15 254 D7
Suffolk Way DE11 255 E1
Sugworth Rd S6 31 F6
Sulleys Field DE22 204 D7
Summerbottom SK14 16 A8
Summerbrook Ct DE22 218 F4
Summer Cross
Tideswell SK17 69 B4
Wheston SK17 68 F3
Summer Dr DE4 165 E7
Summerfield Cres S43 96 E8
Summerfield Rd
Chesterfield S40 266 A1
Dronfield S18 57 B3
Summer Fields Dr DE11 256 D6
Summerfields Way DE7 194 D3
Summerfields Way S DE7 194 D2
Summerhill La SK17 103 C4
Summerhouse Drive S8 43 C1
Summer La
Sheffield S17 55 D4
Wirksworth DE4 165 E8
SUMMERLEY 57 E2
Summerley Lower Rd S18 57 F2
Summerley Rd S18 57 F2
Summerskill Gn S43 97 C7
Summerville Cl DE23 231 B6
Summerwood Croft S18 56 F2
Summer Wood Ct DE23 231 D7
Summerwood La S18 56 F3
Summerwood Pl S18 56 F2
Summit Dr NG20 119 E4
Sumners Pl SK13 10 B1
Sumner St SK13 17 C8
Sunart Cl DE24 231 F2
Sunday School La SK23 47 B6
Sunderland Close 4 DE11 255 E1
Sundew Cl DE21 220 F4
Sundew Court DE24 231 B3
Sundial Cl DE6 201 E8
Sundial Wlk DE6 201 E8
Sundown Ave DE23 231 D6
Sundown Cl SK22 33 A8
Sundown Pl S13 44 F8
Sundown Rd S13 44 F8
Sunflower Cl
Derby DE24 220 A1
Shirebrook NG20 119 D3
Sunflower Gr DE12 262 F3
Sun La DE4 156 F1
Sunlaws Ct SK13 17 B8
Sunlaws St SK13 17 B8
Sunlea Cres NG9 223 F5
Sunlight DE56 190 F1
Sunningdale Ave
Derby DE21 220 D5
Heanor DE75 193 F8
Sunningdale Cl
Burton upon Trent DE13 240 C1
Chesterfield S40 114 E8
Sunningdale Dr
Glossop SK13 10 E1
Ilkeston DE7 208 B5
Sunningdale Pk S42 115 C1
Sunningdale Rise S40 114 C8
Sunninghill Cl DE7 207 D8
Sunnybank DE4 110 F1
Sunny Bank
Great Longstone DE45 90 A4
Mayfield DE6 184 C7
Tibshelf DE55 147 F5
Sunny Bank Gdns DE56 178 F2
Sunny Bank La SK17 69 C4
Sunny Banks 3 SK13 17 B8
Sunny Brook Cl S43 80 E3
Sunnydale Park Nature Reserve★ DE23 231 C7
Sunnyfield SK17 85 F1
Sunny Gr DE21 220 A5
SUNNY HILL 231 D5
Sunny Hill DE56 190 F7
Sunnyhill Ave DE23 231 E6
Sunny Hill Gdns 1 DE56 190 F7
Sunnyside
Swadlincote DE11 255 E7
Whitwell S80 82 A6
Sunnyside Ct DE11 255 F7
Sunnyside Rd ST14 210 B1
Sunnyside Terr DE4 143 A8
Sunny Springs S41 266 B4
Sunnyvale Ave S17 55 E4
Sunnyvale Rd S17 55 D4
Sunset DE12 265 F1
Sunset Gdns DE12 262 F3
Sunshine Cl NG16 160 D4
Sun St
Derby DE22 267 A2
Woodville DE11 256 F2
Surbiton Cl DE22 218 A6
Surbiton Ct DE7 207 D8
Surgery La DE4 157 A1
Surprise Villas S32 53 A7
Surrey St
Derby DE22 218 D6
Glossop SK13 10 C1
Sussex Cir DE21 219 E8
Sussex Cl NG16 195 A8
Sussex Rd DE15 254 E6
Sussex Way NG10 223 B5
Sustainability Dr DE21 220 E2
Sutherland Farm View S44 99 B4
Sutherland Rd
3 Derby DE23 218 F8
Derby DE23 219 A1
Sutton Ave DE73 232 F3
Sutton Cl DE22 218 D6
Sutton Cres S43 97 C7
Sutton Ct NG16 182 F2
Sutton Dr DE24 232 E4
Sutton Hall Rd S44 117 E8
Sutton Ho DE24 233 C5
SUTTON IN ASHFIELD 148 F1
Sutton La
Burntheath DE65 228 C4
Etwall DE65 229 B5
Hatton DE65 227 E4
Hilton DE65 228 D2
Hilton DE65 228 D3
Long Duckmanton S44 116 F7
Longford DE6 214 C5
Sutton on the Hill DE6, DE65 228 B6
Sutton Scarsdale S44 117 A6
SUTTON ON THE HILL 228 B8
Sutton Rd
Church Broughton DE65 227 D7
Sutton in Ashfield NG17 148 F3
Suttons Ave 5 DE11 256 E1
Suttons Bsns Pk DE11 256 E3
Sutton Scarsdale Hall★ S44 117 A6
Suttons La SK6 23 A5
SUTTON SPRINGS WOOD 116 C6
Sutton View
Bolsover S44 118 B8
Temple Normanton S42 116 B4
Sutton Way SK13 10 A5
Swaddale Ave S41 96 B6
Swaddale Cl S41 96 B6
SWADLINCOTE 256 D4
Swadlincote La DE11 255 E2
Swadlincote Rd DE11 256 E3
Swadlincote Ski & Snowboard Ctr DE11 256 C3
Swaines Mdw DE4 165 D8
Swains Cl DE12 262 C5
SWAINSPARK 262 B7
Swainspark Ind Est DE12 262 B6
Swalebank Cl S40 115 B8
Swaledale Ct 2 DE24 233 C6
Swallow Cl DE3 218 A3
Swallow Ct DE5 180 D6
Swallowdale Rd DE24 231 D4
Swallow Fold SK13 16 F8
Swallow Ho DE1 218 E5
Swallow House Cres SK22 25 C3
Swallow House La SK22 25 C3
Swallow Rd DE11 256 F3
Swanbourne Cl 1 S41 96 C1
Swan Dr DE14 253 D7
Swan Hill DE3 230 B6
Swan La NG19 136 B3
Swanmore Rd DE23 231 A8
Swann Yd NG17 148 F3
Swan Rake SK17 104 C1
Swanson Ave NG17 148 F3
Swans Rest DE11 255 F6
Swan St S43 98 A7
SWANWICK 169 E8
Swanwick Ave NG20 119 F3
Swanwick Ct DE55 158 F2
Swanwick Gdns DE21 206 A1
Swanwick Hall Sch DE55 169 F7
Swanwick Hill
Swanwick DE55 169 E6
Swanwick DE55 169 E7
Swanwick Junc Sta★ DE5 170 A5
Swanwick Prim Sch DE55 169 D6
Swanwick Rd
Ilkeston DE7 194 F5
Somercotes DE55 170 B7
Swanwick Sch & Sports Coll DE55 169 F7
Swanwick St S41 77 A2
Swanwick Way S45 131 C5
SWARKESTONE 244 D6
Swarkestone Bridge DE73 244 E4
Swarkestone Dr DE23 231 C5
Swarkestone Rd
Barrow upon Trent DE73 244 B6
Chellaston DE73 244 F8
Swarkestone DE73 244 F6
Swartling Dr DE11 256 D4
SWATHWICK 114 D4
Swathwick Cl S42 114 E4
Swathwick La S42 114 D4
Swayfield Cl DE3 217 C3
Sweeney Dr DE14 253 C8
Sweetbriar Cl DE24 233 A5
Sweethill DE12 262 F5
Sweet Leys Way DE73 252 C8
Swift Bank SK13 16 F8
Swift Cl
Bradwell S33 51 A7
Derby DE3 218 A3
Woodville DE11 256 F3
Swift Ct NG16 182 F2
Swinburne St DE1 267 B1
Swindells Yard SK22 33 C7
Swinderby Dr DE21 206 B1
Swindon Cl NG16 195 C7
Swiney Way NG9 223 F2
SWINGATE 195 F5
Swing Bridge Wharf DE12 262 F3
Swinger La S45 129 C7
Swinney Bank DE56 179 A5
Swinney La DE56 179 A5
Swinscoe Hill DE6 172 B2
Swinscoe Ho 3 DE1 267 B2
Swinscoe Way S40 95 A5
Swinson Cl ST14 197 A3
Swithland Cl S41 115 C7
Sycamore Ave
Chesterfield S40 95 E2
Creswell S80 81 E2
Derby DE22 204 D3
Dronfield S18 57 A3
Findern DE65 230 E1
Glapwell S44 134 B8
Ripley DE5 180 D8
Swadlincote DE11 256 A7
Sycamore Cl
Bolsover S44 99 C2
3 Borrowash DE72 221 A1
Burton upon Trent DE15 254 E5
Buxton SK17 66 B1
Etwall DE65 229 C4
Linton DE12 261 D5
Mapperley DE7 193 F3
New Mills SK22 24 E1
Pinxton NG16 160 D3
Selston NG16 171 D7
Shirland DE55 146 C4
Sycamore Cotts DE6 151 D1
Sycamore Cres NG10 223 A7
Sycamore Croft DE56 179 B2
Sycamore Ct
Belper DE56 179 F1
Derby DE21 220 E5
Willington DE65 242 B5
Sycamore Dr
Calow S44 96 E3
Ilkeston DE7 209 B7
Killamarsh S21 60 C5
Sycamore Gdns 7 DE75 181 D1
Sycamore La
Barlborough S43 80 B6
Brimington S43 78 A1
Sycamore Rd
Awsworth NG16 195 C5
Brimington S43 78 A1
Burton upon Trent DE15 254 F6
Castle Donington DE74 247 B5
Chapel-en-le-Frith SK23 47 B4
Hayfield SK22 24 F2
Long Eaton NG10 236 C5
Mansfield Woodhouse NG19 136 C5
Matlock DE4 143 B6
Mayfield DE6 184 C7
Sycamore St
Church Warsop NG20 120 F6
Sheffield S20 59 C8
Sycamores The
Eastwood NG16 182 E1
Glossop SK13 9 F3
Sheffield S13 44 C6
South Normanton DE55 160 B5
Tutbury DE13 239 E6
Sycamore Terr SK22 25 D3
Sycamore Way DE6 201 F8
Syda La
Old Brampton S42 93 E1
Upper Loads S42 112 D7
Sydall Rise S45 131 D5
Syday La S21 60 D1
Sydenham Rd DE22 218 A7
Sydney Cl
Derby DE3 217 F3
Mansfield Woodhouse NG19 136 C6
Sydney Rd DE72 235 A7
Sydney St S40 95 E3
Sydnope Hall DE4 128 A5
Sydnope Hill DE4 128 A5
Syerscote La
Clifton Campville B79 263 B2
Haunton B79 263 B2
Sylvan Cl S41 266 C1
Sylvan Cliff SK17 85 C7
Sylvan Dr S42 131 A6
Sylvan Pk SK17 85 C8
Sylvester Cl DE1 267 C2
Sylvia Rd S18 76 D5
Sywell Cl DE55 169 F8

T

Tabley Gdns SK6 23 A4
TADDINGTON 88 B3
Taddington Cl 2 DE21 219 E8
Taddington Pl 3 SK13 9 E1
Taddington & Priestcliffe Sch SK17 87 F3
Taddington Rd
Chesterfield S40 95 B5
Derby DE21 205 F1
Taft Ave NG10 223 B6
Tagg La
Crowdicote SK17 121 E7
Moneyash SK17 122 C8
Monyash DE45 107 A1
Taggs Knoll S33 40 B4
Taghole La DE6 188 E2
Tailby Dr DE65 242 A5
Talbot Cres S41 115 D7
Talbot Dr NG9 209 D2
Talbot Meadows DE65 228 D2
Talbot Pl DE12 265 E8
Talbot Rd SK13 10 C2
Talbot St
Buxton SK17 85 D4
Chesterfield S41 115 D7
Derby DE1 267 A3
Glossop SK13 10 C1
Pinxton NG16 160 C2
Swadlincote DE11 256 A1
Talgarth Cl DE21 206 C2
Tallys End S43 80 A6
Tamar Ave DE22 204 D4
Tamworth Rd
Appleby Magna DE12 265 E2
Castle Donington DE72, NG10 235 E1
Long Eaton NG10 236 C5
Tamworth Rise DE56 190 E4
Tamworth St DE56 190 E3
Tamworth Terr DE56 190 E4
Tanglewood DE56 179 A6
Tanner's La DE65 242 C3
TANSLEY 144 B4
Tansley Ave DE7 193 A1
Tansley Ct S41 95 E6
Tansley Dr S40 95 A5
Tansley House Gdns DE4 144 A4
TANSLEY KNOLL 144 A5
Tansley Prim Sch DE4 144 A4
Tansley Rd S42 131 F5
Tansley Rise 4 DE21 205 F1
Tansley Way S43 97 C6
Tansley Wood Ho DE4 143 E5
Tansy Ct DE24 231 C3
Tants Mdw DE56 191 F6
Tantum Ave DE75 181 C4
Tanyard Cl DE74 247 B4
Tapestry Wlk S45 131 E5
Tap La S40 266 A3
Taplow Cl DE3 217 C2
TAPTON 96 C6
Tapton Bsns Pk S41 266 C4
Tapton La S41 266 C3
Tapton Lock Hill S41 96 B6

Tapton Lock Visitor Ctr★
  S41..................96 B6
Tapton Park Bsns Pk **11**
  DE11................256 E1
Tapton Park Ind Est **10**
  DE11................256 E1
Tapton Terr S41......266 C4
Tapton Vale S41.......96 C5
Tapton Way S44........96 F3
Tarina Cl DE73.......233 A1
Tarmac Way NG20.....120 D8
Tarn Cl NG16.........182 R4
Tarnside Fold **1**
  SK13................17 A7
Tarquin Cl DE13......240 E2
Tarragon Cl DE3......217 D4
Tarrat Street **3**
  DE7................194 E2
Tasman Cl DE3.......217 F3
TATENHILL...........253 A8
Tatenhill La
  Branston DE14......253 D7
  Tatenhill DE13.....253 A8
Tatham's La DE7.....194 E4
Tattersall Wlk **5**
  NG19...............136 E4
Tattle Hill DE7......207 F2
Tatwin Ct DE73.......252 F2
Taunton Cl DE24.....233 C8
Tavern Cl **10** DE7...194 E1
Taverners Cres
  DE23...............231 C8
Tavern Rd SK13........9 E3
Tavistock Ave DE5...169 D2
Tavistock Cl **14**
  DE24...............231 D3
Tavistock Ct **14** S41..95 F8
Tavistock Sq DE55...159 B5
Tawney Cl DE4.......144 A4
Tawny Way DE23......231 A7
TAXAL................45 D4
Taxal & Fernilee CE Prim
  Sch SK23............45 D6
Taxal Mews SK23.....45 D6
Taxal Moor Rd SK23..45 C3
Taxhall Rd SK23......45 D5
Tayberry Cl DE24....232 E7
Tay Cl
  Derby DE24.........231 D2
  Dronfield S18.......56 D2
Taylor Cres
  Chesterfield S41....96 D1
  Stapleford NG9.....223 F8
Taylor Ct DE6........173 C1
Taylor La DE75.......181 D4
Taylors La ST14......196 D4
Taylor's La
  Spout DE4..........166 B4
  Trusley DE6........215 E6
Taylor St
  Derby DE24.........219 E2
  Hollingworth SK14....9 D4
  Ilkeston DE7........194 F1
Taylor Way DE55....158 F1
Tayside Cl DE24......231 D3
Tay Wlk DE22.........204 E3
Tealby Wlk **10** NG19.136 E4
Teal Cl NG20.........119 D3
Tean Cl DE15.........248 A1
Teasel Dr DE11.......256 F4
Teasel Gro **3** DE3...217 C4
Tedder Ave SK17......85 D3
Tedgness Rd S32......53 E1
Tedworth Ave DE24..231 D2
Teesdale Rd
  Long Eaton NG10....236 A6
  Sheffield S12........58 F8
Telford Cl DE3.......217 E1
Telford Cres S43.....78 F2
Telford Rd SK6........23 A4
Telmah Cl DE13......240 D1
Temperance Hill
  DE55...............145 E7
Temperance Sq SK14...9 A4
Temperance St **5**
  SK14................16 A8
Templar Cl DE24.....231 C3
Templar Road LE66..258 A1
Temple Ave DE55.....10 C5
Templebell Cl DE23..231 A6
Temple Ct SK17.......85 A6
TEMPLE
  NORMANTON.......116 B3
Temple Normanton Bsns
  Pk S41.............116 A4
Temple Normanton Prim
  Sch S42............116 C4
Temple Rd
  Buxton SK17.........85 A6
  Matlock Bath DE4...143 A1
Temple St
  6 Derby DE23....218 F3
  Derby DE23.........219 A3
  Glossop SK13........10 C5
Templeton Close
  DE3................217 F3
Temple View SK17....85 C7
Tenant St DE1........267 B3
Tenby Dr DE21.......206 C2
Tennessee Rd DE22..220 B7
Tennyson Ave
  Chesterfield S40....266 A3
  Mansfield Woodhouse
  NG19...............136 C2
  Swadlincote DE11...256 C6

Tennyson Rd S80......81 D1
Tennyson Sq NG16...195 C4
Tennyson St
  Derby DE24.........232 D7
  Holmewood S42.....116 D1
  Ilkeston DE7........194 E3
  Shirland DE55.......146 C5
Tennyson Way S42...115 E3
Tenter Cl NG10......236 D5
Tenter La DE56.......168 D1
Terminus Dr DE5.....180 F7
Tern Ave DE11........256 F3
Terrace La NG19.....134 F5
Terrace Rd
  Buxton SK17.........85 B7
  Chapel-en-le-Frith
  SK23................47 B6
  Tideswell SK17......69 C4
Terret Gr SK17........84 D5
Terrey Rd S17.........55 E5
Terr The DE21.......219 E7
Terry Pl DE24........232 F6
Tetford Wlk **13**
  NG19...............136 E4
Tetron Point DE11...255 E3
Tetron Way DE11....255 D3
Teversal Ave NG19..135 B4
Tevery Cl NG9.......223 E8
Teviot Pl DE21.......206 A2
Tewkesbury Ave
  NG19...............136 D4
Tewkesbury Cres
  DE21...............219 D8
Tewkesbury Dr
  NG16...............195 E7
Tewkesbury Rd
  NG10...............236 E4
Thackeray Rd DE55..146 F3
Thackeray St DE24...232 A5
Thame Ct **2** S43....96 E8
Thames Ave **8** S2...43 C8
Thames Cl DE22.....217 F5
Thames Way DE65...228 D1
Thanet Dr DE24......233 A6
Thanet St S41........131 D3
Thatch Cl DE22......204 F2
Thatchers Croft
  DE4................144 A3
Thatchers La DE4....144 A3
Thatchmarsh Cl
  NE7................194 F6
Theatre La S41.......266 C3
Theatre Wlk DE1.....267 C3
Theatre Yd S40......266 B3
Thickley Bank NG20.119 F4
Thimble Hill DE6....189 A2
Thirlmere Ave DE22.204 E3
Thirlmere Cl **3**
  NG10...............223 B2
Thirlmere Dr S18......57 A2
Thirlmere Rd
  Chesterfield S41.....95 C7
  Long Eaton NG10...223 B2
Thirlwell Rd S8.......43 A6
Thirsk Pl DE24.......232 D7
Thirteen Row S44....118 A6
Thistle Bank NG19...136 F4
Thistle Cl
  Eastwood NG16.....195 B8
  Woodville DE11.....256 F4
Thistledown Cl
  DE22...............205 A2
Thistle Gr DE73......232 E1
Thistlegreen Cl
  DE75...............182 B1
Thistle Rd DE7.......209 A4
Thomas Chambers **3**
  SK13................17 C7
Thomas Cl NG16.....170 F3
Thomas Cook Cl
  DE73...............252 A7
Thomas Ct DE1......218 E4
Thomas Mdws SK23...47 A5
Thomas Meadows
  SK23................47 A5
Thomas St
  Compstall SK6.......15 B2
  Glossop SK13........10 E1
Thompson Cl
  4 Chesterfield S41..96 A8
  Derby DE3.........217 B3
  Swadlincote DE11...256 E4
Thompson St
  Chesterfield S41....96 A7
  Langley Mill NG16..182 B3
Thomson Dr DE5.....181 B7
Thomson Wlk DE5...181 A8
Thoresby Ave
  Clowne S43..........81 A4
  Shirebrook NG20...119 C4
Thoresby Cl
  Derby DE21.........206 B1
  Ripley DE5..........169 C1
Thoresby Cres DE72.234 F7
Thoresby Pl S43......97 C6
Thoresby Rd
  Long Eaton NG10...236 C6
  Mansfield Woodhouse
  NG19...............136 A3
Thorn Ave NG19.....135 F1
Thornborough Cl S2..43 C7
Thornborough Pl S2..43 C7
Thornborough Rd S2.43 C7
Thornbridge Ave
  S12.................44 D3
Thornbridge Cl S12...44 D3
Thornbridge Cres
  Chesterfield S40....115 A6

Thornbridge Cres
  continued
  Sheffield S12........44 E3
Thornbridge Dr S12...44 D3
Thornbridge Gr S12..44 E3
Thornbridge La S12...44 E3
Thornbridge Pl S12...44 D3
Thornbridge Rd S12..44 D3
Thornbridge Rise
  S12.................44 E3
Thornbridge Way
  S12.................44 E3
Thornbrook Cl S23....47 C5
Thornbrook Rd S23...47 C6
Thorn Cl
  Buxton SK17.........85 E8
  Derby DE22.........204 D4
Thorncliffe Ave
  DE4................127 A6
Thorncliffe Rd SK13...9 F4
Thorncliffe Terr
  SK17................69 C3
Thorncliffe Vale SK14..9 C6
Thorndene Cl S41.....96 A6
Thorndike Ave
  DE24...............233 A7
Thorndon Cl DE3.....230 D8
Thorndon Way S40..114 C8
Thorn Dr NG16.......195 B8
Thorne Cl S42.........94 F4
Thornecliffewood
  SK14.................9 D5
Thornell Cl S23.......47 C5
Thornescroft Gdns
  DE14...............254 B8
Thorness Cl DE24....233 C5
Thornewill Dr DE13.240 F1
Thorneywood Rd
  NG10...............236 F8
Thornfield Ave S40...95 B1
Thornfield Ct S41.....96 A5
Thornfield Pl S43......80 D2
Thornfield Sq NG10.236 E8
THORNHILL...........39 F3
Thornhill Ave DE56..179 B2
Thornhill Dr DE55....160 B6
Thornhill La S33.......39 F4
Thornhill Rd DE23...218 C1
Thornley Pl DE6.....173 C1
Thornsett...........24 F3
Thornsett S22.........24 E2
Thornsett Ave SK17...85 E8
Thornsett Cl SK17.....85 E8
Thornsett Gdns S17..55 F8
Thornsett La S22......25 B3
Thornsett Prim Sch
  SK22...............24 E3
Thornsett Trad Est
  SK22...............24 E2
Thornsett Trading Estate
  SK22...............24 F2
Thorn St
  Derby DE23.........218 F2
  Woodville DE11.....256 F2
Thorn Street Mews
  DE11...............256 F2
Thornton Dr DE65...240 E8
Thornton Pl **1** S18..56 E2
Thornton Way DE56.179 C6
Thorntree Cl
  Breaston DE72......222 F1
  Breaston DE72......235 E8
Thorntree Cotts
  DE4................154 F2
Thorntree Ct S40....114 F7
Thorntree Gdns
  NG16...............182 F4
Thorntree La
  2 Branston DE14..253 E7
  2 Branston DE14..256 E7
  Derby DE1.........267 B3
Thorn Tree La DE11,
  DE15...............255 F7
Thorn Tree Rd **1**
  DE6................201 E8
Thornway SK6.........32 A7
Thornwood Ct SK17..85 A8
Thorp Cl S2...........43 A8
THORPE.............161 C1
Thorpe Ave
  Dronfield S18........57 C4
  Whitwell S80........81 F5
Thorpe Cl
  Burton upon Trent
  DE15...............248 C2
  26 Chesterfield S41..95 F8
  Stapleford NG9.....223 D7
Thorpe Croft DE4....156 B5
Thorpe Downs Rd
  DE11...............256 B1
Thorpe Dr DE3.......217 B3
Thorpe Hill Dr DE75.193 E8
Thorpe House Ave
  S8..................43 B4
Thorpe House Rd S8..43 B4
Thorpe House Rise
  S8..................43 B4
Thorpe La
  Clifton Campville
  DE9................263 L1
  Shireoaks S80, S81..63 D6
Thorpelands Ave
  NG19...............136 E1
Thorpelands Dr
  DE22...............204 E1
Thorpe Leys NG10...236 D5
Thorpe Rd
  Eastwood NG16....182 F4

Thorpe Rd continued
  Harthill S26.........62 A7
  Ilam DE6...........161 A2
THORPE SALVIN......62 F6
Thorpe's Rd
  Heanor DE75.......181 D1
  Shipley DE75.......193 D8
Thorpe's Rd Ind Est
  DE75...............193 D8
Thorpe St
  Glossop SK13........10 E2
  Ilkeston DE7........194 E3
Thorpe View DE6....185 C8
Thorpe Way DE56....179 B5
Thorpleigh Rd S43....79 B2
Three Gates DE56...178 F2
Threeshires Rd
  SK11...............102 D5
Thrift Cl DE3.........217 C5
Thrift Rd DE14......254 B8
Throstle Nest Way
  DE6................201 F8
THRUMPTON..........237 C3
Thrumpton Ave
  NG10...............237 A7
Thrumpton Hall★
  NG11...............237 B3
Thrushton Cl DE65..230 C2
Thruxton Cl DE24....233 C6
THULSTON...........233 F4
Thunderpit La S32....71 A3
Thurgarton Ct DE6..173 D1
Thurgaton Way
  DE55...............148 A3
Thurlby Ct **9** NG19..136 E4
Thurlow Booth DE4..167 E7
Thurlow Ct DE21....206 A1
Thurman St DE7.....209 A6
Thurrows Way
  DE73...............233 B2
Thurstan Ave S8......56 E8
Thurston Ave DE55.170 D8
Thurstone Furlong
  DE73...............232 F1
THURVASTON
  Longford...........215 C8
  Marston Montgomery.197 F1
Thurvaston La
  Lower Thurvaston
  DE6................214 F6
  Thurvaston DE6.....215 A8
Thurvaston Rd DE6..197 F1
Thyme Cl DE23......231 D4
Thyme St
  Branston DE14......253 E6
  Branston DE14......256 E6
Tiber Cl DE24.......233 D5
Tib Meadow Cl **7**
  DE7................208 C5
TIBSHELF...........148 A6
Tibshelf Bsns Pk
  DE55...............148 C6
Tibshelf Com Sch
  DE55...............147 E5
Tibshelf Inf Sch
  DE55...............148 A7
Tibshelf Rd
  Blackwell DE55.....147 C1
  Holmewood S42.....132 C1
TIBSHELF WHARF...148 D7
Tickham Ave DE24...231 C2
Tickhill Dr **1** S2.....44 A7
TICKNALL...........251 A4
Ticknall Cl DE56.....180 B1
Ticknall Rd
  Hartshorne DE11...250 C1
  Hartshorne DE11...257 B7
  Repton DE65.......250 B6
Ticknall Wlk DE23...231 A6
Ticknal Rd DE65....243 A1
TIDESWELL..........69 D4
Tideswell Bank **15**
  SK13.................9 E1
Tideswell Ct S43......97 C8
Tideswell Ct **5** S40..95 D5
Tideswell Gn DE11...255 E5
Tideswell La S32......71 C5
Tideswell Moor
  Tideswell SK17......50 A3
  Tideswell SK17......69 A8
  Wheston SK17.......68 F8
Tideswell Rd DE21..205 F1
Tideswell Wlk **13**
  SK13.................9 E1
Tiger Yd **6** DE6.....173 B2
Tilbury Pl DE24......233 A5
Tilford Gdns NG9...223 F3
Tiller Cl DE23........231 B6
Tilley Gn DE11.......255 F6
Tillotson Cl **1** S8....43 A6
Tillotson Rise S8......43 A6
Tilton Gr DE7........208 C5
Timber La S45.......132 D5
Timbersbrook Cl
  DE21...............206 A1
Timor Ct DE24......219 E2
Timsbury Ct DE21...205 E2
Tinderbox La DE65..229 F5
Tinker Croft DE7....208 E7
Tinkerley La DE6....165 D1
Tinkley La S42.......130 D2
Tinsell Brook
  Hilton DE65........228 D1
  5 Hilton DE65....240 E8
Tinsell La DE6.......183 A8
Tinsley Rd DE756,
  NG16...............182 D1

Tintagel Cl
  Burton upon Trent
  DE13...............240 E2
  2 Derby DE23...219 B2
Tintagel Way NG19..135 D1
TINTWISTLE..........10 B8
Tintwistle CE (Aided)
  Prim Sch SK13.......9 F6
Tipnall Rd DE74.....247 A3
Tipper's La S41......227 A8
Tip Tree Cl NG16....195 F7
Tiree Cl
  Derby DE24.........231 F4
  Stapleford NG9.....209 D2
  Tibshelf DE55.......147 F5
TISSINGTON.........162 B6
Tissington Bank **27**
  SK13.................9 D1
Tissington Cl S40.....95 B5
Tissington Dr DE21.206 B3
Tissington Gn **26** SK13.9 D1
Tissington Terr **28**
  SK13.................9 D1
Titchfield St
  Creswell S80.........81 F1
  Whitwell S80........81 F6
Tithe Barn Cl SK17...69 C3
Tithebarn Dr DE12..262 B3
Tithe Barn Gdns
  DE65...............242 D2
Tithebarn La DE6...215 C5
Titterton La
  Alstonefield SK17...149 A8
  Clay Cross SK17....131 A2
Tiverton Cl DE4.....167 E3
Tiverton Ct **22** S41...95 F8
Tivey Rd S21.........59 D2
Tivey Way S3.........252 C8
Tivoli Gdns DE1.....218 E2
Toad Hole Cl **4**
  DE7................208 C6
TOADHOLE
  FURNANCE..........158 C6
Toad La DE21........191 E2
TOADMOOR..........167 F3
Toadmoor La DE56..167 F3
Tobermory Way
  DE24...............231 D3
Todbrook Cl SK23....45 D6
Todd St SK13.........17 D8
Toll Bar Ave S12......43 E5
Toll Bar Cl S12........43 E5
Toll Bar Dr S12.......43 E5
Toll Bar Rd S12.......43 E5
Tollbridge Rd S43....79 B2
Tollemache Cl SK14...9 A5
Tollemache Rd SK14...9 A5
Tollgate Cotts DE6..184 E8
Toll House Mead
  S20.................59 C7
Tom Brads Croft
  SK23................45 E8
Tom La
  Chapel-en-le-Frith
  SK23................46 D5
  Staveley S44........97 F5
Tomlinson Bsns Pk
  DE65...............226 F4
Tomlinson Ct DE24..232 F7
Tomlinson Ind Est
  DE21...............205 B8
Tomlinsons Cotts
  DE21...............205 C2
Tom Mead Cl **3**
  DE11...............255 F5
TOMTHORN...........66 E4
Tom Will Way LE65..258 A1
Tomwood Rise SK13.16 C6
Tonbridge Dr DE24..233 A5
Tonge La DE73.......252 F3
Tongue La S17........85 E7
Tongue Lane Ind Est
  SK17................85 E7
Tooth St **3** DE11...256 F1
Top Cotts SK17........88 F7
Top Farm Ct DE56..191 F8
Top Farm Mws S21...60 C1
Top Hagg La DE56...56 A6
Tophill La DE4.......153 D8
Tophole Rd S33.......50 F4
Top La
  Crich DE4..........156 D1
  Mansfield NG19....135 A3
  Old Brampton S42...93 E3
  Shottle DE56.......166 C1
  Tideswell SK17......69 B5
  Wadshelf S42........93 D5
Topley Gdns DE21...205 F2
Top Lons DE6........176 B8
Top Manor Cl DE72.221 C5
Top Mdw DE11.......256 B7
Top of Hope DE6....149 D3
Top o' th' Edge La
  SK17...............121 C7
Toppham Dr S8.......56 F6
Toppham Rd S8........56 F6
Toppham Way S8......56 F6
Top Pingle Cl S43.....96 E7
Top Rd
  Calow S44...........97 A3
  Pilsley DE45.........91 C2
  Wingerworth S42...114 D2
Top Row
  Mansfield NG19....135 A3
  Pilsley DE45.........91 C2
  Somercotes NG16..171 A5
Topshill La DE6.....165 B2

Tor Ave DE55........170 C6
Tor Cl DE4...........143 B2
Torfield Cotts DE4..127 B3
Torksey Wlk **11**
  NG19...............136 E4
Torquay Ct **6** S41...95 F8
Torrance Cl DE14...254 A6
Torrani Way S42.....131 F2
Torridon Cl DE24....231 E4
Tor Rise DE4........143 B3
Torr St SK17.........85 B7
Torrs Valley S22......33 C7
TORR TOP............33 C7
Torr Top St SK22......33 C7
Torrvale Rd S22......33 B7
Torr View S17.........85 E1
Torside Mews SK13..10 A6
Torside St
  Tintwistle SK13.....10 A6
  Tintwistle SK14......9 F6
Torside Visitor Ctr★
  SK13.................6 D1
Torside Way SK13....10 A5
Tors Spring DE4....168 A8
Tors The DE4........156 F1
Tor View Rise DE4..155 A6
Torwood Dr S8........56 E2
TOTLEY..............55 D4
Totley All Saints CE VA
  Prim Sch S17........55 D4
Totley Ave **42** SK13..9 D1
TOTLEY BROOK.......55 E5
Totley Brook Cl S17..55 D5
Totley Brook Croft
  S17.................55 D5
Totley Brook Glen
  S17.................55 D5
Totley Brook Gr S17.55 D5
Totley Brook Rd S17.55 E5
Totley Brook Way
  S17.................55 D5
Totley **47** SK13......9 D1
Totley Gdns **46** SK13..9 D1
Totley Gn **23** SK13...9 D1
Totley Grange Cl
  S17.................55 D4
Totley Grange Dr
  S17.................55 D4
Totley Grange Rd
  S17.................55 D4
Totley Hall Croft S17.55 D3
Totley Hall Dr S17...55 D4
Totley Hall La S17...55 D4
Totley Hall Mead
  S17.................55 D3
Totley La S17........56 A5
Totley Lanes **43** SK13..9 D1
Totley Mews **20** SK13..9 D1
Totley Mount S43.....96 D8
Totley Mws S17.......55 D4
Totley Pl **48** SK13....9 D1
Totley Prim Sch S17.55 D4
TOTLEY RISE.........55 F5
TOTON.............223 E2
Toton Bispham Drive
  Jun Sch NG9.......223 E3
Toton La NG9.......223 E6
Touchstone Ct
  DE73...............232 D2
Toulmin Dr DE11....256 B4
Tower Cl
  Sheffield S2.........43 C8
  Somercotes DE55..170 C8
Tower Cres S44......118 B8
Tower Dr DE3........217 D6
Tower Ho S2..........43 C8
Tower La
  Bonsall DE4........141 F3
  Bonsall DE4........142 A3
Tower Rd
  Burton upon Trent
  DE15...............248 B2
  Hartshorne DE11...257 A6
Tower Rise **11** S2....43 C8
Towers La S32........40 E1
Tower St DE24.......232 D7
Tower View Prim Sch
  DE15...............248 C3
Towle Cl DE72.......221 C1
Towles Pastures
  DE74...............247 A3
Towle St NG10.......236 A4
Town Cres NG16....160 D4
TOWNEND...........47 C7
TOWN END
  Eyam...............71 E6
  Tideswell...........69 C3
Town End
  Apperknowle S18....58 A1
  Bolsover S44........99 A1
  Buxton SK17.........66 E1
  Crich DE4..........156 F2
  Kirk Ireton DE6....165 B1
  Shirland DE55......146 D2
  Taddington SK17....88 B2
Town End Jun Sch
  DE55...............147 E5
Town End La DE6....172 A4
Town End Rd DE72..235 B7
Townfield La S33......39 E1
Town Fold S43........47 C7
Town Gate S33.......51 A7
Town Hall Yd **3**
  DE6................173 C2

TOWNHEAD 55 C7
Townhead S32 ....71 C6
TOWN HEAD
Eyam................71 C6
Tideswell 69 C5
Town Head
Ashbourne DE6...... 173 C3
Bonsall DE4 .... 142 D2
Townhead La S33 ....39 F4
Townhead Rd S17 ....55 C7
Town La
Bradwell S33 ....51 A7
Broadbottom SK13.....16 D6
Newton DE55 .... 148 A3
Townscliffe La SK6 ..23 C6
Townsend Gr DE73 . 233 A2
Townside Cl NG10 .. 236 B4
Town St
Brassington DE4..... 153 A1
Duffield DE56........190 F3
Holbrook DE56...... 191 C6
Marple SK6...........23 B7
Pinxton NG16........160 E3
Sandiacre NG10......223 B5
Town The DE21..... 205 C7
Town View NG16 ....195 F7
Towpath Way DE21 . 220 D3
Towson Ave NG16 .. 182 C2
Trafalgar Parkway
DE24.............. 232 B6
Trafalgar Rd NG10 .. 236 D6
Trafalgar Sq NG10 .. 236 E7
Trafalgar Terr NG10 .236 F7
Trafalgar Way
NG19 .... 136 C7
Traffic St DE1 ...... 267 C2
Traffic Terr
Barrow Hill S43 ....78 B4
2 Chesterfield S41 ...115 B7
Trafford Way DE23 . 231 C8
Trail View
Alfreton DE55........147 F6
Glossop SK13.........10 B5
Tramway The DE11 ..255 F7
Tranmere Ave S45 .. 131 D3
Transport Way
4 Ironville NG16.....170 F4
Ironville NG16 ...... 171 A5
Transvaal Terr S44 . 118 B5
Trapper Way S20.....60 A6
Traso Bsns Pk S18....57 C1
Travellers Cl S44 .....98 F6
Traversgate S44......97 B3
Travers Rd NG10.... 223 B6
Travey Rd S2.........44 A7
Treak Cliff Cavern*
S33..................37 E3
Tredcroft St SK13.....17 B8
Tredegar Dr DE21 .. 206 B2
Treeneuk Cl S40.......95 B3
Treeneuk Gardens
S40..................95 B3
Trefoil Ct DE23 ..... 231 A7
Tregaron Cl DE21... 206 C2
Tregony Way DE24.. 231 D3
Trelawney Rd S45 .. 131 D3
Trenchard Dr SK17 ..85 D3
Trent Ave
Buxton SK17..........85 C4
Willington DE65 ..... 242 C5
Trent Bridge Ct
DE23.............. 231 C8
Trent Bsns Ctr
NG10 .... 223 C2
Trent Cl
Derby DE24 .... 231 D2
Willington DE65 ..... 242 C5
Trent Coll NG10 .... 236 C8
Trent Cotts NG10 ....236 F6
Trent Dr DE23 ...... 231 D6
Trent Gr
Alfreton DE55....... 159 A2
Dronfield S18.........57 B3
Trent Ho NG10 ..... 236 A4
Trent La
Castle Donington
DE74............. 247 A5
King's Newton DE73.. 245 C1
Long Eaton NG10 .....236 F5
Newton Solney DE15 ..248 E8
Weston-on-Trent
DE72..............245 F4
Trent Lane Ind Est
DE74..............247 B5
TRENTLOCK 236 E3
Trenton Dr
Derby DE21 ....220 B6
Long Eaton NG10 .... 237 A8
Trenton Gn DE21 ... 220 B6
Trent Rd DE7....... 208 D4
Trent Rise DE21 .....220 F4
Trent Side
Barrow upon Trent
DE73.............. 244 D6
Barton In Fabis NG11. 237 D6
Trent St
Derby DE24 .... 233 A7
Long Eaton NG10 .....236 E8
Trent Way DE3 ..... 217 B1
Trent Wlk 1 NG19.. 136 E4
Tresillian Cl DE22... 204 E2
Tressall Cl DE7 ..... 209 A8
Trevelyn Cl DE15 ... 248 C2
Treveris Cl DE21.... 220 E4
Trevone Ave NG9... 223 E6
Trevone Ct DE24.... 233 C5
Trevorrow Cres S40 266 B1
Trevose Cl S40 ..... 114 C7
Triangle The
Belper DE56.........178 F4
Ilkeston DE7........ 209 A6
Trickett Cl S33 ....38 C3
Trinity Cl
Ashford in the Water
DE45..............108 F8
Chesterfield S40..... 266 A4
Ilkeston DE7.........194 E3
Trinity Ct S41 ...... 266 A4
Trinity Gr DE11 ..... 256 B3
Trinity Mews S41... 266 A4
Trinity Passage 6
SK17.................85 C7
Trinity St DE1 ...... 267 C2
Trinity View NG10 .. 236 E8
Trinity Way
3 Heanor DE75......181 F1
4 Heanor DE75......193 E8
Trinity Wlk DE1..... 267 C2
Trinkey La S32 ....72 A3
Tristram Gr DE13 ... 240 E2
Trocadero Ct DE23 . 267 B1
Troon Cl
Burton upon Trent
DE13............. 240 C1
Chesterfield S40..... 114 C8
Derby DE23 .... 231 A8
Kimberley NG16......195 E7
Trot La
Great Hucklow SK17....69 F7
Great Hucklow SK17....70 A5
Troughbrook Hill
S43..................97 B8
Troughbrook Rd S43 .78 B1
Trough La
Hulland Ward DE6 ... 175 D2
Kimberley NG16......195 F8
Trough Rd NG16.....195 F8
Troutbeck Gr DE23 . 231 A7
TROWAY 58 B4
Trowbridge Cl DE21 205 E2
TROWELL.......... 209 C5
Trowell Ave DE7.... 209 A5
Trowell CE Prim Sch
NG9 .... 209 D4
Trowell Gr
Long Eaton NG10 .... 223 C1
Stapleford NG9...... 209 D3
Trowell Marsh Nature
Reserve* DE7.......209 B4
Trowell Park Dr
NG9 .... 209 D2
Trowell Rd NG9 .... 209 D2
Trowels La DE22.... 218 C4
Trueblue La DE45... 108 B5
Trueman St DE7 .....194 F4
Truman St
Cossall DE7 .... 195 A1
Kimberley NG16..... 195 D7
Truro Cl DE11 ...... 256 E5
Truro Cres DE21.... 219 E8
TRUSLEY...........215 F4
Trusley Brook DE65. 228 D1
Trusley Gdns DE23.. 231 D5
Trusley Wlk 7
NG19 .... 136 E4
Trustley Cl DE14.... 254 B7
Tudor Cl NG10...... 223 E1
Tudor Court DE13 .. 239 B6
Tudor Ct
Borrowash DE72 .....221 E1
3 Derby DE22........204 F3
Selston NG16....... 171 D6
Tudor Falls DE75 ... 181 E3
Tudor Field Cl DE73 233 A1
Tudor Gdns 6
DE13.............. 239 C5
Tudor House Cl
DE11.............. 256 A7
Tudor Pl DE7....... 208 C5
Tudor Rd DE21 ..... 220 A6
Tudor Rise B79..... 263 E2
Tudor St 2 S43 ......78 F2
Tudor Way DE11.... 256 A6
Tufnell Gdns DE22.. 218 B7
Tulip Rd
Awsworth NG16......195 B5
Tutbury DE13 .... 239 C5
Tulla Cl DE24....... 231 E1
Tumbling Hill DE56 . 168 E1
Tunicliffe Ct DE11 .. 256 D4
Tunnel Yd 7 DE6.... 173 B2
Tunstall Gn S40 ....95 D1
Tunstall Way S40.....95 D1
TUNSTEAD 67 F2
Tunstead Dr DE72 .. 245 B8
TUNSTEAD MILTON ..46 C5
Tuphall Cl DE73 .... 233 B2
TUPTON........... 131 D8
Tupton Hall Sch
S42.............. 131 D7
Tupton Moor Cl
S42.............. 115 D1
Tupton Prim Sch
S42.............. 115 D1
Tupton Rd S45 ..... 131 C5
Tupton Way S42.... 116 D1
Turf Lea Fold SK6 ....23 B1
Turf Lea Rd
Disley SK6 ....32 B8
Marple SK6...........23 B1
TURLOW FIELDS ... 175 C7
Turlowfields La
Hognaston DE6.......164 B1
Turlowfields La *continued*
Hognaston DE6...... 175 C7
Turnberry Cl
Chesterfield S40..... 114 C8
Ilkeston DE7........ 194 C2
Turnbull Cl S40.... 266 A1
Turnbury Cl DE14... 254 A7
Turncliffe Cl SK17 ....84 F6
TURNDITCH 177 B1
Turnditch CE Prim Sch
DE56...............177 B2
Turner Ave NG16 ... 182 A3
Turner Cl
Dronfield S18.........56 F1
Stapleford NG9.......223 E6
Turner Dr
Eastwood NG16 ......195 B7
Staveley S43..........97 B7
Turner Rd
Buxton SK17..........84 E5
Long Eaton NG10 ... 236 C4
Turner's Almshouses
DE22.............. 218 D6
Turners Cl 1 DE55 ..158 F1
Turners La DE55.... 170 A7
Turner St DE24 ..... 232 E6
TURNERWOOD S81 ...63 B7
Turnlee Cl SK13 ......17 C7
Turnlee Dr SK13......17 C7
Turnlee Rd SK13......17 C7
Turnley Rd DE55.... 160 C6
Turnoak Ave NE7 ....194 F5
Turnoaks Bsns Pk
S40............... 115 A6
Turnoaks La S40.... 115 A7
Turnpike Bsns Pk
DE55...............158 F2
Turnpike Cl
Alfreton DE55........158 F2
Matlock DE4 .... 143 C5
Turnpike Way DE6.. 185 E7
Turton Cl NG16..... 182 A3
TUTBURY.......... 239 C5
Tutbury Ave DE3.... 230 E5
Tutbury Bypass
DE13.............. 239 D7
Tutbury Castle*
DE13...............239 B7
Tutbury Dr 4
DE15.............. 248 A1
TUTBURY, FAULD .. 238 C6
Tutbury & Hatton Sta
DE65.............. 239 D8
Tutbury Hollow
1 Ashbourne DE6.... 185 C8
Spitalhill DE6 .... 185 C7
Tutbury Rd DE13.... 240 A1
Tutbury Rd Rural
DE13...............239 F2
Tuxford Cl DE21 .... 206 B1
Twayblade DE14.... 254 B8
Twayblade Cres
SK23.................46 F6
Tweeds Muir Cl 5
DE21...............205 F2
Twentylands DE13 .. 240 D4
Twentywell Ct S17 ...56 A7
Twentywell Dr S17 ...56 B6
Twentywell La S17 ...56 B6
Twentywell Rd S17 ...56 B5
Twentywell Rise
S17..................56 B6
Twentywell View
S17..................56 B6
Twickenham Cl 11
S20..................59 E6
Twickenham Cres
S20..................59 F6
Twickenham Ct 8
S20..................59 E6
Twickenham Dr
DE22.............. 218 A6
Twickenham Glade 10
S20..................59 E6
Twickenham Glen
S20..................59 F5
Twickenham Gr 9
S20..................59 E6
Twiggs Row DE4 ... 143 A7
Twin Oaks Cl DE23...230 F7
Twisses Bank DE6 .. 213 A2
TWO DALES 127 E3
TWYFORD 243 B6
Twyford Cl
Heanor DE75 .... 193 C8
Swadlincote DE11 ....255 F2
West Hallam DE7 .... 207 D8
Willington DE65 ..... 242 C5
Twyford Rd
Barrow upon Trent
DE73.............. 244 A6
Long Eaton NG10 .....235 F4
Twyford DE73....... 243 C6
Willington DE65 ......242 B6
Twyford St DE23.... 267 B1
Tylney Rd S40 ...... 114 B8
Tyndale Chase
DE24.............. 231 C2
Tynedale Cl NG10.. 236 A6
Tynefield Ct DE65... 229 B2
Tynefield Mews
DE65.............. 229 B2
Tynsel Parkes (VC) CE
Fst Sch 4 ST14 ... 210 A1
Tyrian Street
NG16 .... 195 B8
Tythe Barn La DE6.. 215 C5
Tythe The DE11..... 256 B7

U

Uffa Magna DE3 .... 217 C1
Uldale Gr DE11 ..... 256 C1
Ulley Cres S13........44 B7
Ulley Rd S13 ....44 B7
Ullswater Ave S20....59 E6
Ullswater Cl
Derby DE21 .... 205 D2
Dronfield S18.........56 E2
Sheffield S20 ....59 E6
Ullswater Dr
Derby DE21 ....220 E5
Dronfield S18.........56 E2
Ullswater Pk S18 .....56 E2
Ullswater Pl
Chesterfield S41.......95 C7
Dronfield S18.........56 E2
Ulverston Rd S41 .....95 D7
Undercliffe DE45 ... 109 D6
Underhall DE4...... 127 D2
Underhill Ave DE23 ..231 F7
Underhill Cl DE23... 231 E6
Underhill Rd S43 .....80 B6
Underpass The DE1. 267 C4
Undertown La DE6.. 197 D6
Underwood CE Prim Sch
NG16 ....171 F1
UNDERWOOD
GREEN 171 F2
Underwood Terr
Chelmorton SK17.... 106 A8
Darley Dale DE4..... 143 A7
Union Rd
Ilkeston DE7.........208 F7
New Mills SK22........33 C7
Swadlincote DE11 ....256 B5
Union St
Ashbourne DE6.......173 B2
Glossop SK13.........17 C8
Harthill S26 ....61 E6
Long Eaton NG10 ....236 E8
Melbourne DE73..... 252 A7
South Normanton
DE55...............159 F5
Unistates Bsns Pk
S41..................77 B2
Unity Cl DE11....... 256 A1
Unity Wlk SK13.......17 C7
Univ of Derby (Britannia
Mill) DE22..........218 E6
Univ of Derby (Buxton
Campus) SK17 ....85 D3
Univ of Derby (Kedleston
Rd) DE22.......... 204 D1
Univ of Derby
(Markeaton St)
DE22.............. 218 D6
Univ of Sheffield
(Research Labs)
SK17................85 B1
UNSTONE............76 E7
Unstone Dronfield By-
Pass S18.............56 F3
UNSTONE GREEN 76 E6
Unstone Hill S18 .....76 D7
Unstone Jun Sch
S18..................76 E7
Unstone Rd S41 ......76 F4
Unstone St Mary's Inf
Sch S18..............76 F7
UNTHANK 74 D5
Unthank La S18 ....74 C4
Upchurch Cl DE3 ... 217 C3
Upland Dr DE4 ..... 143 A7
Upland Rise S40.......95 D1
Uplands Ave DE23 .. 231 C6
Uplands Gdns DE23. 218 E2
Uplands Rd
Compstall SK14 ....15 A6
Glossop SK13.........17 D8
Upper Albert Rd S2...43 B4
Upper Bainbrigge St
5 Derby DE23.......218 F3
Derby DE23 .... 219 A3
Upper Barn Cl DE75. .181 F2
UPPER BIGGIN...... 175 E4
Upper Blindlow La
SK17.............. 106 A6
UPPER BOOTH.......36 E7
Upper Boundary Rd
DE22.............. 218 E4
UPPER BRADWAY....56 B5
Upper Croft
Clay Cross S45 ....131 E3
Tupton S42...........131 D8
Upper Croft Cl S43 ...96 E7
UPPERDALE 89 B5
Upper Dale Rd
DE23...............218 F1
Upper Derwent Visitor
Ctr* S33.............30 A7
Upper Dunstead Rd
NG16 .... 182 B4
UPPER
ELLASTONE....... 183 B4
UPPER END..........67 B5
Upper End Rd
Buxton SK17..........67 C4
Peak Dale SK17 ....67 B5
Upper Greenhill Gdns 5
DE4............... 143 C6
UPPER HACKNEY ... 143 A8
Upper Hall Cl DE56 . 191 C6
UPPER HARTSHAY . 169 A2
Upper Hartshay
Heage DE56 ....168 F1
Upper Hartshay *continued*
Heage DE56 .... 169 A1
Upper Hollow DE23. 218 C1
UPPER
HOLLOWAY....... 156 C5
Upper King St S43....77 F1
Upper La DE6 ...... 175 E4
UPPER LANGWITH . 119 D8
Upper Lum Cl S41 ....96 D2
Upper Lumsdale
DE4............... 143 E7
Upper Mantle Cl
S45............... 131 C4
Upper Marehay Rd
DE5............... 180 D6
UPPER MAYFIELD.. 172 B1
UPPER MIDWAY ... 256 C7
Upper Moor Rd
DE24.............. 232 E6
Upper Moor St S40 ...95 B2
Upper Nelson St 3
DE75.............. 181 D2
UPPER NEWBOLD....95 A8
Upper Newbold Cl
S40..................95 B7
Upper Northfield Cl 6
DE56...............178 F5
Upper Orchard St 2
NG9 .... 223 E7
UPPER PADLEY......53 D2
UPPER PILSLEY.... 132 D2
Upper School La
5 Dronfield S18 ......57 A1
Dronfield S18.........76 B8
UPPERTHORPE 60 E5
Upperthorpe Rd S21. .60 D4
Upperthorpe Villas
S21..................60 D5
UPPERTOWN 129 A7
UPPER TOWN
Birchover 141 C8
Bonsall............ 142 C1
Hognaston 164 B4
Uppertown La DE4.. 142 C1
Upper Town La DE4. 126 B1
Upper Valley Rd S8...43 B5
Upper Wellington St
NG10 .... 223 C1
UPPERWOOD 155 A8
Upper Wood Cl 6
DE7............... 208 E5
Upperwood Rd DE4. 143 A1
Upton Cl
Castle Donington
DE74..............247 B4
Heanor DE75 .... 182 A1
Upton Mount NG19 . 135 E1
Upwood Cl S40.......95 A5
Upwoods La DE6 ... 211 B3
Upwoods Rd
Doveridge DE6.......210 F4
Doveridge DE6...... 211 A1
Utah Cl DE65 .... 228 E2
UTTOXETER 210 C1
Uttoxeter New Rd
DE22.............. 218 C3
Uttoxeter Old Rd
DE22.............. 218 E5
Uttoxeter Rd
Birch Cross ST14 .... 224 A2
Derby DE3 ....217 E1
Hatton DE65.........227 B2
Hilton DE65 .... 228 C2
Scropton DE65...... 226 C4
Scropton, Foston
DE65...............226 F3
Uxbridge St DE14... 254 C8

V

Vale Cl
Bolsover S44 ....99 A1
Dronfield S18.........57 B1
Vale Ct NG19 .... 136 B3
Vale Dr NG20........119 F2
Valehouse Cl 7
DE65.............. 240 E8
Vale House Dr SK13 ..10 A5
Valehouse Way SK14 ..9 F6
Vale Mills DE22......218 F3
Valemount SK13.......10 A5
Valentine Ave NG16. 171 E7
Vale Rd
Hartshorne DE11 .... 257 A3
Mansfield Woodhouse
NG19 ....136 B4
Swadlincote DE11 ....256 B6
Valerian Cl SK17......85 C7
Valerie Rd DE72 .... 246 A7
Vale Rise
Matlock DE4.........142 F7
3 Matlock DE4 ..... 143 A7
Vale The DE7....... 194 E3
Vallance St NG19 ... 136 B4
Valley Cl S45 .... 132 B4
Valley Cres S41.......96 C2
Valley Dr
Chapel-en-le-Frith
SK23.................47 C6
Killamarsh S21........60 D7
Valley Gdns SK14.....15 E8
Valley Park Com Prim
Sch S14..............43 F2
Valley Rd
Barlow S18...........75 D3
Bolsover S44 .... 118 A8
Broadbottom SK14.....15 E8
Valley Rd *continued*
Chesterfield S41.......96 C2
Clay Cross S45 ...... 131 A4
Derby DE23 .... 218 D1
Derby, Cherrytree Hill
DE21...............220 B5
Glossop SK13.........16 F8
Hayfield SK22.........25 E2
Ilkeston DE7.........208 E5
Killamarsh S21........60 D7
Kimberley NG16..... 195 D7
Mastin Moor S43 ......79 C4
Overseal DE12 ...... 262 A3
Sheffield, Heeley S8....43 A6
Shirebrook NG20 .....119 E5
Valley Rise
Barlow S18...........75 D3
Swadlincote DE11 ....256 B5
Valley View
Alton S42 .... 130 C5
Belper DE56......... 179 A2
Ilkeston DE7.........208 E5
Valley View Cl
Chesterfield S41......115 E7
Eckington S21.........59 C2
Valley View Dr DE7 . 193 B1
Valley View Rd
DE55.............. 170 D4
Valley View Wlk
ST14.............. 197 A3
Vancouver Ave
DE21.............. 220 D4
Vancouver Dr DE15 . 248 C3
Vanguard Rd NG10 . 236 D5
Vanguard Trad Est
S40................115 B7
Varley Cl NG16 ..... 182 A2
Varley Ho S41 ....96 B6
Varley St DE24...... 232 D6
Vaughan Pl NG20... 119 E6
Vaughan Rd SK23.....45 E5
Vauxhall Ave DE22.. 218 A7
Velvet Mill SK17 ......69 B4
Venice Cl DE73 ..... 232 E2
Ventnor Ho DE24 ... 233 C7
Ventura Ct SK22.......24 D1
Venture Ave NG17 ...160 F8
Venture Cres DE55.. 159 A2
Venture Ho S41 ....76 F1
Venture Way S41 .....76 F1
Verbena Dr DE23 ... 231 D4
Vere Cl DE65 .... 242 B5
Vermont Dr DE21... 220 C6
Verney St NG19......134 F7
Verney Way NG19 ...134 F7
Vernon Cotts DE4....154 F1
Vernon Ct
Bakewell DE45 ...... 109 D5
Shirebrook NG20 .... 120 A4
Vernon Dr
Bakewell DE45 ....109 B7
Derby DE21 ....220 F4
Vernongate DE1.... 218 E5
Vernon Gn DE45.... 109 B7
Vernon La S45..... 129 D4
Vernon Oaks La
DE6............... 212 C5
Vernon Rd
Chesterfield S40.......95 D3
Sheffield S17 ....55 F6
Vernon Rise S42.....115 F2
Vernon St
Derby DE1 ....218 E5
Ilkeston DE7.........194 F4
Shirebrook NG20 .... 120 A4
Vernon Street Ind Est
NG20 .... 120 A4
Verona Way DE73... 232 E2
Veronica Dr NG16 .. 195 C8
Vestry Rd DE21 ..... 205 E3
Vetchfield Cl DE24...231 F2
Viadevana DE12 .... 262 E3
Via Gellia Rd
Bonsall DE4 .... 154 C7
Upperwood DE4..... 155 A7
Vicarage Ave
Derby DE23 ....218 E2
Ilkeston DE7........ 194 D4
Vicarage Cl
Belper DE56........ 179 A4
Blackfordby DE11.... 257 C1
Burton upon Trent
DE15...............248 B4
Heath S44...........117 B2
Holmesfield S18.......75 A8
Shirebrook NG20 .....119 E3
Smalley DE7.........192 F6
Swanwick DE55 ......169 E7
Vicarage Croft DE4 . 110 E1
Vicarage Ct
Derby DE3 .... 217 D1
Mansfield NG19 ......135 E1
Vicarage Dr
Derby DE21 .... 220 A7
Uttoxeter ST14...... 210 A4
Vicarage Gdns
Clay Cross S45 ...... 131 C2
Heanor DE75 ....181 F1
Swadlincote DE11 ... 256 C4
Vicarage La
Ashford in the Water
DE45...............89 E2
Ashford in the Water
DE45...............108 E8
Duffield DE56........190 E4
Hayfield SK22.........25 D1
Ironville NG16 ....170 F4
Little Eaton DE21 .... 205 C8

Vicarage La *continued*
Sheffield S17 ....55 D7
Vicarage Mews
DE55 ....170 E6
Vicarage Rd
Belper DE56 ....190 F8
Chellaston DE73 ....232 F2
Derby DE3 ....217 C2
Swadlincote DE11 ....256 C4
Woodville DE11 ....256 E2
Vicarage St DE7 ....194 D4
Vicarage Wlk
Clowne S43 ....80 E4
Rosliston DE12 ....260 C6
Vicar La
Chesterfield S40 ....266 B3
Tibshelf DE55 ....148 A6
Vicarwood Ave
Derby DE22 ....204 F1
Holbrook DE56 ....191 C7
Victor Ave DE22 ....218 F8
Victor Cres NG10 ....223 C4
Victoria Ave
Borrowash DE72 ....221 B2
2 Buxton SK17 ....85 D8
Draycott DE72 ....235 A7
Glossop SK13 ....10 A5
Heanor DE75 ....181 D1
Ilkeston DE7 ....207 B3
Staveley S43 ....79 A3
Victoria Cl DE3 ....217 E4
Victoria Cotts DE45 ....109 D6
Victoria Cres NG16 ....170 F4
Victoria Ct
6 Glossop SK13 ....17 C8
Long Eaton NG10 ....236 D7
Matlock DE4 ....143 C6
Overseal DE12 ....262 A5
Victoria Dr
Blackwell DE55 ....147 E1
Woodville DE11 ....256 E1
Victoria Gr S43 ....96 F5
Victoria Hall Gdns
DE4 ....143 C6
Victoria Ho S80 ....81 F1
Victoria Mews 2
SK13 ....17 C8
Victoria Park L Ctr
DE7 ....194 E1
Victoria Park Rd
Buxton SK17 ....85 D7
Calow S43 ....96 F5
Victoria Rd
Bamford S33 ....40 B3
Draycott DE72 ....235 A7
Pinxton NG16 ....160 D3
Ripley DE5 ....169 D2
Sandiacre NG10 ....223 B6
Selston NG16 ....171 F6
Victoria Sq 13 DE6 ....173 C2
Victoria St
Alfreton DE55 ....159 B4
Bolsover S44 ....118 B8
Brimington S43 ....77 F1
Castle Donington
DE74 ....247 B5
Chesterfield S41 ....266 B4
Clay Cross S45 ....131 C3
Creswell S80 ....81 F1
Derby DE1 ....267 B3
Dronfield S18 ....56 F2
Glossop SK13 ....17 C8
Ilkeston DE7 ....194 F3
Ironville NG16 ....170 F4
Langley Mill NG16 ....182 C3
Long Eaton NG10 ....236 B5
Melbourne DE73 ....252 A7
New Mills SK22 ....33 B6
Pye Hill NG16 ....171 A4
Ripley DE5 ....169 F2
Shirebrook NG20 ....119 F4
Somercotes DE55 ....170 C8
South Normanton
DE55 ....160 A6
Stapleford NG9 ....223 D7
ictoria Street
North S41 ....76 F2
ictoria Street
West S40 ....95 C2
ictoria Terr
Great Longstone
DE45 ....89 F4
Selston NG16 ....160 E1
Tibshelf DE55 ....148 B7
ictoria Way DE24 ....219 E3
ictoria Wlk S42 ....115 D1
ictor Rd S17 ....55 F7
ictory Ave DE5 ....169 F1
ictory Cl NG10 ....236 E5
ictory Dr NG19 ....136 F1
ictory Park Way
DE24 ....232 B6
ictory Rd
Derby DE24 ....232 B6
Derby DE24 ....232 C5
ewdales Cl DE6 ....175 F2
iew Rd S2 ....43 A7
king Bsns Ctr
DE11 ....256 F3
kinglea Cl S2 ....44 B8
kinglea Dr S2 ....44 B8
illage Ct DE56 ....190 F3
illage Prim Sch
DE23 ....231 F7
illage St DE23 ....231 F8
illage The
Dale Abbey DE7 ....207 F2
West Hallam DE7 ....207 E7
Villas Rd
Ambergate DE56 ....167 F3
Bolsover S44 ....98 E2
Villa St DE72 ....235 B7
Villas The
Bolsover S44 ....99 B2
Burton upon Trent
DE16 ....254 E7
Whaley Thorns NG20 ....101 A2
Villa The SK14 ....9 A5
Villiers Cl S2 ....43 E6
Villiers Dr S2 ....43 E6
Vincent Ave
Derby DE21 ....220 E3
Ilkeston DE7 ....208 F8
Vincent Cl DE56 ....192 A8
Vincent Cres S40 ....95 B2
Vincent La S40 ....95 B2
Vincent St DE23 ....218 F1
Vine Cl DE23 ....231 B7
Vine Cres NG10 ....223 B6
Vine Farm Cl DE7 ....208 D5
Vine Gr Ct S20 ....59 D7
Vine Gr Gdns S20 ....59 D7
Vine Wlk Pk NG19 ....136 C6
Vineyard Terr DE4 ....127 C4
Viola Cl DE21 ....206 C3
Violet Ave NG16 ....195 B8
Violet Cl
Donisthorpe DE12 ....262 E1
Shirebrook NG20 ....119 D3
Violet La
Burton upon Trent
DE15 ....254 F8
Burton upon Trent
DE15 ....255 A7
Violet St
Derby DE23 ....218 F1
Derby DE23 ....219 A1
Violet Way DE15 ....255 A8
Violet Way Acad
DE15 ....254 F8
Virginsalley La DE6 ....184 D2
Virtue Cl DE3 ....217 D6
Vista The NG9 ....223 E5
Vivian St
Derby DE1 ....219 B8
Shuttlewood S44 ....98 F6
Vulcan St DE23 ....219 B1
Vulcan Way DE74 ....246 F4
Vyse Dr NG10 ....236 C6

W

Wade Ave
Derby DE23 ....218 C2
Ilkeston DE7 ....209 B7
Wadebridge Gr
DE24 ....233 C5
Wade Dr DE3 ....217 E2
Wade St DE23 ....218 C1
Wadham Close DE3 ....217 F3
WADSHELF 93 E3
Wadsworth Ave S12 ....44 D5
Wadsworth Cl S12 ....44 D5
Wadsworth Dr S12 ....44 D5
Wadsworth Fields Prim
Sch NG9 ....223 F8
Wadsworth Rd
Sheffield S12 ....44 C5
Stapleford NG9 ....223 F8
Wagon La
Bretby DE11 ....256 A8
Bretby DE15 ....249 A1
Wagstaff La NG16 ....171 B4
Wagtail Cl
Derby DE24 ....231 D4
1 Stapleford NG9 ....209 E2
Wain Ave
Chesterfield S41 ....266 C3
North Wingfield S42 ....132 A7
Wainfleet Cl DE7 ....194 C3
WAINGROVES 181 A7
Waingroves Prim Sch
DE5 ....181 A7
Waingroves Rd
Codnor DE5 ....181 B6
Ripley DE5 ....181 A8
Wainhouse Brow
SK22 ....25 D3
Wains Cl SK17 ....47 F1
Wain Way S42 ....132 A7
Wainwright Ave
Mansfield NG19 ....135 D1
Sheffield S13 ....44 D8
Wainwright Cres
S13 ....44 D8
Wainwright Dr
DE11 ....256 F4
Wakami Cres DE73 ....233 A3
WAKEBRIDGE 156 D3
Wakefield Ave DE13 ....239 B6
Wakefield Croft
DE7 ....194 C3
Wakefield Ct
Castle Donington
DE74 ....247 C4
Derby DE74 ....247 B4
Wakelyn Cl
Hilton DE65 ....228 C2
Shardlow DE72 ....234 F1
Walbrook Rd DE23 ....218 F1
Walcote Cl DE56 ....179 D5
Walden Cl DE72 ....245 A8
Waldene Dr DE24 ....233 A6
Walden Rd S2 ....43 B7
WALDLEY 211 C7
Waldley La DE6 ....211 D7
Waldorf Ave DE24 ....233 A7
Waldorf Cl DE24 ....233 A7
Walford Rd
Killamarsh S21 ....60 C6
Rolleston DE13 ....240 D3
Walgrave Cl DE56 ....179 B6
Walgrove Ave S40 ....95 E1
Walgrove Rd S40 ....95 D1
Walk Cl DE72 ....235 A7
Walkdale Brow SK13 ....17 B7
Walker Ave DE5 ....169 E2
Walker Brow SK17 ....47 F1
Walker Brow Rd
SK23 ....45 C5
Walker Cl DE7 ....209 A4
Walker Gr 2 NG9 ....223 E6
Walker La DE1 ....267 A4
Walkers La S21 ....60 D6
Walker St SK13 ....10 A4
Walk Mill Rd SK22 ....25 D2
Walk The DE56 ....192 B8
Wallace Gdns NG9 ....223 F1
Wallace St DE22 ....218 C5
WALLASH 184 C7
Wall Ditch DE6 ....149 B2
Wallef Rd DE6 ....201 E8
Wallfields Cl DE65 ....230 D2
Wallis Cl
Draycott DE72 ....235 A7
4 Ripley DE5 ....180 E8
Wallis Ho DE11 ....256 E3
Wall Rd DE14 ....254 A7
Wallsend Cl DE7 ....194 F4
Walls La S80 ....81 A8
Wall St
Buxton SK17 ....85 D8
Ripley DE5 ....169 D2
Walmsley Cl S45 ....131 C5
Walnut Ave
Derby DE24 ....233 B7
Shireoaks S81 ....63 F7
Walnut Cl
Aston-on-Trent
DE72 ....246 B8
Barrow upon Trent
DE73 ....244 A6
Burnaston DE65 ....229 F5
Chellaston DE73 ....245 A8
Ilkeston DE7 ....209 A6
Repton DE65 ....242 F2
Repton DE65 ....243 A2
Swadlincote DE11 ....256 A5
Walnut Dr
Hilton DE65 ....228 D2
Killamarsh S21 ....60 C5
Walnut Rd DE56 ....179 B3
Walnut St DE24 ....232 C7
Walpole St DE21 ....219 D6
Walseker La S26 ....61 C7
Walsham Ct DE21 ....205 D1
Walter Evans CE (Aided)
Prim Sch DE22 ....204 F2
Walter Evans CE (Aided)
Prim Sch DE22 ....205 A2
Walters Ave NG16 ....182 E6
Walters Cres NG16 ....171 D6
Walter St
Derby DE1 ....218 E7
Draycott DE72 ....234 F8
Walters Wood SK23 ....45 F5
Waltham Ave DE24 ....231 F4
Waltham Croft S41 ....115 C7
Walthamstow Dr
DE22 ....218 B6
Waltheof Rd S2 ....44 A8
WALTON 114 D8
Walton Ave DE24 ....232 E4
Walton Back La
Chesterfield S40 ....114 B7
Holymoorside S42 ....113 F7
Walton Cl
Chesterfield S40 ....114 B8
Dronfield S18 ....56 C2
Swadlincote DE11 ....256 A3
Walton Cres
Ashbourne DE6 ....173 D1
Chesterfield S40 ....95 E1
Walton Ct
Sheffield S8 ....56 E8
West Hallam DE7 ....207 D8
Walton Dr
Chesterfield S40 ....95 E1
Derby DE23 ....231 E7
Walton Drive Ct S40 ....95 E1
Walton Fields Rd
S40 ....95 D2
Walton Hill
4 Castle Donington
DE74 ....246 F4
Castle Donington
DE74 ....247 A4
Walton Holymoorside
Prim Sch S42 ....113 E8
Walton Hospl S40 ....114 E8
Walton La DE14 ....253 C1
WALTON-ON-
TRENT 253 D1
Walton-on-Trent
CE Sch DE12 ....259 D8
Walton Rd
Burton upon Trent
DE15 ....254 D5
Chesterfield S40 ....95 D1
Derby DE21 ....219 F5
Walton St NG10 ....223 D1
Walton Way S42 ....114 E4
Walton Wlk S40 ....266 A2
Wansfell Cl DE3 ....217 E1
Wapentake La DE6 ....165 C2
Warburton Cl S2 ....43 C7
Warburton Gdns S2 ....43 C7
Warburton Rd S2 ....43 C7
Ward Cl DE4 ....165 E6
Ward Dr DE55 ....170 D7
Wardgate Way S40 ....95 A5
Ward La
Barlborough S43 ....80 B8
Disley SK12 ....32 F4
WARDLOW 70 C2
Wardlow Ave
Derby DE21 ....220 A8
17 Gamesley SK13 ....9 D1
Wardlow Cl S40 ....114 F8
Wardlow Fold 21
SK13 ....9 D1
Wardlow Gdns 19
SK13 ....9 D1
Wardlow Gr 22 SK13 ....9 D1
Wardlow Mews 16
SK13 ....9 D1
WARDLOW MIRES 70 C4
Wardlow Rd
Ilkeston DE7 ....194 E3
Sheffield S12 ....44 D5
Wardlow Wlk 18 SK13 ....9 D1
WARDS END 143 C2
Ward's La
Barrow upon Trent
DE73 ....244 F3
Breaston DE72 ....235 D8
King's Newton DE73 ....245 A2
Ward St
Derby DE22 ....218 E4
Tupton S40 ....115 D1
Tupton S42 ....131 D8
Wards Yd S18 ....57 A1
Wardwick DE1 ....267 B3
Warehouse La S33 ....38 D4
WARHILL 9 A3
Warhurst Fold 2
SK13 ....10 A5
Warke Flatt DE74 ....247 B6
WARMBROOK 165 E8
Warmbrook DE4 ....165 F8
Warmbrook Rd SK23 ....47 C6
Warminster Cl S8 ....43 A4
Warminster Cres S8 ....43 B4
Warminster Dr S8 ....43 A3
Warminster Gdns S8 ....43 A3
Warminster Pl S8 ....43 B2
Warminster Rd S8 ....43 A3
Warmwells La DE5 ....180 D6
Warner St
Chesterfield S41 ....266 C1
Derby DE22 ....267 A1
Derby, Markeaton
DE3 ....217 D1
Warney Rd DE4 ....127 D2
Warren Ave NG9 ....223 D7
Warren Ave Extension
NG9 ....223 D7
Warren Cl
Burton upon Trent
DE13 ....240 E1
Pilsley S45 ....132 C2
Warren Cres S21 ....58 E2
Warren Ct NG9 ....223 D7
Warrendale Ct
DE73 ....233 A2
Warren Dr DE12 ....261 C6
Warren Hill 7 DE11 ....255 E5
Warren La
Branston DE14 ....253 F7
Castle Donington DE74,
NG10 ....236 B2
Warren Lea SK6 ....15 B2
Warren Rd 5 DE5 ....170 A1
Warren Rise S18 ....57 C3
Warren St DE24 ....232 F8
Warren Wlk S21 ....58 E2
Warslow Rd SK17 ....121 B4
Warsop Rd NG19 ....136 D3
WARSOP VALE 120 D4
Warwick Ave DE23 ....218 D1
Warwick Cl
Branston DE14 ....253 F8
Glossop SK13 ....17 F8
Swadlincote DE11 ....256 E5
Warwick Ct
Somercotes DE55 ....170 C8
Swanwick DE55 ....170 B8
Warwick Dr DE7 ....194 C3
Warwick Gdns
DE56 ....179 D5
Warwick Rd
Long Eaton NG10 ....237 A7
Somercotes DE55 ....159 C1
Warwick St
Chesterfield S40 ....115 B7
Derby DE24 ....219 D2
Warwick Street Ind Est
S40 ....115 B7
Wasdale Ave 5 S20 ....59 E6
Wasdale Cl S20 ....59 E6
WASH 35 C1
Washbrook La DE6 ....161 F4
Washford Rd DE65 ....240 E8
Washgate La SK17 ....104 C6
Wash Gn DE4 ....166 B8
WASHGREEN 155 A1
Wash Hills Cl DE4 ....153 A1
Washhouse Bottom
SK17 ....69 E8
Wash House Bottom
SK17 ....50 E1
Wash House La S40 ....95 C2
Washington Ave
DE21 ....220 B6
Washington Cl
DE73 ....252 A7
Washington Cotts
DE72 ....221 D1
Washington Dr NG9 ....209 F1
Washington Terr
DE4 ....143 E7
Wash Meadow Cl 5
DE7 ....208 E5
Watburn Rd SK22 ....24 D1
Watchorn Cl DE11 ....256 D5
Watchorn Cotts
DE55 ....158 F3
Watchorn La DE55 ....158 F2
Watchorn Lawns
DE55 ....158 F2
Watercress La S45 ....131 D2
Waterdown Cl
NG19 ....136 D5
Waterfall Cl S8 ....43 C1
Waterfoot Cotts SK14 ....9 A4
Waterfoot La SK23 ....45 D6
Waterford Dr DE21 ....220 B4
Watergo La DE3 ....230 C7
Wateringbury Gr 1
S43 ....78 F2
Watering La DE56 ....191 D6
Water La
Bakewell DE45 ....109 D6
Bamford S33 ....40 A3
Bolsover S44 ....117 E8
Cromford DE4 ....155 A6
Eyam S32 ....71 E6
Hollingworth SK14 ....9 D5
Middleton DE4 ....154 C5
Pleasley NG19 ....135 B3
Sheffield S17 ....55 F7
Shirebrook NG19 ....118 E1
South Normanton
DE55 ....160 B6
Tideswell SK17 ....68 F6
Wirksworth DE4 ....165 F7
Waterlagg La
Hulland Ward DE56 ....188 D8
Hulland Ward DE6 ....176 C1
Water Lily Gdns S80 ....81 E3
WATERLOO 132 C3
Waterloo Cl DE55 ....160 C8
Waterloo Ct
Derby DE1 ....267 C5
Waterloo S45 ....132 B4
Waterloo La NG9 ....209 F6
Waterloo Pl DE11 ....256 B4
Waterloo Rd
Mansfield NG19 ....136 B2
Matlock Bath DE4 ....143 A1
Waterloo St
Clay Cross S45 ....131 C4
Doe Lea S44 ....117 F1
Watermeade S21 ....59 B2
Water Meadow La
S40 ....95 B7
Watermeadow Rd
DE24 ....233 A5
Watermeadows The
NG10 ....236 A8
Watermint Cl DE23 ....231 B6
Watermint Rd S40 ....115 D2
Water Orton Cl NG9 ....223 E3
Waterpark Rd DE6 ....224 B8
Waters Edge SK6 ....23 B8
Waters Edge La SK23 ....47 C5
Waterside
Burton upon Trent
DE15 ....254 E7
Disley SK12 ....32 E7
Furness Vale SK23 ....33 E3
Glossop SK13 ....10 A6
Ironville NG16 ....170 F4
Marple SK6 ....23 A5
Willington DE65 ....242 A6
Waterside Ave SK6 ....23 A5
Waterside Bsns Pk
SK13 ....9 F6
Waterside Cl
Derby DE22 ....205 A2
Sandiacre NG10 ....223 B3
Waterside Ho DE1 ....267 B4
Waterside Rd
Ashbourne DE6 ....185 A8
Burton upon Trent
DE15 ....254 D7
Disley SK12, SK22 ....32 E7
Waterside Ret Pk
DE7 ....195 A1
Water St
Bakewell DE45 ....109 D5
Buxton SK17 ....85 B8
Glossop SK13 ....10 E2
WATER SWALLOWS 67 A3
WATERSWALLOWS
GREEN 66 F3
Waterswallows Ind Pk
SK17 ....67 A3
Waterswallows La
SK17 ....66 F4
Waterswallows Mews
SK17 ....66 E1
Waterswallows Rd
Buxton SK17 ....66 E1
Peak Dale SK17 ....67 C3
Waterthorpe Cl 4
S20 ....59 F8
Waterthorpe Cres
S20 ....59 F8
Waterthorpe Gdns 3
S20 ....59 F8
Waterthorpe Glade 5
S20 ....59 F8
Waterthorpe Glen 2
S20 ....59 F8
Waterthorpe Rise 1
S20 ....59 F8
Waterton Cl DE13 ....241 A1
Waterway The
NG10 ....223 C4
Watery La
Bretby DE15 ....249 C3
Clifton DE6 ....184 E7
Ellastone DE6 ....183 B4
Holme HD9 ....2 F8
Scropton DE65 ....226 E2
Scropton DE65 ....227 A3
Swadlincote DE11 ....255 D5
Thurvaston DE6 ....215 D5
Watford Bridge Ind Est
SK22 ....24 D1
Watford Bridge Rd
SK22 ....24 D1
Watford La SK22 ....24 C2
Watford Lodge SK22 ....24 C1
Watford Rd
Buxton SK17 ....84 F8
New Mills SK22 ....24 C2
Watkin Ave SK13 ....9 E4
Watkinson St DE75 ....181 D2
Watson Ave DE75 ....181 F2
Watson La S42 ....114 C3
Watson Rd DE7 ....194 C2
Watson St
Derby DE1 ....218 E6
Derby DE22 ....218 E7
Watten Cl DE24 ....231 F2
Watts Gn DE45 ....108 F8
Waveney Cl DE22 ....205 B5
Waverley Ct 2 S41 ....96 A6
Waverley St
Derby DE24 ....232 D7
Long Eaton NG10 ....236 E8
Tibshelf DE55 ....148 A7
Wayfaring Rd DE21 ....206 A1
Wayford Ave S41 ....266 C1
Wayside S43 ....96 D8
Wayside Cl S42 ....132 A7
Wayside Ct S43 ....96 D8
Wayzgoose Dr
DE21 ....219 C6
Weaddow La
Middleton DE45 ....124 F2
Middleton DE45 ....140 A8
Weakland Cl S12 ....44 F3
Weakland Cres S12 ....44 F3
Weakland Dr S12 ....44 F3
Weakland Way S12 ....44 F3
Weather Hill La HD9 ....3 E8
Weathern Field
DE12 ....261 D5
Weaver Cl
Ashbourne DE6 ....185 C8
Crich DE4 ....156 F1
Weaver Rd ST14 ....210 B2
Weavers Cl
Belper DE56 ....179 C5
Borrowash DE72 ....221 D1
Weavers Court
DE55 ....148 A3
Weavers Croft DE5 ....180 E8
Weavers Ct SK14 ....9 A4
Weavers Gn DE3 ....217 C1
Weavers The ST14 ....196 D6
Weavers Way DE55 ....160 B6
Weaving Ave S33 ....38 C2
Webb Dr DE74 ....246 E3
Webbs Orch SK23 ....45 D8
Webster Ave NG16 ....182 F1
Webster Croft S41 ....77 B2
Webster Ct S40 ....95 E5
Webster St DE1 ....267 A2
Webster's Terr DE4 ....143 D4
Wedgewood Cl
DE15 ....248 B1
Wedgewood Way
DE11 ....256 F1
Wedneshough SK14 ....9 C5
Wedneshough Green
SK14 ....9 C5
Weighbridge Rd
NG20 ....119 F2
Weightman Dr
NG16 ....195 B7
Weir Bank DE15 ....254 E6
Weirfield Rd DE22 ....205 A2
Weirside DE6 ....184 D7
Welbeck Ave
Buxton SK17 ....85 C6
Ilkeston DE7 ....208 D5
Welbeck Cl
Alfreton DE55 ....170 D7
Dronfield S18 ....56 C2
Staveley S43 ....97 D6
Welbeck College La
S80 ....82 F1
Welbeck Ct
1 Chesterfield S40 ....95 C2
Clowne S43 ....80 F3
7 Staveley S43 ....78 E2
Welbeck Dr S42 ....114 E4
Welbeck Gdns
Beeston NG9 ....223 F3
Bolsover S44 ....99 C2

Welbeck Glade S44 99 B2
Welbeck Gr DE22 204 D3
Welbeck Rd
Bolsover S44 99 B2
Long Eaton NG10 223 C3
Mansfield Woodhouse NG19 136 C3
Welbeck St
Creswell S80 81 E1
Whitwell S80 82 B6
Welburn Cl NG19 136 F2
Welbury Gdns S20 59 E6
Welch Ave NG9 223 E8
Welfare Ave S40 95 D3
Welfare Cl NG20 119 E3
Welfitt Gr NG20 101 B2
Welland Cl
Burton upon Trent DE15 248 A5
Derby DE3 217 D4
Welland Rd DE65 228 D1
Well Banks
Kirk Ireton DE6 165 B1
Kirk Ireton DE6 176 B8
Wellcarr Rd S8 43 A2
Well Cl DE6 175 E3
Wellcroft DE4 126 B1
Wellcroft Grange DE6 183 D8
Welldon St DE5 181 A4
Wellesley Ave DE23 231 D7
Wellfield DE4 143 C6
Wellfield Cl S12 44 E1
Wellfield Ct 2 DE4 143 C6
Well Gate SK13 10 E2
Wellgate La DE45 109 B1
Well Green S32 72 C1
Wellhead La DE4 142 B2
Wellhead Rd 4 S8 43 A6
Wellington Cl DE4 143 D7
Wellington Court DE74 246 F4
Wellington Cres DE1 267 D2
Wellington Ct
1 Belper DE56 178 F3
Eastwood NG16 182 F2
Wellington Mews DE55 146 D2
Wellington Pk
Burton upon Trent DE16 254 A8
Shirland DE55 146 D2
Wellington Pl NG16 182 F2
Wellington Rd DE14 253 E8
Wellington St
Chesterfield S43 77 D3
Derby DE1 267 D2
Eastwood NG16 182 F3
Heanor DE75 181 D3
Long Eaton NG10 223 C2
Matlock DE4 143 C6
Ripley DE5 169 E1
Stapleford NG9 223 C6
Well La
Belper DE56 190 F7
Blackfordby DE11 257 B1
Holymoorside S42 112 F7
Repton DE65 242 C1
Shirland DE55 146 C3
Well Rd S8 43 A6
Well Row SK14 16 A8
Wells Cl NG19 136 D4
Wells Ct DE23 230 E7
Wellspring Cl
Barlborough S43 80 B6
Wingerworth S42 115 B4
Well Spring Cl S43 96 E7
Wellspring Dale NG9 223 E5
Wells Rd DE3 217 E2
Wells St S44 118 C8
Well St
Brassington DE4 152 F1
Derby DE1 267 B5
Elton DE4 140 E7
New Mills SK22 33 B8
Ripley DE5 169 D1
Wellwood Rd DE11 256 A6
Well Yd
Belper DE56 179 A5
Holbrook DE56 191 C6
Welney Cl DE3 230 D8
Welshpool Pl S40 95 D3
Welshpool Rd DE21 205 D1
Welsted Rd DE74 246 E2
Welton Ave DE56 179 B6
Welwyn Ave
Derby DE22 204 D3
Derby, Allenton DE24 232 E4
Mansfield Woodhouse NG19 136 E4
Welwyn Cl
Chesterfield S40 95 D3
Sheffield S12 44 B4
Welwyn Ct S12 44 B4
Welwyn Rd S12 44 B4
Wembley Gdns DE22 218 A6
Wendover Cl DE3 217 C1
Wenham La NG17 148 F4
Wenlock Cl
Chesterfield S40 95 D4
Derby DE3 217 E1
Eastwood NG16 195 C8
Wenlock Cres S40 95 D4
Wenlock Dr S42 115 F3
Wenlock Wlk S42 115 F3
Wenslees DE4 116 C1
WENSLEY 142 A7
WENSLEY DALE 142 B6
Wensleydale Cl NG19 136 E1
Wensleydale Rd NG10 236 B6
Wensleydale Wlk DE24 233 C7
Wensley Dr DE21 220 F3
Wensley Rd
North Wingfield S42 131 F5
Winster DE4 141 D6
Wensley Way S43 97 C8
Wentworth Ave S40 114 E8
Wentworth Cl
Derby DE3 217 F2
Mansfield NG19 136 F2
Wentworth Croft DE75 182 A3
Wentworth Dr DE13 240 D1
Wentworth Ho 1 DE1 218 E5
Wentworth Pl ST14 197 A3
Wentworth Rd S18 56 C1
Wentworth St DE7 195 A2
Werburgh Cl DE21 220 D4
Werburgh St DE22 267 A2
Werneth Low Ctry Pk★ SK14 15 A7
Werneth Low Rd SK14 15 B6
Werneth Rd SK13 17 A7
Wesleyan Chapel La SK17 88 A3
Wesleyan Chapel Wlk NG9 223 D7
Wesley Cl 2 DE6 211 C1
Wesley Ct SK23 47 C6
Wesley Ho 3 SK17 85 D8
Wesley La DE72 221 C5
Wesley Pl NG9 223 E7
Wesley Rd
Ambergate DE56 167 F3
Derby DE24 233 B5
Stonebroom DE55 146 F3
Wesley St
Glossop SK13 10 E2
Hadfield SK13 10 A5
Ilkeston DE7 194 E4
Langley Mill NG16 182 C3
Wessex Cl 5 S43 96 F8
Wessex Dr NG16 195 A8
Wessex Gdns S17 55 D5
WESSINGTON 157 E8
Wessington Bank 9 SK13 9 E2
Wessington Dr S43 97 C8
Wessington Fold 12 SK13 9 E2
Wessington Gn 11 SK13 9 E2
Wessington Green Nature Reserve★ DE55 157 E8
Wessington La DE55 158 A6
Wessington Mews
Derby DE22 204 E1
Gamesley SK13 9 E2
Wessington Prim Sch DE55 157 E8
Westacre Dr DE11 255 F2
Westanes Gn DE55 145 D1
West Ave
Chellaston DE73 232 E3
Derby DE1 267 A4
Draycott DE72 234 F8
Hilton DE65 228 C2
Ripley DE5 169 C1
Sandiacre NG10 223 A6
Stapleford NG9 223 E8
West Ave S DE73 232 E2
West Bank
Matlock Bath DE4 143 A1
Toadmoor DE56 168 A2
Winster DE4 141 B5
West Bank Ave
Crich DE4 156 F1
Derby DE22 218 F8
Mansfield NG19 136 B1
Westbank Cl S18 57 B4
West Bank Cl DE22 218 E8
Westbank Ct S18 57 C4
West Bank Lea NG19 136 B1
West Bank Link NG19 136 B1
West Bank Rd DE22 204 E5
West Bars S40 266 A3
Westbourne Ave DE55 147 A4
Westbourne Cl NG19 136 E4
Westbourne Ct NG9 209 F1
Westbourne Gr S40 95 B3
Westbourne Pk DE22 217 F7
Westbridge Rd S43 80 A7
Westbrook Cl
Chapel-en-le-Frith SK23 47 C5
Chesterfield S40 94 F2
Westbrook Dr S40 94 F2
West Brook La 1 DE55 147 F6
WEST BROUGHTON 225 A6
Westbury Ct DE22 218 E3
Westbury Gdns DE56 179 C5
Westbury St DE22 218 E3
Westby La NG16 195 D3
West Cl DE22 204 E2
West Cres
Duckmanton S44 98 A5
Matlock DE4 143 A6
West Croft Ave DE23 231 D5
West Croft Cl DE45 125 B5
Westcroft Cres S20 59 E8
West Croft Ct S43 97 B5
Westcroft Dr S20 59 E7
West Croft Dr S43 97 B5
Westcroft Gdns S20 59 E8
Westcroft Glen S20 59 E7
Westcroft Gr S20 59 E7
Westcross Ave NG9 223 E8
Westdale Cl NG10 236 A5
Westdale Rd
Mansfield NG19 136 B1
Westwood NG16 171 C4
Westdene Ave DE24 232 D5
West Dr
Derby DE3 217 D2
Doveridge DE6 211 B1
Glossop SK13 9 E7
West Edge Cl S45 129 D4
West End
Alfreton DE55 159 A3
Barlborough S43 80 A7
Baslow DE45 91 E5
Brassington DE4 152 F1
Broadbottom SK14 15 F8
Elton DE4 140 E6
Pinxton NG16 160 C4
Wirksworth DE4 165 E8
West End Cl DE55 159 A3
West End Cres DE7 208 D8
West End Dr
Ilkeston DE7 208 D8
Shardlow DE72 234 E1
West End St NG9 223 C5
West End View S21 59 C2
West End Way SK14 15 F8
Westerlands NG9 223 F6
Western Ave DE55 169 D7
Western Dr DE75 193 F8
Western La SK23 46 A8
Western Mere Cl DE72 235 C7
Western Rd
7 Derby DE23 218 F3
Derby DE3 217 E2
Derby, Rose Hill DE23 219 A3
Western View DE45 90 A4
Western Villas DE56 167 F3
WESTFIELD 59 F8
Westfield Ave
Chesterfield S40 95 B1
5 Heanor DE75 181 F1
West Field Bank S43 80 A7
Westfield Cl
Chesterfield S40 95 B2
Ilkeston DE7 208 C6
Westfield Cres S20 59 C8
Westfield Ctr S20 59 E8
Westfield Derby (Sh Ctr) DE1 267 C2
Westfield Dr
Blackwell DE55 147 E1
Ilkeston DE7 194 D2
Westfield Gdns S40 95 B2
Westfield Gr DE22 218 D4
Westfield Inf Sch S40 95 B2
Westfield La
Barlborough S43 79 F7
Chesterfield S21 77 E8
Westfield Northway S20 59 E8
Westfield Rd
Dronfield S18 76 C8
Killamarsh S21 60 C5
Swadlincote DE11 256 B6
Westfield Southway S20 59 E8
Westgate DE1 218 E6
West Gate
Holme HD9 3 F8
Long Eaton NG10 236 E7
Westgate Cl ST14 196 F3
West Gr DE24 232 D5
Westgreen Ave DE24 232 D5
WEST HALLAM 207 F8
WEST HALLAM COMMON 207 D8
West Hallam Ind Est DE7 207 E6
Westhall Rd DE3 217 D3
WEST HANDLEY 77 D8
West Hill DE5 181 B7
Westhill La S42 115 E3
West Hill Pk NG19 136 B3
West Ho S8 43 A4
West Horderns SK23 47 B5
Westhorpe Dr NG10 236 C8
WESTHOUSES 159 C8
Westhouses Prim Sch DE55 147 C1
Westland Dr NG16 160 C3
Westland Gdns S20 59 D8
Westland Gr 3 S20 59 E8
Westland Rd 1 S20 59 E8
Westlands The ST14 196 D6
West Lawn DE65 230 D2
Westlea DE4 143 D6
West Lea
Chesterfield S40 95 B2
Clowne S43 80 D4
West Lea Cotts S43 80 D4
Westlea View S43 80 D4
West Lees Rd S33 40 B4
Westleigh NG19 136 D6
Westleigh Ave DE22 218 C6
Westleigh Ct S40 95 E5
Westley Cres DE21 191 D2
West Meadow Rise DE74 246 E4
Westminster Ave 1 NG10 223 C5
Westminster Dr DE11 255 E1
Westminster St DE24 232 F8
Westmoor Rd S43 96 F4
Westmoreland Rd S41 76 D1
Westmorland Cl DE21 219 C6
Westmorland Way NG16 171 B3
Weston Bank DE6 197 F1
Weston Cl S40 95 A5
Weston Cres NG10 235 F4
Weston Ct DE72 245 E4
Weston Hall Dr DE72 245 E5
Westonhill Chalet Pk DE72 245 C4
WESTON-ON-TRENT 245 F5
Weston-on-Trent CE (Aided) Prim Sch DE72 245 F5
Weston Park Ave DE24 232 E3
Weston Park Gdns DE24 232 D3
Weston Rd
Aston-on-Trent DE72 246 A7
Weston-on-Trent DE72 245 F6
Weston Rise DE73 245 A8
Weston Spot Cl DE5 180 D7
Weston St
Heanor DE75 194 A8
Swadlincote DE11 256 B3
WESTON UNDERWOOD 189 A2
West Park Ct NG10 236 D7
West Park L Ctr NG10 236 B7
West Park Mdw Nature Reserve★ DE21 220 C5
West Park Rd DE22 218 E8
West Park Sch DE21 220 D5
West Rd
Buxton SK17 85 B6
Derby DE21 220 D5
West Road Ho 2 SK17 85 B6
West Row DE22 205 A1
West Service Rd DE21 220 B3
West St
Bramley-Vale S44 117 D1
Burton upon Trent DE15 248 B3
Chesterfield S40 266 A4
Clay Cross S45 131 A4
Clowne S43 81 A5
Creswell S80 81 D1
Dronfield S18 56 F2
Eckington S21 59 C2
Glossop SK13 9 F7
Heanor DE75 181 D2
Ilkeston DE7 208 F7
Langley Mill NG16 182 B3
Shirebrook NG20 120 D4
Somercotes DE55 170 C6
South Normanton DE55 159 F5
Stonebroom DE55 146 F3
Swadlincote DE11 256 B4
Whaley Thorns NG20 101 A3
West Terr 6 DE7 194 F1
WESTTHORPE 60 D4
Westthorpe Fields Rd S21 60 C4
Westthorpe Rd S21 60 D5
West Towers Mews SK6 23 A4
West View
Barlborough S43 80 A6
Bolsover S44 118 B8
Hulland Village DE6 175 E2
Mayfield DE6 184 D6
Parwich DE6 151 E1
Rocester ST14 197 A3
Staveley S43 78 D1
Tibshelf DE55 147 F6
West View Ave DE23 231 B7
West View Cl S17 55 F6
West View La
Sheffield S17 55 F6
Sheffield S17 56 A6
West View Rd S41 95 E6
Westward Cl ST14 210 B1
West Way DE55 159 C1
Westwell Ct S21 59 C6
Westwell Pl S20 59 D6
Westwick Cres S8 56 D7
Westwick Gr S8 56 E7
Westwick La S42 94 D2
Westwick Pk S41 76 D3
Westwick Rd S8 56 E7
Westwick St DE7 209 B6
WESTWOOD 171 C3
Westwood Ave S43 97 C8
Westwood Cl S43 97 C5
Westwood Dr
Derby DE24 232 D5
Staveley S43 97 C5
Westwood Drive Gdns S43 97 B5
Westwood Gdns DE55 147 B5
Westwood Inf Sch NG16 171 C4
Westwood La S43 96 F4
Westwood Pk DE11 255 F5
Westwood Rd S44 97 A4
Wetherby Cl NG16 195 E7
Wetherby Ct DE14 253 F7
Wetherby Rd DE24 232 E7
Wetherel Rd DE15 248 C2
Wetlands La S43, S44 96 E4
Wetsough La DE4 141 D6
WETTON 149 A3
Wetton La DE55 148 A6
Weyacres DE72 221 C1
Weybridge Cl DE7 207 D8
WHALEY 100 D4
WHALEY BRIDGE 45 D7
Whaley Bridge Prim Sch SK23 45 E7
Whaley Bridge Sta SK23 45 E8
Whaley Common NG20 100 D4
Whaley La SK23 45 C8
Whaley Rd
Bolsover S44 99 F3
Holbeck NG20 101 B5
Whaley NG20 100 F5
Whaley S44 100 B3
Whaley Thorns NG20 100 E2
WHALEY THORNS 101 A2
Whaley Thorns Her Ctr★ NG20 101 A3
Whaley Thorns Ind Est NG20 100 F2
Whaley Thorns Prim Sch NG20 101 A3
Wharf Ct SK23 45 E7
Wharfedale Cl DE22 205 B4
Wharfedale Rd NG10 236 A6
Wharf Hos DE13 253 A1
Wharf La
Chesterfield S41 266 B4
Staveley S43 78 F3
Tibshelf DE55 148 C7
Wharf Rd
Pinxton NG16 160 D2
Whaley Bridge SK23 45 E7
Wharf Road Ind Est NG16 160 D2
WHARF THE 210 C1
Wharf The DE72 235 A2
Wharmby Ave NG19 135 D3
Wharncliffe Cl SK13 9 E4
Wharncliffe Rd DE7 208 E8
Wharton Dr S41 266 C3
WHATSTANDWELL 156 C1
Whatstandwell Sta DE4 156 C1
Wheal La SK17 107 D7
Wheatbridge Rd S40 266 A3
Wheatbridge Ret Pk S40 266 A2
WHEATCROFT 157 A7
Wheatcroft SK13 9 E4
Wheatcroft Cl
Clay Cross S45 131 D2
Wingerworth S42 115 A4
Wirksworth DE4 165 F6
Wheatcroft Dr DE56 168 B5
Wheatcroft La
1 Castle Donington DE74 246 E3
Crich DE4 157 A7
Wheatcroft Way DE21 205 C2
Wheatfield Cres NG19 136 E5
Wheatfield Ct DE65 242 D5
Wheatfields SK23 47 C7
Wheatfield Way S42 94 F5
Wheathill Cl
Calow S43 96 F4
Chesterfield S42 94 F5
Wheathill Gr DE23 231 A6
Wheathill La S41 96 D4
Wheatland Cl DE24 231 C2
Wheatlands DE11 256 B7
Wheatlands La DE45 91 C5
Wheatlands Rd
Burton upon Trent DE15 254 E7
Wingerworth S42 114 E4
Wheatley Ave DE55 159 C1
Wheatley Cl NG19 136 F1
Wheatley Gdns DE4 127 D2
Wheatley La DE15 248 C4
Wheatley Rd DE4 127 D3
Wheatsheaf Cl
Derby DE21 206 C2
Horwich End SK23 45 E6
Wheatsheaf La DE4 156 F1
Wheatsheaf Rd SK23 45 E6
Wheatsheaf Way S43 80 D2
Wheeldon Ave
Belper DE56 179 B4
Derby DE22 218 E7
Wheeldon Cl NE7 194 F6
Wheeldon Cres S43 96 D7
Wheeldon Manor DE22 218 E8
Wheeldon Way DE6 175 E3
Wheelton Farming Office Buildings DE12 259 B7
Wheelwright Way DE24 219 D3
Whenby Cl DE3 217 C2
Whernside Cl DE24 233 D6
WHESTON 68 F5
Wheston Bank
Tideswell SK17 69 B4
Wheston SK17 68 F5
Wheston Ct 7 S40 95 D5
Wheston La
Peak Forest SK17 49 D1
Wheston SK17 68 E7
Whetmorhurst La SK6 23 E4
Whilton Cres DE7 207 D8
Whilton Ct DE56 179 D4
Whinacre Cl S8 57 B6
Whinacre Pl S8 57 A6
Whinacre Wlk S8 57 A6
Whinbush Ave DE24 232 E5
Whinfell Rd
Chesterfield S41 76 D1
Chesterfield S41 95 C8
Whinney Bank NG19 136 D4
Whinney Hill NG19 136 D4
Whippet Way S40 96 C7
Whisperwood Cl S44 98 A5
Whistlestop Cl DE3 217 D4
Whiston St DE23 219 A2
Whitaker Gdns DE23 218 E2
Whitaker Mews ST14 196 F3
Whitaker Rd DE23 218 E2
Whitaker St DE23 219 A2
Whitburn Rd NG9 223 E3
Whitby Ave DE21 205 C1
Whitcombe Pl DE5 169 D2
White Ash Rd DE55 159 E4
Whitebank Cl S41 266 C1
Whitecarr La DE55, S45 145 B4
White Carr La S45 145 B5
Whitecotes Cl S40 114 E8
Whitecotes La S40 114 E8
Whitecotes Pk S40 114 F8
Whitecotes Prim Sch S40 114 F
Whitecroft Rd SK6 23 C
Whitecross Ave SK17 69 C
Whitecross Gdns DE1 218 E
Whitecross Ho DE1 218 E
Whitecross Ind Est SK17 69 D
Whitecross Rd SK17 69 D
Whitecross St DE1 218 E
White Edge Cl S40 95 D
White Edge Dr DE45 91 E
Whitefield La
Ashover S45 129 A
Chelmorton SK17 106 E
White Gate Rd HD9 3 D
Whitegates SK14 9 A
White Gates DE5 181 B
Whitegates Way NG17 148 F
Whitehall Terr SK23 34 D
White Hart Cl DE7 207 D
White Hart Cnr S21 59 E
White Hart Yd DE56 191 F
Whitehaven Gr DE73 233 A
Whitehead Cl DE7 194 D
Whitehead Dr NG16 182 D
Whitehead St 4 S43 78 F
White Horse La DE55 145 D
WHITEHOUGH 46 D
WHITEHOUGH HEAD 46 E
Whitehough Head La SK23 46
Whitehouse Cl DE24 232
Whitehouse Rise DE56 178 F
Whitehouses S41 266
Whitehurst St DE24 232

White Knowle Cl SK17 85 C5
White Knowle Pk SK17 85 C5
White Knowle Rd SK17 85 C5
White La
Eckington S12 44 C2
Shottle DE56 177 D4
Whitelands Cl DE72 246 A7
Whitelea La DE4 144 B6
White Leas S40 95 B4
White Leas Ave S42 132 A7
Whiteleas Rd SK23 45 D3
WHITELEY 180 F6
Whiteley Rd DE5 180 F7
White Lion Sq DE7 208 F7
White Lodge La DE45 91 E6
Whitelow La
Ible DE4 153 E7
Sheffield S17 55 B7
Whitely Ave DE7 194 F5
Whitely Cl 3 NG9 223 E8
WHITE MOOR 179 C5
Whitemoor Hall DE56 179 D5
Whitemoor La DE56 179 D5
White Rd
New Mills SK22 24 C2
Staveley S43 79 A3
White Rock Ct DE4 143 D6
Whites Cl DE55 159 A2
Whites Croft View S43 80 B6
Whites La
Blackwell DE55 147 F1
Somercotes DE55 170 B8
Whitesmead Cl SK12 32 D5
White St DE22 218 E7
White Thorns Cl S8 57 B5
White Thorns Dr S8 57 B5
White Thorns View S8 57 B6
White Tor Rd DE4 143 C2
Whiteway DE22 204 E2
Whitewell Gdns DE24 233 C5
Whitewells La DE56 178 C8
Whitewells Rd DE56 167 E2
Whitewood Way DE4 143 B3
WHITFIELD 17 D8
Whitfield Ave SK13 17 C7
Whitfield Cross SK13 17 D7
Whitfield La DE45 124 E2
Whitfield Pk SK13 17 C7
Whitfield Wells SK13 17 D7
Whiting Ave 2 NG9 223 F2
Whiting St 8 S8 43 A6
White Bank Rd SK22 24 B2
White Rd SK22 24 C1
Whitley Way DE6 185 E8
Whitley Wlk SK13 16 F8
Whitmore Ave S42 115 E2
Whitmore Rd DE21 219 F6
Whitsome Rd DE23 231 E1
Whitstable Cl DE23 231 D7
Whittaker La DE21 191 D2
Whitt Cl DE72 221 C1
Whittinglands Cl DE73 233 A3
Whitting Mews S41 76 F2
Whittington Green Sch S41 77 B3
Whittington Hill S41 77 A2
Whittington La S18 76 F5
WHITTINGTON MOOR 96 A7
Whittington Moor Inf Acad 9 S41 96 A8
Whittington Rd S43 77 F4
Whittington St DE24 232 D6
Whittington Way S41 77 A1
Whitting Valley Rd S41 77 B1
Whittlebury Dr DE23 230 F7
Whitton Pl S44 98 A6
WHITWELL 81 E6
Whitwell S80 82 A5
Whitwell Bank 5 SK13 9 D2
Whitwell Cl
4 Gamesley SK13 9 D2
Ilkeston NE7 194 E6
Whitwell Fold 1 SK13 9 D2
Whitwell Gn 2 SK13 9 D2
Whitwell Lea 3 SK13 9 D2
Whitwell Prim Sch S80 82 A5
Whitwell Rd S80 63 A4
Whitwell Sta S80 82 A5
Whitworth Ave DE4 127 C3
Whitworth Cl DE12 262 E4
Whitworth Hospl DE4 142 F8
Whitworth Rd
Chesterfield S41 95 F6
1 Chesterfield S41 96 A6
Darley Dale DE4 127 B4
Ilkeston DE7 208 F7
Wholey Pl S45 131 C3
Whysall Rd NG10 236 B7
Whysall St DE75 181 E2
Whyteleafe Gr DE21 206 B1
Whytes La ST14 196 F5
Wibben Cl DE21 205 F3
Wichal Farm Cl DE5 180 D7
Wicken La SK23 35 A4
Wickenlow La SK17 103 D1
Wickersley Cl 1 DE22 204 F2
Wickets The DE15 254 F8
Wickfield Cl S12 44 F5
Wickfield Dr S12 44 F5
Wickfield Gr S12 44 E4
Wickfield Pl S12 44 F5
Wickfield Rd S12 44 F5
Wickins Pl S43 79 B3
Wicksteed Cl DE56 179 D5
Widdop Cl S13 44 D8
Widdop Croft S13 44 D8
Widdowson Rd 2 NG10 236 B5
Widdybank Cl DE22 204 C2
Widecombe Ct 24 S41 95 F8
Wideshaft DE11 256 C4
Widmerpool St NG16 160 C2
Wifel Green DE73 252 E5
WIGLEY 93 F4
Wigley Prim Sch S42 93 E4
Wigley Rd S43 97 C6
Wigmore Cl DE3 217 C3
Wikeley Way S43 96 D7
Wilberforce Rd NG19 135 D2
Wilcock Ho DE21 219 C6
Wilcox Ave NG19 136 B5
WILDAY GREEN 75 A2
Wildaygreen La S18 75 B2
Wilday Green La S17 74 F3
Wilden Croft S43 96 C8
Wilderbrook La DE56 178 A8
Wilders Lea Ct DE56 179 A2
Wildersley Rd DE56 179 A1
Wilders Way DE74 247 E2
Wildflower Cl S44 97 A3
Wildhay Brook DE65 228 C1
Wildhay La DE6 183 C7
Wild Hill NG17 148 E7
Wild La DE4, DE55 157 B4
Wildpark La DE6 202 D6
Wildsmith St DE24 233 A8
Wild St DE22 218 D5
Wilfred St DE23 219 B2
Wilhallow La NG16 171 E2
Wilkin Hill S18 75 E2
Wilkins Dr DE24 232 E7
Wilkinson Cl
Chesterfield S40 115 A6
Pleasley NG19 135 A5
Wilkinson Dr S43 97 B7
Willbury Dr S12 44 A6
Willcock Rd DE14 254 A7
Willersley Castle★ DE4 155 B7
Willersley Ct 3 S41 95 D7
Willersley Ho NG10 236 A5
Willersley La
Matlock DE4 143 C1
Matlock Bath DE4 155 C8
Willesden Ave DE22 218 A7
Willetts Rd DE21 220 A7
William Allitt Sch The DE11 255 E7
William Ave NG16 182 F2
William Brown Square S40 266 B1
William Cl
Duffield DE56 190 D4
Sheffield S20 59 D6
William Cres S20 59 D6
William Gilbert CE Endowed Prim Sch DE56 190 E4
William Gregg VC L Ctr DE75 181 F1
William Holmes Almshouses DE5 169 F2
William Levick Prim Sch S18 56 C2
William Lilley Inf Sch NG9 223 D6
William Nadin Way DE11 255 F4
William Newton Cl DE65 241 B5
William Rd NG9 223 D7
William Rhodes Prim Sch S40 266 A2
Williams Cl DE55 170 D6
William Shrewsbury County Prim Sch DE13 240 E1
Williamson Ave SK17 66 C1
Williamson Cres SK23 45 D8
Williamson Gdns NG16 182 A2
Williamson Rd SK23 45 D8
William St
Belper DE56 178 F4
Chesterfield S41 96 A6
Derby DE1 218 E6
Eckington S21 59 D3
Long Eaton NG10 223 C2
William Street N S41 76 F2
WILLIAMTHORPE 132 C8
Williamthorpe Cl S42 132 A7
Williamthorpe Ind Pk S42 116 D2
Williamthorpe Ponds★ S42 116 E2
Williamthorpe Rd S42 132 B7
William Wood La NG20 120 C5
WILLINGTON 242 A6
Willington Prim Sch DE65 242 B5
Willington Rd
Etwall DE65 229 D3
Findern DE65 242 D8
Repton DE65 242 B4
Willington Sta DE65 242 A6
Willn St DE23 218 F1
Willoughby Almshouses NG16 195 C1
Willoughby Ave NG10 223 C3
Willoughby Cl DE72 235 F8
Willoughby Ct DE72 222 D4
Willoughby Ho DE11 256 C4
Willow Ave
Long Eaton NG10 223 D1
Ripley DE5 180 D7
Shirebrook NG20 119 D5
Stapleford NG9 223 D6
Willow Bank
Somersal Herbert DE6 211 F3
Somersal Herbert DE6 212 A2
Willowbath La DE4 165 F7
Willowbrook Cl DE65 228 C2
Willowbrook Grange DE73 233 A1
Willow Cl
Aldercar NG16 182 B4
Alfreton DE55 159 B5
Aston-on-Trent DE72 246 B7
Creswell S80 81 F1
Derby DE72 204 F2
Pilsley S45 132 C1
South Normanton DE55 160 B5
Stanley Common DE7 193 A2
Willow Croft DE24 233 C4
Willowcroft Rd DE21 220 E4
Willow Ct
Ashbourne DE6 185 D7
Calow S44 97 A3
Swadlincote DE11 256 C4
Willow Dr
Chapel-en-le-Frith SK23 47 B5
Mastin Moor S43 79 C4
Swadlincote DE11 255 F7
Willow Farm Bsns Pk DE74 247 B6
Willow Farm Ct DE65 230 D2
Willowfields DE65 228 D2
Willow Garth Rd S41 95 C8
Willow Gr
Belper DE56 179 A2
Willington DE65 242 A6
Willow Grove DE73 232 F1
Willowherb Cl DE24 231 F2
Willow Ho DE21 219 C6
Willow Meadow Rd DE6 185 D7
Willow Park Way DE72 246 A7
Willowpit La DE65 228 E5
Willow Pl DE15 254 E7
Willow Rd
Castle Donington DE74 247 B5
Killamarsh S21 60 C5
Willow Rise NG10 223 B5
Willow Row DE1 267 A4
Willows Ave DE55 159 B5
Willows Ct DE5 169 C1
Willowsend Cl DE65 230 D1
Willowside Gn DE21 220 D3
Willow Sq S42 115 C1
Willows Sports Ctr DE1 267 A4
Willow St DE55 146 C1
Willows The
Chesterfield S40 95 B1
Hulland Ward DE6 175 F3
Pleasley NG19 135 A6
Shirland DE55 146 C3
Willow Stream SK22 33 D8
Willow Tree Ct DE3 217 D2
Willowtree Dr DE21 220 B7
Willow Tree Dr S43 80 F2
Willow Way DE4 127 B3
Willridding La DE6 183 C7
Will Shore's La DE4 142 D6
Willson Ave DE23 231 D8
Willson Dr DE55 170 C7
Willson Rd DE23 231 C8
Wilmans Wlk SK13 10 A6
Wilmington Ave DE24 233 B5
Wilmore Rd DE24 232 B5
WILMORTON 219 E2
Wilmot Ave
Derby DE21 219 F5
Weston-on-Trent DE72 245 E5
Wilmot Dr DE7 192 F6
Wilmot Rd
Belper DE56 179 A4
Swadlincote DE11 256 B3
Wilmot St
Derby DE1 267 B2
Heanor DE75 181 E1
3 Heanor DE75 193 E8
Ilkeston DE7 194 E1
Long Eaton NG10 236 A5
Matlock DE4 143 B6
Wilmslow Dr DE21 206 B1
Wilne Ave NG10 236 A4
Wilne Cl NG10 235 F4
Wilne La
Breaston DE72 235 D4
Shardlow DE72 235 B2
Wilne Rd
Draycott DE72 235 B5
Long Eaton NG10 235 F4
Wilshaw Bottom La SK17 104 B2
Wilshaw Cl SK23 47 C5
WILSON 252 F6
Wilson Ave
Blackwell DE55 147 E1
Clowne S43 80 F5
Heanor DE75 181 B4
Wilson Cl
Burnaston DE3 230 C8
Clay Cross S45 131 D2
Wilson La S44 117 B2
Wilson Pl 6 S8 43 A7
Wilson Rd
Derby DE21 219 F8
Dronfield S18 57 C4
Eastwood NG16 182 F1
Wilson Rise DE73 252 E6
Wilson St
Alfreton DE55 159 B4
Derby DE1 267 B2
Dronfield S18 76 B8
Mansfield NG19 135 D2
Pinxton NG16 160 D3
Wilson's Terr SK13 17 B8
Wilson Way DE13 240 B1
WILSTHORPE 236 B7
Wilsthorpe Rd
Breaston DE72 235 F8
Derby DE21 220 A7
Long Eaton NG10 236 B7
Wilsthorpe Sch NG10 223 B1
Wilton Cl DE24 231 C2
Wilton Pl DE7 194 F1
Wilton St 5 DE7 194 F1
Wiltra Gr DE56 190 F3
Wiltshire Ave NG16 171 B4
Wiltshire Dr SK13 17 F8
Wiltshire Rd DE21 219 E7
Wimbledon Rd DE22 218 A7
Wimborne Cres S41 95 F7
Wimbourne Cl DE73 233 A2
Wimpole Gdns DE22 218 B6
Wimsey Way DE55 159 B2
Wincanton Cl DE24 219 D1
Winchcombe Dr DE15 248 B1
Winchcombe Way DE21 206 B2
Winchester Cl S42 131 F6
Winchester Cres DE7 209 A8
Winchester Dr
Burton upon Trent DE14 254 C8
Linton DE12 261 D5
Mansfield Woodhouse NG19 136 D4
Swadlincote DE11 256 D6
Winchester Rd S41 95 E7
Wincobank Way DE55 160 C7
Winder Ave
Killamarsh S20 60 A6
Sheffield S21 59 F6
Windermere Ave
Dronfield S18 56 E1
Ilkeston DE7 208 D5
Windermere Cl NG19 136 E3
Windermere Cres DE22 204 E3
Windermere Dr DE21 220 E5
Windermere Drive DE65 228 E1
Windermere Gdns NG10 223 B2
Windermere Rd
Chesterfield S41 95 D7
Clay Cross S45 131 B3
Long Eaton NG10 223 B2
Winders Cnr S43 80 B5
Windgather Rd
Kettleshulme SK23 45 A1
Oldfield SK23 64 E8
Winding Wheel The★ S41 266 C3
Windlass Way DE21 220 F2
Windlea Rd DE55 170 C6
WINDLEY 189 D7
Windley Cres DE22 204 F1
Windley Dr DE7 194 D3
Windley La
Idridgehay DE56 176 E5
Turnditch DE56 177 A1
Windley DE56 189 E7
WINDMILL 70 A8
Windmill Ave DE56 192 A8
Windmill Cl
4 Albert Village DE11 256 F1
Bolsover S44 99 A3
Castle Donington DE74 247 B2
Elvaston DE24 233 D4
Ockbrook DE72 221 C5
Ripley DE5 181 A8
3 Uttoxeter ST14 210 B1
Windmill Dr ST14 224 E3
Windmill Greenway S20 59 E5
Windmill Hill La DE22 218 C6
Windmill La
Alderwasley DE56 166 F6
Ashbourne DE6 173 C4
Belper DE56 179 A4
Eyam S32 71 C6
Snelston DE6 184 E2
Unstone S18 77 A6
Windmill Mdw DE21 220 D5
Windmill Pl DE21 205 D3
Windmill Rd DE65 229 B3
Windmill Rise
Belper DE56 179 A5
Somercotes DE55 170 D7
South Normanton DE55 159 F5
Windmill St DE11 256 A1
Windmill View DE56 179 E8
Windmill Way S43 96 C8
Windrush Cl DE22 205 B5
Windrush Ct 4 S43 96 E8
Windrush Rd DE65 240 D8
Windses Est S32 53 D2
Windsmoor Rd NG16 182 D8
Windsor Ave
Derby DE23 231 B8
Hatton DE65 227 D2
Melbourne DE73 252 A8
Windsor Cl
6 Ashbourne DE6 173 D3
Borrowash DE72 221 C1
Chesterfield S40 95 C1
Heanor DE75 181 E3
Swadlincote DE11 256 A6
Swanwick DE55 170 A7
Trowell NG9 209 B5
Windsor Cres
Ilkeston DE7 208 E4
Stapleford NG9 223 E7
Windsor Ct
Derby DE3 217 D3
Long Eaton NG10 236 E7
Sandiacre NG10 223 B4
West Hallam DE7 207 D8
Windsor Dr
Derby DE21 221 A6
Dronfield S18 56 C1
Wingerworth S42 114 E4
Windsor Park Rd SK17 85 D8
Windsor Rd
Buxton SK17 85 C8
Linton DE12 261 D5
Uttoxeter ST14 210 A1
Windsor St NG9 223 E7
Windsor Wlk 7 S41 96 C1
Windwhistle Dr 4 S41 115 F2
Windy Arbour DE6 202 D5
Windy Fields Rd S42 113 D7
Windy House La S2 44 A8
Windy Knowle SK22 25 A3
Windy La DE21 191 C1
Windyridge SK17 121 B6
Winfield Gr SK6 15 B1
Winfield Way DE11 257 B1
WINGERWORTH 114 F4
Wingerworth Ave S8 56 D8
Wingerworth Cotts S42 115 E3
Wingerworth Park Rd DE21 220 E5
Wingerworth St S42 115 E3
Wingerworth Way S40 114 F7
Wingfield Cl 6 S18 56 C1
Wingfield Cres
Harpur Hill SK17 85 D1
Sheffield S12 44 C5
Wingfield Dr
Derby DE21 205 F1
Ilkeston DE7 194 D3
Wingfield Gr SK13 17 F7
Wingfield Hall DE55 157 F3
Wingfield Manor House★ DE55 157 E2
Wingfield Pk
Crich Common DE55 168 C8
Fritchley DE56 168 F5
Wingfield Rd
Alfreton DE55 158 E3
Tupton S42 131 D8
Wingfield View S45 131 E4
Winhill Rd SK22 24 C1
Winkpenny La DE55 147 F5
Winnat Pl S43 97 C7
Winnats Cl
Chesterfield S40 95 D5
Glossop SK13 17 F8
Winnats Pass S33 38 A2
Winnats Rd S33 37 E2
Winney Hill S26 61 E5
Winney La S26 61 E3
Winnings The S80 101 E8
Winnington Rd SK6 23 A7
Winn La DE6 174 F7
WINSHILL 248 B3
Winshill Village Prim Sch DE15 248 C3
WINSICK 115 E6
Winslow Ave SK14 9 A2
Winslow Gn DE21 220 C6
WINSTER 141 C5
Winster CE Prim Sch DE4 141 D6
Winster Cl
Belper DE56 179 B5
Clay Cross S42 131 A5
Winster Ct S41 96 A5
Winster Gn 3 DE11 255 E5
Winster Gr SK17 85 E7
Winster La DE4 140 F7
Winster Market House★ DE4 141 C6
Winster Mews SK13 9 E2
Winster Rd
Derby DE21 205 E1
Staveley S43 97 C8
Winster Sq SK17 85 E7
Winster Way NG10 235 F5
Winston Cl NG9 223 E8
Winterbourne Dr NG9 209 E1
Winter Closes NG16 171 F1
Wintercroft La DE6 161 E1
Wintergreen Dr DE23 230 F6
Winyard Ct 9 S40 95 D5
Wire La DE55 148 B3
Wirestone La
Ashover S45 128 D7
Ashover S45 129 A3
Wirksmoor Rd SK22 33 B7
WIRKSWORTH 165 E8
Wirksworth CE Inf Sch DE4 154 F1
Wirksworth Dale DE4 153 B2
Wirksworth Hall Gdns DE4 165 F8
Wirksworth Heritage Ctr★ DE4 154 F1
Wirksworth Ind Ctr DE4 154 F3
Wirksworth Inf Sch DE4 154 F1
Wirksworth Jun Sch DE4 155 A1
Wirksworth L Ctr DE4 165 F8
Wirksworth Rd
Duffield DE56 190 B4
Holloway DE4 156 B2
Idridgehay DE56 176 F6
Ilkeston DE7 208 C4
Kirk Ireton DE6 165 B2
Shottle DE56 177 C3
Windley DE56 189 F6
Wirksworth Sta★ DE4 155 A1
Wisbech Cl S40 114 E8
Wisgreaves Rd DE24 232 F8
Wishing Stone Way DE4 143 E6
Wistanes Gn DE55 145 D1
Wisteria Way SK13 10 C3
Wiston Way S41 115 C7
Witham Cl
Chesterfield S41 96 C6
Hilton DE65 228 E2
Witham Ct S40 95 C3
Witham Dr DE23 231 D6
Witney Cl DE24 232 C8
Witney St S8 43 A8
Wittering Cl NG10 236 E5
Witton Ct DE24 231 D4
Woburn Cl
Blackwell DE55 147 E1
Swanwick DE55 169 F7
Woburn Cotts DE4 143 B7
Woburn Croft NG10 223 A4
Woburn Ho DE55 147 E1
Woburn La NG19 135 C4
Woburn Pl
Derby DE22 218 B5
Pleasley NG19 135 C4
Woburn Rd NG19 135 C4
Wolds Rd DE4 143 D7

Wolds Rise DE4 143 C7
Wolfa St DE22 267 A2
Wolfcote Cl S45 131 D1
Wolfe Cl S40 95 D1
Wolfscote Cl DE21 205 F3
Wolfscote Dale DE11 255 F2
Wollaton Ave S17 56 A5
Wollaton Dr S17 56 A5
Wollaton Rd
Derby DE21 219 F8
Sheffield S17 56 A5
Wollaton Road N 5
DE21 205 F1
Wollen Cl S80 81 F1
Wolseley Rd 2 S8 43 A7
Wolverley Grange
DE24 233 D6
Woodale Cl DE23 230 F6
WOODALL 61 C6
Woodall La S26 61 D6
Woodall Rd S21 60 F5
Woodall Way S21 60 F5
Wood Ave
Creswell S80 81 D1
Sandiacre NG10 223 A6
Woodbank Ct S17 56 A7
Woodbeck Ct DE21 206 B2
Woodbine Cl DE14 253 E6
Woodbine Terr SK23 47 A6
Woodborough Rd
NG19 135 E1
Woodbourne Rd
SK22 33 A5
Woodbridge Cl
Chellaston DE73 232 F1
Heanor DE75 182 B1
Woodbridge Jun Sch
DE55 159 A3
Woodbridge Rise
S40 114 B8
Woodbrook SK23 45 E8
Woodbrook Ct SK23 45 E7
Woodbrook Rd SK6 23 C6
Woodchester Dr
DE24 233 D6
Wood Cl S42 114 D4
Woodcock Gr SK13 10 E1
Woodcock Sq DE3 230 C8
Woodcote Way
Chesterfield S42 114 E8
Derby DE23 231 A7
Wood Croft DE23 231 D8
Wood Cutters Way
SK23 46 F5
WOODEND
Disley 32 E8
Hanbury 238 A1
Wood End DE4 156 B6
Wood End La DE73 244 D1
Wood End Rd DE75 181 E2
Woodfall La
Duffield DE56 190 A1
Windley DE22 189 E3
Wood Farm Ct
NG11 237 D2
Wood Farm La
DE11 256 E4
Woodfield Cl SK13 9 F5
Woodfield Dr
4 Ripley DE5 170 A1
Swadlincote DE11 256 C5
Woodfield Rd
Pinxton NG16 160 D4
South Normanton
DE55 159 F4
Woodfield The SK17 85 D4
Woodford Rd DE22 218 A7
Woodford Way S43 78 B4
Woodgate Dr DE73 233 A1
Wood Gdns SK22 25 C3
Woodhall Dr DE23 230 E8
Woodhall House Farm
S26 61 C6
WOODHEAD
Crowden 7 C4
Littlemoor 130 E2
Woodhead La S45 130 D1
Woodhead Rd
Charlesworth SK13 6 C1
Charlesworth SK13 11 A8
Glossop SK13 10 D5
Holme HD9 2 E6
Sheffield, Highfield S2 43 A8
Tintwistle SK13 5 E1
Tintwistle SK13 10 B8
Woodhead Way 6
DE65 240 E8
Woodhouse Ct
NG19 136 C2
Woodhouse La
Barlborough S43 79 E5
Bolsover S44 98 E3
Heathtop DE65 227 A6
Mastin Moor S43 79 C5
Scropton DE65 226 F7
South Normanton
DE55 159 E5
Winster DE4 141 C6
Woodhouse Rd
Kilburn DE56, DE7 192 A7
6 Mansfield NG19 136 B1
Rowsley DE4 126 F7
Sheffield S12 44 B6
WOODHOUSES 252 A5
Woodhouse St
DE11 256 D3
Woodhouse Station Ent
Ctr NG19 136 B3
Woodhouse West Prim
Sch S13 44 F6
Woodhurst Cl DE21 219 D8
Wood La
Belper DE56 190 F7
Church Warsop NG20 120 F7
Creswell S80 100 C8
Crich DE4 157 B3
Hanbury DE13 238 A4
Hayfield SK22 25 C3
Holloway DE4 144 A1
Horsley Woodhouse
DE7 192 D5
Ible DE4 153 E6
Idridgehay DE6, DE56 176 E8
Kniveton DE6 163 A1
Nether Langwith
NG20 101 D1
Pleasley NG19 119 D1
Ripley DE5 169 A4
Scarcliffe S44 118 F6
Shirebrook NG20 119 E1
Swadlincote DE11 256 A7
Woodland Ave
Borrowash DE72 221 C2
Breaston DE72 235 F8
Ilkeston DE7 194 D4
Sutton in Ashfield
NG17 148 E4
Woodland Cl
Hodthorpe S80 82 C6
4 Smalley DE75 193 C8
Woodland Dr
Rocester ST14 196 F3
Scropton DE6 226 D4
Sheffield S12 44 B2
Woodland Gr
Barlborough S43 80 A6
Clay Cross S42 131 B6
Clowne S43 81 A4
Mansfield Woodhouse
NG19 136 C4
Woodland Gro
NG20 119 D2
Woodland Pl S17 55 F5
Woodland Rd
Derby DE22 218 E8
Mansfield NG19 136 F1
Sheffield S8 43 B3
Swadlincote DE15 255 B4
Woodlands
Brimington S43 96 D7
Great Longstone DE45 89 F3
Wirksworth DE4 165 E8
Woodlands Ave
Breaston DE72 235 F8
Derby DE24 232 E4
Woodlands Brow
DE6 173 D4
Woodlands Cl
Castle Gresley DE11 255 E2
Glossop SK13 9 F6
Little Eaton DE21 205 B8
Melbourne DE73 252 A8
Thorpe DE6 161 D1
Woodlands Cres
DE12 262 B4
Woodlands La
Chellaston DE73 245 A8
Quarndon DE22 204 D6
Woodlands Rd
Chapel-en-le-Frith
SK23 47 B4
Derby DE22 204 E5
High Lane SK12 32 A6
New Mills SK22 33 A8
Overseal DE12 262 B4
Woodlands Sch
DE22 204 D4
Woodlands The
5 Mansfield NG19 136 B1
Melbourne DE73 252 B8
Tatenhill DE13 253 A8
Whaley Thorns NG20 101 A3
Woodlands View
DE7 193 A2
Woodlands Way
Melbourne DE73 252 B8
Spion Kop NG20 120 F1
Woodlands Yd DE73 245 A8
Woodland View
Buxton SK17 85 C8
Chilcote DE12 264 F3
Crich DE4 167 E8
Hathersage S32 53 A7
Horwich End SK23 45 F2
Sheffield, Abbeydale Park
S17 56 A7
Sheffield, Charnock Hill
S12 44 B2
Whaley Thorns NG20 101 A3
Woodland Views
ST14 224 E2
Woodland Way
Clay Cross S42 131 B6
Eastwood NG16 182 E2
Woodland Wlk S40 94 F5
Woodlark Cl SK17 85 D2
Woodlea Gr DE21 205 C8
Woodlea Rd SK13 17 B7
Woodleigh Cl S40 94 F5
WOODLINKIN 181 E6
Woodmans Croft
DE65 227 C1
Woodmere Dr S41 77 C4
Woodminton Dr
DE73 232 F3
WOODNOOK 94 E5
Woodnook Cl S42 95 A4
Wood Nook Cl
NG16 171 F6
Woodnook Gr S21 58 E2
Woodnook La
Chesterfield S42 94 F5
Ingmanthorpe S18 94 C7
Woodnook Way S42 94 F4
Woodpecker Hill
DE7 208 A2
Woodpigeon Ct S43 98 A7
Wood Rd
Derby, Chaddesden
DE21 220 A8
Derby, Oakwood
DE21 205 F1
Derby, Spondon DE21 221 A6
Woodridge The
DE56 190 F6
Woodrising Cl DE21 206 B3
Woodroffe Wlk
DE23 231 E7
Woodrove Ave S13 44 B7
Woodrove Cl S13 44 B7
Woods Cl DE15 248 A1
Woodsea Level
ST14 210 D8
Woodseat Gr ST14 197 A4
Woodseat Level
ST14 196 E2
WOODSEATS 16 A6
Woodseats La SK13 16 B6
Woodsford Drive
DE24 233 D4
Woodshop La DE73 244 D6
WOODSIDE 192 D4
Woodside
Buxton SK17 85 C7
Carsington DE4 164 E7
Crich DE4 168 A7
Eastwood NG16 182 E3
Horsley DE7 192 D3
Woodside Ave
Holmesfield S18 75 A8
Killamarsh S21 60 F7
Ripley DE5 180 D8
Woodside Cl
Bakewell DE45 109 D5
Chesterfield S40 95 B4
Woodside Cres
Ilkeston DE7 194 D5
Long Eaton NG10 236 B8
Woodside Ct S45 131 B4
Woodside Dr
Bakewell DE45 109 D5
Derby DE22 205 A4
Woodside La S17 56 E2
Woodside Pl S45 131 B4
Woodside Rd
Sandiacre NG10 223 B5
Shirebrook NG20 119 E5
Shireoaks S81 63 F7
Woodside St SK22 33 B6
Woodside View S18 75 A8
Woods La
Burton upon Trent,
Stapenhill DE15 254 F8
Derby DE22 267 A1
Woods Mdw DE72 233 D5
Woodsome Pk S42 116 D1
Woodsorrel Dr
DE21 206 B3
Wood St
Alfreton DE55 159 C5
Codnor DE5 181 B8
Derby DE1 267 C4
Eastwood NG16 182 F3
Glossop SK13 17 C8
Hollingworth SK14 9 D5
Holmewood S42 116 E1
Ilkeston DE7 194 F1
New Mills SK22 33 B7
Ripley DE5 169 D2
Somercotes DE55 170 C8
Swadlincote DE11 256 B2
Wirksworth DE4 165 F8
Woodstock Cl
DE22 204 D4
Woodstock Ct 5
S41 96 A6
Woodstock Dr S41 115 C8
Woodstock Rd NG9 223 F3
Woodstock Rise 2
S41 115 C8
Wood Street North
DE55 159 C5
Woodthorne Ave
DE24 232 E4
WOODTHORPE 79 C2
Woodthorpe Ave
Clay Cross S45 131 A4
Derby, Chaddesden
DE21 219 F6
Woodthorpe CE Prim
Sch S43 79 C1
Woodthorpe Cl S44 98 F7
Woodthorpe Com Prim
Sch S13 44 C7
Woodthorpe Cres
S13 44 C8
Woodthorpe Rd
Sheffield S13 44 C7
Shuttlewood S44 98 F8
Staveley S43 79 C2
Woodvale Cl S40 114 A8
Wood View S21 79 A8
Woodview Cl S42 114 F2
Woodview Gdns
DE22 218 F8
Wood View Ho S21 59 C3
Woodview Rd
Swadlincote DE11 255 E4
Swadlincote DE11 255 E5
WOODVILLE 256 E3
Woodville CE Jun Sch
DE11 256 F2
Woodville Inf Sch
DE11 256 F2
Woodville Rd
Hartshorne DE11 257 A5
Overseal DE12 262 B4
Woodville DE11 257 A4
Woodwards Cl
DE72 221 D1
Woodward's Pl
DE11 256 C3
Woodward Way
DE11 256 D4
Woodyard Ave S41 96 B5
Woodyard Cl DE11 255 F1
Woodyard La
Church Broughton
DE65 227 C6
Scropton DE65 226 F5
Wooley Cl S42 131 B7
Wooliscroft Cl DE7 194 C2
Woollaton La SK17 138 D2
WOOLLEY 145 E5
Woolley Bridge Rd
Glossop SK13 9 F5
Hadfield SK13 9 F5
Woolley Cl SK14 9 D4
Woolley La SK14 9 D4
Woolley Mill La SK13 9 E7
WOOLLEY MOOR 145 D7
Woolley Rd DE4 143 B6
Woolley's Yd DE4 141 C6
Woolrych St DE23 218 F2
Woolsthorpe Cres
DE7 208 D4
Woolstitch Pk DE12 264 E7
Woosnam Cl DE14 254 A6
Wootton Cl DE55 170 C7
Wootton Rd DE6 183 A4
Worcester Ave
NG19 136 C6
Worcester Cl S45 131 E4
Worcester Cres
DE21 219 E8
Worcester Gr SK13 17 F8
Worcester Mews
NG19 136 C6
Worcester Rd DE15 254 E6
Wordsworth Ave
Derby DE24 231 F5
Mansfield Woodhouse
NG19 136 B4
Swadlincote DE11 256 C6
Wordsworth Dr
DE24 232 A5
Wordsworth Pl S18 76 C7
Wordsworth Rd
Awsworth NG16 195 C5
Chesterfield S41 95 F8
Works La S44 97 B3
Worksop Rd
Barlborough S43 80 D7
Belph S80 82 D2
Darfoulds S80 63 C1
Holbeck Woodhouse
S80 101 E7
Mastin Moor S43 79 D4
Thorpe Salvin S80 62 E7
Whitwell S43 81 C7
Whitwell S80 81 F6
Whitwell S80 82 A8
Works Rd S43 78 B2
WORMHILL 68 C1
Worrall Ave NG10 223 E1
Worthington La
DE73 252 F1
Wortley Ave NG9 209 D3
Wortley Cl DE7 209 A8
Wortley Ct S33 51 B7
Wragley Way DE24 231 D2
Wreakes La S18 56 F2
Wren Cl DE11 256 F3
Wren Ct NG10 236 A3
Wren Nest Cl SK13 17 B8
Wren Nest Rd SK13 10 B1
Wren Nest Ret Pk
SK13 10 B1
Wren Nest Terr SK13 10 C1
Wren Park Cl
Belper DE56 178 E5
Chesterfield S40 114 F7
Eckington S12 58 E8
Findern DE65 230 D1
Wren Park Prim Sch
DE3 218 A2
Wrenpark Rd S42 114 D4
Wren Way DE3 230 B7
Wretham Cl DE3 230 D8
Wright Ave DE5 169 F1
Wright Cres DE6 185 D8
Wright St DE5 181 B8
Wroxham Cl DE24 232 D4
Wulfric Cl S2 43 F8
Wulfric Pl S2 43 F8
Wulfric Rd
Eckington S21 59 C3
Sheffield S2 44 A8
WYASTON 185 D2
Wyaston Cl DE22 204 E1
Wyaston Ct DE6 185 D1
Wyaston Gdns DE6 185 D7
Wyaston Rd
Ashbourne DE6 185 C6
Yeaveley DE6 199 D6
Wyatts Way DE5 169 F3
Wyatville Ave SK17 84 E5
Wybersley Rd SK6 32 A8
Wychwood Dr NG9 209 D2
Wycliffe Rd DE55 159 A4
Wycombe Grange
NG19 136 F2
Wye Bank DE45 109 E5
Wye Bank Gr DE45 109 E4
Wye Cl
Hilton DE65 228 D1
Hilton DE65 240 D8
Wye Croft Ct DE45 109 D5
Wye Dale
Castle Gresley DE11 255 F2
Swadlincote DE11 255 F2
Wyedale Cl
Bakewell DE45 109 E4
Buxton SK17 85 B6
Wyedale Cres DE45 109 E4
Wyedale Ct 5 S41 95 E7
Wyedale Dr DE45 109 E4
Wyedale View DE45 109 E4
Wye Gr SK17 85 A7
Wye Head Cl SK17 84 F7
Wye Ho SK17 66 B1
Wyelands Cl SK17 84 F7
Wye Mill SK17 89 A6
Wye St
Buxton SK17 85 C8
Derby DE24 233 A8
Wye Terr DE4 126 F8
Wylam Cl S45 131 D5
Wyming Brook Dr
S10 42 B8
Wyndale Dr DE7 208 C6
Wyndham Cres
DE15 248 C3
Wyndham Prim Acad
DE24 233 A6
Wyndham St DE24 233 A7
Wyndham Way
NG19 135 B4
Wynd The S21 79 C7
Wynton Ave DE24 232 F8
Wyntor Ave DE4 141 C6
Wynyard Cl DE7 194 C3
Wysall Cl NG19 135 E1
Wystan Ct DE65 242 D2
Wyston Brook DE65 228 D1
Wythburn Rd S41 95 C7
Wyver La DE56 178 F6
Wyvern Ave NG10 236 D5
Wyvern Bsns Pk
DE21 220 A4
Wyvern Cl
Eastwood NG16 195 A8
Matlock DE4 143 A6
Wyvern Gdns S17 55 E6
Wyvernside DE21 219 F4
Wyvern Way DE21 220 A4
Wyvil Close LE66 258 B1

Y

Yard Cl DE11 256 B4
Yardley Cl DE55 169 F8
Yardley Way DE56 179 D4
Yard The 4 SK13 10 C1
Yarmouth Ho DE24 233 C7
Yarncliff Cl S40 95 D5
Yarrow Cl
Burton upon Trent
DE15 248 B2
Derby DE24 231 E2
Yarwell Cl DE21 205 D1
Yates Ave DE72 246 A7
Yates Rd SK22 33 C7
Yates St DE23 219 A1
Yeardsley Ave SK23 33 D3
Yeardsley Gn SK23 45 D8
Yeardsley La SK23 33 D3
Yeats La DE4 155 A5
YEAVELEY 199 D5
Yeld Cl DE45 109 C4
Yeldersley Cl S40 95 B5
YELDERSLEY
HOLLIES 186 F4
Yeldersley La
Brailsford DE6 187 B2
Ednaston DE6 201 C8
Osmaston DE6 186 E6
Yeld Rd
Bakewell DE45 109 C4
Bakewell DE45 109 D4
Bakewell DE45 109 D5
Yeld The DE45 109 C5
Yelt La
Doveridge DE6 224 D6
Doveridge DE6 224 D8
Yeoman Park Sch
NG19 136 C4
Yeoman St DE4 142 D1
Yeovil Cl DE24 233 C7
Yerley Hill DE6 172 C6
Yewdale Gr DE21 206 C3
Yews Cl DE73 233 A1
Yews The ST14 197 A3
Yew Tree Ave DE72 221 D5
Yew Tree Cl
Ashover S45 129 F3
Darley Dale DE4 127 B3
Derby DE24 233 C7
3 Smalley DE75 193 C8
Yew Tree Cottages
SK6 15 B3
Yew Tree Cotts
DE72 222 E3
Yewtree Cres DE15 254 F7
Yew Tree Ct DE65 227 C2
Yew Tree Dr
Chesterfield S40 114 A8
Clay Cross S42 131 B6
Killamarsh S21 60 C5
Shirebrook NG20 119 D5
Sutton in Ashfield
NG17 148 F2
Yew Tree Gdns
DE12 260 C6
Yew Tree Hill DE4 156 B5
Yew Tree La
Bradley DE6 186 E8
Elvaston DE72 233 F4
Yewtree Rd DE11 255 F7
Yew Tree Rd
Hatton DE65 227 D1
Rosliston DE12 260 C6
Yokecliffe Ave DE4 165 E8
Yokecliffe Cres DE4 165 E8
Yokecliffe Dr DE4 165 E8
Yokecliffe Hill DE4 165 E8
Yokecliffe La DE4 165 E8
York Ave
Jacksdale NG16 171 B4
Sandiacre NG10 223 A5
York Cl DE11 256 D6
York Cres S44 117 E1
Yorke St NG19 136 B2
York Pl
North Wingfield S42 132 B7
Shireoaks S81 63 F7
York Rd
Derby DE21 219 F7
Long Eaton NG10 223 C1
Shirebrook NG20 119 E3
Swadlincote DE11 256 B2
Yorkshire Way SK13 17 F8
York St
Chesterfield S41 115 C7
Derby DE1 218 E5
Glossop SK13 10 E1
York Terr
Glossop SK13 17 C8
Pinxton NG16 160 C1
Youlgrave Rd
Over Haddon DE45 109 D1
Over Haddon DE45 125 C8
YOULGREAVE 125 B5
Youlgreave Cl DE21 205 F1
Youlgreave Cres SK13 9 D1
Youlgreave Dr S12 44 D5
Young St DE23 218 F1
Yoxall Dr DE22 218 C4
Ypres Rd DE22 204 C2

Z

Zetland Cres DE24 231 C2
Zion Ho DE11 256 C1
Zouche Cl DE75 181 C2